BLACK SAGA

THE AFRICAN AMERICAN
EXPERIENCE

ALSO BY CHARLES M. CHRISTIAN

Baltimore: A Perspective on Urban Development

Modern Metropolitan Systems: An Urban Geography

Alcohol Use Among U.S. Ethnic Minorities

BLACK SAGA

THE AFRICAN AMERICAN EXPERIENCE

CHARLES M. CHRISTIAN
WITH THE ASSISTANCE OF SARI J. BENNETT

HOUGHTON MIFFLIN COMPANY
BOSTON   NEW YORK
1995

For information about permission to reproduce selections from
this book, write to Permissions, Houghton Mifflin Company,
215 Park Avenue South, New York, New York 10003.

Library of Congress Cataloging-in-Publication Data
Christian, Charles Melvin, date.
Black saga : the African American experience /
Charles M. Christian with the assistance of Sari J. Bennett.
p.   cm.
Includes bibliographical references (p. 567) and index.
ISBN 0-395-68717-9
1. Afro-Americans — History — Chronology.   I. Bennett, Sari.
II. Title.
E185.C519   1995
973'.0496073'00202 — dc20   95-3599   CIP

Book designed by Anne Chalmers
Text type: Trump Medieval (Adobe)
Display type: Trajan (Adobe); Lithos Bold (Adobe)
Ornaments: Afrika Borders and Afrika Motifs (Castle Systems)

For information about this and other Houghton Mifflin
trade and reference books and multimedia products, visit
The Bookstore at Houghton Mifflin on the World Wide Web at
http://www.hmco.com./trade/.

Printed in the United States of America
DOC 10 9 8 7 6 5 4 3 2 1

In memory of
the dearest mother in the world,
PAULINE JEFFREY,
who taught her six sons
the value of hard work
and encouraged us to make
positive contributions to the community.

I also dedicate *Black Saga* to
Charles Jr., Fairbanks III, Charla Junee, Charles III, Shaun, and Mariah,
that they may find ways to improve American society.

CONTENTS

MAPS VIII

PREFACE IX

INTRODUCTION XI

BLACK SAGA 1

SELECTED BOOKS FOR
FURTHER READING 567

INDEX 575

MAPS

❖❖❖❖

African Kingdoms, 1000 BC–AD 1967   2

Jamestown   6

Triangular Trade Routes   11

Western Lands   63

Geographical Distribution of
Slave Population in the United States, 1790   66

The Underground Railroad   101

Internal Slave Trade, 1810–1860   148

Status of Slavery after the Compromise of 1850   150

Distribution of Slavery, 1860   173

Cotton Production, 1859 and 1899   176

PREFACE

FROM 1619 TO THE PRESENT, African Americans have grown in number to more than 31 million, or about 12.4 percent of the U.S. population. Far from being a homogeneous group, however, these millions of Americans represent the even greater millions of stories, historical and contemporary, that constitute the African American experience. *Black Saga: The African American Experience* represents the culmination of more than seven years of intensive research into African American history in an attempt to uncover these stories, so often misinterpreted, suppressed, or denied.

This search has been both intellectual and personal. The facts I have collected about people, places, and events in African American history, as interesting as they are in themselves, have served me as signposts to a more complete understanding of my own family's history. I relate some of this personal history here by way of inviting you, the reader, to delve into your own family chronicle and to see in it a compelling, essential component of our nation's history.

I have traced my paternal ancestors to the plantation of the slaveowners Gideon and Carrie Christian, who migrated with thirty-two slaves from South Carolina to Upshur County, Texas, in 1860. After the Civil War, a large number of Black families with the surname Christian lived in that county, and many descendants of Gideon Christian's original thirty-two slaves still live today in the Shiloh area of Upshur County.

My maternal ancestry can be traced to the 1850s, when "Granny" Dora was born a slave somewhere in Louisiana. At the age of seven, Dora was sold in the New Orleans slave market to a white landowner in Gilmer, Texas, for whom she worked as a house slave until the Juneteenth emancipation made her free. But like many ex-slaves, she then had to contend with another kind of enslavement — finding a way to make a living. Dora, although free, continued to live at the home of her former owner. She hired out her labor and after a few years married, and eventually gave birth to four sons and a daughter.

Her youngest son, Sam, my grandfather, was the son of a white landowner who had forced himself on Dora while she was in his employ. My grandfather, "Papa," recounted to me many times how his half-brothers beat him and refused to play with him because he was a "white nigger." He ran away from home when he was about ten years old and hid beneath a white man's house for several days before he was discovered. After he was found, he was asked to stay on and was promised that as long as he did what he was told, he would be well fed — but he would have to live in the barn. Papa led an eventful life, and sadly, many of his stories were as painful as this one and fill me with anger even today.

My mother, too, encountered many difficulties, but her determination to overcome racial discrimination through hard work and loyalty to and belief in her family has served as a model for my own life. After my mother and father separated in Hawkins, Texas, in 1947, she packed our essential belongings onto Papa's pickup truck, with its wooden sideboards, and headed for Black Jack, a small Black farming community in Oklahoma, about seven miles west of Muskogee. On the second trip, she loaded me and my five brothers into the back of the pickup and moved us to our new home on Papa's farm. On her third and last trip, she and three of my brothers loaded and moved Ole Lynch, one of the best milk-producing cows in the county.

In Black Jack, we farmed my grandfather's 160 acres from sunup to sundown. We grew peanuts, cotton, corn, and headfeed and sold milk from several cows we acquired over time. We had an orchard of peach, plum, apple, and apricot trees, and beneath the canopy of trees we grew watermelons, cantaloupes, cucumbers, and squash.

In 1951, as it became harder to make a living on a small farm, my mother, brothers, and I moved to Jerusalem, a small Black community outside the city limits of Muskogee. In Jerusalem we were poor if measured by "dollars and cents," but we were never hungry. We grew an acre garden, canned almost everything we could put in a jar, raised chickens and several pigs, and had steady, but limited, incomes provided by my mother and oldest brother. Mother worked as a hotel elevator operator and cook, and my brother worked as a field hand on a large farm nearby. As we children grew older, we hired out as dayworkers or field hands each summer and on many weekends. We would board trucks at 4:00 or 4:30 in the morning with as many as thirty-five or forty other Black women, children, and men and travel between twenty and fifty miles to work on a farm.

Everyone in our family was a hard worker. Some families in the community accepted welfare; we never did. Mother figured that if everyone in the family worked, we could make much more than the $75 a week paid by welfare. Mother was a model to me, in the fields and at home. She was strong and never complained, and she many times found humor in what appeared to me and my brothers as painful experiences. By the time I was eighteen, I had worked at just about every field job you could name: I had chopped cotton and corn; cut spinach; picked cotton, corn, green beans, strawberries, peaches, tomatoes, watermelons, and cantaloupes; pulled onions; and

helped irrigate hundreds of acres for tomatoes and other crops.

Meanwhile, I continued my education, and I graduated with honors from Manual Training High, an all-Black school in Muskogee, in 1959. Between 1962 and 1968, after a three-year tour of duty in the U.S. Army, I earned a bachelor's and a master's degree and worked as a geography teacher at Byrd Junior High, an all-white school in what was at the time the newest, most prestigious community in Tulsa, Oklahoma. By 1975 I had earned another master's degree and a Ph.D. in social and urban geography from the University of Illinois at Champaign-Urbana. My subsequent work as a professor of social geography at the University of Maryland has led me to explore many scholarly aspects of the African American experience and has aroused my personal interest in the relationship between that broader experience and my own.

Despite the sorrow and anger I often feel when thinking about my family's experiences, there is also much cause for pride. I hunger and continue to search for more and more clues to connect my family's history to the wider African American experience. *Black Saga* is part of that search. By constructing and reexamining this chronology, I have attained a greater sense of perspective and a fuller context for understanding my ancestors', my family's, and my own history and experience. I believe that *Black Saga: The African American Experience* can provide readers of all races with a better understanding of the roles played by African Americans in the development of the United States.

INTRODUCTION

Black Saga is a comprehensive reference book that documents the African American experience in the United States from colonial times to the present in brief entries arranged in chronological order. The people, places, and events that created Black America and the Black perspective are interwoven with concise analyses of the demographic, social, economic, and political trends that affected Blacks — and those that Blacks themselves shaped to win freedom, respect, and prospects for a promising future in a country that often took the most extreme measures to deny them basic rights.

Black Saga begins with a brief overview of African peoples in the kingdoms of Ghana, Mali, and Songhai and then details the participation of Africans in the exploration of the Americas and the settlement in Jamestown, Virginia. The conditions experienced by Black and white indentured servants provide a context for the growth and nature of slavery — the lifelong, involuntary, uncompensated servitude of Blacks — in America. Well-known and less familiar figures of the antislavery movement, both Blacks and whites, are presented through their actions and writings. Telling details such as selections from newspapers that published death threats to abolitionists and advertisements for the sale of slaves and the heartwrenching depiction of a fugitive slave being returned to his owners by the courts of Boston as crowds cried "Shame! Shame!" describe the conflicts that resulted in the Civil War. The faithful service of underpaid, often maligned Black regiments and the refugee camps teeming with "contraband" (slaves under the protection of advancing Union troops) show both the disciplined courage and the dispossessed dependence that complicated Black Americans' transition from enslaved people to free citizens.

The period of Reconstruction after the Civil War combined the government's genuine efforts to secure real citizenship for Blacks with the determination of Blacks to make good on such opportunities. The Freedmen's Bureau provided many former slaves with some of the tools of self-sufficiency: homesteading opportunities, land grant colleges, assistance in obtaining food and clothing, and the most basic instruction in life skills, including reading and managing money — the minor, almost mundane human dignities that slaveholders had carefully withheld from their "property." Blacks eagerly entered the political process, as their almost immediate achievements in state and national government amply prove.

These gains were sadly short-lived; Reconstruction drew to a close as the nation turned its attention to other matters. As federal enforcers of the Thirteenth and Fourteenth Amendments were withdrawn from the South, former slaveholders devised new strategies to "reenslave" Blacks. The enactment of grandfather clauses to prevent Blacks from voting, the terror caused by lynchings and intimidation, and an oppressive system of sharecropping weakened the full citizenship of Blacks and reestablished their dependence on whites, a situation with chilling similarities to slavery.

Living conditions in the South worsened. Black people heard of better opportunities elsewhere, and many decided to migrate, some — the "Exodusters" — to new settlements in the West and others to northern and midwestern cities. The "Great Migration" after the turn of the century powerfully shaped contemporary Black America. *Black Saga* examines Blacks' experiences in this massive population shift and its effects on their destinations. The newcomers often found unemployment, job discrimination, poor housing, and outright racial abuse waiting for them; cities such as Chicago, East St. Louis, New York City, and Philadelphia exploded in racial violence, which included death, injuries, and property losses. Still, the resilience and resourcefulness of Blacks resonated in the Harlem Renaissance, an artistic and intellectual movement in which Black artists, poets, novelists, musicians, and actors achieved national prominence during this turbulent period.

The urbanization of African Americans and racial segregation ordinances and practices created a concentration of Blacks in cities — a powerful tool for protest. Emerging civil rights organizations used a number of strategies, including marches, sit-ins, and boycotts, to gain access to previously segregated institutions and job opportunities. Black organizations such as the Southern Christian Leadership Conference, the Student Non-Violent Coordinating Committee, the Congress of Racial Equality, and the Black Panthers were formed to express the full range of strategies for protest, from nonviolence to direct confrontation. Leaders such as Dr. Martin Luther King, Jr., and Rosa Parks echoed the eloquence and brave actions of earlier freedom fighters such as Frederick Douglass and Harriet Tubman.

Black Saga outlines the emergence and growth of political and economic empowerment among Black Americans since the death of Dr. King. The number of Blacks elected to public offices has increased dramatically, particularly among mayors of large cities, state legislators, and members of the U.S. Congress. *Black Saga* examines the economic advances that have boosted large numbers of Black families into the middle and upper classes and notes the growing number of Black professionals, white-collar employees, and owners of businesses. The volume also charts the growth of social problems that plague the Black community: increasing poverty, particularly among households headed by women with children; the increasing number of children born out of wedlock; the concentration of children in poor areas; escalating drug-related homicide rates among young Blacks; the relatively high proportion of AIDS cases among Blacks; the overall increase in de facto segregation; and the reemergence of violent racism. These serious problems remain to challenge our society, and solving them deserves the best and most immediate efforts of all races.

The four-century trajectory of *Black Saga* is punctuated with the varied, impressive, and delightful accomplishments of Blacks in many fields — the poetry of Phillis Wheatley, the music of William Still, the industrial inventions of Jan Matzeliger, the business acumen of Madame C. J. Walker, the sensational plays and home runs of Jackie Robinson, the political skills and power of Adam Clayton Powell, and the movies of Spike Lee. These and others enliven the story of Black America with their virtuosity and verve.

It is impossible to include every event and person that has contributed to the African American experience. Entries were selected to provide a comprehensive map showing several enriching byways to help the reader chart the journey African Americans have made through history. The author believes that *Black Saga* can help Black Americans understand the richness of their history and the myriad contributions Blacks have made to American society. It can also help white Americans understand variants of the Black perspectives, the Black culture, and history, which are so closely interwoven with their own.

ACKNOWLEDGMENTS

THE AUTHOR GRATEFULLY WISHES to acknowledge the contributions of hundreds of writers who have documented the history of African Americans, whose valuable work is detailed in the bibliography. In addition, I appreciate the work of those who performed valuable research for this volume: Baron Bell, Tess Wingo, Carolyn Kelly, and Asta Urbancic, graduate assistants at the University of Maryland, College Park; Sophia Saks, an intern from the University of Washington; Dr. Ronald Robeson, of Bowie, Maryland; the staff of the Photographs and Prints Division of the Library of Congress; the staff of Special Collections at the University of Maryland, College Park; and the research librarians from countless libraries who willingly answered thousands of questions. I would also like to thank Joel Garreau of the *Washington Post*, and Drs. Curtis C. Roseman of the University of Southern California, Vince Marando of the University of Maryland, College Park, and Lenneal Henderson of the University of Baltimore for their encouragement and helpful suggestions during the early stages of this document.

A special thanks is extended to Dr. Sari J. Bennett of the Department of Geography, University of Maryland Baltimore County, who provided invaluable assistance during the entire production of *Black Saga*. Her assistance was so crucial to the document that she is acknowledged on the title page — a small gesture to recognize her immense contributions.

The author is deeply indebted to Liz Kubik, editorial director for general reference at Houghton Mifflin. She saw the promise of this work, a promise I had seen for more than seven years during the writing of *Black Saga*. Her expertise, probing insight, and rigor were necessary to make *Black Saga* the comprehensive document I had initially envisioned. Her accessibility was of great value in working through many difficult moments. I would also like to thank Senior Editor Borgna Brunner for stepping in at a crucial time and providing the necessary guidance during the final stages of this book.

A special thanks is extended to Dr. Shirley Moore of the University of California, Sacramento, who read the entire document and provided important comments and guidance to improve our coverage of African American women. I also extend thanks to Dr. DeWitt Davis of the University of the District of Columbia, who gave helpful comments on ways to strengthen the work.

I would like, too, to express my sincere thanks to Patricia Robeson, Patricia Garrett, Karen Wyatt, and the other fourth-, fifth-, and sixth-grade teachers at Beltsville Academic Center, Prince George's County, Maryland, and to their innovative principal, William Veater, who assisted the implementation of the annual Black Saga Competition, which has over the past three years helped to teach hundreds of young students about the African American experience. In addition, my thanks go to Yvonne Crawford, principal of Longfields Elementary School in Prince George's County, and to her staff, including Calette Adams and Greta Thomas, who coordinated a Black Saga Competition in their school. I am particularly indebted to the approximately one thousand students who studied hard and competed to make the Black Saga teams. These students inspired me to make *Black Saga: The African American Experience* one of their most important learning resources. I, too, am grateful to many other teachers at various schools throughout the state who offered encouragement and the potential use of *Black Saga* in their classrooms. Further, as a teacher I am gratified when I see young students, of all races and ethnic backgrounds, become excited learning about people, places, and events and the thousands of stories of the African American experience. They have confirmed me in the hope that the publication of *Black Saga* will allow other children and their parents and family members to enjoy and appreciate the richness of our heritage.

Finally, I would like to extend my thanks and appreciation to Dr. John Townshend, chairman of the Department of Geography, University of Maryland, College Park, and to Dr. Irwin Goldstein, dean, and Dr. Stu Edelstein, associate dean, of the Division of Behavioral and Social Sciences, University of Maryland, College Park, for their support.

BLACK SAGA

THE AFRICAN AMERICAN
EXPERIENCE

BLACK SAGA

BEFORE 1492

THREE EMPIRES FLOURISH IN WEST AFRICA

In West Africa three great empires — Ghana, Mali, and Songhai — emerged between A.D. 500 and 1600. Each had a powerful army and controlled great wealth, which included an abundance of gold and also fine manufactured goods, thriving agriculture, and profits from trading. Strong rulers, surrounded by competent, loyal government officials and military leaders, were able to unify empires composed of diverse peoples with different languages, cultures, and geographic locations, including the Kru, Ashanti, Fante, Ewe, Yoruba, and Ibo peoples. Each empire's economic strength and centralized political control made it easy to suppress revolt.

GHANA The Ghana empire was founded along the Niger River between the third and fifth centuries. Ghana was established by the Soninke people of West Africa, who quickly developed an economic life comprising agriculture, manufacturing, and international trade. They were superior metalworkers and produced iron swords and other weapons by which they conquered neighboring peoples and maintained control over their territory. The empire's growth and development were relatively slow until Ghana began to trade with Arab ports on the Mediterranean coast and with other kingdoms of East Africa on the Red Sea.

Ghana's ascent to great power was directly related to its acquisition of gold. Although the name *Ghana* meant "warrior king," it later was used to refer to the empire and its gold. It was written that Ghana's gold was so abundant that the king's dogs wore gold collars. Al-Bakri, an Arab geographer who wrote of Ghana in 1067, mentioned that the king owned a nugget of gold so big that he could tether his horse to it. At its height in the eleventh century, Ghana had a judiciary system and other institutions to govern its people. A king ruled the empire, supported by several provincial governors and viceroys. Ghana dominated the Sudan for almost three hundred years.

MALI The Mali empire differed substantially from the Ghana empire. Its rise to power began in the seventh century, when a small Mandingo state on the upper Niger River was transformed by two great African leaders — Sundiata Keita and Mansa Musa. Although Sundiata Keita began to transform the state into a great empire, its growth was slow until about 1307, when Mansa Musa became ruler. Mansa Musa, a devout Muslim, set out in 1324 on a pilgrimage to Mecca, the holy city for Muslims. His entourage included about sixty thousand persons, including twelve thousand servants. As many as five hundred servants each carried a staff of pure gold weighing six pounds. Eighty camels carried an average of three hundred pounds of gold each. These riches were to be distributed as alms and gifts.

When he returned from his pilgrimage, Mansa Musa directed his architect to design buildings in Timbuktu and other cities under his control. At times, the Mali empire numbered far more than one hundred thousand people. For a while, Timbuktu itself had a population of more than one hundred thousand people. It was a busy place where merchants displayed their merchandise to local and international consumers. Caravans from distant places frequently came to Timbuktu to exchange their exotic goods for gold. Mali's power derived from strong rulers, centralized government, and a successful economic base of agriculture, manufacturing, trade, and amazing wealth in gold.

When Mansa Musa died in 1332, the Mali empire began to disintegrate. Squabbling local rulers could not agree on a central form of government, and neighboring peoples led attacks on the kingdom's cities. By the mid-1400s, the sons of the king of the city of Gao led a successful revolt and began building an empire that would be known as Songhai.

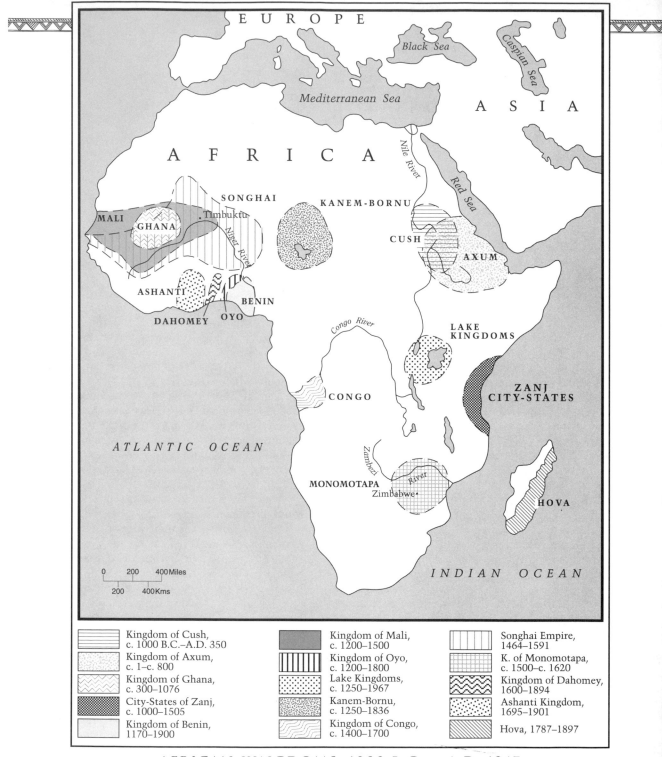

AFRICAN KINGDOMS, 1000 B.C. — A.D. 1967

Africa was the home of many great Black civilizations. This map shows the major kingdoms on the continent, including those in West Africa, where most slaves were eventually captured and sold.

Legend:

Kingdom of Cush, c. 1000 B.C.–A.D. 350

Kingdom of Axum, c. 1–c. 800

Kingdom of Ghana, c. 300–1076

City-States of Zanj, c. 1000–1505

Kingdom of Benin, 1170–1900

Kingdom of Mali, c. 1200–1500

Kingdom of Oyo, c. 1200–1800

Lake Kingdoms, c. 1250–1967

Kanem-Bornu, c. 1250–1836

Kingdom of Congo, c. 1400–1700

Songhai Empire, 1464–1591

K. of Monomotapa, c. 1500–c. 1620

Kingdom of Dahomey, 1600–1894

Ashanti Kingdom, 1695–1901

Hova, 1787–1897

Timbuktu rose to its highest level of development during the Songhai empire, particularly between 1493 and 1529, under Askia Mohammed. During this time, the University of Timbuktu produced more than forty books, on subjects such as logic, theology, ethics, mathematics, and rhetoric. Akmed Baba, the last chancellor of the university, was considered one of the great intellectuals of the sixteenth century.

SONGHAI (SONGHAY) The Mali empire was decisively destroyed by the sons of the king of Gao. Their revolt set into motion the formation of another major empire: Songhai (or Songhay). Although the Songhai empire inherited a solid economic base from its predecessor, its growth was substantially accelerated when Askia Mohammed, a general who had been prime minister, gained power in 1493. In his thirty-six-year quest to make Songhai the most powerful empire in the world, Askia Mohammed embarked on an effort to expand trade to include European countries. It was during his rule that the sale of Black slaves became a major business. He eventually controlled most of West Africa — an area larger than Europe.

Askia was a master politician and a superior leader of people. He restructured the army, secured a stronger system of banking and credit, and established the cities of Gao, Walata, Timbuktu, and Nenne as major intellectual centers where scholarship was encouraged. Timbuktu was a grand city of

about one hundred thousand residents. Its wealth in gold and its stories of intrigue and mystery made it one of the most celebrated cities of its time. It flourished as a business district with many shops, a religious site with the Great Mosque, and an intellectual center with the University of Sankore.

Although many of the peoples of the Songhai empire worked at making tools, weapons, ceremonial items, and artworks of bronze, tin, copper, and gold, the overwhelming majority were farmers and warriors. The farmers grew millet and other crops and spent much of their time tending cattle. Artisans included goldsmiths, wood sculptors, brass casters, cotton spinners, linen weavers, leatherworkers, and iron fabricators. Traders specialized in exchanging ivory, iron, gold, cattle, and clothes for salt, medicine, books, jewels, and other goods from traders to the north and along the Red Sea and the Indian Ocean.

Songhai achieved many military conquests, and the empire reached its zenith in the fifteenth and sixteenth

3

centuries. The decline of the Songhai empire marked the end of the great West African empires. Some claim that the collapse came from the collision of two great religions, Islam and Christianity, and the corrupting influence of the slave trade.

1492 BLACK EXPLORER NIÑO JOINS COLUMBUS
Blacks were among the first explorers of the Western Hemisphere. Pedro (Peter) Alonzo Niño, a pilot on Christopher Columbus's ship the *Santa Maria*, was identified as a Black man.

1501 SPAIN PERMITS AFRICAN SLAVES IN THE AMERICAS
The Spanish government authorized the use of African slaves in the Americas.

1502 NEGRO SAILS WITH COLUMBUS
Diego el Negro (James the Black or Diego Mendez) was the cabin boy on the *Capitana* during Columbus's fourth and last voyage to the Americas.

PORTUGAL DELIVERS SLAVES
Portugal was the first country to land a cargo of slaves in the Western Hemisphere.

1510 SPAIN BEGINS SLAVE TRADE
King Ferdinand ordered 250 African slaves to be taken from Spain to the West Indies.

1512 AFRICAN SLAVE PLANTS WHEAT IN THE AMERICAS
John Garrido, a slave, initiated the cultivation of wheat in the Americas by planting three grains of wheat.

BLACK MAN TRAVELS WITH PONCE DE LEÓN
Peter Mexia, a Black man, searched Florida with Juan Ponce de León for the fountain of youth.

1513 AFRICANS ACCOMPANY EXPLORERS
Africans were members of the exploring parties of Hernando Cortés, Francisco Pizarro, and Pedro Menéndez de Avilés.

AFRICAN SLAVES IN CUBA
Spanish colonists were authorized to use slaves in Cuba.

BLACK EXPLORERS ACCOMPANY BALBOA
Nuflo de Olano accompanied Vasco Núñez de Balboa in claiming the "South Sea" (the Pacific Ocean) for Spain.

Olano and twenty-nine other Blacks were among the explorers who later traveled with Balboa across Panama.

1515 SLAVE-GROWN SUGAR SHIPPED FROM WEST INDIES TO SPAIN
The first shipment of sugar grown by slave labor was shipped from the West Indies. In 1517 Bartolomé de Las Casas, a Spanish missionary, urged bringing more African slaves to the area to replace Indian slaves and laborers. He was a protector of the Indian peoples and advocate of more humane treatment of them. Las Casas later regretted enslaving Africans.

1518 SPANISH AMERICAN COLONIES LICENSED TO RECEIVE SLAVES
King Charles of Spain, successor to King Ferdinand, granted a license (called the *asiento*) for the shipment of Black slaves directly from Africa to the Spanish American colonies. Previously, they had been taken to Europe and Christianized before being sent to the West Indies.

This act was to have major consequences in the Americas, since it allowed companies or individuals to supply African slaves as labor to the colonies. Spanish settlers in the West Indies had tried unsuccessfully to use conquered Indians for labor in the fields and mines. The Indian peoples had succumbed to diseases introduced by Europeans and were considered by the settlers unsuitable for demanding agricultural labor.

1519–1520 AFRICANS TRAVEL WITH CORTÉS IN MEXICO
An estimated three hundred Africans accompanied the Spanish explorer Hernando Cortés in his conquest of Mexico.

1522 SLAVE REVOLT IN HISPANIOLA
The first slave revolt in Hispaniola occurred in 1522. Reports noted that approximately forty African slaves, apparently reacting to harsh laws passed to control them, killed their masters and escaped to the hills.

Later, new legislation was passed to ensure that slaves were treated with more consideration. For example, slave families could not be separated by sale. Planters in Hispaniola were required to baptize their slaves and send them to mass on Sunday. On paper, at least, it seems that slaves could buy their freedom for three hundred dollars, but this law, like many others, was ignored in practice.

1526 FIRST SLAVE REVOLT ON THE NORTH AMERICAN MAINLAND

The first successful slave revolt in territory that would become part of the United States occurred in the San Miguel settlement near the Pedee River in present-day South Carolina. The settlement had been founded by the Spanish colonizer Lucas Vasquez de Ayllon. In the winter of 1526 the slaves revolted, set fire to the settlement, and fled to live among Native Americans.

1528 ESTEVANICO BECOMES EXPLORER

Estevanico, or Esteban, or Estevan de Dorantes (1500?–1539), one of America's most famous Black-Spanish explorers, arrived in America as a member of Pánfilo de Narváez's expedition. On the way to the western Gulf of Mexico, Narváez's ships were blown off course and landed near Tampa Bay, Florida. Narváez and some of his men then walked to what is now Tallahassee. Many men were lost along the way. After building makeshift boats, the survivors drifted westward in the Gulf and were shipwrecked off the coast of Texas (Galveston Island). Only Estevanico and three others survived.

For almost eight years, Estevanico and the other survivors wandered across miles of uncharted territory and lived among Native Americans. When they finally came upon a Spanish outpost in 1536, they were almost unrecognizable as Spaniards except for the fact that they spoke the Spanish language. After they told of their shipwreck and subsequent explorations, they were taken to Culiacán on the Pacific coast; thus they became the first explorers to cross the continent north of the Isthmus of Panama.

1538 FIRST BLACK SETTLEMENT ON THE CONTINENT

Escaped slaves founded Gracia Real de Santa Teresa de Mosé, a settlement near present-day St. Augustine, Florida. The king of Spain granted liberty to all slaves who reached the settlement.

1538–1539 ESTEVANICO EXPLORES ARIZONA AND NEW MEXICO

Estevanico led an advance party in search of the fabled Seven Cities of Cibola into the territory that later became New Mexico and Arizona. After finding the Zuni Pueblo, thought to be the Seven Cities, Estevanico was killed by the Zuni who may have feared he was a spy sent by nations who wished to conquer them.

1539–1542 AFRICANS EXPLORE THE MISSISSIPPI RIVER WITH DE SOTO

An unknown number of Africans assisted Hernando de Soto on his expedition from Florida westward in search of gold. They crossed the river the Native Americans called the Mississippi and continued their search into present-day Arkansas and Oklahoma. After traveling back to the Mississippi River, de Soto fell ill and died.

1540 AFRICANS INVOLVED IN CORONADO'S EXPEDITION

An unknown number of Africans accompanied the Spaniard Francisco Vásquez de Coronado on his explorations of southwestern North America in search of the fabled Seven Cities of Cibola and their gold. Earlier, Estevanico had acted as interpreter and guide for the advance party. The explorers spent several years in the areas now known as Texas, Kansas, Arizona, and Colorado before giving up their search. He and his followers were the first Europeans to see the Grand Canyon. Eventually, Coronado gave up his search for the cities of gold.

1559 TOBACCO REACHES EUROPE

The first tobacco grown by slaves in the West Indies was shipped to Europe; it became a cash crop that demanded large supplies of labor.

1560 AFRICANS OUTNUMBER EUROPEANS IN CARIBBEAN ISLANDS

More Africans than Europeans inhabited the larger Caribbean islands. For example, Hispaniola had thirty thousand Africans and two thousand Spaniards; Puerto Rico had fifteen thousand Africans and only five hundred whites.

1562 BRITISH GOVERNMENT DENIES TRADING IN SLAVES

The British government denied that it had entered the slave trade, even though John Hawkins of Great Britain had sold a large cargo of Africans to planters in Spanish Hispaniola.

1565 AFRICANS HELP FOUND SETTLEMENT IN FLORIDA

Africans were among the expedition led by Pedro Mendez that founded St. Augustine, Florida, the oldest city in the United States.

1592 SLAVE SHIPMENTS FROM SPAIN TO THE NEW WORLD INCREASE

Beginning in 1592 and for nine more years, about 4,250 slaves were delivered annually to the Americas.

The license to transport them was issued by the court of Spain to Gomes Reynal. According to the agreement, 3,500 (about 80 percent) of the slaves shipped each year had to arrive alive.

1600   AFRICAN SLAVES IN LATIN AMERICA

Records indicate that slave trading was a brisk business in Latin America. By this time, more than nine hundred thousand slaves had been brought there. Slave revolts increased, reflecting both the number of slaves sold in this part of the Western Hemisphere and the harsh and cruel treatment they received. Slaves were regarded as "money-making machines." They worked in almost every area of business — mines, ranches, plantations, docks, and industry shops — and in the homes of their owners. Because Africans were plentiful and could be acquired cheaply, the slave trade flourished in the Americas. Portugal, Spain, and France — nations that controlled most of the American waters — controlled most of the trade.

1612   TOBACCO PLANTED IN VIRGINIA

Tobacco, introduced by Captain John Rolfe, was first planted in Virginia in this year. The tobacco was a mild species brought from the West Indies. It became especially popular in the colony, and by 1619 about twenty thousand pounds were harvested. It became an important cash crop for the Jamestown settlement, though King James of England declared tobacco "dangerous to the Lungs."

1619   FIRST AFRICAN SETTLERS REACH NORTH AMERICA

On **AUGUST 20**, a Dutch ship arrived in Jamestown, Virginia, carrying Captain Jope and a cargo of twenty Africans. Though no one really knows why the ship anchored off Jamestown, it is believed that the captain needed food, in exchange for which he offered his cargo of Africans. When the deal was consummated, Antoney, Isabella, and eighteen other Africans disembarked. Although they were not the first Africans to arrive in North America, they were the first African settlers. Regarded as indentured servants rather than slaves, fifteen were purchased to serve their redemption time working for Sir George Yardley, the governor of Virginia and proprietor of the thousand-acre Flowerdew Hundred plantation.

◆ Thousands of whites used indentured servitude (that is, they sold their labor for a number of years in payment for passage) as their means of coming to the colonies. Some came of their own free will, others in-

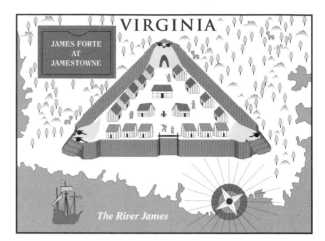

JAMESTOWN

The Jamestown colony, England's first permanent settlement in North America, is shown as it was laid out in 1607. The settlement's marshy land was poor for agriculture and was a breeding ground for malaria-carrying mosquitoes. Only thirty-two of the approximately one hundred original settlers survived the first seven months. A dozen years after the colony was founded, twenty Africans were left there by a Dutch ship. By the 1630s, the colony had established a successful economy based on tobacco.

voluntarily. Enterprising individuals, paupers, dissenters of all kinds, prisoners, prostitutes, vagabonds, and others were sold to the highest bidder as soon as they arrived. If a ship was not filled, many captains encouraged their crew to kidnap people from the streets of London and Bristol.

Life for the white indentured servant was similar to that of the Black indentured servant. They worked side by side as they planted, weeded, suckered, cut tobacco or cleared forest, and were allowed to cultivate small private gardens.

Africans captured by other Africans and sold to white slave traders, who in turn sold them to the highest bidder in Virginia, became part of the social structure of the colony. For about forty years, Black settlers purchased and sold land, voted in elections, testified in court, and moved about without restrictions. In fact, some of the early Black settlers who survived their indentured servitude purchased the services of other Blacks, and some even purchased the services of white indentured servants. This social structure began to break down as more and more Africans entered the

The landing of twenty Africans at Jamestown from a Dutch man-of-war in 1619 marked the beginning of the African American experience. Although most African Americans were probably indentured servants during this period, their status changed quite dramatically by the middle of the seventeenth century, by which time they were clearly servants for life — that is, slaves.

colonies and as slaving became profitable for both the slave trader and the slave owner.

1620   PUBLIC EDUCATION BEGINS IN VIRGINIA

A public school for Native Americans and Blacks was established in the Virginia colony in this year.

1623   FIRST BLACK CHILD BORN IN AMERICA

It is believed that William Tucker (1623?–?), was the first Black child born in America, and the first baptized in the Church of England at Jamestown, Virginia. His parents were Antoney and Isabella, Africans who were sold to the British colony in 1619 as indentured servants. Little is known of Tucker's life or how long he lived.

1624   CHRISTIANIZED BLACKS GRANTED PRIVILEGES

In Virginia, the baptism of Blacks conferred special privileges. Since Virginia was a royal colony, the laws of England generally governed the colony. English law declared that a slave who had been "christened or baptized" became "infranchised." Thus, John Phillip, a Black "christened" man, could testify in general court against a white man. Phillip was considered a free man because he had been baptized twelve years before, in England.

DUTCH COLONY OF NEW AMSTERDAM FOUNDED

As many as eleven Black male slaves were among the founding settlers of New Amsterdam in the Hudson River Valley. They were considered so necessary to the survival of the settlement that when these slaves took part in a murder, the local white settlers asked them to draw lots to determine who would be hanged for the crime. When the unlucky one was hanged, he was so heavy that the rope broke. The small group of settlers decided he should go free rather than endure the ordeal again.

POPULATION OF VIRGINIA INCLUDES SMALL NUMBER OF BLACKS

According to a census of the Virginia colony taken in 1624 and 1625, Africans made up about 2 percent of the total resident population of 1,227. These 23 Black residents (11 men, 10 women, and 2 children) lived in three of the six settlements and among seven planters, five of whom were officers of the colony. The rest of the population included 487 white and Native American indentured servants and 608 "free" white men and women. Even though several ships, the *James,* the *Swan,* and others, had docked at Jamestown since the arrival of the first Black indentured servants, only two Black adult males had been added to the population; one Black child had been born.

VIRGINIA BECOMES A ROYAL COLONY

On **MAY 24**, the Virginia Charter was revoked because of the colony's years of unprofitability; it became instead a royal colony. A charter was given by the Crown to companies or private individuals to establish and control colonies in America. A royal colony was controlled by officials appointed by the Crown.

1625   VIRGINIA COURT DISTINGUISHES BETWEEN BLACK SERVITUDE AND BLACK SLAVERY

In **SEPTEMBER**, the Virginia court not only made a distinction between Black servitude and Black slavery, but also showed the value of tobacco in this statement regarding a Black servant:

> The Negro that cam in with Capt. Jones shall remaine with the Lady Yardley till further order be taken for him and that he shalbe allowed by the Lady Yardley monthly for his labor forty pownd waight of good merchantable tobacco for his labor and service so lone as he remayneth with her.

1626   FRANCE BEGINS WEST INDIAN EMPIRE

The island of Guadeloupe, captured by the French, formed the basis for the French empire in the West Indies. Like the English, Dutch, and Spanish, the French would import slaves as labor for the plantation economies.

1627   TOBACCO PRODUCTION REQUIRES ADDITIONAL LABOR

Tobacco exports soared to about five hundred thousand pounds in this year, up from eighteen thousand pounds. Tobacco remained the most profitable crop for several colonies. King Charles I was heard to say that Virginia was "wholly built upon smoke." Tobacco was so important in Maryland, Virginia, and the northern portion of the Carolina colony that it was used as a medium of exchange. Because growing tobacco required considerable labor, its cultivation led to the importation of more slaves.

1630   DUTCH CLEAR LAND IN WEST INDIES FOR PLANTATIONS

Dutch colonization efforts on Curaçao and other islands began with the clearing of land for plantations. Soon after, slaves were imported for labor.

MASSACHUSETTS PROTECTS RUNAWAY SLAVES

A law was enacted in Massachusetts to protect African slaves who escaped from their owners because of abusive treatment.

VIRGINIA RESTRICTS RELATIONS BETWEEN BLACKS AND WHITES

In Virginia, a white man, Hugh Davis, was ordered publicly whipped before Blacks and whites "for abusing himself to the dishonor of God and the shame of Christians by defiling his body in lying with a Negro, which fault he is to acknowledge next Sabbath Day."

Legislation prohibiting miscegenation was not enacted in Virginia until 1662.

1634 MARYLAND COLONY IMPORTS SLAVES

The demand for labor in the tobacco fields of the Chesapeake region fueled the importation of a growing number of white and Black indentured servants as well as African slaves. Servants were treated harshly by planters who wanted to get the most from their labor. Half of all servants died during their indenture. As long as there were plenty of white indentured laborers, most colonists did not want to bother with importing a large number of Africans since they were more costly and required "conditioning" before they could be productive.

1636 ALL BLACKS AND NATIVE AMERICANS CONSIDERED SLAVES IN BARBADOS

Although scholars agree that there is no record of an actual slave code in the West Indies until 1663, by 1636 Blacks were arriving in Barbados in large numbers, so that the governor's council felt it necessary to control them. From that time on, all Blacks and Native Americans imported onto the island would be considered slaves, bound to work there for the rest of their lives.

INDENTURED SERVANTS A MAJORITY IN VIRGINIA

Approximately three thousand of the five thousand persons living in Virginia in 1636 came to the colony as servants. In 1627, about fifteen hundred kidnapped children had been sent to Virginia, and another shipment of "friendless boyes and girles" had been requested by authorities of Virginia. The system of indentured servitude was firmly established in Jamestown before Blacks arrived. It is estimated that at least eighty thousand indentured servants were imported by Virginians during the colonial period.

1638 CAPTAIN OF THE *Desire* SAILS FIRST AMERICAN SLAVE SHIP TO THE WEST INDIES AND STARTS NEW ENGLAND SLAVE TRADE

According to Governor John Winthrop's journal, Captain William Pierce sailed the *Desire* into Boston Harbor on **DECEMBER 12** with a cargo of salt, cotton, tobacco, and Africans.

Pierce had sailed earlier from Salem, Massachusetts, to the West Indies, with a cargo of Native American slaves he wished to trade for Black slaves and goods. On the basis of Winthrop's journal, it is believed that the first Black slave arrived in New England at about this time.

The successful slave trade involving the ship *Desire* encouraged many ship owners in New England to participate in the developing trade. They faced stiff competition from the European slave traders, but by the latter 1600s, New England traders had become major competitors in the business. Their success, however, was related in part to the Dutch, who diverted much of Europe's attention to the Anglo-Dutch wars, and in part to the breaking up of the powerful slave-trading monopoly enjoyed by the English Royal African Company. Such events allowed New England slave traders to seek slaves more freely in West Africa.

1639 MARYLAND LEGISLATES HARSH TREATMENT FOR RUNAWAYS

Maryland passed a law declaring that a servant convicted of running away should be executed, the most severe law of its kind at the time. See also 1642–1643.

1640

POPULATION OVERVIEW

GENERAL POPULATION IN NORTH AMERICAN BRITISH COLONIES The total population in the colonies was estimated at 26,634 residents in 1640. Approximately 10,442, or about 39 percent, of the colonial population resided in Virginia. Massachusetts had the second largest number of residents, 8,932. These two colonies encompassed about 73 percent of the total colonial population. No other colony had more than 2,000 residents.

BLACKS IN NORTH AMERICAN BRITISH AND DUTCH COLONIES Blacks made up only about 597 residents in colonial North America. Approximately 39 percent of them lived in New Netherland (later called New York), another 25 percent each lived in Virginia and Massachusetts. Smaller numbers and percentages were found in the areas of present-day New Hampshire, Maryland, and Connecticut.

SOCIAL CONDITIONS OVERVIEW

STATUS FOR BLACKS CHANGES Many Blacks were probably indentured servants in the North American colonies until 1640, although some researchers have put the date later. It is the majority view, however, that slavery was becoming the most common condition of Blacks in America at this time, and fewer were accepted as indentured servants. Although some of the colonies had not yet specifically legalized slavery of Blacks, the de facto institution was well established.

BLACK RUNAWAYS PUNISHED MORE HARSHLY THAN WHITES

Three servants of Hugh Gwyn, a Virginia landholder, ran away but were caught in Maryland and returned to their owner. The Virginia court ruled on the case as follows:

> Whereas Hugh Gwyn hath . . . brought back from Maryland three servants formerly run away . . . the court doth therefore order that the said three servants shall receive the punishment of whipping and to have thirty stripes apiece one called Victor, a Dutchman, the other a Scotchman called James Gregory, shall first serve out their times with their master according to their indentures, and one whole year apiece after the time of their service is Expired . . . and after that service . . . to serve the colony for three whole years apiece, and that the third being a negro named John Punch shall serve his said master . . . for the time of his natural life here or elsewhere.

1641 BLACK ELECTED TO MARYLAND GENERAL ASSEMBLY

Mathias De Sousa, a former Black indentured servant, was elected to the Maryland General Assembly.

SLAVERY RECOGNIZED AS LEGAL IN MASSACHUSETTS

Massachusetts was the first colony to recognize slavery as a legal institution. Sanctions concerning slavery are found in Section 91 of the *Body of Liberties*, which reads:

> There shall never be any bond slaverie, villinage or Captivitie amongst us, unless it be lawful Captives taken in just warrs, and such strangers as willingly sell themselves or are sold to us. And these shall have all the liberties and Christian usages which the law of God established in Isreall . . . . This exempts none from servitude who shall be Judged thereto by Authoritie.

These words authorized not only African slavery, but slavery of Native Americans and Europeans as well.

Other colonies followed with statutory recognition of slavery: Connecticut, 1650; Virginia, 1661; Maryland, 1664; New York and New Jersey, 1664; South Carolina, 1682; Rhode Island and Pennsylvania, 1700; North Carolina, 1715; and Georgia, 1750.

1642 VIRGINIA PASSES FUGITIVE SLAVE ORDER

Virginia passed legislation to stop assistance to runaway slaves. Individuals could be fined twenty pounds of tobacco for each night he or she harbored a runaway.

1642–1643 VIRGINIA LEGISLATES HARSH TREATMENT FOR RUNAWAYS

Virginia passed legislation in 1642 and 1643 requiring a servant who escaped for the second time to be branded on the cheek or shoulder with the letter *R*.

DUTCH ARM BLACKS TO PROTECT SETTLEMENTS

In New Amsterdam, Dutch India Company officials armed Black slaves with "tomy hawks and half pikes" to assist them in protecting the settlement against Native Americans.

Virginia, in contrast, had passed legislation in 1639 that excluded "Negroes" from being provided with arms or ammunition.

1643 FOUNDATION LAID FOR FUGITIVE SLAVE LAWS

The New England Confederation entered into an intercolonial agreement that a simple statement of certification from any government magistrate can convict a suspected runaway slave.

1644 BLACK PERSON ISSUED LAND GRANT IN NEW NETHERLAND

On **DECEMBER 15**, Lucas Santomee was issued a Dutch land grant in New Netherland that included major property in what eventually became Brooklyn and Greenwich Village. Santomee was the son of Peter Santomee, one of the first eleven Africans brought to the area. Lucas Santomee, a free Black, became a well-known physician in New Amsterdam.

BLACKS PETITION FOR FREEDOM IN NEW NETHERLAND

Eleven Blacks petitioned for freedom in New Netherland (later called New York). This was probably the first organized Black protest in America. The Blacks were freed by the Council of New Netherland because they had completed their seventeen to eighteen years of servitude. Their names were Paul d'Angola, Big Manuel, Little Manuel, Manuel de Gerrit de

Liverpool, London, Bristol

TOBACCO, RICE, FISH, TIMBER, TAR

CLOTH, TOOLS, AXES, MUSKETS, FURNITURE

New York
Philadelphia
Boston

GRAIN, MEAT, BUTTER

SUGAR, COFFEE, MOLASSES,

SUGAR, COFFEE, CACAO

IVORY, SILVER, INDIAN TEXTILES, BEADS

Cuba
Jamaica
Hispaniola
Puerto Rico
Windward Islands

SLAVES

Gulf of Guinea

TRIANGULAR TRADE ROUTES

Beginning in the mid-1600s, trade routes connected North America, Africa, and the West Indies. Manufactured goods were traded in Africa for slaves; slaves were taken to the West Indies and "broken in" before being taken to mainland North America. Over time, many complex variations of this basic triangular pattern of trade evolved.

Rens, Simon Congo, Anthony Portuguese, Garcia, Peter Santomee, John Francisco, Little Anthony, and John Fort Orange. Each received a parcel of land in what is presently Greenwich Village.

1645 AMERICA ENTERS SLAVE TRADE DIRECTLY WITH AFRICA

The first American slave ship bound for Africa, the *Rainbow*, sailed from Boston. Slaving quickly became a major profit-making industry. A triangular trade route emerged, with slave ships leaving American ports for the west coast of Africa, where Africans, captured largely by neighboring or enemy peoples and sold to Muslim traders in exchange for a variety of goods, were purchased by traders from the Americas and taken to the West Indies — usually to Jamaica and Barbados — where the slaves were traded for salt, tobacco, sugar, and wine. In turn, these goods were sold in the American colonies. Slaves delivered to the West Indies worked on the sugar plantations.

1646 LEGALITY OF TAKING SLAVES QUESTIONED IN MASSACHUSETTS

On **NOVEMBER 4**, the Massachusetts Bay Colony ordered the return of two slaves to Africa at public expense, in the earliest known legislative protest against the stealing of human beings. The slaves had been brought from the Guinea coast by John Smith. According to the legislation:

> The General Court, conceiving themselves bound by the first opportunity, to bear witness against the

CONDITIONS ABOARD SLAVE SHIPS

A typical slave ship traveling from Gambia, the Gold Coast, Guinea, or Senegal would take four to eight weeks to reach New England, Chesapeake Bay, the Gulf of Mexico, or the West Indies. Africans from Senegal were the most prized because many were skilled artisans. Ibos from Calabar were considered the most undesirable because of their high suicide rate.

Women, men, and children were crammed so tightly in the ships that out of a load of seven hundred slaves, three or four would be found dead each morning.

Most ships had three decks, the lower two used for transporting slaves. The lowest deck extended the full length of the ship and was no more than five feet high. Slaves were packed into it side by side to utilize all available space. In the next deck, wooden planks, like shelves, extended from the sides of the ship, where slaves, chained in pairs at the wrists and ankles, were crammed side by side. Men occupied middle shelves and were most often chained in pairs and bound to the ship's gunwales or to ringbolts set into the deck. Women and children were sometimes allowed to move about certain areas of the ship. Although buckets were provided for use as toilets, they were not emptied regularly. The ships smelled of excrement, disease, and death. It is estimated that between 15 and 20 percent of the slaves died en route to the colonies, mostly from diseases associated with overcrowding, spoiled and poisoned food, contaminated water, starvation and thirst, and suicide. Others were thrown overboard, shot, or beaten to death for various reasons.

Slave trading became big business during the seventeenth century. Slaves were acquired in Africa for an average price of about twenty-five dollars each, paid primarily in merchandise. They were sold in the Americas for about one hundred fifty dollars each. As the price of slaves increased, so did the inhumane overcrowding of the ships.

During the latter 1600s and throughout the 1700s, most English ships coming directly to the American mainland from Africa carried about two hundred slaves and weighed about one hundred to two hundred tons, although some were slightly larger. Slave ships were eventually built especially for human cargo. They were long, narrow, and fast, and were designed to direct air below decks. Shackling irons, nets, and ropes were standard equipment. These slave ships could carry as many as four hundred slaves and a crew of forty-seven, as well as thirteen thousand pounds of food. After 1750, the competition at slaving markets on the African coast grew exceptionally keen, and European vessels either left without full loads of slaves or waited several months to purchase a full cargo.

heinous and crying sin of man-stealing, and also to prescribe such timely redress for what is past, and such a law for the future, as may sufficiently deter all others belonging to us to have to do in such vile and most odious courses, justly abhorred of all good and just men — do order that the negro interpreter, with others unlawfully taken, be, by the first opportunity, (at the charge of the country for present) sent to his native country of Guinea, and a letter with him of the indignation of the Court thereabouts, and justice hereof — desiring our honored Governor would please to put this order in execution.

(*Massachusetts Records*, vol. 2, 168)

At this time, Blacks living in Massachusetts (and Rhode Island) were considered servants completing a number of years of service, and not slaves. The term of service for Black servants was later extended from a specified number of years to life.

1650

POPULATION OVERVIEW

GENERAL POPULATION IN NORTH AMERICAN BRITISH AND DUTCH COLONIES It is estimated that 50,368 persons resided in the American colonies at this time. The combined population of Virginia and Massachusetts stood at 32,768 persons, or about 65 percent of the total colonial population. Another 12,759 residents were about equally divided among Maryland, New Netherland, and Connecticut. Other colonies had less than 2,000 residents.

BLACKS IN NORTH AMERICAN BRITISH AND DUTCH COLONIES Approximately 1,600 Blacks lived in the American colonies in 1650. The Black populations of New Netherland, Virginia, Maryland, and Massachusetts together comprised 1,500 persons, or about 94 percent of the total Black population. More than 500 Blacks lived in the New Netherland colony — up from 232 a decade earlier. As many as 405 Blacks lived among the 15,000 residents in the Virginia colony — 255 more than in 1640.

1651　BLACK COMMUNITY ESTABLISHED ACCORDING TO HEADRIGHT SYSTEM

On **JULY 24**, Anthony Johnson, a Black indentured servant who arrived in Jamestown in 1621, was given a grant of 250 acres for importing five persons as indentured servants. This system, whereby planters could claim 50 acres of land for each individual brought into the colony, was called the "headright" system. Johnson settled on the banks of the Pungoteague River in Northampton County, Virginia. The following year, John Johnson, the son of Anthony, received more than 650 additional acres for importing thirteen persons.

In 1654, Richard Johnson, a Black carpenter free of his indentured services, received 100 acres for transporting two persons to the settlement. Other Blacks secured land in different parts of the colony under the headright system — Benjamin Dole, John Harris, Phillip Morgan, and others. The Johnson landholdings in Northampton County amounted to more than 1,000 acres. As many as sixteen Blacks and two whites served as indentured servants there. This settlement constituted one of the first permanent Black communities in the American colonies.

1652　MASSACHUSETTS REQUIRES BLACKS TO SERVE IN MILITIA

Massachusetts passed legislation requiring that "all Negroes and Indians from sixteen to sixty years of age, inhabitants or servants to the English, be listed and hereby enjoined to attend [militia] trainings as well as the English."

Sometimes permission was granted to an individual or several individuals to bear arms. For example, in 1643, Abraham Pearse, a Black man, was listed among men capable of bearing arms in Plymouth colony.

By 1656, however, conditions had changed. In this year, Massachusetts barred Blacks and Native Americans from military service because colonists feared these groups would revolt.

SLAVERY LIMITED IN RHODE ISLAND

On **MAY 18**, the earliest statute for the suppression of slavery in the colonies was noted in the *Rhode Island Records*. Rhode Island ruled that "no black mankind or white" should be a slave for more than ten years, or after the age of twenty-four. This legislation became the first colonial law limiting slavery, but ironically, it was never enforced.

SLAVERY REGULATED IN NEW NETHERLAND

On **MAY 18**, the Dutch permitted the export of Black slaves to the New Netherland colony, where legislation regulated the treatment of slaves by their masters. For example, slaves could be whipped only with the permission of colonial authorities.

1655　SLAVE SUES AND WINS FREEDOM

Elizabeth Key, a slave since birth, sued for her freedom. Born the daughter of an influential Virginia planter and a slave woman, Key had been sold to

Humphrey Higginson, and after a period of nine years, to Colonel John Mottron, a county justice of the peace. When Mottron died, Key sued for her freedom. Her suit was based on three arguments: (1) her father was a free man, and by common law she inherited her father's condition; (2) she had been baptized, the implication being that a Christian could not be a slave for life; and (3) she had been sold to another planter even after she had served nine years.

1657–1661 INCREASING NUMBER OF STATUTES AFFECT SLAVES AND SLAVE TRADE IN VIRGINIA

Beginning in this year, Virginia passed a series of statutes related to slaves and slave trade. One statute (1657) authorized the establishment of a militia to pursue runaway servants. Another (1659) reduced import duties on merchants bringing slaves into the colony. Servants who ran away with slaves became liable for the loss of any slaves (1660). The Virginia Assembly exempted Dutch ships from local duties when they brought in African slaves.

1660

POPULATION OVERVIEW

GENERAL POPULATION IN NORTH AMERICAN BRITISH COLONIES It is estimated that 75,058 persons resided in American colonies at this time. Two colonies, Virginia (27,020) and Massachusetts (20,082), made up

---

ADVANTAGES OF AFRICAN LABOR

From the standpoint of the colonial ruling class, Africans had at least four advantages over Native American and white immigrant labor. First, they were strong. In the words of one observer, "One African is worth four Indians." Second, they were cheap — to buy an Irish or an English servant for seven years cost the same as buying an African for life. Unlike the Irish, the supply of Africans seemed inexhaustible. Third, Africans were black — they could not blend into the dominant white population. Thus, they could more easily be recaptured if they escaped. Fourth, they had no government protection; they could appeal to no monarch nor to white public opinion. These advantages influenced the decisions that based a large segment of the colonial economy in the Americas on African slavery.

Slave ships arrived regularly along the African coast to pick up their cargo of humans. Captains of slavers inspected the Africans in order to select those who were most likely to survive the inhumane Middle Passage and bring a decent price in the American colonies.

about 63 percent of the total population. Maryland and Connecticut had the next largest populations, 8,426 and 7,980, respectively.

BLACKS IN NORTH AMERICAN BRITISH AND DUTCH COLONIES Approximately 2,920 Blacks were estimated to live in colonial America. The largest number, 950, resided in Virginia, followed by Maryland, 758; New Netherland, 600; and Massachusetts, 422. The number of Blacks in Virginia and Maryland more than doubled between 1650 and 1660. Other colonies had fewer than 50 Blacks.

STATUS OF BLACK SERVANTS AND WHITE SERVANTS DETERMINED IN MARYLAND AND VIRGINIA
Maryland and Virginia colonies passed laws concerning Black and white servants. White servants could buy their freedom, but Black servants became slaves.

TAX ON SLAVES REGULATED IN VIRGINIA
On **MARCH 13**, Virginia passed a statute limiting taxes on the sale of slaves. It is considered by many historians to be the first law defining African slaves as chattel.

"BREAKING IN" SLAVES IN THE WEST INDIES

During the early years of the slave trade, most slaves who survived their voyage from Africa were sold in the West Indies. Here, they were trained to work and to obey masters. This process, which lasted three to four years, was called a "breaking-in" period. Harsh and cruel punishments, including frequent floggings, were used against Africans who resisted. Slaves worked from sunup to sundown, cutting, crushing, and boiling sugar cane. Women and men were whipped if they did not work fast enough. Slaves who were very resistant might even be killed, since it was easier and cheaper to replace a slave than to persist in trying to train one. Slaves were fed an inadequate diet — usually poor quality fish and a little grain, often cornmeal. It has been estimated that almost one-third of the slaves died during the breaking-in process. After the slaves were "broken," many were resold to British, Spanish, and Portuguese colonies throughout the Americas.

The breaking-in process was dismantled as the huge demand for labor in the southern colonies required direct importation of slaves into these areas.

Many slaveholders were so conditioned by the institution of slavery that they frequently and harshly flogged their slaves, and many of them justified this abusive behavior with Christian principles. A paddle was sometimes used, but whips, with a lead ball sewed to the end, were most often used in the field. Thus, a flogging and a whipping differed; a whipping was more severe and was usually employed to restrain or alter the behavior of particularly unruly slaves.

1661 COUPLE PETITION FOR FREEDOM IN NEW AMSTERDAM

A slave couple petitioned the government in New Amsterdam for the freedom of their son. Peter Stuyvesant granted the petition. When the British secured control of the colony in 1664, however, the status of Black servants was amended to perpetual slavery.

1662 ROYAL COMPANY OF ADVENTURERS FORMED

The Royal Company of Adventurers was chartered by King Charles II for the importation of African slaves — an indication of the British Crown's expectation that slaves would become the labor force of the future. The fact that slaves already accounted for roughly one-quarter of the servant population in the colonies, and that this proportion was increasing, caused the Crown to become involved in the slave trade. This occurrence coincided with the first laws on perpetual servitude. The formation of the Royal Company provided for "profitable enterprises" in slave trade and slavery.

VIRGINIA DECLARES STATUS OF MOTHER DETERMINES CONDITION OF CHILD

The Virginia House of Burgesses reversed the English common-law precedent that children took on the status of their fathers. In light of the increase in the number of children born of Black mothers and white fathers, Virginia passed legislation providing that children would take on the status of their mothers — bond or free. Therefore, children born of African slave women and free white men would be enslaved.

1663 BONUS OFFERED FOR SLAVE PURCHASE IN CAROLINA

Proprietors in the Carolina colony offered a bonus of twenty-five acres of land for every male African slave purchased by settlers and ten acres for every female African slave.

SLAVE CONSPIRACY REPORTED IN VIRGINIA

On **SEPTEMBER 13**, the first recorded major conspiracy of persons in servitude in colonial America occurred in Gloucester County, Virginia. The plot of white servants and Black slaves to escape from their masters was betrayed by one or more indentured servants.

1664 INTERRACIAL MARRIAGES BANNED IN MARYLAND

On **SEPTEMBER 20**, Maryland became the first colony to pass legislation prohibiting marriage between Black men and white women. The preamble of the statute mentions that "divers freeborn English women, forgetful of their free condition, and to the disgrace of our nation, do intermarry with Negro slaves." Children of such marriages were to be considered slaves.

◈ Similar laws were passed in Virginia, in 1691; Massachusetts, in 1705; North Carolina, in 1715; South Carolina, in 1717; Delaware, in 1721; and Pennsylvania, in 1725.

SLAVERY RECOGNIZED AS LEGAL IN NEW YORK

Colonists in New York (which then included present-day New Jersey) passed legislation condoning slavery. In the New Jersey area, English land proprietors not only authorized slavery but strongly encouraged it by offering a headright of up to sixty acres to any settler who brought a slave into the colony. By the end of the century, Perth Amboy had become one of the leading ports of entry for slaves en route to colonies in the North.

SLAVERY RECOGNIZED AS LEGAL IN MARYLAND

In **SEPTEMBER**, the Maryland colony passed a law that recognized slavery as legal. A law passed the previous year had recognized that Black service was usually perpetual. The law of 1664, however, clearly decreed that all Blacks currently in Maryland and all who would arrive later would be considered slaves. The law defined slavery in the following manner:

Be it enacted by the Right Honorable the Lord Proprietary by the advise and consent of the upper and lower house of this present Generall Assembly, that all Negroes or other slaves already within the province, and all Negroes and other slaves to be hereafter imported into the province, shall serve *durante vita*. And all children born of any Negro or other slave shall be slaves as their fathers were, for the term of their lives. And forasmuch as divers freeborn English women, forgetful of their free condition and to the disgrace of our nation, do marry Negro slaves, by which also divers suits may arise touching the issue of such women, and a great damage befalls the masters of such Negroes for prevention whereof, for deterring such freeborn women from such shameful matches. Be it further enacted by the authority, advise, and consent aforesaid, that whatsoever freeborn woman shall marry any slave from and after the last day of this present Assembly shall serve the master of such slave during the life of her husband. And that all the issue of such freeborn women so married shall be slaves as their fathers were. And be it further enacted, that all the issues of English or other freeborn women that have already married Negroes shall serve the masters of their parents till they be thirty years of age and no longer.

1667 LEGISLATION TO REGULATE NEGROES ON THE BRITISH PLANTATION

The British passed legislation entitled "Act to Regulate the Negroes on the British Plantation" that restricted the movement and behavior of Blacks. According to the act, slaves could not leave a plantation without a pass and never leave on a Sunday; they could not arm themselves or possess horns or other signaling devices. For striking a Christian, punishment could include a whipping for the first offense and branding on the face for a second.

SLAVE SUES FOR FREEDOM BECAUSE HE IS CHRISTIAN

In **AUGUST**, Fernando, a slave for his lifetime, sued his slaveholder for his freedom in the lower Norfolk court, claiming he "was a Christian and had been several yeares in England." He further claimed that he should serve no longer than an English bondsman. He offered papers documenting his conversion to Christianity, but they were written in a language the court did not understand, so his suit was dismissed. Although there were appeals, the final disposition of his case is not known. Many Blacks who converted to Christianity felt they deserved a higher status and more rights than other slaves.

SLAVE LAW PASSED IN VIRGINIA

On **SEPTEMBER 23**, the House of Burgesses passed a law stipulating that Christian baptism did not alter a person's condition of bondage or freedom.

1669 VIRGINIA STATUTE ALLOWS KILLING OF SLAVE

Virginia's assembly passed a law, "An Act About the Casuall Killing of Slaves," that declared it was not a felony for a master or overseer to kill a slave who resisted punishment "since it cannot be presumed that prepense malice should induce any man to destroy his own estate."

SLAVERY RECOGNIZED AS LEGAL IN CAROLINA

The Fundamental Constitutions of Carolina accepted slavery as a legal institution. It stated, "Every Freeman of Carolina shall have absolute power and authority over Negro slaves of what opinion or Religion soever."

1670

POPULATION OVERVIEW

GENERAL POPULATION IN NORTH AMERICAN BRITISH COLONIES From 1660 to 1670, the population in colonial America increased by about 49 percent, from 75,058 to 111,935 total residents. Three colonies comprised the majority of residents: Virginia, 35,309; Massachusetts, 30,000; and Maryland, 13,309. Together, these colonies made up slightly more than 70 percent of the total population.

BLACKS IN NORTH AMERICAN BRITISH COLONIES Approximately 4,535 Blacks lived in colonial America, up 55 percent over the previous decade. The largest concentrations of Blacks were still in Virginia, with a total of 2,000, and Maryland, with 1,190. Virginia had more than doubled its Black population since 1660, and Maryland's increased by 57 percent. Although the Black population grew faster in other colonies, their overall Black populations were considerably smaller. For example, northern Carolina's Black population grew from only 20 in 1660 to 150 in 1670, a 650 percent increase over the decade, and Rhode Island's Black population increased from 65 to 115, a 77 percent increase.

POPULATION IN CHARLESTON, CAROLINA The town of Charleston, Carolina, had a population of roughly 400, many of whom were Blacks from Barbados.

For almost the first 30 years of its existence, southern Carolina was a "child of Barbados," an English island in the Caribbean. It received its first settlers from the island, its economy was closely tied to exporting provisions there, and its lifestyle mirrored that of Barbadian planters. When overcrowding occurred on the island in 1650, many planters, freed servants, and slaves of African descent migrated to other English colonies. In the Carolina colony, a mix of these immigrants settled on the Ashley River near Charleston.

FRANCE ALLOWS SLAVERY IN COLONIES

A royal order permitted slavery in the French colonies. Within the next three years, ten thousand slaves were shipped to the French Caribbean islands.

LAND GRANTS OFFERED TO SLAVE OWNERS IN CAROLINA

Almost from the start, southern Carolina's economy and society involved slaves. Proprietors granted land to all who brought slaves into the colony. One such declaration stated:

To the Owner of every Negro-Man or Slave, brought thither to settle within the first year, twenty acres; and for every Woman-Negro or Slave, ten acres of Land; and all Men-Negro's or slaves after that time, and within the first five years, ten acres, and for every Woman-Negro or slave, five acres.

CHRISTIAN BLACKS NOT CONSIDERED LIFELONG SLAVES IN VIRGINIA

On **OCTOBER 13**, Virginia passed legislation that disallowed lifelong servitude for any Black person who had become a Christian before arriving in the colony. The law was passed to address the difficult moral issue raised as Christians enslaved other Christians.

The law further divided all non-Christian servants into two groups: those coming by sea who "shall be slaves for their lives," and those coming by land who were to serve indentured terms. Thus, Africans, who virtually all arrived by sea, could be enslaved, but Native Americans could not.

1671 IN MARYLAND SLAVE STATUS NOT AFFECTED BY CONVERTING TO CHRISTIANITY

In the Maryland colony, an act was passed declaring that a slave's conversion to Christianity did not affect his slave status.

1672 VIRGINIA IMPOSES BOUNTY ON FUGITIVE SLAVES

A new law put a bounty on the heads of "maroons," fugitive slaves who settled in mountains, swamps, and forests of the southern colonies.

BRITISH CROWN GRANTS SLAVING CHARTER

On **SEPTEMBER 27**, the Royal African Company, a new corporation, was granted an exclusive slaving charter by the English to compete with the Dutch and the French. The company covered an area from the coast of Morocco to the Cape of Good Hope. Although the business plan stipulated that slaves had to be in good health, between the ages of twelve and forty, and sold for fifteen pounds in Barbados and eighteen pounds in Virginia, the business plan also called for satisfying the investors (who gave more than one hundred thousand dollars to finance the venture), a priority that often outweighed other considerations.

1673 BLACK JOINS EXPEDITION INTO TENNESSEE

Gabriel Arthur (1775–1800), a Black indentured servant, and nine Native Americans accompanied James Needham on a four-month expedition into the area of present-day Tennessee. They were the first to explore this region.

INDENTURED SERVANT SUES FOR FREEDOM

When Andrew Moore of Virginia, a Black person whose term of indenture was five years, was not freed after the expiration of his contract, he petitioned the court for relief. The General Court ordered the following:

That the Said Moore bee free from his said master, and that the Said Mr. Light pay him Corne and Clothes according to the Custome of the Country and four hundred pounds tobac and Caske for his service done him Since he was free, and pay costs.

1680

POPULATION OVERVIEW

GENERAL POPULATION IN NORTH AMERICAN BRITISH COLONIES As many as 151,507 persons lived in the American colonies in 1680. Approximately 55 percent of all residents lived in Virginia (43,596) and Massachusetts (39,752). Two other colonies had relatively large populations: Maryland (17,904) and Connecticut (17,246). All other colonies had fewer than 10,000 residents.

Between 1670 and 1680, the largest absolute population increase occurred in Massachusetts, where more than 9,700 residents were added. Virginia gained an additional 8,300 residents. Other large increases were noted for Maryland (4,678), Connecticut (4,638), and New York (4,076).

BLACKS IN NORTH AMERICAN BRITISH COLONIES In 1680, an estimated 6,971 Blacks resided in the American colonies. Their distribution among the colonies was quite different than that of the general population. A large proportion of Blacks (43 percent; 3,000 residents) lived in Virginia. Maryland and New York followed with 1,611 (23 percent) and 1,200 (17 percent), respectively. No other colony was thought to have more than 210 Blacks at the time.

As the next decade progressed, the Black population became more geographically dispersed. Although Virginia, New York, and Maryland received the largest increases in Blacks over the decade — 1,000, 510, and 421, respectively — percentage increases of Blacks in other parts of the colonies were considerable. For example, southern Carolina's Black population grew from 30 to 200, a 566 percent increase, and New Jersey (then a part of New York) experienced a 233 percent increase when its Black population jumped from 60 to 200. Black residents increased in all American colonies.

1681 STATUS OF CHILDREN DETERMINED IN MARYLAND

In the Maryland colony, a law was passed providing that children born of white servant women and Black men were free.

1682 MOVEMENTS OF SLAVES RESTRICTED IN NEW YORK

The General Court in New York City forbade slaves to leave their owners' property without written permission or to buy or sell goods. Up to this time, slaves in New York seem to have been governed by the same judicial processes and criminal code that held for whites.

SLAVE LAW PASSED IN VIRGINIA

On **NOVEMBER 10**, Virginia passed a law that prohibited slaves from possessing weapons, leaving their owners' plantations without permission, or lifting a hand against a white person, even in self-defense. The law stipulated that runaway slaves refusing to surrender might be killed without penalty. (Later, Virginia's slave code was in essence copied by Maryland, Delaware, and North Carolina.) Further, the Virginia slave law of 1670 was also repealed. Thus, the conversion of slaves to Christianity before arriving in the colony no longer kept them from lifelong servitude.

1684 SLAVES IMPORTED INTO PHILADELPHIA

In this year, 150 Africans were imported to work with Philadelphia Quakers in clearing trees and erecting houses. By 1700, approximately one in every fourteen Philadelphia families owned slaves. Although no slaves resided in the colony when William Penn arrived (168), he eventually used them on his own estate. In fact, Philadelphia ship owners brought slaves as part of the return cargo from the Caribbean. Although the Quakers in Pennsylvania were the first religious group to denounce the slave trade and slavery, it became a thriving business in Pennsylvania.

1688 QUAKERS PASS ANTISLAVERY RESOLUTION IN PENNSYLVANIA

On **FEBRUARY 18**, Mennonites (Quakers) in Germantown, Pennsylvania (a small town near Philadelphia), adopted the first formal antislavery resolution in American history. The Society of Friends called slavery the "traffic of mensbody." Their main opposition to slavery was a matter of "liberty of body," which they claimed to be due to all people except those who have done evil.

1690

POPULATION OVERVIEW

GENERAL POPULATION IN NORTH AMERICAN BRITISH COLONIES According to estimates of the Bureau of the Census, about 210,372 persons lived in the American colonies at this time. The largest colonies were Virginia (53,346) and Massachusetts (49,504). Medium-sized colonies (between 10,000 and 25,000 residents) included Maryland, Connecticut, New York, and Pennsylvania.

Over the previous decade, the American colonies experienced a population growth rate of about 39 percent. Although the large colonies continued to have the largest absolute population increases, their rates of growth were rather low, ranging from 21 percent for Virginia to 25 percent for Massachusetts and 34 percent for Maryland. The highest growth rates occurred in the smaller colonies, an indication of population dispersal. In some of the smaller colonies such as New Hampshire, New Jersey, Pennsylvania, and southern Carolina, the population had more than doubled over the previous decade.

BLACKS IN NORTH AMERICAN BRITISH COLONIES Blacks in the colonies numbered about 16,729, or about 8 percent of all colonial residents — up from 6,971 a decade earlier and an increase of more than 140 percent. In contrast to the widespread dispersion of the general population among the colonies, the Black population was rapidly concentrating in the South. For example, Virginia's share of all Blacks in the colonies increased from 43 percent in 1680 to 56 percent in 1690. The number of Blacks in the colony increased from 3,000 to 9,345 over the same period, a 211 percent increase. Southern Carolina's Black population soared from 200 in 1680 to about 1,500 in 1690, a 650 percent increase. Southern colonies increased their share of the Black population over the previous decade from 73 percent to 80 percent.

ECONOMIC CONDITIONS OVERVIEW

PARLIAMENT REVOKES ROYAL AFRICAN COMPANY'S MONOPOLY The demand for slaves in the British colonies was so great in the 1690s that the Royal African Company was unable to satisfy the demand. Parliament responded to the colonies' demands and revoked the company's monopoly on the African coast in 1698. This action opened the slave trade to independent merchants and traders. Fueled by the potential profits from slavery, the number of slave-trading enterprises grew. Because many slavers directed their efforts toward securing slaves from Africa, the annual flow of white servants to many colonies soon dropped sharply, and by 1710, the flow had decreased to a negligible level.

SOCIAL CONDITIONS OVERVIEW

SLAVE CODES ENACTED IN NEW ENGLAND Slave codes, some specific and some general, came into force in the New England colonies. For example, in Massachusetts, Rhode Island, and Connecticut, slaves needed written permission to leave their owners' property. Slaves and free white persons were treated similarly in cases involving the death penalty, and in Massachusetts and Connecticut, slaves and whites were governed by the same courts and procedures. Massachusetts recognized the right of slaves to own property and to sue their masters if it was taken away. No colony in New England denied the right of owners to manumit (free) their slaves, although many imposed some restrictions on manumission. In all colonies, slaves who struck a white person were severely penalized. The sale of alcoholic beverages to slaves was prohibited, as was trading with slaves and harboring runaways.

1691 MARRIAGE BETWEEN BLACKS AND WHITES PROHIBITED IN VIRGINIA

Although penalties had been previously imposed for intermarriage, this was one of the first laws in Virginia that explicitly restricted intermarriage. Whippings and other penalties were imposed for fornication. The Virginia legislature passed a law stating that any free Englishwoman who had a child by a Black or a mulatto would be fined the sum of fifteen pounds sterling. If she defaulted, she would be taken into possession of the church warden and bound into service for five years. Illegitimate children were to be bound out as servants until they reached the age of thirty. Women already in servitude were penalized with an additional five years of service.

VIRGINIA ACTS TO FORCE BLACK FREEDMEN OUT

Virginia passed a law that prohibited any slave owner from freeing Black slaves without paying for their travel out of the colony.

1692 MORE SLAVE LAWS ENACTED IN VIRGINIA

In this year, Virginia passed legislation modifying a 1682 law allowing sheriffs to arrest runaway slaves. The sheriff was permitted to shoot or kill slaves if they resisted or ran away. A new law imposed banishment from the colony of any free white man or woman who married a Black, a mulatto, or a Native American. Later, the penalty was changed to six months' imprisonment and a fine of ten pounds. Slaves could not keep horses, cattle, or hogs. Slaves charged with a capital offense were to be tried without a jury and could be convicted on the testimony of two witnesses under oath. Maryland, Delaware, and North Carolina eventually copied the Virginia laws of 1682 and 1692.

SLAVE WOMAN AMONG THOSE ACCUSED OF BEING WITCHES IN SALEM, MASSACHUSETTS

After several young girls began to behave strangely, Tituba, a West Indian slave woman, and a number of white men and women were accused and tried for being witches. According to some accounts, Tituba initially confessed to being a witch but later admitted that she had been beaten until she confessed. Tituba was jailed for more than a year but was finally sold to pay her jail fees. A year later, the witch hysteria finally abated when the wives of high officials were accused. Judge Samuel Sewell, one of the best-known judges in the trials, later repented his part in the death of the nineteen men and women hanged as witches.

1693 MOVEMENTS OF BLACKS RESTRICTED IN PHILADELPHIA

Philadelphia passed an ordinance ordering the constable to arrest all Blacks "gadding about" on the first day of the week and to imprison them until the next morning. Those arrested were also to receive thirty-nine lashes.

1697 CONDITIONS DETERIORATE FOR SLAVES IN HISPANIOLA

Spain gave up half of the island of Hispaniola to France. French sugar planters soon occupied the land, with the intention of making a quick fortune and then returning to France. They proved to be especially harsh and cruel slave owners. Since they viewed themselves as temporary residents, the planters cared nothing for the local population. They grew increasingly fearful as Black slaves increased, outnumbering whites by twenty to one. Slave codes that prohibited slaves from

INDENTURED SERVANT STATUS GROWS UNCERTAIN FOR BLACKS

It is believed that the first Blacks to arrive in Jamestown, Virginia, in 1619, were indentured servants. By 1648, Black and white indentured servants worked for a specified number of years and were then freed. Most whites worked from four to seven years. Blacks, however, often served longer terms. For example, a Massachusetts court recorded that Jno. G. Hamander, a Black man, was indentured for ten years.

> Be it thought fitt & assented unto by Mr. Steph. Charlton in Court that Jno. G. Hamander Negro, his servant, shall from ye date hereof (1648) serve ye sd Mr. Charlton (his heyers or assns.) until ye last days of November wh shall be in ye year of our Lord . . . one thousand six hundred Fifty & eight and then ye sd Negro is to bee a free man.

Although it was understood that those who bought the services of indentured persons were expected to free them when the contract expired, in fact, some Blacks were held beyond their contracts.

By 1652, indentured servants formed a distinct social class in colonial society. Some laws protected the rights of those who owned the contracts. For example, runaway servants were punished by having extra time added to their terms of service. Other laws protected servants from physical abuse and abuse of contract. The courts could award damages to servants if they were worked beyond their contracted time. Generally, there were "freedom dues" that stipulated the amount of money, clothes, land, and other property that servants would receive when their service contracts expired.

The indentured servant population grew over the years. In fact, from the mid-1600s and into the eighteenth century, many Black and white orphans and children born out of wedlock were routinely indentured until they reached twenty-four or thirty years of age. The following is such a contract:

> This indenture witnesseth yt I Capt. Francis Pott have taken to service two Daughtgers of my negro Emanuell Dregis to serve & bee to me my heyers Exors. Adms. or Assigns. The one whose name is Elizabeth is to serve thirteene years whch will be compleat & ended in ye first part of March in ye yeare of our Lord God one thousand six hundred Fifty & eight . . . And ye other child whose name is Jane Dregis (being about one yeare old) is to serve ye said Capt. Pott as aforesaid untill she arrive to ye age of thirty years old wh will be compleate & ended . . . [May, 1674], And I ye said Francis Pott doe promise to give them sufficient meate, drinke, Apparel & Lodging and to use my best endeavor to bring them up in ye fear of God and in ye knowledge of our Saviour Christ Jesus. And I doe further testify yt the Eldest daughter was given to my negro by one who brought her upp by ye space of eight years and ye younger he bought and paid for to Capt. Robert Shephard (as maye bee made appear). In witness whereoff have hereunto sett my hands & seale in ye 27th of May one thousand six hundred forty & five.
>
> *Mr. Francis Pott.*
> *Witness the names of*
> *Thom. P. Powell & John Pott.*

meeting, carrying arms, striking or insulting whites, or moving from a plantation were imposed. Thousands of slaves ran away to escape such wretched treatment. Conditions were ripe for revolt.

1699–1845 MANY SLAVE MUTINIES AT SEA

As many as fifty-five slave mutinies at sea took place between 1699 and 1845. One of the most noteworthy took place aboard the *Amistad.* (See 1839.)

1700

POPULATION OVERVIEW

GENERAL POPULATION IN NORTH AMERICAN BRITISH COLONIES The colonial population, numbering about 250,888, continued to grow, but not always steadily. In 1699, the first reported yellow fever epidemic killed about one-sixth of the population in Philadelphia. Between 1655 and 1699, some 4,500 convicts arrived from England. Although cities were growing,

RICE REVOLUTION IN SOUTH CAROLINA

In 1694, rice, introduced from Madagascar, became commercially successful in South Carolina. Slaves from Madagascar and other rice-growing areas of Africa, such as the Gambia River valley, brought about the adoption of this crop in the low-lying areas where the climate and conditions were suitable for production.

Rice soon revolutionized South Carolina's agriculture, which had previously experimented unsuccessfully with almost every major cash crop — cotton, silk, tobacco, indigo, sugar cane, and ginger — and had attempted to produce wine. In 1700, South Carolina had one of the most diversified colonial economies, but from that time on, a single crop — rice — increasingly dominated the economy. The colony exported about 100,000 pounds of rice in 1700, 1.5 million pounds in 1710, 6 million pounds in 1720, and 20 million pounds in 1730. Much of the colony's rice was produced in the low country where slaves were heavily concentrated. It is estimated that by 1761, rice accounted for 60 percent of all exports of the region. By the eve of the American Revolution, South Carolina and Georgia (the primary producers) exported more than 65 million pounds annually.

Rice, like tobacco, is a labor-intensive crop. In order to maximize profits and the use of labor, rice was grown by using a "task system." Gangs of slaves cleared swampland of cypress, gum trees, and undergrowth. Then, an outside bank or levee was constructed around the field, made by piling up mud and dirt obtained by digging a ditch about five feet deep and wide; the ditch later served as a canal for the flatboats used during harvesting. Every effort was made to keep saltwater out of the fields during floods because it would damage the soil inside the levee. Fields ranging from ten to twenty acres were subdivided into one-acre plots, to ensure that every acre was flooded and drained properly. A force of thirty to forty laborers under the direction of a slave driver was used to cultivate rice fields ranging in size from 150 to 200 acres.

even doubling between 1690 and 1700, most colonists lived in small towns and on farms. Virginia and Massachusetts remained the largest colonies, with 58,560 and 55,941 residents, respectively.

BLACKS IN NORTH AMERICAN BRITISH COLONIES Blacks in the colonies numbered about 27,817, or about 11 percent of the total colonial population of about 250,888. They continued to be imported into the colonies in large numbers. In Charleston, South Carolina, the number of Blacks had doubled from about 1,000 in 1690. In other cities, the number of Blacks grew rapidly as well. Among the colonies, Virginia had the largest number, with 16,390 Blacks, or about 59 percent of all Blacks in the colonies. Of the 11,088 Blacks added to the colonies between 1690 and 1700, Virginia accounted for 7,045, or almost 64 percent of the increase.

BLACKS IN NEW ENGLAND COLONIES About 1,680 Blacks lived in the New England colonies, out of a population of approximately 93,000. The port of Boston was the hub of American slave trading. Ships filled with food and other products left Boston for the West Indies, where the goods were traded for rum, which was then shipped to Africa to be traded for slaves. Slaves were transported back to the West Indies, and the ships returned to Boston.

NATIVE AMERICANS BECOME SLAVE OWNERS

During the latter part of the 1700s, the Native American peoples of the southeast (Cherokee, Choctaw, Chickasaw, Creek, and Seminole) became slave owners. The Cherokees held the largest number of slaves. Before their removal to Indian Territory (now Oklahoma), the Cherokees used Black slaves on their farms and plantations in Tennessee and Georgia.

In the years prior to the Civil War, abolitionists were particularly active among Native American peoples, teaching Christianity and consequently influencing Native Americans to free their slaves. Because of language barriers and sometimes geographical isolation, abolitionists found it difficult to effect change among Native Americans. It is unlikely that we will ever know the number of Blacks among Native American tribes, particularly since Blacks frequently went into hiding when census takers appeared.

Blacks who lived among Native Americans as slaves had much more freedom than those living among white slave owners. In fact, some Blacks owned land, and several occupied important positions as warriors, political leaders, and even interpreters for the Native Americans in their negotia-

Rice growing involved a number of labor-intensive steps, each requiring large numbers of slaves. The steps are identified in this sketch by James E. Taylor, showing rice culture on Cape Fear River, North Carolina.

tions with the U.S. government. Former slaves were numerous among the Seminoles and frequently intermarried with them. Native Americans, in general, viewed ancestry differently than whites. A child born of an Indian mother and a Black father might be considered Indian; if the father was Indian and the mother Black, the child most likely would be considered "half-Black and half-Indian." In contrast, no matter what the relationship of a white and a Black, whites considered any offspring to be Black (a view still generally held in this country).

PENNSYLVANIA IMPOSES DIFFERENTIAL PENALTIES FOR SLAVES
Pennsylvania had relatively few slaves, and prior to 1700, their legal status was uncertain. In this year,

however, slaves were distinguished as a separate group, and laws were passed that applied only to them. For example, slaves could not be tried in a regular court, but rather by two justices of the peace and six freeholders; slaves could be put to death for murder, burglary, and rape, and whipped for robbing and stealing.

SLAVE-TRADING PATTERNS EMERGE
A number of trading arrangements, including variations of the triangular trade, emerged in the 1700s. A slave ship would leave Liverpool, England, for the coast of Africa with a cargo of textiles, arms, and other smaller items, which were used to purchase Africans. The ship would then sail to Barbados or Jamaica, where it would dispose of the slaves in

SLAVE TRADING BECOMES AN INTERNATIONAL BUSINESS

By the year 1700, slaves were being imported into the Virginia colony at the rate of one thousand per year. Although many companies participated in slave trading in the Americas, a few made a significant mark in this commercial activity. These included the Dutch West Indies Company and the West Indies Company in France, which was succeeded by the Senegal Company. The Guinea Company received the *asiento* for supplying slaves to the Spanish colonies in 1701, and the South Seas Company became an important slave trader when it acquired the *asiento* after the Peace of Utrecht in 1713. In England, the Royal African Company held a monopoly on the slave trade until 1698. Although Danish, Swedish, and Prussian slave-trading companies did a successful business, they did not supply the colonies with large numbers of slaves. In most cases, each company supplied slaves to the American colonies it possessed at the time. Frequently, however, slaves supplied to one colony had to be supplemented by legally or illegally purchased slaves from other countries. As such, the commercial slave-trading business became international in scope, connecting Europe, Africa, South America, the Caribbean, and North America.

It is said that the slave trade was the most profitable enterprise in the world during the eighteenth century. Many wealthy families of the time owed their fortunes to this lucrative business. Even today, some wealthy families can trace their inherited fortunes directly to slave trading and slave ownership.

The slave trade was extremely competitive throughout the 1700s, as the Portuguese, Spanish, Dutch, and British competed for dominance. Slaves were gathered in staging areas such as the Shaka market, shown here, until there were enough to fill a cargo ship.

This picture of a coffle illustrates the enslavement and brutal treatment of prisoners taken in one of many wars among African tribes. Slave traders encouraged these wars to increase the number of Africans kidnapped or captured for sale into slavery. Africans who violated tribal laws were also sometimes sold into slavery.

exchange for sugar to be sold in England. It was thus possible for the slave ship to make three different profits on the original investment. A general rule emerged that successful delivery of one-third of the slave cargo was enough to cover the total cost of the expedition and net a 200 to 300 percent profit. Although the most well known triangular trade is said to have involved trading rum for Africans, there were many other products traded for slaves, including fish, trinkets, and so on.

SEWELL DENOUNCES SLAVERY
On **JUNE 24**, Judge Samuel Sewell of Massachusetts became one of the first public officials to "outrightly" denounce slavery. On this day, he published a three-page statement, entitled *The Selling of Joseph,* in which he drew a parallel between slavery and the Old Testament story of Joseph, whose brothers sold him into slavery for twenty pieces of silver. Sewell courageously handed out copies himself. It be-

came the first antislavery tract distributed in the colonies.

1701 SOCIETY FOR THE PROPAGATION OF THE GOSPEL FOUNDED
The Society for the Propagation of the Gospel in Foreign Parts was chartered by the English Crown as a vehicle to educate slaves and Native Americans.

The society operated in Virginia, Maryland, North Carolina, Pennsylvania, and New Jersey. In New England, the education of slaves and servants was largely the obligation of the master.

1702 SLAVE CODES PASSED IN NEW YORK
New York passed a law that imposed restraints on slaves, stipulating that no more than three slaves could assemble without the consent of their owners, and that a slave striking a free person could be confined for fourteen days and whipped. Slave owners were given broad discretion in punishing their slaves.

1703 POPULATION OF SLAVES IN NEW YORK CITY

According to a census, as many as 43 percent of all whites in New York City owned one or two slaves.

1704 SCHOOL FOR SLAVES OPENS IN NEW YORK CITY

One of the first schools in the colonies to enroll Black slaves was opened in New York City by Elias Neau, a Frenchman. It was called the Catechism School for Negroes and was associated with Trinity Church.

1705 DEATH PENALTY FOR RUNAWAY SLAVES IMPOSED IN NEW YORK

New York passed a law that prescribed the death penalty for all slaves caught beyond a line forty miles north of Albany.

VIRGINIA ENACTS SLAVE CODE

On **OCTOBER 23**, all existing laws dealing with Blacks were collapsed into a slave code called "Act Concerning Servants and Slaves." It defined "who shall be slaves" and clearly stipulated that servants "who could not make due proof of their being free in England, or any other Christian country, were to be accounted slaves." Such language was designed to limit slavery only to Blacks. The legislation also restricted the movement of Blacks within the colony, prohibited intermarriage, and disallowed Black persons from holding a civil or military office. Under this law, slaves were attached to the soil, so that the heir to a plantation was entitled to purchase the inherited interests of others in the slaves. Virginia declared that "all negro, mulatto, and Indian slaves in all courts of jurdicature, and other places, within this dominion, shall be held, taken, and adjudged to be real estate."

STATUS OF FREE BLACKS DETERIORATES

Virginia passed a law that placed legal restrictions on the purchase of white servants by free Blacks. The statute restricted Black ownership of white Christian servants and declared automatically free any white Christian servant whose master married a Black. This act reinforced a previous 1670 statute that stated the same but did not restrict Blacks from buying "any of their owne nation."

1706 BLACKS PERMITTED TO SERVE IN NORTH CAROLINA MILITIA

Although Black slaves generally had far more restrictions on their behavior than free Blacks, North Carolina passed legislation specifying that all free men were required to be organized into militia units, and that in the event of attacks by Native Americans, all able-bodied men, slave and free, were required to serve.

CHILDREN TO TAKE ON STATUS OF MOTHER IN NEW YORK

New York passed legislation requiring that the legal status for children be determined by the condition of the mother: "All and every, Negro, Indian, Mulatto or Mestee, shall follow ye state and condition of the mother and be esteemed reputed taken & adjudged a Slave & slaves to all intents and purposes whatsoever." A similar measure was in effect in North Carolina and Georgia, and it became the law in other parts of the South as well.

NEW YORK DENIES SLAVES RIGHTS AS WITNESSES

New York passed legislation denying slaves the right to testify in any case involving whites.

1707 LABOR COMPETITION BETWEEN SLAVES AND WHITES IN PENNSYLVANIA

In Philadelphia, white mechanics formed a guild to protest what they considered unfair labor competition from Black slaves.

1708 SLAVE REVOLT IN NEW YORK

During a slave revolt in Newton, Long Island, in New York, as many as seven whites were killed. Three slaves (two Black and one Native American) were hanged, and a Black woman slave was burned alive.

1710

POPULATION OVERVIEW

GENERAL POPULATION IN NORTH AMERICAN BRITISH COLONIES A total of 331,711 persons were estimated to be living in American colonies at this time. Virginia, Massachusetts, Maryland, and Connecticut were by far the most populous colonies, with 78,281, 62,390, 42,741, and 39,450 residents, respectively; they made up 222,862 total residents, or about two-thirds of all persons living in the American colonies.

BLACKS IN NORTH AMERICAN BRITISH COLONIES In this year, Blacks comprised an estimated 44,866 residents in the colonies. They were clearly more numerous in the southern colonies, where 36,563, or about 81.5 percent, of all colonial Blacks lived, a proportion equal to that of the previous decade. Although all colonies experienced a relatively large increase in their Black populations between 1700 and 1710, the proportional distribution of Blacks among the regions shifted minimally.

THE PLANTATION ECONOMY IS ESTABLISHED IN SOUTHERN COLONIES

The plantation was becoming a fixture of the landscape in the agricultural colonies. The plantation was a large farm on which, generally, a single cash crop was planted, tended, and harvested by slaves and/or indentured servants. The most frequently grown crops included cotton, tobacco, rice, indigo, and sugar cane. Most plantations specialized in one crop because of climatic conditions; soil quality; the skill, cost, and availability of workers; and the amount of profit to be made.

1711 SLAVE RAIDS IN SOUTH CAROLINA

A number of armed, escaped slaves joined together and raided various plantations and farms from their base in the undeveloped frontier. The raids caused so much fear that whites petitioned the governor to pass legislation offering a reward of fifty pounds for Sebastian, the slaves' Spanish Black leader, who was finally captured.

1712 NEW YORK DENIES SLAVES ACCESS TO COURTS

Slaves were denied access to ordinary courts and other judicial processes. The traditional guarantees of English law did not pertain to slaves, which was also the case in the southern colonies.

SOUTH CAROLINA ADOPTS MODEL SLAVE CODE

South Carolina introduced the basic slave code written by the English for Barbados in 1688. It was revised in 1739 and several times thereafter until slavery was abolished. The code became the model that other English colonies adopted and modified.

The slave code included the following provisions:

- Baptism in the Christian faith does not alter the status of the slave.
- Slaves are forbidden to leave the owner's property without written permission, unless accompanied by a white person.
- Every white person in the community is charged to chastise promptly any slave apprehended without such a pass to leave the owner's property;
- Any person enticing a slave to run away and any slave attempting to leave the province receives the death penalty as punishment.
- Any slave absconding or successfully evading capture for twenty days is to be publicly whipped for the first offense, branded with the letter *R* on the right cheek for the second offense, and lose one ear if absent thirty days for the third offense; and for the fourth offense, a male slave is to be castrated, a female slave is to be whipped, branded on the left cheek with the letter *R*, and lose her left ear.
- Owners refusing to abide by the slave code or inflict specified punishment are to be fined and forfeit ownership of their slave(s).
- The slave owner is obligated to pay the sum of four pounds for all fugitives returned to the owner dead or alive by the commander of any patrol company.
- Slave houses are to be searched every fortnight for weapons and stolen goods. For theft, the owner must punish the slave by whippings, and for each additional theft, the punishment escalates — loss of one ear, branding and nose slitting, and for the fourth offense, death.
- No owner shall be punished if a slave dies under punishment; intentional killing of a slave shall cost the owner a fifty-pound fine.
- No slave shall be allowed to work for pay; to plant corn, peas, or rice; to keep hogs, cattle, or horses;

Tobacco plantations used large numbers of slaves to perform the many jobs necessary to produce this crop — from preparing hotbeds for early cultivation of plants to rolling the hogsheads to market.

to own or operate a boat; to buy or sell; or to wear clothes finer than ordinary "Negro cloth."

The following revisions were made in 1739:

◈ No slave shall be taught to write, work on Sunday, or work more than fifteen hours per day in summer and fourteen hours in winter.
◈ Willful killing of a slave exacts a fine of 700 pounds, and "passion" killing, 350 pounds.
◈ The fine for concealing runaway slaves is one thousand dollars and a prison sentence of up to one year.
◈ A fine of one hundred dollars and six months in prison are imposed for employing any Black or slave as a clerk.
◈ A fine of one hundred dollars and six months in prison are imposed on anyone selling or giving alcoholic beverages to slaves.
◈ A fine of one hundred dollars and six months in prison are imposed for teaching a slave to read and write, and death is the penalty for circulating incendiary literature.
◈ Manumissions are forbidden except by deed, and after 1820, only by permission of the legislature. (Georgia required legislative approval after 1801.)

In 1770, Georgia adopted the South Carolina slave code, and then Florida adopted the Georgia code. Slavery in these colonies produced the most abusive aspects of the system — perhaps because in each of them, slaves outnumbered whites, and the fear of insurrections and conspiracies was great. Also, plantations in these colonies had the highest rate of owner absenteeism, and overseers thus exercised enormous abusive powers. Unhealthy conditions for slaves were frequently ignored because there was little contact between slaves and owners. Overall, the laws were severe, and the owner's power over the slave was boundless.

Other modifications of the South Carolina slave code of 1712 and 1739 were made, often in response to specific circumstances that emerged over time. The adoption of another restriction by one colony led others to adopt it as a preventive or precautionary statute. For example, the Georgia code of 1770 forbade more than six slaves from assembling at any place without the presence of a white person. It also imposed the death penalty for insurrection, rape, murder, poisoning, burglary, arson, and assault upon a white person. All southern colonies denied due process of law to slaves; Blacks did not enjoy the ben-

efits of jury trial, testimony of witnesses, or counsel. No court records were kept. These conditions allowed for hasty judgments based on insufficient evidence, effectively denying justice to the slave.

The slave codes in the tobacco colonies (Virginia, Maryland, Delaware, and North Carolina) were somewhat different from those modeled after the South Carolina code. Here the model was first implemented in Virginia (see 1667, 1682, 1692, and 1705).

SLAVE INSURRECTION IN NEW YORK CITY

On **APRIL 7 AND 8**, a slave revolt in New York City killed nine whites. On July 4, at least twelve slaves were executed (hanged or burned) for their participation, and six others committed suicide before they were brought to the gallows.

It is alleged that twenty-seven armed slaves had set fire to a white man's outhouse and that when whites attempted to extinguish the fire, they were shot by the slaves. The state militia was called out to capture the fleeing slaves. In response to this and other attempted revolts in New York, the Catechism School for Negroes at Trinity Church was closed because slave owners feared that the school's French founder, Elias Neau, was inciting Blacks to revolt or that education for Blacks in itself would inspire riots. More restrictive slave codes were enacted, and the number of slave crimes punishable by death increased. Conspiracy to murder was made a capital offense.

SLAVE IMPORTATION PROHIBITED IN PENNSYLVANIA

On **JUNE 7**, Pennsylvania passed a law preventing importation of slaves into the colony by imposing a duty of twenty pounds per head. The law was repealed in England. Another unsuccessful attempt to control the slave trade in Pennsylvania was made in 1715, when the assembly imposed a five-pound duty on each slave imported. This law was also disallowed in England.

1713 PHILADELPHIA QUAKERS FORM MANUMISSION PLAN

The Quakers developed a plan for the liberation of Africans and their restoration to their native lands in Africa. One of the plan's major components was religious instruction and fundamental education.

Protests by Quakers had seriously curtailed the slave market activity in Philadelphia and had led to legislative action in 1712 and 1715 that attempted to prohibit slave importation into the colony.

1715 POPULATION AND ECONOMIC CONDITIONS OVERVIEW

BLACKS IN NORTH AMERICAN BRITISH COLONIES The census of the colonial population revealed that Virginia had the largest slave population, followed by South Carolina. South Carolina, however, had the largest proportion of Blacks in the population, slightly more than 60 percent.

Slavery was adapted to meet the labor requirements of the plantation agricultural system. In the areas of present-day New Hampshire, Massachusetts, Rhode Island, Connecticut, Pennsylvania, and Delaware, where small-scale agricultural systems predominated, less than 6 percent of the population was Black. Most of the slaves here worked in the towns in domestic and other service occupations.

In the area of New York and New Jersey, the proportion of Blacks in the population was slightly higher: 13 percent and 7 percent, respectively. Although the Dutch government and Dutch East India Company, a major slave trader, had founded the New Netherland colony with the hope of developing large-scale plantations based on slave labor, the system had failed. Blacks here took on a variety of occupations — domestic service, mining, cooperage, carpentry, tanning, and shoemaking.

Maryland and Virginia had much larger proportions of Black residents (19 percent and 24 percent,

respectively). The number of Blacks in these two colonies was directly related to tobacco growing. At least 39 separate days of labor were required to produce 1,000 pounds of the crop. Labor was needed for tending the seedbeds, plowing, harrowing and hilling, cultivating, hoeing, topping, worming, harvesting, curing, sorting, and stripping. No other staple crop in this region was so labor-intensive. A planter would have to pay almost £6 to hire a paid worker for these tasks. In contrast, a slave cost about £3 per year to maintain, after the initial purchase.

Blacks made up one-third of North Carolina's population at this time. The colony's agriculture was more diversified than that of Maryland and Virginia, and included cultivation of rice, tobacco, and indigo — labor-intensive crops that used large numbers of slaves. Black slaves worked in both small-scale and plantation agricultural systems.

In contrast to North Carolina, South Carolina's economy was based on a single crop — rice — which had become a profitable plantation crop in the mid-1690s. Its cultivation required substantial labor, making slave labor essential.

SOCIAL CONDITIONS OVERVIEW

SLAVE RIGHTS IN NEW ENGLAND New Hampshire had only 150 slaves and 9,500 whites. Respective figures for Massachusetts were 2,000 and 94,000; for

Blacks were never safe, even when they had purchased or were given their freedom and could prove it. Because they had no access to the judicial system and few places to hide, many were kidnapped by slave catchers and sold back into slavery.

Rhode Island, 500 and 8,500; and for Connecticut, 1,500 and 46,000. Because slaves were so few in number and constituted such a small proportion of the total population, slave codes in New England were less harsh than those in the South but nevertheless had many similar provisions. In the New England colonies, slaves needed written permission to be away from their owners' property. Laws imposed penalties for harboring runaway slaves, trading with slaves, and selling alcoholic beverages to them. Slaves in general could get little justice in the courts, although the situation varied among the colonies.

Court procedures were similar for slaves and whites in the region except in Rhode Island. In Massachusetts and Connecticut, whippings were imposed for theft, striking a white person, profanity, and stealing; but in Rhode Island, theft brought a whipping and/or banishment. In New Hampshire, slave owners could be liable to grand jury investigation for cruelly treating their slaves. Massachusetts granted marriage rights and placed relationships among slaves on the same basis as for free whites. In essence, a master here could not deny the right of marriage to a slave. Also in Massachusetts, slaves had the right to own property and to sue their masters if it was taken away. All colonies provided the right of manumission, but restrictions on this applied everywhere except in New Hampshire. In most cases, the master had to post security of fifty pounds to ensure that the slave would not become a public charge. In 1728, Rhode Island raised the amount to one hundred pounds, and to as much as one thousand pounds in 1755. In New York in 1712, the owner was required to pay twenty pounds annually to a manumitted slave. The law was changed in 1717 to require only security. New Jersey allowed manumission in 1769, but required surety of two hundred pounds; Pennsylvania in 1726 required an amount equal to thirty pounds.

MARYLAND SHERIFFS ENCOURAGED TO ARREST RUNAWAYS

Maryland passed legislation giving sheriffs unrestrained power over the imprisonment of suspected "runaway slaves and the fees associated with their capture and disposition." In the act passed during the May session of this year, it was declared:

> That, &c. every sheriff that now hath, or hereafter shall have, committed into his custody any runaway servants or slaves, after one month's notice given to

the master or owner thereof of their being in his custody, if living in this province, or two months' notice if living in any of the neighboring provinces, if such master or owner of such servants or slaves do not appear within the time limit as aforesaid, and pay or secure to be paid all such imprisonment fees due to each sheriff from the time of the commitment of such servant or slaves, and also such other charges as have accrued or become due to any person for taking up such runaway servants or slaves, such sheriff is hereby authorized and required (such time limited as aforesaid being expired) immediately to give public notice to all persons, by setting up notes at the church and courthouse doors of the county where such servant or slave is in custody, of the time and place for sale of such servants or slaves, by him to be appointed, not less than ten days after such time limited as aforesaid being expired, and at such time and place by him appointed as aforesaid, to proceed to sell and dispose of such servant or slave to the highest bidder, and out of the money or tobacco which such servant or slave is sold for to pay himself all such imprisonment fees as are his just due for the time he has kept such servant or slave in his custody, and also to pay such other charges, fees or reward as has become due to any person for taking up such runaway servant or slave; and after such payment made, if any residue shall remain of the money or tobacco, such servant or slave was sold for, such sheriff shall only be accountable to the master or owner of such servant or slave for such residue or remainder as aforesaid, and not otherwise.

A lien on the body of the prisoner guaranteed the reward to the capturer and imprisonment fees to the sheriff. A large number of sheriffs saw that it was in their best interest to apprehend and imprison many "colored persons who might be detained for a longer period than six months, whether the person [is] free or slave." If the prison term was prolonged, the fees swelled to nearly the value of the prisoner. When that occurred, the master might be unable or unwilling to redeem the slave. In this instance, the authorized sheriff's sale could easily work to the advantage of an associate working in collusion with the sheriff. Seventy-five years later, on December 22, 1792, the Maryland General Assembly passed an act "to restrain the ill-practices of sheriffs, and to direct their conduct respecting runaways."

SEPARATE MEETINGHOUSES FOR SLAVES FORBIDDEN

In North Carolina, slaves were forbidden to have separate religious meetinghouses.

1716 FIRST SLAVES REACH FRENCH LOUISIANA

On **JUNE 6**, several ships owned by the Company of the West unloaded the first slaves in the French territory of Louisiana. The introduction of labor-intensive crops, particularly sugar and cotton, soon made slaves indispensable to the local economy.

1717 INTERMARRIAGE RESTRICTED IN MARYLAND

Maryland adopted the following provisions: "If any free negro or mulatto intermarry with any white woman, or if any white man shall intermarry with any negro or mulatto woman, such negro or mulatto shall become a slave during life, except mulattoes born of white women, who, &c. shall become servants for seven years."

MARYLAND IMPOSES WHIPPING AS PUNISHMENT FOR SLAVES

The assembly of Maryland declared that "any negro, Indian, or mulatto slave" charged with misdemeanor crimes was not allowed a jury trial. The county court had jurisdiction:

> It shall and may be lawful for any of the justices of the principal or county courts, upon complaint made before him, to cause such negro, Indian or mulatto slave so offending to be brought immediately before him or any other justice of the peace for the county where such offence is committed, who, upon due proof made against any such negro or (Indian) or mulatto slave of any of the crimes as aforesaid, such justice is hereby authorized and empowered to award and cause to be inflicted, according to the nature of the crime, such punishment by whipping as he shall think fit, not exceeding forty lashes.

MATHER FOUNDS SCHOOL FOR BLACKS

The Reverend Cotton Mather (1663–1728) opened a school for Blacks in Boston. The school scheduled night classes for Blacks and Native Americans.

SLAVES BARRED FROM TESTIFYING AGAINST WHITES

In Virginia and Maryland, legislative enactments provided that "any negro or mulatto, bond or free, shall be a good witness in pleas of the commonwealth for or against negroes or mulattoes, bond or free, or in civil pleas where free negroes or mulattoes shall along be parties, and in no other cases whatever." With few modifications, this provision was later enacted in Mississippi, Missouri, Alabama, North Carolina, and Tennessee.

1718 NEW ORLEANS FOUNDED

In **NOVEMBER**, Governor Sieur de Bienville established a settlement at the mouth of the Mississippi River. He named it New Orleans in honor of the regent of France, Philippe, duke of Orléans. The city later became one of the busiest slave markets in the country.

1720

POPULATION OVERVIEW

GENERAL POPULATION IN NORTH AMERICAN BRITISH COLONIES The colonial population was estimated to be about 466,185 residents, of which 68,839, or about 14.7 percent, were reported as Black persons. Massachusetts was the largest colony, with 91,008 residents, followed by Virginia, with 87,757; Maryland, with 66,133; and Connecticut, with 58,830. These colonies together made up 303,728 total residents, or about two-thirds of the entire colonial population. As many as 197,556 residents, or about 42 percent, lived in the southern colonies.

BLACKS IN NORTH AMERICAN BRITISH COLONIES In contrast, the Black population was overwhelmingly concentrated in the southern colonies — 54,758, or about 80 percent, of the 68,839 total Black population lived there. Virginia had the largest number of Blacks (26,559). Maryland followed with 12,499, and South Carolina with 12,000. Other colonies had Black populations less than half that of South Carolina. Fully 70 percent of South Carolina's total population was Black, and 30 percent of Virginia's total population was Black as well.

ECONOMIC CONDITIONS OVERVIEW

SLAVE TRAFFIC (MOLASSES TO RUM TO SLAVES) It was estimated that 171 ships engaged in the slave traffic sailed from Bristol, Liverpool, and London. Commodities, such as iron bars, rum, cloth, brass pans, shells, crystal beads, and foreign coins were shipped from manufacturing centers like Bristol and Liverpool in England and Newport and Boston in New England to areas along the Gold Coast of Africa to be traded for slaves. In order to ensure profits, particularly when England demanded more and more taxes, Americans developed what was called the "three cornered," "round about," or "triangular" trade. Slave traders could secure a slave in Africa for about 100 to 120 gallons of rum, valued at about fifty or sixty dollars. In the islands of the West Indies, which produced cane sugar, slaves were sold for one hundred to

This scene of a slave market on the African coast at the Kambia River shows the confusion that typically accompanied the loading of Africans onto slave ships. Drunken Europeans were sometimes violent and sexually assaulted both men and women, and slaves often cried out, trying to learn the fate of family members.

two hundred dollars each, or for molasses valued at that amount. The molasses was taken to colonial ports where rum was manufactured. Newport, Rhode Island, for example, had as many as twenty-two distilleries making rum to be shipped to Africa in exchange for more slaves.

SLAVES SOLD ON EASY TERMS Slaves could be bought for a small down payment and reasonable terms of three, six, nine, or twelve months' credit. Orders for slaves could also be placed through the mail.

SLAVE REVOLT IN CHARLESTON, SOUTH CAROLINA
A large-scale slave revolt occurred near Charleston, South Carolina; many slaves were banished, some were hanged, and others were burned alive.

1721 "NEGRO WATCH" ESTABLISHED IN CHARLESTON, SOUTH CAROLINA
As the number of slaves grew, and their proportion to free persons rose, fear of them among whites esca-

lated. Slave codes were not enough to allay the fear of serious slave revolts. In this year, suspicious gatherings of Blacks in the streets of Charleston caused such fear among whites that they established a "Negro Watch" to stop slaves on sight and to shoot them if they did not stop on order. In addition, Blacks found on the streets after 9:00 P.M. could be confined. Patrolmen were given almost unlimited power, including the right to arbitrarily administer twenty lashes to a slave found off the plantation without authorization, to search slave dwellings indiscriminately, and to kill suspected runaways who resisted or fled.

SMALLPOX INOCULATIONS SUCCESSFUL IN BOSTON
In MAY, Dr. Zabdiel Boylston successfully used smallpox inoculations to treat a smallpox epidemic responsible for 844 deaths in the Boston area. Boylston was encouraged to experiment with the inoculation by the Reverend Cotton Mather, who had learned of im-

munization from Onesimus, his slave. Onesimus had described to Mather the manner in which his people would deliberately infect themselves to establish immunity to the virus. Boylston used Onesimus's method of inoculation on his son, Thomas, and two slaves. He later inoculated as many as 240 others, of whom 6 actually contracted the disease.

1722 SLAVES PLOT TO KILL WHITES IN VIRGINIA

As many as two hundred Blacks assembled at a church near Rappahannock River, Virginia, to retaliate against abuses by whites. Their plot to kill whites was uncovered, and the Blacks escaped.

1723 BLACKS PUNISHED FOR STRIKING WHITES IN MARYLAND

Maryland legislation permitted barbarous punishment of any slave who struck a white person, upon trial and conviction before a justice of the peace. The offender's ears might be cropped as punishment. Such punishment might also be imposed on free Blacks. Further, "a negro shall be punished with stripes (not exceeding thirty-nine) if he uses provoking language or menacing gestures to a white person." Similar provisions were enacted in the codes of other slaveholding colonies.

VIRGINIA DISFRANCHISED FREE BLACKS

The Virginia Assembly passed legislation that deprived free Blacks of many rights, including trial by peers, serving on juries, and being a witness in any court case. Lieutenant Governor William Gooch made it clear that this new legislation resulted from a slave conspiracy and that there was a need to punish Free Blacks even if they were not involved in the plot.

1724 SLAVE CODES ENACTED IN LOUISIANA

Black codes were introduced in Louisiana, making it legal for slave owners to punish runaway slaves by cutting off their ears, hamstringing them, or branding them.

1725 SLAVES GRANTED SEPARATE CHURCH IN VIRGINIA

Black slaves were granted the right to have a separate Baptist church in Williamsburg, Virginia. The First Church of Colored Baptists was thus established.

SLAVE POPULATION INCREASES

Black slaves numbered about seventy-five thousand in the colonies at this point.

1726 PENNSYLVANIA IMPOSES ADDITIONAL LAWS ON SLAVES

Pennsylvania passed laws that further curtailed the activities of slaves. They could not travel more than ten miles from their masters' property without a pass. They could not be out after 9:00 P.M., and no more than four slaves could assemble together. Racial intermarriage was forbidden. These were the last major changes to the slave code of this state.

1729 SAVAGE PUNISHMENTS PERMITTED IN MARYLAND

Maryland passed a law that allowed justices to mete out brutal punishments upon the conviction of slaves for certain crimes. According to the preamble of the act, such severe punishment was necessary because Blacks had shown no sense of shame for past crimes, and existing laws offered no deterrent from committing future violent acts. The new punishments included hanging, decapitation, and severing the body into four quarters for display in public places.

1730

POPULATION OVERVIEW

GENERAL POPULATION IN NORTH AMERICAN BRITISH COLONIES The total population in the colonies was estimated at 629,445 residents. Among colonial cities, Boston housed the largest number (13,000), followed by New York City (8,500), Philadelphia (8,500), and Charleston (4,000).

BLACKS IN NEW ENGLAND COLONIES The largest concentration of Black residents in New England could be found along the Atlantic seaboard. Massachusetts had the largest and the busiest cities in the colonies. In 1735 the colony had a white population of 141,400 and 2,600 Black residents. Connecticut followed, with 37,300 whites and 700 Blacks. The largest percentage of Blacks could be found in Rhode Island, 9.7 percent of all residents. New Hampshire had the smallest number of Blacks — only 200. In sum, Blacks remained a relatively small proportion of the New England population. In fact, the total number of Blacks there never numbered more than 20,000 during the entire colonial period, and only in Rhode Island did their proportion of total residents reach more than 5 percent.

ECONOMIC CONDITIONS OVERVIEW

RICE PRODUCTION IN SOUTH CAROLINA At the beginning of this decade, a single crop — rice — came to increasingly dominate South Carolina's economy.

The colony exported 6 million pounds of rice, up from 1.5 million pounds in 1710. The increase in rice yields was directly related to the introduction of irrigation in 1724. During the following decade, rice exports surpassed those of pitch and tar, the naval stores that had previously been the top export. Much of the colony's rice was produced in the low country, where slaves were heavily concentrated.

SLAVE AREA IN AFRICA Most of the African immigrants were secured from the subtropical and equatorial regions of West Africa, although some traders penetrated farther into the interior to search for slaves. The "slave area" is generally considered as having two zones — a northern zone called the Sudanese and a southern zone called the Bantu. Some African slaves came from the east coast of Africa, particularly Mozambique.

The decade from 1730 to 1740 marked the beginning of the high point of importation of slaves to the Americas. As earlier monopolies disappeared in favor of more competition among the French, English, and Dutch merchants, the English and Anglo-American merchants began playing a more dominant role in the slave trade.

SOCIAL CONDITIONS OVERVIEW

SLAVES AS SOLDIERS IN FRENCH COLONY OF LOUISIANA

Approximately two thousand Black slaves were brought to the French colony of Louisiana at this time. They constituted more than one-third of the total resident population. The Company of the Indies, a slaving company, sold many slaves to white settlers but retained some to work for the company. To keep order among such large numbers of slaves, some were organized into quasi-military units to control other groups of slaves. In 1729, the governor used such a company of Black slaves to destroy a Chawasha village as a lesson to other Native Americans, warning them not to join a revolt led by the Natchez. In 1730, a force that included about 10 percent Black slaves defeated Natchez warriors near Pointe Coupee.

◈ A memorial praising members of the Black militia for their involvement in this conflict was presented in 1730. It recommended freeing all slaves who had risked their lives for the French. Some of the participants were freed.

1732 MUTINY BY SLAVES ABOARD SHIP

A slave mutiny occurred on a ship commanded by Captain John Major of Portsmouth, New Hampshire.

Major and his entire crew were killed. Although slave uprisings aboard slavers were quite common at this time, generally only those that resulted in the death of the captain or crew members were documented. Little is known about uprisings that failed and of the large numbers of slaves thrown overboard into the sea.

1733 SLAVES ESCAPE TO ST. AUGUSTINE

Many slaves attempted to escape to Florida, particularly to St. Augustine, because a Spanish decree in 1733 stated that slaves who escaped to Spanish territory would be considered free.

GEORGIA COLONY INITIALLY BARS SLAVES

On **JANUARY 13**, James Edward Oglethorpe, a member of the British parliament, arrived in Charleston Harbor with 130 individuals to settle the colony he had founded the previous year. In 1732, Oglethorpe, with thirty-five families, had selected a site on a high bluff along the Savannah River for his settlement. This became the site of modern Savannah.

Georgia was thus established as the last of the original thirteen colonies. It was a haven for the indebted and oppressed. The Crown also established the colony as a barrier between the Carolinas and the Spanish in Florida. Trustees of the colony disapproved of slavery, believing it would corrupt the egalitarian society envisioned by the small landholders. Further, Georgia's proprietors believed slavery to be an unsound mercantile endeavor, and they restricted the importation of slaves to the colony by way of an enactment, signed by the Georgia Trustees in England and accepted by the Crown in 1734. The document supported "rendering the Colony of Georgia more Defensible by Prohibiting the Importation and use of Black Slaves or Negroes into the same." Yet the white colonists failed at almost everything they attempted to produce (wine, silk, and other products) as desired by the trustees, and the idea of slavery became more and more favorable. In 1750, the act prohibiting the slave trade was repealed. Only 349 Blacks were reported to be living there at the time. Ten years later, there were 3,578 Blacks; by 1773, more than 15,000 Blacks lived in Georgia.

1735 SLAVE REVOLT ABOARD THE *Dolphin*

The crew and captain of the slave ship *Dolphin* were overtaken by slaves. Both the captives and captors were killed in an explosion.

SLAVE WHIPPED TO DEATH FOR VIOLATING CURFEW

In the New York colony, a Black slave was whipped to death for violating the city curfew. A coroner's jury investigating the death attributed it to "a visitation of God." Cruel and excessive punishment of slaves, including lynchings of Blacks suspected of rape or theft, was frequent as they became a larger proportion of the colony's population. At the time, 20 percent of the colony's population was Black.

1736 BLACKS FIGHT ALONGSIDE SPANISH

A Spanish force was assembled in Mobile to suppress "rebellious" Natchez Native Americans. About 19 percent of the force was composed of Blacks. Free Blacks served as officers of a separate all-Black company — perhaps the first time that Blacks served as officers during the colonial period.

1739 SLAVE UPRISINGS IN SOUTH CAROLINA

In early **SEPTEMBER**, serious slave uprisings occurred in Charleston, Stono River, and St. John's Parish, South Carolina. Spanish missionaries were blamed. The first of these uprisings occurred in Charleston when a group of slaves set out to find freedom in St. Augustine. Twenty-one whites were killed along the route. The slaves were eventually overtaken and massacred. Another revolt occurred on September 9. It was led by a Black called Cato and started at Stono, west of Charleston. The armed slaves marched to the beat of drums and killed all whites who tried to interfere with their escape to Florida. About thirty whites were slain, and more than thirty Blacks were killed for alleged participation in the revolt. Another dozen slaves escaped capture. The revolt at St. John's Parish in Berkeley County was much smaller.

Slave revolts were blamed on the attraction of St. Augustine, where many slaves had sought refuge and safety. They were also blamed on the disproportionate size of the Black slave population in South Carolina, which amounted to 60 percent of the colony's population. Slave uprisings prompted changes in the slave code.

1740

POPULATION OVERVIEW

BLACK POPULATION IN SELECTED COLONIES Just under 1 million people (905,563) resided in the colonies in 1740. Virginia had the largest population (180,440), followed by Massachusetts (151,613), and Maryland (116,093). These colonies made up just under one-half of the total colonial population.

Blacks, however, were distributed differently, with the largest number in Virginia (60,000), followed by South Carolina (30,000), and Maryland (24,031). These three colonies housed 76 percent of all Blacks in American colonies in 1740. Blacks were the majority population in the South Carolina colony, where they made up about two-thirds of the total population. They composed about one-third of Virginia's total population.

In the northern colonies, Blacks represented a considerably smaller proportion of the total residents. New York had the largest number of Blacks, 8,996, accounting for 14 percent of the colony's total population. New Jersey had the next largest number of Blacks, 4,336, constituting 8.5 percent of the total. In Massachusetts, the New England colony with the largest population, Blacks made up less than 2 percent of the total population.

SOCIAL CONDITIONS OVERVIEW

FREE BLACKS SUFFER HARDSHIPS Documents of the time seem to support the generalization that slaves who rose to responsible positions under their masters' employ posed less threat to white society than free Blacks who achieved their positions by themselves. In most cases, free Blacks were not rewarded — as European immigrants were — with assimilation into the larger society for their hard work, thrift, and good behavior. Rather, such free Blacks were considered a threat to the established social and economic order. Free Black shopkeepers had difficulty getting the credit needed to conduct their businesses. Black artisans were made to feel unwelcome in shipyards and at building sites. Because some free Blacks could not prosper under racism and its hardships, they became destitute and as a last resort sought assistance in almshouses or workhouses. In Boston at this time, for example, it was reported that there were 110 free Blacks in the almshouse and 36 in the workhouse, out of the total Black population (slave and free) of 1,500.

FREE BLACKS MAY BE ENSLAVED FOR AIDING RUNAWAY SLAVES IN SOUTH CAROLINA

A legislative act taken by South Carolina declared:

> If a free negro harbour, conceal or entertain a runaway slave, or a slave charged with any criminal matter, he shall forfeit the sum of ten pounds currency for the first day, and twenty shillings for every succeeding day, &c. And in case such forfeitures cannot be levied, or such free negro, &c. shall not pay the

same, together with the charges attending the prosecution, such free negro, &c. shall be ordered by the justice to be sold at public outcry, and the money arising by such sale shall, in the first place, be paid for and applied towards the forfeiture, &c. to the owner, &c.; and the overplus, if any, shall be paid by the said justice into the hands of the public treasurer, &c.

SLAVES DENIED RIGHT TO HOLD PROPERTY IN SOUTH CAROLINA

South Carolina passed legislation making it unlawful for any slave to "buy, sell, or trade, for any goods" without the permission of the owner. Slaves were also prohibited from having any type of boat and from raising horses, cattle, sheep, or hogs. Such goods could be taken from the slave and brought before a local justice of the peace, who would determine whether the goods had been seized legally. If the justice concurred, the goods were sold, with half the profit going to the state and half to those who had seized the property and laid claim to it.

SOUTH CAROLINA DECREES LIFELONG SLAVERY FOR BLACKS

South Carolina made the following decree:

> All Negroes, Indians (free Indians in amity with this government, and Negroes, mulattoes, and mestizoes, who are now free, excepted), mulattoes, and mestizoes, who are or shall hereafter be in this province, and all their issue and offspring born or to be born, shall be and they are hereby declared to be and remain forever after absolute slaves, and shall follow the condition of their mother.

SOUTH CAROLINA PROHIBITS CRUELTY TO SLAVES

South Carolina passed a law that prohibited cruel and inhumane treatment of slaves. The law specifically declared:

> In case any person shall wilfully cut out the tongue, put out the eye, castrate, or cruelly scald, burn, or deprive any slave of any limb or member, or shall inflict any other cruel punishment, other than whipping, or beating with a horsewhip, cowskin, switch, or small stick, or by putting irons on, or confining or imprisoning such slave, every such person shall, for every such offense, forfeit the sum of one hundred pounds current money.

But another South Carolina act passed at this time stated that a slave could be lawfully killed in certain circumstances.

If any slave who shall be out of the house or plantation where such slave shall live or shall be usually employed, or without some white person in company with such slave, shall refuse to submit to undergo the examination of any white person, it shall be lawful for any such white person to pursue, apprehend, and moderately correct such slave; and if such slave shall assault and strike such white person, such slave may be lawfully killed.

SOUTH CAROLINA PROHIBITS EDUCATION OF SLAVES

South Carolina passed legislation that prohibited teaching slaves to write or hiring them as scribes. This legislation stated:

> Whereas the having of slaves taught to write, or suffering them to be employed in writing, may be attended with great inconvenience, Be it enacted, That all and every person and persons whatsoever who shall hereafter teach or cause any slave or slaves to be taught to write, or shall use or employ any slave as a scribe in any manner of writing hereafter taught to write, every such person or persons shall for every such offence forfeit the sum of one hundred pounds current money.

SOUTH CAROLINA SETS LIMITS ON SLAVES' WORKING HOURS

South Carolina passed the "negro act" in response to some slave owners and overseers who were working their slaves too hard. The law stated that an owner or overseer could be fined for working slaves in excess of fourteen or fifteen hours a day (depending on the season), provided a complaint had been made to a justice. Specifically, the law stated:

> Whereas many owners of slaves, and other who have the care, management and overseeing of slaves, do confine them so closely to hard labour, that they have not sufficient time for natural rest: Be it therefore enacted, That if any owner of slaves, or other person who shall have the care, management or overseeing of any slaves, shall work or put any such slave or slaves to labour more than fifteen hours in twenty-four hours, from the twenty-fifth day of March to the twenty-fifth day of September; or more than fourteen hours in twenty-four hours, from the twenty-fifth day of September to the twenty-fifth day of March, every such person shall forfeit any sum not exceeding twenty pounds, nor under five pounds, current money, for every time he, she or they shall offend herein, at the discretion of the justice before whom the complaint shall be made.

UPRISING FOILED IN SOUTH CAROLINA

In **JANUARY**, as many as fifty slaves were hanged in Charleston after alleged insurrection plots were uncovered.

1741 MAROON SETTLEMENT DESTROYED IN FLORIDA

Soldiers sent from Georgia destroyed an established settlement in St. Augustine, Florida. The settlement of Garcia Real de Santa Teresa de Mosé had housed Negro fugitives from the English plantation of St. George in South Carolina. In addition to having their own public officers, priest, and other officials, the maroons had supported a militia to defend their community.

SLAVE REVOLT IN NEW YORK

Starting about **FEBRUARY 28** and continuing throughout much of this year, suspicious fires and reported slave conspiracies created fears in New York City. On December 31, a slave revolt was suspected when fire broke out in the Manhattan area. Some whites alleged that slaves were seeking to take control of the city. Twenty-nine to 31 Blacks and 5 poor whites (2 of them women) were executed for their participation in the alleged uprising.

According to some accounts, 13 conspirators were burned alive, 18 hanged, and 80 more deported. Another account stated that as many as 400 whites took part in the uprising, and 125 Blacks were arrested. A prosecutor later revealed that there was no evidence of a conspiracy or slave revolt.

1744 SCHOOL FOR BLACKS OPENED IN SOUTH CAROLINA

Samuel Thomas, an Anglican missionary, opened a school for Blacks in South Carolina. Whites were generally opposed to the education of Blacks because "the more knowledge they have, the more likely they are to revolt."

1745 INDIGO FIRST MARKETED IN SOUTH CAROLINA

Indigo, another labor-intensive crop, was successfully marketed by Eliza Lucas Pinckney. The crop had been introduced in the 1660s, but early experiments had not resulted in a profitable crop. Indigo produces blue dye, which was much in demand by the woolen industries in England at the time. Its cultivation took place in seasons when the slaves had finished working in the rice paddies.

Of the thirteen colonies, only South Carolina cultivated indigo as a major crop. During the early stages of indigo production in the colonies, Parliament placed a bounty on the crop to stimulate production. When indigo became a cash crop, the South had a full complement of products — including tobacco, rice, furs, and forest products — to export in exchange for manufactured products from Europe. As the southern economy gathered momentum, English agents managed the sale of the crops. These agents (called factors) filled orders from manufacturers and secured credit for the planters.

1750

POPULATION OVERVIEW

GENERAL POPULATION IN NORTH AMERICAN BRITISH COLONIES The population in the colonies slightly exceeded 1 million residents (1,170,700) in 1750. Immigration continued to cause much of the increase, as it had since 1660. The colonies averaged a 37 percent population increase in each decade throughout the past century. Settlements were becoming more and more dispersed, and land once considered worthless was brought into use. Many claim that these less dense and scattered settlements fostered population growth by reducing the spread of contagious diseases.

Of the total population counted in the American colonies in 1750, approximately 56 percent lived in Virginia (231,033), Massachusetts (188,000), and Maryland (141,073). This contrasted with 1740, when a larger number, about two-thirds of the total population, lived in these colonies. Although the colonial population grew by about 29 percent between 1740 and 1750, several colonies grew faster than others. For example, Georgia, the newest colony, more than doubled its population over the decade. Delaware's population jumped by 44 percent; South Carolina's, by 42 percent; North Carolina's, by 41 percent; Pennsylvania's, by 40 percent; New Jersey's, by 39 percent; and Rhode Island's, by 32 percent.

BLACKS IN NORTH AMERICAN BRITISH COLONIES The number of Blacks in the colonies grew by 36 percent over the decade, from 150,024 to 236,420. Slaves probably accounted for about one-fifth of the total population. It was estimated that about 2,500 slaves had been imported into the colonies annually over the past 35 years.

Virginia continued to house the largest number of Blacks, 101,452, or about 43 percent of the entire Black colonial population. Although there had been some dispersion of the Black population since 1740, Virginia, Maryland, and South Carolina together maintained the overwhelming proportion of Blacks,

Both slave traders and slave owners branded slaves. The procedure helped them distance themselves from the barbarity of slavery by dehumanizing the slaves. It also made it easier to recapture fugitive slaves, since they could identify them as being from a particular ship or plantation.

almost 78 percent. Maryland experienced an 81 percent increase in Blacks over the decade; North Carolina, 80 percent; and Virginia, 69 percent. South Carolina, where Blacks composed almost two-thirds of the colony's population in 1740, recorded only a 30 percent increase in Black population between 1740 and 1750. In addition, Blacks made up 61 percent of the colony's population in 1750, which was down almost 5 percentage points.

BLACKS IN NEW ENGLAND In this year, fully three-quarters of Massachusetts's Black population (approximately 2,700) lived in port cities. In Rhode Island, Blacks were heavily concentrated in the ports on Narragansett Bay. The Black population distribution here was closely related to the strong tie between slave imports and colonial shipping.

SOCIAL CONDITIONS OVERVIEW

MORTALITY AMONG SLAVES A review of the entire series of events by which Africans became slaves in the colonies reveals a high death rate for the slaves. The process had not changed appreciably in the more than one hundred years of slave importation to the Americas. It started with African peoples who waged war on other Africans and took the losers captive, ultimately to be sold into slavery. The captives, often tied together by their necks, traveled day after day in hot sun through difficult terrain and with minimal food and water to the crowded trading stations on the West African coast. After being inspected by European slavers, the healthiest slaves were selected, branded, given numbers inscribed on lead tags, and herded on board. Those rejected were left to die of

Although African captives were shackled on board slave ships, the conditions were so abominable that slave merchants constantly feared rebellion. To ensure their own safety, the captains would punish unruly slaves severely, sometimes throwing them overboard, or arbitrarily punish weaker Africans to discourage others.

starvation. Then came the Middle Passage (the journey to the West Indies), during which the slaves suffered brutal and inhumane treatment during the two-month trip. Once in the West Indies, they were "seasoned," that is, taught the work associated with plantation agriculture, before being shipped north.

About one-third of the Africans first taken, out of a total of fifteen million over the years, died on the march and at the trading stations; another third died during the Middle Passage and the seasoning. Only one in three eventually worked in the American slave system. Once in the Americas, poor conditions and brutal treatment made the Africans' survival difficult.

SLAVE REVOLTS ON THE OPEN SEAS

Slave revolts remained one of the many hazards faced by the captains of slave ships. Some believed that the "Negroes ignorance of navigation" provided a safeguard against mutiny, but the shock and misery associated with their passage to the West became too much for many Africans to endure. Slavers attempted to suppress revolts by severely punishing those involved. Frequently, the punishment meted out was death.

GEORGIA PERMITS SLAVERY

On **OCTOBER 26**, the trustees of the Georgia colony bowed to growing pressure and reversed their anti-slavery position.

Settlers from slaveholding colonies, especially South Carolina, had increasingly settled in Georgia and had petitioned the trustees to allow slavery so that the colony's economic growth would parallel that of the others. The trustees had initially denied the petition, but by 1750, they felt they could no longer ignore the pressure to implement slavery, particularly on the large rice estates. When the decision came, South Carolinians poured into Georgia with their slaves, who were familiar with the methods of rice production. Although this act allowed the importation of Blacks into the colony, it imposed specific restrictions: all Blacks had to be registered; a ratio of four Black males to each white male servant (capable of bearing arms) had to be maintained; interracial marriages were prohibited; and religious instruction for all Black slaves was required.

1751 NEW SLAVE CODE PROVISIONS IN VIRGINIA
Virginia passed legislation giving the church wardens of any parish encompassing power to sell Blacks or slaves residing there one month if they had been emancipated without the consent of the governor and council.

1753 FRANKLIN CONDEMNS SLAVERY
Benjamin Franklin argued that "slavery is a poor economic policy" in a recently published book entitled *Observations Concerning the Increase of Mankind and the Peopling of Countries*. He compared the use of slave labor in the colonies with the system of wage labor in Britain.

1754 BANNEKER MAKES FIRST AMERICAN CLOCK
Benjamin Banneker (1731–1806), son of free Black parents, constructed the first clock made entirely in America.

Banneker had never seen a clock, but his genius and intellect allowed him to use crude tools, including a sundial, to perfect a clock so accurate that it struck the hours with faultless precision for twenty years. Banneker was born on November 9, 1731, in Ellicott Mills, Maryland. He attended a local school and was considered a mechanical genius.

WOOLMAN EMERGES AS LEADING ABOLITIONIST
John Woolman (1713–1772), a tailor and a Quaker, became one of the major figures of pre–Revolutionary War abolitionism with his publication *Some Considerations on the Keeping of Negroes: Recommended to the Professors of Christianity of Every Denomination*. It became the most widely distributed antislavery work before the Revolution. Woolman taught that slavery was unchristian, unjust, and cruel, and had an evil effect upon owners and slaves alike. Woolman noted, "Where slavekeeping prevails, pure

Benjamin Banneker, often referred to as the first African American scientist, was born in Baltimore County, Maryland. Banneker, skilled in mathematics and astronomy, published numerous almanacs and helped to survey and plan the District of Columbia.

religion and sobriety declines, as it evidently tends to harden the heart and render the soul less susceptible of that holy spirit of life, meakness, and charity, which is the peculiar character of a true Christian."

Even before this publication, Woolman had spoken out against slavery and traveled to various cities denouncing the practice. In 1762, Woolman wrote a second volume intended for the general public. He also published *A Word of Remembrance and Caution to the Rich*.

1755   FREEDOM COULD NOT WAIT

Mark and Phillis, the slaves of John Codman of Charleston, South Carolina, were accused of poisoning their master after learning that he had granted them freedom in his will. Mark was hanged, and Phillis was burned alive.

1756–1763   BLACKS SERVE IN FRENCH AND INDIAN WAR

As France and Britain clashed in open warfare over territorial claims in the upper Ohio River valley, Blacks served as scouts, wagoners, and laborers with the regular British forces. Black militiamen served with independent units from almost every colony — Massachusetts, New Jersey, New York, Pennsylvania, South Carolina, and Virginia. Many Blacks received praise for their bravery in a number of battles, including those at Fort Duquesne, Fort Cumberland, and the Plains of Abraham outside Quebec City. A Black man, killed in a fight against Native Americans at "Negro Mountain" in western Maryland, was honored for his bravery.

This war, the last of four between the French and British over control of North America, was known as the French and Indian War in North America and the Seven Years' War in Europe. It ended with a decisive defeat of the French, who were forced out of the North American mainland for good.

1758   QUAKERS TAKE STEPS TO ABOLISH SLAVERY

Following the demand for abolishment of slavery in each of the Quakers' widely distributed documents, Quakers in Philadelphia ceased buying and selling slaves on the grounds that this practice set into motion a demand that stimulated the foreign slave trade. At this "Yearly Meeting" in Pennsylvania, it was agreed that Friends who continue to import, purchase, or sell Blacks would be disowned and suggested that Quakers who owned slaves "sett them at Liberty, seeking a Christian provision for them according to their ages."

Quakers elsewhere followed suit. Those in London, England, followed in 1761; in Maryland, in 1768; in New England, in 1770; and in New York, in 1774. Quakers abolished slavery completely somewhat later — just before the Revolution in New England and the middle colonies and by 1788 in Maryland and Virginia.

SCHOOL FOR FREE BLACKS OPENS IN PHILADELPHIA

An Anglican missionary group, the Associates of Dr. Bray, opened a school for free Blacks. The group was closely associated with the Society for the Propagation of the Gospel in Foreign Parts.

1760

POPULATION OVERVIEW

GENERAL POPULATION IN NORTH AMERICAN BRITISH COLONIES   The population in the colonies was estimated to be 1,593,625 residents. Between 1750 and 1760, the colonial population grew by 36 percent. Blacks numbered 325,806, or about one-fifth of the total population.

BLACKS IN NORTH AMERICAN BRITISH COLONIES   The colonial Black population increased by almost 38 percent between 1750 and 1760. No other colony compared with Virginia's large absolute increase of Blacks (39,118). The largest percentage increase (excluding extremely small population bases) occurred in Georgia, where the Black population increased 258 percent. This was followed by North Carolina, with 69 percent; Pennsylvania, with 54 percent; New York, with 48 percent; and South Carolina, with 47 percent.

The overwhelming majority of the Black population, 75 percent, lived in three colonies: Virginia (140,570), South Carolina (57,334), and Maryland (49,004). Two-fifths of the population of the southern colonies, excluding Maryland, were Black. In South Carolina, Blacks formed 61 percent of the total population and in Virginia slightly more than 41 percent of the colony's population.

ECONOMIC CONDITIONS OVERVIEW

SHIFT OF SLAVES TO THE SOUTH FOR ECONOMIC REASONS   More than 8,000 slaves were sent to the southern colonies annually by private traders. The Royal African Company alone imported as many as 2,500 slaves annually (although its monopoly ended in 1697). In all, it is estimated that there were as many as 386,000 slaves in the colonies; 299,000 were concentrated in the South. Georgia, which had resisted slavery during early stages of its settlement, had acquired a slave population amounting to about one-third of its total residents. Slaves produced the major staples: tobacco, rice, and indigo. Although it is clear that the South was heavily dependent on slave labor, the North was dependent as well. The principal markets and the major sources of revenue for the northern manufacturers were the large slaveholding colonies in the South and in the West Indies.

HAMMON PUBLISHES POETRY

On **DECEMBER 25**, the first known poem authored by an American-born Black, entitled "An Evening Thought: Salvation by Christ with Penitential Cries," was published by Jupiter Hammon (1711–1806?). Hammon's eighty-eight-line poem was not considered an important literary work at the time. In 1787, Hammon published his "Address to the Negroes of the State of New York," in which he advised Blacks to be faithful and obedient to their slave masters until freedom was earned by honesty and good conduct. Hammon lived and died as a slave to three generations of the Lloyd family of Lloyd's Neck, Long Island, New York.

1763   BLACK CHIMNEY SWEEPS ORGANIZE IN SOUTH CAROLINA

On **OCTOBER 29**, Black chimney sweeps in Charleston formed the first union-type organization. They refused to work until the city increased their wages.

1766   BENEZET PUBLISHES ANTISLAVERY TRACT

Anthony Benezet (1720–1784), a schoolteacher from Philadelphia, emerged as one of the great pre-Revolution abolitionists. In this year, he wrote *A Caution and Warning to Great Britain and Her Colonies, in a Sharot Representation of the Calamitous State of the Enslaved Negroes in the British Dominions*. In 1771, he wrote another monumental work on the slave trade, *Some Historical Account of Guinea, Its Situation, Produce, and the General Disposition of Its Inhabitants, with an Enquiry into the Rise and Progress of the Slave-Trade, Its Nature and Lamentable Effects*.

1769   FREE BLACKS AND MULATTOS WIN TAXATION EXEMPTIONS IN VIRGINIA

Free Blacks and mulattos petitioned the Virginia House of Burgesses to exempt freeborn Blacks from the payment of county or parish levies. Free Blacks asked that their wives and daughters be exempt from taxation because of the burdensome and derogatory nature it placed on freeborn subjects. The House of Burgesses approved the measure.

VIRGINIA REJECTS JEFFERSON'S EMANCIPATION BILL

Thomas Jefferson, a new member of the House of Burgesses, introduced a bill calling for the emancipation of slaves. It was soundly rejected.

1770

POPULATION OVERVIEW

GENERAL POPULATION IN NORTH AMERICAN BRITISH COLONIES According to the Bureau of the Census, it is estimated that about 2,148,076 people resided in the American colonies. One-fifth of the colonial population (447,016) lived in Virginia, followed by Pennsylvania, which had 240,057 residents; Massachusetts, with 235,308; and Maryland, with 202,599. These colonies together made up 1,124,980, or slightly over one-half, of all residents in American colonies.

GROWTH IN NUMBER OF SLAVES Approximately 255,000 slaves were brought to the thirteen colonies between 1700 and 1775.

BLACKS IN NORTH AMERICAN BRITISH COLONIES In this year, a total of 459,822 Black people lived in the American colonies, of which almost 41 percent (187,605) could be found on plantations and farms in Virginia. Only three other colonies had relatively large numbers of Black residents: South Carolina, with 75,178; North Carolina, with 69,600; and Maryland, with 63,818. The South contained the overwhelming proportion of Blacks: 411,362, or about 89 percent. Three colonies in New England had sizable numbers of Blacks: Connecticut, with 5,698; Massachusetts, with 4,754; and Rhode Island, with 3,761. Overall, the New England region had only about 15,367 Blacks, or less than 4 percent of all Blacks in colonial America. The middle colonies (New York, New Jersey, and Pennsylvania) had 33,103 Blacks, of which New York had the largest number, with 19,122.

SOCIAL AND ECONOMIC OVERVIEW

BACKCOUNTRY LIFE: LESS DEPENDENT ON SLAVES The backcountry was roughly defined as a block of land between the fall line and the Appalachian Mountains, stretching from Pennsylvania to Georgia. This part of the country followed a way of life that was viewed by others as inferior, crude, and less civilized. By 1776, a large portion of the residents were identified as Scotch-Irish, German, Irish, Welsh, French Huguenots, and other immigrants. Backcountry farms were generally about two hundred acres in size. Corn, peas, beans, potatoes, barley, or rye, and sometimes cash crops such as hemp, flax, and wheat were grown. Tobacco was part of the crop system in the Shenandoah Valley, as was indigo in South Carolina. Some backcountry farmers aspired to modest wealth — though few attained it. It was said that "a few slaves and anything from five hundred to a thousand acres of land carry enough prestige to qualify a man for an appointment as justice of the peace or sheriff or a seat in the assembly."

CHESAPEAKE: THE TOBACCO PLANTATION ECONOMY Perhaps one of the most prevailing aspects of life in Maryland, Virginia, and North Carolina was the dependence on tobacco. The crop was grown on small farms as well as on large plantations, and almost everywhere its cultivation demanded slaves, ranging from a few on the farms to hundreds on the plantations. The plantations greatly influenced the economy of the Chesapeake. They ranged in size from one thousand to six thousand acres and had from fifty to several hundred slaves to work the land. For example, Charles Carroll's plantation, Carrollton, in Maryland, comprised forty thousand acres of land and had as many as 285 slaves. At one time, Carroll was said to be the richest man in America.

The slave population increased without regard to the instability of tobacco prices. For example, there were only about 16,000 Blacks in Virginia in 1700; but by 1770, because of natural increases and heavy importation, the Black population had reached over 170,000, about 42 percent of Virginia's total population.

The Revolutionary War revealed just how dependent this part of the country was on slaves. Prior to the Revolution, tobacco from the Chesapeake region accounted for nearly half of Britain's trade with the colonies. During the war, however, at least 20,000 slaves were lost to British "invaders" who promised them freedom if they enlisted on their side. The postwar decrease in slave labor contributed significantly to a major slump in tobacco exports. One renowned historian noted that this "drastic decline of tobacco exports to Britain marked the most sweeping change in American commerce that occurred immediately after the war." The postwar slave labor shortage took its toll on almost every staple crop in the South.

LOW COUNTRY ECONOMY, SOUTH CAROLINA The low country, a strip of land in South Carolina extending inland from the coast for ten to sixty miles, was estimated to contain about 110,000 people, one-third of the colony's total population. Three-quarters of these were Blacks. Whites who had developed the slave-intensive agriculture system, based on rice and indigo, were the wealthiest members of Charleston's society. A two-hundred-acre plantation in South Carolina cost about two hundred pounds. The forty slaves necessary to cultivate and harvest the rice crop cost an additional eighteen hundred pounds. In an average year, a planter could expect to harvest 350 barrels of rice and sell it for two pounds per barrel. Thus, after only three or four years, a planter could recoup the total initial investment. Although whites living in the low country could make substantial profits, they lived in perpetual fear of an uprising by their oppressed slaves, who sometimes outnumbered their owners three to one, and in some places fifty to one.

By 1770, Georgia's Black population numbered about 15,000 and was about equal to its white population. In the low country, where rice production pre-

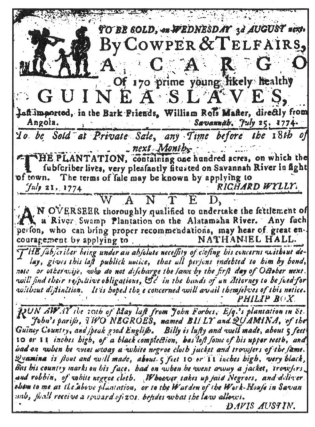

This circular, one of the many that frequently appeared in Savannah, advertises a slave auction. A reward for the return of two runaways who speak "good English" is mentioned.

dominated, Blacks outnumbered whites by a wide margin. Over the years, Georgia's 126-mile-long "Rice Coast" became identified as its "Slave Coast." Throughout much of Georgia's slave history, most of the slaves remained concentrated in the low country.

SLAVES DID MORE THAN FIELD WORK Although the value of slaves as field hands was well documented, their value as craftsmen on a plantation was less well known. Many were put to artisan work, especially as coopers and carpenters. On a large plantation slave artisans also included sawyers, blacksmiths, tanners, tailors, curriers, shoemakers, spinners, iron workers, weavers, stone cutters, and knitters. Such skilled workers made many plantations self-sufficient units.

NORTH CAROLINA PAID MASTERS FOR SLAVES EXECUTED During the period 1751 to 1770, about 22 percent of the colony's contigency funds were spent on

Five patriots were killed in Boston's "Bloody Massacre." The first to die was Crispus Attucks, a Black seaman.

compensating masters for executed slaves. As many as 88 slaves were executed during the 19 years. Execution was cruel and included being roasted or burned alive, hung alive in chains, or dismembered.

ATTUCKS VICTIM OF BOSTON MASSACRE

On **MARCH 5**, Crispus Attucks (1723–1770) of Framingham, Massachusetts, a former slave of mixed African and Native American parentage who had run away to become a seaman, was one of five patriots killed in the Boston Massacre during a demonstration against British import duties. Attucks was reportedly the first man killed.

Attucks was buried along with the other victims in the Granary Burial Ground. Massachusetts later honored him with a statue on the Boston Common. An engraving that portrayed the Boston Massacre by Paul Revere, which hangs in the National Gallery of Art, shows all five victims of the massacre as white men.

NEW SCHOOL FOR BLACKS AND WHITES FOUNDED IN PHILADELPHIA

On **JUNE 28**, Quakers (including Anthony Benezet) opened a school for Blacks in Philadelphia. The school educated both Blacks and whites in a nonsegregated manner. Moses Patterson was selected as the teacher.

Over time, the Quakers established many day schools for Black children, and Sabbath schools and evening schools for Black adults. They eventually participated in almost every aspect of the lives of slaves — planning and advising them on all aspects of living as well as protecting orphans, providing education, and securing employment.

1770s BLACK CHURCHES SUBJECT TO RESTRICTIONS

During this time, Blacks often attended church with their white Christian brothers and sisters. Often, Blacks converted whites just as whites had converted Blacks. As time passed, however, Black men were licensed to preach by the Baptists and the Methodists. In the South, Black churches were prohibited from having too many members to prevent potential slave insurrections. Many times, such assemblies were supervised. Despite occasional white harassment, the church continued to be one of the more focused institutions of the Black community.

1772 VIRGINIA CALLS FOR REDUCTION IN THE IMPORTATION OF SLAVES

Virginia petitioned the throne to stop the importation of African slaves into the colony:

> We are encouraged to look up to the throne and implore your Majesty's paternal assistance in averting a calamity of a most alarming nature. The importation of slaves into the colonies from the coast of Africa hath long been considered as a trade of great inhumanity, and under its present encouragement, we have much reason to fear it will endanger the very existence of your majesty's dominions. Deeply impressed with these sentiments, we most humbly beseech your Majesty to remove all restraints on your Majesty's Governors of this colony, which inhibit to their assisting to such laws as might check so very pernicious a commerce.

No action was taken by the Crown.

MANSFIELD DECISION ABOLISHES SLAVERY IN ENGLAND

On **JUNE 22**, Chief Justice Lord Mansfield abolished slavery in England and thereby gave immediate freedom to 14,000 slaves. His decision in the Sommersett case stated that "by the Common Law no man could have property in another man and that as soon as a Negro came to England he is free; one may be villein in England but not a slave." Penalties were levied on those who did not free their slaves. The English courts did not attempt to apply this decision to their colonies and no official body in America took notice of the decision. Nevertheless some slaves upon hearing of the decision ran away from their owners and attempted to get passage to England.

1773 BLACK BAPTIST CHURCH FOUNDED IN SOUTH CAROLINA

A Black Baptist church was organized at Silver Bluff, South Carolina, twelve miles from Augusta, Georgia. This was probably the first Black Baptist church under Black leadership established in the colonies, although there is some disagreement about this. The date of founding of the Silver Bluff church may have been as early as 1750 or as late as 1775. George Liele and David George, a slave, were early ministers of the congregation.

DuSABLE BECOMES CHICAGO'S FIRST SETTLER

Jean-Baptiste Point DuSable (1745?–1818?), the son of a slave woman and a successful Frenchman from

This rendering shows Jean Baptiste DuSable, the first settler of Chicago, at the lower right, his log cabin at the lower left, and the landscape around the mouth of the Chicago River where the city of Chicago later arose. Also shown is the home of the Potawatomi Indian tribe, which occupied the area before the arrival of DuSable and later settlers.

Haiti, became the first permanent settler in the area that was to become Chicago when he purchased the property of Jean-Baptiste Millet's "Old Peoria Fort." DuSable purchased the property to carry on a fur-trading business on the Chicago River near Lake Michigan. Over time, a successful trading center emerged, and the Chicago settlement was begun.

◈ DuSable was born in St. Marc, Haiti. After being educated in France, he returned to work in his father's business in New Orleans in 1765. DuSable and an associate, Jacques Clemorgan of Martinique, then left Louisiana to establish a fur-trading business along the upper Mississippi River. For two years, they were successful in trading fur with the Native Americans near present-day St. Louis; later, they moved farther north and lived with the Peoria and Potawatomi peoples. Although DuSable's trapping activities extended into areas now known as Chicago and Detroit, and Ontario, Canada, it was not until 1772 that he decided to build a fur-trading post on the Chicago River near Lake Michigan. DuSable sold his property when the territory came under the jurisdic-

tion of the United States. He moved to St. Charles, Missouri, where he died a poor man.

PENNSYLVANIA IMPOSES TAX ON IMPORTED SLAVES
The Pennsylvania legislature passed an act that imposed a 20-pound tax on every slave imported into the colony. The act effectively reduced the involvement of residents in the slave trade.

WHEATLEY PUBLISHES POEMS
Phillis Wheatley (1753–1784), a former slave, became the first African American to have a book of poetry published. *Poems on Various Subjects, Religious and Moral* was published by Archibald Bell, a British printer, after being rejected by American publishing houses.

◈ Wheatley was born in Senegal and brought to Boston in 1761, where she was sold to John Wheatley, a merchant and tailor, and his wife, Susannah. The Wheatleys taught her to read and write, and by the time she was twelve years old, Phillis was writing poetry, some of which described Africa and slavery. She

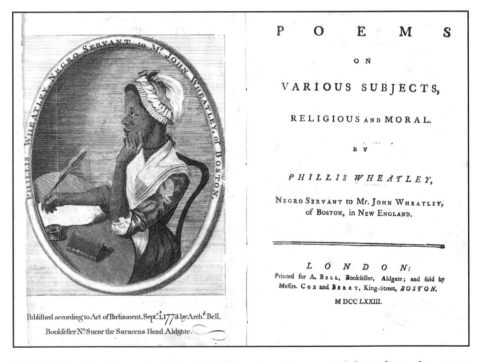

Phillis Wheatley, the most celebrated African American poet of the eighteenth century, published her book, Poems on Various Subjects, Religious and Moral, *while in London, recuperating from an illness. The picture of Phillis Wheatley on the frontispiece is an engraving by Scipio Moorhead, a slave.*

gained her freedom in 1772. Included in her book was the following poem written to the Earl of Dartmouth, the king's representative in North America.

No more American in mournful strain
Of wrongs, and grievance unredress'd complain,
No longer shall thou dread the iron chain,
Which wanton Tyranny with lawless hand
Has made, and which it meant t'enslave the land.

Should you, my lord, while you pursue my song,
Wonder from whence my longe of Freedom
    sprung,
Whence flow these wiches for the common good,
By feeling hearts alone best understood,
I, young in life, by seeming cruel fate
Was snatch'd from Africa's fancy'd happy seat:
What pangs excruciating must molest,
What sorrows labour in my parent's breast?
Steel'd was the soul and by no misery mov'd
That from a father seiz'd his babe belov'd
Such, such my case. And can I then but pray
Others may never feel tyrannic sway?

Wheatley's writings captivated London society. On February 28, 1776, George Washington invited Wheatley to his headquarters in Cambridge, Massachusetts, after she had written a poem in his honor. In his letter inviting her, Washington commented on the poem by noting, "The style and manner exhibit a striking proof of your poetic talents." Wheatley died in Boston on December 5, 1784.

SLAVES IN MASSACHUSETTS PETITION FOR FREEDOM

On **JANUARY 6**, Massachusetts slaves petitioned the colonial legislature and Governor Thomas Hutchinson for their freedom. The petitioners urged the legislature to consider their "unhappy State and Condition: We have no Wives! No Children! We have no City! No Country!" No action was taken by the governor or legislature, which was dominated by commercial interests, including slave traders. Many other such petitions were submitted. On April 20, for example, a letter from four slaves was circulated to delegates of the legislature asking permission for slaves to work one day a week for themselves to earn money to buy their freedom. They also proposed to use the money to leave America and establish a settlement in Africa. The legislature tabled the letter, and the governor said he could not assist them. None of the petitions for freedom based on the "natural rights" of slaves as human beings were granted.

SLAVE SUES FOR HIS FREEDOM

In **NOVEMBER**, Caesar Hendricks of Massachusetts took his master to court and asked to be freed because he had served his time. An all-white jury was convened and rendered a verdict in favor of Hendricks. Hendricks's master was asked to pay damages.

1774 CONNECTICUT, MASSACHUSETTS, AND RHODE ISLAND PROHIBIT IMPORTATION OF SLAVES

Connecticut forbade anyone to bring slaves into the colony "to be disposed of, left, or sold" under penalty of a 100-pound fine. In Massachusetts, Governor Hutchinson and his successor, Governor Gage, refused to sign the law passed by the legislature to prohibit slave trade in that colony.

In Rhode Island, the law prohibiting slave trade was prefaced with a statement of principles noting that "the inhabitants of America are generally engaged in the preservation of their own rights and liberties, among which, that of personal freedom must be considered as the greatest; as those who are desirous of enjoying all the advantages of liberty themselves should be willing to extend personal liberties to others." The law itself stipulated that any slave brought into the colony by an established resident would be free. Persons coming into the colony as visitors or permanent residents could bring their slaves with them, but must take them away when they left. This provision protected southerners who spent the summer in Newport. In addition, slave traders, if unable to sell their slaves in the West Indies, could bring them into the colony under bond for one year.

VIRGINIA PASSES RESOLUTION CONDEMNING SLAVERY

The Virginia Convention of 1774 passed the following resolution:

For the most trifling reasons, and sometimes for no conceivable reasons at all, his Majesty has rejected laws of the most salutary tendency. The abolition of domestic slavery is the greatest object of desire in these colonies where it was introduced in their infant state. But, previous to the enfranchisement of the slaves we have, it is necessary to exclude all further importations from Africa. Yet our repeated attempts to effect this by prohibitions, and by imposing duties which might amount to a prohibition, have been hitherto defeated by his Majesty's negative; thus preferring the immediate advantages of a few African corsairs to the lasting interests of the American states, and to the rights of human nature, deeply wounded by this infamous practice.

CONTINENTAL CONGRESS PLEDGES TO END SLAVE TRADE

On **OCTOBER 20**, the Continental Congress pledged to end the slave trade when it adopted "The Continental Association," which included the following provision:

We will neither import nor purchase, any slave imported after the first day of December next; after which time, we will wholly discontinue the slave trade, and we will neither be concerned in it ourselves, nor will we hire our vessels, nor sell our commodities or manufactures to those who are concerned in it.

Although the resolution was a powerful statement, it proved to mean very little since the desire to gain wealth through slavery was still a potent force in America.

SLAVE REVOLT IN GEORGIA

In **DECEMBER**, a slave revolt took place in St. Andrew's Parish, Georgia. Four whites were killed, and slaves who allegedly participated in the revolt were publicly burned to death.

FAIRFAX RESOLVE SIGNED

On **DECEMBER 1**, George Washington signed the Fairfax Resolve, which prohibited the importation of slaves and resolved to halt all colonial exports to Britain unless the king acted to redress the grievances of the colonists. George Mason was the author of the document. Washington signed it even though he himself owned slaves.

1775 CONTINENTAL NAVY RECRUITS BLACKS

Although the Continental Navy comprised navies, privateers, and vessels sailing under letters of marque, it was considered a formidable force against aggression from the sea. Frequently naval vessels suffered from manpower shortages, and since many Blacks had naval experience in previous wars or by serving on coastal vessels, they were welcomed by the navy.

◈ A recruiting poster of this year, found in Newport, called for "ye able backed sailors, men white or black, to volunteer for naval service in ye interest of freedom." About two thousand Blacks served in the Continental Navy during the Revolution.

SOME COLONIES OPPOSE ENLISTMENT OF SLAVES

Georgia and South Carolina opposed the enlistment of Black slaves as soldiers, primarily on economic grounds. In 1777, the Continental Congress agreed to pay slave owners in these states one thousand dollars for each slave allowed to serve in the Continental Army. At the end of the war, the slaves were to be freed and given fifty dollars. Both colonies rejected the offer. An estimated twenty-five thousand slaves from South Carolina, 20 percent of all the slaves in the colony before the war, and about 75 percent of all slaves from Georgia, ran away during the war, some to British lines.

SLAVES PARTICIPATE IN REVOLUTION

Even though laws and orders specifically restricted the involvement of slaves in the war, they participated in a number of ways. Some substituted for their masters in the army. In Rhode Island, two battalions of slaves were inducted into the war effort. Owners there were paid up to £120 for each slave they freed. New Hampshire, Connecticut, and Virginia also enlisted slaves to fight and gave each enlistee his freedom. In New York, slave owners were given land for each slave they committed to serve in the army, and their slaves received their freedom. British officers noted in their journals the presence of Black slaves in the Continental forces.

FIRST BLACKS INITIATED AS MASONS

On **MARCH 6**, Prince Hall (1748–1807), a caterer and leather dresser, and fourteen fellow Blacks were initiated into British Military Lodge No. 441 of the Masons, a fraternal organization (see also 1787).

PENNSYLVANIA ABOLITION SOCIETY FOUNDED

On **APRIL 14**, the Pennsylvania Society for the Abolition of Slavery, the first antislavery society in America, was founded in Philadelphia. Although originally begun as a Quaker organization, it revised its constitution to include a broader membership. They met four times during this year and decided to work to abolish slavery in Pennsylvania and to protect free Blacks from being sold into slavery. Because of the war, the society did not meet again until February 1784.

BLACKS FIGHT AT LEXINGTON AND CONCORD

On **APRIL 19**, the War of Independence began at Lexington and Concord, Massachusetts. A British militia of seven hundred soldiers, marching to Concord to destroy military stores, was first intercepted at Lexington, where the minutemen had been warned of the British approach by Paul Revere and William Dawes. At the second battle, at Concord, the Americans were initially forced to retreat, but they returned and successfully routed the British at North Bridge. Blacks were among the minutemen who defeated the British

Blacks fought heroically in the Battle of Bunker Hill (actually fought on nearby Breed's Hill), one of the most important battles of the American Revolution.

at Concord. Blacks served as minutemen before they were allowed into the regular army.

COLONIES INITIALLY ALLOW FREE BLACKS TO SERVE IN ARMY

In **MAY**, the Committee on Safety of the Continental Congress permitted free Blacks, but not slaves, to serve in the Continental Army:

> Resolved, that it is the opinion of this Committee, as the contest now between Great Britain and the Colonies respects the liberties and privileges of the latter, which the Colonies are determined to maintain, that the admission of any person, as soldiers, into the army now raising, but only such as are freemen, will be inconsistent with the principles that are to be supported, and reflect dishonor on this Colony, and that no slaves be admitted into this army upon any consideration whatever.

BLACKS FIGHT AT BATTLE OF BUNKER HILL

On **JUNE 17**, several Black soldiers participated in the famous (but misnamed) Revolutionary War battle that actually took place on Breed's Hill, across the

river from Boston. Salem Poor, Peter Salem, Prince Hall, Caesar Brown, Prince Estabrook, Grant Cooper, Barzillai Lew, and George Middleton, among others, fought with the white colonial force. Middleton led an all-Black company called "the Bucks of America," which after the battle was presented with a special company banner by John Hancock. Caesar Brown and Prince Estabrook were killed; Peter Salem (1750–1816) was credited by some with shooting the British commander Major Pitcairn, thus forcing the British troops to regroup and giving the greatly outnumbered colonial troops enough time to retreat rather than surrender.

Salem, who had been freed by his owners so that he could join the Continental Army, had also joined the battle at Lexington and Concord and fought with General George Washington at Valley Forge. After the war, Salem lived near Leicester, Massachusetts, where he wove cane for a living. He died in the poorhouse in 1816. A monument to him was erected in Framingham, Massachusetts.

COLONIES BAR ALL BLACKS FROM SERVING IN THE ARMY

In **JULY**, George Washington ordered recruiting officers to stop recruiting Blacks, although those already in the service were allowed to continue. On October 23, the Continental Congress approved a resolution in line with the action of the council of general officers, barring both slaves and free Blacks from serving in the Continental Army. A month later, General Washington issued orders that prohibited all Blacks from serving, new recruits as well as veterans.

BRITISH RECRUIT BLACKS IN REVOLUTIONARY WAR

On **NOVEMBER 7**, John Murray, Earl of Dunmore, British royal governor of Virginia, offered freedom to Black slaves who would join the British army to put down the rebellion.

> And I do hereby further declare all indented servants, Negroes, or others (appertaining to Rebels) free, that are able and willing to bear arms, they joining His Majesty's Troops, as soon as may be, for the more speedily reducing the Colony to a proper sence of their duty, to his Majesty's crown and dignity.

Dunmore assumed that the colonists would not arm free Blacks lest they organize insurrections and liberate slaves. As many as eight hundred Virginia slaves joined the British. Owners of large plantations opposed Dunmore's offer and tried to get it rescinded

During the Battle of Bunker Hill, Peter Salem shot the British commander, Major Pitcairn.

— many promised their slaves better treatment for not joining Dunmore.

ETHIOPIAN REGIMENT FORMED

By **DECEMBER**, about three hundred Blacks had accepted Lord Dunmore's invitation to join the British army's Ethiopian Regiment, believing it a small price to pay for freedom. Inscribed on their uniforms was the motto "Liberty to Slaves" — a constant reminder of their reason for fighting.

HONORABLE MENTION OF SALEM POOR

On **DECEMBER 5**, a number of distinguished patriots of the Revolutionary War affixed their names to a petition to honor Salem Poor for his bravery.

To the Honorable General Court of the Massachusetts Bay:

The subscribers beg leave to report to your Honorable House (which we do in justice to the character of so brave a man), that, under our own observation, we declare that a negro man, called Salem Poor, of Col. Frye's regiment, Capt. Ames' company, in the late battle in Charlestown, behaved like an experienced officer, as well as an excellent soldier. To set forth particulars of his conduct would be tedious. We would beg leave to say, in the person of this said negro, centres a brave and gallant soldier. The reward due to so great and distinguished a character, we submit to the Congress.

> *Jona. Brewer, Col.*
> *Thomas Nixon, Lt. Col.*
> *Wm. Prescott, Col.*
> *Ephm. Corey, Lieut.*
> *Joseph Baker, Lieut.*
> *Jonas Richardson, Capt.*
> *Eliphalet Bodwell, Segt.*
> *Josiah Foster, Lieut.*
> *Ebenr. Varnum, 2d Lieut.*
> *Wm. Hudson Ballard, Capt.*
> *William Smith, Capt.*
> *John Morton, Sergt.[?]*
> *Lieut. Richard Welsh.*

Cambridge, December 5, 1755
In Council, Dec. 21, 1775 — Read, and sent down.

Perez Morton, Dep'y Sec'y.

ORDER BARRING BLACKS FROM SERVING IN ARMY RESCINDED

On **DECEMBER 31**, Washington reversed his earlier order and commanded recruiting officers to accept free Blacks into the Continental Army. This action was in response to Lord Dunmore's invitation to Blacks to fight for Britain, a heated debate in the Continental Congress, and protests from leaders of the Black community. As a result, more than five thousand Blacks, mostly from the North, fought in integrated units against the British. Slaves were still prohibited from fighting, although many were freed to join the Continental forces.

MARYLAND'S MULATTO POPULATION GROWS DESPITE LAW

In this year, a census reported 8 percent of the Maryland Black population as mulattos. This population continued to grow despite the fact that Maryland prohibited intermarriages by law as early as 1663. In addition, the census showed that Maryland contained about one-sixth of the Black population in the country at the time.

PAINE'S *Slavery in America* IS PUBLISHED

In this indictment against the institution of slavery, Thomas Paine (1737–1809), a Quaker, wrote, "As these people are not convicted of forfeiting freedom, they have still a natural, perfect right to it; and the Governments, whenever they come, should in justice set them free, and punish those who hold them in slavery."

RUSH PUBLISHES ANTISLAVERY ADDRESS

Benjamin Rush (1745–1813), a distinguished Philadelphia physician, chemistry professor, and original member of the Philadelphia College of Physicians, published *An Address to the Inhabitants of the British Settlements in America, Upon Slavekeeping.* Rush presented the case that the Black was intellectually and morally equal to the white, and that any "vices which are charged upon the negroes in the southern colonies and West Indies . . . are the genuine offspring of slavery, and serve as an argument to prove they were not intended by Providence for it." In response to the argument that slaves were necessary to the economic development of the South, Rush countered, "Liberty and property form the basis of abundance, and good agriculture: I never observed it to flourish where those rights of mankind were not firmly established." In rejecting the argument that slavery was a Christian institution and was not condemned by the Bible, Rush commented, "Christianity will never be propagated by any other methods than those employed by Christ and his Apostles. Slavery is an engine as little fitted for that purpose as

Benjamin Rush published An Address to the Inhabitants of the British Settlements in America, Upon Slavekeeping, *in which he argued that Blacks were not intellectually and morally inferior, that slaves were not necessary for the economic development of the South, and that slavery was not a Christian institution.*

Fire or the Sword. A Christian slave is a contradiction in terms."

1776 DRAFT SUBSTITUTION LAWS ENACTED

New York and other colonies passed a law allowing any white who was drafted to serve in the Continental Army to send a free Black in his place.

The number of whites who took advantage of this law remains unknown, since a large number of Blacks, slave and free, volunteered to serve their country.

NEW JERSEY CONSTITUTION GIVES FRANCHISE TO ALL MALES

The New Jersey Constitution declared that "all inhabitants of this colony of full age" shall have the right to vote.

In 1807, the franchise was restricted to free white male citizens twenty-one years of age and older.

DRAFT OF DECLARATION OF INDEPENDENCE CONDEMNS SLAVERY

The final version of the Declaration of Independence signed in Philadelphia omitted the attack on slavery that Thomas Jefferson had written in his draft version. The following is an extract from Jefferson's original draft:

> He has waged cruel war against human nature itself, violating its most sacred rights of life and liberty in the person of a distant people who never offended him; captivating and carrying them into slavery in another hemisphere, or to incur miserable death in their transportation thither. This piratical warfare, the opprobrium of Infidel Powers, is the warfare of the Christian King of Great Britain. Determined to keep open a market where men should be bought and sold, he has prostituted his negative for suppressing every legislative attempt to prohibit or restrain this execrable commerce.

Mr. Jefferson also provided Minutes of Debates in 1776 on the Declaration of Independence:

> The clause, too, reprobating the enslaving of the inhabitants of Africa was struck out, in compliance to South Carolina and Georgia, who had never attempted to restrain the importation of slaves, and who, on the contrary, still wish to continue it. Our northern brethren, also, I believe, felt a little tender under those censures; for, though their people have very few slaves themselves, yet they had been pretty considerable carriers of them to others.

HOPKINS CONDEMNS SLAVERY

Samuel Hopkins, pastor of First Congregational Church in Newport, Rhode Island, published *A Dialogue, Concerning the Slavery of Africans*. In this document, Hopkins called slavery a "scene of inhumanity, oppression, and cruelty, exceeding everything of the kind that has ever been perpetrated by the sons of men." Hopkins vividly presented the evils of slavery: war, death, and destruction in Africa; the slaves' purchase, branding, and the horrible passage; and the thirty thousand deaths attributed to the process of acclimatization, whippings, and other punishment.

POPULATION IN THE COLONIES

Estimates of the population in the British colonies differ at this time. By one count, the population numbered about 2.5 million, of which at least 500,000 were Black slaves and approximately 40,000 were free

Blacks. About one-half of the free Blacks resided in the South. Other estimates went as high as 3 million; these included many non-English European immigrants and from 250,000 to 300,000 Black slaves on the plantations of the West Indies and the southern continental colonies.

CONGRESS FAVORS ENDING SLAVE TRADE

On **APRIL 6**, Congress called for an end to the slave trade.

MASON COMPOSES VIRGINIA BILL OF RIGHTS

On **JUNE 12**, George Mason (1725–1792), a constitutionalist and a slave owner, wrote the Virginia Bill of Rights, which contained the following declaration: "That all men are by nature equally free and inde-

George Mason, a constitutionalist, wrote the Virginia Bill of Rights, which included language to the effect that all men were equal — language that was later used by Thomas Jefferson in the Declaration of Independence.

pendent, and have certain inherent rights, of which, when they enter into a state of society, they cannot by any compact deprive or divest their posterity; namely, the enjoyment of life and liberty, with the means of acquiring and possessing property, and pursuing and obtaining happiness and safety." Just one month later, on July 4, 1776, Thomas Jefferson infused the Declaration of Independence with similar language: "We hold these truths to be self-evident, that all men are created equal, that they are endowed by their Creator, with certain inalienable Rights, that among these are Life, Liberty, and the pursuit of Happiness."

✧ Later, George Mason refused to sign the Constitution because it compromised on slavery. Much of his remaining life was devoted to human rights issues.

1777 CONNECTICUT TOWNS DECIDE WHETHER SLAVE OWNERS CAN MANUMIT SLAVES

Connecticut passed legislation declaring that any slave owner who desired to manumit a slave must submit the case before selectmen of the town who would pass judgment. They were to take into consideration the age, ability, and character of the slave, especially whether the slave could make a living and "would benefit by manumission." If the judgment favored the owner, a certificate freeing the slave and relieving the owner of further responsibility for the care of the slave was provided. An amendment to this law limited such cases to slaves under forty-five years of age.

FREE BLACK SETTLEMENT ESTABLISHED NEAR PLYMOUTH, MASSACHUSETTS

Parting Ways, one of the earliest free Black settlements in America, was established near Plymouth, Massachusetts, when the town gave Cato Howe, a Black Revolutionary War veteran, ninety-four acres of land. The grant specified that the land had to be cleared and settled by Howe and three others who participated in the war. The four men built homes and lived out their lives on this land.

The last owner died in 1840, and the land fell into disuse. Archaeologists today are investigating the settlement area.

STATE CONSTITUTIONS GIVE FRANCHISE TO ALL MALES

New Hampshire followed Vermont in passing no statutes that made a distinction regarding race or color. The New York Constitution declared that "every male inhabitant of full age" had the right to vote, except that Blacks had to secure certificates of freedom certified by a judge. New York, at this time, contained a large number of free Blacks and fugitives.

VIRGINIA TEMPORARILY PROHIBITS IMPORTATION OF SLAVES

Virginia passed legislation prohibiting the importation of slaves within her borders.

This position was later reversed by an act of 1819, which proclaimed the state's willingness to receive all those not convicted of crimes who had been "born within the United States or any territory thereof, or within the District of Columbia."

VERMONT ABOLISHES SLAVERY

From **JULY 2 TO 12**, Vermont took the lead in abolishing slavery and became the first colonial territory to do so. Its action was embodied in its constitution, which made no distinctions among persons on the basis of color in any of its statutes. Its constitution contained the following general proposition: "No male person, born in this country, or brought from over sea, ought to be holden by law, to serve any person, as a servant, slave, or apprentice, after he arrives at the age of twenty-one years, nor female in like manner, after she arrives to the age of eighteen years, unless they are bound by law, for the payment of debts, damages, fines, costs, and the like." Because former owners had habitually taken their former slaves outside the state and disposed of them, the Vermont legislature passed a kidnapping law imposing a fine of one hundred pounds upon anyone convicted of interfering with a legally free Black. Further, the constitution gave the franchise to all males of mature age and extended the rights of trial by jury and habeas corpus to fugitives.

✧ In 1780, Pennsylvania made provisions for gradual emancipation of slaves. In 1783, New Hampshire and Massachusetts prohibited slavery, and a year later Connecticut and Rhode Island followed suit. New York (1799) and New Jersey (1804) lagged in enacting emancipation. By 1804, all the states north of Delaware had taken action to abolish slavery.

1778 BLACKS ENLIST IN CONTINENTAL ARMY

The Continental Army enlisted Blacks for three-year terms. Most of those who served came from the New England states. Black soldiers and white soldiers served in integrated units. By July, each brigade of General Washington's army averaged forty-two Black soldiers. Eventually, all-Black units emerged; for example, a battalion from Rhode Island, a company from Connecticut referred to as "the Colonials," and a company from Boston called "the Bucks of America," which was created from slave volunteers and commanded by a Black.

Black soldiers, including Prince Whipple and Oliver Cromwell, were members of the regiment that crossed the Delaware River with George Washington to attack the British in New Jersey. In 1777, Pompey Lamb's spying efforts assisted General Anthony Wayne's troops in capturing a British fort at Stony Point, New York. Other Black troops also served heroically.

By the end of the Revolutionary War, as many as three hundred thousand persons had fought to protect their liberty and freedom. Among these were five thousand Black soldiers and two thousand Black sailors, many of whom had fought bravely and received high praise from their commanders. Since the overwhelming number of Blacks served as army privates or as navy seamen, they were frequently involved in heavy combat.

VOTERS INITIALLY REJECT MASSACHUSETTS CONSTITUTION
Without calling a convention, Massachusetts wrote a constitution that recognized slavery, excluded Blacks from voting, and did not include a bill of rights. It was rejected by the voters, and a constitutional convention was then called. A bill of rights, one similar to George Mason's bill of rights for Virginia, was included in the new version, which was quickly adopted.

BLACK TROOPS IN RHODE ISLAND
General Nathanael Greene organized the First Rhode Island Regiment, an entirely Black army unit of about 300, after the General Assembly of the colony approved manumission for any slave enlisting in the Continental Army. About two hundred freedmen held the line against three times as many British at Newport in the battle of August 29, 1778, the only battle of the Revolution fought in Rhode Island. The freedmen fought valiantly for almost four hours, enough time to allow the American army to escape a trap. This engagement was referred to as the Battle of Rhode Island.

1779 PROPERTY TO BE TAKEN FROM SLAVES AND SOLD IN NORTH CAROLINA
According to legislation passed by the North Carolina legislature, "All horses, cattle, hogs or sheep, that, one month after the passing of this act, shall belong to any slave or be of any slave's mark, in this state, shall be seized and sold by the county wardens, and by

them applied, to one half to the support of the poor of the county, and the other half to the informer."

RHODE ISLAND PROHIBITS KIDNAPPING OF SLAVES
In 1779, Rhode Island passed substantive antislavery legislation, which forbade persons not residents of the state to purchase slaves for removal from the state. It further declared that any attempt to kidnap a slave from the state without a certificate attesting the slave's consent and signed by two justices of the peace entitled the slave to freedom. In 1778, Rhode Island had forbidden its citizens from participating in the African slave trade in any way. A penalty of one hundred pounds per slave and one thousand pounds per ship was decreed.

SLAVES PETITION NEW HAMPSHIRE LEGISLATURE TO ABOLISH SLAVERY
On **NOVEMBER 12**, twenty slaves signed and submitted a petition asking the New Hampshire legislature to abolish slavery. In their petition, they argued that "the god of nature gave them life and freedom upon the terms of most perfect equality with other men; that freedom is an inherent right of the human species, not to be surrendered but by consent."

1780
POPULATION OVERVIEW
GENERAL POPULATION IN NORTH AMERICAN BRITISH COLONIES The Bureau of the Census estimates that 2,780,369 persons lived in the colonies at this time. Virginia had the largest number of residents and was the first colony to reach the one-half-million mark (538,004). About one-half of the colonial population resided in just four colonies: Virginia, Pennsylvania (population 327,305), North Carolina (population 270,133), and Massachusetts (population 268,627). By region, about 50 percent (1.4 million) of colonial residents lived in southern colonies, 25.6 percent (712,829) lived in New England, and 24.4 percent (677,473) lived in the middle colonies.

Although all colonies experienced population growth between 1770 and 1780, the largest absolute increase occurred in Virginia (90,988), followed by Pennsylvania (87,248), North Carolina (72,933), and South Carolina (55,756). No other colony gained more than 50,000 people over the decade.

BLACKS IN NORTH AMERICAN BRITISH COLONIES As many as one-half million (575,420) Blacks lived in the colonies at this time. Virginia was home to about 38 percent of all Blacks (220,582). Virginia, South Carolina, North Carolina, and Maryland combined to make up 85 percent (489,097) of all Black residents. Over the decade, the colonies gained 115,598 Blacks, of which 89 percent (103,102) were accounted for in the colonies of Virginia (32,977), South Carolina (21,822), North Carolina (21,400), Maryland (16,697), and Georgia (10,206).

Other estimates show that more than half of all slaves resided in Virginia in 1783, nearly two-thirds of them in Virginia and Maryland combined. South Carolina and Georgia together contained less than one-half as many slaves as Virginia.

ECONOMIC CONDITIONS OVERVIEW

ECONOMIC CONDITIONS AND SLAVE PRICES Conditions during this period were such that most learned persons and political leaders predicted an end to slavery in the colonies. Tobacco prices had tumbled, indigo production had dropped, the cost of producing rice had increased, and slave prices had dropped rapidly. All of these factors led George Washington to advise his friends to convert their slave property into some other form of investment.

SLAVES OFFERED AS INCENTIVE TO ENLIST

South Carolina passed legislation offering a slave to each volunteer in the army as an incentive to enlist.

CUFFE AND OTHER BLACKS PROTEST TAXATION WITHOUT REPRESENTATION

On **FEBRUARY 10**, Paul Cuffe (1759–1817) and six other free Blacks of Dartmouth, Massachusetts (Adventure Childe, Pero Coggeshall, Paul Cuve, Samuel Gray, Pero Howland, and Pero Russell), petitioned against taxation without representation and refused to pay their taxes on the grounds that they were denied the right to vote. The court agreed with Cuffe's argument and granted him full legal rights. He was thus the first Black man to be given civil equality in Massachusetts. Cuffe and his brother also started a school for Black children after their own children were barred from attending the village school.
◈ Paul Cuffe, a colonial merchant, was born a free Black on January 17, 1759, near Dartmouth, Massachusetts. The son of a freed slave, Cuffe became one of the wealthiest Black men in America, making his fortune in overseas trade. Paul Cuffe was one of several influential Black leaders who petitioned and encouraged the passage of the 1783 law giving Blacks the right to vote in Massachusetts. Cuffe became a major figure in the movement to colonize Africa. He journeyed to Sierra Leone to help set up a colony for freed slaves. When he found out that backers from the South supported his plan as a way of getting freedmen out of America, he became disillusioned with the venture. He died in 1817 before the founding of Liberia, which was the fruition of his plan.

GRADUAL ABOLITION OF SLAVERY ENACTED IN PENNSYLVANIA

On **MARCH 1**, Pennsylvania passed legislation to abolish slavery. The bill, written by Thomas Paine, George Bryan, and Charles Willson Peale, was watered down before passage to implement a gradual abolition of slavery. Freedom was given to the offspring of slaves only when they reached the age of twenty-eight.

HAYNES COMMISSIONED TO PREACH

On **NOVEMBER 29**, Lemuel Haynes (1753–1833) was commissioned to preach in the Congregational Church, the first Black minister of this church.
◈ Haynes was born in West Hartford, Connecticut, of a white mother and Black father. When very young, he was bound out as a servant to Deacon David Rose in Granville, Massachusetts. The end of his service to the deacon coincided with the outbreak of the Revolution. Haynes saw action with the minutemen at Lexington on April 19, 1775, and later was among the elite group of Ethan Allen's Green Mountain Boys at the capture of Fort Ticonderoga.

After the war, he returned to his preparation for the ministry, and in 1785 he was officially ordained by an association of ministers in Litchfield County, Connecticut. His first call was to Torrington, Connecticut, where he had to overcome the issue of prejudice. In 1804, the faculty of Middlebury College awarded him an honorary master of arts degree, the first ever such degree to be conferred on a Black person in America.

Haynes was an active member of local, regional, and national Congregational Church bodies. He was elected to several official positions and was respected as one of the most intelligent ministers in the church councils and associations. In his older years, Haynes traveled and preached to various congregations.

1781 **JEFFERSON PUBLISHES** *Notes on Virginia*
In this publication in opposition to slavery, Thomas Jefferson asked the following question:

> Can the liberties of a nation be thought secure when we have removed their only firm basis, a conviction in the minds of the people that these liberties are the gift of God? That they are not to be violated but with His

SKETCHES
OF THE
LIFE AND CHARACTER
OF THE
REV. LEMUEL HAYNES, A.M.,
FOR MANY YEARS PASTOR OF A CHURCH IN RUTLAND, VT., AND LATE IN
GRANVILLE, NEW-YORK.

BY TIMOTHY MATHER COOLEY, D.D.,
PASTOR OF THE FIRST CHURCH IN GRANVILLE, MASS.

WITH SOME INTRODUCTORY REMARKS BY
WILLIAM B. SPRAGUE, D.D.,
PASTOR OF THE SECOND PRESBYTERIAN CHURCH IN ALBANY

Nil desperandum Christo duce.

NEW-YORK:
HARPER & BROTHERS, 82 CLIFF-ST.
1837.

Lemuel Haynes is shown in the frontispiece to Sketches of the Life and Character of the Rev. Lemuel Haynes, A.M., *by Timothy Mather Cooley, published in 1837. Cooley wrote that Haynes's life story could "hardly fail to mitigate the unreasonable prejudices against the Africans in our land."*

wrath? Indeed I tremble for my country when I reflect that God is just; that His justice cannot sleep forever.

ARMISTEAD SPIES FOR CONTINENTAL ARMY

In **MARCH**, James Armistead (1760–1832) was granted permission by his owner, William Armistead, to serve in the Continental Army, and became one of the most important spies of the American Revolution. The information he acquired helped his commander, Marquis de Lafayette, a Frenchman serving in the American army, to defeat the British at Yorktown, Virginia, on October 19, 1781.

◇ Whereas Lafayette became an immediate hero, Armistead returned to being a slave. Although Lafayette wrote a letter urging Armistead's freedom, it was not until 1786 that the Virginia General Assembly intervened and granted it. Armistead later adopted Lafayette's name.

INSURRECTION IN WILLIAMSBURG

On **JULY 20**, slaves in Williamsburg, Virginia, rebelled. They set fire to many buildings, including the capitol.

LOS ANGELES FOUNDED BY BLACKS

On **SEPTEMBER 4**, forty-four men and women founded Los Angeles, California; as many as twenty-six were of African descent, and two of Spanish descent. Los Angeles, Nuestra Señora la Reina de los Angeles de Porciuncula, became the second settlement established in California.

1782–1783 SLAVES LEAVE AMERICA WHEN THE BRITISH TROOPS LEAVE

It is estimated that twenty thousand Blacks, four times the number that served with the American army, left with the British troops after the American Revolutionary War. Twelve thousand departed with the British from Charleston and Savannah. The British army offered many slaves, especially those in the South, freedom and other opportunities denied them by Americans. Some Blacks were brought to freedom in England, Nova Scotia, and Jamaica. Others, however, were taken to the British West Indies and sold back into slavery.

Some time later, several key leaders in the founding of Sierra Leone could trace their ancestors to former slaves who had left with the British.

1783   BLACK POPULATION REACHES ONE MILLION

As many as one million Blacks lived in the colonies at this time. More than half of all slaves resided in Virginia.

HONORABLE DISCHARGE FOR CROMWELL

On JUNE 5, Oliver Cromwell (1753–1853), a Black soldier in the Revolutionary War for six years and nine months, was honorably discharged by his commander in general, George Washington. He received the "Badge of Merit."

Born in Columbus, New Jersey, Cromwell joined the Second New Jersey Regiment. He served longer than the average time and saw action in several important battles. He served in the battles of Trenton and Princeton (1776–1777), Brandywine (1777), Monmouth (1778), and was present at the surrender of Cornwallis at Yorktown in 1781. One of Cromwell's most celebrated actions was accompanying George Washington when he crossed the Delaware River in 1776.

MASSACHUSETTS SUPREME COURT ABOLISHES SLAVERY

On JULY 8, the Massachusetts Supreme Court's decision in the case of *Commonwealth* v. *Jennison* abolished slavery in the commonwealth by virtue of the Declaration of Rights of 1780.

The Massachusetts Supreme Court had been petitioned to rule on a case involving Quaco Walker, a slave held by Nathaniel Jennison. After being severely beaten by Jennison, Walker ran away to a neighbor's home in search of protection. He was then hired to work by this neighbor and protector. Jennison petitioned the supreme court, saying that his slave was enticed to leave, but he lost the case. Walker charged Jennison with assault and battery and false imprisonment. Jennison's response was that Walker was his slave and thus subject to correction at the discretion of his owner. Chief Justice William Cushing (later an associate justice of the U.S. Supreme Court) gave the court's opinion in this case:

[The Constitution of Government] sets out with declaring that all men are born free and equal — and that every subject is entitled to liberty, and to have it guarded by the laws, as well as life and property — in short is totally repugnant to the idea of being born slaves . . . the idea of slavery is inconsistent with our own conduct and Constitution; and there can be no

such thing as perpetual servitude of a rational creature, unless his liberty is forfeited by some criminal conduct or given up by personal consent or contract.

The colonial assembly of Massachusetts had passed legislation in 1774 that prevented the importation of slaves into the commonwealth, but it had not been signed by either Governor Hutchinson or Governor Gage. Five years after Chief Justice Cushing's declaration that slavery was illegal and thus abolished in the state, the legislature passed a law forbidding all citizens of Massachusetts from engaging in buying, selling, or transporting slaves, declared insurance void on all ships used in violation of the law, and imposed heavy fines upon anyone convicted of kidnapping free Blacks.

SLAVES RETURNED TO OWNERS AFTER REVOLUTION ENDS

On SEPTEMBER 3, the Treaty of Paris brought the American Revolution to an end. It stipulated that escaped and captured slaves would be returned to their owners.

SLAVES EMANCIPATED IN VIRGINIA

On OCTOBER 23, Virginia emancipated slaves who fought with the patriots of the Continental Army.

1784   CONNECTICUT ABOLISHES SLAVERY

The Connecticut legislature passed a law giving all children born of slave mothers after May 1, 1784, freedom at age twenty-five. Birth certificates had to be filed by the owners before the child reached six months of age.

METHODIST EPISCOPAL CHURCHES IN AMERICA DENOUNCE SLAVERY AND ISSUE MANDATE TO MEMBERS

At the conference of Methodist Episcopal Churches in America, under the leadership of Bishop John Wesley, the church adopted the following strong antislavery statement:

Every member in our Society who has slaves in those States where the law will admit of freeing them, shall, after notice given him by the preacher, set them free within twelve months, (except in Virginia, and there within two years,) at specified periods according to age. Every person concerned who will not comply with these rules shall have liberty to withdraw within twelve months after the notice is given, otherwise to be excluded. No person holding slaves shall in future be admitted into the Society until he previously comply with these rules respecting Slavery.

♦ The adopted regulations were angrily debated at a subsequent conference held in Virginia, and although defended at the time, they were defeated and suspended a year later.

PETITIONS OPPOSE MANUMISSION FOR SLAVES IN VIRGINIA

In this year and in 1785, the Virginia General Assembly was overwhelmed by petitions bearing more than twelve hundred signatures protesting a 1782 Virginia law that allowed masters to free their slaves without legislative approval. Their resistance to this law appeared to be based on the right to "private property."

RHODE ISLAND EMANCIPATES SLAVES

Emancipation of slaves in Rhode Island was solidified, after many feeble efforts, when the General Assembly agreed upon legislation that declared:

> All men are entitled to Life, Liberty, and the Pursuit of Happiness, and the holding of Mankind in a state of Slavery, as private Property, which has gradually obtained by unrestrained Custom and Permission of the Laws, is repugnant to the Principle, and subversive of the Happiness of Mankind, and the great End of all civil Government.

It continued by stating that all children born of slave mothers after March 1, 1784, were to be held as apprentices — males until twenty-one years of age, females until eighteen — and then freed.

JEFFERSON'S PLAN TO BAN SLAVERY DEFEATED

On **MARCH 1**, a congressional committee headed by Thomas Jefferson proposed banning slavery everywhere in the United States after 1800. The proposal was narrowly defeated.

♦ It is unclear what specifically Jefferson had in mind for Black people if his proposal had been accepted. In his *Notes on Virginia*, there was a distinction between his philosophical opposition to slavery and his personal views. In his *Notes*, he described Blacks as lazy, slow, unable to reason, and limited in imagination. Although Jefferson eloquently denounced slavery, he continued to own more than two hundred slaves, who built and maintained Monticello.

1785 SOCIETY FOR ABOLISHING THE SLAVE TRADE ESTABLISHED IN RHODE ISLAND

The Rhode Island Society for Abolishing the Slave Trade was founded in Providence. Its purpose was to organize antislavery activities, assist free Blacks in

Negroes for Sale.

A Cargo of very fine stout Men and Women, in good order and fit for immediate service, just imported from the Windward Coast of Africa, in the Ship Two Brothers.— Conditions are one half Cash or Produce, the other half payable the first of January next, giving Bond and Security if required.

The Sale to be opened at 10 o'Clock each Day, in Mr. Bourdeaux's Yard, at No. 48, on the Bay. May 19, 1784. JOHN MITCHELL.

Thirty Seasoned Negroes
To be Sold for Credit, at Private Sale.

AMONGST which is a Carpenter, none of whom are known to be dishonest.

Also, to be sold for Cash, a regular bred young Negroe Man-Cook, born in this Country, who served several Years under an exceeding good French Cook abroad, and his Wife a middle aged Washer-Woman, (both very honest) and their two Children. Likewise, a young Man a Carpenter. For Terms apply to the Printer.

In order to attract the largest possible number of potential buyers and traders, advertisements announcing slave auctions were printed and circulated widely. This one advertised both the sale of a fresh cargo of slaves from Africa and the sale of domestic slaves for cash or credit.

finding employment, provide education, register deeds of manumission, and discourage the slave trade.

NEW YORK ESTABLISHES SOCIETY FOR PROMOTING THE MANUMISSION OF SLAVES

On **JANUARY 25**, New York became the first state officially to organize an antislavery society. Like many other societies at the time, the New York group promoted freedom for Blacks through publicizing laws relating to slavery, distributed antislavery literature, and sponsored lectures by noted abolitionists. It attracted the membership of distinguished persons who spoke strongly against the slave trade and slavery. John Jay was elected the society's first president and Alexander Hamilton its second. Jay's participation was limited first by virtue of his position as first chief justice of the United States and later because of his role as a diplomat. Jay's two sons, Peter A. (1776–

1834) and William (1789–1858), as well as his grandson, John Jay (1827–1894), were also members.

1786 FREEDMEN HARASSED IN PHILADELPHIA

Since Philadelphia was located only several miles from the Mason-Dixon Line (the border between slave and free states before the Civil War), freedmen there were often harassed. Slavers frequently came north to kidnap freed Blacks at random on the pretext of capturing fugitive slaves. One such victim was the Reverend Richard Allen, founder of the African Methodist Episcopal Church, who was seized by a trader who had made a sworn affidavit that Allen was an escaped slave. After the testimony of many prominent Philadelphians on Allen's behalf, Allen was freed, and the slave trader was imprisoned for perjury.

LAFAYETTE EXPRESSES ANTISLAVERY VIEWS

In a letter to John Adams, Marquis de Lafayette, a hero of the Revolution, said,

> I would never have drawn my sword in this cause of America, could I have conceived that thereby I was founding a land of Slavery.
>
> In the cause of my black brethren, I feel myself warmly interested, and most decidedly side, so far as respects them, against the white part of mankind. Whatever be the complexion of the enslaved, it does not, in my opinion, alter the complexion of the crime which the enslaver commits — a crime much blacker than any African face. It is to me a matter of great anxiety and concern, to find that this trade is sometimes perpetrated under the flag of liberty, our dear and noble stripes, to which virtue and glory have been constant standard-bearers.

PASSAGE OF ANTISLAVERY LEGISLATION IN NEW JERSEY DIFFICULT

In New Jersey, the passage of antislavery legislation was a somewhat cumbersome process. In 1786, the legislature declared: "The Principles of Justice and Humanity require that the barbarous custom of bringing the unoffending Africans from their native country and Connections into a State of Slavery ought to be discountenanced, and as soon as possible prevented." A penalty was imposed on any person who imported a slave from Africa into the state, but the law permitted persons to remove slaves from the state.

PRODUCTION OF SEA ISLAND COTTON BEGINS

"Sea Island" cotton was introduced in 1786. This extremely profitable variety could not be grown more

Cotton production required continuous work. Among the most labor-intensive tasks were picking the cotton and removing the seeds.

than forty miles away from the coast. Its production was to remain concentrated in Georgia and South Carolina.

Sea Island cotton did not much change the economy of the low country area, as it remained a fairly minor specialty crop. In contrast, short-staple cotton changed the economy throughout the South, causing slavery to spread into new areas. Short-staple cotton could be grown widely throughout the South, but its seeds were difficult to remove (before the invention of the cotton gin). Thus, early production of short-staple cotton was largely restricted to small patches for family use.

RUNAWAYS CAUSE CONTINUING DISTURBANCES IN SAVANNAH

A group of runaway Blacks, led by a person trained in military tactics by the British, continued to harass and alarm residents of Savannah. The runaways still referred to themselves as the "King of England's soldiers." They intentionally aroused fear among slaveholders to produce an environment that could lead to a general insurrection by the slaves in that vicinity. They were viewed by many as "the most dangerous and best disciplined bands of marauders which ever infested its borders."

1787 COLONY OF FREE BLACKS ESTABLISHED
IN SIERRA LEONE

The British established a colony of free Blacks in Sierra Leone in West Africa. Trade between the United States and Sierra Leone was established by Paul Cuffe, a mulatto ship captain from Massachusetts. Although Cuffe was the visible leader of the project (not the movement) to resettle many Blacks in Sierra Leone, he personally transported only one shipload of such settlers. The movement was continued by the American Colonization Society.

CONNECTICUT RESTRICTS RESIDENTS
FROM SLAVE TRADE

Connecticut restricted its residents from engaging directly or indirectly in the slave trade and imposed a fine of one hundred pounds for kidnapping any Black covered by the provisions of the emancipation act.

CONSTITUTIONAL CONVENTION CONSIDERS
SLAVERY ISSUE

Since slavery had been such a profitable business in the colonies, it was one of the major items on the agenda of the Constitutional Convention in Philadelphia in 1787. Here slave trade was extended for twenty years by Article 10, Section 9, of the new Constitution of the United States. Article 4, Section 2, called for the extradition of fugitive slaves. It stated, "No person held to Service or Labour in one State, under the Laws thereof, escaping into another, shall . . . be discharged from such Service or Labour, but shall be delivered up on Claim of the Party to whom such Service or Labor may be due." These provisions were to be strengthened by the Fugitive Slave Law of 1793.

During the debate of Article 1, Section 9, of the Constitution, which forbade Congress from prohibiting the importation of slaves before the year 1808, George Mason eloquently argued against the provision:

> It [the importation of slaves] was one of the great causes of our separation from Great Britain. Its exclusion has been a principal object of this State, and most of the States of the Union. The argumentation of slaves weakens the States; and such a trade is diabolical in itself, and disgraceful to mankind: yet, by this Constitution, it is continued for twenty years. As much as I value a union of all the States, I would not admit the Southern States into the Union, unless they agree to the discontinuance of this disgraceful trade, because it brings weakness, and not strength, to the Union.

SLAVES RESTRICTED FROM HIRING THEMSELVES
OUT FOR WORK

By an act of the Maryland General Assembly during its April session, slave owners would be fined if they allowed a slave to hire himself or herself out for work. This law was passed to keep slaves from earning money to purchase both goods and their freedom. Specifically, the act stated that "any person who shall permit and authorize any slave belonging to him or herself, &c. to go at large or hire himself or herself, within this state, shall incur the penalty of five pounds (thirteen and one-third dollars) current money per month, except ten days at harvest."

BLACKS PETITION FOR FUNDS TO RETURN TO AFRICA

On **JANUARY 4**, Blacks in Massachusetts, including Prince Hall, petitioned the Massachusetts General Court for funds to return to Africa. The petition was refused, but it was recorded as the first such effort by Blacks to return to their homeland.

FREE AFRICAN SOCIETY FOUNDED

On **APRIL 12**, Richard Allen and Absalom Jones organized Philadelphia's Free African Society, one of the first official organizations of Blacks in the country. The society was organized as a mutual aid society, a church, and a political structure. Societies were also formed in New York City, Boston, and Newport, Rhode Island. On July 7, 1791, Allen and Jones, with the help of Benjamin Rush, organized "the African Church." Although both leaders wanted to affiliate this new church with the Methodists, their followers preferred affiliation with the Episcopal Church.

◈ Allen left the group and in 1794 organized the Bethel African Methodist Episcopal Church. Jones stayed with the African Church that became the St. Thomas African Episcopal Church. W. E. B. Du Bois later called the Free African Society "the first wavering step of a people toward a more organized social life."

BLACK MASONIC ORDER ESTABLISHED

On **MAY 6**, Prince Hall (1748–1807), a Revolutionary War veteran, organized the Negro Masonic Order in the United States — African Lodge No. 459, in Boston. This became the first Black self-help fraternal institution in the United States.

◈ Hall had presented his petition to form a lodge to the Grand Lodge of England on March 2, 1784. His petition was granted, but its implementation was delayed until 1787. Hall and his associates worked to form Masonic lodges in a number of other cities, making it the first interstate institution in this country. The second American Negro Masonic Lodge was established in Providence, Rhode Island, in 1797; a third was formed in Philadelphia in 1798 (with Absalom Jones and Richard Allen as officers). A lodge in New York was opened in 1812, followed by lodges in the District of Columbia and Maryland in 1825. These fraternal organizations were important to Blacks at the time; along with churches and schools, they constituted an important part of the self-help movement. More than 150 years later, the Negro Masonic Order had 40 grand lodges, 5,500 lodges, and more than 500,000 members.

Hall dedicated much of his life to fighting against slavery and the slave trade. In 1777, he was among eight Black petitioners requesting that Massachusetts abolish slavery. He was instrumental in getting the state legislature to end the slave trade. In 1787, Hall launched an unsuccessful "back to Africa" colonization scheme, more than twenty-three years before Paul Cuffe sailed to Africa. On October 17, 1787, Hall led other Blacks in a petition to the Massachusetts General Court for equal school facilities:

> To the Honorable the Senate and House of Representatives of the Commonwealth of Massachusetts Bay, in General Court assembled.
>
> The petition of a great number of blacks, freemen of this in Commonwealth, humbly sheweth, that your petitioners are held in common with other freemen of this town and Commonwealth and have never been backward in paying our proportionate part of the burdens under which they have, or may labor under; and as we are willing to pay our equal part of these burdens, we are of the humble opinion that we have the right to enjoy the privileges of free men. But that we do not will appear in many instances, and we beg leave to mention one out of many, and that is the education of our children which now receive no benefit from the free schools in the town of Boston, which we think is a great grievance, as by woeful experience we now feel that the want of a common education. We, therefore, must fear for our rising offspring to see them in ignorance in a land of gospel light when there is provision made for them as well as others and yet can't enjoy them, and for not other reason can be given this they are black. . . . We therefore pray your Honors that you would in your wisdom some provision may be made for the education of our dear children. And in duty bound shall ever pray.

◆ There is no reliable information about Prince Hall's birthplace, year of birth, or parentage. Simi-

larly, there are questions about his early life and career. It is known that he died in 1807 and was about seventy-two years of age at the time. Documented evidence indicates that Hall was the slave of William Hall in Boston in the 1740s. He was manumitted in 1770 as a reward for his twenty-one years of faithful service. His military record during the American Revolution is uncertain, because other soldiers were also named Prince Hall. Further, there is no firm evidence that this Prince Hall fought at Bunker Hill or served as a soldier during the war.

THREE-FIFTHS COMPROMISE INCLUDED IN U.S. CONSTITUTION

On **JULY 12**, delegates to the Constitutional Convention in Philadelphia accepted the plan offered by James Madison that determined a state's representation in the U.S. House of Representatives. The issue of how to count slaves split the delegates into two camps. The northerners generally regarded slaves as property who should, therefore, receive no representation. The governor of Pennsylvania stated that the people of his state would revolt if their status were to be considered equal to that of slaves. Southerners, on the other hand, demanded that Blacks be counted equally with whites. The compromise clearly reflected the strength of the proslavery forces at the convention. The "Three-Fifths Compromise" allowed states to count three-fifths of the Black population in determining political representation in the House. Some northerners quickly remarked that the "three-fifths rule" was the most blatant and fateful blunder of the convention. Rather than curtailing and eventually stopping the importation of slaves in South Carolina and Georgia, slavery had been given a new life — a political life. According to the compromise, twenty thousand owners of fifty thousand slaves had a political representation equal to fifty thousand free persons.

Even when the importation of new slaves was eventually stopped by law on January 1, 1808, the South continued to increase its overall political representation and electoral votes by adding slaves through illegal importation and breeding. Thomas Branagan, once a slaveholder, overseer, and slave trader in the West Indies, issued a powerful warning of the growing southern political power in his book entitled *The Penitential Tyrant*, published in 1807. In the book, Branagan noted:

> The tyrants of the South, gain an ascendancy over the citizens of the North, and enhance their paramount rights of suffrage and sovereignty accordingly as they

enslave and subjugate their inoffensive sons of Africa . . . I am astonished at the stupidity of our citizens, in suffering such palpable villainy to be rewarded by political, as well as pecuniary gratifications . . . Unless this villainous inequality is in time remedied, the rights and liberties of our citizens will be eventually swallowed up.

SLAVERY RESTRICTED IN NORTHWEST TERRITORY

On **JULY 13**, the Continental Congress barred the extension of slavery into the Northwest Territory under the Ordinance of 1787. Neither slavery nor involuntary servitude was to be permitted in the region northwest of the Ohio River except as punishment for a crime:

Article 6

There shall be neither slavery nor involuntary servitude in the said territory, otherwise than in the punishment of crimes whereof the party shall have been duly convicted: Provided, always, That any person escaping into the same, from whom labor or service is lawfully claimed in any one of the original States, such fugitive may be lawfully reclaimed and conveyed to the person claiming his or her labor or service as aforesaid.

INTERNATIONAL ANTISLAVERY SOCIETIES ORGANIZED

On **JULY 17**, the London Society, an antislavery group, was organized. It was followed a year later by the Paris Society. Some of the most noble, lettered, and distinguished members of French society applied for membership in the Paris Society. The Marquis de Lafayette was one of its founders.

AFRICAN FREE SCHOOL FOUNDED IN NEW YORK CITY

On **NOVEMBER 1**, in New York City, the Manumission Society organized the African Free School, the first free secular school for Blacks in the city. It was eventually transferred to city authorities.

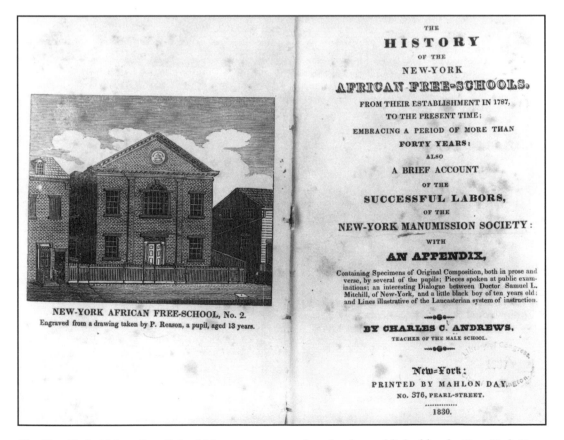

NEW-YORK AFRICAN FREE-SCHOOL, No. 2.
Engraved from a drawing taken by P. Reason, a pupil, aged 13 years.

THE
HISTORY
OF THE
NEW-YORK
AFRICAN-FREE-SCHOOLS,
FROM THEIR ESTABLISHMENT IN 1787,
TO THE PRESENT TIME;
EMBRACING A PERIOD OF MORE THAN
FORTY YEARS:
ALSO
A BRIEF ACCOUNT
OF THE
SUCCESSFUL LABORS,
OF THE
NEW-YORK MANUMISSION SOCIETY:
WITH
AN APPENDIX,
Containing Specimens of Original Composition, both in prose and verse, by several of the pupils; Pieces spoken at public examinations; an interesting Dialogue between Doctor Samuel L. Mitchill, of New-York, and a little black boy of ten years old; and Lines illustrative of the Lancasterian system of instruction.
BY CHARLES C. ANDREWS,
TEACHER OF THE MALE SCHOOL.
New-York:
PRINTED BY MAHLON DAY,
NO. 376, PEARL-STREET.
1830.

The New York African Free School No. 2 was among the schools established by the New York Manumission Society. The history of these schools was presented in this 1830 publication.

ORIGINAL THIRTEEN STATES AND THE ORGANIZATION OF ADJOINING TERRITORIES

WESTERN LANDS

The Northwest Ordinance was a plan to govern the land bounded by the Great Lakes and the Ohio and Mississippi Rivers as the territory evolved into states. Congress placed only two limitations on the five new states created from this territory: the power of the state government had to lie in representatives elected by the people, and slavery was prohibited in all land north of the Ohio River.

1788 ABOLITION SOCIETY ORGANIZED IN DELAWARE

The Delaware Society for Promoting the Abolition of Slavery and for the Relief and Protection of Free Blacks and People of Colour Unlawfully Held in Bondage was organized in 1788. Warner Mifflin was one of the most active and enterprising members of the society. Other members included Isaiah Rowland, Joseph Hodgson, and John Pemberton.

NEW JERSEY PASSES ANTISLAVERY LAW

The New Jersey state legislature passed an antislavery law that stipulated confiscation of ships involved in the slave trade and prohibited the removal of slaves over twenty-one years of age from the state. This law also required slave owners to teach slaves under twenty-one years of age to read and set fines for failure to do so.

PENNSYLVANIA ACTS TO KEEP SLAVE FAMILIES TOGETHER

In Pennsylvania, an act was passed to fine slave owners fifty pounds who separated members of slave families for a distance greater than ten miles without the consent of the family members.

FIRST AFRICAN BAPTIST CHURCH FOUNDED IN GEORGIA

On JANUARY 20, the First African Baptist Church was founded in Savannah, Georgia, by Andrew Bryan, a slave. Bryan had been converted to Christianity by George Liele, another pioneer Black minister. Whites generally opposed Black churches because they feared they promoted opposition to slavery. Slaves were whipped by their owners to stop them from belonging to Bryan's church, but they continued to attend. Bryan was jailed in an unsuccessful effort to close his church. His white master helped to secure his release. Bryan remained a slave until his owner's death, when he purchased his freedom for 50 pounds. He eventually founded three other churches in Savannah.

FREE BLACKS OF MASSACHUSETTS PROTEST SLAVE TRADE

On MARCH 26, free Blacks petitioned the Massachusetts General Court, protesting the forcible exportation of Blacks from Boston to Martinique. This prompted the assembly to review the issue and declare slave trade illegal.

1789 PENNSYLVANIA ABOLITION SOCIETY IS INCORPORATED

The Pennsylvania Abolition Society was incorporated by the state legislature as the Pennsylvania So-

ciety for Promoting the Abolition of Slavery, the Relief of Free Negroes Unlawfully Held in Bondage, and for Improving the Condition of the African Race. The group continued to have many active Quaker participants. Two signatories of the Declaration of Independence were members. Benjamin Franklin became its first president and Benjamin Rush served as secretary. The organization publicized state laws relative to slavery and free Blacks, printed and distributed antislavery literature, initiated assistance to free Blacks and those illegally held in bondage, and built a network of antislavery societies. The organization is believed to be the first colonial group formed specifically to combat slavery.

PUBLICATION OF OLAUDAH EQUIANO'S *Interesting Narrative*

One of the most vivid accounts of the experiences of an African slave was written by Olaudah Equiano. In his book, *The Interesting Narrative of the Life of Olaudah Equiano, or Gustavus Vassa, the African, Written by Himself*, he wrote:

> The first object which saluted my eyes when I arrived on the coast was the sea, and a slave ship which was then riding at anchor and waiting for its cargo. These filled me with astonishment, which was soon converted into terror when I was carried on board. I was immediately handled and tossed up to see if I were sound by some of the crew, and I was not persuaded that I had gotten into a world of bad spirits and that they were going to kill me. Their complexions too differing so much from ours, their long hair and the language they spoke (which was very different from any I had ever heard) united to confirm me in this belief. Indeed such were the horrors of my views and fears at the moment that, if ten thousand worlds had been my own, I would have freely parted with them all to have exchanged my condition with that of the meanest slave in my own country. When I looked round the ship too and saw a large furnace or copper boiling and a multitude of black people of every description chained together, everyone of their countenances expressing dejection and sorrow, I no longer doubted my fate; and quick overpowered with horror and anguish, I fell motionless on the deck and fainted.

SLAVE POPULATION IN THE NORTH

Of the 740,000 slaves in the country, only about 40,000 (5 percent) lived in the North. Most of these were employed as domestic servants. Slave labor was not an important factor in manufacturing — one of

THE

INTERESTING NARRATIVE

OF

THE LIFE

OF

OLAUDAH EQUIANO,

OR

GUSTAVUS VASSA,

THE AFRICAN.

WRITTEN BY HIMSELF.

Behold, God is my salvation; I will trust, and not be afraid, for the Lord Jehovah is my strength and my song; he also is become my salvation. And in that day shall ye say, Praise the Lord, call upon his name, declare his doings among the people. Isa. xii. 2. 4.

EIGHTH EDITION ENLARGED.

NORWICH:

PRINTED FOR, AND SOLD BY THE AUTHOR.

1794.

PRICE FOUR SHILLINGS.

Formerly sold for 7s.

[*Entered at Stationers' Hall.*]

Olaudah Equiano;

or

GUSTAVUS VASSA,

the African?

The Interesting Narrative of the Life of Olaudah Equiano, or Gustavus Vassa, The African, *was one of the most popular personal accounts of slavery. Vassa's autobiography started with his childhood in Africa and continued with his life as a slave and later as a worker for hire. Printed first in London, the narrative ran through eight editions in five years, and Vassa became an international celebrity.*

the reasons that made it more convenient for the North to oppose slavery.

ABOLITION SOCIETY ORGANIZED IN MARYLAND

On **SEPTEMBER 8**, the Maryland Society for Promoting the Abolition of Slavery and the Relief of Free Negroes and Others Unlawfully Held in Bondage was organized. An excerpt from the preamble of the society's constitution illustrates its abhorrence of slavery:

The common Father of mankind created all men free and equal; and his great command is, that we love our neighbor as ourselves — doing unto all men as we would they should do unto us. The human race, how-

ever varied in color or intellects, are all justly entitled to liberty; and it is the duty and the interest of nations and individuals, enjoying every blessing of freedom, to remove this dishonor of the Christian character from amongst them. From the fullest impression of the truth of these principles; from an earnest wish to bear our testimony against slavery in all its forms, to spread it abroad as far as the sphere of our influence may extend, and to afford our friendly assistance to those who may be engaged in the same undertaking; and in the humblest hope of support from that Being, who takes, as an offering to himself, what we do for each other — We, the subscribers, have formed ourselves into the Maryland Society for Promoting

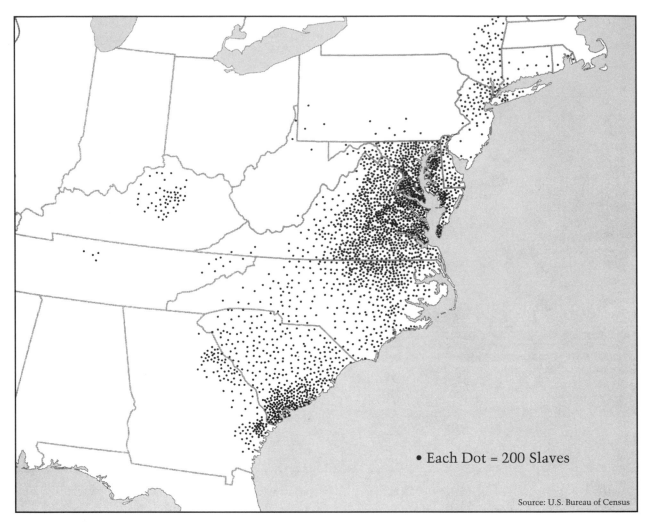

GEOGRAPHICAL DISTRIBUTION OF
SLAVE POPULATION IN THE UNITED STATES, 1790

As much as 91 percent of the slave population at the time of the first U.S. Census was found in the South. The largest concentrations were in the tobacco-growing areas of Maryland and Virginia and along the rice coast of South Carolina.

the Abolition of Slavery, and the Relief of Free Negroes and Others unlawfully held in bondage.

1790

POPULATION OVERVIEW

GENERAL POPULATION IN THE UNITED STATES The first U.S. Census of Population recorded 3,929,214 residents.

Philadelphia was the largest city in the country (42,000 residents), followed by New York City (33,000), Boston (18,000), Charleston (16,000), and Baltimore (13,000).

BLACK POPULATION IN THE UNITED STATES Blacks composed 19.3 percent of the total population, about 757,208 in all. Slaves numbered 697,624, and free Blacks, 59,557. About 67,000 Blacks resided in the

North; 60 percent of these were slaves. Slaves could be found in every state except Vermont and Massachusetts. As many as 21,193 lived in New York, 11,423 in New Jersey, and 3,707 in Pennsylvania. Connecticut had 2,786 slaves (half of its Black population), and Delaware, about 9,000. In the South, slaves were concentrated in the following manner: Virginia, 292,627; South Carolina, 107,094; Maryland and the District of Columbia, 103,036; North Carolina, 100,783. Georgia had 29,264 slaves at this time. In essence, more than 40 percent of the total number of slaves in the United States were concentrated in one state, Virginia. Slaves made up about 42 percent of the total population in both Virginia and South Carolina, the largest slave populations of any states.

BLACK URBAN POPULATION The census revealed that Black communities were developing along the wharves and alleys in many northern cities. In Philadelphia, Blacks resided around Sixth and Lombard Streets; in Boston, on the north side of Beacon Hill in "New Guinea"; in Cincinnati, in "Little Africa" in the first and fourth wards; and in New York City in the notorious integrated slum of Five Points and in the area known today as Greenwich Village. The Black population grew especially large in Philadelphia and New York City. In fact, by the end of the century, these two cities had the largest urban concentrations of Black people.

FREE BLACK POPULATION Of the free Black population, 27,000 resided in the North and 32,000 in the South. Free Blacks rapidly grew in number over the last few decades and were thus considered a major threat by many whites. Therefore, free Blacks began to face restrictions and regulations similar to those governing Black slaves. The probability of slaves becoming free varied from region to region — those in the most southern states found their chances of escaping or purchasing their freedom more difficult than those farther north. South Carolina had fewer than 2,000 free Blacks, mostly in and around Charleston; Georgia had about 400; and these two states together had only 7 percent of the free Blacks of the entire South. In contrast, the middle states of Virginia and Maryland experienced both a large number of escapes and manumissions. As a result, the number of free Blacks among their populations increased.

ECONOMIC OVERVIEW

TOBACCO PRODUCTION PEAKS This year saw the export of 118,000 hogsheads of tobacco, marking the peak of tobacco production in the period before the Civil War. From this time on, tobacco production declined as cotton production increased. A number of factors contributed to the decline of tobacco production, including soil exhaustion in the tidewater area, growth of diversified crops in the piedmont, and the disruption of foreign trade due to the Napoleonic wars.
◈ Exports of tobacco fell to about 58,000 hogsheads in 1797 but rose to 103,000 in 1801. Exports averaged only 7,500 hogsheads between 1811 and 1814, and fell to only about 3,000 in 1814.

INDIGO PRODUCTION PLUMMETS Indigo production plummeted between 1780 and 1790, as competition from the East Indies increased and profitability from growing the crop declined. South Carolina's exports of indigo fell from 839,000 pounds in 1792 to only 96,000 pounds in 1797, and to 3,400 pounds by 1800. In just eight years, production of this crop literally came to a halt. Indigo, once a profitable crop in the American colonies, was no longer favored by planters because of lower prices brought about by increased production in the East Indies.

PRICE OF RICE CONTINUES TO FALL Between 1797 and 1799, the price of rice dropped to only about one-half of its price in 1795 and 1796. Rice required so much labor that it could be produced at a profit only by large-scale plantations with many workers. Controlled flooding of the rice fields was also expensive to maintain. Although production did not cease altogether, as indigo production did, it also did not expand.

ABOLITION SOCIETY FOUNDED IN CONNECTICUT

The Connecticut Society for the Promotion of Freedom and for the Relief of Persons Holden in Bondage was organized to provide education, register deeds of manumission, discourage the slave trade, and assist free Blacks to find employment. Ezra Stiles, president of Yale College, was president of the society, and Judge Simeon Baldwin was its secretary. One of its first efforts was to spread antislavery ideas by distributing literature and sponsoring lectures, including some by the finest orators of the time, such as Noah Webster and Theodore Dwight.

BROWN FELLOWSHIP SOCIETY FORMED

Free Blacks in Charleston, South Carolina, numbering 586 and one of the largest communities of free Blacks in the South, attained a high level of cultural development by working hard to enhance their educational opportunities and overcome isolation on the basis of race. Most of the free Blacks were mulattos whose white fathers had provided for their freedom or

Blacks who had gained freedom through their own efforts. In general, they maintained a behavior as close to the ideals and actions of whites as possible without actually "being white." The Brown Fellowship Society, developed this year, was just one of the organizations established by certain free Blacks to set themselves apart from slaves and other free Blacks. The Brown Society admitted only "brown" men of good character who paid a fifty-dollar membership fee. The society used these funds to educate free Blacks, assist widows and orphans, operate a clubhouse, and maintain a cemetery for its members. Because they identified themselves with the slaveholding aristocracy, they were frequently allowed special privileges.

SOCIETY OF FRIENDS CALLS FOR PROHIBITION OF SLAVERY

On **FEBRUARY 11**, the Society of Friends (Quakers) presented the first petition to Congress calling for the prohibition of slavery in the United States. In less than two weeks after the Constitution became operative, three antislavery petitions — two by the Quakers and one by the Pennsylvania Abolition Society — had been submitted. Benjamin Franklin, head of the Pennsylvania society, signed the petition "to countenance the restoration of liberty" to slaves. Both Quaker petitions denounced the "licentious wickedness" of the international slave trade and called on Congress to immediately abolish it. Congress reported on the petitions by stating that the Constitution prevented it "from passing an act of emancipation" and from abolishing "the slave trade until 1808."

U.S. CONGRESS AVOIDS ISSUE OF SLAVERY IN STATES

On **MARCH 23**, the U.S. Congress decided to leave the issue of slavery entirely up to the individual states. It passed the following resolution after a discussion in committee of the whole House (special deliberation of the committee opened to include all members of the House of Representatives): "That Congress have no authority to interfere in the emancipation of slaves, or in the treatment of them in any of the States, it remaining with the several States alone to provide any regulations therein which humanity and true polity may require."

RESTRICTIONS ON FREE BLACKS ENDED IN PENNSYLVANIA

In **NOVEMBER**, Pennsylvania legislators abolished all restrictions upon free Blacks. In the Pennsylvania

Constitution of 1790, every eligible free man enjoyed the franchise.

◈ Blacks voted under this provision until 1837, when the state supreme court ruled that "Negroes were not freemen and not eligible to vote."

1791 ANTISLAVERY SOCIETIES FLOURISH

The Virginia Anti-Slavery Society was formed, followed by the New Jersey Society in 1792. These were among the last major antislavery societies to be formed. They engaged in many of the same activities as their earlier counterparts in New York, Pennsylvania, Delaware, Rhode Island, and Connecticut.

BANNEKER PUBLISHES ALMANAC

On **AUGUST 22**, Benjamin Banneker of Maryland, a noted astronomer, inventor, and mathematician, became the first Black American to publish an almanac for farmers. It was also the first scientific book written by a Black author.

The almanac was published annually for the next ten years.

BANNEKER SURVEYS WASHINGTON, D.C.

Benjamin Banneker also completed the survey work on the design for the District of Columbia, having been appointed to the commission on the recommendation of Thomas Jefferson. The original planner, Pierre Charles L'Enfant, had grown tired of the criticism of his plan and had returned to France. Banneker had committed the entire plan to memory, and with the help of Charles Ellicott, reconstructed the plan.

BELIEF THAT BLACKS ARE FREE HELD BY ANTISLAVERY ACTIVISTS IN MASSACHUSETTS

At this time, Massachusetts, unlike other colonies, did not have an antislavery society, perhaps because many antislavery activists believed that slavery *had* been abolished there, at least by 1783. Leaders in this state justified this belief by pointing to the Declaration of Independence of 1776, which declared that "all men are created equal"; to the state constitution of 1780, which stated, "All men are born free and equal"; and to the reasoning of Chief Justice Shaw, who said, "How, or by what act particularly, slavery was abolished in Massachusetts, whether by the adoption of the opinion of Somerset's case as a declaration and modification of the common law, or by the Declaration of Independence, or by the constitution of 1780, it is not now very easy to determine; it is rather a matter of curiosity than utility, it being agreed on all

state legislature against certain clauses of the Act of 1740 that restricted their freedom. They specifically protested the clauses that deprived free Blacks — tax-paying, free citizens of the state — of the right to trial by jury and to testify under oath in court.

TOUSSAINT L'OUVERTURE LEADS BLACK SLAVE REVOLT IN HAITI

In **AUGUST**, Toussaint L'Ouverture (François Dominique Toussaint) (1774?–1803), became the first Black to lead a successful revolt against a colonial power in the Americas. He led Black slaves against their French masters in Haiti. Black Haitians fought ruthlessly for more than two years against French masters and soldiers, and many captured Blacks were hanged. The emergence of Haiti as the first independent nation in the Americas ruled by Blacks who had overthrown their owners led to the passage of more stringent laws to control slaves on the mainland.

Toussaint L'Ouverture led slaves in Santo Domingo to revolt against tyranny. The richest of the colonies of the French West Indies, Santo Domingo was home to 28,000 whites, 22,000 free Blacks, and 405,000 slaves on more than 800 sugar plantations. L'Ouverture's successful revolt led to the establishment of Haiti as the first all-Black state in the Americas and to fear among many members of the U.S. House of Representatives that a revolt was impending in the United States.

hands that, if not abolished before, it was by the declaration of rights [part of the state's constitution]."

PENNSYLVANIA ABOLITION SOCIETY PROMOTES BLACK EDUCATION

The Pennsylvania Abolition Society appointed a committee to supervise the instruction of free Black youth and to encourage school attendance.

Five years later, the committee asked the legislature to establish "Free Schools, without Discrimination of Colour, and in populous Towns to promote particular Institutions for the Education of Negroes."

FREE BLACKS OF SOUTH CAROLINA PROTEST

In **JANUARY**, the state's free Blacks, although small in number, pressed for more equality, protesting to the

The revolt in Haiti was bloody, and many French soldiers were hanged or otherwise killed in revenge for the cruel treatment of the slaves by the French. Sketches such as this one fueled the fears of an uprising in the United States.

◈ Eventually, the French government in Paris offered freedom to all Blacks in Haiti who supported France in defeating Spain, which occupied the other half of the island of Hispaniola, and its British allies. L'Ouverture accepted the offer. He joined forces with the French, was made a general, and led the Black forces of Haiti to force the British out. By 1801, he was the powerful head of the government of the island. In 1802, French troops under orders from Napoleon occupied the island in an attempt to reinstitute slavery. They imprisoned L'Ouverture in France, where he died in 1803.

1792   BLACKS BLOCKED FROM MILITIA

Even after Blacks had fought gallantly in the American Revolutionary War, some people questioned whether they should continue to be armed for such service. The issue was settled, to address a growing fear of Blacks, by an act of Congress restricting militia service to "free able-bodied white male citizens." Most of the states that had previously included Blacks in their militias soon passed similar legislation and disbanded their Black militias.

The Yorker's Stratagem, or Banana's Wedding, OPENS

On **APRIL 24**, Blacks were presented on the American stage for the first time in *The Yorker's Stratagem, or Banana's Wedding*, a play by J. Robinson.

FIRST BLACK CATHOLIC SISTERHOOD FOUNDED

On **OCTOBER 11**, Antoine Blanc founded the first Black Catholic order of nuns.

1793   ANTISLAVERY LAW PASSED IN CANADA

The legislature of Upper Canada (now the province of Ontario) passed the colony's first antislavery law. Following this legislation, a small number of slaves from the United States fled to Canada.

RESTRICTIONS IMPOSED ON BLACKS ENTERING VIRGINIA

Virginia passed legislation banning free Blacks from entering the state. Violators were fined or could even be sold back into slavery.

The cotton gin was patented by Eli Whitney in 1793. The gin (short for "engine") had sharp metal teeth that quickly pulled cotton fiber from the seeds when rotated. Whitney earned almost no money from his invention, because its simple process was easily copied by other manufacturers.

COTTON GIN INVENTED

On **MARCH 14**, Eli Whitney received a patent for the cotton gin — a device that removed seeds from cotton far more quickly and cheaply than could be done by hand. The invention revolutionized the cotton industry; soon, vast increases in the amount of land devoted to cotton radically changed the number, status, and distribution of African slaves in America.

◈ Before the invention of the cotton gin, it took a slave an entire day to remove the seeds from one pound of cotton; after the gin, a slave could remove seeds from fifty pounds of cotton in a day. The gin was developed on the plantation of Catherine Green in South Carolina. Whitney manufactured the gin in New Haven, Connecticut.

The introduction of the gin gave cotton production the ultimate technological boost. Its invention created the incentive to clear millions of acres of land, drain swamps, and put idle land into agricultural production.

YELLOW FEVER EPIDEMIC IN PHILADELPHIA

In **AUGUST**, a yellow fever epidemic devastated the city of Philadelphia. More than 24,000 city residents were infected, and the death toll reached 4,044. Dr. Benjamin Rush, who founded the nation's first medical college, believed that Blacks were immune to yellow fever and therefore recruited Black residents to help care for the infected. Blacks, however, were soon stricken, and Black ministers Richard Allen and Absalom Jones helped to secure relief measures to comfort the sick and eradicate disease among Blacks and whites.

FUGITIVE SLAVE ACT

On **FEBRUARY 12**, Congress passed the first federal act making it a crime to harbor an escaped slave or to interfere with the slave's capture or arrest. It was designed to secure enforcement of Article 4, Section 2, of the Constitution, but this law was described as one

The growing number of runaway slaves led to increases in the number of slave catchers. In this sketch, a slave named Scipio is being hunted "as men hunt a deer!" The caption notes that Scipio "fought the dogs right gallantly, and actually killed three of them with only his naked fists."

of the most flagrant "unconstitutional" acts passed by Congress and enforced by the U.S. court system.

Section 2

And be it further enacted, That any agent, appointed as aforesaid, who shall receive the fugitive into his custody, shall be empowered to transport him or her to the state or territory from which he or she shall have fled. And if any person or persons shall by force set at liberty, or rescue the fugitive from such agent while transporting, as aforesaid, the person or persons so offending shall, on conviction, be fined not exceeding five hundred dollars, and be imprisoned not exceeding one year.

◊ The Fugitive Slave Law of 1793, authored by Pierce Butler of South Carolina (often called the father of the fugitive slave clause in the Constitution), strengthened provisions for apprehending, securing, and transmitting a fugitive to the state or territory making a claim. It also provided that anyone rescuing or setting free a fugitive who had been recaptured would, on conviction, be fined an amount not exceeding five hundred dollars and imprisoned for not longer than one year.

Butler, a member of Congress (1789–1796 and 1802–1805), was himself a slaveholder; during his stay in Philadelphia (where Congress then met), slaves staffed his home. During the time that Butler was not a congressman, the Court of Common Pleas in Philadelphia gave freedom to one of his slaves. When the case was brought to the U.S. Circuit Court, its decision upheld the Pennsylvania law giving the state the right to declare free any slaves brought into its boundaries by their owners.

1794 BOWDOIN COLLEGE FOUNDED

Bowdoin College was founded in Brunswick, Maine, and became a center for abolitionist sentiment before the Civil War.

John Russwurm was the first Black graduate of the college in 1826. He later cofounded the first newspaper edited by a Black person. General Oliver Otis Howard (for whom Howard University was named), commissioner of the Freedmen's Bureau, was also a graduate of Bowdoin. Harriet Beecher Stowe's husband taught at Bowdoin, and it was here that she began writing *Uncle Tom's Cabin.*

AMERICAN ABOLITION SOCIETIES HOLD CONVENTION

In **JANUARY**, the American Convention of Abolition Societies took place in Philadelphia. The societies of New York, Pennsylvania, New Jersey, Delaware, and Maryland attended and condemned slavery and restrictions on free Blacks. The societies also formed a federation called the American Convention for Promoting the Abolition of Slavery and Improving the Condition of the African Race.

◊ Over the period of its existence, the federation held twenty-six meetings. The societies from Pennsylvania and New York supplied most of the leadership. Although the federation operated with limited funds, it provided some general guidelines for the state societies. Its last meeting occurred in 1832, and it was officially dissolved in 1837.

FIRST AFRICAN METHODIST EPISCOPAL CHURCH FOUNDED

On **FEBRUARY 4**, Richard Allen organized the Bethel African Methodist Episcopal Church (AME) in Philadelphia.

◊ Allen, a minister and impressive orator, worked especially hard to ensure a growing church membership. His efforts paid off as other AME congregations developed in Wilmington, Baltimore, Camden, New Jersey and Norristown, Pennsylvania. Blacks of great prominence — such as Daniel Coker, Morris Brown, and Nicholson Gilliard — flocked to the AME Church. The various congregations held a conference in 1816 and established the African Methodist Episcopal denomination. They elected Daniel Coker as their first bishop, but when he resigned, Allen was selected to fill the post.

Allen spent his early years as a slave in Delaware. He and his brother earned enough money to purchase their freedom from their owner, whom Allen had converted to Christianity. Allen served as a wagon driver in the American Revolution, and after it was over, he began to preach in the Methodist Church. In 1786, he moved to Philadelphia and tried to establish a separate church for Blacks; but St. George's Methodist Episcopal Church, a white church where he occasionally preached, refused permission. During one prayer service in 1787, Allen, Absalom Jones, and William White were pulled from their knees by a white usher for being in an area that had been reserved for white members of the congregation. Allen, Jones, and other Black members then left the church.

Richard Allen became one of the most influential African Americans in the country when he established the Bethel African Methodist Episcopal Church in Philadelphia — the first church organized and directed by Blacks in the United States.

Seven years later in 1794, Allen left the Free African Society, which he had founded with Absalom Jones, and fulfilled his dream by founding the Bethel African Methodist Episcopal Church.

Allen and Jones continued to work together in a joint effort to abolish slavery in the United States. The Bethel Church was used to hide slaves escaping from the South. Allen died in 1831; he and his wife are buried at the Bethel Church. Allen's prominence has been acknowledged in several ways. Allen University in Columbia, South Carolina, is named after him. In 1876, a monument to him was dedicated in Philadelphia. It may have been the first monument erected to a Black person by other Black persons.

CONGRESS FORBIDS SLAVE SHIPS TO GO TO FOREIGN PORTS

On **MARCH 22**, the U.S. Congress passed legislation forbidding slave trade to foreign ports. The Act of 1794 specifically "forbade any person in the United States, citizen or foreigner, to engage in the carrying of slaves from Africa to countries other than the United States." Abolition societies were credited for influencing Congress to pass this legislation.

FRANCE ABOLISHES SLAVERY

On **FEBRUARY 4**, the revolutionary French government decided to abolish slavery in its colonial territories.

DEDICATION OF ST. THOMAS AFRICAN EPISCOPAL CHURCH

On **JULY 17**, the African Church, founded by Absalom Jones (1746–1818) and several followers, was dedicated by two Episcopal rectors and was received into the Diocese of Pennsylvania on October 17. The African Church was renamed St. Thomas African Episcopal Church — the first Black Episcopal church in the United States.

◆ Jones was born a slave in Sussex, Delaware. His master brought him to Philadelphia when he was sixteen years old. Jones, with the help of his father-in-law and the Quakers, purchased the freedom of his wife in 1770, and in 1784 he purchased his own freedom.

Jones met Richard Allen in Philadelphia in 1786, and together they served as lay preachers for the Black members of St. George's Methodist Episcopal Church. The two were directly responsible for a tenfold increase in Black membership. They left St. George's after a scuffle with a white usher and formed the Free African Society in 1787 (see p. 60). Jones and the majority of the members founded St. Thomas's.

Jones and Allen continued to work together in the community, often with the aid of James Forten, the wealthy Black sailmaker. Jones was ordained a deacon of the Episcopal Church on August 16, 1794, and in 1804, at fifty-eight years of age, Jones became the first Episcopal priest of African descent in the United States.

Although Jones and Allen had gone separate ways (Jones remaining with the Episcopal Church and Allen becoming affiliated with the Methodists), they continued to work together for the abolition of slavery. On April 11, 1816, Jones helped consecrate Richard Allen as the first bishop of the African

Methodist Episcopal Church. In the year before he died, Jones, along with Allen and Forten, organized a convention of about three thousand Blacks to oppose the founding of the American Colonization Society.

1795 FORMER SLAVE GIVES TO COMMUNITY

Amos Fortune, who had been a slave, became a leading businessman in Jaffrey, New Hampshire. Over the years, he founded the Jaffrey Social Library and donated a relatively large sum of money for the town school.

SLAVE REVOLT IN LOUISIANA

In **APRIL**, plans for a slave revolt were uncovered at Pointe Coupee, Louisiana, just north of New Orleans. Twenty-five slaves were executed swiftly, and twenty-three others were put in chains on a riverboat and floated down the Mississippi. At each landing from Pointe Coupee to New Orleans, one slave was hanged, and his head was left on a pole as a lesson for all slaves who dared seek freedom. Whites were alleged to have masterminded the revolt in an effort to overthrow the Spanish rulers; these suspects were banished from the colony.

1796 AFRICAN METHODIST EPISCOPAL ZION CHURCH ESTABLISHED IN NEW YORK CITY

The African Methodist Episcopal Zion Church became the first Black Methodist church to be organized in New York City. Established by a group of Blacks who had separated from the predominantly white John Street Methodist Episcopal Church, it became one of the most influential Black churches in the country. The church actually began as the African Chapel for Methodists and met in a cabinet maker's shop. The Chapel was organized by Peter Williams, Sr., a sexton of the John Street Church. The African Methodist Episcopal Zion Church building was completed in 1800. Its first minister was a white clergyman supplied by the John Street congregation. In 1820 the African methodist Zion Church became the mother church of the African Methodist Episcopal denomination. The designation of "Zion" was officially added to the name of the denomination in 1848. Today, the African Methodist Episcopal Zion denomination has more than one million members.

QUAKERS ACCUSED OF INCITING SLAVE UNREST

A grand jury in Charlotte, North Carolina, accused Quakers of inciting slave unrest and arson.

1797 FOUR BLACK SLAVE FUGITIVES PETITION CONGRESS

On **JANUARY 30**, four Black slaves in North Carolina petitioned Congress in protest against a state law that required illegally freed slaves to be returned to their masters. They asked for freedom for themselves and their people. This was the first recorded antislavery petition to Congress. Congress refused to grant their petition.

The slaves had been freed by their Quaker masters, who had purchased them for the purpose of freeing them, but this practice was illegal.

1798 BANS ON SLAVE IMPORTATION

Georgia passed legislation prohibiting the importation of slaves from Africa.

The state had prohibited the importation of slaves from the West Indies, the Bahamas, and Florida as early as 1793. Other states, including South Carolina, excluded slaves from the West Indies (in particular) and even slaves from some other states. Most states had prohibited the importation of slaves during the latter 1700s: Delaware, in 1776; Virginia, in 1778; Maryland, in 1783; South Carolina, in 1787; North Carolina, in 1794; and Georgia, in 1798.

BLACKS PROHIBITED FROM SERVING IN THE NAVY AND MARINES

On **AUGUST 8**, the secretary of the navy ordered the prohibition of Blacks in the naval service. The newly established Marine Corps declared that "no Negro, mulatto or Indian" could enlist.

JOHNSON ADVERTISES PORTRAIT-PAINTING SERVICES

On **DECEMBER 19**, Joshua Johnson (1765?–1830), a portrait painter, advertised in the Baltimore *Intelligencer*, calling himself a "self taught genius." During his lifetime, Johnson painted portraits of some of the most successful and influential white families in Maryland and Virginia.

1799 EMANCIPATION ACT PASSED IN NEW YORK

New York passed an emancipation act providing that all children born of slaves should be freed after having reached the age of twenty-eight. This legislation was patterned after the first act of gradual emancipation enacted in Pennsylvania in 1780. (Emancipation for all other slaves did not occur until 1827.)

Fourteen years earlier (1785) New York actually had passed legislation that stipulated gradual emancipation, but it was vetoed by the Council of Revision. Although the state senate overrode the veto, the assembly did not. In 1785, New York had already passed legislation to prohibit the bringing of a slave into the state, except under penalty of one hundred pounds and freedom for the slave. Three years later in 1788, the state passed new legislation that prohibited the buying of a slave for export from the state, and any owner wishing to manumit a slave could do so without securing a bond after certifying that the slave was under fifty years of age and self-supporting. The slave population in New York declined gradually.

SLAVE REBELLION IN VIRGINIA

Slaves rebelled in Southhampton County, Virginia, killing two whites. Four to ten Blacks were blamed for the insurrection and were executed.

1800

POPULATION OVERVIEW

GENERAL AND BLACK POPULATION IN THE UNITED STATES The new census reported 5.3 million residents in the United States, an increase of 30 percent since 1790. The most populous state was still Virginia (880,000 residents), followed by Pennsylvania and New York. Tennessee and Kentucky were the fastest growing, more than tripling their populations since 1790. Blacks numbered slightly over 1 million (1,002,037) and made up 18.9 percent of the total U.S. population. Approximately 10 percent of the Black population were free. About half of these lived in the South and half in the North. New Orleans and Charleston were centers of free Black workers, most of whom worked as skilled artisans.

ECONOMIC OVERVIEW

COTTON PRODUCTION AND POLITICAL POWER With the invention of the cotton gin and the plentiful supply of African slaves, cotton was fast becoming the most profitable crop throughout the South. Georgia and South Carolina led the country in cotton production in 1800. More than twenty thousand Africans had been imported into these states largely to work in the cotton fields. The gulf states of Louisiana, Alabama, and Mississippi were quickly shifting their agricultural efforts to cotton. A farmer could make a profit on as little as twelve cents a pound for cotton — and cotton was selling at American ports at an av-

erage of forty-four cents a pound. Thus, even small-scale planters could become prosperous. Their prosperity — and that of the whole South — became increasingly tied to the production of cotton over the next several decades. As textile manufacturers demanded more cotton and paid higher prices, cotton planters needed more workers.

At this time, roughly one million slaves lived in the southern states. In just twenty years, that number jumped to 1,643,000, and by 1860 to almost four million. Many wealthy and politically powerful white southerners owed much of their wealth to the work of Black slaves. For example, Joseph Emory Davis, the brother of Jefferson Davis, produced about three thousand bales of cotton each year on a grand plantation in Mississippi. Other planters — for example, John C. Calhoun of South Carolina, Alexander H. Stephens of Georgia, Joseph E. Brown of Alabama, Albert Gallatin Brown of Mississippi, and Andrew Jackson of Tennessee — held major political positions in the southern states and were representatives in the U.S. Congress. Their power often extended down to the county and local town levels where they determined who won elections and who was appointed to political positions.

PROFITABILITY OF THE SLAVE TRADE Slave trading was big business, earning large sums of money at relatively low risk. For example, a solidly built slave ship that carried three hundred to four hundred slaves and had cost the owner about thirty-five thousand dollars could make from thirty thousand to one hundred thousand dollars on each trip. (A ship could make about five voyages before it became too foul to use.) No trade in any other "commodity" offered such large returns on investment.

SUGAR PRODUCTION EXPANDS Sugar cane, a labor-intensive crop, became an important part of Louisiana's agriculture system. Plantation owners began to import slaves from the West Indies who were familiar with growing sugar cane.

By 1802, seventy-five plantations produced more than 8.5 million pounds of sugar. The center of the new industry was the area just south of the confluence of the Red and Mississippi rivers, which was described as having plantations superb beyond description. Sugar plantations were highly profitable. In 1817, a plantation's yearly income was estimated at twenty thousand to thirty thousand dollars. Sugar planters used more field hands and fewer women and children than did cotton planters. Through the 1820s,

Slaves were used to cultivate sugar at this opulent plantation on the Mississippi River in the same way they were used in the Caribbean. In the early years of the nineteenth century, sugar production increased until it was among the largest industries of the South.

Louisiana dominated the U.S. sugar-producing industry, yielding about 95 percent of the total national output. In southern Louisiana, sugar cane became the dominant cash crop, requiring an estimated sixty thousand slaves in its cultivation.

SOCIAL CONDITIONS OVERVIEW

SLAVERY ENHANCES SOUTHERN POLITICAL POWER

Slavery brought prosperity and power to the South, evidenced by the increased importance of cotton in the southern and national economies, the related growth of the slave population in proportion to the South's total population, and the "three-fifths compromise" (enacted July 12, 1787), which counted slaves in the apportionment population for representation in the U.S. House of Representatives. Virginia, for example, had 514,280 free whites and 365,920 slaves; but according to the three-fifths rule for slaves, the total apportionment population was recorded at 733,832, entitling the state to twenty-two representatives. New York, with a population of 557,000 at the time, had only seventeen representatives. In fact, the slave population nationwide accounted for 17 of the 141 seats of the House. Virginia's large slave population was the result of its position as a "breeding" area for slaves that would later be sold throughout the South.

SULLIVAN'S ISLAND, SOUTH CAROLINA: THE SLAVES' ELLIS ISLAND

It has been estimated that two-fifths of the African Americans who arrived in America during the early 1800s passed through Sullivan's Island across the channel from Charleston, South Carolina. Sullivan's Island was a clearing-house for slaves bound for plantations throughout the South, just as Ellis Island was used to clear foreign immigrants decades later.

ANTISLAVERY PETITION BY FREE BLACKS IN PHILADELPHIA

On **JANUARY 2**, an antislavery petition was presented to Congress by Absalom Jones and Richard Allen on behalf of free Blacks of Philadelphia. The petition opposed the continuation of the slave trade, the Fugitive Slave Law, and slavery as an institution. Congress voted 85 to 1 against the proposal.

SLAVE REVOLT IN VIRGINIA

On **AUGUST 30**, Gabriel Prosser (1775–1800), a Virginia slave, organized about eleven hundred slaves in Henrico County and set out to attack Richmond, Virginia, where he expected widespread support and an appetite for freedom that would enable him to quickly establish a government, which he planned to lead. Prosser, a blacksmith and self-taught preacher, was assisted by his two brothers as well as Jack Bowler, George Smith, Ben Woolfolk, a slave named Gilbert, and a number of other men, some of whom were educated. The slave revolt followed an elaborate plan and was designed along the lines of the Santo Domingo revolt. Gathering six miles outside of Richmond, and armed with clubs, scythes, homemade bayonets, and guns, they reviewed their plans before proceeding to Richmond. The plot was betrayed by two house slaves who wanted to save their master. Many of the slaves were quickly apprehended. In total, as many as ninety-one slaves were convicted for taking part in the revolt. On October 30, Prosser and his family were hanged along with twenty-four other conspirators, near Richmond. Ten other conspirators were deported. The revolt caused significant tension and fear in the area for at least two years, during which another fourteen or more slaves were executed.

1801 SLAVE TRADE REOPENED IN LOUISIANA

Slave trade was reopened in the Louisiana Territory, and it flourished because it had no competition. By this time, every southern state had passed legislation prohibiting the importation of slaves. On October 1, 1800, Spain ceded Louisiana to France in the secret Treaty of San Ildefonso. This treaty was not known of in the United States until May 1801. After the treaty, the French reopened the slave trade to accommodate the successful and profitable 1795 experiment with sugar production in the territory. Many residents in the territory were émigrés from French Santo Domingo, fugitives from earlier slave insurrections. As the number of sugar plantations increased, so did the need for slaves to work the plantations. Between 1801 and 1802, as many as seventy-five plantations were producing an estimated 4 million to 8.5 million pounds of sugar cane. Slaves were used in almost every aspect of sugar production, from plowing the fields into furrows for planting to carrying the brown sugar to the city refinery to be processed into white sugar.

SEVERE PENALTIES FOR FREEING SLAVES IMPOSED IN GEORGIA

According to a new law, anyone in Georgia who freed a slave in any manner other than by special legislative act would be fined two hundred dollars; half of it would go to the county where the "offense" occurred and half to the informer. Further, the manumitted individual would be returned to slave status. The penalty for this offense was later raised to five hundred dollars. Laws such as this one severely limited the possibility of slaves becoming free.

1802 OHIO CONSTITUTION OUTLAWS SLAVERY AND GIVES PROTECTION TO BLACKS

The Ohio State Constitution, enacted in this year, prohibited slavery and involuntary servitude in the state. Article 8, Section 2, stated:

> There shall be neither slavery nor involuntary servitude in the State, otherwise than for punishment of crimes whereof the party shall have been duly convicted. Nor shall any male person arrive at the age of 21 years, or female person arrived at the age of 18 years, be held to serve any person as servant under pretense of indenture or otherwise, unless such person shall enter into such indenture while in a state of freedom, and on condition of a bona-fide consideration received for their service, except as before excepted. Nor shall any indenture of any negro or mulatto, hereafter made or executed out of the State, or made in the State, where term of service exceeds one year, be of the least validity, except those given in case of apprenticeship.

Blacks had the same relationship to the government that Native Americans or unnaturalized foreigners did — they had the right to live in the state and receive the protection of its laws. They did not, however, have the privileges of citizens. For example, the franchise was restricted to white male inhabitants who paid a state or county tax. Other states in the Northwest Territory followed Ohio's lead and restricted Blacks from voting until the time of the Civil War. In 1803, Ohio passed other legislation declaring that Blacks were not to be provided with jury service, which was limited to those who held the franchise.

FRANCE REINSTITUTES SLAVERY

Under the leadership of Napoleon, slavery was reestablished. France also reinstituted the *code noir*, prohibiting Blacks, mulattos, and "colored" people from entering French territory or intermarrying with whites.

The *code noir*, generally more lenient than codes in effect in states along the eastern seaboard, remained in effect in Louisiana until the 1820s, when the slave laws became more harsh.

1803 BLACK SETTLEMENT OF ISLE BREVELLE FOUNDED

Isle Brevelle, a thirteen-thousand-acre settlement of free Black people in Louisiana, was organized by Marie Thérèse, a slave who had gained her freedom in 1778. By 1803, she had accumulated four thousand acres of land and built Melrose Plantation, the centerpiece of the Metoyer landholdings, later known as Isle Brevelle.

Louis Metoyer, one of Marie Thérèse's children, was an architect and designed the main building and the chapel of Melrose Plantation. These buildings still stand, as does Africa House, built in 1800, which is of purely African design. The site is designated a national landmark.

SLAVE TRADE REOPENED IN SOUTH CAROLINA

South Carolina passed legislation that reopened slave trade from South America and the West Indies. Approximately thirty-nine thousand additional Black slaves were imported into the state during the five-year period between 1803 and 1808, the year in which the federal government ended slave importation.

UNREST AND ARSON IN NEW YORK CITY

In **SEPTEMBER**, twenty Blacks were convicted of burning eleven houses in New York City. A plan was revealed showing that these Blacks had called for burning the entire city. Rioting occurred for several days following the arrest of several Blacks.

SLAVERY IN INDIANA TERRITORY DESPITE BAN BY ORDINANCE OF 1787

On **SEPTEMBER 22**, the territorial government adopted "A Law Concerning Servants." The act established a system of indentured servitude whereby any person owning or purchasing slaves outside the territory could bring them into Indiana and bind them to service. Slaves under fifteen years of age were required to serve until the age of thirty-five if they were males, thirty-two if females. Although the law was in

This announcement of the sale of 250 slaves in Charlestown, South Carolina, highlights their arrival from the "rice coast," which might indicate their skill in growing this important cash crop. Also emphasized is the slaves' good health, especially their freedom from smallpox infection.

violation of the Ordinance of 1787, Congress gave tacit approval when it failed to declare such laws null and void.

1804 HAITI WINS INDEPENDENCE

On **JANUARY 1**, Haiti won its independence from France. Many white Haitians fled to the United States.

BLACK LAWS ENACTED IN OHIO

On **JANUARY 5**, the Ohio General Assembly became the first in the country to enact Black Laws, intended to restrict the rights of free Blacks.

These restrictive measures were strongly supported by two groups — white settlers from Kentucky and Virginia, who had settled in southern counties of the state and who despised free Blacks, and a growing group of businessmen whose ventures were tied to slavery in the South. Prompted by pressure from these groups, legislation was passed to keep

Blacks out of the state and discourage those in the state from staying. The laws also appeased many planters in Kentucky and Virginia who had complained that their slaves were escaping to Ohio.

The legislation required Blacks and mulattos to furnish certificates of freedom from a court in the United States before they could settle in the state. All Black residents in the state had to register with the names of their children by June 1, 1805. The fee for registering was twelve and one-half cents per name. It then became a penal offense to employ a Black person who could not present a certificate of freedom. Violators could be fined from ten to fifty dollars. Anyone harboring fugitive slaves, hindering their capture, or aiding in their escape could be fined one thousand dollars; the informer received one-half of the fine. Clearly, the risks associated with helping free slaves escalated.

On January 25, 1807, the Ohio legislature strengthened the Black Laws of 1804 by passing the following amendments: (1) no Black should be allowed to settle in Ohio who could not within twenty days give bond to the amount of five hundred dollars signed by two bondsmen, who should guarantee the good behavior and support of the Black person; (2) the fine for harboring or concealing a fugitive was raised from fifty to one hundred dollars, one-half to go to the informer and one-half to the overseer of the poor in the district; and (3) no Black should be allowed to give evidence in any legal case in which a white person was a party. Other northern states followed Ohio's lead and passed legislation that restricted free Black migration and voting privileges. The Black Laws remained in effect until 1849.

1805 BAPTIST MINISTER EXPELLED FOR ANTISLAVERY VIEWS

David Barrow (1753–1819), a white minister, was expelled from the North District Association of Baptists for his antislavery views and his recently published pamphlet, entitled *Involuntary, Unlimited, Perpetual, Absolute, Hereditary Slavery Examined on the Principles of Nature, Reason, Justice, Policy and Scripture.*

Barrow had previously lived in southern Virginia and northern North Carolina. In 1795, he founded the Portsmouth-Norfolk church, and within a short time installed Jacob Bishop, a Black man, as pastor of this mixed congregation. Barrow was highly criticized for this action, and after being a victim of violence he migrated to Kentucky in 1798. Barrow later served a short time as president of the Kentucky Abolition Society.

Thompson v. Wilmot

In the Kentucky case *Thompson v. Wilmot*, a slave who had been promised his freedom was awarded $691.25 in damages.

The slave had been taken from Maryland to Kentucky to work for a limited time. In Kentucky, he brought suit against his owner when he was held captive beyond the time appointed for his freedom. The court agreed with the slave; the former master appealed, but to no avail.

FREED SLAVES REQUIRED TO LEAVE VIRGINIA

On **MAY 1**, the Virginia legislature passed laws requiring all slaves freed thereafter to leave the state.

BLACK SCOUT SERVES IN LEWIS AND CLARK EXPEDITION

On or about **NOVEMBER 15**, York, an African slave and scout with the Lewis and Clark expedition, reached the mouth of the Columbia River. York, familiar with Native Americans, served as an interpreter and emissary. York's dark skin proved an advantage in his dealings with certain peoples of the Great Plains, whose warriors, when returning from a successful battle, daubed parts of their bodies with charcoal to symbolize bravery. York was the first Black man they had ever seen; they were convinced that he was a very brave man by birth, since his color did not rub off. These Native Americans regarded York as the leader of the expedition because in their culture the warriors led major journeys, rather than tribal leaders.

1806 PARRISH PUBLISHES *Remarks on the Slavery of the Black People*

One of the most complete treatments of slavery and the principles of democracy was presented by John Parrish in his *Remarks on the Slavery of the Black People.* Parrish noted that, although he was not a politician, he knew that "the fundamentals of all good governments, being equal liberty and impartial justice, the constitution and laws ought to be expressed in such unequivocal terms as not to be misunderstood, or admit of double meaning." Parrish indicted the Fugitive Slave Law and stated that in a six-month period, as many as six hundred free Blacks had been kidnapped from the eastern shore of Maryland alone by whites or slave catchers, who acted freely because citizens cast a blind eye on their illegal activities — in order to get rid of the Blacks.

VIRGINIA SLAVE CODE AMENDED

Virginia amended the slave code to provide that all manumitted slaves who did not leave the state within one year of manumission were to be seized and sold. The same legislature declared that slaves could not conduct religious meetings or attend any meetings at night without written permission.

LOUISIANA SETS STANDARDS FOR TREATMENT OF SLAVES

On **JULY 7**, Louisiana passed legislation specifying the quantity and quality of food to be provided for slaves. Every month, owners had to provide slaves with one barrel of Indian corn, or the equivalent in rice, beans, or other grain, and a pint of salt. A fine of ten dollars was imposed for every failure to abide by this law. The law also made the following stipulations:

> The slave shall be allowed half an hour for breakfast during the whole year; from the first day of May to the first day of November, they shall be allowed two hours for dinner; and from the first day of November to the first day of May, one hour and a half for dinner: Provided, however, That the owners who will themselves take the trouble of causing to be prepared the meals of their slaves, be and they are hereby authorized to abridge, by half an hour per day, the time fixed for their rest.

1807 BLACK EDUCATION IN THE DISTRICT OF COLUMBIA

Three former slaves — George Bell, Nicholas Franklin, and Moses Liverpool — built the first schoolhouse for Blacks in the District of Columbia and employed a white teacher. Although the school failed soon after construction, it reopened in 1818. The first Black person to teach in the District of Columbia took charge of this school in 1824.

FIRST ALL-BLACK PRESBYTERIAN CHURCH ORGANIZED

The first all-Black Presbyterian Church, First African, was organized in Philadelphia through the work of John Gloucester, Sr., a freed slave from Tennessee. The second Black Presbyterian was not founded until fifteen years later.

FRANCHISE RESTRICTED IN NEW JERSEY

In New Jersey, the legislature restricted the right to vote to free white male citizens of twenty-one years of age and older. (Everyone, regardless of gender or color, had previously been given the franchise by the constitution of 1776.)

IMPORTATION OF NEW SLAVES RESTRICTED

On **MARCH 2**, Congress passed legislation that barred the importation of new slaves from Africa into U.S. territory, effective January 1, 1808. It stipulated that a person who knowingly purchased an illegally imported slave would be fined eight hundred dollars; equipping a ship for the slave trade would result in a fine of twenty thousand dollars.

◈ Although Congress outlawed the importation of slaves in 1807, the trade continued for some years because of lax enforcement. Slave smuggling intensified as the price of slaves increased with expanding cotton production. For example, in 1859, the *Wanderer* landed on a Georgia dock with more than three hundred slaves. It is difficult to ascertain how many thousands of slaves were smuggled into the United States.

BRITAIN ABOLISHES SLAVE TRADE

On **MARCH 25**, the British Parliament abolished the slave trade.

LOUISIANA DEFINES SLAVES AS "REAL ESTATE"

On **JUNE 7**, an act of the Louisiana legislature stated: "Slaves shall always be reputed and considered real estate; shall be, as such subject to be mortgaged, according to the rules prescribed by law and they shall be seized and sold as real estate."

1808 BLACKS ALLOWED TO TESTIFY IN WASHINGTON, D.C.

In a Washington, D.C., court, Blacks were declared competent witnesses in all court cases.

HAITIAN REFUGEES ARRIVE IN NEW ORLEANS

As many as six thousand refugees fleeing the revolution in Haiti poured into New Orleans after being driven out of Cuba. The refugees comprised a mixture of professionals, artists, and craftworkers, including a number of property owners who arrived with their slaves. Others were free Black men and women. These refugees joined earlier refugees, one of whom was James Pilot, a white man who had become mayor of New Orleans in 1805.

MANUMISSION LAW PASSED IN MARYLAND

In Maryland, the legislature passed a law that facilitated manumission, but children of freed slaves were to remain captive unless freed by their owner.

Those who traded in slaves frequently devised unusual ways to determine the value of female slaves. In this sketch, a woman is being sold by the pound.

SLAVE MARRIAGES DECLARED ILLEGAL IN LOUISIANA
A Louisiana court declares marriages between slaves were illegal until both slaves were freed.

CONGRESS PROHIBITS IMPORTATION OF SLAVES
On **JANUARY 1**, a federal law prohibiting the importation of new slaves into the United States went into effect. Some southern states enacted legislation for disposing of illegally imported Blacks, whereas others took no action at this time. The law also called for the seizure of any importing slave ship and its slave cargo. The federal law was widely ignored, however, since there were no specific mechanisms for enforcement. Some states actively participated in the sale of illegally imported Blacks and channeled the proceeds into their treasuries.

1809 ABYSSINIAN BAPTIST CHURCH FOUNDED IN NEW YORK CITY
On **JULY 5**, a group of eighteen Blacks under the leadership of the Reverend Thomas Paul broke away from the white-dominated First Baptist Church of Gold Street because of discrimination. They established the Abyssinian Baptist Church on Anthony Street in New York City in 1809.

◈ Thomas Paul, a native of Exeter, New Hampshire, and an early worker within the Baptist movement, strongly desired independence and a more congenial atmosphere for worship. He served as the pastor from June to September of 1809. Paul's leadership and missionary work continued on a national and international level. In 1823, he presented a plan for improving the moral and religious conditions of the Haitians to the Baptist Missionary Society of Massachusetts. After being appointed a missionary to Haiti, he was received by the president of the republic and remained there for about six months, winning people to the Baptist Church.

The Abyssinian Baptist Church became one of the most influential and wealthiest Black churches in the city. It eventually became located in Harlem. The Reverend Adam Clayton Powell, Sr., and his son, the Reverend Adam Clayton Powell, Jr., the U.S. representative, both served as pastors of this large congregation from 1908 to 1936, and from 1937 to about 1970, respectively.

THE FIRST AFRICAN BAPTIST CHURCH FORMED
On **MAY 14**, thirteen Philadelphians formed the first African Baptist Church in the city.

1810 POPULATION OVERVIEW
GENERAL AND BLACK POPULATION IN THE UNITED STATES According to the third national census, the national population had soared to just over 7.2 million, a 36.4 percent increase since 1800. About 1.4 million Black persons resided in the United States, composing about 19 percent of the total population. Slaves numbered 1,191,364. Nonwhite free persons numbered 186,446.

ECONOMIC CONDITIONS OVERVIEW

COTTON, THE PLANTATION CROP Upland cotton (short-staple, or green-seed, cotton grown in upland areas) increasingly consumed both the land and the labor of the South. South Carolina, for example, produced about twenty million pounds in 1800 but more than forty million pounds by 1810. Georgia's production jumped from ten million to twenty million pounds in the same period. Significant increases in cotton production were also recorded in North Carolina, four million to seven million pounds; Virginia, five million to eight million; Tennessee, one million to three million; and Louisiana, up to two million. Because cotton was relatively easy to grow and very profitable, even the yeoman farmer could be successful. Although cotton was grown throughout the South, over time the crop was found to be best suited to the "Upper Country," the region extending from the coast of South Carolina and Georgia through the Piedmont and westward through Alabama, Mississippi, and Louisiana, and into Texas. It was in this area, the Cotton Belt, that the link between crop and slave labor was the strongest.

By 1811, as much as three-fourths of the eighty million pounds of cotton produced in the United States was produced in two states — South Carolina and Georgia, with South Carolina producing twice as much as Georgia. Virginia and North Carolina together produced fifteen million pounds of cotton, and Tennessee, three million pounds.

SOCIAL CONDITIONS OVERVIEW

SLAVE INSURRECTIONS Slave uprisings and insurrections were frequent during this time, although they varied significantly in degree of planning, size of endeavor, and number of persons involved. Though they appeared in all slaveholding regions, the larger slave uprisings occurred in South Carolina and Virginia — states with very large slave populations. Several counties in these two states had slave populations exceeding the white population. Slave outbreaks were also frequent around Baltimore, Norfolk, Petersburg (Virginia), and New Orleans. Some plots planned for the destruction of entire cities. The plan to destroy the city of Augusta, Georgia, was designed by a slave named Coo who was executed for his involvement.

SLAVE CHILDREN REQUIRED TO READ BIBLE

New York State passed legislation requiring slave owners to teach slave children to read the biblical scriptures.

BLACK BOXER FIGHTS WORLD CHAMPION

On **DECEMBER 10**, Tom Molineaux (1784–1818), a former slave, challenged Tom Cribb, the heavyweight boxing champion, to a fight in England. Molineaux became the first American boxer to fight for a world championship. A crowd of more than ten thousand spectators watched the fight, apparently won by Molineaux. Because of a biased ruling by a referee (allowing Cribb two minutes to recuperate after being knocked down), however, Cribb was declared the victor after forty-three rounds.

◈ Molineaux was born in Georgetown in the District of Columbia, on March 23, 1784. His father and grandfather were famous boxers among plantation slaves. Tom Molineaux's fighting talents were quickly identified, and after winning enough money to purchase his freedom, he left for London to pursue his boxing career. Molineaux lost to Cribb again in 1811. He eventually gave up boxing, became an alcoholic, and died a pauper in Ireland at age thirty-four.

1811 DELAWARE PASSES LEGISLATION TO BAR FREE BLACKS FROM STATE

The Delaware legislature passed an act that stipulated that any free Black who entered the state was given ten days to leave or else was fined $10 per week. If a free Black was a citizen of the state and left for six months, he or she was no longer considered a resident and could not return.

MAROON COMMUNITY DESTROYED

A group of whites was sent to destroy a maroon (fugitive slave) community in Cabarrus County, North Carolina, and to recover the runaway slaves. Although some slaves escaped, at least two were killed and others captured.

Runaway slaves formed settlements, often called maroon colonies, or joined with Native American groups. Between 1672 and 1864, no fewer than fifty maroon colonies could be found in the South; the largest was located at Dismal Swamp in North Carolina, with about two thousand Blacks, all of whom were runaway slaves.

Large numbers of runaway slaves settled among the Seminole, Cherokee, and Creek peoples. The Seminole wars (1817–1818 and 1835–1842), which displaced Native Americans to the West in order to put their lands into cotton production, served another purpose as well: destroying maroon settlements and stopping runaways.

SLAVE REBELLION IN LOUISIANA

On **JANUARY 8**, a revolt of three hundred to five hundred slaves, led by Charles Deslandes (a free mulatto from Haiti), occurred in St. John the Baptist Parish, Louisiana, approximately thirty-five miles from New Orleans. Whites fled as slaves at Major Andry's plantation armed themselves with cane knives, picks, hoes, axes, and a few firearms. Slaves moved on to several other plantations, wreaking destruction and killing at least one white. The slaves were defeated by a combination of state militia, federal troops, and free Blacks on January 10. Between sixty-six and one hundred slaves were killed; their heads were displayed along the road from New Orleans to Andry's plantation as a lesson for other slaves in the region.

1812 BLACK SEAMEN IN WAR OF 1812

It is estimated that about 15 percent of all seamen in the navy during the War of 1812 were Black. Between 10 and 25 percent of Admiral Oliver H. Perry's naval force in the Battle of Lake Erie were Black seamen.

CUFFE SAILS WITH PASSENGERS TO SIERRA LEONE, AFRICA

Paul Cuffe, a Black sea captain, entrepreneur, and abolitionist, embarked for Sierra Leone at his own expense to resettle thirty-eight Black passengers in an African land. Cuffe also planned eventually to instruct Africans in agriculture and mechanics. Not everyone was enthusiastic about this voyage or the

During the War of 1812, one out of every six seamen in the U.S. Navy was Black. These men served courageously in a number of battles, including the Battle of Lake Erie in 1813, when Admiral Oliver Perry was assured that they "are not surpassed by any seaman we have in the fleet!"

"deportation of free Negroes." Support, however, did come swiftly from prominent slaveholding politicians, who advanced the idea of colonization of Africans back in their "homeland."

ILLINOIS PROHIBITS IMMIGRATION OF FREE BLACKS
In Illinois Territory, the legislature passed a law forbidding immigration of free Blacks into the territory and requiring all those within the territory to register.

1813 FORTEN HELPS DEFEAT ANTI-BLACK LEGISLATION
James Forten (1766–1842), a wealthy sailmaker from Philadelphia and strong opponent of the African colonization movement, gained wide recognition by publishing *A Series of Letters by a Man of Color*, a booklet of essays. The publication, written in protest against a Pennsylvania bill banning Blacks from the state, expressed Forten's "radical" ideas that the races were equal in every way. His efforts helped to defeat the bill.

◈ Forten was born in 1766, and at only fourteen years of age he fought in the American Revolution, serving as a powder boy on the *Royal Lewis*. As a young man, he invented a device to handle sails, making him a wealthy man. By the age of thirty-two, he owned his own sailmaking establishment, which employed forty Blacks and whites. Forten frequently gave funds to support a number of antislavery activities and events, including Garrison's newspaper, the *Liberator*, and he strongly opposed the African colonization movement.

BLACKS SERVE IN BATTLE OF LAKE ERIE
On **SEPTEMBER 10**, as many as fifty Blacks served with Captain Oliver Hazard Perry in the defeat of the British man-of-war in the Battle of Lake Erie. Perry, who initially objected to the "motley set-blacks, soldiers, boys" sent to him, later spoke of his Black crew as "absolutely insensible to danger" after the victory in this major battle of the War of 1812.

JACKSON ATTACKS SEMINOLE INDIANS IN FLORIDA
On **NOVEMBER 9**, Andrew Jackson led a militia of two thousand men in an attack on Native Americans in western Florida; more than five hundred were killed in an attack on the village of Talladega. Some Blacks who had sought refuge from slavery in the area were killed along with the Seminoles.

1814 JACKSON URGES BLACKS TO FIGHT
On **SEPTEMBER 21**, Andrew Jackson issued a proclamation at Mobile, Alabama, urging free Blacks to become more involved in the War of 1812.

◈ Later, in 1815, prior to the final attack by the British on New Orleans, Jackson had the following speech read to the "men of color":

Soldiers: From the shores of Mobile I collected you to arms. I invited you to share the perils and to divide the glory of your white countrymen. I expected much from you, for I was not uninformed of those qualities which must render you so formidable to an invading foe. I knew that you could endure hunger and thirst, and all the hardships of war. I knew that you loved the land of your nativity, and that, like ourselves, you had to defend all that is most dear to man. But you surpass my hopes. I have found in you, united to these qualities, that noble enthusiasm which impels to great deeds.

Soldiers: The President of the United States shall be informed of your conduct on the present occasion, and the voice of the representatives of the American nation shall applaud your valor, as your general now praises your ardor. The enemy is near: his "sails cover the lakes": but the brave are united, and if he finds us contending among ourselves, it will be for the prize of valor and fame, its noblest reward.

By command,
Thos. L. Butler, Aid de Camp

1815 FOUR COTTON CENTERS EMERGE IN THE SOUTH CENTRAL STATES
The growing, processing, and distribution of cotton in the south central states was centered in four areas. Three of these — Nashville, Tennessee; Natchez, Mississippi; and Baton Rouge, Louisiana — were located along the Mississippi River. In each of these areas, cotton production and the number of slaves had increased substantially over the last decade or so. Cotton from these three centers was marketed through New Orleans. The fourth cotton center, located in the valleys of the Tombigbee and Alabama Rivers, was still quite small at this time.

The importance of these four centers is evident in the following statistics. Over the previous fifteen years, cotton production in the Nashville area increased from one million to three million pounds. The number of slaves in the entire state of Tennessee increased from about 14,000 in 1800 to 46,000 a decade later. Natchez not only produced most of Mississippi's cotton but had most of the state's slaves at the time. By 1810, it had about 14,523 slaves. Baton Rouge, one of the most productive cotton plantation regions, shipped thousands of bales of cotton through the New Orleans markets annually. In 1802, the val-

Many Black soldiers, including slaves from nearby plantations, fought in the Battle of New Orleans. After defeating the British, General Andrew Jackson told his Black troops, "You surpassed my hopes. I have found in you . . . that noble enthusiasm which impels to great deeds."

ley region of the Tombigbee and Alabama Rivers had only 2,600 slaves, who produced 2,000 bales of cotton annually.

FREEDOM FOR BLACKS IN CANADA
Returning Black veterans of the War of 1812 carried news of freedom for Blacks in Canada. Such news marked the first stirrings of what would become the Underground Railroad, the system by which runaway slaves were transported to freedom in Canada.

BLACKS FIGHT TO LIBERATE NEW ORLEANS
On **JANUARY 8**, two battalions of five hundred free Blacks fought with Andrew Jackson to liberate New Orleans from the British in the last battle of the War of 1812. Identified as the "Free Men of Color," this was the largest single force of Black men ever assembled to fight for the United States up to that time.

The use of Black troops was the idea of Louisiana governor William C. C. Clairborne. Jackson concurred, noting:

> The free men of colour in your city are inured to the southern climate and would make excellent soldiers. They will not remain quiet spectators of the interesting contest. . . . Distrust them, and you make them your enemies. Place confidence in them and you engage them by every dear and honorable tie to the interest of the country who extends to them the equal rights and privileges of white men.

Jackson accepted the battalion of Free Men of Color plus a battalion of soldiers from Santo Domingo because of the shortage of effective troops. They held their line on the Chalmette Plains and then counter attacked. It was the worst defeat suffered by the British army in years. The British lost more than twenty-six hundred soldiers, whereas American forces lost only twenty-one men. Jackson wrote later that he believed that the British commander, Sir Edward Pakenham, had been killed by a shot fired by a free Black man. Blacks actually fought on both sides of the battle; the First and Second West Indian Infantry Regiments fought with the British. Hopes of freedom for Black Americans were dashed when the Treaty of Ghent (which ended the war) was negotiated. Wording in the treaty called for the mutual restoration of properties; thus, Blacks who had joined the British to secure their freedom were returned to slavery. Some were taken to the West Indies and sold, and their American owners were indemnified. The final Battle of New Orleans was actually fought after the Treaty of Ghent had been signed in Paris.

Ironically, Black soldiers who had fought with Jackson were not permitted to march in the annual parades that celebrated the victory.

1816 BEECHER ESTABLISHES THE AMERICAN BIBLE SOCIETY

Lyman Beecher (1775–1863), a clergyman and theologian, established the American Bible Society, which supported the American Colonization Society's missionary efforts in Africa.

Beecher was the father of Harriet Beecher Stowe. His notes and sermons were especially instrumental in influencing many to turn against slavery. Beecher's skilled oratory and sermons made him one of the most influential figures of his time.

BOXLEY CONSPIRACY UNCOVERED IN PENNSYLVANIA

The Boxley Conspiracy in Spotsylvania, Pennsylvania, was found out. Thirty slaves were arrested, and six were hanged. George Boxley, a white military officer from Virginia who had intended to free slaves in Spotsylvania, escaped.

AFRICAN METHODIST EPISCOPAL CHURCH ESTABLISHED NATIONALLY

On **APRIL 9–11**, Black Methodists from a number of local AME congregations in different cities convened in Philadelphia and consolidated to establish the national African Methodist Episcopal Church. This represented a formal and legal separation and independence of the Black church from the all-white establishment. The assembly elected Richard Allen as its first bishop. Since the establishment of the Bethel AME Church in 1794, the membership had

grown to 9,888, including 14 elders, 26 deacons, and 101 itinerant and local licentiates.

Today, the AME Church has about six thousand churches and more than two million members.

MAROON SETTLEMENT ATTACKED BY U.S. TROOPS AS PRECURSOR TO SEMINOLE WAR

On **JULY 27**, the U.S. government, under pressure from Georgia slaveholders, ordered Colonel Edmund Gaines to attack and destroy Negro Fort on the banks of the Apalachicola River in Florida and to capture the 250 runaway slaves living there. This small, old Spanish fort, about sixty miles from the U.S. border, had been rebuilt by a company of British troops under the leadership of Lieutenant Colonel Edward Nicholls. Nicholls had recruited Native Americans and runaway slaves to perform hit-and-run raids into Georgia, disrupting many Georgia slaveholders. The settlement, led by the Black leader Garcon, had little time to prepare for the fight. One of the government's gunboats fired and hit the fort's powder magazine, which exploded, killing as many as 270 of the 300 women, children, and men in the fort. The attack and destruction of Negro Fort marked the beginning of other attacks by the federal government to recapture runaway slaves, destroy Native American villages, and make way for the ceding of Florida territory to the United States (in 1819).

AMERICAN COLONIZATION SOCIETY FORMED

On **DECEMBER 28**, Robert Finley, a Presbyterian clergyman, founded the American Colonization Society in Washington, D.C., to resettle free American Blacks on the west coast of Africa.

Several prominent Americans were sponsors, including John C. Calhoun of South Carolina, Henry Clay of Kentucky, and John Randolph of Virginia. Judge Bushrod Washington, nephew of the late president, presided. By 1819, the society had received considerable financial support, including one hundred thousand dollars from the federal government. Within the next four years, the first shipload of eighty-eight colonists departed from the United States to colonies along the West African coast. Within five years, the society had a number of state auxiliaries, and county and city societies. Fourteen state legislatures supported colonization efforts. Free Blacks organized to protest and counteract the efforts of the society, raising money for speakers to publicize their cause and reinforce the view that their destiny was on this continent, not in Africa.

Although most of the nation's Black leaders opposed the "anti-free-Black orientation" of the American Colonization Society, a small group backed its efforts. For example, John Russwurm, a coeditor of the first Black newspaper, *Freedom's Journal*, emigrated to Liberia under the auspices of the American Colonization Society. Paul Cuffe and other Blacks who initially supported the society soon disassociated themselves from the group.

1817 DEACON BROWN ORDAINED

Morris Brown (1770–1849) was ordained a deacon in the African Methodist Episcopal (AME) Church.

At this time, the African Methodist Church he had established in Charleston was one of the largest congregations in the country, with a membership in excess of one thousand. By 1822, its membership was

Morris Brown, an influential leader in the Black community, served as both deacon and bishop of the African Methodist Episcopal Church. As the church grew in size and influence, a number of AME ministers became bishops who were important leaders. Several historically Black colleges and universities were named after these bishops.

reported to be three thousand. Brown's religious influence was severely hampered by whites who feared a movement similar to Denmark Vesey's plan to kill slave masters. Because many whites believed Brown was a coconspirator of Vesey's, he had to leave Charleston quickly. Settling in Philadelphia, Brown became a widely respected religious leader and in 1828 was made a bishop in the African Methodist Episcopal Church. He served the church during a period of rapid growth in membership. In 1844 Brown was incapacitated by a stroke, and he died on May 19, 1849, at his home in Philadelphia.

SLAVES TRAINED AS ARTISANS IN FLORIDA

Years after the importation of slaves was prohibited by federal law (1808), slave trader Zephaniah Kingsley illegally imported African men and women to his plantation on Fort George Island in northern Florida. Kingsley taught the slaves to be craftworkers and farmers and then smuggled them into Georgia, selling them at 50 percent above the regular price. Kingsley had an African wife who lived in a separate house and helped him run the plantation.

PROTEST AGAINST AMERICAN COLONIZATION SOCIETY IN PHILADELPHIA

In **JANUARY**, Philadelphia Blacks, led by Richard Allen and James Forten, met at the Bethel AME Church and formally protested against efforts of the American Colonization Society to exile Blacks from the United States. An audience of about three thousand listened as the two leaders termed the colonization an "outrage" formed for the benefit of slaveholding interests. They urged the audience to resist this movement with passion. Forten also used the meeting to denounce the slanderous assertion of the American Colonization Society that Blacks were inherently inferior to whites and that their status was unchangeable. Forten reported that he was outraged at the American Colonization Society's offer to make him ruler of what would be the country of Liberia. The gathering made the following resolution:

> Whereas our ancestors (not of choice) were the first successful cultivators of the wilds of America, we their descendants feel ourselves entitled to participate in the blessings of her luxuriant soil, which their blood and sweat manured; and that any measure or system of measures, having a tendency to banish us from her bosom, would not only be cruel, but in direct violation of those principles, which have been the boast of the republic.

Resolved, That we view with deep abhorrence the unmerited stigma attempted to be cast upon the reputation of the free people of color, by the promoters of this measure, "that they are a dangerous and useless part of the community," when in the state of disenfranchisement in which they live, in the hour of danger they ceased to remember their wrongs, and rallied around the standards of their country.

Resolved, That we never will separate ourselves voluntarily from the slave population in this country; they are our brethren by the ties of consanguinity, of suffering, and of wrong; and we feel that there is more virtue in suffering privations with them, than fancied advantages for a season.

At the same meeting, the leadership put forth an address "to the humane and benevolent inhabitants of the city and county of Philadelphia." The following is a portion of that address:

We have no wish to separate from our present homes for any purpose whatever. Contented with our present situation and condition, we are not desirous of increasing their prosperity but by honest efforts, and by the use of those opportunities for their improvement, which the constitution and the laws allow to all. It is, therefore, with painful solicitude and sorrowing regret, we have seen a plan for colonizing the free people of color of the United States, on the coast of Africa.

We humbly, respectfully, and fervently entreat and beseech your disapprobation of the plan of colonization now offered by the "American Society for colonizing the free people of color of the United States." Here, in the city of Philadelphia, where the voice of the suffering sons of Africa was first heard; where was first commenced the work of abolition, on which heaven has smiled, for it could have success only from the great Master; let not a purpose be assisted which will stay the cause of the entire abolition of slavery in the United States, and which may defeat it altogether; which proffers to those who do not ask for them, what it calls benefits, but which they consider injuries, and which must insure to the multitude, whose prayers can only reach you through us, misery, sufferings, and perpetual slavery.

(Signed)
James Forten, Chairman
Russel Parrott, Secretary.

Those attending the meeting later organized protests and demonstrations in Boston, New York City, Albany, and Hartford. The African colonization issue triggered much debate within the Black community and caused some who supported the movement to be called traitors.

SLAVES ATTACK WHITES IN MARYLAND
On **APRIL 7**, as many as two hundred slaves attacked whites with sticks in St. Mary's County, Maryland. Police moved in to calm the crowds. Abolitionists and free Blacks blamed the slaves' unrest on plans by the American Colonization Society to exile slaves to Africa.

1818 MANUMISSIONS PROHIBITED IN THE SOUTH
The Georgia state legislature prohibited manumissions, irrespective of cause, reason, circumstance, or method. Georgia and other states wanted to reduce and eliminate their free Black populations.

Administrators of estates were fined one thousand dollars when they attempted to comply with manumission provisions in wills. Alabama had legislation that required a posted security when slaves were emancipated to ensure that they could be removed from the state. In South Carolina, free Blacks were prohibited from entering the state. Free Blacks could be forced back into slavery or out of the area if they were not disciplined or submissive in demeanor. The slightest misconduct could bring severe retribution and restrictions. Other states followed with similar prohibitions.

PENNSYLVANIA AUGUSTINE SOCIETY FOUNDED
Free Blacks in Philadelphia formed the Pennsylvania Augustine Society for the education of people of color.

ST. PHILIP'S PROTESTANT EPISCOPAL CHURCH OFFICIALLY ENTERS THE EPISCOPAL DIOCESE
St. Philip's Protestant Episcopal Church in New York was formally received into the Episcopal Diocese. A small group of Blacks had formed St. Philip's in 1809 after they withdrew from Trinity Episcopal Church because of discrimination. The church was relocated with each major wave of migration into the city until it put down permanent roots in Harlem, where it was reported to have built an impressive house of worship.

In 1919, the *Age* reported that St. Philip's was the richest Black church in the world, with holdings estimated at one million dollars.

BATTLE OF SUWANNE TAKES PLACE IN FLORIDA
On **APRIL 18**, the Battle of Suwanne, Florida (one of several battles of the First Seminole War), was fought

between U.S. troops, led by Andrew Jackson, and a force of Native Americans and Blacks. Jackson crushed the force and characterized the hostilities as a "savage and negro war."

1819 ADAMS EXPRESSES HIS SENTIMENTS ON SLAVERY

John Adams's sentiments on slavery were presented in a letter he wrote to Robert I. Evans in **JUNE**:

> Every measure of prudence, therefore, ought to be assumed for the eventual total extirpation of slavery from the United States.
>
> I have, through my whole life, held the practice of slavery in such abhorrence, that I have never owned a negro or any other slave; though I have lived for many years in times when the practice was not disgraceful; when the best men in my vicinity thought it not inconsistent with their character; and when it has cost me thousands of dollars for the labor and subsistence of free men, which I might have saved by the purchase of negroes at times when they were very cheap.

SLAVE SMUGGLING PROHIBITED

On **MARCH 3**, Congress passed the Anti-Slave Trade Act to curtail slave smuggling. Legislation stipulated a fifty-dollar reward per slave to informants and authorized the president to return illegal slaves to Africa. Smuggling had become a highly profitable endeavor and was widespread throughout the South.

1820

POPULATION OVERVIEW

GENERAL POPULATION IN THE UNITED STATES The U.S. population numbered 9,650,000, and the Black population (1,777,254) made up 18.4 percent of the total. About 87 percent (1,543,688) of Blacks were slaves. The nation's population had grown by 30 percent since 1810. Approximately 72 percent of Americans worked on farms. Of U.S. cities, New York City had the largest number of residents (124,000), followed by Philadelphia (113,000). The United States comprised 22 states, 5 more than a decade earlier.

SLAVES AND FREE BLACKS IN SELECTED STATES The largest concentration of slaves was in Virginia, where 425,153 slaves dwelled — more than one-and-a-half times as many slaves as the second largest concentration, in South Carolina, with 258,475 slaves. Four other states had slave populations in excess of 100,000: North Carolina, Georgia, Maryland, and Kentucky. The free Black population in the country stood at roughly 233,600 residents, of which the largest concentration was in Maryland (39,700), followed by Virginia (36,900), Pennsylvania (30,200), and New York (29,300). Free Blacks made up a relatively high proportion of the Black and total populations in Delaware (17.8 percent), District of Columbia (12.3 percent), and Maryland (9.7 percent). Free Blacks were concentrated in these areas because they could find decent jobs more easily than in other places.

ECONOMIC OVERVIEW

COTTON PRODUCTION The South was producing about 335,000 bales of cotton annually; each bale weighed about five hundred pounds. Between 1816 and 1820, cotton accounted for almost 40 percent of the value of all American exports; between 1836 and 1840, almost 63 percent; and thereafter, about 50 percent. In 1821, each of eight individual states — Virginia, North Carolina, South Carolina, Georgia, Alabama, Mississippi, Tennessee, and Louisiana — produced at least five times as much cotton as the whole nation had produced thirty years before.

Slaves were important to the production of cotton because it was a "multiple-day" crop. About 120 days of labor were required over an eight-month period to seed, plant, till, and harvest the crop. The factor that most limited cotton production was the necessity of picking by hand. In the South, farmers rarely hired wage laborers because the cost was high. Cotton production and its profitability were clearly tied to the low cost of slave labor. In the 1820s, a "prime Georgia field hand" had cost about seven hundred dollars; by 1860, one laborer cost eighteen hundred dollars. Small cotton planters, who had formerly expanded production by buying additional slaves, could not continue to do so when slave prices were high. These small planters depended more on their families for labor. Slaveless plantations in the South grew from 39 percent of all plantations in 1850 to 48 percent in 1860. Even in the Mississippi alluvial region, nonslave plantations grew from 20 percent to 36 percent over the decade. Over the years, slaves became numerically concentrated on the largest plantations (those having more than fifteen slaves) and in the highest yield areas, namely, the Cotton Belt of the Mississippi valley and in parts of central Alabama and northeastern Mississippi. Here, each new slave meant fifteen to twenty more acres of cotton production.

Because of the profitability of cotton, planters invested heavily in expanding cotton production in newly cleared areas of the South. Population in southern states grew in relationship to the expansion of the cotton economy. An example of this rapid growth was evidenced in Alabama, one of the newer cotton-producing areas, where population soared from 1,250 in 1800 to 144,300 in 1820 and then doubled during the next decade.

SOCIAL CONDITIONS OVERVIEW

THE CHANGING RELATIONSHIPS BETWEEN SLAVE AND SLAVEHOLDER Slavery became a mode of production and an integral part of southern society. This peculiar institution created a special legal system and paternalistic social patterns. After the importation of slaves had been legally abolished, slaveholders had to maintain their slaves and discourage them from running away. They restricted their slaves' contact with other slaves and the "outside" world in part to isolate them from news that might cause them to revolt and in part to encourage slaves to identify with their plantation. The slaves were not entirely powerless in this situation. They responded to cruel and harsh treatment, long workdays, and inadequate food by staging mini-revolts, deliberately breaking tools to reduce actual work time, stealing food, burning barns and fields, and creating a subculture within the broader slave system. Over the years, some slaveholders came to better understand slave behavior, and many responded by allowing slaves a more livable environment.

ELEMENTARY SCHOOL FOR BLACKS OPENS IN BOSTON

The city of Boston opened an elementary school for Black children. Although a separate school for Negro children had been established by a white teacher in the home of Primus Hall, a prominent Black person, as early as 1798. Blacks had petitioned the city and the state for separate schools, but they had been refused each time until 1820. In 1800, however, Blacks established their own school and employed two Harvard men to instruct students. The school lasted for several years.

MAINE GIVES RIGHT TO VOTE TO ALL MALE CITIZENS

The constitution of Maine gave all of the male citizens the right to vote and the right to an education, regardless of race.

U.S. ARMY RESTRICTS ENLISTMENT

The army prohibited "Negroes and Mulattoes" from enlisting. The bravery and honorable service Blacks had given the country during the Revolution and the War of 1812 had apparently been forgotten.

Mayflower of Liberia SETS SAIL

On **FEBRUARY 6**, the *Mayflower of Liberia* sailed from New York Harbor for Sierra Leone with eighty-six free Blacks aboard. They were to be resettled in a colony of freed slaves founded thirty years earlier by British abolitionists. This marked the first large-scale, organized effort to resettle Africans in their homeland. Influential Black leaders continued to denounce the intentions of the colonization efforts by the American Colonization Society. Martin Delany, the Black abolitionist, labeled the organization "anti-Christian" and "one of the Negro's worst enemies." Many Blacks, particularly free Blacks, questioned why they should leave a land for which many Blacks had given their lives and that they considered their home. Sierra Leone seemed like a foreign country.

MISSOURI COMPROMISE ENACTED

On **MARCH 3**, after a prolonged, acrimonious debate, Congress adopted the compromise arranged by the speaker of the house, Henry Clay. The Missouri Compromise provided for the admission of Missouri into the Union as a slave state and of Maine as a free state. Slavery was prohibited in Louisiana Purchase territory north of the 36° 30′ line and permitted south of that line. Missouri, the first territory within the Louisiana Purchase lands to request statehood, would enter as a slave state since it already held ten thousand slaves. Northern legislators clearly feared that slave states would soon outnumber free states and thereby gain control of Congress. When Maine applied for statehood, Southern politicians made Missouri's admission a necessary condition for Maine's. The heated issues raised in the Missouri debate, such as states' rights and the status of slaves as property, would eventually result in the Civil War.

◈ On March 2, 1821, Congress voted a second time on the Missouri Compromise. Missouri would be admitted to the Union only if the state constitution did not try to limit the rights of citizens, specifically free Blacks. A constitution drafted by inhabitants of the Missouri territory in July 1820 had barred free Blacks and mulattos from the future state.

TRADE IN FOREIGN SLAVES CONSIDERED PIRACY

On **MAY 15**, Congress passed legislation that made the trade in foreign slaves an act of piracy. Any American found guilty of such illegal smuggling could be put to death. Previously, the penalty had been forfeiture of the vessel involved in the smuggling activity.

1821 ALABAMA INTRODUCES SLAVE-HUNTING PATROLS

A patrol system was established in the state of Alabama to prevent the escape of slaves. These patrols were composed of groups of whites who made their living as slave catchers or bounty hunters.

BLACK INVENTOR GRANTED PATENT

The earliest known patent given to a Black person was to Thomas L. Jennings for his invention that dry-cleaned clothes.

BLACK WOMEN ORGANIZE THE DAUGHTERS OF AFRICA SOCIETY

In Philadelphia, a group of Black women founded the Daughters of Africa Society. A benevolent association, the society loaned money to members for rent and other necessities, donated money for burial of a member or of her relatives, provided aid to the sick, gave temporary assistance to survivors of deceased members, and provided a forum for arbitrated disputes between members. To settle extremely serious disputes, the society sometimes expelled members or penalized members by imposing fines. It was common practice for Black churches as well as benevolent associations to function in this manner, rather than relying on the city's white-dominated judicial system.

Hall v. Mullin

In deciding this case, the Maryland State Supreme Court ruled that if a slave was willed property by a master, the slave would be freed because a slave could not legally own property.

LIBERIA FOUNDED BY THE AMERICAN COLONIZATION SOCIETY

The American Colonization Society purchased a site in West Africa to establish a colony for free Blacks from the United States. The following year, the Black Republic of Liberia was founded, and the Reverend Jehudi Ashmun was selected as the leader of the first settlement there, named Monrovia after President James Monroe. The society's leadership believed that racial problems in America could be solved only by encouraging free Blacks to emigrate. Only about twenty thousand Blacks, however, relocated to this colony. Free Blacks were considered by southern whites, particularly slaveholders, to be a likely source of slaves' discontent and rebellion. Some believed that free Blacks were unassimilable into white

society. Among those who supported the colonization plan were James Monroe, Thomas Jefferson, Henry Clay, and Daniel Webster.

The colony was not formed without some conflict. *The Anti-Slavery Record*, published in February 1837, recorded, "In its very infancy the colony was involved in a war, in which the Rev. Mr. Ashmun gained great glory by his courage and conduct."

Although *The Anti-Slavery Record* wrote that "it does not wish to blame the Colonization Society, or Mr. Ashmun, or the colony, for this or any of the subsequent wars with the natives," it provided evidence that "although they were attacked by natives, the colony felt themselves obliged to retaliate by the destruction of a native town." According to the *Record*, "The fault lies in the COLONIZING scheme itself. . . . We do not see how a "new empire" can be built up on the shores of Africa without war — and, if such an empire must be built up by war, we do not see how its building up can possibly aid the conquest of the Prince of PEACE."

The Genius of Universal Emancipation BEGINS PUBLICATION

In **JANUARY**, Benjamin Lundy (1789–1839), a Quaker abolitionist in Mount Pleasant, Ohio, distributed one of the first abolitionist journals — *The Genius of Universal Emancipation*. Lundy followed the first issue with irregular issues until his death.

◈ Lundy, considered one of the most important early members of the antislavery movement, was a saddler by trade. In his business travels to and from Wheeling, Virginia, he saw almost every aspect of slavery and slave trading. At the age of twenty-six, he settled in St. Clairsville, Ohio, where he organized the Union Humane Society, an organization that grew from five to five hundred members. It was one of the first major organizations to discuss openly possible ways to solve the slavery issue. He soon aided Charles Osborn in the publication of Osborn's *Philanthropist*, a paper focusing on antislavery and other reforms.

The *Philanthropist* failed, but Lundy's determination led him to issue a new antislavery paper, *The Genius of Universal Emancipation*. Lundy's ultimate desire was the emancipation of Blacks and their resettlement in self-supporting, respectable colonies. When the American Convention for the Abolition of Slavery was held, he was the first delegate from Tennessee. The next year, he settled a number of freed

Benjamin Lundy, a Quaker abolitionist and the founder of the journal The Genius of Universal Emancipation, *became a major target of slave traders. Lundy, along with other eminent opponents of slavery, contributed significantly to the swell of opposition that eventually abolished slavery in this country.*

North Carolina Blacks in Haiti. In the coming years, he traveled to Canada to secure support for his colonization projects. He also made trips to Texas and parts of Mexico, where he negotiated land grants and agreements for Black settlements.

Lundy's prominence as a major antislavery reformer caused him to be a major target of slave traders. In 1828, he was assaulted and almost killed by slave traders in Baltimore. When Lundy pressed the court for prosecution of the offenders, the judge let it be known that Lundy deserved what he got, and the offenders were free to go unpunished. Throughout his career, Lundy encouraged many others to become involved in the antislavery movement. Sadly,

most of Lundy's papers were lost when Pennsylvania Hall, in Philadelphia, was burned by a mob in 1837, about two years prior to his death.

FREE BLACKS MUST QUALIFY TO VOTE IN NEW YORK
On **NOVEMBER 10**, members of the New York Constitutional Convention extended male suffrage by abolishing nearly all property qualifications for voting. The convention provided that "no man of color unless he shall have been for three years a citizen of this state" could vote; also, a Black man had to have a freehold estate of 250 dollars to be granted suffrage. There were no other legal distinctions between free Blacks and whites.

MURDER OF SLAVE BECOMES A CAPITAL OFFENSE
On **DECEMBER 20**, South Carolina passed legislation that declared "the wilful, malicious and premeditated killing of a slave, by whomsoever perpetrated, is a capital offense." With its passage, the murder of a slave became a capital offense in all slaveholding states since the other states had already passed such legislation.

1822 **FIRST COLORED PRESBYTERIAN CHURCH FOUNDED IN NEW YORK CITY**
Samuel Cornish (1795–1859), a freeborn Black man from Delaware, organized the first Black Presbyterian congregation in New York City, the second founded in the country.

◈ In 1827, Cornish became copublisher of *Freedom's Journal*, the first Black newspaper in the United States. Cornish became one of the major leaders supporting education for Blacks. He further felt that the most effective means of resolving the slavery issue was an economic approach. He strongly urged the establishment of a manual-labor college to train young Black men. Cornish served on several boards, including the American Anti-Slavery Society and the American and Foreign Anti-Slavery Society.

FIRST PUBLIC SCHOOL FOR BLACKS IN PHILADELPHIA OPENS
The first public school for Blacks in Philadelphia, originally called Bird School, was opened. The school eventually changed its name to honor James Forten, a Black entrepreneur and civil rights leader.

MISSISSIPPI LIMITS MANUMISSION
In Mississippi, free Blacks did not make up a large part of the total Black population. In fact, the

supreme court of Mississippi held that "the laws of this state presume a negro *prima facie* to be a slave." The legislature passed a law in this year limiting manumission to cases in which a slave had performed some meritorious act for the owner or state; furthermore, each proposed manumission had to be reviewed and was granted only by a special act of the legislature.

VESEY'S PLAN FOR SLAVE REVOLT DISCOVERED

On **MAY 30**, plans for a slave revolt organized by Denmark Vesey (1767–1822), a former slave, were uncovered. It was one of the most elaborately planned slave revolts on record and reportedly involved nine thousand or more Blacks in the vicinity of Charleston, South Carolina.

Vesey was a brilliant man from Santo Domingo who had purchased his freedom in 1800 from Captain Joseph Vesey, when he was brought to Charleston. Working as a carpenter, Vesey acquired property worth more than eight thousand dollars, traveled rather widely, and became thoroughly familiar with the Bible. He mingled freely among slaves and free Blacks alike and was highly respected by them. Over the years, he inspired slaves to demand their freedom.

Vesey and his coconspirators met in a church in Hampstead, a community near Charleston, to organize the revolt. The plans involved recruiting Blacks within an area of seventy to eighty miles. The revolt was to begin on the second Monday in July 1822, when many of the slaves' masters would be away for summer vacation. One component of the plan appeared to be the complete destruction of the white population of Charleston. Vesey expected aid from Great Britain and Santo Domingo and envisioned the eventual end of slavery as a result. According to some reports, many whites supported Vesey's plan, but their involvement was never revealed. Beginning in December 1821, recruits were identified, money raised to purchase arms, and a blacksmith found to make spikes and bayonets for the attack.

Yet despite Vesey's plans, the plot for the insurrection was betrayed. A house slave leaked the plans to his master, who then alerted officials. They moved quickly to thwart the revolt. The authorities arrested 131 Blacks and 4 whites as conspirators. They were quite surprised to find many respectable free Blacks involved in the conspiracy. Vesey and 35 aides were hanged on July 2 at Blake's Landing, Charleston, South Carolina. Thirty-four other slaves were deported and another 61 or so were acquitted. Records show that torture was used to extract confessions and that some slaves were whipped unmercifully.

Because Vesey had been a free Black, conditions for other free Blacks got worse after the conspiracy. The South Carolina legislature immediately passed a law requiring every free Black to have a respectable white guardian. Another law made it an offense — punishable by imprisonment — to teach a Black to read or write.

SOUTH CAROLINA RESTRICTS FREE BLACKS

In **JULY**, the South Carolina state legislature passed laws to restrict the movement of free Blacks. Whites were especially fearful of free Blacks since the Vesey incident. The laws also provided for the temporary jailing of Black seamen on shore leave.

Richard Furman, the leader of the Southern Baptists, went on record as a strong defender of slavery as a Christian institution. Furman argued that the discovery of the "Charleston Insurrection" (Vesey's revolt) was evidence of God's divine intervention to show approval and protection of slaveholders. Furman advocated religious instruction for slaves, particularly to teach them to respect their masters. Many others from the South preached and supported the compatibility of slavery and Christianity.

BISHOP OF AFRICAN METHODIST EPISCOPAL ZION CHURCH INSTALLED

On **JULY 30**, James Varick (1750–1827) became the first bishop of the African Methodist Episcopal Zion Church (AMEZ) at its first conference. Varick's involvement with the AMEZ Church extended back to 1796, when he formed the first African American church in New York City.

◈ Varick was born in Orange County, New York, and attended the Free School for Negroes. After the American Revolution, he joined the John Street Methodist Episcopal Church and was licensed to preach. Varick and about thirty other Blacks left the John Street Church because of segregated conditions and formed the first Black-established church in New York City. This church was dedicated on September 7, 1800. Varick established the New York African Bible Society in 1817, the African Methodist Episcopal Zion Church in New Haven, Connecticut, in 1818, and helped to establish *Freedom's Journal* in 1827. He was reelected bishop of the AMEZ Church at its second convention in 1824.

1823 CIRCUIT COURT RULES THAT SLAVE ENTERING FREE STATE BECOMES FREE

The U.S. Circuit Court in Washington, D.C., ruled that if a slave was moved to a free state, the slave thereby became free. It also ruled that inhumane treatment of a slave was an indictable offense under common law.

FIRST BLACK AMERICAN COLLEGE GRADUATE

Alexander Lucius Twilight (1795–1857) became the first Black to graduate from an American college. He received an A.B. degree from Middlebury College.

Twilight was born in Bradford, Vermont, to a family of free Blacks. He was indentured at an early age to a neighboring farmer, where he earned enough to purchase his final year of indenture service in 1815.

MISSISSIPPI BARS BLACKS FROM MEETING

Mississippi made it illegal for more than five Blacks (free or slave) to congregate. It also prohibited teaching Blacks to read and write. Punishment for these offenses could be up to thirty-nine lashes.

1824 ILLINOIS REJECTS SLAVERY

The Illinois legislature rejected a proposal to establish slavery in the state.

INDIANA MINISTER ARGUES AGAINST SLAVERY

James Duncan, a minister in Indiana and father of Alexander Duncan, a U.S. representative from Cincinnati, published *A Treatise on Slavery In Which Is Shown Forth the Evil of Slaveholding Both from the Light of Nature and Divine Revelations.* Duncan argued that slavery was not only unconstitutional but also violated fundamental moral law. Slavery, according to Duncan, prevented the slave from performing basic duties owed to God, to family, and to neighbors. Three things were essential to the permanent existence of slavery: First, slaves had to be kept in ignorance to prevent them from pleading their case for freedom or from escaping; second, slaves had to be barred from the courts of law in all cases involving white persons; and third, the master's will was always superior to relative obligations, rights, and privileges. Duncan used the Ten Commandments to reveal slavery as a violation of fundamental law. In addition, he provided "The Slaveholder's Prayer," which later was published as a separate four-page leaflet by the American Anti-Slavery Society and distributed widely. Duncan's treatise was republished in New York and Cincinnati in 1840.

OHIO FURTHER RESTRICTS FREEDOM OF BLACKS

The Ohio legislature passed a law that prohibited a Black from retaliating against abuses by whites. Blacks were also excluded by law from serving on juries, thus allowing whites to abuse Blacks with impunity. The law was approved again in 1828 and 1831.

VIRGINIA EXPANDS SLAVE CODE

The Virginia General Assembly passed a number of laws related to slaves: twelve months' imprisonment for anyone assisting slaves to escape; a fine of fifty dollars and two months' imprisonment for teaching free Blacks to read or write; a fine of fifty dollars for failure to support old or infirm slaves; fines of up to one thousand dollars for written encouragement of insurrection; and a fine of fifty dollars and six months' imprisonment for purchasing anything from slaves or selling alcoholic beverages to them.

WHITES RIOT IN PROVIDENCE, RHODE ISLAND

In **OCTOBER**, the "Hard Scrabble" district of Providence, Rhode Island, was wrecked by a riot. More than four hundred whites attacked Black residents to protest against the employment of Blacks while whites were unemployed. Members of the white mob alleged that Blacks were also working at "white" jobs.

INDIANA ENACTS FUGITIVE SLAVE LAW

In **DECEMBER**, the Indiana state legislature enacted a law that allowed justices of the peace to rule in fugitive slave cases, with both the fugitive slave and claimant having the right to a jury trial.

The law was invalidated in 1850.

1825 JOSIAH HENSON LEADS RUNAWAY SLAVES TO FREEDOM

Josiah Henson led a group of runaway slaves from Maryland to freedom in Kentucky. Henson continued his journey to Canada where he founded a settlement for former slaves. Henson was the alleged model for Harriet Beecher Stowe's character, Uncle Tom, in her antislavery book, *Uncle Tom's Cabin.*

1826 ANTISLAVERY WRITER BECOMES EDITOR IN NEW YORK

William Cullen Bryant (1794–1878), a poet and journalist, took over as editor of the *New York Evening Post.* During his tenure, he argued persuasively against slavery. He became part-owner of the *Post* in 1829, a position he retained and used to fight slavery and racial injustices until his death.

BLACK ACTOR BEGINS PERFORMING

Ira F. Aldridge (1807–1867), a Shakespearean actor, began his stage career. Over the next couple of decades, Aldridge gave command performances before, and was honored by, the monarchs of Sweden, Prussia, Austria, and Russia.

◆ Aldridge was born in New York City probably on July 24, 1807. He attended the African Free School, and in 1821 he joined an African theater company in New York City. When he could not get work in the United States, he moved to Europe and later studied in Glasgow, Scotland. Aldridge became a renowned Shakespearean actor and was best known for his portrayal of Othello. Aldridge died in Poland; he never returned to America.

JONES GRADUATES FROM AMHERST

On **AUGUST 23**, Edward A. Jones (1808–1864) received a bachelor's degree from Amherst College in Massachusetts.

Jones was long considered the first Black college graduate in the United States, because he graduated two weeks before John Russwurm received his degree from Bowdoin College. However, recent research reveals that Alexander Lucius Twilight received his B.A. degree from Middlebury College in 1823, thus making him the first Black college graduate.

WHITE MOB ATTEMPTS TO RUN BLACKS OUT OF CINCINNATI

A mob of hundreds of whites in Cincinnati, Ohio, tried unsuccessfully to rid the city of its approximately 690 Black residents.

RUSSWURM GRADUATES FROM BOWDOIN

On **SEPTEMBER 6**, John Russwurm (1799–1851) received a bachelor's degree at Bowdoin College in Maine. He was the third Black American to graduate from college. He delivered the class oration and was the first Black to join a college fraternity, the Atheneans.

A year after his graduation, Russwurm became copublisher of the first Black newspaper, *Freedom's Journal*, which he steered toward a middle road in the debate on colonization. He became sole editor of the paper when Samuel Cornish, the senior editor, resigned after only six months. The pressure to support colonization may have been too much for Cornish, a more militant and initial nonsupporter of the movement. As editor, Russwurm invited articles supporting the colonization movement. The journal's circulation grew substantially — with distribution in eleven states and as many as twenty-four agents. Russwurm continued to publish *Freedom's Journal* until March 28, 1829, when it ceased to exist. Two months later, on May 29, 1829, *Freedom's Journal* was resurrected as *Rights of All*, by none other than its cofounder — Samuel Cornish.

◆ The following November, Russwurm left for Liberia, where he edited the *Liberia Herald* from 1830 to 1835. He was appointed governor of the Maryland Colony at Cape Palmas in 1836 and served as governor until his death in 1851.

Ira Aldridge, a Black Shakespearean actor, achieved significant acclaim in Europe during a career spanning nearly two decades.

1827 COFFIN MOVES TO INDIANA

Levi Coffin, a Quaker, moved from North Carolina to Newport (now called Fountain City), Indiana, because the community was composed primarily of abolitionists. It was while living in Newport that Coffin became one of the major abolitionists in the nation.

Over the next twenty years, Coffin helped more than two thousand slaves escape to freedom, primarily out of his home on the town's main street. Coffin's involvement in the Underground Railroad became more intense; he became one of the key administrators in organizing escapes and passages for fleeing slaves. To avoid detection, Coffin used a number of different routes to freedom in the North, including connections with Cincinnati, Ohio; Madison, Indiana; and Louisville, Kentucky. Much of what is now U.S. Route 27 was a passageway to freedom. Coffin moved to Cincinnati in 1847, where he used his operation of a dry goods store to help another one thousand slaves in their escape to freedom. Coffin

Levi Coffin, a Quaker abolitionist, was an active member of the Underground Railroad. He helped thousands of slaves escape through Indiana and Ohio to freedom in Canada.

was depicted in Harriet Beecher Stowe's *Uncle Tom's Cabin* as Simeon Halliday, a Quaker who worked unselfishly with the Underground Railroad.

Freedom's Journal BEGINS PUBLICATION

On **MARCH 16**, the first Black newspaper, *Freedom's Journal*, was published in New York City by John Russwurm and Samuel Cornish.

Most Black newspapers prior to the Civil War promoted abolition, and *Freedom's Journal* was no exception; it focused on politics and legislation, people and social events, and messages of hope to African Americans. The first Black newspaper set its publishing agenda as follows:

> We wish to plead our own cause. Too long have others spoken for us. Too long have the publick been deceived by misrepresentations, in things which concern us dearly, though in the estimation of some things which concern us dearly, though in the estimation of some mere trifles; for though there are many in society who exercise toward us benevolent feelings; still (with sorrow we confess it) there are others who make it their business to enlarge upon the least trifle, which tends to discredit of any person of colour; and pronounce anathemas and denounce our whole body for the misconduct of this guilty one. . . .

> Education being an object of the highest importance to the welfare of society, we shall endeavour to present just and adequate views of it, and to urge upon our brethren the necessity and expediency of training their children, while young, to habits of industry, and thus forming them for becoming useful members of society. It is surely time that we should awake from this lethargy of years, and make a concentrated effort for the education of our youth. We form a spoke in the human wheel, and it is necessary that we should understand our pendance on the different parts, and theirs on us, in order to perform our part with propriety.

◈ Cornish was born free in Delaware in 1796. After attending Free Africa Schools in Philadelphia and New York City, he attended Princeton University. He became a minister and founded the first African Presbyterian Church in New York City. Cornish was not only an excellent writer but also was senior editor and overall ambassador for the newspaper. His study was the first office of *Freedom's Journal*. The newspaper ceased publication on March 28, 1829, when Russwurm stepped down as editor. Cornish resumed the editorship of the paper, renamed *Rights of All*, and published the new paper for a year. Other publications subsequently started by Cornish were unsuccessful.

SLAVERY ABOLISHED IN NEW YORK

On **JULY 4**, slavery was officially abolished in New York. More than ten thousand slaves received their freedom. There would be no slaves in the state after this date.

BALTIMORE SLAVE RUNS AWAY

On **AUGUST 8**, Anthony Chase, slave of a Baltimore widow, failed to buy his freedom and escaped from the man to whom he had been hired out. Chase wrote a personal declaration of his feelings:

> I know that you will be astonished and surprised when you become acquainted with the unspected course that I am now about to take, a step that I never had the most distant idea of takeing, but what can a man do who has his hands bound and his feet fettered. He will certainly try to get them lossened in any way that he may think the most adviseable. I hope sir tht you will not think that I had any fault to find of you or your family[.] No sir I have none and I could of hired with you all the days of my life if my conditions could of been in any way bettered which I intreated with my mistress to do but it was all in vain[.] She would not consent to anything that would melorate my condition in any shape or measure[.] So I shall go to sea in the first vesel that may offer an opportunity and as soon as I can acumulate a sum of money suficient I will remit it to my mistress to prove to her and to [the] world that I dont mean to be dishonest but wish to pay her every cent that I think my servaces is worth. . . . I dont supose that I shall ever be forgiven for this act but I hope to find forgiveness in that world tht is to com.
>
> (Anthony Chase to Jeremiah Offman, August 8, 1827. Otho Holland Williams Papers)

In this personal letter, Chase not only revealed his human feelings by wishing his former employer health and happiness, but signed the declaration respectfully — "your most obedient serv[an]t."

1828 BLACKS RESTRICTED AS MAIL CARRIERS

Blacks could carry mail only if supervised by a white man, according to a ruling by the postmaster general.

BLACKFACE ENTERTAINMENT MAKES ITS DEBUT

In Louisville, Kentucky, Thomas "Daddy" Rice, a comedian from New York, painted his face black and then portrayed a character identified as "Jim Crow," a stable boy, who lived behind Rice's theater. The character depicted Blacks as hapless, ignorant, and foolish.

READING ROOM SOCIETY FOUNDED

In Philadelphia, a businessman, William Whipper, founded the Reading Room Society. The Society charged membership fees and monthly dues to finance a library for Blacks and fund programs for educating them. It also provided a center for antislavery activists.

1829 GEORGIA PROHIBITS EDUCATION OF SLAVES

Georgia passed legislation that effectively prohibited education of slaves or free Black persons. Punishments were prescribed for anyone found guilty of teaching a Black — slave or free — to read or write. Other southern states soon enacted similar laws — Louisiana in 1830, Alabama in 1832, and South Carolina in 1834. In North Carolina, it was against the law to give or sell any book or pamphlet to a slave. Although the state laws varied to some degree, in general, slaves convicted of the offense of learning were whipped. Free Blacks were fined and could also be whipped or imprisoned.

Such legislation regarding education of slaves or free Blacks was updated regularly, mostly in response to their demand for learning. Consequently, the punishments for educating Blacks increased. Here is a portion of the South Carolina legislation:

> If any persons shall hereafter teach any slave to read or write, or shall aid in assisting any slave to read or write, or cause or procure any slave to be taught to read or write, such person, if a free white person, upon conviction thereof, shall for every such offence against this act be fined not exceeding one hundred dollars, and imprisoned not more than six months; or if a free person of color, shall be whipped not exceeding fifty lashes, and fined not exceeding fifty dollars; and if a slave, shall be whipped not exceeding fifty lashes; and if any free person of color or a slave shall keep any such school or place of instruction for teaching any slave or free person of color to read or write, such person shall be liable to the same fine, imprisonment and corporal punishment as are by this act imposed and inflicted on free persons of color and slaves for teaching slaves to read or write.

NORTH CAROLINA DEFINES SLAVERY

In its ruling in *The State* v. *Mann*, the North Carolina Supreme Court provided the following description of slavery:

The end (of slavery) is the profit of the master, his security, and the public safety. The subject is one doomed in his own person and his posterity to live without knowledge and without the capacity to make any thing his own, and to toil that another may reap the fruits. Such services can only be expected from one who has no will of his own; who surrenders his will in implicit obedience to that of another. Such obedience is the consequence only of uncontrolled authority over the body. There is nothing else which can operate to produce the effect. The power of the master must be absolute to render the submission of the slave perfect. In the actual condition of things it must be so. There is no remedy. This discipline belongs at once the rights of the master and absolving the slave from his subjection. It constitutes the curse of slavery to both the bond and free portion of our population; but it is inherent in the relation of master and slave.

SCHOOL FOR BLACK CHILDREN OPENS

Daniel L. Payne, a free Black man, opened a school for Black children in Charleston, South Carolina. The school was successful and remained open until 1834, when a state law was passed that prohibited free Blacks from teaching other Blacks, slave or free.

RACE RIOT IN CINCINNATI

On **AUGUST 10**, a race riot erupted in Cincinnati, Ohio, prompting approximately one thousand Blacks to leave the city for Canada, Michigan, western Pennsylvania, and New York.

Although Cincinnati's Black population had increased over the previous several decades, the influence of the Colonization Society had caused many white citizens, particularly the unskilled, to demand the ouster of these new arrivals. As the hostility against Blacks grew more intense, the Cincinnati Colonization Society (founded in 1826 by some of the city's most prominent citizens) influenced local newspapers to join them in agitating against Cincinnati's free Blacks. In the summer of 1829, political officials attempted to enforce Ohio's Black Laws, which required Blacks to post five-hundred-dollar bonds guaranteeing "good behavior." When free Blacks received no legislative reprieve from their petitions against enforcing the laws, white mobs felt justified in attacking defenseless Blacks and burning their homes and communities.

In an effort to repress anti-Black mob violence in other cities, Black leaders, including Samuel Cornish, Richard Allen, and others, called for a national convention in Philadelphia, which was held the following year.

FREE BLACK PUBLISHES *Appeal to the Colored People of the World*

In Boston, on **SEPTEMBER 28**, David Walker (1785–1830), a free Black, published a radical antislavery pamphlet, *Walker's Appeal to the Colored People of the World*. Walker called for Blacks in the South to strike for their freedom, using violence if necessary. Walker's violent thesis was prefaced in the preamble, which stated that Blacks were the most "degraded, wretched, and abject set of beings that ever lived since the world began." The pamphlet was widely distributed and went into its third edition in 1829. Each publication was more militant than the preceding one.

◈ Walker was born in Wilmington, North Carolina, in 1785, to a slave father and free mother. Since Black children inherited the status of their mother, Walker was free. When he left the South, he settled in Boston, where he operated a used-clothing shop. He quickly became a leader in the Colored Association of Boston and was the city's agent for the abolitionist *Freedom's Journal*.

The pamphlet, which came to be known as *Walker's Appeal*, was so inflammatory that the governor of Georgia ordered the ship that brought the pamphlets held in quarantine for forty days. After the state legislature was called into session to consider the consequences of allowing the pamphlet into the hands of slaves, a bill was passed making it a capital offense to circulate literature that might incite slaves to revolt and offering a reward for David Walker's capture — ten thousand dollars alive and one thousand dollars dead. Even though his life was threatened, Walker refused to seek safety in Canada.

Georgia was not unique in its response to *Walker's Appeal*. When the pamphlet was found in some Louisiana communities, the state passed legislation ordering free Blacks who had settled in Louisiana after 1825 to leave the state.

1830–1870 BLACKS HOLD STATEWIDE CONVENTIONS

Throughout this period, Blacks convened in almost every northern state to protest slavery and the abusive treatment of free Blacks (for example, many states denied Blacks the right to protest because they were not considered full citizens). Conventions served as a platform by which Blacks could present

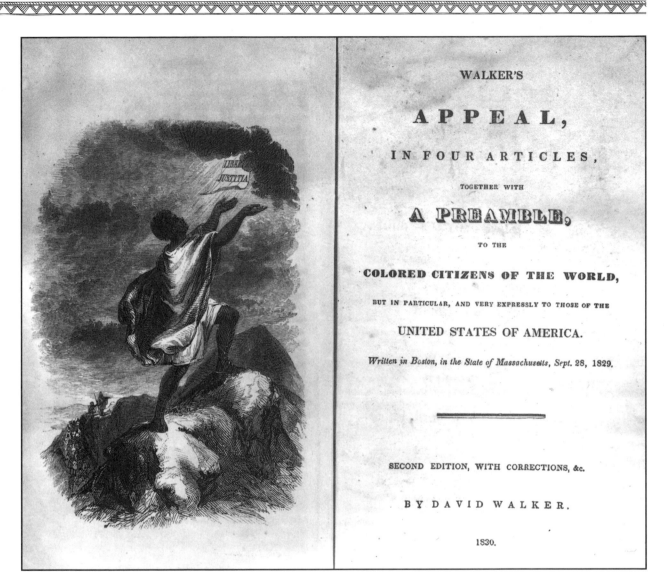

WALKER'S

APPEAL,

IN FOUR ARTICLES,

TOGETHER WITH

A PREAMBLE,

TO THE

COLORED CITIZENS OF THE WORLD,

BUT IN PARTICULAR, AND VERY EXPRESSLY TO THOSE OF THE

UNITED STATES OF AMERICA.

Written in Boston, in the State of Massachusetts, Sept. 28, 1829.

SECOND EDITION, WITH CORRECTIONS, &c.

BY DAVID WALKER.

1830.

David Walker, one of the earliest and most effective abolitionists, first published his Appeal, *a call for "colored citizens" to overthrow slavery with violence, in 1829. Because of the provocative nature of his writing, many abolitionists saw him as too radical and did not support his approach.*

petitions against oppression, particularly against laws prohibiting "basic liberties." Many conventions focused on local and state issues, particularly anti-Black riots and the exclusion of Blacks from juries, militia service, and suffrage. Conventions also protested the widespread oppression of Black people, particularly those still held in slavery.

REWARDS OFFERED FOR "SLAVE STEALERS"

Throughout this period, slave owners offered rewards for white abolitionists and "slave stealers"—brought in dead or alive. One staunch abolitionist who had a bounty of three thousand dollars on her person, dead or alive, was Laura Haviland, a white resident of Adrian, Michigan. Throughout much of her adult life, she harbored fugitive slaves and helped them escape via the Underground Railroad. Known as "Aunt Laura," Haviland was honored with a statue in a public square in Adrian, Michigan.

UNDERGROUND RAILROAD CONTINUES AID TO ESCAPED SLAVES

More than one hundred thousand Blacks escaped slavery between 1825 and 1860, using the network of trails and hiding places known as the Underground Railroad, which stretched from the South to the North, as well as into Canada and Mexico. The Underground Railroad had a profound effect on slavery and its power in this country. Initiated primarily by Quakers, it developed over the decades into a smoothly coordinated organization. In the Midwest, hundreds of Underground Railroad stations in Illinois and Indiana converged on Chicago, where slaves were then moved by boat to Canada. Ohio was the chief center of all Underground Railroad activities. Although estimates vary, some put the number of operators at more than three thousand, of whom half were located in Ohio. In the East, stations were located in and around Philadelphia; some connected northward to Buffalo, and others eastward into New England. Massachusetts emerged as New England's most active state in helping slaves escape into Canada.

1830

POPULATION OVERVIEW

BLACKS IN THE UNITED STATES A total of 2.3 million Black persons lived in the United States. They constituted 18.1 percent of the nation's 12,866,020 residents. About 45,000 free Blacks lived in New York, 38,000 in Pennsylvania, 18,000 in New Jersey, 8,000 in Connecticut, and 7,000 in Massachusetts. As many as 14,000 free Blacks resided in New York City, and as many as 9,700 in Philadelphia. Sizable numbers of Blacks were also found in Boston, Providence, Albany, Newark, and Pittsburgh.

BLACKS AS SLAVE OWNERS The Bureau of the Census reported that 3,777 Black heads of families owned slaves. These slave owners were free Blacks or persons of mixed ancestry.

The overwhelming majority of these Black slave owners had purchased husbands, wives, or children and were not able to emancipate them under existing state laws. One Black slave owner in King George County, Virginia, had seventy-one slaves; another in St. Landry Parish, Louisiana, owned seventy-five

BLACK WOMEN WORK TO IMPROVE WELFARE OF BLACK POPULATION

During the 1830s, Black women worked in a number of activities to improve the overall well-being of the Black community. Black women in Philadelphia were quite aggressive in developing initiatives to improve the welfare of Blacks. In this city, Black women formed a number of societies such as the Philadelphia Anti-Slavery Society (1833), which assisted fugitive slaves; an auxiliary committee of the Vigilance Association, which raised funds to clothe, shelter, and feed runaways; and the Female Literary Society (1831), which focused on education, knowledge, self-improvement, and antislavery activities. In Boston, Black women organized a number of societies including the Afric-American Female Intelligence Society (1832) to improve the education and morals of females and the Colored Female Charitable Society (1832) to assist widows and orphans and provide religious teaching. In New York, education was the major activity that preoccupied Black female societies. In addition to benevolent societies associated with churches, a group of twelve Black women formed an auxiliary (1838) "for the further encouragement of education among our people, and especially securing a more numerous and punctual attendance of colored children at the public schools."

Black women could be found working in many activities. Although Charlotte Forten, Grace Douglass, Sarah McCrummell, Jane Chester, Harriet Hayden, and Nancy Remond were wives or daughters of abolitionist leaders, they contributed significantly to the abolitionist movement by their public speaking, publications, and "upstanding moral, ladylike" behavior. Others such as Maria Stewart, Sarah Douglass, Susan Paul, Sarah Forten, Margaretta Forten, Mary Bibb, and Mary Ann Shadd Cary contributed by educating Blacks as well as providing leadership for the antislavery movement and the community.

slaves; and two Blacks in Collection District, South Carolina, each owned eighty-four slaves. The courts in Delaware and Arkansas refused to sanction the ownership of slaves by "free persons of color."

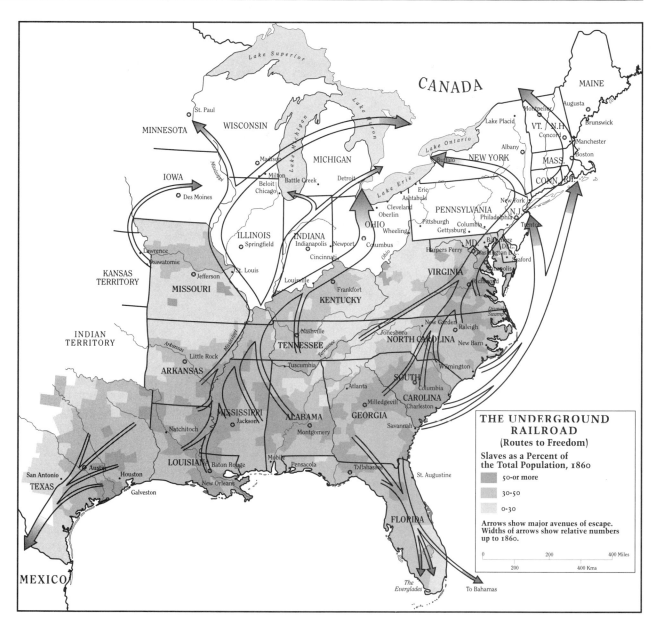

THE UNDERGROUND RAILROAD

Underground Railroad routes enabled thousands of slaves to escape to freedom in Canada, Mexico, Cuba, and the West Indies.

ECONOMIC OVERVIEW

CASH CROPS AND SLAVES IN THE SOUTH Antislavery sentiment met its ugly enemy — profit — during the 1830s. The recent economic recovery in the South quieted many families who believed that Blacks con- stituted an unwelcome element in southern life. The prices of the major cash crops — tobacco and cot- ton — turned sharply upward over the 1830–1840 decade. Tobacco in Virginia more than doubled in price between 1830 and 1836, and the New York price

When slaves brought top dollar, slave owners were more willing to pay for their recapture than to purchase new slaves, and slave catchers enjoyed a brisk business. Dogs were commonly used to track and capture escaped slaves.

for cotton, which had been as low as 9.5 cents per pound in 1832, was 17.5 cents in 1836. The price of a prime field hand in Virginia had risen from $400 between 1825 and 1829, to $650 in 1835, to $1,110 by 1837. In the New Orleans area, the price for a field hand had already reached $1,025 by 1832.

COTTON IN THE MISSISSIPPI RIVER VALLEY The amount of land devoted to cotton in the region increased, and the demand for slaves was high. Wealthy whites built opulent mansions on their successful plantations.

There had been 3,500 slaves in the area in 1800, prior to its being divided into the states of Alabama and Mississippi. By 1830, the number of slaves had soared to 183,000 in the two states combined. This phenomenal growth in slaves was directly related to the production of cotton. By 1835, Alabama and Mississippi, at eighty-five million pounds each, became the two leading producers of the crop. This volume was greater than the combined production of Virginia, North Carolina, South Carolina, and Georgia. Slaves of all ages and both sexes were sold at relatively higher prices at auctions, and many states participated directly in the breeding of slaves for market. In Kentucky, for example, there were only 12,000 slaves in 1800; but by 1830, more than 165,000 slaves lived in cotton-producing areas.

SOCIAL CONDITIONS

BRANDING AND OTHER FORMS OF PUNISHING SLAVES CONTINUE Although the branding of slaves for purposes of identification was common practice during colonial days, it became less common during the nineteenth century. Branding increasingly became a form of punishment rather than identification. In fact, in 1838, a North Carolinian advertised that Bettey, a fugitive, was "burnt . . . with a hot iron on the left side of her face; I tried to make the letter M."

Another incident was recorded in 1848, when a Kentuckian identified his runaway Jane by a brand mark "on the brest something like L blotched."

Cruel punishment, including mutilation, was relatively common in colonial days and had not completely disappeared by this time. In 1831, a Louisiana jailer notified others that he had a runaway in custody: "He has been lately gelded, and is not yet well." Another Louisianian recorded his disgust for a neighbor who had "castrated 3 men of his." Generally, any kind of punishment was tolerated for runaways, and any white person could give such punishment. Many professional slave catchers used shotguns to hunt escaped slaves, and it was not uncommon to find runaways who had marks of shots on hips, thighs, neck, and face. Some even had marks of dog bites, because many slave catchers used "Negro dogs" to catch escaped slaves.

DEMAND FOR SLAVES Because of advances in agriculture and industry, the demand for slaves in the South soared by nearly 25 percent in a short period of time. The demand for slaves was so great that it elicited the worst element of society to participate in the inhuman practice of breeding slaves for market and profit. There were many accounts of slave owners who bred slaves like pigs, cows, and other animals. The older states appeared more likely to participate in this hideous activity.

Slaves were exported from Virginia at a rate of 8,500 annually during the years between 1790 and 1832. During this time, as many as 260,000 slaves were exported to states in the Cotton Belt. Newspaper accounts of slaves sold by producer states to consumer states are many. For example, the Wheeling *Virginia Times* in 1836 claimed that the value of

Slave traders and slave dealers were common between 1800 and 1861. Slaves were usually crowded into large rooms — with women, children, and men in different rooms — where buyers could inspect them. Prices depended on the demand, ranging from a high of $2,800 for a good male worker to about $250 for small children.

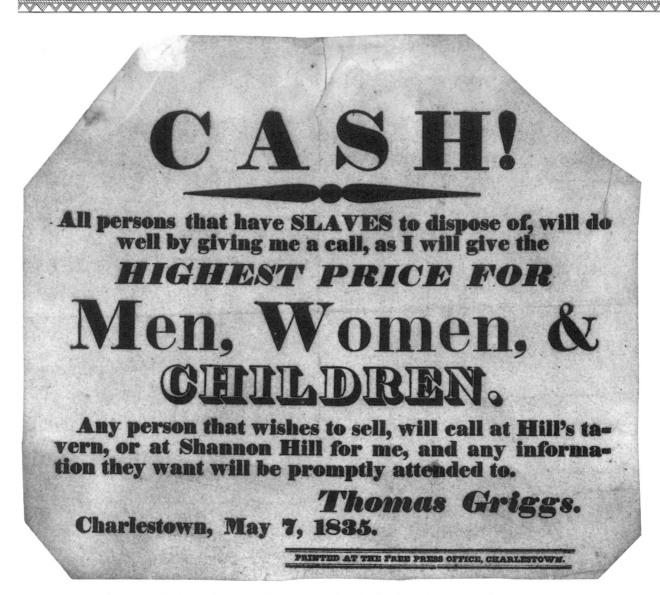

CASH!

All persons that have SLAVES to dispose of, will do well by giving me a call, as I will give the

HIGHEST PRICE FOR

Men, Women, & CHILDREN.

Any person that wishes to sell, will call at Hill's tavern, or at Shannon Hill for me, and any information they want will be promptly attended to.

Thomas Griggs.

Charlestown, May 7, 1835.

PRINTED AT THE FREE PRESS OFFICE, CHARLESTOWN.

Slaves were in such demand in 1830 that agents advertised to buy slaves from their current owners.

slaves taken out of the state put millions in the pockets of slaveholders in Maryland and Virginia. The editor wrote:

We have heard intelligent men estimate the number of slaves exported from Virginia within the last twelve months at 120,000 — each slave averaging at least $600, making an aggregate at $72,000,000. Of the number of slaves exported, not more than one-third have been sold (the others have been carried by their owners, who have removed) which would leave in the state the sum of $24,000,000 arising from the sale of slaves.

According to its records, the offices of Frankoina and Armfield of Alexandria (then part of the District of Columbia) was the largest slave-trading firm in the South from 1828 to 1836. Since tobacco plantations in the state were in decline and it had become illegal to import new slaves, the slavery business in Virginia changed to one of breeding and trading. The Black population in the state dropped from 517,000 to 499,000 in the 1830s, when this trade was at its peak. It has been estimated that about 11,000 Blacks, primarily young men, were exported to the cotton states of the Deep South. The *Natchez Courier* noted that 250,000 slaves were brought into Louisiana, Mississippi, Alabama, and Arkansas during 1836, of which the majority were replacements. The number of slave auctions and slave buyers grew with the demand, and the demand grew steadily as cotton continued to pay handsome profits. The demand for slaves affected their cost. The price for a healthy male field slave rose from about $500 in 1832 to $1300 in 1837. Supporters of slavery increased their bitter assaults on antislavery forces in the North and the South. Free Blacks became targets for much hostility, and Virginia passed laws making it unlawful for groups of Blacks to assemble. Those who violated the "unlawful assembly" law were publicly whipped with at least twenty lashings.

MORE SLAVE CODES PASSED Laws restricting the education and citizenship of slaves were passed in a number of states to counter growing abolitionist sentiment. These slave codes placed legal restrictions on slaves and free Blacks.

OHIO COLLEGES ADMIT BLACKS In the 1830s, both Western Reserve and Oberlin Colleges admitted Blacks. The decision to admit Blacks at Oberlin resulted in student and faculty protest and panic. In February 1835, the board of trustees decided to permit the faculty to rule on entrance requirements for Blacks and thus ensure the admission of qualified Blacks.

SEGREGATION IN CHURCHES Blacks remained segregated in Christian churches. When attending services, they sat in an "African corner," a "nigger pew," seats marked "B.M." (Black Members), or aloft in "nigger heaven." Blacks and whites were segregated in Sabbath schools, and when communion was offered, Blacks had to wait until whites had partaken of the bread and wine.

ABOLITIONISTS LAUNCH LIBERTY PARTY The abolitionist movement gained significant strength with the publication of William Lloyd Garrison's *Liberator* and other influential newspapers, pamphlets, and books. An estimated five hundred abolitionist societies were active in the North in this year. By 1840, membership in these societies numbered 150,000.

PLANS OF AMERICAN COLONIZATION SOCIETY DEEMED IMPRACTICAL The society's plan to buy and free slaves had proved impractical by this time. In 1830, there were about two million slaves and 319,000 free Blacks in the United States. The Colonization Society, which had been founded in 1817, had secured freedom for only about 1,420 slaves, and had sent only 2,228 Blacks to Africa. Not only had the number of slaves increased over the years, but also their average price had risen from four hundred dollars to between one thousand and fifteen hundred dollars — an amount that precluded the society from making many purchases. Although there were 228 auxiliary societies in the United States, the society's income was only forty-three thousand dollars. Ohio had 37 auxiliary societies but had sent out only 55 emigrants by 1860; Kentucky's 32 auxiliary societies sent out fewer than 600 emigrants by 1860. It is estimated that the colonization movement may have sent out 12,000 emigrants by the end of the Civil War.

SLAVES WORK FOR FREEDOM IN OHIO In Ohio, the Black population comprised fugitive slaves, slaves freed by owners to avoid manumission and other restrictive laws, slaves working for their freedom, and southern free Blacks seeking less restrictive environments. About one-third of the seventy-five hundred Blacks in Ohio at this time were slaves working for wages to pay for their freedom.

STATE OF SLAVERY Although it was clear from civil law that a slave was chattel property, the institution of slavery was far more extensive, as is revealed in these twelve general propositions of the South Carolina slave code, incorporated into specific laws there and in other states:

I.   The master may determine the kind, and degree, and time of labour to which the slave shall be subjected.
II. The master may supply the slave with such food and clothing only, but as to quantity and quality, as he may think proper or find convenient.
III. The master may, at his discretion, inflict any punishment upon the person of his slave.
IV. All the power of the master over his slave may be exercised not by himself only in person, but by any one whom he may assign as his agent.
V.   Slaves have no legal rights of property in things, real or personal; but whatever they may acquire belongs, in point of law, to their master.
VI. The slave, being a personal chattel, is at all times liable to be sold absolutely, or mortgaged or leased, at the will of his master.

VII. He may also be sold by processes of law for the satisfaction of the debts of a living or the debts and bequests of a deceased master, at the suit of creditors or legatees.

VIII. A slave cannot be a party before a judicial tribunal, in any species of action against his master, no matter how atrocious may have been the injury received from him.

IX. Slaves cannot redeem themselves, nor obtain a change of masters, though cruel treatment may have rendered such change necessary for their personal safety.

X. Slaves being objects of property, if injured by third persons, their owners may bring suit, and recover damages, for the injury.

XI. Slaves can make no contract.

XII. Slavery is hereditary and perpetual.

BLACK SETTLEMENT IN LIBERIA

By this year, it is estimated that 1,420 Blacks had settled in Liberia.

HORTON PUBLISHES POEMS

George Moses Horton (1797–1883?), a slave in North Carolina, brought out his first book of poems, *The Hope of Liberty*. It was a book that discussed love, religion, and death. In 1845, he published *The Poetical Works of George M. Horton, the Colored Bard of North Carolina*. When his third book, *Naked Genius*, was published, some critics said that his writings were inspired by Milton, Pope, and other English poets. Here is one of Horton's antislavery poems:

How long have I in bondage lain,
And languished to be free!
Alas! and must I still complain —
Deprived of liberty.
                    (From "On Liberty and Slavery")

Horton, a slave in Northampton County, North Carolina, paid fifty cents per day (double the usual price) to his slave owner in order to earn money on the campus of the University of North Carolina, Chapel Hill. His talents were quickly recognized by Carolina Hentz, a professor's wife, author, and abolitionist. She befriended Horton and taught him how to write. She also provided Horton with books of poetry by Homer, Virgil, Milton, and others. In 1828, Horton published poems in the *Lancaster Gazette* (in Massachusetts) and *Freedom's Journal*. In 1834, he published in the *Liberator* and in the *Southern Liter-*

ary Messenger in 1843. Horton was considered by many to be a master poet.

INDIAN REMOVAL ACT SIGNED

On **MAY 28**, President Andrew Jackson signed the bill that forced the Cherokees, Creeks, Chickasaws, Choctaws, and Seminoles off their land in the southeastern United States and moved them over the "trail of tears" to Oklahoma. It is estimated that almost one-third of the members of these tribes were of African-American descent. The U.S. Army reported that 512 Blacks resided in the Choctaw Nation.

"MODEL" FOR STOWE'S UNCLE TOM FLEES TO CANADA

Josiah Henson, an educated slave and minister in the Methodist Episcopal Church, fled from Kentucky to Canada.

Henson, the property of Isaac Riley in Maryland, had been shipped with his family to Riley's brother in Kentucky. Several years later, Henson returned to Maryland, earning $275 on the way by preaching to help buy his freedom. Isaac Riley told him he had not earned enough and sent him back to Kentucky. There, he found his family and with them rowed across the Ohio River, using the Underground Railroad to reach Canada successfully.

At the time, antislavery groups in Canada were concerned with how escaped slaves would earn a living. Henson suggested opening a school for Black men and women that would offer education in trades such as carpentry, blacksmithing, cooking, and sewing. Unfortunately, there were never sufficient funds for his school to operate successfully, and it closed in the 1850s. Henson had written his autobiography to help raise money for his school. After Harriet Beecher Stowe read his story, she incorporated parts of it into her antislavery novel, *Uncle Tom's Cabin*. Henson gained some renown after her book became a success; he made a trip to Britain and was introduced to Queen Victoria. After the Civil War, however, he was largely forgotten. He died in Canada in 1883. It is ironic that Uncle Tom, the character modeled after Henson, represented an individual so much less assertive than the real person.

PUBLISHING AND DISTRIBUTING ABOLITIONIST LITERATURE IS CRIME

The Louisiana Commonwealth passed legislation that anyone found guilty of publishing and distributing abolitionist literature could be imprisoned at hard labor for life or receive the death penalty.

THE UNDERGROUND RAILROAD ESTABLISHED

Almost every year after 1830, the Underground Railroad assisted hundreds of slaves to escape to places in the North. Abolitionists and Quakers had established hundreds of stations of the Underground Railroad in Illinois, Indiana, and Ohio. In Illinois, the routes converged on Chicago, where slaves would leave by ship for Canada. Ohio, with the largest number of stations, was the center of the Underground Railroad activities. After crossing the Ohio River, thousands of slaves were met by friends who assisted them on their journey to Canada. Stations were also found in the eastern part of the country. For example, Philadelphia had numerous stations that led to other stations en route to Buffalo and to New England, particularly Massachusetts. Many of those using the Massachusetts stations to escape into Canada came concealed on ships from southern ports.

It is estimated that overall there were more than three thousand agents of the Underground Railroad, of whom more than half (1,540) were in Ohio. William Still, David Ruggles, Frederick Douglass, J. W. Loguen, Martin Delany, Lewis Hayden, and George DeBaptist were all agents. Still was chairman of the Acting Vigilant Committee of the Philadelphia Branch of the Underground Railroad. Both Levi Coffin and Robert Purvis have been referred to as the "president" of the Underground Railroad because of their dedicated involvement. Harriet Tubman, one of the most famous conductors of the movement, was called the "the Moses of Her People." When John Brown introduced her to Wendell Phillips, she was identified as "one of the best and bravest persons on this continent."

BLACKS DEPORTED FROM PORTSMOUTH, OHIO

On **JANUARY 21**, the Portsmouth, Ohio, city government passed an ordinance allowing Blacks to be forcibly deported from the city.

NATIONAL NEGRO CONVENTION HELD IN PHILADELPHIA

From **SEPTEMBER 15** to **20**, the first National Negro Convention, chaired by Richard Allen, met at the Bethel AME Church in Philadelphia. Attendees devised ways to better their condition and responded to potential mob action against Blacks prompted by colonization propaganda. Thirty-eight delegates arrived from eight states, including Delaware, Maryland, New York, Rhode Island, Connecticut, Pennsylvania, and Virginia. Allen, head of the AME Church, conducted a spirited discussion and led the attendees to approve migration to Canada, oppose African colonization, and call for the founding of a permanent organization to be named American Society of Free Persons of Colour, for Improving Their Condition in the United States, for Purchasing Lands, and for the Establishment of a Settlement in the Province of Upper Canada. Delegates also promoted boycotts of slave-made products. The National Negro Convention met annually for another five years before it was disbanded.

1831 ANTISLAVERY LEADERS PROPOSE COLLEGE

Four antislavery leaders, Simeon S. Jocelyn, a Yale graduate and white minister in a New Haven Black

Simeon S. Jocelyn, the home missionary minister of a Black congregation in New Haven, Connecticut, helped found the American Anti-Slavery Society in 1833.

church; Arthur Tappan, a New York merchant and philanthropist; Samuel Cornish, a noted antislavery activist and Black leader; and William Lloyd Garrison, an abolitionist, proposed a Black college at the annual national convention of Blacks. The college was to be located in New Haven and was to be self-supporting. It would be based on the manual-labor system, "so that the student may cultivate habits of industry and obtain a useful mechanical or agricultural profession, while pursuing classical studies."

Although New Haven appeared to be an ideal site for the college because of its central location, the relative liberality of state laws, and the humane character of the city's residents, the townspeople vigorously protested the establishment of any school that might attract Blacks from other states or threaten the property values and peace of the town.

BLACK WOMAN PUBLISHES FIRST SLAVE NARRATIVE

Mary Prince published *The History of Mary Prince, a West Indian Slave, Related by Herself, with the Supplement by the Editor, to Which Is Added the Narrative of Asa-Asa, a Captured African.* This is the first slave narrative published by a Black woman in the United States.

FEMALE LITERARY SOCIETY ORGANIZED

In Philadelphia, the Female Literary Society, emphasizing "the mental improvement of females," was organized by Charlotte Forten, Sr., and Charlotte Forten (Grimké), her granddaughter, to encourage women to improve their minds to better fulfill their responsibilities. In addition to encouraging education, members promoted antislavery activity. Over the months, the society accumulated a respectable collection of books and pamphlets on the antislavery movement. The society frequently hosted "Mental Feasts," in which members engaged in "moral and religious meditation, conversation, reading and speaking, sympathising over the fate of the unhappy slave, improving their own minds, &c.&c."

FREED SLAVES MUST LEAVE MISSISSIPPI

A Mississippi law stipulated that freed slaves between sixteen and thirty years of age must leave the state within ninety days or be in danger of being sold back into slavery.

THE *Liberator* BEGINS PUBLICATION

On **JANUARY 1**, William Lloyd Garrison (1805–1879) published the first issue of the militant antislavery newspaper the *Liberator*, in Boston. Garrison called for complete and immediate emancipation of all slaves, and his newspaper quickly became a leading newspaper for African Americans in Boston and throughout the East. In fact, Garrison relied heavily on Blacks for support of his paper, which was one of several that provided relevant information for Blacks about politics, social events, employment, racial events, deaths, and forms of discrimination. In Washington, D.C., free Blacks were whipped and imprisoned for picking up copies of the *Liberator*. As the *Liberator*'s readership among antislavery advocates increased, Garrison emerged as the leader of the U.S. abolitionist movement, a position he retained for more than three decades.

Garrison was elected president of the American Anti-Slavery Society in 1843 and served in this capacity until 1865. Garrison was a controversial figure. He favored immediate emancipation, opposed colonization, and opposed violence and insurrections. Some abolitionists believed that Garrison's campaign for women's rights weakened the antislavery movement. Nevertheless, the *Liberator* provided an opportunity for Black leaders to express their views.

NATIONAL CONVENTION OF FREE PERSONS OF COLOR

From **JUNE 6** to **11**, the annual Convention of Free Persons of Color gathered at the Wesleyan Church in Philadelphia. Delegates — free Blacks from five states — studied the conditions of free Blacks, discussed settlement options in Canada, and opposed resettlement policies of the American Colonization Society. There was much discussion of Samuel Cornish's plan for a manual-labor college in New Haven to train young men; the plan for the school was approved despite the fact that both the governor of Connecticut and the U.S. senator spoke against any such action. Simeon S. Jocelyn, Benjamin Lundy, Arthur Tappan, and William Lloyd Garrison attended this meeting, and the group agreed to hold annual meetings.

SLAVE REBELLION IN VIRGINIA

On **AUGUST 21** in Southhampton County, Virginia, Nat Turner (1800–1831) and seventy slaves began a two-day rampage. Turner, a slave preacher, believed that God had chosen him to lead Blacks to freedom. During the revolt, Turner's master was killed, along with about sixty other whites. As troops moved in to capture the slaves, Turner escaped and remained at large until October 30. During his absence, it is estimated

"Horrid Massacre in Virginia" depicts the Nat Turner rebellion. This composite sketch, a woodcut from an 1831 antiabolitionist tract entitled Authentic and Impartial Narrative, *by Samuel Warner, shows (1) Turner attacking a white mother and her children; (2) Turner's master, Mr. Travis, being attacked; (3) Captain John T. Barrow defending himself while his wife escapes; and (4) militia pursuing Turner and the other rebels.*

that as many as fifty-three Blacks were arrested and tried; twenty were hanged, twenty-one acquitted, and twelve transported out of the state. Since there is no official record of the entire event, no one knows for certain how many slaves were killed in the conflict or by self-appointed executioners. Turner himself was hanged in Jerusalem, Virginia, on November 11.

The revolt had a momentous impact throughout the South. It showed that many Blacks were willing to kill and die to achieve their freedom. This uprising led to the adoption of even more rigid slave codes. Not only were slaves even more severely restricted

and harshly punished, but also southerners were prohibited from receiving abolitionist literature. Many southerners believed that this and previous slave revolts were inspired by abolitionists, their literature, and specifically by William Lloyd Garrison. Southern postmasters were advised not to deliver abolitionist literature, and southern U.S. congressmen were successful in passing a "gag rule" prohibiting any representative from reading abolitionist petitions regarding slavery in the District of Columbia. This rule remained on the books for more than eight years, until John Quincy Adams spearheaded its repeal.

Nat Turner was captured on October 29, after eluding his pursuers for more than eight weeks.

1832 **AFRICAN METHODIST EPISCOPAL CHURCH GROWS**
The African Methodist Episcopal Church had grown to eighty-six churches serving as many as 7,594 members in some of the larger cities in the country. It is also estimated that the organization controlled property worth more than $125,000. Because of its rapid membership growth, particularly among influential free Blacks, the church had become one of the most powerful forces against slavery.

BLACK WOMEN ORGANIZE AFRIC-AMERICAN FEMALE INTELLIGENCE SOCIETY IN MASSACHUSETTS
A group of Black women in Boston organized the Afric-American Female Intelligence Society for the purpose of educating "women of color." The preamble to its constitution reinforced a strong commitment to education:

> Whereas the subscribers, women of color, of the Commonwealth of Massachusetts, actuated by a natural feeling for the welfare of our friends, have thought fit to associate for the diffusion of knowledge, the suppression of vice and immorality, and for cherishing such virtues as will render us happier and useful to society, sensible of the gross ignorance under which we have long labored.

FREED SLAVES FROM VIRGINIA SETTLE IN OHIO
Upon the death of Congressman John Randolph of Virginia, 385 freed slaves moved to Mercer County, Ohio, with funds he had left them for transportation,

land, and necessities. Some of Randolph's relatives cheated the freed persons of their land.

SCHOOL FOR BLACKS FOUNDED THAT LATER BECAME CHEYNEY UNIVERSITY OF PENNSYLVANIA

Richard Humphreys, a Philadelphia Quaker, willed $10,000 to establish a school for Blacks. This school, which has been reorganized many times, is now Cheyney University of Pennsylvania. It is sometimes referred to as the oldest Black college in the country. Before the Civil War, the school was known as the Institute for Colored Youth. In 1902, the school was reorganized, renamed, and moved to Cheyney, Pennsylvania, where it became a teacher training school. For several years it was directed by Fannie Jackson Coppin, one of the first Black women college graduates. In 1921, the operation of Cheyney was transferred to the Commonwealth of Pennsylvania, with the promise that Cheyney graduates could teach in either black or white schools in the state. This promise did not become reality until the 1950s.

Today, Cheyney University of Pennsylvania (formerly Cheyney State), a member of Historically Black Colleges and Universities (HBCU), is one of the fourteen institutions of higher learning in the Pennsylvania state system of higher education. Enrollment for the school is about 1,650, of whom 94 percent are Black.

VIRGINIA REWARDS CAPTURE OF FUGITIVE SLAVES

The Virginia legislature passed a law that included the following provision: Anyone apprehending a Virginia fugitive slave in Ohio, Pennsylvania, or Indiana, and returning the fugitive, would receive $50, and twenty cents per mile traveled in returning the slave; anyone returning fugitive slaves from New England or New York received $120 and traveling expenses.

VIRGINIA SETS DEATH PENALTY FOR CERTAIN OFFENSES BY BLACKS

The Virginia legislature imposed the death penalty for both slaves and free Blacks for certain offenses, including rape of a white woman, beating a white person, inciting rebellion, or burning wheat worth fifty dollars.

NEW ENGLAND ANTI-SLAVERY SOCIETY ESTABLISHED

On **JANUARY 6**, the New England Anti-Slavery Society was organized in Boston, Massachusetts. Its constitution was signed by only a dozen men, however, and its membership was small. Blacks played a significant part. Even after three years, the society lacked the widespread acceptance it had expected in the region. It later changed its name to the Massachusetts Anti-Slavery Society.

PENNSYLVANIA REJECTS PETITION OF FREE BLACKS FOR EDUCATION

Free Blacks petitioned the Pennsylvania legislature to admit their children to public schools. They argued that they should have access to public schools because they paid taxes, which supported public school education. Their petition was unsuccessful.

VIRGINIA FREE BLACKS PROHIBITED FROM PURCHASING SLAVES

The Virginia legislature passed a law that prohibited free Blacks from purchasing slaves other than their own parents, spouses, or children.

FLORIDA ALLOWS ENSLAVEMENT OF FREE BLACKS

On **FEBRUARY 10**, Florida passed an act allowing sheriffs to auction the services of any free Black or mulatto who is convicted of a misdemeanor and cannot pay the fine and cost of prosecution. Upon being sold to the highest bidder, the free Black may be "treated as a slave," that is, allowed no rights whatsoever. Specifically, the law stated that if a free negro or mulatto was convicted of any crime or *misdemeanor*, and was unable to pay the fine and costs of prosecution, the sheriff would offer the convicted person's services at public sale, "and any person who shall take such free negro or mulatto for the shortest period of time, paying the fine and costs of prosecution, shall be entitled to the service of such free negro or mulatto, who shall be held and taken *for the said period* of time as a slave to all intents and purposes whatever."

FIRST FEMALE ANTISLAVERY SOCIETY ORGANIZED

On **FEBRUARY 22**, the first female antislavery society was organized by a group of Black women in Salem, Massachusetts. The Female Anti-Slavery Society of Salem sparked the organization of a number of women's antislavery societies. Encouraged by the *Liberator*, Black antislavery societies differed from all-white predecessors in that Blacks called for the immediate, rather than the gradual, abolition of slavery and invited Blacks and women to join. The Female Anti-Slavery Society of Salem focused on mutual improvement as well as antislavery activities. Their constitution follows:

Constitution of the Female Anti-Slavery Society of Salem

We, the undersigned, females of color, of the commonwealth of Massachusetts being duly convinced of the importance of union and morality, have associated ourselves together for our mutual improvement, and to promote the welfare of our color, as far as consistent with the means of this Society, therefore we adopt the following resolutions.

Resolved, That this Society be supported by voluntary contributions, a part to be appropriated for the purchasing of books, &c,: the other to be reserved until a sufficient sum be accumulated, which shall then be deposited in a bank for the relief of the needy.

Mary A. Battys, President
E. A. Drew, Vice President
Charlotte Bell, Corresponding Sec'y
Eleanor C. Harvey, Treasurer
Dororthy C. Battys, Librarian

MARYLAND STATE COLONIZATION SOCIETY INCORPORATED

In **MARCH**, the Maryland State Colonization Society was incorporated by the Maryland General Assembly, and state funds were appropriated for colonization purposes. A census of free Blacks living in Maryland was conducted, and legislation was passed that provided for their forcible expulsion from the state. By December 9, 144 free Black colonists had left for Liberia.

Two years later, in 1834, the Maryland State Colonization Society had purchased land in Liberia at Cape Palmas. The town of Harper was founded by Robert Goodloe Harper. (Later the same year, the Pennsylvania and New York Colonization Societies established a colony at Bassa Cove. Louisiana, and Mississippi societies founded a settlement along the Sinou River in late 1836 and early 1837.)

Maryland's colonization efforts were difficult at best. Society members were frequently attacked by abolitionists when they canvassed northern states for colonists. In 1850, the Maryland General Assembly passed a law lifting restrictions on the importation of slaves into Maryland — an act that clearly hurt colonization efforts. One year later John Russwurm, governor of the colony, died. Maryland in Liberia became independent on June 8, 1854, becoming Maryland County, the fourth territorial division in Liberia. State funds were received for a number of years.

In 1861, the last expedition was sent to Liberia, and in 1862, Liberia was recognized by the United States. A year later, the Maryland Society closed active operations, although financial support for the school at Cape Palmas continued. The society was officially disbanded in 1902, and the remaining money in its treasury was returned to the state.

NEGRO CONVENTION HELD IN PHILADELPHIA

From **JUNE 4** to **13**, the National Negro Convention met in Philadelphia. As at the last convention, the major issue was colonization in Canada and Africa. To provide a better understanding of issues confronting free Blacks and slaves, William Lloyd Garrison and R. R. Gurley, secretary of the American Colonization Society, debated the pros and cons of colonization, after which the convention declared its strong opposition to colonization. Other conventions took place in Philadelphia in 1833, 1834, and (the final one) 1835.

STEWART IS FIRST WOMAN IN UNITED STATES TO GIVE A PUBLIC LECTURE

On **SEPTEMBER 21**, Maria W. Stewart (1803–1879), an ardent abolitionist, educator, and feminist, delivered a public lecture in Boston, the first American woman to do so. Her message that day was called "Daughters of Africa, awake! arise! distinguish yourselves!"

Stewart (née Miller) was born in Hartford, Connecticut, of free Black parents and was orphaned at the age of five. As a young girl she worked as a servant for a minister's family in Connecticut. She was married for three years to James Stewart, who outfitted fishing vessels on Boston's waterfront. Upon his death, Maria was cheated out of a small inheritance by two white men whom her husband had named as executors of his will. This experience led her to urge other women to become educated and accumulate economic power.

She became a strong supporter of and public spokeswoman for women's rights and Black self-help activities. Black male audiences were often hostile to women speakers who publicly criticized their behavior. A group of them jeered Stewart and threw rotten tomatoes at her when she criticized them for failing to be thrifty, sober, and hard working. After numerous such hostile encounters, Stewart moved to New York City, where she joined the Ladies' Literary Society and worked for the North Star Association; she never made another public speech. Stewart later worked at low-paying teaching jobs in Baltimore and Washington, D.C. She also became a matron of Freedmen's Hospital. In the last year of her life, she printed her speeches and writings of the 1830s.

1833 ALABAMA MAKES IT ILLEGAL FOR BLACKS TO PREACH

Alabama passed legislation which made it illegal for free Blacks and slaves to preach the gospel unless five "respectable" slaveholders were present and unless the activity was authorized by some neighboring religious society. The next year, Georgia passed a similar law stating that Blacks were only allowed to preach if they were licensed by a justice.

BLACK WOMEN ORGANIZE THE COLORED FEMALE RELIGIOUS AND MORAL SOCIETY

In Salem, Massachusetts, a group of Black women met to organize the Colored Female Religious and Moral Society of Salem. The organization was established to deal with moral issues including prostitution and temperance, and other issues such as education, care of orphans, and religious training. Clarissa C. Lawrence was selected president of the society. Lawrence also served as vice president of the all-Black Salem Female Anti-Slavery Society.

CRANDALL ARRESTED FOR TEACHING BLACKS

On **JUNE 27**, Prudence Crandall, a white woman, was arrested for teaching Black girls at her academy in Canterbury, Connecticut.

Crandall, of Rhode Island, had opened a boarding school in Canterbury in 1832. After reading the *Liberator* and becoming impressed with the philosophy of William Lloyd Garrison, she accepted Sara Harris, the daughter of a highly respected Black family. After intimidation and constant threats, Crandall was forced to close her school. In February 1833, she reopened it for "colored" girls only. As many as twenty may have enrolled, mostly from well-to-do Black families from large cities in the East. The white citizens of Canterbury boycotted Crandall and her students, refusing to sell anything to them. They also dumped refuse from a slaughterhouse on Crandall's porch, refused her students medical care, shut them out of their church, and even threw stones at them. They also attempted to whip the girls under an obsolete vagrancy law.

Andrew T. Judson, a local politician and leader of the local colonization society, then secured passage of a state law that prohibited harboring, boarding, and instructing any person of color not an inhabitant of the state without the prior approval of the town. This law did not apply to public schools or to incorporated academies and colleges. Crandall refused to obey the state law and was subsequently arrested and taken into custody. Arthur Tappan, an abolitionist, arrived

Prudence Crandall, a teacher, took a stand for the education of Black children when she opened a school for "colored" girls despite threats and intimidation.

in Canterbury to bring attention to the racist act and to provide financial support for her legal fight. Three times members of the jury failed to make a decision. Finally, they convicted Crandall after Judge David Daggett instructed them that Blacks were not citizens of the United States. Daggett had been a major opponent of the Black college proposed for New Haven by Samuel Cornish. His comments to the jury gave Chief Justice Roger Taney judicial precedence for the *Dred Scott* case's decision. Crandall's conviction was later set aside but not reversed. Her case became something of a cause célèbre, and the trial made civil rights history because its arguments struck at the core of rights, justice, and equality.

A mob set fire to Crandall's school, and all the windows were broken. The school was forced to close as assaults and threats against the girls raised the issue of personal safety. Crandall left Canterbury and moved to northern Illinois, where she continued to teach. Many years later, state lawmakers voted her a small yearly pension in atonement for the wrong done to her years before. Her conviction was also erased from the record.

OBERLIN COLLEGE FOUNDED

On **SEPTEMBER 2**, Oberlin College was founded. It was the country's first coeducational college. Two years later, Oberlin was the first college to make nondiscriminatory admissions an official policy. Over the years, Oberlin became one of the most important colleges for educating Blacks — in fact, one of its specific missions was to educate abolitionists. By the Civil War, about one-third of the student body was Black.

CHARLOTTE FORTEN, SR., COFOUNDS PHILADELPHIA FEMALE ANTI-SLAVERY SOCIETY

In **DECEMBER**, Charlotte Forten, Sr., (1784–1884), and seventeen other women founded the Philadelphia Female Anti-Slavery Society. Of the cofounders who signed the constitution, at least seven were Black. Black women expressed their commitment to community activism as well as antislavery activity, leading to debates about goals and tactics. Several of the original members were children of James and Charlotte Forten. Other cofounders and regular attendees included Grace Douglass, Sarah Douglass, Margaretta Forten, Sarah Forten, Harriet Forten Purvis, Sarah Lewis, Sarah McCrummell, Hetty Reckless, and Hetty Burr. Black women frequently served in leadership roles — Margaretta Forten usually served as recording secretary or treasurer, and her sister, Sarah, often presented original poems on slavery. Grace Douglass held leadership positions in the Philadelphia society as well as during the Anti-Slavery Conventions of American Women (in 1837, 1838, and 1839).

In addition to being a leader in abolitionism, community activism, and philanthropy, Charlotte Forten, Sr., was a remarkable mother — she sent her children to private schools and successfully encouraged them to participate in community work, local reform, and abolitionism. She and her daughters devoted much of their time to social causes, frequently hosting white and Black abolitionist friends. Margaretta, Harriet, and Sarah Forten tutored at home and cohosted visits from Harriet Martineau, William Lloyd Garrison, Charles Lenox Remond, John Greenleaf Whittier, and other abolitionists. Whittier wrote a poem called "To the Daughters of James Forten," which was published in the *Liberator*. James, Robert, and William (sons of Charlotte and James Forten) were also educated in social and political activism. Charlotte and her husband, James, had made a fortune by this time and were one of the most influential Black families in Philadelphia.

Two of the most influential white women among the cofounders included Lucretia Mott and Elizabeth Cady Stanton. Mott, with the help of her husband, James Mott, a successful businessman, preached temperance, peace, women's rights, and abolition. In 1848, Mott and Stanton organized the first women's rights convention at Seneca Falls, New York.

Lucretia Mott, a Quaker and an abolitionist, opened her home as a station on the Underground Railroad and served on the executive committee of the Pennsylvania Anti-Slavery Society. After being refused her seat as a delegate to the World Anti-Slavery Convention in London in 1840, she returned to the United States to become a founder of the women's rights movement.

Lewis Tappan, a wealthy dry goods merchant and philanthropist, was one of a small group of men in New York City who opposed slavery and contributed to the aid of Blacks in the tradition of John Woolman and Anthony Benezet. When urged to give up the cause after his store and home were attacked by a mob, Tappan replied, "I will be hung first!" He and his brother Arthur were instrumental in funding a number of antislavery activities.

AMERICAN ANTI-SLAVERY SOCIETY FORMED

On **DECEMBER 4**, Black and white abolitionists in Philadelphia organized the American Anti-Slavery Society, later known as the American Convention for Promoting the Abolition of Slavery and Improving the Condition of the African Race. Three Blacks sat on the executive committee; women were excluded. The three Blacks among the sixty-three delegates were James McCrummell, a dentist; James G. Barbadoes, a Boston reformer; and Robert Purvis, an abolitionist and son-in-law of James Forten. These three delegates plus John B. Vashon, Peter Williams, and Abraham D. Shadd were named to the Board of Managers of the society. Among the white abolitionists, Arthur and Lewis Tappan, wealthy New York merchants, and

Theodore Weld, a minister, were instrumental in forming the society. James Forten, Sr., served on the Board of Managers for years before his death in 1842.

1834 VERMONT ANTI-SLAVERY SOCIETY FORMED

The Vermont Anti-Slavery Society was formed by Quakers and others opposed to slavery. Throughout the state, newspapers opposed slavery and many ministers preached antislavery sermons. Black ministers — including Lemuel Haynes, Samuel Ward, and Henry Highland Garnet — also preached in Vermont.

BLACK LEADERS PROPOSE INCLUSION RATHER THAN SEPARATION

Influential Black leaders in Philadelphia, including Richard Purvis, William J. Whipper, and James Forten, asserted that racial prejudice would continue if Blacks formed special and separate organizations. The first annual report of the American Anti-Slavery Society notes their point of view:

> There is no way to destroy the prejudice which lies at the foundation of slavery, but to invite our colored brethren to a participation with us in all those happy and elevating institutions which are open to others. No efforts, however, powerful or well-intended, which aim only to build up separate institutions for their special benefit, under the denomination so odious to them, of "colored" or "African" can heal the wound. They will end only in conferring upon their objects a keener sensibility to insult, and in establishing between the races an animosity, settled and remediless. Providence seems most kindly to have opened before us the path of safety and success, in creating so strong an anti-slavery sentiment in many of our most hopeful seminaries.

PROSLAVERY MOBS RIOT IN NEW YORK

On **JULY 4**, a meeting of the American Anti-Slavery Society in New York was broken up. A mob burned churches and houses for eight days. The riot was precipitated by proslavery forces angered by the integrated seating of Blacks and whites at the Chatham Street Chapel. A proslavery mob also marched to the house of abolitionist and philanthropist Lewis Tappan, destroying his possessions.

SLAVERY ABOLISHED THROUGHOUT BRITISH COLONIES

On **AUGUST 1**, the abolition of slavery throughout the British colonies came into effect, freeing over 700,000 people, following parliamentary legislation the previous year.

Before slaves in America were emancipated in 1865, they celebrated this date rather than July 4. Free Blacks in the North would hold parades and picnics to mark the occasion. On July 4, 1852, in a speech in Rochester, New York, Frederick Douglass said, "The Fourth of July is yours, not mine. Your sounds of rejoicing are empty and heartless, your shouts of liberty and equality, hollow mockery."

ANTI-BLACK OUTBREAK IN PHILADELPHIA

On **AUGUST 12**, a mob of whites marched into the Black section of Philadelphia and beat numerous blacks; burned, wrecked, and pulled down more than thirty homes; and committed other acts of violence. The next day, whites destroyed the African Presbyterian Church and continued to burn homes and beat Blacks. On the third day, the police became involved and put down the uprising.

White mobs in Philadelphia frequently attacked groups of Blacks, particularly if they were performing "white" jobs or were involved in abolitionist activities. For example, when Blacks gathered to celebrate the abolition of slavery in the West Indies, whites attacked Blacks and went on a rampage throughout the Black community, burning homes and meeting places. During this anti-Black outbreak, the New African Hall and Presbyterian Church were burned. State troops were called to help local police bring quiet to the city.

◈ During the next two decades, Philadelphia was the scene of much race-related violence. In addition to the above riot, it is recorded that in October of the same year, anti-abolitionist crowds destroyed forty homes belonging to Black residents and threw abolitionist literature into the Delaware River. In 1837, a proslavery mob burned abolitionist-built Pennsylvania Hall. And in 1847, fighting between whites and Blacks erupted again. To address these outbreaks of violence, delegates to Pennsylvania's Constitutional Convention in 1838 engaged in heated debates over a number of issues, including miscegenation — an issue that sparked a riot in the city in 1849. That reactions to miscegenation may have caused some of the proslavery activity in the city is borne out by statistics: Mulattos made up about one-fifth of all Blacks in the city in 1800, but about one-third in 1860.

BLACK GRANTED PATENT

On **OCTOBER 14**, Henry Blair, a U.S. slave, became the second Black to hold a U.S. patent. He invented a mechanical corn planter (1835) and later, a cotton planter (1836). In 1858, it was ruled that slaves could not hold federal patents, a situation that remained in effect until after the Civil War.

1835 NORTH CAROLINA DEBATES FREE BLACKS' RIGHT TO VOTE

A debate arose in the North Carolina Constitutional Convention concerning whether free Blacks were citizens and whether the state was obliged to permit them to vote. The majority opinion held that free Blacks were only citizens "by necessity" and subject to "civil slavery" and thus were not allowed to vote. North Carolina became the last southern state to deny free Blacks the right to vote.

SECOND SEMINOLE WAR BEGINS

Because of increasing white settlement in the Florida territory, the federal government engaged in a war to remove the Seminoles from the region. Between one-quarter and one-third of the Seminole people were Blacks. The Second Seminole War ignited when slave catchers captured Osceola's Black wife. Osceola was put in jail after striking an American officer who had tried to restrain him. Osceola vowed revenge, and a guerrilla war ensued for eight years. The war involved other tribes as well. The Creeks, for example, had been told that they could keep as slaves any Blacks they captured, and joined the federal troops in conquering the Seminoles. The Second Seminole War was the costliest Indian war ever waged in this country, costing $20 million and the lives of 1,500 American troops and an unknown number of Blacks and Seminoles. When the war ended in 1842, only a few Blacks were allowed to relocate with the Seminoles to Indian Territory. Fearing that they would be resold into slavery, many Blacks escaped to Mexico. Others were returned to their former white owners or resold into slavery to new owners.

SCHOOL FOR BLACK CHILDREN OPENS IN BOSTON

One of the city's first schools built for Black children was opened. It was named the Abiel Smith School, after a white merchant who had bequeathed money to the city for the purpose. There had been other schools for Black children in the city. In 1798, Primus Hall opened a school in his home on Beacon Hill. In 1808, the first "public" school opened in the African Meetinghouse. The Smith school was the first structure built specifically for the education of Black children.

Ten years after the founding of the Abiel Smith School, Black parents, protesting segregation of their children in all-Black schools, boycotted the school. In 1848, Benjamin Roberts sued the city of Boston because his daughter was forced to attend Smith School, despite the fact that another school was closer to her home. The Smith School operated until 1855.

VIRGINIA EXPORTS SLAVES
According to a Richmond newspaper, Virginia alone exported 120,000 slaves in this year; but most historians believe this figure was exaggerated. During the first half of the nineteenth century, the slave population of the country increased from less than one million to over three million.

NATIONAL NEGRO CONVENTION MEETS AGAIN
From **JUNE 1** to **5**, the annual National Negro Convention met in Philadelphia and urged Blacks to abandon the use of the terms "African" and "colored" when referring to Black institutions and organizations and to themselves. It also opposed migration to Canada and advocated stronger political action against slavery. This was the fifth and last meeting of the National Negro Convention.

MOB DESTROYS INTEGRATED SCHOOL IN NEW HAMPSHIRE
On **AUGUST 10**, a mob of white citizens used one hundred yoke of oxen to pull Noyes Academy, an integrated school, into a swamp just outside of Canaan, New Hampshire.

PROSLAVERY MOB ATTACKS ABOLITIONISTS
On **OCTOBER 21**, William Lloyd Garrison was paraded through the streets of Boston at the end of a rope after a proslavery mob disrupted a meeting of the Boston Female Anti-Slavery Society. The episode started when English abolitionist George Thompson, the scheduled speaker at the abolition meeting, denounced slavery and slaveholders in an eloquent and impassioned manner. After searching for Thompson in vain, the mob found Garrison and dragged him through the streets with a rope around his body. Garrison was rescued by city officials and locked up in the city jail for his own safety. City officials were quickly denounced for the lack of protection they afforded abolition meetings.

PROSLAVERY RIOT IN UTICA
On **OCTOBER 21**, about six hundred antislavery activists from throughout New York State assembled in Utica to form the New York Anti-Slavery Society. Included

John Greenleaf Whittier's poem "My Countrymen in Chains!" was published in 1835, with this drawing as its heading. "Am I Not a Man and a Brother?" was first carved on a cameo by Josiah Wedgwood, the English abolitionist and potter, who made the cameo in 1787 for the London Society for the Abolition of Slavery. Several reproductions were shipped to Benjamin Franklin for distribution to those who were against slavery.

were some of the state's most distinguished men. Because the meeting had been advertised so widely, it encouraged Samuel Beardsley, a city leader, to arrange a protest meeting. It was reported that Beardsley said that "the disgrace of having an Abolition Convention held in the city is a deeper one than that of twenty mobs, and that it would be better to have Utica razed to its foundations, or to have it destroyed like Sodom and Gomorah, than to have the convention meet here." Expecting to meet in the common council chambers, the antislavery convention was forced to find another place when a proslavery mob took possession of the chambers. The abolitionists shifted their meeting to the Second Presbyterian Church, and when they had completed adopting their constitution, their meeting was disrupted by a proslavery mob.

They drove the delegates from the church, followed them to their rooming houses, and continued their agitation until most of the abolitionists had left the city. ◈ Wealthy landowner Gerrit Smith was brought into the antislavery community when he took besieged abolitionists into his home to protect them from a mob.

The leader of the Utica mob, Samuel Beardsley, had been a member of Congress, a U.S. attorney, and was a close friend of President Andrew Jackson. Two weeks after the Utica incident, Beardsley was appointed attorney general of New York by Governor William L. Marcy and subsequently became chief justice of the New York Supreme Court.

PRESIDENT INITIATES BAN ON MAILING ANTISLAVERY PUBLICATIONS

On **DECEMBER 7**, President Andrew Jackson, in his annual message, recommended a law that would prevent the circulation of antislavery materials by mail. He called for the law in response to increased violence over abolitionist activities and requests from proslavery supporters in Charleston, South Carolina.

1836 GRIMKÉ SISTERS PUBLISH ABOLITIONIST TRACTS

Angelina Grimké (1805–1879), of South Carolina, became the most outspoken female abolitionist when she published her *Appeal to the Christian Women of the South*. Her sister, Sarah Moore Grimké (1792–1873) also a famous abolitionist, published *Epistle to the Clergy of the Southern States* in this year as well. Grimké's *Appeal* was widely distributed and brought forth a turbulent storm of criticism and insults. The Quakers threatened to disown her for having published it. Grimké often voiced her opposititon to slavery independently of the position taken by the Quakers, who objected to her acting in ways they considered improper for women. Postmasters in the South publicly burned her *Appeal*. Charleston authorities instructed police to prevent her from entering the city and to ensure that she did not communicate by letter with any person in the city. Officials were authorized to have her arrested and imprisoned until the return of her vessel if she succeeded in entering the city.

Angelina and Sarah were the daughters of Oxford-educated judge John F. Grimké of the South Carolina Supreme Court. As early as 1829, Angelina wrote in her diary: "Yesterday was a day of suffering. Many depths of it, I cried unto the Lord that he would make a way for me to escape from the land of slavery." When Catherine Beecher wrote *An Essay on Slavery and Abolitionism, with Reference to the Duty of American Females*, in which she argued that slavery was a domestic concern of the South, Grimké wrote a strong counterargument. In *Letters to Catherine E. Beecher*, she made several key points:

> The great fundamental principle of abolitionists is, that man cannot rightfully hold his fellow man as property. Therefore, we affirm, that every slavehold is a man-stealer. . . . We sert that it is a national sin. . . . Our main principle of action is embodied in God's holy command: Wash you, make you clean, put away the evils of your doings from before mine eyes, cease to do evil, learn to do well; seek judgment, relieve the oppressed, judge the fatherless, plead for the widow.

Angelina Grimké married Theodore Weld, a noted abolitionist, in 1838. She soon followed him in becoming an eloquent speaker. Although their marriage did not last, she continued her work on behalf of the antislavery movement. Grimké's arguments against slavery were always based on the Bible, fundamental law, moral principles, and the immorality of slavery. Grimké's quarrel with the ranks of the antislavery societies over the women's rights issue (she was an ardent feminist) was intense. In fact, her financial independence allowed her to infuse the antislavery movement with the influence of the women's movement. Her lectures and related missionary efforts were paid, not by the American Anti-Slavery Society, but from her own wealth. She accepted no salary for her work as one of the agents of the society.

LARGEST FREE BLACK POPULATION EXISTS IN LOUISIANA

By this time, Louisiana had more free Black residents than any other southern state. About 855 free Blacks resided there, of whom 620 owned Black slaves. They paid taxes on properties assessed at $2,462,470.

THE *Philanthropist* BEGINS PUBLICATION

James Birney (1792–1857), born to a large slave-owning family, launched one of the most significant abolitionist newspapers — the *Philanthropist* — having freed his slaves two years earlier. He became one of the most outspoken abolitionists in this country. In 1837, he became the executive secretary of the American Anti-Slavery Society and was frequently called upon by both Black and white groups to speak.

TWILIGHT ELECTED TO VERMONT LEGISLATURE

Alexander Lucius Twilight, the first U.S. Black college graduate, was elected to the Vermont legislature, becoming one of the first American Black state representatives. He served only one year at Montpelier, Vermont.

Twilight spent much of his life as a teacher and minister. He held a preceptorship of the Orleans County Grammar School at Brownington, Vermont, and then became its principal; he also served as minister of the local church from 1829 to 1834. In 1847, Twilight retired from the school, but he continued to teach in nearby schools. In 1852, he was headmaster of Brownington Academy and a local minister, a position he held until 1855 when he suffered a stroke. Twilight died in 1857 and is buried near the church.

WOMEN'S ANTI-SLAVERY SOCIETY BARS BLACKS

In New York, the Women's Anti-Slavery Society barred Blacks from membership. Although the group worked to abolish slavery, it is clear that the mixing of whites and Blacks in public was not one of its goals. Even a request to have a Black minister address the Women's Anti-Slavery Society was rejected by its members on the basis that it conflicted with "correct social mores." The white and Black members of some antislavery societies, however, forged excellent relationships.

ABOLITIONISTS PRESENT PETITIONS TO CONGRESS

On JANUARY 11, abolitionists attempted to ban slavery in the District of Columbia through petititons to Congress. Senator John C. Calhoun, a staunch advocate of slavery as an economic necessity and a positive moral good, rejected the petitions and called them "foul slander" against the South.

TEXAS CONSTITUTION LEGALIZES SLAVERY

On MARCH 17, Texas officially adopted a constitution that legalized slavery. This action provoked heated debate in the U.S. Congress between proslavery and antislavery forces.

HOUSE ADOPTS GAG RULE ON ANTISLAVERY PETITIONS

On MAY 26, the U.S. House of Representatives adopted a "gag rule," whereby antislavery petitions were simply tabled with no further action. This action was prompted by the passage of a resolution stating that Congress had no authority over state slavery laws. John Quincy Adams (a leader in the House since the end of his presidency) mounted a nonstop assault against this rule. He made impromptu speeches on every possible occassion, and in doing so angered many members.

◈ Representatives who wanted to keep antislavery petitions from becoming a disruptive issue on the floor of the House attempted to censure Adams. The censure attempt failed, and Adams won a minor victory. Joshua Giddings, a major ally of Adams from Ohio, was successfully censured during the same 1842 session. Still, his district reelected him, and in 1844 the gag rule was abolished.

PROSLAVERY MOB DESTROYS PROPERTY IN CINCINNATI

On JULY 28, a committee of thirteen Cincinnati citizens confronted James Birney and other members of the Ohio Anti-Slavery Society, declaring that "unless they desisted from the publication of the *Philanthropist*, an anti-slavery newspaper [printed in the city], the committee would not be responsible for the consequences." The committee's chairman, Judge Jacob Burnet of the supreme court of Ohio, stated that the mob would consist of as many as five thousand persons, including two-thirds of the property holders of the city. Birney and members of the society were given until the next day to consider the threat. When they decided to ignore the demands, the offices of the society were sacked, and the press of the *Philanthropist* was thrown into the Ohio River.

1837 FIRST BLACK OBTAINS MEDICAL DEGREE

James McCune Smith (1811–1865) was the first American Black to earn an M.D. He received his early education at the African Free School in New York City. Because he could not pursue his higher education in the United States, Smith went to Scotland, where he earned his bachelor's, master's, and medical degrees at the University of Glasgow. He returned to New York City and opened a successful medical practice and two pharmacies. Smith was an avid abolitionist and was a pioneer in the scientific study of race.

NEWSPAPER STUDY REVEALS SUFFERING OF SLAVES

In a study of seventy-two newspapers and their advertisements concerning slaves, done in this year by antislavery activists, the following facts were revealed:

When placed in a larger geographic context, the above findings are especially revealing. For example, it is estimated that there were more than five hundred papers (including dailies) printed in southern states each week at this time, or about twenty-six thousand dailies printed in a year. The seventy-two newspapers thus represent only about a fraction of one percent of the total number of papers published in the South in 1837. One can simply multiply the findings from the seventy-two newspapers by twenty and derive a conservative estimate of the suffering endured by these runaway slaves.

5,400 total fugitives;
960 female fugitives;
360 child fugitives;
80 women with young children;
880 men with scars;
140 women with scars;
260 separated from families;
80 men in irons;
40 women in irons;
40 men marked with shot;
20 men branded.

Other statistics from the same set of newspapers include:

20 licenses to kill;
30,500 total persons advertised for sale;
3,580 females for sale;
2,000 children for sale;
900 women with young children for sale;
8,400 persons sold in estates of deceased slave-holders;
880 persons sold by the sheriff;
13,400 persons sold by auctioneers.

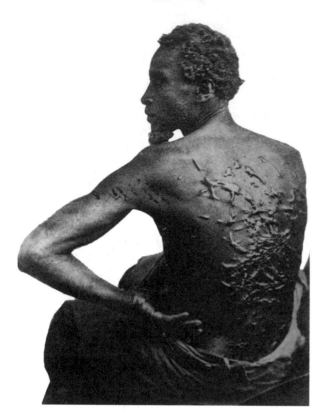

Punishment of slaves was frequently brutal and inhumane. Since slaves had no recourse, masters and overseers could punish as they saw fit. This photograph reveals the scars from countless whippings on a slave's back.

SUICIDE UNDERSCORES TRAGEDY OF SLAVERY

One revelation about slavery was cited in the *Rutherford Gazette*, a paper printed in the western part of North Carolina, and then later reprinted in the *Southern Citizen* of **SEPTEMBER 23**. It is reproduced here:

Suicide.

The negro woman, [Lucy] confined in our jail as a runaway, put an end to her existence on the 28th ult. by hanging herself. Her master came to this place the day on which it occurred, and going to the jail, was recognized by the woman as her master. He had left the jail but a short time, when it was discovered that the woman had de-

◈ 270 persons tried to escape from slavery — 122 of these were males, 48 of these were females, 18 were children and youths less than fourteen years old;

◈ 44 of the men and 7 of the women were described as scarred;

◈ 22 had been brought from distant markets;

◈ 13 were from separated families;

◈ 4 men and 2 women had irons on, or were marked;

◈ 6 men and 1 woman had been freed but were later imprisoned and sold back into slavery;

◈ the ages of the fugitives varied from six months to sixty years;

◈ 2 men were marked with shot, and 1 was branded;

◈ 1 slave's master had given permission to *kill* his slave.

THE GEOGRAPHICAL DISTRIBUTION OF BLACKS IN CANADA

According to a report of the conditions and prospects of the Black population by the American Anti-Slavery Society, in 1837 there were more than ten thousand Blacks in Upper Canada, many of them refugees from the mob violence of the 1820s and 1830s in the United States. Enough Blacks are believed to have left Cincinnati in the spring of 1829 (the year of rioting in the city) to establish the town of Wilberforce, near London, Ontario. Some estimates show that as many as twelve hundred refugees settled in Canada every year during the decade 1850–1860. By 1860, as many as sixty thousand Blacks were estimated to reside in Upper Canada, of whom forty-five thousand were fugitive slaves. Henry Bibb, noted abolitionist and successful businessman in Canada, estimated that about four thousand fugitives had come into Upper Canada in less than a year.

The interlake region of Upper Canada was not the only destination of fugitive slaves, but it was the safest. Settlements of former slaves were located in Essex and Kent counties and in the towns of Windsor, Sandwich, Amherstburg, New Canaan, Colchester, and Buxton. These destinations had Underground Railroad connections through Detroit. Another group of destinations included Fort Erie, St. Catherines, Niagara, Hamilton, and Toronto. In the Thames River valley, fugitive slaves found safety in Chatham, Dresden, Dawn, Sydenham, London, and Wilberforce. Although Blacks experienced prejudice in Canada, it was quite different and less extreme than what they had experienced in the United States. Furthermore, in Canada they were free — a right they were willing to die for. Canada would not surrender any of these persons to claimants, no matter what their justification. Escaped slaves were, however, potential victims of professional or U.S.-authorized slave catchers.

stroyed herself. We have never known an instance where so much firmness was exhibited by any person, as was by this negro. The place from which she suspended herself was not high enough to prevent her feet from touching the floor, and it was only by drawing her legs up and remaining in that position, that she succeeded in her determined purpose.

Lucy chose the ultimate shelter from the American slave owner — death.

Weekly Advocate BEGINS PUBLICATION

On **JANUARY 4**, the *Weekly Advocate*, a Black newspaper, was established in New York by Samuel Ennalls and Philip A. Bell. On January 7, the *Weekly Advocate* presented the following vigorous opposition to colonization:

We need scarcely say, we are opposed to Colonization. It matters not to us what features it may assume whether it present itself in the garb of philanthropy, or assumes the mild and benign countenance of Christianity, or comes with the selfish aspect of Politics; we will believe, assert and maintain (So help us God!) that we are opposed to the exclusive emigration and colonization of the People of Color of these United States. We hold ourselves ready, at all times to combat with opposite views, and defend these our principles to the last!

A month later, this publication reemerged as the *Colored American*, with Samuel Cornish as editor. The immediate name change may have reflected the debate within the Black community concerning its identity and the proper way to refer to Blacks — as Negroes, colored Americans, Anglo-Africans, Africans, or Afro-Americans. The name *Colored American* probably represented a compromise at the time. Like many Black newspapers, the *Colored American* dedicated itself to developing pride and unity within the Black community. It, too, was interested in creating a greater awareness of civil rights and the political means for achieving those rights. The paper had a strong religious and moral basis. In 1839, Cornish resigned and Charles B. Ray, a former general agent and pastor of the Bethesda Congregational Church, became editor. Throughout the history of the *Colored American*, it received generous support from Arthur Tappan, a white abolitionist.

COTTON PRICES FALL, PRECIPITATING SALE OF SLAVES

In **MARCH**, the price of cotton fell by nearly one-half on the New Orleans market. Many businesses that

RUNAWAYS REVEAL WIDE RANGE OF INHUMANE TREATMENT

Runaways were mostly young male slaves under thirty years of age. Some were "habitual or notorious" runaways. Most of the runaways were mulattos or of predominantly white ancestry, although some were described as "Black" or "pure" African. The manner in which slave owners advertised for their return shows some bewilderment concerning slaves' desire for freedom. Below are some excerpts from advertisements seeking runaway slaves.

"always appeared to be in a good humor, laughs a great deal, and runs on with a good deal of foolishness"
"very industrious and answers with a smile"
"very humble with his hand to his hat"
"humbly and respectfully with a smile"
"the slave left without provocation"
"for what do they run away?"

Slaves generally behaved in the deferential manner expected: it ensured that they would be less likely to be abused. Yet this "humbly and respectfully" behavior masked a deeper desire to be free. Many slaveholders believed that "good" treatment of slaves was sufficient for them to be content to remain as slaves. In fact, slave owners generally depicted the slave as "showing ingratitude" when attempting to escape, rather than acknowledging an innate human desire for freedom. Other slaveholders believed that "harsh and inhumane" treatment was necessary to "keep them in their place."

A selection of advertisements concerning runaway slaves, from 1837, reveals the treatment and conditions to which slaves were subjected:

$40 Reward

RANAWAY from my residence near Mobile, two negro men, Isaac and Tim; Isaac is from 25 to 30 years old, dark complexion, scar on the right side of the head, and also one on the right side of the body occasioned by BUCK SHOT. Tim is 22 years old, dark complexion, scar on the right cheek, as also another on the back of the neck. Captains and owners of Steamboats, Vessels, and water Crafts of every description, are cautioned against taking them on board under the penalty of the law, and all other persons against harboring or in any manner favoring the escaped of said negroes under the like penalty. Mobile, Sept. 1.

SARAH WALSH

Committed

TO the Jail of Pike county, a man about twenty-three or four years old, who calls his name John; the said negro has a clog of iron on his right foot which will weigh 4 or 5 pounds. The owner is requested, &c.

B. W. HODGES, Jailer.
[*Montgomery Advertiser*, Sept. 29, 1837]

Ten Dollars Reward

RANAWAY from the subscriber, a negro girl named POLLY. The above reward will be paid for her apprehension and delivered to the subscriber — or $200 if found harbored by any white man, so that the act can be proved.

J. B. WALKER, Water St.
[*Montgomery Advertiser*, Sept. 29, 1837]

Reward

Ranaway from the subscriber, a negro fellow named DICK, about 21 or 22 years of age, dark mulatto, has MANY SCARS on his back from being WHIPPED. The boy was purchased by me from Thomas L. Arnold, and absconded about the time the purchase was made.

JAMES NOE.
[*Sentinel and Expositor*, Vicksburg, Mississippi, Oct. 10, 1837]

depended on cotton were financially hurt, and some were forced to close. In May, the "panic of 1837" began. As many as 618 banks failed in this year alone. Unemployment increased, especially in the southern and western states. High rates of unemployment continued for the next seven years. Since slaves were directly tied to cotton production, any major drop in the price of cotton could force farmers on marginal land to

The sale of estates, pictures, and slaves occurred almost daily during periods when cotton prices plummeted. This slave mart at New Orleans was the scene of thousands of slave sales.

sell their slaves for economic reasons. Even large-scale planters sold their slaves to pay off debts.

ABOLITIONIST KIDNAPPED IN OHIO
In **JUNE**, after giving an antislavery lecture in Berlin, Ohio, Marius Robinson (1806–1876) was kidnapped, tarred and feathered, and dumped beside a road. He never recovered completely from the attack.

Several years earlier, Robinson had left Lane Seminary with Augustus Wattles to set up a school for

Blacks in Cincinnati. He assisted James Birney in editing the *Philanthropist*, an antislavery newspaper. Robinson also edited the *Anti-Slavery Bugle* in Salem, Ohio, and served as president of the Ohio Mutual Insurance Company.

ABOLITIONIST KILLED BY PROSLAVERY MOB
On **NOVEMBER 7**, Elijah P. Lovejoy, editor of an abolitionist newspaper, the *Alton Observer*, was killed in

Marius Robinson, an agent of the American Anti-Slavery Society, pressed for immediate emancipation, spoke out about the broad problems of racial prejudice, and opposed colonization.

Alton, Illinois, by a mob of proslavery activists, who then dumped his printing press into the Mississippi River.

Lovejoy had previously published the *St. Louis Observer*, another antislavery newspaper. He advocated immediate abolition, and his views had so enraged some Missouri residents that he was forced to flee across the Mississippi River to Alton, where he continued to publish. Lovejoy was one of the major organizers of the Illinois Antislavery Society. Lovejoy's murder became a cause célèbre among journalists. A monument to Lovejoy stands today in Alton, and the remains of his printing press, salvaged from the river, are also on display.

SEMINOLES DEFEAT U.S. TROOPS AT OKEECHOBEE

On **DECEMBER 25**, a Seminole force defeated U.S. troops in the Battle of Okeechobee in Florida during the Second Seminole War. Chief John Horse (a Black) shared command with Alligator Sam Jones and Wild Cat. Blacks had a reputation as "fearless" fighters in the numerous battles and skirmishes with U.S. troops. Blacks also served with the American troops as scouts, interpreters, and even spies.

In 1849, John Horse founded the city of Wewoka in Mexico. It served as a refuge for runaway slaves.

Elijah Lovejoy, the abolitionist editor of the Alton Observer, *died defending his right to publish antislavery material, thus combining abolitionism and freedom of the press in a single cause. The picture shows the Godfrey Gilman & Co. warehouse where Lovejoy was killed defending his press.*

1838 PURVIS NAMED PRESIDENT OF UNDERGROUND RAILROAD

In Philadelphia, Robert Purvis (1810–1898), a leading abolitionist, was given the honorary title of president of the Underground Railroad, a network of private homes and establishments that helped slaves escape and protected fugitive slaves from their pursuers. Although it is not known how many slaves actually ran away each year, slave owners estimated that they lost approximately two hundred thousand dollars annually from slaves escaping across the Mason-Dixon Line. Rewards for the return of a runaway were often quite high.

◈ Purvis was born in Charleston, South Carolina. His father was a cotton broker and his mother a freeborn daughter of a slave. In 1826, his father died, leaving him $120,000, some of which he used to help fund antislavery causes. Purvis and his close friend,

Robert Purvis, a wealthy Black abolitionist, became one of the most effective members of the Underground Railroad. He is said to have had a secret trapdoor in his home, behind which fugitives from slavery would hide on their way to freedom.

William Lloyd Garrison, helped form the American Anti-Slavery Society in December 1833. Purvis, however, gave more time to his own state, Pennsylvania, than to the national group. From 1845 to 1850, he was president of the Pennsylvania Anti-Slavery Society. Purvis used his home as a refuge for runaway slaves. He also opposed the colonization movement and refused to pay taxes when the public schools in his township excluded Black children. Since Purvis was subject to heavy taxes, the public schools reversed their decision. After the Civil War and emancipation, Purvis's activities diminished. His son, Charles, became surgeon-in-chief at the Freedmen's Hospital in Washington, D.C.

CALHOUN RESOLUTIONS PASSED

From **JANUARY 3** to **12**, John C. Calhoun introduced resolutions in the U.S. Senate that affirmed slavery as a legal institution, in response to abolitionists' efforts to abolish slavery in the District of Columbia and slave trading across state lines. Calhoun, a strong supporter of states' rights, contended that each state had the right to control domestic institutions, and slavery was an important domestic institution of the southern states. Calhoun said:

> Any intermeddling of any one or more States, or a combination of their citizens, with the domestic institutions and policy of the others, on any ground or under any pretext whatever, political, moral or religious, with a view to their alteration, or subversion, is an assumption of superiority not warranted by the Constitution, insulting to the States interfered with, tending to endanger their domestic peace and tranquility, subversive of the objects for which the Constitution was formed, and by necessary consequence, tending to weaken and destroy the Union itself.

The Senate agreed that the institution of slavery should not be interfered with. Further, they agreed that any attempt to eliminate slavery in the District of Columbia constituted an attack on institutions of slaveholding states. The Senate, however, refused to automatically approve annexations that would expand slave territory.

◈ John C. Calhoun (1782–1850), a native of South Carolina, became one of the most eloquent speakers on the virtues of slavery. He served in the U.S. House of Representatives, as secretary of war, and as vice president under John Quincy Adams and Andrew Jackson. After resigning as vice president of the United States under Andrew Jackson in 1832, he was elected to the U.S. Senate, where he supported nullification (the right of states to nullify federal laws) and promoted slavery as an economic necessity.

MORRIS ATTACKS CALHOUN RESOLUTIONS

In **JANUARY**, Senator Thomas Morris, a vehement antislavery advocate, vigorously argued with John C. Calhoun and others in the U.S. Senate regarding slavery and attacked the Calhoun resolutions with one of the most effective arguments for civil rights. Morris believed slavery was wrong "in principle, in practice, in every country, and under every condition of things." Further, "American slavery is the most obnoxious of its kind, a libel upon our republican institutions, and ruinous to the best interest of our country."

Interestingly, Morris was also a strict advocate of states' rights. In fact, he agreed that slavery was created by state law and that the Constitution did not guarantee or prohibit it. He did not support abolishing slavery in the District of Columbia and did not oppose admitting a slave state into the Union.

Morris, a native of Virginia, had moved to Ohio in 1795 and studied law at night while working as a brickmaker during the day. He served in the Ohio legislature from 1806 to 1830, was chief justice of the state between 1830 and 1833, and was a U.S. senator from 1833 to 1839. Morris was eventually pushed out of his party. Afterwards, he concentrated on the political movement to abolish slavery.

BLACKS PROTEST DISFRANCHISEMENT

On **MARCH 14**, a mass meeting of Blacks took place in Philadelphia to protest disfranchisement of Blacks in Pennsylvania.

Mirror of Liberty BEGINS PUBLICATION

On **AUGUST 30**, the first Black magazine, *Mirror of Liberty*, was published in New York City by David Ruggles, an abolitionist.

DOUGLASS ESCAPES FROM SLAVERY

On **SEPTEMBER 3**, Frederick Augustus Washington Bailey (1817–1895) escaped from slavery in Baltimore, Maryland, to freedom in New Bedford, Massachusetts, by disguising himself as a sailor. In New York City, on his way to New Bedford, he took the name Douglass, the hero of Sir Walter Scott's poem *The Lady of the Lake.*

In 1841 Douglass embarked on his long career as a noted abolitionist, orator, and political activist by lecturing for the Massachusetts Anti-Slavery Society.

This drawing shows Frederick Douglass as a young man, perhaps after his escape from slavery in 1838 and during his early work as an abolitionist.

Over the next several years, he gave lectures in churches, on trains, in fraternal halls, and at conventions. His lectures were not only intellectually challenging but also emotionally moving, and he aroused anger and violent attacks from antiabolitionists on a number of occasions.

◆ Frederick Douglass was born a slave in February 1817, in Tuckahoe, Maryland. At the age of eight, he was sent to Baltimore, where he spent eight years before escaping to freedom. Douglass experienced hard times in New Bedford. He joined a Black abolition society and later became a full-time agent of the Massachusetts Anti-Slavery Society. In Massachusetts, Douglass was influenced by William Lloyd Garrison, Wendell Phillips, and other abolitionists whom he met.

1839 BLACK MINISTER CALLED THE "BLACK DANIEL WEBSTER"

The Reverend Samuel Ringgold Ward (1817–1866), a Presbyterian minister and one of the country's most active abolitionists, was employed as a lecturer by the American Anti-Slavery Society. Because of his stirring and provocative lectures, he was called the "Black Daniel Webster."

Cinque, the son of a Mendi chief from Sierra Leone, West Africa, was captured and chained in the hold of a Portuguese ship bound for Cuba. Placed aboard the Amistad *after being sold to two Spaniards, he and fifty-two other Africans mutinied. During his trial for murder, Cinque made an impassioned speech in his native language, and although no American could understand it, his demeanor helped to influence the verdict in his favor. The decision was appealed to the U.S. Supreme Court, where former president John Quincy Adams argued successfully in Cinque's defense.*

MUTINY ABOARD THE *Amistad*

The best-known slave mutiny in U.S. history occurred in July aboard the *Amistad*, a Spanish ship. Led by a Black named Joseph Cinque, fifty-three African slaves took over the ship, killing the captain and several members of the crew.

The slaves were being shipped from Havana to plantations along the Cuban coast when the mutiny occurred. Two of the crew members were spared by promising to sail the ship back to Sierra Leone. During the day, they sailed the ship northeast toward Africa; at night, when Cinque was sleeping, they turned back to the northwest. The ship finally sailed into Monatauck (Montauk), Long Island, where U.S. sailors boarded the ship and immediately arrested the slaves. While awaiting trial, the slaves were taken to Farmington, a strongly abolitionist town, where they were schooled and given religious instruction. Former president John Quincy Adams defended the group before the U.S. Supreme Court, tearing apart the contention that the slaves were Cubans, not covered by the provisions of the treaty with Britain that had outlawed the slave trade in Spain's colonies in the West Indies. In 1841, the slaves won their freedom. Cinque and others raised money for their return to Africa, but when they arrived there, they found that many of their families had been sold into slavery while they were gone.

RAY BECOMES EDITOR OF *Colored American*

Charles B. Ray (1807–1886) assumed the position of editor of the *Colored American*, where he became a voice for the emancipation of slaves. He remained editor of this important newspaper until 1842.

Ray was born in Massachusetts in 1807, graduated from Wesleyan University in 1832, and then became a merchant in New York City. Over the years, Ray had been chairman of the city vigilance committee and secretary of the state vigilance committee. In addition, he was pastor of the Bethesda Congregational Church for twenty-two years.

WELD PUBLISHES ANTISLAVERY BOOK

Theodore Weld (1803–1895), a white abolitionist, published *Slavery As It Is* on **JUNE 13**. His book was one of the most factual ever written on the nature of slavery.

Weld, who was of Connecticut Puritan stock, elevated his beliefs concerning abolition into a crusade. As a student at Lane Seminary, he worked among the Blacks of Cincinnati. He worked as an agent of the American Anti-Slavery Society in Ohio, going into areas where others dared not go. Weld was often threatened by mobs, and stones were hurled at him during one of his lectures. Nevertheless, he continued his daring crusade. As a result of his work in Ohio, the state's antislavery society had four thousand members, the largest in the nation. Because of Weld's successful lecturing, Ohio had one-third of the membership of all the antislavery societies in the country. Weld spent many hours lecturing to students at New England colleges and seminaries, and he trained many agents at Cleveland and Oberlin for the cause. These agents were sent directly into the

Theodore Weld, a crusader for the abolition of slavery, carried the message to people in both rural and urban areas. His book Slavery As It Is *shocked thousands out of their complacency.*

field to work. Weld gave his final antislavery address on July 4, 1836. Afterwards, he moved into a New York office where he and Henry B. Stanton directed the growing antislavery efforts. He married Angelina Grimké in 1838.

LIBERTY PARTY FORMED IN NEW YORK
On **NOVEMBER 13**, a group of moderate abolitionists met in Warsaw, New York, to form the Liberty Party, the first antislavery political party. The membership selected James Birney, a former Kentucky slaveholder, to be their presidential candidate. Birney had been converted to the abolitionist point of view by Theodore Weld. The vice-presidential nominee was Thomas Earle of Pennsylvania. Members of the Liberty Party opposed the more radical views of William Lloyd Garrison and others who advocated dissolution of the Union. Two Black abolitionists, Samuel Ringgold Ward and Henry Highland Garnet, were among the founders. Other prominent members included Gerrit Smith and Salmon P. Chase, who voiced the party's opposition to the annexation of Texas as a slave state. In both 1840 and 1844, Birney ran unsuccessfully for the presidency. In 1848, the Liberty Party merged with other organizations to form the Free-Soil Party.

1840
POPULATION OVERVIEW
THE UNITED STATES The Bureau of the Census counted 17 million residents in the Untied States; 2,874,000 (16.8 percent) of these were Blacks. New York remained the most populous state, increasing by more than 500,000 over the previous decade to 2.4 million. Virginia lost population over the decade. Free Blacks made up about 5 percent of the total population in the South. Approximately 93 percent of free Blacks in the North were disenfranchised.

BLACKS IN MISSISSIPPI In Mississippi, Blacks outnumbered whites. The population imbalance resulted primarily from the demand for cotton throughout the world and the use of slaves to produce it.

INDIANA IMPLEMENTS "GRANDPARENTS' CLAUSE" TO RESTRICT INTERMARRIAGES
Indiana passed legislation that made it illegal for whites to marry persons who had a great-grandparent who was Black. Violating this law carried a fine of $5,000 and imprisonment of up to twenty years. Ministers who performed such marriages could be fined up to $10,000 per violation.

NORTHEASTERN CITIES SWEPT BY RIOTS
During the 1830s and 1840s, anti-Black riots occurred in Philadelphia, New York City, and other northeastern cities. Many of these riots were sparked by increasing competition between free Blacks and foreign immigrants for manual jobs.

PHILLIPS ATTENDS ANTISLAVERY CONVENTION IN ENGLAND
Wendell Phillips (1811–1884), a lawyer, gave up his law practice and became a noted orator and abolitionist. He joined with William Lloyd Garrison in his campaign against slavery. In 1840, he frequently spoke up at the World Anti-Slavery Convention in England. He continued to work to gain equal rights for Blacks and women even after the Civil War. Phillips also worked to bring about major social reforms.

WOMEN ADVANCE IN ANTISLAVERY CAMPAIGN

Black and white women took part in the antislavery movement from the start; they were barred, however, from administrative and executive positions. Black families, including the Fortens, the Remonds, and the Douglasses, were cofounders of antislavery organizations. But antislavery leadership was considered the work of men for men.

Black women, however, had already founded antislavery societies and been influential in interracial societies. Grace Bustill Douglass, for example, was elected vice president of the first antislavery convention of women, held in 1837 in New York. As many as 10 percent of attendees were Black. Lewis Tappan, one of the strongest supporters of the American Anti-Slavery Society, voiced strong opposition when Abby Kelley, a white woman, was appointed to the business committee at the 1840 convention. Tappan, the other men on the committee, and about three hundred members of the convention left the society to form a new group, the American and Foreign Anti-Slavery Society. Tappan's leaving was critical because he had financially supported many of the society's causes. After the Tappan defection, Lucretia Mott, Lydia Maria Child, and Maria W. Chapman were elected to the executive committee of the American Anti-Slavery Society.

Lydia Maria Child, one of the most widely known women writers of children's stories, caused a racial storm when she wrote *An Appeal in Behalf of That Class of Americans Called Africans*. The book was banned in southern bookstores. Child used the *National Anti-Slavery Standard* to communicate her forceful denunciation of slavery and its consequences.

WORLD ANTI-SLAVERY CONVENTION

On **JUNE 12**, the World Anti-Slavery Convention took place in London, England. Women delegates were denied seats. Charles Lenox Remond (an African American delegate), William Lloyd Garrison, and others boycotted the meetings because of this discrimination. American women delegates, including Lucretia Mott and Elizabeth Cady Stanton, planned to organize their own conferences on women's rights.

AFRICAN AMERICANS INVOLVED IN WHALING INDUSTRY

In New England, particularly in the port areas of Nantucket and New Bedford, African Americans were active in the whaling industry at this time. Black seamen worked on the whaling ships, often as harpooners. A Black metalsmith, Lewis Temple, redesigned the existing harpoon to more securely fasten lines to the whale. His "toggle harpoon" increased the profits of the whalers, allowing them to almost double their catches. Temple never patented his invention and died in poverty.

1841 DOUGLASS MAKES FIRST ANTISLAVERY SPEECH

Frederick Douglass made a speech in Nantucket, Massachusetts, in which he recounted his life as a slave. This was his first antislavery speech. He was immediately employed as an agent by the Massachusetts Anti-Slavery Society. He later joined with white abolitionists to protest successfully against the Dorr Constitution in Rhode Island, which would repeal the right to Blacks to vote in that state.

NEW ENGLAND ANTI-SLAVERY SOCIETY PUBLISHES *Almanac*

The New England Anti-Slavery Society stepped up its attack on slavery by publishing an almanac identifying actions that abolitionists could take to help the cause:

Things for Abolitionists to Do

1. *Speak for the slave.* Plead his cause everywhere, and make everybody feel that you are in earnest.
2. *Write for the slave.* Do you take a religious paper? Write a short article for it, a fact, an argument, an appeal.
3. *Petition for the slave.* Begin at once to circulate petitions for the immediate abolition of slavery.
4. *Work for the slave.* Distribute anti-slavery publications, circulate them in your neighborhood, take them with you on journeys.
5. *Work for the free people of color.* See that your schools are open to their children and that they enjoy in every respect all the rights to which as human beings they are entitled.

SUPREME COURT FREES CINQUE AND FELLOW SLAVES

On **MARCH 6**, the U.S. Supreme Court ruled that African mutineer Joseph Cinque and his fifty-two fellow slaves were free. President Martin Van Buren had urged the Court to turn these Blacks over to the Spanish authorities, but Justice Joseph Story ruled that they were kidnapped free men and thus had the same rights as other kidnapped persons. As free Africans rather than slaves, they were, therefore, free to return to their homelands in Africa. Below are excerpts from Justice Story's opinion:

> This is the case of an appeal from the decree of the circuit court of the district of Connecticut, sitting in admiralty. The leading facts, as they appear upon the transcript of the proceedings, are as follows: On the 27th of June 1839, the schooner "L'Amistad," being the property of Spanish subjects, cleared out from the port of Havana, in the island of Cuba, for Puerto Principe, in the same island. On board of the schooner were the master, Ramon Ferrer, and Jose Ruiz and Pedro Montez, all Spanish subjects. The former had with him a negro boy, named Antonio, claimed to be his slave. Jose Ruiz had with him forty-nine negroes, claimed by him as his slaves, and stated to be his property, in a certain pass or document, signed by the governor-general of Cuba. Pedro Montez had with him four other negroes, also claimed by him as his slaves, and stated to be his property, in a similar pass or document, also signed by the governor-general of Cuba. On the voyage, and before the arrival of the vessel at her port of destination, the negroes rose, killed the master, and took possession of her. On the 26th of August, the vessel was discovered by Lieutenant Gedney, of the United States brig "Washington," at anchor on the high seas, at the distance of half a mile from the shore of Long Island. A part of the negroes were then on shore, at Culloden Point, Long Island, who were seized by Lieutenant Gedney, and brought on board. The vessel, with the negroes and other persons on board, was brought by Lieutenant Gedney into the district of Connecticut, and there libelled for salvage in the district court of the United States. A libel for salvage was also filed by Henry Green and Pelatiah Fordham, of Sag Harbor, Long Island. On the 18th of September, Ruiz and Montez filed claims and libels, in which they asserted their ownership of the negroes as their slaves, and of certain parts of the cargo, and prayed that the same might be "delivered to them, or to the representatives of her Catholic Majesty, as might be most proper." On the 19th of September, the attorney of the United States for the district of Connecticut filed an information or libel, setting forth, that the Spanish minister had officially presented to the proper department of the government of the United States, a claim for the restoration of the vessel, cargo, and slaves, as the property of Spanish subjects, which had arrived within the jurisdictional limits of the United States, and were taken possession of by the said public armed brig of the United States, under such circumstances as made it the duty of the United States to cause the same to be restored to the true proprietors, pursuant to the treaty between the United States and Spain; and praying the court, on its being made legally to appear that the claim of the Spanish minister was well founded, to make such order for the disposal of the vessel, cargo and slaves, as would best enable the United States to comply with their treaty stipulations. But if it should appear, that the negroes were persons transported from Africa, in violation of the laws of the United States, and brought within the United States, contrary to the same laws; he then prayed the court to make such order for their removal to the coast of Africa, pursuant to the laws of the United States, as it should deem fit. . . .

> On the 7th of January 1840, the negroes, Cinque and others, with the exception of Antonio, by their counsel, filed an answer, denying that they were slaves, or the property of Ruiz and Montez, or that the court could, under the constitution or laws of the United States, or under any treaty, exercise any jurisdiction over their persons, by reason of the premises; and praying that they might be dismissed. They specially set forth and insisted in this answer, that they were native-born Africans; born free, and still, of right, ought to be free and not slaves; that they were, on or about the 15th of April 1839, unlawfully kidnapped, and forcibly and wrongfully carried on board a certain vessel, on the coast of Africa, which was unlawfully engaged in the slave-trade, and were unlawfully transported in the same vessel to the island of Cuba, for the purpose of being there unlawfully sold as slaves; that Ruiz and Montez, well knowing the premises, made a pretended purchase of them; that afterwards, on or about the 28th of June 1839, Ruiz and Montez, confederating with Ferrer (master of the Amistad), caused them, without law or right, to be placed on board of the Amistad, to be transported to some place unknown to them, and there to be enslaved for life; that, on the voyage, they rose on the master, and took possession of the vessel, intending to return therewith to their native country, or to seek an asylum in some free state; and the vessel arrived, about the 26th of August 1839, off Montauk Point, near Long Island; a part of them were sent on shore, and were seized by Lieutenant Gedney, and carried on board; and all of them were afterwards brought by him into the district of Connecticut. . . .

> If then, these negroes are not slaves, but are kidnapped Africans, who, by the laws of Spain itself, are entitled to their freedom, and were kidnapped and illegally carried to Cuba, and illegally detained and restrained on board the Amistad; there is no pretence to say, that they are pirates or robbers. We may lament

the dreadful acts by which they asserted their liberty, and took possession of the Amistad, and endeavored to regain their native country; but they cannot be deemed pirates or robbers, in the sense of the law of nations, or the treaty with Spain, or the laws of Spain itself; at least, so far as those laws have been brought to our knowledge. Nor do the libels of Ruiz or Montez assert them to be such. This posture of the facts would seem, of itself, to put an end to the whole inquiry upon the merits.

It is also a most important consideration, in the present case, which ought not to be lost sight of, that, supposing these African negroes not to be slaves, but kidnapped, and free negroes, the treaty with Spain cannot be obligatory upon them; and the United States are bound to respect their rights as much as those of Spanish subjects. The conflict of rights between the parties, under such circumstances, becomes positive and inevitable, and must be decided upon the eternal principles of justice and international law. If the contest were about any goods on board of this ship, to which American citizens asserted a title, which was denied by the Spanish claimants, there could be no doubt of the right of such American citizens to litigate their claims before any competent American tribunal, notwithstanding the treaty with Spain. A fortiori, the doctrine must apply, where human life and human liberty are in issue, and constitute the very essence of the controversy. The treaty with Spain never could have intended to take away the equal rights of all foreigners, who should contest their claims before any of our courts, to equal justice; or to deprive such foreigners of the protection given them by other treaties, or by the general law of nations. Upon the merits of the case, then, there does not seem to us to be any ground for doubt, that these negroes ought to be deemed free; and that the Spanish treaty interposes no obstacle to the just assertion of their rights. . . .

LIBERTY PARTY HOLDS NATIONAL CONVENTION IN NEW YORK CITY

On **MAY 12** and **13**, the Liberty Party held a national convention in New York City to reaffirm its militant antislavery position and to invite the participation of antislavery supporters disenchanted with President John Tyler's annexation of Texas as a slave state.

Alvan Stewart, one of the most militant abolitionists, presided over the meeting. Because of his absolute belief in "higher-law" philosophy (the belief that every person is born free because freedom is the natural state of all persons), he was able to give firm

direction to the party. In fact, almost everyone in the party subscribed to the higher-law doctrine. Levi Coffin, William Goodell, and Joshua Leavitt were secretaries of the party and early pioneers of the higher-law doctrine. The party platform included the demand for immediate emancipation, equal educational opportunity for Blacks, access to the franchise, exclusion of slavery from the territories, nondiscriminatory economic policies, and election of the president and vice president by popular vote.

ANTI-BLACK RIOTING IN CINCINNATI

On **AUGUST 29**, street skirmishes escalated into five days of anti-Black riots in Cincinnati.

SLAVE MUTINY ABOARD THE *Creole*

On **NOVEMBER 7**, a group of slaves being carried from Hampton Roads, Virginia, to New Orleans aboard the slave trader *Creole* revolted. Slaves overpowered the crew, seized the ship, and sailed it to the Bahamas, where all except those accused of murder were immediately freed.

REMOND RETURNS FROM IRELAND

On **DECEMBER 3**, Charles Lenox Remond, an abolitionist orator, returned to the United States from Great Britain with an "Address from the People of Ireland" and as many as sixty thousand signatures urging Irish Americans to "oppose slavery by peaceful means and to insist upon liberty for all regardless of color, creed, or country."

1842 BLACKS AND IRISH FREQUENTLY COMPETE FOR JOBS

The Irish, fearing emancipation in the South would cause large numbers of job-seeking free Blacks to rush into northern cities, joined proslavery mobs to drive out Black competitors. In 1842, violence broke out between Irish and Blacks seeking to control coal-mining jobs in Pennsylvania.

◈ Blacks and Irish workers frequently fought for jobs. In 1853, Blacks replaced Irish on the Erie Railroad when the Irish went on strike. In 1855, they fought for jobs on the New York docks. In 1863, the worst battle occurred between Irish and Blacks during the New York Draft Riots.

SECOND SEMINOLE WAR ENDS

The Second Seminole War ended in defeat for Chief Osceola, who, with the Seminoles and many runaway Black slaves, had battled the U.S. Army for more than five years. The Seminoles' defeat allowed the implementation of the Indian removal policy, which required that the Seminoles move west of the Mississippi River.

RESOLUTIONS INTRODUCED IN CONGRESS IN WAKE OF THE *Creole* MUTINY

In **MARCH** Joshua Giddings, the abolitionist representative from Ohio, introduced several resolutions in Congress to resolve issues raised by the *Creole* mutiny of 1841. Some, including Secretary of State Daniel Webster, demanded that the British return the slaves. Giddings strongly opposed this step, but southern representatives gathered enough support to have Giddings censured. On March 23, Giddings resigned, but was reelected to his seat the following May.

Prigg v. *Commonwealth of Pennsylvania*

On **MARCH 1**, the U.S. Supreme Court ruled in *Prigg* v. *Commonwealth of Pennsylvania* that owners might recover their fugitive slaves from any state and that the states could neither help nor hinder the slaves. In essence, the Court held that the states had no power over cases that arose out of the Fugitive Slave Act of 1793.

REMOND ADDRESSES MASSACHUSETTS LAWMAKERS

Charles Lenox Remond (1810–1873), one of the first Blacks selected and employed as a lecturer by an antislavery society and one of the most sought-after abolitionist speakers, became the first Black to address the Massachusetts House of Representatives. He protested against segregated railroad accommodations and other injustices.

◈ Remond was born on February 1, 1810, in Salem, Massachusetts. His father was a native of Curaçao. Remond was an active member of the Massachusetts Anti-Slavery Society. He lectured every day, sometimes twice a day for three-week periods. He persistently urged the "immediate, unconditional emancipation for every human regardless of tongue or color." Regarded by many as the most forceful abolitionist of his day, he argued in a way that rarely failed to move the crowd. He quickly attained a national and international reputation and was appointed an American delegate to the World Anti-Slavery Convention in London in 1840. Despite his oratorical ability, he received little salary and had to supplement his income by working in a variety of jobs. For example, he worked as an agent to enlist men for the

Charles Lenox Remond, a successful merchant and abolitionist, was the first African American lecturer for the Massachusetts Anti-Slavery Society. His lectures were so powerful and compelling that he was asked to address the Massachusetts legislature, before which he appealed for "immediate, unconditional emancipation."

Fifty-fourth Massachusetts Regiment in the Civil War. He died of tuberculosis at the age of sixty-three.

FUGITIVE SLAVE CAPTURED IN BOSTON

On **NOVEMBER 17**, George Latimer, a fugitive slave, was captured in Boston, and his case became one of the first fugitive slave cases to incite northern and southern abolitionists.

Latimer had escaped from his Virginia slaveholder, who, upon hearing of his capture in Boston, arrived to claim him. Because Boston was fast becoming a hotbed of antislavery protest, it was no wonder that Latimer was quickly surrounded by lawyers ready to defend him. To ensure the broadest support, abolitionists promoted the publication of his case in the *Latimer Journal and North Star*, issued three times weekly. In addition, Frederick Douglass spoke frequently of the case and reported his speeches to the *Liberator*, starting on November 18. Boston abolitionists raised money to purchase Latimer from his owner for four hundred dollars. The celebrated case had a significant impact, particularly in Boston and throughout Massachusetts. Supporters gathered as many as sixty-three hundred signatures on a petition to forbid state officials to arrest or detain fugitives. Further, the use of state property would be denied for such detentions. Latimer's supporters urged passage of federal laws to sever free states from any connection with slavery.

1843 ANTISLAVERY MEETING DISRUPTED IN INDIANA

Antislavery meetings were frequently the targets of proslavery mobs. Frederick Douglass wrote about one such incident in Indiana:

> At our first meeting we were mobbed, and some of us had our good clothes spoiled by evil-smelling eggs. This was at Richmond.... At Pendleton this mobocratic spirit was even more pronounced. It was founded impossible to obtain a building in which to hold our convention, and our friends, Dr. Fussell and others, erected a platform in the woods, where quite a large audience attended. As soon as we began to speak a mob of about sixty of the roughest characters I ever looked upon ordered us, through its leaders, to be silent, threatening us, if we were not, with violence. We attempted to dissuade them, but they had not come to parley but to fight, and were well armed. The tore down the platform on which we stood, assaulted Mr. White and knocked out several of his teeth, dealt a heavy blow on William A. White, striking him on the back part of his head, badly cutting his scalp and felling him to the ground. Undertaking to fight my way through the crowd with a stick which I caught up in the melee, I attracted the fury of the mob, which laid me prostrate on the ground under a torrent of blows. Leaving me thus, with my right hand broken, and in a state of unconsciousness, the mobocrats hastily mounted their horses and rode to Andersonville, where most of them resided.
>
> [From *The Life and Times of Frederick Douglass*, 1892]

RILLIEUX RECEIVES PATENT FOR VACUUM PROCESS

Norbert Rillieux (1806–1894) became a noted U.S. engineer and inventor when he received a patent for inventing the "multiple effects vacuum evaporation process" for refining sugar. (In 1846, he received his second patent for an improved vacuum process.) His invention, which used a vacuum evaporator that cheaply and effectively dehydrated sugar cane into granules, revolutionized the sugar industry. Rillieux's process has also come to be used throughout the world in manufacturing soap, glue, condensed milk, and gelatin.

◆ Rillieux was born in New Orleans on March 17, 1806, to Constance Vivant, a slave, and Vincent Rillieux, a wealthy Frenchman, engineer, and plantation owner. Rillieux's early preoccupation with science led his father to send him to Paris to be educated. As a student at L'Ecole Centrale, Rillieux displayed extraordinary talent in engineering, and at age twenty-four, he became an instructor of applied mechanics at the school. In 1830, he published several papers on the mechanics of steam and steam engines. He developed a theory of "multiple-effect evaporation" that became the basis of his revolutionary invention. Rillieux's work finally reached the United States, and he was offered several jobs, including that of chief engineer in a major New Orleans sugar factory. Within a short time, factories throughout Louisiana were installing his refining system.

In 1854 he returned to Paris, where he turned his attention to experimenting with sugar beets. In 1881, he patented a process of heating juices with vapors, still used in many factories today. The inventions of Rillieux have been heralded as "the most significant, precedent-making inventions in the sugar industry," "the greatest in the history of American chemical engineering," and "the invention that brought the greatest savings to all branches of chemical engineering."

UNITED STATES AND BRITAIN BEGIN INTERCEPTING SLAVE SHIPS ALONG AFRICA'S WEST COAST

In the Webster-Ashburton Treaty, the U.S. and British governments jointly agreed to patrol Africa's west coast to intercept vessels involved in smuggling slaves to their territories.

VERMONT BLOCKS ENFORCEMENT OF FUGITIVE SLAVE ACT

The Vermont legislature blocked enforcement of the Fugitive Slave Act of 1793, which allowed owners to recover runaway slaves.

TRUTH BECOMES ANTISLAVERY ACTIVIST

On **JUNE 1**, Sojourner Truth (1797?–1883) left Manhattan to begin a career as an antislavery activist. She offered her services to the abolitionist movement as a speaker on religion and against slavery. Sojourner

Sojourner Truth's wit, gift of song, and force of logic made her one of the most popular lecturers on slavery, women's rights, temperance, prison reform, and conditions for working people.

Truth thereafter devoted her life to helping slaves. As an ardent speaker for temperance, prison reform, improved conditions for working people, and women's suffrage, she became one of the most famous abolitionists.

◈ Truth, born Isabella Baumfree in about 1797, was owned by a Dutch master in New York, from whom she learned to speak English. While a child, her parents died, and she was subsequently sold and resold until she finally became the property of John Dumont of New York. She was a slave for more than forty-six years and saw most of her thirteen children sold into bondage. When New York freed slaves in 1827, Dumont refused to free Baumfree, so she ran away.

In 1843, Baumfree decided that she had important things to accomplish, so she left her job as a domestic servant, gathered her belongings, and set out to teach and preach against slavery. She later took the name "Sojourner" because of her travels. It is said that she asked the Lord for another name, and he gave her "Truth," because, as she remarked, "I was to declare truth unto people." Truth impressed her audiences with her oratorical abilities. Few would guess she was illiterate.

Truth eventually settled near Battle Creek, Michigan. There were many Underground Railroad stations in this area of western Michigan, and Truth helped escaped slaves flee to Canada. During the Civil War, she helped nurse wounded soldiers and urged President Abraham Lincoln to allow northern Blacks to serve in the Union forces. In 1864, she met with Lincoln in the White House. Truth advised freed slaves to purchase land and get an education. She died at the age of eighty-six and was buried in Battle Creek.

CONVENTION OF COLORED MEN MEETS IN BUFFALO

From **AUGUST 15** to **22**, the National Convention of Colored Men convened in Buffalo, New York. Henry Highland Garnet, one of the supporters of the Liberty Party, delivered "An Address to Slaves of the United States," a controversial speech that supported a slave revolt and general strike. Frederick Douglass, one of the delegates, strongly condemned Garnet's speech. Other leaders, such as Samuel Ward and Charles B. Ray, participated in the convention activities. Amos G. Beman of New Haven, Connecticut, was elected president of the convention.

Garnet's powerful address called upon Blacks to disrupt slavery:

> Brethren, arise, arise! Strike for your lives and liberties. Now is the day and the hour. Let every slave throughout the land do this, and the days of slavery are numbered. You cannot be more oppressed than you have been — you cannot suffer greater cruelties than you have already. Rather die freemen than live to be slaves. Remember that you are FOUR MILLION! . . . Let your motto be resistance! resistance! RESISTANCE!

Garnet was criticized for being badly advised by the Garrisonians, who affirmed working to abolish slavery through established means. Garnet was quite disappointed when the Garrisonians steered the convention delegates away from physical violence by a vote of nineteen to eighteen. In response to a lack of endorse-

Henry Highland Garnet, a former slave educated at Oneida Theological Institute in New York, became one of the most influential African Americans between 1840 and 1870. Garnet urged slaves to rebel and even to die rather than to continue to live as slaves. Such remarks were condemned by more conservative abolitionists, including Frederick Douglass.

ment, Garnet replied, "If it has come to this, that I must think as you do, because you are an abolitionist, or be exterminated by your thunder, then I do not hesitate to say that your abolitionism is abject slavery."

LIBERTY PARTY NOMINATES BIRNEY FOR PRESIDENT

On **AUGUST 30** and **31**, the antislavery Liberty Party met in Buffalo, New York, and nominated James Birney of Michigan for president and Thomas Morris of Ohio for vice president. The party's platform opposed extension of slavery into new territory but made no statement about annexing Texas, which would bring another slave state into the Union.

CONVENTION OF BLACKS MEETS IN DETROIT

From **OCTOBER 23** to **27**, a state convention of Michigan Blacks met in Detroit. The convention discussed many of the problems confronting free Blacks through-

out the state and region and ended with a strongly worded petition against oppression and a call for Blacks to strongly "defend our liberties, prove to our oppressors, and the world, that we are determined to be free." In addition, it strongly condemned laws designed to discriminate against Blacks and poll taxes designed to "tax without representation."

1844 FIRST BLACK AMERICAN TO PASS THE BAR

Macon B. Allen (1816–1874) passed the bar examination in Maine, becoming the first licensed African American attorney in the United States. The following year, he became the first Black attorney to practice law in Boston, having been admitted to the bar in Suffolk County, Massachusetts, in May 1845.

Allen became a justice of the peace in 1848 and practiced law in the state until 1870.

KNIGHTS AND DAUGHTERS OF TABOR ESTABLISHED

Blacks in Cincinnati formed Knights and Daughters of Tabor, organizations dedicated to the eradication of slavery by any means. This secret society spread to a few other cities, including St. Louis, where the members called themselves the Knights of Liberty. It is believed that the order may have grown to as many as 50,000 members.

PROTEST AGAINST "JIM CROW" SCHOOLS IN BOSTON

Boston Blacks held mass meetings to protest segregated "Jim Crow" schools and other instances of inequality.

LEGISLATORS DEBATE ANNEXATION OF TEXAS

On **JUNE 8**, the U.S. Senate overwhelmingly rejected the Texas annexation treaty, which would have brought another slave state into the Union. Henry Clay and Martin Van Buren, both presidential candidates, opposed the treaty. The proslavery and southern wing of the Senate was outmaneuvered by the large and growing group of antislavery legislators. But on December 3, President John Tyler appealed to Congress in favor of the annexation of Texas.

ALABAMA BAPTIST CONVENTION CALLS FOR DISCUSSION OF SLAVERY

In **DECEMBER**, the Alabama Baptist Convention called for a meeting of the Southern Baptists to discuss the slavery issue, in response to the northern-controlled Foreign Mission Board of the church, which had declared slaveholding a barrier to appointment as a missionary.

GAG RULES ON ANTISLAVERY PETITIONS REPEALED

On **DECEMBER 3**, the so-called gag rules, a set of resolutions from 1836 preventing members of the U.S. House of Representatives from debating antislavery petitions, were repealed.

Arguing that such rules were unconstitutional (violating the right of petition), John Quincy Adams and Joshua Giddings had hammered away at these restrictive resolutions until they were repealed in this year.

1845 CLAY FOUNDS *True American*

Cassius M. Clay (1810–1903) founded the antislavery journal *True American*, in Lexington, Kentucky.

Clay, a devout abolitionist, became one of the founders of the Republican Party in 1854. In 1861, he was selected to be U.S. ambassador to Russia; he was reappointed and remained in the position until 1869.

DOUGLASS BEGINS SPEAKING TOUR IN ENGLAND

In 1845, in Liverpool, England, Frederick Douglass spoke on an antislavery campaign. Many who heard him questioned whether such an eloquent speaker could really be an ex-slave. Douglass had left for England to escape violent reaction to his just-published autobiography, *Narrative of the Life of Frederick Douglass*, which revealed his treatment as a slave in Baltimore. Even on the steamer *Cambria*, Douglass was refused cabin accommodations. Abolitionist supporters resolved the problem, and he was asked to lecture on the ship. One speech so angered some passengers that they threatened to throw him overboard. Douglass spent two years in England on the speaking tour.

FLORIDA AND IOWA ENTER UNION

On **MARCH 3**, Florida joined the Union as a slave state, and Iowa joined as a free state. The two new states were admitted at the same time by Congress to continue the principle of balanced representation between slave and free states.

SEGREGATED SCHOOLS CONTINUE TO OPERATE IN BOSTON

By 1845, Massachusetts Blacks had a high degree of political and legal equality with whites, including being able to send their children to the public schools in Salem, New Bedford, Nantucket, Worcester, and Lowell. Only Boston maintained segregation. Boston Blacks, rejected at almost every local level in their attempt to achieve equal school rights, turned to legislative appeals.

MARYLAND SLAVES REVOLT

In **JULY**, as many as seventy-five slaves from three counties in Maryland armed themselves and started marching to freedom toward the Pennsylvania state line when they were surrounded by whites near Rockville, Maryland. The bloody encounter left many slaves dead and thirty-one captured. Several managed to escape.

FIRST BLACK U.S. DIPLOMAT APPOINTED

In **OCTOBER**, William A. Leidesdorff (1810–1848) was named subconsul to the Mexican territory of Yerba Buena (San Francisco), becoming the first U.S. Black diplomat and public official.

◆ Leidesdorff became one of San Francisco's leading citizens during the first half of the nineteenth century. He arrived in San Francisco as a seaman from the Virgin Islands, became a naturalized citizen, and within a short time was regarded as one of the city's most prominent businessmen. In 1847, Leidesdorff launched the first steamboat on San Francisco Bay. In September 1847, he was elected to San Francisco's first town council. He became the town treasurer in 1848, and served on the three-person committee that established San Francisco's first school. He built the first hotel in the city and organized the first horse races in the state. He died in San Francisco at the age of thirty-eight. The city of San Francisco has recognized the contributions of William Leidesdorff by naming a street in the financial district in his honor.

1846 BLACKS GRANTED LAND IN NEW YORK

Gerrit Smith, an ardent abolitionist, granted forty to sixty acres of land in northern New York State to each of three thousand Blacks. It is believed that this generous grant was an experiment to encourage independent farming as well as a way to help Blacks secure suffrage, since land ownership was a requirement for voting. Two years later, only about thirty families had been successful. Poor soil and lack of funds contributed to widespread failure.

NEW JERSEY FINALLY ABOLISHES SLAVERY

In this year, the New Jersey legislature, after repeated unsuccessful efforts, finally passed a law to abolish slavery. The law declared "that slavery in this state be and it is hereby abolished." Just two years before, in 1844, a state constitutional convention failed to abolish slavery, and unlike Massachusetts, the state courts had made no definitive decisions that effectively abolished slavery.

BOSTON SCHOOL BOARD RULES
ON SEGREGATED SCHOOLS

The segregation of schools in Boston, Massachusetts, continued to provoke protest among Blacks in the city. Blacks challenged the school board to provide equal educational opportunity to its Black students. The school board responded by providing justification for segregation with the following declaration:

In applying these principles to the case of colored children we maintain,

1. That their peculiar physical, mental and moral structure, requires an educational treatment, different, in some respects, from that of white children. Teachers of schools in which they are intermingled, remark, that in those parts of study and instruction in which progress depends on memory, or on the imitative faculties, chiefly, the colored children will often keep pace with the white children; but, when progress comes to depend chiefly on the faculties of invention, comparison, and reasoning, they quickly fall behind.

2. That the number of colored children, in Boston, is so great, that they can be advantageously placed in separate schools, where all needful stimulus, arising from numbers and competition, may be felt, without their being degraded or discouraged.

3. That they live so compactly, that in very few (if in any) cases, is it at all inconvenient to attend the special Schools provided for them.

4. That the facts, connected with the origin and history of these Schools, show, that, without them, the colored people would have remained ignorant and degraded, and very few would have been found in the Schools.

5. That if these special Schools were now abolished, the number of colored children in the Public Schools would be greatly diminished, while serious injury would also be done to the other Schools, and no benefit would result.

6. That the majority of the colored, and most of the white people, prefer the present system.

As, then, there is no statute, nor decision of the civil Courts, against classifying children in schools according to a distinction in races, color, or mental and physical peculiarities, the Committee believes that we have the right to classify on these principles; nor do we believe, that, by so doing, we defeat the intent, or violate the spirit, of the law, the Constitution, or the invaluable common-school system established by our fathers; nor in any way infringe the rights of the colored child, or degrade the colored people. These Schools were established for their special benefit: for the same reason we would have them vigorously sustained. No man, colored or white, who understands their real value to the colored people, would seek their destruction.

While, therefore, your Committee proposed no change in the policy of this Board, they recommend the adoption of the annexed Resolution, as expressive of their opinions.

Respectfully submitted,
WILLIAM CROWELL,
JOSEPH W. INGRAHAM,
DAVID KIMBALL

Resolved, That, in the opinion of this Board, the continuance of the separate Schools for colored children, and the regular attendance of all such children upon those Schools, is not only legal and just, but is best adapted to promote the education of that class of our population.

SLAVE HUNTERS ARRESTED IN MICHIGAN

When a band of slave hunters demanded that a family of escaped slaves be turned over as fugitives, the slave hunters were arrested and charged with attempted kidnapping. They were seeking Adam Crosswhite and his family, who had escaped from slavery in Kentucky and settled in Marshall, an area of Michigan where many antislavery New Englanders had settled. While the slave hunters were held, the Crosswhites escaped to Canada. News of the arrest received national attention. Henry Clay and other southerners denounced Michigan in Congress and demanded punishment for those who had let the slaves escape. The case led to passage of the Fugitive Slave Act of 1850, whereby slave hunters could retrieve escaped slaves anywhere in the United States.

WILMOT PROVISO DEBATED IN CONGRESS

When President James K. Polk asked Congress for funds to purchase land from Mexico after the Mexican War ended, an amendment known as the Wilmot Proviso was appended to the appropriations bill in the U.S. House of Representatives. In this proviso, David Wilmot of Pennsylvania used language taken directly from the Northwest Ordinance of 1787: "Neither slavery nor involuntary servitude shall ever exist in any part of" the land acquired from Mexico. Although the bill passed the House, the Senate adjourned before acting on the legislation. Southern senators, led by John C. Calhoun, insisted that Congress could not

A SLAVE FATHER SOLD AWAY FROM HIS FAMILY.

Children in abolitionist families were often informed at an early age about the conditions of slavery through publications such as this primer.

pass such a law and that it was up to the residents of the territory to decide. The question of slavery in the territory thus remained undecided.

AMERICAN MISSIONARY ASSOCIATION FOUNDED

On **SEPTEMBER 3**, the American Missionary Association (AMA) was organized to train and educate slaves. It was the first such organization to educate southern slaves in an organized, consistent manner. Before the Civil War, the AMA was both a missionary and an abolitionist society. After the war began, it focused more heavily on providing education to freed slaves.

◈ On September 17, 1861, the AMA opened its first school on the grounds of Chesapeake Female College,

across the Hampton River in Virginia. On July 23, 1863, it opened its first school for Blacks in North Carolina in New Bern. Other schools were opened in Morehead, Roanoke Island, and Beaufort by autumn. Although the AMA had goals to educate both Black and white students in the same school, it deviated from its plan when it opened an all-white school in Beaufort in December 1866. Blacks wanted this school closed, but the AMA resisted, because it believed it had a mission to educate Blacks and whites, even if in separate schools.

By 1868, the AMA had more than five hundred teachers and missionaries in the South and border states. AMA teachers often lived and worked with

Black families, but they often failed to recognize the richness of the Black culture. It was not uncommon to find racial prejudice among some AMA teachers. The AMA's most lasting contribution was the many colleges it established, including Fisk University, Berea College, Atlanta University, Talladega College, Hampton Institute, Tougaloo College, Tillotson College, LeMoyne Institute, and Straight University (now Dillard University).

1847 ANTISLAVERY ALPHABET PUBLISHED

Many young children learned their alphabet from a book called *Anti-Slavery Alphabet*, published in this year, in which letters were associated with the evils of slavery. For example:

A is for Abolitionist,
A man who wants to free
The wretched slave, and give to all
An equal liberty.

W is for Whipping post,
To which the slave is bound,
While on his naked back, the lash
Makes many a bleeding wound.

Later, *Uncle Tom's Cabin* was produced in a picture-book format for younger readers, and the American Anti-Slavery Society published a free children's magazine, *The Slave Friend*, to evoke sympathy for the plight of slaves. Young people joined junior antislavery societies, boycotted cotton clothing, and refused to eat candy, because cotton and sugar cane were produced by slaves. Children accompanied their parents to antislavery lectures and some made clothing for escaped slaves. Children of "conductors" on the Underground Railroad also helped escaping slaves.

FIRST BLACK GRADUATES FROM AMERICAN MEDICAL SCHOOL

David John Peck graduated from Rush Medical College in Chicago. He was the second African American to receive a medical degree. Dr. James McCune Smith was considered the first.

LIBERIA DECLARES INDEPENDENCE

On JULY 26, President Joseph Jenkins Roberts declared his country, Liberia, an independent republic about twenty-five years after the first free African Americans journeyed to the colony of Cape Mesurado. Roberts was a native of Virginia.

KENTUCKY SLAVES ESCAPE TO FREEDOM

On SEPTEMBER 6, the *Louisville Democrat* reported that nearly fifty Kentucky slaves had escaped across

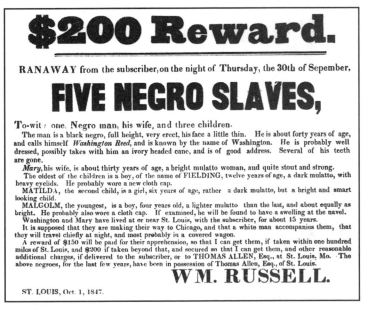

By 1847, when this broadside was issued, entire families were escaping to freedom together.

the Ohio River. The article mentioned that slave property was becoming "entirely insecure" in the river counties.

North Star BEGINS PUBLICATION

On **DECEMBER 3**, in Rochester, New York, Frederick Douglass and Martin Delany began publishing the *North Star*, an abolitionist newspaper. As the most sought-after speaker on slavery, women's suffrage, and other subjects, Douglass had raised thousands of dollars to help found the paper. The *North Star* became one of the most widely read antislavery newspapers in the country. Douglass finally had a forum by which to address the Black population in this country. Douglass's cofounder, Martin Delany, was a militant abolitionist and agent on the Underground Railroad. Douglass used his own home in Rochester as an Underground Railroad station.

1848 KENTUCKY SLAVES ATTEMPT ESCAPE

About seventy-five slaves from Fayette County, Kentucky, made a break for the Ohio River. Led by a white college student, the slaves were pursued by slaveholders. They were finally surrounded, and after several encounters, were forced to surrender. A number of slaves were killed, and as many as forty were tried for making a "public insurrection." Three of them were executed, and their white leader was sentenced to twenty years in prison.

SLAVEHOLDERS TRY TO STOP RUNAWAYS

Maryland slaveholders met to adopt measures to stop runaway slaves. It was believed that more slaves escaped to the North through Maryland than through any other state. For example, the *Baltimore Sun* reported that "in Cecil County, slaves are running away in droves." In Charles County, a "strange and singular spirit" appeared to have engulfed the bondservants; more than eighty fled in a single group.

SLAVES WIN SUIT FOR MALTREATMENT

In the case of *State* v. *Bowen* in South Carolina, the state brought a complaint under the 1740 act against an owner of twenty-one slaves for not supplying them with sufficient food and clothing. In this unique situation, the magistrate decided against the owner. When the owner appealed to the supreme court, the following circumstances of the case were revealed:

> The defendant did not give his negroes enough even of meal — the only provisions which he did give them.

Five bushels of meal weekly, the largest quantity stated by any witness, was clearly insufficient for a family of eight whites and twenty-one slaves. It appears by the testimony of Jackson, the defendant's overseer, that even this supply was not regular. The grown negroes had only a quart of meal a day. Many days, he says, they had no meal. Sometimes it gave out on Thursday and sometimes on Friday. They would then have a quart to last them till Monday evening. The stinted allowance, when withheld, must have reduced the wretched slaves to famine. For seventeen months, Jackson did not know that shoes had been given to them. Their feet were frostbitten and sore. During the same period no clothes were given to them.

WOMEN'S RIGHTS CONVENTION HELD AT SENECA FALLS

On **JULY 19** and **20**, the world's first Women's Rights Convention was held at Seneca Falls, New York, linking women's rights and antislavery causes for the first time. Frederick Douglass was in attendance; he seconded the women's suffrage motion introduced by Elizabeth Cady Stanton, the convention organizer. He was the only prominent man at this convention.

FREE-SOIL PARTY FORMED

On **AUGUST 9**, the Free-Soil Party, resulting from a merger of all antislavery groups, including the Liberty Party, was formed in New York to oppose the extension of slavery into the territories secured during the Mexican War and to support free homesteads for settlers. Many Black abolitionists attended the organizational meeting of this political party. A number of well-established politicians and businessmen were also attracted to the party, including Martin Van Buren, the party's first presidential candidate. The campaign slogan was "Free Soil, Free Speech, Free Labor, and Free Men."

The party was active during both the 1848 and 1852 elections, but by 1854, it had merged with the Republican Party.

CRAFTS MAKE INGENIOUS ESCAPE FROM SLAVERY

On **DECEMBER 26**, William and Ellen Craft escaped from slavery in Georgia. Ellen (1826–1897) impersonated a slaveholder and William pretended to be her servant in one of the most celebrated slave escapes in history.

Ellen was the daughter of a slave master, and her light skin enabled her to pass as a white person. The slave master's wife had given Ellen to her daughter as a wedding present. After Ellen married William Craft, they decided to escape to the North. They traveled for four days by train from Georgia to Philadelphia. Ellen dressed as a man; she faked ill health by walking with a limp, carrying her arm in a sling, and covering her face with a bandage. When asked, William explained that he was accompanying his master north to seek medical care. Abolitionists in Philadelphia protected them from slave hunters until the Crafts could sail to England, where they learned to read and write. They wrote a book about their escape, entitled *Running a Thousand Miles for Freedom*. They returned to the United States with their five children in 1868, bought a plantation, and opened a trade school for Black people.

1849 AMERICAN BAPTIST FREE MISSION SOCIETY FORMS COLLEGE

The American Baptist Free Mission Society established New York Central College in McGrawville, New York. The college admitted both races and sexes, appointed a Black to the faculty, adopted the manual-labor system of education, and forbade the use of tea, coffee, alcohol, and tobacco. Some whites opposed an integrated, state-supported school. They charged that the college promoted a "mottled conglomerate of insanities" — miscegenation, women's rights, abolitionism, and socialism. By 1858 the college was bankrupt.

BLACK PROFESSOR TEACHES AT WHITE UNIVERSITY

Charles L. Reason (1818–1893) became the first Black professor at a predominantly white university. He was named professor of belles-lettres, Greek, Latin, and French at New York Central College, in McGrawville, New York. He was also an adjunct professor of mathematics.

CIVIL RIGHTS LEADER ARRIVES IN CALIFORNIA

Mary Ellen Pleasant arrived in San Francisco with her husband during the Gold Rush. She opened a restaurant and boarding house, where many prominent Californians stayed. She also managed estates and made loans and is said to have run houses of assignation.

During the 1850s and 1860s, Pleasant was active in rescuing slaves who were illegally held in rural areas. She helped secure passage in 1863 of a state law in California that gave Blacks the right to testify in court and the right to ride on San Francisco's streetcars. Later, Pleasant returned to the East and was believed to have contributed funds toward John Brown's raid at Harpers Ferry. She then returned to California

and secured employment with Thomas Bell, a banker. Pleasant died in 1904. She remains a mysterious and controversial figure in California's history.

DEGRASSE BEGINS MEDICAL CAREER

John V. DeGrasse received his medical degree from Bowdoin College. Although he was considered by some sources to have been the first African American to receive a medical degree, he was preceded by Dr. James McCune Smith (1837) and Dr. David John Peck (1847). On August 24, 1854, John V. DeGrasse became the first Black physician to be admitted to the Massachusetts Medical Society. DeGrasse served in the Army Medical Corps during the Civil War and was one of eight African Americans commissioned as surgeons.

Roberts v. *City of Boston* DEBATES INTEGRATION IN SCHOOLS

Benjamin Roberts filed the first school integration suit on behalf of his daughter, Sarah, who tried to

Charles Sumner, one of the most outspoken opponents of slavery, argued for desegregated schools in 1849, and when he was elected to the U.S. Senate, he became a powerful voice in Congress in favor of abolition.

enter an all-white Boston school the previous year. A Boston city ordinance provided for segregation of Black and white students. Education was one of the most sought-after privileges of free Blacks, but most free public schools were closed to them. Charles Sumner, a white attorney, and his Black assistant, Robert Morris, represented Sarah Roberts. Sumner argued that the Massachusetts constitution declared all men free, equal, and entitled to equal protection of the laws and that to deprive Blacks of equal education denied them their rights as defined in the state constitution. The Massachusetts Supreme Court ruled in favor of the city of Boston in 1850 and thus established a "separate but equal" precedent. Although Sumner and Roberts lost the case, their argument was so compelling that in 1855 the Massachusetts legislature declared that "no person shall be excluded from a public school on account of race, color, or religious opinion."

SEVERAL BLACK CONVENTIONS HELD

State conventions of Blacks were held in Ohio, New Jersey, and Connecticut to discuss the conditions of free Blacks and slaves. The conventions also evaluated progress and how to target resources appropriately.

VIRGINIA DEFINES STATUS OF BLACKS

The Virginia code of 1849 declared that "every person who has one-fourth part or more of negro blood shall be deemed a mulatto, and the word 'negro' . . . shall be construed to mean mulatto as well as negro."

In South Carolina, the terms "negroes, mulattoes, and persons of color" had no specific definitions. According to the court of appeals, there had to be a "visible mixture," but that depended upon a person's "reputation" among his neighbors. In Alabama, the term *mulatto* was used to identify a person "of mixed blood, descended, on the part of the mother or father, from negro ancestry, to the third generation inclusive, though one ancestor of each generation may have been a white person." Throughout most of the other states, the term *mulatto* included a person with one Black grandparent (a quadroon, with one-quarter Black ancestry) or great-grandparent (an octoroon, with one-eighth Black ancestry).

LINCOLN INTRODUCES ANTISLAVERY LEGISLATION

In **JANUARY**, Illinois representative Abraham Lincoln introduced antislavery legislation into Congress. He was blasted by South Carolina senator John C. Calhoun, who argued, "To destroy the existing relation between the free and servile races in the South would lead to consequences unparalleled in history." Lincoln planned to introduce a bill that would free children born of slave mothers in the District of Columbia. Lincoln's term as a representative in Congress ended in this year.

MISSOURI SUPPORTS POPULAR SOVEREIGNTY

On **MARCH 10**, the Missouri legislature went on record in support of "popular sovereignty," seeking to exclude Congress from intervening in slavery issues in territories. The legislature stated, "The right to prohibit slavery in any territory belongs exclusively to the people thereof."

TUBMAN ESCAPES FROM SLAVERY

In **JULY**, Harriet Tubman (1821?–1913) escaped from slavery in Maryland. It had been rumored that slaves on her plantation were to be sent into the Deep South. Tubman and two of her brothers escaped, but the brothers turned back, fearing the consequences if they were caught. Tubman made as many as nineteen trips into Maryland to rescue other slaves, including three of her brothers and sisters and her mother and father. She became one of the most venturesome conductors of the Underground Railroad, leading more than three hundred slaves to freedom.

Slave masters offered a reward of forty thousand dollars for Tubman's capture. She was clearly the most celebrated of the conductors, but there were many conductors, Black and white, who risked their lives to help slaves escape. During the thirty years prior to the Civil War, an estimated seventy-five to one hundred thousand slaves escaped to freedom.

Tubman supported John Brown's plan to seize the arsenal at Harpers Ferry. During the Civil War, Tubman worked as a nurse and a spy. She eventually settled in Auburn, New York, where she helped raise money for African American schools. She spent many of her last years in poverty before finally receiving a twenty-dollar monthly government pension for her work during the Civil War. She used much of her pension to help establish (in 1908) a home for elderly and poverty-stricken African Americans.

SLAVEHOLDER FOUND GUILTY OF MURDERING SLAVE

On **SEPTEMBER 1**, one of the most "wilful, malicious and deliberate" murders of a slave by a master occurred in Virginia. It was written that the slave's

Anticipating that she and her siblings might be sold to a chain gang in the Deep South, Harriet Tubman escaped from Maryland to Pennsylvania. She became one of the most celebrated agents of the Underground Railroad. If any slave in her parties faltered, she drew her gun and said, "You'll be free or die." This photograph shows Tubman, at the far left, with a group of people she conducted to freedom.

offenses, according to the master's allegation, were "getting drunk and dealing with two persons — white men" who were present and witnessed the whole of the horrible transaction, without interfering in any way to save the life of the slave. The opinion of the court provided the following narrative:

> The indictment contains fifteen counts, and sets forth a case of most cruel and excessive whipping and torture. The negro was tied to a tree and whipped with switches. When Souther [the master] became fatigued with the labour of whipping, he called upon a negro man of his and made him cob Sam with a shingle. He also made a negro woman of his help to cob him. And, after cobbing and whipping, he applied fire to the body of his slave, about his neck, belly and private parts. He then caused him to be washed down with hot water in which pods of red pepper had been steeped. The negro was also tied to a log, and to the bedpost, with ropes, which choked him, and he was kicked and stamped by Souther. This sort of punishment was continued and repeated until the negro died under its infliction.

The jury found Souther guilty of murder in the second degree. Under an act of 1847, the crime would have been murder in the first degree. However, Virginia passed a new act on August 15, 1849, defining murder to be "by poison, lying in wait, imprisonment, starving, or any willful, deliberate and premeditated killing, or in the commission or attempt to commit arson, rape, robbery or burglary." Omitted from the newer legislation were the words "wilful, malicious, and excessive whipping, beating, or other cruel treatment or torture," which had appeared in an 1819 law, or the "wilful and excessive whipping, cruel treatment" wording in the law of 1847. In both of these laws, the Souther case might have exacted a first-degree murder pronouncement on the master.

1850–1860 BLACKS SUBJECT TO SUMMARY EXECUTIONS

In this decade, of the forty-six Blacks known to have been executed for the murder of masters or overseers, twenty-six were summarily executed. Of the seventeen put to death for rape or attempted rape, twelve were killed by mobs.

PRODUCING THE "IDEAL SLAVE"

In order to produce the "ideal slave," the master performed a number of steps to reduce the slave to a "helpless and dependent" condition.

The first step was to establish and maintain strict discipline. Slaves were to obey at all times, in all circumstances, cheerfully and with alacrity. "Unconditional" submission was the goal. Slaves were not allowed to exercise will or judgment in opposition to a master's order; they were taught that the master governed absolutely.

The second step was to create a sense of personal inferiority. Slaves had to "know their place." They were made to feel the difference between "the place of the master and the slave," and that their African ancestry was a curse and their color a badge of degradation. All white people, no matter their position, had to be respected; slaves had to give way on the streets to whites of the lowest social position.

The third step was to train slaves to be in awe of the master's enormous power, instilling fear in the minds of the slaves. Slaveholders often responded to abolitionist challenges by increasing their authority over slaves and heightening this sense of fear. They required that slaves adhere to rigid rules and punished them severely if they were not followed. Some slaveholders on large plantations carried and used a whip or cane frequently, to create fear and to convey a sense of their own power.

The fourth step included teaching the bondservants to take an interest in the master's enterprise. It was important for the master to show the slaves that his improved status directly influenced their well-being. Many slaves accepted the master's standards of work and conduct.

The fifth step was to reconstruct the slave as a helpless and perfectly dependent individual. The master thus set out to keep the slave ignorant of all things that would encourage independence. Slaves were not allowed to "take care of themselves." The most dependent slaves were those kept on the land. Factory slaves were given a bit more space to roam about, which sometimes gave them a taste for independence. Slaves were encouraged to direct afterwork hours to rest and simple entertainment rather than education, so they would be less likely to develop or pursue their own ambitions or think of ways to provide for themselves.

These methods of producing the "ideal slave" were followed on many plantations. By exercising such control over their slaves, slave owners believed that they had little to fear as long as the law supported their peculiar institution.

1850

POPULATION OVERVIEW

TOTAL NUMBER OF BLACKS More than 3.6 million Blacks resided in the United States. They made up 15.7 percent (3,638,808) of the 23,191,876 million total residents.

FREE BLACKS AND SLAVES According to the Bureau of the Census, about 37 percent of the free Black population (434,495) were classified as mulattos. There were 3,204,313 Black slaves. Only about 1 in 8 Blacks was free. As many as 347,725 American families reported owning slaves in this year.

SLAVES IN RURAL AND URBAN AREAS The largest number of slaves lived on farms and plantations. Of the 3.2 million slaves in the United States in this year, no less than 2.8 million lived on farms and plantations. About 1.8 million lived on cotton plantations; the remainder worked on farms and plantations devoted to producing tobacco, sugar, and rice. About 400,000 (11 percent) of all slaves lived in towns and cities. Many worked in factories, most of which were located in small towns. Between 160,000 and 200,000 slaves (about 5 percent of all slaves) worked as industrial slaves. Four-fifths of these were owned by the manufacturers, who used their servants as laborers; others were rented out for specified time periods. In several major cities in the South, large numbers of slaves worked in iron, processed tobacco, and worked in the mills. In general, slaves worked as domestic servants, in shops, in factories (where health hazards were great), and as laborers building streets, bridges, and municipal installations (when cheap labor was necessary).

BLACK SETTLERS IN OREGON TERRITORY Blacks were among the emigrants traveling west on the Oregon Trail looking for better economic opportunities in

Washington and Oregon. George William Bush, a wealthy Black cattle owner, and his family headed for Oregon on a wagon train in 1844. Years later, a former slave named George Washington accompanied his adopted white family to Oregon. He ultimately founded a town in Washington called Centerville, now called Centralia. To encourage new settlers, Washington laid out two thousand lots and built churches, streets, and a public park. During the panic of 1873, Washington helped save his town by buying and importing food from other cities and providing jobs for the unemployed; Washington was seventy-six years old at this time.

ECONOMIC CONDITIONS OVERVIEW

BLACKS MINE FOR GOLD IN CALIFORNIA Half of California's two thousand Blacks worked in the gold-mining area. Most were free Blacks. As of 1850, these Blacks had come from three geographic regions: the free states, mainly New York and Massachusetts; the slave states of the South and the Deep South; and the border states of the South. Black prospectors were scattered throughout the mining district in places such as Downieville, Placerville, Grass Valley, Negro Bar, and Mormon Hall. Whites strongly resented their presence and often would not dig alongside them. The "jumping" of Black claims also occurred. At Mokelumne Hill, white miners directed a Black miner to a hillside they thought was worthless. The Black miner, however, later returned with a sack of gold.

◈ Two Black men, Kelsey from Massachusetts and a Black Methodist minister, discovered a sizable gold deposit on what was subsequently called "Negro Hill." It was located on the American River, not far from where it forks. Two years later, another strike occurred in the same general area. A sizable Black mining community began to grow, comprising Negro Hill and Little Negro Hill. The community had a store, boarding house, and homes of Black residents. By 1854, a white Methodist minister offered Sunday services; a year later, the Negro Hill community numbered four hundred.

Black miners, including slaves, increasingly became major figures in the Gold Rush. David Rogers of Arkansas found enough gold to purchase his freedom for one thousand dollars. When his master kept the money and refused to release Rogers, some whites raised enough money for him to buy his freedom and that of his family. They moved back to California. Coffey, a slave from Missouri, earned five thousand dollars in the mines and seven hundred dollars working at night. When he offered to buy his freedom, his owner took the money and sold him to another slave owner. Coffey made an agreement with his new master, guaranteeing his freedom if he could find enough gold to make the master rich. His plan succeeded. By 1860, Coffey and his family were living in Tehama County, California. Not all slaves were as fortunate; the Fugitive Slave Law extended into the mining districts as well as into the California cities.

COTTON PRODUCTION Two-thirds of the world's cotton crop was produced by the slave states at this time. About one-third of the crop went to the northern textile mills; the rest was exported to Europe. The demand for cotton in the North and in Europe caused some plantation owners to work the slaves night and day to meet demands.

SOCIAL CONDITIONS OVERVIEW

DEATH FROM "FEVER" HIGHER AMONG BLACKS According to the 1850 census, deaths from "fever" were substantially higher for Black people than for whites. This health problem was most acute in the lowlands of the Deep South, where many Blacks lived along the malarial riverfronts. Malaria often headed the list of causes of death enumerated by masters. In addition to malaria, yellow fever affected a large number of Blacks and whites. Epidemics took a large toll on whites in Charleston, Savannah, and New Orleans.

In 1853, about one-sixth of the entire population in New Orleans died from yellow fever, and, in 1855, about one-sixth of Norfolk's population died when a yellow fever epidemic ravaged the city. Blacks were spared from similar death tolls because of their greater resistance to the toxin of the yellow fever virus. Although many Blacks were affected by yellow fever, they did not die from it as often as whites did. On the other hand, Asiatic cholera, first identified in the United States in 1832, was more deadly to Blacks than to whites. It spread throughout the Mississippi Delta from New Orleans to the plantations of Louisiana and Mississippi. In 1833, cholera caused three hundred deaths in Lexington, Kentucky; killed many slaves in Savannah, Georgia; and caused many masters to abandon both crops and property to avoid the disease.

EDUCATION AVAILABLE TO BLACKS BEFORE THE CIVIL WAR Prior to the Civil War, education was relatively inaccessible to Blacks. Slaveholders strongly resisted educating their slaves because it was generally believed that educated slaves were a source of discontent

This etching shows slaves shipping cotton by torchlight along the Alabama River.

that could destroy the institution of slavery. In a number of cases, Quakers and others established schools to educate and "Christianize" slaves as well as free Blacks. Some of these early efforts were heroic and included the work of Cotton Mather, Thomas Bray, Anthony Benezet, Benjamin Franklin, Thomas Paine, Richard Allen, Absalom Jones, Primus Hall, and others. In addition to these outspoken and daring leaders, countless thousands of Blacks, slave and free, taught themselves and one another to read and write. Although such education was outlawed in many places, particularly throughout the South, clandestine schools were formed for slaves or free Blacks who craved education.

The overwhelming proportion of African Americans remained illiterate prior to the Civil War. A few attended college, but mostly in foreign countries. Before the Civil War, several Black schools (which later became colleges) were established, including Cheyney State (1837), Lincoln (1854), and Wilberforce (1856). It is no mystery that the first two of these schools were located in areas where large numbers of Quakers lived. It is also not surprising that the oldest known Black college, Wilberforce, was found in Ohio, the home of the largest number of antislavery societies and the largest number of Underground Railroad stations.

INTENSE RACIAL HATRED AMONG WHITE SETTLERS TO-WARD BLACK MIGRANTS IN WEST As free Blacks and runaway slaves moved westward, they found many of the same customs and laws they had left in the South. Parts of the West had laws prohibiting the migration of Black people. Many constitutional conventions of western states had heated debates concerning whether Blacks should be allowed to settle there. In 1844, antislavery members of the Iowa Constitutional Convention had to contend with opposing views such as these: "We would never consent to open the doors of our beautiful state and invite him [the Black] to settle our land." "The negro not being a party to the government, has no right to partake of its privileges." "There are strong reasons to induce the belief that the two races could not exist in the same government upon an equality without discord and violence."

In 1850, the Indiana Constitutional Convention was so overwhelmingly anti-Black that when a delegate proposed equal suffrage, his resolution was voted down by 122 to 1. One delegate argued, "The same power that has given him a black skin, with less weight or volume of brain has given us a white skin, with greater volume of brain and intellect; and that we can never live together upon an equality is as certain as that no two antagonistic principles can exist together at the same time." When a provision was introduced to exclude Black emigrants from Indiana, the members overwhelmingly approved it by a six-to-one margin.

By 1860, Nebraska, New Mexico, and Utah had passed legislation barring Blacks from voting or serving in the militia. Even the territory of Washington had limited voting rights to whites by 1853. It was made clear in newspapers that the West was "the land for the white man." Oregon's exclusion provision, passed in 1857, remained on the books until 1927. It is said that Oregon entered the Union in 1859 as a free state but with a Black exclusion provision acceptable to Congress.

MIGRATION TO CANADA For the most part, the number of slaves escaping to Canada was relatively small until 1850, when the Fugitive Slave Act was passed in the United States. It was then that fugitive slaves living in the northern part of the United States were no longer safe from bounty hunters. The only place where they could continue to live safely was in Canada.

PLANTATION CULTURE The distribution of plantations that grew cotton, tobacco, sugar, and rice was dictated primarily by climatic and soil conditions. A particular way of life, known as "plantation culture," developed among the slaveholding whites. Also, because so many slaves performed the labor on these plantations, the geography of the plantation became

the hearth of Black culture. Geographically, this culture took root in Virginia, the Carolinas, Georgia, Florida, Alabama, Mississippi, Louisiana, Kentucky, Tennessee, Arkansas, Missouri, and Texas. These states were "slave" states; that is, slave trading was legal in their boundaries.

Slaves were so entrenched in the southern economy by 1850 that advertisements for their sale could be found in many cities and towns from Maryland to Texas. Price was determined by a slave's age and ability to perform work. As the demand for agricultural products increased, workers were badly needed to clear land and cultivate crops. And as the demand for slaves increased, so did their price. Interstate slave-trading businesses were established to profit from this growing demand. Slave-trading firms in New Orleans, for example, were particularly aggressive, and within a short time, the city became one of the busiest slave markets in the South. New Orleans traders journeyed to other cities throughout the South to secure slaves. Some companies that sold hardware, dry goods, furniture, and agricultural implements also sold slaves — for slaves were considered goods, not human beings.

"SOLD DOWN THE RIVER" ENTERS AMERICAN LEXICON The phrase "sold down the river" derived from a reference to slavery. At this time, slaves from the older areas of the South could be sold to masters in the newer areas of the Cotton Belt, especially along the Mississippi River. Life in these areas was considered exceptionally harsh, as new planters attempted to make great profits from the labor of their slaves.

STATES PROHIBIT ENTRY OF BLACKS Constitutional conventions and legislatures in Illinois, Indiana, Iowa, and Oregon agreed to prohibit the entry of more Blacks. White voters gave these laws their overwhelming approval.

AMERICAN LEAGUE OF COLORED LABORERS FORMED
Samuel R. Ward became president of the newly founded American League of Colored Laborers, a union of skilled workers in New York. The League was organized to develop Black craftworkers and encourage Black-owned businesses.

BLACK PIONEER DISCOVERS PASS THROUGH ROCKIES
James P. Beckwourth (1798–1866?), a legendary Black pioneer, fur trader, army scout, and rancher, discovered a pass through the Sierra Nevada.
◈ Beckwourth, a mulatto, was born in Fredericksburg, Virginia. He explored many parts of the western

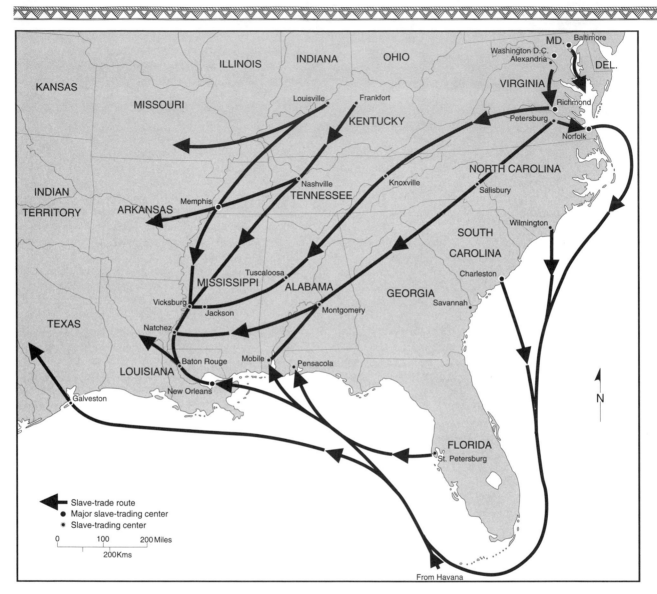

INTERNAL SLAVE TRADE, 1810-1860

The internal slave trade flourished after 1808, when the legal slave trade between the United States and Africa ended. Eastern farmers generally found it more profitable to sell their slaves than to own them. Slaves were transported by boat or marched along roads to towns along the lower Mississippi River and the Gulf coast.

United States, but he greatly expanded his expertise when he joined General William Ashley's Rocky Mountain Fur Company. Working as a hunter, trapper, and scout, Beckwourth acquired a unique knowledge of the territory and the people who lived there. He became a trusted friend of several Native American peoples, married first a woman of the Blackfeet

people and later a woman of the Crow people. It is believed he lived with the Crow people from 1826 to 1837. The Crow made him a chief, giving him the name Bull's Robe.

Beckwourth was most famous for his discovery of a valley in Nevada, later called the Beckwourth Pass, which became the main passageway for migrants moving to the West. Beckwourth built a combination home and trading post in the Sierra valley in 1852. Here, he sold food and fresh horses to those traveling west. Today, the pass he discovered can be found on California Route 70, also known as the Feather River Highway, north of Lake Tahoe, California. A town near the pass also bears Beckwourth's name. Beckwourth continued exploring for many years after he discovered the pass. He died among the Crow while on a mission for the U.S. government.

IRISH OUTNUMBER BLACKS AS SERVANTS

Irish servants outnumbered Black servants in New York City by ten to one. This proportion contrasted with data for 1830, which showed Blacks as the majority of New York City's servants. Blacks and Irish vied for jobs in many cities of the Northeast.

INDIANA UPHOLDS SEGREGATION

An Indiana court upheld segregation "because Black children are deemed unfit associates of Whites, as school companions."

CLAY PROPOSES RESOLUTIONS TO PRESERVE THE UNION

On JANUARY 29, Senator Henry Clay proposed a series of compromise resolutions that he hoped would enable the North and the South to preserve the Union. These resolutions eventually led to the Compromise of 1850.

TESTIMONY OF NONWHITES DENIED IN CALIFORNIA

In APRIL, the California legislature passed a law barring testimony by nonwhites in any case involving whites: "No Black or mulatto person or Indian shall be permitted to give evidence in favor of or against any white person. Every person who shall have one-eighth part or more of Negro blood shall be deemed a mulatto, and every person who shall have one-half Indian blood shall be deemed an Indian."

Within one year, the legislature amended the law to read that "Negroes or persons having one half or more Negro blood" could not testify in cases "to which a white person is a party." This law affected not only Blacks but also Native Americans and Chinese. It was clear that if no whites were willing to testify on behalf of an injured party who was Black, then Blacks could be victimized easily. In the *Pacific*, a San Francisco religious paper, an article ridiculed the legislation. It stated: "M. Dominguez, one of the signers of the Constitution of this state, is prohibited by the present law from giving testimony in our courts, being half Indian." This would apply to the Pico family, a highly influential and politically involved family, who had some African ancestry. Pio Pico was appointed governor of California in 1845, when it was still under Spanish rule.

COMPROMISE OF 1850 ADOPTED

From SEPTEMBER 9 to 12, Congress adopted five bills based on Henry Clay's original resolutions made in January. Known as the Compromise of 1850, the legislation admitted California to the Union as a free state but strengthened the Fugitive Slave Law, encouraging the apprehension of runaway slaves. The bill contained these provisions: (1) immediate admission of California as a free state; (2) organization of the other areas taken from Mexico into the territories of New Mexico and Utah without any restrictions on slavery; (3) the assumption of Texas's debt by the federal government; (4) abolition of the slave trade in Washington, D.C.; and (5) the passage of a stronger fugitive slave law. Some believe that this legislation precipitated increased migration of Blacks from the South. California contained only 972 Blacks at the time it was admitted to the Union.

FUGITIVE SLAVE LAW STRENGTHENED

On SEPTEMBER 18, President Millard Fillmore signed into law a stronger fugitive slave bill, providing for federal jurisdiction over runaway slaves and the prompt return of slaves to slave owners, and denying fugitive slaves trial by jury or the right to testify on their own behalf. Any white who attempted to help a slave escape became subject to a fine and/or imprisonment. In addition, the federal commissioner who awarded an escaped slave to his owner received a fee of ten dollars; if the commissioner did not return the slave, he received five dollars. Some called the law a "slaveholder's dream," since it required citizens and federal officers to become diligent slave catchers. Resistance was widespread. On October 21, the Chicago City Council passed an ordinance refusing to enforce the federal Fugitive Slave Law.

1851 CARY STARTS NEWSPAPER FOR BLACKS IN CANADA

Mary Ann Shadd Cary (1823–1893), born to free parents, moved to Windsor, Ontario, and started the *Provincial Freeman*, a weekly newspaper serving Blacks and their economic betterment in Canada.

Before moving to Canada, Cary had taught and had established schools for Blacks in Delaware,

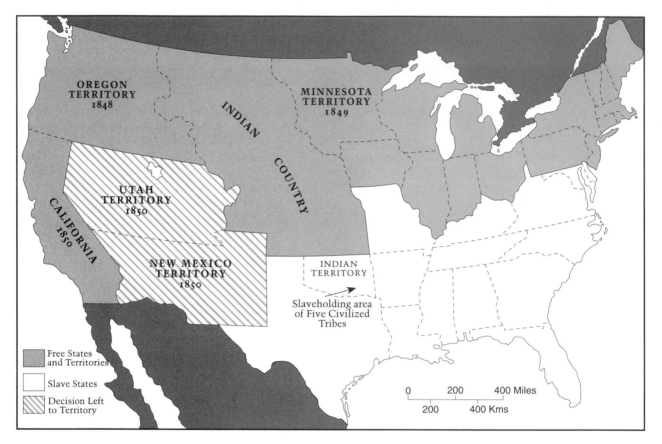

STATUS OF SLAVERY AFTER THE COMPROMISE OF 1850

The Compromise of 1850 was intended to end the conflict between free and slave states over the land acquired after the Mexican-American War. California was admitted to the Union as a free state; slavery was not restricted in the Utah and New Mexico territories.

Pennsylvania, and New York. The Fugitive Slave Act of 1850 angered Cary so much that she began helping slaves, particularly those who had escaped to Canada. In 1869, Cary moved to Washington, D.C., where she taught school and received a law degree from Howard University. She continued to be an activist — this time in the women's suffrage movement.

EMANCIPATED SLAVES LOSE RIGHTS IN VIRGINIA

According to the Virginia Constitution, "If any emancipated slave (infants excepted) shall remain within the state more than twelve months after his or her right to freedom shall have accrued, he or she shall forfeit all such right, and may be apprehended and

sold by the overseers of the poor, &c. for the benefit of the literary fund." In North Carolina, a slave could be sold by order of the court, the proceeds being equally divided between the wardens for the poor and the informer.

NELL PUBLISHES BLACK MILITARY HISTORY

Black abolitionist William C. Nell (1816–1874) published *Services of Colored Americans in the Wars of 1776 and 1812*, the first extended work on the history of American Blacks.

His book was revised in 1855 and published as *The Colored Patriots of the American Revolution*. In 1861, Nell was appointed a postal clerk in the U.S.

Henry Bibb was one of many former slaves who wrote about their lives as slaves.

Postal Service in Boston, Massachusetts. He was the first African American to hold a federal civilian job.

REFUGEES' HOME COLONY ESTABLISHED

Henry Walton Bibb (1815–1854), a slave, organized the Refugees' Home Colony in Canada, purchasing about thirteen hundred acres of land for the settlement of escaped slaves. Bibb wrote an autobiography entitled *Narrative of the Life and Adventure of Henry Bibb, An American Slave in 1849*. Bibb wrote of the brutality of slavery in answer to his former master:

> You may perhaps think hard of us for running away from slavery, but as to myself, I have but one apology to make, which is this: I have only to regret that I did not start at an earlier period. . . . To be compelled to stand by and see you whip and slash my wife without mercy when I could afford her no protection, not even

by offering myself to suffer the lash in her place, was more than I felt it to be the duty of a slave husband to endure, while the way was open to Canada. My infant child was also frequently flogged by Mrs Gatewood, for crying, until its skin was bruised literally purple. This kind of treatment was what drove me from home and family to seek a better home for them.

Strader v. *Graham* DECIDED

The U.S. Supreme Court ruled that slaves returning to Kentucky from Ohio had to be governed by Kentucky law.

SUMNER ELECTED TO U.S. SENATE

Charles Sumner (1811–1874), a lawyer and abolitionist, was elected to the U.S. Congress as a senator from Massachusetts. Sumner continued to denounce slavery during his tenure in Congress.

"THE BLACK SWAN" LAUNCHES HER CAREER

Elizabeth Greenfield (1808–1876), perhaps the first African American musical artist to gain recognition outside the United States, launched her career with a concert before the Buffalo Musical Society. Her concert caused a sensation both because it was relatively unknown for a Black woman to give a concert and because of the remarkable quality of her voice, which had the unusual range of baritone G on the bass clef to high C above the treble clef. A Buffalo newspaper called her "the Black Swan" in comparison to the famous white singer, Jenny Lind, who was known as "the Swedish nightingale."

◆ Born a slave in Natchez, Mississippi, Greenfield was taken to Philadelphia before her first birthday to be raised in the home of a white Quaker, Mrs. Greenfield, who gave her the family name. Her vocal talents were recognized early, and she gave solo performances at private parties in Philadelphia. After her patron died, Greenfield went to Buffalo, New York, where several philanthropic women provided opportunities for her to perform. Rave reviews followed each performance. Greenfield went to England in 1853 but was stranded when arrangements for her tour failed. Fortunately, Harriet Beecher Stowe, who was in London at the time, helped Greenfield make contact with the city's musical establishment. She then gave a number of concerts under the patronage of royalty, and eventually a command performance before the queen in 1854. Her concerts were enthusiastically reviewed by the London newspapers. She returned to the United

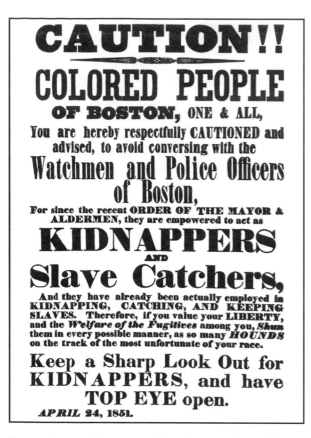

In reaction to the return of the fugitive slave Thomas Sims to Georgia, the Reverend Theodore Parker produced this broadside warning Black people in Boston to be wary of watchmen and police officers, who were acting as kidnappers and slave catchers.

States in 1854 and set up residence in Philadelphia, where she taught voice and performed occasionally.

FUGITIVE SLAVE IN BOSTON RETURNED TO GEORGIA

In **APRIL**, a Georgia slaveholder arrived in Boston to claim Thomas Sims, a seventeen-year-old Black male, as his fugitive slave. Sims had been arrested and placed in a federal building with an armed guard. Excitement and emotion ran high as abolitionists saw an opportunity to show the injustice of slavery, particularly the Fugitive Slave Law. City and federal officials assumed that mob action was imminent and put the military on watch to ensure that Sims was not res-

cued. The cost of securing Sims for his return to his master was astronomical.

In most such cases, particularly in the North, a trial was held to ensure the slaveholder's rights to his "property." During Sims's trial, every effort was made to control a growing crowd of Black and white citizens opposed to slave hunters, kidnappers, catchers, and the Fugitive Slave Law itself. Rather than use violence to rescue Sims, the crowd prayed. The commissioners held that Sims was to be returned to his master, despite Sims's pleas for freedom.

Just before dawn, about three hundred armed constables convened at the courthouse to escort Sims to a southbound ship. Along the route, abolitionists prayed aloud and expressed their shame at Boston's support of the Fugitive Slave Law. Throughout the city, church bells rang loudly to signal support for Sims's freedom as he was returned to slavery.

Antislavery proponents increasingly made daring efforts to help fugitive slaves, even when they had been arrested and imprisoned. Although the Fugitive Slave Law had recently been strengthened, abolitionists were not deterred. Abolitionists and residents of New York City, for example, came together to buy the freedom of James Hamlet, a free Black who had been arrested under the new Fugitive Slave Law. They were instrumental in preventing his return to slavery in the South. In Syracuse, thousands of citizens raided the sheriff's office, freed William "Jerry" Henry, a runaway slave, and helped him to escape to Canada. In many instances abolitionists were not afraid to storm the courtrooms and jails to free fugitive slaves.

WOMEN'S RIGHTS CONVENTION HELD

On **MAY 29**, the second Women's Rights Convention gathered in Akron, Ohio. Former slave, abolitionist, and women's rights advocate Sojourner Truth addressed the convention, delivering her famous "Ain't I a Woman?" speech.

SLAVE CATCHERS THWARTED IN PENNSYLVANIA

On **SEPTEMBER 11**, Blacks turned back a group of slave catchers in Christiana, Pennsylvania. One white person was killed and another was wounded. Blacks had been warned that the slave catchers were on their way, so that when the slave catchers arrived, they were confronted by armed Blacks. When the slave catchers asked the group to turn over their slave, the armed Blacks replied that "no such slave was among them." The standoff continued, and more Blacks from the surrounding areas came to lend support. As the situation escalated, the slave catchers decided to act before the standoff turned irrevocably in favor of the Blacks. They assaulted the Blacks, thinking that the Blacks would not risk their lives for the fugitive slave. But the Blacks beat back the assault with almost every kind of weapon (including guns) and chased the slave catchers away.

FUGITIVE SLAVE RESCUED IN SYRACUSE

On **OCTOBER 1**, as many as ten thousand Black and white abolitionists in Syracuse, New York, stormed a courtroom and rescued a fugitive slave, William "Jerry" Henry, who had been arrested by a U.S. marshal and readied for return to his master. After freeing Henry, the citizens of Syracuse helped him escape to Canada.

1852 DELANY ADVOCATES BLACK COLONY IN LATIN AMERICA

Martin Delany (1812–1885), a physician, abolitionist, colonizationist, and cofounder of the *North Star*, published *The Condition, Elevation, Emancipation and Destiny of the Colored People of the U.S., Politically Considered.* The work indicted the abolitionists for their failure to consistently fight for integration of Blacks into American society. He called for the establishment of a Black "Promised Land" in Central or South America as an answer to discrimination. The book was attacked by the white antislavery press and ignored by Frederick Douglass. But Delany's call for emigration received a warm response from some Blacks, and Delany became a major proponent of the colonization movement.

◇ Delany was born in Charles Town (in what is now West Virginia), the son of a slave father and a free Black mother. His grandparents had been brought from Africa as slaves. One grandfather was a Mandingo prince and the other a Golah village chief. When he was nineteen years old, Delany went to Pittsburgh, where he studied medicine with a white physician, became a leader of the city's Black community, and published the *Mystery*, the first Black newspaper west of the Allegheny Mountains. After the *Mystery* failed for financial reasons, he copublished the *North Star*. When the paper could not support two publishers, Delany left. He attended the medical school of Harvard College but left after the winter term because students protested his presence. He simply returned to Pitts-

burgh as Dr. Delany, since there were no licensing requirements for doctors at the time.

Delany served meritoriously as an army surgeon during the Civil War. During his tenure, he was promoted to the rank of major, the first African American to reach this rank. After the war, he worked with the Freedmen's Bureau and later became a trial judge in Charleston, South Carolina.

BLACKS PETITION FOR RIGHT OF TESTIMONY

Having been denied the right to testify in cases involving a white person, the Black leadership in California, particularly in San Francisco, began a petition drive to persuade state legislators to repeal the provisions denying Blacks the right of testimony on an equal basis with whites. The petition, organized and written by Mifflin W. Gibbs, Jonas Townsend, and William Newby, read as follows:

> To the Honorable the Legislature of the State of California:
>
> Your memorialists beg leave to represent, that by the Third Division of the Ninety-ninth Chapter of the Statutes of this State, entitled "An Act concerning Crimes and Punishments," passed April 16TH, 1850, Black and mulatto persons are rendered incompetent as witnesses to give evidence against white persons;
>
> That this provision of the Statute in effect denies to all such colored persons, the protection of law in the enjoyment of the rights of property and personal security; and the vicious and unprincipled take advantage of this disability and prey upon those rights with impunity.
>
> In the name of republicanism and humanity, we pray your Honorable body to repeal the aforesaid provision of the Statute, and restore to the colored people the right of protection which that provision withholds from them. And your memorialists, as in duty bound, will ever pray.
>
> *San Francisco, March 10, 1852*

Black leaders in other major cities of the state, including Sacramento, similarly responded to the restrictions of the testimony law. On January 10, a white Sacramento lawyer wrote, "The colored men of Sacramento County called upon me some days ago to draw up a petition to the legislature of California, requesting the repeal of the law which disqualify them as witnesses against white persons in civil and criminal actions."

SCHOOL FOR BLACK INDIGENT ORPHANS OPENS IN NEW ORLEANS

The Catholic Indigent Orphan's School formally opened in New Orleans. It was founded by a bequest for this purpose by Madame Bernard Couvent, the widow of Gabriel Bernard Couvent, a wealthy Black carpenter in the city.

Little is known for certain about the early life of Madame Couvent (née Justine Fervin). It is believed she was born in Africa and brought to New Orleans as a slave. After her marriage, she wanted to share her wealth with the poor, particularly by founding a school for orphans of free Blacks, many of whom had white fathers. She died in 1837, but more than fifteen years passed before the school was opened. The Couvent school was coeducational and taught the classics as part of its academic program. The teachers, who were all Black, were considered some of the best educators in the city. The school educated a number of writers, poets, artists, and leaders of the time. During Reconstruction (1865–1877), enrollment fell as Black children attended public schools, but the school never closed. Several local leaders were instrumental in saving the institution from economic ruin. It operates today as the Holy Redeemer School, under the auspices of the Catholic church.

Uncle Tom's Cabin PUBLISHED

In **MARCH**, Harriet Beecher Stowe published her novel *Uncle Tom's Cabin*. It was serialized in the antislavery newspaper *National Era* in June, and its immediate popularity was proven by its record-breaking sales — three hundred thousand copies by August 23 and more than one million copies in its first year.

The novel evoked sympathy for slaves among readers in the North and enraged readers in the South. It presented the cruelties of slavery through the selfless character of Tom, who rescued a white child but was then sold to a sadistic master, Simon Legree. Legree, incensed with Tom's virtue and quiet strength, had him whipped to death.

Uncle Tom's Cabin helped the antislavery movement build momentum. When challenged by critics stating that the book exaggerated the conditions of slavery, Stowe defended her claims through evidence presented in another book, *Key to Uncle Tom's Cabin*.

Stowe was born in 1811, and during her childhood she was greatly affected by her father's prayers for Africans and slaves. She visited a Kentucky plantation and had seen firsthand the conditions slaves were forced to endure. Stowe had also read about slavery from the writings of Josiah Henson, Lewis Clark, and Frederick Douglass. She was further encouraged to write *Uncle Tom's Cabin* by the passage of the Fugitive Slave Act of 1850.

MEANING OF FOURTH OF JULY FOR SLAVES

On **JULY 5**, Frederick Douglass delivered his well-known speech "What to the American Slave Is Your Fourth of July?" For the slave, Douglass propounded, "the Fourth of July is a sham . . . to cover up crimes which would disgrace a nation of savages. There is not a nation of the earth guilty of practices more shocking and bloody than are the people of the United States at this very hour."

1853   BLACKS PETITION FOR RIGHT TO JOIN MILITIA

Blacks petitioned the Massachusetts Constitutional Convention for the right to join the state militia.

BLACK WOMAN SETTLES IN CALIFORNIA

One of the most famous and prosperous settlers in California during the early 1850s was Biddy Mason, a forty-niner who rose from slavery to affluence. Mason, a thirty-two-year-old woman, traveled from Mississippi to California with three hundred wagons commanded by her master, Robert Smith. Mason's job was to drive and ensure the well-being of the cattle during the long trip. When they arrived in California, Smith decided to move again, to Texas. En route, the Smith party stopped to rest in Santa Monica. It was here that Smith's slaves, Biddy and Hannah, and their twelve children and grandchildren, submitted a legal petition and summoned local officials in Los Angeles to help secure their freedom. All were taken into custody by the sheriff, and their petition was presented before a judge. Biddy convinced the judge that they did not want to go to Texas. The judge declared that they were free and reproved Smith for promising them that their "condition" would be no different in Texas than in San Bernardino. (Four of the children had been born free in California but would be considered slaves in Texas.)

Although little is known of Hannah from this point, Biddy officially took the name of Biddy Mason and moved from Santa Monica to Los Angeles. She took up housecleaning and nursing to make a living. She also became well-known as a midwife. Biddy earned enough money in ten years to buy land just outside of Los Angeles. As the city grew, her land became valuable, and she became a wealthy woman. Over the years, she saved for and soon owned her own homestead. She used her wealth in many good causes — giving land and money to communities to establish schools, churches, and nursing homes. She often gave generously to help victims of disaster.

BLACK YMCA ORGANIZED
Anthony Bower organized the first Black Young Men's Christian Association (YMCA) in Washington, D.C.

BROWN PUBLISHES NOVEL
Clotelle, or The President's Daughter, the first novel by an African American writer, was written by historian William Wells Brown (1814–1884) and published by a British company. *Clotelle* describes the plight of a mulatto born in Thomas Jefferson's household.

Brown later published other works, including *The Escape* (1858) — the first play written by an African American — *The Black Man,* and *The Negro in the American Rebellion* (1867).

William Wells Brown trained as an apprentice printer with Elijah Lovejoy and was an agent of the Western Massachusetts Anti-Slavery Society. Often called America's first Black man of letters, Brown was a pioneer in writing Black history.

DOUGLASS TEACHES BLACK CHILDREN
In this year, Sarah Mapps Douglass (1806–1882) took charge of the girls' primary department of the Institute for Colored Youth in Philadelphia. She continued to teach at the Quaker-supported institute until her retirement in 1877. The institute, which later was reorganized as Cheyney State College, was noteworthy for the number of public school teachers who received their training there.

◈ Douglass was the daughter of a Quaker family. Her maternal grandfather had been a member of the Free African Society, and her father was one of the founders of the First African Presbyterian Church of Philadelphia. In the 1820s, Douglass had opened a school for Black children in the city, which later was supported by the Philadelphia Female Anti-Slavery Society. Through this society, Sarah met and became friends with many abolitionists, including Lucretia Mott, Charlotte Forten Grimké, and Sarah and Angelina Grimké. When Douglass and a number of other Blacks attended the wedding of Angelina Grimké and Theodore Weld, the noted abolitionist, the press in the city condemned their attendance as an intolerable incident of "amalgamation practice." Sarah exemplified what a Black woman could accomplish in the segregated society of the mid-1800s. She later married the Reverend William Douglass, rector of the St. Thomas Protestant Episcopal Church.

REMOND FORCES THEATERS TO ADMIT BLACKS
In this year, Sarah Parker Remond (1824–1894), an active member of the Salem Female Anti-Slavery Society and the Massachusetts and Essex County Anti-Slavery Societies, was handled so roughly by a policeman ejecting her from a Boston theater that she fell down the stairs. She sued for damages and forced the theater owners to admit Black spectators.

◈ Remond, the youngest daughter of John and Nancy Remond, grew up in the antislavery movement. Her father was a life member of the Massachusetts Anti-Slavery Society, and her brother, Charles, was the society's first Black lecturer. Nancy and her other daughters were members of the Salem Female Anti-Slavery Society, and because of their wealth, they met and were influenced by many major figures of the antislavery movement — William Lloyd Garrison, Wendell Phillips, and William Wells Brown. Like many wealthy Black families during this time, the Remonds encouraged their children to become educated and to "work against the traffic in human flesh." In 1835, Sarah was refused admission, after passing the examination, to Salem's high school. Her parents responded by moving to Newport, Rhode Island, where Sarah attended a private school for Blacks. In 1856, she was appointed a lecturing agent of the American Anti-Slavery Society working with a team of lecturers — including her brother Charles, Wendell Phillips, Abby Kelley, and Stephen Foster — who toured New York. Her success as a lecturer led her to be invited, in 1858, to speak before the National Women's Rights Convention.

In 1858, Sarah was invited to lecture in England. She toured England, Scotland, and Ireland under the sponsorship of Ladies and Young Men's Anti-Slavery societies. In a speech in 1859, Remond spoke eloquently of the suffering of slaves in America, and she extracted from the theme of sexual exploitation a common bond of womanhood between Black and white women: "If English women and English wives knew the unspeakable horrors to which their sex were exposed on southern plantations, they would freight every westward gale with the voice of their moral indignation, and demand for the Black woman the protection and rights enjoyed by the white." She spoke frequently of the "slave status" of the Black woman and worked to break down racial barriers within the abolitionist circles. While in England, she was encouraged to attend Bedford College for Ladies (now a part of the University of London). She remained in London, began her college education, and continued lecturing as a member of the London Emancipation Society and the Freedmen's Aid Association. She made a brief trip to the United States in 1866 to lecture on behalf of the Equal Rights Association, but she returned to Europe and then entered medical school in Florence, Italy. After completing her education, Sarah practiced medicine in Florence. Her strong opposition to racism in America compelled her to encourage her sisters, Maritcha Remond and Caroline Remond Putnam, to join her in Florence. She died there in 1894.

Uncle Tom's Cabin PERFORMED ON NEW YORK STAGE
On **MARCH 15**, *Uncle Tom's Cabin* opened in New York City at Purdy Theater, which provided a separate viewing area for "respectable" Blacks.

NATIONAL COUNCIL OF COLORED PEOPLE ESTABLISHED
On **JULY 6**, delegates from several states convened to form the National Council of Colored People. One of the primary items on their agenda was to encourage vocational training of Blacks.

Frances E. W. Harper, a Black poet, protested slavery and the unequal treatment of people on the basis of race and gender in her work. The following two stanzas are taken from "The Slave Auction," which appeared in her volume Poems of Miscellaneous Subjects.

> *The sale began — young girls were there,*
>   *Defenseless in their wretchedness,*
> *Whole stifled sobs of deep despair*
>   *Revealed their anguish and distress.*
>
> *And mothers stood with streaming eyes,*
>   *And saw their dearest children sold;*
> *Unheeded rose their bitter cries,*
>   *While tyrants bartered them for gold.*

1854 HARPER PUBLISHES POEMS
Frances Ellen Watkins Harper's volume of verse, *Poems on Miscellaneous Subjects*, was published in this year and within five years sold ten thousand copies.

Harper was born the daughter of free Blacks in Baltimore, Maryland. She published her first volume of poems, *Forest Leaves*, when she was only twenty years old. Despite her literary successes, Harper was best known as an antislavery lecturer and women's rights advocate. She was so eloquent that many did not believe she was a Black woman. Some thought she was a man; others, that her skin was painted black. *Iola Leroy,* her only novel, was published when she was sixty-seven years old. It has been rediscovered largely due to the work of Black feminists who hold her work in high regard.

FIRST BLACK UNIVERSITY CHARTERED

On **JANUARY 1**, Ashmun Institute, named after Jehudi Ashmun, a white emigrationist and the first president of Liberia, became the first Black college chartered in the United States. In 1866, it was renamed Lincoln University. The university, located in Lincoln University, Pennsylvania, was founded by the Reverend John Miller Dickey, a white merchant from Philadelphia, and his wife, Sara Emlen Cresson, "for the scientific, classical, and theological education of colored youth of the male sex." Lincoln was known originally as the "Black Princeton" because of its demanding curriculum and the fact that many of its first instructors came from the faculty of Princeton Theological Seminary.

No Black professors taught at Lincoln until 1932. For the first one hundred years of its existence, Lincoln had only male students; the first woman graduated in 1953. Since 1972, Lincoln has been part of the Pennsylvania Commonwealth System of Higher Education. Among its distinguished alumni are U.S. Supreme Court Justice Thurgood Marshall and actor Roscoe Lee Browne. In the school's first one hundred years, it graduated 20 percent of all Black physicians and 10 percent of all Black lawyers practicing in the United States. More recently, Lincoln has produced 25 percent of all Blacks receiving bachelor's degrees in physics. In 1987, Lincoln appointed its first Black female president — Dr. Niara Sudarkasa. Enrollment is currently about eleven hundred students.

REPUBLICAN PARTY FOUNDED, WITH ABOLITION ITS MAJOR GOAL

On **FEBRUARY 28**, a group of Whigs, Free-Soil Democrats, and members of the Liberty Party gathered in Ripon, Wisconsin, to discuss the Kansas-Nebraska bill. They agreed to form a new party if the bill was passed. Alvan E. Bovay, a lawyer in attendance, suggested that the new party be called "Republican" after the party of Jefferson, a champion of the small landholder and an opponent of slavery. After the Kansas-Nebraska Act became law, a Republican state convention was held in 1856 in Wisconsin to organize the party. John C. Frémont was selected as the presidential candidate; he campaigned to abolish slavery and to restrict polygamy in the territories.

FUGITIVE SLAVE RETURNED FROM BOSTON

In **MAY**, approximately two thousand federal troops suppressed mob attacks on the federal courthouse in Boston, Massachusetts, where Anthony Burns, a fugitive slave, was being held. On May 24, Anthony Burns had been arrested by a U.S. deputy marshal and held for his former slave owner, Colonel Charles Suttle of Alexandria, Virginia. Abolitionists were angered by federal and city police collusion in the incident. The next day, three distinguished civil rights and antislavery lawyers — Charles M. Ellis, a member of the Boston Vigilance Committee; Richard Henry Dana, Jr., known for successfully defending fugitive slaves; and Robert Morris, the most prominent Black civil rights lawyer in the country — joined forces to defend Burns. Morris had been a law clerk for Charles Sumner when he was the defense attorney in *Roberts* v. *City of Boston.*

That evening, Fanueil Hall was packed with citizens protesting Burns's arrest. A steady stream of abolitionist speakers echoed the urgent need to dismantle the Fugitive Slave Law. After speeches by Wendell Phillips and Theodore Parker, the angry crowd moved to Court Square, joining another crowd led by the Reverend Thomas Wentworth Higginson and Lewis Hayden, to break down the courthouse door to rescue Burns. When the door gave way, constables and deputies fired their pistols, and Higginson was wounded. In the scuffle, one deputy was killed. Military reinforcements were summoned, and the abolitionist crowd scattered. Many were arrested.

The abolitionists, seeing their hopes of rescuing Burns dashed, raised twelve hundred dollars to purchase him, but the federal government held fast to the Fugitive Slave Law and refused any such transaction.

As emotions escalated, police and soldiers surrounded the courthouse and guarded every conceivable entry or escape route. President Franklin Pierce himself told federal officials to spare no cost in supporting the Fugitive Slave Law. The court ruled that Burns had to return to slavery. To ensure his delivery, the entire Fifth Regiment of Artillery was called upon to escort him through the streets of Boston to a waiting ship. An additional fifteen hundred dragoons, marines, lancers, and almost the entire police force of Boston joined the parade that marched Burns to the dockside. The opposition had gathered as many as fifty thousand supporters of Burns's release. They cried "Shame!" as they started their march. At least one skirmish occurred when the crowd tried to

The case of Anthony Burns encouraged many states to pass personal liberty acts that would block the enforcement of the Fugitive Slave Law.

break through the police barricade to rescue Burns. As he was led onto the cutter *Morris*, the crowd began to pray.

Although Burns was returned to his owner, the incident was so intense that no fugitive slave was ever again returned from Massachusetts. The government spent in excess of forty thousand dollars to protect and return Burns to his slave owner, though the cost of any slave on the open market was about twelve hundred dollars. This disparity led many abolitionists to claim some degree of success from the incident.

KANSAS-NEBRASKA ACT

On **MAY 26**, Congress passed the Kansas-Nebraska Act, allowing settlers of these territories to choose whether to permit slavery there.

The act was introduced in the U.S. Senate by Stephen A. Douglas of Illinois. Douglas apparently had several reasons for sponsoring this legislation: He wanted southern support for his own political ambitions, he supported the idea of self-government, and he wanted to build a transcontinental railroad through the territory. The act repealed the Missouri Compromise of 1850, which prohibited slavery north of the southern boundary line of Missouri. The Kansas-Nebraska Act essentially opened northern territory to slavery.

BLACK CATHOLIC PRIEST ORDAINED

On **JUNE 10**, James A. Healy (1830–1900) was ordained a Catholic priest in Notre Dame Cathedral in Paris, France. Healy was the first Black American ordained a Catholic priest and later became the first Black American Roman Catholic bishop.

SUPREME COURT RULES FUGITIVE SLAVE LAW INAPPLICABLE IN CANADA

On **JULY 17**, the Supreme Court declared the Fugitive Slave Law inapplicable in the case of Joshua Glover, a fugitive slave who was freed from jail by an abolitionist mob and helped to Canada.

BLACK DELEGATES ATTEND NATIONAL EMIGRATION CONVENTION OF THE COLORED PEOPLE

On **AUGUST 24**, delegates from eleven states convened in Cleveland, Ohio, to discuss and develop a national plan for Black emigration. Although the delegates were primarily from Pennsylvania and Ohio, some of the most outspoken emigrationists were present — Dr. Martin Delany, James T. Holly, James M. Whitfield, and H. Ford Douglas. Delany, a physician and journalist, was perhaps the most prominent emigrationist at the meeting, and thus his views heavily influenced the convention's deliberations. The platform of the convention echoed that Blacks had been doomed to constant "disappointment, discouragement, and degradation." And because Blacks had no political power, and statutes and customs relegated them to inferior positions, they would never attain equality with whites. It was pronounced that the American Black must consider emigration or "face deterioration." The convention established a National Board of Commissioners, headed by Delany, to implement an emigration policy.

Delany's views were opposed by Frederick Douglass, who called colonization "unwise, unfortunate, and premature." Douglass argued, "We are Americans. We are not aliens. We are a component part of the nation. Though in only some of the States, are we an acknowledged necessary part of the 'ruling element,' we have no disposition, to renounce our nationality. We do not wish to form a separate nation in these United States." Douglass believed that whites would eventually grant full citizenship rights to Blacks.

DOUGLASS PROPOSES SOLUTION TO KANSAS CRISIS

On **SEPTEMBER 15**, Frederick Douglass, after evaluating the fighting among proslavery and antislavery forces, suggested that the Kansas issue could be solved by sending families of free Blacks there:

> Let it be known, throughout the country, that one thousand Colored families, provided with all the needful implements of pioneers, and backed up by the moral influence of the Northern people, have taken up their abode in Kansas, and slaveholders, who are now bent upon blasting that fair land with Slavery, would shunt it, as if it were infested with famine, pestilence, and earthquakes. They would stand as a wall of living fire to guard it. The true antidote, in that Territory, for black slaves, is an enlightened body of black freemen — and to that Territory should such freemen go.
>
> To the question, Can this thing be accomplished? we answer — Yes! Three cities can, at one, be named, in which, if proper means be adopted, nine hundred of the one thousand families can be obtained in three months, who would take up their abode as permanent settlers in Kansas the coming spring. New York City and its vicinity could send three hundred families. Philadelphia and its vicinity would gladly spare three hundred families more. Cincinnati and vicinity could afford three hundred families for such a purpose; and

Boston, with the aid of New England, could easily send the additional one-hundred — making an army of One Thousand families. . . . The line of argument which establishes the right of the South to settle their black slaves in Kansas, is equally good for the North in establishing the right to settle black freemen in Kansas.

LINCOLN CONDEMNS KANSAS-NEBRASKA ACT

On **OCTOBER 16**, Abraham Lincoln gave a speech in Peoria, Illinois, in which he condemned the Kansas-Nebraska Act and called for the gradual emancipation of southern slaves. Lincoln's reputation began to grow with this speech and others relating to slavery.

1855 BEREA COLLEGE ADMITS BLACK
AND WHITE STUDENTS

Kentucky, a slave state, became the location of the first college specifically founded for the purpose of educating both Black and white students. Berea College was founded by two Kentucky abolitionists, Cassius M. Clay and John G. Fee. They believed that racial equality had to begin with educational equality. Students at the school worked for the college in return for their education.

Four years after its founding, the small school was forced to close by a group of armed men, but it opened again in 1865. For the next fifty years, about half of the students were Black and half white. In 1904, the Kentucky legislature passed a law forbidding racial mixing and thus barring Blacks from Berea. A separate Black facility was founded near Louisville, and Berea operated as a whites-only school until 1954.

DOUGLASS PUBLISHES ANTISLAVERY WORKS

In 1855, Frederick Douglass published *My Bondage and My Freedom*, followed by *The Life and Times of Frederick Douglass* in 1881. Douglass's publications were strongly worded antislavery documents that aroused many to support the cause. These two publications were actually major revisions of his autobiography.

MORMONS PROCLAIM BLACKS UNFIT TO BE PRIESTS

Brigham Young, leader of the Mormon Church, issued a proclamation that a "single drop" of Black blood rendered a man unfit to enter the Mormon priesthood.

KANSAS ELECTS PROSLAVERY LEGISLATURE

On **MARCH 30**, several thousand proslavery Missourians crossed into Kansas and voted in the territorial election; thus, a proslavery legislature was elected. The federal governor of the territory recognized this election as valid, in the hope of curtailing further violence over the slavery issue.

LANGSTON ELECTED TOWN CLERK IN OHIO

On **APRIL 2**, John M. Langston (1829–1897), the first known Black elected to office in a settled community in the United States, was voted in as clerk of Brownhelm Township, Lorain County, Ohio. Later, Langston was elected clerk of the township of Russia, near Oberlin, and then went on to become a member of the council of the incorporated village of Oberlin. In 1889, he was elected to the U.S. House of Representatives from Virginia.

MASSACHUSETTS RULES AGAINST
"JIM CROW" SCHOOLS

On **APRIL 28**, the governor of Massachusetts signed a bill legally ending "Jim Crow" schooling in Boston. The bill prohibited racial or religious distinction in admitting students to any Massachusetts public school.

ANTISLAVERY SETTLERS IN KANSAS
HOLD CONVENTION

On **SEPTEMBER 5**, Kansas settlers opposing slavery held a convention at Big Springs and petitioned for admission to the Union as a free state. They declared that the territorial proslavery legislature was illegal because Missourians supporting slavery had voted in the election.

KANSAS FREE STATERS MEET
TO ESTABLISH GOVERNMENT

While Kansas was engulfed in bloody skirmishes that reflected the views of pro- and antislavery camps, antislavery leaders known as "Free Staters" met in Topeka from **OCTOBER 23** to **NOVEMBER 12** to draw up plans for an antislavery government with specific antislavery legislation. They elected James H. Lane as their president. In his address to the group, Lane predicted that Kansas would favor the "exclusion of blacks." Lane's prediction became fact when the electorate voted three to one on December 15 in favor of excluding Blacks from Kansas.

BLACK CONVENTION HELD IN CALIFORNIA

On **NOVEMBER 21**, as many as forty-seven Black delegates attended a convention in Sacramento. Delegates represented almost every vocation — business, law, the ministry, teaching, community leadership, and journalism. One of the most pressing issues facing Black residents was the Black Laws, particularly the rule prohibiting Blacks from testifying against whites in court. Speakers condemned this law, which in effect allowed Blacks to be driven off their land without legal recourse. State conventions held in 1856 and 1857 also addressed this pressing issue.

1856 CALIFORNIA'S FIRST BLACK NEWSPAPER, *Mirror of the Times*, STARTED

The state's first Black newspaper, *Mirror of the Times*, was founded and published by California businessman Mifflin W. Gibbs (1828–1903) just before the 1856 Black convention. The newspaper immediately became a vehicle that leaders used to publicize issues of importance to Blacks. As the state legislature continued to ignore the petitions of California's Black leaders concerning the right to give testimony, Gibbs made the *Mirror of the Times* more and more militant. He became one of the most powerful crusaders for equal rights in the state.

◊ Gibbs was born in Philadelphia. His father, a Methodist minister, died when he was eight. While in his teens, Gibbs joined the Underground Railroad and Philadelphia's antislavery society. At the age of twenty, he was encouraged by Frederick Douglass and Charles Lenox Remond to become an antislavery lecturer. Instead, he joined the rush to California in search of gold. Starting out by shining shoes, he eventually opened a clothing business and then a store to sell imported shoes and boots from London and New York. His hard work made him a successful businessman, which led him into politics.

As early as 1851, Mifflin and other Black Californians published a series of resolutions denouncing the state's Black Laws. It was the state's rejection of these resolutions that prompted Gibbs, in 1855, to start the *Mirror of the Times*. In 1858, Gibbs became frustrated with escalated racism in the state and joined the Gold Rush to the Fraser River Valley in British Columbia. In Canada, he opened a store and became a councilor in 1866. Although he was elected again the next year, Gibbs's interest in law led him to study in Arkansas; he later graduated from Oberlin College in Ohio. In 1870, he was admitted to the Arkansas bar, and in 1873, he was elected the city of Little Rock's first Black judge. In old age, he received minor appointments by Presidents Rutherford Hayes and Chester Arthur, including an appointment as a U.S. consul to Madagascar.

Daily Creole of New Orleans FOUNDED

J. M. Weymout established the first Black daily newspaper, the *Daily Creole of New Orleans*.

SONG REFLECTS ABOLITIONIST SENTIMENT

Benjamin Hanby, a schoolteacher and theological student, published the song "Darling Nelly Gray," which helped raise the national consciousness about slavery. Hanby based his song on the story of Joe Selby, an escaped slave. Hanby's ballad, sung by Nelly's lover after she had been sold by their Kentucky plantation owner, reflects Selby's story. The chorus of the song captures the sentiment:

> O my poor Nelly Gray, they have taken you away
> And I'll never see my darling anymore
> I'm sitting by the river, and I'm weeping all the day
> For you've gone from the old Kentucky shore

The publishing company paid Hanby no royalties, telling him that the fame he received was reward enough. Hanby composed several other politically inspired songs before his death at the age of thirty-four in 1867.

SOUTH CAROLINA SEEKS REPEAL OF LAW ABOLISHING SLAVE TRADE

The governor of South Carolina, James H. Adams, argued for repeal of the 1807 law prohibiting slave trade into the United States. He believed that farmers and planters in the state would not have enough slave labor to maintain the agricultural economy.

WILBERFORCE UNIVERSITY FOUNDED IN OHIO

Wilberforce University was founded by the African Methodist Episcopal (AME) Church. It was named in honor of William Wilberforce, an Englishman who vehemently opposed slavery and the slave trade. Wilberforce was the first college to be owned and operated by African Americans in this country. The university's first students were freed or escaped slaves. Mulatto children of southern planters were also students at Wilberforce.

Today the school has numerous undergraduate programs, including a cooperative education program for all degrees. The school is still church-related. Enrollment is about twelve hundred students.

Wilberforce University, pictured here in 1856, the year of its founding, provided free Blacks with an excellent education. Although it started with a staff of white professors, Sarah Early, an African American professor, was hired during its first three years of operation. In 1863, Wilberforce was purchased by the AME church and Bishop Daniel L. Payne became its president, thus becoming the first African American college president.

BATTLE IN KANSAS BETWEEN ABOLITIONIST AND PROSLAVERY FORCES

Some scholars note that the Civil War actually began in Kansas, where abolitionist and proslavery forces earned the state a nickname — Bleeding Kansas. On **MAY 1**, supporters of slavery pillaged Lawrence. Four days later, abolitionists murdered five proslavery settlers. John Brown, a fervent abolitionist, was blamed for the murders. On May 21, several hundred advocates of slavery from Missouri arrived with a U.S. marshal and warrants for citizens accused of treason against the government. As the warrants were being served, proslavery forces turned into a mob, burning the Free State Hotel, wrecking the newspaper, and ransacking homes. At least one man was killed.

Three days later, John Brown and his followers retaliated by shooting and killing five slaveholding settlers on Pottawatomie Creek.

ATTACK ON SENATOR SUMNER

On **MAY 22**, Representative Preston Brooks of South Carolina attacked and severely beat Senator Charles Sumner at his Senate desk in the Capitol.

Brooks used his walking stick to batter Sumner unconscious in retaliation for a speech that Sumner made denouncing slavery and proslavery congressmen, including Brooks's uncle, South Carolina senator Andrew Butler, whom Sumner compared to a "chivalrous knight" who had chosen "harlot Slavery" as a mistress. Sumner had also charged that But

John Brown, a minister from Connecticut, went to Kansas to battle proslavery forces. Some scholars consider that the Civil War began in Kansas, where abolitionists and those in favor of slavery first came into open conflict. On May 21, 1856, several hundred supporters of slavery arrived in Lawrence, the center of antislavery sentiment in the region, with a U.S. marshal and warrants for the arrest of abolitionists whom they accused of treason. These people turned into a mob which burned the Free State Hotel, wrecked the newspaper office, ransacked homes, and killed one person.

ler was preparing to "conduct the state of South Carolina out of the union." Sumner did not know his assailant prior to the attack.

PROSLAVERY FORCES ATTACK BROWN'S STRONGHOLD

On **AUGUST 30**, more than three hundred proslavery men attacked Oswatomie, Kansas, the stronghold of abolitionist John Brown. Brown and about forty supporters drove off the attackers. Governor Daniel Woodson, a proslavery advocate, declared Kansas to be in a state of open insurrection.

1857 CURRY ELECTED TO U.S. HOUSE OF REPRESENTATIVES

Jabez L. M. Curry (1825–1903) was elected to the U.S. House of Representatives. Curry served from 1857 to 1861, during which time he supported and promoted legislation to educate Black and white children in the South.

In 1865, just after the Civil War, Curry, a white man, was selected to guide the early development of Howard University as its president. He served in this position from 1865 to 1868. After 1890, because of his relationships with the Peabody Fund and the Slater Fund, two major philanthropic foundations, Curry was influential in the establishment of Black schools, particularly in the South.

NEW HAMPSHIRE GRANTS FULL CITIZENSHIP TO BLACKS

In response to the *Dred Scott* decision in 1857 (see entry at March 6), which held that Blacks were not citizens of the United States, the New Hampshire General Assembly passed legislation that did not deprive any person, regardless of color, of citizenship within the state nor of the rights associated with that citizenship. Specifically, the legislature provided: "Neither descent, near or remote, from a person of African blood, whether such a person is or may have been a slave, nor color of skin, shall disqualify any person from becoming a citizen of this State, or deprive such person of the full rights and privileges of a citizen thereof."

DISUNION CONVENTION MEETS

On **JANUARY 15**, the Disunion Convention met in Worcester, Massachusetts. Delegates adopted the slogan "No union with slaveholders." The convention supported a split between slave states and free states. William Lloyd Garrison, founder of the New England Anti-Slavery Society, was the main speaker.

BUCHANAN INAUGURATED AS PRESIDENT

On **MARCH 4**, James Buchanan was sworn in as the fifteenth president. In his inaugural address, he called for tolerance of slavery for the purpose of keeping the states united. Buchanan had defeated the antislavery platform of John C. Frémont.

Dred Scott v. *Sanford* DECISION ANNOUNCED

On **MARCH 6**, in the case of *Dred Scott* v. *Sanford*, the U.S. Supreme Court held that Blacks were not citizens

When proslavery forces went on a rampage and burned the Free State Hotel in Lawrence, Kansas, they intended to intimidate antislavery settlers and introduce slavery in the territory.

of the United States, thus upholding the Fugitive Slave Law and further denying to Congress the power to prohibit slavery in any federal territory. The Court declared that Blacks had no rights that a white man was required to respect. Thus, Dred Scott had no right to sue his owner in a federal court. The case further weakened the Missouri Compromise and caused outrage in the North and jubilation in the South.

Montgomery Blair (1813–1883) defended Dred Scott before the court. Dred Scott was born a slave in Virginia. He was taken by his master from Missouri into the free state of Illinois and then into Minnesota. He lived for four years outside Missouri before being returned there. Scott sued for his freedom on the basis that he had become a free man while living on free soil.

Chief Justice Roger Taney wrote that the Declaration of Independence and the U.S. Constitution were never meant to include "Negroes." The *New York Tribune* wrote that the Court "has draggled and polluted its garments in the filth of pro-slavery politics." Some say that the *Dred Scott* decision made it clear that a civil war was imminent.

THE *Golconda* SAILS FROM CHARLESTON TO LIBERIA
On **MAY 30**, the Colonization Society's packet ship *Golconda* set sail from the port of Charleston, with 321 emigrants en route to Liberia. Most were from South Carolina — as many as 116 were from Marion County, 19 from Aiken, 49 from Newberry, and 72 from Charleston; Georgia Blacks included 45 from

After the U.S. Supreme Court decision in the Dred Scott case, Scott became the best-known Black person in the country. Mass protests by abolitionists in the North and West decried the case and other outrages suffered by Blacks. The decree pulled many whites into the ever-expanding antislavery movement.

1858 KANSAS REJECTS SLAVERY

On **JANUARY 4**, voters in Kansas Territory voted down a "constitution with slavery." All but 112 of the 10,388 voters rejected the proslavery constitution. Three weeks before, Kansas citizens had voted for a special article on slavery in the constitution.

FREE BLACKS CHOOSE BETWEEN SLAVERY AND EXILE

In **FEBRUARY**, the Arkansas legislature required free Blacks to choose between exile and enslavement.

ANTISLAVERY CONVENTION HELD BY BROWN

On **MAY 8**, John Brown held an antislavery convention in Chatham, Canada. Twelve whites and thirty-four Blacks attended. The group drew up a constitution for a nation of liberated slaves to be set up in the mountains of Virginia. Brown laid out his plan for freeing the slaves: First, he would strike at a point in the South, provoking a general slave uprising. Then he would lead slaves and free Blacks into the mountains, from which they would fight.

The convention adopted a provisional constitution to guide the new Black nation while a government was being formed. This government would exist side by side with the U.S. government and would explicitly prohibit slavery. John Brown was elected commander in chief of the army to be formed. The target of the first strike was to be Harpers Ferry, Virginia. This site was selected for a number of reasons: it contained an armory and arsenal of arms; the nearby mountains provided a staging and hiding area; and Virginia, though a slave state, was only forty miles from Pennsylvania, a free state.

OBERLIN-WELLINGTON RESCUE

On **SEPTEMBER 13**, the Oberlin-Wellington rescue occurred when Black fugitive John Price, seized by slave catchers, was rescued by Professor Simon M. Bushnell and two dozen Black and white students, all from Oberlin College, Ohio. After stealing Price from three U.S. marshals, they swiftly sent him to safety in Canada. After the incident, Charles Langston (brother of John M. Langston) and Bushnell, a white man, were tried and convicted for the crime. Charles Langston wrote:

> Names must not be mentioned. The conduct of particular individuals must not be described. It is enough for us to know, just now, that the brave men and women who came together in hot haste, but with well-defined

Macon and 8 from Columbus; and 6 were from Philadelphia and 1 from Baltimore. Most of these emigrants were destined for Grand Bassa County (122); others were bound for Sinou (76), Cape Palmas (60), Carysburg (53), and Monrovia (10).

Three emigrants were native Africans returning to their own country, one taken into Savannah on the celebrated *Wanderer*. Among the émigrés were thirty-one farmers, five bricklayers, five laborers, four carpenters, four engineers, three painters, three waiters, two shoemakers, two coopers, two cooks, two plasterers, one blacksmith, one barber, one butcher, one druggist, one stonecutter, one upholsterer, one cabinetmaker, one minister, and one clerk. Thirty-one could read, and eighteen could read and write.

This photograph shows twenty of the Oberlin Rescuers standing in front of the Cuyahoga county jail. The Rescuers, most of whom were students, helped fugitive slaves in their flight to freedom.

intention, returned as the shades of the night came on bringing silence and rest to the world, bearing in triumph to freedom the man who, but an hour before, was on the road to the fearful doom of slavery.

John M. Langston, the first elected Black official in the country, also took part in the slave rescue. He published the address his brother gave before an Ohio court in the *Anglo-African Magazine* in July 1859:

> I was tried by a jury, who were prejudiced; before a Court that was prejudiced; prosecuted by an officer who was prejudiced. . . .
>
> One more word, sir, and I have done. I went to Wellington, knowing that colored men have no rights in the United States, which white men are bound to respect; that the Courts had so decided; that Congress has so enacted; and that people had so decreed.

LINCOLN-DOUGLAS DEBATE TAKES PLACE

On **OCTOBER 15**, in Galesburg, Illinois, Abraham Lincoln and Stephen A. Douglas completed their seventh and final debate as they campaigned for U.S. Senate. Douglas supported a state's power to choose whether or not to allow slavery. Lincoln argued that all people are born with the right to life, liberty, and the pursuit of happiness. In one debate, Lincoln made the prophetic statement "A house divided against itself cannot stand." Yet Lincoln at the time was not an abolitionist, taking a moderate stand on the slavery issue. He opposed expansion of slavery in the West but did not oppose it in states where it already existed, believing it would eventually die a "natural death."

SEWARD CALLS NORTH-SOUTH DISPUTE OVER SLAVERY "IRREPRESSIBLE"

On **OCTOBER 25**, in a speech in Rochester, New York, Republican senator William H. Seward vehemently characterized the dispute over slavery: "It is an irrepressible conflict between opposing and enduring forces, and it means that the United States must and will, sooner or later, become either entirely a slave-holding nation or an entirely free-labor nation."

Seward had been elected governor of New York in 1838. He became a strong abolitionist while in office. In 1848, he was elected to the U.S. Senate, where he actively debated issues concerning the Compromise of 1850. He strongly supported the abolition of slavery and the slave trade in the District of Columbia and the exclusion of slavery entirely from the western territories. From 1855 to 1860, Seward was an ardent spokesperson of the antislavery movement.

Seward hoped to become the presidential candidate of the Republican Party in 1860, but Lincoln was chosen because Seward was too outspoken against slavery. Upon election, Lincoln selected Seward as his secretary of state.

1859 BLACK FAMILY MAY HAVE WRITTEN CONFEDERATES' ANTHEM

"Dixie," the anthem of the Confederacy, was first sung publicly in Mechanics Hall in New York City.

It was believed at the time that a white minstrel performer, Dan Emmett, was the composer. New evidence, however, suggests that the song may have been written by a Black family. In a book published by the Smithsonian Institution Press (1993), authorship of the song was credited to a family of Black musicians, the Snowdens, who lived in Mount Vernon, Ohio, but missed their family home in Maryland. It is alleged that Emmett learned the song from the Snowdens. The debate surfaced when cemetery markers of Dan and Lew Snowden were discovered, inscribed with the statement "They taught 'Dixie' to Dan Emmett." Evidence showed that the Snowdens wrote many songs for minstrel shows and frequently passed their songs along to other performers. Emmett founded the first blackface minstrel troupe in 1843 and often returned to Mount Vernon to visit relatives who lived next door to the Snowdens.

Why would a freed slave wish "to be in the land of cotton"? Perhaps the Snowdens' loss of contact with family, tradition, and culture explains these lyrics. "Dixie" was played at Jefferson Davis's inauguration in Montgomery, Alabama, and has been performed at social and political rallies in the South for more than one hundred years.

DELANY SECURES TREATIES FOR RESETTLEMENT OF BLACKS

During this year, Dr. Martin Delany, a fervent emigrationist, traveled throughout Africa signing treaties with African kings to secure land for a permanent settlement for Blacks. Delany persuaded eight kings of Abeokota to grant land in the Yoruba area. Before these areas could be secured, however, the kings broke the treaties and reneged on the grants.

As early as 1854, Delany had helped organize the first Black National Emigration Convention in Cleveland, Ohio. Delany had also led an emigration party to Africa and later explored the Niger River valley. Delany noted, "I had but one object in view — the moral, social, and political elevation of ourselves, and the Regeneration of Africa." Delany was an early organizer of the Liberian Exodus Joint Stock Steamship Company in 1878. The company purchased the bark *Azor* and sailed on April 23, 1878, with 206 Black emigrants to Liberia. Even with the support of the American Colonization Society and several Black leaders who supported colonization — Henry Highland Garnet, Henry Turner, and others — Delany's mission failed.

FREE BLACKS WORK AS WHALERS

According to a survey of the free Black population published in this year, about twenty-nine hundred of the six thousand Black men in the U.S. merchant marine based in Atlantic ports served on board whaleboats. Blacks could find work in this industry, and wages were paid according to rank, not color. Integration among the races varied from vessel to vessel — as many as one out of every six crewmen may have been Black. Blacks had a more equal footing with white coworkers aboard the ship than ashore.

By 1863, the industry had changed considerably, and the position of Blacks had deteriorated to the point where most worked as cooks and stewards. At its peak in the 1840s, the U.S. whaling industry comprised about 731 vessels; by 1856, the number had dwindled to about 650 whaleboats.

LAST SLAVE SHIP DOCKS IN ALABAMA

The *Clothilde* was the last slave ship to stop (illegally) at an American port. The slaves aboard, numbering 130 men, women, and children, had been stolen from a Tarkar village in West Africa. The ship's captain, William Fowler, eluded federal boats patrolling the Mississippi Sound, unloaded his ship in Mobile, Alabama, and then burned it.

Fowler was unable to sell the slaves, and they were set free when the Civil War started. The Tarkars, under the leadership of Ka Zoola (Cudjoe Lewis), were able to stay together and formed a village, Africa Town, in an area known as the Plateau, near Mobile. Here, they kept their African customs, names, and language. Descendants of these Blacks can still be found in East Mobile. Cudjoe Lewis, the last of the original Tarkars, died in 1935.

MISSISSIPPI THREATENS SECESSION

The Mississippi legislature resolved to secede from the Union immediately if a Republican was elected president of the United States.

STATE COURTS NOT ALLOWED TO FREE
FEDERAL PRISONERS

On **MARCH 7**, the U.S. Supreme Court reversed a decision of the Wisconsin Supreme Court in *Ableman* v. *Booth* and declared that state courts had no jurisdiction to free federal prisoners.

Sherman M. Booth had been convicted in federal court of rescuing a fugitive slave. The decision of the Supreme Court thus confirmed the constitutionality of the Fugitive Slave Act of 1850, and the federal government rearrested and imprisoned Booth.

SOUTHERN COMMERCIAL CONVENTION MEETS

On **MAY 9 THROUGH 19**, the Southern Commercial Convention met in Vicksburg, Mississippi. The meeting called for reinstitution of legal slave trade.

ANTHONY SPEAKS OUT FOR RIGHTS
OF BLACKS AND WOMEN

In New York City, on **MAY 12**, Susan B. Anthony (1820–1906) addressed the ninth National Women's Rights Convention. Here she posed the question, "Where, under our Declaration of Independence, does the Saxon man get his power to deprive all women and Negroes of their inalienable rights?" Anthony was a member of the national committee of the Anti-Slavery Society.

BROWN ARRIVES IN COLORADO

In **JUNE**, "Aunt Clara" Brown arrived in Denver, Colorado, at the age of fifty-nine, employed as a cook for a wagon train. She moved to Central City, opened a laundry, and worked as a nurse, hoping to earn enough money to buy freedom for her family, who remained in slavery.

By 1866, Brown had earned ten thousand dollars and had invested in several mining claims. She found many of her family members after the Civil War and purchased wagons to help them move west. She eventually sponsored other wagon trains for Blacks.

Clara Brown, reportedly the first free Black resident of the Colorado Territory, opened a laundry to wash the shirts of gold seekers in Central City, Colorado. Charging fifty cents for every shirt, she made a fortune. She brought her family to Colorado and worked to improve the conditions of other Blacks.

Clara Brown is respectfully remembered in Central City. She was buried with honors, and a chair at the opera house was named in her memory.

BROWN RAIDS HARPERS FERRY

In **AUGUST**, John Brown, a white abolitionist minister from Kansas, met with Frederick Douglass in Chambersburg, Pennsylvania, to enlist his support for the planned Harpers Ferry raid. Brown wanted Douglass to organize the slaves who would be freed as a result of his raid. Douglass refused, believing that Brown's mission was suicidal and would ultimately turn the whole country against Blacks (slave and free). Despite Douglass's refusal, Brown continued with his plan for the October raid.

On October 16, Brown attacked, seized, and took arms from the United States Arsenal at Harpers Ferry, Virginia. He was accompanied by about a dozen white men, and five Black men — Shields Green,

Dangerfield Newby, Sherrard Lewis Leary, Osborne P. Anderson, and John A. Copeland. Brown sent out word for slaves to rise up against their masters, but slaves did not respond in large numbers. Federal troops led by Colonel Robert E. Lee attacked and recaptured the town and the arsenal. Brown was wounded, and a few of his followers were captured. Two of Brown's sons and six others were killed; about a half dozen escaped. Brown and the captured raiders were taken to Charles Town and jailed. After their arraignment, they were tried and found guilty of treason against the Commonwealth of Virginia. Brown was

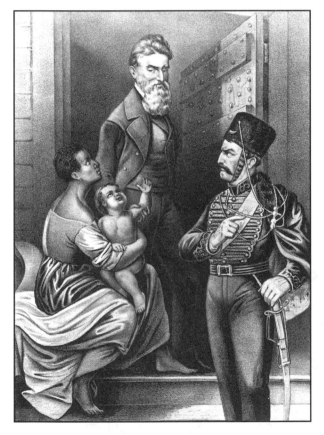

John Brown, shown here being directed to the gallows, was hanged for leading an attack on the federal arsenal at Harper's Ferry. The poet Frances E. W. Harper wrote, "Already from your prison has come a shout of triumph against the giant sin of our country." Brown's death was mourned by almost every noted abolitionist. Henry Thoreau commented, "Old John Brown is dead — John Brown the immortal lives."

also found guilty of murder and conspiring with slaves to create an insurrection. Other captured conspirators were sentenced to death by hanging. Brown was executed on December 2. Of those who had escaped, two whites (John Cook and Albert Hazlett) were captured in Pennsylvania and returned to Charles Town, where they, too, were tried, found guilty, and hanged.

Osborne P. Anderson, one of the coconspirators, escaped and later served with distinction in the Civil War.

Our Nig PUBLISHED

In **SEPTEMBER**, Harriet Wilson published *Our Nig*, the first novel published in the United States by an African American woman.

VAGRANT BLACKS CAN BE SOLD INTO SLAVERY

On **DECEMBER 17**, the Georgia legislature passed a law designed to maintain the number of slaves in the state. The law declared that any Black indicted for vagrancy could be sold into slavery.

1860

POPULATION OVERVIEW

BLACKS IN THE UNITED STATES The U.S. Census recorded a total of 4,441,830 Black residents, 14.7 percent of the 31,443,790 total residents. About 92 percent of the Black population resided in the South. In general, the concentration of Blacks in the South was directly tied to cotton production and plantation farming.

URBAN POPULATION The only southern city with a population greater than 100,000 was New Orleans. Charleston followed, with 41,000 residents; then Richmond, with 38,000; and Mobile, with 29,000.

FREE AND SLAVE POPULATIONS Census figures showed the increase in the number of slaves in the United States from almost 698,000 in 1790 to almost 3,953,760 in 1860. Foreign slave trade (illegal after 1808), slave breeding, normal excess of births over deaths, and a booming domestic slave trade contributed to the steady growth of the slave population during the first half of the nineteenth century. Even with this increase, slaves remained relatively costly: $1,000 for a healthy male field slave in Virginia; $1,500 for one in New Orleans.

Major concentrations of free Black residents were found in Baltimore, Washington, D.C., New Orleans, Charleston, and Richmond. The geographic breakdown showed that the majority of free Blacks (52.9 percent) still lived in the South, but almost one-quarter resided in cities, mostly in the North. Overall, though, the overwhelming proportion of Blacks (about 92 percent) lived in the South — a proportion that did not change much until the 1900s.

When the foreign slave trade was officially closed in this country, slaves numbered about 1,000,000. By 1830, the census counted 2,000,000, and in 1860, 3,953,760. Virginia led all other states, with more than 500,000 slaves, followed by Georgia, with 465,000; Alabama and Mississippi came next, with slightly more than 435,000 each. From 1850 to 1860, the most significant increase in slave population occurred in the states of the cotton kingdom — Georgia, Alabama, Tennessee, Mississippi, Arkansas, Louisiana, and Texas. By 1860, 2,200,000 Blacks, more than half of the entire Black population, lived and worked in this region.

The free Black population in the country continued to grow, but more slowly than the slave population did. In 1790, some 59,000 free Blacks were counted by the census. They accounted for about 8 percent of the Black population. By 1830, they

numbered 319,000, or about 14 percent of all Blacks; and by 1860 they amounted to 488,000, but their percentage of the total Black population had slipped to about 11 percent.

An assessment of the free Black and slave populations by regional divisions shows the spatial variation in their location since 1790. According to the 1790 census, 92 percent of the slave population lived in the South Atlantic division, 2.3 percent in the East South Central division, and 5.7 percent in the North. Although the South as a whole continued to hold more than 94 percent of all slaves up to 1860, the changing distribution of slaves within the region is worth noting. The South Atlantic division, where 92 percent of all slaves lived and worked in 1790, had only three-quarters of all slaves in 1820, just over one-half in 1850, and about 47 percent in 1860. The East South Central division's slave population soared from 2.3 percent in 1790 to more than 34 percent of all slaves in 1860.

This etching shows a slave ship being pursued off the coast of Cuba. Trade in African slaves continued until the Civil War, even though the slave trade was outlawed in the United States in 1808. The profits and thus the motive for the business remained extremely high, and a relatively brisk illegal trade continued because the law was seldom enforced.

The caption of this etching of a slaver reads, "At sunset the slaves are stowed for the night; the officers, with whip in hand, ranging the slaves — those on the right side facing the bows, those on the left side facing the stern — so as to bring each negro on his right side, and thus allow better action for the heart."

In the West South Central area, the slave population rose gradually from 2.9 percent in 1810 to 7.6 percent in 1840. By 1860, the slave population there had almost doubled, to 15.8 percent of total slaves. In each of these three subdivisions, the slave population increased every decade up to 1860.

SLAVEHOLDING IN SLAVE STATES AND DISTRICT OF CO-LUMBIA About 384,000 white families owned slaves. Eighty-eight percent of slave owners held fewer than 20 slaves; 72 percent, fewer than 10; and 50 percent, fewer than 5 slaves. About 3,000 families owned more than 100 slaves. Many researchers claim that it was impossible to operate a plantation efficiently with fewer than 20 slaves.

FREE BLACKS AND SLAVES IN BALTIMORE, MARYLAND In this year, Baltimore, Maryland's largest port and major city, had grown so large that it could boast not

only of being the largest city in Dixie, but also the country's fourth largest.

In 1820, Baltimore had 62,738 total residents. Blacks numbered 14,683, or about 23 percent of the total. In contrast to other southern urban centers, where slaves outnumbered free Blacks, Baltimore's free Black population made up about 70 percent of the total Black population. Baltimore's total population jumped to 80,620 in 1830 and to 102,313 in 1840. In each of the two decades before the Civil War, Baltimore's total population increased by an average of 55,000. The number of free Blacks in the city grew from 14,790 in 1830 to 25,680 by 1860. In contrast, the slave population declined each decade during the period, from 4,120 in 1830 to 2,218 in 1860. Overall, the Black population (free and slave) constituted a smaller proportion of the city's population in 1860 than it did

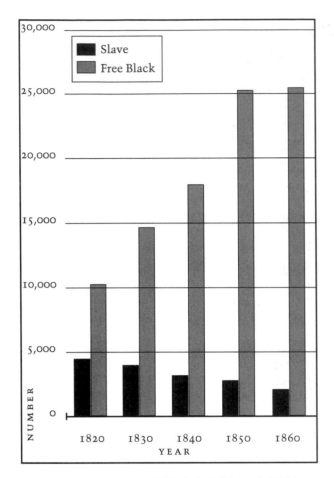

30,000

Slave
Free Black

25,000

20,000

15,000

10,000

5,000

0

NUMBER

1820   1830   1840   1850   1860

YEAR

FREE AND SLAVE POPULATIONS
IN BALTIMORE, MARYLAND,
1820–1860

Nevertheless, the city's population doubled between 1820 and 1860. Although much of this growth could be attributed to Charleston's manufacturing and railroad development, it depended in large part on cotton production. When cotton production began to shift westward, Charleston's competitive advantage over other cities began a gradual decline.

Few visitors to Charleston could miss the city's racial diversity. Because Blacks outnumbered whites in the city, it was common for writers to make statements such as that "two-thirds of the people one sees in town are negroes." In 1820, Blacks constituted more than 58 percent of all residents, but on the eve of the Civil War, Blacks were estimated to make up less than half of Charleston's residents. Slightly more than one-third of Charlestonians were slaves. Slaveholding was relatively higher in Charleston than in other large cities. In 1830, the census counted 2,873 "heads of families"; 379 of them had no bondservants and 401 had at least 10. Eighty-seven slave owners had 20 or more slaves, and 19 had more than 30. Among the largest slave owners in the city were business partnerships or corporations. Two mills, Canonboro and Chrisolus, each had more than 70 slaves in 1840. By 1860, however, the number of slaves and slave owners had dropped substantially. The gender imbalance among free Blacks can be attributed to the fact that slave owners sold younger males to planters in cane and cotton country, leaving behind a disproportionately large female population. For example, in 1860, there were 2,000 free Black women and 1,200 free Black men in Charleston. For whites, there was no marked gender differential.

FREE BLACKS AND SLAVES IN LOUISVILLE, KENTUCKY Louisville, the most prosperous urban center in Kentucky, enjoyed early growth because of its location on the falls of the Ohio River. Founded in 1778, the city grew swiftly up to about the year 1830 because the break in river transportation at the falls made it necessary for travelers to stop there. In 1830, the Louisville and Portland Canal opened, and Louisville no longer monopolized the river-borne commerce of the West. Louisville's population doubled every decade between 1820 and 1850, from 4,012 to 43,194 total residents. The next decade revealed a slowing of population growth; 68,033 residents were recorded in the city in 1860. Overall, Louisville's Black population grew steadily, from 1,124 in 1820 to 6,970 in 1850, but during the decade before the Civil War, the number of Black residents dropped to 6,820. The free Black population grew from less than 100 in 1820 to

in 1830 — 13 percent versus 23 percent. Baltimore's free Black population favored females, outnumbering males by 1,600 in 1820 and by almost 5,000 in 1860 (out of a total of 25,680 free Blacks). Although the slave population was considerably smaller during the 1820–1860 period, female slaves consistently outnumbered male slaves in each decade. In 1860, there were 2.28 female slaves for every male slave in Baltimore.

FREE BLACKS AND SLAVES IN CHARLESTON, SOUTH CAROLINA Charleston could no longer claim to be the largest and richest metropolis in Dixie. The city that had been the fifth largest metropolis in the United States in 1810 had fallen to twenty-second largest at this time.

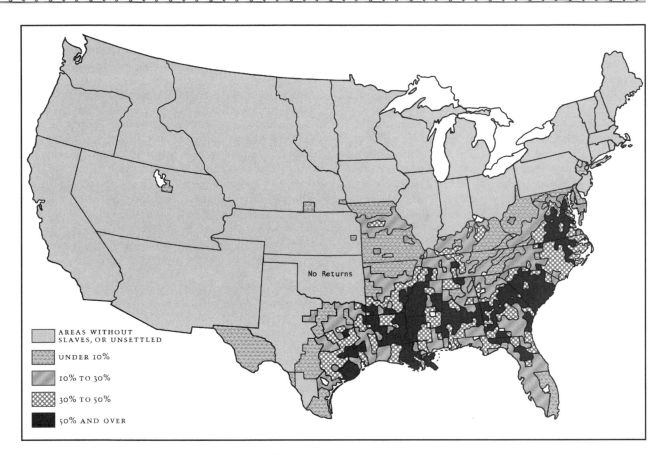

DISTRIBUTION OF SLAVERY, 1860

The greater the number of slaves there were in a state, the more likely it was to secede from the Union. South Carolina was the first. Slaves were concentrated in the tobacco-growing areas of Virginia; the Cotton Belt, which ran through South Carolina, Georgia, and Alabama; and the fertile cotton-growing region of the Mississippi River and its delta.

more than 1,917 in 1860. By this time, free Blacks made up about 28 percent of the total Louisville Black population, up from 22 percent a decade earlier.

FREE BLACKS AND SLAVES IN MOBILE, ALABAMA In this year, Mobile, located on the bay at the mouth of the Alabama River and the Gulf of Mexico, became one of the major ports in the Deep South. Influenced by both the French and the Spanish, the city's old, influential, wealthy families had for many decades controlled the growth and development of the city.

Mobile's population growth was relatively rapid, jumping from 300 to almost 2,700 in the nine years preceding the 1820 census. In 1820, fully 38 percent of the city's residents were Black, and 31 percent were slaves. The next decade revealed an almost even dis-

tribution of Black and white residents. During these decades (1820–1840), the city's population jumped to 12,672 residents, then up to 20,515 in 1850, and up to 29,259 in 1860. The striking growth in total population over these four decades was generally mirrored in the Black population. The number of Black residents, free and slave, more than quadrupled, increasing from about 1,000 to 4,410 during the 1820 to 1840 period. Whereas the free Black population increased from 183 in 1820 to 541 in 1840, the overwhelming proportion of Black population growth occurred among slaves. In 1840, Blacks made up 35 percent of the city's population; slaves alone accounted for 31 percent. Over the next twenty years (1840–1860), the Black population grew to 8,404 residents, but their proportion of the city's total population fell to 29 percent. In the Black population, the larger increase occurred among slaves, who increased in number from 3,869 to 7,587, up 96 percent. The free Black population in the city grew by 276, up only 51 percent. Free Blacks composed only about 10 percent of the entire Black population in 1860 — only a slightly larger proportion than in 1820.

Mobile's development from 1820 to 1860 was heavily tied to its involvement in cotton production. The city acted as a transfer point from producer to manufacturer. One visitor to the city reported that people in Mobile "live in cotton houses and ride in cotton carriages. They buy cotton, sell cotton, think cotton, eat cotton, drink cotton, and dream cotton. They marry cotton wives, and unto them are born cotton children. ... It has made Mobile, and all its citizens." About half of all whites owned slaves, and some corporations owned relatively large numbers of slaves. For example, the Factor's Press Company ranked as the largest slaveholder in the city, with 95 slaves in 1860.

FREE BLACKS AND SLAVES IN NEW ORLEANS, LOUISIANA

By 1860 New Orleans had become the most populous city in the Deep South. Founded by the French in 1718, the city retained a distinctly French character. Americans of various ethnic groups enriched the city in many ways. New Orleans had emerged, too, as one of the wealthiest cities in the South. Much of the city's wealth was attributable to its location at the mouth of the great Mississippi River, a geographic position that made it one of the busiest ports in the country — and the world. Sugar from nearby plantations, cotton from elsewhere in the South, and grain and livestock from the interior all passed through the city. In addition, it was the port of entry for imports from Europe, Latin America, and the Orient.

In 1820, New Orleans's volume of exports was second only to New York City's, and in certain years of the 1830s and 1840s, exports from the city actually surpassed those of New York City. The population soared from 27,176 residents in 1820 to more than 102,000 in 1840 and more than 168,000 by 1860, making it the sixth largest city in the nation.

New Orleans's Black population followed a pattern similar to that of several cities of the South. In 1805, Blacks made up more than one-half of the city's residents. During the unprecedented growth over the next couple of years, the Black population maintained its majority. By 1820, Black residents, almost equally divided between slave and free, still constituted about one-half of New Orleans's population of 27,176. Although the slave population increased by

only about 2,000 between 1820 and 1830, over the next decade the number of slaves soared to 23,448, up more than 150 percent. In 1840, slaves alone composed about one-fifth of the city's population, but the combined slave and free Black populations (42,674) made up about 42 percent of all residents. Over the same period, the number of free Blacks jumped from 6,237 to 19,226, an increase of 208 percent. The next decade (1840–1850) saw a drop in both Black populations. The free Black population declined by more than 48 percent between 1840 and 1850, and it increased only slightly during the next decade (1850–1860). Slaves, on the other hand, continued to decrease in number more gradually from 1840 to 1860, when they numbered 13,385.

The number of slave owners in the city dropped during this period. In 1830, the census counted 215 residents with more than 10 slaves; 22 of these had more than 20 slaves. In 1860, the city recorded only 83 heads of families owning from 1 to 10 slaves; 20 families owned more than 20. Among the largest slave owners in the city, James Higgings claimed 155; I. A. Blanc, 69; and Walter Campbell and Isaac Cubrer, 59 each. Corporations such as the New Orleans Canal and Banking Company, the Fireproof Cotton Press, and L. A. Garidal & Company owned relatively large numbers of slaves. As in other major southern urban centers, there was a gender disparity among free Blacks in New Orleans, with 1,750 more free Black females than free Black males.

FREE BLACKS AND SLAVES IN RICHMOND, VIRGINIA

Richmond, the state capital of Virginia, was a major industrial center of the South, with several factories and warehouses concentrated along the James River. Away from the river, the city's mansions bespoke both old and new wealth.

Richmond's early growth depended heavily on the growing and processing of tobacco. Later, as the home of Tredegar Iron Company, it quickly became a producer of iron for a number of other cities in the region. The success of Richmond's iron furnaces was due not only to the extensive coalfields on the city's edge but also to the heavy use of slaves. The coalfields provided fuel for New York City, Baltimore, Newark, and a number of other smaller urban centers. Not only a major manufacturing center, Richmond claimed a commercial and political edge over its sister cities, maintaining its traditional early industries and fostering new industrial diversity.

In 1820, Richmond claimed a resident population of 12,067, of whom Blacks comprised about 47 percent. The city's overall population growth was quite steady up to 1850, but only about 15,500 additional residents had been added during this thirty-year period — less than 520 residents annually. The decade 1850–1860 saw more impressive growth, however, as the population increased by slightly more than 10,000 residents, to 37,910. Black residents, although representing just under one-half of the city's population in 1820, actually made up the majority of the population (52 percent) in 1830. Slightly more than 76 percent of Blacks in the city were slaves. From 1830 to 1860, the number of Black residents continued to grow, and the largest component continued to be the slave population. Whereas the free Black population grew from 1,960 in 1830 to 2,576 in 1860, the slave population increased from 6,345 to 11,699. Roughly 88 percent of all Blacks in the city in 1860 were slaves — a proportion that had increased gradually over the entire period. Blacks, both slave and free, made up a smaller proportion of Richmond's total population at the end of this time period (38 percent) than at the beginning. Although slaves in Richmond were accustomed to urban living, they were still sold to plantations in the West despite their strong objections. Many eventually escaped from their new owners and returned to Richmond.

The slaveholding population decreased between 1820 and 1860; most of this decrease was among small slave owners. Those owning 10 to 20 slaves actually increased in number from 14 to 47, and owners of more than 20 slaves increased from 7 to 93. Almost all of this growth occurred among corporations, which increased their holdings of slaves for manufacturing. On the eve of the Civil War, no less than 54 corporations owned at least 10 slaves each. At least 274 slaves were owned by the Virginia Central Railroad.

In contrast to other urban centers in the South, Richmond's gender disparity among slaves actually favored the male, rather than the female, slave population. After 1820, male slaves increased at a faster rate than females; there were 1,573 more males than females in 1860. In the free Black population, however, females outnumbered males in each decade, though the gender disparity was not especially large. The substantial gender disparity among the slave population may be explained by the increasing number of slaves held by corporations and manufacturers.

FREE BLACKS AND SLAVES IN SAVANNAH, GEORGIA In this year, the value of cotton exports from Savannah amounted to more than $17 million. Yet Savannah

was far less dependent on the business of cotton production than cities to the west, such as Mobile, Alabama.

A strong manufacturing orientation had encouraged the early use of steam power in Savannah. As early as 1818, the city sent a steamship to Liverpool in an effort to promote the city's "business enterprise." In 1848, a city official noted that no less than 18 establishments were using steam power; 14 of these had been started less than 10 years earlier. Savannah's boosters were quick to adapt steam to a number of enterprises, including the completion of a 190-mile railroad project to Macon — considered the longest railroad in the country at the time. The city's entrepreneurial spirit made its port one of the most competitive on the east coast.

As manufacturing and cotton production increased, so did the city's population. In 1820, Savannah had a population of 7,523, of whom about 47 percent were Black residents. Of these, slaves were by far the most numerous, composing 84 percent. The 1830 census listed only the total population, showing an increase of only about 250 residents over the decade. By 1850, both the total and the Black populations had more than doubled — to 15,312 and 6,899, respectively. Blacks made up 45 percent of the city's total population, and slaves constituted about 41 percent. Although the slave population had more than doubled between 1820 and 1850, the number of free Blacks increased only by 104, less than 18 percent. During the next decade (1850–1860), Savannah's total population increased by about 7,000, mostly among whites. The combined Black population grew from just under 6,917 to 8,417, an increase of only 1,500. As a result, the proportion of Blacks declined to 38 percent of the city's total residents, down from 45.2 percent in the previous decade. Over the entire 1820–1860 period, the number of free Blacks in the city increased by only 123, but the slave population rose by 4,637. By 1860, Blacks made up just over 25 percent of Savannah's total residents. Slaves outnumbered free Blacks by almost 10 to 1. During this decade, cotton production shifted westward, and many wealthy Savannah residents, recognizing the importance of cotton to their wealth, chased it with railroads and river steamboats.

ECONOMIC CONDITIONS OVERVIEW

COTTON PRODUCTION According to the census, cotton production had reached almost 4 million bales annually by 1860.

COTTON PRODUCTION, 1859 AND 1899

During the four decades between 1859 and 1899, as cotton became more valuable than any other crop or land use, the amount of land devoted to its production increased dramatically in three areas: eastern Texas, the Mississippi River Valley, and the older cotton-growing areas of the Piedmont. (*Source:* U.S. Department of Agriculture, *Atlas of American Agriculture,* part 5, sec. A (Washington, D.C.: Government Printing Office, 1918), 17).

As cotton production soared and the cotton-growing areas shifted toward the Mississippi Valley, thousands of slaves were auctioned and exported from the older cotton-producing areas to the newer ones.

Production rose from 6,000 bales in 1792 to 73,000 bales eight years later, then to more than 1.4 million bales in 1840 and almost 4 million bales in 1860. Although the geographic area devoted to cotton expanded considerably over the decades, the belt from Alabama and Tennessee westward to Texas produced almost three-quarters of all cotton in 1860, up from one-sixteenth in 1811. As cotton became "king" in this area and throughout the South, it demanded more and more intensive labor. By this time, approximately three-quarters of all slaves were working in cotton agriculture, and the slave population was increasingly concentrated in these cotton-producing areas. Slaves made up almost half the population of Alabama and Mississippi, but in the coastal areas of Georgia and South Carolina, they made up more than half, sometimes almost three-quarters, of all residents. Virginia remained the leading exporter of slaves up to about 1860, exporting nearly 300,000 slaves between 1830 and 1860 alone. Other states, — including Maryland, the Carolinas, Kentucky, Tennessee, and Missouri — also exported slaves to satisfy the demand that cotton production had caused. The selling of slaves was big business; however, the small slave owner often sold a slave at a reduced price to pay off debts. In 1860, one of the largest recorded slave sales occurred when executors of the estate of James Bond of Georgia sold 566 slaves for a total of $580,000. In the previous year, another Georgia estate had sold as many as 400 slaves to pay off debts.

SLAVE GANGS PRODUCE MORE THAN FREE FARMERS

By this time, about 50 percent of the adult slave population worked as gang laborers, a form of labor that was believed to be roughly 70 percent more productive than employing free farmers or slaves on small plantations. Gangs worked intensely to produce more in thirty-five minutes than free farmers could produce in one hour.

SOCIAL CONDITIONS OVERVIEW

BLACK COLLEGES FOUNDED

Between the end of the Civil War and 1870, twenty-two historically Black colleges and universities (HBCUs) were formed to meet the overwhelming demand of freed Blacks for an education. Some colleges started as primary schools and gradually expanded to offer the higher grades and college courses. Some started with only one or two teachers in a one- or two-room structure. One was even set up in a railroad car. The new colleges opened in the Black Belt and on its edges: Maryland, Washington, D.C., Tennessee, and Virginia. The Freedmen's Bureau as well as religious organizations and private individuals were instrumental in founding these colleges. They were staffed largely by northerners, especially white women. Several of the largest and most prominent historically Black colleges were established in this era: Atlanta University, Fisk University, Howard University, Morehouse College, and Hampton Institute. (See Appendix.)

PRIMARY, SECONDARY, AND COLLEGE EDUCATION FOR BLACKS

Between 1830 and 1860, education for Blacks was limited partly because whites feared slave uprisings. Denmark Vesey's rebellion (1822) and Nat Turner's insurrection (1831) heightened such fears. Many states passed legislation prohibiting educational opportunities for Blacks. Despite these laws, some whites, especially women, continued to educate their slaves. Margaret Douglass kept a Sunday school for slave children in Norfolk, Virginia, in 1854. Douglass spent time in jail for her "crime." Mary S. Peake of Hampton, Virginia, a mulatto seamstress, dared to keep school for Blacks in her home. In 1861, the American Missionary Association collaborated with Peake to open a day school for about fifty students in Hampton, Virginia.

Prior to the Civil War, education for Blacks was generally provided by white philanthropists and free Black volunteers. Many schools for Blacks in the South were conducted in a clandestine fashion. In the North, education was more freely offered. Both Black and white women staffed many schools for Blacks, including the Institute for Colored Youth in Philadelphia, which itself became a training institute for additional Black teachers. As many as twenty-six Blacks had earned degrees from recognized colleges by 1860, and many others had been admitted.

REIGN OF TERROR IN SOUTHERN STATES

Both the *New York Times* and a number of the *Anti-Slavery Tracts* published by the American Anti-Slavery Society stated, "There exists at this moment, throughout the Southern states, an actual Reign of Terror." According to testimony, no northern man was safe in the South: "He cannot visit the region without a rigid watchfulness over all his expressions of opinions; with the risk of personal indignity, and danger even to life and limb." The editor of the *Southern Confederacy*, James P. Hambleton, published a "Black List of the Confederacy," which identified persons and businesses considered to hold opinions contrary to slaveholding. Several examples of this terror, taken from publications of the American Anti Slavery Society, appear below.

Exclusion of Free Negroes from Mississippi

The bill for excluding free negroes from the State of Mississippi passed the House on the 7th December, by a vote of 75 to 5. It provides that they shall leave the State on or before the 1st of July, 1860; or, if they prefer to remain, that they shall be sold into slavery, with a right of choice of masters at a price assessed by three disinterested slaveholders, the proceeds to go into the treasury of the county in which the provisions of the bill may require to be executed.

A Blacksmith Driven Away

Benjamin F. Winter, a blacksmith by trade, has been ordered to leave the town of Hamilton, Harris Country, [Georgia], by a meeting of citizens, for avowing Abolition and incendiary sentiments.

Expulsion of Free Negroes from Arkansas

At the late session of the Arkansas Legislature, an act was passed giving the free negroes of that state the alternative of migrating before January 1st, 1860, or becoming slaves. As the time of probation has now expired, while some few individuals have preferred servitude, the great body of the free colored people of Arkansas are on their way northward. We learn that the upward bound boats are crowded with them, and that Seymour [Indiana] on the line of the Ohio and Mississippi Railroad, affords a temporary home for others.

A party of forty, mostly women and children, arrived in this city last evening by the Ohio and Mississippi Railroad. They were welcomed by a committee of ten, appointed from the colored people of the city, by whom the refugees were escorted to the Dumas House, on McAllister street, at which place a formal reception was held. They were assured by the Chairman of the Reception Committee, Peter H. Clark, that if they were industrious and exemplary in their conduct, they would be sure to gain a good livelihood and many friends. The exiles, as before stated, are mostly women and children, the husbands and fathers being held in servitude. They report concerning the emigration, that hundreds of the free colored men of Arkansas have left for Kansas, and hundreds more are about to follow.

A Trap to Catch Hon. Joshua R. Giddings

A correspondent of the Cincinnati *Commercial*, who has lately visited Richmond, writes from Mayfield [Kentucky] that while in Kentucky, he learned of a deep-laid scheme to capture J. R. Giddings, for the purpose of trying him for treason, etc., in view of his connection with the Harpers Ferry insurgents. This scheme is founded upon the reward offered recently, anonymously, for the bringing of his person to Virginia. This amount has been raised for this purpose, and the object will be to seize him and cross the line into Kentucky and Virginia immediately. The correspondent, who writes anonymously, says further: "I would have addressed Mr. Giddings directly, but do not know his post-office. I would advise him to be ever on his guard, and keep as far from the Ohio River as possible. I offer no apology for not giving my name, living as I do in the South."

A Reward Offered for the Head of Mr. Giddings

Ten Thousand Dollars Reward. Joshua R. Giddings, having openly declared himself a traitor in a lecture at Philadelphia, on the 28th of October, and there being no process, strange to say, by which he can be brought to justice, I propose to be one of one hundred to raise $10,000 for his safe delivery in Richmond, or $5,000 for the production of his head. I do not regard this proposition, extraordinary as it may at first seem, either unjust or unmerciful. The law of God and the Constitution of his country both condemn him to death.

For satisfactory reasons, I withhold my name from the public, but it is in the hands of the editor of the Richmond *Whig*. There will be no difficulty, I am sure, in raising the $10,000, upon a reasonable prospect of getting the said Giddings to this city.

$100,000 REWARD. — MESSRS. EDITORS,

I will be one of one hundred gentlemen, who will give twenty-five dollars each *for the heads of the following traitors:*

Henry Wilson, Massachusetts; Charles Sumner, Massachusetts; Horace Greeley, New York; John P. Hale, New Hampshire; Wendell Phillips, Henry Ward Beecher, Brooklyn; Rev. Dr. Cheever, New York; Rev. Mr. Wheelock, New Hampshire; Schuyler Colfax, Anson Burlingame, Owen Lovejoy, Amos P. Granger, Edwin B. Morgan, Galusha A. Grow, Joshua R. Giddings, Edward Wade, Calvin C. Chaffee, William H. Kelsey, William A. Howard, Henry Waldron, John Sherman, George W. Palmer, Daniel W. Gooch, Henry L. Dawes, Justin S. Morrill, L. Washburn, Jr., J. A. Bingham, William Kellogg, E. B. Washburn, Benjamin Stanton, Edward Dodd, C. B. Tompkins, John Covode, Cad. C. Washburn, Samuel G. Andrews, A. B. Olin, Sidney Dean, N. B. Durfee, Emory B. Pottle, DeWitt C. Leach, J. F. Potter, T. Davis, Massachusetts; T. Davis, Iowa; J. F. Farnsworth, C. L. Knapp, R. E. Fenton, Philemon Bliss, Mason W. Tappan, Charles Case, James Pike, Homer E. Boyce, Isaac D. Clawson, A. S. Murray, Robert B. Hall, Valentine B. Horton, Freeman H. Morse, David Kilgore, William Stewart, Samuel B. Curtis, John M. Wood, John M. Parker, Stephen C. Foster, Charles J. Gilman, C. B. Hoard, John Thompson, J. W. Sherman, William D. Braxton, James Buffington, O. B. Matteson, Richard Mott, George K. Robbins, Ezekiel P. Walton, James Wilson, S. A. Purviance, Francis E. Spinner, Silas M. Burroughs. And I will also be one of one hundred to pay five hundred dollars each ($50,000) *for the head of William H. Seward,* and would add a similar reward for Fred. Douglass, but regarding him head and shoulders above these traitors, will permit him to remain where he now is.

The Rockville [Maryland] *Journal* says that a man was arrested near the Great Falls, in that country, on Wednesday last, for the expression of a feeling of sympathy with the late rebellion at Harpers Ferry. He is now in the county jail.

The Warrentown [Virginia] *Flag,* having been informed that over twenty copies of the *New York Tribune* are taken at the post-offices of Prince William county, suggest that those receiving them should not only be presented before the Grand Jury and fined heavily, but dealt with even more severely.

Mr. Ashley, a Republican member of Congress from Ohio, went to Charlestown, Va., and witnessed the

Many important antislavery activists were targeted for assassination by proslavery forces. Among those whose deaths were most eagerly sought were (clockwise from top left) Frederick Douglass, Wendell Phillips, Joshua Giddings, and William Seward.

execution of John Brown. Some hours before the execution, he was discovered to be a spy, and he plainly avowed himself to the crowd to be a Republican member of Congress. His intrepidity alone saved his life. He was insulted, his life was threatened a hundred times, but by cool bearing, he put his panic-stricken foes to shame, and they did not venture to attack him.

CIVIL WAR SPLITS INDIAN TERRITORY

Each of the five Native American peoples in Indian Territory (the Cherokee, Choctaw, Chickasaw, Creek, and Seminole peoples) sent soldiers to fight, some for the North and some for the South, during the Civil War. This split reflected slaveholding practices of the tribes, as well as abolitionists' efforts to spread antislavery sentiment among them. Like the rest of the nation, Native Americans were divided by the issue of slavery. All of the Native American peoples in Indian Territory owned slaves. Since each group treated their slaves differently, it is not surprising that their views on slavery also varied. In general, large landowners supported the South and slavery, whereas most of the smaller landowners supported the North.

ILLEGAL SLAVE TRADE CONTINUES

On **APRIL 30**, the Spanish galleon *Wildfire* was intercepted off the coast of Cuba and its illegal slave cargo seized by the U.S. Navy's *Mohawk*.

Although slave trade had been illegal in the United States since 1808, slavers continued to illegally transport slaves into the Americas. Slavers were legally defined as "pirates" after 1820 and thus were subject to legal search and seizure.

REPUBLICAN PARTY NOMINATES LINCOLN

On **MAY 16**, Abraham Lincoln was nominated as the presidential candidate of the Republican Party. Hannibal Hamlin of Maine was chosen as Lincoln's running mate. Lincoln defeated New York abolitionist William H. Seward on the third ballot at the convention in Chicago. As a northern Republican, Lincoln represented a party committed since its origins to preventing any extension of slavery. To capture the nomination, Lincoln presented himself as a moderate on the question of slavery. The party's platform called for prohibiting slavery in the territories but was against interfering with slavery within the states.

These illegal slaves were found aboard the Wildfire. *The continued demand for slaves and the consequent profits encouraged many slavers to violate the 1808 law.*

DEMOCRATS SPLIT OVER SLAVERY

In **MAY**, southern delegates at the Democratic National Convention in Charleston, South Carolina, walked out in protest against a plank in the platform that assured federal protection of slavery in the territories. The convention later adjourned after failing to get a two-thirds majority for a presidential nominee. Northern Democrats regrouped in early June and nominated Senator Stephen A. Douglas to run for president and Herschel V. John of Georgia for vice president. On June 28, southern Democrats countered at their own meeting in Baltimore, where they named John C. Breckinridge of Kentucky to run for president and Joseph Lane of Oregon for vice president. The Democratic Party's split over the issue of slavery was irreversible, and the party broke into two separate political entities. Both northern and southern Democratic slates were expected to oppose Lincoln and Hamlin in November.

CONGRESSIONAL RESOLUTION REINFORCES SLAVERY

On **MAY 24** and **25**, the U.S. Congress adopted a set of resolutions sponsored by southern congressmen clarifying the status of slavery in the United States:

Slavery is lawful in all territories under the Constitution; neither Congress nor a local legislature can abolish it there; the federal government is in duty bound to protect slave owners as well as the holders of other forms of property in the territories; it is a violation of the Constitution for any state or any combination of citizens to intermeddle with the domestic institutions of any other state "on any pretext whatever, political, moral, or religious, with a view to their disturbance or subversion"; open or covert attacks on slavery are contrary to the solemn pledges given by the states on entering the Union to protect and defend one another;

the inhabitants of a territory on their admission to the Union may decide whether or not they will sanction slavery thereafter; the strict enforcement of the fugitive slave law is required by good faith and the principles of the Constitution.

SCHOOL ESTABLISHED FOR BLACKS IN NEW ORLEANS

In **SEPTEMBER**, Mary D. Brice, an Ohioan and a student of Antioch College, opened a school for "colored children and adults," at the corner of Franklin and Perdido Streets.

Although Brice and her husband were poor when they came to New Orleans in December 1858, they felt it their "duty to teach colored people." Brice was forced to close the school in June 1861, after enduring threats and criticism. Believing that she had a mission to teach, she opened another school in November, nearby, on Magnolia Street. Although Brice was repeatedly warned to stop teaching, she continued. Threats such as "death to nigger teachers" were posted on the gateposts in front of her home. She was again forced to close her school but continued teaching at night when she was less likely to be observed. She taught at the houses of her pupils even when it was clear that she faced possible imprisonment, banishment, or death.

When the city was occupied by Union forces, Brice's school

"Southern Ass-stock-crazy": This cartoon ridicules South Carolina's break from the Union.

was opened and thrived, and was subsequently placed under the guidance of the state board of education. Brice was employed as an "efficient and honorable principal."

SLAVE CONSPIRACY BETRAYED IN NORTH CAROLINA
In **OCTOBER**, a slave conspiracy occurred in Plymouth, a small community in eastern North Carolina. A score of slaves met in a swamp to plan an insurrection in which they would encourage hundreds of bondservants to join them and march on Plymouth. They planned to burn the town, take money and weapons, escape by ship through Albemarle Sound, and kill all whites who tried to stop them. Like many other slave conspiracies, this one was betrayed by a slave.

LINCOLN ELECTED PRESIDENT
On **NOVEMBER 6**, Abraham Lincoln was elected president of the United States. Although he failed to win a majority of the popular vote, he carried eighteen states and 180 of the total 303 electoral votes. The Black vote was almost solidly Republican. Many southerners, who called Lincoln "That Black Republican," were expected to support the breakup of the Union as a result.

DOUGLASS AND SUPPORTERS ATTACKED BY MOB AT RALLY
On **DECEMBER 3**, a proslavery mob attacked a rally in Boston organized by abolitionist Frederick Douglass in memory of abolitionist John Brown, who was executed for his leadership of the raid on Harpers Ferry. Police helped the mob in driving off Douglass and his supporters.

SOUTH CAROLINA SECEDES
On **DECEMBER 20**, South Carolina's political leaders met for less than half an hour in St. Andrew's Hall in Charleston and voted to secede from the Union, declaring South Carolina an "independent commonwealth." Within days of the secession, Major Robert Anderson moved seventy-three soldiers to Fort Sumter, a massive brick and concrete fortress rising high above sea level on an island in the harbor. In response to this federal action, the South Carolina militia seized other federal installations in the city. President James Buchanan refused to yield to mounting pressure to return Fort Sumter to South Carolinians.

1861 AMERICAN MISSIONARY ASSOCIATION EDUCATES SLAVES
Lewis Tappan, a noted abolitionist and treasurer of the American Missionary Association (AMA), wrote to General Benjamin Butler of Fortress Monroe, in Virginia, offering the services of the AMA in educating the slaves. Butler accepted the aid, and the Reverend Lewis C. Lockwood was sent to develop an educational program. Lockwood enlisted Mary Peake to teach the children at Fortress Monroe. He later opened a Sunday school for slaves in the home of former president John Tyler.

BLACK CREWMAN RETURNS SHIP AFTER CAPTURE
William J. Tillman, a cook on the Union ship *S. J. Waring*, was captured along with the rest of the ship's crew by the Confederate ship *Jefferson Davis*. Tillman escaped, killed his captors, and helped sail the ship to New York. It is reported that he received a reward of $5,000 for his service.

BLACKS AND NATIVE AMERICANS FIGHT IN CIVIL WAR
For months prior to the mustering of the First South Carolina Volunteers (the first sanctioned Black regiment) into the Union army, a large number of Blacks in Kansas and Oklahoma fought, together with Native Americans, against Confederates. In 1861, a regiment of one thousand Blacks and Native Americans led by Chief Opothayohola left Indian Territory for Kansas. They sustained three attacks from the Confederates; without food and ammunition, many scattered to save themselves from freezing cold and starvation. Those who remained retreated and were later recruited by James H. Lane and James Montgomery into a special "red and black jayhawking" regiment to carry out raids and attacks in Missouri. Six Killer, a Black Cherokee, was honored by his fellow soldiers for his bravery after he shot two Confederates, bayoneted another, and clubbed a fourth with the butt of his rifle. Other heroic acts were noted among these soldiers at the Battle of Island Mound, Missouri.

BLACKS REJECTED BY UNION ARMY
After the attack on Fort Sumter, President Lincoln called for seventy-five thousand volunteers to serve in the Union army. Although many free Blacks attempted to enlist, government policy forbade their participation. Lincoln based this policy on his belief that allowing Blacks to enlist would drive slaveholding border states, such as Kentucky, Tennessee, and Missouri, into the Confederacy. Richard Harvey

Early in the Civil War, Blacks worked in a variety of jobs in military camps, including burying the dead.

BLACKS AS LABORERS IN UNION AND CONFEDERACY WAR EFFORTS

Although Blacks could not formally enlist in the Union's war effort until January 1, 1863, they served in a variety of support services, starting in the first year of the conflict. Blacks worked as camp cooks, barbers, and teamsters. They also built fortifications and buried the dead. Blacks had moved into semimilitary and military support positions in the Union army by the end of 1861.

Severe shortages of manpower in the South caused the Confederacy to use slaves in a variety of jobs. At the onset of the war, Blacks made up about one-third of the South's population; most of them were slaves. Slaves built fortifications, repaired railroads, and worked in factories to make weapons and on plantations and farms. They also worked as cooks, teamsters, and nurses. They could not, however, be armed to fight. In one case, when free Blacks in New Orleans volunteered to serve with the Confederacy, they were given broomsticks.

From 1863 on, the South seriously considered arming slaves, but the idea sharply contradicted the basic Southern belief in Black inferiority. On March 15, 1865, conditions were so desperate that the Confederate Congress allowed slaves to be armed. Two weeks later, Lee surrendered.

Cain, who would later serve as a congressman from South Carolina, was turned away by Union recruiters while a student at Wilberforce University. Jacob Dodson, who had accompanied John C. Frémont in his explorations of the West, wrote to Secretary of War Simon Cameron in support of Cain's petition.

Several reasons are offered for the rejection of Black volunteers. Those who continued to believe that the Civil War was over secession rather than slavery felt it was inappropriate for Blacks to fight in a war that concerned whites. Others, including Lincoln, did not believe that Blacks would make good soldiers. Such views were quickly dispelled by the heroic action of Blacks at Fort Sumter and in other battles. Official government policy relegated most Blacks to serve as laborers, nurses, cooks, scouts, or spies. Regardless of policy, some Union commanders informally used Blacks to supplement their forces. In 1862, critical manpower shortages in Port Royal,

South Carolina; New Orleans; and Bates County, Missouri led the local commanders to recruit Blacks to protect their positions.

FORTEN TEACHES EX-SLAVES

When the Civil War broke out, many slaves escaped to the Sea Islands off the coast of South Carolina. Charlotte Forten volunteered to teach the ex-slaves there. The granddaugher of James Forten, a wealthy Black Philadelphia shipbuilder, Charlotte Forten grew up wealthy and attended integrated schools in Massachusetts, where she lived with the Charles Lenox Remond family and aspired to be an abolitionist. She graduated with honors from Salem Normal School in 1856 at the age of nineteen and became the first Black woman to teach white students in Massachusetts when she accepted a position at the Epes Grammar School in Salem. When Forten left the Sea Islands in 1864, thousands of children were enrolled in schools, and adults were learning to read. In 1873, Forten became a clerk in the U.S. Treasury, and five years later she married the Reverend Francis Grimké.

KING OF DAHOMEY PETITIONED

The African Aid Society of New York appealed to the king of Dahomey in West Africa to cease the sale of slaves and to use his people to produce crops for export, particularly cotton. The plea, part of a letter addressed to the king, was published in the January 26,

1861, issue of *Freedom's Journal.* The king of Dahomey sold ten thousand slaves in 1860 for fifty thousand dollars, an amount he could exceed if he chose to employ his people in making products to sell to foreign countries.

LAST FUGITIVE SLAVE RETURNED TO SOUTH

Lucy Bagby Johnson of Cleveland, Ohio, was the last fugitive slave returned to the South under the Fugitive Slave Act of 1850.

Lucy Bagby was taken by a group of law officers from the home where she was employed. A mob gathered to protest her removal to the South. Three prominent white lawyers worked on her behalf, and the court decided that she should be set free. She was then immediately arrested by U.S. marshals and taken before the federal commissioner. He decided that although he found the duty distasteful, Bagby had to be returned according to law. The commissioner offered to contribute to a fund that would purchase Bagby from her master, but the master refused. Bagby was escorted to the train, surrounded by special marshals to prevent her from being freed by local citizens. Bagby was returned to West Virginia. After the Civil War began, her master tried to move her farther south, but Bagby was rescued by a Union army officer. After emancipation, she married a former Union soldier by the name of Johnson and returned to Cleveland, where she died in 1906.

CONFEDERATE STATES OF AMERICA FORMED

Beginning on **JANUARY 10**, Southern states followed South Carolina in seceding from the Union and joining the Confederacy: Mississippi on January 9, Florida on January 10, Alabama on January 11, Georgia on January 19, Louisiana on January 26, Texas on February 23, Virginia on April 17, Arkansas on May 6, North Carolina on May 20, and Tennessee on June 8. On February 4, delegates from the states that had already seceded met in Montgomery, Alabama, and formed the government of the Confederate States of America. On May 21, Richmond, Virginia, was designated the capital of the Confederacy. Missouri and Kentucky did not join the Confederate states, although they had many supporters of slavery. Western Virginia formed a Unionist government in June and became the state of West Virginia on June 20, 1863. It was the Union's thirty-fifth state, and its constitution mandated gradual emancipation of slaves.

CONFEDERATE FORCES OPEN FIRE ON FORT SUMTER

On **APRIL 12, 1861**, Confederate forces opened fire on Fort Sumter in Charleston Harbor, the act that began the Civil War. President Lincoln's decision to use military force to preserve the Union forced several states to choose between the Union or the Confederacy. Virginia, Arkansas, North Carolina, and Tennessee joined with the secessionist states (South Carolina, Florida, Georgia, Alabama, Mississippi, Louisiana, and Texas) to form the Confederate States of America. The slave states of Delaware, Missouri, Kentucky, and Maryland remained with the Union.

FORT SUMTER ATTACK DEEMED "INSURRECTION"

On **APRIL 15**, Lincoln declared the Fort Sumter attack, led by General Pierre Beauregard, commander of the Provisional Forces of the Confederate States of America, an insurrection, not a war.

FIRST INJURY SUSTAINED BY BLACK IN UNIFORM

On **APRIL 18**, Nicholas Biddle, a sixty-five-year-old former slave who had volunteered for the Union, was the first Black person in uniform to be injured in the Civil War. He was struck by a thrown rock while traveling with Pennsylvania troops through Baltimore.

◆ Biddle, an escaped slave and resident of Pottsville, Pennsylvania, had volunteered to serve the Union just two days after a call for volunteers. Rather than wait to be officially inducted, Biddle attached himself to a unit of white troops who gave him a uniform. When the company marched through Baltimore, a slaveholding city, proslavery supporters threw stones, and Biddle was struck and felled. The next day, Baltimore proslavery forces mobbed a Massachusetts regiment and killed four white soldiers.

SIXTH MASSACHUSETTS REGIMENT ATTACKED

On **APRIL 19**, a proslavery, pro-Confederacy mob attacked soldiers of the Sixth Massachusetts Regiment, who had stopped at Baltimore while en route to Washington. The incident began when Southern sympathizers blocked the right of way of the eight-hundred soldiers. A riot erupted when someone shot a gun, and as many as twelve Baltimore residents were killed.

CONFEDERATE CONGRESS DECLARES WAR

On **MAY 6**, the Confederate Congress officially declared war on the United States.

On April 12, 1861, Confederate forces attacked Fort Sumter, starting the Civil War.

SLAVES SEEK FREEDOM AT FORTRESS MONROE

On **MAY 23**, General Benjamin Butler declared slaves who entered his lines to be "contraband." Previously, under the Fugitive Slave Act, escaped slaves had to be returned to their owners. This policy changed when Butler, a lawyer from Massachusetts, was placed in charge of Fortress Monroe in Virginia. An ardent antislavery abolitionist, Butler declared, "The fugitive slave act does not affect a foreign country, which Virginia claims to be. . . ." His decision was approved by the War Department. Some historians note that Butler's action was the first crack in the policy to keep the slavery issue out of the war.

Within two months, about nine hundred runaway slaves sought freedom at the fortress. Butler used the former slaves to build roads and fortifications, unload vessels, and store provisions. Some of them were eventually organized into the Army of the James, and others served on the USS *Minnesota*. Fugitive slaves were not always treated well by the Union forces. Some were worked harshly and received low pay.

CONFISCATION ACT PASSED

On **AUGUST 6**, Congress passed the first Confiscation Act, providing that runaway slaves who had been used to aid the Confederacy could be granted freedom once under the control of the Union army.

FREEDOM FOR MISSOURI SLAVES REJECTED BY LINCOLN

On **SEPTEMBER 2**, President Lincoln declared null and void General John C. Frémont's decree freeing Missouri slaves. On August 30, General Frémont had issued a proclamation of emancipation, freeing the slaves of disloyal (Confederate) Missourians. General Frémont did not share the view that Blacks were not

Hundreds of Blacks made their way to Fortress Monroe in search of freedom.

Contraband slaves provided the Union army at Fortress Monroe with cheap labor for a variety of work details. Although the sketch shows the "contrabands" going merrily off to work, they were often badly treated.

This photograph shows several Black seamen on the deck of a Union gunboat. A large number of Blacks served in the Union navy for a number of reasons: they were experienced seamen, the navy was short of men, and Blacks were prohibited from serving in the army.

suited to the military. At this time, Lincoln felt that Blacks should be used as laborers only. Frémont justified his action with the plea of military necessity: His requests for more men had been consistently denied by the government. His action also reflected his ties with Radical Republicans who hated slavery and had pressed Lincoln to allow individual commanders to emancipate the slaves of rebels.

As punishment for independently freeing the slaves, Lincoln removed Frémont from command on October 24, 1861. He was reinstated in March 1862 with a command in the Mountain Department in western Virginia.

Although others saw the need for enlisting Blacks into the military, no other military leader went as far as Frémont. General David Hunter raised a regiment of Black troops on the Sea Islands off the coast of Georgia. Senator James H. Lane accepted Blacks in two Kansas volunteer units, and in Cincinnati, a Black brigade was raised in 1862 to build fortifications for protecting the city.

PEAKE TEACHES IN FIRST AMERICAN MISSIONARY ASSOCIATION SCHOOL

On **SEPTEMBER 17**, Mary S. Peake opened the first school sponsored by the American Missionary Association for the teaching of Blacks. When Confederate forces occupied the town of Hampton, Virginia, Peake and her husband fled to Brown Cottage on the grounds of Chesapeake Female College, across the Hampton River. Peake used Brown Cottage for the school. Hampton University had its roots in this school.

◈ Although Peake is sometimes credited with being the first Black teacher in a day school after the beginning of the Civil War, others had preceded her in teaching in areas controlled by Union forces. In the years prior to the Civil War, Peake, who had been born free in Norfolk County, established the Daughters of Zion in Hampton for the care of the needy. She also taught Black children and adults in her home. Peake died of tuberculosis a few years after opening her school in Hampton.

SLAVES ENLIST IN NAVY

On **SEPTEMBER 25**, the secretary of the navy authorized the enlistment of slaves to fight in the Civil War. The Union had never barred Blacks from Naval service, in part because of critical manpower shortages. Because Blacks were not allowed to enlist in the army, and a large number of Blacks had experience as seamen, many rushed to enlist. However, Blacks were often confined to duties as servants, cooks, or powder boys.

By 1862, Blacks could be promoted to regular seaman ranks, and by the end of the war, about 30,000 Blacks out of a total of 118,000 enlistees had served in the navy — a proportion higher than in the army. In general, crews aboard navy vessels were integrated; there were no separate all-Black units. But prejudice and discrimination remained, and sometimes officers segregated their crews according to jobs. For example, Admiral David D. Porter, a Union officer from the South, would not allow Blacks to be lookouts because he believed they lacked the requisite intelligence.

1862 BLACKS CONFER WITH LINCOLN

At the first meeting ever held between Blacks and a U.S. president, Abraham Lincoln advocated the emigration of free Blacks to Central America. At the time, Lincoln believed that the two races could not live together peacefully. "There is an unwillingness on the part of our people, harsh as it may be, for you free colored people to remain among us." He asked the Black leaders to recruit volunteers for a government-sponsored colonization project in Central America. Frederick Douglass was outraged by Lincoln's request. He

responded angrily, "This is our country as much as it is yours, and we will not leave it."

In the next year, the United States actually transported 453 Blacks to an island near Haiti. This experiment failed. By the end of the Civil War, Lincoln had changed his opinion about encouraging Black emigration.

KING SERVES WITH FIRST SOUTH CAROLINA VOLUNTEERS

Susie King (later known as Susie King Taylor) (1848–1912) joined the First South Carolina Volunteers, an all-Black regiment raised by General David Hunter, a Union commander. Still in her teens, she taught soldiers to read and write and nursed their wounds after battle. The wife of Edward King, a member of the First South Carolina Volunteers, she became unit laundress and volunteer nurse, traveling with her husband's unit throughout the Civil War. Susie King was one of thousands of Black women who served in a number of ways to support Black soldiers during the war. Because many worked in supportive roles, their activities were not decorated nor were their stories well recorded.

◈ Susie King Taylor began life as a slave on one of the Georgia Sea Islands. She grew up in Savannah and learned to read and write from a free Black woman when it was illegal to teach slaves. She escaped slavery when the Union army occupied the Sea Islands in 1862. At the age of fourteen, she volunteered as a teacher of freed Blacks on St. Simon's Island and later married Edward King and moved to Port Royal Island in South Carolina. It was here that she and her husband joined the First South Carolina Volunteers.

In February 1866, after the war was over, she moved to Savannah, where she operated a night school for freed Blacks. When the school closed in 1868 and her husband died, she was forced to secure employment as a house domestic and laundress. She moved to Boston and married Russell Taylor. In 1886, Susie King Taylor helped organize the Boston branch of the Women's Relief Corps, an auxiliary of the Grand Army of the Republic. In 1898, she returned to Louisiana to care for her ill son. Because Jim Crow laws prohibited her from taking her son to Boston for specialist care, her son died. In 1902, she was encouraged by Colonel Thomas Wentworth Higginson to write her wartime memoirs — the first documentation of duties performed by a Black nurse in the Civil War.

NATIONAL FREEDMEN'S RELIEF ASSOCIATION FORMED

In New York, free Blacks organized a National Freedmen's Relief Association to help slaves adjust to their new freedom. Similar associations formed in Chicago, Cincinnati, and Philadelphia. These groups later consolidated as the American Freedmen's Aid Commission.

SCHOOL FOR FREED SLAVES OPEN ON SEA ISLANDS

Two Quaker abolitionists from Philadelphia, Laura Towne and Ellen Murray, established Penn School on St. Helena Island off South Carolina, within weeks of its capture by Union troops. Here, Blacks received training in agriculture and home economics. The school established the state's first farming co-op. The two women ran the Penn Normal Institute for forty years. The school is now a national historic landmark.

As the Civil War intensified and Union forces swept across the South, they had to contend with a larger number of contraband slaves. Slave families, the slave populations of plantations, and entire communities picked up their belongings and fled to safety behind Union lines.

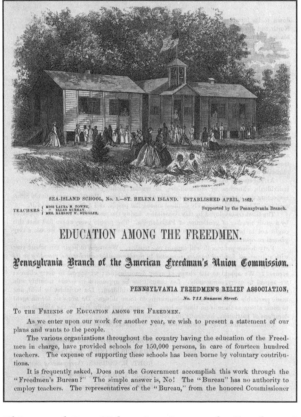

This open letter, "Education Among the Freedmen," demonstrates that some abolitionists did not wait until the end of the Civil War to establish schools in the South for freed slaves.

SLAVES AND FREE BLACKS SWELL UNION RANKS

Former slaves, considered contraband of war, and free Blacks sought protection and freedom within Union forces. Their numbers swelled as the Union army penetrated deeper into the South. After almost every victory, the Union forces had to contend with increasing numbers of human contraband. Union commanders quickly adjusted rations and living quarters to accommodate the Blacks' immediate need for food, clothing, and shelter. In most cases, education was one of the most sought-after services in Black refugee camps. Education helped to provide internal order, as well as a means for easing the transition from slavery to freedom. Contraband arrived from all corners of the South, in families, groups, and even communities.

PRESIDENT OF CONFEDERACY ELECTED

On **FEBRUARY 22**, Jefferson Davis was elected president of the Confederacy. Davis, who was raised on a large cotton plantation in Mississippi, had become a successful planter himself, after attending the U.S. Military Academy at West Point and completing a distinguished military career. Davis was elected to the presidency of the Confederate states as a compromise candidate. A strong supporter of states' rights, Davis was perceived by some as a moderate.

NASHVILLE FALLS TO UNION FORCES
On **FEBRUARY 25**, Nashville became the first Confederate state capital to fall under Union control. Ironically, Tennessee was the last of the states to secede, the last to join the Confederacy, and one of the most divided in its support for the Confederacy.

AID OFFERED TO STATES THAT GRADUALLY ABOLISH SLAVERY
On **MARCH 6**, Lincoln recommended a plan to Congress that would offer aid to any state promising gradual abolition of slavery. Congress declared that the United States would compensate owners for any slave freed in states that adopted this policy.

DISTRICT OF COLUMBIA ABOLISHES SLAVERY
On **APRIL 16**, Lincoln proposed, and the Senate passed, a bill abolishing slavery in the District of Columbia. Slave owners were to be compensated at the rate of

On April 19, 1862, thousands of Black people gathered to celebrate the abolition of slavery in the District of Columbia by the U.S. Congress.

three hundred dollars per slave. A total of $993,407 was allocated as compensation to slave owners for their lost property. In addition, $100,000 was allocated for the voluntary emigration of these freed slaves to Haiti or Liberia. An estimated thirty-one hundred slaves were freed in the district. Seven Black residents received cash compensation in the amount of $5,978.20 for freeing their twenty-six slaves. Robert Gunnell, who owned the most slaves, freed ten; Gabriel Coakley freed eight.

NEW ORLEANS FALLS
On **APRIL 28**, the Union fleet sailed into New Orleans. The largest seaport in the South was now in Union hands.

SLAVES AND FREE BLACK REFUGEES CONCENTRATE IN NORFOLK
In **MAY**, Union forces took Norfolk, Virginia, and it became a center for Black refugees from the countryside. One study estimated that seventy-thousand former slaves were in Norfolk when the Civil War ended.

FIRST SOUTH CAROLINA VOLUNTEERS MUSTERED
On **MAY 9**, the first Black Civil War regiment (made up chiefly of ex-slaves) was formed at Hilton Head by Abram Murchison, a Black minister. At the suggestion of General David Hunter, Murchison had called upon Blacks to volunteer for the Union. Many of the initial volunteers were from the Sea Islands and "contained scarcely a freeman, not one mulatto in ten, and a far smaller proportion who could read or write when enlisted." The regiment was called the First South Carolina Volunteers and commanded by Colonel Thomas Wentworth Higginson. Higginson, like many others, had doubts about the fighting abilities of slaves.

In late 1861, the Union forces captured Sea Island near Beaufort, South Carolina. The slaves stayed on the plantations, including that of J. J. Smith, which was later occupied by the First South Carolina Volunteers.

SMALLS TURNS THE *Planter* OVER TO UNION
On **MAY 13**, Robert Smalls (1839–1915), a Black pressed into Confederate service, sailed the steamer *Planter*, which had been converted to a gunboat, out of Charleston and turned it over to the Union forces.

Following his Civil War heroics, Smalls later became important in South Carolina business and politics, serving five terms in the U.S. House of Representatives.

Robert Smalls, born a slave, became a hero when he captured the Planter, *a Confederate steamer, and turned it over to Union forces. Smalls later became a member of the U.S. House of Representatives.*

HOMESTEAD ACT PASSED
On **MAY 20**, President Lincoln signed into law the Homestead Act, which granted tracts of land at minimal cost to settlers of the West. Citizens could buy up to 160 acres of public property at one dollar and twenty-five cents per acre, as long as they settled on the land for five years. Although free Blacks took advantage of this act, major settlement in the West did not occur until immediately after the Civil War.

SLAVERY OUTLAWED IN TERRITORIES
On **JUNE 19**, President Lincoln signed a bill outlawing slavery in the territories but not in the states.

COME AND JOIN US BROTHERS.

This colorful recruiting poster bore the slogan "Come and Join Us Brothers."

MORRILL LAND GRANT ACT SIGNED

On **JULY 2**, President Lincoln signed into law the Morrill Land Grant Act. It provided thirty thousand acres of land to each state for the establishment of colleges devoted to agriculture, engineering, and military science. The act was named for Representative Justin Morrill, who worked several years to secure its passage. Although this particular act had little direct relation to the African American experience, it set the precedent for the funding of many Black colleges after the Civil War.

CONGRESS AUTHORIZES USE OF BLACKS IN UNION ARMY

On **JULY 17**, Congress authorized and Lincoln signed an act that allowed the use of Blacks in the Union army, in response to demands from Northerners. The new Militia Act permitted the president to use "as many persons of African descent" as needed "for suppression of the Rebellion." This act repealed a 1792 ordinance barring "persons of color" from serving in the militia. Free Blacks and ex-slaves could thus be recruited but were to be regarded as laborers and paid ten dollars per month, less clothing expenses. (Whites were paid thirteen dollars per month, plus clothing expenses.) Black soldiers faced even greater danger than their white counterparts — if captured, they were usually shot or sold into slavery, regardless of their status before the war. Few were taken as prisoners of war. Blacks initially were not allowed to serve as officers but eventually, about one hundred Blacks received commissions in the Union army, and two thousand became noncommissioned officers. Blacks could not be formally recruited until January 1, 1863, following the Emancipation Proclamation.

FIRST KANSAS COLORED VOLUNTEERS BATTLE CONFEDERATES

In **AUGUST**, James H. Lane began organizing the First Kansas Colored Volunteers. The unit was given official recognition in November, thus becoming the first all-Black regiment in a northern area. The First Kansas Colored Volunteers actually saw their first action on October 28, when they battled a superior force of Confederate soldiers at Island Mount, Missouri. It was the first engagement involving Black troops, and the volunteers were victorious.

At the end of the war, the First Kansas Colored Regiment ranked twenty-first among federal regiments in percentage of total enrollment killed in action.

BLACKS FORM FIRST LOUISIANA NATIVE GUARDS

On **AUGUST 22**, General Benjamin Butler called upon free Blacks in New Orleans to serve the Union. Hundreds came forward, including skilled workers, professionals, entrepreneurs, and land owners. Some were descendants of Blacks who had fought with Andrew Jackson at the battle of New Orleans in 1815. On September 27, this group became the first Black regiment to receive official recognition in the Union army. Unlike other units, the First Louisiana Native Guards had Black captains and lieutenants.

LINCOLN QUESTIONED ON AIMS OF WAR

On **AUGUST 22**, Horace Greeley, editor of the *New York Tribune,* questioned Abraham Lincoln about the purpose of the Civil War. Lincoln replied, "My paramount object in this struggle is to save the Union, and not either to save or destroy slavery. If I could save the Union without freeing any slaves I would do it; if I could save it by freeing all the slaves, I would do it, and if I could do it by freeing some and leaving others alone, I would do that."

1863 DOUGLASS RECRUITS FOR UNION FORCES

Noted abolitionist Frederick Douglass became a major recruiter for the Union forces. After meeting several times with President Lincoln, he advised Blacks to join in large numbers as an expression of their patriotism and love of country. Douglass and others believed that Blacks had everything to win (freedom) by joining the Union cause. Two of Douglass's sons, Lewis and Charles, enlisted and served with Union forces. Lewis became a Sergeant Major, and both fought with Colonel Robert Shaw at Fort Wagner. At a meeting at National Hall in Philadelphia, Douglass eloquently appealed to Blacks to enlist in the service of the Union:

> I say at once, in peace and in war, I am content with nothing for the black man short of equal and exact justice. The only question I have, and the point at which I differ from those who refuse to enlist, is whether the colored man is more likely to obtain justice and equality while refusing to assist in putting down this tremendous rebellion than he would be if he should promptly, generously and earnestly give his hand and heart to the salvation of the country in this its day of calamity and peril. Nothing can be more plain, nothing more certain than the speediest and best possible way open to us to manhood, equal rights and elevation, is that we enter this service.
>
> . . . Now, I think there can be no doubt as to the attitude of the Richmond or confederate government. Wherever else there has been concealment, here all is frank, open and diabolically straightforward. Jefferson Davis and his government make no secret as to the cause of this war, and they do not conceal the purpose of the war. That purpose is nothing more nor less than to make the slavery of the African race universal and perpetual on this continent. . . . View it any way you please, therefore, the rebels are fighting for the existence of slavery — they are fighting for the privilege, the horrid privilege, of sundering the dearest ties of human nature — of trafficking in slaves and the souls of men — for the ghastly privilege of scourging women and selling innocent children.

BLACKS FIGHT IN BATTLE OF HUNDRED PINES

In **JANUARY**, the first real clash between the Union army's officially recruited Black troops and Confederate soldiers occurred at the Battle of Hundred Pines. Black soldiers held their ground and repelled Confederate troops.

EMANCIPATION PROCLAMATION ISSUED

On **JANUARY 1**, President Lincoln signed the Emancipation Proclamation out of military necessity. Its

Black leaders were instrumental in recruiting young Black men to serve in the Union forces. These recruits were marching up Beekman Street in New York City.

purpose was to deplete Southern manpower reserve in slaves. The proclamation stated that "all persons held as slaves within any State, or designated part of the state, the people whereof shall be in rebellion against the United States, shall be then, thenceforward, and forever free." It freed only those slaves residing in the territory in rebellion. The president had no constitutional authority to abolish slavery in loyal states. In addition, the proclamation stated, "And I further declare and make known that such persons of suitable condition will be received into the armed service of the United States to garrison forts, positions, stations and other places, and to man vessels of all sorts in paid service."

FREEDMEN'S AID SOCIETIES ASSIST REFUGEES
In **MARCH**, the first large missionary expedition to aid the "contraband" of the Civil War was constituted and sailed from New York to Hilton Head, South Car-

olina. Led by Edward L. Pierce, a representative of the Freedmen's Aid Societies of Boston, New York City, and Philadelphia, as many as forty-five men and fifteen women joined together to assist the ex-slaves in industry, religion, education, agriculture, and "other useful measures." Over the months, the number of teachers and superintendents increased, but proportionately more slowly than the number of freed slaves. By the summer growing season, freed slaves were working fifteen thousand acres of corn, potatoes, and cotton, and thousands were being educated on the responsibilities of citizenship.

CONSCRIPTION ACT ISSUED
On **MARCH 3**, President Lincoln signed an executive order, the Conscription Act, which compelled American citizens to report for duty in the war. All males between the ages of twenty and forty-six were compelled to serve. The act made the Civil War a war of

the poor, since wealthier citizens could buy their way out of serving. For a fee of three hundred dollars, one's military obligation could be waived. This latter provision raised revenue for the war effort but allowed the rich to avoid the dangers of war. The desertion rate was quite high, about 10 percent for each side.

PAYNE PURCHASES WILBERFORCE UNIVERSITY

On **MARCH 10**, Daniel L. Payne (1811–1893), a bishop of the African Methodist Episcopal Church, purchased Wilberforce University in Xenia, Ohio, for ten thousand dollars. Wilberforce had been founded by the Methodist Episcopal Church in 1856. Payne became the first president of a Black institution of higher learning in the country. In 1876, he became chancellor of the university and dean of its theological seminary. He later offered W. E. B. Du Bois a position at Wilberforce.

◆ Payne was born on February 24, 1811, of free parents in Charleston, South Carolina. His father was of mixed English and African parentage and his mother was of Native American and African extraction. He attended Minor's Moralist Society School, maintained by free Blacks, where he studied the Bible and other literature. He was judged as a person of superior intellectual ability. Payne then served as an apprentice to several artisans. In 1828, he began a small school with just three pupils, and in the evening, he instructed adults. He built a school the following year, where he taught a variety of courses. Payne had to close his school in 1834 when the South Carolina legislature made such studies illegal and their teachers subject to whipping and a fine. He then left the state and later studied at the Lutheran Theological Seminary in Gettysburg, Pennsylvania. He was licensed to preach in 1837. He opened a school in Philadelphia in 1840 and joined the African Methodist Episcopal Church a year later. Payne became a minister, educator, and bishop of the AME Church. He organized perhaps the first Black pastors association and founded a school for young preachers. Payne was a noted author; his writings include *Treatise on Domestic Education* and *Recollections of Seventy Years*, an important memoir of this time.

THOMPSON BECOMES FIRST BLACK WOMAN PRINCIPAL IN NEW YORK PUBLIC SCHOOLS

On **APRIL 30**, Sarah Thompson, the daughter of landowners and successful farmers on Long Island, became the first Black woman principal in the New York public school system.

Thompson had previously taught in an African Free School, after receiving her early education from her maternal grandmother and at normal schools in the New York area. At the time of her appointment, Thompson was married to the Reverend James Thompson, rector of the St. Matthew Free Church in Brooklyn. After his death, Thompson married Henry Highland Garnet, the prominent abolitionist. Sarah founded the Equal Suffrage Club, a small club of Black women in New York, and was an early member of the National Association of Colored Women. She opposed discrimination against teachers in public schools. Sarah Thompson Garnet died in 1911. Her younger sister, Susan Maria McKinney Steward, was one of the first Black women to graduate from medical college.

BUREAU OF COLORED TROOPS ESTABLISHED

In **MAY**, the U.S. War Department established the Bureau of Colored Troops to handle all recruitment and organization of Black regiments. Ironically, most of its officers were white, although some Blacks served as noncommissioned officers. Blacks were to be mustered directly into the military, and all such units were to be organized under the United States Colored Troops (USCT). Within several months, thirty Black regiments became part of the Union forces.

CAPTURED BLACK UNION SOLDIERS ENSLAVED OR EXECUTED

On **MAY 1**, the Confederate Congress in Richmond, Virginia, passed a resolution that permitted enslavement or execution of captured Black Union soldiers.

BLACK SOLDIERS PROVE TO BE CONSEQUENTIAL FORCE

Blacks proved themselves brave soldiers in several heroic battles. On **MAY 27**, five Black regiments were ordered into an almost suicidal attack against a Confederate stronghold of almost seven thousand troops at Port Hudson, Louisiana, the last important Confederate stronghold on the Mississippi River. None of the Black troops were seasoned in combat; one regiment had been formed only three months earlier. Six times, more than one thousand Black soldiers charged over difficult terrain in the face of severe enemy fire. In this major battle, Blacks suffered 37 dead, 116 missing, and 155 wounded. Although the Black soldiers did not kill a single Confederate in this defeat, the battle was a turning point in the attitude toward them. They were now seen as brave, courageous, and steadfast. Six weeks later, the Confederate garrison surrendered.

Black soldiers fought heroically at Milliken's Bend, Louisiana.

Blacks distinguished themselves in other battles at this time. On June 6, at Milliken's Bend in Louisiana, Black troops fought heroically against a Confederate force of Texans twice the size of their own. About half of the Black soldiers were killed or wounded. And in July, Black soldiers fought bravely in the Battle of Fort Wagner in South Carolina. Black soldiers participated in at least 39 major battles and 410 minor ones during the Civil War. The blood of Blacks and whites mixed as the battlefield casualties mounted, and Black and white regiments began to depend more and more on one another.

TUBMAN AIDS UNION FORCES
In **JUNE**, Harriet Tubman, a former slave whom many called "Moses," led a group of soldiers up the Comba-hee River in South Carolina, where they moved onto plantations, set them afire, and liberated slaves. About eight hundred slaves were set free. Tubman provided various types of assistance to Union forces — nursing, acting as a scout in the South, and providing information on the behavior of Southerners, plantation owners, and slaves.

Tubman knew firsthand where food and other supplies were stored on plantations — essential intelligence she had gained from more than ten years as a conductor for the Underground Railroad. This infor-mation allowed many Union soldiers to live off the land during their raids on key Southern cities. Clearly, Tubman's knowledge of the South and her contacts via the Underground Railroad and among Southern slaves made her one of the most important "soldiers" of the Civil War.

CONFEDERATE FORCES SURRENDER AT VICKSBURG
On **JULY 4**, Commanding General Ulysses S. Grant ac-cepted the unconditional surrender of General Joseph Pemberton at Vicksburg, Mississippi.

Vicksburg was so strongly defended that Grant had decided to dig in and use continuous artillery bom-bardment lasting for more than six weeks. Some two hundred Union guns bombarded Vicksburg, and gun-boats fired twenty-two thousand shells at the Con-federate defenders between May 22 and July 4. When Pemberton sent word asking Grant to talk, Grant refused, saying he only wanted an "unconditional" surrender and nothing less. As Grant expected, the Confederate troops had suffered heavy losses and had no choice but to surrender. With victories here and at Port Hudson on July 9, the Union gained control of the most strategic geographic position of the war at the time — the Mississippi River — and thus split the Confederacy into two wings. The control of the north-south waterway literally cut off Texas,

Arkansas, and most of Louisiana from other states of the Confederacy. The almost two-month Battle of Vicksburg resulted both in the loss of many lives and the overall destruction of the city. It was reported that civilians hid in caves for safety and ate dogs, cats, and mules to stay alive.

DRAFT RIOTS OCCUR IN NEW YORK CITY

On **JULY 13**, riots against the draft erupted throughout New York City. Demonstrators chanted "Rich man's war, poor man's fight" during a period of four days in which racial and class emotions culminated in rioting, lynchings, and arson. As many as twelve hundred people, including many Blacks and abolitionists, were killed. Some Blacks were hanged on lampposts. The riots actually stemmed from the widespread belief among whites, especially the Irish, that they were

being forced to fight for Blacks whose freedom would then threatened their jobs. In addition, poor whites were angry about military service exemptions allowing wealthy whites to pay three hundred dollars in lieu of service, a price many poor whites could not afford.

UNION FORCES WIN BATTLE AT HONEY SPRINGS IN INDIAN TERRITORY

On **JULY 17**, at Honey Springs (in Indian Territory, now Oklahoma), federal troops led by General James Blount and made up of whites, Blacks, and Native Americans defeated a larger force of Confederate troops commanded by Brigadier General Douglas Cooper in the most important battle fought in Indian Territory.

Troops of the Fifty-fourth Massachusetts Colored Infantry Regiment stormed Fort Wagner.

Sergeant William H. Carney, a member of the 54th Colored Infantry regiment, was badly wounded in his legs, arms, and chest, and thirty-seven years later was awarded the Congressional Medal of Honor for his bravery in battle at Fort Wagner.

FIFTY-FOURTH MASSACHUSETTS VOLUNTEERS STORM FORT WAGNER

On **JULY 18**, the Fifty-fourth Massachusetts Volunteers led the charge against one of the most impenetrable strongholds of the South — Fort Wagner, South Carolina — which guarded the approach to Charleston Harbor. Although their assault was turned back, the Black regiment displayed extreme bravery. Their leader, Colonel Robert Gould Shaw, a young white Harvard alumnus and son of abolitionist parents, was killed during the assault, and by some accounts, along with more than fifteen hundred of his men. Many of them were mangled horribly by exploding artillery shells. Sergeant William H. Carney (Company C), wounded two or three times during the engagement, led the final charge after picking up the fallen flag when the standard-bearer was killed. Thirty-seven years later, Carney was awarded the Congressional Medal of Honor for his bravery.

The Fifty-fourth Massachusetts Volunteers was the first Black regiment raised in the North after the War Department authorized Massachusetts governor John Andrew to recruit Black troops. Massachusetts was successful in enlisting enough Black troops to create the Fifty-fourth Volunteer Infantry and then the Fifty-fifth. The Fifty-fourth included two sons of Frederick Douglass.

The battle at Fort Wagner and the heroism of the Fifty-fourth were dramatized in the 1988 film *Glory*.

QUANTRILL'S RAIDERS STAGE ATTACK IN KANSAS

On **AUGUST 21**, a band of pro-Confederates known as Quantrill's Raiders descended on Lawrence, Kansas, where they looted stores and pistol-whipped any resident in their path. They killed some 150 residents, including every man in two squads of Black federal troops stationed there.

FIFTY-FOURTH MASSACHUSETTS VOLUNTEERS PROTESTS UNEQUAL PAY FOR BLACK SOLDIERS

On **SEPTEMBER 28**, Corporal James Henry Gooding of the Fifty-fourth Massachusetts Volunteers wrote a letter to President Lincoln protesting unequal pay for Black troops. The following is an excerpt of that letter.

Morris Island
Department of the South

September 28, 1863

Your Excelency Abraham Lincoln: Your Excelency will pardon the presumtion of an humble individual like myself, in addressing you, but the earnest Solicitation of my Comrades in Arms, besides the genuine interest felt by myself in the matter is my excuse, for placing before the Executive head of the Nation our Common Grievance: On the 6th of the last Month, the Paymaster of the department informed us, that if we would decide to receive the sum of $10 (ten dollars) per month, he would come and pay us that sum [white soldiers were paid $13]. . . . Now the main question is, Are we Soldiers or are we LABOURERS. We are fully armed, and equipped, have done all the various Duties, pertaining to a Soldiers life, have conducted ourselves, to the complete satisfaction of General Officers, who were, if any, prejiced against us, but who now accord us all the encouragement, and honour due us: have shared the perils, and Labour, of

Reducing the first stronghold, that flaunted a Traitor Flag: and more, Mr. President, Today, the Anglo Saxon Mother, Wife, or Sister, are not alone, in tears for departed Sons, Husbands, and Brothers. The patient Trusting Decendants of Africs Clime, have dyed the ground with blood, in defense of the Union, and Democracy.

For eighteen months, the Fifty-fourth served without pay rather than accept discriminatory wages. Gooding was later captured at the Battle of Olustee, Florida. He died at Andersonville Prison in Georgia, one month before equal pay for Black soldiers was authorized. Thus, when Gooding died, he had received no pay for his service.

GETTYSBURG ADDRESS GIVEN
On **NOVEMBER 19**, President Lincoln delivered his famous address in Gettysburg, Pennsylvania, during the dedication of a military cemetery for soldiers. Edward Everett, a renowned orator, was the main speaker; Lincoln spoke briefly, and his speech was given little attention at the time (except by Everett, who applauded Lincoln for saying more in a few minutes than he had said in his two-hour speech).

The Gettysburg Address grew in significance as historians evaluated the Lincoln years, his life, and his importance in the experience of Black people and the nation. The "three-minute speech" expressed Lincoln's profound support for democracy and the Union.

FREDERICK DOUGLASS
In **DECEMBER**, Frederick Douglass addressed the Third Decade Anniversary Celebration of the American Anti-Slavery Society. The primary questions discussed among abolitionists at the time were: what would be the future of Negroes in the United States? Would they become full-fledged citizens? What would be the responsibility of abolitionists? Douglass addressed these questions in the following manner:

I am . . . of those who believe that the work of the American Anti-Slavery Society will not have been completed until the black men of the South and the black men of the North, shall have been admitted, fully and completely, into the body politic of America. . . . A mightier work than the abolition of slavery now looms up before the Abolitionists. This society was organized, if I remember rightly, for two distinct objects: one was the emancipation of the slave, and the other the elevation of the colored people. When we have taken the chains off the slave, as I believe we

shall do, we shall find a harder resistance to the second purpose of this great association than we have found even upon slavery itself.

1864 BLACK SOLDIER SHOT FOR PROTESTING UNEQUAL PAY
William Walker, a Black sergeant in the Third South Carolina Regiment, was shot by order of a court-martial for leading a protest against unequal pay for Black soldiers.

PRISONERS OF WAR AT INFAMOUS ANDERSONVILLE
Conditions in prisoner-of-war camps in both the North and South were horrendous. Andersonville Prison in Georgia was one of the most notorious camps of the Confederacy. More than one-quarter of the men imprisoned there died of starvation, disease, or exposure.

BLACK REGIMENTS FIGHT IN OLUSTEE, FLORIDA
On **FEBRUARY 20**, in the largest Civil War battle fought in Florida, three Black regiments — the First North Carolina Colored, the Fifty-fourth Massachusetts Volunteers, and the Eighth U.S. Colored of Pennsylvania — joined at least six others of the Union force. Among the first in battle were the Eighth U.S. Colored troops, many of whom were raw recruits without even an hour's practice in loading their guns. More than 300 of their force of 550 were killed. The more combat-experienced Fifty-fourth Massachusetts regiment arrived and managed to hold the area while the rest of the corps retreated. The Fifty-fourth's soldiers were the last to leave the battle. Sergeant Stephen A. Swails of the Fifty-fourth was cited for bravery and became the regiment's first Black commissioned officer shortly afterwards.

LEE IS FIRST BLACK WOMAN PHYSICIAN
On **MARCH 1**, Rebecca Lee graduated from the New England Female Medical College. She became the first African American woman, along with Rebecca Cole and Susan McKinney, to work as a physician.

BLACK TROOPS MASSACRED AT FORT PILLOW
On **APRIL 13**, in an event that is still shrouded in controversy, about fifteen hundred Confederate troops attacked and slaughtered 238 Black soldiers, several dozen white soldiers, and every woman and child at Fort Pillow, Tennessee. Black troops belonging to the Sixth Heavy Artillery were slain even after surrendering. Forty percent of the 557-man force, including

On April 12 and 13, 1864, Confederate forces overran the Sixth Heavy Artillery at Fort Pillow, Tennessee, and killed 238 Black soldiers and several dozen white soldiers after they had surrendered. Revenging the massacre became a rallying cry for Black soldiers.

white troops of the Thirteenth Tennessee Union Cavalry, were killed.

The massacre occurred when Confederate Major General Nathan B. Forrest called a truce but then seized the fort after Union troops had surrendered. Forrest, who had been a slave trader before the war, was vilified throughout the North for his actions. Forrest had previously been decorated several times by the Confederate cavalry for his bravery and leadership.

When the news of Fort Pillow reached Washington, D.C., the cabinet considered executing Southern prisoners in retaliation. Lincoln, however, opposed the plan, noting that "blood cannot restore blood and government should not act for revenge." Although General William Tecumseh Sherman was instructed to punish any of Forrest's troops if caught, there is no evidence that this was ever done. "Fort Pillow" became a rallying cry among Black soldiers for the remainder of the war.

FIRST KANSAS COLORED VOLUNTEERS BATTLE CONFEDERATES IN ARKANSAS

On **APRIL 18**, the First Kansas Colored Volunteers stormed the Confederate lines at Poison Spring,

Arkansas. Not only did they suffer heavy casualties, but those who were captured were murdered by Confederate soldiers. Some were tortured prior to being murdered. African American troops were not taken prisoner as their white counterparts were.

BLACK SOLDIERS ACTIVE IN LONGEST SIEGE OF CIVIL WAR

In JUNE, a ten-month siege started in Petersburg, Virginia, involving Generals Ulysses S. Grant and Robert E. Lee. Grant wanted a quick engagement to cut off rail supplies to Richmond, the Confederate capital. Lee wanted to prolong the siege, believing that the North would tire of the casualties and accept a peace settlement. Black soldiers accounted for twelve hundred of the sixty-three hundred casualties of the entire engagement, which ended only one week before the final Southern surrender at Appomattox.

FUGITIVE SLAVE LAWS REPEALED

On JUNE 28, Congress passed legislation repealing the Fugitive Slave Laws passed by the U.S. Congress in 1793 and 1850.

BLACK TROOPS AT BATTLE OF THE CRATER

On JULY 30, Black troops suffered large losses at the Battle of the Crater near Petersburg, Virginia.

The battle was so named because Union troops built a tunnel under Confederate lines and exploded four tons of powder, creating a huge crater. Black troops of the Ninth Corps had been trained to lead the charge through the crater, but General George Meade feared he would be charged with sacrificing these troops if the attack failed. Therefore, he sent poorly trained white troops in first. Black troops followed. Instead of rushing through the crater, the troops piled up in it and were killed or captured. Almost three thousand Union soldiers of the twenty thousand involved in the assault died or were wounded. It was an egregious failure for the Union army.

LINCOLN CALLS FOR FIVE HUNDRED THOUSAND SOLDIERS

In AUGUST, President Lincoln called for five hundred thousand more soldiers. The conscription law caused many riots. Impoverished Irishmen rioted against Blacks, believing that Blacks were responsible for the war. Tensions eased when exemptions were reduced.

SLAVES DISLOYAL TO CONFEDERACY ARE HANGED

In AUGUST, a public meeting of twelve convened in Brooks County, Georgia, to examine evidence of a conspiracy to rebel by slaves disloyal to the Confederacy. At 6:00 P.M., three Blacks were hanged. Disorder and unfaithfulness among slaves were common during the Civil War, but the Confederate answer (influenced by limited manpower) was severe, swift, and publicized to provide an example to other "bad niggers."

ATLANTA DESTROYED BY GENERAL SHERMAN

On SEPTEMBER 3, General William Tecumseh Sherman wired President Lincoln: "So Atlanta is ours, and fairly won." The city lay in ruins, the result of several months of shelling by Union troops. Sherman's strategy was to destroy Atlanta completely so that it could no longer function as a major supply center for the Confederacy. A foundry, an oil refinery, the Atlanta Hotel, theaters, stores, and public government buildings had gone up in flames. It was reported that only about four hundred houses and a few larger buildings, most of them churches, remained standing after the battle.

The battle for Atlanta began on July 20, when Sherman's forces were attacked at Peachtree Creek, north of the city. The lives of many Black civilians and soldiers on both sides were lost. The capture of Atlanta brought thousands of refugees (men, women, and children just out of slavery) off the plantations into the army camps and cities in search of food, clothing, work, and freedom. Sherman immediately called for the services of philanthropic societies to aid the refugees.

BATTLE FOR CHAFFIN'S FARM, RICHMOND, VIRGINIA

On SEPTEMBER 29, General Benjamin Butler, disgusted that many Union commanders, including Ulysses S. Grant, hesitated to use Black troops in combat, decided to demonstrate their fighting ability. He included nine Black regiments in the attacking force against Fort Harrison, near Chaffin's Farm southeast of Richmond. Most of these regiments were composed of former slaves from Maryland, Virginia, and North Carolina. The Union forces were victorious, although they paid a heavy price. So many white officers were killed that several units ended up being led by Black sergeants. Nine of these noncommissioned officers were among the thirteen Black soldiers who received the Congressional Medal of Honor for bravery during the battle. More than five hundred Black soldiers were killed or wounded.

Christian Fleetwood was one of the Union soldiers who won the Congressional Medal of Honor for his bravery at the Battle of Chaffin's Farm.

Butler later wrote that after seeing so many fallen Black troops, "I swore to myself an oath, which I hope and believe I have kept sacredly, that they and their race should be cared for and protected by me to the extent of my power as long as I lived."

BLACKS HOLD NATIONAL CONVENTION IN SYRACUSE
In **OCTOBER**, 150 Black men, primarily from the North, gathered in Syracuse, New York, to discuss the future of their race. They elected Frederick Douglass as their chairman. High on their agenda was the call for the ballot, and they also exhorted the freedmen to moral, educational, and economic elevation. They recommended that Blacks from all over the country settle "as far as they can, on public lands." The participants concluded the meeting by establishing a program of action for the future and organizing a National Equal Rights League with J. Mercer Langston as the president.

New Orleans Tribune PUBLISHED IN FRENCH AND ENGLISH
On **OCTOBER 14**, the *New Orleans Tribune,* one of the earliest Black daily newspapers, began publication in French and English. Founded by Dr. Louis C. Roundanez in July, it was initially printed three times a week and later became a daily. It was an official organ of the Republican Party. The platform of the *New Orleans Tribune* was presented in a March 5, 1865, issue:

> For colored soldiers who partake of the perils of our armies on the battlefields, we want equal treatment with the white soldiers. We claim for them fair chance for promotion, fair board of examination, and admission of colored officers to all positions and ranks, according to their merit and valor.
>
> For colored laborers who want entire freedom and self-disposal of themselves, we want that they be as free as white men in contracting for their labor, going from place to place and enjoying the earnings of their toils.
>
> For colored ministers, we claim the same respect that is accorded to white clergymen.
>
> For colored children, we want that they shall be received in the common schools. . . .
>
> For the colored woman, we claim the same regard as for the white one. . . .
>
> For the colored men generally, we claim the right of suffrage, and thereby the right of self-taxation and self-government. . . .

LINCOLN REELECTED
On **NOVEMBER 8**, President Lincoln was reelected, carrying twenty-two states and 212 electoral votes. His opponent, General George B. McClellan, won only Delaware, Kentucky, and New Jersey (21 electoral votes).

SHERMAN CAPTURES SAVANNAH
On **DECEMBER 24**, General William Tecumseh Sherman sent a telegram to President Lincoln: "I beg to present you as a Christmas gift the city of Savannah."

Sherman and his army had just captured the city, the second largest in Georgia and one of the key supply points for the Confederacy. Sherman also captured 150 heavy guns, plenty of ammunition, and twenty-five thousand bales of cotton. Since the Confederate soldiers had already retreated, Sherman spared the city. It was Sherman's intent to end the war swiftly by doing whatever was necessary to deny supplies to Lee's troops. On his march from Atlanta to Savannah and from Savannah into the Carolinas, he pursued this strategy while also trying to prevent indiscriminate pillage by his troops; he was not always successful.

DISCRIMINATION PROHIBITED

On **DECEMBER 28**, a law was enacted forbidding racial discrimination by the U.S. postal service in the hiring of letter carriers.

1865–1877 RECONSTRUCTION ERA FOLLOWS
CIVIL WAR

During the period known as Reconstruction, Blacks attended constitutional conventions and participated in all aspects of political life. The Fifteenth Amendment, ratified in 1870, secured the vote for Black Americans.

Blacks voted en masse for the first time, and dozens of Blacks were elected to office. During Reconstruction, there were four Black lieutenant governors, twenty U.S. congressman, two U.S. senators, three secretaries of state, a state supreme court justice, two state treasurers, and numerous minor public officials. The highest positions were attained by Hiram R. Revels, who represented Mississippi as a U.S. senator for the two-year unexpired term of Jefferson Davis, former president of the Confederacy, and Blanche K. Bruce, who represented Mississippi for one full term as a U.S. senator. Fourteen Blacks sat in the U.S. House of Representatives between 1869 and 1877. No other Black was elected to the senate until 1966, when Edward W. Brooke III was elected from Massachusetts. Twenty Blacks served at least one term in the U.S. House of Representatives between 1869 and 1901. Both Joseph H. Rainey and Robert Smalls of South Carolina served five consecutive terms.

The highest state office held by Blacks was that of lieutenant governor — P. B. S. Pinchback of Louisiana, A. K. Davis of Mississippi, and R. H. Gleaves of South Carolina served in that position. Pinchback also served as acting governor. Blacks served as secretaries of state in Florida, Louisiana,

Mississippi, and South Carolina. In Arkansas, Florida, Louisiana, and Mississippi, Blacks were superintendents of education, and in Florida and South Carolina, state treasurers. Some Blacks held a number of positions — Jonathan C. Gibbs held office as secretary of state and later as superintendent of public instruction in Florida; Francis L. Cardozo served as secretary of state and later as state treasurer in South Carolina; John R. Lynch served as Speaker of the Mississippi House of Representatives and later as a congressman. By the 1880s, violence, intimidation, and fear had effectively disfranchised Blacks as southern whites managed to eliminate political and social equality. Consequently, few Blacks held political office after 1877.

1865 AMERICAN COLONIZATION SOCIETY PRESENTS
PROGRESS REPORT

Created in 1817, the American Colonization Society, a group devoted to the resettlement of Blacks in Africa, reported that between 1820 and 1865, it had transported 6,301 former slaves and 4,501 free Blacks to Liberia. In 1847, it was successful in transforming its colony into an independent nation. The overwhelming proportion of emigrants were from the South, although many Blacks from the North also left the country for new homes in Liberia. Of the 1,094 northern Blacks who emigrated to Liberia between 1820 and 1865, no less than 70 percent emigrated in the last fifteen years of the period. For many Blacks, slave and free, northern and southern, the only way to rid themselves of oppression was to leave the country. This was the message promoted by members of the Colonization Society as well.

BLACK OFFICERS SERVE IN THE CIVIL WAR

About seventy-five Blacks held commissions in the army during the Civil War. Units from Massachusetts had ten commissioned Black officers and units from Kansas, three. Many of these officers served with distinction. For example, Lieutenant Colonel William N. Reed of the First North Carolina was mortally wounded in the battle of Olustee after making a gallant charge with his unit. Two of the courageous Louisiana Native Guards killed during the battle at Port Hudson were Captain Andre Cailloux, a prominent free Black from New Orleans, and Second Lieutenant John Crowder.

A number of Blacks also served as surgeons with units of the U.S. Colored Troops, including Major Martin R. Delany, Captain O. S. B. Wall, and Dr.

Alexander T. Augusta, who was breveted with lieutenant colonel in 1865; Dr. John V. DeGrasse was an assistant surgeon. Charles B. Purvis, Alpheus Tucker, John Rapier, William Ellis, Anderson R. Abbott, and William Powell were hospital surgeons in Washington, D.C. Augusta, who later taught at Howard University's department of medicine, was paid $7 per month, the same as a Black enlisted man. He brought pressure on the army through Senator Henry Wilson and the secretary of war to receive appropriate compensation.

BLACK TROOPS AT END OF CIVIL WAR

By the end of the war, the Union army had enlisted more than 386,000 Blacks: 186,000 in combat troops and 200,000 in support units. Of the 186,000 Blacks serving with the Union combat troops in the Civil War, about half came from seceded states, and about 40,765 from Kentucky, Maryland, and Missouri. Blacks represented 10 percent of all Union forces, although they made up only 1 percent of the North's population. Blacks were organized into 166 all-Black regiments (145 infantry, 7 cavalry, 12 heavy artillery, 1 light artillery, 1 engineering). Blacks were assigned to white regiments as well. Fewer than 100 Blacks served as officers. White officers commanding Black troops were carefully selected. Some of the best military leaders commanded Black troops. On the other hand, a great leader is often made by the bravery of the troops. Black troops fought courageously in a number of crucial battles. About 29,000 Blacks served in the Union navy, about one-quarter of all its seamen. Blacks served in all ranks below that of petty officer, including fireman, landsman, and seaman.

Over the duration of the war, more than 37,000 Black soldiers died, almost 20 percent of all Blacks who served in combat. Blacks suffered heavy casualties because they were often used as assault troops. In addition, many of the casualties were caused by poor equipment and medical care. The following list summarizes the service of Blacks in the Civil War:

- Black soldiers participated in 449 battles, including 39 major engagements;
- 2,800 Blacks died in combat;
- 34,000 Blacks died of diseases (a rate nearly twice that of whites);
- 800 Black seamen were casualties (one-quarter of the total casualties);
- 24 Blacks received the Medal of Honor for bravery (17 from the army and 7 from the navy);

- Between 75 and 100 Blacks became officers, the highest rank being lieutenant colonel. There were no Black officers in the navy.

Geographically, the largest number of Black soldiers in the Civil War came from Louisiana (24,052), Kentucky (23,703), and Tennessee (20,133).

BLACKS RECEIVE MEDALS OF HONOR

By war's end, twenty-four Blacks had received the Congressional Medal of Honor, seventeen in the army and seven in the navy. Thirteen of those in the army received their medals for bravery during the Battle of Chaffin's Farm on September 29, 1864. Decatur Dorsey, a Black sergeant, and John Lawson, a Black gunner on the flagship of Admiral David Farragut in the Battle of Mobile Bay, were among the seamen to win the Medal of Honor. Although such bravery was commonplace throughout the war, it was sometimes difficult for white officers to acknowledge the heroic actions of Black troops.

CONVENTION OF NEGROES HELD IN TENNESSEE

The Tennessee State Convention of Negroes convened in Nashville. A petition was submitted to the U.S. Senate protesting the seating of the Tennessee delegates in Congress until the state legislature secured the rights of Blacks as freemen.

EQUAL RIGHTS MASS MEETINGS HELD

Blacks in Norfolk, Virginia, held mass meetings and demanded equal rights and ballots. Other equal rights mass meetings were held by Blacks in Petersburg, Virginia; Vicksburg, Mississippi; Nashville, Tennessee; Raleigh, North Carolina; Richmond, Virginia; Jackson, Mississippi; and Charleston, South Carolina.

JACKSON BECOMES TEACHER AT PHILADELPHIA INSTITUTE FOR COLORED YOUTH

Fannie Jackson, born a slave in Washington, D.C., in 1837, graduated from Oberlin College and became a teacher at the Institute for Colored Youth, in Philadelphia. She later served as its principal. Jackson initially taught the classics at the institute, but a growing demand for public school teachers who could teach reading, writing, mathematics, and social studies persuaded her to begin a "normal school" program at the institute. In 1879, she was instrumental in starting an industrial department to train Black students in trades. After the Civil War, vocational training was available only at a small number of schools, including

Hampton Institute, Tuskegee Institute, and the Philadelphia Institute for Colored Youth. Jackson used her considerable oratorical skills to gather support and funds for the vocational program. She also organized an Industrial Exchange for Black women where they could display their sewing, cooking, and other goods. In 1881, Jackson married the Reverend Levi J. Coppin, later a bishop in the AME Church. After her marriage, Fanny Jackson Coppin became active in the AME Church, especially its missionary work. She traveled with her husband to Africa when he was assigned to Cape Town, South Africa. She died in Philadelphia in 1913. A Black liberal arts college in Baltimore, Maryland, bears her name.

FREEDMEN'S SAVINGS AND TRUST COMPANY OPENS IN WASHINGTON, D.C.

The Freedmen's Savings and Trust Company, the first bank for Blacks, opened in Washington, D.C. It was chartered by the U.S. government to encourage financial responsibility among ex-slaves. One month after its charter, the Freedmen's Bank opened its headquarters in New York City, and soon opened branches in Louisville, Nashville, Vicksburg, and New Orleans. By 1872, there were thirty-four branches, all but two located in the South.

The Bank failed and closed its doors on June 28, 1874.

HEALY RECEIVES DOCTORATE

Patrick Francis Healy (1834–1910) passed the final examinations on July 26 and received a Ph.D. degree from Louvain University in Belgium to become the first Black American to receive an earned doctor of philosophy degree.

NUMBER OF BLACK ARTISANS DECLINES

Near the end of the Civil War, an estimated 100,000 of 120,000 artisans in the South were Black — about five of every six (83 percent); by 1900, only about 5 percent of them were. The reduction in Blacks as artisans reflected the increased opposition by whites to Blacks in skilled trades. As the number of skilled whites increased, they established craft unions and apprentice systems to exclude Blacks from certain trades. If Blacks were to hold on to any of the trades, they had to accept considerably lower wages than white workers. Over the years, certain jobs came to be identified as "Negro jobs," and others as "white men's work" or "clean work."

The Reverend Patrick F. Healy, the first Black American to receive a Ph.D. degree, became an important educator.

ILLINOIS REPEALS BLACK LAWS

In **JANUARY**, the Black Laws were repealed in Illinois. These laws had restricted the freedom of movement and limited the civil and political rights of free Blacks. Several months later, the Illinois legislature became the first to adopt the Thirteenth Amendment, which abolished slavery.

John Jones, a free Black who had become an activist against racial discrimination in the state and for the repeal of its repressive Black Laws, did much to influence this legislative action. Jones had been a supporter of the Underground Railroad and a financial backer of John Brown's activities. When the state passed legislation in 1853 that prohibited Blacks from emigrating to the state, Jones used the wealth he had gained as a tailor to fight these additional restrictions on Blacks. In 1864, he published a pamphlet entitled

The Black Laws of Illinois and a Few Reasons Why They Should Be Repealed. His publication was directed primarily at rich white men, arguing that the Black Laws negatively affected them. For example, he noted that those whites who used Black wagon drivers stood to lose money if their drivers could not provide evidence in the courtroom to convict thieves. Jones's support in the Black community won him election to the Cook County Board of Commissioners, a post to which he was reelected several times. Jones became involved in a number of racial issues in the city, including the integration of schools.

FIRST BLACK ATTORNEY APPEARS BEFORE U.S. SUPREME COURT

On **FEBRUARY 1**, John Rock (1825–1866) became the first Black attorney to practice before the U.S. Supreme Court.

Rock was barred from medical schools and later turned to dentistry in Philadelphia. He finally became a physician in Boston in 1853. In 1861, he became a lawyer and a justice of the peace in Boston.

GARNET PREACHES TO CONGRESS

On **FEBRUARY 12**, Henry Highland Garnet, a renowned abolitionist, became the first Black person to deliver a message in the nation's capitol when he preached a sermon on abolition of slavery.

FIFTY-FIFTH MASSACHUSETTS REGIMENT LIBERATES CHARLESTON

On **FEBRUARY 21**, Black troops of the Fifty-fifth Massachusetts Regiment marched into Charleston, South Carolina. Regiment leader Colonel Charles B. Fox wrote of the experience: "It was one of those occasions which happen but once in a lifetime, to be lived

The Fifty-fifth Massachusetts Colored Infantry Regiment liberated Charleston, South Carolina, and received a warm reception from the city's Black residents.

over in memory forever." Fox was responding to the swift manner in which whites left the town as they heard news of the advancing regiment. When the Black troops arrived, Charleston's Black people quickly surrounded them and cheered. They sang, prayed, and shook the hands of their liberators.

FREEDMEN'S BUREAU ESTABLISHED

On **MARCH 3**, the U.S. Congress established the Bureau of Refugees, Freedmen, and Abandoned Lands to help Blacks adjust to their new freedom. It was created within the War Department to ensure that millions of dollars would be spent on jobs, education, and medical treatment for free Blacks and ex-slaves. State bureaus were set up to aid Blacks in contractual relationships, education, and other life skills. Although a bill to establish the Freedmen's Bureau had been introduced in Congress in 1863, it was not until the Freedmen's Aid Societies petitioned Congress for

action that the bill was given serious consideration. In 1864, Charles Sumner and others had joined together to support a bill that would provide for a permanent department to deal with problems of citizenship for freed slaves. Rejecting Sumner's approach as too extreme, a bill was passed to create the Freedmen's Bureau. Originally it was to remain in operation during the war and one year after. The establishment of the Freedmen's Bureau allowed the secretary of war to "direct such issues of provisions, clothing, and fuel, as he may deem needful for the immediate and temporary shelter and supply of destitute and suffering refugees and freedmen and their wives and children." The president appointed a commissioner vested with broad powers and authority:

> To set apart, for the use of loyal refugees and freedmen, such tracts of land within the insurrectionary states as shall have been abandoned, or to which the United States shall have acquired title by confisca-

The Freedmen's Bureau provided a number of services to impoverished Blacks and whites and helped former slaves in their transition from slavery to independence. Among the most immediate needs of freed Blacks were food and clothing; rations were distributed at various bureau sites.

One of the most sought-after services was education, since only one-tenth of the newly freed slaves could read or write. At this Freedmen's Union Industrial School in Richmond, Virginia, women were taught sewing skills. By the time the Freedmen's Bureau was abolished, nearly 21 percent of freed Blacks were literate.

tion or sale, or otherwise, and to every male citizen, whether refugee or freedman, as aforesaid, there shall be assigned not more than forty acres of such land, and the person to whom it was so assigned shall be protected in the use and enjoyment of the land for the term of three years at an annual rent not exceeding six per centum upon the value of such land, as it was appraised by the state authorities in the year eighteen hundred and sixty, for the purpose of taxation, and in case no such appraisal can be found, then the rental shall be based upon the estimated value of the land in said year, to be ascertained in such manner as the commissioner may by regulation prescribe. At the end of said term, or at any time during the said term, the occupants of any parcels so assigned may purchase the land and receive such title thereto as the United States can convey, upon paying therefor the value of the land, as ascertained and fixed for the purpose of determining the annual rent aforesaid.

The social and economic conditions of freedmen were desperate and required immediate and aggressive attention. General Oliver O. Howard was appointed to head the Freedmen's Bureau. He made the following remarks regarding his work:

In every state many thousands were found without employment, without homes, without means of subsistence, crowding into town and about military post, where they hoped to find protection and supplies. The sudden collapse of the rebellion, making emancipation an actual, universal fact, was like an earthquake. It shook and shattered the whole previously existing social system. It broke up the old industries and threatened a reign of anarchy. Even well-disposed and humane landowners were at a loss what to do, or how to begin the work of reorganizing society and of rebuilding their ruined fortunes. Very few had any knowledge of free labor, or any hope that their former slaves would serve them faithfully for wages. On the other hand, the freed people were in a state of great excitement and uncertainty. They could hardly believe that the liberty proclaimed was real and permanent. Many were afraid to remain on the same soil that they had tilled as slaves lest by some trick they might find themselves again in bondage. Others supposed that the Government would either take the entire supervision of their labor and support, or divide among them the lands of the conquered owners, and furnish them with all that might be necessary to begin life as an independent farmer.

When the bill to continue the Freedmen's Bureau came before Congress in 1866, it passed, but President Andrew Johnson vetoed the legislation. Congress successfully overrode the veto and, in addition, passed the Civil Rights Bill. The combination of these two actions not only furthered the work of the Freedmen's Bureau but also set the stage for the freedmen's entry into society as full citizens.

In its five years of existence, the bureau issued more than twenty million rations, resettled more than thirty thousand persons, established more than fifty hospitals, and spent about $5.3 million on more than 4,000 schools, including Atlanta University, Fisk University, Hampton Institute, and Howard University. In 1870 alone, more than 9,000 teachers and 247,333 pupils were in day and night schools established or supported by bureau funds.

CONFEDERATE ARMY AUTHORIZED TO USE SLAVES AS SOLDIERS

On **MARCH 13**, just three weeks before the end of the war, Jefferson Davis signed a bill authorizing the use of three hundred thousand slaves as soldiers in the Confederate army, implying that the slaves would be set free after the war ended. The order, however, was never put into effect. The Black enlistment bill came too late to influence the outcome of the war. General Robert E. Lee encouraged the use of Black slaves as troops. He noted that it was "not only expedient but necessary" that the Confederate army use Black slaves as soldiers.

Although this was the first time the South had considered using Blacks as soldiers, both slaves and free Blacks had been used behind the lines to build fortifications. The Confederacy could not bring itself to use slaves as soldiers until its plight was desperate. It was absurd to ask slaves to fight for the system that enslaved them, and slaves fighting alongside white men would have certainly destroyed the notion of Black inferiority on which the entire slavery system was founded.

BLACK SOLDIERS FIGHT AT BATTLE OF FIVE FORKS

On **MARCH 29**, Union soldiers attacked Confederate soldiers at Five Forks, south of Petersburg, Virginia. General Lee had instructed General George Pickett to hold Five Forks at all costs, but General Grant's assault caused Pickett's Confederate troops to collapse and retreat. Lee configured his troops to attack on several fronts. In each case, the Union troops, including many Blacks, were victorious, and they moved on to the Appomattox River. Union troops seized Petersburg on April 3 and then approached Richmond, the capital of the Confederacy.

UNION FORCES WITH BLACK REGIMENTS SACK RICHMOND

On **APRIL 5**, Union forces marched into Richmond, Virginia. The city was still smoldering from the artillery bombardment it had received over the previous weeks. Although Union troops destroyed much of the city in their assault, Confederate soldiers actually burned many parts of the city to ensure that nothing was left that would be useful to the Union. Several regiments of Black soldiers were involved in the sack of Richmond, and as they marched through the city, crowds of slaves greeted them with cheers and congratulations. Lincoln visited the city with his son Tad, and as he walked through the streets, Black citizens cheered and cried.

GRANT ACCEPTS LEE'S SURRENDER

On **APRIL 9**, General Robert E. Lee met General Ulysses S. Grant at Appomattox Courthouse to surrender the Northern Virginia Army, the act that ended the Civil War.

The fall of Richmond apparently dashed all Confederate hopes of continuing the war. When Lee and his army retreated from Richmond, they found their escape to Lynchburg and its railroad blocked by General Philip Sheridan and his cavalry, and fifty thousand soldiers under General George Meade. Grant and more soldiers blocked other paths. With twenty-seven thousand Confederate soldiers surrounded and starving, Lee appealed for surrender; Grant accepted an unconditional surrender. The surrender ceremony took about three hours. When it was finished, Lee was free to go; he was not a prisoner of war, nor were his starving troops. After four bloody and destructive years, millions of broken families, and more than half a million deaths, the Civil War was over.

SIXTY-SECOND U.S. COLORED INFANTRY FIGHTS WITH TEXAS REBELS

On **MAY 13**, several days after Confederate president Jefferson Davis was captured and imprisoned at Fortress Monroe, the Sixty-second U.S. Colored Infantry fought with resistant Confederate troops at White's Ranch, Texas. The skirmish left Sergeant Crocket, a Black soldier, dead. He is believed to be the last soldier killed in the Civil War.

JOHNSON'S SOUTHERN RESTORATION PLAN REVEALED

Six weeks after taking office, President Andrew Johnson began to formulate his own reconstruction plan, which he called "Restoration." The principal difference between his plan and the one that Congress would eventually devise was its lack of protection for the civil rights of Blacks. The congressional plan would include punishment for the rebellion and a strong federal presence in the South to prevent abuse of Blacks. Johnson's plan included amnesty to all who swore allegiance to the Union. States were to repudiate the Confederate debt, declare secession null and void, and ratify the Thirteenth Amendment. The military government would then be removed, and the state could once again send representatives to Congress. Johnson named a provisional governor of North Carolina to help prepare the state for reentry into the Union. It was the first of many steps he took to restore the South quickly.

PLANTER ASSOCIATIONS SEEK TO CONTROL BLACK LABOR

In **JUNE**, citizens of various communities of Nelson County, Virginia, convened to agree on a set of labor requirements regarding Blacks. They decided to pay no more than five dollars per month for field hands and not to hire any freed slave without permission from the slave's previous employer, to secure evidence that the employee had fulfilled previous contracts. A month later, planters and farmers met in Franklin County, Virginia, and agreed on the same requirements. These and similar meetings to fix wages and set the conditions of employment forced the Freedmen's Bureau to intervene and declare a ban on planters' meetings. Such meetings occurred in a number of counties in other states, mostly in areas where Black labor was plentiful.

SLAVERY ENDS IN TEXAS

On **JUNE 19**, slavery ended in Texas when General Gordon Granger arrived in Galveston with Union forces. The news spread rapidly throughout the state. African Americans commemorate this day — June 19, or "Juneteenth" — by celebrating the emancipation of African Americans.

CAMP NELSON ENCLAVE PHASED OUT

In **JULY**, General Oliver O. Howard decided to "break up" Camp Nelson, Kentucky, and perform a "careful distribution" of its refugees.

During the Civil War, Camp Nelson had been established to recruit and train Black soldiers. As the war moved farther into the South, Camp Nelson became a refuge for Black soldiers' wives and children as well. At the end of the war, no fewer than three thousand Black refugees lived in the camp, supported by the Union and the Freedmen's Bureau. Because of its size, Camp Nelson posed a problem when the time came to distribute the large number of Black refugees at the close of the war. John G. Fee, the camp's chaplain and a devout abolitionist, wanted to resettle the refugees on land they could purchase rather than distribute them among the local population. He was acutely aware of the local residents' hatred of these refugees and felt that they would not be accepted in the community. When Fee grew frustrated that a decision had not been made concerning the settlement of inhabitants of Camp Nelson, he decided to borrow five hundred dollars. He and his wife also sold some land she owned in a free state, and together they purchased 130 acres of land in Kentucky. The land was set up to accommodate families who would repurchase the land on a long-term basis. Within twenty-five years, forty-two Black families were living in the community established by Fee and his wife.

This settlement plan still left thousands at the camp. With pressure from Washington to close Camp Nelson before winter, a special agent, R. E. Farwell, was given the task of finding homes for the remaining refugees. When General Banbridge and his partners made an offer to take as many as five hundred laborers to their Mississippi plantation, Farwell agreed; three days later, Banbridge began transporting all refugees who agreed to go with him. It was stipulated that the children of the party would be apprenticed at Vicksburg by the assistant commissioner of the Freedmen's Bureau there.

NATIONAL EQUAL RIGHTS LEAGUE FORMED IN CLEVELAND

On **OCTOBER 19**, the first annual meeting of the National Equal Rights League convened in Cleveland. The main objective of the League was the removal of all "invidious distinctions" based on color. The league drew up resolutions urging Black Americans to acquire property, educate their children and themselves, and conduct themselves in a manner that would win respect.

BLACK CODES INTRODUCED IN MISSISSIPPI

On **NOVEMBER 24**, Mississippi established Black Codes restricting the rights and movement of Blacks. In response to the Johnson administration's Restoration program, legislatures in a number of southern states began to enact Black Codes to formalize restrictions already in place: Blacks were forbidden to testify against whites, serve on juries, bear arms, or hold large meetings. Blacks without work could be arrested and hired out to employers. Blacks were to be educated in separate facilities. Other laws penalized Blacks for "seditious" speeches, insulting gestures, and curfew violations. A Chicago newspaper summarized northern sentiment toward these codes: "We tell the men of Mississippi that the men of the North will convert . . . Mississippi into a frog pond before they will allow such laws."

CONGRESS CONVENES WITH REPRESENTATIVES FROM THE SOUTH

On **DECEMBER 4**, the Thirty-ninth Congress convened. All Confederate states, except Mississippi, had accepted President Johnson's requirements for readmission to the Union. Each of these states had sent an all-white delegation as its representatives in Congress. Delegates included four Confederate generals, several colonels, and members of the Confederate Congress. Georgia sent Alexander Stephens, former vice president of the Confederacy, as one of its representatives. Northern congressmen were furious, and, led by Thaddeus Stevens, the House of Representatives omitted the southerners from the roll call, thus denying them admittance. Some congressmen, particularly Radical Republicans, believed that the Confederate officers and other officials should have been punished more severely and denied seats in Congress. The House then moved to discuss punishment for the southern states. Congress insisted that the states had to change their attitudes before readmission and

meet a set of conditions, including ratification of the Thirteenth and Fourteenth Amendments. Further, the South was divided into five military districts under the command of the army. Federal troops protected Blacks and whites as they began to rebuild after the war.

COMMITTEE ON RECONSTRUCTION ESTABLISHED

On **DECEMBER 12**, the U.S. Senate agreed to form the Joint Committee on Reconstruction. Senator William Fessenden of Maine was appointed chairperson of the Senate committee. Congressman Thaddeus Stevens, a Republican abolitionist from Pennsylvania, was selected to head the Committee on Reconstruction in the House of Representatives. Stevens was an uncompromising advocate of civil rights for Blacks. Most Republicans felt that President Johnson was moving too quickly to repair the Union. He had offered amnesty to most Confederate citizens and parole to several southern political leaders, as well as lifting the blockade of southern ports. Republicans were fearful that their majority in Congress would be threatened by an increase in Democrats from the South.

SLAVERY MADE ILLEGAL IN THE UNITED STATES

On **DECEMBER 18**, slavery became illegal in the United States, with the passage of the Thirteenth Amendment to the Constitution. It stated that "neither slavery nor involuntary servitude . . . shall exist . . ." Congress was given powers to ensure that slavery was eliminated. The amendment, proposed by Senator John Henderson in January of the previous year, received the required ratification from twenty-seven states on December 18.

In a "right to vote" petition sent to President Andrew Johnson, North Carolina Blacks included this statement: "In many respects we are poor and greatly despised by our fellowmen; but we are rich in the possession of the liberty brought us, and our wives and our little ones." This statement echoed the great importance of freedom — to be a person and not property; to learn and earn, and enjoy personal success. Many former slaves believed that since they had fought for these freedoms and had given their lives to save a democratic nation, they would eventually share equally in its growth and development. Freedom, many soon found out, required many obligations and sacrifices, and often had to be fought for. Many saw freedom as possible only in another place and quickly left the South for the North and the

One of the ways in which newly freed slaves found relief from persecution was by moving out of the South. Baltimore, a border city with a long history of offering opportunities to free Blacks, was a popular destination for these migrants.

West. Some went from town to town looking for family members before making new lives for themselves.

KU KLUX KLAN ORGANIZED

On **DECEMBER 24**, an anti-Black group, the Ku Klux Klan (KKK), was organized in Pulaski, a small town in central Tennessee. Former Confederate general Nathan B. Forrest, one of Robert E. Lee's cavalrymen and commanding officer of the Fort Pillow Massacre, is considered the founder of the KKK, along with six former Confederate soldiers. The Klan was formed to resist Reconstruction in Confederate states. Its actions became more vicious as northern troops left the South. Members rode at night in hooded white robes,

intimidating, harming, and murdering freed Blacks. The group took its name from the Greek word *kuklos*, meaning "circle." Many of their crimes against former slaves went unpunished and, in fact, may have had the sanction of local and state political officials, including the law. In many cities, counties, and states in the South, these terrorist groups controlled the electoral and governing processes. In Oklahoma and Indiana, the Klan became well represented in state government. The outrageous terrorist behavior of the Klan led Congress to pass several Enforcement Acts designed to protect Blacks from such groups. The KKK was labeled an illegal organization, and the president therefore had the power to suspend the writ

Ku Klux Klan members wore hoods to hide their identity and dark clothing to hide their movements at night. They used intimidation, physical abuse, destruction of property, and murder to achieve their goal — the undermining and denial of racial equality.

of habeas corpus and to proclaim martial law in certain areas to suppress the Klan's criminal activity.

1866 BLACK SHAKESPEAREAN ACTOR EMIGRATES

Morgan Smith, a celebrated Shakespearean actor, emigrated to England to advance his acting career. Smith felt that his talents would not be fully developed or appreciated if he remained in the United States. Over the next several decades, Smith became one of the most sought-after performers of Shakespeare, starring in *Hamlet*, *Macbeth*, *The Merchant of Venice*, *Othello*, and *Richard III*.

BUREAUS OF IMMIGRATION ESTABLISHED IN SOUTHERN STATES

In response to the nullification of Black Codes, particularly those relating to the control and abuses of Black labor, Louisiana and South Carolina established bureaus of immigration. The bureaus encouraged the settlement of foreign immigrants in their respective states. Emigration agents and immigration societies such as the Eastern North Carolina Immigration Association (1868), the Arkansas River Valley Immigration Company (1869), and the Immigration Society of Newberry, South Carolina (1869), were established to assist states in their efforts to attract foreign labor, but for a fee.

Although many immigrants came to the United States over the next several decades, they were not attracted to the South, and the agents and societies were totally unsuccessful in their efforts to secure foreign laborers. In cases where immigrants were successfully recruited and delivered, they often stayed in their new jobs for only a short while. Of one hundred Germans recruited to work on a sugar plantation in Louisiana, thirty deserted on the day of their arrival. The climate, work, and social environment of the South seemed unfavorable to most Europeans.

CONVICT LAWS PASSED BY FORMER CONFEDERATE STATES

Between 1865 and 1866, many southern states passed laws regarding the treatment of prisoners. Such legislation was relatively uniform, allowing convicted Black lawbreakers who could not pay their fines and court costs to be hired out. In a number of states (Alabama, Georgia, South Carolina, Texas, and Virginia) it was legal to have county prisoners work on public projects, including roads, bridges, and sewers. The system closely resembled slavery in its control of the labor of Black people, but this time the authority was not a slave master but the southern courts, who created "labor" by convicting Blacks of crimes and determining punishments. Many of these laws were declared null and void by the commissioners of the Freedmen's Bureau in the districts.

FIRST BLACK ELECTED OFFICIALS SERVE IN MASSACHUSETTS LEGISLATURE

Edward (Edwin) Walker, son of abolitionist David Walker, and Charles L. Mitchell became the first Blacks in the post–Civil War period to be elected to an American legislature, in Massachusetts.

FISK UNIVERSITY FOUNDED

Fisk University opened in Nashville, Tennessee. Known as Fisk Free School, it offered primary to normal education. Founded by E. M. Cravath and E. P. Smith of the American Missionary Association and John Ogden of the Freedmen's Bureau to produce qualified Black teachers, Fisk School was incorporated in 1867 as Fisk University. Fisk was promoted as the best normal school in the South, and it attracted many scholars from major colleges.

Faced with near financial ruin during the period 1870–1915, Fisk sent the Fisk Jubilee Singers on tours across the country and throughout the world to earn money for the school. Their first tour took place in 1871. The group, seven women and four men, was so enthusiastically received that the tour was extended to Europe. Their concerts raised $150,000 for the college. The tours also established the importance of Black music as an art form to be studied, preserved, and appreciated as part of American culture. Generations later, some Black musicians charged the Jubilee Singers as being "Europeanizers" of the culture because they sang Black music with crisp diction and in a formal fashion.

By 1915, Fisk had expanded its infrastructure, its curriculum, and its faculty. In 1940, Charles Johnson became the school's first Black president. Today, Fisk is a private, coeducational, independent school, offering bachelor's and master's degrees. Enrollment is about fifteen hundred. It remains one of the most prestigious Black colleges in the nation.

SHARECROPPING SYSTEM ACCEPTED BY PLANTATION MANAGERS

By this time, the shift to sharecropping was well under way throughout the South. For many Blacks who could not buy or rent land but were willing to work under a plantation superintendency, sharecropping became a way of making a living. The increasing acceptance of sharecropping among ex-slaves reinforced the beliefs of many whites that freed slaves needed supervision in the production of crops. The reality, however, was that freed slaves had nothing to offer but their labor, and they had to accept the system available to them or possibly face starvation. In this year, regional offices of the Freedmen's Bureau from Memphis to Louisiana reported that freed Blacks working for shares outnumbered their counterparts working for wages by more than two to one. In the Memphis area alone, 20,836 freedmen were reported working as sharecroppers, compared with 8,539 working for wages. Many laborers who worked on plantations found themselves poorer at the end of the year than at the beginning, because of heavy charges for negligence or incidental expenses. From the reporting offices of the Freedmen's Bureau came evidence that sharecropping had become the replacement for slavery.

SOUTHERN HOMESTEAD ACT PASSED

Congress passed the Southern Homestead Act, opening federal lands in Florida, Alabama, Mississippi, Louisiana, and Arkansas for homesteading. Settlement could be made on eighty-acre plots. Although the law was structured to provide land to help some Blacks become self-sufficient, it also drained the surplus Black laboring population in Virginia and Georgia. Former Confederates were prohibited from purchasing land under this act until January 1, 1867. Many freed slaves, however, had no capital and were not able to take full advantage of the bill, and the Freedmen's Bureau could not provide stock, tools, and means of subsistence for the new settlers. The Freedmen's Bureau did provide one month's subsistence and free transportation to any settler who chose to settle on land under this law. Over the life of the act, about six years, as many as four thousand Black families secured land. About three-quarters of these families settled in Florida, but few were able to hold on to their land. Because of limited capital, many Black settlers hired themselves out to other planters during regular hours and tried to make their farms successful after hours.

DELEGATION OF BLACK LEADERS PRESENTS VIEWS TO PRESIDENT

In **FEBRUARY**, a delegation of Black leaders called on President Andrew Johnson to discuss civil rights and voting. The delegation included Frederick Douglass, George T. Downing of Rhode Island, and John Jones, a wealthy Illinois politician. After presenting their views on the personal safety and protection of the rights of Black people, they solicited the views of the president. Johnson opposed any federal laws to protect freed slaves and felt that the states had to solve problems within their own boundaries. He urged Blacks to migrate from the South and asserted that Blacks had no "natural" right to vote. The delegation summarized their meeting on a discouraging note — that the president was "delivering them back into the hand of their old enemies." It was believed that Johnson, a southern poor white, despised both slaveholders and Blacks.

Within a short time after the meeting, anti-Black mobs escalated their attacks on Blacks. Before the summer, anti-Black mobs in Memphis and New Orleans had killed or wounded hundreds of Blacks. When General Philip Sheridan reviewed the New Orleans riot, he concluded, "It was an absolute massacre."

FREEDMEN'S BUREAU EXTENDED

On **FEBRUARY 12**, President Johnson vetoed the extension of the Freedmen's Bureau, believing that former slaves should make it on their own. Congress passed the extension over his veto. The extension included provisions to strengthen the authority of the bureau, giving it jurisdiction over anyone who deprived Blacks of their civil rights. It continued to provide food, clothing, shelter, and education to freed slaves.

"FORTY ACRES AND A MULE"

On **FEBRUARY 22**, freed Blacks popularized a slogan, "Forty Acres and a Mule," to sum up the help they hoped to receive from the Freedmen's Bureau. Instead, the bureau provided legal aid, food, and land for schools and other institutions.

REGULAR ARMY ESTABLISHED WITH SIX BLACK REGIMENTS

In **MARCH**, the U.S. Senate passed legislation that established a regular army with sixty-seven regiments, six of which would be composed of Black troops with white officers. The regular army was reorganized in 1869 with four Black regiments rather than six. The four regiments existing at the time included the Ninth and Tenth Cavalry and the Twenty-fourth and Twenty-fifth Infantry. These four regiments were scattered across the West to protect settlers, suppress hostile Native Americans, guard the mail, and protect the railroads that were under construction. The Black regiments were charged with building their own quarters and forts. The Ninth and Tenth Cavalry became the hardest-fighting and best-disciplined mounted forces on the western frontier, despite the fact that they were often given equipment and horses rejected by more favored white units.

It has been estimated that one-fifth of the soldiers who patrolled the western frontier were Black men. Fourteen Black soldiers received the Congressional Medal of Honor by the end of the Indian wars in 1890. The Native Americans called Black troops "buffalo soldiers" as a mark of respect. The Tenth Cavalry also served with distinction in the Spanish-American War. Despite their accomplishments, the Ninth and Tenth Cavalry were almost invisible in most historical accounts of the West. History generally recorded that the heroes of the West were white.

CIVIL RIGHTS BILL OF 1866 PASSED

On **APRIL 9**, the Civil Rights Bill of 1866 granted to Blacks the rights and privileges of American citizenship. The act was passed over the veto of President Andrew Johnson. Blacks were given the privilege to make contracts, hold property, and testify in court, and were made subject to the laws, punishments, and penalties of the United States. The act was passed to strengthen the provisions of the Thirteenth Amendment. Northerners had been concerned by southerners who flagrantly denied citizenship to Black people.

RACE RIOT ERUPTS IN MEMPHIS

On Monday, **APRIL 30**, four policeman in Memphis, Tennessee, confronted three or four Black men on Cousey Street. A policeman struck one of the Blacks with a pistol and was subsequently struck by a Black with a cane. The next day, as word of the incident spread throughout South Memphis, fifty to seventy-five Blacks, mostly discharged soldiers, congregated on the corner of Main and South Streets. Six policemen approached and arrested two Blacks (presumably for intoxication and boisterousness). As they proceeded toward the jail, a growing crowd followed. The crowd grew more threatening, and eventually shots were fired in the air. The police fired into the crowd, and one prisoner escaped; the other was released. Blacks returned the fire, wounding one policeman. Within a short time, the police and a large crowd of whites gathered in the vicinity of South Street. They indiscriminately shot, beat, and threatened every Black they confronted. By midnight on Tuesday, a small detachment of U.S. army troops seemed to have restored calm.

On Wednesday, however, a large mob of armed white citizens, including the police, congregated in South Memphis. Scattered by the soldiers, the whites reconvened in the Black community and burned several Black shanties. Late that night, mounted whites roamed through the Black community, setting fires to schools, churches, and homes. Many Blacks were beaten and wounded; many others lost their homes. Forty-eight people, mostly Blacks, were killed, and five Black women were raped.

According to Major General George Stoneman, the rioters were "police, firemen, and rabble and negro-haters in general, with a sprinkling of Yankee-haters,

Although Black veterans were the target, a white mob that entered the Black community in Memphis, Tennessee, burned schools, churches, and homes. Almost fifty Blacks were killed.

all led on and encouraged by demagogues and office hunters, and most of them under the influence of whiskey."

FORMER CONFEDERATE STATES LIMIT THE MOBILITY OF BLACK LABOR FORCE

In **JUNE**, eight of the former Confederate states had enacted laws to limit the freedom of the Black labor force, as former slaveholders attempted to regain control over Blacks. Because of the importance of labor in the southern economy, the former slaveholders were instrumental in making "Black labor" a major issue in state legislatures. Mississippi's Black Code, the first enacted after the Civil War, included a system of involuntary servitude by requiring that after the second Monday in January of each year, all Blacks had to show written evidence that they had homes and occupations; those that had none could be pressed into servitude. Furthermore, civil officials had the authority to arrest and return any Black who abandoned a contract "without good cause," limiting Blacks' ability to move or change jobs. Mississippi's contract and vagrancy laws imposed fines of up to fifty dollars and imprisonment for up to ten days on violators; Blacks unable to pay such fines within five days were hired out by the sheriff "to any person who will, for the shortest period of service, pay said fine or forfeiture of all cost." These laws made it easy to convict Blacks, and it was always easy to find planters to hire them. Although the Mississippi code was criticized as another means of enslaving Blacks, opposition was not vocal enough to keep South Carolina, Florida, Alabama, Louisiana, and Texas from following Mississippi's lead. In each of these states, legislatures made it a criminal offense for Blacks to violate labor contracts. In Alabama, Louisiana, and

Texas, contract laws were either vetoed by governors or deleted from legislation as a result of increased northern pressure. Although many southern states feared antagonistic northern opinion, many planters saw their continued success dependent upon "control of labor" and persisted in passing legislation to meet this need. By 1867, almost every former Confederate state, except Tennessee, had passed an enticement law (structured to protect white planters from competition with one another in the labor market) and a vagrancy statute (structured to allow planters and sheriffs to coerce Blacks into making and keeping their contracts). Arkansas did not pass a vagrancy law until 1905. Tennessee finally followed the southern lead and passed a vagrancy law in 1875.

FOURTEENTH AMENDMENT SUBMITTED

On **JUNE 13**, Congress proposed the Fourteenth Amendment. This amendment provided for federal protection of the civil rights of Blacks. More specifically, it guaranteed citizenship and equality — particularly the right to vote. The Joint Committee on Reconstruction, led by Radical Republicans, felt that it was necessary to define clearly the civil rights of Blacks and of all people because of continual abuses. President Andrew Johnson opposed the Fourteenth Amendment because it could not be applied to the former Confederate states who were not represented in Congress.

The amendment was sent to the states for ratification. With the exception of Tennessee, all former Confederate states refused to ratify the amendment. Congress reacted by making ratification of the Fourteenth Amendment a condition for readmission into Congress.

EVANGELIST BECOMES MILITANT EMIGRATIONIST

On **JULY 18**, Henry Turner wrote to a colleague, "I became a convert to emigration five weeks ago. I expect to advocate it hereafter as much as I can."

◈ Born in South Carolina in 1834, Turner became a traveling evangelist in his twenties. In the years before the Civil War, Turner was already convinced that Blacks would never share equally in American society, and that emigration was the answer. When his own talents and unbridled ambition frequently went unrecognized because of racial discrimination, his support of emigration grew stronger. He worked to expand the AME Church, and he became fully engaged in building the Republican Party in Georgia. For a while, he was one of the most powerful elected delegates to the convention of 1867 and later was prominent in the state legislature. In September 1868, the Georgia legislature refused to seat Black legislators, including Turner. He continued his activities in the AME denomination. In 1876, he was head of publishing; four years later, he was elected one of the denomination's twelve bishops. Turner used the *African Repository* and a number of other newspapers to articulate his frustration with racial injustices throughout the country. "So long as we are a people within a people vastly our superiors in number, wealth, & c., having no government of our own, we shall be nothing, and be so treated by the civilized world." Turner's conviction had grown so strong that his "crusade to Africa" became angry and militant. Turner traveled to Africa and continued his church-building activities by setting up AME churches in Sierra Leone and Liberia. He eventually became vice president of the American Colonization Society. As Turner aged, he continued to urge Blacks to return to Africa:

In this 1867 engraving, a former slave proudly casts his first ballot. Although ex-slaves were encouraged to vote during Reconstruction, intimidation by whites frequently reduced the number of Blacks who registered or voted by a significant margin. It was not uncommon for federal troops to be called in to secure the rights of newly freed Blacks at the polls.

But for the Negro as a whole, I see nothing here for him to aspire after. He can return to Africa, especially to Liberia where a Negro government is already in existence, and learn the elements of civilization in fact; for human life is there sacred and no man is deprived of it or any other thing that involves manhood, without due process of law. So my decision is that there is nothing in the United States for the Negro to learn or try to attain to.

FIRST FORMER CONFEDERATE STATE READMITTED TO UNION

On **JULY 24**, Tennessee became the first former Confederate state to meet congressional requirements for readmittance to the Union. Requirements included passage of the Fourteenth Amendment and adoption of a new state constitution. Tennessee was followed by Arkansas, North Carolina, South Carolina, Florida, Alabama, and Louisiana later that year.

RIOT FLARES IN NEW ORLEANS

On **JULY 30**, a large-scale race riot occurred in New Orleans in which thirty-five persons were killed and more than one hundred wounded. The outbreak was sparked by the "racist attitudes and actions of the police." Many other accounts of this riot list as many as two hundred killed or wounded.

1867 ATLANTA UNIVERSITY CHARTERED

Atlanta University, established to teach children of slaves, received its charter. The first classes were held in a church and then in a railroad boxcar. Its first normal class graduated in 1873, its first college class in 1876.

Over the years, Atlanta University became the first traditionally Black college to have an accredited graduate school. In 1929, Atlanta University joined with Morehouse and Spelman Colleges to create a university system whereby Atlanta University provided graduate and professional education, and Morehouse and Spelman provided undergraduate courses. More recently, Clark College, Interdenominational Theological Center, and Morris Brown College have joined this university system. Today, Atlanta University remains independent and has an enrollment of about eleven hundred students.

BLACK WOMEN PHYSICIANS BEGIN PRACTICING

There is some dispute as to whether Rebecca Lee or Rebecca Cole was the first Black woman doctor to practice in the United States. Lee graduated first, from New England Female Medical College; Cole graduated in 1867 from Woman's Medical College of Pennsylvania.

Cole went to work with Elizabeth Blackwell, the first white woman to receive her medical degree, (1849). They worked in the New York Infirmary for Women and Children. Blackwell established the first medical social service program in the country, Blackwell's Tenement House Service. Cole worked for the service by going into the slums and teaching women about hygiene and childcare. A spokesperson for health among Black people, Cole practiced social medicine in Philadelphia until 1881. She later became the superintendent of the Home for Destitute Colored Women and Children in Washington, D.C. Cole disagreed with W. E. B. Du Bois, who believed that the high rate of consumption among Blacks was due to ignorance of hygiene practices. Cole instead blamed the slumlords for the housing conditions that led to high mortality rates in poor areas.

BLACK MINORITY FORMS MAJORITY IN VOTER REGISTRATION

Since many whites who served in the Confederacy during the Civil War were prohibited from voting, the Black minority became the majority of registered voters in some parts of the South, including South Carolina, Georgia, Florida, Alabama, Mississippi, and Louisiana. Blacks formed majorities or significant portions of constitutional conventions involved in writing new state constitutions.

FIRST BLACK MAYOR ELECTED IN LOUISIANA

Monroe Baker, a businessman, became the mayor of St. Martin, Louisiana, the first Black person to serve as a town mayor.

FORT SHAW OPENS

Fort Shaw, named after Colonel Robert Gould Shaw, the commander of the Fifty-fourth Massachusetts Volunteers, opened on the remote Montana frontier. The all-Black Twenty-fifth Infantry was posted there for a time.

HOWARD UNIVERSITY FOUNDED

Howard University opened in Washington, D.C., chartered by an act of Congress and established under the aid and assistance of the Freedmen's Bureau. It was named after General Oliver O. Howard, a Union general and commissioner of the bureau. It started with two academic departments, four students, and one teacher. Its original charter called for Howard to educate students, regardless of race. In fact, its first students were white girls, the daughters of faculty members. Howard, however, soon became a center for education for free Blacks.

By 1900, 88 percent of the student body was Black. Over the years, Howard continued to attract both the best faculty and students. In its first century of operation, Howard graduated at least half of the nation's Black physicians, dentists, pharmacists, engineers, and architects. Howard University drew students who were activist and politically involved. In the 1930s, Howard students demonstrated at the segregated restaurant of the U.S. House of Representatives. Its law school has been regarded as the cradle of the civil rights movement because most of the attorneys involved in the movement received their training at Howard. Today, the university includes seventeen schools and colleges and twelve research centers; it offers bachelor's, master's, and doctoral degrees in liberal arts, teacher education, professional curricula, and dozens of specializations. The school has an interracial faculty and student body and a large number of international students. The largest predominantly Black school in the country, Howard's student body numbers more than ten thousand.

TRUTH SPEAKS OUT ON WOMEN'S SUFFRAGE

Sojourner Truth, one of the leading African American abolitionists, spoke forcefully in a debate between abolitionists and feminists, which centered on whether abolitionists should combine their efforts with the cause of women's suffrage. Many male abolitionists were not ready to modify their position to include women's suffrage. Truth reacted to this position by speaking about the double oppression of the Black woman concerning her race *and* gender:

I want women to have their rights. In the courts women have no rights, no voice; nobody speaks for them. I wish woman to have her voice there among the pettifoggers. If it is not a fit place for women, it is unfit for men to be there.

I am above eighty years old; it is about time for me to be going. I have been forty years a slave and forty years free, and would be here forty years more to have equal rights for all. I suppose I am kept here because something remains for me to do; I suppose I am yet to help to break the chain. I have done a great deal of work; as much as a man, but did not get so much pay. I used to work in the field and bind grain, keeping up with the cradler; but men doing no more, got twice as much pay.... We do as much, we eat as much, we want as much. I suppose I am about the only colored woman that goes about to speak for the rights of colored women. I want to keep the thing stirring, now that the ice is cracked. What we want is a little money. You men know that you get as much again as women, when you write, or for what you do. When we get our rights, we shall not have to come to you for money, for then we shall have money enough in our own pockets; and maybe you will ask us for money. But help us now until we get it. It is a good consolation to know that when we have got this battle once fought we shall not be coming to you any more....

I am glad to see that men are getting their rights, but I want women to get theirs, and while the water is stirring I will step into the pool. Now that there is a great stir about colored men's getting their rights it is the time for women to step in and have theirs. I am sometimes told that "Women ain't fit to vote. What, don't you know that a woman had seven devils in her: and do you suppose a woman is fit to rule the nation?" Seven devils ain't no account; a man had a legion in him. The devils didn't know where to go; and so they asked that they might go into the swine. They thought that was as good a place as they came out from. They didn't ask to go into the sheep — no, into the hog; that was the selfish beast; and man is so selfish that he has got women's rights and his own too, and yet he won't give women their rights. He keeps them all to himself....

Truth used her position to advocate many issues, including women's rights, protection of the poor, brotherly love, and Christianity. Although she lived for a time in Washington, D.C., where she dedicated much of her time helping to improve the conditions of Black people in the city, she eventually bought a home in Battle Creek, Michigan.

BLACKS ENFRANCHISED IN DISTRICT OF COLUMBIA

On **JANUARY 8**, the U.S. Congress passed legislation, over President Andrew Johnson's veto, providing suffrage to Blacks in the District of Columbia. Johnson believed that each state must enfranchise its own citizens.

PEABODY FUND FORMED

On **FEBRUARY 6**, the Peabody Fund was established to provide financial support for the construction of buildings, endowment funds, and scholarships for the education of newly freed slaves. The fund specifically undertook to prepare teachers and provide industrial education.

MOREHOUSE COLLEGE FOUNDED

On **FEBRUARY 18**, Morehouse College was founded as the Augusta Institute in Augusta, Georgia. It was founded by Edmund Turney, Richard Coulter, and William Jefferson of the American Baptist Home Mission Society. The school started with thirty-seven students, who were former slaves, and three teachers in a basement of Springfield Baptist Church in Augusta. Morehouse grew rapidly and acquired academic prestige. The school was noted for its rigorous academic standards and for instilling in its students a desire to serve the Black community. The mission of the college was largely formed under the direction of its president, Benjamin Mays.

In 1879, the school moved to Atlanta and changed its name to the Atlanta Baptist Seminary. In 1913, it became Morehouse College, named after the Reverend Henry L. Morehouse, secretary of the society. The school has a distinguished alumni body, including Dr. Martin Luther King, Jr., and filmmaker Spike Lee. One out of every ten Morehouse graduates has an academic or professional doctorate. The school offers a bachelor's degree and a liberal arts curriculum. It remains an independent college for men, and enrollment is currently about twelve hundred students.

BLACK PIONEERS SETTLE IN NEBRASKA

On **MARCH 1**, Nebraska became the thirty-seventh state in the Union. Settlers flocked to this area, once called "the Great American Desert," because land was cheap. The first Blacks arrived in Nebraska shortly after the Civil War. They settled in many counties, including Custer, Hamilton, Harlan, and Cherry. Some, like their white counterparts, were not successful in their new homes. One noteworthy success was Robert Ball Anderson, a former slave, who acquired some of the largest land holdings in the state.

Prior to the Homestead Act of 1862, which provided free land to settlers, only twenty-eight thousand settlers lived in the Nebraska territory; by 1867, more than one hundred thousand settlers resided there. Nebraska's application for statehood was originally vetoed in 1866 by President Johnson because he feared that additional Republican representation from the state could add support to those seeking to impeach him. Congress overrode his veto.

RECONSTRUCTION ACTS PASSED

Congress passed several Reconstruction Acts to provide for political participation of Blacks in southern state politics. These acts inaugurated an air of democracy and equal rights for Blacks and whites in the South that lasted about a decade. The first act, passed in March, provided for military rule in the South until certain political conditions were met. Divided into military districts, the southern states were to call for new elections to fill state offices and ratify the "Civil War amendments" to the Constitution. Each state had to pass a new constitution that guaranteed Blacks the right to vote before military forces would be removed. Since the states continued to refuse to ratify the Fourteenth Amendment, subsequent Reconstruction Acts were passed to force compliance.

On **MARCH 23** and **JULY 19**, additional Reconstruction Acts were passed to impose social and political reform throughout the South. Black Codes had been enacted to restrict the civil rights of freed Blacks and actually instituted a new form of slavery. Hundreds of Blacks had been killed while exercising their new civil rights, and many were too intimidated even to attempt to exercise their rights. Radical Republicans, who had won large victories in both houses of Congress, incorporated major enforcement measures in the Reconstruction Acts. Military governors were given significant power to decide voter eligibility, remove local officials, impose martial law, pass laws deemed necessary to ensure the rights of Blacks to vote, and initiate constitutional conventions, since no state had yet done so. Blacks could be elected as representatives to these conventions. Ultimately, Blacks would be represented in formulating all new state constitutions.

With such broad powers, Republicans were despised and resented by southerners, who called northerners who administered such programs "carpetbaggers," because they came with a few possessions that could fit in a satchel. Southerners used the term "scalawags" to identify white southerners who cooperated in the Reconstruction programs and the term "satraps" to identify the five major generals in charge of each of the five southern regions. These northern generals had almost unlimited power to enforce the Reconstruction Acts.

KU KLUX KLAN (KKK) HOLDS NATIONAL CONVENTION

In **APRIL**, the first national convention of the anti-Black organization Ku Klux Klan convened in the Maxwell House in Nashville, Tennessee. Those in attendance included Confederate generals, colonels, and influential men of both church and state. Ex-Confederate general Nathan B. Forrest, the leader and Grand Wizard, presided. The meeting resulted in a plan to reduce the political importance of Blacks throughout the country through a number of activities, including murder, assassination, terrorism, rape, and intimidation. The Klan reinforced its purpose: to keep the southern Black ignorant and under white control and to destroy the Republican Party. Other groups soon sprang up to assist in destroying the freedom and equality of Blacks: Knights of the White Camellia, the Red Shirts, the White League, Mother's Little Helpers, and the Baseball Club of the First Baptist Church.

KNIGHTS OF THE WHITE CAMELLIA

On **MAY 22**, a secret society called the Knights of the White Camellia was formed in Franklin, Louisiana. The purpose of the society was to preserve white supremacy and to fight "carpetbag" involvement in southern politics. Alcibiade DeBlanc was appointed the grand commander.

THE *Golconda* SAILS FOR LIBERIA

On **MAY 30**, the *Golconda* left Charleston with 321 Black colonists bound for Liberia. As many as 116 of these colonists were led by Cornelius Reeves, a Black Baptist preacher from Mullens Depot, South Carolina.

The story of these colonists was perhaps not unlike those of other groups who were persuaded "to leave this land of oppression and sorrow." In November 1866, Reeves had written to William Coppinger, the corresponding secretary of the American Colonization Society, wanting to know "when we can leave this country on any of your Ships bound for Liberia." Reeves indicated that he and his group of 286 wanted to leave as soon as their labor contracts expired on January 1, 1867. Whatever the motives of Reeves and his followers, it was clear that their poverty and the availability of free transportation influenced their decision. By January 1867, planters urged their employees to sign new agreements, but the Black colonists wanted agreements only up to mid-May — the time when they expected to sail for Liberia. The white planters, "envious against those wishing to emigrate," forced them to sign an annual

contract or no contract at all. Feeling compelled to sign, Reeves wrote to Coppinger, asking him to extend the sailing date until the end of the year. Coppinger responded that he would sail for Liberia in May as planned.

As the time to sail grew near, planters encouraged their workers not to sail, and many told their workers horrible stories of sickness and death in Liberia. Some of the workers defected; Reeves wrote to Coppinger about the decreasing number of applicants who were still committed to making the trip. In April, Coppinger traveled to Mullens Depot to make plans for the trip and to encourage others to join. After meeting with various groups, he journeyed back to Charleston, where he met with Richard Harvey Cain, one of the most powerful Black leaders in the city and pastor of the Emanuel AME Church. Coppinger received the support of Cain and even a commitment that he would supply replacements if there were last-minute defectors. After making the final arrangements for the trip, Coppinger waited for the applicants to arrive. In mid-May, Reeves brought 116 persons with him. Another 205 Black colonists then joined, so that a total of 321 boarded and waved farewell as the *Golconda* sailed on May 30. In November, the *Golconda* made another voyage from Charleston, carrying 312 Blacks to Liberia.

HORTON COMPOSES POEM AS HE EMBARKS FOR LIBERIA

On **DECEMBER 5**, George Horton, the former slave of James Horton of Chatham County, North Carolina, left New York for Liberia.

Although Horton could not write, he arranged his thoughts in rhyme, and when he spoke them aloud, others wrote them down. Over the years, his poems attracted attention and several were published in the *Raleigh Register*.

SONG FOR THE EMIGRANT

Almost as soon I'd be a slave,
As struggling with a treacherous wave,
A friend is but a foe;
Then fearless let us spread our sail,
To meet the unmolesting gale,
Come, *Brother*, let us go!

Let us desert this friendless place,
To stay is nothing but disgrace;
Few are our friends we know;
LIBERIA! break from every mouth,

To leave the North and travel South,
Come, *Sister*, let us go!

Suffer no tear to wet the eye,
Nor heave a melancholy sigh
For leaving vales of snow;
There vegetation ever thrives,
There corn in winter still revives,
Come, *Father*, let us go!

LIBERIA, flow from every tongue,
For there the old are waxing young,
No lasting pain they know;
Where milk and honey flow along,
And murmurs kindle into song,
Come, *Mother*, let us go!

This place is nothing but a strife,
Distressing all the peace of life,
We nothing have to show;
Let others scorn me or degrade,
I'll take my hatchet and my spade,
Come, *all*, and let us go!

1868 CARDOZO BECOMES SECRETARY OF STATE FOR SOUTH CAROLINA

Francis L. Cardozo (1837–1903) was the first Black elected to a state cabinet office. He served with distinction as secretary of state in South Carolina from 1868 to 1872. Cardozo was applauded for his successful organization of a "badly mismanaged" state land commission.

◇ Cardozo, born free in Charleston, South Carolina, was the son of a white economist and journalist, Jacob Cardozo. He attended schools in Charleston until he was twelve, at which time he became a carpenter's apprentice and later, a journeyman. At age twenty-one, he left for the University of Glasgow, Scotland, where he studied for four years. Afterwards, he studied at Presbyterian seminaries in Edinburgh and London.

It was in 1868 that Cardozo became an influential delegate to the South Carolina Constitutional Convention. An eloquent speaker and brilliant economist, he proposed breaking up the large plantations as the best hope of ensuring democracy. This measure was considered too radical and was not supported.

It is a patent fact that, as colored men, we have been cheated out of our rights for two centuries, and now that we have the opportunity, I want to fix them in the Constitution in such a way that no lawyer, however cunning or astute, can possibly misinterpret the

Francis L. Cardozo, one of the best educated Reconstruction politicians, became the first Black person elected to a state cabinet office.

meaning. If we do not do so, we deserve to be, and will be, cheated again.

◇ In 1872 and 1874, Cardozo was elected treasurer of the state. Cardozo's political fortune waned with the declining power of the Republican Party in the South. Although he was recommended for a number of positions, including president of Howard University, he was not selected. In 1878, he accepted a position in the Treasury Department in Washington, D.C., and afterwards, worked as an educator at various schools in the area. He died on July 22, 1903.

MENARD ELECTED FIRST BLACK U.S. CONGRESSMAN

John W. Menard (1839–1893) of Louisiana was the first Black elected to Congress, but he was never seated.

Even though Menard was awarded his full salary, the committee on elections ruled that it was too soon to admit a Black person to Congress. Menard was also the first Black representative to speak on the floor of the House of Representatives when he rose to plead his own case. Menard was the son of French Creole parents. He moved to Louisiana after the Civil War to work for the Republican party. After he was refused his seat in Congress, Menard was appointed inspector of customs for the port of New Orleans.

RACE RIOTS ERUPT IN LOUISIANA
Race riots broke out in various parts of Louisiana: New Orleans (September 22); Opelousas (September 28); and St. Bernard Parish (October 26). In St. Landry Parish, the Ku Klux Klan chased Republicans through the countryside for two days, killing and wounding as many as two hundred.

BLACK DELEGATES MAJORITY AT SOUTH CAROLINA CONSTITUTIONAL CONVENTION
On **JANUARY 14**, the South Carolina Constitutional Convention met in Charleston. It was the first assembly of its kind having a Black majority — more than 60 percent of the 124 members were Black; most of these were former slaves. On July 6, when the General Assembly of the South Carolina Reconstruction government met at Janney's Hall in Columbia, 85 of the 157 legislators were Black. Although Blacks formed a majority in the house, whites controlled the senate.

Blacks formed a majority in South Carolina legislatures between 1868 and 1877. The composition of the South Carolina legislature changed quite rapidly over the years. In 1873–1874, the lower house contained 63 whites and 61 Blacks; in 1876, there were 70 whites and 54 Blacks. By 1876, the Black vote was no longer a significant element in the structure of state government, and the ballot was increasingly limited to whites only.

HAMPTON INSTITUTE FOUNDED
On **APRIL 1**, Hampton Institute, an agricultural and industrial college for Blacks, primarily freed slaves, was founded in Hampton, Virginia. It was established by Samuel Chapman Armstrong, a twenty-seven-year-old brevet brigadier general who had commanded Black troops in the Civil War. Armstrong, the head of the eastern district of the Freedmen's Bureau, bought the site and started the school, called Hampton Nor-

This photograph shows the radical members of South Carolina's first legislature after the war. Their specific contributions to government, often cited as small, have yet to be fully assessed.

mal and Agricultural Institute, in an old federal hospital, with two teaching assistants and fifteen students.

Armstrong borrowed the fundraising technique of Fisk University's Jubilee Singers and sent musicians from the school to the North to tour and raise money. Prominent white northerners — including Andrew Carnegie, James Garfield, and William Howard Taft — served on the institute's board of trustees. Fundraising was very important to the institute, which charged no tuition to its largely penniless student body. Booker T. Washington, founder of Tuskegee Institute, graduated from Hampton in 1881 and took the school's philosophy of practical education and community service with him to Tuskegee.

The school is now known as Hampton University. It is a privately supported coeducational college with an enrollment of more than five thousand. About 94 percent of the student body is Black.

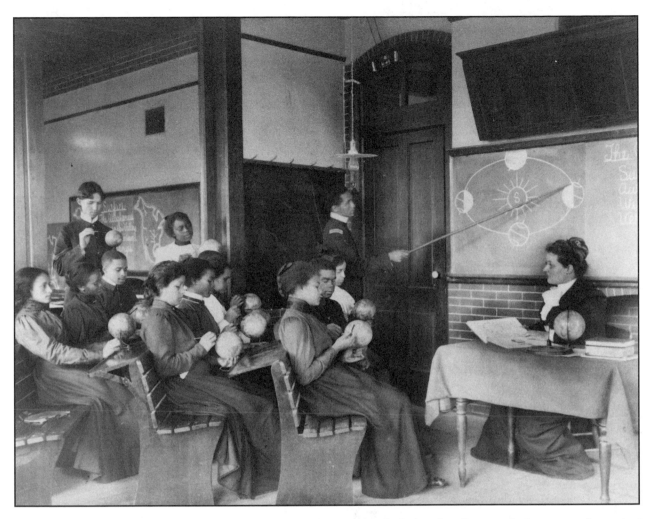

Hampton Institute became one of the major centers for educating freed Blacks. This photograph shows a mathematical geography class in which students are learning the relationship of the sun to the seasons.

BLACK DELEGATES AT THE REPUBLICAN CONVENTION

On **MAY 20**, P. B. S. Pinchback and James J. Harris became the first Black American delegates to a Republican convention. They supported the nomination of Ulysses S. Grant for president.

CONGRESSIONAL COMMITTEE RELEASES STATISTICS ON SLAIN FREED SLAVES

In **JUNE**, the Congressional Committee on Lawlessness and Violence released statistics on slain freed slaves. Using data for the years 1866–1868, the committee reported that 373 freed slaves had been killed by whites, and 10 whites had been killed by freed slaves. The committee acknowledged that since the Civil War, the Ku Klux Klan had killed thousands of Blacks and others. Florida and Louisiana were plagued by excessive violence in this year. Governor Harrison Reed of Florida had requested federal troops to curb the killing in his state, but the federal government had not responded.

LOUISIANA ELECTS BLACK LIEUTENANT GOVERNOR

On **JUNE 13**, Oscar J. Dunn (1821–1871), a former slave, assumed the office of lieutenant governor of Louisiana, the highest elective office held by an American Black up to this time.

◈ It is known that Dunn was born in Louisiana, but his early life is relatively obscure. Some accounts indicate that he was born a slave and ran away when he was a boy; other accounts say he was born a free Black. Dunn learned to read and write on his own, and during his early years, he played the violin, a skill he used to become a music teacher. During the Civil War, Dunn enlisted in the first regiment of Black troops raised by General Benjamin Butler. He rose to the rank of captain, the highest rank open to Black soldiers. But when a white soldier, considered to be incompetent, was promoted above him to the rank of major, Dunn resigned his commission.

Dunn's rapid rise in politics started when he was appointed by General Philip Sheridan to the city council of New Orleans. He was later elected as delegate to the Louisiana Constitutional Convention in 1867. In April 1868, he was elected lieutenant governor, and Henry C. Warmoth, a youthful white carpetbagger, governor. Dunn slowly gained a reputation as an effective public servant and an eloquent speaker. As lieutenant governor, Dunn was president of the Board of Police Commissioners and worked diligently to integrate New Orleans public schools.

On August 9, 1870, Dunn emerged as the chairman of the Republican State Convention after a bitter dispute among Louisiana Republicans. In particular, Dunn's fight was with Governor Warmoth, whom Dunn accused of selling out the interests of enfranchised Black voters to further his political ambition among white Democrats. Dunn's position as the presiding officer made him a powerful figure in the state, and many expected he would be the Republican nominee for governor in 1872. His political career was cut short with his untimely death on November 22, 1871. After a sudden violent illness lasting two days, Dunn died. It was speculated that he might have been a victim of poisoning, but there was insufficient evidence to confirm this.

MORE STATES READMITTED TO THE UNION
As of **JUNE 25**, Alabama, Arkansas, Florida, Louisiana, North Carolina, and South Carolina had been readmitted and had sent representatives to Congress. Texas, Virginia, Mississippi, and Georgia had not yet met readmission standards.

FOURTEENTH AMENDMENT RATIFIED
On **JULY 28**, Secretary of State William H. Seward announced the ratification of the Fourteenth Amendment and declared Blacks to be full citizens. As a result, Blacks were given constitutional guarantees.

Earlier in the year, the U.S. Congress had been presented with an amendment proposed by a group of congressmen, the Joint Committee of Fifteen. The committee had worked for several years to draft an amendment that was relatively simple but covered a host of highly complicated issues. The first draft of the amendment, presented in 1866, contained language that guaranteed citizenship of Black Americans, but the use of the term *male* angered many suffragists. Since the final amendment did not mention males, women believed that they could therefore claim the legal right to suffrage. The amendment was rewritten several times before being presented to Congress.

Congress passed the amendment, but some southern politicians boycotted the vote. Congress then sent it to the states for the three-fourths ratification required for constitutional amendments. The amendment included provisions for representational apportionment, status of Confederate soldiers, the right to vote, and the rights of newly freed slaves. More specifically, apportionment of congressmen was to be directly tied to each state's population. Any person who took the constitutional oath but fought against the Union was banned from holding national office. In contrast to what many southern states expected, the amendment stated that the Confederate debt would not be absorbed by the nation. Several southern states refused to ratify the amendment. When Congress made ratification of the Fourteenth Amendment a requirement for representation in Congress, southern states reluctantly accepted it.

BLACK GEORGIAN LEGISLATORS EXPELLED
In **SEPTEMBER**, the Georgia legislature expelled all twenty-eight Black members on the basis that although Blacks had the right to vote in Georgia, they did not have the right to hold public office. Military rule was then reimposed and the state's readmission to Congress was revoked.

Georgia was readmitted in 1870 after the Reconstruction Acts and the Fourteenth Amendment were fully enforced there, the Fifteenth Amendment had been ratified, and the expelled Black legislators reseated.

1869   BLACK MAN EARNS LAW DEGREE FROM HARVARD
George L. Ruffin (1834–1886) became the first Black person to earn the LL.B. degree from Harvard Univer-

sity. He is thought to be the first American Black to graduate from a university law school and obtain a law degree.

◆ Ruffin was born in Richmond of free parents. He went to school in Boston and worked as a barber. After his graduation from Harvard, Ruffin developed a thriving practice in Boston with the firm of Harvey Jewell. In 1876 and 1877, he was elected to the Boston Common Council. He attended Black conventions and presided over the one held in New Orleans in 1872. His friend, Frederick Douglass, asked Ruffin to write the introduction to the 1881 revision of his autobiography. In November 1883, Ruffin was appointed as judge of a municipal court in Charlestown. In the same year, he was also appointed consul resident in Boston for the Dominican Republic. Ruffin and his wife were considered prominent Black citizens of Boston; however, when Ruffin died of Bright's disease, he was almost penniless, having contributed much of his money to charities.

BLACK TEACHERS AND STUDENTS CONFIRM IMPORTANCE OF EDUCATION

In a letter written by M. A. Parker, a Black woman, the craving of Blacks for education was revealed:

It is surprising to me to see the amount of suffering which many of the people endure for the sake of sending their children to school. Men get very low wages here — from $2.50 to $8 per month usually, while a first rate hand may get $10, and a peck or two of meal per week for rations — and a great many men cannot get work at all. The women take in sewing and washing, go out by day to scour, etc. There is one woman who supports three children and keeps them at school; she says, "I don't care how hard I has to work, if I can only sen[d] Sallie and the boys to school looking respectable." Many of the girls have but one decent dress; it gets washed and ironed on Saturday, and then is worn until the next Saturday, provided they do not tear it or fall in the mud; when such an accident happens there is an absent mark on the register. . . . One may go into their cabins on cold, windy days, and see daylight between every two boards, or feel the rain dropping through the roof; but a word of complaint is rarely heard. They are anxious to have the children "get on" in their books, and do not seem to feel impatient if they lack comforts themselves. A pile of books is seen in almost every cabin, though there be no furniture except a poor bed, a table and two or three broken chairs.

The letter above is typical of the experiences of more than nine thousand teachers who taught freed Blacks in the South. As much as 45 percent of the teachers were women; most of the white women came from the North, the Black women from the South. There are no accurate numbers of Black women who taught freed Blacks, but it is estimated to be substantial.

DILLARD UNIVERSITY FOUNDED

Straight University and the Union Normal School, the predecessors of Dillard University, were founded in New Orleans. Dillard University, a private liberal arts institution affiliated with the United Church of Christ and the Methodist Church, was established in 1930 by a merger of New Orleans University (previously called Union Normal School — Methodist affiliated) and Straight College (previously called Straight University — Congregational affiliated). The school was named in honor of James Hardy Dillard, a white man who promoted the education of Blacks throughout the South.

UNION PACIFIC RAILROAD EMPLOYS BLACK WORKERS

The Union Pacific Railroad, which built a portion of the transcontinental railroad, employed the notably large number of three hundred Black workers.

NATIONAL CONVENTION OF COLORED MEN MEETS

On **JANUARY 12**, the National Convention of Colored Men was held in Washington, D.C. This group formed to address the alarming directions race relations were taking in the North and the South. Frederick Douglass was elected as its president.

BLACK DIPLOMAT REPRESENTS UNITED STATES IN HAITI

On **APRIL 16**, Ebenezer Don Carlos Bassett (1833–1908) was appointed U.S. minister to Haiti. He was the first Black diplomat to represent the United States and the first to receive a major governmental appointment.

◆ Bassett was born in Litchfield, Connecticut, and received his early education at Wesleyan Academy in Wilbraham, Massachusetts. He graduated with honors from the Connecticut State Normal School. Between 1857 and 1869, Bassett was principal of the Institute for Colored Youth in Philadelphia. Bassett was an excellent administrator and teacher, often teaching mathematics, natural sciences, and classics. Bassett's intellect and reputation influenced President

Ulysses S. Grant to appoint him to be U.S. minister to Haiti and the Dominican Republic. Bassett served as a diplomat for eight years. According to Frederick Douglass, Secretary of State Hamilton Fish had mentioned that "he wished one-half of his ministers abroad performed their duties as well as Mr. Bassett."

Although Bassett resigned in 1877 because of a new presidential administration, it was just two years later that he was appointed to serve as consul general for Haiti in New York. He served in this position from 1879 to 1888. In 1889, Bassett acted as secretary and interpreter for Frederick Douglass when he was appointed minister to Haiti and the Dominican Republic. In his older years, Bassett moved to Philadelphia, where he wrote *A Handbook on Haiti* for the Pan American Union. In ill health, complicated by malaria, Bassett died of a heart condition in 1908.

BLACK CONGRESSMAN DEFENDS RIGHT TO BE SEATED IN GEORGIA'S LEGISLATURE

On **SEPTEMBER 6**, Henry Turner, an elected member of the Georgia House of Representatives, spoke before the state representatives who had denied him and twenty-five Black representatives and two Black senators their seats.

MR. SPEAKER: Before proceeding to argue this question upon its intrinsic merits, I wish the members of this House to understand the position I take. I hold that I am a member of this body. Therefore, sir, I shall neither fawn or cringe before any party, nor stoop to beg them for my rights. Some of my colored fellow members, in the course of their remarks, took occasion to appeal to the sympathies of Members on the opposite side, and to eulogize their character for magnanimity. It reminds me very much, sir, of slaves begging under the lash. I am here to demand my rights, and to hurl thunder bolts at the men who would dare to cross the threshold of my manhood. There is an old aphorism which says, "Fight the Devil with fire," and if I should observe the rule in this instance, I wish gentlemen to understand that it is but fighting them with their own weapon.

The scene presented in this House, today, is one unparalleled in the history of the world. From this day, back to the day when God breathed the breath of life into Adam, no analogy for it can be found. Never, in the history of the world, has a man been arraigned before a body clothed with legislative, judicial or executive functions, charged with the offence of being of a darker hue than his fellowmen. I know that ques-

tions have been before the Courts of this country, and of other countries, involving topics not altogether dissimilar to that which is being discussed here today.

But, sir, never in all the history of the great nations of this world — never before — has a man been arraigned, charged with an offence committed by the God of Heaven Himself. Cases may be found where men have been deprived of their rights for crimes and misdemeanors; but it has remained for the State of Georgia, in the very heart of the nineteenth century, to call a man before the bar, and there charge him with an act for which he is no more responsible than for the head which he carries upon his shoulders. The Anglo-Saxon race, sir, is a most surprising one. No man has ever been more deceived in that race than I have been for the last three weeks. I was not aware that there was in the character of that race so much cowardice, or so much pusillanimity. The treachery which has been exhibited in it by gentlemen belonging to that race has shaken my confidence in it more than anything that has come under my observation from the day of my birth. . . .

Whose Legislature is this? . . . They question my right to a seat in this body, to represent the people whose legal votes elected me. This objection, sir, is an unheard of monopoly of power. No analogy can be found for it, except it be the case of a man who should go into my house, take possession of my wife and children, and then tell me to walk out. I stand very much in the position of a criminal before your bar, because I dare to be the exponent of the views of those who sent me here. Or, in other words, we are told that if black men want to speak, they must speak through white trumpets; if black men want their sentiments expressed, they must be adulterated and sent through white messengers, who will quibble, and equivocate, and evade, as rapidly as the pendulum of a clock. If this be not done, then the black men have committed an outrage, and their Representatives must be denied the right to represent their constituents.

The great question, sir, is this: Am I a man? If I am such, I claim the rights of a man.

◆ By this time, white Democrats had regained the legislature and passed laws weakening the radical Reconstruction constitutions. By 1876, only South Carolina, Florida, and Louisiana retained their Reconstructionist governments. This became one of Turner's major defeats, influencing him later to call for mass emigration of Blacks to Africa.

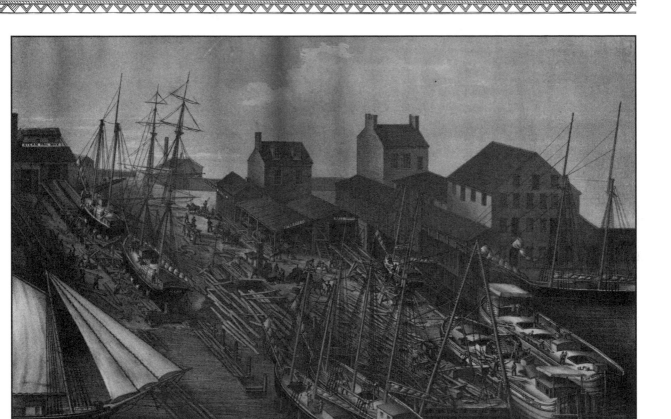

One of the largest and most successful Black businesses was the Chesapeake Marine Rail Way & Dry Dock Company of Baltimore, Maryland. It was organized with the help of Isaac Myers, a prominent Black labor leader who was also an officer of the company. At the time of incorporation, it had capital of $100,000.

NATIONAL NEGRO LABOR CONVENTION HELD

On **DECEMBER 12**, the National Negro Labor Convention met in Washington, D.C., and established the Colored National Labor Union. Isaac Myers, a ship caulker and carpenter from Baltimore, became the first important Black labor leader when he assumed leadership of the Colored National Labor Union. The union attempted to improve conditions for Black workers. But, like the Knights of Labor and the International Workers of the World, who also demanded better working conditions for Blacks, its efforts were largely unsuccessful. Myers also helped organize a Black-operated shipyard in Baltimore, the Chesapeake Marine Railway and Dry Dock Company. Blacks had organized one of their first labor unions in Baltimore in 1838, the Caulkers' Association.

1870

POPULATION OVERVIEW

BLACK POPULATION IN THE UNITED STATES The Bureau of the Census recorded a total of 4,880,009 Black residents in the country. They made up 12.7 percent of the total population of 39,818,449. Population figures rose dramatically from 1860 to 1870 as a result of the arrival of 2.3 million immigrants.

URBAN POPULATION There were only 14 cities in the entire country with a total population over 100,000. Only 27 percent of all U.S. residents lived in cities at this time. Black residents were still heavily concentrated in rural areas but were beginning to move into cities at a more rapid rate than whites. Living conditions in cities were not necessarily better than in the rural areas they had fled. Crowding was

RECONSTRUCTION CONSTITUTIONS GUARANTEE POLITICAL AND CIVIL RIGHTS TO ALL

Constitutional conventions were held throughout the South during the period from 1867 to 1869. Southern Republicans, both Black and white, created documents that addressed numerous social, economic, and political issues. The resulting constitutions reflected both moderate and radical elements within the party.

The largest group of delegates were southern white Republicans, especially in the states of North Carolina, Georgia, Arkansas, Alabama, and Texas. Most of these were farmers, small merchants, and professionals, most of whom had never held political office. This group had almost unanimously opposed secession. Carpetbaggers made up about 17 percent of the delegates, and many of them had served in the Union army, were the best educated of all the delegates, and generally wrote the most important provisions of the new constitutions. Blacks were underrepresented in most states, although they did form a majority of delegates in Louisiana and South Carolina and about 40 percent of the delegates in Florida. They formed almost one-fifth of the delegates in Georgia, Alabama, and Mississippi. Although biographical data of the Black delegates are incomplete, about 107 had been born as slaves, 28 had spent most or all of their lives in the North, and 40 had served in the Union army; the largest occupational groups were ministers, artisans, farmers, and teachers. Regardless of background, Black delegates were unified on issues of civil rights and access to education; they differed on economic policy and disfranchisement of former Confederates.

The constitutions produced by these delegates set up free public school education; established penitentiaries, orphanages, and insane asylums; and abolished property qualifications for office and jury service. They all guaranteed political and civil rights to Blacks, incorporating language addressing the equality of all people. Delegates could not agree, however, on racially integrated schools and the social equality of Blacks. On the highly charged issue of school integration, no state constitution required separate schools, and Louisiana and South Carolina actually prohibited them. Blacks objected in every state to any constitutional language that required racial segregation in schools.

The constitutions were voted on in 1868; all but two were approved by the majority of voters. In Alabama, whites boycotted the elections so that there was no majority of registered voters. In Mississippi, a clause that disfranchised most former Confederates kept nearly all whites from voting for the constitution. These new state constitutions remained in effect during Reconstruction. But the withdrawal of federal troops from the South in 1877 gave a signal to white supremacists that there would be few impediments to disfranchising Blacks and reversing the provisions of equality embodied in these state constitutions.

commonplace, and diseases such as yellow fever and typhoid were rampant.

SOUTHERN BLACK RESIDENTS IN THE NORTH AND THE WEST Most of the Black residents who moved from the South to the North and the West were previously residents of Virginia. Kentucky and Tennessee ranked second as the place of origin of Black emigrants. The fewest number of southern Black emigrants, only about 3,600, originated in Louisiana, Texas, or Arkansas.

BLACK RESIDENTS IN CALIFORNIA The state of California claimed 4,272 Black residents. Most lived in the gold-mining areas of the Sierra Nevada and in Sacramento and San Francisco.

ECONOMIC CONDITIONS OVERVIEW

BLACK STRIKEBREAKERS USED IN COAL AND STEEL INDUSTRIES In the 1870s, Blacks faced a deteriorating labor market. Although industrialization was gaining force, Blacks were not considered for employment in the growing skilled jobs market. Blacks monopolized jobs as coachmen, footmen, valets, chambermaids, chefs, and waiters. Yet competition for even these jobs grew as foreign-born whites sought them, too. In 1874, about five hundred Blacks were brought into Hocking Valley in Ohio to break a coal strike. The success of Blacks as strikebreakers encouraged their use by management. Blacks were not always told that they were to serve as "scabs." Blacks were recruited from Memphis, Richmond, Louisville, and other border and southern cities to break strikes in Braidwood, Illinois, in 1877; in Ohio's Tuscarawas Valley in 1880; and in Pittsburgh in 1880. Following the success in the coal industry, the use of Black strikebreakers spread to the iron and steel industry.

SOCIAL CONDITIONS OVERVIEW

BLACK COLLEGES FOUNDED No fewer than twenty-three historically Black colleges and universities (HBCUs) were founded during the 1870–1880 decade. All but one of these new schools were established in the South; three or more each were founded in Mississippi, Alabama, Tennessee, and North Carolina in this decade. Others were established in Arkansas, Florida, and Kentucky. In general, these colleges were located on the periphery of the Black Belt, the cultural hearth of the Black population at the time, with some established in areas newly settled by Blacks.

BLACK LITERACY IN THE SOUTH Black illiteracy in the South had been reduced to 79.9 percent, largely as a result of teachers engaged by the Freedmen's Bureau. Union troops had actually opened schools for Blacks as they invaded the South during the Civil War. By 1867, the Freedmen's Bureau had set up almost forty-five hundred schools. Not all were free; some had tuition costs as high as one-tenth of typical monthly incomes for Blacks. By 1870, bureau schools enrolled 250,000 students. The growing literacy of Blacks gave some a chance to participate in Reconstruction, especially in the political process. Several educated Blacks served as state legislators and in the U.S. Congress. Most Blacks who sat in Congress during the 1880s and 1890s had more formal education than did Warren G. Harding, president of the United States from 1876 to 1880.

BLACK MIGRANTS IN KANSAS The reign of white terrorism against Blacks throughout the South caused many Blacks and whites to leave. By the late 1870s, Reconstruction had ended, federal troops had been withdrawn, and the rights that Blacks had enjoyed were being abused and legislated out of existence by both state and national Jim Crow laws. Many Blacks feared a return to a type of slavery. As the social and political structure of the South continued to favor white supremacists, individuals, families, and colonies of Blacks migrated west. Kansas quickly became a major destination for many of these migrants because of the possibility of land ownership. Anyone with a filing fee of ten dollars could claim 160 acres of public land under the Homestead Act of 1862, gaining title after living on the land and working it for five years.

Posters invited Blacks to leave their homes in the South for places in Kansas. Such was the start of the major exodus of Blacks that many attribute to Benjamin "Pap" Singleton but which was clearly influenced by many others. Singleton organized three communities in Kansas: Dunlap, Singleton, and Nicodemus. Nicodemus, which was founded in 1877, is the only one of these that survives. It attracted about six hundred to seven hundred colonists in 1877 and 1878, about 530 of them from Kentucky. Most of the Blacks moving to Kansas ultimately settled in the larger urban Black communities, such as Kansas City and Topeka. Sixty thousand blacks were believed to have left the South and headed for Kansas from 1875 to 1881.

Blacks from Kentucky and Tennessee established no fewer than four Black colonies in Kansas. The total population of these colonies was about two thousand individuals. Before 1879, most of the Black immigrants to Kansas were self-sufficient, but afterwards, they were no better off than the white immigrants who were also pouring into Kansas.

EXPATRIATION OF BLACKS TO LIBERIA The American Colonization Society sent an average of only 98 Blacks annually to Liberia in the 1820s, and about 74 per year in the 1880s. Between 1820 and 1864, the Colonization Society sent a total of 10,764 Blacks to Liberia. Between 1865 and 1869, it transported 2,394; over the next thirty years, it transported only 2,013. The Colonization Society was becoming outdated. Loss of white support rendered the society ineffective. Supporters of the colonization movement included Henry Turner, William J. Whipper, Richard Harvey Cain, and Martin Delany.

KU KLUX KLAN USES INTIMIDATION TO REGAIN GOVERNMENT FOR DEMOCRATS According to a congressional report concerning nine South Carolina counties in 1870, the Klan had murdered thirty-five men and whipped as many as 262 men and women. The Republican hold on the political structure in the South had weakened considerably over the past several years. Conservative Democrats had regained control over many of these states by using various tactics, including intimidation, violence, and murder by the Ku Klux Klan to secure political power. A separate study by the Florida secretary of state documented

153 murders by Klan members in Jackson County in that state.

SOUTHERN STATES TAKEN OVER BY DEMOCRATIC PARTY

White supremacists forced Virginia, Tennessee, Texas, Mississippi, and North Carolina back to the Democratic Party. Terror and violence against Blacks spread, and there was no longer any pretense of enforcing the Thirteenth, Fourteenth, and Fifteenth Amendments. Congress had lost the strong supporters of Reconstruction, including Thaddeus Stevens, who had died. Only Benjamin Butler remained.

TERROR IN THE SOUTH

Before the U.S. Senate, Senator Adelbert Ames, a white Republican of Mississippi, spoke eloquently of the consequences of the first reign of terror in the South, from 1868 to 1870:

> It must not be forgotten that, as a general thing, it is the prominent Republican who is killed, and not the obscure or insignificant. Now, I would ask, what political party in the North can retain its vigor and lose yearly in each State by murder of eight hundred of its best and most reliable workers? It is not so much in the diminution of their numbers by so many that the great political harm is done as in the demoralization consequent thereto. Whole counties become paralyzed, and inaction falls on recognized leaders, who, there, because of the want of universal education, are much more depended upon than in the North. It can very easily be understood how cities, counties, and whole states change their political complexion under such opposition as this.

ALLEN UNIVERSITY FOUNDED

Allen University was established as Payne Institute in Cokesbury, South Carolina, by the AME Church. The school was named after Daniel Alexander Payne, an apostle of African American education.

In 1880, the school relocated to Columbia, South Carolina, and in a new charter, was renamed Allen University in honor of Bishop Richard Allen, founder of the AME Church. Allen University was the first Black institution of higher learning in South Carolina, and its functions continually expanded. It taught from the first grade to the college graduate level. Today, the school is coeducational and offers bachelor's degrees in programs in liberal arts and teacher education. Enrollment is about 460 students.

BLACK ELECTED LIEUTENANT GOVERNOR OF SOUTH CAROLINA

Alonzo J. Ransier (1834–1882) was elected lieutenant governor of South Carolina. Born in Charleston, Ransier moved up the political ladder quite quickly despite his limited education. Following the Civil War, he was appointed registrar of elections. He journeyed to Washington, D.C., in 1868 with other delegates to deliver a petition from the Friends of Equal Rights of Charleston. He was a delegate to the 1868 state constitutional convention, chaired the Republican state central committee, and served in the South Carolina House of Representatives. Ransier used the office of lieutenant governor to support Republican candidates. An honest and hard-working politician, he was nominated by the Second District Republicans to run for Congress in 1872. He was elected and served one term, until 1874. He was appointed a collector of internal revenue in South Carolina. Later, he became impoverished after the death of his wife and worked as a day laborer for the city government of Charleston until his death in 1882.

BLACK LEADER LYNCHED IN NORTH CAROLINA

Wyatt Outlaw, a Black leader in Alamance County, North Carolina, was lynched. Racial violence and intimidation was so intense that Governor William W. Holden declared the county to be in a state of insurrection.

BLACK MERCHANT REPRESENTS ALABAMA IN CONGRESS

Benjamin S. Turner (1825–1894) was elected U.S. representative from Alabama's First Congressional District — the first Black member of the House from Alabama. In the Forty-second Congress, Turner pushed through two private pension bills, one providing an eight-dollar-per-month pension to a corporal of a Civil War Black regiment. He presented a petition requesting a refund of the cotton tax collected from southern states, decrying its harmful impact on primarily Black fieldworkers. Turner also called for the federal government to purchase large private tracts of land and resell divided parcels of 160 acres to freed Blacks. Neither of these proposals received the support of his colleagues.

◈ Turner was born a slave in Halifax County, North Carolina. After the Civil War, Turner settled in Selma, Alabama, where he became a merchant and owner of a livery stable. He became a tax collector of Dallas County in 1867, and two years later, he became a city councilor of Selma.

Although Turner won the renomination of his party, Philip Joseph, another Black candidate, ran as an Independent and split the Black and Republican vote, allowing the white Democrat to win. Turner retired from national politics. One of his last political activities occurred in 1880, when he was a delegate to the Republican National Convention in Chicago. Turner died in Selma.

BLACKS HOLD SEATS IN MISSISSIPPI LEGISLATURE

Mississippi's first legislature after Reconstruction was convened in Jackson. Of the 106 elected representatives, 31 were Black. In the 33-member senate, Blacks numbered 5.

ELLIOTT RUNS FOR U.S. CONGRESS

Robert Brown Elliott (1848–1884) was nominated by the Third District Republicans in South Carolina to run against John E. Bacon, the Democratic candidate for Congress.

After winning the election, Elliott served on several key committees in the U.S. House of Representatives, including the Committee on Education and Labor. He was an outspoken advocate of education and Black voting rights. He challenged an amnesty bill for Confederates, urging a delay in the restoration of political rights to ex-Confederates, and he spoke eloquently in support of an act restricting the Ku Klux Klan's influence.

◈ Elliott was probably born in Liverpool, England, in 1848, although there is some uncertainty about his early life. Some evidence suggests that he was born in Boston, but it seems more likely that he was born in England and educated in both England (at Eton College) and Boston, where he learned the typesetter's trade. He arrived in Boston about 1867, moved to Charleston within the year, and worked for Richard Harvey Cain (U.S. representative, 1872–1874) as associate editor of the *South Carolina Leader*. Elliott had attended the 1868 state constitutional convention, where he spoke up for compulsory public education. In the same year, Elliott was elected to the South Carolina House of Representatives. During his tenure, he studied law and was admitted to the state bar.

In 1872, Elliott was reelected to Congress without opposition, capturing 93 percent of the vote. He continued his forthright support for civil rights. On January 5, 1874, he gave a speech supporting the omnibus Civil Rights Bill sponsored by Senator Charles Sumner. He revealed his keen knowledge of constitutional law by interpreting the recent *Slaughterhouse* cases of the U.S. Supreme Court as obligating Congress to legislate against discrimination. After he returned to South Carolina, Blacks acclaimed him a hero. In response to this outpouring of support and the widespread corruption and intimidation tactics that Democrats used to suppress the Black vote throughout the state, Elliott resigned his House seat and won a seat in the South Carolina General Assembly.

Elliott rose to become Speaker of the General Assembly. Although he had significant legislative power among his peers, the state was experiencing a rise in Ku Klux Klan violence and a shift toward Democratic power. Hoping to make a difference, Elliott made another political move. In 1876, he was elected state attorney general. His power in this position weakened considerably as conservative white Democrats became more powerful throughout state government and the end of federal Reconstruction approached. In May 1877, Elliott was forced out of office.

Elliott practiced law for a while but eventually accepted an appointment as special customs inspector for the U.S. Treasury Department in Charleston. He continued to be active in the Republican Party. In 1881, Elliott was transferred by the U.S. Treasury Department to New Orleans. He responded to the move with such disgust that he was removed from his duties a year later. Elliott lapsed into poverty before his death in New Orleans on August 9, 1884.

FIRST BLACK HIGH SCHOOL OPENS IN WASHINGTON, D.C.

By some accounts, the first Black high school in America opened in this year in the basement of the Fifteenth Street Presbyterian Church in Washington, D.C. The church had many distinguished leaders, including the Reverend Henry Highland Garnet and the Reverend Francis J. Grimké.

FIRST BLACK STUDENT ADMITTED TO WEST POINT

James W. Smith of South Carolina became the first Black student admitted to West Point. However, he did not graduate. He was court-martialed and forced to leave the academy for breaking a coconut dipper over the head of another cadet. It would be another seven years before the first Black cadet, Henry O. Flipper, graduated from West Point. Cadet Smith wrote to a friend about his treatment at West Point:

I have been so harassed with examinations and insults and ill treatment of these cadets that I could not write or do anything else scarcely. I passed the examination all right, and go in, but my companion Howard failed and was rejected. Since he went away I have been lonely indeed. And now these fellows appear to be trying their utmost to run me off, and I fear they will succeed if they continue as they have begun. We went into camp yesterday, and not a moment has passed since then but some one of them has been cursing and abusing me. . . . It is just the same at the table, and what I get to eat I must snatch for like a dog. I don't wish to resign if I can get along at all; but I don't think it will be the best for me to stay and take all the abuses and insults that are heaped upon me.

GEORGIA LEGISLATURE RECONVENES WITH BLACK REPRESENTATIVES

The Georgia state legislature was reconvened, and elected Black representatives and senators previously barred from membership were admitted.

In addition to seating the elected Black legislators, Georgia (like all other former Confederate states) had to reratify the Fourteenth Amendment and ratify the Fifteenth Amendment (which made it illegal to deny the right to vote on racial grounds) before gaining readmission to the Union and the return of its delegation to Congress. Already, violence and intimidation directed toward Blacks and Republican politicians ensured conservative Democratic control of state offices.

New Era FOUNDED

The *New Era* newspaper, edited by J. Sella Martin, was founded in Washington, D.C. Frederick Douglass was its corresponding editor. The paper became a leader in exposing the nature of racism in the country.

Douglass purchased the *New Era* in 1870, and it was renamed the *New National Era* in 1872. He took over as editor with the help of his two sons. When Douglass was elected president of the National Colored Labor Union, the *New National Era* became the organization's official paper.

LAST FORMER CONFEDERATE STATES READMITTED TO UNION

The last former Confederate states were readmitted to the Union after meeting federal requirements. Virginia was readmitted on January 26, Mississippi on February 23, Texas on March 30, and Georgia on July 15.

BLACK TAILOR REPRESENTS GEORGIA IN CONGRESS

On **JANUARY 1**, Jefferson F. Long (1836–1900) was elected to the U.S. Congress from the state of Georgia. Although he served only one term, until March 3,

1871, while in Congress, he became known for his support of the enforcement of the Fifteenth Amendment.

◆ Long, born near Knoxville, Georgia, was a self-educated man who worked as a tailor in Macon, Georgia, before he won the Republican Party's nomination to fill a vacancy in the U.S. House of Representatives. When he left Washington, he resumed his business in Macon and later served as a delegate to the Republican National Convention in 1880. Long was the only African American from Georgia to serve in the U.S. Congress during the nineteenth century. The next Black congressman from Georgia was Andrew Young in 1972.

MISSISSIPPI READMITTED TO THE UNION

On **FEBRUARY 23**, Mississippi was readmitted to the Union and sent representatives to Congress. However, violence against Blacks in the state increased, with more than sixty murders in two months, leading to the passage by Congress of additional Enforcement Acts in 1871 to support and enforce the Fourteenth Amendment.

REVELS BECOMES FIRST BLACK SENATOR

On **FEBRUARY 25**, Hiram R. Revels (1827–1901), born a free man in Fayetteville County, North Carolina, took his seat in the U.S. Senate. Revels became the first Black U.S. senator, and the first Black in Congress. He had been elected to Congress by the Mississippi legislature by a vote of 85–15 to fill the unexpired term of Jefferson Davis in the U.S. Senate. There was much opposition to Revels's membership in this exclusive body of white men. Some claimed he was not a citizen; others claimed that the election was null and void because Mississippi was under military rule when it was held; still others asserted that his credentials were invalid because they were signed by an unelected military governor. Other objections included outright racism. On March 16, in the first official speech by a Black person in Congress, Revels voiced his opposition to the readmission of Georgia to the Union without adequate safeguards for Black citizens. Revels served for only one year but was instrumental in defeating segregation in the public schools of the District of Columbia.

◆ Before his election, Revels served as a pastor of African Methodist Episcopal (AME) churches in Illinois, Missouri, and Indiana. Revels championed the Union cause by recruiting other Blacks and serving as chaplain of his regiment. In 1863, he established a school for freed Blacks in St. Louis. After settling in Natchez in 1866, he was elected alderman in 1868 and was elected to the state senate a year later.

After retiring from politics, Revels served as editor of the *Southwestern Christian Advocate*, and in 1871, he became the first president of Alcorn College, the first land grant college in the United States for Black students. He resigned in 1873 to avoid being dismissed by Mississippi's Governor Adelbert Ames, a political enemy. Revels reentered politics with some anger for Republicans and campaigned heavily for Democratic candidates for state offices in 1875. His racial conservatism was revealed when he testified before the Senate's Select Committee to Inquire into Alleged Frauds in Recent Elections in Mississippi. Revels said that elections had been peaceful without widespread violence. Black Mississippians were inflamed with his remarks, and members of the Holly Springs Church dismissed him as their pastor. Although Revels was reappointed president of Alcorn College by Democratic Governor John M. Stone, he never regained the high level of respect and admira-

tion he had enjoyed as senator. He retired in 1882 but continued to serve as a teacher at Shaw University (later Rust University).

FIFTEENTH AMENDMENT RATIFIED

On **MARCH 30**, the Fifteenth Amendment to the U.S. Constitution, granting Blacks the right to vote, was ratified by states. The amendment barred voting discrimination on "basis of race, color, or previous condition of servitude." Because the Republican Party had championed Black rights and the passage and ratification of the Fifteenth Amendment, Black voters became Republicans in large numbers.

CONGRESS PASSES ENFORCEMENT ACT

On **MAY 31**, Congress passed the first Enforcement Act to enforce the Fifteenth Amendment because terrorist tactics were being used throughout the South to keep Blacks from voting. It stipulated penalties for public officials and other citizens who deprived others of suffrage and civil rights. It also authorized the use of the U.S. Army to protect the right of Blacks.

STANCE AWARDED MEDAL OF HONOR

On **JUNE 28**, Sergeant Emanual Stance, Company F, Ninth Cavalry, was the first Black American to receive the Medal of Honor during the Indian campaigns.

While stationed at Fort McKavett, Texas, Stance and nine other troopers commanded by Captain Henry Carroll left the fort in search of Native Americans who had stolen two

Hiram R. Revels, the first Black U.S. senator, represented the state of Mississippi. He was elected by the Mississippi legislature to replace Jefferson Davis.

children during a raid. On their way back to the fort, they were attacked by about twenty Native Americans who were stalking a herd of government horses. Stance and several of his men outflanked and defeated the attackers. Captain Carroll recommended Stance for the Medal of Honor because of his courage and skill.

Stance remained in the army for many years afterwards. Over a period of sixteen years, he was promoted to the rank of first sergeant. He was reassigned to the all-Black "F" Troop in Fort Robinson, Nebraska. Here, soldiers with hot tempers and time on their hands frequently brawled. Although some noncommissioned officers lost control of their men, Stance remained a strict disciplinarian. In December 1887, his body was found along the road to Crawford, Nebraska, with four bullet wounds — the presumed victim of his own men.

KLAN VIOLENCE ERUPTS IN NORTH CAROLINA

KKK activities intensified in many counties throughout North Carolina as Democrats sought to suppress Black participation in politics. Governor William W. Holden continued to denounce Klan activities. On **JULY 8**, he declared Caswell County to be in a state of insurrection. Still, white conservative Democratic politicians used the Klan to win elections throughout the state and gain control of the legislature, and their victories signaled the end of Reconstruction in North Carolina. On December 14, the conservative legislature voted to impeach anti-Klan Governor Holden.

DELARGE ELECTED TO CONGRESS

On **OCTOBER 19**, Robert Carlos DeLarge (1842–1874), a Republican, was elected U.S. representative from South Carolina. Although the election was challenged, DeLarge was seated in the Forty-second Congress, which convened on March 4, 1871. In Congress, DeLarge supported appropriations for an orphan asylum and enforcement of the Fourteenth Amendment, but his tenure was shortened when he took a leave of absence to prepare his defense against charges of election irregularities. On January 18, 1873, the House Committee on Elections reported that so many abuses and irregularities had occurred during the election that it was impossible to determine a winner. The committee decided that neither DeLarge nor his opponent, Christopher Bowen, was entitled to the seat and declared the seat vacant. DeLarge chose not

to run for reelection, but another Black South Carolinian, Alonzo J. Ransier, won the seat.

◈ Born as a slave in Aiken, South Carolina, DeLarge had little formal education but gained a wealth of experience in various vocations — farmer, tailor, agent with the Freedmen's Bureau, and organizer with the South Carolina Republican Party. He chaired the credentials committee at the Colored People's Convention in Charleston and the platform committee of the 1867 Republican State Convention. He was a member of the Committee on Franchise and Elections at the South Carolina Constitutional Convention, a member of the South Carolina House of Representatives, and chairperson of the Committee on Ways and Means. DeLarge was appointed land commissioner, responsible for allocating more than two thousand small tracts of land for homeowners. After leaving Congress, DeLarge was appointed a magistrate in the city of Charleston, where he died at the age of thirty-one.

KU KLUX KLAN VIOLENCE CONTINUES

In **DECEMBER**, a U.S. army officer arrived in York County, South Carolina, to investigate Klan activities; by July 1871, he reported that more than three hundred persons had been whipped and six murdered by the Klan during his stay.

WOOD ELECTED MAYOR OF NATCHEZ

In **DECEMBER**, Robert H. Wood was elected mayor of Natchez, Mississippi. Wood was one of several Black mayors who served in southern cities during Reconstruction.

BLACK JUSTICE APPOINTED IN SOUTH CAROLINA

On **DECEMBER 1**, Jonathan Jasper Wright (1840–1887) was elected associate justice of the South Carolina Supreme Court. He was the first Black to be elected to a major judicial position, though he initially took over the position in February when he filled the unexpired term of a justice. He was elected to a six-year term on the bench and was the highest-ranking Black justice in the nation. Wright left the judiciary in 1877.

FORTY-FIRST CONGRESS CONVENES

On **DECEMBER 5**, the Forty-first Congress convened. For the first time since 1860, all southern states were represented. Members included one Black senator (Hiram R. Revels of Mississippi) and two Black U.S. representatives — Jefferson F. Long of Georgia and Joseph H. Rainey of South Carolina (elected the following week).

RAINEY REPRESENTS SOUTH CAROLINA

On **DECEMBER 12**, Joseph H. Rainey (1832–1887) was elected to the U.S. House of Representatives from South Carolina, thus becoming its first Black member. He won a special election to fill the vacancy created when Congressman Benjamin F. Whittemore resigned after being charged with selling appointments to U.S. military academies.

◈ Rainey was born a slave in Georgetown, South Carolina. In 1846, his family moved to Charleston after Rainey's father purchased their freedom. In 1862, Rainey was drafted by South Carolina, made to work as a messman on a Confederate blockade runner, and assigned other menial tasks. Within months, he and his wife, Susan (whom he had married in 1859), escaped to freedom in Bermuda.

In 1866, after the war was over, Rainey and his wife returned to South Carolina where he was selected to be a member of the executive committee of the South Carolina Republican Party. In 1868, Rainey was a representative to the South Carolina Constitutional Convention, and in 1870, he was elected state senator.

After his election to the Forty-first Congress, Rainey was placed on several key committees. On the Freedmen's Affairs Committee, he was an outspoken advocate of Senator Charles Sumner's civil rights legislation and supported the use of federal troops to protect Black voters from KKK threats and violence. Rainey was reelected in 1872, and as a member of the Committee on Indian Affairs, he replaced Speaker James G. Blaine during the debate on the Indian Appropriation Bill. He thus became the first Black representative to preside over a House session. In 1874, he won the congressional election by only 669 votes. The election was contested, but the House Committee on Elections declared Rainey the winner. Rainey strongly condemned the overt racism of the savage massacre of Black militiamen in Hamburg, South Carolina, before the U.S. House of Representatives.

In 1876, Rainey won a fourth term in the U.S. Congress. The election was appealed with charges that white voters were intimidated by members of armed Black political clubs, the Black militia, and the large contingent of federal soldiers in Hamburg because of the massacre. Rainey received a favorable vote from the committee and was later sworn in. He continued to support the use of federal troops to protect Black voters and was a strong supporter of the Freedmen's Savings and Trust Company.

In May 1878, the House Committee on Elections declared Rainey's congressional seat vacant because of election irregularities in the First District. The full House refused to accept the committee's report, thereby allowing Rainey to remain seated. Later that year, however, Rainey lost the election to John Richardson, and his opportunities for a noteworthy political appointment were significantly reduced when Democrats gained control of the House of Representatives. Rainey accepted a job as an Internal Revenue Service agent in South Carolina. In 1881, he returned to Washington when the Republicans regained the Congress. He was disappointed when fellow Republicans passed him over for an appointment. He later worked at several jobs, including establishing a brokerage and banking firm, which later failed.

1871 ALABAMA NEGRO LABOR UNION ESTABLISHED

About ninety-eight Black farmers formed the Alabama Negro Labor Union to consider the plight of Black workers in the state and to evaluate social and economic inequities faced by Blacks, including their voluntary removal to the West. George F. Marlowe was elected president and charged with finding out about opportunities for Blacks in Kansas. When Marlowe reported to the group in January 1872, he mentioned that opportunities for work and education were plentiful and that Blacks could purchase land for one dollar and twenty-five cents an acre. Some opposed the migration of Blacks to Kansas and other western destinations, instead "trusting in God and the federal government for the protection to which they [Blacks] were entitled."

BLACKS MASSACRED IN MISSISSIPPI

About thirty Blacks were massacred in Meridian, Mississippi. State laws offered Blacks no protection. Although Congress passed a law to end the Ku Klux Klan menace, there was little enforcement; other similar organizations sprang up to continue the violence.

BLACKS SERVE IN FORTY-SECOND CONGRESS

The Forty-second Congress convened, including five Black congressmen: Joseph H. Rainey, of South Carolina; Robert Carlos DeLarge, of South Carolina; Robert Brown Elliott, of South Carolina; Benjamin S. Turner, of Alabama; and Josiah T. Walls, of Florida.

HARPER PUBLISHES POETRY

Frances Ellen Watkins Harper (1825–1911) published *Poems*, a collection of poetry that focused on anti-slavery sentiment and aspects of slavery.

Harper had written poetry from her childhood about growing up in Baltimore. Many years later, in 1892, Harper published a novel titled *Iola Leroy*, which was much praised by white critics at the time. Although Harper was born to free parents, she wrote eloquently about slavery, probably because she began lecturing on issues of race and slavery while quite young. As an abolitionist, she traveled broadly throughout the United States and Canada. She was also active in the Women's Christian Temperance Union and a strong supporter of women's suffrage.

COLORED NATIONAL LABOR UNION PETITIONS CONGRESS

On **JANUARY 19**, the Colored National Labor Union petitioned Congress to implement a national system of educational and technical training. The union, which assembled two hundred delegates at its first convention in 1869, considered it absolutely necessary to use its growing power immediately, since it had tied its future to the Republican Party. Isaac Myers of Baltimore, the key leader of the movement at the time, admitted this when he said of the Republican Party: "By its success, we stand; by its defeat we fall." The union failed in 1872.

REPRESENTATIVE LONG SPEAKS IN HOUSE

On **FEBRUARY 1**, Jefferson F. Long, U.S. representative of Georgia, gave a speech opposing leniency for ex-Confederates before his peers of the U.S. House of Representatives. Long became the first Black to make an official speech before this body.

CONGRESS PASSES SECOND ENFORCEMENT ACT

On **FEBRUARY 28**, Congress passed another Enforcement Act, or Ku Klux Klan Act, giving federal officers and courts control of voter registration and voting in congressional elections. The law was designed to help enforce the Fifteenth Amendment.

TURNER AWARDED POST IN LIBERIA

On **MARCH 1**, James Milton Turner (1844–1915) was appointed U.S. minister to Liberia, thus becoming the first Black American diplomat to an African country and the second Black in the diplomatic corps. Turner's post was a reward for his support of Ulysses S. Grant's election.

Turner had been born a slave in Missouri and was essentially self-educated. He served in the Civil War, and when it ended, became active in public life. He later established a refugee depot in Missouri for the "Exodusters" — Blacks migrating to the West — on their way to Kansas. Turner later served as an attorney for Black members of the Cherokee people who had been denied a fair share of the grant given to the tribe at the end of the Civil War as payment for land.

WALLS FIGHTS FOR SEAT IN CONGRESS

On **MARCH 4**, Josiah T. Walls (1842–1905), born a slave in Winchester, Virginia, presented his credentials to Congress as Florida's sole representative. The election was disputed by his opponent, Silas L. Niblack. Walls agreed that infractions to voting procedure had occurred and that voters had been intimidated at the polls by Democrats. The House Committee on Elections unseated Walls and declared Niblack the winner on January 29, 1873. He held office for less than two months. Walls had already defeated him in the November 1872 election.

As a congressman, Walls supported public education, particularly a national educational fund to be financed with money from public land sales. He supported pensions and local improvements for his state. Walls ran for reelection in 1874 and won by only 371 votes. His opponent, Jesse J. Finley, appealed to the House Committee on Elections that votes in Columbia County had been tampered with and should not be counted. Although Walls received support from his colleagues concerning the legality of votes, the House rejected his position and seated Finley. Although Walls ran for the House seat in 1876, Horatio Bisbee defeated him by a wide margin. Walls turned his attention to state politics and was elected to the Florida Senate in November 1876. He retired from politics in 1879. In 1884, he tried again for the U.S. House of Representatives, but lost.

KU KLUX KLAN FORCES WHITE TEACHER OUT OF BLACK SCHOOL

On **MARCH 18**, the Ku Klux Klan forced Sarah A. Allen, a white woman, to leave the school where she taught Black children in Cotton Gin Port, Mississippi.

CONGRESS PASSES THIRD ENFORCEMENT ACT

On **APRIL 20**, Congress passed a third Enforcement Act, defining Klan conspiracy as rebellion against the United States and giving broad powers to the president to suspend the writ of habeas corpus and declare martial law in rebellious areas.

KU KLUX KLAN TRIALS HELD IN THE SOUTH

The federal courts were deluged with KKK trials. In Oxford, Mississippi, many whites from all professions (doctors, lawyers, ministers, politicians, and college professors) were members of the Klan. The federal government's major anti-Klan campaign had been somewhat successful in rounding up, jailing, and convicting Klansmen for murder, violence, and interfering with the rights of Black and Republican voters. A total of 930 indictments had been handed down in Mississippi, resulting in the trial and conviction of 243 Klansmen. As many as 1,180 Klan members had been indicted in South Carolina, and 1,849 in North Carolina. Because of continued Klan disturbances in South Carolina, President Ulysses S. Grant, on **OCTOBER 17**, suspended the writ of habeas corpus and declared martial law in nine South Carolina counties. On November 26, KKK trials started in the Federal District Court in Columbia, South Carolina.

PINCHBACK BECOMES LIEUTENANT GOVERNOR OF LOUISIANA

On **NOVEMBER 22**, P. B. S. (Pinckney Benton Stewart) Pinchback (1837–1921) assumed the position of lieutenant governor of Louisiana when Oscar J. Dunn died. Pinchback had been serving as president pro tempore of the Louisiana senate, the next in succession to the lieutenant governor's position.

◈ Pinchback was born in Mississippi on May 10, 1837; his father (William Pinchback) was a white planter, his mother (Eliza Stewart) a free Black woman. P. B. S. Pinchback, the eighth of ten children, was born free because William had taken Eliza to Philadelphia and emancipated her before she gave birth to Pinckney.

Pinckney and an older brother, Napoleon, were sent away to Cincinnati for education. When their father died in 1848, the family moved to Cincinnati to prevent any attempts by white relatives to reenslave them. Pinckney worked as a cabin boy and steward on boats in the South and the Midwest. In May 1862, he arrived in New Orleans behind Union lines and quickly volunteered for service. As part of his official duty, he organized several companies of Black volunteers to fight in the Civil War. After rising to the rank of captain, he resigned the position because of racist treatment of Black officers and troops.

After the war ended, Pinchback organized a Republican club, joined the state central committee,

and was known as one of the most influential Republicans in Louisiana. In 1868, he was elected to the Louisiana senate, where he fought against racial discrimination in public accommodations. Pinchback was a delegate to the Republican convention in 1868, and the next year, Pinchback founded the *New Orleans Louisianian* newspaper.

In 1871, Pinchback was elected president pro tempore of the state senate. When Oscar J. Dunn died, Pinchback became the lieutenant governor. During the impeachment proceedings of Governor Henry C. Warmoth, Pinchback assumed the leadership role in the state (see 1872).

1872 BLACK HARVARD GRADUATE APPOINTED PROFESSOR IN SOUTH CAROLINA

Richard T. Greener, the first Black graduate of Harvard University, was appointed to the faculty of the University of South Carolina as professor of metaphysics. Upon his appointment, white faculty and students left in protest. Greener later served as the dean of Howard University Law School from 1879 to 1882. Greener was outspoken on a number of major issues affecting Blacks. He defended the Black Exodus to western destinations such as Kansas, Nebraska, and Oklahoma against Black leaders such as Frederick Douglass, who believed that migration from the South permitted the federal government to dismiss its responsibility to protect the rights of southern Blacks.

In 1898, Greener was appointed U.S. consul at Bombay and Vladivostok. He remained a staunch advocate of migration to western lands and encouraged Blacks to leave the South.

BLACK LABOR CONDITIONS IN THE SOUTH DESCRIBED

A letter from A. W. Shadd, a graduate of Howard University Law School and brother of A. D. Shadd, Speaker of the House in the Mississippi legislature in 1871, described the condition of Black labor in the South during this time:

> The Southern gentleman rents the land to his former slave at about the whole value of the land each year, and thus practically sells his land each year, recovering it at the end. This high-toned gentleman, this soul of honor, does more — he "furnishes" the people on his plantation, buys provisions, and sells to the poor colored man at an advance of 50 to 100%, agreeing to wait for his pay until the crop is picked out and ready for market. A little judicious exaggeration of the account usually attends these operations, and at

the end of the year, the colored man frequently finds that he has nothing due him for his year's labor.

BLACK OFFICIALS ELECTED IN SOUTH CAROLINA

Republicans (four Blacks and four whites) won a slate of state offices. Blacks were elected as lieutenant governor — Richard H. Gleaves; secretary of state — Henry E. Hayne; treasurer — Francis L. Cardozo; and adjutant general — Henry W. Purvis. In addition, Blacks won 97 of the 157 seats in the South Carolina General Assembly and four of the five national congressional districts.

BLACKS ELECTED TO OFFICE IN LOUISIANA

Blacks were elected to several major offices in the state of Louisiana. Among these were C. C. Antoine, lieutenant governor; P. G. Deslonde, secretary of state; W. B. Brown, superintendent of public education; and P. B. S. Pinchback, congressman at large. Antoine Dubuclet, state treasurer, was a carryover from the 1870 elections; he won again in 1874, however.

CAIN ELECTED U.S. REPRESENTATIVE

Richard Harvey Cain (1825–1887) was elected to an at-large seat in the U.S. House of Representatives. In the House, Cain supported civil rights for freed slaves, particularly Charles Sumner's Civil Rights Bill of 1870. Cain's seat was eliminated in 1874, but he remained active in the Republican Party, and was reelected to Congress in 1876. Although his opponent charged election irregularities, the House voted in Cain's favor, and he was seated in the Forty-fifth Congress. Here, Cain supported compulsory education, an educational fund apportioned by population, and the emigration of Blacks to Liberia.

◈ Born to free parents in Greenbrier County, Virginia, on April 12, 1825, Cain moved to Gallipolis, Ohio, six years later. In 1844 he entered the ministry, but because of segregation in the Methodist Episcopal Church, he switched to the African Methodist Episcopal Church. In 1865, the AME Church sent Cain to South Carolina as pastor of Charleston's Emmanuel Church, where he successfully increased the church's membership. He also established other churches throughout the state.

As a political and economic leader, Cain served as a delegate to the South Carolina constitutional convention of 1868 and as a state senator from 1868 to 1870. He was a strong advocate of Black business development and owner-operated farms among freed Blacks. As editor and publisher of the *South Carolina Leader*, he frequently encouraged freedmen to purchase tracts of land for farming.

After Cain failed to gain reelection in 1880, he was elected bishop of the African Methodist Episcopal Church, overseeing the Texas-Louisiana area. He later was instrumental in establishing Paul Quinn College in Waco, Texas; he served as its president until July 1884. Cain later served as bishop of the New Jersey AME Conference (which included New England, New Jersey, New York, and Philadelphia).

HILL SAILS FOR LIBERIA

The Reverend Elias Hill of York County, South Carolina, left with 165 followers for Liberia, Africa. A local paper indicated that the group comprised the "most industrious negroes in that section of the country, many of whom, since their emancipation, have shown themselves to be thrifty and energetic, and not a few of them had accumulated money."

RAY IS FIRST BLACK WOMAN LAW GRADUATE

Charlotte E. Ray, the first Black woman lawyer in the United States, graduated from Howard University Law School. Although she was an excellent law student, she found it difficult to overcome the gender barriers to setting up a legal practice. Ray eventually took a teaching job in the Brooklyn schools.

KU KLUX KLANSMEN ARRESTED

In **MARCH**, as many as five hundred Klansmen in South Carolina were arrested as part of the anti-Klan campaign, but only fifty-five were convicted in federal court of offenses against Blacks.

CONGRESS PASSES AMNESTY ACT

On **MAY 22**, the Amnesty Act allowed all but a few hundred former Confederate leaders to hold elective office. Their participation had previously been precluded by the Fourteenth Amendment.

FREEDMEN'S BUREAU CLOSES

On **JUNE 10**, the Freedmen's Bureau closed. Liberal Republicans believed it was time for Blacks to stand on their own. The action reflected a broad feeling of weariness in the nation with the effort to enforce better treatment of Blacks in the South — a situation that promised no change.

During its period of operation, the bureau appropriated land and leased it to freed Blacks at low rent. It founded schools, provided education and health care, and even issued clothing and rations when necessary.

BLACK ADMITTED TO U.S. NAVAL ACADEMY

On **SEPTEMBER 21**, John Henry Conyers of South Carolina became the first Black to enter the U.S. Naval Academy in Annapolis; he later resigned. Although little was written about this appointment, documents show that it was rejected outright by midshipmen, faculty, and the general public. The press questioned not only whether a Black man could command a crew but also whether he could "maintain the discipline and enforce the respect incident thereto from the crew." Although Conyers dealt with many racial abuses, he remained undaunted until found deficient in two courses, math and French, and was asked to resign in 1873.

Other Blacks followed Conyers to the academy: Alonzo McClennan of South Carolina was appointed in September 1873 but resigned after six months; Henry E. Baker, Jr., entered in September 1874 but was dismissed for disciplinary reasons after only two months. It was not until 1936 that another Black entered the academy.

◇ In June 1936, James Johnson from Illinois entered the academy, attended classes for eight months, and resigned because of poor health; George Trivers entered in 1937 but resigned within a month. At this time, Black leaders and their respective organizations were angered by the academy's racism and discrimination. In the Johnson case, they alleged that fellow midshipmen discriminated against him and that white faculty discriminated in giving him low grades. Blacks were not appointed to the academy again until 1945, when Wesley A. Brown entered (see 1949).

RAPIER ELECTED TO CONGRESS

In **NOVEMBER**, James Thomas Rapier (1837–1883) was elected U.S. representative from Alabama after fighting a hard campaign to defeat Democrat William C. Oates. He became the second Black representative from this state.

◇ Rapier, born in Florence, Alabama, was educated in a Black school in Nashville. In 1856, he attended school at Buxton, Ontario, an experimental Black community. Rapier became a teacher in Buxton in 1863, but a year later he returned to Nashville and began to farm two hundred acres of rented land in Maury County, Tennessee.

Rapier yearned for the political life, and in August 1865, he gave the keynote address at the Tennessee Negro Suffrage Convention in Nashville. He became disappointed with the speed of change in Tennessee and decided to return to Alabama, where he rented land and became a successful cotton planter. He used his success to offer sharecroppers low-interest loans, established a newspaper in Montgomery, and began organizing Blacks into political blocs. When the first Alabama Republican State Convention was held, he was platform committee chairperson, a position that he used to oppose total disfranchisement of white former Confederates.

Rapier was elected a delegate to the Alabama constitutional convention and worked for the national Republican ticket. As his visibility as a rising politician increased, he was accused of conspiring to burn the Tuscumbia Female Academy. This false charge forced Rapier to go into hiding in Montgomery for at least a year. When he was cleared of these charges, he attended the founding convention of the National Negro Labor Union.

In 1870, Rapier ran for secretary of state, but lost. He was given an appointment as internal revenue assessor while helping to organize the Alabama Negro Labor Union.

As a congressman, Rapier was successful in securing passage of the Montgomery Port Bill. He sponsored legislation to fight illiteracy among Blacks, supported land grant colleges, and was a strong supporter of the Civil Rights Act.

When Rapier decided to seek reelection in 1874, he found the political environment drastically changed. Voters were intimidated, bribed, and sometimes murdered. Federal authorities could provide only minimal protection. The campaign and election were especially marred as his opponent, Jeremiah Williams, an attorney and former Confederate army major, used violence and vote tampering to defeat Rapier. After the loss, Rapier moved to Lowndes County and ran for a house seat in the state legislature, representing the Fourth District — a predominantly Black district. Rapier and Jeremiah Haralson split the Black vote, and Democrat Charles Shelley, a white, won the seat. In 1878, Rapier was appointed collector of internal revenue for the Second District; but his consuming interest at this time was his support of Black emigration to the West. In May 1879, he chaired the migration committee of the Southern States Negro Convention and encouraged Blacks to join the "Exodusters." Rapier used his own funds to promote the migration of Blacks to the West. Between 1882 and 1883, white Democrats began an assault on Rapier to remove him from the collector's position, and he was forced to resign.

BLACKS PARTICIPATE IN SOUTH CAROLINA GENERAL ASSEMBLY

On **NOVEMBER 26**, the South Carolina General Assembly convened in Columbia. Among the Blacks holding important positions were Stephen A. Swails, elected president pro tempore of the senate, and Samuel J. Lee, Speaker of the House. The assembly appointed four Blacks to the seven-person governing board of the University of South Carolina: Samuel J. Lee, J. A. Bowley, Stephen A. Swails, and W. R. Jarvay.

PINCHBACK BECOMES GOVERNOR OF LOUISIANA

On **DECEMBER 9**, P. B. S. Pinchback was sworn in as governor of Louisiana after Henry C. Warmoth was impeached "for high crimes and misdemeanors." Pinchback used his temporary status as governor to influence and strengthen the Republican Party throughout the state and to serve *all* citizens of Louisiana.

On January 13, 1873, he relinquished the office. Later in this year, Pinchback was elected congressman at large on the Republican ticket. His seat was contested, and he ultimately lost to the Democratic candidate. Pinchback was the only Black to serve as governor of a state until 1990, when L. Douglas Wilder was elected governor of Virginia.

1873 ALLEN ELECTED JUDGE

Macon B. Allen was elected judge of the Inferior Court of Charleston, South Carolina. Allen, a Black lawyer and partner with William J. Whipper and Robert Brown Elliott, was the second Black to hold a major judicial position in the country and the first Black with a major judicial position in a city.

BLACK MEMBERS IN THE FORTY-THIRD CONGRESS

A total of seven Black congressmen were elected to the Forty-third U.S. Congress (1873–1875): Richard Harvey Cain, of South Carolina; Robert Brown Elliott, of South Carolina; Joseph H. Rainey, of South Carolina; Alonzo J. Ransier, of South Carolina; James Thomas Rapier, of Alabama; Josiah T. Walls, of Florida; and John R. Lynch, of Mississippi.

STRUGGLE FOR CONTROL OF TEXAS STATE GOVERNMENT

In **JANUARY**, after an election marred by fraud and violence, Democrats took over the Texas legislature as the majority party. Governor Edmund J. Davis refused to recognize the validity of the election and called upon the state's predominantly Black militia to secure the state capitol in Austin. Open conflict erupted; Democrats controlled the upper floors of the building, and the governor and Black militia controlled the lower floors. Governor Davis summoned federal troops, but President Grant refused to intervene.

LYNCH ENTERS CONGRESS

On **APRIL 4**, John R. Lynch (1847–1939) took his seat in the U.S. Congress, representing the Sixth District of Mississippi.

◈ Lynch was born a slave on Tacony Plantation in Concordia Parish, Louisiana. His father, the manager of the plantation, died less than two years later, but not before he had made arrangements to purchase freedom for his wife and three sons. However, his untimely death allowed the slaveholder to ignore the agreement and to sell Lynch's family to another planter in Natchez, Mississippi.

Lynch, freed with the emancipation of 1863, became a photographer and real-estate manager in Natchez. In 1869, he was elected justice of the peace and several months later a state representative. In 1872, he was chosen to be Speaker of the House, a powerful position that he used to redraw boundaries of six districts to ensure Republican victories.

In Congress, Lynch worked diligently to ensure the passage of the Civil Rights Act of 1875 and to introduce legislation to benefit local interests. In 1875, Lynch sought reelection, but he faced the "Mississippi Plan," whereby Democrats tried to eliminate the Black vote via economic strangulation and physical violence. The Democrats implemented a plan to defeat Lynch, but Lynch narrowly won. He then started a campaign directed against white racist groups. In Congress, he attacked the Democrats and their violence, while defending the Republicans against corruption. He was defeated in the 1876 election, and the House Committee on Elections refused to hear his complaint about the validity of the election results.

In 1880, Lynch was unsuccessful in unseating the Democratic incumbent, but when he challenged the election, the Committee on Elections heard his appeal and awarded Lynch the seat as a member of the Forty-seventh Congress on April 29, 1882. During his term, which lasted only until August 1882, Lynch sponsored legislation to benefit his constituents, particularly funds for the Protestant Orphan Asylum and a National Board of Health. He lost his reelection bid to Henry S. Van Eaton, a Confederate veteran, by nine hundred votes. In 1884 and again in 1886, Lynch lost his bid to regain his seat in the House. Between 1881 and 1892, Lynch became chairman of the Republican State Executive Committee and a member of the Republican National Committee. In 1884, Lynch was selected as temporary chair of the Republican National Committee and delivered the keynote address before the Republican National Convention in Chicago — the first Black person to do so. He later served as auditor of the treasury for the Navy Department, practiced law, and was appointed paymaster for the army by President William McKinley. He retired from the regular army in 1911 and moved to Chicago, where he practiced law and wrote avidly. Many of his works were published. During the late 1930s, he wrote his autobiography, *Reminiscences of an Active Life*, a book that was not published until 1970.

BLACKS KILLED IN COLFAX MASSACRE

On **APRIL 14**, Easter Sunday, the Colfax Massacre occurred in Grant Parish, Louisiana. Armed whites killed more than sixty Black men, women, and children in the small Black village.

U.S. SUPREME COURT ERODES FOURTEENTH AMENDMENT

On **APRIL 14**, the U.S. Supreme Court, in a 5-4 decision, started to chip away at the power of the Fourteenth Amendment. In a number of decisions in the *Slaughterhouse* cases, the Court ruled that the Fourteenth Amendment protected federal civil rights, not the "civil rights heretofore belonging exclusively to the states."

◆ The *Slaughterhouse* cases arose from actions by the state of Louisiana in 1869. To protect citizens' health, the state had chartered a meat-packing company, giving it a monopoly. A group of white butchers sued, claiming that the action violated the Fourteenth Amendment by depriving them of life, liberty, or property, without due process.

HAYNE ENTERS UNIVERSITY OF SOUTH CAROLINA

In **OCTOBER**, Henry E. Hayne, secretary of state of South Carolina, applied for admission as a student at the University of South Carolina. Hayne was accepted, and as a result, he opened the door for many other Black students. Hayne's enrollment in the university precipitated the resignation of three white professors — M. LaBorde, A. N. Talley, and R. W. Bibbes. Their resignations were accepted by the predominantly Black board of trustees.

BLACKS ELECTED TO OFFICE IN MISSISSIPPI

On **NOVEMBER 16**, several Blacks were elected to offices at the state level: secretary of state, superintendent of education, commissioner of immigration, commissioner of agriculture, and lieutenant governor. Alexander K. Davis was lieutenant governor; James Hill, secretary of state; and T. W. Cardozo, superintendent of education. In addition, Blacks were elected to 55 of the 115 seats in the house and 9 of 37 seats in the senate. Blacks served as employees in many other state offices as well.

At the local level, Blacks held important offices in areas where they composed a majority of the local population. In Natchez, for example, the sheriff, county treasurer and assessor, and a majority of the magistrates and county affairs officers were Blacks. The board of aldermen had three Black members. The first Black U.S. senator and the first and only Black congressman from Mississippi were residents of this center of Black power. Robert H. Wood, a Black man, was mayor of Natchez.

The same pattern existed elsewhere. In Marshall, Yazoo, and Warren Counties, three of the five supervisors were Black. In Madison and Amite, four of the five were Black. In Issaquena, all five supervisors were Black. Issaquena's members of the legislature and its sheriff, clerks, justices of the peace, and constables were all Black. In Issaquena County, only two public officials were white.

GIBBS ELECTED JUDGE IN ARKANSAS

In **DECEMBER**, Mifflin W. Gibbs, who had just graduated with a law degree from Oberlin College in Ohio, was elected city judge in Little Rock, Arkansas. He was the first Black city judge in U.S. history. Gibbs's background as a businessman, founder of the *Mirror of the Times* (California's first Black newspaper), and a civil rights activist made him one of the most qualified judges in the country.

1874 BLACK ELECTED SPEAKER IN MISSISSIPPI LEGISLATURE

I. D. Shadd was elected Speaker of the House of the Mississippi legislature.

BLACKS REPRESENTED IN ALABAMA STATE LEGISLATURE

At this time, thirty-five Blacks were members of the Alabama legislature (26 percent of the total members).

BOUCHET ACHIEVES PHI BETA KAPPA AT YALE

Edward A. Bouchet was the first Black inducted into Phi Beta Kappa, a national honor society. He received this honor at Yale University.

HARALSON ENTERS U.S. CONGRESS

Jeremiah Haralson (1846–1916?) was elected to the U.S. Congress as a Republican representative from Alabama. He won the election by a wide margin, but his opponent contested his victory, charging vote fraud and other illegal tactics. Although the House Committee on Elections found the charges valid, they were not considered significant enough to discount the margin of Haralson's victory. Congress seated Haralson.

◈ Haralson was born a slave on a plantation near Columbus, Georgia. When he was thirteen years old, John Haralson, his slaveholder, took him to Alabama. Two years after securing his freedom in 1867, Haralson ran for Congress but was defeated. Although Haralson was a farmer, he had acquired skill as an orator and debater and a passion for politics. In 1870, he was elected to the Alabama legislature and was later selected as the presiding officer of the First Congressional District convention, which successfully nominated and elected Benjamin S. Turner to the U.S. Congress.

In the Forty-fourth Congress, Haralson supported education and health-related legislation and initiated legislation to use monies from public land sales for education. He deviated from the expectations of his fellow Black members and other Republicans when he supported amnesty for former Confederate soldiers. Haralson also refused to support the use of federal troops to suppress violence and oversee the rights of persons, particularly Blacks, to vote.

In the 1876 election, Haralson was opposed by former U.S. representative James Thomas Rapier (Republican) and Charles M. Shelley (Democrat). In a newly gerrymandered district that was predominantly Black, Haralson and Rapier split the Black majority, and Shelley won the election. Although Haralson contested the election, Shelley was seated. Haralson worked at several low-level jobs until 1878, when he decided to run against Shelley; he lost again. Haralson later moved to Arkansas, Oklahoma, and Colorado in search of decent employment. There are no records confirming the date or place of his death.

HYMAN ELECTED TO CONGRESS

John A. Hyman (1840–1891) became the first Black U.S. representative from North Carolina.

◈ Although Hyman was born a slave in Warrenton, North Carolina, he was taught to read and write by a Warrenton jeweler. But because of laws prohibiting the teaching of reading and writing to slaves, the jeweler, his wife, and Hyman were forced to flee the community. Hyman was subsequently sold to an Alabama slaveholder. As a slave, Hyman was so preoccupied with securing an education that his owners were prompted to sell him as many as eight times to avoid harm or jail. In 1865, after emancipation, Hyman returned to Warrenton and became active in politics, particularly in securing the voting rights of Blacks.

At age twenty-six, Hyman attended the Freedmen's Convention of North Carolina, and two years later he became a delegate to the 1867 Republican State Convention, where he secured a position on the state executive committee. In January 1868, he was one of 15 Black delegates to the 133-member North Carolina Constitutional Convention. He was elected to the North Carolina senate the same year and became a strong voice supporting the voting rights of Blacks.

In 1872, Hyman ran as a Republican to represent the predominantly Black Second Congressional District for the U.S. House, but lost to Charles Thomas. He was the Republican nominee again in 1874, but this time he defeated his Democratic opponent, George W. Blount. The election was contested, and Hyman spent almost the entire term preparing his defense against Blount's allegations. On August 1, 1876, the House declared Hyman the winner.

Hyman became a member of the Committee on Manufacturers, where he sponsored legislation to compensate constituents for losses during the Civil War, financial relief for the resettled Cherokee people, and the erection of a lighthouse on Pamlico Sound in his district. None of his proposals received adequate attention.

Hyman tried to secure the renomination for the 1876 election, but it went to former governor Curtis Brogden. Hyman left politics and became a farmer and retail businessman (owner of a grocery and liquor store). Hyman eventually moved to Maryland, where he worked as a mail clerk's assistant. In 1889, he moved to Washington, D.C., to take a job in the Department of Agriculture. Hyman died in Washington, D.C.

NASH ELECTED TO CONGRESS

Charles E. Nash (1844–1913) was elected to the U.S House of Representatives from the Sixth Congressional District of Louisiana.

◆ Nash, born in Opelousas, Louisiana, attended school in the same area and became a bricklayer in New Orleans. In 1863, he joined Company A of the Eighty-second Regiment of the United States Volunteers. Sergeant Major Nash (after several promotions) was wounded and lost much of his right leg in April 1865, in a battle at Fort Blakely, Alabama. Republicans capitalized on Nash's military background by pushing him into the political arena. Without much political background, Nash was elected to the House without a challenger. He became one of the few Blacks to be present when his term convened; others had to wait until the House Committee on Elections made decisions in their favor.

Nash spoke before the House regarding the deteriorating political conditions in the South, the need to protect freed slaves, and the need for public education. In 1876, Nash ran for the House seat again but was defeated by about forty-three hundred votes. He decided to leave political life altogether and returned to the bricklayer's trade. He did, however, serve as a postmaster in St. Landry Parish in 1882.

SMALLS ELECTED TO CONGRESS
Robert Smalls (1839–1915) was elected to the U.S. Congress. Smalls made significant contributions to his country through his career as a soldier and politician.
◆ Born a slave in Beaufort, South Carolina, in 1851, Smalls moved to Charleston. Having worked on the waterfront as a stevedore, foreman, sailmaker, rigger, and sailor, he eventually became a boat pilot. Because of his expertise, South Carolina called him into service when the Civil War erupted.

In 1864, Smalls was rewarded for his heroism by being selected one of several free Blacks sent to the Republican convention. Between 1868 and 1874, Smalls was elected to a number of important state positions — delegate to the state constitutional convention, state representative, and state senator.

In Congress, Smalls opposed racial discrimination in the armed forces and was against moving federal troops from the South. In 1876, he won reelection, but his opponent, George Tillman, charged irregularities in an attempt to have the results invalidated. In the Forty-fourth Congress, Smalls called for an "honest ballot" by condemning the efforts of Democrats and the Klan to deprive Blacks of their political rights. Smalls became a target of Democrats around the country, particularly those in South Carolina. In 1877, they gained control of state political offices and planned to drive Smalls out of office by convicting him on false charges of having received a five-thousand-dollar bribe while in the state senate. He was jailed but then pardoned by the Democratic governor, William D. Simpson.

Democrats gerrymandered and abolished voting precincts with Republican majorities and stationed armed whites at Smalls's election meeting. In the 1878 and 1880 elections, Smalls lost both times. He challenged the latter election before the House Committee on Elections, which ruled in his favor. He was seated in the Forty-seventh Congress on July 19, 1882. Later that year, Smalls was defeated for the Republican nomination by Edmund Mackey, but after Mackey died in 1884, Smalls filled the vacancy. Smalls won the election in 1886. In the Forty-ninth Congress, he supported equal accommodations for all passengers on interstate railroads, spoke in favor of integrating eating establishments in the District of Columbia, and asked the House to override President Grover Cleveland and vote for a fifty-dollar monthly pension for the widow of General David Hunter, who in 1862 had issued an order freeing slaves in Florida, Georgia, and South Carolina.

In 1886, the congressional contingent of South Carolina successfully unseated Smalls. He lost his challenge before the House Committee on Elections. Although he remained a political force in the Black community, Smalls's political base had dwindled because the Democrats controlled both the state and the congressional representatives. In 1889, President Benjamin Harrison appointed Smalls collector of the port of Beaufort, but he was forced to give up the job in June 1913.

WHITE DEMOCRATS BATTLE BLACK MILITIA FOR CONTROL OF ARKANSAS GOVERNMENT
The predominantly Black militia of Arkansas was called upon to secure the state capitol after white Democrats sought to take it by force. The battle spread to the streets of Little Rock, then to a naval engagement on the Arkansas River. According to most historians, the battle resulted in a standoff, but the long-term victory was won by the white Democrats, who effectively continued to employ fraud, internal subversion, and intimidation to gain control of state government. President Grant refused to intervene.

RECONSTRUCTION ENDS IN TEXAS
On **JANUARY 17**, Democrats carrying firearms seized the Texas capitol to wrest control of the state government, thereby terminating Reconstruction in Texas.

BRUCE ELECTED TO CONGRESS

In **FEBRUARY**, Blanche K. Bruce (1841–1898), born a slave in Farmville, Virginia, was elected U.S. senator by the Mississippi legislature. He became the first African American to serve a full six-year term (1875–1881) in the U.S. Senate.

◈ As a slave, Bruce worked as a field hand and printer's apprentice. The slaveholder's son taught him to read and write. At the beginning of the Civil War, Bruce escaped to freedom. Believing that serving in the Civil War would earn his freedom, he tried to enlist, but the Union army refused to accept him. Instead, Bruce taught, attended college, and worked on a steamboat. After settling in Hannibal, Missouri, Bruce established the state's first school for Blacks in 1864. Between 1866 and 1868, he attended Oberlin College. He subsequently moved back to Mississippi, where he became a wealthy landowner and planter involved in local politics.

Bruce's political career started at a relatively young age. Before age thirty, Bruce had been appointed registrar of voters in Tallahatchie County, tax assessor of Bolivar County, and sheriff and tax collector of Bolivar. In 1870, his political talents were recognized by powerful whites in Mississippi's Reconstructionist government. At age thirty-four, Bruce was elected by the Mississippi legislature to represent the state as a senator in the U.S. Congress, thus becoming the second Black senator.

In the Forty-fifth Congress, Bruce fought hard to seat Louisiana Black leader P. B. S. Pinchback, made numerous appeals to his colleagues to curb violence and intimidation in Mississippi elections, encouraged the desegregation of U.S. armed forces, and spoke vigorously for more land grant assistance to Black emigrants. In 1879, Bruce presided over a Senate session that debated the Chinese Exclusion Bill, and he later chaired the Select Committee to Investigate the Freedmen's Savings and Trust Company.

Bruce's tenure in the U.S. Senate was short. In 1880, white Democrats controlled the political environment, and they chose James George to succeed Bruce. Bruce later accepted an appointment by President James A. Garfield to be registrar of the U.S. Treasury, where he served until 1885. He then became a lecturer and a writer for several magazines. In 1889, President Benjamin Harrison appointed Bruce recorder of deeds for the District of Columbia. He later was reappointed registrar of the U.S. Treasury by President William McKinley, a position he retained until his death.

FREEDMEN'S BANK FAILS

In **MARCH**, Frederick Douglass was appointed president of the failing Freedmen's Savings and Trust Company (also known as Freedmen's Bank). On June 28, the bank failed, and thousands of Blacks lost their savings. Blacks had deposited about three million dollars in the bank, which had headquarters in Washington, D.C., and branches in thirty-three cities throughout the country. At the time of its closing, the bank had only thirty-one thousand dollars on hand to cover sixty-one thousand depositors. The bank's directors had not been prudent in their investments, speculating in real estate in Washington, D.C., and making unsecured loans to a number of companies. When Douglass realized the bank's situation, he attempted to get additional funds, even using some of his own money. Many urged that freedmen be repaid with federal funds, even though the bank was a private corporation, since advertisements for the bank showing Lincoln had made many Blacks believe that the federal government stood behind the bank's activities. Eventually, about one-half of the depositors received compensation averaging $18.51 per person; the rest received nothing. The changing political structure (from Republican to Democrat) of the Congress and the attitudes of white citizens forced the bank's closure.

"WHITE LEAGUE" FOUNDED

On **APRIL 27**, the "White League," a paramilitary white supremacist, racist organization, was founded at Opelousas, Louisiana.

BLACK PRIEST BECOMES PRESIDENT OF GEORGETOWN UNIVERSITY

On **JULY 31**, Father Patrick Francis Healy, S.J., Ph.D., a Black priest, was installed as president of Georgetown University, the oldest Catholic college in the United States. He thus became the first Black president of a predominantly white university, over which he presided until 1883.

BLACKS LYNCHED IN TENNESSEE

On **AUGUST 26**, sixteen Blacks were lynched in the state of Tennessee. They were first taken from a jail and tortured.

BLACKS MASSACRED IN LOUISIANA

On **AUGUST 30**, in Coushatta, Louisiana, several Blacks and Republican officeholders were slain by white Democrats. It is estimated that more than sixty Blacks and whites were killed in the Coushatta Massacre. The governor declared martial law to prevent further violence.

COLONIZATION COUNCIL FORMED IN LOUISIANA

In **SEPTEMBER**, out of desperation and fear for their lives, Blacks in Louisiana formed a new organization called the Colonization Council. An epidemic of violence had spread throughout the South. In a petition signed by one thousand Blacks, Louisiana Blacks asked President Ulysses S. Grant to remove them to a territory "where they could live by themselves" because it was "utterly impossible to live with the whites of Louisiana." They also expressed a willingness to go to Liberia because of their fear of rising violence and the inability of the federal government to halt it. Blacks wanted to prevent a recurrence of the massacre that took place at Coushatta.

Grant ordered the Seventh Cavalry to situate itself in the northern part of Louisiana. He dispatched General Philip Sheridan on an inspection tour, instructing him to take command wherever he saw fit.

In January 1875, Sheridan took control of the Louisiana legislature when armed white conservatives attempted to take it over. Sheridan told the secretary of war that the situation in the South was so bad that Congress should declare the white terrorists in Louisiana, Arkansas, and Mississippi "banditti" who could be arrested, tried, and punished by the military authorities.

LOUISIANA STATEHOUSE SEIZED

On **SEPTEMBER 14**, an angry mob of white Democrats seized the Louisiana statehouse in an attempted coup d'état. As many as twenty-seven persons (sixteen whites and eleven Blacks) were killed in close combat among Democrats, Republicans, and Blacks. President Grant ordered the Democratic mob to disperse. The rebellion finally collapsed, but only after Democrats made their point: intimidation and even murder would continue to be used to suppress the political activities of Black and Republican voters.

RIOT BREAKS OUT IN VICKSBURG

On **DECEMBER 7**, as Blacks attempted to prevent the forcible ejection of Sheriff Crosby, a Black man, in Vicksburg, Mississippi, seventy-five Blacks were killed by white Democrats and Klan members. KKK members had stirred up intense hatred for Blacks in public office throughout Mississippi. This riot appar-

ently stemmed from a struggle between white Democrats and Republican county officials over political control of Warren County. When it was time for paying and collecting taxes, the white Democrats refused, citing the indictment of officials for forgery and embezzlement. White Democrats met and voted to demand the resignation of the sheriff, chancery clerk, treasurer, and coroner. Anticipating trouble, all these officials left town, except Sheriff Crosby who had, in fact, already signed his resignation. In an effort to stir up trouble, KKK members circulated false information, including a poster claiming that Sheriff Crosby had called white and Black Republicans in the county to aid and support him.

White Democrats, including Klansmen, armed themselves for outright conflict because they expected Blacks to rise up and defend Sheriff Crosby. Many Blacks left their farms to come and support Crosby. Heavily armed white Democrats and Klan members began their march to meet unarmed Blacks. On Grove Street, they met and fired upon about 200 Blacks, who dispersed and retreated. The groups engaged again, and as many as 15 Blacks were killed, several wounded, and more than 20 captured. On Hills Ferry Road, whites fired on about 250 Blacks. The Blacks fired back but were routed; several were killed, and many were wounded and captured. On Baldwin's Ferry Road, a similar incident occurred. After questioning some of the captured and jailed Blacks, the *Vicksburg Herald* mentioned that Crosby had summoned Blacks and white Republicans to come to the city. Crosby, however, even after being jailed, continued to deny his involvement. In fact, the whole incident may have been incited by Klansmen, who had started similar riots and participated in the killing of Blacks throughout Mississippi, most recently in Meridian and Clinton. Evidence presented to the senate in the following year revealed the extent to which whites intimidated Blacks:

> We are intimidated by the whites. We want to hold meetings, but it is impossible to do so; if we does, they will say we are making an invasion on the city and come out [to] kill us. When we hold church meetings, they breakes that up; our lives are not safe in our houses. Now we ask you who shall we look to for protection.... We are in the hands of murderers. There will not be peace here until troops come to unarm them.
>
> (Letter from three hundred Black voters in Vicksburg)

1875 BLACK JOCKEY WINS FIRST KENTUCKY DERBY

Oliver Lewis became the first winner of the Kentucky Derby, riding the horse Aristides. Thirteen of the fourteen horses entered in the first Kentucky Derby were ridden by Black jockeys. Black jockeys dominated horseracing during the last part of the nineteenth century, in part because they had become experienced trainers and riders in Kentucky before the Civil War. Unfortunately, the accomplishments of these jockeys were not highly regarded. The first names of several Derby-winning jockeys were never recorded.

BLACKS ELECTED TO FORTY-FOURTH CONGRESS

When the Forty-fourth Congress convened, it included a total of eight Black members, including one U.S. senator: Senator Blanche K. Bruce, of Mississippi; and Jeremiah Haralson, of Alabama; Josiah T. Walls, of Florida; John R. Lynch, of Mississippi; John A. Hyman, of North Carolina; Charles E. Nash, of Louisiana; Joseph H. Rainey, of South Carolina; and Robert Smalls, of South Carolina.

JIM CROW LAWS ADOPTED IN TENNESSEE

Although the Thirteenth, Fourteenth, and Fifteenth Amendments to the U.S. Constitution gave Black Americans the same rights and privileges as other citizens, new state laws emerged to render them unequal in all respects. In this year, the Tennessee legislature passed the first Jim Crow legislation segregating public transportation. Tennessee also passed two other pieces of legislation: (1) a "contract labor law" that prohibited anyone from encouraging a laborer to break a work contract; and (2) a "vagrancy law" that made it a misdemeanor to "neglect to engage in an honest calling" or "to tramp or stroll" in rural areas without visible means of support. These laws were easily subject to the interpretation of whites, who often charged Blacks with vagrancy when additional labor was needed. Blacks paid off the fine for vagrancy by working without pay. In essence, these two pieces of legislation were designed to make the labor of Blacks subject to the control of whites.

JONES ELECTED COUNTY COMMISSIONER

John Jones (1816–1879), one of the wealthiest Blacks in America, was elected a commissioner in Cook County, Illinois. Jones was instrumental in a successful effort to repeal the Black Laws of Illinois and in fighting school segregation in Chicago. Later, he became the first Black elected to the Chicago Board of Education.

Jones made his fortune as a tailor, and his home had served as a station on the Underground Railroad.

WHIPPER ELECTED JUDGE

William J. Whipper, a lawyer and state legislator, was elected judge of the Circuit Court of Charleston by the South Carolina General Assembly.

◈ Whipper, born in Michigan, had served in a volunteer regiment in 1865 during the Civil War. After moving to the South and becoming a lawyer, he was elected to the state legislature in 1868 and 1870. Between 1882 and 1888, Whipper served as probate judge of Beaufort County. He refused to vacate his position after being defeated in the 1888 election and was subsequently jailed. As owner of the *Tribune*, a newspaper in Beaufort, and one of three administrators who managed the *New South*, another newspaper, Whipper was one of the most influential Blacks in the state.

FEDERAL TROOPS SENT TO RELIEVE RACIAL TENSIONS IN VICKSBURG

On **JANUARY 5**, continuing racial tensions and violence provoked President Grant to send federal troops to Vicksburg, Mississippi. Troops were only partially effective, as white Democrats and KKK members openly used intimidation tactics and other measures to prevent Blacks and Republicans from participating in political activities. On July 4, white Democrats killed several Blacks in the city. Federal troops were requested again in September in response to the Clinton and Yazoo City massacres, but the U.S. attorney general refused to send them.

CIVIL RIGHTS ACT PASSED

On **MARCH 1**, Congress passed a Civil Rights Act prohibiting discrimination in public accommodations (hotels, theaters, and public carriers) and President Grant signed it into law. Eight years later, it was ruled unconstitutional by the U.S. Supreme Court. The text of the act is presented below:

*An Act to Protect All Citizens
in Their Civil and Legal Rights*

Whereas it is essential to just government we recognize the equality of all men before the law, and hold that it is the duty of government in its dealings with the people to mete out equal and exact justice to all, of whatever nativity, race, color, or persuasion, religious or political; and it being the appropriate object of legislation to enact great fundamental principles into law: Therefore,

Be it enacted.

SECTION 1

That all persons within the jurisdiction of the United States shall be entitled to the full and equal enjoyment of the accommodations, advantages, facilities, and privileges of inns, public conveyances on land or water, theaters, and other places of public amusement; subject only to the conditions and limitations established by law, and applicable alike to citizens of every race and color, regardless of any previous condition of servitude.

SECTION 2

That any person who shall violate the foregoing section by denying to any citizen, except for reasons by law applicable to citizens of every race and color, and regardless of any previous condition of servitude, the full enjoyment of any of the accommodations, advantages, facilities, or privileges in said section enumerated, or by aiding or inciting such denial, shall, for every such offense, forfeit and pay the sum of five hundred dollars to the person aggrieved thereby. ... and shall also, for every such offense, be deemed guilty of a misdemeanor, and upon conviction thereof, shall be fined not less than five hundred nor more

than one thousand dollars, or shall be imprisoned not less than thirty days nor more than one year. ...

SECTION 3

That the district and circuit courts of the United States shall have, exclusively of the courts of the several States, cognizance of all crimes and offenses against, and violations of, the provisions of this act. ...

SECTION 4

That no citizen possessing all other qualifications which are or may be prescribed by law shall be disqualified for service as grand or petit juror in any court of the United States, or of any State, on account of race, color, or previous condition of servitude; and any officer or other person charged with any duty in the selection or summoning of jurors who shall exclude or fail to summon any citizen for the cause aforesaid shall, on conviction thereof, be deemed guilty of a misdemeanor, and be fined not more than five thousand dollars.

SECTION 5

That all cases arising under the provision of this act. ... shall be renewable by the Supreme Court of the U.S., without regard to the sum in controversy.

FIRST BLACK CATHOLIC BISHOP APPOINTED
On **JUNE 2**, Pope Pius IX named James A. Healy bishop of Portland, Maine (a primarily white

James Healy, the first Black Catholic bishop in the United States, presided for twenty-five years over a diocese in Maine and New Hampshire, where he founded sixty parishes and eighteen schools.

diocese), making him the first African American Catholic bishop in the United States.

◊ Healy was born in Macon, Georgia, and attended Quaker elementary schools in Flushing, New York, and in New Jersey. After graduating from the College of Holy Cross and attending Sulpician seminaries in Montreal, Canada, and in Paris, France, he was ordained as priest at the Cathedral of Notre Dame in Paris in 1854. After eleven years of service in Boston, Massachusetts, Healy became pastor of St. James Church in South Boston in 1866. In 1900, Bishop Healy served as assistant to the papal throne. He served only two months before he died. He was the brother of Father Patrick Francis Healy, who served as president of Georgetown University from 1874 through 1882.

BLACK JOURNALISTS HOLD CONVENTION

On **AUGUST 4**, the first convention of Black journalists convened in Cincinnati, Ohio. The Convention of Colored Newspapermen was attended by representatives from a number of influential African American newspapers. Among these were J. Sella Martin (*True Republican*), Henry Turner (*Christian Recorder*), L. H. Douglass (*Elevator*), Henry Scroggins (*American Citizen*), and Mifflin W. Gibbs (*Pacific Appeal*). Other newspapers represented included the *Baton Rouge Grand Era, Carroll Parish* (Louisiana); *Concordia* (Louisiana); *Cincinnati Colored Citizen, Galveston Spectator, Lexington American Citizen* (Kentucky); *Los Angeles Pacific Appeal, Memphis Planet, New Orleans Louisianian, New York Progressive American*, and *Tand Bonne Republican* (Louisiana).

RACE RIOT FLARES UP IN CLINTON, MISSISSIPPI

In **SEPTEMBER**, racial conflict erupted in Clinton, Mississippi. Between twenty and eighty Black leaders and Black Republicans were killed. Four days later, the Mississippi governor requested federal troops to protect the rights of Black voters; his request was refused. The Grant administration's refusal was based on the reasoning that federal troops were generally ineffective against these types of outbreaks.

RACE RIOT ERUPTS IN YAZOO CITY, MISSISSIPPI

On **SEPTEMBER 1**, serious racial conflict occurred in Yazoo City, Mississippi. White Democrats and KKK members attacked Blacks and Republicans and killed ten to twenty Blacks.

"MISSISSIPPI PLAN" SUCCEEDS

On **NOVEMBER 2**, the Democrats celebrated as they won many state and local governmental offices throughout the South. They effectively suppressed the Black vote in Mississippi through fraud and violence. The tactics of the Mississippi Democrats were known as the "Mississippi Plan." They involved staged riots, political assassinations, massacres, social and economic intimidation, and murder. The plan succeeded in defeating the Reconstruction governments in South Carolina and Louisiana, thus restoring white supremacy.

One of the most effective techniques involved the organization of "rifle clubs" among whites. Rifle clubs used methods analogous to those used in the American Revolution by colonists to "supplement and circumvent the regular government." One observer gave the following account:

> Armed usually with pistols they would invade Republican political meetings, heckle the speakers, and insist on their own speakers being heard. In the course of the meeting they would move about in the crowd, persuading Negroes and white Radicals that the healthy course would be to vote Democratic. If forced to disband they would reorganize as missionary societies or dancing clubs and carry on as before. ... By such means Negroes in large numbers, and a great many white Republicans as well, were induced, usually without actual violence, to "cross Jordan."

1876   BOUCHET RECEIVES DOCTORATE

Edward A. Bouchet, a physicist, was the second Black to be awarded the degree of doctor of philosophy by a major American university — Yale. Bouchet, the principal of a high school in Gallipolis, Ohio, died in 1918.

DORMAN FIGHTS ALONGSIDE CUSTER

Isaiah Dorman was a member of the company headed by General George Custer at Little Big Horn. Dorman was one of the 264 men who died with him there. The Sioux did not scalp and mutilate Dorman as they did the white soldiers.

Dorman had served as a courier for the War Department in the Dakota Territory. Probably because he knew the territory, the language, and may have been part Sioux, he was requested by Custer to serve as an interpreter.

GRANT SENDS FEDERAL TROOPS TO SOUTH CAROLINA

In response to widespread racial rioting and white terrorism, President Grant sent federal troops to restore calm and stabilize the state government.

MEHARRY MEDICAL COLLEGE FOUNDED

The first all-Black medical school in the United States, Meharry Medical College, was established in Memphis, Tennessee, by the Freedmen's Aid Society of the Methodist Episcopal Church as the medical department of Central Tennessee College. Samuel Meharry and his four brothers contributed a large portion of their combined fortune to establish the medical department of the college.

Samuel Meharry had been befriended by a slave family years earlier when, as a teenager, he was stranded when his wagon got stuck on a back road in Kentucky. He promised to repay the debt when he had the funds. When he became a prominent businessman in Indiana, Meharry, who held strong abolitionist views, proposed the establishment of a medical school at Central Tennessee College. When Central Tennessee College was reorganized and renamed Walden University in 1900, the medical department became Meharry Medical College of Walden University. Meharry opened a teaching hospital and a school of nursing in 1910. In 1915, however, Walden University failed. Meharry was granted a separate charter by the state of Tennessee and moved to its present location in Nashville in 1931. Today, it is the only fully accredited, privately endowed, predominantly Black medical college in the United States. Over the years, it has included a number of medical programs, and it has built relationships with both Black and white schools to ensure students the best education possible. Enrollment is about 680 students. Meharry and Howard University are the only two all-Black medical schools in the country today.

United States v. Reese REVIEWS RIGHT OF SUFFRAGE

The U.S. Supreme Court decided in *United States* v. *Reese* that "the 15th Amendment to the Constitution does not confer the right of suffrage" but only allows the government to provide a punishment for denying the vote to anyone based on "race, color, or previous condition of servitude."

PINCHBACK LOSES SEAT IN SENATE

On **MARCH 8**, the U.S. Congress refused to seat P. B. S. Pinchback of Louisiana in the senate. Pinchback defended his election and record:

Several Senators (I hope they are not Republicans) think me a very bad man. If this be true I fear my case is hopeless, for I am a bad man in the eyes of the democracy [and] weak-kneed Republicans. But of what does my badness consist [?] I am bad because I have dared on several important occasions to have an independent opinion. I am bad because I have dared at all times to advocate and insist on exact and equal justice to all Mankind. I am bad because having colored blood in my veins I have dared to aspire to the United States Senate, and I am bad because your representatives dared express the will of the people rather than obey the will of those who thought they were the people's Masters, when they elected me.

Friends I have been told that if I dared utter such Sentiments as these in public that I certainly would be Kept out of the Senate, all I have to say in answer to this, is that if I cannot enter the Senate except with bated breath and bended knees, I prefer not to enter at all.

Pinchback had been elected to the U.S. Senate by the state legislature in 1873. The senate vote (after three years of debate and controversy) was 32–29 against his seating. This was the second time Pinchback was denied a seat in Congress. In 1872, he had been elected to the U.S. House of Representatives as a congressman at large on the Republican ticket. His seat was contested, and his Democratic opponent was seated.

United States v. Cruikshank ERODES BLACKS' RIGHT TO MEET

On **MARCH 27**, in the case of *United States* v. *Cruikshank*, the U.S. Supreme Court denied punishment to persons who had broken up a meeting of Blacks discussing the forthcoming Louisiana election. The Court ruled that breaking up such a meeting was a crime only if the meeting had been concerned with a national election. The Court decided that the "right of suffrage is not a necessary attribute of national citizenship . . . [and that] the right to vote in the states comes from the states."

BLACKS MASSACRED IN SOUTH CAROLINA (TWO ACCOUNTS)

ACCOUNT #1 On **JULY 8**, it was alleged, two whites were impeded on their trip to the town of Hamburg by a Black militia company. Thomas Butler, one of the whites, complained about the militia's behavior to Prince Rivers, a Black man and trial justice. Justice Rivers questioned Captain "Doc" Adams, the company commander, who was arrested when he became "insolent." The Black militia rescued Adams from the courthouse. Justice Rivers requested his return and asked the militia to disarm. When they refused, he called on whites and the state militia to disarm the Black militia by force. The Black militia occupied a building and refused to surrender their captain and disarm. After shots were fired by both sides for several hours, one Black was reported killed, nine Blacks taken prisoner, one white killed, and another white wounded.

While rifle shots were being exchanged, the state militia had a piece of artillery delivered from Augusta. When it arrived, the soldiers fired all their rounds of ammunition. Several members of the Black militia were killed instantly; others retreated to nearby buildings; some escaped. Although Justice Rivers was legally in charge of the citizens' assault, many whites (KKK members) took a special satisfaction in routing the Black militia because of their "uppity" behavior. Members of the Black militia apparently refused to surrender because they knew what the outcome would be. For example, many of the captured Black militiamen were not tried in court — they were shot. Racial unrest continued, and President Grant eventually ordered federal troops to restore order after five to six Blacks had been killed (Based on information in the *New York Times*, July 9 and 10, 1876).

ACCOUNT #2 The massacre in Hamburg, South Carolina, is still considered one of the most cruel incidents in the Black experience. On July 3, Thomas Butler and Henry Getzen interfered with the drill of the local Black militia on a back street in Hamburg. The next day, the two white men brought charges in the local court of a Black justice of the peace against the Black militia for blocking the street. General M. C. Butler, an ex-Confederate soldier and now an agent of disorder, organized and assembled whites to descend upon the town to force a trial. As the trial before the Black justice of the peace took place, Butler called on the Black militiamen to apologize for their offense and to surrender their arms. When they refused, Butler set out for Augusta to secure a cannon and other munitions. The Black militiamen, surrounded and outnumbered, asked for protection if they gave up their arms. They even inquired whether Butler would let them ship the arms to the governor of the state. When this request was refused, the militia secured the armory for their own protection, for the whites had already begun firing. When the can-

non was turned on the militiamen, they tried to escape; several were killed, and twenty-seven were captured. Five were shot in cold blood after surrendering. James Cook, the Black chief of police of the town, was also shot in cold blood.

◇ Ex-Confederate soldier General M. C. Butler was elected to the U.S. Senate from South Carolina. He participated in many disturbances throughout the state but was most famous for his participation in the Hamburg Massacre. He was a strong advocate of "providing for the migration of persons of color from the Southern States."

LIBERIAN EXODUS JOINT STEAMSHIP COMPANY CREATED

On **JULY 26**, as many as four thousand Blacks joined in a celebration of Liberian independence, in Charleston, which was becoming a center of activity supporting emigration to Liberia. Several Blacks took advantage of this momentum and formed the Liberian Exodus Joint Steamship Company. Martin Delany, Henry Turner, and other prominent Blacks supported the enterprise.

RACE RIOT OCCURS IN CHARLESTON

On **SEPTEMBER 6**, a race riot erupted in Charleston, South Carolina.

TERRORISM AGAINST BLACKS IN SOUTH CAROLINA

On **SEPTEMBER 15** through **20**, white Democrats and Klan members attacked Blacks and Republicans in Ellenton, South Carolina. When calm was restored, a total of thirty-nine Blacks and two whites were dead.

RACE RIOT BREAKS OUT IN SOUTH CAROLINA

On **OCTOBER 16**, a race riot erupted in Cainhoy, South Carolina; five whites and one Black were killed.

1877 FORTY-FIFTH CONGRESS HAS THREE BLACK MEMBERS

The forty-fifth Congress convened with three Black members: Blanche K. Bruce, senator from Mississippi, and representatives Richard Cain and Robert Smalls of South Carolina.

DOUGLASS NAMED U.S. MARSHAL

Frederick Douglass became the first Black to receive a major government appointment in the United States when he was named U.S. marshal for the District of Columbia. He was confirmed by the senate after some difficulty.

For almost sixty years, Henry Flipper, the first African American graduate of West Point, worked to clear his name of the trumped-up charges that had led to his court-martial. Although his efforts were unsuccessful, his name was cleared posthumously.

FLIPPER IS FIRST BLACK TO GRADUATE FROM WEST POINT

Henry O. Flipper (1856–1940), born in Thomasville, Georgia, became the first Black to graduate from the U.S. Military Academy at West Point. He was only the second Black to enter West Point (James W. Smith had attended in 1870, but he did not graduate). Flipper was nominated by James Freeman from Georgia and received the rank of second lieutenant, thus becoming the first Black officer in the regular army. He was assigned to the all-Black Tenth Cavalry in the West, and at various times, he was stationed at Fort Sill, Fort Elliott, Fort Concho, Fort Davis, and Fort Quitman.

Ironically, if there had not been all-Black regiments at the time, Flipper would have had no place to serve in the highly segregated and racist army. After successfully serving four years with the Tenth Cavalry, Flipper came under intense attack from his white fellow officers and the press, and in 1881, he was court-martialed on charges of mishandling company funds. Although acquitted of these charges, he was discharged from the service for "conduct unbecoming an officer and a gentleman." The U.S. Army ignored Flipper's contention that he had been falsely accused by a prejudiced colonel. Angered by these events, Flipper moved to Mexico, where his civil engineering and mining engineering skills were in great demand. He also helped translate Spanish land grant documents for the Department of Justice in 1895 and helped to build a railroad in Alaska. For more than fifty years, Flipper worked as a leading mining engineer in the Southwest, becoming the first Black expert in this field. In 1921, Flipper was appointed an assistant to the secretary of the interior. He also worked as a historian, examining, among other things, the role of the explorer Estevanico in the Southwest. Flipper later went to Washington, D.C., as an assistant to Secretary of the Interior Albert Fall. Flipper was considered an expert on Mexican government policy.

Until his death, Flipper tried in vain to clear his name in the military. In 1976, the army, at the behest of the first Black graduate of the U.S. Naval Academy, Commander Wesley A. Brown, and the historian Ray O. MacColl, analyzed records and events surrounding his court-martial. They concluded that the charges were not warranted and that Flipper deserved an honorable discharge. Flipper was given a posthumous honorable discharge, and his body was reinterred with full military honors. In 1977, H. Minton Francis, deputy assistant secretary of defense (equal opportunity), successfully encouraged the U.S. Military Academy to dedicate a memorial bust and alcove in the cadet library in honor of Flipper on the one hundredth anniversary of his graduation.

FEDERAL TROOPS LEAVE SOUTH CAROLINA AND LOUISIANA

On **APRIL 10**, federal troops withdrew from Columbia, South Carolina, and Democrats took over the state government. Ten days later, federal troops were withdrawn from the public buildings in New Orleans, where they had protected the rights of Republicans and Blacks. Here, too, the Democrats took over state government. On February 26, just months prior to the withdrawal, representatives of President Rutherford B. Hayes and representatives of the South worked out an agreement concerning the withdrawal of the last federal troops from the South.

BLACK MILITIAS FORMED

After the federal government withdrew its soldiers from the South, leaving Black citizens unprotected from white racist societies, Blacks sought to arm themselves for self-protection. In an advertisement in the *Colored Citizen* on **NOVEMBER 9**, the Black community in Topeka, Kansas, followed the lead of several other Black communities in organizing a local militia for self-defense.

> Many of the prominent colored citizens of this city having signified their desire to organize and maintain a militia company we have determined to go ahead and perfect such an organization, and we invite all colored men to favor such a step to call at the *Colored Citizen* printing office and leave their names and when a sufficient number have done so we will call a meeting and consummate the organization.
>
> *W. L. Eagleson*

1878 BLAND ACHIEVES FAME AS SONGWRITER

Songwriter James A. Bland published the song "Carry Me Back to Ole Virginny," one of more than seven hundred songs he wrote. His other important pieces included "Oh, Dem Golden Slippers" (1879) and "In the Evening by the Moonlight" (1879). (It is believed that many state legislators who selected the song "Carry Me Back to Ole Virginny" as the state song of Virginia in 1940 may not have known that James A. Bland was an African American.)

Bland was the most popular Black minstrel performer of the nineteenth century, earning as much as ten thousand dollars per year. After the Civil War, minstrel shows were very popular; the music was usually written by whites and performed by whites in blackface. In 1875 an all-Black minstrel company was formed and Bland, a composer who had graduated from Howard University, joined. Previously, when Bland had served as a page in the U.S. House of Representatives, he had performed at the private gatherings of some prominent politicians. Although "Virginny" was perhaps his most popular song, Bland never lived in Virginia. The popularity of minstrel shows eventually faded, but not before Bland had toured Europe, giving a command performance for

Queen Victoria and being acclaimed as the "Prince of Negro Song Writers." Bland died penniless and was buried in Bala-Cynwyd, in suburban Philadelphia. The American Society of Composers and Performers (ASCAP) provided a headstone for his grave in 1939.

Hall v. *De Cur* DECISION ALLOWS SEGREGATION

On **JANUARY 14**, the U.S. Supreme Court overturned a Louisiana law of 1869 prohibiting racial segregation on public carriers. The Court noted, "If the public good requires such legislation, it must come from Congress and not from the states." Thus, the plaintiff, a Black woman, was held to have no right to get cabin space on a Mississippi steamboat plying from New Orleans, Louisiana, to Vicksburg, Mississippi. In 1883, the Court reversed this decision.

1879 EXODUS OF 1879

Escalating violence and the revelation that the sharecropping system was just another form of slavery caused thousands of Blacks to seize the slightest opportunity to leave the Deep South for the North and the West. Benjamin "Pap" Singleton successfully organized mass migrations of thousands of Blacks to Kansas. When the Black Exodus reached large numbers, white farmers realized they were losing cheap labor. Politicians were summoned to restrict the movement of Blacks out of their areas. Not only were transportation companies forbidden to sell tickets to Blacks, but also Black travelers were arrested under vagrancy laws. Labor agents were charged high registration fees for recruiting Blacks, and those "agitators" of Black migration were horsewhipped, driven away, or jailed.

Singleton was so successful in his resettlement efforts that he was summoned to Washington, D.C., in December to testify before a Democratic Congress on whether he was part of a Republican scheme to increase Black voting strength in the North. Singleton presented evidence that Blacks were actually moving to escape mob action, KKK terror, plantation trickery, high commissary prices, and the fact that their children were forced to work in cotton fields rather than attend school. Many Southern Democrats remained convinced that the exodus was a Republican plot.

The conditions of settlers in Kansas were mixed. Many Blacks settled on public lands, bought cattle, and started farming. Others practiced their professions as doctors, druggists, barbers, and businessmen. Although the Homestead Law allowed Black migrants to purchase land, many had few funds to buy anything else. Among these were the very poor, who had left the South with nothing more than a dream and the desire for freedom.

Los Angeles Eagle BEGINS PUBLICATION
The *Los Angeles Eagle*, the oldest continuously printed Black newspaper in the United States, was founded. During its early years, the *Eagle* detailed problems and prospects of living in California and the West.

"TO LEAVE, OR NOT TO LEAVE"
The issue "whether or not to leave the South" became a matter of debate among Black leaders. Frederick Douglass advised Blacks to remain in the South, so that they would retain sufficient numbers to wield political power. Promoters of the movement west, such as Richard T. Greener and John M. Langston, were convinced that the federal government would not actively support Blacks in the South and that they should leave to pursue freedom and opportunities in the West.

FORTY-SIXTH CONGRESS CONTAINS ONLY ONE BLACK
The death of Reconstruction was revealed when the Forty-sixth Congress convened in **MARCH**. Only one Black congressman was present — Blanche K. Bruce, U.S. senator from Mississippi.

NATIONAL EMIGRANT AID SOCIETY FORMED
In **MARCH**, the National Emigrant Aid Society was formed in Washington, D.C., to regulate immigration from the South to the West. Senator William Windom was elected the society's first president. Senators, congressmen, religious leaders, and a host of prominent Black and white citizens were members.

THE *Azor* CARRIES BLACK EMIGRANTS TO LIBERIA
Although the plan to raise three hundred thousand dollars to establish the Liberian Exodus Joint Steamship Company had disappointed expectations — only six thousand dollars had been received from the sale of stock — the enterprise proceeded with the purchase of the bark *Azor*, which was dedicated in a festive ceremony before more than five thousand Blacks.

On **APRIL 21**, the *Azor* sailed from the port of Charleston carrying 206 emigrants; the voyage was a disaster. The "ship physician" actually had no medical training — he had only assumed the title to get the boat through customs. As many as twenty-three passengers died en route for want of medical attention. Because of limited financial resources, the ship sailed without many of the essentials for long trips. For example, it had supplies for only three weeks rather than for six months. The mission was a terrible failure, and in November 1879, the company auctioned off the *Azor* to meet its debt. By December 1879, nineteen of the emigrants had returned to the United States.

BLOCKADE FORMED TO STEM WESTWARD MIGRATION
In **MAY**, a mob of white terrorists, led by General James R. Chalmers, a Confederate hero, set up a military-style blockade of the Mississippi River, with the specific intent of closing it to Black migrants. The white South feared the long-term consequences of losing its cheap labor to Kansas and other western places. Black leaders and local agents of the exodus were driven out of town or beaten. In an effort to keep Blacks from leaving, the mob threatened to destroy or sink any boat with Black migrants daring to move beyond the vicinity. Consequently, ship owners stranded more than fifteen hundred Blacks along the banks of the Mississippi River. General Thomas Conway wrote to President Hayes, "Every river landing is blockaded by white enemies of the colored exodus; some of whom are mounted and armed, as if we are at war."

General Conway, a former Freedmen's Bureau official, threatened to charter a fleet of steamers, arm them, and sail to rescue Blacks stranded at ports along the Mississippi if the policy was not abandoned. Conway made it appear that he had the official approval of President Hayes to intervene. Steamboat companies rescinded their ban against Black passengers in the spring of 1879. The price of the trip from the Deep South to St. Louis, generally costing from two dollars and fifty cents to four dollars, jumped to five dollars between June and September. The price was raised to cover the extra danger associated with confronting white "rifle clubs" and other mob violence.

BLACKS AND WHITES MEET AT VICKSBURG
In reaction to the threat of economic ruin posed by the exodus of their labor force for better opportunities in the West, whites met with Blacks throughout the South to influence them to stay. On **MAY 6**, at the most important of these meetings in Vicksburg, Mississippi, whites promised to improve conditions for Blacks to keep them from leaving. Some whites, however, took more drastic and punitive measures to

achieve their goals, denying Blacks transportation and imprisoning some. Heavy migration ceased, although gradual emigration continued; but promises of better conditions were soon forgotten.

MAYOR WARNS BLACK MIGRANTS NOT TO COME TO ST. LOUIS

In **JUNE**, numerous migrants crossed the Mississippi River and headed for St. Louis to escape the growing violence directed toward Blacks in the South. The mayor stated that he could not provide for them. The crush peaked in the summer and then subsided. The migrants, some seven thousand in number, pushed on to Kansas, where many settled in hot, dusty camps.

MAHONEY BECOMES FIRST BLACK WOMAN NURSING GRADUATE

On **AUGUST 1**, Mary E. Mahoney graduated from the nursing program at New England Hospital for Women and Children. She was the first African American woman to graduate from a nursing program in the United States.

Although Black women served as volunteer civilian nurses during the Civil War, they were not trained as nurses. A separate school for Black nurses was not established until 1891.

1880

POPULATION OVERVIEW

BLACK POPULATION IN THE UNITED STATES A total of 6,580,793 Blacks were recorded as residents in the United States. Blacks made up 13.1 percent of the nation's 50,155,783 total residents. The Black population doubled during each of the 30-year periods from 1790 to 1850. During the 1850–1880 period, the Black population increased by only 80.9 percent, from 3,638,808 to 6,580,793. Although Blacks did not improve their proportion of total residents in the South over this period, some states showed an increase in the proportion of Blacks in their population. For example, Mississippi, Georgia, and Alabama experienced the largest increases, whereas North Carolina, South Carolina, and Louisiana recorded relatively small increases. Significant decreases in the proportion of Blacks occurred in Delaware, Maryland, and Kentucky, whereas the District of Columbia and Virginia had marked increases over the same period. During the 1880s, the proportion of Blacks in the South began to decline rapidly. In fact, in each of the states of the lower South, except South Carolina,

Mississippi, and Louisiana, there was a decrease in the percentage of Blacks in the population. In the 1880s, the first time since 1790 (the earliest census), the Black population dropped below 35 percent of the southern population.

URBANIZATION OF BLACKS In 1880, the largest concentration of Black residents could be found in New Orleans, followed by Baltimore, Washington, D.C., and Philadelphia. Each of these urban centers had more than 30,000 Black residents. Of the 30 largest Black-populated cities in this year, the cities of Baltimore, Washington, D.C., and Philadelphia had the largest absolute growth over the previous decade. The largest percentage growth occurred in Indianapolis, Indiana (121.9 percent); Kansas City, Missouri (116 percent); and Montgomery, Alabama (91.6 percent). Overall, as many as 18 cities grew by more than 30 percent. Only 3 cities lost population over the decade, and each of these was located in the South — Vicksburg lost 14.2 percent of its Black residents, followed by Mobile (12.1 percent), and Memphis (3.7 percent). Six of the 30 cities had Black population majorities — New Bern, North Carolina, had the highest percentage of Black residents, followed by Wilmington, North Carolina; Montgomery, Alabama; Charleston, South Carolina; Petersburg, Virginia; and Savannah, Georgia.

ECONOMIC CONDITIONS OVERVIEW

KNIGHTS OF LABOR RECRUITS BLACKS The Knights of Labor, a national labor union, actively recruited Blacks as members. Its Black membership numbered ninety thousand, out of a total membership of seven hundred thousand. Other labor unions resisted inducting Black members because they felt white workers would refuse to work with Blacks. The Knights of Labor was formed as a secret society in 1869 but went public in 1878. Membership was open to "men and women of every craft, creed and color."

LABOR AGENTS Many labor agents were listed in city directories and recruited Black laborers for almost every type of work. For example, C. H. L. Pierre, who advertised in directories in New Orleans from 1875 through 1887, boasted on his letterhead that "at the shortest notice" he could furnish "Cane-cutters, Plough and Hoe Hands, Woodchoppers, Cotton Pickers, Levee and Rail-Road Hands and Mechanics of all Trade." In a postscript, he noted, "P.S. — I have made arrangements in different states for the emigration of Colored Families for the Sugar and Cotton Planters." Black workers were provided primarily to large plantations, many owned by politicians. Although only a few Blacks were listed as labor brokers and labor agents, some did act on behalf of white brokers and agents, often making the contacts with Blacks in the communities; that is, the Black men would "round up the hand for the labor agent," and the labor agent then negotiated the work arrangement, wages, and pay advances.

SOCIAL CONDITIONS OVERVIEW

BLACK COLLEGES FOUNDED Nineteen historically Black colleges and universities (HBCUs) were established between 1880 and 1890, slightly fewer than the number established during the previous two decades. About half were public institutions, created by an act of the state legislature. Other schools were established through the efforts of religious and philanthropic groups to educate specific segments of the Black population. Tuskegee Institute, Spelman College, and Southern University represented philanthropic efforts of Blacks and whites to implement an educational philosophy. A large number of the smaller colleges (Lane, Paine, Kittrell, Daniel Payne, and Morris Brown) were founded as religious training schools or as vocational centers. Geographically, these colleges were located primarily in the newer areas of Black occupancy rather than in the traditional core areas. A larger number of smaller institutions were founded in small but growing urban centers of Virginia, Alabama, Arkansas, and Tennessee. Georgia, which added no major HBCUs in the previous decade, saw the founding of three in this decade; two were established in Atlanta near several other Black institutions.

BLACK MILITANCY IN THE PRESS T. Thomas Fortune, the editor of the New York *Globe*, was one of the most outspoken militant members of the Black press. Throughout his career, he advocated a militant stance toward oppression and racism. The Afro-American League was one of the organizations that arose from his influence. In the editorial below, Fortune expresses a militancy that was growing among the Black press:

When murder, usurpation, intimidation, and systematic wrong are practiced in open violation of law; when the Negro who steals from society what society steals from him under the specious cover of invidious law is hung upon the nearest oak tree, and the white villain who shoots a Negro without provocation is not so much as arrested — when society tolerates such an abnormal state of things, what will the harvest be?

The question of illegal suppression of a tremendous voting population is not a race question; it is a national question, defined minutely in the federal constitution.... A people invite destruction or violent contention by permitting fundamental laws to be abused, by permitting common rights to be usurped by an arrogant and violent class. The people of the United States will find all too soon that they are playing on top of a volcano which is liable to erupt at any moment.

BLACK VOTER PARTICIPATION DECLINES Over the 1880s, the voting participation of Blacks in Georgia, South Carolina, and Florida declined substantially. In Georgia and South Carolina, more than half the Blacks who voted in 1880 did not vote in 1888. In Florida, Black voting participation dropped by 27 percent. Decreases in these states were indicative of Black voting behavior throughout the South.

EDITORIALIZING ABOUT LYNCHING During the 1880s, Blacks who spoke out against lynching often faced the possibility of being lynched themselves. Jesse B. Duke, the editor of the *Montgomery Herald*, a Black newspaper, editorialized against lynching, citing that many of the rapes for which Blacks were lynched had involved consenting white women. His remarks so angered whites that Duke had to flee Montgomery to avoid being lynched himself.

INJUSTICE OF CONVICT-LEASE SYSTEM DESCRIBED On **FEBRUARY 13**, the *Kansas Herald* printed details of one of the cruelest systems in the South, the convict-lease system. Millions of Black men, women, and children were drawn into this legal form of slavery. Blacks were often arrested on any charge, convicted, and sentenced to work on farms, where companies bought their labor for pennies. When planters and farmers needed labor, the judicial system simply made more arrests and convictions. The *Kansas Herald* described the process:

The convict slaves are leased out to men who entirely control them, who have to pay but $.06 cents per day for their hire, and only $200 if one escapes. A white man with money could bribe his way out, but there is no chance for the poor unfortunate colored people. ... If the colored man breaks a contract, he is sentenced to 12 months on the chain gang.... We hope that so long as these outrages continue, the colored people will continue to leave the South until those in power will see the error of their ways and repent in sackcloth and ashes and accord equal justice to all.

POLL TAXES IMPOSED IN THE SOUTH Between 1877 and 1889, all former Confederate states passed statutes to restrict suffrage. Poll taxes were introduced in

Georgia in 1871 and 1877, and in Virginia in 1877. In 1881, Virginia repealed the tax but adopted more stringent restrictions in 1884, which clearly shifted political power to whites. Mississippi imposed poll taxes in 1876, North Carolina in 1877, South Carolina in 1882, and Florida in 1888.

Although most southern states adopted this easy and obvious method of disfranchisement, it was not wholly satisfactory; a money requirement (one dollar and fifty cents in Alabama, for example) for the privilege of voting worked against the poor of both races. It was common practice, however, for politicians to ignore or pay the poll taxes for needy whites.

RACIST WORDS IN THE PRESS Many terms used to describe Blacks in magazines, newspapers, and other print media revealed different degrees of racism, from condescension to outright hatred. These terms included *nigger, niggah, darkey, coon, pickaninny, mammy, buck, uncle, aunt, highyaller, yaller hussy,* and *light-complected yaller man.* In addition, a number of names were used to poke fun at Blacks — for example, Colonel, Senator, Sheriff, Apollo Belvedere, George Washington, Abraham Lincum, Napoleon Beneyfidy Waterloo, Lady Adeliza Chimpanzee, Prince Orang Outan, Anainias, Piddlekins, Asmodeus, and Bella Donna Mississipp Idaho.

SEGREGATION LAWS INTRODUCED Tennessee began the trend toward modern segregation by passing a Jim Crow law requiring racial segregation in railroad cars. Other states in the South followed suit by passing legislation requiring segregation of public accommodations: Florida in 1887; Mississippi, 1888; Texas, 1889; Louisiana, 1890; Alabama, Kentucky, Arkansas, and Georgia, 1891; South Carolina, 1898; North Carolina, 1899; Virginia, 1900; Maryland, 1904; and Oklahoma, 1907.

AGRICULTURAL CO-OPS SUCCEED ON SEA ISLANDS

The first successful agricultural cooperative association settlement was established with the colonization of the Sea Islands. General Samuel Armstrong, president of Hampton Normal and Agricultural Institute of Hampton, Virginia, wrote about the success of this experiment in the *Southern Workman:*

> The relations between the races, and the condition of the colored people on the Islands is reported as the most gratifying and progressive. Day labor is becoming scarce, owing to the improvement in the condition of the laborers. Colored men who ten years ago worked as field hands for 50 cents a day now own

their own lands and earn a comfortable support from them. Every inducement is offered by the planters to the colored laborers to settle on their places. On some of the Islands laborers work two days a week for the planter who gives them a house and 7 or 8 acres for himself; on another he worked one and a half acres of the planter's land for the use of acres for himself. On John's Island, the colored people own 4,300 acres; on James Island 1,600 acres; on Wadmala, 500 acres; and on Edisto, 4,000 acres and make two thirds of the entire crop of the island. In 1872 a co-operative association of 35 colored men purchased a tract of 750 acres on Edisto Island, for $6,000. Their agent, Mr. John Thorne, is now one of the most prominent colored planters on the Island.

BLACK COAST GUARD FACILITY ESTABLISHED

A former slave, Captain Richard Etheride, established an all-Black Coast Guard facility on Pea Island on the Outer Banks of North Carolina, near Roanoke Island. It operated for seventy-two years, but no trace of the facility exists today.

SINGLETON HELPS BLACK MIGRANTS TO KANSAS

Benjamin "Pap" Singleton and others created a wave of enthusiasm among Blacks for leaving the South and migrating to places in the West. But, as the movement continued, the conditions of migrants grew worse. A letter from Singleton, reprinted in the *Kansas Herald,* revealed a new social, economic, and political landscape in the West:

> I have received a letter from Tennessee. There are a thousand people that have sent here for me to come after them.... They have sent for "Old Pap" but I find that the city is overrun with exodusters at this time and I think it would be inexpedient to bring more here at present. But still they want to come here and nowhere else; and there is no way of getting around it as Kansas is their destiny and they are bound to come. I am getting too old and I think it would be better to send someone more competent, and identified with the immigration, and has the interest of his race at heart and not his own pocket; someone that has heretofore directed and established colonies in the State and is known in the South. They should be sent to turn the tide of immigration.

Two years later, the *Colored Patriot* in Topeka printed an editorial depicting the accomplishments of "Pap" Singleton:

> The friends of Pap Singleton, the father of the great exodus, have decided to celebrate his next birthday, the

15th of August. Pap was born in 1809. . . . He was the prime mover of the Real Estate Association formed in Nashville, Tenn. in 1868. In this association was inaugurated the movement which resulted in the great hegira. Pap led out a colony and located them at Baxter Springs, Kansas in 1875. All the party have done well. Several other colonies were subsequently located by him, among which are Singleton colony in Morris and Lyons County. Between 1875 and 1880, Pap travelled back and forth repeatedly between Tennessee and Kansas, until he had conducted hither, according to statistics gathered from railroad and steamboat officials, 7,432 exodusters. On the 19th. of May, 1876, Pap and others called the first Emigration Convention ever assembled in America, in Nashville, Tennessee.

SOUTHERN UNIVERSITY AND A & M COLLEGE FOUNDED

Southern University and Agricultural and Mechanical (A & M) College was chartered in New Orleans by the Louisiana legislature for "persons of color" and opened the following year with twelve students.

In 1892, it was designated a land grant college, and in 1914, it moved to Baton Rouge, Louisiana. The school expanded significantly beyond its early emphasis on serving agricultural and mechanical need in the state. It implemented an arts and sciences department in 1940, a graduate school in 1958, and established branch campuses in New Orleans (SUNO) in 1956 and Shreveport-Bossier (SUSBO) in 1964. It remains one of the largest predominantly Black institutions in the United States.

Strauder V. *West Virginia* RULES ON JURY DUTY FOR BLACKS

On **MARCH 1**, the Supreme Court declared it unconstitutional to exclude Blacks from jury duty. The ruling was based on the Fourteenth Amendment.

BLACK JOCKEY WINS DERBY

On **MAY 18**, George Lewis rode the horse Fonso to the finish line to win the sixth Kentucky Derby.

1881 "BUFFALO SOLDIERS" GIVE CITIZENS ULTIMATUM

Black soldiers, apparently fed up with the abusive behavior of townspeople of San Angelo, Texas, posted this handbill in the town:

> We, the soldiers of the United States Army, do hereby warn cowboys, ttc., of San Angelo and vicinity, to recognize our rights of way as just and peacable men. If we do not receive just and fair play, which we must

have, someone will suffer; if not the guilty, the innocent. It has gone too far; justice or death.
>   U.S. Soldiers, one and all

These soldiers were diligent in their duties and military charge. They not only faced the maltreatment from the townspeople, but also they had to contend with Native Americans who engaged the soldiers because they represented the "Americanization of the West."

In fact, Black soldiers probably faced off with Native Americans in more than one hundred battles. They earned the sobriquet "buffalo soldiers" from the Native Americans and received 18 of the 370 Medals of Honor awarded by the U.S. government up to this time.

DOUGLASS APPOINTED RECORDER OF DEEDS

Frederick Douglass was appointed recorder of deeds for the District of Columbia.

"EXODUSTERS" LEAVE EDGEFIELD COUNTY

As many as five thousand Blacks packed their belongings and migrated from racially tense Edgefield County, South Carolina, to settle in Arkansas.

FORTY-SEVENTH CONGRESS INCLUDES TWO BLACKS

When the Forty-seventh Congress convened, two Black U.S. representatives were present as members — Robert Smalls of South Carolina and John R. Lynch of Mississippi.

SPELMAN COLLEGE FOUNDED

Spelman College was founded in Atlanta, Georgia, by Sophia B. Packard and Harriet E. Giles, two white women from New England. The school was related to the American Baptist Home Mission Society and was the first college for Black women.

The college traced its growth from the basement of the Friendship Baptist Church pastored by the Reverend Frank Quarles. Originally called Atlanta Baptist Female Seminary, its name was changed to Spelman Seminary in 1884 when it moved to nine acres of land and several frame buildings that had previously served as grounds and barracks for Union troops during the Civil War. The school was sponsored by the Rockefeller family and named after the Harvey Buel Spelman family, the parents of Mrs. John D. Rockefeller. In 1924, it became Spelman College.

In 1988, actor Bill Cosby and his wife Camille gave Spelman a gift of twenty million dollars, the largest single donation to any historically Black college.

An engraving by Frederic Remington shows several Black soldiers at a watering hole in the desert. Black soldiers primarily from the Ninth and Tenth Cavalry and the Twenty-fourth and Twenty-fifth Infantry made up the first all-Black regular army regiment, known as the Buffalo Soldiers. Their duties included guarding settlers in the West. Despite discrimination against them in acquiring horses, rations, and equipment, the Buffalo Soldiers had the army's lowest desertion rate and its highest rate of reenlistment.

Spelman is part of the Atlanta University system, a conglomerate that provides students with access to courses offered at affiliated colleges of the system. Spelman's current enrollment is approximately twelve hundred.

GARNET APPOINTED MINISTER TO LIBERIA

On **JUNE 30**, Henry Highland Garnet, a Presbyterian minister and abolitionist leader during the years of slavery, was appointed minister to Liberia. Garnet became ill shortly after his arrival and died on February 13, 1882, in Monrovia, Liberia, at the age of sixty-six.

TUSKEGEE INSTITUTE FOUNDED

On **JULY 4**, thirty young men and women joined twenty-five-year-old Booker T. Washington in a one-room shanty to open Alabama's first normal school for the training of Black teachers. The school, Tuskegee Institute, now called Tuskegee University, was established by an act of the Alabama legislature.

In 1882, Washington bought a one-hundred-acre abandoned plantation near Montgomery, which became the nucleus of the present campus. The original brick buildings, including Washington's home, the Oaks, were built and designed by the students. They ate food they raised on the school's land — the first balanced meals that many of the students had ever eaten. The school survived at first through hard work and donations from poor Blacks across the state, who gave food, livestock, and a little money. In its early years, the school was a leader in agricultural and industrial inventions and innovations.

In time, hundreds of thousands of dollars were donated to Tuskegee by philanthropists like Rockefeller and Carnegie. By 1970, Tuskegee comprised six schools and colleges with more than three thousand students and one of the largest Black faculties ever assembled. George Washington Carver was the best known of Tuskegee's faculty. (Both Carver and Washington are buried in the University Cemetery.)

Today, Tuskegee Institute is a coeducational, independent, and state-related comprehensive university. It offers undergraduate, graduate, and first professional degree–granting programs. It is estimated that 75 percent of the Black veterinarians in the nation are graduates of Tuskegee. Enrollment is now about 3,500, of whom 88 percent are Black.

LATIMER RECEIVES PATENT FOR ELECTRIC LIGHT BULB
On **SEPTEMBER 13**, Lewis H. Latimer (1848–1928), with Joseph Nichols, received a patent for his invention of the first incandescent electric light bulb with a carbon filament, an improvement upon the incandescent electric lamp invented by Thomas Edison in 1879. In 1882, Latimer received another patent for a process to manufacture the filaments cheaply. Latimer invented both of these while employed by the United States Electric Lighting Company in Bridgeport, Connecticut.

◈ Latimer was born in Chelsea, Massachusetts, the son of an escaped slave whose freedom had been purchased by several famous abolitionists including Frederick Douglass and William Lloyd Garrison. Latimer later sold copies of the *Liberator* to help support his family after his father disappeared. He served in the Union navy and was honorably discharged in 1865. He then went to work for Crosby and Gould, patent solicitors in Boston, who reluctantly gave him a chance to make patent drawings. His work proved so excellent that he worked as the chief draftsperson of the company for about ten years. Latimer's most famous drawings came with his work for Alexander Graham Bell, whose school was not far from Latimer's office. Bell asked him to make drawings of each part of the telephone to be submitted with the patent application. Bell received the patent in 1876.

In 1883, Latimer began working with Thomas Edison as chief draftsperson, engineer, and expert witness in defending Edison's patents in court. As a member of the Edison Electric Light Company, he was the only Black American member of the famous Edison Pioneers, a group of people who had worked with Edison before 1885. In 1890, Latimer wrote the first textbook on the incandescent lighting system used by the Edison Company. From 1896–1911, Latimer was chief draftsperson and expert witness of the Board of Patent Control of the General Electric Company and Westinghouse, which protected their patents from other companies. After his retirement, he published a volume of poetry, *Poems of Love and Life.* After his death, the Edison Pioneers noted, "Broadmindedness, versatility in the accomplishment of things intellectual and cultural, a linguist, a devoted husband and father, all were characteristic of him, and his genial presence will be missed from our gatherings."

1882 BILL PROPOSES EQUAL EDUCATION IN THE SOUTH
A bill was introduced in the U.S. Congress that proposed using federal funds to equalize educational opportunities for Blacks and whites in the South. Opponents of the bill defeated it by raising concern about unwelcome federal intervention in the schools and the mixing of the races.

BLACK JOCKEY TRIUMPHS AT SARATOGA
Isaac Murphy, a Black jockey, won forty-nine of his fifty-one races at Saratoga, riding the horse Buchanan.

When Murphy was finally given the opportunity to ride in the Kentucky Derby, he won it three times — in 1884, 1890, and 1891. No other jockey would win the derby three times until Eddie Arcaro in 1948.

Murphy started to ride professionally at the age of fourteen. His career extended for twenty-two years. He participated in more than fourteen hundred races and won 44 percent of them, including four of the first five American Derbies and five Latonia Derbies, which were more prestigious than the Kentucky Derby at the time.

CONVENTION OF COLORED MEN CALLS FOR LAND FOR BLACKS
The Convention of Colored Men convening in Parsons, Kansas, requested distribution of public lands in Oklahoma to Black people.

Gray v. *Cincinnati and Southern Railroad Company* DECISION AFFIRMS SEGREGATION
In *Gray* v. *Cincinnati and Southern Railroad Company*, a federal court ruled that separation of races on trains was legal as long as accommodations provided for Blacks were equal to those provided for whites.

LYNCHING CONTINUES IN THE SOUTH
Forty-nine Blacks were lynched during this year, in a continuation of the ugliest and deadliest form of vigilantism in the nation.

LYNCHING IN THE UNITED STATES, 1882–1950

PERIOD	AVERAGE NUMBER OF LYNCHINGS PER YEAR
1882–1900	150.4
1901–1910	84.6
1911–1920	60.6
1921–1930	27.5
1931–1940	11.4
1941–1950	3.0

In the 1850s, vigilantes in Louisiana and Texas lynched those suspected of plotting slave uprisings. Lynching spread during Reconstruction, when it was specifically directed at former slaves who were perceived as a threat to whites. Data show that between 4,000 and 6,000 lynchings occurred between 1882 and 1950, most between 1885 and 1915. The year with the infamous distinction of having the most lynchings was 1892, when 230 took place. Although the number of lynchings decreased after 1892, the percentage of Black victims increased, as did the number of victims tortured, dismembered, and burned at the stake. The average annual number of lynchings for the period 1882 to 1900 was about 150.

The decrease in lynchings after 1892 was probably due to three factors: increased public awareness, fear of legal consequences, and the crusade against lynching by individuals such as Ida Wells Barnett, editor and co-owner of the *Memphis Free Speech.*

After 1882, 82 percent of all lynchings occurred in the South. Three-quarters of all victims nationwide were Black, and in the South, 84 percent were Black. Ninety-five percent of all victims were male. The most lynchings after 1882 took place in Mississippi, with 581 (93 percent were Black), followed by Georgia, with 530 (93 percent Black); Texas, with 493 (71 percent Black); and Louisiana, with 391 (86 percent Black).

Most often the crime of the victim was cited as murder or attempted murder. Other alleged crimes included arson, burglary, slapping a white person, and theft. About one-third of all those lynched were accused of rape, or attempted rape, of a white woman. Whites believed that the threat of lynching was a de-

terrent, especially for rape. Very few individuals involved in lynch mobs were ever caught or prosecuted.

O'HARA ELECTED U.S. REPRESENTATIVE

James O'Hara (1844–1905), running unopposed, was elected to the Forty-eighth Congress from North Carolina. This was the fourth time he had campaigned for the seat — he had been defeated in 1874, 1876, and 1878. O'Hara was reelected in 1884 by about seven thousand votes. He lost the election of 1886, when he ran against a white Democrat, Furnifold M. Simmons, and a Black Republican, Israel Abbott. Simmons was elected by two thousand votes.

While in Congress, O'Hara was one of the most outstanding Black legislators serving after the Civil War. Active and articulate, O'Hara introduced legislation to reimburse depositors of the Freedmen's Bank, which that had failed a decade earlier. This legislation was defeated both times he introduced it. O'Hara was also unsuccessful in increasing the military benefits of Robert Smalls and his crew, in getting a constitutional amendment passed that would guarantee civil rights for Blacks, and in passing a bill that would allow equal accommodations for Blacks in restaurants and other public facilities in the District of Columbia. O'Hara did have a number of successes, however. He secured greater funding for river and harbor projects in North Carolina and inserted a provision into the Interstate Commerce Bill of 1884 to require nondiscrimination in interstate railroad travel. In his argument, he noted that Congress had already protected animals in transit, and it was time for the national government to "throw a shield about citizen's rights." Democrats who opposed this legislation weakened the amendment before final passage. ❖ O'Hara was born in New York of an Irish father and a West Indian Black mother. His family moved to the West Indies in the 1850s, but he returned to teach school in North Carolina before the Civil War. He served in the state house of representatives from 1868 to 1869. He received a law degree and served as chairperson of the Halifax County Board of Commissioners and as county attorney, and he was one of six Blacks elected to the state constitutional convention of 1875. After his congressional defeat, O'Hara returned to practicing law in New Bern, North Carolina.

SLATER FUND ESTABLISHED

John F. Slater contributed one hundred thousand dollars to establish the Slater Fund, which supported the education of Blacks throughout the South.

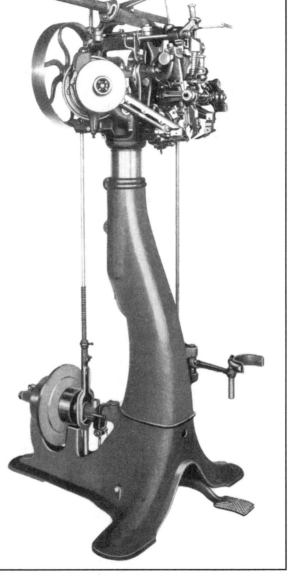

Jan Matzeliger, a worker in a Lynn, Massachusetts, shoe factory, was among several nineteenth-century Black inventors who greatly influenced the lives of Americans. Matzeliger invented the lasting machine, which both revolutionized the shoe industry and enabled the United Shoe Machinery Corporation, which bought his invention, to capture fully 98 percent of the shoe machinery trade. The picture on the right shows a modified operational version of Matzeliger's lasting machine.

Washington Bee BEGINS PUBLICATION

The *Washington Bee*, a Black-owned newspaper, was established in Washington, D.C., by attorney William Calvin Chase.

Cairo, Illinois Gazette BEGINS PUBLICATION

On **APRIL 23**, the *Cairo, Illinois Gazette*, a Black daily, was founded. It was published by W. S. Scott until white arsonists destroyed the plant six months later.

1883 *Cleveland Gazette* BEGINS PUBLICATION

The *Cleveland Gazette*, a Black newspaper, was established in Cleveland, Ohio, by Harry C. Smith.

COLORED INDEPENDENT PARTY ORGANIZED

Blacks in Pennsylvania organized a state party, the Colored Independent Party. It primarily served to inform the Black public and the general public of issues facing the Black community.

MATZELIGER RECEIVES PATENT

Jan Matzeliger (1852–1889) received a patent for a "lasting" machine that revolutionized the American shoe industry. At the time, there were machines for all parts of the shoemaking process except the last step: sewing the upper part of the shoe to the inner sole. This part was done by hand by skilled workers who stretched the leather over a wooden mold of a foot called a last. Matzeliger believed he could design a machine that would perform the lasting process. It took him more than two years to build a metal model of his machine. He ultimately received financing from two Lynn businessmen but in return forfeited two-thirds of the interest in any profit that might result from his invention. When he finally demonstrated his machine, it produced a perfectly sewn shoe in one minute. His invention produced seven hundred pairs of shoes in a ten-hour day, compared with the fifty pairs made by a skilled laster. Shoes could thus be mass-produced and made available at lower cost to most people. Matzeliger eventually gave up the rights to his patent to finance a large-scale shoemaking operation. In return, he received stock in the new company.

◈ Matzeliger was born in 1852 in Dutch Guiana of a Dutch father and a Black mother. As a young man, he became a skilled machinist by working in his father's shop. When he was nineteen years old, Matzeliger left Dutch Guiana (now Suriname), sailed for two years to the Far East, and came to Philadelphia in 1873. Despite his skills, Matzeliger had difficulty finding work, as did most skilled Blacks at the time. He finally became an apprentice shoemaker and deftly operated the machine that sewed soles. Four years later, he moved to Lynn, Massachusetts, then the shoe-manufacturing center of the United States, with more than 170 shoe factories. He found a job sewing soles at one of the factories and worked evenings studying mechanical science.

In 1886, Matzeliger was diagnosed with tuberculosis, often called the "shoemaker's disease." Doctors believed it came from working in factories with little or no ventilation. Years of overwork had weakened him, and he died at thirty-seven years of age. A bridge in Lynn is named in honor of Matzeliger.

RUFFIN APPOINTED JUDGE

George L. Ruffin of Boston, the first Black to earn a law degree from Harvard University, was appointed city judge of the District Court of Charlestown, the first Black to hold this position. Although Ruffin served as a judge until his death, there was evidence that he served also as a member of the Boston City Council in 1876 and 1877.

ST. BENEDICT THE MOOR CHURCH OPENED IN NEW YORK

St. Benedict the Moor became the first Black Roman Catholic church in New York City. It was located in the Greenwich Village neighborhood.

CIVIL RIGHTS ACT OF 1875 DECLARED UNCONSTITUTIONAL

On OCTOBER 15, the U.S. Supreme Court declared the Civil Rights Act of 1875 unconstitutional. Thus, discrimination was allowed in public facilities. Exceptions were made for interstate travel and jury duty.

RACE RIOT BREAKS OUT IN VIRGINIA

On NOVEMBER 3, a race riot erupted in Danville, Virginia, and four Blacks were killed.

FORTY-EIGHTH CONGRESS INCLUDES TWO BLACKS

On DECEMBER 3, the Forty-eighth Congress convened with two Black representatives — James O'Hara of North Carolina and Robert Smalls of South Carolina.

BLACKS HOLD STATE CONVENTION IN OHIO

On DECEMBER 22, a meeting of Black citizens convened in Columbus to discuss continued white terrorism in the South and protection of the rights of Black citizens. The *State Journal of Harrisburg*, Pennsylvania, a Black newspaper, commented:

> The object of the convention is to take into consideration the educational, moral, civil, and political interests of the colored race, and particularly the question of the equal rights of the colored people of the South. The recent decision of the Supreme Court annulling the Civil Right bill, as well as the murder of colored men at Danville, Virginia, are the principal reasons for the assembling of the convention.

1884 AME *Church Review* FOUNDED

Benjamin Tucker Tanner founded the AME *Church Review*, a leading magazine of the day. Tanner had served as an AME bishop and as editor of the *Christian Recorder*, one of the influential newspapers during this time.

MEDICO-CHIRURGICAL SOCIETY FOUNDED

The Medico-Chirurgical Society of the District of Columbia, the first African American medical society, was founded. The society was formed so that Black physicians could acquire additional medical knowledge at monthly meetings. The society grew out of the exclusion of Black physicians from the American

Medical Association. A national body of Black physicians, the National Medical Association, was formed in 1895. The Medico-Chirurgical Society still exists today.

RACE RIOT IN MISSISSIPPI ELICITS MILITANT BLACK RESPONSE

T. Thomas Fortune, a noted Black publisher, used the riot in Yazoo City to develop a basis for self-defense among free Blacks:

At Yazoo City, Mississippi, last week, a white merchant and a colored butcher had an altercation. The white merchant acting upon the natural cowardice of his race in such matters, declined to settle this dispute in an honorable hand-to-hand fight, but posted off after his friends. The colored butcher did the same. When the white man returned with his friends, the colored man and his friends, without standing to be shot proceeded to stand and shoot. As a consequence, "three of the best citizens of the place were killed outright," and others were wounded. And the whole gang of them, on murder bent, should have been killed outright. When a man takes violence as his weapon he should die by violence. "An eye for an eye, a tooth for a tooth," the accepted law of retaliation.

But the matter did not rest here. The citizens "rose up as a man," took the law in hand, and lynched the colored men, who had been lodged in jail. The colored men fought the mob to the bloody end, and died like heroes. And so brave men always die.

Two hundred white men flooded Yazoo City to defy the law and to avenge men who had invited the death they deserved. In a warfare of this nature, where brute force and cruelty are the only rules observed, let both sides carry to its logical result the cowardice of the fight. Let the torch vindicate the outrages of the mob and the shotgun....

The Supreme Court of the United States, a beggarly apology for wisdom and fairness, declares that such lawlessness and murder are without the justification of the National Government; that if the State affords the victim no protection he need not look to the National Government. Then, where shall he look, pray? To the mercy of the mob, the humanity of the murderer? No; let him use the same weapons that other oppressed people use — let him use the dagger, the torch and the shotgun. There is no other appeal; no other argument will avail. The State denies protection; the National Government declares it has no jurisdiction. Then shall black men, free and independent, made in the image of their Maker, stand up as cowards to be shot by ruffians made of the same clay, with no more rights, human or Divine? Perish the thought! A race of cowards would thus sink their manhood, but free men never!

SONS OF NEW YORK FORMED

A group of Blacks born in New York organized the Sons of New York. The society believed that its members were superior to other Blacks, particularly those born in the South. Such thinking prevailed throughout New York. For example, T. Thomas Fortune, publisher of the *New York Age*, criticized the Black migrant from the South as a "threat to law and order." In 1907, the *New York Age* depicted the southern Black migrant in New York City in this manner: "loud of mouth, flashy of clothes, obtrusive and uppish southern Negro."

NEWSPAPERS PUBLICIZE BLACK SETTLEMENTS IN WEST

Letters and advertisements encouraging Black migrants to settle in communities of the new West could be found in almost every Black newspaper. On **JANUARY 19**, in the *People's Advocate* of Washington, D.C., I. B. Burton described the Black settlement at Crete, Nebraska, and encouraged similar cooperative ventures:

A large company can emigrate and purchase railroad lands for about half of what it would cost single persons, or single families, and the fact is, single persons are by no means as desirable as families or large settlements.... Wholesale goods and machinery can be shipped the same way in large lots for the colony with wide-awake agents. Windmills are indispensable in the far west, and one windmill could be made to answer four or five farmers — each having an interest in it....

On February 23, 1884, the same newspaper published a description of a Black settlement in Iowa:

Muchachinock is a town five miles south of Oskaloosa, Iowa in a rich coal region. The output is about 120 cars daily. The population is about 20,000 of which 1,500 are colored, mostly from Virginia. They have two churches, one Methodist, the other Baptist; two frame school houses attended by about 200 children. There is one large dry goods store, quite a number of ice cream and eating saloons, and confectioneries and boarding houses kept by colored men. They have a colored brass band, an Odd Fellows hall, a goodly number of Masons, and a Mutual Benefit association. None have ever been buried by the county. There is no Justice of the Peace, no constable, or police force to support. All offenses, according to mutual agreement, are tried before a committee, and fines enforced thereunder go to the Mutual Benefit association. There are but three billiard halls in the town.

The colored miners average $70 per month, as many as much as $80.

BLACK BASEBALL PLAYER MAKES DEBUT

On **MAY 1**, Moses Fleetwood Walker made his debut as a catcher on the Toledo team of the American Baseball Association, becoming the first Black player in major league baseball — and the only one until Jackie Robinson in 1947.

FORTUNE FOUNDS NEWSPAPER

In **NOVEMBER**, T. Thomas Fortune (1856–1928), one of the most prominent Black journalists and clearly the most militant in his day, founded the *New York Freeman*, a daily newspaper, which became the *New York Age* in 1887. Fortune was active in Republican politics and closely identified with the ideas of Booker T. Washington. In fact, he served as an adviser, confidant, and ghost writer for Washington. Fortune subsequently edited the *Negro World*, the publication of Marcus Garvey's Black nationalism movement.

◆ Fortune, born a slave in 1856 and freed by proclamation in 1865, was trained as a printer. He moved to New York City in 1879 and became part owner of the weekly tabloid *Rumor*, which later became the *Globe*. That paper failed in 1884. The *New York Age* was regarded as the leading Black newspaper of its day, primarily because of Fortune's editorials, which condemned racial discrimination. To supplement his income, Fortune also wrote for the *Boston Transcript* and the *New York Sun*, both general-circulation newspapers.

Fortune also authored pamphlets and several books, including *Black and White: Land, Labor, and Politics in the United States* (1884), *The Negro in Politics* (1886), and *Dreams of Life, Miscellaneous Poems* (1905). Mental illness drove Fortune out of the public spotlight, and although he was frequently referred to as "the dean of Negro newspapermen," he died in relative obscurity. Fortune was considered by some as the most articulate spokesperson for his race in the North in the early 1900s. He was the first to advocate use of the term *Afro-American* instead of *Negro*.

Philadelphia Tribune BEGINS PUBLICATION

In **NOVEMBER**, the *Philadelphia Tribune* was founded by Christopher J. Perry. The newspaper was one of five papers founded in the nineteenth century that still survive.

1885 FIRST BLACK BASEBALL TEAM ORGANIZED

Frank Thompson, a headwaiter at the Argyle Hotel in Babylon, New York, organized the first Black baseball team composed of paid players. The other waiters at the hotel made up the team. The team was called the Cuban Giants, and members feigned speaking Spanish.

FORTY-NINTH CONGRESS INCLUDES TWO BLACKS

The Forty-ninth Congress convened with two Black congressmen — James O'Hara of North Carolina and Robert Smalls of South Carolina.

MINISTER TO HAITI NAMED

George Washington Williams, a Black minister, lawyer, and historian, was named minister to Haiti.

Born in Pennsylvania in 1849, Williams had enlisted in the Union army when he was fourteen years old. He achieved the rank of sergeant major before the Civil War ended. He became a minister, helped found a journal, and worked in the U.S. Post Office Department. He served in the Ohio legislature before being named minister to Haiti. He was the author of the two-volume *History of the Negro Race in America, 1619–1880*, considered the definitive work of African American history in the nineteenth century. He also wrote a history of Black troops in the Civil War. With a change in administrations, Williams was succeeded as minister to Haiti by Dr. John E. W. Thompson, a graduate of Yale University Medical School.

FERGUSON CONSECRATED PROTESTANT EPISCOPAL BISHOP

On **JUNE 24**, Samuel D. Ferguson was consecrated bishop of the Episcopal Church and named bishop of Liberia. Ferguson became the first Black American with full membership in the House of Bishops.

HOPKINS NAMED MINISTER TO LIBERIA

On **SEPTEMBER 11**, Moses Hopkins was named diplomatic minister to Liberia. Hopkins was a minister and educator.

1886 AMERICAN NATIONAL BAPTIST CONVENTION HELD

As many as six hundred delegates convened in St. Louis and organized the American National Baptist Convention. They elected the Reverend William J. Simmons as their president.

LYNCHING CONTINUES IN LOUISIANA

As many as seventy-four Blacks were lynched in the United States this year. The Black community was outraged by the abuses and racist actions of white mobs common throughout the South. The lynching of Robert Smith in St. Bernard's Parish of Louisiana was typical:

> In St. Bernard's Parish, La., May 4, a plantation overseer by the name of Green, known to be a Louisiana desperado who had figured in two or three killing scrapes, had a quarrel with Robert Smith, a colored laborer, and threatened his life with a knife in his hand, advancing on Smith, who picked up a stick laying near by and stood Green off. Green became enraged and armed himself, and at night, accompanied by two other white companions, went to Smith's cabin and broke open the door. Smith knew Green's voice and suspected his mission and as the door fell in he opened fire on the first man who appeared and Green received the contents of Smith's revolver, and was mortally wounded from which he died. The other two white men returned the fire and ran, slightly wounding Smith. Smith was arrested next morning. At noon a lynching party composed of white men went to the jail and demanded the keys which were surrendered to them without trouble. They took Smith out and hung him to a tree in broad daylight without being masked. Smith is the seventh colored man mobbed in the South last week as follows: Kentucky mobs one and shoots one, Georgia one, Louisiana one, Mississippi one and Virginia one. There are from six to eight colored men or women murdered by white men in the Southern States weekly. There seems to be no other redress for us but to organize into protective unions in defense of our parents, wives and children, whose lives are in jeopardy every day at the hands of those Southern white desperadoes. The white press doesn't publish half the crimes committed upon colored people by their white brothers. Premise they are ashamed to put them on record.

NORTH CAROLINA TEACHERS DEMAND EQUALITY

The North Carolina State Teachers' Association for Negroes presented demands for Blacks in higher education, federal aid to education, and the establishment of uniform requirements and salaries for Black and white teachers.

TOLTON ORDAINED PRIEST

Augustine Tolton (1854–1897) is considered by some to be the first fully Black African American to be ordained a Catholic priest, because both of his parents were African Americans. (Although James A. Healy and Patrick Francis Healy are usually considered the first Black priests, they were both the sons of an Irish father and a mulatto mother.) Tolton's parents escaped from slavery in Missouri, fleeing to Quincy, Illinois, before the Civil War. After he was ordained, Tolton became pastor of St. Joseph's Church in Quincy, where he held interracial services, a most uncommon practice at the time.

BLACKS MASSACRED IN MISSISSIPPI

On **MARCH 17**, more than twenty Blacks were killed in Carrollton, Mississippi.

COLORED FARMERS' ALLIANCE ESTABLISHED

On **DECEMBER 11**, the Colored Farmers' Alliance was formed in Texas by a white man, General R. M. Humphrey. It grew rapidly throughout the South, claiming as many as one million members by 1890. The Colored Farmers' Alliance was similar in structure to the white Southern Farmers' Alliance. The Colored Farmers' Alliance favored the Federal Elections Bill, which would guarantee the voting rights of Blacks in the South in national elections through the use of federal troops.

Several Black newspaper editorials spoke out strongly against the alliance even though it continued to enroll members. The *American Citizen* of Topeka, Kansas, included material from the Selma, Alabama, *Independent* with its own criticism of the alliance:

> The Farmers' Alliance is making great efforts to get the colored people to vote their ticket in the coming election. . . . Is it not plain to every colored man that this alliance intends to plot the oppression of colored farmers? . . . But the Alliancemen are now saying they are going to organize a "nigger alliance." This was never thought of until this election when they needed our votes. It is too late to fool us in this way.
>
> We hope the colored people of Alabama will stand by their color and exercise their rights as citizens. Let them contend for a free ballot and a fair count, in such a manner that all who prize and wish to preserve the liberties of the people will come to their rescue.

In 1891, the alliance initiated a major cotton pickers strike, a move that angered the white Southern Farmers' Alliance, whose members employed Black cotton pickers. Just before the strike, Blacks accused the Southern Farmers' Alliance of keeping wages low and

Cotton, cotton, cotton — hundreds of bales of cotton await shipment on a wharf in New Orleans. More than 18 million acres of land were devoted to cotton production, and more than 6.3 million bales of cotton were produced annually.

influencing legislatures to pass discriminatory laws. By 1891, the Colored Farmers' Alliance had organizations in twenty states and nearly 1,250,000 members. It organized a cotton pickers strike for higher wages in Texas. Shortly afterwards, the alliance collapsed.

1887 FIFTIETH CONGRESS HAS NO BLACK MEMBERS
For the first time in seventeen years, Congress had no Black members. The continued intimidation of Black voters kept most away from the polls.

LYNCHINGS REPORTED IN BLACK PRESS
Seventy Blacks were reported lynched during the year. Five of these lynchings occurred at Yorkville, South Carolina in April. One important function of the Black press was to report on lynchings and other forms of oppression. The following is an editorial of the *Weekly Pelican* of New Orleans on the Yorkville lynchings:

> The lynching of five colored men at Yorkville, S.C. . . . by armed men is but another heinous crime which, from time to time, have been practiced upon the

Negro. Even the judge on the bench, in instructing the Grand Jury, said that "It [the lynching] was one of these things which the law could not reach, and therefore it would be useless for them to lose their time in attempting to ferret out the perpetrators." Well, if the law can't reach the rascals, if justice can't overtake the ruthless slayers of black men and women, the only recourse the colored man has is to protect himself and to remember the old law, "an eye for an eye, and a tooth for a tooth."

WOODS INVENTS INDUCTION TELEGRAPH SYSTEM
Granville T. Woods (1856–1910), an inventor, was credited with many inventions (he received more than sixty patents) relating to the railway system and electrical industries. In this year, he invented the induction telegraph system, which allowed communication between moving trains and between trains and stations. This invention significantly reduced accidents.

In 1888, Woods designed an overhead conducting system for railway cars. The sight of streetcars connected to these overhead wires became common in American cities. He also invented the "third rail," which is still used in subway systems today. Among his other inventions are an automatic safety cutout for electric circuits, an incubator, and automatic air brakes that increased the safety of the railroads. His patents were sold and assigned to General Electric, Westinghouse, and American Bell Telephone. Woods entered court on several occasions to claim the rights to inventions claimed by Edison and was successful several times. After Woods secured a second court victory, Thomas Edison offered Woods a position, which he turned down. In 1888, the *American Catholic Tribune* referred to Woods as "the greatest electrician in the world."

BLACK WESTWARD MIGRATION ATTRIBUTED TO ECONOMIC MOTIVES
On **JANUARY 22**, the reason for the large migration of Blacks from the South to the West was explained by Will M. Clemens of Jacksonville, Florida, in an article written in the *Freeman*:

> There is going on an exodus of Negroes to the Western States. Over 3000 have already left North Carolina alone. It is not an organized movement but there is a manifest method in it. I can but see one valid reason for this exodus. The Negro is not virtually a lazy, shiftless individual. He will work, and work hard, if paid for his labor. All about him here in the South the lack of thriftiness and industry. He has

little to inspire him to labor for a home when his white brother is an indolent creature, who prefers to wander idly about the streets rather than work. The Negro wants an air of prosperity all about him. He seeks it in the West, and thus I can readily see a reason for the Western exodus. The condition of white labor in the South is largely the cause of the depressing conditions of all classes in the South. The Negro is poorly paid for his labor, as compared with the labor in the North. And the white laborers and mechanics in the South are the ones to blame.

There are other reasons why the colored man should seek pastures new, notwithstanding that he is more prosperous here than his shiftless white brother. In every southern state there are laws on the statute books which give the white landlord almost absolute control of the interests of the colored renter or laborer. The "crop mortgage" system is only a legalized form of confiscation. A colored man is compelled to pay exorbitant price for the use of land to begin with — often as much per acre as it could be bought for by a white man. In order to get provisions for his family while his cotton is being raised he must pledge his whole crop in advance, and pay for everything he buys at rates two or three times as those which are asked in the regular channels of trade. At the end of the year he is indeed fortunate if he can settle with his landlord and storekeeper by turning over to them all the proceeds of his labor, and more frequently he finds himself in debt after such a transfer.... The Negro is not a free agent in the transaction. He is entirely at the mercy of those who fix the contract. His absolute necessity deprives him of all liberty of choice. He must have land to cultivate and must pay an exorbitant price for it. He must have food and clothing for his wife and children, and he must pay the merchant a double price for the same. This is the prevailing rule throughout the South. I do not speak of any special case. The law is on the side of the white man. The courts are with the white man and so is public sentiment to a certain extent. The Negro is a slave still in a certain sense. He is not treated as the white man, and here lies the secret of success and prosperity in the great South. Her whole labor system is liable to pull to pieces for want of wise and timely action in the direction of assuring the colored people that the wrongs under which they are suffering shall be removed. This is the cause of the immigration to the West. The Negro mechanics and laborers in the towns and cities are prosperous and contented as I have stated. The agricultural class, those who raise cotton and till the soil, are the dissatisfied ones.... Without the Negro, the South is doomed a failure. She will never be prosperous without his aid, and if the South were wise she would hasten to correct her laws and look upon the Negro as her salvation.

ALEXANDER GRADUATES FROM WEST POINT

On **JUNE 12**, John H. Alexander (1864–1894) graduated from the U.S. Military Academy at West Point, becoming the second Black to graduate from this school. Although three other Blacks entered the academy while Alexander was there, none of them graduated.

Alexander, like Henry O. Flipper who graduated ten years before him, had to contend with verbal and physical abuse from his classmates. Nevertheless, he demonstrated his academic ability, especially in languages. After graduating, Alexander was assigned to western frontier duty with the all-Black Ninth Cavalry at Fort Robinson, Nebraska. He was transferred in March 1888 to Fort Washakie, Wyoming, and then to other posts in Utah and Nebraska until he was assigned to be professor of military science and tactics at Wilberforce University in Wilberforce, Ohio, in January 1894. Alexander died of heart disease at the youthful age of thirty, three months later.

MOUND BAYOU FOUNDED

On **JULY 12**, Mound Bayou, a large Black town, was founded by former slaves. The founders, including Isaiah Thornton Montgomery, later a member of the 1890 state convention, hoped that their new community would afford African Americans the social, political, and economic freedom that they could not find in white municipalities. Their plans coincided with those of the Yazoo and Mississippi Valley Railroad, which wanted settlers to form towns along its right of way. Montgomery had been a slave on the plantation of the brother of the Confederate president, Jefferson Davis.

1888 BLACK MIGRATION TO OKLAHOMA TERRITORY BEGINS

As the established settlements in Kansas filled up, Blacks began looking to Oklahoma as the next area of settlement. This was new territory, and Blacks started developing proposals for making Oklahoma Territory an all-Black state. *The American Citizen*, a Black newspaper, kept its readers informed on the proposed settlement:

Let every colored man who wants 160 acres of land get ready to occupy some of the best lands in Oklahoma and should it be open up, there is no reason why at least 100,000 colored men and women should not settle on 160 acres of land each and thus establish themselves so firmly in that territory that they will be able to hold their own from the start.

The discontented and oppressed Europeans have heard of the intended opening of this country and they are now falling over each other, so to speak, to reach America in time to enter the best of these lands. Let the colored American keep his eye on Oklahoma and when the opening alarm shall have been sounded, move forward and take it. We shall keep our readers posted on whatever Congress does on this matter, to the end that they may be prepared to act unitedly and at the proper time.

BLACK TOWN INCORPORATED IN FLORIDA

Eatonville, Florida (north of Ocala), was incorporated. By some accounts, it was the oldest Black-run town in the country. Today, the town is still entirely composed of Blacks. Zora Neale Hurston, the Black novelist, was the town's most famous citizen.

CHEATHAM ELECTED TO CONGRESS

Henry P. Cheatham (1857–1935) was elected to the Fifty-first Congress as a Republican representing North Carolina.

◈ Cheatham, born a slave on a farm near Henderson, North Carolina, attended school in the area, then entered Shaw University in Raleigh in 1875. After receiving an A.B. degree, he became the principal of the Plymouth Normal School. In 1887, he and several others established an orphanage for Black children at Oxford, North Carolina. As a first-term congressman, Cheatham found his fellow House members resistant to issues pertaining to the well-being of Black people. He was unsuccessful in getting any of his proposals accepted or passed. In 1890, he won reelection, and was the only Black member of the Fifty-second Congress when John M. Langston of Virginia and Thomas E. Miller of South Carolina were defeated in their bids for reelection. In an effort to soften the Congress on issues pertaining to Blacks, Cheatham spent much of his time making Congress and the nation aware of the myriad contributions of Blacks to American life since emancipation. He appealed for congressional appropriations to support exhibits of Blacks' contributions, but his proposals were defeated. He lost his bid for reelection in 1892, and two years later, he lost the election to his brother-in-law, George H. White. President William McKinley appointed Cheatham recorder of deeds for the District of Columbia in 1897. Ten years later, he returned home to be superintendent of the Oxford orphanage.

LYNCHING OF BLACKS CONTINUES

Sixty-nine Blacks were reported lynched this year. Although lynching statistics were reported frequently in Black-owned newspapers, there was no systematic accounting nationwide. A more accurate accounting of lynching was started in 1889 by Tuskegee Institute. Although history shows that horse thieves and desperadoes were frequently lynched by vigilante committees in the West, lynching by mobs was a product primarily of the Civil War and the Reconstruction era. Between 1882 and 1888, 595 whites and 440 Blacks were lynched in the United States. These statistics changed drastically over the years as a disproportionate number of Blacks were lynched. In addition, the mob behavior took a turn toward torture. In Paris, Texas, in 1893, a white mob turned away from lynching a Black man, but instead gouged out the victim's eyes with a red-hot poker before burning him to death. The mob allegedly scrambled to secure bones of the victim as souvenirs after the fire burned the flesh from his bones. W. E. B. Du Bois recorded seeing the fingers of a lynched Negro displayed in the windows of a butcher shop in Atlanta. Mob behavior was unpredictable. Some mobs were recorded to have pulled out the teeth of the victim, chopped off the fingers and toes with axes, and castrated or mutilated the body while the victim was still alive.

LANGSTON ELECTED TO CONGRESS

John M. Langston (1829–1897) was elected to the U.S. Congress from Virginia but was denied his seat until Congress declared him the winner on September 23, 1890.

◈ Langston was born in Louisa, Virginia, to Ralph Quarles, plantation owner, and Lucy Langston, a free Black. Langston's parents died when he was five years old. He went to Chillicothe, Ohio, to live with the executor of his father's estate. After receiving an M.A. from Oberlin College, he was denied admission to two law schools. He was fortunate, however, to read law with the respected Judge Philemon Bliss of Elyria, Ohio. Langston was admitted to the Ohio bar in 1854, and in the following year, he became the first Black elected to public office in this country — clerk of Brownhelm Township.

Langston, an astute politician, eventually held a number of local and national positions. During the

Civil War, he served as a Union recruiting agent in the Midwest and chaired the National Equal Rights League; in 1867, he became inspector general of the Freedmen's Bureau. Just prior to 1868, Langston established the law department at Howard University and served as dean from 1868 to 1875.

At the national political level, Langston was widely respected, and he frequently turned down presidential appointments. He accepted the position of vice president and acting president of Howard University, a position he resigned after being refused its presidency. In 1877, President Rutherford B. Hayes appointed Langston as minister to Haiti and chargé d'affaires in Santo Domingo. In 1885, he became president of Virginia Normal and Collegiate Institute in Petersburg, Virginia. Three years later, Langston ran as an independent for the U.S. Congress as representative of the Fourth Congressional District in Virginia. He lost by 641 votes, but charged that the election was blemished by fraud and other irregularities. Because Democrats boycotted the vote, the Republicans voted to seat him.

Because Langston was seated only a week before recess, he had little time to familiarize himself with his duties before returning home to campaign for reelection. When he returned to Congress in December, he fought unsuccessfully to establish a Black industrial university, to get Blacks admitted to the U.S. Naval Academy, and for the observance of Grant's birthday as a national holiday. He was an outspoken advocate of the institution of Lincoln's birthday as a holiday and of the Voting Rights Act of 1870. Langston lost his bid for reelection in 1890 and refused to run in 1892. He remained in the Washington, D.C., area, writing his autobiography, *From the Virginia Plantation to the National Capital*, published in 1894.

SMITH NAMED MINISTER TO LIBERIA
Ezra E. Smith, a minister and educator from North Carolina, was named minister to Liberia.

He later fought in the Spanish-American War. Smith was considered the founder of Fayetteville State Normal School (now Fayetteville State University). He donated the land for the school and served as the principal.

Indianapolis Freeman BEGINS PUBLICATION
On **JULY 14**, the *Indianapolis Freeman*, the first Black illustrated newspaper, was established. It was the brainchild of Edward Elder Cooper, who had worked

for the U.S. mail service and for the Indianapolis *World*. After creating the *Freeman*, he began publishing the *Colored American* in 1893 in Washington, D.C.

FIRST BLACK BANK OPENS IN WASHINGTON, D.C.
On **OCTOBER 17**, the Capital Savings Bank of Washington, D.C., the first Black-created and Black-run bank, opened. It was also the first Black bank with no fraternal organization connections. The Savings Bank of the Order of True Reformers in Richmond, Virginia, opened in April of this year.

1889 LYNCHING ESCALATES
Ninety-four Blacks were reported lynched in this year. Between 1885 and 1889, the number of lynchings of Blacks increased by about 64 percent over the previous five-year period.

MUTUAL TRUST COMPANY ESTABLISHED
The Mutual Trust Company was chartered in Chattanooga, Tennessee, as one of the first Black banks in the country. The bank failed during the panic of 1893.

WELLS-BARNETT BECOMES EDITOR OF
Memphis Free Speech
Ida Wells (later Wells-Barnett) (1862–1931) became editor and part owner of the *Memphis Free Speech*. She wrote such forceful and stinging editorials against racism and Black passivity that she raised the emotions of white racists and local city leaders. She was especially critical of lynchings.

◆ Orphaned during the yellow fever epidemic of 1878, Ida Wells supported her five brothers and sisters as a teacher in Holly Springs, Mississippi. She moved to Memphis in 1882. Although she had endured racism in Mississippi, her experience in Memphis marked a new course in her life. In 1883, she began her war against racial injustice when she was asked by the conductor of the Chesapeake, Ohio and Southwestern Railroad Company to move to the crowded smoking car, a place that was not equal to white facilities. She refused, and when she was physically moved by the conductor, she sank her teeth into the conductor's hands and gripped her chair. Wells lost the battle with the conductor, but she brought suit against the railroad company. Wells ultimately lost her suit, but her disgust and hatred of racial discrimination and the lack of legal protection for Blacks caused her to turn much of her attention to fighting these injustices.

Ida B. Wells-Barnett became one of the most noted Black journalists when she embarked on a crusade to condemn lynching and other forms of racial injustice.

Wells gained a broad audience of Blacks beyond Memphis. In fact, many of her articles and editorials were reprinted in other Black newspapers throughout the Mississippi Valley. Her growing reputation as a freedom fighter caused whites to view her as a serious threat to the social and economic status quo. Local whites responded by attacking Wells's character. She lost her teaching job for being critical of the quality of Black education in Memphis. While she was out of town in May 1892, her newspaper office and equipment were destroyed. Threats on her life were made, and she chose not to return to Memphis. She moved to Chicago instead and continued her sharp, blistering demands for equal rights for Blacks in this country.

In Chicago, she married Ferdinand Barnett, assistant state's attorney for Cook County and editor of the first Black newspaper in Chicago. Wells-Barnett continued to report on race riots during and after World War I. In 1906, Wells-Barnett attended the meeting of the Niagara Movement. Three years later, she was one of two Black women who signed the "Call" for a meeting "To Discuss Means for Securing Political and Civil Equality for the Negro." She was part of the Committee of Forty, which led to the founding of the National Association for the Advancement of Colored People (NAACP). Wells-Barnett also worked diligently for women's suffrage and with Jane Addams to successfully block the setting up of segregated schools in Chicago.

YOUNG GRADUATES FROM WEST POINT

Charles Young (1861–1922) graduated from West Point, the third Black to do so. He was initially assigned to the Tenth Cavalry but then was reassigned

Charles Young, the son of former slaves, became the first African American to attain the rank of colonel in the U.S. Army. A graduate of West Point, Young served on the western frontier and in the Philippines, Haiti, and Liberia.

to the Twenty-fifth Infantry and then to the Ninth Cavalry — all Black units.

◈ Young was born in Mays Lick, Kentucky, and educated in Ohio where he attended Wilberforce University. He became an instructor there after graduation. He was admitted to West Point in 1884 but ran into academic difficulties. Because of deficiencies in mathematics, he was dismissed. He was readmitted in 1885 after passing a reexamination in math.

Young's military career took another turn in 1894 when he was assigned to Wilberforce University as a professor of military science and tactics. He left the army when the war with Spain erupted in 1898 and took a commission as major in the all-Black Ninth Ohio Volunteer Infantry. Although he expected to go to Cuba, he and his troops were not shipped out. In 1899, he rejoined the regular army and was promoted to captain. He was assigned to the Philippines, where he saw combat for almost two years. When he returned to the United States, he was assigned superintendent of Sequoia and General Grant National Parks in California.

In May 1904, Young was appointed as U.S. military attaché to Haiti, the first Black officer to hold this position. He was reassigned in 1911 to the Office of the Army Chief of Staff, and later named military attaché to Liberia, a position he held until 1915. In 1917, Lieutenant Colonel Young was considered for a position as commander of a regiment, or even a larger unit, when American forces were being mobilized for World War I. Young was the highest-ranking Black officer at the start of World War I. Instead of becoming a commander, the War Department forced him to retire from active duty because of medical disabilities, after which they promoted him to full colonel. Although Young objected, he accepted his forced retirement. He protested by mounting his favorite horse and riding from Chillicothe, Ohio, to Washington, D.C., to prove his stamina and to appeal his retirement. Some believe that Young was forced into retirement because of fear that he would have eventually commanded white soldiers. Colonel Young died in January 1922 and was buried in Arlington National Cemetery.

BLACK CATHOLICS HOLD FIRST LAY CONGRESS

On **JANUARY 1**, the Catholic Afro-American Lay Congress convened in Washington, D.C. to discuss a wide range of pressing problems including the lack of Black priests. Only four Black priests had been ordained up to this time.

FIFTY-FIRST CONGRESS INCLUDES THREE BLACKS

When the Fifty-first Congress convened on **MARCH 4**, two Black congressmen were seated as members: Henry P. Cheatham of North Carolina and John M. Langston of Virginia. Thomas E. Miller of South Carolina contested his defeat and would not be seated until 1890.

1890

POPULATION OVERVIEW

BLACK POPULATION IN THE UNITED STATES The Bureau of the Census published data that showed the Black population at 7,488,676. Blacks made up 11.9 percent of the national population of 62,947,714.

ONE HUNDRED YEARS OF POPULATION CHANGE In the 100 years between 1790 and 1890, the proportion of white residents in the country increased from 80.73 percent to 87.80 percent. Correspondingly, the proportion of the Black population declined by slightly more than one-third, dropping from 19.27 percent to 11.9 percent.

BLACK POPULATION IN CITIES Black residents continued to move from rural areas to cities. In fact, of the 20 cities with the largest Black residential population in 1890, most registered relatively large increases in Black residents over the 1880–1890 decade. Chicago recorded a 120 percent increase in its Black residents over the decade, jumping from 7,791 to about 16,000. Eight other cities with impressive increases in their number of Black residents included Memphis (92.7 percent); New York City (86.2 percent); Nashville (79.8 percent); Atlanta (72 percent); Kansas City, Missouri (68.2 percent); Augusta, Georgia (67 percent); Norfolk, Virginia (61.3 percent); and Washington, D.C. (56.2 percent). In most cases, relatively large increases in Black residents occurred in cities with relatively low percentages of foreign-born whites. Washington, D.C., had the largest Black population (75,572) in the country at this time, followed by Baltimore (67,104) and New Orleans (64,691). Of the 20 cities with the largest Black populations, 3 already had Black majorities at this time: Montgomery (59 percent), Charleston (56.4 percent), and Savannah (53.2 percent).

In the decade 1880–1890, the Bureau of the Census documented that only 12.9 percent of the Blacks in the United States resided in urban areas, though Blacks were starting to move to urban areas in large numbers. Many scholars have noted the emergence of the modern urban ghetto in the United States during this decade.

OCCUPATIONS OF BLACKS, NATIVE WHITES, AND FOREIGN WHITES, 1890

	BLACKS	PERCENT	NATIVE WHITES	PERCENT	FOREIGN WHITES	PERCENT
Agriculture, fishing, and mining	1,757,403	57	5,122,613	47	1,305,901	26
Domestic and personal service	936,080	31	1,342,028	12	1,375,067	27
Manufacturing and mechanical industries	172,970	6	2,067,135	19	1,597,118	31
Trade and transportation	145,717	5	1,722,426	16	712,558	14
Professional services	33,994	1	640,785	6	114,113	2

Source: U.S. Bureau of the Census, Occupations, 1890 (Washington, D.C.: Government Printing Office, 1893), 19.

ECONOMIC CONDITIONS OVERVIEW

EMPLOYMENT DISCRIMINATION AGAINST BLACKS

Blacks faced great discrimination in every occupation that paid well. Management in large industries relegated them to unskilled jobs and used them occasionally as strikebreakers. Most organized labor groups refused them membership and had organized only a small number of them into unions. Black workers had little power to remedy the situation. Relative to other populations, such as native whites and foreign whites, Blacks occupied the lowest rung of the economic ladder as shown in the figures in the table.

HIGHER PERCENTAGE OF BLACKS THAN WHITES WORK REGARDLESS OF AGE OR GENDER

In this year, census data showed that Blacks were generally employed at younger and older ages than whites, regardless of gender. For Black men, considerably higher percentages of those under nineteen years of age were gainfully employed than were their white counterparts. Almost one-third of Black male children under age fourteen were gainfully employed, in contrast with less then 10 percent of white children. That both groups had children working probably reflects the fact that many families were still working in agriculture, and on farms everyone's labor was needed. In the prime working ages, twenty to sixty-four years of age, the percentage of Black and white men gainfully employed was almost the same. In the oldest age category, a higher percentage of Black men than white men continued to be gainfully employed, about 90 percent for Black men in contrast to 78 percent for white men.

Among women, African Americans in all age categories were much more likely to be gainfully em-

ployed than white women. The differences were especially great in age categories of more than twenty-five years. Overall, the percentage of Black working women over twenty-five years of age remained at about 40 percent, whereas the percentage of white women working dropped to about 10 percent. In the oldest age group (over sixty-five), almost 30 percent of Black women were still working, but only about 3 percent of white women worked. This may reflect the fact that Black women worked both in agriculture and as domestic workers.

SOCIAL CONDITIONS OVERVIEW

BLACK COLLEGES FOUNDED

Over the decade, as many as fourteen historically Black colleges and universities (HBCUs) were established. About half of the HBCUs were public institutions. Most colleges were located in relatively small towns. The publicly supported institutions seem to have been founded where they would generate or stimulate growth, or provide jobs and concentrate Black residents in particular geographic areas, such as Fort Valley, Georgia; Langston, Oklahoma; Denmark, South Carolina; Crockett, Texas; and Institute, West Virginia. It might also be argued that new state-supported Black colleges were located in small towns to reduce costs and make college accessible to a previously isolated Black population.

GRANDFATHER CLAUSES ADOPTED

Grandfather clauses were introduced in the South in Mississippi to keep Blacks from voting. They restricted voting to those who were descendants of persons who had voted prior to 1866. Of course, no Blacks voted before 1866.

Grandfather clauses were adopted by South Carolina in 1895 and Louisiana in 1897. Other measures to disfranchise Blacks were enacted in North Carolina in 1900, Virginia and Alabama in 1901, Georgia in 1907, and Oklahoma in 1910.

"MISSISSIPPI TESTS" ADOPTED Mississippi adopted a new constitution that placed restrictions on voting and included a poll tax and literacy tests. These measures were designed to disfranchise Blacks. The "Mississippi tests" were adopted by South Carolina in 1895, Louisiana in 1898, North Carolina in 1900, Alabama in 1901, Virginia in 1901, Georgia in 1908, and Oklahoma in 1910.

UNCLE REMUS TALES PUBLISHED Joel Chandler Harris (1848–1908), a journalist with the *Atlanta Constitution*, wrote stories in the African American dialect, based on legends and folktales that had been passed down by slaves through their oral tradition. The stories of Uncle Remus brought many Americans into contact with Black storytelling for the first time. Harris, an advocate of fair treatment for African Americans after the Civil War, based his stories on tales he heard told by George Terrell, an elderly Black man from Eatonton, Georgia, where Harris grew up.

◇ In 1947, the NAACP and other Black organizations protested the film *Song of the South*, which depicted Uncle Remus as the main character, because they believed that the Walt Disney Studio's film perpetuated Black stereotypes.

BLAIR BILL DEBATED IN CONGRESS

The Blair Bill was debated on the floor of the U.S. Senate. The bill proposed providing federal support for education and funds to reduce illiteracy among freed Blacks. It was defeated.

LYNCHING OF BLACKS CONTINUES

Eighty-five Blacks were reported lynched this year.

TANNER, RENOWNED ARTIST, COMPLETES MAJOR WORK

In this year, Henry O. Tanner (1859–1937) completed *The Banjo Lesson*, one of his most famous works, marking his emergence as the most promising Black artist of his day.

◇ Born in Pittsburgh on June 21, 1859, the son of an AME bishop, Tanner chose art over theology as a career. After attending the Pennsylvania Academy of Fine Arts, he taught at Clark University at Atlanta.

In the years following the end of Reconstruction, white terrorism against Blacks took a number of forms, the most heinous of which was lynching. This photograph shows the lynching of George Meadows, a suspected murderer and rapist. From 1882 until 1964, according to records kept by Tuskegee Institute, 4,742 Black people were lynched.

In 1891, Tanner moved to Paris, France, abandoning Black subject matter and concentrating on religious themes. His painting *The Resurrection of Lazarus* won Tanner recognition as an artist of great talent and ability. The French government purchased this painting for a major gallery. Tanner later visited the Holy Land and painted a series of pictures depicting events in the Bible: *Daniel in the Lion's Den, Flight into Egypt,* and *Christ on the Road to Bethany.* These paintings won Tanner significant fame and fortune.

He received many awards, including the Lippincott Prize, the French Legion of Honor, and a silver medal at the Paris Exposition. Tanner exhibited his art in many prestigious places, including the Salon des Artistes Français, Paris, 1894–1924; the Anglo-American Art Exhibition, London, 1914; and the Century of Progress, Chicago, 1933–1934. Retrospective shows after his death were mounted at the Harlem Cultural Council, New York Urban League, 1967; and the Smithsonian Institution, Washington, D.C., 1969–1970. He was the first Black elected to the National Academy of Design. He died in Paris in 1937, having achieved worldwide recognition as a master painter.

FORTUNE ORGANIZES AFRO-AMERICAN LEAGUE

On **JANUARY 25**, in a meeting of influential Black leaders in Chicago, T. Thomas Fortune organized the Afro-American League of the United States, a forerunner of the NAACP. Fortune and the founding members intended the organization to promote rights for Blacks and to encourage industrial education, job training, and overall economic opportunity for Blacks. Joseph C. Price, president of Livingston College, was elected president. Although the league was a national organization, its members worked mostly in northern cities. The organization considered revolution as one of its means for securing equal rights for Blacks. Due to lack of support from important Black leaders such as Frederick Douglass, John M. Langston, and Blanche K. Bruce, the league failed within three years.

SECOND MORRILL ACT PASSED

On **AUGUST 30**, the second Morrill Act was passed by the U.S. Congress, providing for a permanent annual endowment of twenty-five thousand dollars for each land grant college established under the provisions of the Morrill Act of 1862. It also allowed a portion of federal appropriations to be used for the endowment, support, and maintenance of historically Black land grant colleges in states that maintained separate educational facilities.

MILLER ELECTED U.S. REPRESENTATIVE

On **SEPTEMBER 24**, Thomas E. Miller (1849–1938) was sworn in to the Fifty-first Congress as a representative from South Carolina. He actually had been defeated in the election of 1888 by William Elliott, but Miller contested the election, alleging that properly registered Black voters had not been able to vote in the election.

The House Committee on Elections finally ruled in Miller's favor and allowed him to take his seat.

While in Congress, Miller spoke for passage of a bill to authorize the government to oversee federal elections and protect voters from violence and intimidation. He also spoke in rebuttal to a speech by Senator Alfred H. Colquitt of Georgia, who blamed Blacks for slowing economic development in the South. Miller said that white southerners were responsible for the economic problems of the region because they were motivated by bigotry and vengefulness in denying Blacks the full rights of citizenship.

◈ Miller was born of a free Black couple in Ferrebeeville, South Carolina. After the Civil War, he worked as a newsboy on a railroad in Hudson, New York. He earned a scholarship that allowed him to attend Lincoln University in Pennsylvania, where he graduated in 1872. Before being elected to Congress, Miller was a school commissioner, studied law at the University of South Carolina, was admitted to the bar, and served in both the state senate and house of representatives. In 1884, he was Republican state party chairperson.

Miller ran for reelection in 1890 and was the apparent victor until the South Carolina Supreme Court determined that Elliott deserved the seat because the size and color of Miller's ballots were illegal. Miller appealed to the House Committee on Elections, but a majority of the committee gave the seat to Elliott. Miller later lost the primary election for the Republican nomination for the Fifty-third Congress to George Murray.

After leaving Congress, Miller again served in the state house of representatives. He was a delegate to the state convention that established laws requiring that voters be able to read and write and own at least three hundred dollars' worth of property. Miller and several other Black delegates could not stop the adoption of these proposals. Later, Miller helped establish the State Negro College (now South Carolina State) and served as its president. He also worked for the hiring of Black teachers in Black public schools.

ALABAMA PENNY SAVINGS BANK OPENS

On **OCTOBER 15**, the Alabama Penny Savings Bank was established in Birmingham. It was the first Black bank in the state.

1891   GEORGIA SEGREGATES STREETCARS

The Georgia legislature passed laws to segregate streetcars.

LYNCHING INCIDENTS INCREASE

One hundred and thirteen Blacks were reported lynched this year.

PROVIDENT HOSPITAL FOUNDED AS FIRST INTERRACIAL HOSPITAL IN AMERICA

The Provident Hospital in Chicago, the first interracial hospital in America, was established by Black surgeon Daniel Hale Williams. The idea of building interracial hospitals generally meant that many white hospitals would not have to serve Black patients at all, thus reinforcing racial segregation. Provident Hospital provided the first training school for Black nurses. The idea of a Black-run hospital was not universally accepted within the Black community: some Blacks felt that it reinforced segregation of the races. Nevertheless, the hospital opened after a citywide fundraising campaign.

FIFTY-SECOND CONGRESS INCLUDES ONE BLACK

One Black congressman, Henry P. Cheatham of North Carolina, was a member of the Fifty-second Congress, which convened on **DECEMBER 2**.

1892 BLACKS FORM DEMOCRATIC CLUBS IN SOUTH CAROLINA

Blacks formed Democratic clubs and subsequently cast large blocs of votes to ensure the election of Blacks in the Charleston City Council and the South Carolina state legislature.

LEWIS BECOMES FIRST BLACK ALL-AMERICAN ATHLETE

William H. Lewis of Harvard University was chosen the first Black all-American athlete from a major college. He was selected as the center on Walter Camp's football team in this year and also in 1893. He completed his law degree from Harvard and in 1911 was appointed assistant attorney general of the United States by President William Howard Taft. Lewis was the first Black person to serve in a subcabinet position.

LYNCHING OF BLACKS CONTINUES

As many as 161 Blacks were reported lynched this year. This was the largest recorded number of lynchings.

Baltimore Afro-American BEGINS PUBLICATION

On **AUGUST 13**, the first issue of the *Baltimore Afro-American* was published. It continues to be published more than one hundred years after its founding.

1893 DUNBAR PUBLISHES POEMS

Paul Laurence Dunbar (1872–1906) published his first volume of poems, *Oak and Ivy*. It was followed by *Majors and Minors* (1895), *Lyrics of Lowly Life* (1896), and *Complete Poems* (1913).

◈ Born in Dayton, Ohio, Dunbar was giving public recitals of his poems at the age of thirteen. While in high school, Dunbar was the only Black in his class. He held a number of school positions, including president of the literary society and editor of the newspaper. When he graduated, Dunbar could not afford to go to college, so he took a job at four dollars per week, running an elevator. Dunbar raised money to help offset the cost of his first volume of poetry by selling the book to his elevator customers. Dunbar's poetry was written in African American dialect, which became very popular with the public. After a noted literary critic gave rave reviews of Dunbar's work, he emerged as a major American poet and also enjoyed

Unlike many Black writers, Paul Laurence Dunbar gained national acclaim while he was still living. He was also an early promoter of African American studies.

popularity in Britain. Perhaps his best-known volume of poems, *Lyrics of Lowly Life*, published in 1896, went through eleven printings and was a best-seller at the time. Dunbar later grew frustrated because there was little demand for his poetry that was not written in dialect. The pressure to publish finally took its toll on this frail man. When he caught tuberculosis, doctors prescribed whiskey; this caused Dunbar to develop a drinking problem that caused his health to deteriorate. Dunbar never recovered fully, but during his illness, he wrote three novels, including *The Sport of the Gods*. On February 9, 1906, Dunbar died at the age of thirty-four.

FIFTY-THIRD CONGRESS INCLUDES ONE BLACK
When the Fifty-third Congress convened, it had only one Black member, George W. Murray, U.S. representative from South Carolina.

LYNCHING DRAWS LARGE CROWDS
The lynching of a well-known Black person was a special affair and often attracted whites from some distance to watch and participate in the mob violence. Some came by special train for the occasion. A public lynching might include torture and mutilation before the lynching. The lynching of Henry Smith, in Paris, Texas, drew a crowd of ten thousand, among them people of all classes and women of "social and intellectual" culture.

WILLIAMS PERFORMS HEART SURGERY
Dr. Daniel Hale Williams (1856–1931), one of the nation's most noted surgeons, performed the world's first successful heart operation at Chicago's Provident Hospital.
◈ Williams, formerly a barber and law clerk, attended Chicago Medical College (now Northwestern University Medical School), which was one of the best in the country at that time. When he graduated in 1883, the germ theory of medicine, antiseptic surgery, and anesthetics were just being accepted. Operations often took place in private homes, especially for Blacks who were generally not admitted to hospitals. Williams's surgical skills were soon recognized, and he was appointed to the surgical staff of a dispensary and to the Illinois State Board of Health in 1889. Although this was a prestigious appointment, as a Black man, Williams still had no hospital appointment. This ended in 1891 when Williams founded Provident Hospital.

In 1893, a young Black, James Cornish, was brought to Provident with a knife wound in his chest. Without x-rays, blood transfusions, or antibiotics (none of which had yet been developed), Williams surgically opened Cornish's chest and sutured a tear in the pericardium surrounding the heart. This was the first surgery of its kind. Cornish lived for another fifty years.

Williams was appointed chief surgeon of Freedmen's Hospital in Washington, D.C., in 1894. He was accused of professional misconduct while there, and although he was later exonerated, he never recovered from the disgrace. In 1912, Williams was appointed associate attending surgeon at St. Luke's Hospital in Chicago, the largest and most important hospital in the city at the time. No other Black held such a position until twenty-five years after Williams's death.

MURRAY WINS SEAT IN CONGRESS
On MARCH 4, George W. Murray (1853–1926) took his seat in the Fifty-third Congress as a representative from South Carolina. He became a member of the Committee on Education.
◈ Murray was born of slave parents in Sumter County, South Carolina, and attended the University of South Carolina and the State Normal Institute at Columbia. After he graduated in 1876, Murray farmed, taught school, and lectured for the Colored Farmers' Alliance. He was rewarded for his work in local Republican politics by being appointed inspector of customs for Charleston in 1890. In the same year, he lost his race for the Republican nomination to Congress but was successful two years later in the general election.

While in his first term of Congress, Murray backed an appropriation for a federal exhibit at the Cotton States and International Exposition that would highlight the achievements of Black Americans. To substantiate his point, he showed Congress a partial list of ninety-two patents that had been granted to Black Americans, including eight for agricultural tools that he himself had patented. In 1895, Murray asked that the body of Frederick Douglass be allowed to lie in state in the Capitol, but his request was denied by Speaker of the House Charles F. Crisp of Georgia.

Murray ran for election in 1894 from a gerrymandered district where Blacks had difficulty getting registered to vote. He was defeated by William Elliott but appealed the election, charging voting irregularities. The House Committee on Elections supported his charge, and he was seated in the Fifty-fourth Congress on June 4, 1896. New restrictions on voting rights for Blacks in South Carolina severely cut the number of registered Black voters, and in November, Murray lost the election to Elliott. Murray wanted Congress to conduct an investigation of South Carolina politics, but Congress adjourned without taking action.

Murray returned to farming and invested in land that was resold to Black tenant farmers. He left South Carolina to avoid three years of hard labor after he had been convicted of forgery in a contract dispute with two tenants. Murray settled in Chicago where he worked for the Republican Party and wrote two books: *Race Ideals: Effects, Cause and Remedy for the Afro-American Race Troubles* (1914) and *Light in Dark Places* (1925).

BLACK JOCKEY WINS NEW YORK RACES
On **JUNE 23**, Willie Simms won five of six races at Sheepshead Bay in Brooklyn, New York. Simms did this again in 1895. Later, Simms won two Kentucky Derby races and two Belmont Stakes races. During this period, Simms was one of the country's most successful jockeys.

1894 AFRO-AMERICAN DEMOCRATIC LEAGUES FORMED
Black Democrats begin operating Afro-American Democratic Leagues in an effort to pull Black voters away from the Republican Party. A Black Democratic club was formed in Boston in this year.

BURLEIGH BECOMES SOLOIST AT ST. GEORGE'S, MANHATTAN
In this year, Harry T. Burleigh became featured baritone soloist at one of the most aristocratic churches in Manhattan, St. George's Episcopal Church, which claimed J. P. Morgan among other wealthy and powerful members.

Burleigh, a composer of more than three hundred songs, was credited with popularizing the Black spiritual and adapting the music to the concert stage. He toured both the United States and Europe and performed for the British royal family. He held his position as soloist at St. George's for more than fifty years. In 1917, the NAACP awarded Burleigh the Spingarn Medal for excellence in creative music.

Mary Church Terrell devoted much of her life to women's issues and Black causes. She remained actively involved in fighting injustice, including picketing segregated restaurants in Washington, D.C., into her eighties.

1895 BLACK SERVES ON SCHOOL BOARD IN WASHINGTON, D.C.
Mary Church Terrell (1863–1954), a civil rights leader, became the first African American to serve on the Washington, D.C., School Board.

Terrell, who graduated from Oberlin College in 1884, dedicated significant time to social and equal rights issues. In 1896, she helped form the National Association of Colored Women. She continued to fight for the rights of African Americans in general and of African American women in particular. In 1940, she wrote her autobiography, *A Colored Woman in a White World*.

DU BOIS RECEIVES DOCTORATE

W. E. B. Du Bois became the first Black American to obtain a doctorate at Harvard University.

LYNCHING OF BLACKS CONTINUES

One hundred thirteen Blacks were reported lynched this year.

NATIONAL MEDICAL ASSOCIATION FORMED

The National Medical Association, a Black medical association, was founded in Atlanta, Georgia, at the Cotton States and International Exposition. Dr. Miles Vardahurst Lynk, who had called for such an organization to be founded, was among the twelve physicians present at the founding.

SOUTH CAROLINA RESTRICTS BLACK VOTING

South Carolina adopted a new constitution that severely restricted the voting rights of Blacks.

DOUGLASS DIES

On **FEBRUARY 20**, Frederick Douglass, the Black abolitionist, died at age seventy-eight. President Abraham Lincoln had called him "the most meritorious man of the nineteenth century." The North Carolina legislature, composed primarily of Black Republicans and white populists, adjourned to mark his death. Five state legislatures adopted resolutions of regret. At his last rites, held in Washington, D.C., two U.S. senators and a Supreme Court justice were among the honorary pallbearers.

HEARD NAMED MINISTER TO LIBERIA

On **FEBRUARY 23**, William H. Heard, an AME minister, educator, and former member of the South Carolina House of Representatives, was named minister to Liberia. Heard also served as trustee of Wilberforce University and Payne Theological Seminary.

BLACK LABORERS ATTACKED IN NEW ORLEANS

On **MARCH 11** and **12**, Black laborers in New Orleans were attacked by whites. Six Blacks were killed in the two-day clash.

BLACKS SAIL FOR LIBERIA

On **SEPTEMBER 18**, about two hundred Blacks embarked from Savannah, Georgia, to settle in Liberia.

WASHINGTON DELIVERS "ATLANTA COMPROMISE" SPEECH

On **SEPTEMBER 18**, Booker T. Washington made his famous "Atlanta Compromise" speech. Washington, the only Black American invited to speak at the Cotton States and International Exposition in Atlanta, called upon Blacks to work and develop themselves into useful members of society. An advocate of racial solidarity, he dismissed the importance of discrimination, focusing instead on developing the Black community, particularly supporting Black business. Because Washington's approach to southern whites was accommodating, he was able to influence white philanthropists to contribute hundreds of thousands of dollars for fighting discrimination and segregation laws. Washington's philosophy of accommodation was challenged by many Black leaders, some of whom sought a more militant program of Black advancement. William Monroe Trotter, George Forbes, and W. E. B. Du Bois were among the most influential Black leaders who disagreed with Washington.

◈ Washington was born in Franklin County, Virginia, the son of a slave cook and an unknown white man. His mother named him Booker and he adopted the name "Washington" when he first enrolled in school. Washington spent his first nine years as a slave. At the age of sixteen, he entered Hampton Normal and Agricultural Institute in Virginia. He worked as a janitor to pay the cost of room and board, and the Institute's principal, Samuel Chapman Armstrong, found a white benefactor to pay his tuition. At Hampton, Washington studied academic subjects and agriculture. He graduated with honors in 1875.

Washington learned much of his educational philosophy from Armstrong, who believed that the progress of freedmen and their descendants depended on a practical, utilitarian education.

NATIONAL BAPTIST CONVENTION HELD IN ATLANTA

On **SEPTEMBER 28**, three Baptist organizations — the Foreign Mission Convention of the United States, the American National Baptist Convention, and the Baptist National Education Convention — convened in Atlanta and formed the National Baptist Convention (NBC).

SOUTH CAROLINA HOLDS CONSTITUTIONAL CONVENTION

On **DECEMBER 4**, the South Carolina Constitutional Convention adopted a new constitution, which included an "Understanding Clause" designed to strip Blacks of any remaining political rights, particularly the vote.

1896 BLACK BANKS OPEN IN RICHMOND

The Nickel Savings Bank was established in Richmond, Virginia. In the same year, another Black-owned bank, the St. Luke's Savings Bank, also opened in the city.

CARVER BECOMES DIRECTOR AT TUSKEGEE

George Washington Carver (1861?–1943) was selected to be the director of agricultural research at Tuskegee Institute, Alabama. Here, Carver began to teach and experiment with agricultural production and the chemical derivatives of various agricultural products.

Carver was one of the first botanists to encourage crop rotation, and he developed several hundred industrial and household uses for peanuts and sweet potatoes. Carver was born to slave parents on the plantation of Moses and Susan Carver near Diamond, Missouri. Carver showed an interest in plant life as a youth, and he pursued this interest throughout his education. After completing high school, he homesteaded in Kansas for two years and then attended Simpson College in Indianola, Iowa, from 1890 to 1891, when he was admitted to Iowa State College. Carver studied systematic botany and graduated three years later at the top of his class, the first Black to graduate from that institution. Carver then worked at Iowa State as an assistant in the agriculture experiment station and studied for his master's degree, which he received in 1896. After taking the position at Tuskegee, Carver was invited by Thomas Edison to work with him in Menlo Park, New Jersey, but Carver refused the offer, saying that he preferred to stay in the South where he could be of help to southern farmers. During his tenure from 1896 to 1943 as a chemist and botanist at Tuskegee, Carver built an international reputation. When he died, he left his entire life savings, about sixty thousand dollars, to establish a research foundation at the institute.

CURTIS JOINS COOK COUNTY HOSPITAL STAFF

Austin M. Curtis, physician, became the first Black on the medical staff of Cook County Hospital in Chicago. He later became the chief surgeon of the Freedmen's Hospital in Washington, D.C., and head of surgery at Howard University Medical College.

JUSTICE HARLAN DISSENTS ON JIM CROW LAWS

Justice John Marshall Harlan (1833–1911) became an important figure in African American history when he dissented concerning the legality of Jim Crow laws. Harlan wrote the dissenting opinion, stating that Jim Crow laws deprived Black citizens of equal protection of the law. Harlan served as an associate justice of the U.S. Supreme Court from 1877 to 1911.

LYNCHING OF BLACKS CONTINUES

In this year alone, 78 Blacks were lynched. Between 1887 and 1896, 1,035 Blacks were lynched in the South.

NATIONAL ASSOCIATION OF COLORED WOMEN ORGANIZED

The National League of Colored Women and the National Federation of Colored Women combined to form the National Association of Colored Women. Mary Church Terrell, a civil rights leader and equal rights activist, was most instrumental in the formation of this group, which was concerned mainly with educational and health issues and ending the practice of lynching. The association is the oldest women's organization still in existence.

Oriental America PERFORMED ON BROADWAY

The first Broadway production with an all-Black company was John W. Isham's production of *Oriental America*.

WHITE ELECTED TO CONGRESS

George H. White (1852–1918) was elected to the U.S. House of Representatives from North Carolina and was reelected in 1898.

◆ White became a noted politician after the Civil War. A former slave, White was educated at Howard University and studied medicine before he transferred to the study of law in North Carolina. He was admitted to the North Carolina bar in 1879 and elected to the state house of representatives the next year. He was instrumental in passing legislation that established four normal schools for training Black teachers. After serving as a principal at a school at New Bern, he was elected to the state senate in 1884. White also served as solicitor and prosecuting attorney for the Second Judicial District of North Carolina.

In 1894, White decided to run for Congress from the Second District but lost the Republican nomination to his brother-in-law, Henry P. Cheatham. Two

George White, elected to the Fifty-fifth Congress, sponsored the country's first antilynching legislation.

years later, White defeated Cheatham for the nomination and was elected. He was the only Black representative sworn in when the Fifty-fifth Congress met on March 15, 1897. In 1900, White sponsored America's antilynching bill, which proposed to make lynching a federal crime. White tried in vain to secure financial relief for Civil War hero and former congressman Robert Smalls and former Louisiana governor P. B. S. Pinchback. In February 1898, after the Black postmaster of Lake City, South Carolina, and his son were murdered by a white mob, White presented a resolution to secure financial relief for the victim's wife and five surviving children, all of whom had been wounded. Southern white congressmen objected to his request, and it never came to a vote. In his last days in Congress, White spoke before his congressional colleagues, noting the absence of Black congressmen.

After leaving Congress, White developed a Black town (Whitesboro) in Cape May County, New Jersey,

and by 1906, the town had more than eight hundred residents. White soon opened a bank in Philadelphia, the People's Savings Bank, but had to close it because of his poor health.

Plessy v. *Ferguson* DECISION CREATES DOCTRINE OF "SEPARATE BUT EQUAL"

On **MAY 18**, the segregation laws related to public carriers were tested in the U.S. Supreme Court case of *Plessy* v. *Ferguson*. The case concerned Homer Adolphe Plessy, a Black who had purchased a first-class ticket on an intrastate railroad and refused to accept a seat in a coach assigned to Black passengers. He had been arrested and convicted of violating a Louisiana statute mandating railroads to provide separate facilities (coaches) for Black and white passengers. Plessy's lawyer, Albion W. Tourgee, argued the case on the basis of the Thirteenth and Fourteenth Amendments, noting, "Justice is pictured blind and her daughter, the Law, ought at least to be color blind." The U.S. Supreme Court decided against Plessy, declaring the "separate but equal" doctrine constitutional as it related to the civil rights of American Blacks. The Court added, "If one race be inferior to the other socially, the Constitution of the United States cannot put them upon the same plane." The decision allowed racism to be institutionalized and marked the beginning of Jim Crow laws and acceptance of overt racist behavior. Justice John Marshall Harlan dissented.

WASHINGTON AWARDED HONORARY DEGREE BY HARVARD

On **JUNE 24**, Harvard University awarded an honorary master of arts degree to Booker T. Washington, the first ever awarded to an African American.

WILLIAMS AWARDED CONGRESSIONAL MEDAL OF HONOR

On **NOVEMBER 12**, Moses Williams was awarded the Congressional Medal of Honor. Williams was cited for his bravery in the Battle of Curchillo Negro Mountains, New Mexico.

1897 BEARD INVENTS "JENNY COUPLER"

Andrew J. Beard, a Black inventor from Alabama, designed a railroad-car coupling device, for which a New York railroad paid him fifty thousand dollars. This device is now commonly known as the "Jenny coupler." In 1892, Beard had received a patent for a rotary engine.

BLACK TOWN OF LANGSTON FOUNDED

Edwin P. McCabe founded the town of Langston, Oklahoma, named in honor of John M. Langston, a well-known Black antislavery worker, educator, inspector general for the Freedmen's Bureau, and U.S. representative from Virginia.

McCabe, a successful Kansas politician and a state auditor from 1883 to 1887, moved to Oklahoma Territory in 1887. He originally envisioned an all-Black state in Oklahoma Territory and was instrumental in moving three hundred families from North Carolina and five hundred Black families from South Carolina into Oklahoma. Other plans called for more than five thousand families to migrate to Oklahoma. His town was given life with the purchase of 160 acres (forty miles northeast of Oklahoma City) from a white man. McCabe purchased another 160 acres, set up the McCabe Town Company, and sent agents into many parts of the South to encourage settlers to move to his town. The federal government and President Benjamin Harrison provided no support for his "all-Black state" enterprise, and the movement failed.

When McCabe, the town's visionary, accepted the position of deputy auditor for Oklahoma and moved to the state capital, much of the excitement for growth left with him, and the town languished.

FIFTY-FIFTH CONGRESS INCLUDES ONE BLACK

Only one Black congressman was a member of the Fifty-fifth Congress — George H. White of North Carolina.

LOUISIANA'S GRANDFATHER CLAUSE BECOMES MODEL FOR THE SOUTH

The "grandfather clause" in Louisiana's 1897 constitution specified that a person might register and vote if his father or grandfather had been eligible to vote on January 1, 1867, or if he or an ancestor had served in either the Confederate army or the Union army. This provision, which effectively barred Blacks in the South from voting, became a model for other southern states.

LANGSTON UNIVERSITY FOUNDED

Langston University was established by the Oklahoma territorial legislature as the Colored Agricultural and Normal University. Because it was located in the Black town of Langston, the school was often called Langston. The school and town derived their names from John M. Langston, a congressman from Virginia during Reconstruction.

The school's name was formally changed to Langston in 1941. Today, the school is state supported and offers a bachelor's degree in liberal arts, teacher education, and vocational curricula. Enrollment is about 1,250 students.

LYNCHING OF BLACKS CONTINUES

One hundred and twenty-three Blacks were reported lynched this year.

NEW CONTRACT LAW ACCEPTED IN SOUTH CAROLINA

South Carolina adopted a new contract law providing that any laborer, working for a share of the crop or for wages, who takes advances and then "willingly and without just cause fails to perform the reasonable service required of him" could receive a fine or imprisonment. It was relatively easy to convict Blacks of breaking this law and to benefit from their free labor as they worked off fines or prison sentences.

The system was extremely profitable to white planters. In general, private companies or the state itself could use the labor of prisoners while they served their terms. Although the U.S. Supreme Court eventually outlawed the convict-lease system along with peonage (which allowed debtors to be bound to work for their creditors until the debt was paid) in 1911, neither system was stopped. Blacks were still routinely locked up for trivial offenses and sentenced to outrageously long terms. In 1903, for example, Missouri made chicken stealing a *felony* punishable by five years in prison and/or a $200 fine. In Mississippi, the infamous "pig law" exacted up to five years in prison for stealing a pig. Under these conditions, Blacks always formed a disproportionately large segment of the jail population.

In 1904, stiffer penalties were added to extract more unpaid labor from Blacks — even conviction and time spent in jail would not release the worker from the unpaid debt that caused imprisonment in the first place. In 1907, the South Carolina Supreme Court and a federal district court ruled this statute unconstitutional.

In a short time, peonage and contract labor practices were modified to become "no indebtedness due" — thus a case of involuntary servitude or "pure and simple" slavery existed. Blacks who were so unfortunate to be imprisoned for any charge could be released to planters for unspecified work times. In Mississippi, many Blacks (individuals and families) were held in involuntary servitude and peonage, but owing to the "peculiar labor conditions existing in the Delta section," the courts usually chose to take no action on the situation.

AMERICAN NEGRO ACADEMY FOUNDED

On **MARCH 5**, the American Negro Academy was founded by Alexander Crummell for the purpose of promoting African American literature, science, art, and higher education.

1898 *A Trip to Coontown* PRODUCED

A Trip to Coontown, a musical comedy written by Bob Cole, was produced, directed, and managed by Blacks. The first musical comedy written by a Black for Black talent, it opened in New York and ran for three seasons.

BLACK JOCKEY WINS KENTUCKY DERBY

Willie Simms won the Kentucky Derby. He is thought to be the first American jockey to shorten his stirrups and ride in the crouch style, which is now the norm.

BLACK LONGSHOREMEN STRIKE IN TEXAS

In Galveston, Texas, Black longshoremen went on strike for higher wages and better working conditions.

BLACK TROOPS FIGHT IN SPANISH-AMERICAN WAR

At the time of the Spanish-American War, only about twenty-eight thousand troops constituted the regular army. Congress authorized the call for volunteers and the activation of ten regiments of Black troops, but only four were actually formed: the Seventh, Eighth, Ninth, and Tenth United States Volunteers. None saw action because the war lasted only ten weeks. The four Black regiments already in the regular army (Ninth and Tenth Cavalry and Twenty-fourth and Twenty-fifth Infantry) compiled excellent records during this war. Some states permitted Blacks to organize volunteer units such as the Third Alabama, Third North Carolina, Sixth Virginia, Ninth Ohio, Eighth Illinois, and Twenty-third Kansas regiments. Some had Black officers, but their presence upset many whites, who regarded them as unfit for leadership. Of all the Black units in Cuba during the war, only the four Black regular regiments saw combat. Members of the Black Ninth and Tenth Cavalry rescued the Rough Riders from near annihilation. On June 24, the Tenth Cavalry drove Spanish forces from positions at La Guasimas, Cuba. On July 1, the Tenth Cavalry charged El Caney and relieved Theodore Roosevelt's Rough Riders.

Blacks in the navy played an active part in the war. About twenty-two Black sailors went down when the battleship *Maine* was sunk in Havana Harbor in February. Blacks, in general, were sympathetic to the ideals of Cuban rebels, who were fighting against Spain for their independence.

LYNCHING OF BLACKS CONTINUES

As many as 101 Blacks were reported lynched this year.

MOB ATTACKS BLACK FAMILY IN SOUTH CAROLINA

On **FEBRUARY 22**, a Black postmaster was murdered by a mob of whites in Lake City, South Carolina; his wife and daughters were shot and maimed for life.

According to the *Cleveland Gazette*, the postmaster had been threatened and shot at several times in attempts to make him quit his federal job. An official of the federal government, he was assured that he would be protected, even when he was forced to move the post office into his house. In 1898, on George Washington's birthday, a mob of more than one hundred whites rushed his home and set it on fire. As they watched it burn, they shot rounds of bullets into the house. The postmaster tried to escape the flames but was shot dead as he opened the door. He was followed by his wounded wife who was carrying their dead baby. A second child was fatally wounded and two other children were seriously injured. The house burned to the ground. In it, the bodies of the postmaster and an infant were burned to ashes.

MOB TERRORIZES BLACKS IN PHOENIX

A reign of terror was directed against Blacks in and around Phoenix, South Carolina.

NATIONAL BENEFIT LIFE INSURANCE COMPANY FOUNDED

Samuel W. Rutherford organized the National Benefit Life Insurance Company in Washington, D.C. It quickly became the largest Black insurance company in the nation and remained the largest for several years.

NORTH CAROLINA MUTUAL AND PROVIDENT INSURANCE COMPANY ESTABLISHED

Dr. John Merrick and six associates founded the North Carolina Mutual and Provident Insurance Company in Durham, North Carolina. Other founders included Dr. Aaron M. Moore, P. W. Dawkins, D. T. Watson,

W. G. Pearson, E. A. Johnson, and James E. Shepard, each of whom invested an initial fifty dollars. The business rather than the fraternal aspects of insurance were emphasized.

The company failed in 1899, at which time Merrick and Moore bought out the interests of the other five founders. The company was reorganized in 1900 by the pair and Charles Spaulding as the North Carolina Mutual Life Insurance Company. At one time it was the largest Black-owned business in America. When Merrick died in 1918, the company had more than sixteen million dollars of insurance in force. It had more than eight billion dollars of insurance in force in 1991 and operates in almost every state.

RACE RIOT FOMENTED IN NORTH CAROLINA
A race riot erupted in Wilmington, North Carolina. Eight Blacks were killed when white supremacists drove Black officeholders and plain citizens out of town.

SEGREGATION ON TRAINS REQUIRED IN SOUTH CAROLINA
South Carolina passed legislation requiring racial segregation aboard trains.

BLACK WOMEN NURSES SERVE DURING SPANISH-AMERICAN WAR
In JULY, the Surgeon General authorized Namahyoke Sockum Curtus, wife of the chief surgeon at Freedmen's Hospital, Washington, D.C., to recruit Black women nurses, who were considered to be immune to typhoid and yellow fever. (It was generally believed by whites at the time that Blacks were immune, both because of their long residence in warm wet climates, where these diseases were easily transmitted, and because of their "thicker dark skin.") As many as thirty-two Black recruits were dispatched to Camp Thomas in Chickamauga Park, Georgia, to care for typhoid fever patients. The nurses performed admirably, and the U.S. Congress introduced legislation after the war to create a permanent nursing corps in the army. The Army Nurse Corps was authorized in 1901; a Navy Nurse Corps was established in 1908.

NATIONAL AFRO-AMERICAN COUNCIL FOUNDED
On SEPTEMBER 15, the National Afro-American Council was founded in Rochester, New York. The organization proposed a program of protest. Bishop Alexander Walters of the AME Zion Church was elected president.

1899   BLACKS MASSACRED IN GEORGIA
Eight Blacks were massacred in Palmetto, Georgia.

CHESNUTT PUBLISHES STORIES ABOUT SLAVERY
Charles W. Chesnutt (1858–1932) published *The Conjure Woman*, a collection of short stories about slavery. It was written in a dialectic, folktale style that related to the times. Chesnutt wrote several other books of fiction — *The Wife of His Youth and Other Stories of the Color Line* (1899), *The House Behind the Cedars* (1900), and *The Marrow of Tradition* (1901). Although Chesnutt's first book, *The Conjure Woman*, was his best-known work, the Spingarn Medal was awarded to Chesnutt for his recording of the nature and struggles of Black people.

DU BOIS PUBLISHES *The Philadelphia Negro*
W. E. B. Du Bois (1868–1963), an educator, author, and major Black social activist, published his most famous document, *The Philadelphia Negro*, a study of the Black community. In 1944, Du Bois's work was praised by the Swedish sociologist Gunnar Myrdal, in

W. E. B. Du Bois, the first Black to earn a Ph.D. in the field of history, published The Philadelphia Negro, *which became one of the most famous historical works about an African American community.*

An American Dilemma, as a model study of a Black community.

◈ Du Bois was born on February 23, 1868, in Great Barrington, Massachusetts. His father left the family when Du Bois was young, and he was virtually left penniless in 1884 when his mother died. He graduated from high school in that same year and went on to earn a B.A. degree from Fisk University in 1888. In 1895, he became the first Black to receive a Ph.D. from Harvard University. In 1897, Du Bois accepted a position as professor of economics and history at Atlanta University, where he taught until 1910. In 1903, Du Bois published another of his important works, *The Souls of Black Folk*. In 1905, he founded the Niagara Movement to oppose the policies of Booker T. Washington. Du Bois was one of the founders of the National Association for the Advancement of Colored People (NAACP) and served as its director of publicity and research and as editor of its magazine, *Crisis*.

Du Bois is often remembered for his opposition to Washington's accommodationist stance. In fact, Du Bois had maintained cordial relations with Washington for some years. The controversy apparently related to the control that Tuskegee had over political appointments and foundation grants for education, and its opposition to organizations such as the Niagara Movement and the NAACP. When Washington died, Du Bois called him "the greatest Negro leader since Frederick Douglass, and the most distinguished man, white or black who has come out of the South since the Civil War. . . . On the other hand, in stern justice, we must lay on the soul of this man, a heavy responsibility for the consummation of Negro disfranchisement, the decline of the Negro college and the firmer establishment of color caste in this land."

Du Bois bitterly feuded with Marcus Garvey, calling him a "lunatic or a traitor." Garvey, in return, called Du Bois "a white man's nigger."

Du Bois held strong views about racial segregation. He preferred a separate training camp for colored officers at Fort Des Moines in 1917 rather than no camp at all. In a series of editorials in *Crisis*, Du Bois presented the case for voluntary segregation. The disagreement between Du Bois and the board of the NAACP led to his resignation as editor of *Crisis* in 1934.

Du Bois returned to Atlanta University to head the department of sociology. He grew increasingly critical of the United States and its treatment of Black people. In 1961, Du Bois joined the Communist Party and moved to Ghana, where he lived until his death in 1963. He was buried in Accra.

FIFTY-SIXTH CONGRESS INCLUDES ONE BLACK

When the Fifty-sixth Congress convened, the only Black congressman, George H. White of North Carolina, was present.

JOPLIN RELEASES *Maple Leaf Rag*

Scott Joplin (1868–1917), a noted composer and pianist, released one of his finest works, *Maple Leaf Rag*. Joplin was best known for his ragtime music.

In 1911, Joplin wrote an opera, *Treemonisha*. In the 1980s, the music of Scott Joplin was rediscovered by a number of singers and pianists, who revealed the musical genius of this African American to the present generation.

LYNCHING OF BLACKS CONTINUES

Eighty-five Blacks were reported lynched in this year.

NORTH CAROLINA SEGREGATES TRAINS

The North Carolina legislature passed a law that stipulated racial segregation aboard trains.

RACE RIOT ERUPTS IN ILLINOIS

On **APRIL 11**, white and Black workers rioted over mining jobs at Pana, Illinois. Six persons were killed.

NATIONAL AFRO-AMERICAN COUNCIL CALLS FOR DAY OF FASTING

On **JUNE 2**, the National Afro-American Council began its program of protest with a call for Black Americans throughout the country to observe a day of fasting to protest against lynchings and racial massacres.

BAILEY RECEIVES PATENT

On **JULY 18**, L. C. Bailey received a patent for his invention of a folding bed. It was recorded as patent number 629,286.

1900

POPULATION OVERVIEW

BLACK POPULATION IN THE UNITED STATES According to the Bureau of the Census, there were 8.8 million Blacks in the United States, of whom all but 900,000 resided in the South. Blacks made up 11.6 percent of the 75,994,575 total residents.

BLACK POPULATION IN SELECTED CITIES The 1900 census showed that 72 cities had a population of more than 5,000 Blacks. More important, however, there were 14 cities with Black populations in excess of 25,000, and 5 of these had more than 50,000. The cities with the largest Black populations (50,000 or more) included Washington, D.C., with 86,700; Baltimore, with 79,300; New Orleans, with 77,700; Philadelphia, with 62,600; and New York City, with 60,700.

CITIES WITH HIGH BLACK POPULATION GROWTH RATES AND BLACK MAJORITIES

Of the 30 cities with the largest Black populations, 8 experienced growth over the previous decade in excess of 50 percent. Pittsburgh and Chicago had Black population growth rates of 117.1 percent and 111 percent, respectively. Other relatively high rates of Black population growth occurred in Indianapolis, with 74.4 percent; Memphis, with 73.9 percent; New York City and Birmingham, each with 65.7 percent; Philadelphia, with 59 percent; and Little Rock, with 50.9 percent. The 1900 census showed that Blacks outnumbered whites in Charleston, Savannah, Montgomery, Jacksonville, Shreveport, Vicksburg, Baton Rouge, and several other smaller southern cities.

URBANIZATION OF THE BLACK POPULATION

The urban percentage in the Black population increased from 19.8 percent in 1890 to 22.7 percent in 1900. An increase in urbanization in the white population occurred over the same period, from 38.4 percent to 43.0 percent. Overall, the proportion of total urban residents who were Black amounted to only 6.5 percent, about the same proportion as in 1890. Of all rural residents, Blacks composed 15.1 percent in 1900, up slightly from 14.9 percent in 1890. The movement of Blacks from rural into urban communities was gathering momentum. For example, the proportion of Blacks in the South living in urban communities actually increased from 15.3 percent in 1890 to 17.2 percent in 1900; in the North, from 61.8 percent in 1890 to 70.5 percent in 1900; and in the West, from 54 percent in 1890 to 67.4 percent in 1900. Overall, about 80.2 percent of the Black population lived in rural areas in 1890, a figure that dropped to 77.3 percent in 1900. Still 69 percent of all urban Black residents lived in the South, as did 96.6 percent of all rural Black residents.

ECONOMIC CONDITIONS OVERVIEW

BLACK BANKS FLOURISH

By 1900, four Black banks were operating: the Savings Bank of the Grand Fountain United Order of True Reformers, in Richmond, Virginia, founded in 1888; the Capital Savings Bank, in Washington, D.C., founded in 1888; the Mutual Trust Company, in Chattanooga, Tennessee, founded in 1889; and the Alabama Penny Savings and Loan Company, in Birmingham, Alabama, founded in 1890.

BLACK-OWNED FARMS INCREASE IN NUMBER

The number of Black-owned farms reached 193,000. Thirty-five years after emancipation, Blacks had made significant progress in agriculture. In the South Central states, they had acquired 95,624 farms, and there were 348,805 Black tenants of land (21.5 percent of all the farms within this region). In the South Atlantic states, Blacks had acquired 287,933 farms; 70.4 percent were tenant farmers and 29.6 percent were owners outright.

◈ The number of Black-owned farms continued to increase until 1910, when it reached 218,467. Black ownership of farms remained relatively steady until 1920, when it began to decline rapidly, falling to 182,019 in 1930 and 176,263 in 1940.

SOCIAL CONDITIONS OVERVIEW

BLACK COLLEGES FOUNDED

Only nine historically Black colleges and universities (HBCUs) were established in the first decade of the twentieth century — down from fourteen during the previous decade. The trend toward establishing HBCUs in smaller towns continued. Of the nine new institutions, only two were located in large urban areas: Coppin State College in Baltimore, Maryland, and Miles College in Birmingham, Alabama. Newly established HBCUs tended to be located near the edges of the Black cultural hearth. Three new HBCUs were located in Mississippi, and the others were scattered from Maryland to Florida and then west to Louisiana. Grambling College in Grambling, Louisiana, fostered the town's growth. Several of the colleges had specific purposes: Grambling, to teach improved farming methods; Mississippi Industrial and Prentiss Normal and Industrial, to educate teachers and ministers; Miles, to improve the welfare of Black residents of Birmingham.

BLACK EXODUS FROM SOUTH BEGINS

The exodus of Blacks from North Carolina, South Carolina, Mississippi, and Arkansas, as well as other southern states, was believed to be directly related to the lien laws. This new system of involuntary servitude became quite common throughout the South at the turn of the century. In 1901, it was even backed up by a number of state laws supporting servitude and the increasing virulence of racism and violence. Blacks made major efforts to eliminate laws and practices that limited their liberty.

BLACK URBAN LIFE IN THE ALLEY

In Charleston, Savannah, Washington D.C., and other cities throughout the South at this time, the nucleus of the Black population was found along "the alley." In general, the alley had the most deplorable housing environment of any city. Landlords used this space, not suitable for other profitable purposes, for Black housing. Little two-room dwellings were crammed into these "backyard spaces," generally behind decent houses. They were poorly constructed, badly lighted, inadequately ventilated, and without decent sanitation. Because of poor drainage and unfinished sewer systems, alley houses were the most unhealthy when rains made the streets smelly and muddy.

The poorest Blacks in the city lived in the alleys. Their homes had an open fireplace, no ceiling, and no windows. The dwellings had no foundations, so the floors were just above the ground. Heavy rains, flooding, and cold winter temperatures contributed to disproportionate rates of disease and death among Black residents. Four to five persons often lived in a one-room alley dwelling and six in a two-room dwelling. Depending on vacancy rates, the whim of the landlord, and amenities, monthly rent for a two-room dwelling ranged from one dollar and fifty cents to four dollars.

CONVICT-LEASE SYSTEM REMAINS PROFITABLE IN GEORGIA The leasing of convicts to private farms or industries continued to increase state revenues. For example, in 1906, Georgia made a profit of $354,853.55 from leasing out convicts, most of them Black.

EDUCATIONAL OPPORTUNITY EXPANDS INTO COLLEGES Between 1870 and 1900, 2,177 Black persons graduated from American colleges. By contrast, during the period 1820 to 1870, only sixty-six Blacks graduated from American colleges.

ILLITERACY RATE AMONG BLACKS DROPS For the first time in history, the illiteracy rate of the Black population dropped below 50 percent. At 44.5 percent, it was down from 57.1 percent in 1890, and from 70 percent in 1880.

JAZZ EMERGES IN NEW ORLEANS Although the precise date of origin is unknown, it is clear that by the start of the twentieth century, the musical form known as jazz was emerging in New Orleans.

Some believe it originated in Congo Square, where Black slaves had performed music and chants from their African roots. Others claim the music originated in Storyville, an area of prostitution, where Black musicians entertained white clientele. Jazz is thought to borrow from a number of sources: the blues, religious hymns and spirituals, and parts of old French and Spanish music heard in Louisiana. It seems only fitting that it was in this year that one of

the world's most famous jazz musicians, Louis Armstrong, was born in New Orleans.

By 1917, the regional music of New Orleans was known throughout the nation. Within the next decade, New Orleans jazz was being modified by musicians in Chicago, New York, and Kansas City. Original New Orleans jazz almost died out. Today, the legacy of New Orleans jazz can be found in the nightly performances given in Preservation Hall in the city's French Quarter.

"NADIR" IN NEGRO LIFE AND HISTORY Scholars on the Black experience called the period between 1877 and 1900 the "nadir" in Negro life and history. This period was characterized by a disputed election of 1876; the Compromise of 1877, which settled it; the abandonment of Black people by the Republican Party; and the national acceptance of the return of white supremacy in the South.

In the 1876 election, Democrat Samuel J. Tilden was one electoral vote short of victory over Republican Rutherford B. Hayes. Twenty votes from four states (Louisiana, Florida, South Carolina, and Oregon) were in dispute because of alleged intimidation of voters and other illegal practices. A commission of eight Republicans and seven Democratic congressmen and senators gave all twenty votes to Hayes. To soothe southerners' feelings, the Republicans removed all federal troops from the South and agreed to appoint a southerner to the Cabinet. Conservative white southerners thereby essentially regained their states' governments, and although they said they would guarantee Blacks their rights and not prevent them from voting, the promise was never kept. Legalized segregation, discrimination, and political disfranchisement were ushered in with almost full support of federal, state, and local governments.

SEGREGATION UBIQUITOUS IN OKLAHOMA AND ARKANSAS Segregation could be found in just about every arena of life — even the state and county jails, workhouses, convict camps, and other correctional institutions were segregated. In some places, separate phone booths were the rule.

"SWEET AUBURN" DISTRICT BECOMES ATLANTA'S PREMIER BLACK AREA Auburn Avenue in northeast Atlanta was called the "richest Negro street in the world."

◈ Over the next few decades, this street would become the location of the Atlanta Life Insurance Company; WERD, the nation's first Black-owned commercial radio station; the street where Dr. Martin

Luther King, Jr., grew up; the location of the Ebenezer Baptist Church, where King, his father, and his grandfather preached; and the place where Dr. King was buried. The Auburn Avenue district became a national park in 1980.

POLITICAL CONDITIONS OVERVIEW

BLACK REPRESENTATION IN CONGRESS DWINDLES

During the 1869–1901 period, twenty-two Blacks served in the U.S. Congress, sitting in every Congress from the forty-first to the fifty-sixth, with the exception of the Fiftieth Congress. About half were former slaves and half were college educated; all were committed to protecting the civil rights of all Americans.

POLITICAL POWER OF BLACKS IN SOUTHERN STATES

From 1879 to 1901, Blacks served a total of fourteen terms in Congress. Of these, two involved disputed elections (Mississippi and Virginia). The other twelve terms all were served by congressmen from two districts: North Carolina's Second Congressional District and South Carolina's Seventh Congressional District. Blacks were a majority in these two districts, but both were gerrymandered to limit Black political power.

ANTILYNCHING BILL INTRODUCED

Black congressman George H. White of North Carolina introduced the first antilynching bill in Congress. It proposed making lynching a federal crime. Although the bill received support, it never came to a vote.

BLACKS DISFRANCHISED IN ALABAMA

In Alabama, only three thousand of the 181,471 Black males of voting age were registered — less than 2 percent. The lack of political participation by Blacks was related to the state's use of the grandfather clause, poll tax, literacy or understanding requirements, and other means such as intimidation to ensure that Blacks did not vote.

GRANDFATHER CLAUSE DISFRANCHISES VOTERS IN LOUISIANA

In Louisiana, as a result of the grandfather clause and other devices enacted in the new constitution in 1897, only 5,320 Blacks were registered to vote in the national elections; in no parish did they form a majority of the electorate. Yet in the 1896 national election (the last election before disfranchisement), more than 130,344 Blacks were registered to vote, outnumbering white voters in twenty-six parishes. This figure represented a 96 percent decrease in Black voters after only two years under the new constitution. During this time, the number of white voters in the state fell from 164,008 to 125,437, or by about 24 percent. Politicians saw the loss of these white votes as insignificant compared to the net gain of effectively stopping the Black vote.

LYNCHING OF BLACKS CONTINUES

A total of 106 Blacks were reported lynched in this year. Between 1882 and 1900, there were 3,011 lynchings — an average of one every other day. About 85 percent of the victims were Black.

MORTON HEADS NEW YORK POLITICAL MACHINE

Upon the retirement of John H. Nail, Ferdinand Q. Morton became the boss of the New York City Black political machine (the United Color Democracy). He remained a major figure in the organization until the 1930s. During this time, he established the American Labor Party.

NEGRO BUSINESS LEAGUE ORGANIZED

Booker T. Washington organized the National Negro Business League in Boston, Massachusetts. In response to an increase in the number of Black-owned businesses throughout the nation, Washington intended to organize businesses and eventually form larger corporations. Within five years, more than one hundred chapters had been formed in cities around the country. An indication of the goals shared by members of the National Business League was embodied in a 1905 resolution, leading to the formation of the Colorado Springs, Colorado, chapter:

> Whereas, we believe that the time has come for the colored people to enter more largely into business pursuits by means of individual as well as co-operative efforts as the surest and most speedy way to gain earnings from invested capital, and to afford employment for our race, and for the further purpose of stimulating our people in this community to engage in such industrial pursuits as may be practical and possible, therefore be it
>
> Resolved, That we form a local business league — and invite the cooperation of all who desire to better the material condition of our people in this city.
>
> Resolved, That we take steps to present the wonderful undeveloped agricultural and mineral resources of Colorado to desirable colored citizens who

Booker T. Washington here addresses Black people at the opening of a cotton seed mill in Mound Bayou, Mississippi, an all-Black town.

may be induced to settle in this state, bring with them capital, brains and pluck for the purpose of seeking permanent homes and helping to develop the natural resources of this state.

RACIAL DISTURBANCE IN FLORIDA

An encounter between a Black man, Jack Trice, and a white mob occurred in Palmetto, Florida, after Trice's fourteen-year-old son had fought with the son of Palmetto's white town marshal. The marshal's son reported the incident to his father, who quickly summoned fourteen of his fellow citizens. They arrived at Trice's house at 3:00 A.M. and demanded that the boy come outside for punishment. When Trice refused to give up his son, the mob opened fire on the house. Trice returned the fire, fatally striking the marshal

with his first bullet. One of the mob then tried to burn the house, but Trice shot him in the head. When the mob rushed the house, Trice mortally wounded another. As the mob retreated for reinforcement, Trice fired, shooting another white in the back. In a few hours, a larger mob returned, but Trice and his son had fled.

VIRGINIA SEGREGATES TRAINS

Virginia passed legislation requiring segregation on trains.

BLACK NATIONAL ANTHEM PERFORMED

"Lift Ev'ry Voice and Sing," the Black national anthem, was first performed on **FEBRUARY 12** at a celebration of Abraham Lincoln's birthday. Written especially for the occasion by James Weldon Johnson and his brother J. Rosamond Johnson, it was sung by a chorus of five hundred schoolchildren. The anthem continues to be widely sung by Blacks.

McCOY RECEIVES PATENT

On **MARCH 26**, Elijah McCoy (1843–1929) applied for a patent for his invention of the graphite lubricator. He applied for another in December.

McCoy's invention made it possible for engines to be lubricated while in motion. Previously, engines had to be stopped to be lubricated. McCoy eventually held more than twenty patents on lubricator-related inventions.

◈ Elijah McCoy was born in Colchester, Ontario, in 1843 of runaway slave parents. After the Civil War, his family moved to the United States. McCoy hoped to study engineering, but he was unable to receive the proper training because engineering was considered an unsuitable job for Blacks at the time. McCoy subsequently moved to Scotland and successfully completed his education there. Upon his return to the United States, McCoy took a job with the Michigan Central Railroad as a fireman (a job frequently held by Blacks), shoveling coal into the engine. He was astonished that the engine had to be stopped every time it needed lubrication. McCoy designed a lubricating cup that allowed oil to drip onto the engine (or other machinery) when needed. This invention was credited with saving factory owners a fortune in lost time. Imitations of his product soon emerged, but all were inferior. As customers often asked whether a lubricating machine was the "real McCoy," the term eventually came to mean something genuine and dependable. McCoy invented many other devices, including a lawn sprinkler, and started his own company, the Elijah McCoy Manufacturing Company, in Detroit, Michigan. Many of McCoy's inventions are displayed at the Henry Ford Museum in Dearborn, Michigan. Ford's auto business was helped by several of McCoy's inventions.

PAN-AFRICAN CONGRESS HELD IN LONDON

On **JULY 23** through **25**, the Pan-African Congress convened in London. Several national and international Black leaders were in attendance, among them, W. E. B. Du Bois, Bishop Alexander Walters, and H. Sylvester Williams, a lawyer with a London practice. Two women educators, Anna Julia Cooper and Anna H. Jones, also addressed the congress.

RACE RIOT OCCURS IN NEW ORLEANS

On **JULY 24**, a race riot erupted in New Orleans and continued for five days. Several persons were injured; a Black school and thirty Black homes were burned. The riot began when two policemen were murdered, allegedly, by Robert Charles, a Black man. Frustrated by their inability to catch the murderer, policemen and white racists congregated at Lee Monument in the well-to-do section of the city to incite mob action. The group, which quickly grew to five hundred in number, marched up St. Charles Avenue, stopping streetcars and taking Black passengers off and beating them. The police did not intervene, despite hundreds of appeals by women and children. In an effort to protect its riders, the Carrollton and New Orleans Street Car Company ordered all Blacks off the cars before they reached the mob. As soon as members of the mob heard this, they marched farther into the Black area, attacking any Black in their path, regardless of age or disability.

The mob then changed its course and moved toward the parish prison to lynch a Black man named Pierce, who was with Robert Charles when the incident occurred. After meeting several hundred armed deputies, members of the mob turned back and reentered the Black section, where they killed one Black man and a newsboy. The police marched behind the mob as vocal supporters and interfered only to protect certain stores from being looted. People broke into a number of stores on Rampart Street to secure guns and ammunition, however, without police intervention. When the streets were cleared of Black people, the mob eventually dispersed.

The following day started with isolated mistreatment of Blacks, but as Blacks began to arm themselves and show resistance, the mayor swore in five hundred special policemen and called for fifteen hundred members of the state militia. By nightfall on July 26, Blacks had been removed from the streets. The police, state militia, and to some extent, the mob, had gained control of the city. Because the police visibly supported the white mob, it was not surprising that no white person was arrested or even taken into custody for murder, assault, or disturbing the peace.

On **JULY 27**, the police located Robert Charles in a residential section of the city. During a gun battle lasting several hours, hundreds of shots were fired. Charles allegedly killed several policemen and wounded other citizens. He eventually was smoked out and literally shot to pieces.

On **JULY 28**, the mob sought still more vengeance, roaming through the Black community and setting fire to more than thirty residences. Thomy Lafon School, one of the few Black schools in the city, had already been torched. Again, the police expressed outward sympathy with the mob, and some police officers actively participated in the violence.

RACE RIOT OCCURS IN NEW YORK CITY
On **AUGUST 15**, a racial disturbance occurred in the West Side Tenderloin district of New York City when white residents, mostly Irish, moved into the district, assaulting and beating Blacks. The violence escalated when a Black man, Arthur J. Harris, killed a policeman in a scuffle. White mobs assaulted Blacks and pulled them from trolley cars. Police participated in clubbing and kicking Blacks. Many Blacks retaliated by throwing objects from their apartment windows. Police responded by firing their guns in the direction of those windows. During the first three hours of this mob violence, the *New York Age* noted not a single white was arrested, but many Blacks were taken into custody. Clashes between whites and Blacks continued for several days. Both Blacks and whites condemned the abuse by police during the riots. The Urban League published a pamphlet detailing some seventy-eight acts of police brutality committed during the riot.

BLACK DUO MAKES RECORDS
On **OCTOBER 11**, Bert Williams and George Walker made several records for the Victor Talking Machine Company. They were the first Black recording artists.

1901 *Boston Guardian* FOUNDED
The *Boston Guardian* was founded, edited by William Monroe Trotter and George Forbes, both of whom opposed Booker T. Washington's hegemony over the Black community. Although many agreed with Washington's view on industrial education, Trotter and Forbes saw it as limiting. The *Boston Guardian* gathered together a group of Black intellectuals and formed the Niagara Movement. W. E. B. Du Bois was selected to head the group.

GRAMBLING COLLEGE FOUNDED
Grambling College was founded as the Lincoln Parish Training School, an industrial education school. In response to a request for help, Booker T. Washington sent Charles P. Adams to assist in founding the school. The school was patterned after Tuskegee Institute, with a strong emphasis on industrial education.

Fidelia Jewett, a philanthropist, later donated funds to move the school to its present site and improve its industrial school curricula. By 1918, it was controlled by the Lincoln Parish School Board, and in 1940, it instituted a four-year program, with additional emphasis on training teachers for small rural schools. By 1954, the school provided training for the study of medicine, law, and dentistry. The school continues to offer professional programs, as well as degrees in teacher education and liberal arts. Grambling currently has an enrollment of about thirty-six hundred students.

WASHINGTON INVITED TO WHITE HOUSE
President Theodore Roosevelt invited Booker T. Washington to dine at the White House on **OCTOBER 16**. Roosevelt was criticized by whites throughout the nation, particularly in the South. In this year, Booker T. Washington also published his autobiography, *Up from Slavery*, examining his life and philosophy.

ALABAMA ADOPTS NEW CONSTITUTION
On **NOVEMBER 28**, Alabama adopted a new constitution that included literacy and property tests, along with a grandfather clause, that effectively disfranchised Blacks. In 1903, the U.S. Supreme Court upheld these clauses.

1902 DISPUTE OVER BLACK POSTMISTRESS IN MISSISSIPPI
Minnie Cox, a Black postmistress in Indianola, Mississippi, offered to resign after whites protested her reappointment. They claimed that the reappointment allowed for "nigger domination." President Theodore Roosevelt refused to accept her resignation and suspended postal service to the town. Cox left Indianola in 1903 but returned a year later after the controversy had faded.

VIRGINIA IMPOSES "UNDERSTANDING TEST" AND "TAX REQUIREMENT" ON BLACK VOTERS
In Virginia, a total of 147,000 Black men of voting age were registered prior to this time. With the implementation and enforcement of the "understanding test" and the "tax requirement," the number of Black registered voters was reduced to only 21,000 by 1905.

1903 FEDERAL COURT ATTACKS PEONAGE
A secret service report on peonage in Alabama, submitted in 1903, revealed widespread, flagrant abuses

of Blacks, particularly of Black men. The study was initiated by Thomas G. Jones, a white federal district judge for the Middle District of Alabama, with the support of Booker T. Washington.

After reviewing the secret service report, Jones impaneled a federal grand jury to continue investigating. The grand jury concluded that a widespread pattern of peonage existed, involving the collaboration of wealthy landowners, local constables, justices of the peace, and plantation overseers. The system worked as follows: A Black was often arrested on a baseless charge and sentenced to pay a fine he could not afford. The offender was then given the opportunity to pay the fine by working off the time. By odd circumstance, a planter just happened to be in court. An agreement would later be signed, and the offender taken to the large plantation to work off the fine.

Judge Jones finally declared the Alabama law violated the constitution of Alabama and the Constitution of the United States. Before his investigation was complete, Jones uncovered extensive and abusive forced labor in Coosa, Tallapoosa, and Lowndes Counties. Although many were brought to trial and convicted of breaking state and federal laws against forced labor, Jones exacted minimal jail terms and fines on those convicted. His efforts were geared more toward exposing a heinous crime in the hope that public awareness would result in preventing its recurrence. Booker T. Washington worked behind the scenes to stimulate and encourage the research and its outcome.

The Souls of Black Folk INTENSIFIES RIFT BETWEEN DU BOIS AND WASHINGTON

W. E. B. Du Bois published *The Souls of Black Folk*, which crystallized opposition to Booker T. Washington's program of social and political subordination to whites. The division between the supporters of Du Bois and Washington grew acrimonious. The poet James Weldon Johnson, who was a friend of Du Bois, wrote, "One cannot imagine the bitterness of antagonism between these two wings."

WALKER OPENS ST. LUKE PENNY SAVINGS BANK

Maggie Lena Walker (1867–1934) of Richmond, Virginia, became the first African American woman in America to own and operate a bank when she opened the St. Luke Penny Savings Bank in Richmond, Virginia.

Walker had worked as a secretary for the Order of St. Luke, a Black fraternal organization. She started

Maggie Lena Walker, the founder and leader of the Saint Luke Penny Savings Bank in Richmond, Virginia, argued for and promoted Black economic self-reliance for many years before she herself achieved it. With only $9,000 in initial deposits, Walker increased her bank's holdings until it had more than $376,000 in deposits in 1919. Saint Luke's Bank and Trust Company, as it was eventually called, helped Blacks secure educational, housing, and other loans.

the bank and insurance company as a way for Black businessmen to get credit or insurance that they could not obtain from white firms. The Penny Bank eventually became the Consolidated Bank and Trust Company, the largest Black-owned bank in the country.

BLACK TOWN OF BOLEY FOUNDED IN OKLAHOMA

By this time, Black towns had developed throughout Oklahoma. Their number increased with heightened racism in the South. Among these settlements were Arkansas Colored, Bailey, Bookertee, Canadian Colored, Chase, Ferguson, Foremen, Gibson Station, Lewisville, Liberty, Lima, Lincoln City, Lincoln (later called Clearview), Marshalltown, North Folk Colored, Overton, Red Bird, Rentiesville, Summit, Taft, Tatums, Tallahassee, Wernon, Wellston Colony, Wild Cat (later called Grayson), and Wybark.

In **AUGUST**, Boley was established as an all-Black town. Located about ninety miles southwest of Tulsa, this new settlement was the product of Black migrants from the South and the Midwest. They settled here because of heightened racism in their areas of origin and the lure of land ownership. The Fort Smith and Western Railroad played an important part in the development of Boley, and the town was actually named for the road master of the railroad. As the railroad expanded toward the territorial capital of Guthrie, it encouraged settlements along the route.

The area that was to become Boley was also selected as the Black town site because of its proximity to Creek territory. The Creek, like other Native American peoples that were forced to move to Oklahoma Territory, had kept slaves. The Creek had the largest number of freed Blacks after the Civil War, and many moved the short distance to Boley.

Booker T. Washington, visiting Boley in 1905, described it as a thriving town of approximately two thousand residents, "with two banks, two cottongins, a newspaper, a hotel, and a 'college,' the Creek-Seminole College and Agricultural Institute." In an article in 1908, a year after Oklahoma had become a state, Washington described Boley as "on the edge of civilization." Although the city was on the railway, it was some distance from a large city. Blacks practiced law and order and self-government in Boley. The city had a cadre of government officials, and residents included people of all classes. T. R. Ringe, the mayor, was born a slave in Kentucky. E. L. Lugrande, a stockholder in the new bank, was from Denton, Texas. D. J. Turner, owner of the drugstore, grew up among Native Americans in Indian Territory.

Many of Boley's citizens were farmers from Texas, Arkansas, and Mississippi, drawn to the area by plentiful cheap land. The town attracted doctors, lawyers, and craftworkers from other places as well. Today, Boley remains an all-Black town, but its representation of the struggle of the "Negro for moral, industrial and political freedom" may be disappearing as opportunities elsewhere lure townspeople away. Over the last couple of decades, the town has almost become a ghost town, and as the population in the surrounding area declines and small farmers sell their land to larger landholders, its survival is uncertain.

1904 BETHUNE ESTABLISHES NORMAL INDUSTRIAL INSTITUTE FOR GIRLS

Educator Mary McLeod Bethune (1875–1955) opened the first Black institution in Florida to offer education beyond the elementary grades. She started her school for the training of teachers in Daytona Beach, a community where one-third of the population was Black. Most of the residents worked in the resort business. Her school opened with just five students. Bethune hoped to find a benefactor for her school among the millionaires who vacationed in Daytona Beach.

James Gamble of Proctor and Gamble supported the school in its early years. He had been asked by Bethune to come and see her school. When he arrived, he found her sitting on a chair next to a crate. When asked where the school was, she responded, "In my mind . . . and in my soul." Bethune and her students were resourceful fundraisers. For example, they sold sweet potato pies and ice cream to railroad crews. They eventually bought the city dump and reclaimed it as the new school campus. The school merged with Cookman Institute, a male school, in 1922. Many of the workers who built the campus facilities took part of their pay in tuition credits after the merger.

BLACK ATHLETE COMPETES IN OLYMPIC GAMES

The first Black to compete and win a medal in the Olympics was George Poage of the Milwaukee Athletic Club. Poage participated in the 400-meter race and won the bronze medal in the 400-meter hurdles in the Games held in St. Louis.

DEPRIEST ELECTED COUNTY COMMISSIONER

Oscar DePriest was elected to the County Board of Commissioners in Cook County, Illinois. He was re-elected in 1906. In 1928, DePriest was elected to the U.S. House of Representatives.

LEAGUE FOR THE PROTECTION OF COLORED WOMEN ESTABLISHED

The League for the Protection of Colored Women was established to combat unethical practices by northern employment agencies. The league gathered evidence showing that irresponsible agencies were using false claims to entice Black girls to the North. It provided aid in the form of jobs and lodging for women who arrived and found no job as promised.

NATIONAL LIBERTY PARTY FORMED

The National Liberty Party, an all-Black national political organization, was formed.

WHITE MOB TERRORIZES BLACKS IN STATESBORO, GEORGIA

When two Black men were convicted of murdering a white family, a white mob gathered in this small town to avenge the crime. The mob seized and burned the two Black men who allegedly committed the crime and then went on a rampage, beating and whipping Black citizens and destroying their property. Several persons were killed.

CREDO PUBLISHED BY W. E. B. DU BOIS

In **OCTOBER**, W. E. B. Du Bois published his credo in the *Independent*, a New York journal. In his words, "I believe in liberty for all men; the space to stretch their arms and their souls; the right to breathe and the right to vote, the freedom to choose their friends, enjoy the sunshine and ride on the railroads, uncursed by color; thinking, dreaming, working as they will in a kingdom of God and love." The credo was so well received that it was printed in scroll form and Black Americans hung it on their walls.

1905 JEANNES DONATES MONEY FOR BLACK EDUCATION

Anna T. Jeannes, a Philadelphia philanthropist, donated two hundred thousand dollars to the General Education Fund to enhance the education of Blacks in the South.

RACE RIOT ERUPTS IN NEW YORK CITY

A racial riot occurred in the San Juan Hill district of New York City. It stemmed from police abuse of Black citizens and poor relations between the predominantly Irish police and the Black community. The *New York Age* and *New York Post* rebuked the police for their brutality against Black citizens. Blacks re-created the Citizens' Protective League to protect the rights of Black citizens. Later, the NAACP established the New York Vigilance Committee to investigate police brutality against Blacks. According to most newspaper accounts, including the *New York Times*, the *Weekly Anglo African*, the *New York Globe*, and others, the Irish abused Black residents because they competed for similar housing and jobs. The papers reported that the Irish practiced bigotry to maintain control of labor unions in the city.

WETMORE ELECTED TO JACKSONVILLE, FLORIDA, CITY COUNCIL

J. Douglas Wetmore, a Democrat, became the first Black elected to the Jacksonville City Council in Florida.

Chicago Defender FOUNDED

On **MAY 15**, Robert Sengstacke Abbott published the first issue of the *Chicago Defender*. It sold only three hundred copies.

The *Defender* became a national newspaper with circulation of 250,000 in 1929. The *Defender* was well known for its attacks on racial injustice in the South, specifically discrimination, segregation, and lynching. The newspaper was also credited with encouraging much of the migration from southern states by providing information about opportunities in the North. Within a couple of decades, the *Defender* became one of the most influential newspapers in the country.

Abbott, born the son of former slaves in Savannah, Georgia, graduated from Kent Law School in Chicago in 1899. When he was told he was "too dark" to practice law in this country, he turned his energies toward newspaper publishing.

NIAGARA MOVEMENT ORGANIZED

On **JULY 11** through **13**, twenty-nine Black intellectuals from fourteen states, headed by W. E. B. Du Bois, met in Fort Erie, Canada, and organized the Niagara Movement, which demanded the abolition of all forms of racial discrimination. In addition, the organization called for school integration, voting rights, and the election of Blacks to political offices. Those present included William Monroe Trotter, J. Max Barber, and John Hope. The Niagara Movement remained operational for only five years, perhaps because it did not gain widespread acceptance. It is frequently cited as the precursor to the National Association for the Advancement of Colored People (NAACP), organized in 1909.

ATLANTA LIFE INSURANCE COMPANY FOUNDED

On **SEPTEMBER 3**, Alonzo F. Herndon opened the Atlanta Life Insurance Company in Atlanta, Georgia. The firm grew rapidly with business from the city's growing Black middle class.

Herndon began life as a slave near Social Circle, Georgia. After emancipation, he moved to Atlanta and opened a barbershop. At one time, Herndon was the wealthiest Black businessman in the country.

1906 BLACK FRATERNITY FOUNDED AT CORNELL

Alpha Phi Alpha Fraternity, the first Black fraternity, was founded at Cornell University in Ithaca, New York. Membership today exceeds seventy-five thousand. The fraternity promotes academic excellence and supports community service activities.

GEORGIA EQUAL RIGHTS CONVENTION HELD

The Georgia Equal Rights Convention was held in Macon, Georgia. Approximately five hundred delegates attended.

RACE RIOT OCCURS IN ATLANTA

Atlanta erupted in racial violence; ten Blacks and two whites were killed. Martial law was proclaimed. The riot grew out of sensational reporting in the newspapers of a "crime wave" of rape and murder committed by Blacks. Newspaper stories depicted planned aggression by Blacks against whites.

SOLVENT SAVINGS BANK AND TRUST FOUNDED

Robert Church, Sr., a former slave, founded the Solvent Savings Bank and Trust Company in Memphis, Tennessee. It was one of the fastest growing Black-owned banks of the early twentieth century. Church was the father of Mary Church Terrell, first president of the National Association of Colored Women. At the time of his death in 1912, Church was probably the first Black American millionaire.

HOPE BECOMES PRESIDENT OF MOREHOUSE COLLEGE

John Hope (1868–1936), an educator and civil rights leader, was selected to be president of Morehouse College in Atlanta, Georgia. Hope was the first African American to hold this position. Hope supported education for Blacks similar to that received by whites, rather than the manual and technical education advocated by Booker T. Washington.

RACE RIOT FLARES UP IN TEXAS

On AUGUST 13, racial insults provoked a group of Black soldiers to raid Brownsville, Texas; one white man was killed, and two others were wounded. President Theodore Roosevelt dishonorably discharged three companies of the Black Twenty-fifth Regiment for alleged involvement in the raid. This action changed Blacks' perception of President Roosevelt as supportive of their cause.

NIAGARA MOVEMENT MEETS

On AUGUST 15–19, the Niagara Movement held its second meeting at Harpers Ferry, West Virginia, to commemorate John Brown's raid. W. E. B. Du Bois, one of the founders, demanded full citizenship rights for African Americans.

1907 LOCKE BECOMES FIRST BLACK RHODES SCHOLAR

Alain Locke, an educator and writer with a Ph.D. from Harvard University, became the first Black Rhodes scholar.

NATIONAL PRIMITIVE BAPTIST CONVENTION HELD

In this year, Black Baptist churches formed after the Civil War met to organize specific Christian themes to be followed by its members. They agreed to follow three religious rites: baptism, Holy Communion, and foot washing. Among other items agreed upon by the members were a publishing house, women's auxiliaries and missions, training unions, and schools. Today, as many as two thousand Black churches are members of this organization.

OKLAHOMA SEGREGATES STREETCARS

The Oklahoma legislature passed state laws adopting segregated streetcars.

THE *Union* BEGINS PUBLICATION

On FEBRUARY 13, Wendell P. Dabney published the *Union*, a Black newspaper in Cincinnati, Ohio. The paper, according to Dabney, was printed to unite Black people.

PEOPLE'S SAVINGS BANK INCORPORATED

On SEPTEMBER 26, the People's Savings Bank was officially incorporated in Philadelphia. Its founder was George H. White, a former U.S. congressman, who wanted the bank to build self-sufficiency among African Americans by lending money for homes and businesses.

It closed in 1918 after White became seriously ill.

1908 BLACK SORORITY FOUNDED

Alpha Kappa Alpha, the country's first Black sorority, was founded at Howard University in Washington, D.C. The organization's primary goal was to improve quality of life for Blacks throughout the world. Current membership is estimated at one hundred thousand.

Jack Johnson, the first Black heavyweight boxing champion, became the center of racial controversy after he defeated Tommy Burns. The white public demanded that the former champion, Jim Jeffries, come out of retirement and take the title from Johnson.

BLACK TOWN OF ALLENSWORTH FOUNDED IN CALIFORNIA

Colonel Allen Allensworth, a former slave from Kentucky, and his family and friends founded the town of Allensworth in the San Joaquin Valley, north of Bakersfield, California. Allensworth hoped that the town would provide a means for Black self-sufficiency and enable Black residents to escape the racial animosities they faced elsewhere. The small agricultural community prospered until a water shortage forced the settlers to leave.

◈ Allensworth once rode as a jockey in many races in Louisville. During the Civil War, he served in the Union navy and later was chaplain of the Black Twenty-Fourth Infantry Regiment.

Today, Allensworth, the only town in California founded, financed, and governed by Blacks, survives as a historical state park.

BLACKS LYNCHED IN HOUSTON

Six Blacks were lynched in Houston. They were suspected of plotting a murder.

CURFEW IMPOSED ON BLACKS IN MOBILE, ALABAMA

The Mobile City Council passed a curfew law applying exclusively to Blacks and requiring them to be off city streets by 10:00 P.M.

JOHNSON BECOMES FIRST BLACK HEAVYWEIGHT BOXING CHAMPION

Jack Johnson (1878–1946) defeated Tommy Burns in Sydney, Australia, to become the first Black heavyweight boxing champion, knocking Burns out in the fourteenth round. The search for a "great white hope" to reclaim the heavyweight title got under way immediately.

◈ In 1912, Jack Johnson jumped bail and left the United States after being arrested on charges of violating the Mann Act (a law prohibiting the transportation of women across state lines for immoral purposes). Many Blacks saw this as just another form of discrimination and racism against outspoken and visible Blacks. Johnson was not only flamboyant but also was frequently found in the company of white women — a behavior that provoked many white supremacists. In 1915, Jess Willard (a white boxer) defeated Johnson. Sometime later, Johnson claimed that the fight had been fixed.

RACE RIOT ERUPTS IN ILLINOIS

On **AUGUST 14** and **15**, a race riot occurred in Springfield, Illinois. Blacks were lynched within half a mile of Abraham Lincoln's home. Troops were called in to calm the situation. This riot, a pivotal event in the founding of the NAACP, began with a white woman's false accusations of rape by a Black handyman. Tensions ran high because a group of Blacks had recently arrived in the area, previously settled by white southerners. The whites resented the use of Blacks as strikebreakers in the coal mines and felt that Blacks were competing with them for jobs. The state militia quelled the riot after two days, during which eight Blacks died and two thousand fled the city. Whites tried to drive all remaining Blacks out of the community, and whites who did not fire their Black employees received death threats.

1909 ATTAWAY FOUNDS BLACK LIFE INSURANCE COMPANY

Dr. William A. Attaway established the Mississippi Life Insurance Company with a loan of fifty thousand dollars.

NATIONAL ASSOCIATION OF COLORED GRADUATE NURSES

The National Association of Colored Graduate Nurses (NACGN), the first professional organization of Black women, was founded by Martha M. Franklin, Ada Thoms, and more than fifty other nurses. The purpose of the association was to work for professional recognition of Black nurses and to increase the number of Blacks entering nursing schools throughout the country and to improve the quality of their training.

U.S. SENATE INVESTIGATES BROWNSVILLE RIOTS

The U.S. Senate investigated the race riot in Brownsville, Texas, after which an entire battalion of Black troops was dishonorably discharged. As a result, all qualified soldiers were allowed to reenlist. Their records, however, still contained dishonorable discharges.

NATIONAL ASSOCIATION FOR THE ADVANCEMENT OF COLORED PEOPLE (NAACP) FOUNDED

On **FEBRUARY 12**, the National Association for the Advancement of Colored People (NAACP) was founded in New York City. Its founding began with the publication of a document, "The Call," supported by forty-seven whites and six Blacks. It was published in newspapers across the country, urging leaders to address issues important to Blacks. The NAACP absorbed the Niagara Movement. Moorfield Storey, a white Boston attorney, was named its first president. W. E. B. Du Bois was named director of publicity and research. Du Bois edited *Crisis*, the official journal of the NAACP, from 1910 to 1933. On May 31, the NAACP held its first conference in New York City. Approximately three hundred Blacks and whites attended. A number of civil rights leaders spoke at the conference, identifying an agenda for the organization.

HENSON PLACES U.S. FLAG AT NORTH POLE

On **APRIL 6**, Matthew Henson (1866–1955), a member of Admiral Robert E. Peary's expedition, placed the American flag at the North Pole. Records show that Henson was actually the first person to reach the North Pole. Henson twice saved Peary's life.

◈ "Plant the Stars and Stripes over there, Matt — at the North Pole," directed Peary. Peary and Henson had finally reached their goal after seven previous expeditions. Henson and Peary had built a great companionship over their twenty-three years of joint exploration. Henson had traveled with Peary to the Arctic seven times, knew the Inuit language, and had become skilled at many tasks needed for survival in this region. In 1912, Henson wrote of his experiences in *A Negro Explorer at the North Pole*. For thirty years after his journey, Henson worked as a clerk in the federal customs house in New York. In 1945, Congress awarded Henson a medal for "outstanding service to the Government of the United States in the field of science." In 1955, President Dwight D. Eisenhower honored Henson at the White House. A decade later, Henson's home state, Maryland, placed a plaque in his memory in the state house — the first time a Black person was honored in such a manner in all of the South.

When Henson died, he was initially buried in a shared grave in New York because there was not enough money for a separate grave. In 1988, seventy-nine years to the day after Henson reached the North Pole, his remains were reinterred in Arlington National Cemetery, next to those of Admiral Robert E. Peary, and Henson was recognized equally as the first to reach the North Pole.

Amsterdam News FOUNDED

On **DECEMBER 4**, the New York *Amsterdam News* was founded by James Anderson. Today it has a circulation of almost thirty-five thousand and is one of the oldest continuously published African American newspapers in the country.

1910

POPULATION OVERVIEW

BLACK POPULATION IN THE UNITED STATES The U.S. population numbered 93,402,151 residents, of which 10.7 percent (9,827,763) were Blacks.

IMMIGRATION INFLUENCES MIGRATION OF BLACKS Between 1870 and 1910, almost 19 million immigrants came to the United States. During the same 40-year period, the North and the West experienced a net migration gain of only about 386,000 Blacks. Racism, riots, and the intense competition for jobs with new immigrants, particularly the Irish, caused a mere sluggish flow of Black migrants to these regions.

CULTURAL HEARTH OF BLACK AMERICA STILL LOCATED IN SOUTH The South contained about 89 percent of the entire Black population in this country. The cultural hearth of Black America remained concentrated within the geographic boundaries of the plantation areas and the Cotton Belt in the South.

BLACK MIGRATION, NORTH AND SOUTH The Bureau of the Census showed that Blacks numbered 9.8 million; only 1 million resided outside the South. In the next decade, the "Great Migration" of more than 2 million southern Blacks began, as large numbers migrated north and west in search of new housing and employment opportunities. Before the decade 1910–1920 was over, the South had experienced an estimated net migration of 454,000 Blacks.

BLACK RESIDENTS IN CITIES In 1910, Washington, D.C., had the largest concentration of Black residents of any city in the country, almost 95,000 Blacks. It was followed by New York City, New Orleans, Baltimore, and Philadelphia. Baltimore, which ranked first in number of Black residents in 1860 and second during the next 4 decades, had thus dropped to fourth. Only 1 of these 5 cities was located in the Deep South. This distribution highlighted the continuing exodus of Blacks from the South and into northeastern and border cities. Only 8 cities had more than 50,000 Black residents; 10 cities had between 25,000 and 50,000 Black residents; and 25 cities had between 10,000 and 25,000 Blacks.

Of these Black population centers, Birmingham recorded the highest percentage growth during the 1900–1910 decade, 215.6 percent. It was followed by Dallas, whose Black population grew by 99.5 percent; Jacksonville, by 80.4 percent; Houston, by 63.8 per-

cent; and Shreveport, by 62.7 percent. Birmingham also had the largest absolute growth of Black residents (35,730); it was followed by New York City, with 31,000; Philadelphia, with 21,846; and Atlanta, with 16,175. Black residents held a majority in five large cities — Charleston, Savannah, Jacksonville, Vicksburg, and Montgomery — but in each of these cases, the Black population's share of the city total population had declined. Black residents in 20 cities made up between 33 percent and 50 percent of the total population.

BLACK RESIDENTS IN CALIFORNIA As many as 43.4 percent of Blacks living in California resided in Los Angeles County.

ECONOMIC CONDITIONS OVERVIEW

BLACK FARMERS AND FARM WORKERS The Bureau of the Census recorded that more than half of gainfully employed Blacks worked in agriculture. Half of the remainder (one-fourth) worked in domestic occupations. The number of Black farmers had increased over the past decade from 769,528 to 924,450. Of these, 26 percent were farm owners and 74 percent tenant farmers. Of the tenants, just over 42 percent were sharecroppers. The three-quarters of Black farmers who were sharecroppers or cash tenants formed an integral part of the southern economy. They produced 53 percent of all the cotton, 29 percent of the sweet potatoes, 28 percent of the dry peas, 27 percent of the peanuts, 19 percent of the corn, 16 percent of the tobacco, and 11 percent of the potatoes harvested in the South, for an estimated annual yield value of $373 million.

BOLL WEEVIL TRIGGERS ADDITIONAL BLACK MIGRATION NORTH Toward the middle of the decade, the cotton crop in much of the South was devastated by the boll weevil, which burrowed into the cotton boll and destroyed it. With little chance to make money off the crop, large numbers of Blacks sought economic opportunities by moving north.

LABOR AGENTS RECRUIT BLACKS Steel mills, stockyards, ammunition depots, automotive industries, and the Pennsylvania Railroad sent labor agents into Black areas of Georgia, Florida, Mississippi, and other southern states to recruit Black workers to offset losses of white workers to the military. The *Chicago Defender* encouraged many southern Blacks to migrate north after being promised jobs by agents. The Pennsylvania Railroad recruited as many as twelve thousand Black men to work on rail tracks and in the yards. Black women were also recruited to work in factories.

SOCIAL CONDITIONS OVERVIEW

BLACK COLLEGES FOUNDED Only five historically Black colleges and universities (HBCUs) were established in the decade in which the Great Migration of Blacks from the South to the North began. All but one of these colleges was located in a moderately sized urban area, perhaps to enhance the opportunities, including teaching, for the increasing number of Blacks living in rapidly growing urban America. California got its first HBCU, Compton State. Only one of the five new HBCUs, Tennessee State, was started as a state-supported institution. The others were private colleges with a principal focus on educating teachers.

NAACP DECLARES RESIDENTIAL SEGREGATION GREATEST RACIAL ISSUE According to the NAACP, the greatest issue facing Blacks in this year was residential segregation. According to their own report in the March issue of *Crisis*, "This discriminatory practice arose in three forms: attempts at residential segregation through property-holders' covenants; efforts toward that end through mob violence; legislation designed to force Negroes to live in restricted areas." Property holders' covenants were contracts agreed upon by residents of a block or district not to sell or rent to Blacks for a specified number of years. Segregation ordinances were passed by city councils to prohibit whites and Blacks from living together.

COMMITTEE ON URBAN CONDITIONS FOUNDED

The Committee on Urban Conditions was founded in New York by Ruth Standish Baldwin and Dr. George E. Haynes, who was one of only three trained Black social workers in the nation.

The primary purpose of the committee was to assist rural Blacks to adjust to city life. Haynes was selected to serve as its executive director. In 1911, it merged with several organizations to become the National Urban League.

Baldwin, a wealthy white woman, had previously been active in the League for the Protection of Colored Women. She was also the widow of the late William Baldwin, Jr., president of the Long Island Railroad.

BRITISH PEOPLE HEAR TWO VERSIONS OF "NEGRO CRISIS"

Both Booker T. Washington and W. E. B. Du Bois spoke about the "Negro crisis" in the United States as they separately toured Great Britain. Whereas Washington asserted that Blacks were making some progress toward elevating their status in the country, Du Bois presented evidence of injustices against Blacks and claimed that the federal government was not prepared to address their interests. Upon his return, Du Bois joined the Socialist Party and published a novel entitled *The Quest of the Silver Fleece*, which highlighted the relationship between racism and economics.

LYNCHING OF BLACKS CONTINUES

During this year, sixty-seven Blacks were reported lynched in this country.

SICKLE CELL ANEMIA IDENTIFIED

Sickle cell anemia, a hereditary blood disease that almost exclusively affects Black people, was identified and described by J. B. Herrick in this year. It was not fully understood until 1949, when Linus Pauling and several of his associates showed that the disease was related to abnormal hemoglobin in red blood cells. It was frequently called hemoglobin S, or sickle hemoglobin, because the red blood corpuscle had a distorted shape when its oxygen level was low. There is still no cure for the disease.

STATE CONSTITUTIONS EFFECTIVELY DISFRANCHISE BLACK PEOPLE

By this time, the Black population had been effectively disfranchised by new constitutions adopted in states throughout the South. The provisions in the constitution adopted by whites in Mississippi provided the legislative model followed by other southern states. In the Mississippi constitution, every effort was made to rewrite every clause that enfranchised Black people. Although retaining clauses directly related to progress (such as public education), the new white Democratic legislators wrote a suffrage amendment that imposed a poll tax of two dollars and excluded voters convicted of the crimes of theft, arson, perjury, bigamy, bribery, burglary, and murder. The amendment also prohibited suffrage to any person who could not read any section of the state constitution, understand it when read, or give a reasonable interpretation of it. Threatened by Mississippi's Black majority, white supremacists acted to restrict Blacks from participating in government. Isaiah T. Montgomery, the only Black delegate at the constitutional convention, voiced his objection by noting that the poll tax and the education requirement would effectively disfranchise 123,000 Blacks and only 11,000 whites. After what many white legislators called an excellent session, the convention declared the new constitution to be in effect.

Madame C. J. Walker, one of the most prominent citizens and business leaders of Indianapolis, is shown here on the steps of the new Black YMCA with (front row, from the left) Freeman *publisher George Knox, Booker T. Washington,* Indianapolis World *publisher Alex Manning, and YMCA executives R. W. Bullock and Thomas Taylor. Madame Walker contributed $1,000 to the YMCA building fund, the largest sum donated by any Black benefactor.*

Following Mississippi's example, South Carolina and Louisiana adopted new constitutions in 1895; North Carolina amended its constitution in 1900 and 1905; Alabama did so in 1901; Virginia, in 1902; Georgia, in 1908; and Oklahoma, in 1910. These new constitutions ignored the protests of Black delegates and forged ahead with legislation to circumvent the Fifteenth Amendment and completely disfranchise Blacks. Although a major goal of these new constitutions was to take the vote away from Blacks, their broader purpose was to exclude Blacks completely from political life and to reduce them to a subordinate status.

The new constitutions had an immediate effect on Black voting and office holding. In 1896, as many as 130,344 Blacks were registered in Louisiana; by 1900,

only 5,320 Blacks were on the registration books. In Alabama, registered Black males of voting age declined from 181,471 to only 3,000 after the new constitution went into effect. In each of the southern states, the newly crafted constitutions had completely disfranchised the Black population; the gains made during Reconstruction had been lost. These new constitutions set the stage for violent racial relations.

WALKER FOUNDS MANUFACTURING FIRM

Madame Walker (1867–1919) established the Madame C. J. Walker Manufacturing Company in Indianapolis — the largest Black-owned business in the state.

For thirteen years, Sarah McWilliams, a widow, worked as a washerwoman in St. Louis, Missouri, for one dollar and fifty cents per day. She had a vision of owning her own business and providing a better life for herself and her daughter A'Lelia. Using a day's wages, she invested in herbs and other natural products and mixed them into a hair ointment to make Black women's hair softer and easier to style. Up to that time, Black women had often pressed their hair with heavy, hot irons to straighten it, often resulting in burns and scorched hair. McWilliams's conditioner, used with a metal heating comb that she also invented, formed the basis of an industry employing more than three thousand people and producing annual sales of five hundred thousand dollars.

◇ Born in Delta, Louisiana, on December 23, 1867, of former slaves, McWilliams had been orphaned, married, borne a daughter, and widowed by the time she was twenty years old. She used the French title "Madame" after her marriage to newspaperman Charles J. Walker, because its glamorous overtones seemed appropriate for beauty products. At first, Madame Walker personally sold her products, traveling throughout much of the Midwest and throwing advertising leaflets from the train to people standing at station platforms. Madame Walker advertised widely in Black newspapers and magazines and promoted her business by giving demonstrations of her hair treatment system. Her business flourished through mail orders, and she expanded by developing a correspondence course on skin and hair care. Upon graduation, each woman received the right to sell Walker products and equipment. In 1913, she established Lelia College to train young women about the Walker beauty system and the use of her products. It is recorded that Madame Walker was the first American woman to become a millionaire by her own efforts.

Madame Walker used her wealth in charitable ways, sponsoring community clubs and educational causes, including scholarships for women and funds for Bethune-Cookman College. She sponsored Black artists and writers and contributed to the NAACP and to homes for the aged and needy. In her later years, Madame Walker moved to New York City, where she built a resplendent mansion in the exclusive area known as Irvington-on-the-Hudson. When she died at the age of fifty-two, she left an estate valued at more than one million dollars. She willed a considerable amount to charitable organizations and the remainder to her daughter.

JOHNSON DEFEATS JEFFRIES

On **JULY 4** in Reno, Nevada, Jack Johnson, the Black heavyweight boxing champion, knocked out his opponent, Jim Jeffries, in the fifteenth round. This victory by a Black boxer set off several racial riots across the country. As many as eight Blacks were killed after the bout — in which many whites wished that "the great white hope" would emerge victorious. Numerous excuses were made for Jeffries's loss — "out of shape," "just came out of retirement," and "must have been sickly." Few whites actually admitted that Johnson was the better fighter and a worthy champion.

◇ Johnson was born in Galveston, Texas. When he finished the fifth grade, he left school and took on a number of odd jobs and activities, including gambling and dock fights, to make a living. His break came when he knocked out a professional boxer while traveling with a circus. Johnson had become the heavyweight champion by defeating Tommy Burns in Sydney, Australia, in 1908. Johnson lost his title when he was knocked out by Jess Willard in the twenty-sixth round in 1915. Although he tried to make a number of comebacks, he was not successful.

Crisis BEGINS PUBLICATION

On **NOVEMBER 1**, *Crisis*, the journal of the National Association for the Advancement of Colored People (NAACP), made its debut with the publication of one thousand copies. W. E. B. Du Bois, one of the NAACP founders and the organization's director of publicity and research, was the editor. According to Du Bois, the journal highlighted the dangers of racial prejudice and supported the rights of all people, regardless of color.

CITIES PASS SEGREGATION ORDINANCES

On **DECEMBER 19**, Baltimore passed a residential segregation ordinance stipulating that white and Black residents were not to live on the same streets or in the same residential areas. Other cities followed Baltimore's lead. Winston-Salem adopted residential segregation ordinances in 1912, followed in 1913 by Madisonville, Kentucky; Birmingham, Alabama; Atlanta, Georgia; Richmond, Virginia; and Norfolk, Virginia. Louisville, Kentucky, followed in 1915; St. Louis, Missouri, in 1916; and Dallas, Texas, in 1916.

1911 ARKANSAS INTRODUCES RACE LAWS

Arkansas passed legislation that made cohabitation between the races a felony.

LYNCHING OF BLACKS CONTINUES

In this year, sixty Blacks were lynched.

KAPPA ALPHA PSI FOUNDED

On **JANUARY 5**, the Kappa Alpha Psi fraternity was founded at Indiana University by Elder Watson Diggs, Byron Kenneth Armstrong, and eight others. It was the first African American fraternity chartered as a national organization. On May 15, it became incorporated.

LEWIS MADE ASSISTANT ATTORNEY GENERAL

On **MARCH 26**, William H. Lewis was appointed assistant attorney general of the United States. He was the first Black person to hold this government position.

NATIONAL URBAN LEAGUE FORMED

In **OCTOBER**, the Committee on Urban Conditions merged with the Association for the Protection of Colored Women, the Committee for Improving the Industrial Conditions Among Negroes, and the National League for the Protection of Colored Women, to form the National League on Urban Conditions Among Negroes. Booker T. Washington, with the help of wealthy whites, was instrumental in founding the organization. In addition to setting a mission to enhance the social and economic situation of Blacks, it focused on the training of social workers and worked to change housing, health, sanitation, recreation, and employment conditions. The league's first chairman of the board was Edwin R. A. Seligman of Columbia University. Economist George E. Haynes and sociologist Eugene Kinckle Jones served as executive officers. Jones became executive secretary in 1914 and particularly concentrated on integrating Blacks into industry.

The league differed from the NAACP in that it dealt with social and economic needs, whereas the NAACP focused on civil rights. Years later, its name was shortened to National Urban League. By 1991, the league had 114 affiliates in thirty-four states and the District of Columbia. The National Urban League is now headquartered in New York City.

OMEGA PSI PHI FRATERNITY INCORPORATED

On **OCTOBER 28**, Omega Psi Phi fraternity was founded at Howard University by three students — Frank Coleman, Oscar J. Cooper, and Edgar A. Love — and their faculty adviser, Ernest Everett Just. The fraternity was incorporated in 1914.

1912 FOSTER DIRECTS FIRST BLACK FILM

The Railroad Porter became the first Black film. It was a comedy directed by Bill Foster, a pioneer Black filmmaker.

IDLEWILD, MICHIGAN, BECOMES RESORT FOR BLACKS

In the midst of segregated America, members of the growing Black middle class were barred from white resorts. In the Midwest, a group of white developers sought to take advantage of the situation by purchasing and developing twenty-seven hundred acres of land in Lake County, Michigan, about eighty miles north of Grand Rapids. They hired Black salespeople to sell lots in the new resort community of Idlewild to Blacks in cities like Detroit and Chicago. Among the prominent Blacks who bought property in Idlewild were W. E. B. Du Bois and Daniel Hale Williams.

Idlewild was highly successful and attracted some of the most famous Black entertainers to perform

One of the founders of the National Urban League, Eugene Kinckle Jones served as its executive secretary for more than twenty years. Jones was also a member of President Franklin Roosevelt's "Black Cabinet."

there during the summer season. Singers such as Della Reese and Sarah Vaughan both got their starts in the Paradise Club there. In this respect, Idlewild was similar to the Catskills in New York, where many Jewish entertainers got their start.

Idlewild was most popular from the 1920s to the 1950s. When segregation legally ended, many residents sold their property and left the community. Nevertheless, Idlewild still exists, and many old-time property owners continue to live there.

JOHNSON PUBLISHES NOVEL

James Weldon Johnson (1871–1938), a politician, diplomat, songwriter, and civil rights activist, published a novel entitled *The Autobiography of an Ex-Colored Man*.

◈ Born on June 17, 1871, Johnson was influenced by Booker T. Washington, Joseph C. Price, T. Thomas Fortune, and other influential Black civil rights leaders at the time. Probably no other African American took advantage of as many opportunities or overcame as many barriers as Johnson. After being educated at Atlanta University, he taught school in rural Henry County, Georgia, in 1891 and 1892. He worked as a carpenter during the World's Columbian Exposition in Chicago in 1893, where he was introduced to Frederick Douglass and listened to poetry by Paul Laurence Dunbar. From 1894 to 1901, he was the principal at Stanton School in Jacksonville, Florida, during which time he founded the *Daily American*, a newspaper in which he editorialized about various racial issues and problems. In 1898, Johnson became the first African American lawyer admitted to the bar in Duval County, Florida. In 1900, he wrote the words to "Lift Ev'ry Voice and Sing," which became known as the Black national anthem. In 1901, Johnson and his brother teamed up with Stern and Company and produced a number of successful songs — "Under the Bamboo Tree" was part of the musical comedy *Sally in Our Alley*. They wrote music for a number of other concerns, including *The Evolution of Ragtime: A Musical Suite of Six Songs Tracing and Illustrating Negro Music* (1903). They wrote two songs especially for Theodore Roosevelt's presidential campaign, "You're All Right, Teddy" and "The Old Flag Never Touch the Ground."

Johnson's songwriting was put on hold when, in 1906, he was appointed consul in Venezuela. In 1908, he was assigned and promoted as consul to Nicaragua, a position he resigned in 1913. During his tenure as consul, he used some of his leisure time to

James Weldon Johnson, intellectual, educator, poet, and civil rights activist, published his novel The Autobiography of an Ex-Colored Man *in 1912. Johnson is most often remembered as a civil rights activist and as the lyricist for "Lift Every Voice and Sing."*

write his anonymous novel, *The Autobiography of an Ex-Colored Man*. The novel was not well received by either Black or white audiences until the 1920s (the Harlem Renaissance era), when it was reprinted in 1927. In 1914, Johnson assumed the editorship of the *New York Age*, where he made his militant, intellectual voice known. He used the *Age* to promote his novel. In November, Johnson was offered the post of field secretary of the NAACP by Joel Spingarn, the chairman of the board. After accepting the position, Johnson became an effective organizer for the NAACP, increasing the membership and number of chapters. In a short time, Johnson organized a silent march in New York City as a protest against lynching in the country. He spoke frequently against Jim Crow laws, mob violence, and lynching. In addition, he used journalism to promote civil rights causes, writing many articles for mainstream newspapers. In 1925, he and Walter White raised funds to support the *Sweet* case, and later, Johnson worked hard to win the *Texas White Primary* case. In 1927, he published *God's Trombones*.

Johnson left the NAACP because of exhaustion and overwork. After the publication of *Black Manhattan* in 1930, he accepted the Adam K. Spence Chair at Fisk University — a chair established specifically for him. Over the next few years he lectured at a number of universities, and in 1933, he wrote his autobiography, *Along This Way*, in which he provided a vivid picture of the African American experience as it related to his own life.

Johnson died in a tragic accident. While he and his wife were driving from Great Barrington, Massachusetts, to their summer home in Maine, they were struck by a train at an unguarded railroad crossing. Johnson was killed immediately, and his wife died several weeks later.

LYNCHING OF BLACKS CONTINUES
Sixty-one Blacks were reported lynched in this year.

NAACP NEGOTIATES LABOR AGREEMENT
The NAACP won an agreement from the Southern Railway Corporation to employ Blacks in skilled trades. This agreement followed a recent strike by white firemen of the Cincinnati, New Orleans, and Texas Pacific Railroad to protest that Blacks had been hired for the same jobs as whites.

VIRGINIA ALLOWS RESIDENTIAL SEGREGATION
The Virginia legislature gave its cities the right to designate neighborhoods as Black or white, thereby approving residential segregation of races.

HANDY PUBLISHES "MEMPHIS BLUES"
In SEPTEMBER, W. C. Handy (1873–1958), a noted bandleader and songwriter, published his best-known composition, "Memphis Blues," originally called "Mr. Crump" and composed as part of the political campaign of Edward H. "Boss" Crump. In 1914, Handy published "St. Louis Blues," and became a prolific songwriter and music publisher in the late 1920s.

St. Louis Argus ESTABLISHED
In NOVEMBER, one of the important Black-owned newspapers, the *St. Louis Argus*, was established, founded by J. E. Mitchell and William Mitchell. The newspaper remains a source of information for Black citizens of the St. Louis area today, where its circulation is estimated to be 32,500.

1913 LYNCHING OF BLACKS CONTINUES
In this year, fifty-one Blacks were lynched.

STANDARD LIFE INSURANCE FOUNDED
In this year, Herman Perry started the Standard Life Insurance company of Atlanta with a capital sum of one hundred thousand dollars. Within a short time, the company became one of the largest Black-owned legal reserve companies, and by 1922, it claimed assets worth two million dollars and annual premium income of about $1.2 million.

However, growth proved to be too rapid for the company, and although it absorbed the Mississippi Life Insurance Company (started in 1909) and subsequently resold it to a white-owned company to improve revenue, Standard defaulted on mortgage payments and was taken over by whites. Efforts to revive Standard Life in 1925 failed, and it ceased operations in 1931.

WILLIAMS BECOMES MEMBER OF AMERICAN COLLEGE OF SURGEONS
Dr. Daniel Hale Williams, pioneer heart surgeon and founder of Provident Hospital, became the first Black member of the American College of Surgeons.

Williams had resigned from the staff of Provident Hospital because of internal leadership problems, and he had become the first and only Black doctor on the staff of Chicago's St. Luke Hospital.

DELTA SIGMA THETA FOUNDED
On JANUARY 13, the Delta Sigma Theta sorority was founded at Howard University by twenty-two undergraduates. The sorority now has more than eight hundred chapters throughout the United States and other countries.

ALPHA KAPPA ALPHA SORORITY INCORPORATED
On JANUARY 29, the Alpha Kappa Alpha Sorority, founded at Howard University in 1908, was incorporated. It was one of several Black fraternities and sororities to be formed in the early twentieth century.

Cleveland Call & Post FOUNDED BY WALKER

In **SEPTEMBER**, the *Cleveland Call & Post* was established by William O. Walker in Cleveland, Ohio. Walker used the newspaper to criticize injustices against Blacks and to advance the civil rights movement.

The *Cleveland Call & Post* has been a voice for Black people during every political campaign. In 1939, Walker was elected to the Cleveland City Council, where he served for six years. He then became a member of the State Central Committee for the Twenty-first Congressional District. He became the first Black person to hold a state cabinet position, as director of the Department of Industrial Relations in Governor James A. Rhodes's administration. Among his community service activities, he served as president of the Negro Business League, the Cleveland Urban League, and the Cleveland Branch of the NAACP. In addition, he sat on the boards of the National Urban League, the NAACP, and the Legal Defense Fund of New York. In 1945, Walker was named as one of three Black publishers to accompany President Franklin D. Roosevelt on a tour of military bases in Europe. As the president of the National Newspaper Publishers' Association in 1958, Walker called for a "Summit Meeting of Negro Leaders" in Washington, D.C., to identify and map out a civil rights strategy. At this meeting, attended by more than three hundred top Black leaders and addressed by President Dwight D. Eisenhower, the "whole civil rights movement [was] delineated." The *Cleveland Call & Post* continues to publish and is supported by the Black community.

TUBMAN DIES

On **MARCH 10**, one of the nation's important heroes, Harriet Tubman (1821?–1913), died. Tubman was an important leader of the Underground Railroad and Black suffrage movements. In her capacity as conductor of the Underground Railroad and the "Black Moses" to her people, she would take off several months whenever she was running low in funds and work as a domestic servant to raise money. Tubman served her country and her people in a number of other important ways — as a scout, spy, cook, and nurse during the Civil War. Although many Blacks performed services for the Union army, many white officers relied heavily upon the information that Tubman supplied. After her death, as well as during her life, Tubman was a great inspiration. During her life, Frederick Douglass wrote the following in a letter to Tubman:

You ask for what you do not need when you call upon me for a word of commendation. I need such words from you far more than you can need them from me, especially when your superior labors and devotion to the cause of the lately enslaved of our land are known as I know them. The difference between us is very marked. Most that I have done and suffered in the service of our cause has been in public, and I have received encouragement at every step of the way. You, on the other hand, have labored in a private way. I have wrought in the day — you in the night. I have had the applause of the crowd and the satisfaction that comes of being approved by the multitude, while the most that you have done has been witnessed by a few trembling, scarred, and foot-sore bondmen and women, whom you had led out of the house of bondage.... The midnight sky and the silent stars have been the witness to your devotion to freedom and of your heroism....

Much that you have done would seem improbable to those who do not know you as I know you.

Politicians, abolitionists, and Black leaders mourned her death, and many, then and now, see in the life of this "poor Black woman" an exceptional spiritual richness. She remains a symbol of the resilient and ever-present spirit to be free and to challenge inequities anywhere and against anyone.

1914 BULLARD JOINS FOREIGN LEGION

Eugene J. Bullard enlisted in the French Foreign Legion as soon as war broke out in Europe. He joined the regiment known as the "Swallows of Death" and became known as the "Black Swallow."

After he was wounded at the front line, he volunteered for service with the aviator corps. He was accepted and trained as a pilot. Upon graduation, he won a one-thousand-dollar bet offered by an American who alleged that he was incapable of learning to fly. Bullard was credited with downing two German planes, though neither incident was recorded in his official records. Although Bullard stayed in France for several years after the war, he returned to the United States during World War II.

IMMIGRATION BEGINS TO DECLINE

The number of foreign immigrants to the United States started to decline. The resulting shortage of unskilled labor created the need to employ Blacks. Immigrants dropped from 1,218,480 in this year to 326,700 in 1915, and to 110,618 in 1918. Over the decade 1910–1919, a total of 6.3 million immigrants entered the country. This figure contrasted sharply with the 8.2 million who came to the United States in the previous decade.

LOUISIANA SEGREGATES AMUSEMENT ACTIVITIES

The Louisiana legislature passed a law requiring segregated amusement activities. Specifically, it required separate entrances, exits, and ticket windows, twenty-five feet apart, at recreational facilities.

MORGAN WINS PRIZE FOR GAS MASK DESIGN

Garrett Morgan (1875–1963), a scientist and inventor, presented his "smoke inhalator" at the Second International Exposition of Sanitation and Safety. Described as a breathing helmet and smoke protector, his device won First Grand Prize. It proved successful in 1916 when he rescued a number of men trapped in a tunnel.

SPINGARN MEDAL INSTITUTED FOR
BLACK ACHIEVEMENT

Joel E. Spingarn, former chairman of the Board of Directors of the NAACP, instituted a medal to be given annually to the African American man or woman who attained the highest achievement during the preceding year or years. Winners have been honored for their work in art, music, literature, theater, dance, photography, science, medicine, business, politics, public service, law, education, the military, civil rights, and sports. The award has been given annually since 1915, with the exception of 1938.

OMEGA PSI PHI FRATERNITY ESTABLISHED

On **OCTOBER 28**, the Omega Psi Phi Fraternity, was incorporated at Howard University, Washington, D.C.

1915 AGENTS RECRUIT BLACK WORKERS
FROM THE SOUTH

Labor agents from the North were sent south to recruit Black workers. Foreign immigration had dropped steadily during the war in Europe.

DEPRIEST ELECTED TO CITY GOVERNMENT

In Chicago, Oscar DePriest, a Black man, was elected to the city council. Black men gained elective office in Chicago and St. Louis a little earlier than in other eastern, northern, and western cities.

In 1924, DePriest became the first Black person to be elected a ward committeeman. DePriest was later elected to the U.S. Congress, becoming the first Black person ever elected to Congress from outside the South.

FUNDS FOR EDUCATION UNEQUAL

By this year, the amount of state funds provided by South Carolina to educate white pupils was more than ten times the amount of public money spent on Black children. Records showed that the disparity had widened significantly since the 1890s, when per capita expenditures for education for the two groups were two dollars and seventy-five cents for white pupils versus two dollars and fifty-one cents for Blacks. Even in 1895, the increasing racial disparity was evident, when per capita expenditures for white pupils had increased to three dollars and eleven cents, whereas the amount for Black pupils had declined to one dollar and five cents per capita.

LINCOLN MOTION PICTURE COMPANY FOUNDED

The Lincoln Motion Picture Company was founded in Los Angeles by Clarence Brooks and Noble Johnson, two Black actors, James T. Smith, a Black druggist, and Harry Grant, a white cameraman. This was the first serious Black movie production company in the country.

LYNCHING OF BLACKS CONTINUES

During the year, fifty-six Blacks were reported lynched.

MORE BLACKS BECOME DEMOCRATS

The growth of Blacks in the Democratic Party in New York was notable. Only one thousand Black Democrats were recorded in 1915. By 1930, the number had increased to 327,000; nineteen of the twenty-two Black political clubs were Democratic.

NAACP AWARDS SPINGARN MEDAL TO JUST

The NAACP awarded the Spingarn Medal to Ernest Everett Just (1883–1941) for his contributions to the sciences despite racial prejudice and a host of other barriers.

◇ Just was a native of Charleston, South Carolina. He received his B.A. degree from Dartmouth College in 1907 and a Ph.D. in zoology and physiology from the University of Chicago in 1916. He became a noted marine biologist and served for thirty-two years as a faculty member at Howard University, Washington, D.C., where he also headed the physiology department from 1912 to 1920. Just worked for twenty summers at the Marine Biological Laboratory in Woods Hole, Massachusetts. Just's research focused on fertilization, cellular physiology, and experimental embryology. He was the author of two major books, *General Cytology* and *Jerome Alexander's Colloid Chemistry*. He spent most of the last ten years of his life working in institutes and universities in Germany, Italy, and France. Just died of cancer in Washington, D.C.

NAACP LEADS PROTEST AGAINST *Birth of a Nation*

The NAACP actively protested against the film *Birth of a Nation*, produced by D. W. Griffith and written by Thomas Dixon. Although the film utilized state-of-the-art technology, it was offensive to Blacks because it portrayed emancipation, Reconstruction, and the general morality of Black people in a negative manner. It also glorified organizations like the Ku Klux Klan.

OKLAHOMA BLACKS MOVE TO GHANA

Led by a Ghanaian, Alfred C. Sam, about sixty Blacks from Oklahoma attempted without success to establish a colony in Ghana.

OKLAHOMA SEGREGATES TELEPHONE BOOTHS

The Oklahoma legislature authorized segregation of telephone booths by requiring telephone companies to provide separate booths for "whites and colored patrons."

WASHINGTON DIES

Booker T. Washington (1856–1915), Black leader and educator, died. Washington emerged as a Black leader when he delivered an address (the "Atlanta Compromise") at the Cotton States and International Exposition in Atlanta. Washington became Frederick Douglass's successor as the prominent Black leader; he made the speech on September 18, 1895, about seven months after Douglass's death. Washington spoke to Black people of ways to move into "material and moral betterment." His book *Up From Slavery* detailed his experience as a Black person; it was a best-seller. One of the most persuasive orators among Black leaders, Washington presented his views in articles, books, and speeches. In addition, he used this skill to gain support for the education of African Americans. His contributions to education began when General Samuel Chapman Armstrong recommended him for the position of principal of a new school for African Americans in Macon County, Alabama — Tuskegee Institute.

SUPREME COURT RULES "GRANDFATHER CLAUSES" ILLEGAL

On **JUNE 21**, the U.S. Supreme Court ruled in *Guinn* v. *United States* that the grandfather clauses in the Maryland and Oklahoma constitutions were unconstitutional and repugnant to the Fifteenth Amendment. The NAACP had earlier assumed the responsibility for influencing the Supreme Court to declare such grandfather clauses unlawful.

KU KLUX KLAN CHARTERED

On **DECEMBER 4**, the Superior Court in Fulton County, Georgia, accepted the charter for the establishment of the new Ku Klux Klan. The organization had been revived on November 26 in Atlanta by Colonel William J. Simmons. The organization, whose membership peaked at about five million, spread rapidly throughout the country and was highly influential in the local and state governments of Oklahoma, Indiana, California, Oregon, and Ohio.

1916 FLOODS CAUSE BLACK MIGRATION FROM MISSISSIPPI DELTA

Floods destroyed much of the cotton crop in the Mississippi Delta, where a large part of the nation's total crop was grown, greatly contributing to the migration of Blacks out of the region.

GARVEY ESTABLISHES U.S. UNIVERSAL NEGRO IMPROVEMENT ASSOCIATION

Marcus Garvey (1887–1940), a Jamaican Black nationalist, set up the first branch of the Universal Negro Improvement Association (UNIA), begun in Jamaica several years earlier, in the United States in this year. Membership in UNIA grew slowly in the United States until World War I, but after the war membership reached six million: two million in the United States and the rest scattered around the world. Garvey tried to foster a sense of nationhood among Black Americans. A central tenet of the movement involved emigration to Africa, to bind the United States and Africa more closely together. UNIA created many self-help Black institutions and ran many business enterprises, including the Black Star Line, a shipping company used by Garvey and UNIA to trade with Africa. In addition, it published the largest Black weekly newspaper in the world — appropriately named *World*.

Garvey was indicted by the U.S. government in January 1922 for fraudulent use of the mail in raising funds. In 1925, he was convicted and sentenced to five years in the federal penitentiary in Atlanta. After serving two years, Garvey was pardoned in 1927 by President Calvin Coolidge but was deported to Jamaica as an undesirable alien.

PERSHING LEADS TENTH CAVALRY IN PURSUIT OF PANCHO VILLA

The all-Black Tenth Cavalry pursued the Mexican bandit, Pancho Villa, into Mexico after his raid on a New Mexican border town. Brigadier General John Pershing, placed in charge of the mission, specifically requested the Tenth Cavalry. (He had previously led the Tenth in 1896 and through the Spanish-American War and recognized their fighting abilities.) It was from his leadership of Black troops that Pershing's nickname, "Black Jack," was derived.

WOODSON PUBLISHES *Journal of Negro History*

On **JANUARY 1**, Dr. Carter G. Woodson published the first issue of *Journal of Negro History*. Woodson became one of the most important Black persons in the country.

Carter Woodson devoted his life to preserving the history of the African American community. He noted, "If race has no history, if it has no worthwhile tradition, it becomes a negligible factor in the thought of the world, and it stands in danger of being exterminated." Because of Woodson and his prolific, authoritative research and writings, "Negro history" became a legitimate topic for academic study.

◆ Woodson established the Association for the Study of Negro Life and History, and Black History Month, and he has been called the "father of Negro history." He earned degrees from the University of Chicago and Harvard, even though he did not attend high school until he was twenty years old. He spent his teen years working in coal mines in Virginia. He came to Washington, D.C., in 1909 and worked as a schoolteacher and principal. He was concerned that the history books his students read included no information on the role of Black people in the nation's history. He originally proposed a Black history week to be held in February near the birthdays of Frederick Douglass and Abraham Lincoln. The first Black History Week was celebrated in 1926. It was expanded to Black History Month in 1976. Woodson also worked until his death in 1950 to develop and provide materials that could be used to teach Black history in the elementary and secondary schools.

MORGAN RESCUES TRAPPED MINERS USING GAS MASK

On **JULY 25**, Garrett Morgan (1875–1963) was called to the scene of an underground explosion. Twelve men were trapped in Tunnel Number Five at the Cleveland Waterworks, about 228 feet below Lake Erie. Morgan, who had just invented a gas mask, was asked to prove its value by going deep into the gaseous tunnel. He entered the tunnel and rescued a number of men.

ROBESON FACES DISCRIMINATION

On **OCTOBER 14**, Paul Robeson, a sophomore tackle and guard with the Rutgers University football team, was benched when the team from Washington and Lee University refused to play against an African American. Robeson experienced significant discrimination throughout his football career but was named a football all-American twice. He later went on to achieve international fame as a singer.

1917 BLACKS FIGHT WITH THE FRENCH IN WORLD WAR I

Black combat troops were almost always assigned to the French as soon as they arrived. Even the French did not know what to do with them but considered them "on loan" for combat purposes. The 369th Infantry joined the French Fourth Army at the front and spent 191 days in trenches, the longest front-line service of any American regiment. More than 170 of its men and officers received the French croix de guerre or the Legion of Honor for their bravery in action. The Germans called them "Hell Fighters," but they referred to themselves as "Black Rattlers."

BLACKS SERVE IN SOS UNITS

One of the first units of American troops to arrive in France were several hundred Black stevedores, who became known as Services of Supply (SOS) units. Usually working day and night to set up docks and warehouses, they formed the core of the supplies logistics system. Blacks were often denied promotions beyond the rank of corporal for what many praised as hard and essential work.

LYNCHING OF BLACKS CONTINUES

In this year, thirty-eight Blacks were reported lynched.

PUBLICATIONS STIR BLACK CONSCIENCE

Several major publications were founded in this year that spoke forcibly to issues affecting the equal rights of Black people. Marcus Garvey, an emerging Black leader, founded the *Negro World* as a militant voice for the self-development of Black people. Other publications included James Weldon Johnson's protests in his *Fifty Years and Other Poems,* and A. Philip Randolph and Charles Owens's socialist journal *The Messenger.*

SUPREME COURT DECLARES RESIDENTIAL SEGREGATION UNCONSTITUTIONAL

In *Buchanan* v. *Warley,* the U.S. Supreme Court declared unconstitutional the Louisiana and Kentucky ordinances requiring Blacks to live in certain sections of the city. The Court decision declared unconstitutional all city segregation ordinances mandating that Blacks and whites reside on separate blocks.

UNITED STATES ENTERS WORLD WAR I

When the United States entered World War I, it was preoccupied with many social, economic, and educational disparities between Blacks and whites. As in almost every war, Blacks had to use pressure and petition for a role. After establishing a policy of segregating Black and white manpower, the army formed two Black divisions, the Ninety-second and the Ninety-third. The Ninety-third was composed of four infantry regiments, three National Guard units, and one unit of draftees. When they arrived in Europe, General John Pershing assigned them to French divisions. Thus they fought with French weapons and under French leadership until the war ended.

The Ninety-second was composed of Black draftees. They were segregated from white draftees, who received better training and better equipment. Part of the division was located at Camp Funston, Kansas, where state law prohibited segregated facilities. A Black soldier exercised this right by trying to enter a theater in Manhattan, but was denied entry. After learning about the incident, General Charles C. Ballou, the division commander, chastised his troops for starting trouble. When the Black community heard of the treatment of soldiers in this incident, they openly protested. But before anything happened, the Ninety-second, poorly trained and poorly led, was on its way to France. Both weaknesses plagued the division during its stay in France. Most of the soldiers did not see combat, and the majority were shifted to labor battalions, stevedore companies, and depot brigades. About one-third of all labor troops in the army were Black.

RACE RIOT IN ILLINOIS

From **JULY 1** to **3,** in the industrial and railroading community of East St. Louis, Illinois, one of the most serious race riots in the nation occurred. At least forty Blacks and eight whites were killed. Martial law was declared in the community.

The riot stemmed from the recruitment of Blacks to meet a severe labor shortage. Upon their arrival, they were paid low wages, poorly housed, and experienced hostility from the white laborers. Blacks were often used as strikebreakers. For example, when white workers went on strike at the Aluminum Ore Works, Black workers were brought in from other states to fill these jobs. Employers refused to negotiate with unions because of the availability of Blacks. On one day, three hundred Blacks were estimated to have arrived for work. White hostility against Blacks escalated as they saw this relatively large number of Blacks enter the town. Although local union leaders tried to stop the flow of cheap Black labor into East St. Louis, as well as remove many who were already there, they were generally unsuccessful. A headline in the *East St. Louis Journal* helped to spread fear and hostility: "Make East St. Louis a Lily White Town."

In May, tension mounted as Blacks were beaten and National Guardmembers were called into the city to keep peace. On Sunday, July 1, white joy riders rode through the Black section of town shooting at residences. When Blacks gathered to resist, the police were informed that an armed Black mob had formed. White plainclothes policemen in an unmarked car rushed to the scene and were fired upon by Blacks who thought they, too, were joy riders. One policeman died, and three were wounded. Large white mobs quickly formed to avenge the death of the policeman.

Although no attempt was made to invade the Black section of town, fires were started on the edges of the district, and Blacks where shot as they fled burning buildings. Many were burned alive, and most of the Black district was destroyed. Many who were on their way home were pulled from streetcars and beaten; others were caught in white areas and killed. The riot continued until July 3.

In the aftermath of the riot, some estimates claim that as many as half of the Black population left East St. Louis, some returning to the South and others fleeing across the river to St. Louis. Also, a total of four hundred thousand dollars worth of property was destroyed — almost all of it owned or occupied by Black residents. In general, local and state troops were ineffective in quelling the violence, and many took no steps to halt the melee. Few whites were ever convicted of any crime, and those who were received minor punishment. In an ironic twist, the German Nazis used the incidence of race riots such as this one and of lynchings of Blacks to spread antiwar sentiment among Blacks during World War II. Why should Blacks support a war out of which they gained nothing? Such propaganda had no noticeable effect on the morale of Black citizens or Black members of the armed forces.

BLACKS MARCH TO PROTEST VIOLENCE

On **JULY 28**, between ten thousand and fifteen thousand Blacks silently marched down Fifth Avenue in New York City to protest continued lynchings and discrimination in the South and elsewhere in the country. Organized by the NAACP, the march was explained in a leaflet entitled *Why We March*:

We march because by the grace of God and the force of truth the dangerous, hampering walls of prejudice and inhuman injustices must fall.

We march because we want to make impossible a repetition of Waco, Memphis, and East St. Louis by arousing the conscience of the country, and to bring the murderers of our brothers, sisters, and innocent children to justice.

We march because we deem it a crime to be silent in the face of such barbaric acts.

We march because we are thoroughly opposed to Jim Crow cars, segregation, discrimination, disfranchisement, lynching, and the host of evils that are forced on us. It is time that the spirit of Christ should be manifested in the making and execution of laws.

We march because we want our children to live in a better land and enjoy fairer conditions than have fallen to our lot.

The parade was led by Dr. W. E. B. Du Bois.

RACE RIOT OCCURS IN TEXAS

On **AUGUST 23**, the most serious riot involving Black soldiers occurred in Houston, Texas. The riot was sparked by racial tension caused by the presence of Black soldiers who resisted traditional southern rules of behavior. The specific incident that provoked the riot involved a Black soldier who intervened in the arrest of a Black woman by two white policemen and then was beaten, arrested, and later released. When another Black soldier attempted to find the white police officers and ascertain what had happened to his Black colleague, he was chased, captured, beaten, and arrested. Word of the ill-treatment of the soldiers by the policemen spread throughout the military camp, and rumors circulated that the second soldier had been shot and killed. To avenge the alleged killing, more than one hundred armed Black soldiers of the Twenty-fourth Infantry marched on the city.

By one account, the riot between soldiers and Houston citizens culminated in thirteen known deaths, including one Black, and nineteen wounded, including five soldiers. Another account showed that a total of thirty-five whites, four Blacks, and one Mexican American were killed in the rioting. Sixty-four Black soldiers were tried for murder; thirteen were sentenced to death and hanged publicly. Forty others were given life imprisonment. Soldiers were denied the right of appeal. The NAACP and James Weldon Johnson appealed to President Woodrow Wilson to intervene on behalf of the soldiers. Texas requested that the remaining Black soldiers be expelled from the state immediately. Although neither of the requests received positive action from President Wilson at the time, several newspapers, including the *Enquirer*, retracted the story that Black soldiers had actually started the riot. In fact, they later provided evidence that the troops were "goaded into attacking civilians." The newspaper also reported the slogan of the troops before the riot: "To hell with going to France, let's clean up this dirty town."

◈ On September 3, another five Black soldiers were hanged for their alleged participation in the Houston

Sixty-four Black soldiers of the Twenty-fourth Infantry were tried for mutiny and murder after the race riot in Houston, in what was the largest murder trial in U.S. history.

riot of 1917. The NAACP lobbied for more than twenty years on behalf of the imprisoned soldiers. Not until 1938 was the last soldier released.

BLACK OFFICERS COMMISSIONED

On **OCTOBER 15**, a total of 639 Blacks received army commissions: 106 were appointed captains, and the remainder were promoted to the rank of first or second lieutenant. All were graduates of the all-Black officers' training school in Fort Des Moines, Iowa, commanded by a white colonel, which was created as a result of NAACP lobbying efforts led by Joel E. Spingarn and James Weldon Johnson.

1917–1918 DISTINGUISHED MILITARY SERVICE BY BLACKS

From **JUNE 5, 1917**, to **SEPTEMBER 12, 1918**, about 2,290,529 Black men registered for service with the U.S. Army. Approximately 400,000 Blacks served during World War I. As many as 200,000 saw action in France, and 42,000 served as combat troops. Although the overwhelming majority served as stevedores, cooks, and laborers, more than 1,300 Blacks were commissioned as officers (still less than 1 percent of all officers), and most of the Blacks held the rank of First and Second Lieutenant. The highest-ranking Black officer, Colonel Charles Young, was forced to retire at the beginning of the war for medical reasons.

The first two Americans to win France's croix de guerre for bravery were Henry Johnson of Albany, New York, and Needham Roberts of Trenton, New Jersey. Both men served with the all-Black 369th Infantry. Johnson and Roberts were serving on guard duty on May 14, 1918, when attacked by twenty Germans. Although both were wounded, they were able to kill four Germans, wound several others, and send the rest fleeing. Johnson received the French croix de guerre and star and palm because he saved Roberts from being taken prisoner. It was Johnson, who after firing his last bullets, used his bolo knife and the butt of his rifle to wound several Germans and put the others to flight. Johnson and Roberts were credited with smashing a German surprise attack.

1918 DAWSON RUNS IN REPUBLICAN PRIMARY

William Dawson (1886–1970), a graduate of Fisk University and Northwestern University Law School, ran against Martin B. Madden, who had represented Illinois's First Congressional District since 1904. The issue of race was brought to the forefront in the campaign, and when the votes were counted, Dawson recorded 29 percent of the Republican primary vote, a portion significant enough to signal the emergence of Black political muscle in Illinois, and particularly in Chicago.

LYNCHING OF BLACKS CONTINUES

As many as sixty Blacks were reported lynched this year.

MICHEAUX DIRECTS FIRST FULL-LENGTH BLACK FILM

Oscar Micheaux (1884–1951), a pioneer filmmaker, produced and directed *Birthright*, the first full-length Black film. *Birthright* was adapted from a Pulitzer Prize–winning novel by T. S. Stribling.

Micheaux was born in Metropolis, Illinois, and worked as a Pullman porter during his early adult life. He wrote a number of books and worked in publishing before entering film production. His corporation, Oscar Micheaux Corporation, made more than thirty movies, including a treatment of his own novel, *The Homesteader*, and *Body and Soul*, the film in which Paul Robeson made his debut. Micheaux made many low-budget films.

NAACP RECORDS THIRTY YEARS OF LYNCHINGS

In **APRIL**, the NAACP issued a pamphlet entitled *Thirty Years of Lynching in the United States — 1889–1918*. During this thirty-year period, a total of 3,224 persons had been lynched in the United States, 2,522 Blacks and 702 whites. Of the 2,522 Blacks

Reacting to the 1917 race riot in East St. Louis, Blacks (organized by the NAACP) protested racism by silently walking down Fifth Avenue.

lynched, 2,472 were men and 50 were women. The NAACP published a record of lynching for each year since 1918.

Only 219 of the lynchings occurred in the North and 156 in the West; thus, the overwhelming majority of lynchings (2,834) occurred in the South. Georgia led all states in the number of Blacks lynched there (386), followed by Mississippi (373), Texas (335), Louisiana (313), Alabama (276), Tennessee (296), Arkansas (214), Florida (178), and Kentucky (169).

The lynchings were performed to avenge charges of murder (900), rape (477), attacks upon women (237), crimes against the person (253), crimes against property (210), and miscellaneous crimes (303). As many as 142 lynchings were unclassified or carried out with the "absence of crime." These Blacks were lynched for behavior such as testifying against whites or suing whites.

369TH, 370TH, AND 371ST INFANTRY REGIMENTS SERVE HONORABLY

In **APRIL**, the 369th Infantry, the first Black combat unit sent overseas, saw action against the Germans. For 191 days from the time of its engagement, the 369th never had a man captured or was forced to retreat. Their superior training and bravery allowed them to be victorious against the Germans at Bois d'Hauza, at Maison-en-Champagne, and along the Rhine River. The unit was cited for heroism eleven times and received the French croix de guerre for

The 369th Infantry joined the French in fighting the Germans and spent 191 days in the trenches.

bravery. A total of 171 of the officers and enlisted men of the 369th Infantry were decorated with the croix de guerre or the Legion of Honor.

The all-Black 370th Infantry, Ninety-third Division, was noted for bravery during the war. Men of this unit fought in the Battle of the Argonne Forest and pursued Germans into Belgium. Twelve members of the unit received the Distinguished Service Cross for extraordinary heroism, and sixty-eight of the men received the croix de guerre from the French government.

The 371st Infantry Regiment served honorably in the War. The 371st Regiment participated in frontline combat against the Germans for more than three months. Under the command of General Goybet, the regiment was successful in capturing Montfauxelle —a place held by the Germans for almost a year. Not only did the 371st capture many prisoners, but they also seized munitions and railroad cars filled with food, clothing, and other supplies. The 371st took heavy casualties. As many as 2,384 men — almost half the regiment — lost their lives.

In spite of the bravery shown by the Black men of these units, white officers, many of them from the South, often taunted them for cowardice.

RACE RIOTS ERUPT IN PENNSYLVANIA

In JULY, two separate race riots occurred in Pennsylvania. From July 25 to July 28, a race riot occurred in Chester that resulted in the deaths of three Blacks and two whites. From July 26 to July 29, a race riot in Philadelphia left three whites and one Black dead.

ARMY "EXPERIMENTS" WITH BLACK NURSES BEFORE THEY ARE ACCEPTED

Ada Thoms of the National Association of Colored Graduate Nurses encouraged Black nurses to enroll in the American Red Cross when the United States declared war on Germany in 1917. Even though there was a shortage of nurses, the Red Cross rejected all Black applicants. But since the Surgeon General had to approve the Red Cross's decision, Blacks registered in large numbers anyway, in the hope that the Surgeon General would rule in their favor. Black nurses were finally accepted into the Army Nurse Corps in September 1918, two months before the Armistice.

During this time, the nation and the world were affected by the first wave of an eventual epidemic of influenza, which was killing thousands of people worldwide. Because soldiers were increasingly affected, the army recognized that the shortage of nurses had

reached an acute level. In response, the army decided to "experiment" with Black nurses, accepting only eighteen Black women in DECEMBER. They were assigned to base hospitals at Camp Sherman, Ohio, and Camp Grant, Illinois. They worked in integrated facilities but lived in segregated ones. The first Black nurses proved themselves to be professional and competent. The eighteen nurses are listed here:

Lillian Ball
Pearl Billings
Marion Brown
Susan Boulding
Eva Clay
Aileen Cole
Edna DePriest
Magnolia Diggs
Sophia Hill
Jeanette Minnis
Anna Oliver Ramos
Clara Rollins
Lillian Spears
Virginia Steele
Frances Stewart
Nettie Vick
Jeanette West
Mabel Williams

1919 DU BOIS PONDERS RACIAL HATRED

According to W. E. B. Du Bois, the conditions in northern industrial centers were hellish and reflected intensified racial hatred. In his autobiography, *Dusk of Dawn*, he wrote:

The facts concerning the year 1919 are unbelievable as one looks back on them today. During that year, seventy-seven Negroes were lynched, of whom one was a woman and eleven were soldiers; of these, fourteen were publicly burned, eleven of them being burned alive. That year there were race riots large and small in twenty-six American cities including thirty-eight killed in a Chicago riot in August; from twenty-five to fifty killed in Phillips County, Arkansas; and six killed in Washington. For a day, the city of Washington in 1919, was actually in the hands of a Black mob fighting the aggression of the Whites with hand grenades.

Kansas City Call FOUNDED

Chester Franklin founded the *Kansas City Call*. He aimed to make his newspaper an integral part of the Black community by promoting racial justice and working toward the economic, political, and social development of the community.

The newspaper was considered one of the best Black-owned newspapers in the country. From 1923 to 1931, the managing editor was Roy Wilkins (later head of the NAACP). After the death of Chester Franklin in 1955, the paper was continued by his widow, Ada Crogman Franklin, publisher, and Lucile H. Bluford, editor. Ada Franklin, a dramatist and college educator — she taught at Alabama State College and Tennessee A & I State University — continued to improve the newspaper. In 1973, she won the Distinguished Publisher Award of the National Newspaper Publishers Association. The *Kansas City Call* is still operating and is delivered to as many as fifty thousand subscribers each week.

LYNCHING OF BLACKS CONTINUES
Seventy-six Black persons were reported lynched this year

MOBS LYNCH BLACK IN NEBRASKA
In Omaha, Nebraska, a white mob, incited by alleged Black attacks on white women, burned the courthouse and lynched one Black.

Negro Trail Blazers of California
Delilah Beasley (1872–1934), a columnist, chronicled an important part of the African American experience in *The Negro Trail Blazers of California*. The book detailed the racial problems in the state and the heroic achievements by Blacks to overcome them.

POLLARD BECOMES FIRST BLACK AMERICAN PROFESSIONAL FOOTBALL PLAYER
Fritz Pollard coached and played for the Akron Indians of the American Professional Football League. He was the first Black player in professional football and became the first Black coach of a major professional team. He coached the team to the World Professional Championship in 1920.

PROGRESSIVE FARMERS AND HOUSEHOLD UNION OF AMERICA ORGANIZE
In this year, Black farmers of Phillips County, Arkansas, were finally successful in organizing and formally protesting against the cruel dependency of their sharecropper and tenant farmer relationships. Their union called for landlords to be accountable so that members could calculate their own earnings. Although Black farmers had tried for several decades to improve their economic and social status, previous Black organizations had met with overwhelming intimidation and were immediately dissolved. The organization of the Progressive Farmers and Household Union alarmed whites, who tried to suppress this organizational "rebellion." They attacked Black farmers in Elaine, Arkansas. Whites from Arkansas, Mississippi, and Tennessee indiscriminately attacked Black farmers, and although some Blacks fought back, they were no match when federal troops poured in to help the white farmers suppress the Blacks' "rebellious" actions. Many Blacks arrested by Arkansas officials were quickly tried and convicted; twelve were sentenced to death, and fifty-four were sentenced to from one to as many as twenty years in prison. Because of the sweeping, unsubstantiated nature of the convictions, the U.S. Supreme Court and the Arkansas governor later released the twelve who had been sentenced to death.

RACIAL DISCRIMINATION SHOULD BE OUTLAWED
William Monroe Trotter, a noted civil rights leader, argued strongly but unsuccessfully at the Paris Peace Conference that the treaty to end World War I should include an end to racial discrimination. Trotter had some difficulty getting to Paris. When his application for a passport was denied, he had to take a job as a cook on a transatlantic ship. His frustration apparently added fire and poignancy to his speech before the delegates.

"RED SUMMER" OF VIOLENCE RESULTS IN MANY DEATHS
As many as eighty-three Blacks were lynched during the "Red Summer of Hate," as the Ku Klux Klan held more than two hundred meetings throughout the country to launch arbitrary lynchings, shootings, and other acts of violence on Black people. Mobs hanged seventy-eight Blacks, including several World War I veterans, and burned eleven men at the stake.

Race riots occurred in twenty-five cities from April to early October. The largest took place in Chicago, where thirty-eight persons of both races died and five hundred were injured. Other serious riots occurred in Elaine, Arkansas; Charleston, South Carolina; Knoxville, Tennessee; Longview, Texas; Omaha, Nebraska; and Washington, D.C.

Several factors led to this flood of violence. A growing number of Blacks were pitted against whites in obtaining jobs and housing in northern cities. Blacks in turn had new aspirations of political power

This photograph shows a Black victim of the Chicago race riot, one of the nation's worst. Burgeoning Black migration to northern cities caused increased competition for housing and jobs and consequently increased racial tensions.

and wealth. Those returning from the war in particular believed that they would be rewarded for their efforts in defeating Germany, but these hopes were, in general, not realized. The country in general wanted to push Blacks to the bottom of the social, political, and economic ladders. Legal avenues to equality also seemed cut off, and many formerly nonviolent Blacks became aggressive. Never before had retaliatory violence been so widespread. Some suggested that a "New Negro" was emerging, one who would retaliate if attacked.

These circumstances were compounded by the prevailing mistrust in postwar America of all things "alien," including Blacks. The "Red Scare" translated into beatings of the foreign-born, mass arrests of radicals, and raids on left-wing organizations. Americans searching for "enemies within" directed their hatred toward foreigners, nonconformists, radicals, and Blacks.

In an article in *Crisis*, Walter White cited the following causes of the riot in Chicago as applicable to any of the major cities with large Black populations: racial prejudice, economic competition, political corruption and exploitation of Negro voter, police inefficiency, newspaper lies about Negro crime, unpunished crimes against Negroes, housing, and reaction of whites and Negroes from war.

State v. *Young* ADMITS BLACKS TO JURIES IN VIRGINIA

The Virginia Supreme Court declared in *State* v. *Young* that Blacks should be admitted to juries in the state. The ruling derived from a case in which a Black man had been sentenced to life in prison by an all-white jury.

SUPREME COURT STRIKES DOWN SEGREGATION IN KENTUCKY

The U.S. Supreme Court struck down the Louisville ordinance requiring Blacks and whites to live on separate blocks.

PAN-AFRICAN CONGRESS CONVENES

On **FEBRUARY 19** through **21**, the first Pan-African Congress, organized by W. E. B. Du Bois, met at the Grand Hotel in Paris, France. Du Bois's goal was to promote unity and peace in the world. The meeting, which was attended by representatives from as many as sixteen countries and colonies, was the first convention of the world's Black people. A total of fifty-seven delegates, including sixteen from the United States and fourteen from Africa, spoke passionately about peace and brotherhood. Blaise Diagne of Senegal was elected president, and Du Bois, secretary.

ASSOCIATED NEGRO PRESS FORMED

On **MARCH 2**, the Associated Negro Press (ANP) was established by Claude A. Barnett. The ANP became the first national news service for African American newspapers.

RACE RIOT SPARKED IN CHICAGO

From **JULY 27** through **30**, Chicago was the scene of one of the nation's worst riots. The city had experienced a large immigration of southern Blacks and whites, and tensions between the two groups had worsened as crowding and demand for housing escalated. (In the short time between 1915 and 1919, the Black population in Chicago had tripled, increasing from just over 50,000 to roughly 150,000.) Many of these new arrivals were concentrated in the so-called Black Belt — the city's south side. The large influx of southern whites brought with them their traditional racism.

The riot started on Sunday afternoon as hundreds of whites and Blacks crowded the beaches at Twenty-sixth and Twenty-ninth Streets along Lake Michigan. These beaches formed the eastern boundary of Chicago's Black Belt. Blacks and whites had hitherto observed an invisible line in the water separating the two beaches: the Twenty-ninth Street beach was considered the white beach, and the Twenty-sixth Street beach was considered the Black beach. They were sometimes referred to as the southern beach and the northern beach. There are several accounts of how the riot actually started.

ACCOUNT 1: On Sunday afternoon, July 27, four Black youths walked through the white section of the bathing beach and decided to enter the water. When white men ordered them to leave and they refused, whites threw stones at the Black youths. They were consequently chased from the white beach. The Blacks went to their own beach and returned with re-inforcements; the conflict escalated. During the conflict, a seventeen-year-old Black youth strayed from the Black side of the beach onto the white side. Perhaps frightened, rather than swimming back to the Black side, he managed to find a piece of wood to float on in the deep water. When a white man started to swim toward the Black youth, he let go of the wood and went down. Blacks charged that the youth had been struck by someone and pointed out a white man who was throwing stones. The white policeman refused to arrest him. News spread that the young boy had been stoned to death. Police reinforcements were called in, and when they arrived, they found a crowd of angry Blacks. A shot was heard, and a Black policeman was believed shot by a member of the crowd; the policeman returned fire and killed his assailant.

ACCOUNT 2: The incident started when a seventeen-year-old Black male, Eugene Williams, strayed over the line separating the beaches as he floated on a railroad tie. When pelted with stones, he lost his grip on the tie and drowned. Police refused to arrest those who threw the stones that hit Williams. The drowning and the refusal by police to arrest the offender incited the riot. According to the coroner's jury, Williams had drowned from "fear of stone throwing."

Later in the afternoon, a Black fired a shot into a group of policemen at the beach and was killed by a Black policeman.

Both accounts are generally similar from this point on. Larger and larger crowds gathered, and during the remainder of the afternoon, evening, and fol-lowing morning, clashes occurred near the beach and in white districts to the west. It was reported that twenty-seven Blacks were beaten, seven stabbed, and four shot. That morning, Blacks went to work as usual. On their way home, they were attacked by white ruffians. Many were pulled from streetcars, dragged into the street, and shot. Police were unable to cope with these attacks, as whites rode through Black residential areas shooting at random into Black homes. Black residents retaliated by sniping. Hostilities continued into Tuesday and Wednesday. On Wednesday, Mayor William Hale Thompson called in the militia to patrol the south side. Rioting abated as rain fell Wednesday night and Thursday.

The riot resulted in more than thirty-eight deaths — fifteen whites and twenty-three Blacks; 537 people were injured, including 178 whites. As many as one thousand individuals were left homeless after the riot. About one-third of the clashes during the riot occurred in the Black Belt, and 40 percent in white neighborhoods near the stockyards. The mobs were made up, for the most part, of boys between the ages of fifteen and twenty-two. Subsequent investigation showed that violence was intermittent, not continuous. Most rioting occurred after work hours. Police had insufficient forces for handling the riot.

LINCOLN MOTION PICTURE COMPANY RELEASES FIRST FILM
On **SEPTEMBER 3**, Noble Johnson and Clarence Brooks, owners of the Lincoln Motion Picture Company, a film company wholly owned by African Americans, released their first feature-length film, *A Man's Duty.*

1920
POPULATION OVERVIEW
BLACK POPULATION IN THE UNITED STATES The Black population in the United States exceeded the ten million mark — 10,463,131 total residents. They made up 9.9 percent of the national population (105,710,620). Overall, the Black population had increased by 6.5 percent over the previous decade; but the urban Black population had grown by 32.6 percent. Rural communities had 224,876 fewer Blacks in 1920 than in 1910. On the other hand, urban communities gained 870,244 more Blacks than were present in 1910. These shifts reflected massive migration of Blacks.

MULATTO POPULATION The 1920 census counted only 1,660,554 mulattos, a considerable drop from the 1910 figure of 2,050,606. This decrease reflected the racist conditions of the time, which made mulattos unwilling to report themselves as such. Also, those who could "pass" for white may have done so. Both situations could have caused a drop in the actual number of mulattos counted.

GEOGRAPHIC DISTRIBUTION OF BLACK RESIDENTS The Black population was unevenly distributed. For example, only about 79,000 Blacks resided in the entire New England region; 78,000 in the Mountain and Pacific states (the Far West); 1,393,000 in the Middle Atlantic, East North Central, and West North Central states (the industrial heartland of the country); and 8,900,000 in the South. Although Blacks made up less than 3 percent of the population in each of the other census regions, they composed about one-fourth of the total population in the South. Blacks' continued concentration in the South was a result of the limits poverty set on mobility but also reflected a lack of knowledge about opportunities elsewhere and the intimidating tactics by whites that inhibited migration.

Georgia had the largest Black population of any state at this time — 1,206,365 out of a total population of 2,895,832. Blacks composed 41.7 percent of the state's population. In fact, Georgia's Black population was larger than the Black population residing in the Middle Atlantic and East North Central states together. Eight southern states had Black populations greater than those in the Middle Atlantic states or the East North Central states. Ten southern states had Black populations constituting more than 25 percent of the state population — six of these had Black populations that exceeded 33 percent of total residents.

Within these states, the Black population was quite unevenly distributed. Some counties had Black majorities, whereas others were primarily white. The Black population was concentrated in agricultural areas where labor was used intensively for cotton, rice, tobacco, and sugar. Counties with heavy concentrations of Blacks were frequently referred to as the Black Belt.

BLACK MIGRATION During the 1920s, an estimated 749,000 Blacks migrated from the South. Prior to 1900, more than 90 percent of the Black population lived in the South, but their migration increased with each decade. The North offered greater opportunities in employment and better race relations. The South continued to undergo significant changes as whites assumed greater control over political systems and regained the superior positions they had lost during Reconstruction. Rigid Jim Crow segregation patterns and disfranchisement were legislated, and white in-

timidation, including lynchings, increased. With jobs declining in the cotton industry and whites competing for many of the same jobs that were once traditionally "Negro jobs," many Blacks, perceiving themselves as "surplus labor," set out for employment opportunities in the North.

URBANIZATION AND THE BLACK POPULATION IN THE UNITED STATES

A census report showed that for the first time, the urban population was greater than the rural population in the United States. The northeastern region was considerably more urban than the other regions. Fully three-quarters of all residents in the Northeast lived in cities. The South lagged behind — only about one-third of the residents there resided in cities. Large cities such as New York City and Chicago were growing more than 7 times faster than rural areas. The Chicago Commission on Race Relations reported that during an 18-month period, more than 50,000 Blacks had arrived in the city.

Most major northern cities experienced marked increases in Black population during the 1910–1920 decade. For example, the Black population of Chicago increased by 148.2 percent (from 62,355 to 109,458); Columbus grew by 74 percent (from 12,739 to 22,181); and New York's jumped by 66.3 percent (from 60,758 to 152,467). Philadelphia and St. Louis each experienced growth in Black population in excess of 50 percent; Indianapolis, Kansas City, and Columbus saw similar percentage growth rates. This growth was at least partially influenced by labor recruiters who circulated throughout the South during this period, offering both free transportation and high wages to Blacks willing to work in industrial plants of the North. Northern industrial firms were forced to recruit large numbers of Blacks when World War I immigration restrictions reduced their supply of cheap immigrant labor.

Social scientists have discerned three major migration streams that characterized the movement of Blacks from the Deep South. The first wave came from the Carolinas, Georgia, and Florida. Blacks from these states moved up the east coast to the big cities of Washington, D.C., Philadelphia, New York City, and Boston. A second stream was composed of migrants from Mississippi, Arkansas, and part of Alabama who headed for the midwestern cities of St. Louis, Detroit, Chicago, and Milwaukee. The third group migrated from Texas and part of Louisiana and moved to Los Angeles and other cities on the West

Coast. New streams of migration developed as opportunities occurred in other cities.

The census reported that New York City was the largest city in the country, with 5.6 million residents. It was followed by Chicago, Philadelphia, Los Angeles, and San Francisco. Of these, Philadelphia had the largest proportion of Blacks, 7.4 percent.

ECONOMIC CONDITIONS OVERVIEW

BLACK ENTERPRISES CONSTITUTE SMALL PERCENTAGE OF U.S. BUSINESSES According to the census, about 70,000 Blacks were engaged in business enterprises at this time. This number was quite small when compared to the total number of businesses in the United States at the time (2,258,423). Although Blacks made up about 10 percent of the total national population, they controlled about 3 percent of its business concerns. More important, the majority of Black business concerns were concentrated in retail trade and personal services that served Blacks largely or exclusively. The scope of their investment, business activity, and client base was often limited. The most common enterprises are shown in the table.

NUMBER OF BLACK-OWNED BUSINESS ENTERPRISES, 1920

BUSINESS	NUMBER
Restaurant and Lunchroom Keepers	7,511
Grocers	6,339
Truck farmers	6,242
Hucksters and peddlers	3,194
Butchers and meat dealers	3,009
Miscellaneous retail dealers	1,754
Poolroom keepers	1,582
Undertakers	1,558
Contractors and builders	1,454
Real-estate dealers	1,369
Junk dealers	1,132
Hotel keepers and managers	1,020

Source: U.S. Bureau of the Census, 1920.

BLACK FARMING PEAKS AMID UNCERTAIN CONDITIONS Black farmers (owners, tenants, and sharecroppers) reached their greatest number in 1920. Black farmers numbered almost 1 million (925,710) and represented about 14 percent of the 6.5 million farmers in the United States. About half were tenant farmers who were paid with a share of the harvested crop.

The boll weevil, an insect that destroys the cotton plant, spread rapidly through the South at this time, reducing cotton production and consequently the number of Black laborers needed. Soil erosion and depletion in many cotton-producing areas, particularly Georgia and South Carolina, as well as the use of machinery to plant, weed, and pick the cotton, further reduced the need for labor.

LAND OWNERSHIP IN THE SOUTH In a special census of agriculture issued in 1927, the following characteristics of land ownership in 1925 were noted for the South:

❖ There were 2,299,963 white farmers and 831,455 Black farmers. Black farmers made up about one-third of all southern farmers. Nine-tenths of all Black farmers resided in the South.

❖ Fewer than one-fifth of Black farmers owned their farms (159,651), compared to one-half of white farmers who owned their farms in full (1,173,778).

❖ There were 636,248 Black tenant farmers in the South, compared to 965,051 white tenant farmers. Although Blacks constituted one-fourth of all farmers in the South, they made up two-fifths of all tenant farmers in the South.

❖ In South Carolina and Mississippi only, there were more Black farmers than white farmers. South Carolina had 90,581 Black farmers and 82,186 white farmers. Nearly half of the white farmers (37,925) owned their farms; fewer than one-sixth of the Black farmers (14,476) owned theirs. Black tenant farmers numbered 72,179; whites numbered 40,251. For Mississippi, the proportions were quite similar except that only about one-ninth of the Black farmers owned their land, and the number of Black tenants (130,796) was three times higher than the number of white tenants (44,946). Clearly, the statistics show that Black farmers rarely owned land. Over the 1900–1920 period, the percentage of farm tenancy among Blacks increased: 74.6 percent in 1900, 75.3 percent in 1910, and 76.3 percent in 1920.

This tenant farmer with a plow and two mules farmed in the way that southern Blacks had farmed for decades. The uncertainties of farming and abuse from landlords sent many tenant farmers deeper into debt every year.

LIFE AS A TENANT FARMER Most Black farmers did not own land but lived precariously from the wages they received from the sale of contracted portions of the crops they planted, cared for, and harvested. Two types of tenant farmers had emerged over the years: (1) those who controlled all aspects of farming (what to plant, when to harvest, when to sell, and who to sell to) and who often made a small amount of money; and (2) those whose actions were entirely controlled by the landowners. As sharecroppers, members of this latter group borrowed supplies from the landowner, merchants, and the company store for subsistence and for raising the crop. The sharecropper furnished the labor. Because of high interest rates on rented implements, the rented shack, overpriced goods, and deceitful landowners, sharecroppers often fell into heavy debt for many years.

For most Blacks, tenant farming was a most uncertain way of life. Usually the landlord kept the books and sold the crop, and the Black farmer, often illiterate or semiliterate, was easily shortchanged. In fact,

even if the farmer was aware of being shortchanged, there was often very little the farmer could do about it. Sometimes, the landlord would broker the crop — buying it at a low price and selling it at a higher price. Because most Black farmers were poor, they borrowed from the landlord for equipment and personal necessities. These loans were secured against the crop yield and were often inflated and frequently modified so that the landlord would eventually get a larger proportion of the crop yield. The tenant farmers got deeper in debt and were prevented from leaving the land or held on the land against their will until the debt had been paid. The law allowed the sheriff or other law officials to arrest farmers who left without paying off debts. There is evidence that Black tenant farmers left the land many times, only to be returned to the same dependencies by the law officials.

In some cases, the tenant farmer was paid a wage that was secured by a contract. Even with a contract, employers would pay Black workers what they chose to. This type of abuse was frequent. When Blacks left because of being shortchanged, they were frequently arrested and brought back to fulfill the contract (generally for terms of five to seven years). Sometimes, the Black employee was severely whipped as punishment for leaving the farm. Governor Hugh Dorsey of Georgia, in a public statement issued on April 22, 1921, noted that a Georgia planter actually killed eleven Black laborers to prevent them from revealing the conditions under which they were forced to work. In many cases, Blacks were no better off than they had been during slavery.

MORE BLACKS WORK IN MANUFACTURING According to the Bureau of the Census, as many as 566,680 Blacks were engaged in manufacturing and mechanical pursuits, up from 406,582 in 1910. Blacks could be found in a wide range of industrial activities.

STRIKES ENLARGE BLACK EMPLOYMENT OPPORTUNITIES During the first part of this decade, strikes occurred in almost every major industrial city, creating opportunities for many Blacks who were brought up from the South as strikebreakers. In fact, for the first time, Blacks entered industries that had previously excluded them and secured jobs that had been wholly monopolized by white workers. Cities such as Boston, New York City, Philadelphia, Pittsburgh, Cleveland, Cincinnati, Detroit, Indianapolis, Chicago, St. Louis, and Kansas City employed the overwhelming majority of Blacks in manufacturing industries. Unfortunately, most of the jobs Blacks obtained

OCCUPATIONS OF BLACKS IN MANUFACTURING, 1920

OCCUPATION	NUMBER
Blacksmiths	9,046
Boilermakers	1,402
Brick masons	10,736
Carpenters/cabinetmakers	34,916
Cigar/tobacco workers	19,849
Clay, glass, stone workers	3,596
Clothing workers	13,888
Coopers	2,252
Dressmakers	27,160
Electricians	1,411
Stationary engineers	6,353
Firefighters	29,640

Source: U.S. Bureau of the Census, 1920.

during strikes were only temporary. Eventually, however, Blacks were able to secure permanent jobs in manufacturing in large northern cities.

SOCIAL CONDITIONS OVERVIEW

APOLLO THEATRE BECOMES PREMIER ENTERTAINMENT CENTER The Apollo Theatre in Harlem became the most prestigious Black entertainment center of the country — a position it held until the 1960s. No Black entertainer "made it" without playing the Apollo. Its popularity peaked in the days when Blacks were barred from white hotels, theaters, and other entertainment spots. Whites, too, came to the Apollo Theatre, as well as to the Cotton Club, to see Black performers.

One of the historic features of the Apollo Theatre was the "Tree of Hope." Aspiring artists, including Paul Robeson, Ethel Waters, and Bill Robinson, would gather under an old elm tree in the heart of Harlem before entertaining. It was said that many entertainers stroked the bark of the tree for good luck. The Tree of Hope stood near the Lafayette Theater and the Cotton Club at Seventh Avenue and 132nd Street. When the tree was cut down in 1934, the stump was placed in the Lafayette Theater. Today, the stump is housed in the Apollo Theatre, where young amateur performers still stroke it for luck.

BEALE STREET IN MEMPHIS EMERGES AS HEART OF BLACK COMMUNITY This street, formerly the home of wealthy cotton planters before the Civil War, became the center of the Memphis Black community in the 1920s.

After the Civil War, epidemics of yellow fever drove the wealthy to healthier areas of the city. The area became a Jewish commercial hub in the 1890s and later became the center of the Black neighborhood. It was here that Black musicians flourished, including W. C. Handy, who described the area in his "Beale Street Blues." The Daisy Theatre attracted the top Black entertainers of the time. The area thrived during prohibition but by the 1950s had begun to decay. About twenty years later, the street was restored as a tourist attraction.

BLACK COLLEGES FOUNDED Most Black colleges and universities established since 1920 had been publicly supported, and the majority were junior and community colleges. Although only a few of these were founded as Black colleges, many evolved as such because of their locations in predominantly Black areas, including Black neighborhoods of Los Angeles, Chicago, Detroit, Atlanta, Newark, and Houston. Black students are also in the majority at Wayne County Community College (Michigan) and Essex County College (New Jersey).

BLACK RESORT BUILT IN FLORIDA The Afro-American Life Insurance Company purchased twenty acres of oceanfront land near Jacksonville, Florida, as a resort area for Blacks, who were generally barred from white resorts and public beaches in the state. The community was developed with modern homes and electric street lighting. Many original property owners still live in the community.

INTERMARRIAGE BETWEEN RACES PROHIBITED Marriages between the races in the South were illegal and unconstitutional. In six southern states — Alabama, Florida, North Carolina, South Carolina, Mississippi, and Tennessee — it was unconstitutional for any white person and a Black, or a descendant of a Black, to marry. Other states adopted laws under which intermarriages between whites and Blacks were prohibited, including Delaware, Maryland, Virginia, West Virginia, South Carolina, Georgia, Florida, Alabama, Louisiana, Kentucky, Tennessee, Arkansas, Oklahoma, and Texas. In Arizona, California, Mississippi, Missouri, Montana, Utah, and Oregon, intermarriages between whites and Asians were prohibited. In its annual report, the NAACP in 1927 noted that six states — Connecticut, Maine, Massachusetts, Michigan, New Jersey, and Rhode Island — had introduced anti-intermarriage bills. They were all defeated.

NEGRO BANNER DISPLAYED first used by Marcus Garvey in the 1920s, the banner employed colors selected to represent the "new Negro." Black was for "our race," red for "our blood," and green for "our hope."

KANSAS CITY, MISSOURI, BECOMES JAZZ CENTER A particular kind of jazz, Kansas City jazz, emerged in the 1920s and 1930s. This style, which included solo improvisations and riffs by the brass section, was epitomized by the Count Basie Band, which was organized there. Charlie "Bird" Parker was also part of this movement.

"TOO DAMNED PROSPEROUS AND BIGGITY FOR A NIGGER" It was not necessarily a positive thing for Blacks to be prosperous or successful at this time. In many parts of the South, whites wanted Black people to be dependent, helpless, and "childlike." They promoted numerous measures to create this type of behavior. But when Black farmers saved, purchased land and livestock, practiced efficiency in farming, and became quite prosperous, white neighbors often became jealous and took revenge. Blacks who were thrifty and prosperous were often labeled "uppity niggers" or "too biggity for a nigger." When word of their wealth spread through a farm community, trouble often followed.

Governor Hugh M. Dorsey of Georgia eloquently described a case in point, which began when a Black man saved money, purchased a farm of 140 acres, and lived there with his wife and twelve children. Three of his daughters were schoolteachers, and their contributions allowed the family to live quite well and have a prosperous farm. When the farmer became active during the war in the sale of Liberty Bonds and Thrifty Stamps, an action praised by the local press, his white neighbors saw things quite differently — he was getting "too damned prosperous and biggity for a nigger." His white neighbor had the Black's land surveyed and later drove stakes at least twenty-five feet over into the Black man's property. The Black man, knowing where his property ended, disregarded the new boundary and plowed to his old line.

On a Saturday afternoon when the Black farmer, his three daughters, and one son went into town, he was handed an arrest warrant by the town marshal. An altercation occurred, and the marshal struck and knocked the Black man to the ground. Almost immediately, several other white men rushed to assist the marshal. They beat the Black man severely. Part of Dorsey's statement follows:

> Two of his daughters started to him. A man kicked one girl in the stomach. The other reached her father and began to wipe the blood from his face. The three were quickly overpowered. The third daughter and the son were caught. All were locked in jail. The girl who was kicked became deathly sick. She lay in jail moaning and begging that something be done for her, and for her father, who was bleeding badly from his wounds. The sheriff locked them in and left them without medical attention and ignorant of the charge against them.
>
> Next morning the Negro learned that his neighbor had sworn out a warrant against him for trespass. The marshall refused to tell him what the charge was against his son and daughters. The Negro employed a lawyer. Then he found that he and his daughters were charged with resisting an officer in the discharge of his duty, his son with carrying a pistol. Only one witness claimed to have seen the pistol. This was the white neighbor who said that he had seen the son put the pistol in the buggy while the crowd was on his father. The buggy was searched. The pistol was not found.
>
> Talk of lynching the Negro and his family caused their removal to another county. . . .
>
> The man, his daughters and son were tried in the Superior Court. The father was sentenced to serve twelve months in the chain gang and pay a fine of $250. The girls were fined $50 each. The son was fined $100. The Negro paid the fines of his children.
>
> The man's smaller children and wife were in his home while he was in jail. A mob, led by the town marshal, went to the house, kicked open the door and demanded admittance, then shot up the house and went away. This was night.
>
> Next morning, the woman with her children fled from her home, never to return.
>
> A friend went by night and removed the livestock belonging to the family, and sold it for them at a great sacrifice. Their crop was a total loss. They will be lynched, it is said, if any of them ever return to their home.
>
> The education of his children and the success of his thrift seem to be the sole offense of the Negro.

For many Black farmers, success brought a high social cost — being punished for success or being run out of town.

BLACK WOMEN RECEIVE DOCTORATES

The distinction of being the first Black woman to receive a Ph.D. degree was shared by Eva B. Dykes, who received a Ph.D. in English from Radcliffe College; Sadi T. Mossell, with a Ph.D. in economics from the University of Pennsylvania; and Georgiana R. Simpson, with a Ph.D. in German from the University of Chicago.

DEPRIEST ELECTED ALDERMAN IN CHICAGO

Oscar DePriest (1871–1951) gained the support of Chicago's Second Ward Republicans. He defeated his competition in the general election to represent this ward, which was 70 percent Black, in the city council.

DETT'S MUSICAL GENIUS HONORED

During this year, Robert Nathaniel Dett (1882–1943), a Black composer and conductor, was honored for his talent and his wide-ranging contributions to music. An educator at Hampton Institute and leader of the famed Hampton Institute Choir, Dett was awarded the Bowdoin Prize by Harvard University for an essay entitled "The Emancipation of Negro Music."

Dett had studied music at the University of Chicago, Columbia University, Harvard University, Oberlin College, and the University of Pennsylvania. He was known as one of the most gifted and learned scholars of piano performance. Under his leadership, the Hampton Institute Choir performed at Carnegie Hall in New York, Symphony Hall in Boston, and in a number of European locations. Among his compositions were *Magnolia* (1912), *Music in the Mine* (1916), *Enchantment* (1922), and *The Ordering of Moses* (1937). Among a string of awards, Dett was awarded honorary degrees from the Eastman School of Music, Oberlin College, and Harvard University.

THREE BLACKS LYNCHED IN MINNESOTA

In Duluth, Minnesota, a mob of more than five thousand whites gathered and lynched three Blacks. Race riots also occurred in Independence, Kansas, and Ocoee, Florida.

WHITES KILLED DURING LYNCHING ATTEMPT IN KENTUCKY

In Lexington, Kentucky, five white persons were killed while attempting to lynch a Black man accused of murder.

NATIONAL NEGRO BASEBALL LEAGUE ORGANIZED

On **FEBRUARY 20**, the constitution of the National Negro Baseball League, organized by Andrew "Rube" Foster, was signed. Over the years, a large number of talented Black baseball players had moved from one small Black community to another in search of a team to play. Foster succeeded in assembling eight midwestern clubs: the Chicago American Giants (his team), the Chicago Giants, the Cuban Stars, the Detroit Stars, the St. Louis Stars, the Indianapolis ABC, the Kansas City Monarchs, and the Dayton Marcos. Only the owner of the Kansas City Monarchs, J. L. Wilkinson, was white.

Blacks were excluded from playing on white teams and in their leagues during the early twentieth century. In 1906, however, a league of two white and four Black teams was formed, but it received little support and folded the next season. In the late 1800s, however, there were several baseball teams composed of Black players. In fact, in the summer of 1887, the Cuban Giants, a Black baseball team, played Cincinnati, a major-league team, and beat them 11–5. In the same season, the Gorhams, another Black team, beat the Metropolitans, a major-league team in New York, by a score of 2–1.

Foster hoped that one day the Black and white champions would play each other in the World Series. Foster planned to develop Black baseball so that when integration finally occurred, "we would be ready."

Foster had been an outstanding pitcher with a number of Black teams before organizing the Chicago American Giants, who won several pennants. He was also credited with inventing the hit-and-run bunt, a strategy never adopted in the white leagues. His players were well paid for the time, receiving about two thousand dollars per year. Thirty-six of the players in the Negro leagues eventually played in the majors. Foster was elected to the Baseball Hall of Fame in 1981.

ZETA PHI BETA INCORPORATED

On **MARCH 30**, the Zeta Phi Beta sorority was founded and incorporated at Howard University.

UNIVERSAL NEGRO IMPROVEMENT ASSOCIATION (UNIA) HOLDS INTERNATIONAL CONVENTION

On **AUGUST 1**, the pioneer Black nationalist Marcus Garvey inaugurated the International Convention of the Universal Negro Improvement Association (UNIA) in the Liberty Hall of Harlem in New York City. The next day, as many as twenty-five thousand Blacks crowded into Madison Square Garden to hear Marcus Garvey speak on the goals of UNIA. Garvey's movement had already spread to a number of cities in the United States and claimed millions of members. In addition to publishing the *Negro World*, Garvey founded the Universal Black Cross Nurses, the Universal African Motor Corps, the Black Star Steamship Line, and the Black Eagle Flying Corps. UNIA reached its greatest influence during the years 1920 through 1922.

O'NEILL'S *The Emperor Jones* PREMIERES WITH BLACK ACTOR

On **NOVEMBER 3**, Charles Gilpin starred in the role of Brutus Jones in the play *The Emperor Jones* by Eugene O'Neill, which premiered with the New York–based Provincetown Players. His performance was given excellent reviews by the critics. The *New York Times* and the *Tribune* called it "a performance of heroic stature."

JOHNSON BECOMES SECRETARY OF NAACP

On **NOVEMBER 6**, poet James Weldon Johnson became the first Black executive secretary of the NAACP.

1921 COLEMAN BECOMES LICENSED INTERNATIONAL PILOT

Bessie Coleman (1893–1926) became the first person to receive an international pilot's license when she graduated from the Federation Aeronautique Internationale in France. She was also the first Black woman pilot and the first Black woman stunt pilot. She died in an air crash.

FILIBUSTER BLOCKS ANTILYNCHING BILL

Southern Democrats filibustered to block the Dyer antilynching bill in the U.S. House of Representatives. The NAACP had worked to secure a sponsor for the bill. James Weldon Johnson, secretary of the NAACP, had persuaded L. C. Dyer, representative from Missouri, to introduce a bill "to assure to persons within the jurisdiction of every state the equal protection of the laws, and to punish the crime of lynching."

HARLEM RENAISSANCE BLOSSOMS

The Harlem Renaissance — a period of creativity among Black artists, writers, musicians, orators, dramatists, and entertainers — was centered in Harlem, the largest urban Black community in the country, which had grown substantially with the arrival of thousands of southern Black migrants. It was an exciting time — with the end of World War I, the economy had improved, and the Black middle class prospered. Black artists flourished, and both Black and white Americans eagerly received their work. At the time, the movement was referred to as the "New Negro" movement and then the "Negro Renaissance." The term *renaissance* was used because the movement built on the heritage of Black Americans. More books were published by Black authors during the 1920s than in any previous decade in American history. The artists who participated in the Harlem Renaissance were brought together by their common cultural experience. They did not create a formal organization but rather were friends and colleagues. For the most part, they maintained strong relationships with white patrons who were instrumental in publicizing their works. As the Great Depression of the late 1920s deepened and extended into the next decade, the renaissance slowed — little money was available to support the artists.

LYNCHING OF BLACKS CONTINUES

In this year, fifty-nine Blacks were lynched.

MOSSELL PRACTICES LAW

Sadi T. Mossell, one of the first Black women to receive a doctoral degree in the United States, became the first Black woman to practice law in Pennsylvania.

RACIAL TURBULENCE CONTINUES IN CHICAGO

From 1917 to 1921, an average of one racially motivated bombing every twenty or so days took place in Chicago. Many of these bombings served the same purpose as racially restrictive housing covenants formed in other cities — they prevented Blacks from moving into white neighborhoods by terrorizing them. In many cases, too, the bombings were the work of the Ku Klux Klan, which had expanded significantly to the North and the West.

Shuffle Along OPENS ON BROADWAY

On **MAY 23**, *Shuffle Along*, one of the most popular Black musicals, opened at the Sixty-third Street Music Hall in New York City. Eubie Blake (James Hubert Blake), a ragtime pianist and composer, and Noble Sissle produced the musical, using scenery and costumes left over from other shows. This was the first Broadway show to be written, produced, and performed by Blacks. It was also the first to include jazz compositions.

It is sometimes speculated that the Harlem Renaissance may have come about because of the success of *Shuffle Along*. The show launched a number of Black performers, including Florence Mills, who later

HARLEM RENAISSANCE AUTHORS

AUTHOR	WORK	YEAR PUBLISHED
Bontemps, Arna	*God Sends Sunday*	1931
Cullen, Countee	*Color*	1925
	The Black Christ	1929
Du Bois, W. E. B.	*The Souls of Black Folk*	1924
Fausett, Jessie	*There Is Confusion*	1922
	Plum Bun	1929
Fisher, Rudolph	*The Walls of Jericho*	1928
Gordon, Taylor	*Born to Be*	1929
Handy, W. C.	*The Blues: An Anthology*	1926
Hughes, Langston	*The Weary Blues*	1926
Johnson, Georgia Douglass	*Bronze*	1922
	An Autumn Love Cycle	1928
Johnson, James W.	*Book of American Negro Poetry*	1922
Larsen, Nella	*Quicksand*	1928
	Passing	1929
Locke, Alain	*The New Negro*	1925
McKay, Claude	*Harlem Shadows*	1922
	Home to Harlem	1928
	Banjo	1929
Thurman, Wallace	*The Blacker the Berry*	1929
Toomer, Jean	*Cane*	1923
Waldron, Erick	*Tropic Death*	1926
White, Walter	*The Fire in the Flint*	1922
	Flight	1926
	Rope and Faggot — A Biography of Judge Lynch	1929

starred in musicals in New York City and Europe, and Paul Robeson, who became known for his magnificent singing voice and acting abilities. William Still and Hall Johnson composed music and played in the orchestra. One of the important songs from the hit was "I'm Just Wild About Harry," which later became the campaign theme song for Harry Truman.

◈ Like other Black performers of the time, Blake (1883–1983) suffered the indignities of segregation. He was forced to stay at poor hotels, even while appearing on stage and drawing large white audiences. Blake was an accomplished jazz musician and com-

poser. For many years during the height of the Jazz Age, he collaborated with Noble Sissle on many songs and shows, some of which starred major entertainers like Josephine Baker. His ragtime hits included "The Charleston Rag" (1899), "Chevy Chase" (1914), "Fitz Water" (1914), and "Bugle Call Rag" (1926). Blake was rediscovered again in the 1970s when there was a renewed interest in ragtime music, especially the music of Scott Joplin, a friend and associate of Blake's in the early 1900s. Blake performed almost until the end of his life. The Eubie Blake Cultural Center has been established in his hometown of

HARLEM RENAISSANCE MUSICIANS

ARTIST	TALENT
Anderson, Marian	opera singer
Armstrong, Louis	jazz musician, orchestra leader
Bledsoe, Jules	singer, actor
Burleigh, Harry T.	singer
Carter, Benny	musician, orchestra leader
Christian, Charlie	jazz guitarist
Collette, Buddy	jazz musician
Dawson, William L.	writer, composer, director of Tuskegee Choir
Dett, Robert Nathaniel	writer and composer
Ellington, Edward Kennedy "Duke"	pianist, composer, orchestra leader
Fitzgerald, Ella	jazz singer
Gillespie, John Birks "Dizzy"	jazz trumpeter
Gordon, Taylor	singer
Hamilton, Chico	jazz musician
Hampton, Lionel	jazz vibraphonist, orchestra leader
Handy, W. C.	composer, cornetist, "Father of the Blues"
Hayes, Roland	concert singer
Johnson, Hall	violinist and leader of Hall Johnson Choir
Johnson, J. P.	musician (famous for the Charleston)
Johnson, J. Rosamond	singer
Kirby, John	musician, composer, orchestra leader
Mingus, Charlie	jazz bass player, band leader, composer
Mitchell, Abbie	singer, actress
Monk, Thelonious	jazz pianist, composer
Morton, Ferdinand Joseph "Jelly Roll"	pianist, composer
Parker, Charlie	jazz alto saxophonist
Powell, Earl "Bud"	jazz pianist, composer
Robeson, Paul	singer, actor
Still, William	writer and composer
Sullivan, Maxine	singer
Waller, Thomas "Fats"	musician
Webb, Chick	jazz drummer, composer, orchestra leader
Williams, Clarence	musician
Williams, Spencer	musician
Wilson, Teddy	musician, orchestra leader
Work, John W., III	writer, composer
Young, Lester	jazz tenor saxophonist

Louis "Satchmo" Armstrong (center rear) delivered a new jazz sound as the trumpeter of King Oliver's band. Armstrong and other Black American musicians made jazz popular among both whites and Blacks.

Baltimore, Maryland. It houses a collection of his belongings and musical memorabilia.

RACE RIOT SPARKED IN OKLAHOMA

Blacks and whites in Tulsa, Oklahoma, engaged in a "race war" in which more than eighty-five Blacks and whites were killed and several hundred injured. The riot followed the arrest of a Black man named Rowland on **MAY 31** on charges of attacking a white woman. Upon being taken to the courthouse, rumors circulated within the Black community that he was to be lynched. Armed Black citizens gathered at the

Tulsa County Courthouse to prevent this crime. Police attempted to disperse the crowd, but in the process, a volley of shots was fired. Blacks retreated to their neighborhoods, where they held off the pursuing white mob. Because of the size of the white mob and the lack of police control, the mayor called upon the governor for assistance. Three companies of the National Guard were dispatched to Tulsa, and in the midst of the commotion, Rowland was moved from the courthouse. On June 1, major violence erupted when armed whites directly assaulted the Black section of the city. Despite some resistance, whites set fire to every home they encountered as they penetrated deeper into the Black community, turning the disturbance into one of the bloodiest massacres this nation has witnessed.

In addition to the many Blacks killed, some whites were killed by Blacks, who were defending their homes and neighborhood. Early estimates listed sixty Blacks and twenty-five whites dead. Densely populated blocks of the Black community were completely destroyed, leaving thousands homeless and without any assistance. More than six thousand Blacks were rounded up, arrested, and placed in detention camps under heavy guard. The downtown Black section was completely burned, and only the chimneys remained standing.

According to the 1920 census, Tulsa had 8,878 Black residents out of a total population of 72,075. Based on its past, Tulsa was very much a "southern city." In fact, Tulsa County and the entire state of Oklahoma had been under siege by the KKK just a few years before the race riot. Race relations in the city and the state had reached a low point. Probably the most important aspect of this and other riots of the 1915–1935 period was the militancy associated with the "new Negro," who both demanded rights and opportunities and was prepared to fight and die for them.

Although business leaders quickly started to rebuild the Black section of town, many Blacks moved to other parts of Oklahoma or to other states.

Major race riots also broke out in Springfield, Ohio; Coatesville, Pennsylvania; Springfield, Illinois; Chester, Pennsylvania; Rosewood, Florida; Johnstown, Pennsylvania; and East St. Louis, Illinois. Major casualties occurred in Knoxville, Tennessee; Washington, D.C.; Millen, Georgia; Longview, Texas; Omaha, Nebraska; and rural Phillips County, Arkansas.

Clouds of smoke indicate where residential and downtown Black sections of Tulsa were burned during the 1921 race riot. Tulsa was a major center of KKK activity, and abuses of Blacks were common.

LIBERTY LIFE INSURANCE COMPANY FOUNDED

On **JULY 25**, the Liberty Life Insurance Company was founded by Frank L. Gillespie. Gillespie guided the growth and development of the company until 1926, when it merged with Supreme Life and Casualty of Columbus, Ohio, and Northeastern Life of Newark, New Jersey, to become the Supreme Life Insurance Company. For a while, it was one of the largest Black-owned companies in the nation.

1922 BLACK YOUTH BURNED AT THE STAKE

A Black youth was tortured and burned at the stake for allegedly killing a white woman in Georgia.

BLACK COMMITTEE MEMBERS ELECTED IN ST. LOUIS

Robert T. Scott was elected Republican committee member in St. Louis's Sixth Ward, becoming the first Black to serve on the city's Republican City Central Committee. Elizabeth Gamble became the first Black woman on the committee when she was appointed to succeed a white woman in the Seventeenth Ward.

BLACK-OWNED PROFESSIONAL BASKETBALL TEAM FORMED

Robert Douglas, an entrepreneur from Harlem, formed the first all-Black, Black-owned professional basketball team, the New York Renaissance, commonly referred to as the Rens. They played their first game in the Renaissance Ballroom and beat their opponents, the Collegiate Big Five, by a score of 28–22.

By the end of their second season, the Rens began playing almost all their games on the road. They played between 125 and 150 games a year, traveling across the country on their team bus. At the time, Black players could not compete on white teams, and there were no all-Black leagues. Therefore, the Rens played many white professional teams in exhibitions. The Rens were the world's best team throughout the 1930s, amassing an eighty-eight-game winning streak. The team's success peaked in 1939 when they won professional basketball's first integrated tournament. John Wooden, who later coached the University of California's basketball team to ten national championships, once played against the Rens. He called them "the best team I ever saw."

LYNCHING OF BLACKS CONTINUES

A total of fifty-one Blacks were lynched in this year.

MCKAY BECOMES MAJOR FIGURE IN HARLEM RENAISSANCE

Claude McKay (1890–1948) released *Harlem Shadows*, a collection of poetry. Although McKay had written several volumes of verse, *Songs of Jamaica* (1912), *Constab Ballads* (1912), and *Spring in New Hampshire* (1920), it was not until the publication of *Harlem Shadows* that McKay became significant in the new Black renaissance.

◈ Claude McKay was born in central Jamaica. At the age of six, he moved into the home of his brother, a schoolteacher, where Claude was exposed to literature, science, and the radical thinking of his brother. After a short apprenticeship at the age of sixteen,

Claude McKay, one of the important young writers of the Harlem Renaissance, was encouraged by a cadre of more established writers that included Charles Johnson, Alain Locke, and Jessie Fauset.

McKay joined the island constabulary. In this capacity, he met a number of people who influenced his life, including an Englishman, Edward Jekyll. Jekyll introduced McKay to major literary authors who inspired him to write two volumes of verse, *Songs of Jamaica* and *Constab Ballads*. In 1912, McKay studied agriculture at Tuskegee Institute, and later at Kansas State College, where he remained for about two years. By this time, writing had replaced agriculture as his vocation. Throughout the next several years, McKay published in *Pearson's Magazine* and the *Liberator*; he became the associate editor of the latter. In 1919, he traveled to England and worked with Sylvia Pankhurst, daughter of suffragist Emmeline Pankhurst, to publish *Workers Dreadnaught*. Upon his return to New York, he published his most important work, *Harlem Shadows*.

In 1922, McKay left for Russia to publicize this book. Before returning to the states in 1934, he traveled to France, Spain, Morocco, and a number of other countries. During this time, he published three novels: *Home to Harlem* (1928), *Banjo* (1929), and *Banana Bottom* (1933). In 1937, he wrote his autobiography, *A Long Way from Home*; in 1940, he published *Harlem: Negro Metropolis*.

In 1943, McKay had a stroke and died on May 23, 1948.

ANTILYNCHING BILL PASSED; BUT DEFEATED BY SENATE

On **JANUARY 26**, the U.S. House of Representatives passed the Dyer antilynching bill. However, the bill was defeated by a southern filibuster in the Senate, despite the fact that as many as fifty lynchings of Blacks had already occurred during the first six months of this year. Of the fifty lynchings, thirty were the result of mobs storming jails and taking prisoners. One of the most vivid of these incidents occurred in Kirvin, Texas, where more than five hundred whites gathered to watch the burning of three Black men.

The bill actually called for only mild punishment — the fining of law officers who allowed lynching to take place — for such a heinous crime.

BLACK FATHER OF WHITE WOMAN'S CHILD IS LYNCHED

On **JULY 14**, a Black man by the name of Jake Davis of Colquitt, Georgia, was lynched as punishment for being the father of a white woman's child.

When the woman gave birth to a Black child, her neighbors insisted that she reveal who was the father of the child. When she did so, a mob formed and the lynching was carried out.

ANTI–KU KLUX KLAN ACTIVITY ORGANIZED IN OKLAHOMA

In **SEPTEMBER**, anti–Ku Klux Klan activity was organized in Oklahoma in response to a rash of incidents led by the Klan. It had been reported that thousands of whippings had occurred and hundreds of Blacks had been run out of town, lynched, or wounded.

SIGMA GAMMA RHO SORORITY FOUNDED

On **NOVEMBER 12**, the Sigma Gamma Rho sorority was founded in Indianapolis, Indiana, by Mary Lou Allison, Bessie Mae Downey, Hattie Mae Annette Dulin, Nannie Mae Gahn, Dorothy Hanley, Cubena McClure, and Vivian White.

1923 BLACKS CONTINUE TO FLEE THE SOUTH

A spokesperson for the Department of Labor reported that as many as five hundred thousand Blacks had left the South in the previous twelve months.

Chandler v. *Neff* UPHOLDS DISFRANCHISEMENT OF BLACKS

In *Chandler* v. *Neff*, a federal court preserved the statute holding that the denial of the right to vote in a Democratic primary did not violate the "privileges and immunities of the Constitution."

HAYES IS FIRST BLACK PERFORMER AT CARNEGIE HALL

Opera singer Roland Hayes was the first Black performer to appear at Carnegie Hall in New York.

Hayes was widely known in Europe before being accepted by American audiences and was instrumental in opening up opportunities for other classical singers, including Marian Anderson, his protégé.

DUE PROCESS VIOLATED WHEN WITNESSES ARE INTIMIDATED

In *Moore* v. *Dempsey*, the U.S. Supreme Court declared that the due process of the law is violated when and if a trial is interfered with by mobs, or if witnesses are physically threatened or beaten.

JOHNSON FOUNDS *Opportunity* MAGAZINE

Dr. Charles S. Johnson (1893–1956) founded and became editor of the National Urban League's magazine,

Opportunity: Journal of Negro Life. This magazine published the works of writers and others who became part of the Harlem Renaissance.

◆ In 1917, Johnson received his doctorate in sociology from the University of Chicago. He was appointed in 1919 to the Governor's Committee to Investigate the Chicago Riots, which he had witnessed. In 1920, Johnson directed the National Urban League's research and investigation division. He coauthored a book entitled *The Negro in Chicago*, in 1922. Sub- sequently, Johnson held a number of positions, including that of consultant to the U.S. Department of Agriculture, director of the Swarthmore Institute for Race Relations, and director of the Julius Rosenwald Fund's Interracial Relations Program; he was also a member of the League of Nations team that investigated slavery in Liberia. Johnson, the son of a freed slave, was appointed the first Black president of Fisk University in 1946, a position he held until his death.

Charles Spurgeon Johnson, a writer and scholar, founded the journal of the National Urban League, Opportunity, *which aided many new Black writers by sponsoring literary contests.*

MORGAN RECEIVES PATENT FOR TRAFFIC LIGHT

Garrett Morgan (1875–1963) received a patent for the automatic traffic light. He sold the rights for this invention to General Electric for forty thousand dollars.

SMITH RECORDS FIRST SONG

Bessie Smith (1894–1937), "the Queen of the Blues," recorded her first song, "Down Hearted Blues," written by Alberta Hunter and Lovie Austin. The song sold about eight hundred thousand copies almost immediately — the first major hit for Columbia Records. It eventually sold more than one million copies. Smith became known for her emotional style and stage performances.

◈ Smith was born in a poor community in Tennessee. She eventually became the leading lady of blues, performing with many of the great bands in the country, including those of Louis Armstrong and Benny Goodman. Before this, she appeared in Black theaters throughout the North and in tent shows in the South.

Bessie Smith appealed to jazz and blues lovers with her magnificent voice and dramatic style. By 1927 she had become the highest-paid Black performer in the world. The continuing popularity of her music encouraged Columbia Records to reissue all of her songs on compact disc almost sixty years after her death.

Ten years after her first recording, Smith made her final and perhaps most famous recording, "Nobody Knows You When You're Down and Out." It summarized her later years, when the misery of the Great Depression left many blues singers without work. Smith became a heavy drinker as her popularity faded. She died in an automobile accident in Mississippi in 1937. The legend that she died after being refused admission to a nearby all-white hospital is untrue. Actually, she was taken immediately to a Black hospital, where she died. She was buried in Mt. Lawn Cemetery in Sharon Hill, Pennsylvania. For many years her grave was neglected. Finally, the singer Janis Joplin purchased a tombstone for it.

TEXAS BARS BLACKS FROM VOTING IN PRIMARIES

A statute barring Blacks from voting in any Democratic party primary in the state was enacted by the Texas legislature. The statute was authored by D. A. McAskill, who had been defeated in an election in Bexar County in 1922 by an opponent who was widely supported by Blacks.

KKK INFLUENCES IMPEACHMENT OF OKLAHOMA GOVERNOR

On **AUGUST 13**, Oklahoma governor J. C. Walton declared war on the Ku Klux Klan and late that day issued a proclamation that placed the city of Tulsa under martial law. The Klan responded on August 18 by setting up more than two hundred KKK cross burnings throughout the state. By August 31, absolute martial law existed in all of Tulsa County. On September 15 at midnight, the governor placed the entire state under martial law.

According to the governor's office, for almost a decade, Blacks had been run out of Oklahoma towns. Secret societies had whipped thousands of Black citizens, and Blacks had been murdered for being in the wrong place at the wrong time. Statistics from the governor's office showed that during 1922, as many as twenty-five hundred "whipping parties" had occurred in Oklahoma.

The governor called out more than six thousand National Guardmembers to "put down insurrection and rebellion against state authorities by the KKK." The governor had become the target of irate legislators opposed to his attacks on the Klan. Walton was finally suspended from office pending an impeachment trial and then was ousted by the state senate in response to his anti-Klan measures.

KU KLUX KLAN DOMINATES THREE STATES

As of **OCTOBER 31**, the *New York Times* reported that the Klan dominated Texas, Arkansas, and Oklahoma. In Texas, the Klan controlled the state government and the legislature and was a major influence in the large cities and most of the counties. Dallas and Fort Worth were completely dominated by these masked knights. In Oklahoma and Arkansas, the Klan's power was also visible. Not only did it threaten serious violence, but also its tactics of intimidation kept many people from the polls. Although bigotry and hatred may not have been supported by the majority of residents of these states, the large number of Klan-related incidents of violence indicated a certain level of general acceptance of the Klan. The Klan's strength was demonstrated at a meeting of twenty thousand members in Dallas. Included on the agenda was building a more active membership drive in areas where Blacks were making notable advances, especially in areas outside the South, and greater activism within the political structures of local and state governments.

1924   IMMIGRATION RESTRICTIONS FEED DEMAND FOR BLACK WORKERS

The National Origins Act of 1924 restricted foreign immigration, thereby increasing demand for Black workers in northern industry.

BLACKS KILLED BY KU KLUX KLAN IN ILLINOIS

Six Blacks were killed by KKK terrorists during violence at Herrin, Illinois.

RACE RIOT QUELLED IN OHIO

Federal troops were called to Niles, Ohio, where twelve Blacks were wounded in KKK riots.

RESIDENTIAL SEGREGATION ORDINANCE ENACTED IN NEW ORLEANS

In New Orleans, a residential segregation ordinance, enacted under authority of a state statute, forbade the establishment of a residence by a white person in a Black community or by a Black in a white community "without the written consent of a majority of the persons of the opposite race in the community affected." Each seven days' residence in violation of these provisions constituted a separate offense, and each offense could be punished.

SUPREME COURT DECLINES TO RULE IN *Corrigan* V. *Buckley*

The case of *Corrigan* v. *Buckley* concerned thirty whites who had entered into a restrictive covenant whereby each agreed not to sell or lease properties to a Black for a period of twenty-one years. The suit arose when Irene Corrigan, one of the signers of the agreement, contracted to sell her property to Helen Curtis, a Black woman. Buckley, another covenantor, sued to prohibit the sale of Corrigan's property to a Black. The Court asserted, "It is our duty to decline jurisdiction. . . ." The decision, read by Justice Edward T. Sanford, stated, "It is State action of a particular character that is forbidden, individual invasion of individual rights is not the subject-matter of the [Fourteenth] Amendment. We therefore conclude that neither the Constitution nor statutory questions relied on as ground for the appeal to this Court have any substantial quality or color of merit, or afford any jurisdictional basis for the appeal."

U.S. DISTRICT COURT DISMISSES ATTEMPT TO INVALIDATE FOURTEENTH AMENDMENT

In *Bolte* v. *Cohen*, the U.S. District Court of Eastern Louisiana dealt with a legal attack on the validity of the Fourteenth Amendment. Bolte sought to prevent Walter Cohen, a Black man, from exercising his employment duties as comptroller of customs for the Port of New Orleans, a position to which he had been appointed. It was alleged that Cohen was not a citizen of the United States because he was Black. The case further alleged that the Fourteenth Amendment, the basis upon which Blacks claimed citizenship, was invalid because it had never been proposed by two-thirds of both houses of Congress nor ratified by three-fourths of the states. Judge Foster dismissed the bill of complaint and quickly disposed of Bolte's argument.

HUBBARD WINS OLYMPIC GOLD MEDAL

In **JULY**, DeHart Hubbard, a track-and-field athlete of the University of Michigan, won the broad jump with a leap of 24 feet, 5½ inches, at the Olympic games in Paris, thus becoming the first Black to win an Olympic gold medal.

Hubbard held the national championship in broad jumping from 1922 to 1927. In 1922 and 1923, Hubbard won the National Amateur Athletic Union hop, skip, and jump championship. Hubbard became a public official in Cleveland, Ohio, and later an employee of the Federal Housing Administration in Washington, D.C.

COLORED WORLD SERIES INAUGURATED

On **OCTOBER 20**, the first Colored World Series of baseball took place in Kansas City, Missouri, between the Kansas City Monarchs of the National Negro League and the Hilldale Club of Philadelphia of the Eastern Colored League. The Monarchs won the series, five games to four, with one tie. Attendance was not especially high for the ten-game series, drawing only 45,857 fans. The following year, the Hilldale Club avenged its loss to the Monarchs.

Rube Foster was responsible for the Colored World Series. The series continued for a few years, even though it drew fewer and fewer fans. It was canceled after the 1927 series and recommenced in 1942.

1925 ANDERSON'S *Appearances* PERFORMED ON BROADWAY

The first Broadway production of a play by a Black writer was that of Garland Anderson's *Appearances*.

CULLEN'S POETRY INFLUENCES HARLEM RENAISSANCE

Countee Cullen (1903–1946) became an influential voice in the Harlem Renaissance when he published his volume of poetry *Color*. His later works include *Copper Sun* (1927), a second volume of poetry, and *One Way to Heaven* (1931), a novel.

◈ Born Countee Porter in Baltimore, Cullen was adopted by the Reverend and Mrs. Frederick Cullen after the death of his grandmother, in about 1918. The Reverend Cullen was pastor of Salem Methodist Episcopal Church, one of the largest and most influential churches in Harlem. Countee Cullen went to public school in New York, where he wrote poetry and distinguished himself academically. He went on to earn a B.A. degree from New York University in 1925 and an M.A. from Harvard in 1926. Cullen was among the best-known writers of the Harlem Renaissance and won a number of prizes for his poetry. Cullen served as assistant editor of *Opportunity* magazine between 1926 and 1928 and taught French at Frederick Douglass High School. He received a Guggenheim Fellowship in 1928.

GOLDEN STATE LIFE INSURANCE COMPANY FORMED

George Beavers, Jr., William Nickerson, Jr., and Norman O. Houston formed the Golden State Life Insurance Company, headquartered in Los Angeles, California. It became the third largest Black-owned life insurance company.

GRAND DRAGON OF KKK SENTENCED

The grand dragon of the KKK, D. C. Stephenson, was sentenced to life for the rape, assault, and kidnapping of a young Indianapolis woman named Madge Oberholtzer, who was able to give evidence that directed police to Stephenson before she died. He was sentenced to another twenty years for her murder.

KLANSMEN MARCH IN NATION'S CAPITAL

More than forty thousand Klansmen paraded through the streets of the nation's capital, as two hundred thousand spectators watched. The Klansmen wore their robes and hoods but not their masks. It was estimated that KKK membership had reached more than four million, though other estimates showed their membership to be twice that number. Founded in Tennessee in 1865, the Klan had grown significantly in number and had spread racial hatred in almost every part of the country.

MEMPHIS JOURNALIST DESCRIBES LYNCHING

In the autumn of 1925, as many as six hundred whites gathered to watch the lynching of a Black man. A correspondent of the *Memphis News Scimitar* wrote the following description:

> I watched an angry mob chain him to an iron stake. I watched them pile wood around his helpless body. I watched them pour gasoline on this wood. And I watched three men set this wood on fire. I stood in a crowd of 600 people as the flames gradually crept nearer and nearer to the helpless Negro. I watched the blaze climb higher and higher, encircling him without mercy. I heard his cry of agony as the flames reached him and set his clothing on fire.
>
> "Oh, God! Oh, God!" he shouted. "I didn't do it. Have Mercy!" The blaze leaped higher. The Negro struggled. He kicked the chain loose from his ankles but it held his waist and neck against the iron post that was becoming red with the intense heat.
>
> "Have mercy, I didn't do it. I didn't do it!" He shouted again and again. . . .
>
> Soon he became quiet. There was no doubt that he was dead. The flames jumped and leaped above his head. An odor of burning flesh reached my nostrils. I felt suddenly sickened. Through the leaping blaze I could see the Negro sagging and supported by the chains.

When the first odor of the baking flesh reached the mob there was a slight stir. Several men moved nervously.

"Let's finish it up," someone said.

Instantly about 12 men stepped from the crowd.

They piled wood on the fire that was already blazing high. The Negro was dead, but more wood was piled on the flames. They jumped higher and higher. Nothing could be seen now for the blaze encircled everything.

Then the crowd walked away. In the vanguard of the mob I noticed a woman. She seemed to be rather young, yet it is hard to tell about women of her type, strong and healthy, apparently a woman of the country. She walked with a firm, even stride. She was beautiful in a way.

The crowd walked slowly away.

"I'm hungry," someone complained. "Let's get something to eat."

RANDOLPH FORMS BROTHERHOOD OF SLEEPING CAR PORTERS

A. Philip Randolph (1889–1979) organized the Brotherhood of Sleeping Car Porters Union (an all-Black union) to bargain with the Pullman Company, which held a virtual monopoly on sleeping car facilities. It took Randolph ten years to achieve a real collective-bargaining agreement.

◆ Randolph, the son of a minister and a seamstress, both of whom were slaves, was educated at Cookman Institute, Florida, and City College, New York. He joined the Socialist Party as a young man because of his hatred of racial injustice in this country. He founded the *Messenger*, a socialist magazine, for which he organized students and workers against domestic, economic, and social injustices. Randolph became one of the most important Black leaders in this country in the 1940s, when he organized the March on Washington. Randolph remained

The Ku Klux Klan's growing membership was revealed by this 1925 march on Washington.

president of the Brotherhood of Sleeping Car Porters until 1968 and used his position to influence civil rights in the country.

STOCKADE HOUSING PROVIDED FOR BLACK EMPLOYEES

At Sparrow's Point, Maryland, the Bethlehem Steel Corporation provided housing for single Black men in two extensive stockades separated from the rest of the town by wire. Within the stockade, small wooden shacks were arranged in rows. They were heated by stoves and generally housed four workers, mostly from the South, per shack. The workers ate in a common dining room and shared common laundry. These facilities were cleaned by company janitors. This temporary housing provided no opportunities for social life.

THE *Sweet* CASE WON BY A BLACK

Ossian Sweet, a Black medical doctor in Detroit accused of murder, was successfully defended by Clarence Darrow. Darrow, a nationally known criminal lawyer with liberal sympathies, had just defended John Scopes, the Tennessee teacher who had taught Darwin's theory of evolution. Through the cases Darrow took and through his lectures and writings, he debated before the public many important issues, including racism, capital punishment, and child labor.

The *Sweet* case arose out of mob action by whites to prevent Sweet and his family from occupying a house that Sweet had purchased in an all-white Detroit neighborhood. Sweet postponed moving into the house on Garland Avenue until September 8. But that evening, a mob gathered to prevent his occupancy. They demonstrated and threw stones at the house. As the morning came and the mob grew larger, more stones were thrown at the house. Eventually shots were fired; one member of the mob was killed and another wounded. The police moved in and arrested eleven occupants of the house for first-degree murder. When the case went to trial in November, the jury disagreed with the charges, and Sweet was freed.

WOMEN AMONG LYNCHING VICTIMS

Between 1889 and 1925, ninety lynchings of women occurred. Of these, the largest number occurred in Mississippi (16), followed by Texas (11), Alabama (9), Arkansas (9), Georgia (8), Tennessee (7), and South Carolina (6). Among the charges leveled at the victims were murder, implication in murder, resisting arrest, relationship to criminals, and disorderly conduct.

FIRST BLACK IN TWENTY-FIVE YEARS ELECTED STATE LEGISLATOR

In **JANUARY**, the Illinois legislature swore in Adelbert H. Roberts, the first Black state legislator of any state assembly in the previous twenty-five years. Although there were many reasons for Blacks' long absence from this office, it can be largely attributed to the terrorist activities of white hate groups, including the KKK.

GARVEY SENT TO FEDERAL PRISON

On **FEBRUARY 8**, Marcus Garvey was escorted to federal prison in Atlanta, Georgia, to begin a five-year sentence for mail fraud. Garvey claimed that the charges were "political" and that his attempts to raise money for his steamship line were legitimate. Garvey, one of the most talented mass leaders at this time, may have collected as much as ten million dollars in a single two-year period, making UNIA the most powerful international Black organization. Although Garvey continued to insist he was innocent, he was subsequently deported to Jamaica in December 1927.

Many established Black leaders, including W. E. B. Du Bois, disliked Garvey. But Du Bois later remarked that Garvey was an important catalyst of "a mighty coming thing."

NATIONAL BAR ASSOCIATION ORGANIZED

On **AUGUST 1**, the National Bar Association was organized by a group of twelve African American lawyers in Des Moines, Iowa. Among these pioneer lawyers were George H. Woodson, S. Joe Brown, and Gertrude E. Rush. This organization of Black lawyers was established "to advance the science of jurisprudence."

Crisis MAGAZINE AWARDS PRIZES IN LITERATURE AND ART

On **OCTOBER 25**, *Crisis* magazine, under the editorship of W. E. B. Du Bois, awarded first prizes in literature and art to Arna Bontemps's poem "Nocturne at Bethesda," Countee Cullen's poem "Thoughts in a Zoo," Aaron Douglass's painting *African Chief*, and a portrait by Hale Woodruff.

Body and Soul RELEASED

On **NOVEMBER 9**, Oscar Micheaux released his film *Body and Soul*, in which Paul Robeson made his film debut.

1926 DISCRIMINATION IN TEACHERS' PAY

Throughout much of the South and even in border states, pay for Black and white teachers differed, regardless of the work performed, preparatory work, certificates and diplomas, or years of experience. Blacks received lower pay than whites. According to the report of the Maryland Inter-Racial Commission, white elementary schoolteachers in Maryland with third-grade certificates and four to five years of experience received $650 annually; Blacks with equivalent qualifications received $360 annually. Those with first-grade certificates and nine or more years of experience received a maximum of $1,150 if white and $680 if Black. Among high-school teachers, the racial disparities were just as great.

Such racial disparities could be found in cities as well, but frequently they were not as marked as in rural areas and small towns. For example, in Memphis, the minimum salary for white elementary teachers was $1,000; the maximum was $1,600. For Black elementary teachers holding similar certificates, the minimum pay was $720; the maximum was $1,020. In some cities, the maximum salary for Black teachers was the minimum for white teachers with the same certificates and same teaching obligations.

DREW GRADUATES FROM MEDICAL SCHOOL

Charles R. Drew (1904–1950) graduated from Amherst Medical School. Drew later became head of the Freedmen's Hospital in Washington, D.C., and a leading authority on blood plasma.

HUGHES PUBLISHES WELL-RECEIVED POETRY

Langston Hughes (1902–1967) took his place as one of the nation's leading poets when he published *The Weary Blues* in this year. Hughes became a key figure in the intellectual growth and development of the African American community during the Harlem Renaissance.

◈ Hughes first began to write poetry while a high-school student in Cleveland. While studying at Columbia University in 1921, he published several poems in *Crisis*, the publication of the NAACP. He left college after one year and embarked on a trip to Africa and to Paris, France, often working as a steward, doorman, dishwasher, and cook to pay his way. He returned to the United States and continued to write poetry, although he could not find steady work. In 1925, he received his break when the noted poet Vachel Lindsay praised his work. Almost instantly he became famous, winning literary prizes, publishing

Langston Hughes, a poet, novelist, and playwright, wrote about the African American experience. His play Mulatto enjoyed a long run on Broadway.

widely, and amassing a collection of poems, which he titled *The Weary Blues*. Hughes, like other writers of the Harlem Renaissance, expressed feelings about discrimination and prejudice in his work. He often employed humor and jazz rhythms in his writing. In 1930, he published a novel, *Not Without Laughter*, and in 1949, he published *One-Way Ticket*. On October 24, 1935, Hughes's play *Mulatto* opened on Broadway. It became a success and for many years held the record for the longest run of any play by an African

American. Throughout his career, Hughes traveled across the country, in part to make ends meet by giving poetry readings at Black schools, colleges, and churches. He also traveled around the world and used his experiences as a basis for his literary work.

LAWNSIDE, NEW JERSEY, INCORPORATED

This former station on the Underground Railroad and almost all-Black community was incorporated as a town.

One of Lawnside's most famous residents was William Still, one of the founders of the Pennsylvania Society for the Abolition of Slavery. Still was a free Black and a successful businessman who later wrote a definitive history of the Underground Railroad.

With many famous all-Black nightclubs, Lawnside emerged as an entertainment center during the 1930s. Lawnside exists today as one of the few historically all-Black towns in the country.

NEGRO HISTORY WEEK ESTABLISHED

Negro History Week was established by Dr. Carter G. Woodson and other Black leaders of the Association for the Study of Negro Life and History, Inc.

RESIDENTIAL SEGREGATION IN INDIANAPOLIS

Indianapolis enacted an ordinance limiting Black residence to particular districts of the city. The ordinance also forbade whites from residing in Black districts.

TEACHERS DEMAND RIGHT TO VOTE

In **JANUARY**, Indiana Little, a Black woman school-teacher in Birmingham, led as many as one thousand Black women and a few men before the Board of Registrars and demanded the right to vote as American citizens. She was immediately arrested and charged with vagrancy. Although no Black person was allowed to register to vote at this time, Little's brave action encouraged others to organize one protest campaign after another until they were registered.

ANDERSON APPEARS BEFORE SUPREME COURT

On **JANUARY 29**, Violette N. Anderson became the first African American woman admitted to practice before the U.S. Supreme Court.

SAVOY BALLROOM OPENS

On **MARCH 12**, the Savoy Ballroom opened in New York City and almost immediately attracted a number of top performers, including several dance groups that got their start there. It was sometimes called the "Home of Happy Feet," because jitterbug dancing was created at the Savoy.

JOHNSON BECOMES PRESIDENT OF HOWARD UNIVERSITY

On **JUNE 20**, Mordecai W. Johnson became the first African American president of Howard University, one of the most important educational institutions for Blacks in the country.

1927 DISPARITIES CITED IN EDUCATION OF WHITES AND BLACKS

According to a report by the Commission on Interracial Cooperation in Atlanta, Georgia, average annual expenditures for school-age children differed significantly for Blacks and whites. In Texas and Tennessee, average annual expenditure for education per school-age child was about half as great for Black children as for white children. In Georgia, Florida, Mississippi, Louisiana, North Carolina, and Virginia, expenditure per school-age child was four, five, or six times as great for white children as it was for Black children. In South Carolina, the discrepancy between expenditures for white and Black school-age children was as much as ten times in favor of white children.

HARLEM GLOBETROTTERS FOUNDED

In **JANUARY**, the Harlem Globetrotters, a sensational traveling basketball team, was formed by Abe Saperstein in Chicago. The team was originally called the Savoy Big Five, because they played at the Savoy Ballroom. (The owners of the Savoy Ballroom in New York had opened a second ballroom on the south side of Chicago.) The team was used by the ballroom owners to attract business when three members of the Savoy Big Five grew unhappy with their low pay and left the team. They asked Saperstein to be their coach. He changed the team name to "Saperstein's Harlem, New York, Globetrotters" because he had dreams of being successful in New York City. The word *Harlem* indicated that it was a Black team, and the term *Globetrotters* suggested world travelers, although the team initially traveled only locally. Saperstein acted as owner, manager, coach, chauffeur, and the only substitute the team had. He suited up for the games and substituted to give the regular team members a rest. When the Globetrotters played, they were serious competitors and soundly beat most opponents. The humorous antics associated with the team today came much later. The names of the original team players have been lost; more recent team stars included Reece "Goose" Tatum, Marques Haynes, "Meadowlark" Lemon, and "Curley" Neal. Wilt Chamberlain played for the team at one time. The team is still an outstanding box-office attraction and is known throughout the world.

Nixon V. *Herndon* STRIKES DOWN WHITES-ONLY PRIMARIES

On **MARCH 7**, the U.S. Supreme Court struck down whites-only primaries in *Nixon* v. *Herndon.* The Court found that "white primaries are a denial of equal protection under the law." Justice Oliver Wendell Holmes, Jr., noted, "It is hard to imagine a more direct and obnoxious infringement of the Fourteenth Amendment." The case emerged as a result of the Texas law barring Blacks from voting in "white primaries."

ELLINGTON PERFORMS AT THE COTTON CLUB

On **DECEMBER 4**, Edward Kennedy "Duke" Ellington debuted at the Cotton Club in Harlem. Ellington went on to write more than two thousand songs, including scores for ballets and films, musicals, and choral works, and became known internationally as a bandleader and pianist.

◈   Ellington was born in Washington, D.C., in 1899, the son of middle-class parents. He acquired his father's taste for elegant clothes, and before he was in high school, the neighborhood boys were calling him "Duke." An accomplished musician, Ellington picked up piano-playing skills from the ragtime artists who appeared in the District. He formed a band and moved to New York in 1923, where the band played in a variety of clubs and speakeasies. The Cotton Club, the most prestigious night spot in

After opening at the famous Cotton Club, where most successful Black entertainers got their start, Edward Kennedy "Duke" Ellington and his ten-piece band played there for five years. Unlike other band leaders, Ellington mostly played his own compositions, scoring and arranging them in his own unique style.

Harlem, gave Ellington his big chance. His band became world renowned, perhaps reaching its peak between 1938 and 1942. Its performances of "swing" music, a sophisticated form of jazz, were broadcast across the country. He preferred to call his music "American music" because it could not be categorized. For twenty-eight years, Ellington collaborated with composer-arranger Billy Strayhorn.

Ellington was always a dignified performer. He never presented the "caricature" style that Black performers during the time of Jim Crow were forced to use to appeal to patronizing white audiences.

After being diagnosed with lung cancer in 1972, Ellington turned toward religious music, although it had been an interest of his for some time. One of his last performances was the premiere of a religious program of music at Westminster Abbey in London.

Among Ellington's most famous songs are "It Don't Mean a Thing If It Ain't Got That Swing," "Sophisticated Lady," "Mood Indigo," and "Don't Get Around Much Anymore."

1928 LYNCHING OF BLACKS CONTINUES

Nine Blacks were known to have been lynched in 1928, the lowest number in forty years.

ROBESON STARS IN *Show Boat*

Paul Robeson (1898–1976), one of the most gifted American stage actors, starred in the musical *Show Boat*, in which he sang his famous rendition of "Ol' Man River." Robeson played a former slave and sang several spirituals. He and the musical received top reviews.

◆ Robeson's singing talents had first been praised when he appeared in the stage play *The Emperor Jones* in 1925. He gave his first concert of Black spirituals in April of the same year. He subsequently starred in the film versions of *The Emperor Jones* and *Show Boat*. He also became an accomplished Shakespearian actor, starring in a stage production of *Othello* that ran for 296 performances in New York City between October 1943 and July 1944, the longest run a play by Shakespeare has ever had in America. Presented with racial barriers, he joined the Communist Party in the hope that it would remedy racism. The American public ostracized him for this decision, so he left the country and lived in Europe from 1958 to 1963. After returning to the United States, he retired from an active stage career. Robeson began his career not as an actor but as an athlete. While attending Rutgers University, he was twice named an all-American

football end and earned twelve letters in four different sports. He was a member of Phi Beta Kappa and the valedictorian of his class in 1919. He then earned a law degree at Columbia University in 1923.

TAYLOR PUBLISHES AUTOBIOGRAPHY

Marshal "Major" Taylor published his autobiography, *The Fastest Bicycle Rider in the World*. He was the first Black champion in any sport. Taylor was the American sprint champion in bicycling from 1898 through 1900. During this time he participated in championship meets in Europe and Australia, where bicycling was a major sport. During championship races, white riders ganged up on Taylor, but because of his excellent physical condition, he was able to outstrip them.

FATS WALLER COMPOSES SCORE FOR *Keep Shufflin'*

Fats Waller (Thomas Wright Waller) (1904–1943) became one of the most successful and well-known African American entertainer-composers in the country when he wrote the score for *Keep Shufflin'*. For the next decade, Waller worked in cabarets, theaters, and eventually on Broadway. In the late 1920s, Waller appeared in many Broadway revues, singing many of the hundreds of songs he had recorded. Several of his songs have become musical standards, for example, "Ain't Misbehavin'," "Honeysuckle Rose," and "Blue Turning Gray over You." Waller appeared in *Stormy Weather*, a major film, in 1943.

Atlanta Daily World FOUNDED

In **NOVEMBER**, the *Atlanta Daily World* was founded by William A. Scott III. This Black newspaper became a daily in 1932, the first Black daily since Reconstruction.

DEPRIEST ELECTED TO CONGRESS

The Chicago political machine selected Oscar DePriest (1871–1951) for the congressional vacancy in the First Congressional District created by the death of Congressman Martin B. Madden, a white who had represented the district since 1904.

On **NOVEMBER 6**, DePriest defeated two other candidates and was elected to the Seventy-first Congress, thus becoming the first Black U.S. congressman from a northern state and the first Black representative since 1901 — the year Representative George H. White left the Congress.

◆ DePriest was born in Florence, Alabama, on March 9, 1871. Like many other Black families, the DePriests

Oscar DePriest, a U.S. congressman, owed much of his political success to the growing voting power of southern Blacks in Chicago.

left the South and moved to Kansas. DePriest learned bookkeeping in high school, and after settling in Chicago in 1889, he worked at odd jobs in the building construction industry. He ultimately set up his own business — a real-estate firm. In 1904, DePriest gained a seat on the powerful Cook County Board of Commissioners. Later, he served two years on the Chicago City Council but resigned when charges surfaced that he had accepted "protection" money. Charles Darrow, the famous lawyer, represented DePriest and won his acquittal. DePriest's political base softened in the Black Second and Third Ward, and he lost a bid to regain a council seat. By 1924, DePriest had regained sufficient power to become the Third Ward committee member.

In the Seventy-first Congress, DePriest called for a reduction in congressional seats for states that disfranchised Blacks. He also called for a monthly pension to ex-slave citizens over seventy-five years of age, the declaration of Lincoln's birthday as a legal public holiday, and fines and imprisonment of local officials who allowed their prisoners to be lynched. DePriest served in the Seventy-first through Seventy-third Congresses. Because many Blacks had abandoned the Republican Party in favor of Franklin D. Roosevelt, the New Deal, and the Democratic Party,

DePriest lost his bid for reelection in 1934. Arthur W. Mitchell, a Black supporter of Roosevelt's New Deal, won the House seat. DePriest ran against Mitchell in 1936 but lost. In 1943, DePriest was elected as alderman of the Third Ward, a post he held until defeated for reelection in 1947. DePriest died in Chicago on May 12, 1951.

1929 "NEGRO ZONES" ESTABLISHED IN ST. LOUIS

Real-estate dealers in St. Louis entered into private contracts to establish "Negro zones" in response to the rapid migration of Blacks into the city. "Negro zones" effected segregated housing.

TIBBS WINS FAME AS OPERA SINGER

Lillian Evans Tibbs became the first Black American opera singer to gain an international reputation. Nevertheless, she was not permitted to sing at the Metropolitan Opera in New York City because of her race.

URBAN LEAGUE ORGANIZES BOYCOTTS IN ST. LOUIS AND CHICAGO

As the number of Blacks in northern cities increased, Blacks protested the economic and political limits placed upon them. In this year, the Urban League sponsored "Jobs for Negroes" boycotts in St. Louis and "Don't Buy Where You Can't Work" boycotts in Chicago.

NEW ATLANTA UNIVERSITY CREATED

On **APRIL 1**, Morehouse College, Spelman College, and Atlanta University, all historically Black schools, agreed to affiliate and offer an exciting new intellectual experience for Black students in the newly created Atlanta University. John Hope, president of Morehouse, was selected as president of the new university. New courses, programs, and additional degrees were created as a result of the merger.

Hot Chocolates PREMIERES

On **JUNE 20**, the show *Hot Chocolates* premiered at the Hudson Theatre in New York City. The team of Fats Waller (music) and Andy Razaf (lyrics) was a success, and several of the songs from the show, notably "Ain't Misbehavin'" and "Black and Blue," became popular hits.

BLACKS SUFFER AFTER STOCK MARKET CRASH

On **OCTOBER 29**, the stock market collapsed, sending businesses, industries, and personal fortunes into ruins. This event heralded the Great Depression, and because Blacks had been the last hired in a number of occupational classes, they were the first to be fired. Unemployment among Blacks reached disproportionately high levels relative to whites. Unemployment rates among Black men may have been three to four times as high as those of whites, and Black unemployment definitely remained at least two to three times higher than that of whites. Racism and discrimination in the job market made matters worse, and the National Urban League instituted a number of movements to better the conditions of Blacks in major cities.

1930

POPULATION OVERVIEW

BLACK POPULATION IN THE UNITED STATES The Bureau of the Census reported that the U.S. population had reached 122,775,046. Blacks made up 9.7 percent (11,891,143 residents) of the national population.

BLACK POPULATION IN THE NORTH AND THE SOUTH Between 1910 and 1930, the number of Blacks in the North increased by 1,381,545. However, over the 1900–1930 period, more than 4 million Blacks moved from the South primarily to urban centers of the North. Their proportional representation by region shifted considerably — from roughly 90 percent to 79 percent still concentrated in the southern region. Migration from the South most commonly involved Blacks from Mississippi, South Carolina, Georgia, and Alabama.

BLACK URBANIZATION In the decade 1920–1930, the number of urban Blacks increased from about 3.6 million to 5.2 million, showing that urbanization was increasing among Blacks in both southern and northern states. Census statistics showed that 43.7 percent of the total Black population resided in urban areas, compared with 56.2 percent of the national population. Blacks made up only 7.5 percent of urban dwellers. Blacks in Los Angeles increased by 31,295, or 412 percent, over the decade.

SOCIAL CONDITIONS OVERVIEW

THE DISTRIBUTION OF BLACK PHYSICIANS AND OTHER PROFESSIONALS The 1930 census revealed that there were 3,805 Black physicians and surgeons in the United States. Nearly 40 percent of these professionals lived in seven northern states and the District of Columbia, where the combined Black population was less than 19 percent of the entire Black population in the country. Illinois had more Black physicians than Alabama, Arkansas, and South Carolina combined.

There were more Black dentists in Pennsylvania than in Arkansas, Georgia, Mississippi, and South Carolina combined. The number of trained Black nurses was almost evenly distributed among New York, New Jersey, and Pennsylvania (combined Black population of one million). In contrast, Black clergy were heavily concentrated in the South, where 76 percent of all Black clergy resided, a proportion almost matching the 78 percent of Black residents who were concentrated in the South.

JUDICIAL RACISM IN SCOTTSBORO BOYS' TRIAL PRODUCES DECADES OF PROTEST On **APRIL 6**, nine Black youths were brought to trial before an all-white jury in Scottsboro, Alabama, for allegedly attacking and raping two white girls who were riding on the same freight train. Although the girls were examined by doctors who found no evidence of rape, eight of the boys were convicted and sentenced to death. It took the jury only twenty-five minutes to find Heywood Patterson, the first to be tried, guilty. These young men had no legal counsel available to them until two lawyers volunteered on the day of the trial.

The case became a cause célèbre because of the speed with which the young men were convicted, despite the lack of evidence. The case was appealed three times to the U.S. Supreme Court between 1931 and 1937. In December 1931, Clarence Darrow, who had volunteered his help, dropped his commitment because of "communist exploitation of the case." The case attracted the attention of Black leaders, Black organizations, liberal whites and their organizations, and the Communist Party.

The first Scottsboro case appeal, *Powell* v. *Alabama*, reached the U.S. Supreme Court in 1932. The Supreme Court declared that due process had not been carried out and that the youths had not been provided adequate counsel. Their defense, now headed by Samuel Liebowitz, a noted lawyer from New York, was also supported by the International Labor Defense, an organ of the Communist Party. Their involvement in the case immediately brought international attention. The International Labor Defense exploited this attention and supported demonstrations against the convictions in more than twenty-eight countries. U.S. embassies in Europe and Latin America were attacked with stones and picketed. More than one million dollars were raised to help the Scottsboro Nine.

In another appeal, *Norris* v. *Alabama*, the U.S. Supreme Court stated that trials before all-white juries were unfair and ordered a retrial of each defendant. On

In this 1933 photograph, the "Scottsboro Boys" are shown meeting with their lawyer, Samuel Leibowitz. The defendants, ranging in age from thirteen to twenty-one, were charged with raping two white girls. Consistently denied their constitutional rights during the many years they sought to regain their freedom, these young men had their lives completely ruined by false accusations.

March 27, 1933, a retrial of the Scottsboro case began. On April 10, Blacks protested and rioted on Broadway in New York City to show their anger at the previous day's conviction of Scottsboro defendants in Alabama. By December 1, Heywood Patterson, one of the young "Scottsboro Boys," was given the death penalty by a jury. On March 17, 1934, as many as five thousand Black New Yorkers battled police in protest over the Scottsboro trial. On April 1, 1935, the U.S. Supreme Court ordered a new trial in the case. By the end of 1937, five of the young Black men were freed when earlier convictions were reversed by the U.S. Supreme Court. By 1950, all of the Scottsboro Boys were free either by parole, appeal, or escape. The last one to be cleared, Clarence W. Norris, had escaped while on parole in 1948. He was pardoned on October 25, 1976, by an order signed by Governor George C. Wallace of Alabama.

DELTA SIGMA THETA SORORITY INCORPORATED

Delta Sigma Theta, founded at Howard University in 1913, was incorporated this year.

HAMPTON PLAYS VIBRAPHONE FOR RECORDING

Lionel Hampton (1913–) became recognized as one of the great jazz vibraphonists when he made a recording in this year. Hampton, a drummer with the Louis Armstrong band, became a proficient vibraphonist. He played with the Benny Goodman quartet from 1936 to 1940 and became a bandleader later.

HOLIDAY STARTS SINGING CAREER AT POD'S AND JERRY'S

Billie Holiday (1915–1959) stopped in at a speakeasy called Pod's and Jerry's and asked to see the manager about a job as a dancer. But before she had finished auditioning, a pianist yelled, "Well, then, can you sing?" Holiday nodded and asked the pianist to play "Trav'ling All Alone," a popular song at that time. When she had finished singing, the eyes of the auditioners were filled with tears. She got the job, and that same night, Holiday raked in more than one hundred dollars in tips. Her professional singing career would lead to recognition as one of the most gifted blues singers of all time.

◈ Holiday was born Eleanora Fagan on April 7, 1915, in Baltimore, Maryland. In her autobiography, *Lady Sings the Blues*, she stated that her parents were not married — they were just a couple of kids in love and were unprepared for parenthood. Her childhood was difficult. She was raised by a cousin who frequently abused her. She found friendship with her elderly great-grandmother. When her great-grandmother died, Eleanora became emotionally insecure and was confined to a hospital for a month. As a child, she skipped classes to watch movies at the Royal Theater. She began calling herself Billie because she wanted to be a Hollywood actress like Billie Dove.

On her way home from school one evening, Holiday was attacked by a man who tried to rape her. Although the police arrived in time to arrest her attacker, she was taken to the police station and put in jail. Refusing to release her in the custody of her mother, the judge sentenced her (then a ten-year-old) to an institution for wayward girls until she reached the age of twenty-one. At the age of twelve, she was allowed to leave the institution. She moved to New York with her mother, but her troubles did not end. Within a short time, a well-known madam who ran a brothel had secured Holiday's services as a "strictly twenty-dollar call girl." She was almost killed by one of her clients. In court at the age of thirteen, Holiday was given prison time in an adult correctional institution on Welfare Island in New York's East River. When released, she worked as a prostitute for a short while but wanted a better life. It was when she and her ill mother were about to be evicted that she went out in search of a job as a dancer.

Billie's professional career began about the same time that Harlem was reaching its height as a musical and theatrical center. Holiday's demeanor was unusual. She took many liberties as an entertainer, and when she waited on tables, she took only tips that were handed to her — the reason that some gave her the name "Lady." Some entertainers noted that Holiday's singing was a "kind of communication" that only she had because she had lived many of the lyrics. Holiday's singing became known as a "blues-inspired jazz." When she sang "Wouldja for a Big Red Apple?" music producer and promoter John Hammond was convinced that she was the best jazz singer he had ever heard. In his column in *Melody Maker*, he gave her enthusiastic reviews. On November 27, 1933, Holiday joined popular jazz band leader Benny Goodman to record her first song. She finally got her chance to perform at the Apollo Theatre on April 19, 1935, just a few days before her twentieth birthday. She was a great success. Her second engagement at the Apollo occurred on August 2, 1935.

In the 1930s, Holiday recorded "Summertime" and "Billie's Blues." She appeared in a short musical film, *Symphony in Black*, with Duke Ellington and his orchestra. Holiday was in demand and could sing wherever she wanted to. In 1937, Holiday joined Count Basie on a tour throughout the South. Within eight months, she and Basie had parted company, and she joined the Artie Shaw Band (one of the first Black vocalists to be a member of a white jazz band). During performances in the South, she found this a major problem, noting in her book, "Almost every day there was an incident."

While performing at the Café Society, a poet, Lewis Allen, showed her a poem he had written entitled "Strange Fruit." With the help of Sonny White, she adapted it into a song that became the trademark of Holiday's manner of communicating with her audience. Although she wanted to record the song, her record company thought it too provocative — the strange fruit referred to Black people hanging from trees. The song was eventually cut for the Commodore label. It was an immediate success and became Holiday's best-known record. Her songs were increasingly about loneliness and lost love. "Gloomy Sunday" and "God Bless the Child" were released in 1941. By the mid-1940s, Holiday had jumped to another record label, Decca, and was recording with the jazz greats.

At the top of her career, she suffered a tragic setback — drug addiction. Long gloves became part of her attire to hide the needle marks on her arms. Although she was voted the best vocalist by jazz critics in 1943, her addiction was becoming more apparent and destructive. Drug withdrawals produced violent illnesses, and in 1947, she checked into a New York sanatorium to beat the habit. When she returned to the stage, she was followed by several agents of the U.S. Bureau of Narcotics. On May 16, they raided her hotel room. She was arrested and pleaded guilty to narcotics possession with the hope of being sent to a rehabilitation center. Instead, she was sent to the Federal Reformatory for Women at Alderson, West Virginia, for a year and a day.

On March 27, 1948, Holiday performed at Carnegie Hall. Prison had not been kind to her, and she was not at her best. Over the next year, she appeared at many places including the Mansfield Theater, the Ebony Club, and the Strand Theater, and she was joined by Count Basie's orchestra. Although people stood in line to see Holiday perform, some of her best friends began to abandon her because she was constantly under the watchful eye of local police and fed-

eral narcotics agents. On January 22, 1949, Holiday was arrested on narcotics charges in San Francisco after being duped by a close friend who had given some opium to Holiday to get rid of it. After much abuse by her family, the men she loved, and the drugs that provided an escape from unhappiness, Holiday died at the age of forty-four.

JULIUS ROSENWALD FUND OPENS FIVE-HUNDREDTH SCHOOL

In this year, the Julius Rosenwald Fund built its five-hundredth Black school.

Julius Rosenwald had contributed twenty-five thousand dollars in 1883 to be used for the construction of buildings at Tuskegee Institute and schools in Macon County, Alabama. Rosenwald later became head of the Sears, Roebuck, and Company mail-order house. Black education in the South was greatly helped by the work of the fund. The new school buildings helped to elevate the quality and interest in education among Blacks in every state in the South. The literacy rate among Blacks in the South had improved substantially, increasing by about 94 percent, whereas the rate for the South overall increased by only 32 percent.

NAACP PROTESTS JUDGE PARKER'S APPOINTMENT TO THE SUPREME COURT

On **MARCH 31**, President Herbert Hoover nominated Judge John J. Parker of North Carolina as associate justice of the U.S. Supreme Court. Because Parker was a known racist, the appointment was considered an affront to Black people. Black leaders joined with the NAACP to launch a national campaign to derail his appointment. The NAACP succeeded, and the U.S. Senate refused to confirm Parker's appointment.

GIBSON LAUNCHES BASEBALL CAREER

On **JULY 25**, Josh Gibson, who would be called "the Black Babe Ruth" because of his bashing of home runs for the Pittsburgh Homestead Grays, was called out of the stands to substitute for the catcher of the Grays. This incident kicked off the career of one of the best players in the history of baseball. He played for about fifteen years and finished with a lifetime batting average of .384 (though some sources have claimed it was .423). Gibson played with a number of teams, including the Crawfords, Trujillo All-stars (in the Dominican Republic), and even a team in Puerto Rico. His batting average was .457, .435, and .480, re-

Josh Gibson, a six-foot, one-inch catcher for the Pittsburgh Homestead Grays, led his team to hundreds of victories, nine straight pennants, and World Series titles in 1943 and 1944. He led the Negro leagues in home runs ten times.

spectively, for these teams. In 1972, his career as a professional player with a number of all-Black professional baseball teams was recognized at his induction into the Baseball Hall of Fame. He was one of ten African American ball players in the Baseball Hall of Fame, although he was not given an opportunity to play in the major leagues.

1931   BONTEMPS BECOMES LEADING FIGURE IN HARLEM RENAISSANCE

Arna Bontemps (1902–1973) became one of the leading writers of the Harlem Renaissance with the publication of *God Sends Sunday*, the story of Little Willie, a Black racehorse jockey, and the racetrack and gambling worlds of New Orleans and St. Louis.

◊   Bontemps was born in Alexandria, Louisiana. She received a B.A. from Pacific Union College of California in 1923 and in 1943, with the aid of two Rosenwald fellowships, earned an M.A. degree from the University of Chicago. In 1926, she was awarded the *Crisis* Magazine Prize for poetry; in 1927 and 1928, she was awarded the Alexander Pushkin Prize by *Opportunity* magazine. Bontemps's first publication, *God Sends Sunday*, was adapted as a Broadway stage musical comedy in 1946, called *St. Louis Woman*. Bontemps wrote more than thirty books on the African American experience. Three especially outstanding novels were *Black Thunder*, about the 1800 slave rebellion led by Gabriel Prosser in Virginia; *Drums of Dusk*, describing a slave revolt in Haiti; and *The Old South* (1973), about Black life in the South.

MUHAMMAD FOUNDS NATION OF ISLAM

Elijah Muhammad (1897–1975), born Elijah Poole on a Georgia farm, founded the Nation of Islam in Detroit. The organization, initially called the Lost-Found Nation of Islam, later moved from Detroit to Chicago. By 1940, Chicago had surpassed New York as the center of Black nationalism in the United States. The Nation of Islam's goal of separate self-sufficiency for African Americans often set the group outside the mainstream civil rights movement. When Elijah Muhammad died, his son, Wallace J. Muhammad, assumed leadership. In 1978, Louis Farrakhan formed a new Nation of Islam, and the faction led by Wallace J. Muhammad renamed itself the American Muslim Mission.

SHARECROPPERS ORGANIZE IN ALABAMA

In Alabama, the Sharecroppers' Union was organized. Its membership was primarily composed of Black farmers, who, with the assistance of the Communist Party, demanded an improvement in the conditions of sharecroppers and tenant farmers. The Sharecroppers' Union also demanded the right to raise gardens for their own food, to seed and sell their own crops, to enjoy a three-hour rest period during the middle of the day, to receive wages in cash for picking cotton, and to receive advances of food until pay settlement time. Because Blacks cherished education, they demanded that the school year be extended to nine months and that a free school bus be provided for Black children.

White landlords immediately organized to suppress this threat to their control over Black labor. Many white farmers and landlords called upon the local law enforcement officials to harass members of the union, and in Camp Hill and Reeltown, they actually murdered several tenant farmers. In the Camp Hill confrontation of this year, members of the Sharecroppers' Unions failed to prevent the lynching of a young Black man who had wounded a number of deputy sheriffs in a gun battle several hours earlier. Black members fought with whites for several hours before their ammunition ran out. In Reeltown, Alabama, members of the Sharecroppers' Union battled both landlords and deputy sheriffs who came to confiscate the livestock of a Black tenant farmer. Because Blacks had little chance of winning a case in the local courts and ran the risk of hanging for being "uppity," they increasingly resorted to direct clashes with whites to defend themselves. Despite terrorism and intimidation by white groups and law officials, the Sharecroppers' Union remained active. By 1933, the organization had fifty-five hundred members, and in 1934 and 1935, it sponsored a cotton pickers' strike. The union remained active until 1939.

WHITE BECOMES SECRETARY OF NAACP

Walter White (1893–1955), author of one of the definitive books on lynching of Black folk, *Rope and Faggot*, was selected to succeed James Weldon Johnson as secretary of the NAACP. White used his position to speak out against racism and inequality.

1932   FRAZIER PUBLISHES *The Free Negro Family*

E. Franklin Frazier (1894–1962) made his mark as an important African American sociologist with the publication of *The Free Negro Family*. Frazier, who earned a Ph.D. from the University of Chicago, was the head of the sociology department at Howard University, Washington, D.C. In 1939, Frazier published another important book on the African American experience, *The Negro Family in the United States*. In 1957, he published *Black Bourgeoisie*. Frazier built a first-rate sociology department at Howard University during his tenure of twenty-five years.

Walter F. White, a light-skinned Black who could have crossed the color line into white America, chose instead to remain among his race and fight against segregation and discrimination. White became a powerful leader of the NAACP. His theme was "Now is the time."

RENS WIN WORLD BASKETBALL CHAMPIONSHIP

On **MARCH 30**, the New York Rens, an African American basketball team, defeated the Boston Celtics, a predominantly white team, by three points, to win the World Basketball Championship. Although the Rens had been successful throughout their history, this was the first time they had won this championship.

CHI ETA PHI SORORITY FOUNDED

On **OCTOBER 16**, Chi Eta Phi sorority was founded by Aleine Carrington Ewell and eleven other women in Washington, D.C. The nursing sorority expanded quickly to more than seventy-two chapters throughout the United States.

1933　DUNHAM HAS FIRST LEAD DANCE ROLE

Katherine Dunham (1910–94) danced her first lead rold in Ruth Page's West Indian ballet *La Guiablesse*. Dunham, often referred to as the mother of African American dance, was born in Glen Ellyn, Illinois. She received a degree in anthropology from the University of Chicago in 1936. Her thesis investigated the *Dances of Haiti*, which she had studied while in the West Indies. In 1944 she founded the Katherine Dunham School of Dance in New York City, which performed dances largely based on those of the West Indies and Africa. In 1963, she became the first Black choreographer to work at the Metropolitan Opera when she choreographed *Aida*. In 1967, Dunham began the Performing Arts Training Center in the poor Black community of East St. Louis, Illinois.

JARBORO PERFORMS WITH CHICAGO OPERA COMPANY

Caterina Jarboro, a soprano, became the first Black to perform with an American opera company. She was featured in a Chicago Opera Company production of Äida.

Jarboro studied voice in Paris, France, and then in Milan, Italy, under the supervision of Nino Campino.

Los Angeles Sentinel FOUNDED

In this year, the *Los Angeles Sentinel* was founded by Leon H. Washington. The *Sentinel* became one of the most powerful voices fighting racial injustices in the city and throughout California.

MARTIAL LAW DECLARED IN OKLAHOMA CITY

Governor Johnston C. Murray declared martial law in Oklahoma City to calm the threat of rioting and bloodshed in response to the establishment of Black residences in white neighborhoods. Using his emergency powers, Murray identified segregated residential zones for Blacks and whites with a "nontrespass" zone between the two. Martial law continued until the city enacted a "segregation" ordinance identical to those found unconstitutional by the Supreme Court in the 1920s; however, this ordinance was supported by the valid military powers of the governor. But the Oklahoma Supreme Court held the ordinance invalid and criticized the city authorities for this action, stating that "the exercise of wrongful police power to defeat illegal martial law is police power wrongfully employed."

NAACP MOUNTS ATTACK ON SEGREGATION

The NAACP initiated court attacks on segregation and discrimination in education. Its first suit was filed against the University of North Carolina on behalf of Thomas Hocutt. It was lost because a president of a Black college refused to certify the records of the plaintiff.

LYNCHERS GO FREE IN MARYLAND

In Maryland on **MARCH 18**, a white mob of two thousand lynched a Black man accused of attacking a white woman. On November 29, the court freed the four held as lynchers.

Emperor Jones IS RELEASED

On **SEPTEMBER 16**, United Artists released the film *Emperor Jones*, starring Paul Robeson as Brutus Jones. This was the first major movie starring an African American, with whites in supporting roles.

1934　BLACK-OWNED BANKS DECLINE

In 1934, there were only twelve banks owned by Blacks in this country — despite the fact that more than 134 had been created since 1888. Beginning with the establishment of the True Reformers' Bank in Richmond, Virginia, and the Capital Savings Bank in Washington, D.C., in 1888, Black banks had spread to every state in the South by 1930. Although they expanded and proliferated rapidly, they were also short-lived. Most of these banks failed in the same year they were established.

HURSTON PUBLISHES NOVEL

Zora Neale Hurston (1891–1960) published *Jonah's Gourd Vine* in 1934. The novel was widely acclaimed for its literary interpretation of the African American experience (particularly in the South) and its folklore. The next year, she published *Mules and Men*; in 1937, *Their Eyes Were Watching God*; and in 1938, *Tell My Horse*. The blend of folktales, southern history, and interpretation of folklore was the distinctive hallmark of Hurston's books.

Hurston was born and raised in Eatonville, Florida, a self-governing Black town. Here, Hurston developed a love for folktales listening to the town's residents tell stories as they gathered at the general store. She received her B.A. in anthropology from Barnard College in 1928 and later studied folklore with Franz Boas at Columbia University before going on to collect folktales during her travels in the South and the

Zora Neale Hurston, a novelist and folklorist, published most of her famous works between 1934 and 1942. Although she was living in relative obscurity and poverty when she died, six of her works have since been reprinted.

Caribbean. Hurston died in poverty and obscurity. Years later, the writer Alice Walker discovered and marked Hurston's grave. Since Hurston's death, there has been renewed interest in her work, and several of her books have been reprinted.

KU KLUX KLAN SUPPORTS HITLER
In Westchester, New York, the KKK was revitalized and spoke up in support of Hitler's Nazi Party in Germany.

SOUTHERN TENANT FARMERS UNION ORGANIZED
In response to a large number of evictions, both Black and white tenant farmers and farm laborers organized the Southern Tenant Farmers Union (STFU) in Arkansas. The primary objectives of the union were to secure a fair share of federal payments to farmers and to prevent tenants from being evicted because of federal agricultural policies. By 1937, the STFU had more than 30,827 members in Arkansas and surrounding states. Although it held a number of unsuccessful cotton chopper and cotton picker strikes, it was most successful in exposing the evils of the sharecropping system, notably peonage, forced labor, and the absence of civil liberties. In addition, the STFU was able to show the "almost slaverylike" conditions that existed throughout much of the South as "croppers" and tenants suffered poverty, illiteracy, and disease. The federal government responded to these conditions by passing a number of laws to curb such abuses. Because of racial conflict within the organization, flight from the region, and heightened violence and threats from agents of landlords, STFU membership had by 1942 dropped to less than half its level in 1937.

MOTEN SINGS AT WHITE HOUSE
On **JANUARY 31**, Etta Moten, a stage and screen star, became the first African American actress to sing at the White House, performing before President and Mrs. Franklin D. Roosevelt at a dinner party of family and friends. Moten sang a number of songs from her role in the films *Gold Diggers of 1933* and *Swing Low, Sweet Chariot*.

NAACP LAUNCHES MAJOR ATTACK ON DISCRIMINATION AND RACIAL INJUSTICES
On **OCTOBER 26**, representatives of the NAACP and members of the American Fund for Public Service convened in New York City to wage an organized campaign against discrimination and segregation. Charles H. Houston, the vice dean of the Howard University Law School, was selected to direct the NAACP legal campaign.

FIRST BLACK DEMOCRATIC CONGRESSMAN ELECTED
In **NOVEMBER**, Black Democrats had grown so much in strength in the city of Chicago that they solicited a novice in city politics, Arthur Mitchell (1883–1968), to run against the well-known Black Republican congressman Oscar DePriest. Blacks had been abandoning the Republican Party in large numbers over the past several decades. On November 7, Mitchell received 53 percent of the Black vote in the Illinois First Congressional District, becoming the first Black Democrat in the U.S. Congress.

Mitchell, born in Lafayette, Alabama, attended public school and later Tuskegee Institute, where he worked as an office assistant for Booker T. Washington. After teaching school in Georgia and Alabama, Mitchell founded and served as president of Armstrong Agricultural School in West Butler, Alabama. Mitchell studied law and passed the bar examination in 1927. After practicing law in Washington, D.C., and then moving to Chicago in 1929, he opened a real-estate business. He quickly became a major player in the Republican political machine of Chicago, but he shifted his allegiance to the Democrats when the policies of the New Deal were articulated. When Mitchell first sought the Democratic nomination for Congress from the First District, he was defeated by Harry Baker; but he was selected to run when Baker died.

Mitchell used his congressional position to denounce Italy's invasion of Ethiopia and to denounce the U.S. Supreme Court's failure to enforce the Fourteenth Amendment to uphold the rights of Black people. When Mitchell sued the Chicago, Rock Island and Pacific Railway because he was prohibited from using its first-class service, the U.S. Supreme Court decided in his favor.

In 1942, Mitchell decided not to run for reelection. He moved to a farm in Petersburg, Virginia, where he died in 1968.

HAWKINS ELECTED TO CALIFORNIA STATE ASSEMBLY

In **NOVEMBER**, Augustus F. Hawkins (1907–?) was elected to the California Assembly from Los Angeles.

Hawkins, a native of Shreveport, Louisiana, moved to Los Angeles at the age of eleven and attended local schools. After graduating from the University of California in 1931, he attended the University of Southern California Institute of Government. In 1962, Hawkins was elected to the Eighty-eighth Congress from California's Twenty-first Congressional District. He remained a noted advocate of civil rights for Blacks.

1935 AFRICAN AMERICANS MOUNT RELIEF EFFORTS FOR ETHIOPIA

After the invasion of Ethiopia by the Italian facist dictator Benito Mussolini, Black churches and other organizations organized relief efforts for Ethiopians.

BETHUNE ORGANIZES NATIONAL COUNCIL OF NEGRO WOMEN

Mary McLeod Bethune (1875–1955) established the National Council of Negro Women (NCNW) to fight

Mary McLeod Bethune, who was chosen from among her sixteen siblings to go to school, became a leader in support of literacy for Blacks. A friend of Eleanor Roosevelt's, Bethune was probably the most influential member of FDR's "Black Cabinet." As a Black leader, she demonstrated in support of antilynching legislation, jobs and job training for women and youth, and equal rights.

racial and gender discrimination. The goals of the NCNW were eventually expanded to include eliminating all types of discrimination — whether based on race, creed, color, gender, or national origin. The organization grew rapidly; by the mid-1970s, it was one of the largest organizations of African American women, with as many as three million members and one hundred affiliates in forty states.

Bethune was born in the small rural cotton-growing community of Mayesville, South Carolina. In 1888, she left home to attend Scotia College in North Carolina. In 1895, she attended the all-white Moody Bible Institute in Chicago. In 1904, with only one dollar and fifty cents in cash, five students, and a rented building, Bethune founded the Normal and Industrial School for young Black women in Daytona Beach, Florida.

During the 1930s and 1940s, Bethune served as a member of Hoover's Committee for Child Welfare and as director of the National Business League, the National Urban League, the Commission on Interracial Cooperation, and president of Roosevelt's Division of Negro Affairs of the National Youth Administration. In this latter capacity, which she accepted in 1936, Bethune became the first Black woman to head a federal office and the first to head an "informal" Black cabinet. A national memorial was erected in her honor in Washington, D.C., in July 1974, almost twenty years after her death.

BLACKS IN HARLEM RIOT AGAINST EXPLOITATION BY MERCHANTS

In late **MARCH**, Harlem was the scene of a destructive looting rampage that left the community shaken. The riot was precipitated by a rumor that a child had been beaten for shoplifting. The real reason for the riot, however, was later found to be the feeling in the community that Blacks were being exploited by area merchants. Radicals enflamed the situation, encouraging discontented Black residents to express their despair by smashing store windows, looting inventories, and destroying thousands of dollars' worth of goods. Although the riot was spontaneous, looting was limited to stores along 125th Street (Harlem's main retail and theatrical center).

BLACKS LYNCHED IN TEXAS

In Texas, a mob of seven hundred lynched two Blacks accused of murder.

FITZGERALD BEGINS SINGING CAREER

Ella Fitzgerald (1918–) began her singing career with the Chick Webb Orchestra in New York. She traveled abroad and soon became one of the most sought-after jazz singers throughout the 1940s and 1950s.

HUGHES'S PLAY SUCCEEDS ON BROADWAY

Langston Hughes's play *The Mulatto* opened on Broadway. It was a major success for Hughes, continuing to play on Broadway through 1937. When the play had run its course, efforts to take it to theaters across the country met with bans in several cities because of its alleged "radical" theme. In the 1940s, the play was performed at small neighborhood theaters.

JULIAN DEVELOPS DRUG FOR GLAUCOMA

Percy L. Julian (1899–1975), an industrial chemist, synthesized physostigmine, a drug used in the treatment of glaucoma. The next year, Julian was selected as director of research in the soya products division of the Glidden Company. During his tenure there, Julian and staff were granted more than eighty-seven patents. He was best known for those patents associated with a process for preparing pure soya protein used for coating and sizing paper and also a synthesis of cortisone for the treatment of rheumatoid arthritis.

OWENS SETS LONG-JUMP RECORD

Jesse Owens (1913–1980) set a new long-jump record of 26½ feet in Michigan. At this meet, Owens broke three records, the largest number ever at a single college meet. Owens went on to compete in the 1936 Berlin Olympics.

SERVICE ESTABLISHMENTS OPERATED BY BLACKS

According to the U.S. business census, a total of 22,172 service establishments were operated by Blacks in this year. Of these businesses, 8,710 (39.3 percent) were located in the North, 12,204 (55 percent) in the South, and 1,258 (5.7 percent) in the West. Receipts were skewed more toward the North. Of the $27,281,000 in receipts, 46.2 percent were in the North, 49.1 percent in the South, and 4.7 percent in the West.

WORKS PROGRESS ADMINISTRATION HIRES MANY BLACKS

The Works Progress Administration (WPA), created by executive order of President Franklin D. Roosevelt, hired many unemployed Blacks to work on public projects. Many Black writers were employed to record and document the experiences of Black people in certain states and regions.

The writer Arna Bontemps directed a federal writers unit that included Claude McKay, Richard Wright, Roi Ottley, Zora Neale Hurston, Frank Yerby, Margaret Walker, Marcus Christian, Robert Hayden, Ralph Ellison, and John H. Johnson. Johnson later became the publisher of *Ebony* and *Jet*, successful Black-oriented magazines.

Many young Black actors were employed by other federal projects. All-Black companies were established in Harlem, Chicago, Birmingham, and Los Angeles, where Blacks gained firsthand knowledge of all aspects of producing theater and movies.

GOVERNMENT REPORTS ON PURCHASING POWER OF BLACKS

According to a Department of Commerce report by Eugene Kinckle Jones released in **JANUARY**, the total annual purchasing power of Blacks, based on a study of 5.5 million workers, was estimated to be about two billion dollars.

DUST BOWL DEVASTATES BLACK FARMERS

On **APRIL 11**, a severe dust storm blew over half of the United States. Crops were destroyed, and people fled their homes. The major portion of this storm covered western Kansas, eastern Colorado, Wyoming, western Oklahoma, nearly all of Texas, and parts of New Mexico. Dust pneumonia was an immediate threat to children. Black farmers, most of them barely making a subsistence living from agriculture, were devastated.

LOUIS KNOCKS OUT CARNERA

On **JUNE 25**, Joe Louis (1914–1981), a Black heavyweight boxer, knocked out Primo Carnera in the sixth round before a large crowd at Yankee Stadium in New York.

Louis, born in Lafayette, Alabama, in 1914, later moved to Detroit with his family. After quitting school, he worked for one of the automobile plants during the day, and in his spare time, he boxed. Although Louis was physically gifted, he had trouble getting a chance at the championship despite his record of thirty-four victories in thirty-five bouts.

UNIVERSITY OF MARYLAND ORDERED TO ADMIT MURRAY

On **NOVEMBER 5**, the Maryland Court of Appeals ordered the University of Maryland to admit Donald Murray, a Black graduate of Amherst College who had been

denied admission to the University of Maryland Law School on the basis of race. The university offered to pay Murray's tuition to any law school of his choice that would accept him. The court declared the "choice arrangement" to be de facto inequality, noting, "Equal treatment can be furnished only in the existing (University of Maryland) Law School," and, therefore, that Murray had to be admitted. Thurgood Marshall was Murray's lawyer in this case.

1936 INCOMES OF FAMILIES REPORTED BY RACE

The data on average income of Black and white families (not on relief) showed clearly that Blacks in large cities of the North Central region had median incomes roughly twice that of Blacks in southern cities and rural communities. The average Black family income was about 44 percent of the average white family income in southern rural communities, 34 percent in southern cities of twenty-five hundred or more, and 64 percent in North Central cities of one hundred thousand residents or more.

LOUIS KNOCKS OUT SHARKEY

Joe Louis knocked out Jack Sharkey in the third round. He continued his quest for a championship bout and eventually was scheduled to fight Jim J. Braddock for the heavyweight championship.

VIRGIN ISLANDS GIVEN RIGHT TO ELECT LEGISLATURE

Congress passed legislation that gave the Virgin Islands, a U.S. territory, the right to elect its own legislature.

◈ The Virgin Islands, composed of three main islands — St. Thomas, St. Croix, and St. John — and more than fifty islets in the West Indies,

Donald Gaines Murray (center) and his attorney, Thurgood Marshall (left), confer. Marshall argued before the Supreme Court that since Maryland had no state-run separate-but-equal law school for Blacks, Murray should be admitted to the University of Maryland School of Law.

was purchased by the United States from Spain in 1917. During the sixteenth century, most of the Arawak and Carib Indians had been replaced by African slaves. In fact, during the mid-1800s, the slave population had reached a high of almost forty-three thousand. Because the Virgin Islands' population was overwhelmingly Black (between 85 and 90 percent), and because many of the residents could easily trace their heritage to slave relatives who had worked in sugar cane and cotton fields, the right to select their own legislature was a substantial move toward self-government for Blacks.

SCOTTSBORO DEFENDANT SENTENCED
On **JANUARY 23**, Heywood Patterson was sentenced to seventy-five years in prison in the Scottsboro case.

SCOTTSBORO DEFENDANT SHOT IN ESCAPE
On **JANUARY 24**, Ozie Powell, a defendant in the Scottsboro case, was shot and wounded in an escape attempt.

NATIONAL NEGRO CONGRESS ORGANIZED
On **FEBRUARY 14** through **16**, the National Negro Congress convened in Chicago, attended by 817 delegates representing more than five hundred organizations. A. Philip Randolph, head of the Brotherhood of Sleeping Car Porters, was elected president of the organization.

BETHUNE NAMED DIRECTOR OF NEGRO AFFAIRS
On **JUNE 24**, educator Mary McLeod Bethune became the first Black woman to receive an important federal appointment when she was chosen director of Negro Affairs of the National Youth Administration.

BLACK ATHLETES WIN THIRTEEN OLYMPIC MEDALS
On **AUGUST 4** through **9**, ten Black athletes won medals in track and field at the Summer Olympics in Berlin, Germany. Black track star Jesse Owens won four gold medals, in the 100-meter race, the 200-meter race, the 4 × 400-meter relay, and the long jump, breaking the Olympic record in both the 200-meter race and the long jump. Other Black gold medal winners were John Woodruff (800-meter), Cornelius Johnson (high jump), and Archie Williams (400-meter). In addition, medals were won by Ralph Metcalfe (100-meter); Matthew Robinson (200-meter); David Albritton and Delos Thurber (high jump); James LuValle (400-meter); and Frederick Pollard (110-meter high hurdles). Adolf Hitler, whose racist

Jesse Owens was called the "Ebony Antelope" when he won four gold medals at the 1936 Olympics in Berlin.

ideology held Blacks to be an "inferior race," was chagrined as Blacks easily won in the sprints and hurdles and dominated the field events.

NAACP SUES FOR EQUAL PAY FOR TEACHERS
On **DECEMBER 8**, the NAACP filed suit in *Gibbs* v. *Board of Education* of Montgomery County, Maryland, in an effort to equalize the pay of Black and white teachers. In a landmark decision, the U.S. Supreme Court declared that setting unequal salaries for Black and white teachers was unconstitutional. The decision formed the basis for a series of suits filed by the NAACP throughout the country to eliminate wage differentials between the races.

1937 HUGO BLACK CONFIRMED AS ASSOCIATE SUPREME COURT JUSTICE
The U.S. Senate approved Hugo Black's nomination to the U.S. Supreme Court. Justice Black was reported to be a member of the Ku Klux Klan. He refused to confirm or deny reports that he had ever been a Klan member.

THE "GREAT WHITE FATHER"

Blacks abandoned Herbert Hoover and the Republican Party in favor of Franklin D. Roosevelt, the Democrats, and "bread and butter" issues. When Roosevelt emerged victorious, his liberal Democratic administration appointed many Blacks as advisers in government departments — far more than any other president. FDR was dubbed the "Great White Father" because of these appointments and his visible and outspoken support for Black people. Government agencies such as the Works Progress Administration, the National Youth Administration, the Civilian Conservation Corps, the Federal Theater, and other projects provided many jobs and opportunities for Blacks. In 1936, Roosevelt received overwhelming political support from Black voters. It was during his second administration that Black advisers were given the name "Roosevelt's Black Cabinet." In 1938, the cabinet included the following highly qualified Blacks:

MARY MCLEOD BETHUNE,
National Youth Administration

EDGAR BROWN,
Civilian Conservation Corps

DR. ROSCOE C. BROWN,
Public Health Service

DR. AMBROSE CALIVER,
Department of the Interior

JOSEPH H. EVANS,
Farm Security Administration

CHARLES E. HALL,
Department of Commerce

WILLIAM H. HASTIE,
Department of the Interior

DR. FRANK HORNE,
Housing Authority

JOSEPH R. HOUCHINS,
Department of Commerce

WILLIAM I. HOUSTON,
Department of Justice

HENRY A. HUNT,
Farm Credit Administration

DEWEY R. JONES,
Department of the Interior

EUGENE KINCKLE JONES,
Department of Commerce

EDWARD H. LAWSON, JR.,
Works Progress Administration

RALPH E. MIZELLE,
Post Office

LAWRENCE A. OXLEY,
Department of Labor

J. PARKER PRESCOTT,
Housing Authority

ALFRED EDGAR SMITH,
Works Progress Administration

WILLIAM J. TRENT,
Federal Works Agency

DR. WILLIAM J. THOMPKINS,
Recorder of Deeds

DR. ROBERT C. WEAVER,
Housing Authority

ARTHUR WEISEGER,
Department of Labor

JOHN W. WHITTEN,
Works Progress Administration

By 1930, the Works Progress Administration had affected the lives of more than one million unemployed Blacks, enhanced Black culture, added significantly to the facilities of Black colleges and universities, provided skilled trades to thousands of Black men and women, and made available hundreds of nontraditional employment opportunities for Blacks.

FATHER DIVINE'S HOME BURNS DOWN

Self-styled Father Divine's "Super-super Haven," an eighty-room mansion located in Ulster County, New York, burned to the ground. Father Divine (1882–1965) had created a religious cult based in Harlem. In major cities throughout the country, Father Divine's ministry had set up shoeshine parlors, food stores, restaurants, coal yards, and other cooperatives to assist his followers. His disciples believed that he was an incarnation of God. He advocated racial and economic equality and supported Black business.

RED CAPS UNIONIZE

The International Brotherhood of Red Caps, a group of Black railway baggage porters, was organized by Willard S. Townsend. He later became a vice president of the AFL-CIO. As the union continued to press for membership in the Congress of Industrial Organizations (CIO), it changed its name to the United Transport Service Employees of America.

FIRST BLACK FEDERAL JUDGE APPOINTED

On **MARCH 26**, William H. Hastie became the first Black to serve as a U.S. federal judge. He was appointed to a federal district court in the Virgin Islands by President Franklin D. Roosevelt. He served two years in this position and then accepted a position as assistant solicitor in the Department of the Interior. Although there was bitter opposition to his confirmation as assistant solicitor, support from the NAACP and Harvard Law School alumni insiders helped to win approval.

Hastie later became dean of Howard University Law School and a member of Roosevelt's "Black Cabinet" as a civilian aide to the secretary of war. He served only a short time in this position before resigning because of widespread discrimination in the War Department and its failure to act against segregation in the armed services. Hastie was later appointed governor of the Virgin Islands by President Harry S. Truman in 1946. In 1949, Truman appointed him to the U.S. Court of Appeals, Third Circuit, where he served until 1971.

LOUIS BECOMES WORLD HEAVYWEIGHT CHAMPION

On **JUNE 22**, Joe Louis earned the title of heavyweight boxing champion of the world by defeating Jim J. Braddock. He became the first Black heavyweight champion in twenty-two years. More than forty-five thousand boxing fans paid to see the fight, the largest audience ever to attend a single fight. Louis held the championship from 1937 to 1949, successfully defending the title twenty-five times.

Although he retired in 1949 (having lost only once), he returned to the ring to fight Ezzard Charles and then Rocky Marciano — he lost both fights. Louis may have been the greatest heavyweight champion ever to hold the crown — he held the title longer than anyone else in the history of the competition.

TWO BLACKS LYNCHED IN FLORIDA

In Florida, two Black youths were lynched by a mob on **JULY 20**.

PULLMAN COMPANY RECOGNIZES RANDOLPH'S UNION

On **OCTOBER 1**, the Pullman Company formally recognized A. Philip Randolph's union, the Brotherhood of Sleeping Car Porters. It had taken many years for this to occur.

1938 WHITE MERCHANTS PERSUADED TO HIRE BLACKS IN HARLEM

Due to the efforts of Adam Clayton Powell, Jr., and other leaders, white merchants in Harlem were persuaded to hire Blacks to make up at least one-third of their labor force. The merchants also agreed to work toward equal opportunities for promotion.

JACK AND JILL OF AMERICA INCORPORATES

On **JANUARY 21**, Jack and Jill of America, Inc., was founded in Philadelphia by Marion Turner Stubbs Thomas. The organization was created to develop educational, cultural, civic, and social programs for African American youth. Today, there are as many as 180 chapters throughout the country.

LOUIS KNOCKS OUT SCHMELING

On **JUNE 22**, in a rematch of their 1936 fight, Joe Louis again knocked out the German heavyweight champion, Max Schmeling, in one round to retain his world heavyweight crown. Ironically, during this time when Germans believed in "Aryan superiority," Louis's boxing talents had proved superior to that of any white boxer.

FAUSET ELECTED TO PENNSYLVANIA LEGISLATURE

On **NOVEMBER 8**, Crystal Bird Fauset was elected to the Pennsylvania House of Representatives, becoming the first Black woman elected to a state legislative body.

William Hastie, an influential member of Roosevelt's "Black Cabinet," was the first Black appointed to a federal judgeship.

SUPREME COURT RULES ON EQUAL EDUCATION FOR BLACKS

On **DECEMBER 12**, the U.S. Supreme Court ruled that states had to provide equal if separate educational opportunities for Blacks, in *Missouri ex rel Gaines* v. *Canada.* The case stemmed from Lloyd Gaines's effort to be admitted to the law school of the University of Missouri. Rather than admit him, the state and school offered to pay his tuition to another school or to establish a special school for Blacks. Gaines responded that the offer to go outside Missouri for his education violated the "separate but equal" law, and that attending a separate school would not afford him the desired prestige of having attended the University of Missouri Law School. The U.S. Supreme Court ruled in favor of Gaines, declaring that "the obligation of the state to give the protection of equal laws can be performed only where its laws operate, that is, within its own jurisdiction." The Court also ruled that Gaines could not be denied admission to the law school simply because of his race or color, and that out-of-state tuition scholarships for Blacks to attend institutions in other states did not meet the "separate but equal" requirement.

1939 BLACK INCOMES WELL BELOW THOSE OF WHITES

The average annual wage and salary income of Black men in the United States was $460 — 41 percent of the average income of white men, which was $1,112.

BLACK-OWNED RETAIL BUSINESSES INCREASE SIGNIFICANTLY

According to the Bureau of the Census, there were a total of 29,827 Black-owned establishments in this year, accounting for $71,466,000 in sales. This represented an increase of 49 percent over sales for 1935. However, the 1939 retail sales total was actually 27.5 percent lower than that of 1929, when $98,602,000 in sales was generated by 24,969 — approximately five thousand fewer — retail stores.

BLACK SOLDIERS SQUEEZED OUT

Blacks had suffered many indignities after coming home from World War I. Between 1919 and 1939, they experienced Jim Crow laws, assaults by white mobs, and Klan lynchings. The military leadership felt simply that Blacks should be removed from the peacetime army. They circulated racist literature, which increased resentment of Blacks among white soldiers, and officers began expressing racist attitudes similar to those found in the general public. In this year, there were only about thirty-six hundred Blacks in the regular army; only five were officers, and three of these were chaplains. Widespread efforts were implemented to remove Black soldiers and Black troops from the army.

The army created two new Black units in this year, the Forty-seventh and the Forty-eighth Quartermaster regiments, despite the objections of racists. The army saw the possibility of war on the horizon and started preparing for it.

CARVER GUEST AT WHITE HOUSE

President Franklin D. Roosevelt invited George Washington Carver, the noted botanist, to the White House. The visit created a stir among many whites throughout the country.

CHRISTIAN DEVELOPS UNIQUE GUITAR STYLE

Charlie Christian (1919–1942), after perfecting the use of electrically amplified instruments together with the guitar, joined the Benny Goodman Orchestra. From 1939 to 1941, he worked with Dizzy Gillespie and Thelonius Monk to create bebop, a modern style of jazz. Christian was a sought-after jazz guitarist until his early death from tuberculosis.

HORNE MAKES FIRST FILM

Lena Horne (1917–), who began her career as a chorus dancer at the New York Cotton Club at the age of sixteen, made her first film, *The Duke Is Tops*, in this year. Horne eventually gained international recognition as a blues singer. In 1943, she starred in the movie *Stormy Weather*, which is memorable for her expressive singing. Her career has included tours of Europe and the United States.

MCDANIEL WINS OSCAR

Hattie McDaniel and the Academy of Motion Picture Arts and Sciences made history when McDaniel became the first Black to win an Oscar as best supporting actress for her role as the slave Mammy in *Gone with the Wind*. Noted Black actors and actresses, including Hattie McDaniel, who had roles in white pictures were listed as "featured players" rather than as "stars."

STORY OF A.D. PRESENTS PLIGHT OF TENANT FARMER

Research by scholars such as A. Raper and Ira A. Reid showed the situation of the tenant farmer to be a "completely hopeless dead end of debt and servitude." In a journal article, they presented the case of a Black farmer, code-named A.D., who, after raising seven bales of cotton that sold for $338.74, ended up owing his landlord $14.75. It seemed that no matter how large a crop was produced, the tenant farmer ended the year in debt. After reviewing the situation, A.D. gave his reaction:

> I looked at my cotton receipts and my debt and I said "A.D., you's goin' to town; you had a good year, but you ain't got nothin' and you never will have nothin' as long as you stay here." So me and my old lady and the chillun jes' lef.... I's through with farmin'. Through. Yes sir, through.

A.D.'s decision was not atypical; thousands were moving to town in search of "freedom" from the cropping and tenant systems that had simply produced another form of slavery.

The DAR's refusal to allow Marian Anderson to sing in Constitution Hall provoked Eleanor Roosevelt and Secretary of the Interior Harold Ickes to arrange for her to sing before a large audience at the Lincoln Memorial.

DAR DISALLOWS CONCERT BY BLACK ARTIST

On **FEBRUARY 27**, the Daughters of the American Revolution (DAR) refused to allow Black contralto Marian Anderson (1902–1993) to sing at Constitution Hall in Washington, D.C. First Lady Eleanor Roosevelt furiously resigned from the DAR to protest the organization's action. Others protested through mass meetings and petitions. Anderson herself said, "I am shocked beyond words to be barred from the capital of my country after having appeared in almost every other capital in the world."

The DAR claimed that they could not accommodate her performance because Constitution Hall had been previously booked by the Washington Symphony. However, when Anderson's manager asked for alternate dates that were known to be open, he was again turned down. DAR policy at the time allowed Blacks to sit in the audience but not to perform on the stage. The organization said it was simply following the segregationist policy common in the District of Columbia at the time.

Upon hearing of the DAR incident, Secretary of the Interior Harold Ickes offered the Lincoln Memorial to Anderson for the concert. Introducing Anderson before the concert, Ickes observed, "In this great auditorium under the sky, all of us are free." The crowd that day numbered seventy-five thousand and included members of congress and cabinet members. Anderson opened her program with the song "America." She also sang operatic selections and finished with several spirituals, which were expected of Black singers at the time. For her encore, she sang "Nobody Knows the Trouble I've Seen." Thunderous cheers and applause followed her performance. Immediately after the concert, Anderson said, "I'm just so overwhelmed today, I cannot express myself. . . . The immensity of this affair has done so much to me."

In 1943, Anderson finally sang in Constitution Hall in a charity concert for China relief. Yet the "white artists only" policy of the DAR was reaffirmed in 1947 and continued until 1952. Anderson was not allowed to sing at the Metropolitan Opera in New York until 1955, when she became the first Black singer to perform there. Ten years later, Anderson began her farewell concert tour at Constitution Hall.

◆ Anderson was born in Philadelphia. She received her early training in church choirs; church members set up a trust fund to help pay for her voice lessons. At the age of nineteen, she began to study with the renowned teacher Giuseppe Boghetti, subsequently entering and winning a major voice competition. Anderson made her European debut in Berlin in 1930 and performed concerts in Europe for the next five years, establishing a reputation as one of the world's finest contraltos. Upon returning to the United States, she toured triumphantly, sometimes giving more than one hundred concerts in a season. In 1942, she established the Marian Anderson Award for young singers. President Dwight D. Eisenhower appointed Anderson as a delegate to the Thirteenth General Assembly of the United Nations. She retired from performing in 1965. In 1978, Anderson was one of five performers to receive the first John F. Kennedy Center honors.

BOLIN APPOINTED JUDGE

On **JULY 22**, Jane M. Bolin (1908–) was appointed by Mayor Fiorella La Guardia to the New York City

Court of Domestic Relations, becoming the first African American woman judge.

Bolin, born in Poughkeepsie, New York, graduated from Wellesley College in 1928 and from Yale Law School in 1931. Prior to her appointment as judge, she served as assistant corporation counsel of New York City.

NAACP LEGAL DEFENSE FUND PLEDGES WAR ON DISCRIMINATION

On **OCTOBER 11**, leaders of the NAACP Legal Defense and Educational Fund organized an all-out war on discrimination. Charles H. Houston, a Harvard-educated lawyer, directed the major task of mobilizing the best legal talent in the country to fight racial bias. Thurgood Marshall was selected to be director.

1940–1969 NUMBER OF BLACK FARM OPERATORS DECLINES

The number of Black farm operators declined by 87 percent during this period. The proportion of Black farm operators who were tenant farmers declined from 74.6 percent to 20.1 percent. For a host of reasons, Blacks had been driven off the farms and out of agriculture in great numbers.

1940

POPULATION OVERVIEW

BLACK POPULATION IN THE UNITED STATES The U.S. population numbered 131,669,275 residents, of whom 12,865,518, or 9.8 percent of the total, were Black.

The Black population still remained concentrated in the South, but not to the same degree as at the beginning of the twentieth century, when more than 90 percent of Blacks resided there. The demand for workers in the Northeast and the Midwest, in conjunction with a host of social and economic problems in the South, precipitated waves of Black migration from the South that continued from 1910 to 1970. Although some Blacks did move into the South, a far greater number left, resulting in a net migration of at least 300,000 Blacks in each decade between 1910 and 1970. In 1940, more than three-quarters of the entire Black population resided in the South, compared with only about one-third of total U.S. citizens. Blacks made up only a small percentage of the population in the West and were equally distributed between the Northeast and the Midwest, each with 11 percent of the Black population. In the three decades from 1940 to 1970, Blacks continued to move away from the South.

URBAN POPULATION The census estimated that 56.5 percent of the total U.S. population resided in urban areas. The percentage of the Black population classified as urban was 48.6 percent. Blacks composed 8.4 percent of all urban residents.

BLACKS IN THE BLACK BELT In the Black Belt of the American South, Blacks formed majorities in about 180 counties. In another 290 contiguous counties, Blacks constituted from 30 to 50 percent of the population. This region of the country, the locus of plantation slavery, contained more than 5 million Blacks.

BLACK AMERICANS BECOME HONORARY SHIPMASTERS

Between 1940 and 1950, eighteen Black Americans became honorary shipmasters; that is, they were honored by having their names affixed to one of America's Liberty ships:

SS *Robert S. Abbott* (Founder of the *Chicago Defender*)

SS *George Washington Carver* (Scientist and inventor)

SS *Frederick Douglass* (Abolitionist, writer, publisher, and diplomat)

SS *Paul Laurence Dunbar* (Poet)

SS *John Hope* (Educator and president of Atlanta University and Morehouse College)

SS *James Weldon Johnson* (Writer, teacher, and lawyer)

SS *Toussaint L'Ouverture* (Ex-slave, military leader, and statesman)

SS *John Merrick* (Business and civic leader)

SS *John H. Murphy* (Civil War veteran, journalist, and newspaper owner)

SS *Edward A. Savoy* (Public servant)

SS *Harriet Tubman* (Fugitive slave, Underground Railroad leader, and Union spy)

SS *Robert L. Vann* (Lawyer, founder of *Pittsburgh Courier*, and political strategist)

SS *Booker T. Washington* (Ex-slave, educator, orator, and writer)

SS *Bert Williams* (Entertainer and Broadway star)

USS *Jesse Brown* (First Black pilot in U.S. Navy and first Black officer killed in Korean War)

USS *George Washington Carver* (Scientist and inventor)

USS *Leonard Roy Harmon* (Soldier killed in action trying to save a wounded officer)

USS *Miller* (Recipient of Silver Star for extraordinary courage)

In addition to the Liberty ships, four Victory ships were named after Black colleges:

The *Fisk Victory* (Fisk University, Atlanta, Georgia)
The *Tuskegee Victory* (Tuskegee University, Tuskegee, Alabama)
The *Howard Victory* (Howard University, Washington, D.C.)
The *Lane Victory* (Lane College, Jackson, Tennessee)

DEFENSE INDUSTRIES EXCLUDE BLACKS

Black employees were largely excluded from defense industries. Most plants had no Black employees, and many excluded Blacks outright as a matter of policy. A common excuse, "there are no trained Blacks available," pointed out part of the problem — many training schools did not admit Blacks, and the unions would not admit them whether or not they were trained.

FOUR BLACKS LYNCHED IN THE SOUTH

On the basis of reports by the research department of Tuskegee Institute, the NAACP, and the Association of Southern Women for the Prevention of Lynching, a total of five lynchings occurred in this year. One victim was a white man who was flogged to death by KKK members for beating his wife and being drunk. The other four lynchings had Black victims and are described below:

- On May 8, O'Dee Henderson was shot to death by the police and a mob of whites inside a police station in Fairfield, Alabama. Henderson was accused of engaging in an altercation with a white man;
- On June 20, Elbert Williams's body was fished from the Hatchie River in Brownsville, Tennessee. Williams was kidnapped and killed by local whites for leading a campaign that encouraged Black people to vote;
- On June 22, Jesse Thornton's body was dragged from a river near Tuskegee Institute and Luverne, Alabama. Thornton had been shot to death by a police-led mob because he refused to address a white man as "mister;"
- On September 8, sixteen-year-old Austin Callaway was shot to death by a masked white mob, who forced entry into the La Grange, Georgia, jail and demanded his release. Callaway was accused of attempted rape of a white woman.

The report emphasized that in as many as twenty-two instances — three in the North and nineteen in the South — attempted lynchings were foiled by officers. There were other suspected lynchings not included in the report:

- On August 3, near Dyersburg, Tennessee, Roosevelt Jones was shot to death by a police-led posse that trailed him through three states. Jones was accused of stealing money from another Black man and for shooting a white officer in the hand when apprehended;
- On November 24, Eddie Garrett was shot to death by a posse led by policemen in Hammond, Louisiana. Garrett was accused of killing a white farmer in a robbery attempt.

Federal antilynching legislation was introduced during the Seventy-sixth Congress by Representative Joseph A. Gavagan in the House and by Senator Robert Wagner in the Senate. The Gavagan measure passed the lower body in January. In May, the Judiciary Committee voted 12–4 to place the Wagner bill on the calendar, but it was never called to a vote on the Senate floor.

NAACP PROTESTS EXCLUSION OF BLACKS FROM DEFENSE INDUSTRIES

Blacks protested their exclusion from defense industries. Major organizations such as the NAACP, the Urban League, and other organizations supported A. Philip Randolph's call for a march on Washington to demand jobs and integration of the military.

VIRGINIA SELECTS STATE SONG BY BLACK COMPOSER

The Virginia General Assembly chose "Carry Me Back to Old Virginny," written by Black composer James A. Bland, as the state song of Virginia.

WAR DEPARTMENT OPENS OFFICER CANDIDATE SCHOOLS TO BLACKS

The War Department made history by opening the officer candidate schools to Blacks. Because of the nature of training, the schools were integrated even when the Tuskegee training station remained segregated. In addition, five Blacks graduated from West Point during World War II; none graduated from the U.S. Naval Academy at Annapolis.

WRIGHT'S *Native Son* IS BOOK-OF-THE-MONTH CLUB SELECTION

Richard Wright's *Native Son* was published, the first novel by a Black writer to become a Book-of-the-Month Club selection.

AMERICAN NEGRO THEATER ORGANIZED

On **JUNE 5**, the American Negro Theater was organized in Harlem, New York, by Frederick O'Neal and Abram Hill. It went on to produce a number of plays, some of which played on Broadway, and launched the careers of a number of major actors, including Harry Belafonte, Ruby Dee, and Sidney Poitier. One of the plays adapted by Hill, *Anna Lucasta,* premiered on Broadway in 1944 and ran for as many as nine hundred performances.

COTTON CLUB CLOSES

On **JUNE 10**, the famous Cotton Club in Harlem closed its doors because of low attendance. It had been Harlem's musical and entertainment center for several decades. Many of the great jazz musicians and singers played at the Cotton Club, including Lena Horne and Duke Ellington.

DAVIS BECOMES FIRST BLACK GENERAL IN U.S. ARMY

On **OCTOBER 16**, Benjamin O. Davis, Sr., became the first Black general in the history of the U.S. military. Davis was soon promoted to brigadier general and was the highest-ranking U.S. Black officer during World War II. The next year, he was assigned commander of the Fourth Cavalry Brigade, Fort Riley, Kansas. His son, Benjamin O. Davis, Jr., became the first African American general in the U.S. Air Force.

SUPREME COURT RULES THAT BLACKS CANNOT BE BARRED FROM WHITE NEIGHBORHOODS

On **NOVEMBER 13**, the U.S. Supreme Court declared in *Hansberry* v. *Lee* that it was illegal for whites to bar African Americans from white neighborhoods. The case in question involved a wealthy real-estate broker, Carl Hansberry of Chicago, who moved his family to an all-white neighborhood. Lorraine Hansberry, who was ten years old when the U.S. Supreme Court handed down its decision, wrote about this experience in her powerful play *A Raisin in the Sun.*

1941 LOCKER ELECTED TO CINCINNATI CITY COUNCIL

Jesse Locker, a Black Republican, was elected to the city council of Cincinnati, Ohio. He served from 1941 to 1953, when he was appointed ambassador to Liberia by President Dwight D. Eisenhower.

LOUIS REMAINS UNDEFEATED CHAMPION

Joe Louis won his seventeenth match in defense of his heavyweight championship title. He continued his undefeated reign with a victory over Buddy Baer.

MILLER HONORED FOR SERVICE AT PEARL HARBOR

Dorie Miller was awarded the Navy Cross for shooting down four enemy planes during the attack on Pearl Harbor. Miller was a steward aboard the USS *Arizona.* (Blacks were allowed to enlist in the navy but only as stewards.)

ROOSEVELT OPPOSES MARCH ON WASHINGTON

The March on Washington planned by A. Philip Randolph and others, scheduled for July 1, was publicly opposed by President Roosevelt. The march was expected to draw more than fifty thousand Blacks from throughout the

Benjamin O. Davis, Sr., began his distinguished military career during the Spanish-American War in 1898. He first became an officer in 1901 and was steadily promoted, reaching the rank of brigadier general in 1940.

country to demonstrate against discrimination in defense industries. Roosevelt made his statement after he and members of his cabinet met with Randolph and Walter White, executive secretary of the NAACP. In an effort to postpone the march, Roosevelt promised to appoint a committee to study the problem and recommend solutions.

One week before the march, Roosevelt issued Executive Order 8802 to end discrimination in defense industries and to oversee implementation of the nondiscrimination order. On June 25, Randolph called off the march in response to Roosevelt's order, which set up the Fair Employment Practices Committee (FEPC) to prohibit discrimination based on race, color, creed, or national origin in government defense industries — but not in the armed forces. Little actual progress was made until 1943, and it came only with increased Black protest and pressure.

WEAVER DIRECTS PROGRAM TO INTEGRATE BLACKS
Dr. Robert C. Weaver was appointed director of the government office in charge of integrating Blacks into the national defense program. Weaver, who received his doctorate from Harvard, had come to Washington

Robert Weaver, an economist and a government official, went to Washington, D.C., as a young New Dealer. He served President Franklin Roosevelt as an adviser on minority issues for several government agencies. Weaver later became the first African American cabinet member.

to work in New Deal programs. He became leader of the "Black Cabinet," a group that worked for reforms in government hiring.

ANTILYNCHING BILLS INTRODUCED
On **JANUARY 3**, no less than six specific antilynching bills were introduced into the Seventy-seventh Congress by Black U.S. representative Arthur W. Mitchell and white U.S. representatives Joseph A. Gavagan, Ulysses Samuel Guyer, Lee E. Geyer, Bartel Jonkman, and Louis Ludlow.

TRAINING COURSES IN ENGINEERING FOR DEFENSE INDUSTRIES AT HOWARD UNIVERSITY
On **JANUARY 3**, about eighty students enrolled in a series of intensive short courses in defense-related engineering at Howard University. The program was geared to enhance engineering training in support of the war and was sponsored by the U.S. Office of Education. Howard was the only Black university out of the ninety-one schools authorized to give such training.

SUIT FILED BY BLACK MAN TO ENLIST IN ARMY AIR CORPS
On **JANUARY 15**, Yancey Williams, a Howard University student, filed suit against Henry Stimson, secretary of war, and the army chief of staff to permit his enlistment into the Army Air Corps as a flying cadet. The suit was sent to trial but it became irrelevant when a Black flight squadron was established at Tuskegee, Alabama.

TUSKEGEE ARMY AIRFIELD ESTABLISHED
On **JANUARY 16**, the U.S. Army announced the formation of a training school for Black pilots at Tuskegee, Alabama. The airfield was nicknamed the "Home of Black Aviation." Several days prior to the announcement, the NAACP had stated that it planned to file a suit against the War Department to compel the government to enlist a Black citizen in the Army Air Corps.

Although few records detail the early development of the school, it was noted that on January 17, the National Airmen's Association (Colored) met in Chicago and passed a resolution condemning the War Department's plan to create an all-Black air squadron at Tuskegee. In their protest, they emphasized that they would rather be "excluded than segregated." Students at Tuskegee went on a three-day strike, and forty-nine of them were dismissed.

The allotment of $1.8 million for the establishment of the all-Black Army Air Corps did not come until April 21, and the first U.S. Army flying school for Black cadets was dedicated at Tuskegee Institute on July 19. The first class of Black pilots started with ten members; at the time of graduation, the class had five cadets; one captain, Benjamin O. Davis, Jr., a West Point graduate; and five lieutenants — George Spencer Roberts, Mac Ross, Charles DeBow, and Rodney Curtis. They formed the Ninety-ninth Fighter Squadron, under the command of Captain Benjamin Davis. The Ninety-ninth Squadron served in North Africa and parts of Europe. Black aviators from Tuskegee were referred to as the "Black Eagles." During World War II, approximately six hundred Black pilots received their wings. Black pilots in a number of squadrons served with distinction: 150 earned the Distinguished Flying Cross. Sixty-six were killed and thirty-two shot down and captured as prisoners of war.

GOLDEN GATE QUARTET AMONG ARTISTS AT CONSTITUTION HALL

On **JANUARY 19**, the Golden Gate Male Quartet, a gospel group, performed at the President's Inaugural Concert at Constitution Hall, Washington, D.C. They were the only Black entertainers among the many artists who participated. Blacks still remembered when Marian Anderson was blocked from singing at Constitution Hall two years earlier by the Daughters of the American Revolution. Black patrons also protested their exclusion from the event, and some were not receptive to an all-Black pre-inaugural concert at the Labor Department Auditorium, sponsored by "the Committee on Special Entertainment."

EXCLUSION OF BLACKS FROM JURIES CAUSES BLACK PRISONERS TO BE RELEASED

On **JANUARY 24**, Edgar Smith was released from jail by Judge Langston G. King, because Blacks had been excluded from his jury. Following a celebrated trial in which Smith was convicted of criminal assault upon a white woman in 1939 and sentenced to life imprisonment, the U.S. Supreme Court declared in November 1940 that Smith's conviction was unconstitutional and his sentence void because Blacks had been systematically excluded from jury service in Houston, Texas (the venue of the alleged crime).

NAACP CAMPAIGNS AGAINST U.S. SUPREME COURT APPOINTEE

On **JANUARY 25**, the NAACP started a vigorous campaign to derail the appointment of Senator James Byrnes of South Carolina to the U.S. Supreme Court.

They also telegraphed President Roosevelt, stating that the senator was unfit for the high court appointment because his record had been "absolutely consistent in opposing any and every effort to give colored citizens the protection of the United States Constitution." On June 12, Byrnes was confirmed by the U.S. Senate as an associate justice of the U.S. Supreme Court.

BLACKS REPRESENTED ON GRAND JURIES IN NEW YORK AND ALABAMA

On **FEBRUARY 4**, Robert Braddick was named acting foreman of the February term of the New York County Grand Jury, the first Black to serve in this capacity. Three weeks later, on February 24, the first Blacks were named to a grand jury in Montgomery County, Alabama. They were Dr. Jerome D. Harris, pastor of First Baptist Church, and J. R. Wingfeld, superintendent of the Alabama Reform School at Mt. Meigs. Black representation held out the possibility that Black defendants would be judged more fairly.

SALARY INCREASES FOR BLACK TEACHERS

On **FEBRUARY 19**, the Alabama State Board of Education voted to equalize salaries of Black and white teachers. Although it adopted a minimum salary schedule for all teachers, a step required by the U.S. Supreme Court, Black educators stated the regulations avoided a thorough equalization of salaries.

Several weeks earlier, on January 31, the board of education in Norfolk, Virginia, took steps toward reducing the salary disparity between Black and white teachers. Although the Board admitted to the racial disparity and set up a plan for complete equality of salary by 1943, their actions were viewed as incomplete by Black leaders. On the other hand, the General Assembly of Maryland passed a bill on March 31 authorizing equal pay, and thus, Maryland became the first state in the South to achieve equal salaries for Black and white teachers. Maryland's action influenced others to step up their plans. For example, on April 4, the Portsmouth School Board in Virginia voted to equalize salaries beginning July 1. Louisville, Kentucky, followed on May 16, when its board of education voted to increase its 1941–1942 budget by $205,000 to equalize Black and white teachers' salaries.

BLACK BUSINESSWOMAN BUILDS RECREATION CENTER FOR SOLDIERS

In **MARCH**, Lizzie Lunceford, a Black businesswoman in Columbus, Georgia, started plans for a recreation center for soldiers returning from the war. The project would cost about $15,000.

LYNCHING COSTS DOUGLAS COUNTY MORE THAN ONE MILLION DOLLARS

On **MARCH 1**, Douglas County, Nebraska, paid the last installment of a total of $1,375,250, a debt resulting from the lynching of Will Brown in 1919. The courthouse had been burned to the ground by a white mob in order to get to Brown, the victim. The county had to float a bond issue to pay $550,000 for restoring the courthouse, $200,000 for restoration of public and court records, and $656,250 in interest on the principal.

BAR ASSOCIATION OPENS LIBRARY TO BLACK MEMBERS

On **MARCH 11**, the District of Columbia Bar Association voted to remove restrictions to the use of its library housed in the federally owned District Court Building. After more than two years of work, Black lawyers were victorious in a suit filed by Huver I. Brown, a Black lawyer, against the association and government officials for prohibiting Black lawyers from using the library. The association had considered moving the library to another (nonfederal) building, but on discovering that it would cost more than one hundred thousand dollars to duplicate the services of the District Court Building, members decided to change their policy regarding use of the library by Blacks.

MITCHELL WINS DISCRIMINATION CASE

On **MARCH 13**, Arthur Mitchell argued before the U.S. Supreme Court that he was denied equal treatment when he was ejected from a Pullman car while traveling from Chicago to Hot Springs in 1937. Mitchell contended that he had paid a first-class fare and was given second-class accommodation. Nine southern states petitioned the court to refuse a ruling on the constitutionality of their segregation laws in Mitchell's case.

On April 28, the U.S. Supreme Court ruled unanimously in favor of Representative Mitchell in his case against the Chicago, Rock Island and Pacific Railroad. They found that Mitchell was denied his constitutional rights and that Blacks were entitled to all first-class services on railroad trains. Chief Justice Charles E. Hughes noted that the issue was "not a question of segregation, but one of equality of treatment."

Ironically, Representative Mitchell had not been supported by several governmental agencies, including the Interstate Commerce Commission. Nor did he get a favorable ruling from the Federal District Court of North Illinois, which had heard the case earlier and had chosen to uphold segregated and unequal facilities.

DAR REFUSES TO LET ROBESON SING

On **MARCH 17**, the internationally renowned baritone Paul Robeson was refused permission to sing on the stage of Constitution Hall in Washington, D.C., by the Daughters of the American Revolution, two years after they had refused Marian Anderson permission to perform there. Robeson was to sing in a concert sponsored by the Washington Committee for Aid to China.

NATIONAL URBAN LEAGUE SUPPORTS EQUAL ACCESS TO DEFENSE JOBS

On **MARCH 30**, the National Urban League sponsored a one-hour program on nationwide radio to encourage equal employment opportunities for Blacks in the defense program. Among the participants were Ethel Waters, Bill "Bojangles" Robinson, Joe Louis, Eddie Matthews, Anne Wiggins Brown, Marian Anderson, Kenneth Spencer, and Eugene Kinckle Jones.

HARVARD UNIVERSITY BENCHES BLACK LACROSSE PLAYER

On **APRIL 5**, Harvard University benched Lucien Alexis, Jr., a Black lacrosse player, in its game with the U.S. Naval Academy at Annapolis, which refused to let a Black person play on its grounds. Harvard became the scene of major protest from within the college community and from Black leaders over this action. In response to this protest, Harvard announced on April 21 that it would not play any lacrosse team requesting that a player be benched on the basis of race.

CARVER DEVELOPS DRUG FOR TREATMENT OF PYORRHEA

On **APRIL 10**, Dr. George Washington Carver submitted a new drug to the John A. Andrew Clinical Society in a session at Tuskegee Institute. The new drug was developed from the persimmon for the treatment of the gum disease pyorrhea.

CARVER RECEIVES AWARDS AND HONORARY DEGREE

On **APRIL 22**, Dr. George Washington Carver became the first recipient of an award presented by the Catholic Committee of the South for his "significant contribution to the welfare and progress of the South." A few weeks later, on May 16, Dr. Carver received the

1940 Humanitarian Award by the Variety Clubs of America for his contributions to society. Later, the University of Rochester awarded Carver an honorary doctor of science degree.

ALPHA KAPPA ALPHA SORORITY PROTESTS DISCRIMINATION

On **APRIL 25**, more than three thousand telegrams and telephone calls were made by the Alpha Kappa Alpha sorority to the Office of Production Management, protesting discrimination against Blacks in national defense activities, in one of the most significant demonstrations against racial inequality in recent years.

WILLIAMS LYNCHED — TWICE

On **MAY 13**, a white mob burst into the local jail in Quincy, Florida, and took A. C. Williams. After shooting Williams several times, the mob left him to die. Williams managed to crawl away to his home after the mob had left him for dead. But on his way to the hospital in an ambulance, he was overtaken by the mob, pulled from the ambulance, driven down the road, and killed.

RIOTS OCCUR IN ILLINOIS

On **MAY 27**, a race riot erupted in East St. Louis, Illinois. It continued for several days before police could restore calm. One African American was killed. The riot was reminiscent of the race riots that occurred in the city in 1917, leaving many injured and hundreds homeless.

BLACK TANK BATTALION ACTIVATED

On **JUNE 1**, the 758th, the first African American tank battalion, was activated.

WHITE SNIPER SENTENCED TO DEATH

On **JUNE 6**, John Eklund, a white man accused of shooting to death four Blacks in Washington, D.C., simply because they were Black, was sentenced to death by an all-white jury. His sentenced was postponed pending additional evidence.

ROOSEVELT ORDERS END TO DISCRIMINATION IN DEFENSE INDUSTRIES

On **JUNE 13**, President Roosevelt ordered the Office of Production Management to implement whatever measures were necessary to end the "nationwide discrimination against Negroes in defense industries, at a time when the nation is combating the increasing threat of totalitarianism."

KKK MEMBERS FOUND GUILTY

On **JUNE 20**, three Ku Klux Klansmen were found guilty of violating a South Carolina law that prohibited the wearing of masks and hoods for unlawful purposes. The jury in Spartanburg, South Carolina, also found the men guilty of intimidating Blacks by conducting a parade of masked and hooded men in the Black section of town in October 1940. Judge Thomas Sease sentenced the men to serve prison terms and denied any appeal for a new trial.

TEACHER REINSTATED AFTER WINNING SUIT

On **JUNE 26**, Aline Black, a high school teacher in the Norfolk, Virginia, school system, was reinstated in her position by the city board of education.

Black was dismissed in 1939 for filing a suit against the board, demanding equalization of salaries for Blacks and whites in the same professional category.

BLACKS REMOVED FROM SEGREGATED GOLF COURSES

On **JUNE 29**, policemen escorted three Black golfers off the federally owned East Potomac Golf Course in Washington, D.C. They were the first Blacks to play on this course, and they contended that the segregated golf courses provided for them were not adequate. No violence occurred.

MISSOURI SUPREME COURT QUALIFIES ADMISSION OF BLACKS TO UNIVERSITY

On **JULY 10**, the Missouri State Supreme Court declared that Lucille Bluford, who sued the University of Missouri for admission to its graduate school of journalism, had to be admitted only if Lincoln University (a Black institution) refused to admit her after "proper demand" and "reasonable time." This limited ruling kept the doors of the University of Missouri closed to qualified Black students.

WHITE PROFESSORS AT UNIVERSITY OF GEORGIA DISMISSED FOR "ADVOCATING EQUALITY"

On **JULY 14**, two white educators were dismissed for being "fair-minded" and "practicing equality" on the campus of the University of Georgia. Dr. Walter D. Cockling, dean of the college of education, was dismissed for his interest in the Julius Rosenwald Fund and its support of education for Blacks throughout the South. Dr. Marvin S. Pittman was discharged for permitting a group of Black Tuskegee students to eat sandwiches on the campus with white students. Their dismissals were prompted and encouraged by

Governor Eugene Talmadge, who charged them with advocating equality.

In October, the Southern University Conference of Schools, with a membership of forty-one institutions of higher learning in southern states, voted to drop the University of Georgia from its membership as a result of the dismissals. Faculty and students responded to this vote with a protest against Governor Talmadge. Students burned him in effigy.

GEORGIA BANS BOOKS ABOUT BLACKS
On **SEPTEMBER 11**, Governor Eugene Talmadge of Georgia ordered all public schools to ban from their libraries all books on evolution, adolescence, and Blacks. Talmadge, an outspoken racist, encouraged racist activities against Blacks throughout the state.

AFL REFUSES TO STUDY RACIAL DISCRIMINATION IN ITS UNIONS
On **OCTOBER 14**, the sixty-first convention of the American Federation of Labor (AFL) was presented with a resolution requesting that a committee study evidence of discrimination against Blacks in its unions. The resolution was introduced by A. Philip Randolph, president of the Brotherhood of Sleeping Car Porters, an AFL affiliate, but it was rejected.

POWELL ELECTED TO NEW YORK CITY COUNCIL
In **NOVEMBER**, the Reverend Adam Clayton Powell, Jr., was elected the first Black councilor in New York City. Powell was the minister of the large Abyssinian Baptist Church. In an effort to disseminate political and religious information, Powell founded a newspaper called the *People's Voice* in 1942.

CIVIL ENGINEERING TO BE OFFERED AT STATE COLLEGE FOR NEGROES IN KENTUCKY
On **NOVEMBER 5**, the Kentucky State Board of Education authorized a two-year course in civil engineering at the State College for Negroes. The vote was prompted by a suit filed by Charles Eubanks of Louisville, who sought to be admitted to the engineering school at the white state university. The NAACP filed the case on behalf of Eubanks, but when the board authorized a similar program, even at unequal facilities, the case was considered irrelevant and was not pursued.

NATIONAL NEGRO OPERA COMPANY ESTABLISHED
On **NOVEMBER 12**, the National Negro Opera Company was established in Pittsburgh, Pennsylvania, by Mary Cardwell Dawson, an opera instructor, and Lillian Evanti, a coloratura soprano. They organized the company to improve opportunities for African Americans in opera. Its first performance, Verdi's *Aïda*, was performed at the annual meeting of the National Association of Negro Musicians. The company was credited with launching the careers of a number of famous opera singers, including Minto Cato, Lillian Evanti, and Robert McFerrin.

1942 BLACK ENGINEERS INSTRUMENTAL IN ALLIED EFFORTS IN THE PACIFIC
Black engineers and soldiers were involved in a number of construction projects important to Allied action in the Pacific. They built landing strips on New Caledonia in the Battle of the Coral Sea, a road from India to China, and the Alcan Highway, from the United States to Alaska.

BLACKS ADMITTED TO U.S. NAVY
Blacks were allowed to enlist in all branches of the U.S. Navy for the first time in history. Black seamen were also admitted to the Naval Reserve. Although general service appeared to be open, a Black quota of no more than 10 percent, established in 1940, remained in effect, and Blacks did not go to sea; they were restricted to shore duty or served in small harbor or coastal craft.

BLACKS SERVE IN COMBAT SUPPORT ROLE
Although Blacks enlisted in large numbers, all of the four major services held fast to their 10 percent Black participation quota set in 1940. At this time, Blacks were primarily segregated and assigned only in certain areas.

Almost three-fourths of all Blacks who saw military service in World War II served in the U.S. Army. Participation ranged from 5.9 percent at the time of Pearl Harbor to 8.7 percent in September 1944. Blacks were, however, highly represented in certain units. For example, they made up 15.5 percent of members in combat support, 2.8 percent in combat arms, but 45.6 percent of the quartermaster corps, and 32.3 percent of all transportation units.

Two Black army divisions, the Ninety-second and the Ninety-third, were reactivated from World War I. Although both divisions were viewed negatively by a segregated and racist army, the soldiers of the Ninety-second won more than twelve thousand decorations and citations. Members of this regiment, stationed in the Mediterranean, were awarded at least two Distinguished Service Crosses, sixteen Legion of Merit Awards, ninety-five Silver Stars, and nearly eleven hundred Purple Hearts. The division suffered more than three hundred casualties in six months of fighting. Other all-Black units saw little combat or never fought as a whole unit. A host of small units were created out of divisions that were disbanded. The 761st Tank Battalion fought in Europe. It was the only all-Black unit to win the Presidential Unit Citation. It fought for 183 continuous days in over thirty major assaults. Ironically, the unit was nominated for the award six times between 1945 and 1976 but did not receive its just recognition until 1978.

Booker T. Washington LAUNCHED
The *Booker T. Washington* was launched at Wilmington, Delaware. It was the first U.S. merchant ship to be commanded by a Black captain, Hugh Mulzac.

DAWSON ELECTED TO CONGRESS
William L. Dawson (1886–1970) was elected to the U.S. House of Representatives from Chicago, Illinois. He served in Congress for the next twenty-seven years.

◆ Dawson, born in Albany, Georgia, worked his way through Fisk University, graduating in 1909. After serving in World War I, he returned to Chicago to finish his law degree at Northwestern University.

Dawson's political career began in 1928 as a Republican precinct captain. He then served five terms (1933–1943) on the city council. Mayor Edward Kelly selected Dawson for the position of Democratic ward boss for the Second Ward, but he also organized workers in five other Chicago districts. Dawson controlled the precinct captains and workers and delivered thousands of votes to certain Democratic candidates. In addition, Dawson was selected vice chairperson of the Cook County Democrats and vice chairperson of the Democratic National Committee. When Representative Arthur Mitchell decided not to seek reelection to the U.S. House of Representatives in 1942, Dawson easily won the nomination and the election. Because of his political power in the predominantly Black wards, Dawson played a key role in the larger political machine that selected Richard J. Daley for mayor in 1955. Dawson's wards were particularly important in the election of John F. Kennedy as president in 1960. Kennedy offered him the cabinet post of postmaster general, but he refused. In Congress, Dawson was a powerful force, becoming the first Black to chair a major committee (the Committee on Expenditures in

Executive Departments). He strongly supported issues relating to civil rights and Blacks in federal employment. Although he fought against racist tactics such as poll taxes and tax burdens on the poor, Dawson offered little specific legislation concerning Blacks. In the mid-1960s, his political organization weakened, and he acted quickly to appoint a successor, Ralph H. Metcalfe. Metcalfe won the election on November 9, 1970; six days later, Dawson died.

FARMER FOUNDS CONGRESS OF RACIAL EQUALITY
The Congress of Racial Equality (CORE), an action-oriented civil rights group, was founded by James

James Farmer founded the Council of Racial Equality (CORE), the first protest organization to use nonviolent, passive resistance to achieve its goals. Farmer was appointed assistant secretary of legislation at HEW by President Richard Nixon but later resigned because the post had little substance.

Farmer in Chicago. Its primary goal was to secure civil rights for African Americans through nonviolent, direct-action projects. The group's first major effort was a sit-in against discrimination at a Chicago restaurant.

The organization later implemented a voter registration drive and freedom rides throughout the South. As the organization branched out to more urban areas during the 1970s, it became more militant; by 1980, CORE had virtually died out.

HARMON DIES A NAVAL HERO

Leonard Roy Harmon, a mess steward, died in the Battle of Guadalcanal. He was posthumously awarded the Navy Cross for extraordinary heroism aboard the USS *San Francisco* in that engagement. The U.S. Navy honored Harmon on August 31, 1943, by naming a destroyer escort, the USS *Harmon*, in his name, the first time that the navy had honored a Black American in this manner.

JONES INVENTS VEHICLE AIR CONDITIONER

Frederick McKinley Jones, an engineer, invented the air conditioner for vehicles.

In 1943, Jones invented the self-starting gasoline engine. He held about twenty-four patents, most relating to two-cycle gasoline engines and apparatuses for heating, cooling, and refrigeration. Many of his inventions are still in use today.

RACE RIOTS OCCUR IN MICHIGAN

The city of Detroit erupted in one of the worst riots to date. Sociologist Gunnar Myrdal described it this way:

In trying to move into a government defense housing project built for them in Detroit, Negroes were set upon by white civilians and police. The project (Sojourner Truth Homes) was built at the border between Negro and white neighborhoods but had been planned for Negroes. Encouraged by the vacillation of the federal government and the friendliness of the Detroit police (many of whom are Southern born) and stimulated by the backing of a United States congressman and such organizations as the Ku Klux Klan, white residents of the neighborhood and other parts of the city staged protest demonstrations against the Negro housing project, which led to the riot.

ROBINSON COMMISSIONED NAVAL ENSIGN

Bernard W. Robinson was commissioned as the first Black ensign in the U.S. Navy.

BLACK COMBAT UNITS SERVE IN MARINE CORPS

In AUGUST, the Marine Corps opened its doors to Black soldiers. Still segregated, most Blacks served in depot and ammunition companies. Two Black combat units were created during World War II — the Fifty-first and Fifty-second Defense Battalions. Fully three-quarters of the seventeen thousand Black marines served overseas, but few actually saw combat.

Negro Digest PUBLISHED

On NOVEMBER 1, John H. Johnson published *Negro Digest*. Financed by a loan of five hundred dollars from a small loan office in Chicago, it became the first Black-owned, commercially successful general magazine. *Negro Digest* initially had three thousand subscribers, solicited by a direct-mail campaign to almost twenty thousand people. Johnson purchased much of the first issue himself in order to convince white distributors that there was a large demand for this type of magazine. His plan succeeded. *Negro Digest*, which included articles similar to those in *Reader's Digest* but focused on a Black readership, published articles by many prominent Americans, including First Lady Eleanor Roosevelt.

Negro Digest was published by Johnson's firm, the Johnson Publishing Company of Chicago.

1943   ALL-BLACK NAVY CREWS STAFF TWO SHIPS

Two ships — a destroyer escort, the USS *Mason*, and a submarine chaser, the *PC 1264* — were staffed with all-Black crews.

When each ship was launched, all officers and petty officers were white, but within six months of commission, Blacks replaced the white petty officers on the submarine chaser. Even though there was a plan to replace all the white officers with Blacks, it never happened. It was not until 1945 that the U.S. Navy commissioned a Black officer; he then was assigned to the submarine chaser with the all-Black crew.

BLACK-OWNED BANKS CONTROL MILLIONS

In this year, there were eleven Black-owned banks, with deposits amounting to about fourteen million dollars.

BLACK GROUPS PRESSURE WAR DEPARTMENT TO EMPLOY AND TRAIN BLACKS

In response to the pressures of the NAACP, the Urban League, and other Black organizations and leaders, the War Department initiated a number of programs to increase Black participation in national defense programs. Bethune-Cookman College participated in the National Administration Student Training program for defense work.

BLACK PILOT SHOOTS DOWN NAZI PLANE

Lieutenant Charles Hall of the 99th Pursuit Squadron was credited with being the first Black pilot to shoot down a Nazi plane.

RACIAL DISTURBANCES OCCUR NATIONWIDE

As many as forty persons were killed in serious racial disturbances across the nation. U.S. troops were dispatched to Mobile and Detroit, where disturbances threatened defense production. In the Detroit riot, as many as twenty-nine persons were killed and hundreds were wounded; as many as thirteen hundred Blacks were arrested. A 10:00 P.M. curfew was ordered. Racial conflict occurred in Detroit auto plants because white workers resisted advancement of Blacks into jobs previously allocated to whites. Whites staged "hate strikes" in which they refused to work if Blacks advanced to better jobs. Similar incidents took place in Beaumont, Texas; Los Angeles; and Harlem, where rumor of the murder of a Black man incited a major race riot, in which 5 were killed and 410 were injured.

Black aviators of the Ninety-ninth Squadron were among four units merged into the all-Black 332nd Fighter Group, whose mission was to escort Allied bombers into battle. They set a record unmatched by any other escort unit that flew as many missions — they never lost a bomber to an enemy fighter.

VAUGHAN BEGINS CAREER IN JAZZ

Sarah Vaughan (1924–1990), a native of Newark, New Jersey, entered an amateur contest on a dare at the Apollo Theatre in Harlem. She was immediately hired by Earl "Fatha" Hines.

After singing her soft style of jazz at nightclubs and gaining a fan following, she made her first recording in 1945. Nicknamed "the Divine One," Vaughan went on to become one of the top jazz singers in the country.

BLACK PURSUIT SQUADRON FLIES FIRST COMBAT MISSION

On **JUNE 2**, the Ninety-ninth Pursuit Squadron (the first African American Army Air Corps unit) flew its first combat mission; the Black pilots attacked Pantelleria, an island in the Mediterranean.

ROBESON STARS IN *Othello*

Paul Robeson starred in the title role of *Othello*, which opened at the Shubert Theater in New York City on **OCTOBER 19**. The production ran for 296 performances, setting the record for the longest run of a Shakespearean drama on Broadway.

Stormy Weather PREMIERES

On **JULY 21**, *Stormy Weather*, one of the most successful musical shows, premiered in New York City. Its star-studded cast included Lena Horne, Fats Waller, Cab Calloway, Bill Robinson, the Nicholas Brothers, and Katherine Dunham. It became an immediate success.

1944 BLACK PARACHUTE INFANTRY COMPANY FORMED

The U.S. armed forces' first sixteen Black paratroopers earned their wings as the 555th Parachute Infantry Company, nicknamed the "Triple Nickel." Led by First Sergeant Walter Morris, the company of Blacks trained separately from whites, lived in separate housing, and ate at separate tables.

BLACK WOMEN ADMITTED TO NAVY

The Women's Naval Corps accepted Black women for the first time.

POWELL ELECTED TO CONGRESS

Adam Clayton Powell, Jr. — minister, publisher, and militant — was elected to the U.S. House of Representatives from Harlem. He was the first Black member of the House from the eastern United States. As

Adam Clayton Powell, Jr., was elected to the U.S. House of Representatives by a voting base consisting of the 14,000 members of his Abyssinian Baptist Church in Harlem. As the chairman of the powerful Education and Labor Committee, Powell took fifty pieces of legislation to the House floor and was successful in getting all of them enacted.

chairperson of the powerful Education and Labor Committee, Powell was instrumental in passing laws prohibiting the use of federal funds to build segregated schools. Many of his white colleagues found Powell too intimidating and uncompromising.

In 1967, Powell was temporarily denied his seat in the House because of ethics charges. When the U.S. Supreme Court delivered its findings on the matter, it declared that the "expulsion" was unconstitutional and overturned the House's decision to unseat him. He was reelected by his Harlem constituents in 1968 despite this censure. Charles Rangel, another Black, defeated Powell in 1970.

SS *Frederick Douglass*

The SS *Frederick Douglass*, named in honor of the famous abolitionist and Black leader, was lost in European waters.

SUPREME COURT RULES WHITE PRIMARIES UNCONSTITUTIONAL

In *Smith* v. *Allwright*, the U.S. Supreme Court ruled that a white primary excluding Blacks from voting in the South was unconstitutional. More specifically, the Court stated that Blacks could not be barred from voting in the Texas Democratic primaries. For the first time since Reconstruction, southern Blacks regained the opportunity to participate more actively in politics. Congressmen representing many southern states viewed the decision as "destroying state sovereignty."

UNITED NEGRO COLLEGE FUND ESTABLISHED

The United Negro College Fund, founded by Frederick Douglass Patterson, president of Tuskegee Institute, was established as a nonprofit organization in response to the financial plight of exclusively Black colleges. In its first year, it raised $760,000.

McALPIN IS FIRST BLACK CORRESPONDENT AT WHITE HOUSE

On FEBRUARY 8, Harry S. McAlpin, a writer for the *Daily World* in Atlanta, became the first African American permitted to attend White House press conferences.

BLACK ANTI-AIRCRAFT BATTALION

On JUNE 6, the all-Black 320th Anti-Aircraft Barrage Balloon Battalion played an integral part in the D-Day invasion in Normandy, France.

BLACKS CONVICTED IN "PORT CHICAGO MUTINY"

On JULY 17, an explosion at an ammunitions depot rocked Port Chicago, California. At least 320 persons, including 202 African Americans assigned by the U.S. Navy to handle the explosives, were killed. Because of the danger involved, another 258 African Americans refused to be assigned to this type of work. Fifty were tried and convicted of mutiny. The event became known as the "Port Chicago Mutiny."

MECHANICAL COTTON PICKER INTRODUCED

On OCTOBER 2, a working, production-ready model of a mechanical cotton picker was publicly demonstrated. It could pick up to one thousand pounds (two bales) per hour — a good field hand could pick twenty pounds per hour. Each machine could do the work of fifty people; cotton planters no longer needed large numbers of Black workers. The mechanical picker became a major factor contributing to Black migration from the South.

BLACK AND WHITE SOLDIERS FIGHT TOGETHER IN ARMY FOR FIRST TIME

In DECEMBER, at the Battle of the Bulge in the Ardennes forest of Belgium, Luxembourg, and France, Black and white American soldiers fought together for the first time. About twenty-five hundred Black soldiers volunteered to join the attack against the Germans. When the battle was over, however, the Black troops returned to their all-Black units.

1945   BLACK POSTAL BATTALION ARRIVES IN EUROPE

About eight hundred Black women from the army, air force, and army service forces formed the 6888th Central Postal Battalion to establish a central postal directory in Europe. They arrived in Europe in February and began their duties under the command of Major Charity Adams.

The 6888th's facilities were segregated, but it maintained discipline while accomplishing its mission. Criticism of the battalion's inefficiency failed to take into consideration that it had a backlog of more than three million pieces of mail. In mid-1945, the battalion relocated to France, where its members were praised for excellent work despite their heavy workload and extreme isolation.

BLACKS IN WORLD WAR II BUILD IMPRESSIVE RECORD

The number of Blacks who participated in World War II was impressive:

Registered for service: 3,000,000
Served in the U.S. Army: 701,678
Served in the U.S. Navy: 165,000
Served in the U.S. Coast Guard: 5,000
Served in the U.S. Marine Corps: 17,000
Served in the U.S. WAVES and WACS: 4,000

BLACK SQUADRONS SERVE IN ARMY AIR FORCE

Although the War Department had ordered the abolishment of segregation in army posts, segregation was still the norm throughout every branch of the U.S. military, and the Army Air Force (AAF) was no exception. Approximately 140,000 Blacks joined the AAF, but they never exceeded 8 percent of total AAF members. Five all-Black units were created during World War II — the Ninety-ninth and the One-hundredth Fighter Squadrons, the 332nd Fighter Group, the 477th Bombardment Group, and the 477th Composite Group. All pilots and air crews were trained at Tuskegee Institute in Alabama, the only training facility for Black aviators in the country. These Black pilots and crews won almost one thousand awards and medals for bravery.

COLE HOSTS RADIO SHOW

Nat "King" Cole, the pianist and singer, was the first Black to have his own network radio show. It ran for seventy-eight weeks on NBC radio and retained its sponsor throughout.

GODMAN ARMY AIR FIELD DEDICATED

Godman Army Air Field, near Louisville, Kentucky, was dedicated to the 477th All-Negro Bomb Group, commanded by Colonel Benjamin O. Davis, Jr. This base was built to accommodate Black officers who were not accorded equal treatment at Freeman Army Air Field near Seymour, Indiana.

Colonel Robert Selway, Jr., the commander at Freeman, had decided that although white officers could use the base's main officers' club, Black officers had to use the inferior student officers' club. When Black officers tried to use the main club anyway, they were placed under arrest. After an investigation, the situation was resolved by providing the 477th Bomb Group with its own base.

LOVE ELECTED ALDERMAN IN ST. LOUIS

Walter Love became St. Louis's second Black alderman, joining the Reverend Jasper C. Gaston on the city council, an indication that the ward system was becoming more open to Blacks seeking elective office.

NEW YORK ESTABLISHES FAIR EMPLOYMENT PRACTICES COMMISSION

The New York legislature established the Fair Employment Practices Commission to guard against employment discrimination. It was the first state to form a commission to secure the employment rights of Black Americans.

POLL TAX REPEALED IN GEORGIA

Georgia repealed the poll tax.

ROBINSON SIGNS WITH MONTREAL ROYALS

Jackie (Jack Roosevelt) Robinson, a baseball player from the Kansas City Monarchs of the Negro American League, signed with the Montreal Royals, a Brooklyn Dodgers Triple A affiliate in the International League.

Robinson, the son of a sharecropper and grandson of a slave, earned a four-sport star at the University of California at Los Angeles. He was also an all-American halfback. Branch Rickey, president and part owner of the Brooklyn Dodgers, was credited with the brave ac-

tion of signing an African American. Robinson played with the Montreal Royals, but in less than eighteen months, he was called up to play in the majors.

WHITE STUDENTS PROTEST INTEGRATION

One thousand white students walked out of classes to protest the integration of schools in Gary, Indiana. This incident set the pace for more than two decades of school integration controversy.

DAVIS COMMANDS AIR BASE

On **JUNE 21**, Colonel Benjamin O. Davis, Jr., was appointed commander of the 477th Composite Group of Godman Field, a U.S. Army Air Force base, becoming the first African American to command a base.

GILLEM BOARD REPORT CAUSES CONTROVERSY IN ARMED FORCES

In **OCTOBER**, a three-person board led by Lieutenant General A. C. Gillem, Jr., was directed to "prepare a policy for the use of authorized Negro manpower potential during the postwar period." The Gillem Board issued a report for comment in November, and in January 1946, it issued a supplementary report. The board noted that adequate plans for utilization of Blacks in previous wars had been developed but not implemented. It recommended wider use of Blacks in all occupational specialties within existing quotas. The report caused so much controversy among the top military officers that they requested another board to review the current policies for utilizing Blacks and to recommend any new policies considered appropriate. This board reported in February 1950 and recommended that the 10 percent quota be continued, that segregation of units be maintained, and generally that the status quo be retained. These internal squabbles concerning the nature and use of Black soldiers were cut short by President Harry S. Truman's Executive Order 9981 of 1948 (see 1948).

Ebony MAGAZINE PUBLISHED

In **NOVEMBER**, the premier issue of *Ebony* magazine sold out quickly. Modeled after *Life* magazine, *Ebony* became the most successful and most widely circulated Black magazine in the world. The magazine largely depicted the goals and successes of the Black middle class. It was the first Black-oriented magazine to attract advertising from white companies.

John H. Johnson, the publisher of *Ebony*, started his publishing business with *Negro Digest*. With the

John H. Johnson built a multi-million-dollar publishing, cosmetics, and television empire from an initial $500 investment. He tapped a huge unserved market by producing publications and products for the growing African American population.

success of *Negro Digest* and *Ebony,* Johnson spread his efforts into other areas. The Johnson Publishing Company also published books and *Jet* and *Encore* magazines. The company is now one of the largest Black conglomerates in the country, also controlling Fashion Fair Cosmetics and an insurance company. In 1993, the Johnson Publishing Company was ranked as the third largest Black-owned business by *Black Enterprise Magazine.*

1946   BOSWELL AMENDMENT PASSED
Alabama passed the Boswell amendment, requiring that prospective voters be able to understand and explain any part of the U.S. Constitution to the satisfaction of local registration officers. It became known as the "Boswellian technique" to restrict Black voting participation. A federal district court ruled it to be in violation of the Fifteenth Amendment in January 1949.

JOHNSON BECOMES PRESIDENT OF FISK UNIVERSITY
Charles S. Johnson (1893–1956), an educator and sociologist, became the first African American to be selected president of eighty-year-old Fisk University. Johnson remained president of Fisk until 1956. Johnson also acted as a consultant to the Japanese educational system after World War II and served as a U.S. delegate to UNESCO.

RACE RIOTS OCCUR IN SEVERAL STATES
Racial disturbances broke out in Athens, Alabama; Columbia, Tennessee; and Philadelphia, Pennsylvania — nearly one hundred Blacks were injured.

ROBINSON WINS WORLD WELTERWEIGHT TITLE
"Sugar Ray" Robinson (Walter Smith; 1921–1989) won the world welterweight boxing title. He was considered one of the fastest and most graceful fighters ever to enter the boxing ring.

◈ Robinson went on to win the middleweight title in 1951. In 1952, Robinson announced his retirement.

SWEATT REFUSED ADMISSION TO UNIVERSITY OF TEXAS LAW SCHOOL
Heman Sweatt of Houston, Texas, applied for the February term at the University of Texas Law School. His admission was refused. Sweatt appealed to the Texas courts to reverse the law school's decision, but his plea was denied. The Texas legislature, believing that the NAACP was seeking a separate-but-equal law school, changed the name of the state college to Prairie View State College and adjourned, but it did not allocate any funds for a law school building at the college. Thurgood Marshall, the NAACP attorney representing Sweatt, saw that the state's action provided an opening for a direct attack on segregation. After initial pleadings in the case, the state legislature, now realizing that the NAACP was attacking the principle of segregation, reconvened and appropriated $2.6 million for a Black law school to be built at Texas Southern University. The NAACP saw this action as too little, too late, and proceeded to take Sweatt's case to the U.S. Supreme Court.

TRUMAN APPOINTS COMMITTEE ON CIVIL RIGHTS
President Harry S. Truman appointed a national committee on civil rights to investigate racial injustices and recommend action.

WASHINGTON JOINS LOS ANGELES RAMS

Kenny Washington signed with the Los Angeles Rams on **MARCH 21**. He became the first Black to play professional football. On May 7, the Rams signed a second Black player, Woody Strode. In the same year, Ben Willis and Marion Motley signed with the Cleveland Browns.

Morgan v. *Virginia* DECISION PROHIBITS SEGREGATION ON INTERSTATE BUSES

On **JUNE 3**, in *Morgan* v. *Virginia*, the U.S. Supreme Court prohibited segregation in interstate bus travel.

Irene Morgan, a Black woman, brought suit after she was arrested and fined ten dollars for refusing to move to the back of a bus originating in Gloucester County, Virginia, and destined for Baltimore.

1947 "BEST CITIES FOR NEGROES" PUBLISHED

Negro Digest published a list of America's ten best cities for Blacks: Boston, Detroit, New York City, Chicago, Philadelphia, Seattle, Buffalo, San Francisco, Cleveland, and Los Angeles.

BLACK BASEBALL PLAYERS JOIN MAJOR LEAGUES

Several Black baseball players followed Jackie Robinson into the major leagues. Robinson joined the Brooklyn Dodgers from the farm team on April 10. Larry Doby signed with the Cleveland Indians on July 5 and debuted in his first game the same day. Doby was the first Black to play in the American League. Dan Bankhead became the first Black pitcher to play in the major leagues when he went in on relief on August 26 for the Brooklyn Dodgers against Pittsburgh. He also hit a home run in his first appearance at bat during the same game. Bankhead joined Jackie Robinson on the Dodgers.

Willard Brown and Hank Thompson became the first Black players to appear together when they played for the St. Louis Browns in a game on July 20. Brown was also the first to get a home run when he hit off Hal Newhouser of the Detroit Tigers on August 13. On August 9, two Black players opposed each other for the first time when Thompson, playing for St. Louis, played against Larry Doby, who pinch-hit for Cleveland.

BLACK BECOMES ALL-AMERICAN BASKETBALL PLAYER

Don Barksdale of UCLA became the first Black selected for all-American basketball honors.

PAROCHIAL SCHOOLS INTEGRATED IN ST. LOUIS

Archbishop Joseph E. Ritter threatened excommunication for St. Louis Catholics who protested integration of parochial schools.

TEXAS SOUTHERN UNIVERSITY FOUNDED

Texas Southern University in Houston, Texas, was founded by the Texas legislature in response to pressures to provide equal higher education for Blacks. Facing the real possibility of racial desegregation of predominantly white universities, the state provided Texas Southern with many of the facilities and opportunities found at white schools.

The school grew significantly, and today it offers bachelor's and master's degrees, a liberal arts curriculum, and a multitude of courses related to teacher education, professional work, and occupational programs. Enrollment is about seven thousand students.

TUSKEGEE INSTITUTE PUBLISHES LYNCHING STATISTICS

Statistics collected by Tuskegee Institute indicated that between 1882 and 1947, as many as 3,426 Blacks were lynched in the United States. Of these, 1,217 (or 36 percent) were lynched in the decade 1890–1900.

CORE INSTITUTES FIRST "FREEDOM RIDE"

On **APRIL 9**, the Congress of Racial Equality (CORE) tested the Supreme Court's ban against segregation on interstate bus travel (*Morgan* v. *Virginia*, 1946) by sending freedom riders into the South. Eight Blacks and eight whites began what was called a "Journey of Reconciliation." Bayard Rustin, one of the leaders of the effort, was arrested in North Carolina when he refused to move to the back of the bus. He subsequently served twenty-two days on a chain gang. This first freedom ride served as a model for the freedom rides in 1961, the Montgomery bus boycott, and the student sit-ins of the 1960s.

ROBINSON JOINS DODGERS

Jackie Robinson (1919–1972) joined the Brooklyn Dodgers on **APRIL 10**, and became the first acknowledged Black baseball player in the modern major leagues. Robinson was an excellent athlete in college — he won letters in four sports at UCLA. Because of his hitting, base stealing, and fielding, Robinson was named Rookie of the Year. He became an outstanding player and was the first Black player to enter the Baseball Hall of Fame.

1948 BUNCHE ASSIGNED TO PALESTINE

Professor Ralph J. Bunche, a Black political scientist, was confirmed by the United Nations as temporary UN mediator in Palestine.

CAMPANELLA JOINS BROOKLYN DODGERS

Roy Campanella (1921–1993) joined the Brooklyn Dodgers this year, thus becoming the first Black catcher in the major leagues.

Campanella had played with the Negro leagues since 1936. During his short ten-year career (all with the Brooklyn Dodgers) in the major leagues, he won the National League's Most Valuable Player award in 1951, 1953, and 1955. Campanella's career was cut short by an automobile accident in 1958 that left him paralyzed. He subsequently worked for the Dodgers organization in a variety of roles.

HILL ELECTED TO RICHMOND CITY COUNCIL

Oliver W. Hill was elected to the city council in Richmond, Virginia. This election, and others, signaled that Blacks were making political progress in local politics in the South.

LAW PROHIBITING INTERRACIAL MARRIAGES DECLARED UNCONSTITUTIONAL

The Supreme Court of California declared unconstitutional the state law prohibiting interracial marriages.

About two decades after this decision, the U.S. Supreme Court declared all such state laws unconstitutional.

QUARLES PUBLISHES BIOGRAPHY OF FREDERICK DOUGLASS

Benjamin A. Quarles (1904–), a noted historian and writer, made a major impact on the field of American history when he published *Frederick Douglass*. His work was well received within and beyond academic circles.

Quarles was a professor of history at Dillard University. In 1953, he became head of the de-

Jackie Robinson is shown here signing a major-league baseball contract with Branch Rickey, the general manager of the Brooklyn Dodgers.

partment of history at Morgan State College. At this time, Quarles published *The Negro in the Civil War*. In 1961, he published *The Negro in the American Revolution*, and in 1964, he wrote *The Negro in the Making of America*. His books offer historical accounts of African American culture and its contributions to the growth and development of this country.

SUPREME COURT RULES THAT STATES MUST PROVIDE LEGAL EDUCATION FOR BLACKS

The U.S. Supreme Court declared in *Sipuel* v. *University of Oklahoma* that a state must provide legal education for Blacks at the same time it is offered to whites. The issue in the case was "a citizen's constitutional right to equal protection under the law."

Ada Sipuel had applied to the University of Oklahoma Law School but was denied admission. After the Court decision, she entered the university's law school and was one of its first Black graduates.

SUPREME COURT STRIKES DOWN RESTRICTIVE HOUSING COVENANTS

The U.S. Supreme Court decided in *Shelley* v. *Kramer* that courts could not enforce restrictive housing covenants, agreements that restricted certain homes or tracts of

land from use and occupancy by "people of the Negro or Mongolian Race."

COMMISSION ON CIVIL RIGHTS PROPOSED

On **FEBRUARY 2**, President Truman proposed to Congress a bill to outlaw lynching and to establish a federal commission on civil rights. The idea of such a commission stemmed from a committee headed by Charles E. Wilson, president of General Electric Company, in a report entitled "To Secure These Rights."

"WORST CITIES FOR NEGROES" LISTED

In **MARCH**, *Negro Digest* published "America's Ten Worst Cities for Negroes":

1. Columbia, South Carolina
2. Greenville, South Carolina
3. Alexandria, Louisiana
4. Atlanta, Georgia
5. Jackson, Mississippi
6. Annapolis, Maryland
7. Birmingham, Alabama
8. Miami, Florida
9. Houston, Texas
10. Washington, D.C.

Ollie Stewart, a staff reporter of the *Baltimore Afro-American*, used the following criteria for ranking the

Thurgood Marshall, Ada Lois Sipuel (Fisher), and Amos T. Hall here discuss the integration of the University of Oklahoma Law School with Dr. J. E. Fellows, dean of admissions.

cities: amount of lynching, kidnapping, or other mob activity; access to libraries, schools, hospitals, and parks; number of churches and youth centers; juvenile delinquency level; number of Blacks in public service jobs, especially as police officers and firefighters; and nondiscriminatory access to public transportation.

PAIGE PITCHES FOR CLEVELAND

Only **JULY 7**, Leroy Robert "Satchel" Paige became the first Black baseball player to pitch for the American League. Paige had been a major player in the Negro leagues before signing with the Cleveland Indians. Although Paige was a rookie at forty-two years of age, he pitched a winning shutout in his first game.

Paige began playing baseball in the 1920s with teams of the National Negro League. In 1933, Paige won thirty-one games for the Pittsburgh Crawfords, twenty-one of these in succession and five within the same week. In 1946, Paige pitched for the Kansas City Monarchs, and during that season he threw sixty-four consecutive scoreless innings, probably unmatched by anyone in professional baseball. Paige also became the first Black player to pitch in the World Series. In the fifth game of the 1948 World Series, Paige worked two-thirds of an inning and allowed no hits or walks.

PRESIDENT TRUMAN ISSUES EXECUTIVE ORDER 9981

On **JULY 26**, President Harry S. Truman signed Executive Order 9981 to end discrimination in the armed forces — "as rapidly as possible." All persons in uniform should have "equality of treatment and opportunity regardless of race, color, religion, or national origin." The order established a presidential committee to examine racial policies within the armed services and to determine the best plan to implement the president's policy. Opposition was immediate among many commissioned and noncommissioned officers, and there was swift resistance within Truman's own party, particularly in the Deep South.

Charles Fahy was assigned to chair the presidential committee in early 1949. In May 1950, the Fahy committee issued its final report, which examined two basic questions: (1) Are Blacks mentally and technically qualified to hold all military occupations? and (2) Should segregated units be maintained? Fahy's committee report declared that military efficiency would be improved with full utilization of Blacks and that segregated units were an inefficient use of Black resources.

DEMOCRATS COURT BLACK VOTES

In **AUGUST**, the Democrats began an earnest effort to win the Black vote by banning racial segregation in their national headquarters.

COLEMAN BECOMES CLERK TO SUPREME COURT

On **SEPTEMBER 1**, Justice Felix Frankfurter appointed William T. Coleman as a clerk to the U.S. Supreme Court, the first African American to be appointed to this position. Coleman later became the president of the NAACP Legal Defense and Education Fund, and later, in 1975, he was appointed secretary of transportation by President Gerald Ford.

1949 BROWN GRADUATES FROM ANNAPOLIS

Wesley A. Brown became the first Black graduate of the U.S. Naval Academy in Annapolis, Maryland, and the 20,699th midshipman to graduate. He was appointed by Black U.S. representative Adam Clayton Powell, Jr., of New York, in June 1945.

◊ Brown, a resident of Washington, D.C., was born in Maryland but attended school in the District of Columbia. While he attended Dunbar High School, several of his teachers encouraged him to seek a military career. At the academy, Brown was an active midshipman, participating in tennis, track, chess, and photography. Although he was subjected to racial abuse, severe harassment from upperclassmen, and demerits for the slightest infractions of the rules, he persevered. After graduation, Brown served his country in a number of assignments, eventually earning the rank of lieutenant commander.

The second Black to graduate from the U.S. Naval Academy was Lawrence C. Chambers in 1952. Chambers retired from the navy as a rear admiral.

BUNCHE REFUSES POST OF ASSISTANT SECRETARY OF STATE

Ralph J. Bunche refused the position of assistant secretary of state in Washington because he did not want his family to "risk indignities because of his color."

Bunche had become the first Black division head in the State Department in 1945 and the first head of the Trusteeship Division of the United Nations in 1946.

HASTIE, WILLIAM H.

William H. Hastie, former District Court judge and governor in the Virgin Islands, was appointed a judge of the Third U.S. Circuit Court of Appeals.

FIRST BLACK-OWNED RADIO STATION BROADCASTS IN ATLANTA

WERD-AM in Atlanta, Georgia, became the first Black-owned radio station in the United States. It was founded by Jesse Blanton, Sr.

HOUSING AID CUT IN CASES OF RACIAL BIAS

President Truman signed an order banning federal housing aid in areas where racial or religious bias was found.

MISSISSIPPI COLLEGE TEACHES WHITE SUPREMACY

Jefferson Military College in Mississippi was given a fifty-million-dollar gift on condition that the money be used to teach "white supremacy."

ROBINSON VOTED MOST VALUABLE PLAYER

Jackie Robinson was voted the Most Valuable Player in the National League for his sizzling batting average of .342 — the highest in the league.

U.S. SENATOR PROPOSES GEOGRAPHIC REDISTRIBUTION OF BLACK POPULATION

On JANUARY 28, Senator Richard Russell of Georgia introduced a bill proposing equitable redistribution of the Black population throughout the United States. The bill also proposed to create a racial relocation bureau with a budget of $4.5 billion.

RENS CLOSE A CHAPTER IN THE AFRICAN AMERICAN EXPERIENCE

On MARCH 21, the New York Rens played their last game, against the Denver Nuggets. The team, which dominated the game of basketball during the 1920s, disbanded after twenty-six years of winning play. The Rens' record of 2,318 wins and only 381 losses was the most impressive record of any basketball team.

STILL'S OPERA PERFORMED

On MARCH 31, William Still's opera *Troubled Island* premiered at the New York City Opera. It was the first opera written by an African American to be produced by a major opera company. Robert McFerrin made his debut as the first African American male to sing with the New York City Opera.

CHARLES WINS HEAVYWEIGHT BOXING TITLE

On JUNE 22, Ezzard Charles won the heavyweight boxing championship in a decision over Jersey Joe Walcott.

SAMPSON APPOINTED ALTERNATE U.S. DELEGATE TO UNITED NATIONS

On AUGUST 24, Black attorney Edith Sampson was appointed alternate delegate to the United Nations.

1950

POPULATION OVERVIEW

BLACK POPULATION IN THE UNITED STATES The Bureau of the Census recorded 150,697,361 total residents in the United States. Black people constituted 10 percent (15,042,286) of the total population and 12.3 percent of the population in central cities. New York remained the state with the largest total population in the country (14,743,210). California moved from fifth to second most populous state.

BLACK MIGRATION IN THE UNITED STATES The net migration rate of Blacks was 34 percent for the Northeast, 42 percent for the North Central states, and 61 percent for the West. More than 1.5 million Blacks (16 percent of the entire U.S. Black population) migrated from the South. Mississippi registered the largest losses over the decade — 30.2 percent, or 326,000 Blacks. The proportion of Blacks residing in the South declined substantially over the 1940–1950 decade — from 77 percent to 68 percent of all Black Americans. Over the same period, Blacks increased from 48.6 percent to 62.4 percent of all urban residents. Although the majority of southern Blacks were destined to live in a northern urban center, many Blacks within the South were also moving from rural to urban areas. In fact, the proportion of southern Blacks living in urban areas increased from 36.5 to 47.6 percent.

ECONOMIC CONDITIONS OVERVIEW

INCOME DISPARITY BETWEEN BLACK AND WHITE FAMILIES The median income of Black families increased from 54 percent of the median income for white families in 1950 to 57 percent in 1952 and to 56 percent in 1953 and 1954, but after this, the proportion dropped to 51 percent in 1958, the same level as in 1947 and 1949. As the 1950s ended, Black median family income was only 52 percent of white family income.

SHIFTS IN BLACK EMPLOYMENT AND OCCUPATION The number of Black men in the labor force who were farmers, farm managers, or farm laborers declined from 40.9 to 23.6 percent. The proportion of Black men in white-collar jobs increased from 5.1 to 8.3 percent. The proportion of Black women employed in agriculture decreased as well, dropping from 15.9 to 9.1 percent. The proportion of Black women in white-collar jobs rose from 6.3 percent to 12.7 percent.

SOCIAL CONDITIONS OVERVIEW

MORE BLACKS PURSUE HIGHER EDUCATION Blacks continued to attend colleges and universities at a greater rate each decade. By 1950, there were 28.4 times as many students in historically Black colleges as there were in 1900. As many as 23,000 Blacks attended colleges and universities in 1940, which increased to 113,735 in 1950. Although complete segregation continued in many states of the South, such as South Carolina, Alabama, and Mississippi, institutions of higher education in other states were slowly opening their doors. With barriers still relatively high at predominantly white schools, the great majority of Black college students attended historically Black colleges and universities.

NATIONAL CHANGES FOSTER HOPES OF PROGRESS FOR BLACKS A number of factors in the post–World War II period gave Blacks hope that progress would occur:

◈ Spectacular growth in the economy meant that Black economic advancement did not have to come at the expense of whites;

◈ Rapid industrialization of the South eliminated

During the 1950s and 1960s, African Americans in the civil rights movement fought racial inequality with nonviolent protests and demonstrations. Led by Dr. Martin Luther King, Jr., and other civil rights activists, the demonstrations were frequently met with violence from local and state governments and white citizens. Early in the civil rights movement, National Guardsmen were used to prevent protests and demonstrations; later they were used to protect the rights of demonstrators.

the need for a large number of unskilled workers. Many of the new industries were owned by northern corporations that did not practice segregation;

◈ Mechanization of agriculture, especially cotton, forced rural Blacks to cities, particularly in the North. Thus, the race problem was no longer confined to the South. In cities, Blacks were more likely to develop group solidarity;

◈ The emergence of the United States as a world power meant that white racism adversely affected the country's relationships with people in the rest of the world, the majority of which were non-white;

◈ Racist ideas declined in intellectual respectability.

Those opposed to the progress of Blacks often used the fear of communism to halt their efforts, equating Blacks' quest for equality with communist ideology. The civil rights movements was forced to proceed slowly so as not to appear too radical.

SEGREGATION IN THE INTEGRATED ARMED FORCES DURING THE KOREAN CONFLICT By late 1949 or early 1950, all branches of the military had adopted policies of equal treatment. Implementation was another matter, however. Discrimination and segregation continued. When the ranks of the all-Black Twenty-fourth Infantry Regiment were filled, new Black recruits had no place to go but to an all-white unit. Over time, Blacks were regularly assigned to all-white units, and whites were assigned to all Black-units, but racism still occurred when commanders created pockets of all-Black companies or smaller all-Black units. By mid-1951, Blacks constituted 13.5 percent of the total U.S. military strength, but 80 percent of Black soldiers in Korea were assigned to all-Black units — and more than 60 percent of those units worked as service support units.

BLACK TROOPS SHARE FIRST AMERICAN VICTORY IN KOREAN WAR
The all-Black Twenty-Fourth Infantry Regiment recaptured the city of Yech'on.

BRANCH RECEIVES MARINES COMMISSION
Frederick C. Branch became the first Black to be commissioned in the U.S. Marine Corps.

BROOKS WINS PULITZER PRIZE
On **MAY 1**, Gwendolyn Brooks (1917–) was awarded the Pulitzer Prize for her semi-autobiographical volume of poetry, *Annie Allen*. She was the first African

Gwendolyn Brooks, one of America's most gifted poets and novelists, won the Pulitzer Prize for poetry in 1950 for Annie Allen. *She was poet laureate of Illinois for sixteen years and also served as a consultant to the Library of Congress.*

American to win this prestigious award. Her other notable works include *Bronzeville Boys and Girls* (1956), *Selected Poems* (1963), *In the Mecca* (1968), and *To Disembark* (1981).

◈ Brooks was born in Topeka, Kansas, but during her early childhood, the family moved to Chicago, where she was raised and educated. She published her first poem, "Eventide," when she was thirteen in *American Childhood* magazine. She was encouraged in her writing by a number of successful Black writers, including James Weldon Johnson and Langston Hughes. As a student at Wilson Junior College, she was a regular contributor to the *Chicago Defender*, the influential Black newspaper published by Robert S. Abbott. Later works appeared in *Harper's*, *Common Ground*, *Mademoiselle*, *Poetry*, and *Yale Review*. In 1945, Brooks published her first volume of poetry, *A Street in Bronzeville*.

Brooks's poetry revealed her personal advocacy and commitment to social justice. *Annie Allen* and later volumes — including *Primer for Blacks* (1980), *Mayor Harold Washington and Chicago, The I Will City* (1983), *The Near-Johannesburg Boys and Other Poems* (1986), *Blacks* (1987), and *Winnie* (1988) — expressed her keen sense of contemporary injustices.

BROWN BECOMES FIRST BLACK U.S. NAVAL AVIATOR

Jesse L. Brown was appointed the first Black naval aviator, but in December, he was killed in a combat mission. The U.S. Navy posthumously awarded him the Distinguished Flying Cross and Air Medal for his service.

BUNCHE AWARDED NOBEL PEACE PRIZE

Ralph J. Bunche received the Nobel Peace Prize for his skillful mediation of the 1948 Arab-Israeli dispute. He was the first Black to win a Nobel Prize.

Bunche graduated from the University of California and Harvard University, earning money by working as a janitor and doing errands for a shipping line.

GIBSON PLAYS IN U.S. TENNIS CHAMPIONSHIP

Althea Gibson became the first Black to compete in the U.S. Open tennis championship. Gibson, a twenty-two-year-old student from Florida A & M College, sought her first title at Forest Hills, New York.

UNIVERSITY OF TENNESSEE REJECTS ADMISSION OF BLACKS

The University of Tennessee in Memphis defied Supreme Court rulings and rejected five Blacks seeking admission.

COOPER JOINS BOSTON CELTICS

In **APRIL**, Charles Cooper joined the Boston Celtics, becoming the first Black signed by a National Basketball Association team. The Boston Celtics was the first team to start five Black players — Bill Russell, K. C. Jones, Sam Jones, Satch Sanders, and Willie Naulls. Nat (Sweetwater) Clifton was signed by the Knickerbockers and became the second Black player in the association.

HALL WINS TONY AWARD

On **APRIL 9**, Juanita Hall was awarded a Tony for her role as Bloody Mary in the musical *South Pacific*. Hall was the first African American to receive a Tony Award.

Ralph Bunche was one of the few African Americans in government service who focused on international rather than domestic affairs. His international work marked a resurgence of African American interest in Africa.

RACIAL SEGREGATION WITHIN INSTITUTIONS OF HIGHER LEARNING DECLARED ILLEGAL

On **JUNE 5**, in the case of *McLaurin* v. *Oklahoma*, the U.S. Supreme Court declared that once a Black student was admitted to a previously all-white school, there could be no distinctions made on the basis of race. G. W. McLaurin, a Black student initially denied admission to the University of Oklahoma Law School, was ordered admitted by the Court. The University of Oklahoma complied with the Court only to the extent of admission. They forced McLaurin to live and study in areas isolated from whites, and he was forced to sit in a chair outside classrooms when attending lectures. In essence, McLaurin was physically and intellectually isolated from white students within the university. In 1950, the Supreme Court declared that racial segregation within higher education institutions was illegal.

SUPREME COURT RULES SEPARATE DINING CAR FACILITIES UNCONSTITUTIONAL

On **JUNE 5**, in ruling on *Henderson* v. *United States*, the Supreme Court declared that an Interstate Commerce Commission decision requiring Black passengers in railroad dining cars to eat behind a curtain separating them from other passengers was unconstitutional.

SWEATT V. PAINTER WEAKENS SEGREGATION

On **JUNE 5**, in the case of *Sweatt* v. *Painter*, the U.S. Supreme Court declared that equality of education involved more than identical physical facilities. The Court struck a serious blow to segregation when it declared that the "hastily organized" law school at the historically Black Texas Southern University was substantially unequal to that of the law school of the University of Texas, the largest university in the South. The Court ordered the plaintiff, Heman Sweatt, admitted to the University of Texas Law School because "in terms of number of the faculty, variety of courses and opportunities for specialization, size of the student body, scope of the library, availability of law review and similar activities, the University of Texas law school is superior."

AMERICAN MEDICAL ASSOCIATION OPENS DOORS TO BLACKS

On **JUNE 26**, the American Medical Association accepted African American delegates at its convention for the first time.

LLOYD PLAYS WITH WASHINGTON CAPITOLS

On **OCTOBER 31**, Earl Lloyd became the first African American to play in a National Basketball Association game when he played with the Washington Capitols. The Capitols defeated the Rochester Royals, 78–70.

1951 BUNCHE BECOMES UNDERSECRETARY OF UNITED NATIONS

Ralph J. Bunche was appointed undersecretary of the United Nations. He was the highest-ranking Black American employed by the international organization.

LOOBY ELECTED TO NASHVILLE CITY COUNCIL

Z. Alexander Looby, a Black attorney, was elected to the city council in Nashville, Tennessee. This election was another indication that Blacks were breaking down racial barriers to participation in local politics in the South.

LOUIS FAILS TO REGAIN HEAVYWEIGHT TITLE

Joe Louis's bid to become the first to regain a heavyweight title was stopped by Rocky Marciano. In the same year, Louis knocked out Lee Savold in a comeback bout in New York.

MOORE ASSASSINATED IN FLORIDA

Harry T. Moore, the leader of the Florida NAACP, was assassinated in Mims, Florida, by a racist-inspired bomb explosion.

Moore was a civil rights activist working to increase the number of African Americans registered to vote and was active in the desegregation of the University of Florida.

PETITION CHARGES GENOCIDE AGAINST AMERICAN BLACK PEOPLE

A delegation headed by Paul Robeson and William L. Patterson presented a petition to the United Nations, charging the U.S. government with a "policy of genocide against the American Negro People."

SWANSON WINS NEW YORK MUSIC CRITICS CIRCLE AWARD

The New York Music Critics Circle Award was bestowed on Howard Swanson for his composition entitled *Short Symphony*. Swanson was known internationally for his composition of music for orchestra, solo voice, piano, and chamber ensembles. Swanson was born August 18, 1909, in Atlanta, Georgia.

ROBINSON WINS WORLD TITLES

Sugar Ray Robinson won the middleweight title when he knocked out Jake LaMotta. Robinson had earlier won the world welterweight title in 1946. He was considered one of the fastest and classiest fighters ever to enter the boxing ring. After retiring in 1952, Robinson became a film star.

UNIVERSITY OF NORTH CAROLINA ADMITS FIRST BLACK STUDENT

On **APRIL 24**, the first Black student was admitted to the University of North Carolina.

TERRELL INSTRUMENTAL IN RESTAURANT DESEGREGATION

Mary Church Terrell, a Black feminist leader, was instrumental in getting the Municipal Appeals Court in Washington, D.C., to outlaw segregation in Washington, D.C., restaurants. On **MAY 24**, the Municipal Court of Appeals decided that racial segregation in Washington, D.C., restaurants was illegal.

THOMPSON AWARDED MEDAL OF HONOR

On **JUNE 21**, private William Thompson, first class, was posthumously awarded the Congressional Medal of Honor for bravery in the Korean War; he was the first Black to win this prestigious award since the Spanish-American War.

NAACP AWARDS SPINGARN TO HOUSTON

On **JUNE 25**, the NAACP posthumously awarded the Spingarn Medal to Charles H. Houston (1895–1950) in honor of his long career providing legal services to the NAACP's Legal Defense and Educational Fund.

◈ Houston was born in Washington, D.C., to William and Mary Houston. Houston's father was a member of the District of Columbia bar and taught at the law school of Howard University. His mother was a schoolteacher but later became a hairdresser. Houston graduated from Amherst College with a Phi Beta Kappa key and as one of six valedictorians in 1915. After serving as a first lieutenant in the U.S. Army during World War I, Houston taught briefly before entering Harvard Law School in 1919. The first Black elected editor of the *Harvard Law Review*, Houston graduated cum laude in 1922, earning an LL.B. degree; he continued at Harvard, where he became the first Black to be awarded the doctor of juridical science degree. In 1924, he was admitted to the District of Columbia bar.

By 1929, Houston was an associate professor of law and resident vice dean of the Howard University Law School three-year day program. In 1935, he joined the staff of the NAACP as special counsel.

During his tenure with the NAACP, Houston was instrumental in preparing and arguing a number of important and successful civil rights cases before the U.S. Supreme Court. Included among these cases were *Missouri ex rel Gaines* v. *Canada* (in which the Supreme Court declared that Missouri could not exclude a Black person from its white state university law school in the absence of other and proper provisions for the legal education of Negroes); *Steele* v.

Louisville & Nashville R.R. (in which the Supreme Court declared that a white labor union must represent, without racial discrimination, Black firefighters excluded from union membership); *Hurd* v. *Hodge* and *Shelley* v. *Kramer* (which dealt with restrictive housing covenants in Washington, D.C., and in other states, respectively); and, sharing the argument with Thurgood Marshall, *University of Maryland* v. *Murray* (in which the Supreme Court required the University of Maryland to admit Murray).

When Houston died at the age of fifty-five, five U.S. Supreme Court justices were among the mourners at his funeral.

RACE RIOT BREAKS OUT IN ILLINOIS

On **JULY 12**, Governor Adlai Stevenson of Illinois dispatched the National Guard to calm a race riot in Cicero, Illinois. More than three thousand whites had protested a Black family's efforts to occupy a home in the all-white community. The mob broke windows, mutilated the exterior of the house, and shouted epithets at the couple. The riot was deemed the worst racial disturbance in the North since 1919.

NAACP PICKETS STORK CLUB

On **OCTOBER 23**, the NAACP picketed the Stork Club in New York City for refusing admission to Josephine Baker. Although the city convened a special committee that found Baker's charges to be without basis, Thurgood Marshall blasted the report as a "shameless whitewash" of racist practices of the Stork Club.

1952 BLACK PITCHER WINS WORLD SERIES GAME

Joe Black, pitching for the Brooklyn Dodgers in the first game of the World Series, beat the New York Yankees, 4–2. He thus became the first Black pitcher to win a World Series game.

ELLISON PUBLISHES *Invisible Man*

Ralph Ellison (1914–1994) published his novel *Invisible Man* to great critical acclaim. Ellison wrote about the degree to which Blacks were estranged in a hostile white environment. *Invisible Man* won the National Book Award. In 1964, Ellison wrote *Shadow and Act*, and in 1986, he published *Going to the Territory* — a collection of essays and speeches.

MAYNOR PERFORMS AT CONSTITUTION HALL

Dorothy Maynor, a Black soprano, became the first Black artist to perform commercially in the DAR auditorium, Constitution Hall, since before 1939.

The ban against commercial performances by Black artists came about in 1939 after the DAR refused Marian Anderson permission to sing. Blacks did perform at the hall for benefits.

MIAMI SUED FOR MUNICIPAL COUNTRY CLUB RESTRICTIONS

Joseph Rice sued the city of Miami to gain unrestricted use of Miami Springs Country Club, a city-owned golf course. He contended that he was denied equal protection of the law by being allowed to play golf only on Mondays, when whites could use the course all other days of the week. The Florida Supreme Court ruled in favor of the city, and the U.S. Supreme Court refused to hear an appeal, citing "nonfederal grounds." Justices Hugo La Fayette Black and William O. Douglas voted to hear the appeal.

MOORE WINS LIGHT HEAVYWEIGHT TITLE

Boxer Archie Moore, born Archibald Lee Wright on December 13, 1913, in Benoit, Mississippi, won the light heavyweight crown.

NO LYNCHING RECORDED IN THE UNITED STATES

A Tuskegee Institute report indicated that for the first time in seventy-one years of data compilation, no lynchings of Blacks were reported in the United States.

PRICE SINGS IN *Porgy and Bess*

Leontyne Price (1927–) starred as Bess in George and Ira Gershwin's *Porgy and Bess*. She was a major hit and continued in this role through 1954. In 1955, Price appeared in a number of television operas, and in 1957, she appeared at the San Francisco Opera. In 1961, Price performed works by Verdi and Puccini at the New York Metropolitan Opera in New York City. An international opera star, Price retired in 1985.

RACIST BOMBINGS INCREASE

Racist bombings increased, according to a report of the Southern Regional Council, an interracial civil rights reporting agency. The council reported about forty such bombings since 1951.

ROBINSON AWARDED HIGH SALARY

Jackie Robinson became the highest-paid baseball player in Brooklyn Dodgers history.

UNIVERSITY OF TENNESSEE ADMITS BLACK STUDENT

The University of Tennessee admitted its first Black student.

FBI ARRESTS KU KLUX KLAN MEMBERS

On **FEBRUARY 16**, the Federal Bureau of Investigation arrested ten members of the KKK in North Carolina.

1953 **BALDWIN PUBLISHES** *Go Tell It on the Mountain*

James Baldwin (1924–1987) published his first book, *Go Tell It on the Mountain*. Baldwin, one of the most prolific African American writers, also published collections of essays; the most famous were *Notes of a Native Son* (1955), *Nobody Knows My Name* (1961), and *The Fire Next Time* (1963). His writings reflected the struggle of Blacks for equality in America. In 1965, his play *Blues for Mr. Charlie* opened on Broadway. It was based on the Emmett Till murder case.

◈ Baldwin was born in Harlem and began writing while a high school student in the Bronx. He became a Pentecostal preacher when he was a teenager. As a young man, he published essays and reviews in the *Nation*, the *New Leader*, *Commentary*, and the *Partisan Review*. In 1948, he moved to Paris to escape "the stifling racial bigotry" of the United States. He stayed for almost ten years, with the help of several fellowships. After returning to the United States, Baldwin became a civil rights activist. He wrote about the struggle, raised funds, and organized protest marches. He was also an early opponent of the Vietnam War. On December 1, 1987, Baldwin died of cancer in France at the age of sixty-three. In the previous year, France had bestowed upon him their highest national award — the Legion of Honor — for his writings and activism. Baldwin was eulogized by fellow African American novelist Ralph Ellison, who said, "America has lost one of its most gifted writers."

CAMPANELLA VOTED MOST VALUABLE PLAYER

Roy Campanella, catcher for the Brooklyn Dodgers, was voted the National League's Most Valuable Player. He received 297 votes from the Baseball Writers Association, second only to Stan Musial, who received 303 votes in 1948.

CLEMENT ELECTED TO ATLANTA BOARD OF EDUCATION

Rufus E. Clement, president of Atlanta University, was elected to the Atlanta Board of Education.

EISENHOWER APPOINTS COMMITTEE TO INVESTIGATE DISCRIMINATION

The Government Contract Compliance Committee was appointed by President Dwight D. Eisenhower to investigate discrimination among employers with government contracts. Eisenhower, however, was viewed by Blacks as nonsupportive of desegregation and other Black causes.

PHI BETA KAPPA ESTABLISHED AT BLACK COLLEGE

On **APRIL 4**, the first chapter of the scholastic fraternity Phi Beta Kappa at a Black college was begun at Fisk University in Tennessee.

WARREN APPOINTED CHIEF JUSTICE

On **SEPTEMBER 30**, President Eisenhower nominated Earl Warren to be the fourteenth chief justice of the U.S. Supreme Court; he replaced Frederick Moore Vinson, who had died in office. Warren's liberal outlook influenced decisions relating to school segregation and other labor issues.

JACK INAUGURATED AS PRESIDENT OF BOROUGH OF MANHATTAN

On **DECEMBER 31**, Hulan Jack, a Black West Indian, was inaugurated as president of the Borough of Manhattan, the highest municipal executive post to be held by a Black to date.

1954 COURT-ORDERED INTEGRATION DEFIED BY SOUTHERN LEADERS

In Richmond, twelve southern leaders met and agreed not to comply with court-ordered integration.

DAVIS APPOINTED AIR FORCE GENERAL

Benjamin O. Davis, Jr., was appointed general in the U.S. Air Force, becoming the first Black to hold this rank. Davis commanded the Fifteenth Air Force bombers in their important attacks on Romanian oil fields during World War II. Davis was promoted to major general in 1959, the highest-ranking African American in the U.S. Air Force. His rank as major general was one grade higher than that accomplished by his father, Benjamin O. Davis, Sr., who was the first African American to achieve the rank of brigadier general in the U.S. Army.

DIGGS BECOMES MICHIGAN'S FIRST BLACK CONGRESSMAN

Charles C. Diggs, Jr., was elected to the U.S. House of Representatives from Michigan at age thirty-three. He was the first Black congressman from the state.

Just before completing all the requirements for his law degree from Detroit College of Law, Diggs had been elected state senator. In 1969, Diggs founded and

Benjamin O. Davis, Jr., the commander of the all-Black Ninety-ninth and 332nd Fighter Squadrons and the winner of several medals, including the Silver Star, was the first Black general in the U.S. Air Force.

chaired the Congressional Black Caucus. As chairperson of the Committee on the District of Columbia in 1972, Diggs was successful in gaining partial self-government in the District of Columbia. On December 24, 1973, President Nixon signed the District of Columbia Self-Government and Governmental Reorganization Act. Diggs was later convicted of mail fraud and falsifying payroll forms, and he resigned from the Ninety-sixth Congress on June 3, 1980.

JULIAN FOUNDS SUCCESSFUL LABORATORIES

Percy L. Julian (1899–1975), an African American chemist, founded Julian Laboratories, Inc., in Chicago, Mexico City, and Guatemala. His company successfully developed a synthetic cortisone. His products were in such demand that major chemical and drug companies competed to buy his laboratories. He sold the Chicago laboratories to Smith, Kline & French, but he remained president. Upjohn Company purchased the Guatemala laboratories.

◇ Born in Montgomery, Alabama, Julian received degrees at some of the most prestigious institutions in the world — B.A., DePauw University in Indiana; M.A., Harvard University; and Ph.D., University of Vienna, Austria. Although he received his Ph.D. degree in 1931, he had already served as an instructor at Fisk University (1920–1925); he later became associate professor of chemistry at Howard University. Although Julian had proven himself a talented scientist and had delivered scientific papers and published frequently, he could not secure a faculty position at DePauw University because of racism. He then accepted a position as director of research for the Glidden Company in Chicago, a position he held from 1936 to 1953 and in which he developed a number of commercial products from soya. He developed a synthetic progesterone, used to prevent miscarriages, and physostigmine, a drug used to treat glaucoma. His accomplishments made Julian one of the most successful chemists of his time. During his life, he held no fewer than 105 patents.

MAHONEY NAMED U.S. DELEGATE TO UNITED NATIONS

Charles Mahoney, a Detroit insurance executive, was appointed by President Eisenhower as a permanent delegate to the United Nations, the first Black to hold this position.

MARSHALL BECOMES PRESIDENT OF NEW YORK MEDICAL SOCIETY

Dr. Peter Murray Marshall was the first Black to head a unit of the American Medical Association. He was installed as president of the New York County Medical Society.

MAYS LEADS NEW YORK GIANTS TO VICTORY

Willie Mays won a batting title and led the New York Giants to the National League pennant. Mays also won the National League's Most Valuable Player award after batting .345 and hitting forty-one home runs. Mays stole forty bases in 1956, the best performance in both leagues.

MORIAL RECEIVES LAW DEGREE FROM LOUISIANA STATE

Ernest Nathan Morial was the first Black to receive the LL.D. degree from Louisiana State Law School.

◇ Morial was elected to the Louisiana legislature in 1967, the first Black elected to this body since Reconstruction. Morial became a judge of the Juvenile Court of New Orleans in 1970 — the first Black to sit on this court. In 1974, he was elected to the Court of Appeals for the Fourth Circuit (New Orleans). In 1977, Morial became the first Black to be elected mayor of New Orleans.

SEGREGATIONISTS RESPOND ANGRILY TO *Brown* DECISION

The *Brown* v. *Board of Education* decision precipitated the formation of a monstrous wave of defensive groups in the South, whose purpose was to maintain a decadent southern way of life — one that placed Black people in subordinate roles. A number of resistance groups were formed to denounce the Supreme Court Decision:

> American States' Rights Association
> Federation of Constitutional Government
> Federation of Defenders of State Sovereignty and
>   Individual Liberties
> Grass Roots League
> National Citizens' Protective Association
> The States' Rights Council of Georgia, Inc.
> The Society for the Preservation of State Government and Racial Integrity
> Virginia League
> White American, Inc.
> White Citizens' Council

STUDY PUBLISHED ON SEGREGATION AND INTEGRATION IN THE ARMY

During World War II, the U.S. Army had initiated a study on the effects of segregation and integration in the army. The study, "Project Clear," conducted by the Operations Research Office of Johns Hopkins University, was released in this year; it concluded that racially segregated units limited overall effectiveness, whereas integration enhanced effectiveness. The study also noted that integration throughout the

Earl Warren, chief justice of the U.S. Supreme Court, was instrumental in establishing the constitutionality of Blacks' demands for their civil rights.

army was feasible and that a quota was unnecessary. Because of this study, and others drawing the same conclusions, the last all-Black unit was disbanded, and future enlistments were not to be based on any racial quota.

Still, many vestiges of racism, such as segregated on- and off-post housing and other facilities, were overlooked. These forms of discrimination and segregation changed slowly, and when Blacks tried to speed up the integration process, the military justice system operated swiftly and harshly against them. Because commanders were responsible for implementing equal treatment, there was often no one else responsible to ensure its enforcement. Therefore, while some army bases were eagerly breaking down barriers to equal treatment, others ignored the equal treatment policy.

UNEMPLOYMENT RATIO SKEWED AGAINST BLACKS

For the first time, Black unemployment rates were about twice those of whites, a ratio that remained constant for the rest of the decade.

In 1956, for example, Black unemployment was 8.3 percent, compared to only 3.9 percent for whites. Blacks were more than 2.3 times more likely to be unemployed than whites. The Black/white male unemployment ratio was considerably higher than the Black/white female unemployment ratio. In addition, unemployment rates for Black teenagers were as high as 26.2 percent for females and 24.3 percent for males, versus 11.6 percent and 14 percent, respectively, for white teenagers.

WILKINS NAMED SECRETARY OF LABOR

President Eisenhower named James Ernest Wilkins, Jr., of Chicago, as assistant secretary of labor.

Wilkins, a member of Phi Beta Kappa, received his Ph.D. degree from the University of Chicago at the age of twenty.

Brown v. *Board of Education of Topeka*
RESULTS IN LANDMARK DECISION

On **MAY 17**, the U.S. Supreme Court ruled in the case of *Brown* v. *Board of Education of Topeka, Kansas* that "racial segregation in public schools is unconstitutional." The decision was a major victory for Thurgood Marshall, chief counsel of the Legal Defense and Educational Fund of the NAACP, and other Black civil rights leaders who contributed their efforts to this case. Chief Justice Earl Warren delivered the unanimous decision. This decision reversed *Plessy* v. *Ferguson* (1896) and declared "separate educational facilities . . . inherently unequal." This victory set the tone for the civil rights movement. Chief Justice Earl Warren wrote, "In the field of public education, the doctrine of separate but equal has no place. Separate educational facilities are inherently unequal."

PUBLIC SCHOOLS DESEGREGATED IN WASHINGTON, D.C., AND BALTIMORE, MARYLAND

Desegregation was undertaken in the public schools of Washington, D.C., and Baltimore, Maryland. These efforts represented the most comprehensive desegregation efforts since the Supreme Court decision of May 17 (*Brown* v. *Board of Education*). The District of Columbia moved to end segregation on **JUNE 2**; Baltimore followed later. The *World Book* annual list of new words and phrases for 1954 included the word *desegregate.*

Roy Wilkins, a newspaperman and an articulate spokesman for civil rights, became the executive director of the NAACP in 1955. He was a very powerful force in the passage of the Civil Rights Act of 1964 and the March on Washington.

DISCRIMINATION IN RESTAURANTS MADE ILLEGAL IN WASHINGTON, D.C.

On **JUNE 8**, the U.S. Supreme Court ruled in *District of Columbia* v. *John R. Thompson Co., Inc.* that discrimination in Washington, D.C., restaurants was illegal. The vote in the Court was 8–0, and the ruling specifically declared that restaurants could not legally refuse to serve "well-behaved and respectable" Black patrons. This decision upheld an 1873 law, which made it a criminal act for proprietors of public eating places to refuse to serve anyone solely on the basis of race or color, and a decision of the Municipal Court of Appeals of 1951, which pronounced racial segregation in District of Columbia restaurants to be

illegal. The ruling overturned a U.S. Court of Appeals ruling of January 22.

BLACK UNITS ABOLISHED IN ARMED FORCES

On **OCTOBER 30**, the U.S. Defense Department completely abolished Black units in the armed forces.

1955 AVERAGE INCOME FOR BLACKS REPORTED

The average annual wage and salary income of Black men at this time was $2,342 — about 59 percent of the average $3,986 received by whites.

BERRY ELECTED VICE MAYOR OF CINCINNATI

Theodore Berry was elected vice mayor of Cincinnati, a consequence of coming in second among all candidates. In 1972, he was elected mayor of the city.

BERRY RELEASES "MAYBELLENE"

Chuck Berry (1926–) released his hit "Maybellene." Berry soon became the most significant rock-and-roll singer of his time. He influenced the direction of rock-and-roll with his unique style. A number of other hits followed: "Johnny B. Goode," "Roll Over, Beethoven," "Sweet Little Sixteen," "My Ding-a-Ling," and "Rock and Roll Music." His lyrics and guitar playing inspired a number of singing groups and individuals, such as the Beatles and the Rolling Stones.

BLACKS ELECTED AS LEADERS IN AFL-CIO

A. Philip Randolph and Willard S. Townsend were elected vice presidents of the AFL-CIO, becoming the highest-ranking Black leaders in the labor union umbrella organization.

Willard S. Townsend, perhaps the lesser known of the two labor leaders, was actually the first president of the Auxiliary of Redcaps, which was founded in 1936. The Redcap union represented railroad baggage porters. Because of his long history of labor leadership, Townsend was made one of the first vice presidents when the American Federation of Labor (AFL) merged with the Congress of Industrial Organization (CIO) to become the AFL-CIO.

CHARLES RECORDS HIT SONG

In this year, Ray Charles (Ray Charles Robinson; 1930–) released one of his most successful songs, entitled "I've Got a Woman." Blind since age six because of untreated glaucoma, Charles had recorded a successful song in 1951, "Baby Let Me Hold Your Hand." These songs launched a long career in performing and recording. Charles's albums include *Ray Charles* (1957), *Modern Sounds in Country and Western Music* (1962), and *Wish You Were Here Tonight* (1983).

ICC PROHIBITS SEGREGATION

The Interstate Commerce Commission prohibited segregation in public vehicles operating in interstate travel beginning on January 10. The order also extended to waiting rooms.

WILKINS BECOMES EXECUTIVE SECRETARY OF NAACP

Roy Wilkins was selected as the executive secretary of the NAACP, following the death of executive secretary Walter White. He became the third African American to serve in this position. Wilkins, of St. Louis, Missouri, was a journalist and had served the NAACP both as editor of *Crisis* and as assistant executive secretary. Wilkins used his position to gather support and funding to fight against racial segregation in all aspects of life, as well as for school desegregation throughout the country. Wilkins was an important figure in the passage of the Civil Rights Act of 1964.

ANDERSON DEBUTS AT METROPOLITAN OPERA

On **JANUARY 7**, Marian Anderson became the first Black American to sing on the stage of the Metropolitan Opera in New York. She debuted as Ulrica in Verdi's *Masked Ball*. Anderson had become the first Black American hired by the Metropolitan Opera when she signed a contract with the company the previous October.

BLACK PITCHER ACHIEVES NO-HITTER

On **MAY 12**, Sam Jones of the Chicago Cubs became the first Black pitcher in major league history to pitch a no-hitter. He beat the Pittsburgh Pirates 4–0.

SUPREME COURT ADOPTS "GO SLOW" APPROACH IN SCHOOL INTEGRATION

On **MAY 31**, the Supreme Court rejected the pleas of the NAACP to order instant and total school desegregation. The Court adopted the "go slow" approach advocated by the Justice Department. It assigned local school officials responsibility for developing the school desegregation plans and allowed federal judges to determine the pace of desegregation, despite the fact that the *Brown* decision called for a "prompt and reasonable start toward full compliance" so that desegregation could proceed with "all deliberate speed." A poll showed that more than 80 percent of southern-

ers opposed desegregation at this time. The justices felt that a gradual pace would circumvent southern politicians' attempts to defy federal authority.

States in the South tried to prevent the integration of school in many ways. In Mississippi, Governor Hugh L. White tried to sidestep integration by equalizing aid to all public schools. Governor White encouraged the teachers to accept voluntary separate school attendance, suggesting that the state would abandon its public schools if it had to integrate them. Black teachers adopted resolutions rejecting the governor's proposal, declaring, "We heartily endorse the Supreme Court decision of May 17, 1954, and of May 31, 1955, as being just, courageous and timely. All good citizens have a solemn obligation to abide by the law. As professional educators, our obligation in this regard is even more impelling." In North Carolina, Governor Luther Hodges carried out a similar strategy, which included attending a leadership conference of Black teachers on August 26, at which he attempted to intimidate the teachers.

MORROW APPOINTED AS AIDE TO EISENHOWER

On **JULY 9**, E. Frederick Morrow was appointed as one of several administrative aides to President Dwight D. Eisenhower. Morrow became the first African American to hold an executive position on the White House staff.

TILL KIDNAPPED AND MURDERED

On **AUGUST 28**, Emmett Till, a fourteen-year-old Black youth from Chicago who allegedly made advances toward a white woman, was kidnapped in Money, Mississippi. His body was found four days later in a river. The two white men tried for his murder by an all-white, all-male jury were acquitted. The trial highlighted unequal treatment of Blacks in the courts.

SUPREME COURT BANS SEGREGATION IN RECREATIONAL FACILITIES

On **NOVEMBER 7**, the U.S. Supreme Court banned segregation in public recreational facilities in a Baltimore case.

MONTGOMERY BUS BOYCOTT BEGINS AFTER "ROSA PARKS INCIDENT"

On **DECEMBER 1**, Rosa Parks (1913–), a seamstress and secretary of the Montgomery NAACP, refused to "move back" on a crowded Montgomery bus so that a white person could have her seat. Because segregation on buses was a municipal law, the bus driver had her arrested. This act precipitated a bus boycott by Blacks, beginning on December 5. Over the course of the next 381 days, more than fifty thousand Blacks participated in the boycott, cutting the profit of the bus company by almost two-thirds. Blacks used all modes of transit except buses; they walked, carpooled, and rode on mules.

The treatment of Blacks on Montgomery buses was particularly offensive. Blacks had to pay their fares at the front of the bus, then get off and board again at the back door. There were no Black bus drivers, and because most Blacks depended on bus transportation, they often had to endure harsh treatment from the white drivers twice a day. The boycott was led by twenty-seven-year-old Martin Luther King, Jr., a newcomer to the city. This was King's first experience in leading a major protest. In the speech that initiated the boycott, King said, "But there comes a time that people get tired. We are here this evening to say to those who have mistreated us for so long that we are tired — tired of being segregated and humiliated; tired of being kicked about by the brutal feet of oppression. We had no alternative but to protest."

◈ Parks was raised in Tuskegee and Montgomery, Alabama. She attended Alabama State College and in 1932 married Raymond Parks, a barber and worker for the local NAACP chapter.

Because of the harassment Parks and her family endured during the boycott, they moved to Detroit, where Parks worked on the staff of Congressman John Conyers, Jr., until 1988. She displayed courage in her refusal to leave her seat on the bus. Eldridge Cleaver would later write about her action: "Somewhere in the universe a gear in the machinery had shifted."

1956   BROWN ELECTED COLORADO SENATOR

George L. Brown was elected to the Colorado state senate, the first Black to attain this post in the state. Brown had previously been appointed by the governor to the house of representatives. He served four successive terms (1960 through 1972) in the Colorado Senate. In 1974, he was elected lieutenant governor of Colorado.

DAVIS DEBUTS ON BROADWAY

Sammy Davis, Jr. (1925–1990), made his stage debut on Broadway in the musical *Mr. Wonderful.* Davis was born in Harlem and began his career at the age of three, performing with his father and uncle in vaudeville. Davis, a

Rosa Parks provided fuel for the civil rights movement when she violated a Montgomery, Alabama, ordinance by not giving up her bus seat to a white man. Parks is shown being fingerprinted by the Montgomery Police Department following her arrest.

versatile entertainer, became known for his superb dancing and for his abilities as a musician and impressionist. In 1964, he received a Tony nomination for his role as a young boxer in *Golden Boy*. Davis enjoyed success as a nightclub performer and recording artist (his notable hits included "I've Got to Be Me," 1969, and "Candy Man," 1972). He starred in countless television variety and comedy shows and numerous films, including *Porgy and Bess* (1959), *Oceans Eleven* (1960), *Robin and the Seven Hoods* (1964), and *Sweet Charity* (1969). He hosted his own television series in 1966. Davis wrote two autobiographies, *Yes I Can* (1965) and *Why Me?* (1989). Davis was active in the civil rights movement of the 1960s and sang at fundraisers for Dr. Martin Luther King, Jr. On May 16, 1990, at age sixty-four, Davis died of throat cancer in Los Angeles. Dr. Benjamin L. Hooks, executive director of the NAACP, noted at the time of Davis's death that he was "an American treasure that the whole world loved."

GIBSON WINS FRENCH OPEN

Althea Gibson (1927–) became the first Black to win a major tennis title when she captured the French Open women's singles title.

INTEGRATION CAUSES ANTI-BLACK PROTEST AND VIOLENCE

Efforts to desegregate schools in Mansfield, Texas; Clinton, Tennessee; and Sturgis and Clay, Kentucky, were met with violent anti-Black protests. In Mansfield, the Texas Rangers were dispatched to put down riots protesting Blacks' enrollment in high school. In the Clinton, Tennessee, case, the National Guard calmed riots caused by the admission of twelve Blacks to schools; nine of the twelve were finally admitted. In Sturgis, the situation was so tense that the National Guard charged the mob with bayonets to open the school to Blacks.

LUCY ENTERS UNIVERSITY OF ALABAMA

Autherine Lucy, under court order, was admitted to the University of Alabama. She was suspended after an anti-Black riot occurred at the school, and the day after her admission, she was expelled for making "false" and "outrageous" statements about university officials. Officials claimed they were acting to protect her from "great bodily harm." The NAACP filed a discrimination suit against the university.

MONTGOMERY BUS BOYCOTT ENDS

As many as 115 Blacks were jailed and indicted by a grand jury in Montgomery for participating in the bus boycott. The Supreme Court ruled that segregation on public buses in Montgomery (and in the state of Alabama) violated the Constitution. On **DECEMBER 21**, the boycott ended, and the city buses were integrated. This was the first time Blacks had ridden the buses since December 5, 1955, when the boycott began.

The boycott had many consequences. It was a successful example of how organized efforts of the Black community could challenge racism in the South. It also took the civil rights movement to the streets by encouraging others to take part in marches, boycotts, and sit-ins. It also spurred the organization of Black clergy to lead the protest, particularly as they came together in the Southern Christian Leadership Conference, and it vaulted Martin Luther King, Jr., into prominence as a civil rights leader. It also, however, marked the beginning of massive white resistance to change. The Klan and White Citizens' Councils flourished after the boycott, and the survival of the NAACP was in jeopardy.

NAACP ORDERED TO SHUT DOWN

Because of the effectiveness of NAACP strategies in breaking down racial barriers in Alabama, the state's highest court ordered the NAACP to cease operating in the state. A number of NAACP branches were lost throughout the South in the late 1950s.

The NAACP was a target for white resistance because it was the organization most responsible for mounting efforts for school desegregation. Laws were passed to harass the NAACP branches — for example, requiring the organization to make its membership lists public, making membership a cause for dismissal of public school teachers and state employees, and making it a crime for an organization to cause trouble by attacking local segregation ordinances. Such actions clearly took their toll — by 1958, the South's percentage of NAACP membership dropped from almost 50 percent to 25 percent, and 246 branches had been closed. The Supreme Court eventually struck down all the anti-NAACP laws. The use of the laws for several years, however, managed to divert the attention of the NAACP from desegregation efforts to its own survival.

NEWCOMBE NAMED NATIONAL LEAGUE'S MOST VALUABLE PLAYER

Don Newcombe, pitcher for the Brooklyn Dodgers, was awarded the National League's Most Valuable Player award for the best won-lost record of any pitcher in the league and for his consistent outstanding leadership. Newcombe won twenty games in his 1949 rookie season.

PATTERSON WINS WORLD HEAVYWEIGHT BOXING TITLE

Floyd Patterson, at the age of twenty-one, was the youngest man to hold the world heavyweight boxing title. He won a technical knockout against Archie Moore.

RACISTS ATTACK NAT KING COLE

The popular Black singer Nat King Cole was attacked by racists in Birmingham, Alabama, as he sang to a white audience.

ROBINSON NAMED BASEBALL ROOKIE OF THE YEAR

Frank Robinson, an excellent batter and outfielder for the Cincinnati Reds, won the Rookie of the Year award. Robinson went on to become one of baseball's most versatile players.

STATE FUNDING FOR PRIVATE SCHOOLS APPROVED

The Virginia General Assembly sanctioned state funding of private schools — a way to circumvent court-ordered integration and maintain segregation in education.

SUPREME COURT RULES TO ADMIT BLACK STUDENT TO FLORIDA LAW SCHOOL

The U.S. Supreme Court declared in *Florida, ex rel Hawkins* v. *Board of Control* that Virgil Hawkins had to be immediately admitted to the College of Law of the University of Florida.

TALLAHASSEE BUS BOYCOTT RESULTS IN DESEGREGATION

Segregation on buses was outlawed in Tallahassee, Florida, as a result of six months of boycotting by Blacks.

WHITE RESISTANCE TO SCHOOL INTEGRATION GROWS

Several things led to massive white resistance to school integration in the late 1950s. The "Southern Manifesto," which called for states to decide whether a school should be integrated, combined with the "deliberate speed" mandated by the Supreme Court and the lack of strong leadership from the Eisenhower White House, led many whites in the South into defiance of the law.

◆ Although the president was required to enforce the federal law, Eisenhower never endorsed the *Brown* ruling. He had never approved of school desegregation just as he had not approved of desegregating the military. Similarly, Adlai Stevenson of the Democratic Party asked that the South be "given time and patience."

More than 450 laws and resolutions were enacted to prevent or limit school desegregation. One of the most successful laws was that of "pupil placement." In theory, it allowed every student freedom of choice by prohibiting local school officials from assigning children to schools based on race. However, the school officials could accept or reject applications to schools on a variety of criteria such as "the psychological effect upon the pupil of attendance at a particular school" and "the morals, conduct, health and personal standards of the pupil." They simply used these loopholes to assign Black students and white students to different schools. In 1958, the Supreme Court declared these laws constitutional, although their enforcement led to de facto segregation.

SUPREME COURT AFFIRMS BAN ON SEGREGATION IN SCHOOLS AND ON BUSES

On **MARCH 5**, the U.S. Supreme Court affirmed the ban on segregation in public schools; on April 23, the Court upheld a lower-court ban on interstate bus segregation in South Carolina.

LOUISVILLE PUBLIC SCHOOLS INTEGRATE

On **SEPTEMBER 10**, public schools in Louisville, Kentucky, were integrated.

COLE BEGINS OWN TV VARIETY SERIES

Nat King Cole (1919–1965) became the first Black with his own national network television variety series. *The Nat King Cole Show* ran for sixty-four weeks in 1956 and 1957 on NBC-TV.

Nathaniel Adams Cole was born in Montgomery, Alabama. His music career started early when he and his brother, Eddie, joined the production of *Shuffle Along*. As the leader of the King Cole Trio, Nat was singled out as a balladeer. He became an entertainer of international stature with the release of "Mona Lisa,"

Two baseball legends, Hank Aaron and Willie Mays: "Hammerin' Hank," of the Milwaukee (later Atlanta) Braves, became baseball's all-time home-run king in 1974; Mays, of the New York (later San Francisco) Giants, was the National League's Most Valuable Player in 1954 and 1965. Both were outstanding all-around players.

"The Christmas Song," and "Unforgettable." Although Nat King Cole broke down a number of racial barriers, few gave him appropriate credit for it. In 1989, the National Academy of Recording Arts and Sciences, an organization which he helped found, honored him posthumously with a Lifetime Achievement Grammy.

HOLDER JOINS METROPOLITAN OPERA

On **NOVEMBER 13**, Geoffrey Holder joined the Metropolitan Opera as a dancer with a contract to dance in twenty-six performances. Included among them were the operas *Aïda* and *La Périchole*. Holder later expanded his career into acting and advertising.

SHUTTLESWORTH'S HOME BOMBED

On **DECEMBER 25**, the home of Fred L. Shuttlesworth, a Black minister and civil rights activist, was bombed in Birmingham, Alabama. Blacks responded with massive defiance of bus segregation regulations, and at least forty were jailed.

1957 AARON NAMED MOST VALUABLE PLAYER

The Milwaukee Braves' Hank Aaron received the Most Valuable Player award of the National League for leading his team to the pennant. Over the season, Aaron hit forty-four home runs and became a leader of the team.

Aaron started his baseball career with the all-Black Indianapolis Clowns. He was signed by Milwaukee as a shortstop but was shifted to the outfield. In 1974, Aaron made baseball history when he broke Babe Ruth's record for career home runs (714). Aaron had hit 733 home runs by the end of the 1974 season. During the next season, he added twenty-two additional home runs to this total to complete a career total of 755 home runs.

◈ Aaron was born in Mobile, Alabama, on February 5, 1934. His baseball career started when he signed a two-hundred-dollar-per-month contract with the Indianapolis Clowns of the Negro American League. In 1952, he signed with the Boston Braves and played the next season with Jacksonville of the South Atlantic League. His big break came in 1954 when he was promoted to the big leagues as a member of the Milwaukee Braves. Aaron was one of the most gifted players of the game. In addition to being the home run leader four times, the leader in RBIs four times, and hitting forty or more homers eight times, he was named to twenty consecutive all-star teams. Aaron finished his career in the city where he began. In January 1982, Aaron was voted into the Baseball Hall of Fame, receiving 406 of 415 votes from the Baseball Writers Association.

BASIE GIVES COMMAND PERFORMANCE

In this year, William "Count" Basie gave a command performance for Queen Elizabeth II of England. Basie, a native of Redbank, New Jersey, had become one of the most noted jazz composers in the world. Over the years, Basie played in a number of bands, and during the mid-1930s, when he formed his own band, he attracted some of the most gifted musicians and subsequently became the recipient of many Grammys and other awards. In 1981, he was honored at the Kennedy Center.

CAREY CHAIRS PRESIDENTIAL COMMITTEE

Archibald Carey was appointed chairperson of the president's Committee on Government Employment Policy. He became the first Black to chair this committee.

FAIR HOUSING PRACTICE ORDINANCE PASSED IN NEW YORK

New York City passed the nation's first fair housing practice ordinance to prevent discrimination in housing.

FEDERAL TROOPS AND NATIONAL GUARD DEPLOYED IN ARKANSAS

President Eisenhower ordered one thousand federal troops and ten thousand National Guard members into Little Rock, Arkansas, to halt state interference in desegregation. Governor Orval Faubus of Arkansas issued a series of court orders to block the desegregation of the city's Central High School. Governor Faubus and the mob of whites finally moved aside as the federal troops escorted nine Black children (the Little Rock Nine) to school on September 25. Regular army troops remained as protectors from September 24 to November 27 as violence occurred frequently in front of the school. On one occasion the violence escalated to such an extent that Blacks were forced out of school for safety reasons.

The National Guard remained in Little Rock until May 1958.

GEORGIA ENACTS VOTER REGISTRATION BARRIERS

Voter registration barriers in Colquitt County, Georgia, were enacted to prevent Blacks from exercising their right to vote. In this county, according to representative Peter Zack Geer, the following prospective voters were prohibited from voting by local election officials:

Parents of illegitimate children or parties to common law marriages
Parents accused of child abandonment
Parents accused of possessing and transporting moonshine liquor
Men who failed to register or report for military service
Persons adjudged guilty of bigamy, adultery, false swearing, or a felony

In addition, prospective voters were asked thirty questions regarding Georgia law, the Georgia constitution, and the U.S. Constitution. Judge Walter Geer of Colquitt County Superior Court instructed registrars and other voting officials to prevent investigators of the Commission on Civil Rights (created by the Civil Rights Act of 1957) from seeing the voting rolls, and he threatened to jail both the commission members and FBI agents if they continued probing into local voting matters.

GIBSON WINS TENNIS CHAMPIONSHIP

Althea Gibson became the first Black to win a U.S. national tennis championship — the U.S. Open championship. She won the women's singles title, de-

Althea Gibson was considered the best female tennis player in the world when she captured the singles title at the Wimbledon tennis championships in England in July 1957.

feating Louise Brough, at Forest Hills, New York. She also won the Wimbledon women's singles championship, becoming the first Black woman to hold this title. She garnered the Wimbledon championship again in 1958.

INTERRACIAL ATHLETICS PROHIBITED IN GEORGIA

The Georgia General Assembly passed a law prohibiting interracial athletics.

NASHVILLE SCHOOL BOMBED

A Nashville school was bombed by a white mob to prevent school integration.

POLICE PROTECT BLACKS IN LEVITTOWN

The first Black family to move into Levittown, New York, a white suburban enclave, received police protection.

RACIAL VIOLENCE FOLLOWS ATTEMPTS AT SCHOOL INTEGRATION

Birmingham, Nashville, and other southern cities were scenes of mob violence and bombings as school integration was enforced.

SIFFORD WINS LONG BEACH OPEN GOLF TOURNAMENT

Charles Sifford became the first Black to win a major professional golf tournament when he won the Long Beach Open.

SOUTHERN CHRISTIAN LEADERSHIP CONFERENCE FORMED

The Southern Christian Leadership Conference (SCLC) was organized by the Reverend Martin Luther King, Jr., Bayard Rustin, and several Black ministers, at a meeting in New Orleans. The group's goal was to consolidate the resources of many civil rights groups. Atlanta was selected to be the site of the organization's headquarters. The SCLC was one of the key organizations that helped secure passage of the Civil Rights Bill of 1964 and the Voting Rights Act of 1965. Martin Luther King, Jr., was chosen as its first president.

HOME OF KING BOMBED

On **JANUARY 30**, the home of Dr. Martin Luther King, Jr., was bombed in Montgomery, Alabama. King was a leader of the Montgomery bus boycott. He had given an electrifying speech the previous month that had solidified Black support for the boycott. After the

The integration of Central High School in Little Rock, Arkansas, caused tempers to flare as members of the 101st Airborne Division were brought in to escort the nine Black students to class. After the Brown *decision of 1954, states and counties enacted 145 laws to prevent desegregation.*

bombing, King addressed a small crowd from his front lawn and urged nonviolence.

BLACKS BOYCOTT WHITE MERCHANTS TO PROTEST GERRYMANDERING

In **JUNE**, Black residents of Tuskegee, Alabama, began a boycott of white businesses to protest the state legislature's gerrymandering of electoral districts to reduce the number of Black districts and their overall political power. Charles G. Gomillion, a sociologist at Tuskegee Institute, led the movement. Blacks also took legal action; the case of *Gomillion* v. *Lightfoot* went to the U.S. Supreme Court, which ruled in 1960 that gerrymandering was illegal. Blacks subsequently took political control of Tuskegee and of Macon County.

THURMOND FILIBUSTERS AGAINST CIVIL RIGHTS

On **AUGUST 30**, Senator Strom Thurmond of South Carolina set a new record for a filibuster in the U.S. Congress. He spoke against the civil rights bill for twenty-four hours and twenty-seven minutes.

1958 AILEY FORMS DANCE COMPANY

Alvin Ailey (1931–1989) formed his own dance company — the Alvin Ailey American Dance Theater — and eventually became one of the best-known choreographers in the nation.

A student of Lester Horton, Ailey made his debut in 1950. He began choreographing in 1953 and was best known for *Creation of the World* (1954), *Blues Suite* (1958), and *Revelations* (1960).

BANKS NAMED MOST VALUABLE PLAYER
Ernie Banks won the National League's Most Valuable Player award for hitting 129 RBIs and forty-seven home runs.

Banks gained the distinction of being the first Black player (along with Gene Baker) with the Chicago Cubs (1953), and he became noted for adopting his "slugger's" bat, a relatively light bat that is used by most sluggers today. More important, in a five-year stint (1955–1960), Banks hit more home runs (248) than any other player. In addition, he was the first National League player to win the Most Valuable Player award two years in succession, in 1958 and 1959.

LYNCHING OF BLACKS CONTINUES
Between 1952 and 1958, four lynchings of Blacks were recorded.

NAACP FINED FOR CONTEMPT
The state of Alabama imposed a one-hundred-thousand-dollar contempt fine on the NAACP for failing to provide its membership lists to an Alabama judge. It was a clear attempt to weaken the NAACP's civil rights activities in the state. Through legal maneuvers, the NAACP was kept out of Alabama until a decision was made by the Supreme Court in 1964. In *NAACP* v. *Alabama*, the Court declared that it would not tolerate denial of constitutional rights.

NINE-POINT ANSWER OUTLINES WHAT BLACKS WANT
In Dallas, Texas, 112 Black ministers issued a document highlighting a "nine-point" answer to what the Black population wanted:

1. No special privilege
2. To be respected as a person
3. To live in a truly free society
4. All services rendered on Blacks' behalf be based upon deeper values than humanitarian philanthropy and paternalism
5. The right to live and find free expression for their native endowments as individuals
6. Individual differences neither to be ignored nor accentuated
7. Unity of equal terms
8. Unity of diversity
9. Peace and harmony in an ordered society

ROBINSON WINS ANOTHER MIDDLEWEIGHT TITLE
Sugar Ray Robinson, who came out of retirement to regain the middleweight boxing title in 1955, won

the title for the fifth time. He thus became the only fighter to win a world boxing championship five times. After several other fights, Robinson retired in 1965.

SIT-IN ORGANIZED BY NAACP YOUTH COUNCIL
A segregated restaurant in Oklahoma City, Oklahoma, became the target of sit-ins by members of the NAACP Youth Council.

STUDENTS MARCH FOR INTEGRATED SCHOOLS
Jackie Robinson, Harry Belafonte, and A. Philip Randolph led ten thousand students in the Youth March for Integrated Schools in Washington, D.C.

WHARTON NAMED AMBASSADOR TO ROMANIA
On **FEBRUARY 5**, Clifton R. Wharton, Sr., was confirmed as ambassador to Romania, thus becoming the first Black to head a U.S. embassy in Europe. Wharton was named ambassador to Norway in 1961.

RUSSELL NAMED MOST VALUABLE PLAYER
On **MARCH 24**, Bill Russell, one of basketball's great centers, was voted the National Basketball Association's Most Valuable Player. Russell was the center for the Boston Celtics.

BLACKS GATHER IN SUPPORT OF VOTING RIGHTS ACT
On **MAY 17**, from fifteen thousand to thirty thousand Americans, mostly Black, convened on the steps of the Lincoln Memorial in Washington, D.C., to pray and to demonstrate support for a voting rights act while the bill was being debated. Martin Luther King, Jr., headed the demonstration, leading the chant "Give us the ballot!"

SPINGARN MEDAL AWARDED TO "LITTLE ROCK NINE"
On **JULY 11**, the NAACP awarded the Spingarn Medal to each of the brave students who desegregated Central High School in Little Rock, Arkansas.

LITTLE ROCK APPEALS TO DELAY SCHOOL INTEGRATION
In **AUGUST**, an appeal by the Little Rock school board for a delay in the racial integration of Central High School was rejected unanimously by the U.S. Supreme Court. Thurgood Marshall and other members of the NAACP supported rejection of any delay in opening Little Rock schools. Governor Orval Faubus responded by closing four Little Rock high schools on

Monday (the start of the new term). Nearly half of the white students then enrolled in private schools, about one-third attended schools outside the city, and about six hundred white students did not attend any school that year. Most of the Black high school students, including the Little Rock Nine, also did not attend school. The U.S. Supreme Court ruled that closing the high schools was unconstitutional and that "evasive schemes" such as this one could not be used to delay integration. In August 1959, the public high schools were reopened and integrated according to the federal requirements.

CIVIL RIGHTS ACT OF 1957 BECOMES LAW

On **SEPTEMBER 9**, President Eisenhower signed the first civil rights act since Reconstruction. The legislation declared the disfranchisement of Black Americans illegal; it authorized the Justice Department to seek injunctions against interference with the right to vote, and it established the Commission on Civil Rights to investigate interference with the law.

The act, however, had a limited effect. Over the next three years, less than two hundred thousand Blacks were added to the voting lists in the South, an increase of less than 3 percent. Voting rights activists registered Blacks in a door-to-door campaign, often going to the homes of Blacks living in isolated rural communities — a time-consuming task.

KING STABBED BY BLACK WOMAN

On **SEPTEMBER 20** in Harlem, a Black woman stabbed Martin Luther King, Jr., while he was autographing copies of his book about the Montgomery bus boycott, *Strides Toward Freedom*. The wound was serious, but King recovered. The Black woman was found to be deranged and not connected with any hate group or anti–civil rights organization.

1959 BAYLOR NAMED ROOKIE OF THE YEAR

Elgin Baylor, a six-foot-tall basketball player for the Los Angeles Lakers, was named National Basketball Association Rookie of the Year. Baylor was viewed by many as the most complete basketball player in the game.

In 1960, Baylor scored a total of seventy-one points in a single game. In 1976, Baylor was selected as head coach of the New Orleans Jazz basketball team. He remained the coach until 1979. In 1986, he was chosen to be director of basketball operations for the Los Angeles Clippers, a position he still holds.

CLAY ELECTED ALDERMAN IN ST. LOUIS

William Lacy Clay was elected alderman of the Twenty-sixth Ward, a predominantly Black district in St. Louis. As an active member of several civil rights organizations, Clay had spent several months in jail for demonstrating at a local bank. In 1964 and 1968, he was elected a ward committee member for the same ward.

GORDY FOUNDS MOTOWN RECORD CORPORATION

Berry Gordy, Jr., was encouraged by William (Smokey) Robinson, Jr., to start a recording company. The company was named Motown Record Corporation and released its first record in this year. By 1960, Motown had its first gold record — *Shop Around* — also by Smokey Robinson, who became a vice president of Motown.

Motown was the Black nickname for Detroit, the Motor City. The Motown sound reflected the rhythm of the factories and the life in Black neighborhoods. Most of the early artists who recorded on the Motown label were from Detroit. These included the Supremes, the Four Tops, the Temptations, Martha and the Vandellas, and Mary Wells. As the company became more successful, artists from other cities signed on, including Marvin Gaye, Stevie Wonder, and the Jackson Five.

Gordy's early success was in part related to timing. In the late 1950s, there were many Black rock-and-roll artists who recorded for companies that were owned and operated by white executives. In the early 1960s, some major record companies where found to have paid disc jockeys for playing certain records. These "payola" scandals prompted radio stations to play songs from small, independent record companies that previously would have been ignored. These circumstances allowed Gordy to penetrate the industry and get his records heard by a national audience. Motown was to become a multi-million-dollar enterprise. About a decade after its incorporation in Detroit, Gordy moved Motown's headquarters to Los Angeles.

HANSBERRY WINS AWARD FOR *A Raisin in the Sun*

Lorraine Hansberry (1930–1965) won the New York Drama Critics Circle Award for her play *A Raisin in the Sun*. Hansberry became the youngest American to win this award and the first African American woman writer whose play was staged on Broadway. It ran for about nineteen months. The play was about a Black family living in the poorest section of Chicago.

In 1959, Lorraine Hansberry's play A Raisin in the Sun *opened on Broadway. In addition to having been written by a Black, this award-winning play was produced and directed by Blacks and featured Black actors and actresses in the starring roles. Sidney Poitier (right) played the lead in both the stage and the screen version.*

Lloyd Richards, an African American, directed the play, and Sidney Poitier starred in it. It was made into a film in 1961 and won an award at the Cannes Film Festival. Hansberry wrote one other play, *The Sign in Sidney Brustein's Window*, in 1964, before she died of cancer at age thirty-four.

POVERTY ESPECIALLY PREVALENT AMONG SOUTHERN BLACKS

According to the Bureau of the Census, in the South, 26.6 percent of whites and 67.4 percent of Blacks were reported to be living in poverty. In the North and the West combined, 14.6 percent of whites lived in poverty, whereas 33.4 percent of Blacks lived in such conditions.

RACIAL TROUBLE PERSISTS IN LITTLE ROCK

After the school had been closed by Governor Orval Faubus and later reopened, two Black students walked through a crowd of more than 250 protesting whites gathered by the door of Central High School in Little Rock, Arkansas. White demonstrators were restrained by police and firefighters armed with clubs and water hoses. As many as twenty-one protesters were arrested. Governor Faubus encouraged the segregationists to continue to resist integration of all Arkansas schools.

URBAN RENEWAL PROGRAM BEGINS

The U.S. Congress appropriated $650 million for a pilot "slum clearance" project in New Haven, Connecticut. The program quickly evolved into a "Black removal" project, involving the widespread destruction of housing occupied by Black people and the uprooting and subsequent relocation of entire Black communities into high-rise public housing. This pattern would be followed in other cities as well.

WHITES ABANDON SCHOOL TO AVOID INTEGRATION

The public school system in Prince Edward County, Virginia, was abandoned by whites to avoid integrating the school. In contrast, Arlington and Norfolk schools opened their desegregated public schools without major disturbances.

LYNCHING OCCURS IN MISSISSIPPI

On **APRIL 26**, another lynching was recorded in the South — Mack Charles Parker was hanged at Poplarville, Mississippi. The failure to bring the murderers to justice echoed a lack of progress in race relations throughout the South.

GREEN GRADUATES FROM PREDOMINANTLY WHITE SCHOOL

On **MAY 29**, Ernest Green, one of the Little Rock Nine, graduated from Little Rock Central High School. He was the only African American among the school's six hundred graduates. Green became a public servant and politician in Washington, D.C.

STUDY SHOWS PREVALENCE OF SEGREGATION

The **JUNE** issue of *Southern School News* analyzed 7,677 school districts in eighteen states. It was reported that 2,875 districts were biracial and 742 segregated. A total of 9,658,361 white children and 2,999,157 Black children went to school in the region; 2,261,513 white and 447,022 Black children studied in integrated school environments. Six states — Alabama, Florida, Georgia, Louisiana, Mississippi, and South Carolina — had no desegregated schools at all.

1960–1969 INCOME AND EMPLOYMENT IMPROVE SOMEWHAT FOR BLACKS

By 1960, median income of Black families had reached 55 percent of median family income for white families. After having dipped to a low similar to that in 1941 (51 percent), Black median income edged upward during the latter part of the 1960s. By 1969, Black family median income was 63 percent of white family income. Blacks generally continued to improve their economic status when measured by income.

These statistics do not reveal the high unemployment rate among Black workers during the early 1960s — reaching a high of 12.4 percent in 1961 — which was more than twice as high as white unemployment. Some researchers emphasize that these unemployment statistics understate the true unemployment for Blacks, because they do not reflect involuntary part-time employment and "hidden unemployed" or discouraged Black workers. For example, in 1973, it was estimated that about one-quarter of all involuntary part-time workers were Black. Although hidden unemployment is difficult to calculate, it is generally accepted that the decrease in labor force participation over the previous decade reflects, at least partially, pessimism among Black males about finding decent employment.

The later 1960s, however, showed some improvements in the overall well-being of Black families. Unemployment rates dropped below 10 percent for the first time in seven years. In fact, by 1969, Black unemployment was only 6.4 percent. Still, this rate was not as low as that of the early 1950s.

1960–1975 THE VIETNAM ERA

The commitment of U.S. forces to fight in Vietnam was a difficult decision for military leaders and the commander in chief. After the decision was made, only regulars were used. But as the war escalated, the military turned to draftees to meet troop demands. Because of draft deferment provisions for whites, a disproportionate number of Blacks entered the armed forces. For the first time in history, Blacks comprised 16 percent of all draftees, although they made up only 11 percent of the national population. It was clear to all what was occurring — whites were able to receive deferments, whereas Blacks were not. It was simply a matter of racial discrimination — local draft boards were composed primarily of whites.

Vietnam was a bloody and mean war, and it took a heavy toll on all who participated. Blacks, however, tended to stay longer than whites in the military; and because they volunteered at a higher rate than whites, they were proportionally more likely to see more combat. In addition, Blacks were more likely to volunteer for elite units such as airborne and air cavalry units — those that frequently encountered intense combat. Blacks therefore had a higher proportion of casualties than whites. Military bases experienced discrimination in the same manner as society in general; racism blocked promotional opportunities for soldiers just as it had blocked civilians seeking to move up the corporate ladder. Violence erupted at a number of military installations during the late 1960s and early 1970s.

When the United States concluded its involvement in Vietnam, there were many problems to face at home. Many cities suffered much destruction because demands for civil rights had not been met. Police brutality was frequently the response to the demands of civil rights leaders. Some boycotts, sit-ins, marches, and freedom rides were nonviolent; others employed violent measures, as Blacks accepted and joined the Black Power movement.

1960

POPULATION OVERVIEW

BLACK POPULATION IN THE UNITED STATES The U.S. resident population reached 179,323,175, of whom 18,871,831, or 10.5 percent, were Black residents. Among the Black population, 11.3 million lived in the South, 3 million in the Northeast, 3.5 million in the North Central states, and 1 million in the West.

URBANIZATION OF BLACKS Fully 72 percent of the U.S. population overall lived in urban areas. Blacks were slightly more urbanized than whites — 73 percent lived in urban areas in contrast to 70 percent of whites. In 1890, roughly 80 percent of Blacks lived in rural areas. In 1960, for the first time, a larger proportion of Blacks lived in cities than did whites. In this year, the census recorded for the first time that more than half of southern Blacks were residing in cities. This development reflected the overwhelming nature of Black urbanization, particularly the movement of southern Blacks into cities in the North, the South, and the West. The distribution of population by urban and rural residence for selected years is depicted in the table.

BLACKS IN NORTHERN CITIES With each decade, northern cities continued to gain larger proportions of Black residents. In St. Louis, for example, the percentage of Blacks in the total population jumped from 13 percent in 1940, to 18 percent in 1950, and to 29 percent in 1960.

GEOGRAPHIC DISTRIBUTION OF POPULATION BY URBAN AND RURAL RESIDENCE AND BY RACE FOR SELECTED YEARS, 1890–1960

YEAR	TOTAL POPULATION (THOUSANDS)	PERCENT RESIDING IN		
		URBAN AREAS	RURAL AREAS	
			TOTAL	FARM
BLACK				
1890	7,489	20	80	(NA)
1910	9,828	27	73	(NA)
1940	12,866	49	51	35
1950	15,045	62	38	21
1960	18,871	72	27	8
WHITE				
1890	55,101	38	62	(NA)
1910	81,732	49	51	(NA)
1940	118,702	57	43	22
1950	134,478	64	36	15
1960	158,838	70	30	7

Source: U.S. Bureau of the Census, *The Social and Economic Status of the Black Population in the United States: An Historical View* (Washington, D.C.: Government Printing Office, 1980).

BLACKS IN THE SOUTH The population of the South grew by 17 percent over the 1950–1960 decade. About 48 percent of all Blacks lived outside the states of the former Confederacy. In 1940, the comparative figure was 18 percent. Blacks made up about 20.9 percent of the population of the South; about 52 percent of all Blacks in the United States resided in the South, down from 68 percent in 1940.

BLACK MIGRATION A total of 1.5 million Blacks moved away from the South. Mississippi was the largest loser: 323,000 (32.7 percent) of its Black residents left the state. Net migration rates of Blacks were 26 percent for the Northeast, 24 percent for the North Central states, and 39 percent for the West. Major states that experienced large net migration gains (that is, the total number of migrants arriving, less the total number of migrants departing) included the following: California, 350,000; New York, 280,000; Illinois, 190,000; and Michigan, 190,000.

Although Black migration had slowed during the 1930s because of the Great Depression, World War II and the demands of industry caused a resurgence of Black migration. Between 1910 and 1960, slightly less than 5 million Blacks left the South. Most were destined for large northern cities.

BLACKS LESS MOBILE THAN WHITES From March 1960 to March 1961, about 3.4 percent of the white population moved from one state to another, but only 2.3 percent of the nonwhite population made a state-to-state move.

BLACK POPULATION REACHES MAJORITY IN WASHINGTON, D.C. The Bureau of the Census recorded a Black majority in Washington, D.C.: 54.8 percent of all residents were nonwhites. A review of intercensal estimates shows that Washington, D.C., may have become a majority Black city in 1957, when it was estimated that the city comprised 787,600 residents, of whom 397,600 were estimated to be nonwhite (50.4 percent).

ECONOMIC CONDITIONS OVERVIEW

BLACKS WORK PRIMARILY IN MENIAL JOBS At this time, as many as 75 percent of Blacks held menial jobs.

INCOME DISPARITY BETWEEN BLACK AND WHITE FAMILIES The median income of Black families increased from 54 percent of the median income for white families in 1950 to 57 percent in 1952 and 56 percent in 1953 and 1954. After this, the proportion dropped to 51 percent in 1958, the same level as in 1947 and 1949. As the decade ended, Black median family in-

---

REGIONAL DISTRIBUTION OF U.S. POPULATION, 1940–1960

Although the percentage of Blacks in the total U.S. population had remained about the same since the turn of the century, the regional distribution shifted somewhat, mostly for Black residents. During this twenty-year period (1940–1960), many Blacks continued to leave the South, and their main destinations were the urban centers in the Northeast, the Midwest, and the West. The South was the home of more than three-quarters of all Blacks in the country in 1940, but in 1960, only 60 percent of Blacks resided there. The number and proportional representation of Blacks increased in each of the other regions, from 11 percent to 16 percent in the Northeast; from 11 percent to 18 percent in the Midwest; and from 1 percent to 6 percent in the West. Black migration from the South started anew as Blacks perceived greater social and economic opportunities in wartime industries and later, during the nation's postwar economic boom.

---

come was only 52 percent of white family income. From 1947 (when statistics were first kept) to 1959, Black family median income reached its highest level in the early 1950s.

SOCIAL CONDITIONS OVERVIEW

BLACK CHILDREN LAG IN EDUCATION According to the U.S. census, Black children were three years behind white children in grade level of education. Also, although Blacks made up about one-tenth of the total U.S. population, they made up only one-twentieth of students attending college.

BLACKS DISPROPORTIONATELY AMONG NATION'S POOREST According to Bureau of the Census data on poverty (1959), about 55.1 percent of Blacks lived in poverty, in contrast to 18.1 percent of whites. In 1960, the disparity widened: about 55.9 percent of nonwhites were recorded as living below the poverty level. For whites, the proportion dipped to 17.8 percent. The poverty threshold for a nonfarming family of four was an income of $2,973 in 1959.

SCHOOLS STILL SEGREGATED According to the Southern Education Reporting Service, about 94 percent of the South's Black students still attended segregated classes in spite of the Supreme Court decision of 1954. More specifically, of the 3,029,000 Black children attending public schools in the South, only about 524,425 were in integrated school districts.

POLITICAL CONDITIONS OVERVIEW

BLACK REPRESENTATION IN CONGRESS INCREASES

From 1950 to 1960, the number of Blacks elected to the U.S. Congress increased from four to fourteen. Two of the newly elected members of the House of Representatives came from the South, a first during the twentieth century.

AFL-CIO SUPPORTS BLACK BOYCOTTS

The American Federation of Labor–Congress of Industrial Organizations (AFL-CIO) pledged its support to Black boycotts around the country.

BLACKS REGISTER TO VOTE

About 11.5 million U.S. Blacks were of voting age at this time; 61 percent reported that they were registered to vote.

BLACKS WIN MEDALS AT OLYMPICS IN ROME

At the Olympics in Rome, Black Americans staged some major upsets. Lee Calhoun, Willie May, and Hayes Jones won the gold, silver, and bronze medals in the 110-meter high hurdles, each beating Martin Lauer, the world record holder from Germany. Otis Davis won the gold for the 400-meter run and Glen Davis, the gold for the 400-meter hurdles. Wilma Rudolph ran the 100-meter race in a record eleven seconds (disallowed because of wind) to win the gold medal. Cassius Clay, Willie McClure, and Eddie Crook brought home gold medals in boxing, and Rafer Johnson won the gold for the decathlon to become the world's greatest athlete.

BOYCOTTS PROVEN TO BE EFFECTIVE

In Philadelphia, boycotts by about 400 Black ministers were considered successful when Sun Oil, Gulf Oil, Tastee Baking, and Pepsi-Cola agreed to hire more than 600 Blacks for middle and higher administrative and managerial jobs.

CORE SECURES EMPLOYMENT AGREEMENT

The Congress of Racial Equality (CORE) secured an employment agreement with Bank of America, in California, to recruit and hire eight thousand Blacks over a twelve-month period.

KING AND OTHERS ARRESTED FOR SIT-IN AT ATLANTA RESTAURANT

Martin Luther King, Jr., and about fifty Blacks were arrested for a sit-in at an Atlanta department-store restaurant. A judge in Decatur, Georgia, revoked King's previous parole for conviction on a minor traffic violation and sentenced him to four months in Georgia's maximum security prison. President-elect John F. Kennedy and his brother Robert assisted in obtaining King's release.

NEGRO AMERICAN LABOR COUNCIL

Since the AFL-CIO was slow to desegregate its union leadership hierarchy and many of its union affiliates, A. Philip Randolph founded the Negro American Labor Council to give Blacks equal access to union jobs and to protest the slow pace of desegregation by the unions.

RUDOLPH NAMED FEMALE ATHLETE OF THE YEAR

The Associated Press selected track star Wilma Rudolph as Female Athlete of the Year. Rudolph had overcome the effects of polio to win three gold medals at the 1960 Olympics.

SEGREGATION IN SCHOOLS CONTINUES

Six years after the Supreme Court prohibited segregation in the schools, only 6 percent of the schools in the South had begun to integrate. Several states had not even begun the process, including Alabama, Florida, Louisiana, Mississippi, and South Carolina.

STUDENT NON-VIOLENT COORDINATING COMMITTEE FOUNDED

The Student Non-Violent Coordinating Committee (SNCC) was organized at Shaw University in Raleigh, North Carolina. The group established a nationwide network of student sit-in activities.

VOTING RIGHTS ACT PASSED

President Eisenhower signed the Voting Rights Act at the end of his term. The law, sometimes called the Civil Rights Act of 1960, was designed to bolster the act of 1957. It granted additional protection to Blacks trying to obtain suffrage. Under the new law, whenever the government found a pattern or practice of depriving Blacks of their vote, it could enfranchise the entire affected area. In addition, federal courts were authorized to appoint "voting referees," who were empowered to register Blacks in areas where racial discrimination against voters had been proven.

WARWICK BECOMES SINGING STAR

Dionne Warwick began her solo singing career when she teamed up with Burt Bacharach and Hal David. Their songs became instant hits, and Warwick won three Grammys. Among her successful songs is "What Do You Get When You Fall in Love?"

Warwick was born in East Orange, New Jersey. She started her singing career as part of a gospel trio with her sister Dee Dee and cousin Cissy Houston. Whitney Houston, one of the most popular singers today, is a relative.

WAVE OF SIT-INS BEGINS IN GREENSBORO

On **FEBRUARY 1**, four Black North Carolina Agricultural & Technical State University freshmen occupied seats at a Woolworth's lunch counter in Greensboro, North Carolina; they were refused service. Their action set in motion a wave of nonviolent sit-ins that reached every major city in the country. In less then two weeks, the movement had spread to fifteen cities in five southern states; within two years, it diffused throughout the entire South. Sit-ins provoked strong reactions from whites. In Greensboro itself, it took about seven months of sit-ins to desegregate public facilities there. During this time, more than sixty-eight sit-ins had occurred in thirteen states — from Columbia, South Carolina, to Houston, Texas. In Marshall, Texas, police used fire hoses to break up the sit-in protesters at a lunch counter. Most of these sit-ins met with heavy resistance, sometimes including armed assault. For example, in a wade-in in Biloxi, Mississippi, as many as ten Blacks were wounded by gunfire. In Jacksonville, Florida, a race riot erupted, and as many as fifty persons were injured. And in a kneel-in in Atlanta, Georgia, acid was thrown in a protester's face. Most of these protests were held in variety stores serving inexpensive lunchtime meals. Martin Luther King, Jr., assumed leadership of the movement. The sit-ins were successful, though they entailed major costs; more than seventeen school districts and countless stores, beaches, libraries, and movie theaters were integrated as a result.

PROTEST AGAINST SEGREGATION IN ALABAMA

On **MARCH 9**, about one thousand Black students protested against segregation on the steps of the former Confederate capitol building in Montgomery, Alabama. Elroy Embry, the protest organizer, warned those who could not protest peacefully to stay away because of extreme racial tension in the city.

RACE RIOT BREAKS OUT IN MISSISSIPPI

On **APRIL 24**, a major race riot erupted in Biloxi, Mississippi, after Blacks moved onto a section of the Biloxi beach reserved for whites only. Armed whites gathered, and shots were fired. City leaders blamed the NAACP for inciting the violence, during which as many as eight Blacks and two whites were shot.

RESTRICTIONS ON BLACK VOTING END IN TENNESSEE

On **APRIL 25**, the federal court ended restrictions against Black voting in Fayette County, Tennessee. It was the first voting case under the Civil Rights Act of 1957.

BELAFONTE WINS EMMY

On **JUNE 20**, Harry Belafonte was awarded an Emmy for his television special "Tonight with Harry Belafonte," becoming the first African American to win an Emmy.

BLACK STATE CALLED FOR BY NATION OF ISLAM

On **JULY 31**, Elijah Muhammad, in a meeting of the Nation of Islam in New York City, called for the creation of a Black state in this country. In his rationale for creating this state, he purported that "Blacks and whites do not get along together" in the same residential space.

SCHOOLS INTEGRATED IN VIRGINIA

On **AUGUST 15**, schools in Richmond and Roanoke, Virginia, were integrated.

JOHNSON WINS DECATHLON

On **SEPTEMBER 6**, Rafer Johnson, a six-foot-three African American, made Olympic decathlon history. Johnson had been slightly ahead of his schoolmate C. K. Yang in points, but it was in the 1,500-meter race that Johnson pulled ahead in a dramatic head-to-head competition. He clocked in at only 1.2 seconds less than Yang, to set an Olympic decathlon record of 8,392 points, beating Yang by only 58 points. Yang had won four of the first five Olympic decathlon events, but he trailed Johnson by 55 points. Johnson excelled in the shot put, which put him ahead. With only the 1,500-meter run remaining, Yang was ahead in all six of the running and jumping events, and Johnson dominated the three throwing events; he led by 67 points. It was up to Johnson to remain within 10 seconds of Yang's anticipated victory in the 1,500-meter race. Johnson stayed at the heels of Yang throughout the race and finished only 1.2 seconds behind Yang. As a result, Johnson won the Olympic decathlon by 58 points.

The decathlon is a ten-event track-and-field competition comprising the 100-meter dash; the 400-meter and 1,500-meter races; the 110-meter hurdle race; pole vaulting; discus throwing; shot putting; javelin throwing; and the broad and high jumps. This event has been part of the Olympic Games since 1912.

Johnson was born on August 18, 1934, in Hillsboro, Texas. Johnson was honored by being selected to light the torch in the 1984 Olympic Games in Los Angeles.

HATCHER WINS APPOINTMENT IN KENNEDY ADMINISTRATION

On **NOVEMBER 10**, Andrew Hatcher (1925–), a journalist, was named associate press secretary by President-elect John F. Kennedy, becoming the highest-ranking Black appointee in the executive branch of the federal government to date.

LEGISLATURE INTERFERES WITH DESEGREGATION IN NEW ORLEANS

On **NOVEMBER 10**, U.S. District Judge J. Skelley Wright prohibited implementation of laws against integration. On the same day, the New Orleans school board approved plans to admit five Black children to two previously all-white schools. On November 13, the state legislature acted to prevent integration and took control of the city's schools, fired the school superintendent, and ordered all schools closed on November 14. At the same time, Judge Wright issued a new order, prohibiting interference in the schools by the state. On November 14, four Black children enrolled in the two schools amid the jeering of angry mobs of white parents. White protests and a boycott by whites continued for much of the school year.

SEGREGATION IN BUS TERMINALS ENDED

On **DECEMBER 5**, the U.S. Supreme Court ruled in *Boynton* v. *Virginia* that segregation in bus terminals serving interstate passengers was a violation of the Interstate Commerce Act.

1961 DU BOIS MOVES TO GHANA

Civil rights leader W. E. B. Du Bois, one of the original founders of the NAACP, moved to Ghana in West Africa and became a citizen of that country. He wrote, "My great-grandfather was carried away in chains from the Gulf of Guinea. I have returned so that my dust shall mingle with the dust of my forefathers." Du Bois died in Ghana in 1963 at the age of ninety-five.

HEISMAN TROPHY AWARDED TO DAVIS

The Heisman Memorial Trophy was awarded to Ernie Davis for outstanding play as one of the nation's most gifted football athletes. This award was given to the best college football player by the Downtown Athletic Club (DAC) of New York City. The trophy was named after John W. Heisman, who coached Georgia Tech to the national championship in 1917 and later served as athletic director of the DAC.

MCLENDON NAMED CLEVELAND PIPERS COACH

John McLendon was selected to coach the Cleveland Pipers in the American Basketball League. He became the first Black coach of a predominantly white professional team.

MARSHALL APPOINTED CIRCUIT COURT JUDGE

President Kennedy appointed Thurgood Marshall, chief counsel for the NAACP, as judge of the Second U.S. Circuit Court of Appeals (the area including New York, Connecticut, and Vermont).

PARSONS APPOINTED JUDGE

President Kennedy appointed James B. Parsons (1913–1993) as judge of the District of Northern Illinois. He became the first Black to secure such a position in the continental United States.

Parsons was born in Kansas City, Missouri, and studied music at Milliken University. After his graduation in 1934, he worked at various positions at Lincoln University in Jefferson City, Missouri, including acting head of the music department. Parsons served in the U.S. Navy from 1942 to 1945, and in 1949, he received his law degree from the University of Chicago. Parsons joined a Chicago law firm, taught constitutional law, and served as assistant corporation counsel for Chicago until 1951, when he became assistant U.S. district attorney. He later served as a judge on the Superior Court in Cook County.

POLICE MOVE PROTESTERS BY FORCE IN MISSISSIPPI

City police with clubs and dogs were summoned to the courthouse in Jackson, Mississippi, to move approximately one hundred Black protesters. Several Blacks were injured in the confrontation.

BLACK HEISMAN TROPHY WINNERS

YEAR	PLAYER	COLLEGE	POSITION
1961	Ernie Davis	Syracuse	Halfback
1965	Mike Garrett	Southern California	Halfback
1968	O. J. Simpson	Southern California	Halfback
1972	Johnny Rodgers	Nebraska	Flanker
1974	Archie Griffin	Ohio State	Halfback
1975	Archie Griffin	Ohio State	Halfback
1976	Tony Dorsett	Pittsburgh	Halfback
1977	Earl Campbell	Texas	Halfback
1978	Billy Sims	Oklahoma	Halfback
1979	Charles White	Southern California	Halfback
1980	George Rogers	South Carolina	Halfback
1981	Marcus Allen	Southern California	Halfback
1982	Herschel Walker	Georgia	Halfback
1983	Mike Rozier	Nebraska	Halfback
1985	Bo Jackson	Auburn	Halfback
1987	Tim Brown	Notre Dame	Wide receiver
1988	Barry Sanders	Oklahoma State	Rightback
1989	Andre Ware	Houston	Quarterback

Source: *Sports Illustrated: 1992 Sports Almanac* (Boston: Little, Brown and Company, 1991), 170.

POWELL CHAIRS HOUSE EDUCATION AND LABOR COMMITTEE

Representative Adam Clayton Powell, Jr., of Harlem became chairperson of the powerful House Education and Labor Committee.

PROPORTION OF OUT-OF-WEDLOCK BIRTHS HIGHER AMONG BLACKS

There were almost 4.3 million births in the nation in this year, of which 240,000 (6 percent) were out of wedlock. Of the 667,000 Black births, roughly 22 percent were out of wedlock. Only 2 percent of white births were so classified.

RACE RIOT OCCURS AT UNIVERSITY OF GEORGIA

An anti-Black riot resulted in the suspension of two recently admitted Black students (Charlayne Hunter and Hamilton Holmes) at the University of Georgia.

A federal court ordered the University of Georgia to admit Blacks, including Charlayne Hunter, one of the major complainants. Hunter became the first Black to successfully integrate and graduate from the University of Georgia. Hunter became a news reporter for public television's news program *The MacNeil/Lehrer Report*.

ROBERTSON NAMED ROOKIE OF THE YEAR

Oscar Robertson, already a star basketball player for the Cincinnati Royals of the National Basketball Association (NBA), was voted the NBA Rookie of the Year. Robertson was noted for his scoring and his passing ability.

ROBINSON NAMED MOST VALUABLE PLAYER

Frank Robinson of the Cincinnati Reds was named the National League's Most Valuable Player. He was one of the major reasons the Cincinnati Reds won the pennant. He hit 37 home runs, batted in 127 runs, and attained a .342 batting average.

RUDOLPH NAMED FEMALE ATHLETE OF THE YEAR
Track star Wilma Rudolph was again selected by the Associated Press as Female Athlete of the Year.

SCHOOLS DESEGREGATE PEACEFULLY IN ATLANTA
Four high schools in Atlanta, Georgia, were peacefully desegregated as ten Black children entered classrooms.

SUPREME COURT PROHIBITS GERRYMANDERING
The U.S. Supreme Court, in *Gomillion* v. *Lightfoot,* held that Tuskegee's gerrymandering was an unconstitutional "essay in geometry and geography" that deprived Blacks of their right to vote in city elections.

Gerrymandering transformed this small Alabama town, where the Black electorate outnumbered the white, from a square into a strange, irregular twenty-eight-sided figure, with the intention of redrawing town boundaries to exclude all but four or five of its four hundred Black voters, while not moving a single white voter or resident. The redefining of districts was designed to prevent Blacks from voting in municipal elections.

SUPREMES FORMED
Diana Ross, Mary Wilson, and Florence Ballard formed the Supremes, one of the most dynamic, successful singing groups with the Motown label. The group recorded fifteen consecutive hit singles and was instrumental in developing the "Motown sound" that made Detroit a center of popular music during the 1960s. Ross eventually separated from the group to pursue a number of personal interests, and the group was never really successful without her.

WEAVER FILLS TOP GOVERNMENT POSITION
Robert Weaver, a housing expert with a Harvard Ph.D., assumed the post of administrator of the Housing and Home Finance Agency, the highest federal post ever held by a Black American up to that time.

WHARTON NAMED AMBASSADOR TO NORWAY
Clifton Wharton was appointed U.S. ambassador to Norway. Although many saw Kennedy's appointment as a sign of tokenism, it represented an awareness that Blacks needed to be included as representatives of the United States.

Whitney Young, a moderate, became the executive director of the National Urban League in 1961. Young engaged white business leaders in helping to improve conditions for urban Blacks.

YOUNG BECOMES DIRECTOR OF NATIONAL URBAN LEAGUE
Whitney Young, Jr. (1921–1971), already a noted civil rights leader, was selected to be executive director of the National Urban League, one of the major civil rights organizations in the country. Young dedicated his energies to improving employment and housing for Blacks throughout the country. He remained in the directorship until 1971, when he died while attending a meeting in Africa.

◆ Young was born in Lincoln Ridge, Kentucky. He received a B.S. degree from Kentucky State College in 1941 and an M.A. degree from the University of Minnesota in 1947. In 1950, he assumed the post of executive director of the Omaha Urban League. From

1950 to 1954, Young was on the faculty of the University of Nebraska School for Social Work. After becoming the executive director of the National Urban League, he called for a "domestic Marshall Plan" that would address the economic and educational problems of Black Americans. Young was considered a moderate civil rights leader, preferring to work within the existing system and encouraging businesses and individual whites to help in the struggle:

FREEDOM RIDES BEGIN

On **MARCH 13**, James Farmer of CORE invited volunteers to participate in freedom rides throughout the South to test discrimination in terminals for interstate travel (restaurants, restrooms, and waiting areas). Segregation in these facilities had just been prohibited by the Supreme Court decision in *Boynton* v. *Virginia*. Farmer also wanted to test how the administration in Washington would respond. On May 4, seven Blacks and six whites left Washington, D.C., in two groups, one on a Greyhound bus and the other on a Trailways bus. They traveled to Richmond, Petersburg, and Lynchburg, Virginia, without incident. On May 9, however, violence erupted at the Greyhound station in Rock Hill, South Carolina. Here, Black volunteer John Lewis was clubbed and beaten

Formal colored facilities still existed throughout much of the South despite the U.S. Supreme Court decision intended to abolish them. CORE organized freedom riders to test whether and where segregation still existed.

by whites when he tried to sit in a whites-only wait-ing room. Others in the group were also beaten, and the police intervened only after one of the women had been pushed to the ground. No arrests were made, and the riders were allowed to enter the wait-ing room. The riders then proceeded to Sumter, Cam-den, Augusta, Athens, and Atlanta, Georgia, without further incident. They regrouped there to begin their journey into Alabama and Mississippi. On May 14, a white mob attacked freedom riders (Blacks and whites) at a bus station in Birmingham, Alabama. Six days later, freedom riders were attacked by a white mob of one thousand in Montgomery, Alabama, and as many as twenty were injured. In an effort to curb integration efforts in Mississippi, more than twenty-seven freedom riders were jailed in Jackson on May 24, and another seventeen were jailed four days later for defying a federal injunction prohibiting their ac-tivity. White segregationists, including Ku Klux Klan members, followed freedom riders throughout the South, causing racial violence in many cities. The in-tent of freedom riders was to destroy state and inter-state segregation policies. Attorney General Robert F. Kennedy responded to the violence and political pres-sure by sending U.S. marshals to Alabama. In addi-tion, the governor of Alabama declared martial law and dispatched the National Guard to calm certain areas. The U.S. Supreme Court voided the first group of sit-in convictions.

DISCRIMINATION IN PUBLIC ACCOMMODATION PROHIBITED IN ST. LOUIS

In **MAY**, the St. Louis Board of Aldermen passed a "public accommodation" ordinance prohibiting dis-crimination in public places because of race or reli-gious beliefs. It was to be administered by the St. Louis Council of Human Relations. William Lacy Clay was one of the aldermen involved in the intro-duction and passing of this ordinance. Clay was later elected to the U.S. House of Representatives.

NATIONAL GUARDMEMBERS BATTLE WHITES IN MONTGOMERY

On **MAY 20**, more than four hundred National Guardmembers battled with whites to ensure the safety and security of the Reverend Martin Luther King, Jr., and fifteen hundred people in a Montgomery church.

KING ORGANIZES VOTING REGISTRATION DRIVE IN THE SOUTH

Because of flagrant abuses of Blacks' right to vote, the Reverend Martin Luther King, Jr., officially started a voting registration drive in the South on **SEPTEMBER 25**. Several months earlier, the White Citizens' Council and the Louisiana county registrar had been charged with violating the voting rights of Black citizens.

1962 ALBANY MOVEMENT FORMED TO COMBAT DISCRIMINATION

The Albany Movement, a citywide effort in Albany, Georgia, to abolish discrimination in all public facili-ties was formed. It was supported by the Southern Christian Leadership Conference (SCLC), the Student Non-Violent Coordinating Committee (SNCC), the NAACP, and CORE. Led by Dr. Martin Luther King, Jr., the SCLC sponsored a number of demonstrations to integrate public facilities and open employment op-portunities for Blacks. The local police responded with force — beating and jailing hundreds of demon-strators. Because of the difficulty the movement en-countered here, many civil rights leaders began to question the effectiveness of mass marches, sit-ins, and other traditional forms of protest.

BLACK OFFICIALS ELECTED

Several Blacks were elected to important posts in this year: Otis M. Smith, auditor general of Michigan; Gerald A. Lamb, state treasurer of Connecticut; and Edward Dudley, borough president of Manhattan in New York City.

BLACKS REMAIN DISPROPORTIONATELY POOR

A recent Bureau of the Census publication showed that about 44 percent of all Black families in the country were living in poverty, compared with 17 percent of all white families. In rural areas, 84 per-cent of Blacks on farms lived in poverty; 85 percent of all Black rural farm families lived in the South.

BROOKE ELECTED AS MASSACHUSETTS ATTORNEY GENERAL

Edward W. Brooke III, a lawyer from Boston, was elected attorney general for the state of Massachu-setts, becoming the highest-ranking Black official in New England. He served in this position until 1966, at which time he was elected to the U.S. Senate.

◇ Brooke was born on October 26, 1919, in Wash-ington, D.C. He received a B.S. degree from Howard

University in 1941, served in the U.S. Army with the 366th Infantry Regiment, returned to school, and received an LL.B. from Boston University Law School in 1948. In 1950, he received the LL.M. from the same school. Brooke entered politics in 1960, when he ran for the post of secretary of the commonwealth. Although he lost the election, he was selected chairperson of Boston's finance commission.

Brooke, a moderate, served the U.S. Senate and the Black community in a number of ways. He was a strong supporter of school integration, public housing, affirmative action, minority business development, and expanding minimum wage standards.

Brooke was defeated in the Republican primary of 1978 and returned to practicing law in Washington, D.C.

CHAMBERLAIN BREAKS RECORDS FOR PHILADELPHIA WARRIORS

Wilt Chamberlain, playing center for the Philadelphia Warriors, scored 100 points against the New York Knickerbockers. He broke several records in the Warriors' 169–147 victory, including 36 field goals, most points for a quarter (31), most points for a half (59), and highest percentage of free throws (28 of 32). He also broke his own previous record of total game points (78).

CHURCHES BURNED IN GEORGIA

Two Black churches were burned to the ground by white supremacists in Sasser, Georgia.

GAYE SIGNS MOTOWN CONTRACT

Marvin Gaye (1939–1984) signed a contract with Motown in this year, a relationship that helped make Motown and Detroit, Michigan, one of the major centers of popular music. Teamed with Berry Gordy, Jr., the owner of Motown, Gaye made a number of smash hits throughout his twenty-two-year career. Gaye teamed up with new musicians to promote their work. For example, his performances with Mary Wells and Tami Terrell launched their careers. His song "Pride and Joy" hit the top of the charts. Other songs had crossover audiences, for example, "What's Going On," and "Midnight Love." Gaye received the NAACP's Image Award in 1973 and a UNESCO award in 1975.

GRAVELY COMMANDS DESTROYER ESCORT

Lieutenant Commander Samuel L. Gravely received command of the USS *Falgout*, a destroyer escort. He

Lieutenant Commander Samuel Gravely took command of the warship USS Falgout *in 1962. Nine years later, he became the first African American to earn the rank of rear admiral.*

became the first Black to command a U.S. warship. ◈ Born in Richmond, Virginia, in 1922, Gravely was the first Black ensign commissioned in World War II. He received a B.A. degree from Virginia Union University in 1948 but was recalled by the navy in 1949. In 1971, Gravely became the first Black rear admiral, and five years later, he assumed command of the U.S. Third Fleet. He retired from the navy in 1980.

HAWKINS ELECTED TO CONGRESS

Augustus Hawkins, elected to the U.S. House of Representatives of the Eighty-eighth Congress, became the first Black to represent California. He represented California's Twenty-first District (Los Angeles).

In 1962, Hawkins was elected to the U.S. Congress as the first Black Representative from a western state. Within a short time of taking his seat, Hawkins sponsored legislation on job creation and civil rights. He worked diligently to secure the passage of the Equal Employment Opportunity Commission in Title VII of the Civil Rights Act of 1964. With Hubert

Humphrey, Hawkins cosponsored the Full Employment and Balanced Growth Act (the Humphrey-Hawkins Act) of 1978. In the Ninety-eighth Congress, he became chairperson of the powerful Committee on Education and Labor. He also served as the chair of several other key committees — House Administration, Joint Committee on the Library, and Joint Committee on Printing.

◈ Hawkins was born in Shreveport, Louisiana, on August 31, 1907. At about eleven years of age, he moved with his family to California. Hawkins attended high school in Los Angeles and went on to the University of California at Los Angeles, where he received an undergraduate degree in 1931. Four years later, Hawkins was elected to the California Assembly, where he served until he was elected to Congress. During this relatively long career as a California legislator, Hawkins was successful in securing better housing, employment, and disability insurance for low-income and minority residents.

INCOME GAP BETWEEN BLACKS AND WHITES STILL SIGNIFICANT

According to the Bureau of the Census, the ratio of Black earnings to white among full-time employees was 63 percent, representing a gap of $2,226.

JOHNSON ELECTED TO GEORGIA SENATE

Leroy Johnson, a lawyer, was elected to the Georgia Senate — the state's first Black legislator since Reconstruction.

MEREDITH IS FIRST BLACK STUDENT AT UNIVERSITY OF MISSISSIPPI

James Meredith enrolled at the University of Mississippi in the fall, but the governor of Mississippi, Ross Barnett, blocked Meredith's admission. White segregationists and KKK members made the campus a hotbed of controversy. On the day Meredith entered the university, major violence erupted, and many outsiders came onto the campus. About fifty people were

James Meredith was escorted by U.S. marshals on the campus of Ole Miss.

injured. President John F. Kennedy dispatched three thousand troops after two people died in racial riots.

Meredith, a political science student, had previously attended Jackson State College, after spending nine years in the air force. In August 1963, Meredith became the first Black to graduate from the University of Mississippi. Federal troops remained on campus during his entire stay.

MISSISSIPPI USES FORCE TO MAINTAIN SEGREGATION
Because of Mississippi's stubborn resistance to school integration and its use of the state's National Guard to maintain segregation by force, President John F. Kennedy federalized the Mississippi National Guard and ordered the state to speed integration.

NAACP SUES ROCHESTER, NEW YORK, SCHOOL SYSTEM
The NAACP sued the Rochester school system for de facto segregation. The group claimed that Rochester's housing patterns influenced racial segregation in the school system and that such housing patterns were affected by public policies regarding the location of single-family, multifamily, and public housing throughout the city.

SEGREGATIONISTS EXCOMMUNICATED FROM ROMAN CATHOLIC CHURCH
Joseph Rummel, Roman Catholic archbishop, excommunicated three deacons in Louisiana for their outspoken opposition to his order to end desegregation and integrate parochial schools in New Orleans.

STOKES ELECTED TO OHIO LEGISLATURE
Carl Stokes, at age thirty-five, became the first Black Democrat elected to the Ohio House of Representatives. He was elected from a county whose population was only 8 percent Black.

SUPREME COURT OVERTURNS FREEDOM RIDERS' CONVICTIONS
The U.S. Supreme Court overturned the convictions of six freedom riders.

ROBINSON INDUCTED INTO BASEBALL HALL OF FAME
On JULY 3, Jackie Robinson was inducted into the Baseball Hall of Fame at Cooperstown, New York, becoming the first Black to be a member of this great cadre of famous players. Robinson was credited with breaking the "color barrier" in baseball.

His exceptional hitting and base stealing earned Robinson Rookie of the Year and Most Valuable Player awards; he led the Brooklyn Dodgers to the National League Championship in 1955. Robinson played for the Brooklyn Dodgers from 1947 to 1956.

GOODE BECOMES TELEVISION NEWS COMMENTATOR
On AUGUST 29, Mal Goode was selected as news commentator on ABC-TV. He became the first African American network television news commentator. He was hired to cover the United Nations.

HIGGINBOTHOM APPOINTED TO FEDERAL TRADE COMMISSION
On SEPTEMBER 26, A. Leon Higginbothom, Jr., was appointed a member of the Federal Trade Commission, becoming the first African American on this important domestic policy commission. Later, Higginbothom became a federal district judge and a justice of the Third U.S. Circuit Court.

LISTON KNOCKS OUT PATTERSON
On SEPTEMBER 26, Sonny Liston knocked out Floyd Patterson to become the world heavyweight boxing champion.

RACIAL DISCRIMINATION PROHIBITED IN FEDERALLY ASSISTED HOUSING
On NOVEMBER 20, President John F. Kennedy signed an executive order prohibiting racial discrimination in housing built or purchased with federal assistance.

1963 BLACK CADETS GRADUATE FROM AIR FORCE ACADEMY
Three Blacks who entered the Air Force Academy in 1959 — Charles V. Bush, Isaac S. Payne IV, and Roger B. Sims — graduated in 1963.

Although Blacks were not part of the first class graduating in June 1959 from the newly established Air Force Academy at Denver, Colorado, Black attendance and graduation have been steady since then.

BRADLEY ELECTED TO LOS ANGELES CITY COUNCIL
Thomas Bradley was elected to the Los Angeles city council, becoming the first elected Black official in Los Angeles and only the second California Black elected to public office.

HOWARD NAMED MOST VALUABLE PLAYER
Elston Howard of the New York Yankees became the first Black baseball player in the American League to win the Most Valuable Player award.

JONES ACCLAIMED FOR *Othello* PERFORMANCE

James Earl Jones (1931–) received critical acclaim for his performance in the title role in *Othello.*

In 1968, Jones proved his acting skill when he portrayed Jack Johnson in *The Great White Hope,* a stage production that signaled his rising talents. In 1986, he gave a superior performance in the Broadway production of *Fences,* for which he won a Tony. His distinctively resonant voice and acting skill have kept him in demand both in the theater and in films. He starred in the most acclaimed African American productions of the 1970s, 1980s, and 1990s — *Roots, Queen,* and *Malcolm X.*

KENNEDY CALLS CIVIL RIGHTS A "MORAL ISSUE"

President John F. Kennedy declared that the Black struggle for civil rights was a "moral issue." He called upon Congress to strengthen voting rights, create job opportunities for Blacks, and enforce school integration.

KENNEDY'S CIVIL RIGHTS POLICIES CRITICIZED

Malcolm X, the leader of the Black Muslims, criticized the Kennedy administration's civil rights policies as "inactive" and ineffective. The Reverend Martin Luther King, Jr., James Baldwin, and Malcolm X publicly called President Kennedy's overall leadership during these turbulent times inadequate and misinformed.

POITIER WINS ACADEMY AWARD

Sidney Poitier was the first Black to win an Academy Award for best actor, for his performance in *Lilies of the Field.* Poitier became one of the most sought-after African American film stars.

Poitier turned in outstanding performances in a number of other major films — *Porgy and Bess* (1959), *A Patch of Blue* (1965), which he also directed, *The Blackboard Jungle* (1965), and *In the Heat of the Night* (1967). His powerful performance in *In the Heat of the Night* prompted a television series of the same title. In 1980, he directed *Stir Crazy,* one of the most successful films made by an African American director.

PROTESTERS ARRESTED IN BALTIMORE

Approximately 298 protesters (mostly Blacks) were arrested in an attempt to integrate an all-white amusement park near Baltimore, Maryland. Included among those arrested were the Reverend Eugene C. Blake,

Dr. Martin Luther King, Jr., and Malcolm X held a conference in Washington in 1963 to criticize President Kennedy's civil rights policies.

head of the Presbyterian Church, and other Protestant, Catholic, and Jewish religious leaders. Park owners refused to yield to their demands for integration.

RUSTIN ORGANIZES MARCH ON WASHINGTON

Bayard Rustin (1910–1987), a civil rights leader who helped to found the Southern Christian Leadership Conference, was one of the organizers (with A. Philip Randolph) of the 1963 March on Washington. Rustin contended that the march should concentrate on the need for federal action in securing jobs, housing, and education for Blacks. But in the weeks before the march, the focus changed to more traditional political objectives, in part to secure the support of moderate Blacks such as Roy Wilkins of the NAACP.

Rustin had a long career pursuing equal rights for Blacks. In 1941, he founded the New York branch of the Congress of Racial Equality (CORE). As a conscientious objector during World War II, Rustin served a two-and-a-half-year prison term. He was one of the organizers of the first freedom ride in 1947 to test compliance with the antidiscriminatory interstate travel laws in the South. From 1955 to 1964, Rustin was the chief tactician of the civil rights movement. He worked with Dr. Martin Luther King, Jr., in the Montgomery bus boycott and served as King's assistant for seven years. He emphasized peaceful direct action and was instrumental in developing King's philosophy of nonviolence. In 1964, he became executive director of the A. Philip Randolph Institute.

SUPREME COURT DECISIONS SUPPORT CIVIL RIGHTS MOVEMENT

In the spring of this year, the U.S. Supreme Court's decisions in a number of cases strengthened the civil rights movement. On April 29, it ruled that segregation in courtrooms was unconstitutional. On May 20, it ruled that state and local governments could not interfere with peaceful sit-ins for racial integration of public places of business. On May 27, the court prohibited an "indefinite delay" in the desegregation of public schools.

WHITE COLLAR JOBS CLOSED TO BLACKS

According to information given by former secretary of commerce Luther H. Hodges in an address at the Equal Opportunity Day dinner of the National Urban League, "Negroes, to a very large extent, have been

The F. W. Woolworth store in Birmingham, Alabama, turned its lunch counter into a flower mart to avoid racial integration.

excluded from the white-collar occupations which, since 1947, have accounted for 97 percent of the total increase in United States employment."

WALLACE BECOMES GOVERNOR OF ALABAMA
At his inauguration, on **JANUARY 14**, Governor George Wallace of Alabama declared, "segregation now, segregation tomorrow, and segregation forever." During the year, Wallace made many stands against integrating schools, including the University of Alabama and Tuskegee High School. When the Alabama National Guard was federalized, Wallace gave up. Twenty Black students entered the public schools in Tuskegee and Mobile.

BLACKS ADMITTED TO TULANE UNIVERSITY IN NEW ORLEANS
On **JANUARY 25**, five Black students became the first admitted to Tulane University in New Orleans, Louisiana.

CONVICTION OF PROTESTERS OVERTURNED BY SUPREME COURT
On **FEBRUARY 25**, the U.S. Supreme Court overturned the convictions of 187 Blacks found guilty of illegal protest activities in South Carolina.

PEACEFUL MARCH TURNS VIOLENT IN ALABAMA
On **APRIL 12**, church leaders Martin Luther King, Jr., and Ralph Abernathy, and Fred L. Shuttlesworth led a peaceful march in Birmingham to protest the city's racial barriers. King and Abernathy, along with about fifty-eight others, were arrested for parading without a permit. Their arrests caused a violent confrontation between about two thousand Blacks and police. Hundreds of Blacks and some police were injured. On April 14, as many as thirty protesters were arrested for their part in the violence. Marches and violence became a way of life in many cities of Alabama. A political showdown between Alabama governor George Wallace and President John F. Kennedy and U.S. Attorney General Robert Kennedy threatened as Governor Wallace refused to abide by federal integration orders and used state resources to enforce school segregation. During the first six days of May, more than fifteen hundred Blacks were arrested in protest marches in Birmingham. Some were hurt when the police dispersed crowds with fire hoses.

Fred Shuttlesworth, a clergyman, was an active civil rights leader in Alabama and with the Southern Christian Leadership Conference.

BLACK CHILDREN ARRESTED
On **MAY 31**, some six hundred Black children were arrested and jailed for protesting.

BLACKS ADMITTED TO UNIVERSITY OF ALABAMA
On **JUNE 11**, two Black students (Vivian Malone and James Hood) were admitted to the University of Alabama, although Governor George Wallace physically blocked their entrance to the building where they registered. Later that day, a federal court enabled the two students to register. National Guardmembers were federalized by President Kennedy and ordered to ensure the students' enrollment. This historic moment, captured on national television, marked the crumbling of the walls of segregation that had long

prohibited the entry of Blacks into predominantly white universities throughout the country.

EVERS MURDERED IN MISSISSIPPI

NAACP field secretary Medgar Evers was murdered on **JUNE 12** in the doorway of his home in Jackson, Mississippi. His alleged assailant, Byron De La Beckwith, a white racist and segregationist, was acquitted by a hung jury. Violence erupted in a number of cities throughout the South as a result. In Jackson, Blacks flooded the streets, hurling rocks and bottles and destroying property. As many as twenty-seven were ar-

rested. The NAACP offered a ten-thousand-dollar reward for information leading to the arrest and conviction of the leader's assassin. Evers was buried at Arlington National Cemetery, among others who had fought for America's ideals.

MARCH ON WASHINGTON DRAWS 250,000 AMERICANS

On **AUGUST 28**, the March on Washington attracted more than 250,000 Americans from all walks of life to one of the largest single protest events in American history. The marchers gathered on the steps of

Peaceful demonstrators in Birmingham, Alabama, were met by angry white citizens and police brutality. The police were instructed to use attack dogs as well as any other means necessary to disrupt the protests. Photographs such as this one elicited nationwide sympathy and support for the civil rights movement.

This view from the Lincoln Memorial shows only a small portion of the 250,000 people who gathered for the March on Washington protesting the plight of Black people.

the Lincoln Memorial to dramatize the discontent of many Americans with the plight of Black people. A. Philip Randolph and Bayard Rustin led the march. The Reverend Martin Luther King, Jr., delivered his immortal "I Have a Dream" oration. The slogan of the March on Washington was "Jobs and Freedom Now."

INTEGRATED SCHOOLS CLOSED

In the month of **SEPTEMBER**, many schools scheduled to integrate for the coming school year remained closed. In Birmingham, several schools remained closed for this reason. Alabama's governor, George Wallace, also called the state police to prevent the in-

tegration of Tuskegee High School. Many public schools throughout the states of South Carolina and Louisiana, however, were integrated.

BOMB KILLS FOUR GIRLS IN BIRMINGHAM, ALABAMA

On Sunday, **SEPTEMBER 15**, a bomb exploded in the Sixteenth Street Baptist Church, killing four young Black girls — Addie May Collins, Denise McNair, Carole Robertson, and Cynthia Wesley — who were attending Sunday school. This atrocity was considered by many as the turning point in the civil rights struggle in Birmingham. The vicious act precipitated a day of rioting, during which two Black youths were

The Sixteenth Street Baptist Church in Birmingham, Alabama, was the site of a bombing that killed four young Black girls. It was targeted because many civil rights meetings and voting instruction sessions were held there.

killed. Two white men were arrested for perpetrating the bombing but were later released.

It was not until 1977 that Robert E. Chambliss was convicted of the crime and sentenced to life in prison for the first-degree murder of Denise McNair. Chambliss had been a city employee and a member of the Ku Klux Klan.

◆ Before the bomb blast, Birmingham, which Blacks referred to as "the Johannesburg of America," had been the scene of many civil rights actions. In the spring of this year, the Southern Christian Leadership Conference and Martin Luther King, Jr., had called for an economic boycott of downtown businesses and a series of marches to bring about desegregation of public facilities and jobs. The city was infamous in part because of the actions of Police Commissioner "Bull" Connor and his all-white police force, which used water cannons and dogs against peaceful Black protesters. It was these actions, broadcast on nationwide television, that brought increased attention to and support of the civil rights struggle across the country.

Dr. Martin Luther King, Jr., was arrested in Birmingham during the protests. His belief in nonviolent protest was articulated in "Letter from Birmingham Jail," a defense of his civil rights activities addressed to church leaders of Birmingham. During the summer, pressure from federal authorities, including President Kennedy's federalization of the Alabama National Guard, forced Governor Wallace and city officials to comply with the court-ordered desegregation of the city. Tensions, however, did not abate. It was not until after the church bombing that Birmingham seemed to have had its fill of violence. Most members of the white community then accepted desegregation of the city.

BLACKS BOYCOTT CHICAGO SCHOOLS

On **OCTOBER 22**, a massive boycott, involving nearly a quarter of a million Black students, was staged in Chicago to protest de facto school desegregation. Other boycotts followed.

WELCOME BECOMES FIRST BLACK WOMAN ELECTED TO STATE SENATE

In **NOVEMBER**, Verda F. Welcome became the first Black woman elected to a state senate when she won the election in Maryland. Welcome sponsored many bills supporting equal opportunity, equal pay, and voter registration by mail. She had to overcome two major strikes against her: racial and gender discrimination.

Welcome was born in North Carolina and went to public schools in North Carolina and Delaware. She graduated from Morgan State College in 1939 and received a master's degree from New York University in 1943. She was a member of the Maryland House of Delegates from 1959 to 1963. She served on President Johnson's National Citizens' Committee for Community Relations. Welcome received the *Afro-American* newspaper's award for superior public service. She died in 1990 at the age of eighty-four.

MEDALS OF FREEDOM

On **DECEMBER 7**, President Lyndon Johnson awarded Ralph J. Bunche and Marian Anderson the Presidential Medal of Freedom, the nation's highest civilian decoration, for outstanding contributions to the ideals of freedom and democracy.

1964 CIVIL RIGHTS GROUPS REPORT VIOLENCE IN MISSISSIPPI

Civil rights groups in Mississippi reported that three people had been killed, three wounded, eighty physically assaulted, and over one thousand arrested. Also, thirty buildings (primarily homes and churches) had been bombed in Mississippi during the course of a year's civil rights activity.

CONGRESS PASSES CIVIL RIGHTS ACT

Congress passed the Civil Rights Act of 1964, which included provisions prohibiting discrimination in public accommodations and discrimination in employment. It was hailed by Blacks as the most important piece of civil rights legislation since 1875. President Lyndon Johnson signed the bill in the presence of major civil rights leaders, including Dr. Martin Luther King, Jr.

CONGRESS PASSES ECONOMIC OPPORTUNITY ACT

Congress passed the Economic Opportunity Act, a one-billion-dollar legislative package that included programs collectively known as the War on Poverty. Specific programs that significantly benefited Blacks included Head Start, Upward Bound, and college work-study educational programs.

CONYERS ELECTED TO CONGRESS

John Conyers, Jr., was elected to the Eighty-ninth Congress as representative for the First District in Michigan. As a member of the Judiciary Committee,

Conyers presided over hearings on criminal justice issues. He successfully sponsored legislation to provide literacy and vocational training to inmates of correctional facilities. He was a founder of the Congressional Black Caucus and was a principal sponsor of the Voting Rights Act of 1965, the Humphrey-Hawkins Full Employment Act of 1978, and the Martin Luther King, Jr., holiday bill in 1983. He continues to serve in the U.S. House of Representatives.

◇ Conyers was born in Detroit in 1929. He served with the U.S. Army in Korea and then entered Wayne State University, where he received a B.A. degree in 1957 and an LL.B. degree from the Law School in 1959. He worked as a legislative assistant to Representative John Dingell from 1958 to 1961. Conyers was active in the civil rights movement and was one of the founders of the National Lawyers Committee for Civil Rights Under Law. He also served as general counsel for the Detroit Trade Union Leadership Council.

FRANKLIN BECOMES CHAIRPERSON OF UNIVERSITY OF CHICAGO'S HISTORY DEPARTMENT

John Hope Franklin, one of the nation's foremost educators, was selected to chair the department of history at the University of Chicago.

Franklin received his Ph.D. from Harvard University. He wrote several books, including *The Free Negro in North Carolina, The Militant South 1800–1860, Color and Race*, and *From Slavery to Freedom*. Franklin was the first Black to be elected president of the Southern Historical Association and the American Historical Association.

FREEDOM DEMOCRATIC PARTY FORMED IN MISSISSIPPI

In response to intimidation and other racist tactics that prohibited many poor Blacks from registering to vote and participating in Mississippi politics, a coalition of civil rights organizations organized the Mississippi Freedom Democratic Party (MFDP). The MFDP sent a delegation headed by Fannie Lou Hamer to the Democratic National Convention and challenged the legitimacy of Mississippi's all-white delegation. Although they were not successful in taking the seats of white Democrats, they were able to show the state and the nation that white supremacist intimidation and violence would no longer work to suppress the demands for civil rights.

In a compromise proposed by Hubert Humphrey and Walter Mondale, Mississippi regulars would be seated if they swore loyalty to the national party, and two "at-large" seats were offered to the MFDP. The compromise failed when all but three regulars walked out of the convention and the MFDP delegation was removed from the floor when they attempted to take the seats of the party regulars.

Also during the convention, a split developed between the Student Non-Violent Coordinating Committee (SNCC) and the mainstream of the civil rights movement. Martin Luther King, Jr., James Farmer, Bayard Rustin, and Roy Wilkins had lobbied for the compromise; Hamer and SNCC felt that it was not enough. SNCC no longer worked for interracial plans, nonviolence, and civil rights but for liberation. The group was particularly angry at Dr. King, believing that he had betrayed them. Most African American leaders, embarrassed by SNCC's actions, distanced themselves from the group.

MALCOLM X FORMS ORGANIZATION OF AFRO-AMERICAN UNITY

Malcolm X (Malcolm Little; 1925–1965) broke with the Black Muslim movement of Elijah Muhammad to form the Organization of Afro-American Unity, a Black nationalist party. Also known as El-Hajj Malik El-Shabazz, Malcolm X expressed dissatisfaction with the nonviolent movement and preached "self-defense" against white supremacists. The Organization for Afro-American Unity embraced the mission to seek independence for Blacks throughout the Western Hemisphere.

Believing that his life story might be of some importance to Black people across the country, Malcolm X collaborated with Black author Alex Haley to write *The Autobiography of Malcolm X*, which described his conversion to the Black Muslim faith while in prison from 1946 to 1952 for burglary, and his transformation from Malcolm Little to Malcolm X — a Black Muslim minister — on his release. His autobiography was published in this year, describing various aspects of the Black Power movement in this country in the early 1960s. It became a classic. Malcolm X used his organization to encourage militancy regarding civil rights and equality. He was assassinated at a meeting of the Organization for Afro-American Unity in New York City in February 1965.

Malcolm X, a Black Muslim minister, was one of the most outspoken Black leaders of the early 1960s, advocating separatism and Black pride.

MOTLEY ELECTED TO NEW YORK SENATE

Constance Baker Motley was elected to the New York Senate, becoming the first African American elected to this body. In 1965, the New York City Council elected her president of the borough of Manhattan.

NAACP PROTESTS EMPLOYMENT DISCRIMINATION

The NAACP demonstrated in more than forty-one cities to break the general pattern of employment discrimination in private industry. General Motors was encouraged to employ Blacks in secretarial, manager-

ial, professional, and supervisory capacities for the first time.

NOBEL PEACE PRIZE AWARDED TO KING

Martin Luther King, Jr., (1929–1968), a Black leader who believed in nonviolent resistance to racial oppression, received the Nobel Peace Prize. At thirty-five years of age, King was the youngest man in history and the second Black American to receive the award. King was applauded for achieving the peaceful desegregation of buses during the Montgomery boycott in 1955. He was also cited for leading the nonviolent campaign to dismantle racism and segregation during the 1950s and 1960s.

PUBLIC ACCOMMODATIONS SECTION OF CIVIL RIGHTS ACT UPHELD

The U.S. Supreme Court upheld the constitutionality of the section of the Civil Rights Act of 1964 dealing with public accommodations. In *Heart of Atlanta Motel* v. *U.S.*, the Court declared that a motel could not refuse to rent rooms to Blacks.

RACE RIOTS OCCUR IN NORTHEAST

Racial disturbances occurred in many of the nation's cities. A riot in Harlem was sparked by the shooting of a fifteen-year-old Black by an off-duty white police officer on July 18. During the five days of rioting, at least one Black person was killed, 140 injured, and more than 500 arrested. The violence quickly spread from Harlem to the Bedford-Stuyvesant area of Brooklyn. President Johnson ordered the FBI to inquire into the causes of the Harlem riot.

Many other racial riots resulted from clashes between Blacks and police. Serious racial disturbances took place in Rochester, Brooklyn, Jersey City, Chicago, and Philadelphia. On July 26 and 27, racial violence spread throughout Rochester. Molotov cocktails were hurled at cars and into the windows of stores, looting occurred in some areas, and guns were fired. More than 120 were arrested. Governor Nelson Rockefeller dispatched one thousand National Guard-members to restore calm. Several hundred people were injured in these disturbances, and millions of dollars in property was lost. In most cases, the National Guard was sent in to calm the riots.

ROWAN APPOINTED DIRECTOR OF U.S. INFORMATION SERVICE

Carl T. Rowan, a Black journalist, was appointed director of the United States Information Service by President Lyndon Johnson. Rowan became the first Black to hold this post, which carried membership in the National Security Council. Rowan was thus one of President Johnson's highest-ranking Black appointees. He was known throughout Washington political circles as a fine journalist.

Although Rowan served as deputy assistant secretary of state for public affairs (1961–1963) and as U.S. ambassador to Finland (1963–1964), his journalism career most truly revealed his intellectual breadth. He worked for the Minneapolis *Tribune* (1948–1961), the Chicago *Daily News* (1965–1978), and the Chi-

Carl Thomas Rowan, a journalist, became the head of the U.S. Information Service in 1964. He served in a number of other important political positions under several presidents. Rowan was the first Black to attend a meeting of the National Security Council.

cago *Sun-Times* (1978–). Rowan is still one of the few African American journalists who are syndicated columnists in most major newspapers in the country and on radio. In 1954, 1955, and 1966, Rowan was awarded the Sigma Delta Chi award for excellence in journalism.

SOUTHERN POLITICIANS DISPROPORTIONATELY POWERFUL IN INFLUENCING POLICY

The South consistently exerted a powerful influence on domestic public policy in this country. In this year, southern Democrats chaired 62.5 percent of all U.S. Senate committees. Yet they made up only 31 percent of the U.S. senators. Their influence, solidified because of their seniority, exceeded their representation in the Democratic Party. These representatives regularly gutted sound legislation that they perceived would have a negative impact on southern economics or southern customs. Many U.S. presidents had to give "pork" to these representatives to secure passage of legislative packages, most notably the national budget.

STUDENTS ORGANIZE BOYCOTT TO PROTEST DE FACTO SCHOOL SEGREGATION

In **JANUARY**, **FEBRUARY**, and **MARCH**, a number of demonstrations and protests occurred in which students actually boycotted schools in protest against de facto school segregation. As many as 464,000 students were absent from Harlem schools in February, and as many as 267,000 were absent in March. In Cleveland, 68,000 (about 86 percent) were absent from schools in April; in Cincinnati, 26,455 students were absent from schools in February; in Chicago, as many as 172,300 did not attend Chicago schools in February. Absences and rioting occurred in Cleveland, Ohio, and Chester, Pennsylvania.

TWENTY-FOURTH AMENDMENT RATIFIED

On **JANUARY 23**, the Twenty-fourth Amendment to the U.S. Constitution was ratified. The amendment prohibited the denial or abridgement of the right to vote by "reason of failure to pay any poll tax or other tax." The poll tax was still used by many southern states as a means of discouraging Black voters. Black voting registration in Alabama and Mississippi, the most heavily Black-populated areas of the country, was less than 5 percent of all eligible voters.

CLAY WINS WORLD BOXING TITLE

On **FEBRUARY 25**, Cassius Clay won the world heavyweight championship by defeating Sonny Liston in Miami. Clay, who had won an Olympic medal several years earlier, was considered one of the greatest fighters in the game. Several months later, Cassius Clay converted to Islam and changed his name to Muhammad Ali.

CIVIL RIGHTS WORKERS SLAIN IN MISSISSIPPI

On **AUGUST 5**, three young civil rights workers who had been working on Black voter registration — James E. Chaney (age twenty-one), Michael Schwerner (age twenty-four), and Andrew Goodman (age twenty-one) — were officially declared missing and presumed murdered in Mississippi; they had been missing since June 21. The search party knew only that they had been arrested for speeding, incarcerated, fined, and released. President Johnson sent two hundred naval personnel to assist in the search for the missing civil rights workers. Their bodies were found buried near Philadelphia, Mississippi.

On October 4, two residents of Philadelphia, Mississippi, were indicted and arrested for the slaying of the three civil rights workers. By December 10, a total of twenty-one men, including a sheriff and a deputy, were arrested in connection with the murders. All were members of the KKK or the White Knights. Evidence revealed that the law officers released the three civil rights workers to the KKK. A federal judge released nineteen of the twenty-one men on the grounds that a confession was improperly obtained. Many were arrested again on January 16, 1965.

BLACKS RECEIVE MEDAL OF FREEDOM

On **SEPTEMBER 14**, President Lyndon Johnson presented the Medal of Freedom to Leontyne Price and A. Philip Randolph for their courage and contributions to the ideals of freedom and the well-being of others.

CHURCH BOMBED IN VICKSBURG

On **OCTOBER 4**, a Black church in Vicksburg, Mississippi, was bombed. Two people were killed. The church was used as a center for voter registration.

HAYES WINS OLYMPIC GOLD MEDAL

On **OCTOBER 15**, Bob Hayes was awarded a gold medal at the Olympic Games in Tokyo for the 100-meter dash. He tied the Olympic record of ten seconds.

MANY BLACK OFFICIALS ELECTED IN STATE ELECTIONS

In **NOVEMBER**, Black voters went to the polls to elect 280 Black candidates to public office around the country. Ninety of the victors were state legislators.

1965   BOND DENIED SEAT IN GEORGIA HOUSE OF REPRESENTATIVES

Julian Bond (1940–), son of an ex–college president and himself a leader of the SNCC, was denied his seat in the Georgia House of Representatives by a vote of 184–12. Although he had been duly elected, legislators refused to seat Bond because he opposed U.S. involvement in Vietnam. About one thousand people marched on the state capitol in support of Bond. In December 1966, the U.S. Supreme Court ordered Bond seated.

In 1968, Bond became the first African American to have his name placed in nomination at the Democratic National Convention for vice president of the United States. In 1971, he and others founded the Southern Poverty Law Center, an organization developed to help protect the rights of poor people of all races, particularly in the South.

Bond, a Democrat, served in the Georgia House of Representatives from 1965 to 1975 and in the Georgia Senate from 1975 to 1987. More recently, Bond has narrated several television documentaries on the African American experience.

MARSHALL APPOINTED SOLICITOR GENERAL

President Lyndon Johnson named Thurgood Marshall, an appeals court judge and civil rights lawyer, to be solicitor general of the United States, thus assuming the highest judicial position ever held by a Black.

BOSTON BREAKS WORLD BROAD-JUMP RECORD

Ralph Boston soared through the air at twenty-seven feet and five inches at the California Relays, creating a new broad-jump world record. He broke his old record by three-quarters of an inch.

CIVIL RIGHTS DEMONSTRATIONS TAKE PLACE IN THE SOUTH

Civil rights demonstrations occurred in Jackson, Mississippi, and Bogalusa, Louisiana. Each resulted in massive arrests. Blacks took their issues to the Capitol in Washington, D.C., where they conducted a sit-in demonstration to protest the slowness with which the federal government was moving to protect their rights.

CLEAVER PUBLISHES *Soul on Ice*

Eldridge (Leroy) Cleaver (1935–), Black militant and leader of the Black Panther Party, published his autobiography, *Soul on Ice,* which dealt with his experience in the U.S. penal system and the racial hatred that influenced his life.

COSBY STARS IN *I Spy*

Bill Cosby (1937–), a comedian and entertainer, became the first African American actor to star in a television series — *I Spy.* The series costarred Robert Culp and remained on the air until 1968.

Cosby later starred in *Uptown Saturday Night* (1974), one of his several movie appearances. He is perhaps best known as the producer and costar of the award-winning television series *The Cosby Show,* which first aired in 1984 and ranked as the top television series for many years, receiving several awards. Cosby has written a number of books, including *Fatherhood* (1986). More recently, Cosby took on the role of host on a quiz show, *You Bet Your Life.*

Participants at this sit-in in Washington were protesting the lack of federal protection for Blacks' civil rights.

COUNCIL ON EQUAL OPPORTUNITY FORMED

President Johnson created a cabinet-level Council on Equal Opportunity, chaired by Vice President Hubert Humphrey. The council coordinated the civil rights activities of federal agencies. Vice President Humphrey, discussing his role as chair of the Council on Equal Opportunity, called upon Blacks to help his efforts succeed.

RACIAL RIOTING ERUPTS OVER USE OF FIRE HYDRANT

Rioting broke out in Chicago over disputes between police and Black children concerning the use of a fire hydrant for recreational purposes. When the disturbance ended, two Blacks were dead, many were injured, and more than 370 had been arrested. Mayor Richard J. Daley and Dr. Martin Luther King, Jr., announced new recreational programs for Blacks and the establishment of a committee to study police-citizen relations.

SCHOOL SEGREGATION PROTESTED IN CHICAGO
Civil rights demonstrators protested against school segregation in Chicago, resulting in the arrest of more than 225 protestors, including CORE director James Farmer, Dick Gregory, and nine clergymen.

SULLIVAN FOUNDS OIC
Leon H. Sullivan (1922–), a Baptist minister, founded the Opportunities Industrialization Center (OIC), an organization created for the purpose of securing agreements with major firms in Philadelphia to hire and provide on-the-job training for African Americans. The organization was a direct result of his boycott of Philadelphia firms in 1959 and his success in getting them to hire African Americans. Sullivan's organization became so successful that he was encouraged to implement its programs throughout the nation and in major centers in Africa. In 1971, Sullivan became the

Leon Sullivan, the founder of the Opportunities Industrialization Center in Philadelphia, encouraged corporations to provide job training for African Americans.

first African American to join General Motors as a member of the board of directors. Although Sullivan implemented several plans to secure agreements with American companies doing business in South Africa, his efforts were unsuccessful. In response, he and other African American leaders began a movement to pressure U.S. companies to withdraw their subsidiaries and investments from South Africa because of apartheid's unequal treatment of Black Africans.

VOTING RIGHTS ACT UPHELD BY SUPREME COURT
The U.S. Supreme Court upheld the recent Voting Rights Act, which provided for: (1) the suspension of literacy tests and other devices found to be discriminatory as qualifications for voting in the states of Alabama, Arkansas, Georgia, Louisiana, Mississippi, South Carolina, Virginia, and at least twenty-six counties in North Carolina; (2) the assignment of federal examiners to oversee voter registration to ensure that it was an open process and, if necessary, to conduct the registration themselves; (3) the U.S. attorney general to bring suits to test the constitutionality of poll taxes that abridged the right to vote; and (4) the extension of protection under civil and criminal law to qualified persons seeking to vote and to those urging or aiding others to vote.

WEAVER APPOINTED HUD SECRETARY
President Lyndon Johnson appointed Robert C. Weaver as the first African American secretary of the Department of Housing and Urban Development (HUD). Weaver was the first Black to serve at the presidential cabinet level.

VOTER REGISTRATION DRIVE OPENED IN SELMA
Civil rights activists, led by Dr. Martin Luther King, Jr., opened a voter registration drive in Selma, Alabama. King was attacked as he registered at a formerly all-white Selma hotel. On **JANUARY 19**, Dallas County law enforcement officers began arresting potential Black voters and their supporters. A federal court order was issued prohibiting interference with those seeking the right to vote.

As Black voter registration increased throughout Alabama, whites intensified their resistance. In Dallas County, Alabama, more than seven hundred Blacks, including King, were arrested within a one-month period. Jimmie L. Jackson, a Black demonstrator, died from wounds received at the hands of state troopers in Marion, Alabama. During March, several hundred Black protesters were routed by billy clubs, tear gas, whips, and cattle prods as they attempted to march across the Edmund Pettus Bridge into Selma. The Reverend James Reeb, a white participant in the voting rights protests, died from a beating by three white men.

MALCOLM X ASSASSINATED

On **FEBRUARY 21**, Malcolm X, former Black Muslim and outspoken advocate of Black nationalism, was shot to death in New York City before more than four hundred members of his newly founded Organization for Afro-American Unity. One week earlier, the home of Malcolm X had been bombed, but he was not injured.

In February 1966, Talmadge Thayer was arrested and confessed to slaying the Black leader. Thomas 15X Johnson and Norman 3X Butler were also arrested. The three defendants were found guilty during the subsequent trial and were sentenced to prison. Fourteen years later, Thayer recanted his first confession, stating that Johnson and Butler were innocent, and he named four others as having been involved in the assassination. Despite Thayer's statement, no new trial was held. Johnson, Butler, and Thayer each served more than twenty years in prison before being paroled. The facts surrounding Malcolm X's assassination remain disputed.

MARCH FROM SELMA TO MONTGOMERY BEGINS

On Sunday, **MARCH 7**, civil rights leaders Hosea Williams and John Lewis, together with five hundred

Dr. Martin Luther King, Jr. (in front of flag), was joined by his wife, Coretta Scott King, and other civil rights demonstrators as they marched from Selma to Montgomery, Alabama, in one of the most famous protests of the civil rights movement.

followers, began a fifty-mile march from Selma, Alabama, to the state capital, Montgomery, to protest the denial of voting rights, arouse national indignation for their cause, and spur the federal government into action. At this time, only about 3 percent of Blacks in Selma were registered to vote, although Selma's population was almost half Black. The city had an infamous reputation, largely based on the violent treatment of civil rights activists by the county sheriff, James Clark.

In February, the Reverend Martin Luther King, Jr., had started a series of demonstrations in Selma, to which Clark responded by arresting hundreds of people, including schoolchildren. In March, despite an executive order by Governor George Wallace forbidding them to march, marchers began to cross the Edmund Pettus Bridge over the Alabama River. They were met by state troopers and local police, who fired tear gas and attacked the unarmed group with bullwhips, rubber tubing wrapped in barbed wire, cattle prods, and chains. Fifty marchers were hospitalized. Images of police brutality were broadcast by the major television networks across the country. The White House and the Congress were besieged by calls for intervention; sympathy marches involving thousands of individuals took place across the country.

The march was rescheduled for March 9, although federal judge Frank Johnson issued an order that it should not take place, pending further hearings. King returned to Selma from Atlanta, where he had gone after a series of earlier death threats. He was caught in a dilemma — he had never violated a federal order, yet the protesters were adamant and would march without him. A compromise was reached. King agreed to march with the protesters across the bridge, where they would be met by police. They would stop, pray, and then return to Selma. Thus, they would avoid defying the federal order. King told no other leader or any of the marchers of the agreement. The march took place as planned until, in a move to embarrass King, Major John Cloud, the commander of the state troopers, ordered his troops to stand aside, thus making the road to Montgomery wide open. Nevertheless, King instructed the marchers to return to Selma. Most were aghast at his explanation that they had made their point and could therefore return. He did not tell them of the compromise. This action further split the SNCC activists, who believed that King had betrayed them again, and the SCLC.

The White House finally took action. On March 15, President Lyndon Johnson asked Congress in a televised address to pass a voting rights bill. He also prevailed on Judge Johnson to lift the injunction and let the march proceed. President Johnson also told Governor Wallace that the marchers would be protected by federalized National Guard troops.

On March 21, some thirty-two hundred marchers, led by Martin Luther King, Jr., Ralph J. Bunche, and Ralph Abernathy, again crossed the Edmund Pettus Bridge. They continued their march and arrived without incident in Montgomery on March 25. The march influenced the passage of the Voting Rights Act in August of this year.

ALL-BLACK TEAM WINS BASKETBALL CHAMPIONSHIP

On **MARCH 19**, Texas Western University, with a team made up exclusively of Black players, defeated the University of Kentucky for the National Collegiate Athletic Association (NCAA) Basketball Championship. An all-Black team had never previously played an all-white team in the NCAA title game.

WHITE CIVIL RIGHTS ACTIVIST MURDERED

On **MARCH 26**, Viola Gregg Liuzzo, a white civil rights supporter from Michigan, was killed. Those indicted for her murder were released in May because of a mistrial. On October 22, an all-white jury acquitted Collie Wilkins of her murder. Wilkins, a member of the KKK, was convicted of conspiracy to violate Liuzzo's civil rights. During the first week in December, three members of the Ku Klux Klan were convicted in Montgomery, Alabama, for her murder. Each received ten years in jail. On appeal, a jury cleared Klansman Eugene Thomas in the slaying of Liuzzo.

Another Alabama jury freed all whites accused in the murder of the Reverend James Reeb, a Boston minister slain in the Selma demonstrations.

BLACK WOMAN APPOINTED AMBASSADOR

On **MAY 19**, Patricia Roberts Harris was appointed U.S. ambassador to Luxembourg. Harris became the first African American woman to be an ambassador of the United States. Harris later became one of the most powerful African American women in the country when she was appointed to a presidential cabinet post.

MALONE GRADUATES FROM UNIVERSITY OF ALABAMA

On **MAY 30**, Vivian Malone graduated from the University of Alabama, becoming the first African American to graduate from this predominantly white university.

RACE RIOTS FLARE UP IN NEBRASKA

On **JULY 5**, rioting started in Omaha, Nebraska, and was so serious that the governor called upon the National Guard to calm the Black areas of the city.

RACIAL RIOTING ERUPTS IN WATTS, LOS ANGELES

In **AUGUST**, one of the nation's bloodiest race riots occurred in the Black neighborhood of Watts in Los Angeles, California. More than five days of violence left more than thirty-five dead, more than nine hundred injured, more than thirty-five hundred arrested, and property losses worth more than $225 million. According to civil rights reports, it was the most serious racial disturbance in American history. Records showed that although racial tensions had been high, the spark that ignited the violence was the arrest of a Black man on drunk driving charges and subsequent police brutality. After the news had traveled through the Watts community, young Blacks used the incident to release their suppressed anger. Watts exploded in flames, snipers were heard firing off several rounds, stores were looted, and chaos spread everywhere. Federal troops were called in, and a curfew was imposed to restore calm.

ALI DEFEATS PATTERSON

On **NOVEMBER 22**, Muhammad Ali defeated Floyd Patterson for the world heavyweight boxing title. Ali won in twelve rounds.

1966 ASHE WINS TENNIS TITLES

Arthur Ashe (1943–1993) won the NCAA singles and doubles titles — the first African American to do so. Ashe was a student at UCLA.

ASHFORD APPOINTED MAJOR LEAGUE UMPIRE

Emmett Ashford umpired in the American League from 1966 through 1970. He was the first Black umpire in major-league baseball.

BLACK PANTHER PARTY FORMED

Huey Newton of Grove, Louisiana, and Bobby Seale, of Dallas, Texas, organized the Black Panther Party in Oakland, California. The Panthers' primary goals included self-defense and revolutionary change in the United States. The party branched out to other major cities throughout the country.

Although they were harassed by local, state, and federal authorities, the Panthers emerged as one of the most misrepresented militant segments of the Black movement. For example, their platform included the rights of Black people to determine their own destiny; the rights to full employment, decent housing, and education; and the right to gain knowledge of themselves through their own history. In addition, their platform called for an end to police brutality, equal justice (by their own peers), the exemption of Blacks from all military service, immediate freedom for all imprisoned Blacks, and land and reparations. In their effort to expand the membership and to counter negative press, the Black Panthers worked hard at the community level, setting up breakfast programs for elementary school children, establishing health clinics and "liberation" schools, and collecting clothing for the poor. The Panthers were both a community group and a revolutionary group with a Marxist-Leninist viewpoint. They attempted to create a positive image, but Americans were troubled by the Panthers' Marxist-Leninist perspective and support of the use of violence to protect Blacks from attack by the police and others. Notable members included Eldridge Cleaver and Fred Hampton.

BLACK POWER MOVEMENT SWEEPS BLACK ORGANIZATIONS

During this year, the concept of Black Power engulfed a number of Black organizations and individuals who felt hopelessness, despair, frustration, and outrage at the unwillingness of the United States to support its stated policies and its creed — that all people are created equal. The phrase *Black Power* was first enunciated by Stokely Carmichael, the new head of the Student Non-Violent Coordinating Committee (SNCC). The chanting of "Black Power" could be heard at almost every major protest, but it meant different things to different people. Carmichael and Charles Hamilton wrote a book to delineate the meaning of Black Power:

> [Black Power] is a call for Black people in this country to unite, to recognize their heritage, to build a sense of community. It is a call for Black people to begin to define their own goals, to lead their own organizations and to support those organizations. It is a call to reject the racist institutions of this society and its values.

BLACKS SERVE AS AMBASSADORS

Six Blacks held important government positions as U.S. ambassadors:

Mercer Cook, Senegal
Patricia Harris, Luxembourg

Bobby Seale and Huey Newton, leaders of the Black Panther Party, expressed the new sense of Black identity that arose with the Black Power movement of the late 1960s. The Black Panthers' image, involving leather jackets, berets, and firearms, implied a message of revolution.

Clinton Knox, Dahomey
Hugh Smythe, Syria
Franklin Williams, Ghana
Elliot Skinner, Upper Volta

BRIMMER APPOINTED TO FEDERAL RESERVE BOARD
Andrew F. Brimmer, an economist, became the first Black to be appointed to the Federal Reserve Board. In 1965, Brimmer was appointed assistant secretary of commerce for economic affairs.

◆ Brimmer was born in 1926 in Newellton, Louisiana. He received a B.A. in 1950 and an M.A. in 1951 from the University of Washington. After studying abroad at the Delhi School of Economics and the University of Bombay, he returned to be a teaching fellow at Harvard University, where he received his Ph.D. degree in 1957. From 1955 to 1957, Brimmer worked as an economist for the Federal Reserve Bank in New York. He later taught at Michigan State University and the Wharton School of Finance and Commerce.

Following his work with the Federal Reserve Board, Brimmer served as a visiting professor at Harvard University before going into business. He now owns a consulting company.

BROOKE ELECTED TO U.S. SENATE
On **NOVEMBER 8**, Edward W. Brooke III, attorney general of Massachusetts, was elected U.S. senator from Massachusetts. Brooke became the first Black elected by popular vote to occupy a seat in the U.S. Senate. In addition, Brooke, a Republican, was the first Black to sit in the U.S. Senate since Reconstruction — eighty-five years earlier. Brooke followed Hiram R. Revels and Blanche K. Bruce, both Black senators from Mississippi who were elected by the state legislature.

BURKE ELECTED TO CALIFORNIA LEGISLATURE
Yvonne Brathwaite Burke was elected to the California Assembly, thus becoming the first Black woman to serve in the state assembly. Burke went on to serve in the U.S. House of Representatives in 1972.

HENRY ELECTED MAYOR OF SPRINGFIELD
Robert C. Henry was elected mayor of Springfield, Ohio. He was the first Black to be elected mayor of a midwestern city of significant size.

JORDAN ELECTED TO TEXAS SENATE
Barbara Jordan of Houston was elected to the Texas Senate. She became the first Black to sit in this leg-

Edward W. Brooke was the first Black elected to the U.S. Senate since Reconstruction, eighty-five years earlier.

islative body since 1883. Jordan was elected to the U.S. House of Representatives in 1972.

MASSIE APPOINTED TO U.S. NAVAL ACADEMY FACULTY
In this year, Dr. Samuel P. Massie joined the chemistry department of the U.S. Naval Academy at Annapolis. He became the first Black faculty member in the academy's history.

◆ Massie, a native of Little Rock, Arkansas, graduated from high school at the age of thirteen, received a B.S. degree in chemistry, and graduated summa cum laude from Arkansas AM & N College at the age of eighteen. He received advanced degrees at Fisk University and Iowa State University.

During World War II, Massie performed military research in a number of areas, including chemical warfare agents, antimalarial agents, and the atomic bomb. After the war, he worked for Eastman Kodak and then at Langston University, Fisk University, and Howard University. He later directed a program at the National Science Foundation. In 1963, he was appointed president of North Carolina College at Durham. It was from there that he joined the U.S. Naval Academy, where from 1977 to 1980, he served as chairperson of the chemistry department.

Massie has published almost three dozen scientific papers, received more than forty-five research grants, and chaired a number of state science councils.

OCCUPATIONAL EMPLOYMENT OF BLACKS REFLECTS INEQUALITY

Although nonwhite workers represented 10.8 percent of the total employment in this country, they were underrepresented in jobs that paid well and overrepresented in those that paid poorly and offered limited benefits or none at all. Racial discrimination still blocked access by Blacks to decent jobs and equality of opportunity in this country.

RACIAL AND ETHNIC RIOTING IN BROOKLYN

Racial unrest in the east section of Brooklyn, New York, took a new twist. For almost a week, groups and gangs of Blacks, whites, and Puerto Ricans fought in the streets. Hundreds were injured, at least two were killed, and more than one thousand police tried to bring calm to the area. Mayor John Lindsay appealed to gang leaders to calm the streets and negotiate their differences.

ROBINSON NAMED MOST VALUABLE PLAYER

Frank Robinson won the American League's Most Valuable Player award for his outstanding season, becoming the first player ever to earn the Most Valuable Player award in both the National League (1961) and the American League. He was the first player to win the Triple Crown since 1956 — first in batting (.316), first in runs batted in (122), and first in home runs (49).

Robinson later led the Baltimore Orioles to win the pennant and the World Series. He played with the Baltimore Orioles from 1966 to 1971. He also played with the Los Angeles Dodgers in 1972, the California Angels from 1973 to 1974, and the Cleveland Indians from 1974 to 1976.

MCKISSICK BECOMES HEAD OF CORE

On **JANUARY 3**, Floyd McKissick (1922–1991) was elected director of the Congress of Racial Equality (CORE), when James Farmer resigned. As its director, he traveled throughout the country, stressing the need for economic as well as political power for Blacks.

◆ McKissick, born in Asheville, North Carolina, was active in civil rights as a teenager, when he was arrested for directing traffic around an all-Black roller-skating race. He graduated from North Carolina College at Durham (now North Carolina Central University). He then entered a legal battle to gain admission to the all-white University of North Carolina Law School. Thurgood Marshall, then an NAACP attorney, represented McKissick in the case. McKissick graduated in 1951, the first Black to earn an LL.B. degree from that university. Upon graduation, McKissick set up a law practice in Durham, North Carolina, specializing in civil rights cases, and he served as legal counsel for CORE.

McKissick fought in World War II and received a Purple Heart. He was known for being one of the

Floyd McKissick, a civil rights lawyer, became the head of CORE in 1966. He is shown here testifying at a Senate hearing on the role of the federal government in urban development.

most influential and vocal leaders of civil rights beginning in 1947, when he helped lead the first integrated bus ride through the South.

The outspoken McKissick was one of the first Black leaders to denounce the war in Southeast Asia, saying Blacks were "going over to Vietnam and dying for something that they don't have a right for here." McKissick directed CORE to focus on helping Blacks gain economic and political power. In 1967, he surprised many Black leaders when he refused to heed a call by Dr. Martin Luther King, Jr., for massive demonstrations in the North, and again when he switched from the Democratic to the Republican Party and supported President Richard Nixon. He considered it "foolish" for Blacks to place all their faith in the Democratic Party. In 1968, McKissick left CORE and started Floyd B. McKissick Enterprises. An arm of that company developed Soul City, a new town conceived as a showcase for Black entrepreneurship. When the federal government cut funds to the project, Soul City died.

McKissick died at the age of sixty-nine. He had been appointed a North Carolina district judge by Governor James G. Martin the previous June.

SOUTHERN CHRISTIAN LEADERSHIP CONFERENCE OPENS BRANCH

On **JANUARY 23**, the Southern Christian Leadership Conference opened its first branch in a northern city — Chicago. This branch became the headquarters for Martin Luther King, Jr.

MOTLEY APPOINTED FEDERAL JUDGE

On **JANUARY 25**, Constance Baker Motley, former borough president of Manhattan, became the first Black woman appointed as a federal judge. She was appointed by President Lyndon Johnson to the U.S. District Court for Southern New York State. In 1982, Motley became chief judge of the Federal District Court, which includes Manhattan, the Bronx, and six southern New York counties. In 1986, Motley became senior judge of that court.

Motley, who received her LL.D. in 1946 from Columbia University, had worked for the NAACP Legal Defense and Educational Fund. Between 1960 and 1964, she won nine of the ten cases that she argued before the U.S. Supreme Court. She represented James Meredith in his admission suit against the University of Mississippi.

Constance Baker Motley, a civil rights lawyer, was the first Black woman to be appointed a federal judge. Before achieving that office, she served in a number of other important positions, including senator in the New York state legislature.

RUSSELL BECOMES CELTICS COACH

On **APRIL 18**, Bill Russell, one of basketball's most successful centers, was selected to coach the Boston Celtics basketball team. Russell became the first Black coach of a predominantly white professional NBA basketball team. He received the highest salary ever paid to any coach or manager, $125,000 annually, and he continued to play for the Celtics.

OLIVE AWARDED MEDAL OF HONOR

On **APRIL 21**, Milton Olive III was posthumously awarded the Medal of Honor for bravery in the Vietnam War. Olive saved the lives of many soldiers by falling on a live grenade during a search-and-destroy mission near Phu Coung. Olive was the first African American to be awarded this medal for service in Vietnam.

CARMICHAEL BECOMES HEAD OF SNCC

In MAY, Stokely Carmichael, born in Trinidad, was elected chairperson of the Student Non-Violent Coordinating Committee (SNCC). Carmichael guided the SNCC into a more militant and aggressive position.

Carmichael graduated from Howard University in 1964, and in 1965, he became director of a SNCC voter registration project in Lowndes County, Alabama, where he organized the Lowndes County Freedom Organization, an independent political party with a black panther as its symbol.

COSBY WINS EMMY

On MAY 22, Bill Cosby, costar of *I Spy*, was awarded an Emmy for best actor in a dramatic series, becoming the first African American to receive an Emmy in this category.

BLACK COLLEGE STUDENT SHOT

James Meredith, the first Black to scale the racial barriers to education at "Ole Miss" (the University of Mississippi), was shot in the back on JUNE 6 along U.S. Highway 51 after starting his "one-man pilgrimage against fear" from Memphis to Jackson, Mississippi. Police arrested a white man who admitted to the shooting. The Reverend Martin Luther King, Jr., and approximately two hundred other marchers staged protests and took up the march started by Meredith. Although the marchers were dispersed by tear gas, they regrouped and continued. On June 25, Meredith was well enough to join the marchers near Jackson, Mississippi.

RACIAL VIOLENCE ERUPTS IN NORTHERN CITIES

During the month of JULY, major racial disturbances occurred in Chicago, New York City, and Cleveland.

RACIAL VIOLENCE OCCURS IN CLEVELAND

On or about JULY 21, racial violence erupted in Cleveland, Ohio. It seemed to spread from a neighborhood bar throughout the Black ghetto of Hough on the city's east side. Shootings, fire bombings, and looting occurred. In total, 4 were killed, 50 injured, and 160 arrested; widespread property damage was sustained. Ten buildings were completely destroyed by fire. Several days later, a young mother was killed by police

— an incident that triggered even more rioting, the loss of two more lives, and thirty more injuries.

RACIAL VIOLENCE ERUPTS IN CHICAGO

In Chicago, more than four thousand National Guardmembers were called in to suppress racial unrest and violent clashes between Blacks and police. As many as two Blacks were killed, and several police were wounded. More than fifty people were wounded. Black community leaders attributed the unrest to unemployment and despair. On JULY 31, the Reverend Martin Luther King, Jr., and several hundred protesters were stoned by whites in the Chicago suburb of Cicero, Illinois. They had been demonstrating against residential and employment discrimination in the area. As many as fifty-four protesters were hurt when whites hurled bricks and other objects at them.

CHARLES R. DREW POSTGRADUATE MEDICAL SCHOOL CHARTERED

On AUGUST 2, the Charles R. Drew Postgraduate Medical School was chartered in Los Angeles, California. Later renamed the Charles R. Drew University of Medicine and Science, it was the only predominantly African American medical school west of the Mississippi; Meharry and Howard Universities were the only other predominantly African American medical schools in the country.

RACIAL VIOLENCE ERUPTS IN MISSISSIPPI

On SEPTEMBER 12, the small city of Grenada, Mississippi, (population about 8,000, with about 48 percent Black residents) was overwhelmed by racial hatred and mob behavior in response to integration. A number of Blacks were attacked by a white mob as they sought to integrate the city's schools. Although the police were present, they did nothing to prevent the assault on Blacks. Over the next several days, Blacks and white protesters confronted each other with jeers and profanities. On September 17, thirteen whites were arrested for harassing and physically assaulting Black protesters. Two days later, Joan Baez, singer and civil rights activist, got involved by walking a group of young Black children to the school door. State patrol officers refused to let them enter the elementary school. More and more civil rights leaders and marchers came to Grenada to break the back of racism. Black students were harassed daily as they attended school. On October 24, about two hundred whites were arrested for harassing Black students.

1967 BLACK POWER CONFERENCE HELD IN NEW JERSEY

A four-day Black Power Conference, the largest of its kind in American history, convened in Newark, New Jersey. More than four hundred people representing forty-five civil rights groups from thirty-six cities expressed views on methods to achieve civil rights for Black people, ranging from moderate to militant action. H. Rap Brown (SNCC) and Jesse Jackson (SCLC) were among the leaders at this conference.

BLACKS SERVE IN GEORGIA GENERAL ASSEMBLY

A total of eleven Blacks were members of the Georgia General Assembly. Two were members of the senate.

EMPLOYMENT DISCRIMINATION REMAINS WIDESPREAD

The Equal Opportunities Commission charged that the American pharmaceutical industry had practiced widespread employment discrimination against Blacks, and it demanded that the industry hire and promote more Black workers. Other companies, such as Ford Motor Company, Chrysler Corporation, and the Michigan Bell Telephone Company, had responded to anticipated charges of employment discrimination by opening more jobs to Black Americans in Detroit.

EIGHTEEN INDICTED IN SLAYING OF CIVIL RIGHTS WORKERS

As many as eighteen suspects were indicted in the murder of civil rights workers James E. Chaney, Michael Schwerner, and Andrew Goodman, slain in Mississippi in 1964. Seven were later acquitted.

FREEMAN MAKES ACTING DEBUT

Morgan Freeman (1937–) made his acting debut in a staging of *Hello, Dolly!* produced with an African American cast.

Later, Freeman captured a major role in the television program *The Electric Company*. His break in the movies came in a supporting role in *Street Smart*, for which he was nominated for an Academy Award. Freeman starred in *Clean and Sober* and *Lean on Me*, both of which revealed him as one of America's most versatile actors, Black or white. Freeman received critical praise for his leading roles in *Glory* and *Driving Miss Daisy* and was again nominated for an Academy Award.

Richard Hatcher, elected in 1967 as the mayor of Gary, Indiana, cosponsored the first Black national political convention held in the United States in the twentieth century. The convention encouraged Blacks to stop relying on the two major political parties and to rely instead on "the power of our own Black unity."

HATCHER ELECTED MAYOR OF GARY, INDIANA

Richard B. Hatcher, a Democrat, was elected mayor of Gary, Indiana. Because he was inaugurated at a later date than Carl B. Stokes of Cleveland, Hatcher became the second Black mayor of a major American city in the twentieth century.

Hatcher had been on the Gary city council for several years and had supported a number of civil rights issues. Hatcher was reelected a total of four times and served as mayor for twenty years. He was defeated in 1987.

Demographic changes, which reflected a growing number of Blacks in cities and the suburbanization of the white population, provided Blacks with opportunities for election to political office.

MANY CITIES SUFFER "HOT SUMMER"

Many of the nation's cities experienced what was called a "hot summer," as the worst racial disturbances in American history took place. More than forty riots and at least one hundred similar incidents took place. The most serious racial disturbances occurred in Newark, New Jersey, where twenty-six people were killed, and in Detroit, where at least forty were killed. Other outbreaks happened in New York City, Washington, D.C., Baltimore, Chicago, and Atlanta, as well as in other large and medium-size cities. President Johnson appointed a National Advisory Commission on Civil Disorders to investigate the disturbances and make recommendations. Illinois Governor Otto Kerner headed this commission, known as the Kerner Commission.

MARSHALL APPOINTED SUPREME COURT JUSTICE

President Johnson appointed Solicitor General Thurgood Marshall to the U.S. Supreme Court. Marshall was confirmed by a 69–11 majority vote of the U.S. Senate, becoming the first Black associate justice of the U.S. Supreme Court.

In 1967, Thurgood Marshall became the first Black appointed to the U.S. Supreme Court. Marshall's impressive civil rights record made him extremely well qualified for his role as an associate justice on the nation's highest court.

Marshall won twenty-nine of the thirty-two cases he had defended before the U.S. Supreme Court, most notably *Brown* v. *Board of Education*, the landmark case that set in motion the integration of schools in this country.

PRIDE LAUNCHES CAREER IN COUNTRY MUSIC

Charley Pride (1939–), a baseball player who sang songs between innings at a company-sponsored baseball game, finally got his chance to become a real country singer when he debuted with the Grand Ole Opry.

Although Pride had signed a recording contract in 1964, the bottom line was clear — "you ain't made it in country until you done the Grand Ole Opry." Pride became the first successful Black country music entertainer. In 1972, he was awarded a Grammy. Pride, born in Sledge, Mississippi, originally wanted to be a professional baseball player but was content to become one of the most successful country music singers in the industry.

STOKES ELECTED MAYOR OF CLEVELAND

Carl B. Stokes was elected mayor of Cleveland, Ohio. He was the first Black mayor to take office in a major American city in the twentieth century. Stokes, a lawyer, had previously served in the Ohio General Assembly. He was reelected mayor in 1969. In 1972, Stokes became a newscaster at NBC-TV in New York City.

SUMMARY OF RACE RIOTS, 1964–1968

Urbanologists disagree on the exact number of racially based riots and the amount of destruction they caused during the 1964–1968 period. One estimate included 329 major riots in 257 cities, resulting in 52,629 arrests, 8,371 injuries, and 220 deaths. Another estimate cited more than 400 riots during the period. In 1967 alone, 83 people, mostly Black, were killed, and another 1,897, mostly Black, were injured. Damage to property was in the millions of dollars.

THE URBAN COALITION MEETS

In an effort to tackle the problems associated with racial disturbances in cities throughout the country, civil rights leaders called upon business and labor leaders to participate in their solution. The Urban Coalition held this meeting in Washington, D.C., and offered a forum for some of the most influential leaders in the country to put forward their views and offer solutions.

WALLACE BECOMES VARSITY BASKETBALL PLAYER

Perry Wallace of Vanderbilt University became the first Black varsity basketball player in the Southeastern Conference (SEC).

The SEC had fought integration harder than any other conference. But by the 1991–1992 season, 64 percent of all SEC basketball players and 57 percent of all basketball players were Black.

Wallace is now an attorney in Washington, D.C., and a law professor at the University of Baltimore.

POWELL OUSTED AND THEN REELECTED

On JANUARY 1, Adam Clayton Powell, Jr., was ousted as chairman of the House Education and Labor Committee and was denied his seat in the House by the Ethics Committee. The vote by House members was 307–116 to exclude him. It was the third time in history that the U.S. House of Representatives had denied a seat to one of its elected members. Several days later, the Abyssinian Church in Harlem, where Powell was pastor, rallied in support of its representative. In a special election for the House seat, Powell emerged as the winner.

KING DENOUNCES VIETNAM WAR

On MARCH 24, in Atlanta, the Reverend Martin Luther King, Jr., stated that the Vietnam War was the biggest obstacle to civil rights in the country. Two weeks later, he publicly urged Blacks and whites to resist support of the Vietnam War by seeking conscientious objector status. On April 10, the NAACP voted against King's position on the Vietnam War.

BROWN APPOINTED SNCC CHAIRPERSON

On MAY 12, H. Rap Brown, a militant, succeeded Stokely Carmichael as chairperson of the Student Non-Violent Coordinating Committee (SNCC). Brown was popular among Black youths for his militant rhetoric. He was frequently in trouble with the law. In Maryland, he was accused of inciting a race riot in Cambridge; in Louisiana, he was convicted of transporting firearms across state borders; and in Virginia and New York, he was charged with violating bail. In 1971, Brown was wounded by police after a bar holdup in New York City. In 1973, he began serving a prison sentence during which he converted to the Islamic faith. When he was released from prison, he went to Atlanta, where he opened a grocery store.

RACE RIOT TAKES PLACE IN BOSTON

On JUNE 4, racial violence erupted in Boston. Blacks broke windows, looted, and set fires. Nine people were injured.

SUPREME COURT UPHOLDS RIGHT TO INTERRACIAL MARRIAGES

On JUNE 12, the U.S. Supreme Court, ruling against a Virginia law, declared that states could not interfere with or prevent interracial marriages.

RACE RIOT OCCURS IN BUFFALO

On JUNE 27, racial rioting erupted in Buffalo, New York. The following day, as many as fourteen persons were shot.

LAWRENCE IS FIRST BLACK ASTRONAUT

On JUNE 30, Major Robert H. Lawrence, Jr., of the U.S. Air Force became the first Black astronaut. Lawrence, a research scientist with the Air Force Weapons Laboratory at Kirtland Air Force Base in New Mexico, was one of four pilots chosen to begin training for space flights. He was killed on December 8, 1967, in a plane crash.

RACE RIOT ERUPTS IN NEWARK

Starting on JULY 12, and continuing throughout most of July, Newark, New Jersey, contended with heightened racial conflicts. Over a four-day period (July 12–16), rioting spread throughout several Black neighborhoods and sections of the downtown area. By July 16, as many as twenty-six were dead, more than fifteen hundred were hurt, and about one thousand had been arrested. The magnitude of the destruction — of both lives and property — provoked more than four hundred civil rights leaders to convene to discuss causes and resolutions.

RACE RIOT OCCURS IN DETROIT

On JULY 22, Detroit erupted in one of the worst riots in the history of the city, and perhaps the nation. Although city officials and civil rights leaders quickly convened meetings to find ways to stem the violence, including killings and property destruction, it lasted for several days. Forty-seven hundred federal troops were called in to assist local police, and more than four thousand rioters were arrested. When calm finally returned to the city, forty-three people — thirty-three Blacks and ten whites — had been killed and more than two thousand had been injured. Thousands of fires had been set, and property loss or damage, estimated in initial reports at $250 million, had left about five thousand people homeless.

RACE RIOT TAKES PLACE IN MARYLAND

On **JULY 24**, the sleepy, rural town of Cambridge, on Maryland's east shore, erupted in one of the most violent confrontations experienced in the entire state. Three days of rioting occurred as civil rights demonstrators and white segregationists squared off.

WASHINGTON APPOINTED COMMISSIONER OF WASHINGTON, D.C.

On **SEPTEMBER 21**, President Lyndon Johnson named African American Walter E. Washington as commissioner of the newly organized municipal government of Washington, D.C. Washington headed the nine-member city council. He was the first Black American to govern the nation's capital.

REDDING KILLED IN PLANE CRASH

On **DECEMBER 10**, Otis Redding, a promising R & B singer, was killed in a plane crash. Before his death, he had recorded one of his most famous songs, "(Sittin' on) The Dock of the Bay." It became a number one hit on the popular music charts and earned a Grammy Award for the best R & B song of the year.

1968   BLACK POWER MOVEMENT ENDS

The coalition between the Black Panther Party and the Student Non-Violent Coordinating Committee (SNCC) dissolved, effectively ending the Black Power movement. The relationship had emerged in 1968 when Stokely Carmichael left SNCC to join the Black Panthers. Carmichael was the "prime minister" of the party.

BLACKS ELECTED TO STATE LEGISLATURES

Blacks were elected to several state legislatures for the first time since Reconstruction: Henry Frye, a Greensboro lawyer, won a seat in the North Carolina house; Joe Lang Kershaw, a Miami schoolteacher, was elected to the Florida house; and J. O. Patterson of Memphis and Avon Williams from Nashville were elected to the Tennessee senate.

CALL ME "AFRO-AMERICAN" OR "BLACK," BUT DON'T CALL ME "NEGRO"

A *New York Times* poll of Black Americans found that 59 percent of them preferred to be called "Afro-American" or "Black" rather than "Negro."

Many Black and white female politicians, and women in general, can trace some of their progress in gaining their rights to Shirley Chisholm, of New York. Not only was she the first African American woman to sit in Congress; she set a standard of aggressiveness and intelligence for many women who followed her.

CHISHOLM ENTERS U.S. HOUSE OF REPRESENTATIVES

Shirley Chisholm (1924–) of New York became the first Black woman elected to Congress. She was elected to the U.S. House of Representatives from New York's Twelfth District. She had defeated James Farmer, the well-known civil rights leader. Chisholm served in the Ninety-first through the Ninety-seventh Congresses.

◈ Chisholm was born Shirley Anita St. Hill in Brooklyn. She received a B.A. degree in sociology and then an M.A. degree in 1952 from Columbia University. From 1946 to 1964, Chisholm worked as a nursery school teacher, school director, and educational consultant for New York's Division of Day Care.

In 1964, she was elected to the state assembly from the Fifty-fifth District, serving until 1968, when she was elected to Congress.

Chisholm quickly became a champion for causes affecting children, women, and low-income populations. She criticized the congressional seniority system when she was given a committee assignment that had little to do with inner-city residents and issues. As a result of her criticism, she was transferred to another committee. She served effectively as a member of the Veterans' Affairs Committee, the Rules Committee, and the Education and Labor Committee. She joined a bipartisan coalition to introduce legislation to end the draft and substitute an all-volunteer force. She cosponsored a measure to implement a national commission on consumer protection and product safety. In addition, Chisholm strongly advocated restricting arms sales to South Africa. She introduced and supported legislation affecting the well-being of children and working mothers and cosponsored legislation guaranteeing an annual income to families.

In 1972, Chisholm became the first Black woman to run for the presidency; she entered primaries in twelve states.

Chisholm decided to resign from Congress in 1982, but she continued to speak on issues relating to the health and welfare of working mothers and children.

CLAY ELECTED TO U.S. HOUSE OF REPRESENTATIVES

Democrat William Lacy Clay (1931–), the first Black to represent Missouri, entered the U.S. House of Representatives. He represented the predominantly Black First District.

◈ Clay was born in St. Louis. He earned a B.S. degree in history and political science from St. Louis University. Upon returning from military service, he became active in the civil rights movement in St. Louis. In 1959, he was elected alderman from the Twenty-sixth Ward, and in 1964, he became ward committeeman.

Clay continues to represent this district and has become a powerful member of several congressional committees, including the Education and Labor Committee.

JOHNSON APPOINTS BLACKS TO HIGH POSITIONS

During his second term, President Johnson appointed more Blacks to high-level federal posts than any previous chief executive. Before leaving office, he appointed five Black ambassadors, promoted Wade Mc-Cree, Jr., from the U.S. District Court to the Circuit Court of Appeals, appointed Hobart Taylor to the board of Export-Import Bank, and named Andrew F. Brimmer as a governor on the Federal Reserve Board.

KITT BANNED FROM WHITE HOUSE

Eartha Kitt became persona non grata following her candid expressions at a White House luncheon. Kitt and about fifty other women were invited by Lady Bird Johnson to discuss urban crime, but Kitt's remarks related the escalation of the war in Vietnam to rioting in the streets. She remarked, "You send the best of this country off to be shot and maimed."

KU KLUX KLAN FINED ONE MILLION DOLLARS FOR SLAYING BLACKS

In Mississippi, a federal judge fined the Ku Klux Klan and three Klansmen a total of one million dollars for slaying Blacks.

PHILLIPS NOMINATED FOR PRESIDENT

The Reverend Channing E. Phillips of Washington, D.C., was the first Black nominated for president of the United States at a major national convention. He was the favorite-son candidate of the District of Columbia.

POLICE OFFICERS SHOOT INTO PEACEFUL CROWD

Three Black students were killed and several others were wounded as a result of shots fired by South Carolina police officers during a disturbance at South Carolina State College, Orangeburg. The incident began as a protest against segregation of a local bowling alley. The National Guard was mobilized, and the college was closed. The shooting followed a minor injury to a state trooper (knocked down by a piece of wood). Attempts to indict and prosecute the officers involved in the shooting and killing were unsuccessful.

POWELL CALLS FOR "BLACK REVOLUTION"

Former Congressman Adam Clayton Powell, Jr., on a speaking tour of California college campuses, urged Black and white students to begin a "Black revolution" that would address injustices against Black people. He particularly criticized the continuing use of nonviolent strategies to bring about civil rights.

STUDENT UNREST AFFECTS BOSTON UNIVERSITY

Black students used the sit-in method of protest on university and college campuses. They took over the administration building at Boston University to protest their discriminatory treatment and to demand a Black history major.

CLARK ENTERS MISSISSIPPI LEGISLATURE
On **JANUARY 2**, Robert Clark was seated as the first Black in the Mississippi legislature in seventy-four years.

AMERSON BECOMES SHERIFF IN ALABAMA
On **JANUARY 16**, Lucius D. Amerson was elected sheriff of Macon County, Alabama. He was the first Black sheriff in the South since Reconstruction. He was later indicted by a grand jury in Alabama for beating a Black prisoner in the Tuskegee jail. He was acquitted by an all-white jury in May 1971.

Soul on Ice PUBLISHED
On **FEBRUARY 12**, Elridge Cleaver's book *Soul on Ice* was published. The book reflected his anger at social injustices.

KERNER COMMISSION REPORTS
On **FEBRUARY 29**, the Kerner Commission, headed by former Illinois governor Otto Kerner, reported that "our nation is moving toward two societies; one black, one white — separate and unequal." The federally funded commission compiled the most comprehensive reports on the issue of race ever sponsored by the U.S. government. It concluded that "white racism" was the principal cause of the disturbances that rocked the nation in 1967. It warned of potential catastrophe if the nation did not commit more resources to solving the problems of urban ghettos, including increased resources to ensure better housing and education, more access to a wider range of employment opportunities, and programs for enhancing interracial communication.

STUDENTS PROTEST AT HOWARD UNIVERSITY
On **MARCH 19**, students at Howard University took over the administration building to protest the lack of Black culture in their curriculum and demanded the resignation of certain university officials. Howard was one of the first schools at which students appealed for the formation of Black studies programs.

KING ASSASSINATED IN MEMPHIS
On **APRIL 4**, Dr. Martin Luther King, Jr., who had journeyed to Memphis, Tennessee, to take part in a strike

In 1968, former Illinois governor Otto Kerner and Mayor John Lindsay of New York City released the Kerner Commission Report, which stated that two racially separate and unequal societies were emerging in America.

by Black city workers, was shot by a sniper while standing on the balcony of the Lorraine Motel. King, thirty-nine years old, was rushed to St. Joseph's Hospital, where he was pronounced dead. The assassin, James Earl Ray, managed to escape. Although King's associates pleaded for calm, rioting broke out in different parts of the city as Blacks expressed their rage in the streets. More than four thousand National Guardmembers were activated to restore order and to enforce a curfew on residents. A week of racial rioting ensued in no less than 125 major cities.

CIVIL RIGHTS ACT PASSED
On **APRIL 11**, President Lyndon Johnson signed the Fair Housing Act — the Civil Rights Act of 1968 — pro-

Soldiers patrolled Washington, D.C., in response to the riot that followed the assassination of Dr. Martin Luther King, Jr. Riots occurred throughout the country after his murder in Memphis, Tennessee.

hibiting discrimination on the basis of race in the renting and sale of houses and apartments. It was based on a proposal Johnson had discussed with Dr. Martin Luther King, Jr.

ABERNATHY BECOMES SCLC PRESIDENT
On **APRIL 29**, the Reverend Ralph Abernathy succeeded the Reverend Martin Luther King, Jr., as president of the Southern Christian Leadership Conference (SCLC) and led the Poor People's Campaign. Several days later, in Memphis, a crowd of one thousand people started the Poor People's March on Washington. Later in the year, Abernathy led a group of Blacks, whites, Native Americans, and Mexican Americans to Washington for another Poor People's March. On May 12, as many as three thousand participants gathered in Washington, D.C., to dramatize the magnitude of racism in American society. They lobbied, and they erected a campsite known as "Resurrection City." Protesters remained on the campsite for almost two months to bring attention to the needs of the poor, particularly poor southern Blacks. The protest, however, did not receive the attention nor produce the impact envisioned by King.

LUCAS BECOMES AIR FORCE COLONEL
On **MAY 26**, Ruth A. Lucas was promoted to colonel in the U.S. Air Force, becoming the first African

Ralph D. Abernathy assumed the leadership of the Southern Christian Leadership Conference after the death of Dr. King. One of his first actions was to organize the Poor People's March on Washington.

American to be promoted to this rank in this branch of the service.

HOLLY PLAYS AFRICAN AMERICAN ROLE ON TELEVISION

On **JULY 15**, Ellen Holly joined the cast of ABC-TV's daytime television show *One Life to Live*. She portrayed Carla, an African American who passed for white.

Holly's acting career hitherto consisted primarily of stage productions of Shakespearean plays. She performed a multitude of roles on stage before joining the cast of *One Life to Live*.

RACE RIOT OCCURS IN CLEVELAND

On **JULY 24** and **25**, racial disturbances in Cleveland, Ohio, left eleven dead and about one and a half million dollars' worth of property damage. On July 24, a small organization of armed "Black nationalists" allegedly engaged the Cleveland police in a gun battle in the Glenville ghetto, resulting in widespread looting and burning. Three white police officers and eight Blacks were killed in the disturbances. The city's African American mayor, Carl B. Stokes, ordered the National Guard to restore order in the ghetto.

ASHE WINS U.S. TENNIS TITLES

On **AUGUST 25**, Arthur Ashe won the U.S. amateur men's singles tennis championship. On September 6, Ashe won the men's U.S. Open championship, defeating Tom Okker at Forest Hills Stadium in New York. Ashe, an army lieutenant and the American clay court champion, was the first Black player to win this event. He was unable to accept the $14,000 prize because he was in the service.

MISS BLACK AMERICA PAGEANT HELD

On **SEPTEMBER 8**, the first Miss Black America pageant was held in Atlantic City, New Jersey. Saundra Williams was crowned the first Miss Black America.

NEWTON CONVICTED OF MANSLAUGHTER

On **SEPTEMBER 8**, Huey Newton, a Black Panther leader, was convicted on manslaughter charges in the shooting of an Oakland policeman. He was later given a two- to fifteen-year jail sentence.

TYUS WINS OLYMPIC MEDAL

On **OCTOBER 15**, Wyomia Tyus won a gold medal in the 100-meter race at the Olympic Games in Mexico City, becoming the first person to win this race in two consecutive Olympic competitions

SMITH AND CARLOS WIN OLYMPIC MEDALS

On **OCTOBER 16**, Tommie Smith won the gold medal in the 200-meter dash at the Olympic Games in Mexico City; John Carlos won the bronze medal. During the awards ceremony, Smith and Carlos raised clenched fists to symbolize Black unity. They were suspended from the games two days later.

BEAMON WINS OLYMPIC MEDAL

On **OCTOBER 18**, Bob Beamon won the gold medal in the long jump at the Olympic Games in Mexico City. Beamon jumped 29 feet, 2½ inches, a world record that lasted for many years.

NINE BLACKS ELECTED TO U.S. CONGRESS

On **NOVEMBER 5**, nine African Americans were elected to the U.S. Congress. Shirley Chisholm, the first Black congresswoman, was among them. Together with Massachusetts senator Edward W. Brooke III, they formed the largest number of African Americans to serve in the U.S. Congress since Reconstruction.

1969 AMERICAN BAPTIST CONVENTION SELECTS BLACK LEADER

At the annual conference of the predominantly white American Baptist Convention, Thomas Kilgore, a Black American from Los Angeles, was selected as their president. Kilgore was the first Black to head this religious body.

BLACK CANDIDATES ELECTED TO OFFICE

Voters elected a total of 1,185 Black candidates to political offices around the country. This contrasts with only about 280 Blacks elected to public offices just five years earlier.

CENSUS REPORT ON BLACK POPULATION RELEASED

In a monograph entitled *Changing Characteristics of the Negro Population*, the Bureau of the Census reported that the following factors were involved in the more rapid differential improvements in the occupational status of Black women over Black men:

◈ The women had higher educational levels than the men. During the 1950–1960 decade, the gap in educational achievement between men and women did not decrease (as it did between white men and women) but actually grew larger in each of the four geographic regions;

◈ The occupational gains of the Black woman did not appear to constitute as great a threat to the value system fostered by segregation as did the possible gains of the Black man. This, in turn, led to greater acceptance of the upwardly mobile Black woman than of the Black man;

◈ In job competition with white women, the Black woman was not subject to the economic discrimination encountered by the Black man in competition with white men. Expressed in another way, the sorts of occupational discrimination to which all women were subjected were similar to the discrimination against Blacks, so that the prejudice against Black women was no greater than that against all women;

◈ In some of the occupations reviewed, a greater proportion of nonwhite women worked forty weeks or more in 1959 than did nonwhite men;

◈ In many occupational categories, there was a similarity between the median earnings of white and nonwhite women. This contrasted with the situation for men, where there were significant differences between the median earnings of whites and nonwhites in most of the occupational categories.

COLLINS ELECTED TO FILL OUT CONGRESSIONAL TERM

George Washington Collins was elected to fill out

Tommie Smith and John Carlos brought international attention to the struggle of Black Americans when they gave the Black Power salute after winning medals in the 1968 Olympic games.

MINORITY BUSINESSES IN THE UNITED STATES

A national minority business survey showed 321,958 minority-owned-and-operated business enterprises in the United States in 1969. The volume of business conducted by minority-owned business enterprises in that year represented a small fraction of total business activity. Receipts for this segment of the business community, totaling $10.6 billion, accounted for only 0.7 percent of the 1967 receipts or $1,498 billion reported by all firms combined. The minority-owned businesses represented 4 percent of the total number of enterprises. Nationally, there were 7,489,000 enterprises in the American business community.

❖ Black-owned firms numbered about 163,000, about 2.2 percent of all firms and about 0.3 percent of all receipts;
❖ Black-owned firms employed 151,996 people;
❖ Black-owned firms received 58 percent of their receipts from retail and selected service trades;
❖ Black-owned firms with employees numbered 38,304, with total receipts of $3.6 billion and an average of $95,000.

Source: U.S. Bureau of the Census, 1971.

the unexpired term of Illinois Sixth District U.S. Representative Daniel J. Ronan, who died in August. Later elected to a full term, he tackled issues of concern to his district and to low-income families in general. During his second full term, Collins was killed in an airplane crash on his way to Chicago to help in the annual children's Christmas party.

Collins, born in Chicago, earned a business law degree from Northwestern University and served as deputy sheriff of Cook County and as secretary to Alderman Benjamin Lewis of the Twenty-fourth Ward. When Lewis died, Collins succeeded him as alderman.

DAVIS WINS EMMY

Ossie Davis (1917–), actor, playwright, screenwriter, and director, was awarded an Emmy for his role in *Teacher, Teacher.* Davis, a seasoned and accomplished actor, had starred in a number of successful plays and films. His best known include *Jeb, Purlie Victorious, Let's Do It Again, Do the Right Thing,* and *Jungle Fever.*

EVERS ELECTED MAYOR OF FAYETTE, MISSISSIPPI

James Charles Evers was sworn in as the first African American mayor of Fayette, Mississippi, a small town of about seventeen hundred residents, of whom about three-quarters were Black. His election was a result of the Voting Rights Act of 1968, which allowed the names of Blacks to be placed on registration books. Whites protested by quitting their city jobs and leaving the city. Evers was the first Black mayor of a biracial town in Mississippi since Reconstruction. In 1971 and again in 1983, Evers ran unsuccessfully for the governorship of Mississippi. He is the brother of slain civil rights activist Medgar Evers.

FEW BLACKS AMONG NIXON APPOINTEES

President Richard Nixon appointed only three Blacks to major positions — James Farmer, assistant secre-

Ossie Davis, an actor, playwright, and director, began his career with a small theater group in Harlem. For more than forty years, Davis appeared on the stage and on television. His performances and direction earned him a number of awards, including an Emmy and a Tony.

tary of health, education, and welfare; Arthur A. Fletcher, assistant secretary of labor; and William H. Brown III, chairperson of the Equal Employment Opportunity Commission. He retained Walter Washington as mayor of Washington, D.C.

FISHER WINS EMMY AWARD
Gail Fisher was the first Black actress to win an Emmy. She received the award for her role as Peggy Fair on the *Mannix* television series. Fisher was also the first Black performer to act in a national television commercial with spoken lines.

HOSPITAL WORKERS PROTEST
More than seven hundred Black hospital workers in Charleston, South Carolina struck to protest racial discrimination. The strike was led by Ralph Abernathy of SCLC and was later joined by Coretta Scott King. The workers marched in protest through the city's downtown area. National guardmembers were called in and more than two hundred striking workers were arrested.

JONES WINS TONY AWARD
James Earl Jones earned a Tony Award for his starring role as boxing champion Jack Johnson in *The Great White Hope*. Jones continued to receive top billing in a number of Broadway plays and films.

JUSTICE DEPARTMENT SUES STATE OF GEORGIA
The U.S. Department of Justice sued the state of Georgia for its refusal to implement court-ordered school desegregation plans. Governor Lester Maddox, a staunch racist, responded to the suit by vowing to "win the war against these tyrants." This was the first time the federal government had filed a desegregation suit against an entire state.

MITCHELL FOUNDS DANCE THEATER OF HARLEM
Arthur Mitchell established the Dance Theater of Harlem.

In 1955, Mitchell was the first Black to be a principal dancer in a major American ballet company, the New York City Ballet.

PHILADELPHIA PLAN INSTITUTES AFFIRMATIVE ACTION IN FEDERAL CONSTRUCTION PROJECTS
The "Philadelphia Plan" included guidelines issued by the U.S. Department of Labor for minority employment on federally assisted construction projects. It required contractors on federally assisted construction work exceeding five hundred thousand dollars in cost to hire a specific number or percentage of minority workers.

SLEETS WINS PULITZER PRIZE
Moneta Sleets was awarded the Pulitzer Prize for photographs of Coretta Scott King and her daughter attending the funeral of her husband, Martin Luther King, Jr. Sleets became the first African American to win a Pulitzer Prize for photography.

STUDENTS PROTEST AT BRANDEIS UNIVERSITY
Black student unrest erupted at Brandeis University in Waltham, Massachusetts. Sixty-five Black students invaded Ford Hall, the Brandeis administrative and communication center. They presented a list of demands to Morris A. Abram, Brandeis's president.

SUPREME COURT DECLARES DELAYS IN INTEGRATION UNCONSTITUTIONAL
The U.S. Supreme Court ruled in *Alexander* v. *Holmes* that Mississippi's "continued operation of segregated schools under a standard of 'all deliberate speed' for desegregation is no longer constitutionally permissible.'" The Court also rejected the Nixon administration's appeal for delay in desegregating thirty Mississippi school districts.

SUPREME COURT RULES AGAINST DISCRIMINATION IN HOUSING
The U.S. Supreme Court ruled that cities could not enact ordinances or charter provisions that would have the effect of establishing discrimination in housing. The decision involved a case filed by Nellie Hunter, a Black housewife who had tried to purchase a home in Akron's all-white west side.

KING'S ASSASSIN PLEADS GUILTY
On **MARCH 10**, James Earl Ray pleaded guilty to the assassination of Martin Luther King, Jr., for which he was later sentenced to ninety-nine years in prison. Ray stated that, contrary to the conclusions drawn by U.S. Attorney General Ramsey Clark and FBI chief J. Edgar Hoover, he did not act alone in the assassination. The House Select Committee on Assassinations, too, declared its belief that Ray did not act alone but was part of a larger conspiracy.

BLACK PANTHERS INDICTED
On **APRIL 2**, a total of twenty-one Black Panthers were indicted for a secret plot to kill police officers.

STUDENT UNION AT CORNELL UNIVERSITY CONTROLLED BY BLACK STUDENTS

On **APRIL 19**, Black students took over the student union at Cornell University. They demanded an end to racism and a separate Black college.

No Place to Be Somebody OPENS ON BROADWAY

On **MAY 4**, Charles Gordone's play *No Place to Be Somebody* opened at the Public Theater in New York City. The following year, Gordone was awarded the Pulitzer Prize for drama.

MCLENDON NAMED DENVER NUGGETS COACH

On **MAY 14**, John B. McLendon became the coach of the Denver Nuggets, a professional team in the American Basketball Association (ABA). McLendon became the first African American to coach in the ABA.

JOHNSON PRODUCTS COMPANY INCORPORATES

On **OCTOBER 29**, the Johnson Products Company, a hair care products manufacturing company founded by George Johnson in 1954, was incorporated. In 1971, it became a publicly traded corporation on the American Stock Exchange — the first African American–owned company to be listed on this board.

BLACK PANTHER HEADQUARTERS RAIDED BY POLICE

On **DECEMBER 4**, Chicago police raided the Black Panther headquarters, killing Fred Hampton and Mark Clark and wounding four others. Close to one hundred shots were fired into the headquarters. Evidence suggested that Hampton was not conscious when he was killed. No crime was alleged to have been committed; thus, no police officers were prosecuted. However, a subsequent investigation concluded that the police used undue force.

1970

POPULATION OVERVIEW

BLACK POPULATION IN THE UNITED STATES The U.S. population numbered 203,984,000 residents, of which 22,581,000 (11.1 percent) were Black residents. About 1.5 million Blacks had left the South in each of the previous three decades. Blacks still made up 19 percent of the South's population and 10 percent of the population in the North and the West.

BLACK RESIDENTS IN METROPOLITAN AREAS Almost 28 percent of the residents of the twelve largest metropolitan areas were Black. Black population growth since 1960 had been almost completely concentrated in the central cities of metropolitan areas.

When the 1970 census was taken, four of every ten Blacks were concentrated in just thirty cities. About sixteen cities had Black populations of 50 percent or more, compared to only three such cities in 1960. Blacks made up more than half the population of four large cities: Washington, D.C.; Newark, New Jersey; Atlanta, Georgia; and Gary, Indiana.

The Black trek to the big cities from rural areas was more than matched by the movement of whites to the suburbs. Hence, the cities were becoming increasingly Black, whereas the suburbs were mostly white. In all, Blacks made up only 5 percent of the suburban population, and this group showed only a slight increase in numbers between 1960 and 1970. The trend of business and industry toward relocating into suburban areas would change this pattern somewhat.

No matter how population data were broken out, they showed clearly that the migration patterns of Blacks and whites were different. An examination of city-suburb population and population change for the decade 1960–1970 showed that the white flight from central cities was confined to the largest metropolitan areas, those with over two million people. On the other hand, the data showed that significant white population growth was found in other central cities of the smallest metropolitan areas. In other words, the largest growth of white residents (826,000) was found in the central cities of the smallest metropolitan areas.

The Black population differed significantly in its pattern of population change. Black population growth in central cities showed that the largest metropolises received the largest Black increases (1,755,000). Central cities of the smaller metropolitan areas received smaller numbers of Blacks.

BLACK BELT The Black Belt contributed many Black migrants to urban places in all regions of the country. In 1970, the Black Belt contained about 4,288,911 Black residents.

ECONOMIC CONDITIONS OVERVIEW

BLACK INCOMES INCREASE About one-fourth of the 4.8 million Black families had annual incomes of $10,000 or more. Median family income for Blacks was only 61 percent of median family income for whites. Blacks' median family income reached its highest relative level at this time. The census data showed that the dollar gap between Black and white families was $9,247 annually. The poverty threshold for a nonfarming family of four was recorded at

$3,965 in 1970, up slightly from $3,743 in 1969. By 1970, 7.7 million Blacks and 17.5 million whites were below the poverty level, compared with 7.2 million and 16.7 million, respectively, in 1969. Approximately 34 percent of all Black people were below the poverty level in 1970, compared with 10 percent of whites.

BLACK REPRESENTATION IN ARMED FORCES REMAINS LOW Blacks made up about 293,000 members of the U.S. Armed Forces, 10 percent of the total. Blacks were highly underrepresented among officers, making up only 2 percent of the total. Blacks were more likely to reenlist than were Whites.

EMPLOYMENT OPPORTUNITIES FOR BLACKS There were nine million Black people employed in this country at this time, about 10 percent of the nation's total work force. About one million worked as common laborers on farms, and more than half that number worked as domestics. Blacks had slowly moved into clerical positions — about one million Blacks worked as clerks. Just slightly over half a million Blacks were employed as factory supervisors and craftworkers, and almost a quarter of a million were schoolteachers. Compared with whites, Blacks were disproportionately concentrated in blue-collar jobs. Fully three-fourths of all Black men were in this category, compared with only 53.4 percent of white workers. Black men found in white-collar jobs were heavily concentrated in the lower occupational levels. At the upper end of the job ladder, there were about fourteen thousand Black engineers and fewer than twelve thousand doctors and dentists. Blacks made up only 1 percent of the country's engineers and 2 percent of its physicians and dentists.

Over the decade, the number of Blacks employed in white-collar, crafts, and operative occupations increased by 72 percent, from three million to about five million. For whites, the increase was about 24 percent. Losses occurred in private household jobs and farm labor. Blacks had thus made significant progress over the previous decade, but job equality remained elusive. In fact, within these broad job categories, Blacks continued to hold jobs that paid the least and offered the least opportunity for promotion.

SOCIAL CONDITIONS OVERVIEW

BLACK HOME OWNERSHIP INCREASES Forty-two percent of the nation's 6.2 million Black homes were owner-occupied. Whites, on the other hand, owned 65 percent of the homes they occupied. The pattern varied geographically. The lowest home ownership

among Blacks was found in the Northeast, where only 29 percent were listed as home owners; the highest home ownership for Blacks was in the South, where 47 percent owned homes. In the North Central region, 42 percent of Blacks owned homes; 40 percent of Blacks owned homes in the West. The regional breakdown for whites showed that they were most likely to own their homes in the North Central region (70 percent), followed by the South (68 percent), the Northeast, and the West (each with 60 percent ownership). Home ownership among Blacks, however, was increasing faster than among whites.

EDUCATIONAL LEVEL OF BLACKS ON THE INCREASE Fifty-four percent of young Black men and 58 percent of young Black women completed high school in 1970. Ten years earlier, the figures were 36 percent and 41 percent, respectively.

***Muhammad Speaks* TOPS BLACK NEWSPAPER READERSHIP** Of the total 3.5 million readers of Black publications in 1970, *Muhammad Speaks* had the largest single readership of any Black weekly or daily in the country — more than six hundred thousand readers. Its appeal to Blacks was its emphasis on building self-esteem and improving one's material conditions. Based on the readership figures, the influence of the Black Muslims in the Black community was apparently greater than most researchers have acknowledged.

SOUTHERN PRIVATE SCHOOLS TRY TO AVOID INTEGRATION Since the passage of the Civil Rights Act of 1964, several hundred private schools had opened in the South to circumvent desegregation. Secretary of Housing, Education, and Welfare Robert Finch moved to cut off tax exemptions to these private schools. Finch estimated that as many as four hundred private schools for whites had opened to avoid participation in desegregation of public schools.

BLACKS UNDERREPRESENTED AMONG POLICE IN CERTAIN CITIES

Blacks were underrepresented on city police forces throughout the country. Without doubt, the major obstacle was racial discrimination. Tests used by cities to screen applicants had been found to be racially biased, and if Blacks passed these tests and became police officers, they faced discrimination in assignments and promotions. Of the cities listed in the table, not one had a Black police representation proportionate to the city's Black population. Birmingham had the most disparate representation; Blacks made up 42 percent of the city's residents, but only

1.9 percent of it police officers. New Orleans residents were 45 percent Black, but only 6.1 percent of its police force was Black.

Cotton Comes to Harlem IS MAJOR BOX OFFICE HIT

Ossie Davis produced and directed *Cotton Comes to Harlem*, a movie starring Godfrey Cambridge and Raymond St. Jacques. It grossed more than nine million dollars. Davis thus laid a firm foundation for many other Blacks to produce movies featuring Black actors and actresses only.

COTTRELL OPENS BUSINESS

In this year, Comer Cottrell (1931–) founded a small business that later became known as Pro-Line Corporation. Pro-Line, which produced a number of hair care products, was destined to become the largest Black-owned business in the Southwest.

According to Cottrell, he started the business with six hundred dollars and a borrowed typewriter. The success of Pro-Line allowed Cottrell to invest in a number of other business ventures, including part ownership of a major league baseball team, the Texas Rangers, in 1989.

BROWN HOSTS TELEVISION PROGRAM THAT ADDRESSES BLACK ISSUES

Tony Brown's career in television began in 1970 when he became the executive producer and host of *Black Journal*, the first nationally televised, issues-oriented program produced by a Black person. In 1977, the name of the program was changed to *Tony Brown's Journal.*

In 1971, Brown founded the School of Communication at Howard University and became the school's first dean. As a long-time advocate of community and self-help programming, Brown organized in 1981 the Council for Economic Development of Black Americans, which later launched a "Buy Freedom Network" program encouraging Black consumers to patronize Black-owned businesses.

JOINT CENTER FOR POLITICAL STUDIES FOUNDED

The Joint Center for Political Studies — a nonprofit, nonpartisan organization — was founded in Washington, D.C. The center received a grant from the Ford Foundation to research, collect, and disseminate information on the status of and change in Black politics.

In 1990, the center changed its name to the Joint Center for Political and Economic Studies.

KING WINS GRAMMY

B. B. King (1925–), one of the country's most gifted blues singers, was awarded a Grammy for his hit "The Thrill Is Gone." King and his guitar, Lucille, have had more than fifty hit blues albums during his long career.

LITTLE WINS TONY

Cleavon Little (1939–1993), film and television star, won a Tony for the musical *Purlie.*

In 1989, Little won an Emmy for a guest appearance on the television series *Dear John.* His most visible role was in Mel Brook's *Blazing Saddles.* Little was known for his many roles focusing on the African American experience. His stage credits included *Jimmy Shine, All Over Town, Macbird,* and *The Naked Hamlet.* In 1986, Little was nominated for a Tony as best actor for *I'm Not Rapaport.* The award went to his costar, Judd Hirsch, who called Little to the stage to share the award. His film credits included *What's So Bad about Feeling Good,* and *Cotton Comes to Harlem.*

Essence MAGAZINE PUBLISHED

Essence was founded with the aim of depicting the Black image of the Black woman.

NAACP DENOUNCES NIXON NOMINEE TO SUPREME COURT

The NAACP was successful in pressuring the U.S. Senate to reject President Nixon's nomination of G. Harold Carswell as an associate justice of the U.S. Supreme Court. Civil rights groups believed Carswell was a racist based in part upon a statement he made in 1948 when he expressed a "firm, vigorous belief in the principles of white supremacy."

NATIONAL URBAN COALITION FORMED

The National Urban Coalition was formed by a number of religious, business, labor, and civil leaders who saw the need for an organization to focus national attention on problems and solutions for Blacks in cities. The members identified their main challenges as education, employment, health care, and housing. Operating on funds from private foundations, grants, and contracts, the coalition helped create chapters in a number of major urban centers. Carl Holman served as the executive director of this organization through its early development. Today, Ramona Edelman is the organization's executive director.

NEWSPAPER INDUSTRY DISCRIMINATES AGAINST BLACKS

The major newspapers in the United States had few if any Blacks in decision-making jobs. The *New York Times,* often cited as one of the most liberal newspapers in the country, had only thirteen Black employees among its editorial staff of four hundred. The *Detroit News* had five Blacks among three hundred positions. The *Washington Post* had nineteen Blacks on its editorial staff of two hundred twenty-two. On the basis of these numbers, the *Washington Post* was the "least discriminatory," although many of the jobs held by Blacks were "racially segregated job classifications."

NIXON'S DESEGRATION POLICY CALLED INADEQUATE

The U.S. Commission on Civil Rights issued a report that stated President Nixon's policy on the desegregation of schools in the country was "inadequate, overcautious, and indicative of possible retreat." The NAACP's Legal Defense Fund sued the Department of Health, Education, and Welfare for not enforcing school integration.

RACIAL CLASHES OCCUR AT DESEGREGATED SCHOOLS THROUGHOUT THE COUNTRY

During the early part of the fall school year, a number of schools were closed because of violent racial conflicts. In Pontiac, Michigan, racial conflict left four whites and two Blacks wounded from gunshots; a number of people suffered minor injuries from thrown rocks and bottles. Sniper fire and burning occurred in Henderson, North Carolina. In Trenton, New Jersey, racial violence spread from the school to the downtown area, where major violence against businesses provoked police to arrest hundreds of participants.

Clashes between Blacks and police became more common in northern ghettos. Armed Blacks fired into police stations in Cairo, Illinois, and in Detroit and other big cities; police, Black Panthers, and the National Committee to Combat Fascism continued their violent confrontations.

SCHOOL BUSES BOMBED

In Denver, Colorado, segregationists intent upon maintaining all-white schools dynamited about one-third of the school buses.

SOUTHERN GOVERNORS REJECT BUSING PLANS

The governors of Georgia, Alabama, Louisiana, and Florida pledged to reject all busing plans imposed on their states by the federal government or the courts.

ATLANTA ELECTS BLACK OFFICIALS

In the **JANUARY** elections, Blacks improved their political representation in Atlanta, Georgia. Blacks held five of the eighteen positions on the board of aldermen, and three of the ten members of the board of education were Black. Maynard Jackson was elected vice mayor and president of the board of aldermen, and Benjamin E. Mays was elected to head the school board. The election signaled Blacks' growing political clout in the city.

WHARTON BECOMES UNIVERSITY PRESIDENT

On **JANUARY 2**, Clifton Wharton, Jr., an economist, educator, and administrator, became president of Michigan State University at Lansing, the first African American to preside over a predominantly white public university. (Patrick Francis Healy, as president of Georgetown University in Washington, D.C., had been the first African American to head a predominantly white university.)

◆ Wharton was born in Boston in 1926. He graduated from Harvard University and received an M.A. degree from Johns Hopkins University in Baltimore and a Ph.D. degree in economics in 1958 from the University of Chicago. In 1967, Wharton was selected vice president of the Agricultural Development Council. Wharton's career included visiting professorships at the University of Malaya (1958–1964) and Stanford University (1964–1965) and positions as adviser to the U.S. Department of State (1966–1969) and to the School of Advanced International Studies (1969–1973).

Michigan State experienced the same student unrest as other major campuses. As outrage against injustices and the Vietnam War spread through the university, several buildings were burned. Wharton met with various university groups and entertained their demands, and he met with Blacks and agreed to create an off-campus Black cultural center. He also agreed to double Black enrollment from the 8 percent recorded in May 1970. Through his tenure, Wharton influenced the university to become more responsive to Blacks' needs.

In 1977, Wharton became the chancellor of the State University of New York. In 1993, he served a short time as deputy secretary of state in the Clinton administration.

DESEGREGATION PROCEEDS IN MISSISSIPPI

From **JANUARY 5** to **7**, several school districts in Mississippi desegregated under the watchful eyes of federal marshals sent to ensure compliance with a November 6, 1969, desegregation ruling of the U.S. Fifth Circuit Court of Appeals.

The court ruling ordered thirty Mississippi school districts to desegregate; however, only three opened at this early date for the second semester. Although there was no violence, many white parents picketed the newly desegregated schools. As each day passed, more school districts opened to Blacks. White parents did participate in sit-ins and protested by not sending their children to school, particularly on opening day. Governor John Bell Williams of Mississippi had announced on January 3 that he would work with the state legislature to build a Mississippi private school system and that for the present time, all Mississippians should peacefully accept the ruling. On January 13, Williams asked the state legislature to provide funds to private academies in the form of tax deductions for all who donated money to assist all-white schools in the state.

BIRTHDAY OF KING CELEBRATED

On **JANUARY 15**, Blacks and whites celebrated the anniversary of the birth of Martin Luther King, Jr., and vowed to make this day a national holiday. State governors who supported this measure included Kenneth M. Curtis of Maine, Frank Licht of Rhode Island, and Nelson Rockefeller of New York — all of whom had declared Martin Luther King, Jr., Day in their respective states. Big cities such as Baltimore, Kansas City, New York City, and Philadelphia closed schools in tribute. Coretta Scott King, the widow of Martin Luther King, Jr., dedicated Atlanta's new Memorial Center in the name of her slain husband.

WHITES ATTACK BUS CARRYING BLACK CHILDREN

On **MARCH 3**, angry whites swinging ax handles and baseball bats attacked school buses bringing Black children to integrate an all-white school in Lamar, South Carolina. State troopers used riot clubs and tear gas to disperse the mob of more than two hundred whites. Several children received minor injuries, but state troopers made no attempt to arrest anyone involved in the attack. Later, federal marshals attempted to identify the leaders.

VOTING RIGHTS ACT EXTENDED

On **MARCH 13**, the U.S. Senate voted to extend the Voting Rights Act of 1965 for another five years. Included among the new provisions of the act was a ban on literacy tests.

RACE RIOT OCCURS IN AUGUSTA, GEORGIA

On **MAY 12**, racial rioting erupted in Augusta, Georgia, and police used the ultimate force — killing — to bring calm to the city. Six Black men were killed by local police. In September, a federal grand jury indicted two white police officers for violating the civil rights of two Black men — John W. Stokes, who was killed, and Louis N. Williams, who was wounded during the racial rioting.

BLACK COLLEGE STUDENTS KILLED IN RACIAL DISTURBANCE

On **MAY 14**, police were called to the women's dorm at Jackson State University, Jackson, Mississippi, to bring order. The racial disturbances escalated, and two Black students were killed; twelve were wounded as the police opened fire indiscriminately. Two days later, Blacks reacted to the killings by boycotting white-owned businesses.

STUDENT VIOLENCE ERUPTS AT OHIO STATE UNIVERSITY

On **MAY 21**, the National Guard was called in to calm student violence when Black and white students joined to protest the presence of ROTC programs on the campus and the lack of African American student admissions.

RANGEL DEFEATS POWELL IN CONGRESSIONAL PRIMARY

In **JUNE** of this year, Charles Rangel (1930–) ran against perhaps the nation's most famous Black legislator, the Reverend Adam Clayton Powell, Jr., for the Democratic primary in New York's Eighteenth Congressional District. Powell had held the seat, which included Harlem, almost continuously for twenty-five years. After a narrow victory in the June primary, Rangel was elected by a wide margin in the November general election. Rangel became one of eight African Americans in the U.S. House of Representatives at this time.

◆ Rangel was born in New York City. He did not graduate from high school until after he had served in the U.S. Army in the Korean War. He was discharged as a staff sergeant in 1952. Five years later, he received a B.S. degree from New York University School of Commerce. In 1960, he received his law degree from St. John's University.

His legal career included a year as an assistant U.S. attorney for the Southern District of New York, counsel to the speaker of the New York Assembly, counsel to the President's Commission to Revise the Draft Laws, and legal adviser to many civil rights leaders.

He served two terms in the New York Assembly prior to his election to Congress.

During his more than ten years in Congress, Rangel emerged as a leader in fighting drug addiction and drug-related crime. He opposed any legislation that might lead to the legalization of drugs. He favored decreasing U.S. financial and military aid to countries that did not participate in international efforts to control drug trade. As chairperson of the Select Committee on Narcotics Abuse and Control, he was critical of proposed reductions in the antidrug budget. He was instrumental in amending the Omnibus Drug Bill to increase financial aid to state and local law enforcement agencies.

Rangel also worked to extend tax credits to businesses that employed Vietnam veterans, former prisoners, welfare recipients, and economically disadvantaged workers. He is currently a senior member of the House Committee on Ways and Means and has served as the chairperson of the Congressional Black Caucus. Former Speaker of the House Tip O'Neill, Jr., appointed Rangel a deputy whip in 1983.

In 1992, Rangel was reelected to his twelfth term in the House. He captured 96 percent of the votes in his district.

NAACP DENOUNCES NIXON ADMINISTRATION AS "ANTI-NEGRO"

On **JUNE 29**, the chairman of the NAACP's board of directors, Bishop Stephen Gill Spottswood, denounced the Nixon administration as "anti-Negro" in his address to the annual NAACP convention in Cincinnati, Ohio. Spottswood detailed the Nixon administration's retreat from school desegregation, nomination of conservative southerners to the U.S. Supreme Court, and acceptance of Daniel Moynihan's confidential memo on "benign neglect" of Blacks.

Moynihan was serving as Nixon's domestic adviser. The memo stated, "The time may have come when the issue of race could benefit from 'benign neglect.'" Moynihan later explained that he meant that Blacks could fare better if extremists on both sides

would lower their voices. He said that the purpose of the memo was to update the president on the progress of Blacks over the last ten years and to suggest ways in which these gains could be consolidated.

RACE RIOTS OCCUR IN NORTHERN CITIES

In **JULY**, a number of northern cities experienced racial rioting in response to inadequate housing, high unemployment, and crime. On July 7, Asbury Park, New Jersey, experienced four days of rioting in which as many as forty-three citizens were wounded. Black organizations helped to bring calm to the city and presented white city leaders with demands.

On July 12, New Bedford, Massachusetts, flared up in violence, and on July 31, Hartford, Connecticut, erupted in violence by African Americans and Puerto Ricans. In each of the cities, three to four days of rioting ended with sections of the city shut down because of confrontations among racial groups.

GIBSON ELECTED MAYOR OF NEWARK

On **JULY 1**, Kenneth A. Gibson, a city engineer, was elected mayor of Newark, New Jersey. He was the first African American to be elected to this position. In a city generally known for its corruption, Gibson ran on a platform concerned with cleaning up government.

In 1982, Gibson was elected to a fourth term as mayor, but he admitted to having done little to clean up government corruption.

McGEE BECOMES MAYOR OF DAYTON

On **JULY 15**, James McGee was sworn in as the first African American mayor of Dayton, Ohio. Dayton was the fourth largest city in the United States to elect a Black mayor. McGee, an attorney, had served as city commissioner from 1967 to 1970. He was mayor of Dayton until 1982.

SCOTT APPOINTED SCHOOL SUPERINTENDENT

On **SEPTEMBER 1**, Dr. Hugh S. Scott was appointed superintendent of schools in Washington, D.C., thus becoming the first Black to hold such a position in a major U.S. city.

PRIVATE ALL-WHITE ACADEMIES LOSE TAX-EXEMPT STATUS

On **SEPTEMBER 11**, the Internal Revenue Service (IRS) revoked the tax-exempt status of five all-white private academies in Mississippi when they refused to admit Black children. This effort provoked the federal government and the IRS to review racial discrimination policies of these private schools and academies.

WILSON STARS ON TELEVISION

On **SEPTEMBER 17**, Flip Wilson's program, *The Flip Wilson Show*, premiered on NBC-TV. It was the first time an African American had starred in a prime-time variety show since *The Nat King Cole Show*.

HEW INCREASES AID TO HISTORICALLY BLACK COLLEGES AND UNIVERSITIES

On **OCTOBER 1**, Department of Health, Education, and Welfare (HEW) secretary Elliot L. Richardson announced that historically Black colleges and universities would get a 30 percent increase in federal aid, an amount equal to about $30 million. Richardson noted that the increase came in response to an appeal by Black educators. Although the funds were made available, Black educators complained that qualifications for them required matching provisions and that they were not given enough time to prepare applications.

DELLUMS ELECTED TO CONGRESS

In **NOVEMBER**, Ronald V. Dellums, a psychiatric social worker, was elected to the U.S. House of Representatives from the Seventh Congressional District in California. He represented a district with a population that was less than 30 percent Black. Coretta Scott King actively campaigned for Dellums while Vice President Spiro Agnew worked with local Republicans to defeat him. Dellums was a vocal critic of Nixon's policy in Vietnam.

◈ In Congress, Dellums established himself as an opponent of the growing defense budget. Dellums became a member of the House Armed Services Committee and chairperson of the Subcommittee on Military Installations and Facilities. He became chairperson of the Armed Service Committee in 1993 when Les Aspin left the Congress to become secretary of defense in the Clinton administration. Dellums was also chairperson of the Committee on the District of Columbia. During his terms in the House, Dellums introduced legislation on health care, housing, the environment, and restrictions on nuclear arms deployment. He was elected chair of the Congressional Black Caucus in 1988.

Dellums was born in 1935 in Oakland, the son of a longshoreman and labor organizer. After serving in the Marine Corps, he earned a B.A. degree from San Francisco State College and an M.A. degree in social welfare from the University of California at Berkeley.

Ronald V. Dellums, a social worker, became a member of the U.S. House of Representatives in 1970. In more than twenty years in Congress, he rose to become the chairman of two major committees.

In 1967, he was elected to the Berkeley City Council, where he became a spokesperson for minorities and the disadvantaged.

METCALFE ELECTED TO CONGRESS

In **NOVEMBER**, Olympic medal winner, teacher, and former Chicago city council member Ralph H. Metcalfe (1910–1978) was elected to Congress to represent the First Congressional District of Illinois, a seat that had been held since 1942 by William L. Dawson. Dawson had retired from the seat and had strongly supported Metcalfe's bid. Metcalfe was elected only a few days before Dawson died.

◈ Metcalfe, born in Atlanta, migrated to Chicago with his family. From the time he was fifteen years old, Metcalfe excelled at track. His track career culminated in medal-winning performances at the

Olympic Games of 1932 and 1936. After serving in the U.S. Army, Metcalfe became director of the Chicago Commission on Human Relations' civil rights department. In 1952, he was elected a Democratic committeeman from Chicago's Third Ward. Three years later, he won a seat on the city council.

During his four terms in Congress, Metcalfe worked in a number of areas of interest to Blacks. He fought to eliminate the practice of "redlining" — the withholding of home loan funds and insurance from low-income neighborhoods. He worked to improve opportunities for minority-owned businesses. For example, he was successful in adding an amendment to railroad legislation that would give minority-owned firms the chance to work on projects to revitalize the national railroad system.

After his first term in office, Metcalfe broke his association with Chicago's Democratic machine, led by Mayor Richard J. Daley. Metcalfe charged that Black citizens had been abused by city police, and he held a number of hearings at which victims and witnesses could publicly air their grievances. Metcalfe organized a citizens' group to lobby for reform in city government, and he further emphasized the split by refusing to back machine candidates, including Daley, in his mayoral campaign in 1975. Daley responded by depriving Metcalfe of patronage in the Third Ward and by backing his aide, Erwin A. France, to challenge Metcalfe in the Democratic primary in 1976. Metcalfe defeated France by a large margin, and two years later ran unopposed for renomination. However, one month before the general election in November 1978, Metcalfe died. His seat was captured by Bennett Stewart.

MITCHELL ELECTED TO CONGRESS

In **NOVEMBER**, Democrat Parren J. Mitchell was elected Maryland's first Black congressman.

He had served as executive secretary of the Maryland Human Relations Commission, which was implementing the state's public accommodations law. He was also a professor of sociology at Morgan State University and president of Baltimore Neighborhoods, Inc.

U.S. Congressman Parren Mitchell (at podium), from Maryland, served as the chairman of the Congressional Black Caucus. He is shown here with other members of the caucus, Shirley Chisholm and Cardiss Collins, of Illinois.

Mitchell had run unsuccessfully for the U.S. House of Representatives seat in 1968. During his eight terms in Congress, Mitchell worked toward promoting minority-owned businesses, including supporting a fixed percentage of set-aside work for minority contractors on federal projects.

He became chairperson of the Committee on Small Business in 1981. In 1985, Mitchell announced he would not seek reelection.

Mitchell is the brother of Clarence Mitchell, Jr., a civil rights leader who played a prominent role in promoting the Civil Rights Act of 1968. The entire Mitchell family of Baltimore is known for its civil rights leadership.

1971 BLACK ARTISTS AND ENTERTAINERS ENJOY SUCCESS IN MANY FIELDS

Black authors published numerous works, including Maya Angelou's first book of poetry, *Just Give Me a Cool Drink of Water 'fore I Die*, Gwendolyn Brooks's two volumes of poetry, *Family Pictures* and *Aloneness*, Nikki Giovanni's *Spin a Soft Black Song: Poems for Young People*, and Ernest J. Gaines's *The Autobiography of Miss Jane Pittman*, a novel that was later made into an award-winning television movie.

In the film industry, Melvin Van Peebles wrote, starred in, produced, directed, and distributed *Sweet Sweet Back's Baadaass Song*, which grossed $15 million at the box office. At the time, this was the largest gross for a Black-oriented film. *Shaft*, another Black-oriented film, was released, directed by Gordon Parks. Its theme song, performed by Isaac Hayes, became a pop hit and won an Academy Award for best song.

As many as fifty-eight Black painters and sculptors exhibited their work in "Contemporary Black Artists in America," which opened at the Whitney Museum of American Art in New York. Among those whose works were exhibited were Jacob Lawrence, David Driskell, and Alma Thomas.

ATTICA PRISONERS REVOLT TO END DISCRIMINATION

In Attica, New York, Black and Puerto Rican prisoners rioted to bring attention to widespread racial discrimination and inhumane prison conditions. Both guards and prisoners were held hostage, and forty were killed. Many of the deaths occurred when more than one thousand state troopers, guards, and local policemen stormed the prison. It is considered the worst prison riot in American history.

BLACK PANTHER LEADER TRIED IN NEW HAVEN

The six-month trial in New Haven, Connecticut, of Bobby Seale, chair of the Black Panther Party, and Ericka Huggins, a New Haven Panther, for crimes arising from the death of Alex Rackley, ended with a hung jury.

Rackley, a Panther, died in May 1969. The state contended that Rackley was killed because the party leadership believed he was an informer.

In the same year, thirteen Black Panthers in New York were acquitted of 156 conspiracy charges (including the bombing of police stations and department stores). It was the longest-running trial in New York history — nine months. The U.S. House of Representatives Internal Security Committee reported that the Black Panthers posed a danger to law enforcement officials, but were incapable of overthrowing the U.S. government.

BLACK UNEMPLOYMENT RATE REMAINS TWICE THAT OF WHITES

The average unemployment rate in 1971 was 9.9 percent of the work force. Black joblessness was twice that of whites. It was higher in the central cities than in the suburbs. About 32 percent of Black teenagers were out of work.

BROWN INDUCTED INTO PRO FOOTBALL HALL OF FAME

Jim Brown (1936–), one of the most gifted running backs in the National Football League (NFL), was inducted into the Pro Football Hall of Fame.

Brown played for the Cleveland Browns from 1957 through 1965, during which time he won a record eight league rushing titles and placed second among all-time leading rushers, with 12,312 yards. After his retirement, he became a movie actor and businessman.

JACKSON FOUNDS OPERATION PUSH

The Reverend Jesse Jackson (1941–), addressing four thousand cheering Blacks, announced the founding of a new organization for economic and political action — People United to Save Humanity (PUSH). The announcement followed Jackson's sixty-day suspension by leaders of the Southern Christian Leadership Conference from his post as director of Operation Breadbasket — which he had started in 1966 — and his subsequent resignation from both organizations.

CIVIL RIGHTS ORGANIZATIONS PUT JOBS HIGH ON AGENDA

Civil rights organizations were successful in opening doors to employment opportunities. In an agreement with Bethlehem Steel, a quota system was adopted to ensure fair hiring, training, and promotion of Black workers. In Chicago, Jesse Jackson and his recently organized Operation PUSH (People United to Save Humanity) staged a four-day "Black Expo" exhibition designed to stimulate interest and investment in Black-owned businesses. More than 800,000 people attended.

Blacks made gains at the top levels of the corporate structure. Leon Sullivan was elected to the board of directors of General Motors, the first Black American to hold such a position. James O. Plinton, Jr., became corporate head of Eastern Airlines.

KLAN MEMBERS ARRESTED IN MICHIGAN

In Pontiac, Michigan, six Ku Klux Klan members were arrested for bombing ten school buses.

NIX APPOINTED TO PENNSYLVANIA SUPREME COURT

Robert N. C. Nix, Jr., became the first African American to sit on the Pennsylvania Supreme Court.

In 1984, Nix became the first African American chief justice of a state supreme court. He was selected by his peers as president of the Conference of Chief Justices, an honor which no other African American had received.

Nix was born on July 13, 1928, in Philadelphia.

PAIGE INDUCTED INTO BASEBALL HALL OF FAME

Satchel Paige (1906–1982) was inducted into the Baseball Hall of Fame.

In 1971, Leroy Robert "Satchel" Paige, the first Black pitcher in the American League and the first Black to pitch in a World Series, became the first Black to be elected to the Baseball Hall of Fame.

Paige, a baseball pitcher, played for all-Black teams until he became the first African American pitcher signed to play in the American League. He joined the Cleveland Indians in 1948 and played with them until 1951, at which time he was bought by the St. Louis Browns, with whom he played until 1953. He pitched a number of no-hitters and was considered one of the greatest pitchers in the game. Paige played the game of baseball for more than forty years.

RACE RIOTS OCCUR IN WILMINGTON, NORTH CAROLINA, AND OTHER CITIES

A race riot occurred in Wilmington, North Carolina, and two Black persons were killed. Benjamin Chavis (later executive secretary of the NAACP) and nine other people were arrested and charged with burning a store in the Wilmington riot. They became known as the "Wilmington Ten." Amnesty International and other groups joined together to get the convictions overturned. Other riots erupted in the Brownsville section of New York City and Black areas of Chattanooga, Tennessee; Jacksonville, Florida; and Columbus, Georgia.

SUPREME COURT BARS DISCRIMINATORY EMPLOYMENT PRACTICES

In *Griggs* v. *Duke Power*, the U.S. Supreme Court ruled that a North Carolina firm discriminated against Blacks by requiring that applicants for menial jobs be high school graduates or pass IQ tests. In this case, the Court ruled that tests for hiring and promotion had to be related to job performance and could not be used to exclude minorities.

TOP TEN INSURANCE COMPANIES OWNED BY BLACKS LISTED

In 1971, the National Insurance Association published its "Golden Anniversary Membership Roster," which listed the largest members of the association. In this year, North Carolina Life Insurance Company, with more than ninety-four million dollars in assets, led all others; it was followed by Atlanta Life Insurance Company, Supreme Life Insurance Company of America, Universal Life Insurance Company, and Golden State Mutual Life Insurance Company.

CONGRESSIONAL BLACK CAUCUS BOYCOTTS NIXON'S STATE OF THE UNION ADDRESS

In **JANUARY**, members of the Congressional Black Caucus absented themselves from President Nixon's state of the union address after the president refused to meet with them. The caucus, created in 1970 and composed of twelve Black members of Congress, had asked for the meeting after holding special congressional hearings concerning the killing of Black Panther members Fred Hampton and Mark Clark in December 1969. The caucus was later given the chance to meet with the president.

FLOYD APPOINTED PRINCETON MAYOR

On **JANUARY 1**, James A. Floyd was selected by the five-member Township Committee in Princeton, New Jersey, to be the township's mayor. Floyd became the first Black mayor in the history of this affluent, predominantly white suburban community. Later, the Township Committee appointed Frederick M. Porter, a Black man, as chief of police.

SUPREME COURT RULES IN FAVOR OF BUSING FOR INTEGRATION

On **APRIL 20**, the U.S. Supreme Court ruled in *Swan* v. *Charlotte-Mecklenburg* that busing and redistricting were tools that could be used for integrating American schools. The ruling struck directly at the state-imposed segregation of the South. Many of the northern states were exempt, because barriers to integration reflected housing patterns rather than law, constituting de facto rather than de jure segregation. About 58 percent of northern Black children attended schools that were 80 percent to 100 percent Black, compared with only 39 percent in the South. Almost immediately, the NAACP requested the Court to apply the rulings to northern states. One week before the Court's ruling, northern liberals and southern conservatives teamed up to defeat a twenty-billion-dollar plan to speed desegregation. Democratic Senator Abraham Ribicoff from Connecticut blasted his colleagues in the U.S. Senate for hypocrisy and stated, "I do not see how you can ever point your finger at a Southern senator or a Southern school district and tell them that they are discriminating against Black children when you are unwilling to desegregate schools in your own cities."

RACE RIOTS BREAK OUT IN TENNESSEE

On **MAY 21**, the National Guard was called into Chattanooga to put down riots that had spread through much of the downtown area and adjacent Black sections. One Black person died, and more than four hundred were arrested.

Busing of children met with opposition from whites, which forced the Supreme Court to declare the legality of busing.

PIRATES FIELD FIRST ALL-BLACK TEAM
On **SEPTEMBER 1**, the Pittsburgh Pirates baseball team fielded an African American in every position on the team that played against the Philadelphia Phillies. It was the first time that a major league team fielded only Blacks in professional play.

FAUNTROY ELECTED TO REPRESENT DISTRICT OF COLUMBIA
In **NOVEMBER**, Walter Fauntroy became the first elected representative from the District of Columbia in more than one hundred years.

A native of Washington, D.C., Fauntroy earned a B.A. degree from Virginia Union University and a B.D. degree from Yale University Divinity School. He served as minister of New Bethel Baptist Church in the District of Columbia. Fauntroy had a long history of service in the civil rights movement. He was appointed by Martin Luther King, Jr., as director of the Washington Bureau of the Southern Christian Leadership Conference in 1960. He was the district coordinator for the March on Washington in August 1963 and the coordinator of the 1965 march from Selma to Montgomery, Alabama. Within the District of

Columbia, he had founded and directed the Shaw Urban Renewal Project, which focused on the revitalization of a neighborhood, and the Model Inner City Community Organization.

In 1970, Congress passed the District of Columbia Delegate Act, which provided for the District's representation in Congress. The following year, Fauntroy won the Democratic nomination for the seat and was elected by an overwhelming majority. After his election, he worked for home rule for the District of Columbia. In 1973, the District of Columbia Self-Government and Governmental Reorganization Act became law, thereby allowing limited self-rule, including an elected mayor and city council.

In March 1990, Fauntroy announced he was giving up his seat to run for mayor of the District of Columbia. He found it difficult to generate support for his candidacy while being investigated by the U.S. Justice Department, concerning the employment of a colleague's son in the U.S. House of Representatives. He was defeated in his bid.

BAYLOR RETIRES
On **NOVEMBER 4**, Elgin Baylor retired from the Los Angeles Lakers.

During his fourteen-year career in the NBA, Baylor scored 23,149 points, the third highest lifetime score of any player in the league. Baylor ranked as the fifth highest career rebounder.

1972 ARMED FORCES RACIAL COMPOSITION
BECOMING MORE BALANCED
African Americans made up a larger number of enlistees in all branches of the military. This trend had continued since 1948, when President Harry S. Truman issued an executive order that ended segregation in the armed forces.

BLACK INCOMES INCREASE
Measures of income showed that Blacks had made substantial gains since 1960. In fact, the gap between Black and white incomes over the 1960–1972 period had lessened. The ratio of Black to white median incomes rose from 53 percent to 62 percent for men, from 62 percent to 96 percent for women, and from 56 to 62 percent for families.

Absolute income gains occurred in all regions of the country from 1960 to 1972. The greatest absolute and relative improvements occurred in the South, where median Black family income grew from 46 per-

cent of white income to 55 percent over the period. In the West, it increased from 67 percent to 71 percent. However, in the Northeast and the North Central regions, Black family income as a percentage of white family income was less in 1972 than in 1959.

Black family income improvements were not consistent over this period. After 1966, the gap between Blacks and whites actually widened, both in the United States as a whole and in each of the regions, most notably in the Northeast, where the gap widened by as much as 7 percentage points.

BLACKS ELECTED TO NINETY-SECOND CONGRESS
The ten congressional districts with Black populations in excess of 50 percent were represented by nine Black congressmen and one Black congresswoman. Of the twelve congressional districts with 38 percent to 49 percent Black population, only one — Chicago's First District — was represented by a Black, George Collins. Ronald V. Dellums was the only Black congressman elected from a district with less than a 30 percent Black population.

BLACKS REMAIN DISPROPORTIONATELY POOR
A total of 7.7 million Blacks (31.5 percent of all Blacks) still lived in poverty in 1972 (annual income less than $4,275 for a nonfarm family of four). Another two million were classified as near poor (incomes below 125 percent of poverty level). Those in poverty and those near poverty accounted for 42 percent of Blacks. Blacks were still three times more likely to be poor than whites. The Black poor were more likely to reside in central cities and in the South, although the number of Blacks living in poverty in the South had declined by almost 2.7 million since 1959. In the North and West, the number of Blacks living in poverty had increased by two hundred thousand. Poverty among Blacks in areas outside metropolitan areas had dropped from 50 percent to 38 percent between 1959 and 1971, but in central cities, poverty among Blacks had increased from 38 percent to 49 percent. In 1972, 2.7 million Black children, two-thirds of those in poverty, lived in homes headed by women.

BLACKS USED AS GUINEA PIGS IN MEDICAL EXPERIMENT
It was reported that U.S. health officials had used Blacks as guinea pigs in a forty-year syphilis experiment. Beginning in 1932, the U.S. Public Health Service had used three hundred Black male residents of

Macon County, Alabama, as subjects in what came to be popularly known as the Tuskegee Syphilis Study. In the study, which was essentially nontherapeutic, officials studied morbidity and mortality among untreated Black male syphilis victims: subjects in later stages of the disease received neither new drug therapies nor those already known and in use.

CHISHOLM BECOMES CANDIDATE FOR PRESIDENT
Shirley Chisholm campaigned for the presidency of the United States, becoming the first Black woman to seek the nation's highest political office. She raised the consciousness of the American people on many problems of the poor, women, and minorities.

FREEDOM NATIONAL BANK IN HARLEM IS LARGEST BLACK-OWNED BANK
Although the number of Black-owned banks in the country was growing, most had relatively small assets. As of March 31, the Freedom National Bank in Harlem ranked as the largest Black-owned bank in the country, with assets of $53,871,473. Ranked by assets, the Freedom National Bank did not place among the thousand largest banks in this country.

GIBSON VOTED INTO BASEBALL HALL OF FAME
Josh Gibson was posthumously voted into the Baseball Hall of Fame for his leadership and play of the game with the Homestead Grays, an all-Black baseball team. Some sportswriters still call Gibson the greatest baseball player ever.

Racial discrimination prohibited the nation and world from seeing this talented player, or of measuring his talents against the best in the white leagues. Gibson hit eighty home runs in one season, the most of any player in Black or white leagues. He earned the nickname "the Babe Ruth of Negro Baseball."

HOOKS APPOINTED TO FCC
President Richard Nixon appointed Benjamin L. Hooks to the Federal Communications Commission (FCC). Hooks, a Memphis attorney and minister, became the first Black person to serve as a member of this powerful commission. Later, Hooks was selected to head the NAACP.

MORIAL ELECTED MAYOR OF NEW ORLEANS
Ernest N. Morial, a lawyer, judge, and state legislator, was elected first Black mayor of the city of New Orleans.

NIXON REJECTS BUSING AS MEANS OF INTEGRATING SCHOOLS
The busing of children, Black and white, from one neighborhood school district to another, became a controversial political issue. The Nixon administration supported and signed into law a bill that prohibited busing solely to achieve racial integration. Nixon stated that busing was a "classic case of the remedy for one evil creating another evil." Although Gallup polls showed that the country favored desegregating public schools, the polls also revealed an undercurrent of antipathy toward busing.

PRISON INMATES DISPROPORTIONATELY BLACK
A 1972 jail survey revealed that 42 percent of all inmates were Black. Blacks represented 58,000 of the 141,600 total inmates. The survey showed that of the jailed Blacks, 70 percent had less than a high school education, 46 percent had incomes of less than $2,000 annually at the time of arrest, and 12 percent had been earning less than $3,000 annually.

ROSS CAST IN *Lady Sings the Blues*
Diana Ross, formerly of the Motown singing group the Supremes, continued her film career in the role of Billie Holiday in the film *Lady Sings the Blues.* Her performance received excellent reviews. Ross later received a Tony Award for her Broadway show *An Evening with Diana Ross.*

SUPREME COURT RULES AGAINST SEPARATE EDUCATION DISTRICTS
In *Wright* v. *City of Emporia* and *Cotton* v. *Schotland Neck Board of Education,* the Supreme Court held that these towns (which had a vast majority of white students) could not secede from a largely Black county school system and form another school district to avoid integration.

WASHINGTON ELECTED MAYOR OF WASHINGTON, D.C.
Walter Washington, a public official and lawyer, began his four-year term as mayor of Washington, D.C. Washington received a B.A. degree from Howard University in 1938 and an LL.D. degree from Howard University Law School in 1948.

In 1941, Washington started working his way through the ranks at the National Capital Housing Authority, finally becoming the executive director. In 1966, he was selected chairperson of the New York City Housing Authority by Mayor John Lindsay. In

1967, Washington was encouraged to return to Washington, D.C., to head a nine-member city council.

In 1976, Washington was reelected to a second term as mayor.

CHAMBERLAIN SCORES THIRTY-THOUSANDTH POINT

On **FEBRUARY 16**, Wilt Chamberlain, center for the Los Angeles Lakers, scored his thirty-thousandth point while playing the Phoenix Suns. Chamberlain was the first player in National Basketball Association history to achieve this distinction. Chamberlain retired after the 1972 season.

NATIONAL BLACK POLITICAL CONVENTION HELD IN INDIANA

On **MARCH 10** through **12**, more than eight thousand Black delegates and observers met in Gary, Indiana, at the first National Black Political Convention and voted to establish a permanent representative body to set the direction for Black political and social actions. The convention was almost ignored by the white media but was hailed by the Black media as an important political and cultural event. It signaled to Black people across the country that Black leaders were aware of their plight and frustrated with the American political system, which continued to ignore Black Americans. The convention and its agenda were endorsed by the Black Political Caucus of the U.S. House of Representatives, the Southern Christian Leadership Conference, and several other major groups. The writer LeRoi Jones and the Black mayor of Gary, Indiana, Richard B. Hatcher, were credited with moving the political and social agendas along and helping the group reach agreement on common issues. Thirty-five delegates from forty-four states debated a "National Black Political Agenda," which reflected the frustration of its delegates:

> Our cities are crime-haunted dying grounds. Huge sectors of our youth — and countless others — face permanent unemployment. Those of us who work find our paychecks able to purchase less and less. Neither the courts nor the prisons contribute to anything resembling justice or reformation. The schools are unable — or unwilling — to educate our children for the real world of our struggles. Meanwhile, the officially approved epidemic of drugs threatens to wipe out the minds and strength of our best young warriors. Economic, cultural, and spiritual depression stalk Black America, and the price for survival often appears to be more than we are able to pay.

USS *Jesse L. Brown* LAUNCHED

On **MARCH 18**, Jesse L. Brown, an African American naval pilot killed in the Korean War, was honored when a U.S. naval ship bearing his name was launched in Westwego, Louisiana. It was the first U.S. naval ship to be named after an African American naval officer.

Brown, a pilot, was a member of the U.S. Naval Reserve when killed in the Korean War.

RODGERS NAMED TEACHER OF THE YEAR

On **APRIL 24**, James M. Rodgers, Jr., was named National Teacher of the Year at a ceremony in his honor at the White House. Rodgers, a native of Durham, North Carolina, was the first African American to be honored in this way.

DAVIDSON HEADS ARMY DIVISION

On **APRIL 25**, Major General Frederick E. Davidson was appointed commanding general of the Eighth Infantry Division in Europe, becoming the first African American to be head of a U.S. Army division.

WALLACE SURVIVES ASSASSINATION ATTEMPT

On **MAY 15**, in Laurel, Maryland, an assassination attempt was made on the life of Alabama governor George Wallace, an independent candidate for president of the United States. His campaign had focused primarily on the issue of busing and desegregation. He had already won the Florida Democratic primary. Wallace was hit by bullets in many parts of his body, including the spine. Arthur Bremer, the gunman, was captured moments after he fired the shots.

Bremer, a white person, was found to have planned the assassination for some time. Although Wallace survived the attempt, he was paralyzed for life.

DAVIS ACQUITTED

On **JUNE 4**, Angela Davis, a Black Marxist, was acquitted of conspiracy to kidnap and murder. An all-white jury deliberated for more than thirteen hours before reaching its verdict. Davis, a twenty-eight-year-old philosopher and ex-teacher at the University of California, was elated with the decision.

NATIONAL BLACK MBA ASSOCIATION INCORPORATED

On **JUNE 12**, the National Black MBA [Master of Business Administration] Association was incorporated. The organization was developed to help minorities, primarily Black people, enter the business community as professional employees and as business owners and managers.

DEATH PENALTY SET ASIDE BY SUPREME COURT

On **JUNE 29**, the U.S. Supreme Court set aside the death sentences of two men. The Court ruled in a 5–4 decision that the death penalty imposed cruel and unusual punishment and was thus unconstitutional. Some justices reasoned that if states redrafted legislation to meet nondiscriminatory standards, they might legally be able to carry out the death penalty. The NAACP approved the decision; it had been campaigning for several decades against the death penalty and the highly discriminatory manner in which it had been used. The last execution had occurred in June 1967.

PATTERSON BECOMES VICE CHAIRPERSON OF DEMOCRATIC NATIONAL COMMITTEE

On **JULY 14**, Basil Patterson was elected vice chairperson of the Democratic National Committee, becoming the first African American to hold such a high position in a national political party.

DISHONORABLE DISCHARGES OF BROWNSVILLE SOLDIERS TOO HARSH

On **SEPTEMBER 28**, the secretary of the U.S. Army rescinded the dishonorable discharges given to 167 soldiers after the Brownsville, Texas, riot of 1906.

Soldiers of the Twenty-fifth Infantry had been involved in a riot with city police and merchants. In response to city and state pressure to punish the African Americans soldiers, President Theodore Roosevelt had discharged the soldiers without a trial. The army now found that this action had been improper.

BURKE ELECTED TO CONGRESS

In **NOVEMBER**, Yvonne Brathwaite Burke was elected to the U.S. House of Representatives from California's Thirty-seventh District. She was the first Black woman to represent the state of California in the U.S. Congress. Burke supported many social and economic programs of concern to Black and other minority citizens. Burke's tenure in the Congress extended from the Ninety-third to the Ninety-fifth Congress.

Burke had served the state in various capacities before being elected to the U.S. Congress, including deputy corporation commissioner, hearing officer for the Los Angeles Police Commission, staff attorney of the McCone Commission, which investigated causes of the Watts riots of 1965, and member of the Califor-

nia Assembly. In 1978, she ran unsuccessfully for state attorney general of California. She now practices law in Los Angeles.

JORDAN ELECTED TO CONGRESS

In **NOVEMBER**, Barbara Jordan (1936–) of Texas became the first Black woman representative in the U.S. Congress elected from the South, defeating Republican Paul Merritt to represent Texas's Eighteenth Congressional District.

◈ Jordan was born in Houston. She was educated there and received a B.A. degree in political science and history from Texas Southern University in 1956. After receiving a law degree from Boston College, she began practicing law in Houston.

Upon her election to the U.S. House of Representatives, Jordan became a member of the House Judiciary Committee. It was as a part of this committee, which held hearings on the possible impeachment of President Richard Nixon, that Jordan became nationally prominent. Her belief in the Constitution of the United States was eloquently presented during the hearings. She voted for all five articles of impeachment. Her eloquence led to her selection as the keynote speaker of the Democratic National Convention in 1976. She was the first Black and first woman to be honored in this way.

During her three terms in Congress, Jordan worked diligently in the area of civil rights. She attached civil rights amendments to legislation that authorized cities to directly receive law enforcement assistance grants and voted to extend the Voting Rights Act of 1965 for ten years. She supported legislation to extend the Voting Rights Act to Native Americans, Asian Americans, and Hispanic Americans. She voted against Gerald Ford's confirmation as vice president because she questioned his civil rights record.

Jordan announced that she would not stand for reelection in 1977. Her seat was captured by Mickey Leland in 1978. After leaving Congress, Jordan became a professor at the Lyndon B. Johnson School of Public Affairs at the University of Texas in Austin.

YOUNG ELECTED TO CONGRESS

In **NOVEMBER**, when Andrew Young (1932–) won the election in the Fifth Congressional District of Georgia, he became the first Black person to represent Georgia in Congress in more than one hundred years. This was his second attempt to win a seat in Congress (he had been unsuccessful two years earlier, when he lost to

Republican incumbent Fletcher Thompson). This time, Young beat Republican candidate Rodney M. Cook.

◈ Born in New Orleans, Young earned a B.A. degree from Howard University in 1951 and a B.D. degree from Hartford Theological Seminary four years later. As a minister, he served in Marion, Alabama, and Thomasville and Beachton, Georgia.

Young was very active in the civil rights movement of the 1960s. Martin Luther King, Jr., appointed him director of the Southern Christian Leadership Conference (SCLC) in 1964. He worked with white business and political leaders in a wide range of desegregation activities throughout the South. He was also responsible for a training program for Black leaders to prepare them for public office. Prior to his election to Congress, Young served two years as chairperson of the Atlanta Human Relations Commission.

During his five years in Congress, Young was an advocate of better U.S. relations with Black Africa. He supported legislation to terminate South Africa's sugar quota, feeling that economic pressure could bring about social change in that country. He supported a resolution to halt twenty million dollars in covert aid to groups fighting in Angola's civil war. When foreign ministers of forty-three African countries opposed the nomination of Nathaniel Davis as assistant secretary of state for African affairs, Young tried, unsuccessfully, to persuade the Senate Foreign Relations Committee to reject the nomination. Davis had allegedly been involved in covert political destabilization programs in Latin America. Although Davis was confirmed, he served only several months before accepting an ambassadorial position.

Young continued his civil rights activity in Congress. He favored a one-hundred-twenty-five-million-dollar appropriation that would help local community school districts to design their own desegregation plans for review by the courts. He voted for a ten-year extension of the Voting Rights Act of 1965. In 1976, Young campaigned for Jimmy Carter within the Black community and delivered a seconding speech for Carter at the Democratic National Convention.

After Carter was elected, he appointed Young U.S. representative to the United Nations, a position Young held for two years. Young was elected mayor of Atlanta in 1982 and reelected in 1985.

1973 INCOME OF BLACKS REMAINS BELOW THAT OF WHITES

In 1973, Black families were more likely than whites to be concentrated in the lowest income categories. Blacks were more than three times as likely to have incomes below five thousand dollars annually. About 16 percent of Black families had incomes in excess of fifteen thousand dollars compared with 38 percent of white families.

COLLINS CHAIRS HOUSE COMMITTEE

Cardiss Collins became the first woman and the first Black person to chair the House Government Operations Subcommittee — Manpower and Housing.

Collins had been elected to Congress in a special election to represent the predominantly Black Seventh District in Illinois. She filled the position left vacant when her husband, Democratic Congressman George Collins, was killed in an aircraft accident in December 1972. She served as chairperson of the Congressional Black Caucus from 1978 to 1980.

CHILDREN'S DEFENSE FUND FOUNDED

Marian Wright Edelman, a successful lawyer working on behalf of poor people in Mississippi, founded the Children's Defense Fund to advocate on behalf of the nation's poor, minority, and handicapped children.

Edelman was born Mary Wright in Bennettsville, South Carolina, on June 6, 1939. She became the first African American admitted to the bar in Mississippi. In addition to her work in Mississippi, Edelman directed the NAACP's Legal Defense and Educational Fund in New York and Mississippi.

COMBINED BLACK PERSONAL INCOME ESTIMATED

The Bureau of the Census indicated that there were 5,440,000 Black families who had a mean income of $8,667. On the basis of these statistics, one can estimate the aggregate Black personal income to be more than $47 billion. Not included in this figure were purchases by Black churches, businesses, organizations, and educational institutions. These purchases would constitute relatively large expenditures but were especially hard to estimate. Thus, the forty-seven-billion-dollar estimate was clearly an underestimate of the aggregate consumer income in the Black community.

CRIME SURVEY SHOWS BLACKS VICTIMIZED MORE THAN WHITES

A crime victimization survey showed that Blacks were more likely than whites to be victims of personal crimes. This survey also showed that Blacks were more likely than whites to be victims of rape, robbery, and assault. Victimization rates were eighty-

Marian Wright Edelman, a lawyer and children's rights activist, founded the Children's Defense Fund in 1973.

five per one thousand for Black males and seventy-five per one thousand for white males. Black households were more likely to be targets of burglary than white households in all income groups. In general, the typical victim was Black, male, poor, and under-educated.

EEOC SUES AT&T

In response to a suit brought by the Federal Equal Employment Opportunity Commission, the American Telephone and Telegraph Company (AT&T) agreed to pay $15 million in back pay and to award $23 million in promotion and raises to employees who experienced discrimination.

FOLEY ELECTED MAYOR OF TAFT, OKLAHOMA

Lelia Smith Foley was elected mayor of Taft, Oklahoma, a small all-Black town about forty miles from Tulsa. Foley became the first African American woman to be elected mayor of a U.S. city. She remained mayor of the town for thirteen years.

SUPREME COURT ORDERS INTEGRATION OUTSIDE THE SOUTH

In *Keyes* v. *Denver School District*, the U.S. Supreme Court for the first time ordered integration in a non-southern school system.

SUPREME COURT UPHOLDS VOTING RIGHTS ACT

In *Georgia* v. *United States*, the Court upheld the Voting Rights Act of 1965, which prohibited states that had deprived Blacks of the right to vote (that is, Alabama, Georgia, Louisiana, Mississippi, North Carolina, South Carolina, and Virginia) from making any changes in voting procedures without first submitting the plan to the U.S. attorney for approval.

WILLIAMS BECOMES FIRST BLACK UMPIRE IN NATIONAL LEAGUE

Art Williams was the first Black umpire in the National League. He served in this position from 1973 to 1977.

YOUNG ELECTED MAYOR OF DETROIT

Coleman Young was elected the first Black mayor of Detroit, Michigan. He had been a Michigan state senator from 1964 to 1973. Young was also active in the early organizing efforts of the United Auto Workers. He was leader of the Wayne County CIO and served as executive secretary of the National Negro Labor Council. He was president of the U.S. Conference of Mayors from 1982 to 1983. Young, the first African American to serve on the Democratic National Committee, had received the Adam Clayton Powell Award for Outstanding Political Leadership from the Congressional Black Caucus. Young served as mayor of Detroit from 1974 to 1993. During his term in office, he had wrestled with numerous social problems: unemployment, urban decay, drugs, and crime. He had to contend with the dismantling of the auto industry, the loss of the middle-class population to the suburbs, and the consequent shrinking tax base. At the same time, he attempted to attract business to the city by backing plans to revitalize the downtown area, most notably by building the Renaissance Center.

Coleman Young, a labor organizer and five-term mayor of Detroit, worked with area employers to bring renewal to his economically devastated city.

FIRST BLACK-OWNED TELEVISION STATION GRANTED LICENSE

On **JUNE 1**, WGPR-TV was granted a license to operate a television station in Detroit, Michigan. It was to be the first Black-owned television station in history.

DAVIS SWORN IN AS CALIFORNIA MAYOR

On **JUNE 5**, Doris A. Davis was sworn in as mayor of Compton, California, thus becoming the first Black woman to govern a metropolitan city. Compton is located within the Los Angeles metropolitan area.

ILLINOIS VOTES BIRTHDAY HOLIDAY FOR KING

On **SEPTEMBER 17**, the state of Illinois became the first state to pass legislation honoring Martin Luther King, Jr., with a state holiday.

ALLEN APPEARS ON BROADWAY

On **OCTOBER 18**, Debbie Allen debuted on Broadway in *Raisin*, the musical adaptation of Lorraine Hansberry's play *A Raisin in the Sun*. Her role of Beneatha Younger landed her a role in the movie and television series *Fame*. She later enjoyed a successful career as a choreographer and as a director of *A Different World*, a series on NBC-TV that featured a number of Black actors.

JACKSON ELECTED MAYOR OF ATLANTA

On **OCTOBER 18**, Maynard Jackson was elected the first Black mayor of Atlanta, and the first Black mayor of any major southern city, defeating incumbent Sam Massell. Maynard's political platform was to implement the politics of inclusion — the opening of government to Blacks, women, and younger people. Many white businesspeople were apprehensive about a Black mayor, particularly one wishing to open the government to include a large number of "nonbusiness" interests. Jackson rushed to implement a strong and effective affirmative action program. In a city that had almost a majority of Blacks, Jackson sought to move the proportion of city contracts awarded to Blacks from less than 1 percent to a level close to parity.

Jackson was reelected to the office of mayor of Atlanta in 1978. According to law, Jackson could serve only two consecutive terms. In 1982, Andrew Young, Jackson's choice for the office, was elected and served the maximum two terms. Maynard Jackson was elected mayor again in 1989. Atlanta has continued to be a progressive city with regard to Black business development and successes from affirmative action.

BRADLEY ELECTED MAYOR OF LOS ANGELES

In **NOVEMBER**, Thomas Bradley was elected the first Black mayor of Los Angeles, America's third largest city. He defeated Sam Yorty, who had served three terms and had beaten him in an earlier mayoral race. Only 15 percent of Los Angeles voters were Black. Bradley served as mayor of Los Angeles for five consecutive terms until his retirement in 1993. During the riots that followed the acquittal of four white police officers on charges of beating a Black man, Rodney King, in 1992, Bradley was forced to share some of the blame for his city's racial division and racism within the police department. This negative publicity damaged the mayor's credibility within the African American community.

Bradley was born in Texas and had also served as the head of the Los Angeles Police Department.

1974   BLACK REPRESENTATION INCREASES IN STATE LEGISLATURES

In the early part of this year, as many as 236 Black state legislators served in forty-one state legislatures

Tom Bradley, a native of Texas, spent all of his adult life in the service of the citizens of Los Angeles, California. He spent twenty-one years as a member of the Los Angeles Police Department, a decade as a city councilman, and another two decades as the mayor of the city.

throughout the country. Black political representation in these lawmaking bodies had increased from 209 Black legislators in thirty-seven state legislatures in 1972. Gains made after the elections in November showed a total of sixteen Blacks in the U.S. House of Representatives, of whom four were women. Edward W. Brooke III, the only Black U.S. senator, secured his position in the Senate for another term.

DYMALLY ELECTED LIEUTENANT GOVERNOR

Mervyn M. Dymally became the first Black lieutenant governor in the twentieth century when he was elected to this post in California.

ELDER WINS GOLF TOURNAMENT

Lee Elder became the first Black golfer to win a Professional Golfer's Association (PGA) tournament in the United States when he won the Monsanto Open. As a result, he was the first Black player to qualify for the masters tournament in 1975.

Elder qualified for membership in the PGA in 1967. He won the Houston Open in 1976 and the Greater Milwaukee Open and Westchester Classic in 1978. Elder, whose earnings topped two million dollars, joined the ranks of two other professional African American golfers — Calvin Peete and Charlie Sifford.

ERVING NAMED MOST VALUABLE PLAYER

Julius Erving (1950–) was selected the Most Valuable Player by the American Basketball Association (ABA).

Erving, nicknamed "Dr. J.," played basketball at the University of Massachusetts (1968–1971), then joined with the Virginia Squires of the ABA, where he played from 1971 to 1973. The forward, who is six feet six inches tall, perfected his own style of play and was known for his "dunking." In 1973, Erving signed to play for the New York Nets, for whom he played until 1976, when he moved to the Philadelphia 76ers of the National Basketball Association (NBA). Erving won the Most Valuable Player award again in 1976. In 1981, Dr. J. received the Most Valuable Player award for the third time.

FORD ELECTED TO CONGRESS

Tennessee's first Black member of the U.S. House of Representatives, Harold Ford, was elected at the age of twenty-nine, having already served in the state house of representatives for four years, including a term as majority whip.

Ford is from a prominent Memphis Black family in the mortuary business. One of fifteen children, Ford received a B.S. degree in business administration from Tennessee State University and a degree in mortuary science from John Gupton College. He also received an M.B.A. from Harvard University, a degree he earned after his election to Congress.

Ford holds a seat on the powerful House Ways and Means Committee. As chair of the Subcommittee on Public Assistance and Unemployment Compensation, he oversees programs such as Aid to Families with Dependent Children, Child Welfare and Foster Care, and Unemployment Compensation. He has introduced a comprehensive welfare reform bill. In 1987, Jim Wright, then Speaker of the House, appointed Ford to the Democratic Steering and Policy Committee.

KING'S MOTHER SLAIN IN ATLANTA

The mother of Martin Luther King, Jr., was slain by a gunman who fired into an Atlanta church, killing Mrs. King, a church deacon, and an organist.

MORE BLACK FAMILIES HEADED BY WOMEN HOUSEHOLDS LIVE IN POVERTY

Contrary to general belief, more than half (54.1 percent) of all female heads of families were in the labor force. The median income for families headed by women was relatively low when compared to husband-wife families. In 1973, families headed by Black women had the lowest median income, $4,226, compared to $6,560 for families headed by White women.

The condition of poverty was most prevalent among families headed by women. Between 1973 and 1974, the percentage of families living in poverty rose considerably — by 5.8 percent. For families headed by a woman, the increase was 7.2 percent. The number of white families living below poverty level jumped from 11.4 million in 1973 to 12.5 million in 1974, a 9.6 percent increase. For Blacks, the number dropped to about 6.5 million, a decline of about 1 percent. However, the number of Black families headed by women in poverty increased by 9 percent to about one million, a rate similar to that of white families headed by women (about 1.3 million families). In 1974, families headed by women with children were more likely to be in poverty. The poverty rate for all families headed by women with children was 51.5 percent; for Blacks, it was 65.7 percent; for whites, 42.6 percent.

RIGHTS OF BLACK MEN VIOLATED

A federal court ruled in favor of more than six hundred Black males who were stopped and questioned indiscriminantly by local police during the hunt for the "Zebra" killers.

RUSSELL INDUCTED INTO BASKETBALL HALL OF FAME

Bill Russell (1934–) one of the greatest basketball players ever, was inducted into the Basketball Hall of Fame. Russell was renowned for his rebounding and shot blocking.

Russell, at six feet ten inches tall, was center for the Boston Celtics of the National Basketball Association (NBA) from 1956 to 1968. During that time he led the Celtics to eleven NBA championships — in 1957, 1959 through 1966, 1968, and 1969. Russell was chosen as Most Valuable Player five times during regular season play (in 1958, 1961 through 1963, and 1965) and once during all-star play (1963). He was also named to the all-star team eleven times. Russell also made basketball history by being selected to be both a player and coach of the Boston Celtics in 1966. He became the first African American to coach a U.S. professional basketball team.

VIETNAM WAR ENDS

Between 1965 and 1974, approximately 275,000 Blacks served in the war in Vietnam. Fatalities numbered 5,681.

WOODSON ELECTED TO PRESIDE OVER NEW JERSEY LEGISLATURE

Howard Woodson, a Black minister and representative in the New Jersey legislature from Trenton, was elected the first Black presiding officer in an American legislative body.

AARON BREAKS BABE RUTH'S HOME RUN RECORD

On **APRIL 8**, Hank Aaron of the Atlanta Braves hit home run number 715, thus breaking Babe Ruth's record. He became the leading home run hitter in baseball history. He hit this famous home run in the fourth inning off pitcher Al Downing of the Dodgers.

Aaron, born in 1934 in Mobile, Alabama, started his professional baseball career with the all-Black Indianapolis Clowns of the Negro leagues. He got his break in major league baseball in 1954 when Bobby Thompson broke an ankle and Aaron was put in the lineup. In that year, he batted .280, a good season for a rookie, and was named to the National League all-star team, an honor he then received each year of his career. In 1957, he was named Most Valuable Player in the National League when he led the Braves to victory in the World Series. Many baseball fans considered Aaron the greatest right-handed hitter to ever play the game of baseball.

Aaron retired in 1976 with 755 total home runs. He set a National League record with 2,297 RBIs. Aaron's career ended with the Milwaukee Brewers of the American League.

CURFEW IMPOSED IN NEWARK

On **SEPTEMBER 4**, the city of Newark, New Jersey, implemented a curfew that prohibited any street protest against racism.

MARINO CONSECRATED AUXILIARY BISHOP

On **SEPTEMBER 12**, Eugene A. Marino was consecrated Roman Catholic auxiliary bishop of the United States, thus becoming the first African American auxiliary bishop.

RACIAL VIOLENCE ERUPTS IN BOSTON

On **SEPTEMBER 12**, white students rioted to protest desegregation of Boston public schools. White students attacked Blacks at random, and many boycotted classes. Although the police escorted buses to South Boston High School and helped to defuse the tension, violence flared up again on October 15, mostly because of the beating of Andre Yvon Jean-Louis, a Haitian, by whites on October 7. The fights among students were racially polarized, particularly in the Roxbury neighborhood of the city, where busing had divided the community along racial lines. Within days, scattered incidents of violence broke out in Roxbury. Some Black high school students from South Boston hurled rocks at whites in the streets, supposedly in retaliation for the absence of police protection and isolated beatings by white gangs. The rioting continued until Governor Francis Sargeant obtained help from the National Guard. President Ford denounced the violence but indicated that "federal troops should be used only as a last resort." Civil rights leaders were highly critical of his statement. Black leaders were further disturbed when Mayor Kevin White revealed his strong antibusing position.

TYSON WINS TWO EMMYS

On **MAY 28**, Cicely Tyson was awarded two Emmys for best actress in a special and best actress in a drama for her acclaimed role as Jane Pittman in *The Autobiography of Miss Jane Pittman*.

ROBINSON BECOMES CLEVELAND INDIANS MANAGER

On **OCTOBER 3**, Frank Robinson made history when he was selected to manage the Cleveland Indians. He was the first Black manager in the major leagues. He acted as both player and manager of the Cleveland Indians, positions he held from 1975 to 1977. Robinson later managed the San Francisco Giants (1981–1984) and the Baltimore Orioles (1988).

ALI REGAINS HEAVYWEIGHT CROWN

On **OCTOBER 29**, Muhammad Ali defeated George Foreman in Zaire, Africa, to regain his heavyweight boxing title.

BROWN BECOMES LIEUTENANT GOVERNOR OF COLORADO

On **NOVEMBER 5**, George Brown became the first Black to be elected lieutenant governor of Colorado. In 1956, Brown had been elected to the state senate, the first African American to sit in this body. He was reelected to four successive terms. He also served as the first executive director of the Metro-Denver Urban Coalition.

1975 ASHE WINS AT WIMBLEDON

Arthur Ashe won the All-England Lawn Tennis Men's Singles Championship at Wimbledon by defeating Jimmy Connors. He became the first Black to win this prestigious event.

BLACK PEOPLE UNDER FBI AND CIA SCRUTINY

The nation's newspaper and television media revealed that noted Black leaders had been spied upon by the FBI and CIA. Dr. Martin Luther King, Jr., Eartha Kitt, leaders of the Black Panther Party, and many others were among those targeted for wire-tapping surveillance and background investigations.

COLEMAN NAMED SECRETARY OF TRANSPORTATION

President Gerald Ford appointed William T. Coleman as secretary of transportation. Coleman was the second Black to hold a cabinet-level position.

Coleman had held more than twenty-five federal, state, and community positions. After receiving his LL.B degree from Harvard University Law School in 1946, he worked as secretary to Judge Herbert F. Goodrich of the U.S. Court of Appeals and also for U.S. Supreme Court justice Felix Frankfurter. He served on the boards of several major corporations, including Pan American World Airways and Penn Mutual Insurance Company. Coleman was also president of the NAACP Legal Defense and Education Fund.

FIRST BLACK-OWNED TELEVISION STATION BEGINS BROADCASTING

WGPR-TV in Detroit, the first Black-owned television station, went on the air for the first time. It was organized and owned by a Detroit group headed by Dr. William V. Banks.

HAMILTON WINS NEWBERY MEDAL AWARD

Virginia Hamilton (1936–) won the prestigious Newbery Medal for children's literature and a National Book Award for *M. C. Higgins, the Great*. Hamilton

William T. Coleman, who made a career in public service, was appointed secretary of transportation in 1975.

was noted for her fiction about the African American experience and her retelling of Black folktales. Among her biographies of African Americans for children are *W. E. B. Du Bois* (1972), *Paul Robeson, The Life and Times of a Free Black Man* (1974), and *Anthony Burns* (1988). In 1983, Hamilton received the Newbery Honor Award and the Coretta Scott King Award for *Sweet Whispers, Brother Rush*, and, in 1986, she received the Coretta Scott King Award and a *New York Times* award for *The People Could Fly*, a book of Black folktales.

MANUFACTURING JOBS DECLINE IN NEW JERSEY

In New Jersey, a major manufacturing state, manufacturing jobs declined from nine hundred thousand in 1969 to seven hundred thousand in 1975. New Jersey's strategic location in the shadows of Philadelphia and New York City promoted the shift from manufacturing to service and information-related jobs — a move that the state encouraged. Such a shift generally worked to the disadvantage of Black laborers.

SOUTHERN BLACKS MAKE EDUCATIONAL ADVANCES

Segregation, poverty, and the rural isolation of Blacks acted in concert to reduce their access to formal edu-

cation. In 1940, about 49 percent of southern Blacks had completed less than five years of school. For whites, the proportion was only 16 percent. In 1960, only 32 percent of southern Blacks (and 10 percent of southern whites) had completed less than five years of school. By 1975, less than 5 percent of either race in the South had less than five years of education, indicating the advances Blacks had made to overcome obstacles to their desire for education.

UNEMPLOYMENT RATE AMONG BLACKS DISPROPORTIONATELY HIGH

A government report estimated that 15 percent of Blacks were unemployed, in contrast with 9 percent of whites. The National Urban League disputed these figures, claiming that the Black unemployment rate was actually 26 percent.

VOTING RIGHTS ACT OF 1975 PASSED

The Voting Rights Act, passed by Congress and signed by President Ford, abolished literacy requirements for voting.

PARSONS APPOINTED FEDERAL JUDGE

On **APRIL 19**, James B. Parsons became a chief judge of the U.S. District Court in Chicago. He was the first Black to be a chief judge of a federal court.

Parsons was also the first African American to be a district court judge when he was appointed in 1961.

JAMES PROMOTED TO FOUR-STAR GENERAL

In **AUGUST**, General Daniel "Chappie" James (1920–1978) of the U.S. Air Force became the nation's first Black four-star general. He was also named commander of the North American Air Defense Command (NORAD) at Peterson Air Force Base in Colorado. In this capacity, he was responsible for all U.S. and Canadian strategic aerospace defense forces.

◈ James was born in Pensacola, Florida. He was the youngest of seventeen children. He attended Tuskegee Institute and received a degree in physical education, but then he completed pilot training under the Civilian Pilot Training Program. He was asked to remain at Tuskegee as an instructor pilot in the Army Air Corps Aviation Cadet Program. He later entered the program as a cadet and received his commission as a second lieutenant in 1943.

By 1949, James was stationed at Clark Field in the Philippines. In Korea, in 1950, he flew 101 missions. From 1957 to 1966, James attended the Air Command and Staff College. He was then reassigned to

Headquarters U.S. Air Force, the Pentagon; to the Royal Air Force Station at Bentwaters, England; and to Davis-Monthan Air Force Base in Arizona.

When the Vietnam War began, James was assigned to Ubon Royal Thai Air Force Base, Thailand, in 1966, where he flew seventy-eight combat missions into North Vietnam. He led a flight in which seven MiG-21s were knocked from the skies — the highest total kill of any mission during the Vietnam War.

James was honored many times by his peers as well as the communities where he was assigned. In 1970, he served as deputy assistant secretary of defense (public affairs), and in 1974, he served as vice commander of the Military Airlift Command. On February 1, 1978, General "Chappie" James retired. In less than four weeks, on February 25, he died.

HATCHER BECOMES FLORIDA SUPREME COURT JUSTICE
On **SEPTEMBER 2**, Joseph W. Hatcher was sworn in as a state supreme court justice in Tallahassee, Florida. He became the first African American to be seated on the state's highest court since Reconstruction and the first Black state supreme court justice in the South in the twentieth century.

ALI WINS "THRILLA IN MANILA" BOXING MATCH
On **SEPTEMBER 30**, Muhammad Ali and Joe Frazier fought in the Philippines for the world heavyweight boxing title. The match was billed as "the Thrilla in Manila." Ali won in the fourteenth round when Frazier's trainer refused to let him continue.

NATIONAL ASSOCIATION OF BLACK JOURNALISTS FORMED
On **DECEMBER 12**, a number of African American journalists convened in Washington, D.C., to form the National Association of Black Journalists. Max Robinson, the first Black anchor of a national network news program, and Acel Moore, a future Pulitzer Prize winner, were among the founding members.

1976   BLACKS WIN MORE ELECTIONS
Because of increased voter registration among Blacks, 3,979 Black candidates were elected to public office in the United States, compared with 1,185 in 1969. Seventeen Black congressmen were reelected.

BUSING BRINGS VIOLENCE TO BOSTON
Violence broke out in Boston when Blacks were bused into predominantly white schools. Boston's schools had been ordered to use busing to achieve racial integration by Judge Arthur Garrity of the U.S. District Court.

CARTER APPOINTS MANY BLACK JUDGES
During his presidency, Jimmy Carter took major steps to redress racial imbalances on the federal appellate court, the nation's second highest court. When President Carter took office, only two federal appellate judges were Black. During his administration, he appointed fifty-six judges to the federal appellate court — six of them Black. (This course was reversed during the Reagan and Bush administrations. President Reagan made 83 appointments to the federal appellate court; only one was Black. President Bush made thirty-two appointments; only one was Black.

CARTER'S CHURCH ENDS BAN ON BLACKS
Shortly after Jimmy Carter was elected president of the United States, garnering 94 percent of the Black vote, Carter's church in Plains, Georgia, dropped its eleven-year ban on attendance by Blacks.

FINNEY APPOINTED CIRCUIT COURT JUDGE
Ernest A. Finney, Jr., an attorney in Sumter, South Carolina, was selected as the state's first Black circuit court judge.

HALEY PUBLISHES *Roots*
Alex Haley (1921–1992) achieved instant fame when he published *Roots*. The book told the story of his family, starting with the capture and sale into slavery of one of his African ancestors. It took a critical view of slavery in the mid-eighteenth century. Because of its broad popularity, *Roots* was made into a television miniseries in 1977. It became the most-watched series of all time, drawing approximately eighty million viewers. LeVar Burton, Cicely Tyson, and John Amos were among the stars of the series. It ran an unprecedented eight consecutive nights and drew more than 51 percent of the television audience each night. Haley was awarded the Spingarn Medal for his extensive research. He also won a Pulitzer Prize for his work.

Haley performed much of the research for *Roots* while serving in the U.S. Coast Guard (1939–1959). In 1965, he collaborated with Malcolm X on *The Autobiography of Malcolm X*. Prior to his death, he completed *Queen*, a story about his mother.

Barbara C. Jordan, a U.S. representative from Texas, enhanced her reputation as a great orator when she delivered the keynote address at the 1976 Democratic convention. Jordan was quickly recognized as a Black leader, and women embraced her for her stands on women's rights and other women's causes.

JORDAN FEATURED AS KEYNOTE SPEAKER

U.S. Representative Barbara Jordan became the first Black keynote speaker at a national political convention when she addressed the Democratic National Convention in New York City.

OWENS AWARDED MEDAL OF FREEDOM

President Gerald Ford presented the Medal of Freedom to Jesse Owens for his contribution to the ideals of freedom and democracy.

Owens won four gold medals at the 1936 Olympic Games in Berlin, directly confronting Hitler's belief in Aryan racial superiority.

MINES ATTENDS U.S. NAVAL ACADEMY

In **JUNE**, women were admitted to the U.S. Naval Academy for the first time. A total of eighty-one women enrolled. Of these, only one Black woman, Janie L. Mines, was among the historymakers.

Mines was well prepared because she had been a member of the Navy Junior ROTC unit at her high school. While at the academy, Mines participated as a midshipman drill officer and regimental adjutant while pursuing a political science major. In 1980, she became the first African American woman to graduate from the U.S. Naval Academy. She was assigned to supervise three dining halls at the Naval Training Center at Orlando, Florida.

Mines's sister, Gwen, entered the academy in 1977; she graduated in 1981.

GIBSON HEADS U.S. CONFERENCE OF MAYORS

On **JULY 1**, Kenneth A. Gibson, mayor of Newark, New Jersey, was elected president of the U.S. Conference of Mayors. He was the first African American to hold this post.

DEATH PENALTY REINSTATED BY U.S. SUPREME COURT

On **JULY 2**, the U.S. Supreme Court declared that death penalty statutes in Florida, Georgia, and Texas were constitutional. The Court ruled 7–2 in *Jurek* v. *Texas* to reverse its earlier decision on capital punishment. It was argued that if the cost of crime was death, then the death penalty would deter major crimes. Justices Thurgood Marshall and William Brennan dissented. Both believed strongly that the death penalty was a violation of the Eighth Amendment, which prohibited "cruel and unusual punishment."

SECRETARY OF AGRICULTURE RESIGNS AFTER MAKING RACIAL SLUR

On **OCTOBER 4**, Earl Butz, secretary of agriculture, resigned after a racial slur he made caused public outrage.

LAST OF THE SCOTTSBORO BOYS PARDONED

On **OCTOBER 25**, the last surviving member of the Scottsboro Boys, Clarence "Willie" Norris, was pardoned by Governor George Wallace.

Norris, who had spent about fifteen years of his life behind bars for allegedly raping a white woman, had been a fugitive since fleeing parole in Alabama in 1946.

1977 BLACKS ELECTED TO OFFICE IN CALIFORNIA

In California, Lionel Wilson became Oakland's first Black mayor, and John George becomes the first Black Alameda County supervisor.

BRYANT APPOINTED JUDGE

William Bryant was selected as chief U.S. District Court judge in Washington, D.C. Bryant was the first Black to hold this position.

CARTER ADMINISTRATION APPOINTS BLACKS

President Carter appointed nineteen Blacks to serve in the White House and thirty-seven to executive positions. Wade McCree, Jr., served as solicitor general and Drew Days as assistant attorney general for civil rights in the Justice Department.

EMPLOYMENT PREFERENCES FOR MINORITIES CANNOT OVERRIDE SENIORITY RIGHTS

The U.S. Supreme Court ruled that employment preferences for minorities could not interfere with seniority rights held by employees at the time that the 1964 law was passed.

FARRAKHAN CREATES SEPARATIST GROUP AMONG NATION OF ISLAM

Louis Farrakhan (1933–), Malcolm X's successor at Temple No. 7 in Harlem, New York, created a separatist group of followers within the Nation of Islam. He was earlier known among members of the Nation of Islam as Louis X. As a minister and national representative of Elijah Muhammad, Farrakhan was displeased with the philosophical move of the Nation of Islam toward racial harmony and away from racial separatism after the death of Elijah Muhammad. Farrakhan embraced a philosophy that reinforced the strict separatism and racial exclusiveness that characterized the Black Muslims during their formative years.

Farrakhan was born Louis Eugene Walcott in New York City.

GEORGIA SENATOR SUES TO END USE OF THE WORD *Nigger* IN PUBLIC BROADCASTING

Georgia state senator Julian Bond filed suit in federal court demanding that the word *nigger* on radio and television be declared illegal.

HOOKS BECOMES EXECUTIVE DIRECTOR OF NAACP

Benjamin L. Hooks (1925–) succeeded Roy Wilkins as executive director of the National Association for the Advancement of Colored People. Hooks served the NAACP until 1993, the longest period of service of any director.

MORRISON PUBLISHES *Song of Solomon*

Toni Morrison (1931–) became more widely known as an imaginative novelist when she published *Song of Solomon*. This novel vividly depicted the African American experience. In 1981, Morrison published another novel, *Tar Baby*, and in 1987, she published her Pulitzer Prize–winning best-seller, *Beloved*. Toni Morrison is currently one of the most respected African American authors in the country.

MORTON BECOMES U.S. TREASURER

Azie Taylor Morton was appointed U.S. Treasurer. Although she was the thirty-sixth treasurer for the country, she was the first Black woman to hold this important position. Morton was responsible for U.S. savings bonds, the U.S. Bureau of the Mint, and the U.S. Bureau of Engraving and Printing. Morton, born in Dale, Texas, was a teacher and an investigator with the U.S. Equal Employment Opportunity Commission, and she had served as a special assistant to the chairperson of the Democratic National Committee (1972–1976).

PAYTON SETS RUSHING RECORD

Walter Payton (1954–), famed running back for the Chicago Bears of the National Football League, set the record for yards rushed in a single game, with 275 yards. Payton was known for his powerful, smooth running ability, and during his career for the Chicago Bears (1975–1987), he was their leading rusher.

Payton's total career rushing yards amounted to 16,726. He played his whole football career with the Chicago Bears, and in 1985, Payton led his team to a Super Bowl victory — the first and only one for this great player. When Payton retired from the game of football, he became involved in efforts to secure a football franchise.

RAWLS WINS GRAMMY

Lou Rawls, a versatile and successful singer of blues, jazz, and R & B, was awarded a Grammy for best R & B vocal performance.

A native of Chicago, Illinois, Rawls currently contributes a significant amount of his time and energy to hosting the United Negro College Fund telethon, a position he has held since 1984.

SAYERS INDUCTED INTO PRO FOOTBALL HALL OF FAME

Gale Sayers was inducted into the Pro Football Hall of Fame and became the youngest player ever to be thus honored.

In 1965, Sayers was the first-round pick of the Chicago Bears. He became one of the most outstanding running backs in the National Football League. He played his entire football career with the Bears.

Andrew Young, a civil rights activist, served the public in many capacities, including U.S. congressman from Georgia, U.S. ambassador to the United Nations, and mayor of the city of Atlanta.

YOUNG APPOINTED AMBASSADOR TO UNITED NATIONS

Andrew Young was appointed by President Jimmy Carter to serve as America's ambassador to the United Nations. He was the first Black to serve in this prestigious post. In 1979, he resigned and was succeeded by Donald F. McHenry, a Black career diplomat.

ALEXANDER NAMED SECRETARY OF ARMY

On **JANUARY 19**, Clifford Alexander, Jr., became the first Black secretary of the army. He was named to this position by President-elect Jimmy Carter. Alexander, a graduate of Yale University Law School, had served as assistant district attorney for New York County between 1958 and 1960. In 1965, he was appointed associate special counsel to President Lyndon Johnson and later deputy special counsel. Alexander became the chairperson of the Equal Employment Opportunity Commission in 1967 but left after policy

disagreements with the Nixon administration. He practiced law in Washington, D.C., and ran unsuccessfully for mayor against Walter Washington in 1975.

RAY CAPTURED AFTER ESCAPE

On **JUNE 13**, James Earl Ray and six other convicts were captured after their escape from Brushy Mountain State Prison. Ray had been incarcerated for several years of his ninety-nine-year sentence for the murder of Martin Luther King, Jr. There was national skepticism surrounding his escape. Many believed that Ray did not act alone in King's murder and that his escape was part of an effort to silence him. Governor Ray Blanton requested that the federal government take complete charge of Ray.

KING AWARDED MEDAL OF FREEDOM POSTHUMOUSLY

President Jimmy Carter awarded the Medal of Freedom to Martin Luther King, Jr., posthumously, on **JULY 11**.

BROCK BREAKS RECORD FOR STOLEN BASES

On **AUGUST 29**, Lou Brock of the St. Louis Cardinals broke Ty Cobb's 1928 stolen-base record of 892.

Roots WINS NINE EMMY AWARDS

On **SEPTEMBER 11**, *Roots* captured nine Emmys, the largest number ever awarded to a single television series. Among them was Quincy Jones's award for his musical compositions for *Roots*.

INCREASE IN MINIMUM WAGE HELPS BLACKS

On **NOVEMBER 1**, President Jimmy Carter signed into law a bill that raised the minimum wage to two dollars and sixty-five cents per hour. The bill included a mandatory increase to three dollars and thirty-five cents per hour in 1981. It was a compromise between management and unions; unions had strongly supported a three-dollar minimum wage rate in this year. Since a large percentage of Black workers were unskilled and worked as low-wage earners, it meant a boost in their income.

KLAN MEMBER CONVICTED OF 1963 MURDERS

On **NOVEMBER 18**, a court convicted Robert Edward Chambliss, a former KKK member, for the murder of the four African American teenage girls who were killed in the infamous 1963 bombing of the Sixteenth Street Baptist Church in Birmingham, Alabama. Civil rights leaders called for more convictions for this crime.

FARMER BECOMES FIRST BLACK MEMBER OF DAUGHTERS OF THE AMERICAN REVOLUTION

In **DECEMBER**, Karen Farmer became the first Black member of the Daughters of the American Revolution (DAR). She was a descendant of a soldier who had served in the Revolutionary War.

1978 CHAMBERLAIN INDUCTED INTO BASKETBALL HALL OF FAME

Wilt Chamberlain (1936–) was inducted into the Basketball Hall of Fame.

Chamberlain played his collegiate ball at the University of Kansas, but before completing his eligibility, he signed to play with the Harlem Globetrotters. With a height of seven feet one inch, he dominated the professional game from 1959 through 1972. He played for the Philadelphia Warriors, the Philadelphia 76ers, and the Los Angeles Lakers of the National Basketball Association. During this time, he secured a number of records that still stand today — the most points scored in a season (4,029), most points in a game (100), and the most rebounds per season (2,149). Chamberlain ranked second in all-time regular season scoring with 31,419 points. Only Kareem Abdul-Jabbar scored more points (38,387). Chamberlain was the NBA's Most Valuable Player four times (in 1960, 1966, 1967, and 1968).

DOBY BECOMES WHITE SOX MANAGER

Larry Doby, the first African American to play professional baseball in the American League, became the manager of the Chicago White Sox, the second Black to manage a major-league baseball team.

GREGORY JOINS NASA ASTRONAUT TEAM

Lieutenant Colonel Frederick Gregory was selected to be among the eighth group of NASA astronauts. He remains a NASA astronaut today.

Gregory graduated from Anacostia High School in Washington, D.C. The fourth Black to graduate from the U.S. Air Force Academy, he received a B.S. degree from the academy in 1966 and a master's degree in information systems from George Washington University.

Gregory has served as a helicopter pilot, fighter pilot, and test pilot on more than forty different types of aircraft. He has logged more than forty-one hundred hours of flight time.

Only two other Blacks had been selected as astronauts — Ronald E. McNair and Guion S. Bluford.

MOORE NAMED MONSIGNOR OF CATHOLIC CHURCH

The Right Reverend Emerson Moore, Jr., was named monsignor of the Roman Catholic Church in the United States. He became pastor of St. Charles Borromeo Church in New York City. Moore was the first Black monsignor in the Roman Catholic Church.

MORE BLACKS MOVE TO SUBURBS

Census figures showed that in 1977, 55 percent of Blacks lived in the nation's central cities, a decrease of 4 percent since 1970. The number of Blacks living in suburbs had increased from 2.4 million to 4.6 million.

PETERSEN NAMED MARINE CORPS GENERAL

Frank E. Petersen, Jr., became the first Black general in the Marine Corps. He was promoted to brigadier general at this time.

Petersen joined the U.S. Marine Corps to become a pilot. He was trained at the Marine Corps air station at El Toro, California, and after earning his wings and commission, he became the first Black aviator in the history of this branch of the armed forces. In 1954, Petersen was assigned to Korea, where he flew in sixty-four combat missions. In Vietnam, he commanded a fighter squadron and was awarded the Distinguished Flying Cross. During his tour in Vietnam, he flew no less than thirty-one combat missions. After attending the National War College in Fort Leavenworth, Kansas, in 1973, Petersen had compiled more than enough achievements to be promoted to the rank of general. He was promoted to the rank of lieutenant general in 1986. He retired from the military in 1988. The following year he became a vice president with Dupont.

WATTLETON BECOMES PLANNED PARENTHOOD PRESIDENT

Faye Wattleton was elected president of the Planned Parenthood Federation of America, a position she held until 1992. As the spokesperson for this national organization, she became one of the most influential women in this country. She currently is a television show host for Tribune Entertainment in Chicago.

WILSON PUBLISHES *The Declining Significance of Race*

William J. Wilson, a Black sociologist and chair of the history department at the University of Chicago, published *The Declining Significance of Race*. In this book, Wilson contended that work skills and education were increasingly becoming significant in determining the status of Black Americans in predominantly white America. Race, he noted, was still a chief determinant, but class was becoming more important than race in determining the overall status of Blacks. He was criticized by a number of college and university educators.

MORMON CHURCH OPEN TO BLACK PRIESTS
On **JUNE 9**, the Church of Jesus Christ of the Latter Day Saints announced that it was ready to admit Black men to its priesthood. According to Spencer W. Kimball, president of the church, "all worthy male members of the church may be ordained to the priesthood without regard for race or color." Throughout the existence of their church, Mormons had excluded Blacks because of "reasons known only to God."

SUPREME COURT STRIKES DOWN STRICT MINORITY QUOTAS IN COLLEGE ADMISSIONS
On **JUNE 28**, the U.S. Supreme Court ruled in a 5–4 decision, in *Regents of the University of California* v. *Bakke,* that race might be considered in admissions decisions but that schools could not apply rigid quotas for minorities that disregarded academic qualifications. The justices issued six separate opinions. Although Allan Bakke, the defendant, was ordered to be admitted, the Court gave no clear guidance to university or other governmental institutions regarding affirmative action programs and their use of race in selecting applicants.

Bakke had been rejected (twice) by the medical school at the University of California at Davis. He charged that he was unconstitutionally rejected because preference was given to minority students with lower scores. In a battle to defeat affirmative action, starting in 1974, Bakke challenged the University of California. In 1976, the California Supreme Court ruled that Bakke should be admitted, at which time the university appealed the case to the U.S. Supreme Court.

ALI REGAINS WORLD HEAVYWEIGHT TITLE
On **SEPTEMBER 17**, in New Orleans, Louisiana, Muhammad Ali regained the world heavyweight championship for a record third time when he defeated the reigning champion, Leon Spinks. He became the first fighter ever to achieve this record.

BROOKE DEFEATED IN SENATE RACE
In **NOVEMBER**, Senator Edward W. Brooke III of Massachusetts, the only Black senator since Reconstruction, was defeated by Paul Tsongas.

DIXON ELECTED TO CONGRESS
In **NOVEMBER**, Julian Dixon was elected to the U.S. House of Representatives from California, having previously served seven years in the California Assembly. Dixon holds a law degree from Southwestern University.

While in Congress, Dixon wrote the first economic sanction laws against South Africa and was instrumental in getting increased economic development aid for Africa. He also worked on legislation related to low- and moderate-income housing and health care. He served as chairperson of the Committee on Standards of Official Conduct, frequently referred to as the Ethics Committee. Dixon also chaired the Congressional Black Caucus in the Ninety-eighth Congress.

EVANS ELECTED TO CONGRESS
In **NOVEMBER**, Melvin Evans (1917–1984), the first popularly elected governor of the Virgin Islands, became the islands' congressional representative after defeating Democratic candidate Janet Wattlington.
◊ Born in St. Croix, Evans attended school on St. Thomas and earned a B.S. degree and an M.D. degree from Howard University. He held a number of medical and public health posts in the United States and the Virgin Islands and was the islands' public health commissioner from 1959 to 1967. President Nixon appointed him governor of the Virgin Islands, and he won election to that office in 1970 after Congress passed the Virgin Islands Elective Governor Act. He served as governor until 1975, when he was defeated for reelection.

Evans served only one term in Congress. During his years in office, he secured additional federal funds for the Virgin Islands' public education system and introduced legislation to alleviate the islands' critical shortage of doctors by allowing foreign physicians to practice there. He succeeded in including the Virgin Islands under the definition of a state, so that the islands could receive law-enforcement funding.

Evans was defeated by Democrat Ron DeLugo in 1980. He was then appointed ambassador to Trinidad and Tobago, a position he held until his death in 1984.

GRAY ELECTED TO CONGRESS
In **NOVEMBER**, William Gray (1941–) was elected to the U.S. House of Representatives from the Second Congressional District in Pennsylvania on his second attempt, winning the primary and the general election by large margins. In January 1979, Gray took his

seat in the U.S. Congress and became a member of the Budget Committee, the Committee on the District of Columbia, and the Foreign Affairs Committee. He became one of the most powerful congressmen in the country.

◆ Gray was born in Baton Rouge, Louisiana. His family moved from Louisiana to Florida, and then to northern Philadelphia. In Philadelphia, Gray received a bachelor's degree from Franklin and Marshall College in 1963. Three years later, he earned a master's in divinity from Drew Theological Seminary, and in 1970, a master's in theology from Princeton Theological Seminary.

Gray's church work started in 1964 in Montclair, New Jersey, when he became minister of Union Baptist Church. He left Union Baptist in 1972 and became the leader of Philadelphia's Bright Hope Baptist Church. Gray's efforts were not confined to the pulpit. He became a community activist, working especially to secure low- and moderate-income housing for members of his community.

Although Gray was strongly encouraged to run for the U.S. Congress in the Second Congressional District against Representative Robert N. C. Nix, Sr., in 1972, he was defeated. In 1978, he won the seat.

In 1981, Gray was reelected and joined the Committee on Appropriations and the Democratic Steering and Policy Committee. He was responsible for an "aid package" in the creation of the African Development Foundation, which set aside certain government contracts for minority- and women-owned businesses and supported historically Black colleges. His support for causes in Africa led to the approval of emergency food aid to famine-stricken areas.

In 1985, Gray was elected to the powerful position of chairperson of the House Budget Committee. He became the Democratic spokesperson on issues pertaining to the national budget. Gray was also successful in ensuring passage of anti-apartheid legislation, which banned bank loans and certain exports to South Africa. Congressional colleagues elected him chair of the House Democratic Caucus and, in June 1989, Democratic whip, the highest positions in Congress ever held by a Black person to date. In 1991, Gray abruptly resigned from the U.S. Congress to become head of the United Negro College Fund, a move that he declared was in the best interests of his family and the education of his children. His resignation surprised many Black leaders, who thought Gray's next move in the Congress would be to Speaker of the House, the most powerful position in the U.S. Congress.

LELAND ELECTED TO CONGRESS

In **NOVEMBER**, George Thomas "Mickey" Leland was elected to the Texas congressional seat vacated by Barbara Jordan.

A pharmacist by training, Leland had served six years in the Texas legislature before his election to Congress. During his six terms in the U.S. House of Representatives, he became a national spokesperson for the problems of hunger in the United States and throughout the world. He drew attention to the starvation of Ethiopian and Sudanese refugees and was instrumental in securing relief measures for that region of Africa.

In August 7, 1989, Leland was killed in a plane crash in Ethiopia, following a visit to a UN refugee camp.

MANY BLACKS AMONG SUICIDE VICTIMS IN JONESTOWN

In **NOVEMBER**, at the People's Temple in Jonestown, Guyana, 909 cultists, mostly Black, apparently committed suicide by swallowing a concoction of Kool-Aid and cyanide. Their white leader, James Warren Jones, known as the Reverend Jim Jones, was found dead on the altar in the commune with a bullet wound in his head. Reports say that Jones, believing himself to be God, was upset by a visit from Congressman Leo Ryan of California, who was investigating complaints of kidnapping and bizarre sexual rites. Congressman Ryan was found dead near the airport, about eight miles from Jonestown. He was shot along with four others traveling with him. Jones was said to have ordered the mass suicide after learning that some members of the Ryan party had escaped.

No one was found alive in the camp, and some bodies were found in the Guyana jungle around Jonestown.

STEWART ELECTED TO CONGRESS

In **NOVEMBER**, following the death of Representative Ralph H. Metcalfe, Bennett McVey Stewart (1912–1988) was nominated to represent the First Congressional District of Illinois. He won the November election by defeating former Chicago alderman A. A. Raynor.

◆ Stewart was born in Huntsville, Alabama. He was educated in Huntsville and Birmingham and received a B.A. degree from Miles College in 1936. He served as an alderman in the city council from the Twenty-first Ward from 1971 to 1978.

Although Stewart served only one term in Congress, he made important contributions. He supported federal loan guarantees to Chrysler Corporation, which employed more than one thousand workers in his district. Remembering the segregated schools he had attended in Alabama, Stewart vigorously opposed a proposed constitutional amendment to prohibit public school busing. He believed it subverted the Fourteenth Amendment and was an attempt to reinstitute segregation in the United States.

After his defeat by Harold Washington in 1980, Stewart served for two years as the interim director of the Chicago Department of Inter-Governmental Affairs. He then retired from public life.

FEDERAL BUREAU OF INVESTIGATION TRIED TO DISCREDIT KING

On **NOVEMBER 17**, two FBI agents testified before the House Select Committee on Assassinations that J. Edgar Hoover had held a deep-seated hatred of Dr. Martin Luther King, Jr., and had wanted to discredit him at any cost. Internal papers of the FBI written by J. Edgar Hoover over the years revealed his animosity toward the civil rights leader. Because Hoover had almost unchallenged power, many African Americans believed that the FBI had been involved in the assassination of King.

CONSPIRACIES ALLEGED IN ASSASSINATIONS OF KENNEDY AND KING

On **DECEMBER 30**, the House Select Committee on Assassinations released information that lent credibility to the beliefs of many citizens that President John F. Kennedy and civil rights leader Dr. Martin Luther King, Jr., had not each been killed by a single gunman working alone. The committee, which heard reports from various experts, believed that James Earl Ray might have worked with others, including his two brothers and a businessperson who had offered $50,000 for King's death.

1979 GLOVER NAMED FBI FIELD CHIEF

James Glover was named chief of the FBI's Milwaukee field office. Glover was the first Black to hold such a post. Glover was also the first Black FBI officer to be promoted to the rank of inspector at the agency's headquarters in Washington, D.C.

HARRIS APPOINTED HOUSING SECRETARY

Patricia Roberts Harris served in two cabinet posts in one administration. Following her appointment by

Patricia Roberts Harris, a lawyer and diplomat, became the first Black woman to serve in a number of ambassadorial and cabinet positions.

President Jimmy Carter as secretary of housing and urban development, a position she held from 1977 to 1979, she became secretary of health, education, and welfare. Harris, a lawyer, former dean of Howard University Law School, former ambassador to Luxembourg (1965), and former alternative delegate to the United Nations General Assembly (1966–1967), was sworn in by Thurgood Marshall, the first Black Supreme Court justice. She was the first African American woman to hold a cabinet post in the United States and the first Black woman ambassador.

HAYES IS FIRST BLACK WOMAN PILOT IN U.S. MILITARY

Marcella A. Hayes, a second lieutenant in the U.S. Army, received her aviator wings and became the first Black woman pilot in U.S. armed services history.

JACKSON RELEASES TOP-SELLING ALBUM

Michael Jackson released his album *Off the Wall* in this year. It soared on the charts and sold more than seven million copies worldwide, becoming the most successful album released up to this date.

Jackson, born on August 29, 1958, in Gary, Indiana, initially achieved fame with the Jackson Five, a group made up of his brothers. After signing with Motown Records in 1968, Jackson became the lead singer and dancer of the Jackson Five. The group splintered in 1972 when Michael Jackson released his first solo album. His rhythmic music and dance made him one of the most exciting performers of his time.

LIFE EXPECTANCY OF BLACKS LOWER THAN THAT OF WHITES

The National Center for Health Statistics reported that Black women could be expected to outlive their male counterparts by more than nine years (average life expectancy for the Black woman was 74.2 years; for the Black man, 65.5 years). For whites, the female life expectancy was 78.2 years; male life expectancy was 70.6 years.

MAYS INDUCTED INTO BASEBALL HALL OF FAME

Willie Mays was inducted into the Baseball Hall of Fame in this year. Mays started his career as an outfielder for the New York Giants in 1951. He played twenty-one years with the team. During his career, he hit 660 home runs (the third largest number of home runs of any player in the National League). In addition, he was named the National League's Most Valuable Player in 1954 and 1965.

POVERTY GRIPS TWENTY-FIVE MILLION AMERICANS

According to a Bureau of the Census report, about twenty-five million Americans, 11.6 percent of the population, earned less than $7,412 annually, the official poverty level for a nonfarming family of four. The overall median family income was $19,684, up 11.6 percent from the previous year — much of it attributed to inflation, however. Incomes remained racially stratified. The median family income of whites was $20,520, and that of Blacks $11,651 — only 56.8 percent of that earned by whites.

ROBERTSON INDUCTED INTO BASKETBALL HALL OF FAME

Oscar Robertson (1938–) was inducted into the Basketball Hall of Fame. Robertson, frequently called the "Big O," was known for his scoring and passing from his years of playing for the Cincinnati Royals (1960–1970) and the Milwaukee Bucks (1971–1974).

While playing in the NBA, Robertson was a sensational player — Rookie of the Year (1961), Most Valuable Player (regular season 1964), and Most Valuable Player in three all-star games (1961, 1964, and 1969). During his playing career, Robertson ranked fourth in regular season scoring, with 27,710 career points. In addition, he was the only player to average a triple-double (ten or more assists, points, and rebounds) for an entire season (1961–1962). Robertson retired from the game in 1975.

THOMAS NAMED FORD FOUNDATION PRESIDENT

Franklin Thomas was named Ford Foundation president, becoming the first Black to head a major philanthropic foundation. Thomas, an attorney, had served as deputy police commissioner for legal matters in the New York City Police Department from 1965 to 1967. He was engaged in private legal practice at the time of his appointment to the Ford Foundation.

SUPREME COURT RULES IN FAVOR OF PREFERENCE FOR BLACK WORKERS

In *U.S. Steel* v. *Brian Weber*, the Supreme Court ruled that private employers could give special preference to Black workers to eliminate racial imbalance in traditionally white jobs.

YOUNG TALKS TO PALESTINE LIBERATION ORGANIZATION

Andrew Young resigned as U.S. ambassador to the United Nations after it was reported that he had held unauthorized talks with the Palestine Liberation Organization (PLO). Secretary of State Cyrus Vance distanced himself from Young, indicating that Young had breached American policy.

Young's personal view toward recognition of the PLO was generally known, but he had up to this point followed the Carter administration's policy, which barred any contact with the PLO.

SEGREGATION OF SCHOOLS STILL WIDESPREAD

On **FEBRUARY 13**, the U.S. Civil Rights Commission released a report stating that 46 percent of the nation's minority students were still attending segregated schools. Despite the U.S. Supreme Court rulings that "separate educational facilities are inherently unequal" and that school boards had to integrate "with all deliberate speed," the process continued to drag. The Civil Rights Commission report noted that only token segregation had been implemented in traditionally segregated areas and that many schools had resisted integration altogether.

ROBINSON ANCHORS NATIONAL NEWS PROGRAM

On **MAY 13**, *ABC World News Tonight* debuted Max Robinson. He became the first African American to be a news anchor on a major network.

JOHNSON NAMED BRIGADIER GENERAL

In **SEPTEMBER**, Hazel Winifred Johnson became the first Black woman to achieve the rank of general.

◈ Johnson was born on a farm near Malvern, Pennsylvania. She took a B.A. degree in nursing from Villanova University, an M.A. degree in nursing education from Columbia University, and then a Ph.D. degree in educational administration from Catholic University.

In 1955, she entered the Army Nurse Corps and served in a number of U.S. and overseas hospitals. Over the years, she moved through the ranks and excelled in the duties assigned to her. In 1980, she was appointed chief of the Army Nurse Corps. In recognition of her military career, Johnson was awarded a number of medals, including the Legion of Merit, the Meritorious Service Medal, the Army Commendation medal with Oak Leaf Cluster, and hundreds of other military, professional, and civic awards. Johnson retired as head of the U.S. Army Nurse Corps in 1983.

LAST LIVING FORMER SLAVE DIES

On **OCTOBER 2**, Charlie Smith, who claimed to be America's last living slave, died at the age of 137.

RACIAL VIOLENCE BREAKS OUT IN BOSTON

On **OCTOBER 15**, racial violence erupted again in Boston high schools. It took several days for order to be restored.

ARRINGTON ELECTED MAYOR OF BIRMINGHAM

On **OCTOBER 30**, Richard Arrington was elected the first Black mayor of Birmingham, Alabama.

"DEATH TO KLAN" MARCH HELD IN GREENSBORO

On **NOVEMBER 3**, a relatively small number of participants, mostly members of the Communist Workers Party, marched against the Ku Klux Klan in Greensboro, North Carolina. Four of the demonstrators were killed and several wounded when Klan members fired automatic weapons and shotguns into the crowd. The two vehicles used in the killing were quickly stopped by the police; twelve Klan members and sympathizers were charged with murder and conspiracy to commit murder.

LEWIS WINS NOBEL PRIZE

On **NOVEMBER 17**, Arthur Lewis, a Jamaican-born American, was awarded the Nobel Memorial Prize in Economic Sciences for his pioneering research into economic development in developing countries. He shared the prize with Theodore Schultz.

RACIAL VIOLENCE IN MIAMI FOLLOWS POLICE ACQUITTALS

On **DECEMBER 21**, Arthur McDuffie, a Black insurance agent and father of two children, died of injuries received at the hands of a beating by a Miami police officer. When McDuffie slowed rather than stopped his motorcycle at a stop light in Miami, police who attempted to stop him, found themselves in a high-speed chase that eventually involved no less than a dozen police cars. When McDuffie was finally stopped, police officers beat him severely. Four police officers were accused of crimes ranging from second-degree murder to manslaughter and tampering with evidence. Blacks waited patiently to see if justice would be rendered. At the trial in Tampa in 1980, several police officers who testified described the beating in great detail, but the all-white jury found the police officers not guilty on all counts. Janet Reno, later appointed attorney general by President Bill Clinton, was the state prosecutor in the McDuffie case.

1980

POPULATION OVERVIEW

BLACK POPULATION IN THE UNITED STATES The Bureau of the Census recorded a total of 227,255,000 residents in this country. Blacks composed 26.5 million (about 12 percent) of the total residents. In addition, Blacks constituted more than 20 percent of the population in seven states. Twelve states had Black populations of 1 million or more. Approximately 85 percent of the Black population resided in urban areas, compared with 71 percent of the white population. Although a majority of Blacks still lived in central cities, Blacks were moving to the suburbs in increasing numbers, up 43 percent over the past decade. But Blacks still made up only about 6 percent of the suburban population.

New York City had the largest Black population of any city, followed by Chicago, Detroit, Philadelphia, and Los Angeles. Slightly more than one-third of all Blacks in the country resided in seven major cities: New York City, Chicago, Detroit, Philadelphia, Los Angeles, the District of Columbia, and Baltimore.

Each of these cities had more than one-half million Black residents. Of the 100 cities with the largest percentage of Black residents, East St. Louis, Illinois, had the highest percentage (96 percent), followed by East Orange, New Jersey (83 percent).

Black migration from the South had apparently slowed or even reversed by this time. Although about 220,000 Blacks migrated from the South between 1975 and 1980, about 415,000 Blacks moved into the South, an indication that the long-term exodus from the South had stopped. The proportion of Blacks residing in the South in 1980 remained at about 53 percent, about the same as it was in 1970.

Perhaps one of the most dramatic dimensions of the population shifts among Blacks was the degree to which cities with relatively large proportions of Black residents continued to increase their Black populations. Of the cities with 100,000 or more total residents whose populations were between one-third and one-half Black, all had become proportionately more Black in makeup. The trend in these cities toward a larger percentage of Black residents showed that Blacks and whites generally did not share the same residential spaces for very long. In many of these cities, the Black populations were actually declining in absolute number but were increasing as a proportion of total residents, because whites were moving out at a faster rate than Blacks.

Blacks were gradually shifting their residence from central cities to suburban locations. The proportion of the total Black population residing in suburban areas had increased from 19.2 percent to 23.3 percent of all Blacks. Other residential locations experienced a decrease in the proportion of Black population — the largest proportional loss occurring in the central city — from 60 percent in 1970 to 57.8 percent in 1980.

BLACK MIGRATION For one hundred years after the first U.S. census in 1790, more than 90 percent of the nation's Black population lived in the South. By 1980, the figure had dropped to just a little over 50 percent. Much of this redistribution came about because Blacks migrated from the South to opportunities in the North and the West.

Blacks began migrating from the South in sizable numbers in the decade following the Civil War. Most moved to large cities of the Northeast and the Midwest. The number of migrants increased markedly in the 1920s, following restrictions on foreign immigration imposed in 1921 and 1924. The manufacturing jobs formerly filled by immigrants were taken by southern Blacks, many of whom were actively recruited by northern industrialists.

The decade of the Great Depression saw Black migration from the South decrease, but after World War II, the volume increased as never before. Between 1940 and 1970, more than four million Blacks left the South. The West, as well as the Northeast and the Midwest, offered job opportunities in manufacturing and services.

In the 1970s, the trend reversed, and there was a positive net migration of Blacks to the South. Some of these were "return migrants" who had left the region decades before. Some returned home for retirement, others for economic opportunities. The economic boom in the Sunbelt that began in the 1970s attracted both Blacks and whites to many parts of the South.

BLACK RESIDENTS IN APPALACHIA Blacks in Appalachia numbered about one million, or 9 percent of the total population. Sizable numbers of slaves and free Blacks had lived in Appalachia prior to the Civil War. Between 1800 and 1870, as much as 15 percent of the region's population was Black. Most Blacks lived in the southern part of the area, in Alabama, Tennessee, the Carolinas, and the Virginias. Beginning in the 1870s, large numbers of Blacks and whites moved into Appalachia to work in the coal mines that fueled America's industrial expansion. Blacks made up slightly more than half of the coal miners in Alabama and a quarter of those in West Virginia by 1930.

Mechanization in the mines, especially after 1950, eliminated thousands of jobs. Displaced Black miners often migrated to the industrial cities of the Midwest, cities that also attracted other Black rural migrants. A smaller number of displaced Black miners remained in the South but moved to the growing urban areas of the Piedmont, including Winston-Salem, Roanoke, and Atlanta. In some places, the rate of migration out of Appalachia was substantial. For example, between 1950 and 1970, nearly half of the Blacks in Kentucky left; many of them were miners.

POPULATION GROWTH OF MINORITIES Between 1970 and 1980, the Black population increased by 17.3 percent, the Hispanic population by 61 percent, and the Asian population by 142 percent.

REGIONAL MIGRATION OF BLACKS The Northeast region experienced its greatest level of immigrants in the decades 1880 to 1930; immigrants were mainly Blacks and whites moving in from the South and foreign immigrants, largely from Europe. After 1930, the rate of net immigration fell, culminating in a loss of more than one million migrants who left between 1970 and 1980. It is interesting to note that throughout this entire period, except in the 1940s and 1970s, the Northeast experienced population gains.

Like the Northeast, the North Central region experienced a loss of residents exceeding one million in the decade 1970–1980. From 1870 to 1930, the North Central region gained population, but since 1930, it has recorded a negative net migration rate.

The South experienced seven out of eleven decades of negative migration. Although migration from the South occurred heavily between 1870 and 1880, movement into the South was high enough to have a slight positive migration rate. Although the South continued to lose residents, the net migration out of the South was reversed during the 1960–1970 decade, when the South actually gained 740,000 residents and experienced a positive net migration rate of 1.3 residents per 1,000 residents. During the 1970–1980 decade, the South continued to gain population, with a net migration of more than 7.5 million residents and a positive net migration rate of 11.5 percent.

The West was the only region in the country to experience a positive net migration during each of the eleven decades since 1870. Although the West gained a net migration of two million persons during the 1900–1910 decade, slightly less than the 2.7 million gain of the Northeast, the West had been the leader in net migration growth since then. Since 1940, the West experienced migrations larger than those of any other region. Although the West sustained a net migration of 5.1 million persons during the 1970–1980 decade, the southern region experienced the largest net migration (7.5 million) during this decade.

Clearly, the migration of inhabitants in the United States had shifted. The Northeast and the North Central regions were losing populations to the South and the West. Added together, these two regions (sometimes popularly referred to as the Sunbelt) experienced a net migration of more than 12.6 million persons over the 1970–1980 period. This reversal in migration trends in the United States is not expected to change for some time, and experts note that the South and the West will continue to experience population growth at the expense of the Northeast and the North Central regions.

ECONOMIC CONDITIONS OVERVIEW

BLACK HOME OWNERSHIP CONTINUES TO LAG BEHIND WHITES The census showed that 44 percent of Black households owned their homes, compared with 68 percent of white households.

BLACKS STILL CONCENTRATED IN LOWER-PAYING JOBS DESPITE EDUCATIONAL AND OCCUPATIONAL GAINS Although Blacks made significant improvement in their educational attainment over the 1970–1980 decade, their distribution in the work force relative to white workers did not adequately reflect their educational gains. In general, Black workers were still concentrated in the lower-paying, less prestigious occupations. In this year, about 33 percent of Black men were working as professionals, managers, salespeople, and craftworkers, whereas 59 percent of white men were employed in these job categories. About 32 percent of white women were employed in these categories, compared with 19 percent of Black women.

THE RATIO OF BLACK FAMILY INCOME TO WHITE FAMILY INCOME DROPS Although the Bureau of the Census reported that the aggregate income for the Black population was $127 billion in 1980 (a per capita income of $4,804), whites continued to make a larger share of the aggregate income, $1,590 trillion (a per capita income of $8,233). The fact that Blacks were losing income relative to whites was shown clearly by charting median family income by race over the previous decade. In 1970, the ratio of median family incomes of Blacks to whites was .613; that is, Black families made only 61.3 percent of the average white family incomes. In constant dollars, Black families lost relative income; in 1980, they received only 58 percent of the average family income for whites. Furthermore, the proportion of Blacks in poverty in 1980 was about the same as it was in 1970 — about one in every three Blacks. About 29 percent of Black families were living below the poverty level.

SOCIAL CONDITIONS OVERVIEW

CENSUS REPORTS BLACK MAJORITIES IN NATION'S LARGEST CITIES On April 16, it was reported in census data that Blacks and Hispanics formed majorities, or sizable minorities, in the nation's largest cities because of white flight to the suburbs. A census study of twenty-six of the thirty largest cities in the country showed that central cities lost a substantial proportion of their white middle-class population between 1970 and 1980. These cities were often surrounded by white suburban areas, frequently housing populations larger than those in the cities themselves.

BLACK CHILDREN IMPROVE IN READING ABILITY In a report by the National Assessment of Educational Progress dated April 29, 1980, young Black children were found to have made substantial gains in their reading abilities over the previous decade. In 1980, Black children answered 58 percent of the reading questions correctly, in contrast with 45 percent in 1970. These gains were attributed to remedial education financed by funds through Title I of the Elementary and Secondary Education Act.

BLACKS GRADUATE FROM U.S. NAVAL ACADEMY IN LARGER NUMBERS During the decade from 1970 to 1980, 289 Blacks graduated from the U.S. Naval Academy. This number represented a considerable increase over the 35 Blacks who had graduated from the academy in the previous two decades.

BLACK WOMEN HEAD MANY HOUSEHOLDS On March 13, 1980, a census report stated that about one-third of U.S. households received noncash federal benefits, such as Medicare, food stamps, and low-cost housing. Furthermore, the number of women who functioned as sole heads of their households had increased to 8.5 million, an increase of 53 percent. The Bureau of the Census recorded that 40.4 percent of Black families were headed by women, 4.1 percent were headed by men, and 55.5 percent were headed by a man and a woman. In white families, husband-wife households made up 85.6 percent, households headed by women represented 11.5 percent, and households headed by men constituted 2.8 percent.

CENTERS FOR DISEASE CONTROL REPORTS ON "BEING BLACK IN AMERICA" The Centers for Disease Control reported that being Black in America meant experiencing higher mortality rates, lower levels of education, lower levels of occupational status, lower incomes, and higher levels of marital disruption than the white population. These disturbing trends among Blacks were attributed to racial discrimination.

CHILDREN BORN OUT OF WEDLOCK MORE LIKELY TO BE BLACK Black children were 5.1 times more likely to be born out of wedlock than white children.

DIVORCE RATE AMONG BLACKS INCREASING Census data revealed that over the previous decade, the divorce rate for Black men and women had increased by 144 percent and 147 percent, respectively. The combined divorce rate of Black men and women was 203 per 1,000 marriages, a rate more than double that of whites and Hispanic Americans.

POVERTY DECREASING IN THE SOUTH According to the census, the South was the only region of the country that had experienced a decrease in poverty over the 1970–1980 decade. The proportion of people in poverty there had decreased from 18 percent to 15 percent. The decline had occurred outside the South's metropolitan areas. Southern poor were concentrated in the cities and were more likely to be female heads of households, the elderly, or the handicapped. These populations were more dependent on welfare than they had been in the past.

BURRUS BECOMES EXECUTIVE VICE PRESIDENT OF UNION

William Burrus was elected as executive vice president of the American Postal Workers Union. He had served as business agent of the union from 1978 to 1980. Burrus was reelected to this post several times, and in 1994, he still represented the postal workers.

BROWN NAMED SPEAKER OF HOUSE IN CALIFORNIA

Willie L. Brown of California became the first Black Speaker of the House in state government. He retains that position and is considered by his peers to be the most powerful politician in the state. Brown was first elected to the California Assembly in 1964, representing a San Francisco district.

CROCKETT ELECTED TO CONGRESS

A noted leader of Detroit's Black community, George W. Crockett, Jr., was elected to the congressional seat vacated by the resignation of Charles C. Diggs.

Crockett had had a long career as a lawyer and judge prior to his election. In 1939, he had served as the first Black lawyer in the U.S. Department of Labor, and President Franklin D. Roosevelt had appointed him a hearing examiner with the Fair Employment Practices Commission. As an attorney, he often defended labor unions and civil rights organizers. As a judge, he was known to be reluctant to sentence defendants who might have been victims of police brutality. He served in Congress until 1988.

PIERCE APPOINTED SECRETARY OF HOUSING AND URBAN DEVELOPMENT

President Ronald Reagan named Samuel R. Pierce, Jr., as secretary of housing and urban development (HUD). He was the highest-ranking Black appointee of the Reagan administration. Pierce was later forced to resign from HUD and was investigated for wrong-doings while secretary.

Pierce had served in the Eisenhower administration as assistant to the undersecretary of labor. In 1970, President Richard Nixon appointed him general counsel to the Treasury Department, another first for a Black.

NEW YORK CITY PRESSURED TO HIRE BLACK AND HISPANIC POLICE OFFICERS

On **JANUARY 12**, a U.S. district court judge ruled to correct a pattern of discrimination in hiring police officers in New York City. The ruling required that half of all new police officers hired by the city be Black or Hispanic. Up to this time, Black and Hispanic police officers had made up only about 11.5 percent of the force, although representing 30 percent of the city's labor force. On August 1, the U.S. Court of Appeals altered this ruling, declaring that the written test used to hire officers had "significant disparate racial impact" and that until a new test was implemented, 33 percent of the police officers hired had to be Black or Hispanic.

MINORITY CHILDREN STILL ATTEND SEGREGATED SCHOOLS

On **JANUARY 15**, the U.S. Civil Rights Commission reported that nearly half of all minority schoolchildren remained in "racially isolated" schools, despite the Supreme Court decision outlawing school segregation. The commission attributed the continued segregation to antibusing measures and other legislation used by Congress.

BUSING REPORTED TO RESULT IN "WHITE FLIGHT" AND RESEGREGATION OF SCHOOLS

On **JANUARY 22**, in a review of current policies used by lower courts to achieve school desegregation, Supreme Court justices Lewis Powell, Jr., Potter Stewart, and William Rehnquist contended that in many cities, busing to integrated schools resulted in white flight and the resegregation of schools. They believed that the quality of education was thus further damaged.

BLACK ENTERTAINMENT TELEVISION BEGINS BROADCASTING

On **JANUARY 25**, Black Entertainment Television (BET) began operation in Washington, D.C., the first and only Black-owned cable satellite television network. It was started by Robert L. Johnson after he secured a personal loan of fifteen thousand dollars. In 1991, it became the first Black-owned company to be traded on the New York Stock Exchange. BET, anchored in Washington, D.C., is today a successful cable television network with roughly twenty-five million subscribers.

CALIFORNIA SUPREME COURT APPROVES QUOTA SYSTEM

On **JANUARY 27**, the California Supreme Court, in a split decision (4–3), upheld a Sacramento County quota hiring system designed to increase jobs for minorities. The majority opinion noted, "Such remedial affirmative action measures promote rather than thwart the attainment of the ultimate constitutional and legislative objective: a society in which equal employment opportunity is a reality rather than an elusive dream."

SOUTH BEND, INDIANA, AGREES TO DESEGREGATE SCHOOLS

On **FEBRUARY 9**, the public school system of South Bend, Indiana, agreed to desegregate its teachers and students by the beginning of the 1981–1982 school year. This decision was important because it marked the first time that a school system outside the South had consented to a Justice Department desegregation plan without going to court.

HOOVER CHARGED WITH BLOCKING PROSECUTION OF KLAN MEMBERS

On **FEBRUARY 17**, J. Edgar Hoover (1895–1972), former FBI director, was charged in a Justice Department report with blocking the prosecution of four Ku Klux Klansmen identified as responsible for the 1963 bombing that killed four Black children at the Sixteenth Street Baptist Church in Birmingham, Alabama. The report also revealed the cover-up of the involvement of an FBI informant in other violent attacks on Blacks, civil rights activists, and journalists.

SCHOOL DENIED FEDERAL FUNDS BECAUSE OF ALLEGED SEGREGATION

On **MARCH 4**, the school system of Ferndale, Michigan, was denied four hundred thousand dollars a year in federal funds because of alleged segregation. Although the school system as a whole had a racial mix that paralleled the national average, four of the five elementary schools remained less than 5 percent Black, despite an open enrollment plan that allowed Black families to choose which schools their children would attend.

DESEGREGATION PLAN FOR CLEVELAND PUBLIC SCHOOLS REQUIRES BUSING

On **MARCH 18**, in a 6–3 decision, the Supreme Court approved a Cleveland public school desegregation plan requiring the cross-town busing of fifty-two thousand students. The following April, a federal district judge threatened to impose "serious sanctions" against the school board for not executing a three-phase desegregation plan to achieve racial balance.

HOLMES WINS HEAVYWEIGHT CHAMPIONSHIP

On **MARCH 31**, Larry Holmes fought Leroy Jones for the vacant world heavyweight championship title. He knocked out Jones in the eighth round.

CHICAGO FIRE DEPARTMENT PROHIBITED FROM DISCRIMINATING IN PROMOTIONS

On **APRIL 2**, the Chicago Fire Department was permanently prohibited from discriminating against any candidate for promotion on the basis of race or national origin. This prohibition resulted from a suit charging the fire department with violating provisions of the Civil Rights Act of 1964 and the Federal Revenue Sharing Act of 1972.

WHITES ATTACK BLACK DEMONSTRATORS IN GEORGIA

On **APRIL 10**, a group of seventy-five Blacks protesting against economic and political injustices in the county were attacked by a group of one hundred or more whites outside the county sheriff's office in Wrightsville, Georgia. According to the town's Black leaders, the whites included police officers. Several days later, the FBI began an investigation of the incident.

CHICAGO SCHOOLS FOUND TO BE ILLEGALLY SEGREGATED

On **APRIL 22**, the Justice Department found that the public schools of Chicago were illegally segregated and invited city officials to begin negotiations for a settlement rather than file suit against the system immediately. On September 25, an agreement was reached, ending a twelve-year struggle between the city's school board and the Justice Department. The board received $422,000 to implement the plan.

SUPREME COURT RULES PROOF IS NEEDED TO DECLARE AN ELECTION SYSTEM UNCONSTITUTIONAL

On **APRIL 23**, the Supreme Court voted 6–3 that intentional discrimination had to be proven to declare a local election system unconstitutional. Justices William Brennan, Byron White, and Thurgood Marshall dissented.

This decision reversed the findings of two lower courts that the at-large election system in Mobile, Alabama, was unconstitutional. Despite the fact that Blacks made up 35 percent of the population of Mobile, not a single Black had been elected city commissioner or to the county school board in the city's entire history. According to the Supreme Court decision, it had to be proven that at-large voting systems were established intentionally to exclude Black voters.

SUPREME COURT APPROVES DESEGREGATION PLAN FOR DELAWARE

On **APRIL 29**, by refusing to review a 1978 "massive" desegregation plan for New Castle, Delaware, the Supreme Court in effect approved the plan. The plan required the combination of eleven independent school districts and the busing of twenty-one thousand students to remedy segregation in one school district in Wilmington.

AMOCO PAYS CIVIL PENALTY FOR DISCRIMINATION

On **APRIL 30**, Amoco Oil agreed to pay a record civil penalty of two hundred thousand dollars to settle charges of discrimination against Blacks, Hispanics, and women in the issuance of credit cards. (Applicants living in ZIP code zones with large Black populations had been denied credit.) This was the largest settlement levied to date under the Equal Credit Opportunity Act. In addition to the fine, Amoco had to reconsider the applications of all who had been denied credit.

SETTLEMENT REACHED ON DESEGREGATION IN FLINT, MICHIGAN

On **MAY 1**, in a settlement between the Justice Department and the Flint, Michigan, school board, six more magnet schools would be added to the system to complete desegregation.

WHITE SUPREMACIST CONVICTED OF CONSPIRACY TO BOMB BLACK CHURCH

On **MAY 15**, J. B. Stoner, a self-avowed white supremacist, was convicted of conspiring to bomb the predominantly Black Bethel Baptist Church in Georgia twenty-two years earlier. No one was injured in the blast.

While released on a twenty-thousand-dollar appeal bond, Stoner continued his run for a seat in the U.S. Senate. He was sentenced to ten years in prison.

RACE RIOTING OCCURS IN FLORIDA

On **MAY 17**, after an all-male, all-white jury acquitted white Dade police officers in the beating death of Black insurance executive Arthur McDuffie, Liberty City and the predominantly Black Coconut Grove section of Miami erupted in violence. Sixteen people were killed and 371 injured; stores were looted and property burned, resulting in damage totaling $200 million dollars. National Guard troops were called out to patrol the areas. Attorney General Benjamin Civiletti announced a full-scale federal investigation in response to charges by Blacks of two separate and unequal standards of justice in Miami. The number of deaths and amount of destruction made this the worst race riot since Detroit and Newark in 1967. On July 18, violence erupted again. After three days, a curfew was imposed, and 170 square blocks were cordoned off by police barricades.

JORDAN WOUNDED BY GUNSHOT

On **MAY 29**, Vernon Jordan, president of the National Urban League, was shot and seriously wounded outside his motel room in Fort Wayne, Indiana. The assailant was not found. Jordan survived a shot from a 30.06 rifle that left a hole in his back the size of a fist. The National Urban League offered a fifty-thousand-dollar reward for information leading to the arrest of the assailant.

DIGGS RESIGNS FROM CONGRESS

On **JUNE 4**, Charles C. Diggs resigned the seat in the U.S. House of Representatives that he had held for twenty-six years. He had been convicted of mail fraud and diversion of funds in payroll kickbacks in 1978. In July, he began to serve a three-year sentence at a minimum security facility at Maxwell Air Force Base, where many of the convicted Watergate figures served their sentences.

SUPREME COURT UPHOLDS PERCENTAGE OF FEDERAL PROJECTS SET ASIDE FOR MINORITIES

In **JULY**, the Supreme Court upheld the 10 percent minority "set-aside" of federal public works contracts. In its ruling in *Fullilove* v. *Klutznick*, the Court supported two lower court decisions that had also upheld the provision of the Public Works Employment Act of 1977 requiring that 10 percent of federal public works projects be reserved for minority-owned businesses. It was the first time the highest court in the nation had expressly backed the awarding of federal funds based on the race of the recipients.

Vernon Jordan served as the executive director of the National Urban League.

The majority opinion in the case noted, "Congress had abundant evidence from which it could conclude that minority business had been denied effective participation in public contracting opportunities. . . . We reject the contention that in the remedial context the Congress must act in a wholly color-blind fashion."

POLICE BRUTALITY MAJOR CAUSE OF URBAN DISORDERS

On **JULY 10**, in a study of police brutality, the U.S. Civil Rights Commission found that police brutality was still a serious problem and the major cause of urban disorders. The commission advocated granting the Justice Department additional power to prosecute cases of alleged police misconduct and to initiate suits against local police forces.

WILLS NAMED MANAGER OF SEATTLE MARINERS

On **AUGUST 4**, Maury Wills was selected manager of the Seattle Mariners, becoming the third African American manager in the major leagues.

CENSUS ALLEGEDLY UNDERCOUNTS BLACKS AND HISPANIC AMERICANS

In **SEPTEMBER**, a U.S. District Court judge invalidated the 1980 census in a suit brought by the city of Detroit, because it undercounted Blacks and Hispanic Americans. Such undercounting violated the one-person, one-vote principle. Higher courts later upheld the census count.

SCHOOLS INTEGRATE PEACEFULLY IN ST. LOUIS

In **SEPTEMBER**, the St. Louis schools were integrated peacefully after eight years of struggle.

New York Times EMPLOYEES WIN RACIAL DISCRIMINATION SUIT

On **SEPTEMBER 18**, Black, Hispanic, and Asian American employees of the *New York Times* won an out-of-court settlement in the amount of $685,000 in a racial discrimination suit that they had waged for six years. In addition to the cash settlement, these employees were to receive higher-level managerial positions. The paper also agreed to provide journalism scholarships to minorities. As part of the agreement, a statement was issued contending that there had been no finding of discrimination by the newspaper.

LABOR DEPARTMENT ANNOUNCES NEW HIRING GOALS

On **SEPTEMBER 25**, the Department of Labor set new hiring goals, based upon the percentage of minorities in an area's civilian work force, for federal contractors in 285 major metropolitan and 183 rural areas. Minorities contended that the new rules reduced existing minority hiring goals, whereas contractors claimed that they would have to hire entry-level personnel at higher wages to meet the government's requirement to pay the prevailing wage for a job.

KLAN REVEALS EXISTENCE OF "SPECIAL FORCES GROUP"

On **SEPTEMBER 28**, the Grand Dragon of Alabama's Ku Klux Klan revealed that a "special forces group" had been in existence in Cullman, Alabama, for more than a year. The FBI believed this group to be the most unpredictable and dangerous of all the Klan groups. Trainees in the camp said they were preparing for a race war.

HOLMES STOPS ALI FROM REGAINING WORLD BOXING TITLE

On **OCTOBER 2** in Las Vegas, Muhammad Ali's attempt to regain the world's heavyweight championship for a fourth time was foiled by Larry Holmes, a thirty-year-old undefeated champion. Holmes, a former sparring partner of Ali's, was too quick for the aging Ali.

RACIAL KILLINGS OCCUR IN BUFFALO

On **OCTOBER 13**, Black leaders reported that six Black men, ranging in age from fourteen to seventy-one, had been killed in Buffalo, New York. Blacks believed that the killings were fueled by bitterness over what whites perceived as preferential treatment of Blacks in employment, school desegregation, and other areas. According to one Black community leader, racial tensions were high because the white middle class felt itself to be in an economic pinch. Investigations were conducted by local and state law enforcement agencies and the FBI.

BIRMINGHAM AGREES TO DESEGREGATION PLAN

On **OCTOBER 23**, the Justice Department and the school board in Birmingham, Alabama, agreed on a school desegregation plan, ending a twenty-year battle to bring about school integration. Magnet programs and middle schools would be used to achieve desegregation with a "minimum of voluntary busing."

BLACK MURDERS LABELED "RANDOM ATTACKS" BY FBI

On **OCTOBER 23**, FBI director William Webster contended that there was no evidence of a nationwide conspiracy to kill Blacks, even though twenty-four had been murdered over the past fifteen months in seven cities.

SOUTHERN BANK DISCRIMINATES AGAINST MINORITIES AND WOMEN

On **OCTOBER 24**, a U.S. District Court judge ruled that Republic National Bank, the largest bank in the South, had discriminated against Blacks and women in salaries, promotions, and hirings over a ten-year period. Only 15 of the bank's 570 officers were Black, and none held the rank of vice president or a higher rank.

DYMALLY ELECTED TO CONGRESS

In **NOVEMBER**, Mervyn M. Dymally, a former member of the California Assembly (1963–1966) and the state senate (1967–1975), was elected to the U.S. House of

Representatives from the state's Thirty-first Congressional District, after defeating four other candidates in the Democratic primary.

Dymally, born in Trinidad, was a teacher in California before entering politics.

In 1974, Dymally was elected lieutenant governor of California on the Democratic ticket with Governor Jerry Brown. He lost the campaign for reelection in 1978.

While a member of Congress, Dymally was especially concerned with U.S. economic policies in Africa and the Caribbean. He also worked to increase funding for the education of minority students and for opportunities for firms owned and operated by minorities to develop oil and gas resources on federal land.

From 1987 until 1989, Dymally chaired the Congressional Black Caucus.

SAVAGE ELECTED TO CONGRESS

In **NOVEMBER**, Black journalist and civil rights advocate Gus Savage (1925–) was elected to the U.S. House of Representatives from Chicago's Second Congressional District after defeating three other opponents in the Democratic primary. In the general election, he received 88 percent of the vote. He succeeded Morgan Murphy, who retired in 1979.

◊ Savage, born in Detroit, attended public schools in Chicago, and after doing a tour of duty in the U.S. Army, received a B.A. degree in philosophy from Roosevelt University in 1951. He started his journalistic career in 1954.

In 1965, Savage became owner and editor of a chain of independent community weekly newspapers, the Citizen Newspapers.

Savage opposed the Chicago Democratic machine of Mayor Richard J. Daley. In 1968 and 1970, Savage ran unsuccessfully in the Democratic primary for the congressional seat of Chicago's Third District.

While in Congress, Savage served as chairperson of the Committee on Public Works and the Transportation Subcommittee on Economic Development. He was also the senior Black member of the Committee on Small Business. One of his most important accomplishments was the sponsorship of an amendment to the National Defense Authorization Act of 1987 that implemented the largest federal contract set-aside program in the history of military procurement. Minority-owned businesses and institutions and historically Black colleges could compete for as much as twenty-five billion dollars. Savage lost the Democratic primary in 1992 to Mel Reynolds.

ALL-WHITE JURY ACQUITS KLAN SYMPATHIZERS OF MURDER CHARGES

On **NOVEMBER 17**, an all-white jury acquitted six Klan sympathizers of murder charges in the 1979 killings of five "Death to the Klan" marchers of the Communist Workers Party. After a week of deliberation, the jury concluded that the Klan supporters were acting in self defense and that they were provoked. The Justice Department announced that it would review the case to determine whether federal charges should be brought against the defendants. Five other men who faced murder charges were yet to be tried.

HOWARD UNIVERSITY TELEVISION STATION STARTS BROADCASTING

On **NOVEMBER 17**, WHMM-TV, a television station owned by Howard University, started broadcasting. It was the first African American–owned public broadcasting television station in the country.

LOS ANGELES POLICE DEPARTMENT REQUIRED TO HIRE MORE MINORITIES

On **NOVEMBER 21**, victims of discrimination were awarded two million dollars by the Los Angeles Police Department. Further, in a consent decree reached with the Justice Department, the department was required to hire minorities and women in numbers equal to their proportion in the labor force. Women were also to be hired until they held at least 20 percent of the police officer posts.

FORD MOTOR COMPANY AGREES TO FUND TRAINING PROGRAMS AND PAY COMPENSATION TO MINORITIES AND WOMEN

On **NOVEMBER 26**, in one of the five nationwide discrimination investigations initiated by the Equal Employment Opportunity Commission in the early 1970s, the Ford Motor Company reached an agreement to spend twenty-three million dollars on improved training programs and compensatory payments to minority and women workers. Minorities would also be placed in more than 20 percent of the company's skilled trades, production, and maintenance supervisory positions, and more than 15 percent in general supervisory positions.

ANTIBUSING AMENDMENT VETOED

In **DECEMBER**, one of Jimmy Carter's last actions as president was to veto an antibusing amendment, proposed by Senator Jesse Helms of North Carolina, that would have barred the Justice Department from bringing any legal action to require school busing.

1981 ANTIDISCRIMINATION POLICIES DISMANTLED BY REAGAN

The Reagan administration proposed legislation to exempt employers with fewer than 250 workers and federal contracts of less than one million dollars from federal regulations requiring them to submit written plans for hiring and promoting women and minorities. These changes reversed the antidiscrimination guidelines established in 1964 by President Lyndon Johnson's Executive Order 11246.

In 1983, the Labor Department proposed that the exemptions be expanded to contractors with one hundred employees and one hundred thousand dollars in federal contracts.

BLACK FARMING POPULATION FURTHER DECLINES

According to the Bureau of the Census, the Black farming population was less than 1 percent of all Blacks. The Black farming population was 48.7 percent in 1920.

BLACK MAN LYNCHED IN ALABAMA

Michael Donald, a Black man, was lynched in Mobile, Alabama.

BLACK MIDSHIPMAN HOLDS HIGHEST RANK AT U.S. NAVAL ACADEMY

For the first time in the history of the U.S. Naval Academy, a Black midshipman, Walter Nobles, became the brigade commander for the academic year, for 1981–1982. Nobles had also served as regiment commander the previous summer and was responsible for the initiation and basic training of the entering plebe class. Nobles widened the doors for qualified Blacks at the academy.

BLACK ENLISTMENT IN ARMED FORCES INCREASES

Post-Vietnam participation of Black soldiers in the armed forces increased markedly — the percent of Blacks enlisted increased from 11.4 percent to 22.1 percent, representing almost four hundred thousand Blacks. The percentage of Black officers more than doubled — increasing from 2.3 percent to 5.3 percent — but nevertheless remained proportionally low, accounting for fifteen thousand Black officers. The percentage of Black officers who were women increased from 3.3 percent to 10.3 percent.

One reason that the military had become attractive to Blacks was simply the fact that it offered steady employment. Also, conditions within the military had changed significantly over the previous decade; large-scale equal opportunity programs had been implemented. Also, civilian jobs for workers lacking high school and college diplomas had declined considerably.

Today, Blacks constitute almost 20 percent of all military personnel on active duty, up from 10.2 percent in 1971.

CHARLES BOLDEN NAMED ASTRONAUT

Charles F. Bolden (1946–), a highly qualified pilot who had flown more than one hundred sorties in Southeast Asia, was named an astronaut. He piloted craft in several missions, notably the space shuttle *Atlantis* in a mission in 1992.

BOYCOTT AGAINST COCA-COLA BRINGS INVESTMENT TO BLACK COMMUNITY

The national boycott against Coca-Cola, organized by PUSH (People United to Save Humanity) and Jesse Jackson, ended when the company agreed to invest thirty-four million dollars in Black businesses and communities.

COBB APPOINTED PRESIDENT OF CALIFORNIA STATE UNIVERSITY

Jewel P. Cobb (1924–), a prominent cancer research biologist, was selected president of California State University (CSU) at Fullerton. Cobb was the first African American woman to hold a presidency in the entire CSU system.

Cobb had served as a professor and administrator at Connecticut College and Rutgers University before this appointment.

COLE-ALEXANDER HEADS LABOR DEPARTMENT'S WOMEN'S BUREAU

Dr. Lenora Cole-Alexander was selected to head the U.S. Labor Department's Women's Bureau. She was the first Black to head this important bureau.

JOHNSON BECOMES PUBLISHER OF THE *Ithaca Journal*

Pamela Johnson became the first Black woman publisher of a major newspaper in this country. She is publisher of the *Ithaca Journal*.

The Marva Collins Story AIRS ON TELEVISION

The Marva Collins Story appeared on national television. It told the story of Marva Collins of Monroeville, Alabama, who opened a school in Chicago and became an innovator in teaching inner-city students. Using her pension funds, Collins opened the Westside Preparatory School to reverse the educational deterioration that she had witnessed. Her school and teaching methods became a model used by a number of educators and politicians to show that "all kids can learn if given the opportunity."

BLACKS TRIED FOR KILLING WHITES DURING MIAMI RIOTS

On **JANUARY 7**, the trials of four Blacks began in Miami. They were charged with beating and stomping three whites to death during the riot in May 1980. In February, three of the defendants were convicted of murder. The fourth was acquitted.

CHICAGO SELECTS FIRST BLACK GENERAL SUPERINTENDENT OF SCHOOLS

On **JANUARY 14**, Ruth Love, superintendent of Oakland public schools, was voted the first Black general superintendent of Chicago's public schools, following the rejection of Manford Byrd, Jr., a Black deputy superintendent who had been in the system for twenty-six years.

BUDGET CUTS ANNOUNCED IN PROGRAMS TO AID THE POOR

In **MARCH**, and in a series of announcements throughout the year, the Reagan administration proposed major cuts in aid to the disadvantaged citizens of this nation. T. H. Bell, the secretary of education, announced that he would ask Congress to approve a 25 percent cut ($1.4 billion in 1982) in education assistance programs to the disadvantaged and the handicapped, including Title I programs, in addition to a 20 percent reduction in other school assistance programs. A committee in the House of Representatives revealed in a hearing that 658,000 families out of those receiving Aid to Families with Dependent Children (approximately one-sixth of the total) would be dropped or would have their benefits severely reduced. The administration also called for a seven-hundred-million-dollar reduction in the federal school lunch program and other food programs for the poor, in addition to cuts already announced.

Efforts by some legislators in Congress to restore this aid proved unsuccessful, although the actual cuts made were not as severe as those initially recommended.

WHITE SUPREMACIST CONVICTED IN BLACK JOGGER MURDER

On **MARCH 5**, Joseph Paul Franklin was convicted on federal charges of violating the civil rights of two Black male joggers killed in Salt Lake City, Utah, in August 1980. Franklin was sentenced later in the month to two consecutive life sentences for the murders. In September, Franklin was convicted on first-degree murder charges for the same murders. He received another life sentence, although the state had called for the death penalty. Franklin continued to be the major suspect in the Vernon Jordan sniper attack in Fort Wayne, Indiana, in May 1980.

LOS ANGELES MAYOR BRADLEY WINS THIRD TERM

On **APRIL 16**, Mayor Thomas Bradley garnered almost 64 percent of the vote and beat eighteen opponents to be reelected to his third term as mayor of Los Angeles.

PARENTS OF MURDERED OR MISSING CHILDREN IN ATLANTA PROTEST REMARKS BY FBI AGENT

On **APRIL 17**, the Committee to Stop Children's Murders sent a letter to FBI director William Webster to protest the remarks made by an agent that some of the children killed in a spate of unsolved murders in Atlanta may have been killed by their parents.

Agent Michael Twibell asserted before a civic club meeting in Macon, Georgia, that the children might have been killed by their parents because they were nuisances and that their deaths did not indicate a "great crime wave sweeping Atlanta."

WHITE ARMY PRIVATE INDICTED ON CHARGES OF SLAYING BLACK MEN IN BUFFALO

On **APRIL 30**, Joseph G. Christopher was indicted by a grand jury on charges of murdering three Black men in Buffalo.

Christopher allegedly told army nurses that he had also killed Black men in New York City. In October, against the advice of his two lawyers, Christopher waived his right to a jury trial. Christopher was also the prime suspect in the murder of nine other Black men and a Hispanic man in New York in 1980.

EQUAL EMPLOYMENT OPPORTUNITY ACT CHALLENGES CIVIL RIGHTS ACT

On **MAY 7**, a bill was introduced in the House of Representatives aimed at prohibiting the use of numerical quotas to increase the hiring or school enrollment of minorities and women. The bill, introduced by Representative Robert Walker, was called the Equal Employment Opportunity Act and was intended to amend the Civil Rights Act of 1964.

MIAMI RIOTS OF THE 1980S REPORTED TO DIFFER FROM THOSE OF THE 1960S

On **MAY 17**, a Ford Foundation report asserted that spontaneous uprisings by Blacks to beat or kill whites, like those that occurred in Miami in 1980, had not occurred since the slave uprisings before the Civil War. Unlike the rioters of the 1960s, the report said, the Liberty City rioters were from a more law-abiding and representative group.

BLACK COLLEGE ENROLLMENT DOUBLES IN A DECADE

On **MAY 20**, the Bureau of the Census reported that one million Black students were enrolled at American colleges and universities as of October 1980, up from 522,000 in 1970.

JUSTICE DEPARTMENT NO LONGER ADVOCATES RACIAL QUOTAS OR MANDATES

On **MAY 23**, Attorney General William French Smith announced that the Justice Department would no longer vigorously pursue mandatory busing and the use of racial quotas in employment discrimination cases because these remedies had been found ineffective. The department was also considering an amendment to make "reverse discrimination" (that is, discrimination against whites) illegal under the Civil Rights Act.

BLACK MIDDLE CLASS LIVING IN SUBURBS

On **MAY 31**, census data revealed that Blacks had increased their percentage of the population in suburban areas of large cities. Black middle-class neighborhoods had appeared in cities such as Cleveland and Newark. Nevertheless, only about six million Blacks resided in suburban and rural areas. Almost fifteen million lived in central cities of metropolitan areas.

BUSING ATTACKED BY U.S. HOUSE OF REPRESENTATIVES

In **JUNE**, the U.S. House of Representatives passed a bill that would bar the Justice Department from starting lawsuits to institute school busing to bring about integration. Supporters of the measure believed that this effort would be supported by the new Reagan administration.

A companion bill in the U.S. Senate proposed not only to prohibit federal courts from busing students more than five miles or fifteen minutes from their homes but also to dismantle any such plans already existing. For nearly a year, opponents of the Senate bill, led by Senator Lowell Weicker of Connecticut, filibustered. In March 1982, the bill finally passed. It contained the most restrictive antibusing language ever passed by either house of Congress.

In April, the measure was dropped when the appropriations measure to which it was attached was voted on. The larger bill had to be passed to avoid a shutdown of the government. It would not pass with the antibusing language attached.

EQUAL EMPLOYMENT OPPORTUNITY COMMISSION GETS NEW LEADER

On **JUNE 15**, William Bell was nominated by President Reagan to succeed Elinor Holmes Norton as head of the Equal Employment Opportunities Commission. He would be the second-highest-ranking Black in the administration. His nomination was opposed by the National Urban League, the NAACP, and the League of Women Voters because he lacked administrative experience.

SUPREME COURT UPHOLDS LOWER COURT DECISION ON HIRING BLACK POLICE OFFICERS IN NEW YORK CITY

On **JUNE 16**, by refusing to hear an appeal by New York City, the U.S. Supreme Court effectively upheld a lower court decision that at least one-third of city police officers hired by the city had to be Black and Hispanic. This employment formula was sanctioned by a federal appeals court that found that a 1979 police department test had a "disparate racial impact" on applicants.

ATLANTA KILLINGS STOP

On **JUNE 21**, Wayne B. Williams, a Black man, was charged with the murder of one of the twenty-eight Black children and young adults slain in Atlanta over the past two years. Williams had been a suspect for some time; he was charged on the basis of links between fibers found in his home and those found on the victim, Nathaniel Carter, a twenty-seven-year-old Black man whose body was found in the Chattahoochee River on May 24. Williams claimed he was innocent. On February 28, 1982, Williams was convicted in two of the murders and was sentenced to two consecutive life terms.

REAGAN ADMINISTRATION WEAKENS AFFIRMATIVE ACTION

On **JULY 16**, major cutbacks by the Reagan administration on the enforcement powers of the Justice Department, combined with weakened rules against racial discrimination, sent negative signals to Blacks. A month later, the administration began a review of thirty federal regulations, including civil rights guidelines, to see whether they were "burdensome, unnecessary or counterproductive." The Task Force on Regulatory Relief would review, among other provisions, Title IX regulations that required that companies maintain hiring guidelines and records to prevent job discrimination against Blacks and other minorities.

BLACKS LOSE LAND

On **JULY 31**, the executive director of the nonprofit Emergency Land Fund indicated that Blacks in the Southeast had been losing their traditional land at the rate of five hundred thousand acres per year since 1974.

RELAXATION OF RULES FOR FEDERAL CONTRACTORS ANNOUNCED

On **AUGUST 25**, Secretary of Labor William Donovan announced new regulations that would no longer require a review of an employer's hiring patterns as a prerequisite for awarding a federal contract and would reduce the number of affirmative action steps required for federal contractors. Only employers with 250 employees or more and with contracts of one million dollars or more would have to file formal affirmative action documents. The old regulations pertained to contractors with fifty or more employees and contracts of more than fifty thousand dollars. Donovan stated that 77 percent of women and minority workers were still protected by these proposals.

"ALLIANCE" BETWEEN KLAN MEMBERS AND POLICE OFFICERS REVEALED IN STUDY

On **OCTOBER 3**, the Institute for Southern Studies, after a six-month study, revealed that the Ku Klux Klan and Nazi Party gunmen acquitted in the murder of five members of the Communist Party in Greensboro, North Carolina, in November 1979, had had an "intimate alliance" with the local district attorney and police officials who handled the case.

POLL REFLECTS BLACKS' FEELINGS ABOUT PRESIDENT REAGAN

On **OCTOBER 5**, a *Times*/CBS News Poll found that 74 percent of Blacks and 35 percent of whites felt that President Reagan did "not much" care about the needs and problems of poor people. Regardless of age, income, or education, Black Americans overwhelmingly disapproved of the president and his programs.

EQUAL EMPLOYMENT OPPORTUNITY COMMISSION OPPOSES FURTHER EASING OF REGULATIONS

On **OCTOBER 8**, J. Clay Smith, Jr., acting chairperson of the Equal Employment Opportunity Commission, stated that the government's efforts to ease federal regulations prohibiting job discrimination had gone too far. He opposed a proposal that would exempt all but four thousand of seventeen thousand federal contractors from submitting affirmative action plans.

MARTIN LUTHER KING, JR., LIBRARY AND ARCHIVES OPENS

On **OCTOBER 19**, the Martin Luther King, Jr., Library and Archives opened in Atlanta, Georgia. The facility was founded by King's widow, Coretta Scott King. It housed the hundreds of speeches and resource materials associated with major civil rights organizations and the civil rights movement.

HALF OF BLACK BIRTHS OCCUR OUT OF WEDLOCK

On **OCTOBER 27**, the National Center for Health Statistics reported that the majority of babies born to Black women over the past decade had been born outside marriage. In 1979, 55 percent of Black babies were born outside marriage, compared with 38 percent in 1970.

YOUNG ELECTED MAYOR OF ATLANTA

On **OCTOBER 29**, former U.S. representative and UN ambassador Andrew Young defeated Sidney Marcus in a runoff election to become mayor of Atlanta, Georgia. Young won the election by receiving a majority of the Black vote and a significant percentage of the white vote.

OWENS ELECTED TO CONGRESS

In **NOVEMBER**, Robert Owens was elected to Congress from New York's Twelfth Congressional District to the seat formerly occupied by Shirley Chisholm, who had retired after fourteen years in the House of Representatives. He had run as a candidate independent of the Democratic machine in Brooklyn. He had previously represented the Brownsville and East New York sections of Brooklyn in the state senate.

◈ Born and raised in Memphis, Tennessee, Owens received a B.A. degree from Morehouse College in

1956, and a year later, an M.S. degree in library science from Atlanta University. He was an adjunct professor of library science and director of the Community Media Program at Columbia University from 1973 to 1975.

Owens also became actively involved in politics and civil rights. New York City mayor John Lindsay appointed Owens as commissioner of Community Development, a community action agency that organized and supervised self-help and antipoverty programs.

In Congress, Owens became a senior member of the Education and Labor Committee, working on legislation to restore federal funding to library services, to alleviate problems of high school dropouts, and to assist Black colleges. New York's congressional district boundaries changed after the 1990 election; still, in 1992, Owens was overwhelmingly reelected to his sixth term in Congress, this time representing the Eleventh District. He carried more than 90 percent of the votes.

REAGAN ENDORSES EXTENSION OF VOTING RIGHTS ACT WITH MODIFICATIONS

On **NOVEMBER 7**, President Ronald Reagan endorsed the extension of the Voting Rights Act of 1965 but with qualifications that, civil rights groups charged, would make the act unenforceable. The president said he favored a "reasonable" bailout provision that could free states from the law's requirements on the basis of several years of good conduct. This provision was included in the House of Representatives version of the bill. Reagan also supported a provision requiring proof of intent to discriminate in addition to other evidence in proving violations of the act.

SCHOOL DESEGREGATION POLICY CHANGES

On **NOVEMBER 20**, the U.S. Justice Department announced that it would no longer seek to desegregate an entire school district when discrimination was shown to exist in only a portion of the district. William Bradford Reynolds, head of the civil rights division, said that schoolchildren would no longer be compelled to have an integrated education if they chose against it.

BLACK HOUSEHOLDS RECEIVE FEWER FREE OR REDUCED-PRICE LUNCHES FOR CHILDREN

On **NOVEMBER 26**, a census report indicated that school-age children from half of all Black households received free or reduced-price lunches. These statistics reflected the degree of poverty in the Black community. But poverty was becoming more widespread, and white and Hispanic children were being added to the program at a faster rate than Black children. In 1980, the number of Hispanic households receiving such assistance increased by 15 percent (eight hundred thousand households) and the number of white households by 14 percent (3.4 million households). The comparable rate for Black households was 6 percent.

JACOB SUCCEEDS JORDAN AT NATIONAL URBAN LEAGUE

On **DECEMBER 7**, John E. Jacob (1934–), the Urban League's executive vice president, was selected to succeed Vernon Jordan as president of the organization, effective January 1, 1982. Jordan would become a partner in the law firm of Akin, Gump, Strauss, Hauer, and Feld in Washington, D.C.

John E. Jacob took over the leadership of the National Urban League in 1981.

◈ Jacob was born in Trout, Louisiana. He graduated from Howard University in 1957 and earned a master's degree in social work from that institution in 1963. He was employed as a social worker in Baltimore City from 1960 to 1965. Jacob then became director of education and youth incentives for the Washington Urban League. He was executive director of the San Diego Urban League from 1970 to 1975 and president of the Washington Urban League from 1975 to 1979. He became the executive vice president of the National Urban League in 1979, a position he held until his appointment as president in 1982. Jacob serves on the board of several major corporations and is chairperson emeritus of the board of trustees of Howard University.

JUSTICE DEPARTMENT ANNOUNCES PLANS TO MAKE CASE AGAINST AFFIRMATIVE ACTION

On **DECEMBER 8**, William Bradford Reynolds, head of the Justice Department's civil rights division, announced plans to seek a ruling by the U.S. Supreme Court to find giving minorities and women preference in hiring and promotion unconstitutional. He specifically wanted to reverse the Court's decision in *Weber* v. *Kaiser Aluminum and Chemical Corporation*, which upheld the legality of affirmative action hiring and promotion practices. Reynolds contended that the same set of rules should apply to both the public and private sectors. Under his plan, individuals, the Labor Department, and the Equal Employment Opportunity Commission would be prohibited from seeking such preferences.

1982 GUMBEL ANCHORS TELEVISION NEWS PROGRAM

Bryant Gumbel, formerly sports director of KNBC in Los Angeles, became the first Black in the history of NBC-TV to anchor a national news program.

INCOME GAP GROWS FOR BLACKS

Census data showed that the median income gap between Black and white families was $9,392 annually. In comparison with 1970, Blacks were relatively worse off in 1980.

JACKSON RECORDS *Thriller*

Michael Jackson recorded *Thriller*, the biggest-selling record of all time. In 1983, *Thriller* won eight Grammy Awards, including album and record of the year. It has since sold more than thirty million copies worldwide.

ROBINSON INDUCTED INTO BASEBALL HALL OF FAME

Frank Robinson, one of the most talented players in baseball history, was inducted into the Baseball Hall of Fame. Robinson was honored for his contributions to the game and his many achievements: Rookie of the Year (1956), Most Valuable Player in the National and American Leagues (1961 and 1966, respectively), player and manager of the Cleveland Indians (1975–1977), and manager of the San Francisco Giants (1981–1984) and the Baltimore Orioles (1988). Robinson is a vice president in the Baltimore Orioles organization today.

SMALLER CITIES HAVE FEWER BLACKS

In 1982, 181 cities in the United States had one hundred thousand or more inhabitants. Of these, 56 cities (31 percent) had experienced population decreases between 1980 and 1982. All but 6 of these cities also experienced population decreases between 1970 and 1980. They included Chattanooga, Memphis, and Nashville, Tennessee; Eugene, Oregon; Pueblo, Colorado; and Sterling Heights, Michigan.

Only 8 of the 181 cities had a Black population greater than 50 percent, whereas 67 had a Black population of less than 10 percent. Seven cities had proportionately fewer Blacks in 1980 than in 1970. Five of these cities were in California: Bakersfield, Berkeley, Fresno, Los Angeles, and San Francisco. The other 2 cities were Odessa, Texas, and Lexington, Kentucky.

Thirty of the 181 cities lost population between 1970 and 1980, but according to the 1982 population estimates, they had gained population between 1980 and 1982.

WALKER PUBLISHES *The Color Purple*

Alice Walker (1944–) achieved fame as a novelist when she published *The Color Purple*, which won both the Pulitzer Prize and the American Book Award in 1983. It told the story of Celie, a poor African American girl, and her experiences in a rural community in the South.

Walker's earlier critically praised publications included *Once* (1968) and *Revolutionary Petunias and Other Poems* (1973). In 1970, Walker wrote a novel, *The Third Life of Grange Copeland*, and in 1974, she published a biography, *Langston Hughes, American Poet*. Walker also edited a book on Zora Neale Hurston, her role model.

Walker was born in Eatonton, Georgia, a rural area that informed the setting of *The Color Purple*.

Alice Walker became the first Black woman writer to win a Pulitzer Prize for a work of fiction — The Color Purple.

REAGAN ADMINISTRATION PROPOSES GIVING SEGREGATED SCHOOLS TAX-EXEMPT STATUS

On **JANUARY 8**, a U.S. Treasury Department official announced that the Internal Revenue Service would no longer be allowed to deny tax-exempt status to private schools that discriminated because of race. This departure reversed an eleven-year-old federal policy. The argument for the changing of the tax status provision, according to the administration, was that the decision to confer tax status was the responsibility of Congress, not that of an executive agency.

Within a week, the NAACP filed papers in the Supreme Court to attempt to block the federal government from granting tax-exempt status to Bob Jones University in Greenville, South Carolina, and to Goldsboro Christian Schools of Goldsboro, North Carolina. Four days later, the Reagan administration bowed to pressure and sent a bill to Congress to deny tax exemptions to private schools that practiced segregation. Intense criticism of the proposal held that granting tax exemptions to these schools would be a racist act.

BLACK WOMEN IMPRISONED ON VOTE FRAUD CHARGES

On **JANUARY 12**, Julia Wilder, age sixty-nine, and Maggie Bozeman, age fifty-one, of Carrollton, Alabama, were jailed for vote fraud. The women, who had solicited thirty-nine absentee ballots from elderly and illiterate Blacks, were convicted by an all-white jury on the testimony of one person who arrived to vote and claimed that she had never signed an absentee ballot. Their sentences totaled nine years' imprisonment, considered by some to be the harshest sentences ever handed down by the state for this type of offense. The sentences were upheld by the Alabama Court of Appeals, but after an outcry against their harshness, the women were placed in a work-release program.

STANDARDIZED TESTS FOUND NOT TO DISCRIMINATE AGAINST BLACKS

On **FEBRUARY 3**, a National Academy of Sciences panel found that standardized tests in and of themselves did not necessarily discriminate against Blacks. Their findings, however, did not refute the claim that unequal test scores between Blacks and whites might result from unequal background and preparation caused by low socioeconomic status and other factors.

MARCH HELD IN SUPPORT OF VOTING RIGHTS ACT

On **FEBRUARY 7**, Representative Walter Fauntroy of the District of Columbia began to lead one hundred people on a thirteen-day march to support extension of the Voting Rights Act of 1965. The marchers retraced the route taken by Dr. Martin Luther King, Jr., from Selma to Montgomery. The marchers felt that the Reagan administration would try to weaken the Voting Rights Act and nullify the voter registration progress made over the past seventeen years. By the time the march ended, three thousand to five thousand supporters had taken part. The march had been organized by the Reverend Joseph Lowery of the Southern Christian Leadership Conference.

EQUAL EMPLOYMENT OPPORTUNITY COMMISSION HEADED BY THOMAS

On **FEBRUARY 19**, Clarence Thomas, a conservative Black attorney, was nominated by the Reagan administration to head the Equal Employment Opportunity Commission (EEOC). President Reagan nominated Thomas after he was forced to withdraw his original nomination of William Bell in the face of strongly voiced opposition by civil rights groups and several Democratic senators. Thomas opposed school busing and affirmative action as remedies for discrimination. He had been serving as assistant secretary for civil rights in the Department of Education.

BLACK SPECIAL AGENTS WIN RACE DISCRIMINATION SUIT

On **FEBRUARY 20**, two hundred Black special agents won a case against the Federal Drug Enforcement Agency, charging that they had been victims of race discrimination since 1972. They won two million dollars in back pay.

HOUSTON SELECTS FIRST BLACK CHIEF OF POLICE

On **MARCH 10**, Lee Patrick Brown, former commissioner of public safety in Atlanta, became Houston's first Black chief of police. He had previously achieved prominence in the case of Wayne B. Williams and the deaths of twenty-eight young men in Atlanta.

FULLER WINS PULITZER PRIZE

On **MARCH 12**, Black writer Charles Fuller won the Pulitzer Prize for his celebrated novel *A Soldier's Play.*

U.S. SENATE APPROVES BILL TO OVERTURN COURT-ORDERED BUSING

On **MARCH 13**, Senators J. Bennett Johnson of Louisiana and Jesse Helms of North Carolina sponsored an amendment to prohibit students from being bused to schools more than five miles or fifteen minutes from their homes. In addition, it forbade the Justice Department from initiating suits that proposed busing as a remedy for segregation and allowed the department to dismantle or reduce existing busing plans. After an emotional debate, the Senate approved the bill. The House attached a similar antibusing rider to a nine-billion-dollar appropriations bill.

U.S. CIVIL RIGHTS COMMISSION TO BE HEADED BY PENDLETON

On **MARCH 19**, Clarence Pendleton, former head of the San Diego Urban League, was confirmed by the Senate as the first Black to head the U.S. Civil Rights Commission. A conservative Republican, Pendleton said he had no opinion on busing to achieve school desegregation. He opposed granting tax exemptions to schools practicing racial discrimination and supported the Equal Rights Amendment and extending the Voting Rights Act of 1965.

BLACK PARENTS IN BOSTON WANT ACCESS TO ALL CITY SCHOOLS

On **APRIL 1**, believing that the city's 1974 desegregation plan had not improved the quality of education for their children, Black parents in Boston filed a suit to scrap the desegregation plan and allow "open access" to all city schools. They contended that Black students had all too often been shifted from inferior schools in Black neighborhoods to inferior schools in white neighborhoods. At this time, the city's population was 70 percent white, although the public school population was 66 percent minority.

SUPREME COURT RULES FOR INTENT TO DISCRIMINATE

On **APRIL 6**, in a split decision, 5–4, the Supreme Court found that "intent to discriminate" had to be proven in legal challenges of job seniority and promotion systems reached through the collective bargaining process. The decision came in a suit brought by Black employees of the American Tobacco Company's plant in Richmond, who held that they had been effectively barred from promotion — not because of intentional discrimination but because they had always held low-level jobs.

VIRGINIA ABOLISHES AT-LARGE VOTING DISTRICT

On **APRIL 15**, the U.S. Justice Department approved a redistricting plan for Virginia's House of Delegates. The former citywide, at-large voting districts were replaced by one hundred single-member districts. Black majorities in nine of these districts could result in the election of more Blacks to the house in the November 1982 election.

LOS ANGELES URBAN LEAGUE CALLS FOR SUSPENSION OF POLICE CHIEF

On **MAY 12**, in referring to a choke-hold commonly used by police to disarm suspects, Daryl Gates remarked, "We may be finding that in some Blacks when it is applied, the veins or arteries do not open up as fast as they do in normal people." This comment about "normal people" prompted the president of the Los Angeles Urban League and three members of the city council to demand the suspension and censure of Chief Gates, a thirty-three-year veteran of the police force.

BLACK AIR FORCE GENERAL FORCED INTO EARLY RETIREMENT

On **MAY 15**, Major General Titus Hall, age fifty-four, the highest-ranking Black in the air force, was forced to retire early following allegations of favoritism toward Blacks in his command. He had been serving as commander of Lowry Air Force Base Technical Training Center in Colorado.

ROTARY CLUB OF BIRMINGHAM VOTES TO MAINTAIN WHITES-ONLY MEMBERSHIP

On **MAY 31**, the members of the Rotary Club of Birmingham, Alabama, which included some of the most influential men in the state, voted 120–90 to maintain the club's whites-only membership policy. Several members resigned after the vote, but among those choosing to retain their membership were Lieutenant Governor D. H. McMillan, Jr., and Wilmer Cody, superintendent of public schools.

MISSISSIPPI CREATES FIRST BLACK MAJORITY VOTING DISTRICT IN TWENTY YEARS

On **JUNE 10**, in Oxford, Mississippi, a three-judge federal panel ordered the state to carry out a congressional redistricting plan that created the first district with a Black majority since the 1960s. Civil rights leaders, however, saw the decision as only a partial victory that might not ensure the election of a Black, since only 60 percent of the registered voters in the district were Black.

NEWARK REELECTS MAYOR GIBSON TO FOURTH TERM

On **JUNE 15**, Kenneth A. Gibson beat the city council president, Earl Harris, to secure a fourth term in office. Even though both candidates were Black, race became an issue in the campaign when Gibson accused Harris of having "sold out" to white interests in the city.

"REVERSE DISCRIMINATION" SUIT FILED

On **JUNE 24**, a Boston teachers' union challenged a desegregation order that allowed eleven hundred white teachers with seniority to be laid off while recently hired Black teachers were retained. The union's appeal to the Supreme Court challenged a decision by the U.S. Circuit Court of Appeals that "the elimination of the vestiges of a segregated school system cannot be accomplished until the effects of past hiring discrimination have been eradicated."

MEHARRY MEDICAL COLLEGE SAVED BY PRESIDENTIAL ORDER

On **JUNE 26**, an order issued by President Reagan offered special financial aid for Meharry Medical College in Nashville, Tennessee. The affiliation between Meharry and the Veterans' Administration hospital in Murfreesboro would be expanded and thus would help the school retain its accreditation. In addition, the Department of Health and Human Services would take over the balance of a loan of twenty-nine million dollars that had built Meharry's Hubbard Hospital. Meharry, founded in 1876, had trained half of the nation's Black doctors and dentists.

VOTING RIGHTS ACT OF 1965 EXTENDED FOR TWENTY-FIVE YEARS

On **JUNE 30**, President Ronald Reagan signed into law a bill that extended and strengthened key provisions of the Voting Rights Act of 1965.

SUPREME COURT ALLOWS LOWER COURTS TO ORDER RESTRUCTURING OF ELECTORAL SYSTEMS

On **JULY 2**, the Supreme Court ruled in favor of allowing federal judges to order massive restructuring of racially discriminatory electoral systems. The decision upheld a lower court ruling that had forced Burke County, Georgia, to end its at-large voting system, under which Blacks, who made up more than half of the county's population and about 38 percent of its registered voters, had never elected one Black as a county commissioner. The at-large system was to be replaced by a district system more likely to elect a minority candidate in districts where minorities predominated.

SUPREME COURT SAYS NAACP NOT RESPONSIBLE FOR BOYCOTT DAMAGES

On **JULY 3**, the Supreme Court unanimously overturned a 1979 Mississippi court decision that had ordered the NAACP to pay damages to white merchants whom they had boycotted in 1966 as part of their protest against segregated schools, hospitals, and other public facilities. In *NAACP* v. *Claiborne Hardware Co.*, Justice John P. Stevens III stated, "The political boycott enjoyed the full protection of the Constitution."

POVERTY AT HIGHEST LEVEL SINCE 1967

On **JULY 19**, the Bureau of the Census released discouraging news about poverty in the United States. The report indicated that more Americans were poor than at any time since 1967. About 14 percent of Americans lived in poverty, up from 11.1 percent in 1973. In the past year alone, as many as 2.2 million additional Americans fell into poverty. The official poverty level was set at $9,287 annual income for a nonfarming family of four.

Twelve months of recession combined with cuts in social programs by the Reagan administration contributed to the increase in poverty. Blacks suffered the most dramatic reductions in income. The proportion of Blacks living in poverty rose to 34.2 percent; among whites, the proportion was 11.1 percent; among Hispanics, 26.4 percent. Median annual family income dropped by 3.5 percent to $22,390.

AVOWED RACIST ACQUITTED IN SHOOTING OF JORDAN

On **AUGUST 18**, after eight hours of deliberation, a federal grand jury found Joseph Paul Franklin not guilty of shooting former National Urban League president Vernon Jordan in 1980. Franklin was already serving four life sentences for slaying two Black joggers in Salt Lake City, Utah.

Harvard Law Review EMPLOYS FIRST BLACK WOMAN EDITOR

On **OCTOBER 10**, the prestigious *Harvard Law Review* elected two Blacks and four Asians as editors. Annette Gordon was the first Black woman to be selected as an editor in the ninety-six-year history of the journal.

BLACKS' TEST SCORES IMPROVE

On **OCTOBER 14**, a College Board report indicated that over the last year, Blacks had gained nine points on the verbal portion of the Scholastic Aptitude Test and four points on the math portion. Since 1976, scores had increased an average of twenty-one points for Blacks and decreased an average of seventeen points for whites. Nevertheless, as a group Blacks still scored more than one hundred points below whites on each section of the test.

SETTLEMENT REACHED CONCERNING RAID OF BLACK PANTHERS HEADQUARTERS

On **OCTOBER 25**, a settlement of $1.85 million was reached between the federal government and the survivors and relatives of Black Panther Party members Fred Hampton and Mark Clark, who were shot to death in a police raid of their Chicago apartment in 1970. The settlement, pending approval by the governments of the city of Chicago and Cook County, would be paid by these jurisdictions and the federal government in equal shares. The original suit, filed twelve years earlier, charged that Cook County attorney Edward Hanrahan and his staff, the police, and

the FBI had conspired to violate the civil rights of those in the apartment. Grand juries investigating the case found evidence of whitewashing to make it appear that the Panthers were responsible for the shootings and violence.

HALL ELECTED TO CONGRESS

In **NOVEMBER**, Katie Beatrice Hall (1938–) became Indiana's first Black U.S. representative when she defeated her Republican opponent and assumed the seat vacated by the death of Representative Adam Benjamin, Jr.

◆ Hall was born in Mound Bayou, Mississippi, and received a B.S. degree from Mississippi Valley State University. She then moved to Indiana, where she taught in the Gary public schools until 1975. She worked in the mayoral campaigns of Richard B. Hatcher in 1967, 1971, and 1975. She also was elected to the Indiana House of Representatives and the Indiana Senate, as well as becoming chair of the Lake County Democratic Committee.

Although she served in only two Congresses, Hall was active in a number of areas. She spoke in favor of the passage of legislation to protect the U.S. steel industry from imports and encouraged the export of American-produced steel. This issue was especially important to her because she represented a district that had experienced severe unemployment due to plant closings.

Hall introduced a bill in the House in July 1983 to make the birthday of Martin Luther King, Jr., a public holiday. That bill passed the House in August. The Senate bill was passed in October, and President Reagan signed it into law in November.

Hall lost the Democratic primary in 1984.

TOWNS ELECTED TO CONGRESS

When Representative Frederick W. Richmond of New York's Eleventh Congressional District resigned his seat in August 1982, Edolphus "Ed" Towns (1941–), a former borough president of Brooklyn, entered the race to succeed him. In **NOVEMBER**, he was elected to the U.S. House of Representatives.

◆ Towns, born in Chadbourn, North Carolina, received a B.S. degree from North Carolina A & T University. After serving in the U.S. military, Towns taught in New York City's public schools and at Fordham University and the Medgar Evers College of the City University of New York. For ten years, 1965 to 1975, he worked in hospital administration, first at Metropolitan Hospital and then at Beth Israel Hospital. Towns actively worked with educational and health programs for youth and senior citizens. Between 1972 and 1982, he was the Democratic committeeperson for the Fortieth Assembly District.

Towns has served on the Committee of Government Operations, the Committee on Public Works and Transportation, and the Select Committee on Narcotics Abuse and Control. He has worked to pass legislation that affected bilingual education, 1890 land grant institutions, and animal rights. In 1992, he served as chairperson of the Congressional Black Caucus. He also served as the caucus treasurer and vice chairperson. Towns was reelected to his sixth term in office in 1992, capturing 96 percent of the votes in his district.

WHEAT ELECTED TO CONGRESS

In **NOVEMBER**, Alan Wheat (1951–) became the representative of Missouri's Fifth Congressional District after serving three terms in the Missouri General Assembly, during which he chaired the Urban Affairs Committee.

Prior to his election to the assembly, Wheat had received a B.A. degree in economics from Grinnell College and worked as an economist for the Department of Housing and Urban Development. He had served as an aide to the Jackson County, Missouri, chief executive from 1975 to 1976. Wheat was elected to Congress at the age of thirty-one.

Wheat became the third freshman representative in history to serve on the prestigious House Committee on Rules. He also served on the District of Columbia Committee and the Select Committee on Children, Youth, and Families. He has served as vice chairperson of the Congressional Black Caucus. In 1992, Wheat was reelected to his fifth term, winning 62 percent of the votes cast in his district.

BRADLEY LOSES BID TO BECOME NATION'S FIRST BLACK GOVERNOR

On **NOVEMBER 6**, by seven-tenths of a percentage point, Thomas Bradley lost the California gubernatorial race to Republican attorney general George Deukmejian. Three weeks before the election, polls had showed Bradley with a fourteen-point lead. Willie Brown, California's Speaker of the House, claimed that race was the deciding factor in the election. Other political analysts attributed Deukmejian's victory to an exceptionally large turnout of conservative voters to defeat a gun control measure. In Orange County and towns in the Central Valley with large proportions of Republi-

can voters, the gun control measure was soundly defeated, also bringing down Bradley in its wake.

CONGRESS APPROVES KING MEMORIAL IN CAPITOL

On **NOVEMBER 22**, the U.S. House and Senate approved a resolution to erect a statue of Martin Luther King, Jr., in the Capitol. It would be the first statue in the building recognizing the contributions of a Black American.

CIVIL RIGHTS COMMISSION STATES THAT "JOB DISCRIMINATION IS ALARMING"

On **NOVEMBER 24**, the chairperson of the U.S. Civil Rights Commission released a report stating that despite civil rights legislation, job discrimination against women and Black and Hispanic men continued at an alarming level. The report found job bias "virtually everywhere, at every age level, at every educational level, at every skill level."

BLACK ENROLLMENT IN COLLEGES DECREASES

On **NOVEMBER 28**, a significant drop in Black enrollment was noted in colleges and universities around the country. Among the forty-two historically Black colleges under the United Negro College Fund, freshman enrollment had dropped by 12 percent, with overall enrollment down by about 4 percent. Reasons for the decline included poor economic times, an exceptionally high dropout rate for minority students, and the perception among Black students and their families that a college education could no longer be a reality.

KING ASSASSINATION SITE PURCHASED

On **DECEMBER 14**, the Lorraine Motel in Memphis, Tennessee, the site of the assassination of Martin Luther King, Jr., in 1968, was purchased by the Martin Luther King Memphis Memorial Foundation. The foundation intended to use the property for an international civil rights museum and shrine to King.

RACE RIOTING TAKES PLACE IN OVERTOWN SECTION OF MIAMI

On **DECEMBER 29**, a twenty-year-old Black man was shot by a police officer in a games arcade as the officer attempted to apprehend him. An angry crowd encircled the officer, who had to be rescued by a special weapons team. A short time later, more than one hundred young people rioted in Overtown, a predominantly Black section of Miami, Florida, just north of the city's downtown area. During the riot, rocks and bottles were thrown, two firebombs were thrown into stores, and a car was set on fire.

1983 BLACK MAYORS ELECTED IN SEVERAL BIG CITIES

Blacks became mayors for the first time in several major cities. Former Representative Harold Washington won the mayoral election in Chicago. W. Wilson Goode was elected in Philadelphia, defeating former mayor Frank Rizzo in the Democratic primary. Harvey Gantt won in Charlotte, North Carolina; James A. Sharp, Jr., was elected in Flint, Michigan.

Twenty Blacks became mayors of cities with populations exceeding one hundred thousand. In Los Angeles, Detroit, New Orleans, Atlanta, Hartford, Birmingham, and Washington, D.C., Blacks were re-elected as mayors.

CIVIL RIGHTS COMMISSION COMES UNDER ASSAULT

The White House announced that three members of the U.S. Civil Rights Commission who opposed the administration's policies on racial quotas and busing would be replaced by Democrats who agreed with President Ronald Reagan's policies. Commissioners Mary Frances Berry, Blandina Cardenas Ramirez, and

Mary Berry is shown here fighting to retain her position as a commissioner on the U.S. Civil Rights Commission.

Rabbi Murray Salzman had vocally disagreed with the administration's opposition to racial quotas and busing for school integration.

On **OCTOBER 25**, President Reagan fired Commissioner Berry, a professor of history and law at Howard University, along with two other members of the Civil Rights Commission. Berry, however, chose to fight Reagan's decision in the news media, charging that the president wanted to "shut up" any views different from his own. After she sued, she was reinstated. The "flap" caused many members of the U.S. Congress to question the composition of the Civil Rights Commission as well as the method of appointing commissioners. (Members of the Civil Rights Commission, a bipartisan, independent, advisory body established under President Eisenhower, were subject to Senate approval and served at the pleasure of the president.)

No other president had attempted to drastically change the commission's membership. Critics of the Reagan administration charged that the President was trying to eliminate all opposition to his "racially charged" policies.

The congressional protests that erupted after the dismissal of the three commissioners resulted in a change to the makeup of the commission. In November 1983, Congress passed legislation that made the commission a creature of both Congress and the executive office. Four members would be appointed by the president and four by the Congress.

In January 1984, the newly constituted U.S. Commission on Civil Rights renounced the use of racial quotas for the promotion of Blacks and other minorities. It left the issue of busing to achieve desegregation for future consideration.

ECONOMIC STATUS OF BLACKS IMPROVES

Studies of the economic status of the Black population revealed that the number of Black doctors had tripled since 1960; the number of Black lawyers was six times greater than the 1960 total.

GOSSETT WINS ACADEMY AWARD

Lou Gossett, Jr., won the Oscar for best supporting actor for his role as a drill sergeant in *An Officer and a Gentleman*. Gossett was the first African American to win the supporting actor award and the third African American to win an Oscar for acting. Gossett won an Emmy for his role as Fiddler in *Roots*, and had two television series of his own: *The Lazarus Syndrome* in 1979 and *Gideon Oliver* in 1989.

HAYES ELECTED TO CONGRESS

In a special primary, Charles A. Hayes (1918–) defeated fourteen opponents to win the congressional seat left vacant when Walter Washington was elected mayor of Chicago. Hayes won the election and took his seat in September. He represented the First Congressional District, which included much of south central Chicago.

◈ Born in Cairo, Illinois, Hayes worked for more than forty years as a trade unionist. During his terms in Congress, Hayes introduced legislation to improve education and employment opportunities for American workers. He worked to provide disadvantaged youth with job training and to encourage dropouts to complete their education. He opposed actions of the South African white government and demonstrated at the South African Embassy in Washington, D.C., to protest against that government's apartheid policies. In 1992, Hayes was defeated in the Democratic primary by former Black Panther Bobby Rush. Hayes's loss was at least partly related to the disclosure in the House bank scandal that he had written 716 overdrafts.

LUNG CANCER RATES DIFFERENT FOR BLACKS AND WHITES

From 1977 to 1983, the age-adjusted lung cancer incidence rate was about 40 percent higher for Black men than for white men, 111 compared with 80 per 100,000. In contrast, Black women had a lung cancer incidence rate that was 10 percent lower than white females, 28 compared with 31 per 100,000.

MARCH ON WASHINGTON COMMEMORATED

More than 250,000 people marched in Washington, D.C., to commemorate the 1963 March on Washington led by Martin Luther King, Jr. This second march focused on the theme of "Jobs, Peace, and Freedom" but lacked the single purpose of the 1963 march, during which King gave his famous "I Have a Dream" speech. Some suggested that the theme that emerged most clearly was opposition to the Reagan administration.

PROSTATE CANCER HIGHER AMONG BLACKS

From 1977 to 1983, the age-adjusted incidence rate for prostate cancer was considerably higher for Black men (119 per 100,000) than for any other group, and 71 percent higher than that of white men. The Black survival rate was 10 percent lower than that of white men during the period 1975–1984.

RACIAL QUOTAS ANGER REAGAN

One of the many tools employed to redress racial discrimination was racial hiring quotas. But the Reagan administration let it be known that the president strongly opposed them and, in fact, favored their complete and immediate abolition. Quotas for Blacks were established by the Equal Employment Opportunity Commission created by the Civil Rights Act of 1964. Quotas had erased some of the discrepancies between races resulting from years of racial discrimination, but equality of opportunity had not yet been achieved.

SEGREGATION IN HOUSING PREVALENT IN CERTAIN CITIES

The Citizens Committee on Civil Rights, based in Washington, D.C., released a study on the segregated nature of cities with at least one hundred thousand Blacks.

Using 1980 census data, the survey examined integration block by block. It found Chicago to be the most segregated (receiving ninety-two out of one hundred points, which indicated total segregation). Cleveland came in second, with ninety-one. Oakland, California, had the lowest segregation index score of fifty-nine.

KU KLUX KLAN AND NAZI PARTY MEMBERS FOUND NOT GUILTY

On **APRIL 13**, an all-white jury found six Ku Klux Klan members and three American Nazi Party members not guilty of the murders of five persons in Greensboro, North Carolina, in 1979.

WASHINGTON ELECTED MAYOR OF CHICAGO

On **APRIL 13**, Harold Washington (1922–1987) was elected the first Black mayor of Chicago. A record 82 percent of the 1.6 million registered voters in the city turned out to vote after a racially charged campaign. Washington won 51 percent of the vote; his white opponent, Bernard E. Epton, won 48 percent. Although most whites voted along racial lines, a critical number voted with Blacks to elect Washington. His immediate task as mayor was to unify a racially divided city.

Washington resigned his seat in the U.S. House of Representatives to run for mayor. He served in the U.S. Congress from 1981 to 1983. Prior to this, Washington had served in the Illinois House of Representatives (1965–1976) and in the Illinois Senate (1976–1980).

NAYLOR WINS AMERICAN BOOK AWARD

On **APRIL 28**, Gloria Naylor won the American Book Award for fiction for her first novel, *The Women of Brewster Place*. The novel focuses on the lives of seven female characters and explores the complexity of the Black woman's experience in America. The book was quickly contracted for a television movie, starring Oprah Winfrey, Jackee, and Paula Kelly.

◈ Gloria Naylor was born in New York City in 1950. After receiving an M.A. in Afro-American studies from Yale University in 1983, she taught writing and literature at a number of universities. In addition to *The Women of Brewster Place* (1982), her novels include *Linden Hills* (1985), *Mama Day* (1988), and *Bailey's Cafe* (1993).

COURT RULES ON TAX-EXEMPT STATUS

On **MAY 24**, in a vote of 8–1, the U.S. Supreme Court ruled in *Bob Jones University* v. *United States* that the federal government could not grant tax exemptions to private schools that practiced racial discrimination. The dissenting vote was cast by Judge William Rehnquist.

This ruling upheld the Internal Revenue Service (IRS) policy adopted in 1971. Bob Jones University had lost its tax-exempt status in 1975 when it prohibited interracial dating. Goldsboro Christian School refused to admit Blacks and lost its tax-exempt status from 1969 to 1972. Both schools sued the IRS but lost in the federal district and appellate courts. The Reagan administration had tried to abandon the IRS policy in 1982.

MARSH OUSTED AS MAYOR

On **JULY 1**, Henry A. Marsh III was ousted as mayor of Richmond and was replaced by Roy A. West, another Black. Marsh became one of the nine city council members.

CIVIL RIGHTS AGENCIES ACCUSE REAGAN ADMINISTRATION OF LACK OF ENFORCEMENT

On **AUGUST 13**, as many as thirty-three state agencies responsible for overseeing civil rights signed a letter charging that President Reagan was responsible for a "dangerous deterioration in Federal enforcement of civil rights." They highlighted lack of commitment and support on the part of the administration, as well as lack of support for nominations and appointments to the Civil Rights Commission, Equal Employment Opportunity Commission, and the civil rights division of the Department of Justice.

BLUFORD PARTICIPATES IN SPACE SHUTTLE MISSION

On **AUGUST 30**, Lieutenant Colonel Guion S. Bluford became the first Black American in space. He would later be the mission specialist aboard the space shuttle *Challenger*.

WILLIAMS IS FIRST BLACK MISS AMERICA

In **SEPTEMBER**, Vanessa Williams of New York became the first Black Miss America. She was forced to relinquish her crown in July 1984 when a scandal spread about nude photos taken of her prior to the pageant, which were subsequently published in *Penthouse* magazine. Williams used her singing talent to secure a recording career, and her album *The Right Stuff* became a success. She also starred on Broadway in *Kiss of the Spider Woman*.

Suzette Charles, first runner-up, succeeded Williams as Miss America until the next pageant. Charles, representing New Jersey, was also African American.

SHAW NAMED FLORIDA SUPREME COURT JUSTICE

On **SEPTEMBER 6**, Leander Jay Shaw, Jr., was appointed a justice of the state supreme court in Florida, the first African American to hold this position. In 1990, Shaw was appointed chief justice and became the first African American chief justice of the Florida supreme court.

FEDERAL HOLIDAY FOR KING'S BIRTHDAY SIGNED INTO LAW

On **OCTOBER 20**, President Ronald Reagan signed into law the bill making the third Monday in January a holiday commemorating the life of Martin Luther King, Jr.

The House of Representatives had approved the legislation earlier in the year. The Senate had voted 78–22 to approve the federal holiday after acrimonious debate. The debate in the Senate was largely between Jesse Helms and Edward Kennedy. Helms charged that the holiday would have severe economic consequences and that it was inappropriate to honor King because he had been a Marxist-Leninist. Kennedy charged Helms with conducting a "smear campaign."

JACKSON SEEKS THE PRESIDENCY

On **NOVEMBER 3**, Jesse Jackson, one of the most active and visible civil rights leaders, announced that he would seek the Democratic nomination for president of the United States. The forty-two-year-old Jackson, a Baptist minister, had devoted much of his life to the social, economic, and political development of the Black community. Jackson also had been involved in several international issues and problems.

Jackson, a close friend of Martin Luther King, Jr., was a central figure in many civil rights organizations, notably the Congress of Racial Equality (CORE), the Southern Christian Leadership Conference (SCLC), Operation Breadbasket, and People United to Save Humanity (PUSH). Jackson was most often identified with the cause of voter registration among Blacks.

GANTT ELECTED MAYOR OF CHARLOTTE

On **NOVEMBER 8**, Harvey Gantt was elected mayor of Charlotte, North Carolina, becoming the first African American mayor of this major southern city. Gantt gained a reputation as an astute politician and later sought to oust conservative and racist incumbent Jesse Helms from his U.S. Senate seat.

GOODE ELECTED MAYOR OF PHILADELPHIA

On **NOVEMBER 8**, W. Wilson Goode was elected mayor of Philadelphia, becoming the first Black mayor of this large eastern city. In fact, Philadelphia was the largest city ever led by an African American mayor.

SHARP ELECTED MAYOR OF FLINT

On **NOVEMBER 8**, James A. Sharp, Jr., was elected mayor of Flint, Michigan, becoming the first African American mayor of this northeastern manufacturing city.

1984 BUTLER WINS HUGO AWARD

Octavia Butler, a science fiction writer, was awarded the Hugo Award for excellence in science fiction writing. She was the first African American woman to receive this honor. Butler was born on June 22, 1947, in Pasadena, California.

DICKERSON BREAKS RUSH RECORD

Eric Dickerson of the Los Angeles Rams rushed for 215 yards for a total of 2,007 yards, the most yards rushed during a single season. He thus broke O. J. Simpson's record for yards in one season.

GAYE KILLED BY FATHER

Marvin Gaye, songwriter and musician of the Motown label, was killed by his father, the Reverend Marvin Gaye, Sr. Gaye was known for such hits as "Heard It Through the Grapevine," "Sexual Healing," "Mercy, Mercy, Me (The Ecology)," "What's Going On," and "Let's Get it On."

JACKSON MAKES STRONG SHOWING IN PRESIDENTIAL PRIMARIES

The Reverend Jesse Jackson received strong support among Blacks in his first bid for the presidential nomination. He won the primary in the District of Columbia and Louisiana. He came in third in the New York primary, after Walter Mondale and Gary Hart.

JORDAN NAMED BASKETBALL ROOKIE OF THE YEAR

Michael Jordan (1963–) was awarded the National Basketball Association (NBA) Rookie of the Year award. Jordan, six feet six inches tall, helped North Carolina win the National Collegiate Athletic Association championship in 1982. He also was instrumental in helping the U.S. Olympic basketball team win the gold medal in 1984. After two years in the professional ranks, Jordan won the NBA Most Valuable Player award in 1987; he won it again in 1990. From 1987 to 1990, Jordan averaged 34.6 points per game — the highest average in the league. Jordan helped to carry the Chicago Bulls to the national championship in 1991, 1992, and 1993. Jordan retired from professional basketball in 1993.

JURORS CANNOT BE EXCLUDED BECAUSE OF RACE

In New York City, a federal appeals panel ruled, in the first decision of its kind, that prosecutors could not exclude prospective jurors solely because of race.

In this case, a Black defendant had been convicted of robbery by an all-white jury. The prosecutor had rejected one Hispanic and several Black prospective jurors to finally get an all-white jury.

MARSALIS WINS GRAMMYS

Wynton Marsalis became the first musician to win Grammys for jazz and classical music recordings simultaneously. Marsalis is considered one of the most gifted and outstanding jazz trumpet players in the world.

Marsalis was born in New Orleans on October 18, 1961, to a famous musical family — both his father and his brothers were famous jazz musicians. His career soared after joining Art Blakely's Jazz Messengers.

NIX NAMED PENNSYLVANIA'S CHIEF JUSTICE

Robert N. C. Nix, Jr., became chief justice of the Pennsylvania Supreme Court. He became the first African American to lead a state supreme court.

MOVIE *Purple Rain* OPENS

Purple Rain was released and became the most celebrated rock movie ever made. It was one of the biggest box office successes of 1984 and earned its producer, Prince — one of the nation's most unusual rock stars — an Oscar for best original song score and soundtrack album. Prince's songs had topped the charts for several years.

NUMERICAL QUOTAS NO LONGER SUPPORTED BY COMMISSION ON CIVIL RIGHTS

The U.S. Commission ended its support of numerical quotas as a means of securing greater employment opportunities for Blacks and correcting the discriminatory practices of the past. This reversal disturbed many Black leaders, who denounced the decision and the overall civil rights policy of the Reagan administration.

SUPREME COURT RULES SENIORITY SUPERSEDES AFFIRMATIVE ACTION CONCERNS

In *Firefighters* v. *Stotts,* the U.S. Supreme Court ruled that courts could not upset valid seniority systems in an effort to protect the jobs of minority workers hired under affirmative action.

The case arose when white firefighters in Memphis with many more years' seniority than recently hired Blacks were laid off when the city reduced its public employee payroll.

They brought suit, and their victory in this case marked the most significant victory to date for the Reagan administration's reversal in civil rights policy. The majority opinion stated in part that Title VII of the 1964 Civil Rights Act "protected ... bona fide seniority systems, and it is inappropriate to deny an innocent employee the benefits of his seniority in order to provide a remedy in a pattern suit such as this. ... Even when an [minority] individual shows that the discriminatory practice has had an impact on him, he is not automatically entitled to have nonminority employees laid off to make room for him."

Proponents of affirmative action in hiring viewed this upholding of the "last hired, first fired" doctrine as a major setback for minorities and women.

WONDER WINS GRAMMY

Stevie Wonder (Steeland Judkins Morris) won a Grammy for best song, "I Just Called to Say I Love You."

Wonder was born in Saginaw, Michigan, and became a singing sensation as Little Stevie Wonder at the age of twelve. Wonder released a string of hits, and his albums racked up major sales. More recently, Wonder has contributed to a number of movie soundtracks, including music for the film *Jungle Fever.*

SUPREME COURT DECLINES TO REVIEW *Bratton et al.* v. *Detroit*

In **JANUARY**, the U.S. Supreme Court refused to review *Bratton et al.* v. *Detroit,* thereby upholding the legality of voluntary, race-based quotas in the Detroit police department. This Supreme Court action rebuffed the Reagan administration, which had asked it to find that race-based affirmative action plans were unconstitutional if they included quotas. The administration believed that such plans violated the Fourteenth Amendment's guarantee of "equal protection of the law" for all citizens.

The city of Detroit had agreed to hire and promote an equal number of Blacks and whites after a federal court had found discrimination against Blacks in the city's police department. A Detroit police union had sued to have the plan overturned.

JACKSON HELPS NEGOTIATE RELEASE OF U.S. PILOT IN LEBANON

On **JANUARY 3**, U.S. Navy pilot Robert Goodman, shot down in central Lebanon the previous month, was released from Lebanon. Jesse Jackson had met with Lebanese officials and with Syrian president Hafez al-Assad to ensure Goodman's release.

SUPREME COURT REINTERPRETS NONDISCRIMINATION REQUIREMENTS

On **FEBRUARY 28**, in a 6–3 decision, the U.S. Supreme Court limited the enforcement of civil rights laws in *Grove City College* v. *Bell.* The Court ruled that only the program or activity receiving federal funds was subject to the anti-bias laws, but not the entire institution. Thus, Grove City and other colleges that received financial aid as their only federal assistance could discriminate in programs other than financial aid. The decision affected four categories of persons who had received greater freedom through the Civil Rights Act of 1964: the physically disabled, women, the aged, and minorities. This decision of the Supreme Court was overturned by Congress in 1988 in the Civil Rights Restoration Act.

GEORGETOWN HOYAS WIN NCAA CHAMPIONSHIP

On **APRIL 3**, the Georgetown Hoyas, led by Patrick Ewing, won the NCAA championship. John Thompson, the coach, had worked hard to get these collegiate basketball players to perform at their highest level. This was the first championship won by an African American coach.

The Cosby Show AIRS ON TELEVISION

On **SEPTEMBER 20**, *The Cosby Show*, starring Bill Cosby and Phylicia Ayers Allen (now Rashad), premiered on NBC-TV.

The series was accepted cautiously by NBC after it had been rejected by other network executives. *The Cosby Show* was to become the most popular television series in history, securing a number of awards annually. Included among its talented cast were Malcolm Jamal Warner and Keisha Knight Pullam. *The Cosby Show* continued to feature new and familiar African American talent throughout its successful history. The show ran through the 1992 season.

CIVIL RIGHTS ACT OF 1984 TABLED IN THE SENATE

On **OCTOBER 3**, the U.S. Senate, in a roll call vote of 53–54, failed to reach a compromise on the Civil Rights Act of 1984 and tabled the measure. Proponents of the bill had sought to attach it to an omnibus spending bill for the 1985 federal budget. This was a defeat for civil rights advocates who expected to use the legislation to overturn the Supreme Court decision in *Grove City College* v. *Bell* that had limited the enforcement of discrimination laws. The act had been passed in the House of Representatives.

GOETZ SHOOTS FOUR BLACK YOUTHS

On **DECEMBER 22**, Bernhard Goetz shot four Black youths on the New York City subway. Goetz stated that they were "trying to rip me off." The youths denied his claim, and a police captain said that Goetz "knew what he was doing." Two of the youths were in critical condition. Police did not apprehend Goetz, but he surrendered to police in New Hampshire a few days after the subway attack. On January 25, Goetz,

who confessed to shooting the four youths, was indicted on gun possession charges only.

On June 17, 1987, a jury acquitted Goetz of attempted murder but convicted him of illegal weapons possession. Civil rights activists were enraged with the biased outcome.

1985 CADORIA NAMED BRIGADIER GENERAL

In this year, Sherian Grace Cadoria (1940–) was promoted to brigadier general. She became the highest-ranking African American woman soldier in the U.S. armed forces.

SENATE COMMITTEE REJECTS REAGAN'S NOMINEE

Assistant attorney general William Bradford Reynolds was rejected by the Senate Judiciary Committee for promotion to associate attorney general of the Justice Department.

Civil rights leader had long criticized Reynolds for lax enforcement of civil rights laws.

FOOTBALL COACH ROBINSON BREAKS RECORD NUMBER OF WINS

Eddie G. Robinson (1919–), football coach of Grambling University, became the most successful college football coach in history. He led Grambling State to his 324th win, one more than the record of 323 wins held by Paul (Bear) Bryant. Under Robinson's leadership, Grambling State had won fourteen Southwestern Athletic Conference Championships, and as many as two hundred of his former players had joined professional football ranks.

JONES NAMED PRESIDENT OF NATIONAL MEDICAL ASSOCIATION

Dr. Edith Irby Jones, the first Black graduate of the University of Arkansas College of Medicine, became the first woman president of the National Medical Association (NMA), the Black physicians' association organized in 1895.

NUMBER OF BLACK MAYORS DOUBLES

Since 1975, the number of Black mayors had doubled to total 286. Thirty-one of these Black mayors were elected in 1984, the greatest number in any single year.

WINFREY NOMINATED FOR OSCAR

Oprah Winfrey (1954–), the nation's most-watched television talk show host, was nominated for an Academy Award for best supporting actress for her role in *The Color Purple*.

Winfrey has incorporated Harpo Studios, her own film and television production company in Chicago. Born in Kosciusko, Mississippi, she became the first African American to have her own syndicated talk show.

BLACK RADICAL GROUP BOMBED IN PHILADELPHIA
On **MAY 13**, a bomb was dropped from a state police helicopter on a house in Philadelphia occupied by a Black radical group called MOVE. The resulting fire took the lives of eleven group members and destroyed two city blocks, leaving three hundred people homeless. A ten-million-dollar lawsuit was later filed by members of the community against the city for loss of property.

WILSON NAMED BOSTON SCHOOLS SUPERINTENDENT
On **AUGUST 1**, Dr. Laval Wilson was selected as the first Black superintendent of schools for Boston. About 48 percent of the students in the school system were Black.

1986 BLACK UNITED FRONT ORGANIZED TO PROMOTE AFROCENTRIC EDUCATION
In Portland, Oregon, a group was organized to steer public schools to an Afrocentric curriculum instead of a Eurocentric one. The next year, the public schools of Portland began using an Afrocentric curriculum designed by Asa Hilliard and other African American scholars.

COLLEGE ATTENDANCE OF BLACKS DECLINES
The percentage of Black high school graduates attending college dropped to 36.5 percent, a level 20 percentage points lower than the rate for white high school graduates.

The percentage of Black high school graduates who attended college reached a peak of 48 percent in 1977 — a level that closed the gap between Blacks and whites considerably.

FBI ACCUSED OF TARGETING BLACK OFFICIALS
An eighteen-month bribery probe of Chicago's mayor, Harold Washington, and his political friends, drew fire from the mayor, who stated that the investigation was racially motivated. Washington, seeking to ensure that his high rating with voters in the city was not diminished, requested that former U.S. attorney Thomas Sullivan lead an internal investigation of the scandal allegations. "We are really disturbed over the distinct possibility that there has been a systematic attempt here to set people up," he said.

It all started when Clarence McClain, a business executive and former aide to Mayor Washington, was accused of accepting twenty thousand dollars from an FBI operative and introducing the operative to city officials and aldermen, as a result of which Systematic Recovery Service (an FBI sting operation) won a contract to collect overdue water bills in Chicago.

Jenkins V. *Missouri* UPHOLDS DECISION AGAINST DISCRIMINATORY HOUSING PATTERNS
In *Jenkins* v. *Missouri*, the federal court of appeals upheld the decision of a lower court that discriminatory housing patterns caused segregated schools in Kansas City, Missouri. Evidence in the case revealed that racial "steering" by real-estate brokers, racially restrictive housing covenants, discrimination of lending agencies, and the discriminatory placing of public housing created the housing patterns. The court ordered the state of Missouri to invest three hundred million dollars to enhance educational opportunities for Blacks.

MOB ATTACKS BLACKS IN HOWARD BEACH SECTION OF QUEENS, NEW YORK
Three Black men were brutally beaten by a mob of young white men in predominantly white Howard Beach, a neighborhood of Queens, New York. One of the Blacks, Michael Griffith, died of wounds he sustained when hit by an automobile while being chased by his attackers.

TYSON WINS BOXING TITLE
Mike Tyson (1966–) won the World Boxing Council's heavyweight championship and became the youngest boxer to hold the title. In 1987, he won the World Boxing Association and International Boxing Federation championships. In 1990, he was defeated in a knockout by James "Buster" Douglas for the heavyweight title.

WILDER BECOMES LIEUTENANT GOVERNOR
On **JANUARY 11**, Douglas Wilder became the first Black lieutenant governor of Virginia, having previously served in the Virginia Senate.

BIRTHDAY OF KING OBSERVED
On **JANUARY 20**, the birthday of Dr. Martin Luther King, Jr., was observed as a federal holiday for the first time.

MCNAIR KILLED IN *Challenger* EXPLOSION

On **JANUARY 28**, Black astronaut Ronald E. McNair, a scientist, was among the seven killed when the space shuttle *Challenger* exploded approximately 73 seconds after liftoff from Cape Canaveral, Florida. The explosion was caused by a malfunction of the booster rockets due to the cold weather.

McNair was a graduate of North Carolina A & T University and had earned a Ph.D. in physics from Massachusetts Institute of Technology.

INFANT MORTALITY RATES LINKED TO HEALTH CARE CUTS

In **FEBRUARY**, the Children's Defense Fund released a report showing a rising infant mortality rate — up by 3 percent from 1982 to 1983 — for the first time in eight years; this represented the largest increase in eighteen years. Washington, D.C., recorded the highest infant mortality rate, 19.3 deaths per 1,000 live births in 1983. It was followed by Mississippi, South Carolina, Louisiana, and Georgia; the concentration of deaths within these states was clearly in areas populated by poor Blacks and whites. Respiratory problems and congenital defects caused most of the 14,120 recorded infant deaths. Cutbacks in funding for prenatal and maternal health care, amounting to millions of dollars, contributed to infant mortality.

In fact, between 1983 and 1984, federal block grants to states for maternal and child health had dropped from $478 million to $399 million. According to data from the Robert Wood Johnson Foundation, 63 percent of all poor and near poor families received Medicare in 1975; the foundation estimated that only 43 percent would receive it in 1985.

SUPREME COURT SUPPORTS AFFIRMATIVE ACTION PLANS TO REMEDY PAST DISCRIMINATION

In **MARCH** and again in **JULY**, the Supreme Court ruled in two decisions that affirmative action plans could be used to remedy past discrimination. In its July 2 decision, the Court decided 6–3 that employment preferences on the basis of race, color, or gender could be used to help root out the effects of past discrimination. The Court's decisions were not well received by Reagan administration officials.

WALDON ENTERS CONGRESS

In **JULY**, Alton R. Waldon, Jr., was elected to Congress to fill the seat left vacant by the death of Representative Joseph Addabbo. In this special election, Waldon's victory over Floyd Flake was so close that it was decided by absentee ballots. Waldon took office on July 29, but served for only a few months after losing the Democratic primary in September to Flake, who then won the general election in November.

Despite his short time in Congress, Waldon took action on national and international issues. He sponsored a bill that called for the formation of a national task force on the problem of functional illiteracy. He supported legislation combating drug abuse, especially crack cocaine. On the international front, Waldon called for the House to override President Reagan's veto of legislative sanctions against South Africa. He opposed covert aid to rebels from Angola who supported the white government of South Africa. After leaving Congress, Waldon was appointed to the New York State Investigation Commission.

BLACK ELECTED OFFICIALS REMAIN SMALL MINORITY

On **JULY 26**, a report was released, noting that the number of Black elected officials had increased by 6.1 percent between 1984 and 1985. Nevertheless, Blacks held only 1.3 percent of the total number of elected positions.

PERKINS APPOINTED AMBASSADOR TO SOUTH AFRICA

On **OCTOBER 3** and **4**, President Ronald Reagan appointed Edward J. Perkins, a Black career diplomat, as ambassador to South Africa. The nomination was made in an effort to persuade the Senate to support Reagan's veto of a sanctions bill against South Africa. The veto was overridden by both the House and the Senate.

Brown v. *Board of Education of Topeka* CASE REOPENED

On **OCTOBER 7**, the original plaintiff in the *Brown* v. *Board of Education of Topeka* reopened the case, contending that the school district had not fully complied with the desegregation ruling of 1954.

ESPY ELECTED TO CONGRESS

In **NOVEMBER**, Mike Espy became the first Black congressman from Mississippi in more than a century. (John R. Lynch had served in 1875.) Espy represented the state's only Black majority district. It was predominantly rural and had one of the highest poverty rates in the nation. A Black candidate had been defeated in two previous attempts to win the congressional seat. Espy defeated the incumbent by a narrow margin in this year, even though the district was 60 percent Black. But two years later, he won reelection easily, collecting 46 percent of the white vote.

◆ Espy was born in Yazoo City in the Mississippi Delta, and his family had strong ties to the region. Educated at Howard University and the Santa Clara School of Law, Espy served as assistant secretary of state for the Mississippi Legal Service after graduating from law school. He held two other state offices, including that of assistant state attorney general of the Consumer Protection Division, prior to his election to Congress. He served on several committees important to his constituents, including the Committee on Agriculture and the Select Committee on Hunger. In 1993, President-elect Bill Clinton selected Espy to be secretary of agriculture.

FLAKE ELECTED TO CONGRESS

In **NOVEMBER**, after more than ten years in community service as pastor of Allen African Methodist Episcopal Church in Jamaica, New York, Floyd Flake was elected to the one-hundredth Congress. Flake won his first political office by defeating the incumbent, Alton R. Waldon, Jr., in the Democratic primary in September and his Republican opponent in the general election.

◆ Born in 1945 in Los Angeles, Flake graduated from Wilberforce University and Payne Theological Seminary. Flake first ran for political office in July 1986, when he lost to Waldon in the Democratic primary to fill the congressional seat of Representative Joseph Addabbo, who had died in office. Flake has been reelected three times. In 1992, he captured almost 80 percent of the votes cast in the Sixth Congressional District of New York.

LEWIS ELECTED TO CONGRESS

In **NOVEMBER**, John R. Lewis of Georgia was elected to Congress after a long career as a civil rights organizer. He easily beat his Republican opponent.

◆ Lewis was a minister and one of the founders and chairperson of the Student Non-Violent Coordinating Committee (SNCC) in the 1960s. He had helped Dr. Martin Luther King, Jr., organize the march from Selma to Montgomery, Alabama, in 1965. He was also involved with the freedom rides that challenged segregated bus terminals, and with many voter registration drives. The voter education project that he directed registered over four million Blacks. In 1966, members of SNCC voted Lewis out of office, rejecting his emphasis on nonviolent actions. He was succeeded by Stokely Carmichael.

In 1977, Lewis ran for the House seat vacated when Andrew Young resigned to serve as ambassador to the United Nations. He lost to Wyche Fowler, who later served as U.S. senator from Georgia. Later that year, President Jimmy Carter appointed Lewis a director of ACTION, a federal volunteer agency. In 1981, he won a seat on the Atlanta City Council, where he served for five years.

Lewis currently serves on the Committee on Public Works and Transportation and the Committee on Interior and Insular Affairs.

MFUME ELECTED TO CONGRESS

In **NOVEMBER**, Kweisi Mfume won Maryland's Seventh Congressional District seat following Parren J. Mitchell's retirement the previous year.

◆ Born Frizzell Gray, Mfume adopted his African name in the 1970s. He overcame a troubled youth and economic hardship in inner-city Baltimore to

Kweisi Mfume was elected to the U.S. Congress in 1986. Six years later, he became the chairman of the powerful Congressional Black Caucus.

graduate from Morgan State University with a B.A. degree in urban planning in 1976. In 1984, he received an M.A. degree from Johns Hopkins University and became a member of the faculty at Morgan State, teaching political science and communications. He was elected to the Baltimore City Council in 1979 and served as Baltimore co-chair of Edward Kennedy's presidential campaign in 1980, and as Maryland co-chair of Jesse Jackson's campaigns in 1980 and in 1988.

He has served as vice chairperson of the Congressional Black Caucus and held positions on the Small Business Committee, the Select Committee on Hunger, and the Banking, Finance, and Urban Affairs Committee. In 1992, he was reelected for the third time, winning 84 percent of the votes cast in his district. He subsequently became chairperson of the Congressional Black Caucus.

1987 BATTLE WINS GRAMMY

Kathleen Battle, a gifted operatic soprano, won a Grammy award.

COLE NAMED PRESIDENT OF SPELMAN COLLEGE

Johnetta B. Cole, professor of anthropology and Afro-American Studies at Hunter College, New York, became the first Black woman president of Spelman College in Atlanta, Georgia.

GORDON NAMED WEST POINT CADET COMMANDANT

Brigadier General Fred A. Gordon was appointed commandant of cadets at the U.S. Military Academy at West Point, becoming the first Black to head this prestigious school. The academy's Black enrollment is currently about 8 percent.

JAMISON BEGINS ASTRONAUT TRAINING

Mae Carol Jamison (1956–) became the first Black woman astronaut in training. Jamison was born on October 17, 1956, in Decatur, Alabama. After growing up in Chicago, she became a medical doctor and served in the Peace Corps in Africa. When she returned from Africa, she took up practice in Los Angeles.

JOHNSON NAMED MOST VALUABLE PLAYER

Earvin "Magic" Johnson (1959–) won the National Basketball Association's Most Valuable Player award for his exceptional performance, particularly in as-

Johnetta Cole, the first African American woman to serve as the president of Spelman College, in Atlanta, Georgia, made the historically Black college one of the most prestigious institutions of higher education in the country, Black or white.

sists. Johnson, six feet nine inches tall, was probably the most talented passer in the game.

In 1979, Johnson led Michigan State University to the NCAA basketball championship. He was then signed by the Los Angeles Lakers, with whom he played until his retirement in 1991. During his play with the Lakers, he helped them win five championships (1980, 1982, 1985, 1987, and 1988). Johnson was named Most Valuable Player six times (three times during regular season — 1987–1988, 1988–1989, and 1989–1990 — and three times during playoffs — 1980, 1982, and 1987). He retired when he learned he had the virus that causes AIDS.

PERRY BECOMES MAYOR OF HARTFORD

Carrie Saxon Perry (1931–) was elected mayor of Hartford, Connecticut. She became the first African American woman to be elected mayor of a major U.S. city.

PULITZER PRIZE IN POETRY AWARDED TO BLACK AMERICAN

In this year, Rita Dove (1952–) won the Pulitzer Prize for her collection of poetry titled *Thomas & Beulah.*

◈ Dove was born in Akron, Ohio. She received a B.A. degree from Miami University in Oxford, Ohio, in 1973, and an M.A. degree in fine arts from the University of Iowa in 1977. She received Fulbright scholarships in 1974 and 1975 to study in Germany. In 1981, Dove taught at Arizona State, where she rose to full professorship by 1987. In 1989, she moved to the University of Virginia where she taught creative writing.

Dove's writing includes *Yellow House on the Corner* (1980), *Museum* (1983), *Fifth Sunday* (1985), and *Grace Notes* (1989). Dove has received a number of awards, including the General Electric Foundation Award for Younger Poets (1987), the Ohio Governor's Award (1988), and the Walt Whitman Award (1990). In 1993, Dove was named Poet Laureate of the United States.

RANDOLPH BECOMES HIGHEST-RANKING BLACK GENERAL

Bernard P. Randolph became the highest-ranking Black four-star general currently holding the position. He is stationed at Andrews Air Force Base, near Washington, D.C.

SUPREME COURT UPHOLDS AFFIRMATIVE ACTION

The Supreme Court ruled that women and minorities may be hired based on affirmative action policies, even if they were not the best-qualified applicants. In the case *Johnson v. Transportation Agency, Santa Clara County, California*, the Court stated that the employer need only demonstrate that there was a "conspicuous . . . imbalance in traditionally segregated job categories." Another case in thesame year, *United States v. Paradise*, upheld the use of quotas to remedy "egregious" past discrimination.

REAGAN ADMINISTRATION CONDEMNED AS "INSENSITIVE"

In **JANUARY**, the National Urban League identified the Reagan administration as "insensitive," "morally unjust," and "economically unfair"

In 1987, Dr. Mae Jamison became the first Black female astronaut in the U.S. space program. As a medical doctor with a degree in chemical engineering, she served as an experimental research specialist.

to Blacks. Many leaders believed that the president was ill-advised on issues pertaining to Blacks in this country. In Cumming, Georgia, thousands of civil rights protesters held a rally to protest Reagan administration racial policies.

JUDGE RULES THAT "DISCRIMINATION AND SEGREGATION" HAVE DENIED BLACKS REPRESENTATION ON CITY COUNCIL

On **JANUARY 13**, U.S. District Court judge Harold Parker ruled in favor of Blacks petitioning against five members of the Springfield, Illinois, city council. Parker declared that the effects of seventy-five years of "discrimination and segregation" have denied Blacks an opportunity to gain a seat on the city council.

WHITE TEENAGERS CHARGED WITH MURDER OF BLACK YOUTH IN HOWARD BEACH

On **FEBRUARY 11**, three white teenagers in Howard Beach, Queens, New York, were charged with the murder of a Black youth in 1986.

The white teenagers had attacked the Black youth and, in an attempt to escape, the youth was struck and killed by an automobile.

RIOTING IN FLORIDA FOLLOWS POLICE KILLING OF BLACK

On **FEBRUARY 19**, a young man was killed when he was held by a police chokehold. When the news reached the African American community, rioting erupted. Bottles and rocks were thrown, and some buildings were burned.

SUPREME COURT RULES IN FAVOR OF RACIAL PROMOTION QUOTAS

On **FEBRUARY 26**, the U.S. Supreme Court declared that judges might order racial promotion quotas as a remedy to long-standing, blatant, and pervasive discrimination. The decision stemmed from a judicial ruling requiring the state of Alabama to hire one Black state trooper for each white trooper hired.

BLACK MAYOR OF CHICAGO REELECTED

On **APRIL 7**, Mayor Harold Washington of Chicago won reelection to a second four-year term, defeating Edward R. Vrdolyak, a white alderman who had opposed him on almost every issue during his first term. Washington acquired control of the city council for the first time. On November 25, Washington died of a heart attack. Eugene Sawyer, a Black alderman, was selected to become acting mayor in a compromise among political factions. Some Black citizens were frustrated that a different Black alderman, Timothy Evans, was not selected. In the next election, Michael Bilandic, a white alderman, was elected mayor.

DODGERS FIRE EXECUTIVE FOR RACIST COMMENTS

On **APRIL 8**, the Los Angeles Dodgers fired Al Campanis for his remarks referring to the "limited" ability of African Americans to manage professional baseball teams. Although Campanis publicly apologized, the African American community believed that the problem of racism and employment discrimination in major-league baseball ran deeper than this single incident. Black civil rights leaders, headed by Jesse Jackson, called for an investigation into the hiring and promotion practices within professional baseball.

New York Daily News FOUND GUILTY OF RACIAL DISCRIMINATION

On **APRIL 16**, a federal jury found the *New York Daily News* was guilty of discriminating against four Black editorial reporters in promotions, salaries, and assignments.

WHITE SUPREMACISTS INDICTED

On **APRIL 25**, a federal grand jury in Fort Smith, Arkansas, indicted Girnt Butler, leader of the Aryan Nations Church, and nine other white supremacists on charges of conspiring to assassinate federal officials and to kill members of certain ethnic groups.

Fences WINS FOUR TONY AWARDS

On **JUNE 7**, *Fences* won Tonys for best director (Lloyd Richards), for best play (written by August Wilson), for best performance by an actor (James Earl Jones), and best performance by a featured actress (Mary Alice).

ELECTION GIVES BLACKS MAJORITY ON SELMA'S CITY COUNCIL

On **JULY 29**, Ed Moss was sworn in as a city councilor in Selma, Alabama. Moss's membership on the city council tipped the scales toward a Black majority on the council in Selma, one of the most racially troubled cities during the early days of the civil rights movement.

CARSON SURGICALLY SEPARATES SIAMESE TWINS

On **SEPTEMBER 7**, Dr. Benjamin S. Carson, a Black pediatric neurosurgeon at Johns Hopkins University, led a group of surgeons in an operation that physically separated Siamese twins joined at the head. It was a most delicate operation, and Carson was applauded by his colleagues for his successful leadership.

JACKSON SEEKS PRESIDENTIAL NOMINATION FOR 1988
On **SEPTEMBER 8**, the Reverend Jesse Jackson announced that he would seek the Democratic presidential nomination again in 1988.

U.S. SENATE REJECTS BORK FOR U.S. SUPREME COURT
On **OCTOBER 23**, the U.S. Senate rejected Judge Robert Bork's nomination as associate justice of the U.S. Supreme Court, following an outpouring of opposition from almost every minority and women's rights group in the country, including the NAACP. Liberal members of the Senate stood firm against his nomination.

SCHMOKE BECOMES MAYOR OF BALTIMORE
In **NOVEMBER**, Kurt Schmoke was the first African American to be elected mayor of Baltimore, Maryland. (Clarence "Du" Burns had been the first African American mayor of Baltimore, but he reached the position as a result of Mayor William Shaeffer's being elected governor of Maryland.)

1988 BLACK INFANT MORTALITY RATE DECLINES
The infant mortality rate was ten deaths per thousand live births in 1988. From 1987 to 1988, the infant mortality rate declined by 1.7 percent for Black infants to 17.6 percent, and by 1.2 percent for white infants to 8.5 percent. The Black infant mortality rate remained twice that of white infants.

DRUGS DESTROY BLACK COMMUNITIES
Children living in the inner city were becoming increasingly dependent on drugs, especially crack, an inexpensive and particularly addictive form of cocaine. Because of the widespread use of this drug in the inner city and even among suburban whites, street gangs had been able to secure zones from which they sold drugs. It was rapidly becoming an epidemic in every major city and across the country.

HIGH SCHOOL GRADUATION RATES REMAIN THE SAME FOR BLACKS
In this year, 76.1 percent of Black students completed high school, compared with 75.6 percent in 1985 and 76.5 percent in 1986. The comparable rate for whites

Kurt Schmoke, a former Maryland state's attorney, was elected mayor of Baltimore in 1987 and again in 1991. Like many other big-city mayors, he faced the problems of a dwindling tax base and a decreasing number of jobs for the city's residents.

were 82.1 percent in 1989, 83.6 percent in 1985, and 83.1 percent in 1986.

HOMICIDE LEADING CAUSE OF DEATH FOR BLACK MALES
Homicides claimed twenty-two-thousand lives in the United States in this year, a rate of about nine per one hundred thousand. It was the leading cause of death among Black males from age fifteen to age thirty-four. Firearms were involved in 62 percent of all homicides in the United States in 1988. About 57 percent of Black victims from fifteen to thirty-four years of age were murdered with a handgun, and another 15 percent were killed with other types of firearms.

JOYNER-KERSEE WINS OLYMPIC GOLD MEDALS

Jackie Joyner-Kersee won two gold medals at the Olympic Games in Seoul, Korea — one in the heptathlon and another in the long jump.

JOYNER WINS OLYMPIC GOLD MEDALS

Florence Griffith Joyner proved she was one of the fastest women runners in the world when she won three gold medals at the 1988 Olympic Games in Seoul, Korea, for the 100-meter, 200-meter, and 400-meter races. She also earned a silver medal in the 1,600-meter relay.

KING PUBLISHES AUTOBIOGRAPHY

Coretta Scott King (1927–), the widow of Martin Luther King, Jr., and president of the Martin Luther King, Jr., Center for Social Change, published *My Life with Martin Luther King, Jr.*

LIFE EXPECTANCY FALLS AMONG BLACKS

The Centers for Disease Control (CDC) in Atlanta, Georgia, reported that life expectancy of Black Americans had dropped for the third consecutive year. Using data for 1988, the life expectancy for Blacks was 69.2 years, down from its peak of 69.5 years in 1985. Murder and AIDS reduced life expectancy among Blacks. The life expectancy of a Black man dropped from 65.2 years in 1987 to 64.9 years in this year. For Black women, the life expectancy was 73.4, down from 73.6 years in 1987. Since 1981, life expectancy for white men had risen steadily to a high of 72.8 years. For white women, it was 78.9 years, the same as in 1987. Overall life expectancy for all Americans was now 74.9 years, slightly down from the 1987 high of 75 years.

Life expectancy for whites in America continued to improve, achieving a record 75.6 years. According to the CDC, major causes of death affecting the difference in mortality between Blacks and whites included heart disease, HIV (human immuno-deficiency virus) infection, infant mortality, and homicide. Heart disease continued to be the number one cause of death for Black Americans — 40 percent higher than the rate for whites. Blacks died of AIDS at a rate 3.4 times greater than that of whites. Black homicides continued to escalate to a rate 6.4 times greater than that for whites. Whites tended to have a higher death rate in two of the leading causes of death — chronic lung disease and suicide.

Death rates are affected by a wide range of factors — some controlled by the individual and some not.

Thus, the racial gap in health standards is closely related to economic status. Income influences access to health care and preventive services, the quality of nutrition, and the magnitude of stress in daily life.

TWO SOCIETIES EXIST WITHIN AMERICA

Since 1968, the percentage of Blacks living in poverty has remained constant at about one in three; however, the actual number of poor Blacks increased from 7.6 million in 1968 to more than 9.8 million in 1990. Over the same period, the percentage of whites in poverty remained at about ten percent, while the number of poor whites actually increased by about five million.

LOW-BIRTH-WEIGHT INFANTS HIGHEST AMONG BLACKS

The percentage of low-birth-weight infants was higher among Blacks than among any other racial or ethnic group in the country. Although 13.3 percent of Black mothers delivered low-birth-weight infants, the overall percentage of live infants born weighing less than twenty-five hundred grams had remained at about 7 percent since 1980.

MARINO NAMED ARCHBISHOP OF ATLANTA

Eugene A. Marino became the first Black Catholic archbishop in the United States when he was appointed archbishop of Atlanta by Pope John Paul II. In 1974, when he first became a bishop, he was one of three Blacks to achieve that status within this century.

MORRISON WINS PULITZER PRIZE

Toni Morrison won the Pulitzer Prize for fiction for *Beloved*, a novel portraying a runaway slave who chose to murder her daughter rather than let her be enslaved. Morrison was probably the best-known African American novelist in the country. Ten years earlier, she had been awarded the National Book Award for her novel *Song of Solomon*.

NUMBER OF BLACKS LIVING IN POVERTY SEEMS INTRACTABLE

The Bureau of the Census issued a report indicating that 31.7 million Americans lived in poverty. (The poverty threshold was $12,091 annually for a family of four in this year.) About 10.1 percent of whites lived below the poverty level, compared with 31.3 percent of Blacks. For Blacks, the number in poverty had risen from 8.9 million to 9.4 million persons. The poverty rate for Blacks remained the same, 31.3 percent. For whites, however, the number in poverty dropped from 22.9 million to 20.7 million and the percentage in poverty dropped a full percentage point, from 14 percent to 13 percent. Black children were more than three times as likely to live in poverty as white children. More than 42.8 percent of Black children lived in poverty versus 14 percent of white children.

POWELL NAMED FOUR-STAR GENERAL
Lieutenant General Colin L. Powell was promoted to the rank of four-star general in the U.S. Army, becoming one of only ten four-star generals in the army and the only African American at this rank. Powell's decorations included the Bronze Star and the Purple Heart. Powell became the first African American chairman of the Joint Chiefs of Staff of the armed forces.

General Colin Powell's military career spanned more than thirty years. He became the first Black four-star general and was one of the architects of the American success in the Persian Gulf War in 1991.

WASHINGTON, D.C., BECOMES MURDER CAPITAL OF THE UNITED STATES
Washington, D.C., surpassed Detroit as the "murder capital" of the United States in this year.

WILLIAMS NAMED MOST VALUABLE PLAYER
Doug Williams, quarterback for the professional Washington Redskins football team, was voted the Most Valuable Player in the Super Bowl. Williams led the Redskins to a 42–10 win over the Denver Broncos, becoming the first African American quarterback to play in a Super Bowl game. Ironically, Williams was dismissed by the Redskins the next year because of injuries. Many Blacks believed that he was not treated in the same way as white players with similar injuries.

THOMAS WINS OLYMPIC MEDAL
On **FEBRUARY 27**, Debi Thomas won a bronze medal for figure skating in the Winter Olympic Games in Calgary. Thomas, a medical student in California, was the first Black to win a medal in any Olympic Winter Games. She was also the first African American to win a medal in figure skating.

CIVIL RIGHTS RESTORATION ACT PASSED
In **MARCH**, the Civil Rights Restoration Act was passed by the U.S. Congress, vetoed by President Reagan, and then passed over his veto. The legislation was designed to overturn the 1984 Supreme Court decision (*Grove City College* v. *Bell*) that had limited the enforcement of civil rights laws only to specific programs or activities receiving federal funds. The act specifically required that any institution receiving federal funds, including school systems, corporations, and health facilities, had to comply with the civil rights statutes. Some exemptions were granted to small businesses and to institutions controlled by religious organizations. The Senate had passed the measure by a vote of 75–14 in January, and the House passed it by a vote of 315–98 in March. President Reagan vetoed the bill on the grounds that the exemptions were inadequate and that religious freedoms were being threatened. Congress overrode the veto 73–24 in the Senate and 292–133 in the House.

STOUT SWORN IN AS ASSOCIATE JUSTICE
On **MARCH 3**, Juanita Kidd Stout was sworn in as an associate justice of the Supreme Court of Pennsylvania, becoming the first African American woman to serve on a state supreme court.

the award with three others, Les Fresholtz, Dick Alexander, and Vern Pone.

Jesse Jackson was the most visible Black leader during the 1988 presidential election. As a serious presidential candidate, he focused on urban and social issues.

JACKSON WINS DEMOCRATIC PRIMARIES
On **MARCH 8**, presidential candidate Jesse Jackson took the nation by surprise on "Super Tuesday" by winning the Democratic primaries in Alabama, Georgia, Louisiana, Mississippi, and Virginia, as well as making a good showing in several other states. Jackson emerged as a serious presidential contender. On March 26, he won the Michigan Democratic caucus, the first victory ever for an African American presidential candidate in an industrial state. Overall, Jackson received more than three million votes in the primaries.

BURTON WINS OSCAR
On **APRIL 11**, Willie D. Burton won the Academy Award for best sound in the movie *Bird*. He shared

INCOME GAP WIDENS BETWEEN RICH AND POOR
On **APRIL 30**, the Bureau of the Census released a report that showed a growing gap between the upper and lower income groups in the country. The annual income of people in the top 5 percent rose an average of six thousand dollars during the 1980s, whereas the average income of the bottom 5 percent dropped by more than seven thousand dollars. Such statistics revealed that a large number of Black Americans were drifting into poverty more rapidly than expected. It further revealed that the economy, which was shifting rapidly toward service and high-tech industries, was not providing enough jobs for unskilled workers, many of them Blacks. The direction of the economy and the loss of social programs that provided "safety nets" for the Black poor were forcing many Blacks into the lower fifth of the income strata.

MOTOWN RECORDS SOLD
On **JUNE 29**, Motown Records was sold to an investment group for sixty-one million dollars. Jheryl Busby, a record executive, and other parties, including a venture capital firm, purchased Motown.

SUPREME COURT RULES NO NEED TO PROVE INTENTIONAL DISCRIMINATION
On **JUNE 29**, the U.S. Supreme Court decided in *Watson* v. *Fort Worth Bank and Trust* that women and minorities did not have to prove intentional discrimination in hiring and promotion decisions when the decisions were based on subjective criteria. Clara Watson, the petitioner, had originally brought suit when she was rejected in favor of white applicants for four promotions to supervisory positions at the Fort Worth bank. The bank had not developed any formal selection criteria but instead relied on the subjective judgment of white supervisors.

BLACK JUDGE IMPEACHED
On **AUGUST 3**, the U.S. House of Representatives voted 413–3 to impeach U.S. District Court judge Alcee L. Hastings, the first Black judge on the federal court in Florida, for allegedly soliciting a $150,000 bribe from a defendant being tried on drug-related charges.

Yo! MTV Raps PREMIERES
On **AUGUST 6**, MTV, the twenty-four-hour cable music channel, premiered *Yo! MTV Raps*. The show became

one of the most successful MTV programs and featured a large number of African American rap stars.

HOLMAN DIES

On **AUGUST 9**, M. Carl Holman, a leading civil rights activist and head of the Urban Coalition, a small Black research and civil rights organization, died.

BISHOP COLLEGE CLOSES ITS DOORS

On **AUGUST 15**, Bishop College, a predominantly Black college located in Dallas, Texas, closed its doors because of inability to pay its increasing debts. Bishop had been at one time the largest Black college in the western United States. Started in 1881 in Marshall, Texas, Bishop College had moved to Dallas in 1961 in an attempt to increase enrollment and secure funding. In 1967, more than fifteen hundred students were enrolled. On February 1990, the college campus was auctioned off for $1.5 million.

JOB DISCRIMINATION COMPLAINTS NOT PROPERLY INVESTIGATED

On **OCTOBER 4**, the General Accounting Office reported that the Equal Employment Opportunity Commission (EEOC) had failed to properly investigate about 82 percent of the job discrimination claims filed with the commission during a three-month investigation period. Clarence Thomas was the chairperson of the EEOC.

COSBYS GIVE TWENTY MILLION DOLLARS TO SPELMAN COLLEGE

On **NOVEMBER 4**, Bill and Camille Cosby gave twenty million dollars to Spelman College. The gift arrived within months of Johnetta B. Cole's inauguration as the first woman president of this college. The Cosbys' gift was the largest ever given to a college from a single family donor.

PAYNE ELECTED TO CONGRESS

On **NOVEMBER 8**, Donald M. Payne (1934–) became the first Black elected to the U.S. House of Representatives from New Jersey. He was elected from the Tenth Congressional District, which encompasses much of Newark. Payne succeeded Peter Rodino, who had retired after representing the district since 1948.

◇ Payne was born in Newark, New Jersey. After receiving a B.A. degree in social studies from Seton Hall University, he began work with the Young Men's Christian Association (YMCA). He was elected

the first Black president of the YMCAs of the United States in 1970.

In 1972, Payne was elected to the Essex County Board of Chosen Freeholders. He was elected director of the board by his fellow members in 1977. Payne served on the Newark Municipal Council from 1982 until 1988.

Payne was reelected for the second time in 1992 by a healthy margin, capturing almost 70 percent of the votes.

USE OF TERM *African American* URGED BY JACKSON

On **DECEMBER 21**, Jesse Jackson called upon the Black population to use the term *African American* to describe themselves, because of its reference to a land base and a historical cultural base. There was some resistance by both whites and Blacks to an immediate change from *Black Americans* to *African Americans.*

1989   AIDS INCIDENCE INCREASES

From 1986 to 1989, the annual numbers of cases of AIDS among non-Hispanic Blacks and Native Americans age thirteen years and over had tripled, whereas they increased by factors of 2.4–2.6 for Hispanic Americans, non-Hispanic whites, and Asian Americans. During this year, more than thirty-three thousand adolescent and adult AIDS cases were reported.

In 1988, HIV infection was the fourth leading cause of death among persons twenty-five to forty-four years of age and the sixth leading cause among persons fifteen to twenty-four years of age.

BLACK CONGRESSIONAL REPRESENTATION INCREASES

There were twenty-four Black members of Congress, including a nonvoting delegate from the District of Columbia, in this year. All were members of the House of Representatives, where they constituted 5.5 percent of the membership.

BLACK INCOME ON THE RISE

Black median household income was $18,080 in this year, up 5.1 percent from 1988 in real dollar terms. For the nation as a whole, median household income was $28,910, up 1.3 percent from 1988. White median household income ($30,410) and Hispanic median household income ($21,920) remained relatively unchanged over the same period. Black median household income had risen 6.6 percent in the South, the only region to show a statistically significant increase for Blacks. White household income had risen 3.4 percent in the Northeast, the only region showing a significant increase for whites.

BLACK YOUTH KILLED BY WHITE MOB
A white mob stalked and killed Yusuf Hawkins, a sixteen-year-old Black youth who had traveled into a predominantly white neighborhood in Brooklyn to buy a used car that he had seen in the classified ad section of a newspaper.

CHENAULT NAMED PRESIDENT OF AMERICAN EXPRESS DIVISION
Kenneth I. Chenault, an attorney who had worked for American Express since 1981, was promoted to president of the Consumer Card and Financial Services Group of American Express in this year. Chenault became one of the highest-ranking African Americans within a predominantly white corporation.

COLLEGE ADMISSION TESTS SHOW MINORITIES LOSING GROUND
The American College Testing Company in Iowa City, which administered the American College Test (ACT), and the College Board, which sponsored the Scholastic Aptitude Test (SAT), had been under fire from women and minority groups who claimed that the standardized tests were biased against them. They pointed to the latest scores, which showed wide disparities by gender and race. White students gained points on their combined math-verbal SAT scores, increasing to 937; scores for Blacks, whose combined average score was 737, remained unchanged from the previous year. Women's combined scores fell 2 points to 875. Spokespersons for these tests claimed that "high school preparation, not biased test questions," accounted for test score differences.

DRUG USE AND SMOKING AMONG BLACK AMERICANS
A recent survey by the National Center for Disease Control published the following findings:

◈ Between 1985 and 1989, 5.6 percent of white males reported using cocaine at least once in the previous month, compared to 2.6 percent of Black males. Among females, the gap was even larger: 4.1 percent of white females reported using cocaine, compared to 1.3 percent of Black females;

◈ White high school seniors were much more likely than Blacks to smoke cigarettes and to smoke heavily. Among males, 19 percent, and among females, 13.3 percent reported smoking every day. The figures for Black males and Black females were 8.6 percent and 2.2 percent, respectively;

◈ The proportion of white male high school seniors who reported using marijuana, the most common illegal drug, at least once in the previous year, was 40 percent, compared with 28 percent for Black males. Usage rates were slightly lower among females, 36 percent for whites and 18.4 percent for Blacks;

◈ Among all ethnic groups, Asian Americans had the lowest rates of legal and illegal drug use. Only 9.7 percent of Asian American males reported using marijuana in the previous month, less than half the rate (25.7 percent) among whites. Native Americans had the highest rates of use of illicit and legal drugs; Hispanic Americans reported "intermediate" usage levels;

◈ Religious influence was the only variable that correlated consistently with lower drug use.

JAPANESE "INSENSITIVE" TO BLACK POPULATION
Blacks claimed that Japanese officials and Japanese companies in the United States, particularly carmakers and other manufacturers, practiced discrimination. The Equal Employment Opportunity Commission forced Honda to pay six million dollars to 377 Blacks and women for discriminatory hiring. Discrimination suits had been directed at other Japanese carmakers as well.

◈ The National Association of Minority Automobile Dealers noted that Nissan had only one minority dealership, 0.1 percent of its total number of dealerships. Toyota had three, amounting to 0.3 percent. Overall, Blacks owned only eight of the nearly five thousand Japanese car dealerships in the United States. By contrast, General Motors had 204 Black dealerships, and Ford had 170. (A large proportion of Black-owned firms are car dealerships.)

As late as 1988, the *Washington Post* revealed that Japanese firms were making "Little Black Sambo" dolls and publishing a racist "Little Black Sambo" book. The scope of Japanese racism, according to Blacks, was not limited to isolated incidents. In fact, Japan's justice minister, Serioku Kajiyama, compared a raid on the "Tokyo red-light district" to "America when neighborhoods became mixed because Blacks move in and whites are forced out. Prostitutes ruin the atmosphere of neighborhoods in the same way."

JOYNER-KERSEE NAMED FEMALE ATHLETE OF THE YEAR

The Associated Press selected track-and-field star Jackie Joyner-Kersee as Female Athlete of the Year.

LEE'S MOVIE *Do the Right Thing* BRINGS RACE RIOT TO THE SCREEN

Black filmmaker Spike Lee wrote, produced, directed, and acted in *Do the Right Thing*, the story of a race riot in a Black neighborhood.

MAYOR BRADLEY REELECTED

Mayor Thomas Bradley of Los Angeles won reelection to a fifth term.

NUGGETS BASKETBALL TEAM PURCHASED BY BLACKS

The Denver Nuggets of the National Basketball Association were purchased for fifty-four million dollars by a group of investors led by majority shareholders Bertram M. Lee and Peter C. B. Bynoe, both African American. The Nuggets were the first and are still the only National Basketball Association team to be owned by African Americans.

POVERTY RATE REMAINS ABOUT THE SAME

Blacks still represented the highest proportion of the nation's poor. There were 31.5 million persons living below the official poverty level in 1989, not significantly different from the 31.7 million poor in 1988.

SUPREME COURT RULES AGAINST BLACKS WHO CLAIM VOTING RIGHTS WERE VIOLATED

In *Presley* v. *Etowah County Commission*, the U.S. Supreme Court overruled a decision of the Justice Department, the agency charged with administering the voting rights laws. The Court declared that the Voting Rights Act had not been violated by actions by a white-dominated county board to ensure continued power over the Black minority.

Blacks in Etowah County, Alabama, had finally amassed enough political power to elect a Black to the county board of supervisors. At once, the white board members removed from individual supervisors all power to make decisions regarding their respective districts. Power was reallocated to the board as a whole. Therefore, the people of the Black district would still be governed by the white majority.

SUPREME COURT RULES RACISM INSUFFICIENT GROUNDS TO CHALLENGE CONVICTION

In *McClesky* v. *Kemp*, the U.S. Supreme Court stated that institutional racism in the courts was insufficient cause to challenge a particular conviction or sentence. A Black awaiting execution had to *prove* that racism was the specific cause of conviction or a particular sentence, and this condition was very difficult to meet.

TEMPLE UNIVERSITY INSTITUTES DOCTORATE IN AFRICAN AMERICAN STUDIES

Temple University in Philadelphia became the first university in the country to offer a doctorate degree in African American studies; thirty-five students enrolled in the first class.

GREEN NAMED NEW YORK CITY SCHOOLS CHANCELLOR

On **JANUARY 3**, Richard R. Green, the superintendent of the Minneapolis school system, was named the first Black chancellor of the New York City school system, the nation's largest. Unfortunately, Green died one year later from complications of asthma, before he could fully implement his plans for the school system.

SUPREME COURT RULES MINORITY SET-ASIDE UNCONSTITUTIONAL

On **JANUARY 23**, the U.S. Supreme Court declared the 30 percent set-aside of public works expenditures for minority-owned construction companies unconstitutional. Justice Sandra Day O'Connor wrote the majority opinion, saying that set-asides must redress "identified discrimination."

BLACK WOMAN BECOMES FIRST WOMAN BISHOP OF EPISCOPAL CHURCH

In **FEBRUARY**, Barbara Harris, who had no seminary training, was consecrated as suffragan (assistant) bishop for the diocese of Massachusetts, thus becoming the first woman bishop in the history of the Episcopal Church.

◆ Barbara Harris was born in Philadelphia and worked as a public relations executive before being ordained a deacon in the Episcopal Church in 1979. One year later, she was appointed priest-in-charge of an Episcopalian church in Norristown, Pennsylvania. She was later selected to be executive director of the publishing company associated with the Episcopal Church.

RACIAL VIOLENCE BREAKS OUT IN FLORIDA

On **FEBRUARY 1**, racial violence erupted in Tampa, Florida, when Edgar Allen Price, an alleged drug dealer, died in police custody. According to medical tests, the cause of Price's death was intoxication or suffocation from being laid facedown in the police car. Violence continued for two days.

FEWER BLACK MALES RECEIVE COLLEGE EDUCATION

On **FEBRUARY 7**, the American Council on Education released a report showing a decrease in the number of Black men attending college. The number of women attending college, however, had increased.

In 1976, about 470,000 Black men attended college; ten years later (the latest data available), there were only 436,000. Women's enrollment rose from 563,000 to 645,000 over the same period. The high cost of college education, military enlistment, and the effects of drugs and crime were cited as possible causes for the decreasing number.

BROWN HEADS DEMOCRATIC NATIONAL COMMITTEE

On **FEBRUARY 10**, Ronald H. Brown was elected chairperson of the Democratic National Committee, becoming the first Black to hold this powerful political position.

Brown, a lawyer, worked as a key strategist in the presidential campaign of Senator Edward Kennedy and as the campaign manager for Jesse Jackson's bid for the Democratic presidential nomination.

SULLIVAN APPOINTED HEALTH SECRETARY

On **FEBRUARY 10**, Dr. Louis Sullivan, president of Morehouse School of Medicine in Atlanta, Georgia, was selected by President George Bush as secretary of the Department of Health and Human Services. Sullivan was the only Black in the Bush cabinet.

WHITE NAMED PRESIDENT OF NATIONAL BASEBALL LEAGUE

On **APRIL 1**, Bill White, former St. Louis Cardinal first baseman, became president of the National Baseball League. He was the first Black to head a major sports league.

STALLINGS BREAKS WITH CATHOLIC CHURCH

In **JUNE**, George Augustus Stallings, a Roman Catholic priest in Washington, D.C., broke with the Catholic Church, stating that it was not meeting the needs of the African American community. The

Ronald H. Brown was selected to head the Democratic National Committee in 1989. President Bill Clinton later appointed him secretary of commerce.

Roman Catholic Church, choosing its words carefully, criticized Stallings for his remarks and stressed that it would extend its efforts to meet African American religious needs. In July, the Roman Catholic Church suspended Stallings for "founding an independent Black congregation." On May 13, 1990, Stallings became the first bishop of the church he founded, the African American Catholic church.

POWELL HEADS JOINT CHIEFS OF STAFF

On **AUGUST 10**, General Colin L. Powell (1937–) was named chair of the U.S. Joint Chiefs of Staff, the nation's highest military office. Not only was Powell the first Black to hold this position — he was, at the age of fifty-two, the youngest.

◈ Powell was born to West Indian immigrant parents in the Harlem section of New York City. He received a bachelor's degree from the City College of New York in 1958 and an M.B.A. from George

Washington University in 1971. He attended the National War College. In 1958, Powell was commissioned a second lieutenant in the army through the ROTC program and served in a number of positions, including staff officer at the Pentagon, brigade commander of the 101st Airborne Division, commander of the U.S. Army Fifth Corps in Europe, and deputy assistant and assistant to the president for national security affairs (1987–1989). Prior to heading the Joint Chiefs of Staff, he was commander in chief, Forces Command, Fort McPherson, Georgia. Powell directed the U.S. invasion of Panama to capture and arrest its leader, Manuel Noriega, on drug-trafficking charges, and directed the invasion of Kuwait in the Persian Gulf War of 1991. He was described by former secretary of defense Caspar Weinberger as "the quintessential soldier." He retired from the Joint Chiefs of Staff in 1993.

WOMEN AND MINORITIES MAKE GAINS IN BANKING INDUSTRY

According to information provided by the American Bankers Association (ABA) in **SEPTEMBER**, women and minorities were obtaining high-level management jobs at the nation's top banks at an ever-growing rate. According to the ABA, the advancement of these groups reflected serious recruitment efforts. Their data showed that the number of women filling top management jobs had risen by 166 percent during the previous decade, and the number of Blacks, Hispanic Americans, Asian Americans, and Native Americans had increased by more than 100 percent.

In 1988, minorities in top-level positions held only 15.9 percent of those jobs, compared with 12.3 percent in 1978. Minorities accounted for 20.9 percent of professionals, compared with 15.8 percent a decade earlier. Blacks holding positions as officials or managers increased from 5.4 percent to 6.9 percent of the total over the same period, according to the ABA's report.

BLACKS AMONG HIGHEST-PAID ENTERTAINERS

On **SEPTEMBER 6**, *Forbes* magazine published the 1988–1989 earnings of the world's highest-paid entertainers. According to the magazine, the following African Americans received the highest earnings:

Michael Jackson, $125 million
Bill Cosby, $95 million
Mike Tyson, $71 million

Eddie Murphy, $57 million
Oprah Winfrey, $55 million
Sugar Ray Leonard, $42 million
Prince, $36 million

BLACK WINS MISS AMERICA PAGEANT

On **SEPTEMBER 16**, Debbye Turner was crowned Miss America. Turner, a senior at the University of Missouri Veterinary School, became the third Black woman to be crowned Miss America since the pageant started in 1921.

Emerge IS PUBLISHED

On **SEPTEMBER 19**, Wilmer C. Ames, Jr., published the first issue of *Emerge*, a magazine that covered domestic and international news and issues from an African American perspective.

PERKINS APPOINTED DIRECTOR GENERAL OF FOREIGN SERVICE

On **SEPTEMBER 22**, Edward Perkins, who was the first African American ambassador to the Republic of South Africa, became director general of the U.S. Foreign Service. He was the first African American to hold this position, allowing him to directly influence equal opportunity and affirmative action for African Americans seeking to enter this field of public service.

TEXAS SUPREME COURT ADDRESSES WEALTH DIFFERENTIAL IN FINANCING SCHOOLS

In **OCTOBER**, the Texas Supreme Court voted 9–0 to overturn Texas's education financing system, which had over the years created a "dual" system of educating its young people. The richest school district had fourteen million dollars' worth of property per student versus only twenty thousand dollars' worth for the poorest. This 700–1 wealth disparity trapped many school districts in a web of poverty. School financing had been a major topic among legislators in Texas for several years, but reform had not been implemented. The court's decision required that legislators delineate and employ "equalization formulas" to help historically underperforming school districts — those attended by poor whites and Blacks — recoup the losses they had experienced over the years.

Jump Start PREMIERES

On **OCTOBER 2**, the comic strip *Jump Start* premiered in forty newspapers in the United States. It was the creation of Robb Armstrong, a twenty-six-year-old

African American. Armstrong became the youngest Black to have a syndicated comic strip.

SHELL NAMED RAIDERS COACH

On **OCTOBER 3**, Art Shell was selected by owner Al Davis to be the head coach of the Los Angeles Raiders. Shell became the first African American to be named coach of a National Football League team in more than sixty years.

BLACK JUDGE IMPEACHED

On **OCTOBER 20**, Alcee L. Hastings, a Black U.S. District Court judge, was convicted by the U.S. Senate of eight articles of impeachment concerning conspiracy and perjury. Hastings was acquitted on three articles, and the Senate decided not to take action on the remaining six. His conviction made him the sixth federal official in American history to be removed from office by impeachment.

CIVIL RIGHTS MEMORIAL DEDICATED

On **NOVEMBER 5**, the Civil Rights Memorial was dedicated in Montgomery, Alabama. Standing outside the Southern Poverty Law Center, which commissioned it, the memorial was designed by Maya Lin, who also designed the Vietnam War Memorial in Washington, D.C.

The memorial is composed of two parts, both made of black granite. A nine-foot vertical wall that is constantly washed by water is etched with a quotation of Martin Luther King, Jr.: ". . . until justice rolls down like waters and righteousness like a mighty stream." King used this metaphor on at least two occasions: at the beginning of the Montgomery bus boycott and in his "I Have a Dream" speech.

The other part of the memorial is a round disk, twelve feet in diameter, which is also washed by a continuous flow of water. Engraved on the disk are fifty-three entries that capture the civil rights struggle, from the 1954 Supreme Court decision outlawing school segregation to the assassination of King in Memphis, Tennessee, in 1968. Twenty-one entries are landmark events, and forty are devoted to individuals who died in the civil rights movement. Those individuals included on the memorial all met several criteria: they were killed because of their nonviolent civil rights activism, they were killed by agitators trying to generate opposition to the movement or erect a barrier to the movement, and their deaths created momentum for the movement, usually by focus-

ing attention on the conditions and injustices directed toward Blacks in the South.

The individuals include the following:

◈ Addie Mae Collins, Denise McNair, Carole Robertson, Cynthia Wesley; Birmingham, Alabama, 1963 (killed in the bombing of a Black church);

◈ Emmett Louis Till; Money, Mississippi, 1955 (fourteen-year-old murdered for speaking to a white woman);

◈ Medgar Evers; Jackson, Mississippi, 1963 (civil rights leader killed by an assassin);

◈ Virgil Lamar Ware; Birmingham, Alabama, 1963 (thirteen-year-old killed by white teenagers coming back from a segregationist rally);

◈ The Reverend Bruce Klunder; Cleveland, Ohio, 1965 (white who tried to block the construction of a segregated school);

◈ Jimmie Lee Jackson; Marion, Alabama, 1965 (shot by Alabama state troopers for trying to protect his mother and grandfather from a trooper attack on voting rights marchers);

◈ Viola Gregg Liuzzo; Selma Highway, Alabama, 1965 (white housewife from Michigan);

◈ Samuel Young, Jr.; Tuskegee, Alabama, 1966 (killed in a dispute over a whites-only bathroom);

◈ Vernon Dahmer; Hattiesburg, Mississippi, 1966 (offered to pay poll tax for anyone who could not afford the fee);

◈ Ben Chester White; Natchez, Mississippi, 1966 (caretaker shot to divert attention from a civil rights rally);

◈ Michael Donald; Mobile, Alabama, 1981 (lynched by Ku Klux Klan);

◈ Clarence Triggs; Bogalusa, Louisiana, 1966 (bricklayer shot for having attended a CORE meeting);

◈ The Reverend George Lee; Belzoni, Mississippi, 1955 (killed for leading voter registration drive);

◈ James E. Chaney, Andrew Goodman, Michael Schwerner; Philadelphia, Mississippi, 1964 (civil rights workers abducted and murdered);

◈ Jonathan Daniels; Hayneville, Alabama, 1965 (seminary student killed by deputy);

◈ Warlest Jackson; Natchez, Mississippi, 1967 (killed after promotion to "white job").

BLACK MAYORS ELECTED TO OFFICE

On **NOVEMBER 7**, a number of Blacks were elected or reelected as mayors in major cities. Included among these were Coleman Young (Detroit), Michael White

(Cleveland), Norm Rice (Seattle), Chester Jenkins (Durham), and John Daniels (New Haven). In Detroit, Young won an unprecedented fifth term. Michael White, a city councilor, became the city's second Black mayor. Daniels and Rice became the first Black mayors of their respective cities.

DINKINS ELECTED MAYOR OF NEW YORK CITY

On **NOVEMBER 7**, David Dinkins (1927–), president of the borough of Manhattan, was elected the first African American mayor of New York City, the largest city in the country. Dinkins, a Democrat, defeated his Republican challenger, Rudolph W. Giuliani, and two other candidates. The margin of victory was 898,000 votes for Dinkins, compared to Giuliani's 856,450. Dinkins owed his victory both to overwhelming Black support and to his ability to build an effective multiracial coalition in which Hispanic Americans and Jews supported his candidacy. He was also victorious because he promised to heal the city of the racial and crime problems that had splintered it for several years. Dinkins was defeated in his reelection campaign in 1993 by Giuliani, who claimed that Dinkins had been unsuccessful in dealing with racial and crime problems.

◈ Dinkins graduated from Howard University in 1950 and from the Brooklyn Law School in 1956. He began his career in politics in the 1950s, when he became a Democratic precinct leader, and he was elected a New York state senator in 1966. From 1975 to 1985, he was the city clerk for New York City. In 1985, after two unsuccessful campaigns, Dinkins was elected president of the borough of Manhattan, one of the most powerful positions in the city. Dinkins served in this capacity until 1989.

WILDER ELECTED GOVERNOR OF VIRGINIA

On **NOVEMBER 7**, Douglas Wilder became the first Black American elected to a state governorship — by a margin of just over seven thousand votes. He took the oath of office on January 13, 1990, before a crowd of at least thirty thousand. It is somewhat fitting that the center of slavery and the cradle of the Confederacy would be the first state to elect a Black governor. Wilder had served as lieutenant governor of Virginia and in both houses of the Virginia General Assembly.

RHYTHM AND BLUES FOUNDATION
PRESENTS AWARDS

On **NOVEMBER 10**, the Rhythm and Blues Foundation presented its first lifetime achievement awards to a number of outstanding entertainers, in Washington, D.C. Included among those honored were Charles Brown, Ruth Brown, Percy Sledge, and Mary Wells.

GREGORY LANDS SPACE SHUTTLE

On **NOVEMBER 29**, Colonel Frederick D. Gregory landed the space shuttle *Discovery*, after completing a secret military mission. Colonel Gregory thus became the first African American to command a space shuttle mission.

WASHINGTON ELECTED TO CONGRESS

In **DECEMBER**, Craig A. Washington won a nonpartisan primary and the following special election to fill the congressional seat vacated by the untimely death of Mickey Leland.

◈ Born in Longview, Texas, in 1941, Washington received a B.A. degree from Prairie View A & M University and a law degree from the Thurgood Marshall School of Law at Texas Southern University. He practiced law as a criminal defense attorney before entering politics.

Washington was elected to the Texas House of Representatives along with Leland in 1973. After serving there for ten years, he was elected to the state senate. Washington guided civil rights programs through the legislature, including proposals to increase the participation of women and minorities in state government.

Washington's campaign for the House seat featured the slogan "Pass the Torch," a promise to pursue Leland's political agenda. In 1992, Washington was reelected to Congress; he received almost 70 percent of the votes cast in his district.

DICKERSON WINS AWARD FOR CINEMATOGRAPHY

On **DECEMBER 18**, Ernest Dickerson won the New York Film Critics Circle Award for best cinematography for the movie *Do the Right Thing*.

1990
POPULATION OVERVIEW

BLACK POPULATION IN THE UNITED STATES According to the Bureau of the Census, the U.S. population included 248,709,873 residents, of whom 29,986,060 (12.1 percent) were Black residents. This figure was believed to undercount the Black population by several million. Of the nation's total population, 80.3 percent was white, down from 83.1 percent in 1980. At the same time, the Black population had increased from 11.7 percent to 12.1 percent. Other populations had grown significantly: the Hispanic population was up from 6.4 percent to 9 percent; Asian population had grown from 1.5 percent to 2.9 percent; and Native American population had grown from 0.6 percent to 0.8 percent.

REGIONAL SHIFTS IN THE BLACK POPULATION The Black population in the United States remained concentrated in the South, but not to the same degree as at the beginning of the twentieth century, when more than 90 percent of Blacks resided there. At this time, 52.8 percent (15,828,888) of Blacks lived in the South, 18.7 percent (5,613,222) in the Northeast, 19.1 percent (5,715,940) in the Midwest, and 9.4 percent (2,828,010) in the West. Almost one-quarter of the entire Black population resided in three states: New York (2,859,055), California (2,208,801), and Texas (2,021,632). A total of sixteen states had more than 1 million Black residents. In these states, the total Black population was about 24 million, or about 80 percent of all Black residents. In seven states and the District of Columbia, Blacks represented more than one-fifth of the total residents: District of Columbia, 65.8 percent; Mississippi, 35.6 percent; Louisiana, 30.8 percent; South Carolina, 29.8 percent; Georgia, 27 percent; Alabama, 25.3 percent; Maryland, 24.9 percent; and North Carolina, 22.0 percent.

Migration patterns for Blacks and whites had shifted since the 1940s. Although whites continued to leave cities in large numbers, they began emptying out of the older manufacturing areas of the Northeast and the Midwest. The major shift was to the West: 11 percent of whites resided there in 1940, 21 percent in 1990. The regional shift in Black residents followed a slightly different pattern — they increased proportionally in the Northeast and the Midwest (to 19 percent each), but increased from 1 percent to 9 percent in the West. The South's proportion of total Blacks shifted downward to about 53 percent. Although a greater number of Blacks had been moving into rather than out of the South since the 1970s, the movements of Blacks had not been significant enough to markedly shift the regional proportions. Blacks were distributed in about the same manner as in 1970.

BLACK POPULATION IN THE SOUTH According to the recent census report, the proportion of Black people was increasing in the South for the first time in more than one hundred years. Although the 1970–1980 decade revealed a net migration of Blacks out of the South, the new census data showed a trend toward more rapid growth in the South than in other regions. In fact, during the 1980s, the proportion of the total

Black population residing in the South increased from 52.2. percent to 55.9 percent.

THE URBANIZATION OF AMERICA INCREASES Census data showed that a bare majority of Americans — 50.2 percent — lived in large metropolitan areas of more than 1 million people. During the previous decade, 90 percent of the nation's population growth had occurred in these metropolitan areas. Metropolitan areas in the Sunbelt were the largest gainers: Orlando, Florida, by 53 percent; Phoenix, Arizona, by 41 percent; San Diego, California, by 34 percent; Dallas–Fort Worth, Texas, by 33 percent; and Atlanta, Georgia, by 33 percent.

ECONOMIC CONDITIONS OVERVIEW

BLACK FAMILY INCOME STABLE AS WHITE INCOMES RISE According to a Bureau of the Census publication of this year, between 1982 and 1989, real median family income increased by 13.6 percent. Median income for all families was $34,210. Between 1988 and 1989, the median income of Black families was $20,210 compared with $23,450 for Hispanic families and $35,980 for white families. The ration of Black family income to white family income in 1989 was 0.56, not statistically different from 1988 levels. This simply means that Black families earned fifty-six cents for every dollar that white families earned.

BLACKS LACK AFFORDABLE HOUSING According to a study by the Private Center on Budget and Policy Priorities, adequate housing was beyond the reach of nearly half of the nation's Black and Hispanic families, who were much more likely to live in substandard housing.

The report found that 42 percent of all Black and Hispanic households spent more on housing in 1985 than was considered affordable, compared to only 27 percent of all whites. As many as 37 percent of poor Black households were spending at least 70 percent of their income on housing in 1985, leaving little money for food and other necessities. Although Black and Hispanic households made up 17 percent of all households in the country, they composed 42 percent of those occupying substandard housing and more than half of those living in units with holes in the floor or evidence of rats. According to the report, housing among these two groups had reached a crisis stage.

The Bureau of the Census released data showing that the "American dream of owning a house still is possible but is difficult for some Americans." With conventional financing, some 77 percent of Black Americans could not afford a median-priced home.

With financing through the Federal Housing Authority, this figure dropped to about 74 percent of Black Americans.

NET WORTH HOLDINGS OF BLACKS ARE LOW The Bureau of the Census published in this year a report showing that in 1988, Black households (that is, households with a Black householder) had a median net worth of $4,169. Hispanic households had a median net worth of $5,524, and white households, $43,279. In the lowest income quintile, the median net worth in 1988 for Black households was zero, compared with white households, which had $8,839. Net worth holdings were influenced by the distribution of types of households (married-couple, male householder, or female householder).

NUMBER OF BLACK-OWNED BUSINESSES INCREASES In its 1987 Survey of Minority-Owned Business Enterprises, the Bureau of the Census reported an increase in Black-owned businesses of 38 percent from 1982 to 1987, from 308,000 to 424,000 businesses. The average annual receipts of Black-owned firms was about forty-seven thousand dollars.

SOCIAL CONDITIONS OVERVIEW

BLACK MEN IN TROUBLE WITH THE LAW According to a report by the Sentencing Project, a nonprofit organization in Washington, D.C., which promoted alternative punishments and sentencing reform, about one-quarter of all young Black males were in prison or on probation or parole. The report called for major reforms in the criminal justice system, differentiating treatment of first-time offenders and repeat offenders. The report warned that an entire generation of Black men might never lead productive lives without speedy changes in the criminal justice system.

CHILDREN IN POVERTY According to a study by the Joint Center for Political and Economic Studies, 46.5 percent of all Black children in this country lived in poverty. The youngest children tended to be the worst off: those under three years of age in families headed by women had the highest poverty rate — 87 percent in 1984. In 1979, the rate for this age group was 76 percent. Nearly two-thirds of the mothers associated with this poverty level were in their twenties.

CRIME VICTIMS MORE LIKELY TO BE BLACK According to a National Crime Survey taken between 1979 and 1986, Blacks were more likely than whites to be victims of rape or aggravated assault and were more than twice as likely to be robbery victims. The Justice Department's survey also found that the rate of violent crimes against Black Americans age twelve or older

was 44 per 1,000, compared with 34 per 1,000 for whites of the same age group.

HOUSEHOLDS HEADED BY BLACK WOMEN INCREASE Recent census data showed that this segment of households in the country was growing rapidly. Single-parent households were nearly three times more common among Blacks than among whites. Black families, however, were becoming more stable, and the growth of Black single-parent families had slowed. Over the previous decade, the proportion of households headed by white women had jumped from 13.2 percent of all white households to 17.3 percent, but these numbers still did not approach the proportion of Black households headed by women — 56.2 percent, up from 45.9 percent in 1980.

In the 1950s, more than 82 percent of Black households were classified as two-parent households. The breakup of the family unit, shown by a decline in two-parent households and an increase in households headed by women had become a significant phenomenon in American society. As the number of these households increased, so did their poverty level. As many as 56 percent of Black households headed by women were mired in poverty, compared with 38 percent of their white counterparts. The poverty level was defined as an annual income of $10,530 for a family of three.

INFANT MORTALITY RATE FALLS The nation's infant death rate registered the sharpest decline since 1981, but Black babies continued to fare far worse than white babies. The overall mortality rate for infants was 9.1 per 1,000 in 1990, down from 9.7 deaths a year earlier. The rate for Black infant mortality was 17.6 per 1,000, more than twice the rate of 8.5 for white infants.

LIFE EXPECTANCY FALLS FOR BLACK MEN The National Center for Health Statistics reported that life expectancy for Blacks had fallen — from 69.5 years in 1985 to 69.2 years in 1988. In contrast, life expectancy for whites had continued to rise — from 75.3 in 1985 to 75.6 in 1988. Factors cited included homicides, car accidents, drug abuse, AIDS, inadequate access to medical care, higher infant mortality, and higher death rates from cancer, heart disease, stroke, diabetes, liver trouble, and kidney failure.

MAJORITY OF BLACK CHILDREN BORN OUT OF WEDLOCK Two of every three first births to Blacks under thirty-five years of age were out of wedlock. In 1960, the number was two of every five. As many as 65 percent of never-married Black women had children, compared with 32 percent for whites.

MARRIAGE STATISTICS RELEASED The Bureau of the Census released data that revealed the following information about Black marriages in the United States:

◈ 44 percent of Black adults were married, down from 64 percent two decades earlier;

◈ Among Blacks in their early thirties, 44 percent of the men and 43 percent of women had never married, compared with 25 percent and 15 percent for white men and women, respectively;

◈ Nearly one million of America's fifty-three million married couples were interracial. In 1970, the number was 310,000. This represented an increase of 322 percent;

◈ Nearly three of every five Black children lived with only one parent — usually the mother — compared with one out of every five white children. Twelve percent of Black children lived with a grandparent, compared with 4 percent of white children and 6 percent of Hispanic children.

POVERTY RATE AMONG BLACKS REMAINS HIGH AND UNCHANGED A recent census report showed that the number of poor persons in the country in 1989 remained unchanged between 1988 and 1989: 31.7 million and 31.5 million, respectively. (The average poverty threshold for a family of four was $12,675 in 1989.) The poverty rate for Blacks was more than three times that of whites: 30.7 percent versus 10 percent, respectively. The rate for Hispanic Americans was 26.2 percent, and for Asian Americans, 14.1 percent. Even though the poverty rate for Blacks was highest, whites had the highest proportion of persons in poverty. Whites made up 65.5 percent of all persons below the poverty level; Blacks accounted for 29.5 percent; the remaining 4.6 percent was composed of other peoples.

Households headed by women constituted 73.4 percent of all Black families in poverty. White families headed by a woman, with no spouse present, had a poverty rate of 25.4 percent; the corresponding rate for Blacks was 46.5 percent.

PROPORTION OF BLACK FACULTY IN HIGHER EDUCATION REMAINS SMALL The American Council of Education reported that the number of Black faculty members in institutions of higher education had remained about the same throughout the previous decade. That is, about 4.3 percent of all college professors in 1980 were African Americans; in 1990, they represented about 4.5 percent. What was more revealing, however, was that more than half of all

Black college professors were employed at historically Black colleges and universities (HBCUs).

REPORT SHOWS THAT FINANCING DOCTORATE HAS BECOME HARDER A National Research Council report indicated that financing a doctorate had become harder than it was in the 1970s, when a considerably larger number of students received fellowships, scholarships, and traineeships. Reduction in federal financial assistance over the past decade had negatively affected the number of Black graduate students studying for both master's and doctoral degrees and was the major reason that more than 60 percent of Black and Hispanic graduate students attended graduate school part-time. Even in education, where the demand for Black doctorates was higher than ever before, graduate schools tended to finance more international students than Black students.

STATUS OF THE ALMOST-FORGOTTEN BLACK ELDERLY POPULATION The Bureau of the Census reported that the total elderly population increased by 20.5 percent to 31 million over the 1980–1988 period. Black elderly people numbered about 2.6 million, up about 21.3 percent over the same period. Black elderly people had about the same distribution in poverty as the total Black population, 30.8 percent. Marital status seemed related to poverty level. About 54 percent of elderly Black men were married, compared with 76 percent of elderly white men. About 25 percent of elderly Black women were married, compared with 41 percent of white women.

ABERNATHY DIES

The Reverend Ralph Abernathy, one of the most dedicated civil rights leaders in this century and the most appreciated assistant to Martin Luther King, Jr., died of a heart attack at the age of sixty-four. Abernathy was head of the Southern Christian Leadership Conference, and although he was condemned by King supporters for his controversial autobiography, which was not terribly kind to King, most of those familiar with the civil rights movement agreed that Abernathy had made a great difference in the quality of living for Black people.

ANNENBERG GIVES TO UNITED NEGRO COLLEGE FUND

Walter Annenberg, a wealthy publisher, donated fifty million dollars to the United Negro College Fund (UNCF). This was the largest financial gift ever given to Black colleges. Annenberg was said to have given the gift because UNCF colleges were a "major force for positive change."

ARCHBISHOP MARINO RESIGNS

Archbishop Eugene A. Marino of Atlanta, the highest-ranking Black Catholic priest in the country, resigned his position because of health problems. It was reported that Marino had been undergoing treatment for alcoholism for about twelve years.

Church officials later revealed that Marino had been involved in an intimate relationship with a former lay minister and that this had contributed to Marino's resignation.

BARNETT NAMED PRESIDENT OF UNIVERSITY OF HOUSTON

Marguerite Ross Barnett was selected to be the president of the University of Houston, one of the largest universities in the country, with more than thirty-two thousand students. Barnett, a Black political scientist, was the first woman to hold this administrative position. She had held several important administrative positions, including that of president of the University of Missouri, Kansas City.

Barnett was the first Black woman to head a major university. She remained president of the University of Houston until her death in March 1992.

BELL TAKES PROTEST LEAVE FROM HARVARD

Derrick Bell, a professor of law at the Harvard Law School, took a one-year unpaid leave of absence to protest the school's poor record in hiring women and Blacks. Bell indicated he would not return until the school hired and tenured a woman of color.

BILLINGS NAMED PASTORAL COORDINATOR

Sister Cora Billings was selected as the pastoral coordinator of St. Elizabeth's Roman Catholic Church in Richmond, Virginia, becoming the first Black nun to head a parish in the United States.

BLACKS AT HIGHER RISK FOR DEATH BY CANCER

In a new Atlas of Cancer Mortality Statistics published by the National Cancer Institute, data showed that Blacks were not only at higher risk of dying from cancer than were whites, but also that their death rates were increasing much faster. In some areas of the country, Blacks were dying of cancer twenty to one hundred times more often than whites. Studies by epidemiologists and health researchers were needed to determine causes and suggest ways to eliminate these racial disparities.

BLACK-JEWISH CENTER ESTABLISHED IN NEW ORLEANS

Dr. Samuel Du Bois Cook, president of Dillard University in New Orleans, announced that a National Center for Black-Jewish Relations would be established on the university campus. About one hundred thousand dollars had already been given toward a goal of ten million dollars to improve the relationship between Blacks and Jews.

BLACK MAYORS ELECTED IN LARGELY WHITE CITIES

Blacks had become mayors in a number of large cities with white majorities. Previously, Blacks had been elected in cities where they constituted a majority of voters; there appeared to be a shift toward white voters backing Black voters against white candidates. Blacks were mayors in as many Black majority cities as white majority ones.

BLACK MUSIC INDUSTRY CONTROLLED MORE AND MORE BY BLACKS

As of this year, a record number of African Americans controlled most, if not all, of the day-to-day decisions of the popular music industry. On July 14, Ernie Singleton was selected as president of MCA Records' Black music division. This large company signed Bobby Brown, Havy D. & the Boyz, Gladys Knight, and Patti LaBelle to their record label. Jheryl Busby, president of Motown Records Company, was another influential Black in the music industry. Others included Sylvia Rhone, president of Atco EastWest Records, and Ed Eckstine, president of Mercury Records. Each of these African Americans influenced the direction of Black music in this country and abroad.

BLACK NAMED CEO OF NONMINORITY BANK

The Dime Savings Bank selected Richard Parsons to be its chief executive officer. He became the first African American to hold such a position in a large nonminority savings bank. Parsons was born in New York on April 4, 1942.

BLACKWELL RUNS FOR CONGRESS

J. Kenneth Blackwell, deputy undersecretary of the Department of Housing and Urban Development (HUD), resigned to run for Congress in Ohio. Blackwell had already served as mayor of Cincinnati, the first Black elected to this position. Blackwell, a Republican and the highest-ranking Black official at HUD, was urged to seek the position by President George Bush and Republican party officials. Despite this support, Blackwell was defeated in the Republican primary.

BLACK YOUTH ATTACKED FOR REFUSING DRUGS

David Aupont, a twelve-year-old Black male in New York, was harassed, tied up, beaten with a baseball bat, and set on fire by teenagers who could not get Aupont to smoke crack. He suffered serious second- and third-degree burns over much of his body. The thirteen-year-old who allegedly set Aupont on fire was charged with attempted murder, assault, kidnapping, and weapons possession. Aupont survived the ordeal after extensive treatment and became a hero for young people who avoided using drugs. He became a spokesperson for antidrug campaigns around the country.

BLUE BECOMES SPEAKER OF THE HOUSE

Daniel T. Blue was selected by his peers to be Speaker of the House in the North Carolina House of Representatives. Blue, a forty-one-year-old attorney, was the first Black Speaker of the House of a legislative body in the South since Reconstruction.

BOSTON'S BLACK COMMUNITY OUTRAGED BY MURDER PLOT BLAMING BLACK MAN

Leaders in Boston's Black community requested a formal apology from police, politicians, and news media for their racial insensitivity and blind willingness to accept the story of Charles Stuart, a white man who murdered his wife in a Black neighborhood and then blamed it on a Black man. The racial bias of the Boston police caused them to ignore evidence pointing to Stuart's role as the murderer.

CONGRESSIONAL BLACK CAUCUS HOLDS HEARINGS ON GOVERNMENT HARASSMENT

Michigan congressman John Conyers, Jr., indicated that he would hold hearings to explore whether Black leaders were being investigated fairly by the government. Data were revealed that Black leaders were being investigated, indicted, and convicted far more often than their white counterparts. Over the previous year, U.S. congressmen Harold E. Ford, Walter Fauntroy, and Floyd Flake, and Mayor Marion Barry had been investigated by federal authorities and indicted on charges ranging from fraud to drug use. Conyers wished to explore whether these investigations constituted harassment.

DANIELS BECOMES MAYOR OF NEW HAVEN

On January 1, John C. Daniels, a fifty-seven-year-old former member of the Connecticut state senate was sworn in as the first Black mayor of New Haven, Connecticut.

New Haven was the third largest city in Connecticut, with 130,474 residents. Blacks numbered 47,157 residents, or 36.1 percent of the total city population. In 1980, New Haven's total population was 126,109, of which Blacks made up 31.9 percent, or 40,235 residents. New Haven, like many other medium-to-large cities, had been losing white residents and manufacturing jobs. In addition, the city had experienced an increase in poverty over the past several decades — an issue that the mayor vowed would be at the top of his agenda.

DEATH PENALTY SENTENCING SHOWN TO BE RACIALLY BIASED

The General Accounting Office (GAO) reported that the death penalty was more likely to be imposed by the courts when a white person was killed than when a Black person was killed. Such findings by the congressional agency echoed what many already believed — that the courts valued "white life" more than "Black life." In its evaluation of twenty-eight studies of death sentences, the GAO found that the race of the victim was more important in deciding for the death penalty than the race of the defendant.

DIXON ELECTED MAYOR OF WASHINGTON, D.C.

Sharon Pratt Dixon, an attorney and former utility executive, won the Washington, D.C., mayoral race by an 85 percent landslide. The first Black woman to govern Washington, D.C., she promised to "clean house." Former mayor Marion Barry was defeated in a race for a city council seat.

Dixon selected Vernon Jordan, an attorney and former Urban League president, to chair her transition team.

DOCTORATES AWARDED TO BLACKS

Although African Americans accounted for more than 12 percent of the national population in this year, they were awarded less than 3 percent of the doctorates given out by U.S. universities. The proportion was particularly low for Black men; the total number of doctorates awarded to them was 44 percent less than the number awarded in 1977. Over the same period, the number of doctorates awarded to other minority groups had grown substantially. For example, the number of doctoral degrees awarded to international students had soared by 70 percent. These students received 21 percent of the doctorates awarded by American universities in this year; less than 1 percent were awarded to African American men.

BLACK DOCTORATES ABSENT IN SELECTED FIELDS OF STUDY

In this year, American universities awarded doctorates to international students in a wide range of fields, but these same universities were not attracting Black doctoral students. For example, the 1990 data show that the following fields did not produce a single Black doctorate:

Acoustics
Algebra
Astronomy
Bacteriology
Biology, Molecular
Biophysics
Chemistry, Agricultural and Food
Chemistry, Analytical
Ecology
Engineering, Civil
Engineering, Industrial
Engineering, Nuclear
Engineering, Petroleum
Engineering, Systems
Engineering Mechanics
Geology
Geophysics and Seismology
Materials Science
Mathematics, Applied
Mathematics, General
Microbiology
Neuroscience
Number Theory
Oceanography
Operations Research
Optics
Physics, Atomic
Physics, Molecular
Physics, Nuclear
Topography

EVERS MURDER CASE REOPENED

The murder case of Medgar Evers, a civil rights leader, was reopened. No one had been convicted of the killing of Evers, whose murder had remained unsolved since 1963. Byron De La Beckwith, a white supremacist who had been tried twice for the crime, was expected to face a third murder trial.

FLAKE INDICTED

U.S. Representative Floyd Flake of New York was indicted on charges of misappropriating $75,200 from a federally subsidized housing complex built by his church. Flake was also charged with evading taxes on $66,700 of church money spent for his personal use. Flake, pastor of one of the largest Black churches in the city, denied the charges and was subsequently cleared of wrongdoing.

FLORIDA ATLANTIC UNIVERSITY OFFERS FREE TUITION

Florida Atlantic University (FAU) in Boca Raton announced that it would offer free tuition in the fall to every Black freshman who met admission standards. This policy was part of a dramatic affirmative action plan to increase the number of Black students at the university. FAU was the only school among the nine public state universities to offer such a program. According to forecasts, the school, one of the most progressive in the state university system, could expect the size of the next freshman class to increase by at least 50 percent.

FAU had made history several years earlier, when the faculty hired Dr. Adam Herbert, a Black political scientist, to run the predominantly white university. Herbert has since resigned and is now chancellor of the University of North Florida.

FRANKS ELECTED TO CONGRESS

Gary Franks of Connecticut became the first Black Republican to win a House seat in fifty years. Franks, a graduate of Yale University, was president of a realty company in Waterbury, Connecticut, prior to his election to Congress.

HARPER ELECTED PRESIDENT OF NEW YORK BAR ASSOCIATION

Conrad Harper was elected president of the New York City Bar Association. He became the first Black person to preside over this association. The 120-year-old association was one of the most prestigious legal organizations in the country.

HENDERSON STEALS RECORD NUMBER OF BASES

Rickey Henderson broke Lou Brock's base-stealing record. Henderson, who played for the Oakland Athletics, stole his 939th base in a game against the New York Yankees.

HUNTER BECOMES GENERAL COUNSEL FOR LABOR RELATIONS BOARD

Jerry Hunter was confirmed by the U.S. Senate to be the general counsel of the National Labor Relations Board. He was the first Black to serve in this position. Hunter became responsible for investigating charges of unfair labor practices in this powerful position. He made the final decisions regarding the disposition of all charges.

IDAHO TO CELEBRATE KING'S BIRTHDAY

Supporters finally pushed a bill through the Idaho legislature to officially recognize the birthday of Dr. Martin Luther King, Jr., as a holiday. The bill, signed by Governor Cecil Andrus, identified the third Monday in January as Martin Luther King, Jr.–Idaho Human Rights Day. Supporters of the holiday mentioned that it was necessary to add the words *Idaho Human Rights Day* in order to secure the necessary votes for passage. Civil rights leaders were especially pleased with the outcome, which recognized the importance of King's role in changing civil rights conditions in this country and the world. Three states still had not passed legislation making King's birthday a state holiday — Arizona, Montana, and New Hampshire.

JEFFERSON ELECTED TO CONGRESS

Democrat William Jefferson was elected to the U.S. House of Representatives from Louisiana, replacing Congresswoman Lindsay Boggs. Jefferson's wife, Andrea, was serving in her first year as vice chancellor of Southern University in New Orleans.

JORDAN ELECTED TO WOMEN'S HALL OF FAME

Barbara Jordan, the first Black woman elected to the U.S. House of Representatives from Texas and from the South, was elected to the National Women's Hall of Fame. Jordan, then a professor at the University of Texas, drew admiration when she eloquently presented her views during the House Judiciary Committee's Watergate hearings. The induction ceremony, scheduled for August 26 in Seneca Falls, New York, coincided with the seventieth anniversary of the ratification of the Nineteenth Amendment, which gave women the right to vote.

MAYOR USRY INDICTED

James Usry, mayor of Atlantic City, New Jersey, was indicted along with three others on charges of bribery and corruption associated with the gaming resort. Usry was the first Black mayor of Atlantic City and the president of the National Conference of Black Mayors. Usry pleaded not guilty to all charges and decided to run for reelection. He was opposed by white city councilor James Whelan in the run-off.

PRESIDENT BUSH HONORS JACKSON

Michael Jackson was invited to the White House to receive the honor of Entertainer of the Decade from President Bush for Jackson's enduring success in the music industry. Jackson was named Male Vocalist of the Year in 1971. His numerous hits included the singles "Beat It," "Billie Jean," and "Bad," and the albums *Off the Wall, Thriller, Bad,* and *Dangerous.* He received the ABAA Music Award for efforts to help African famine victims. He published his autobiography, *Moonwalk,* in 1989. Jackson signed a record-setting contract with Sony Music in 1991.

PRESIDENT BUSH NAMES NEW CIVIL RIGHTS COMMISSION HEAD

President George Bush selected Arthur Fletcher to head the Civil Rights Commission. The appointment of this Black Republican, who had served in federal positions under Presidents Nixon, Ford, and Reagan, was viewed by civil rights and other Black leaders as a departure from the hostile and disruptive policies of the Reagan administration.

R. J. REYNOLDS TOBACCO COMPANY PULLS CIGARETTE BRAND

Louis Sullivan, secretary of the Department of Health and Human Services, asked the R. J. Reynolds Tobacco Company to withdraw Uptown, a new brand of cigarette targeted to Black smokers. Sullivan's request was unprecedented but received favorably by the large tobacco company. Reynolds canceled all plans to market the brand to Blacks. The relatively high smoking rate among Blacks was known to have correspondingly adverse consequences on their general health, as well as elevating rates of lung cancer, heart disease, strokes, and other diseases among the Black population.

SHAW NAMED FLORIDA CHIEF JUSTICE

Justice Leander Jay Shaw, Jr., was appointed chief justice of the Florida Supreme Court, becoming the first

Black to attain this position in the state. Shaw had been a member of the court since January 1983.

SUPREME COURT CHARGES KANSAS CITY SCHOOL BOARDS WITH SEGREGATION

In the most sweeping decision of the U.S. Supreme Court concerning school desegregation, the Court ruled 5–4 in *Jenkins* v. *Missouri* that judges could order school boards to increase taxes to achieve racial desegregation. In the initial case, the District Court found that the Kansas City, Missouri, School District was segregated and issued an order that detailed a desegregation remedy and the necessary financing for it through a property tax increase. The state of Missouri appealed the action of the lower court, arguing that a federal court lacks judicial power to order a tax increase.

THOMAS APPOINTED CIRCUIT COURT JUDGE

Clarence Thomas received confirmation from the U.S. Senate to become judge on the U.S. Circuit Court of Appeals for the District of Columbia. Thomas, a Yale Law School graduate, had headed the Equal Employment Opportunity Commission since 1982, before being appointed to the U.S. District Court. Thomas's opposition to quotas and affirmative action was well known, but Black leaders mounted little opposition to his confirmation.

THOMAS HEADS PENNSYLVANIA POLICE DEPARTMENT

Dorothy Thomas became the first Black woman to head the Pennsylvania Capitol Police. The department comprised 117 members, who provided security for all government buildings in Harrisburg as well as state office buildings in Philadelphia, Pittsburgh, Scranton, and other places.

TLC BEATRICE LEADS NATION'S BLACK-OWNED COMPANIES

TLC Beatrice was the largest Black-owned company in the United States, with total revenues of $8.81 billion in 1989, up from $6.79 billion in 1988. The company ranked first among the top one hundred Black-owned companies cited in a special 1990 edition of *Black Enterprise* magazine. The chief executive officer of TLC Beatrice was Reginald F. Lewis.

TOXIC WASTE SITES LOCATED WHERE MINORITIES LIVE

The nation's largest toxic landfill was located in a minority area — Emelle, Alabama. The nation's largest concentration of hazardous waste sites, however, was on Chicago's mostly Black south side.

TURNER APPOINTED SMITHSONIAN UNDERSECRETARY

Carmen Turner became the first Black undersecretary at the Smithsonian Institution. Her job was to manage the day-to-day activities of fifty-six hundred employees and a budget of about $540 million. Turner had previously been the general manager of the Washington, D.C., subway system, the first Black person to run this system.

TYLER DENIED CLEMENCY

Gary Tyler, a Black civil rights advocate who had consistently claimed his innocence in the murder of a white student in Drestrehan, Louisiana, was denied clemency by Louisiana governor Buddy Roemer. The governor rejected the State Pardon Board's recommendation of clemency, a position supported by Amnesty International and other groups. Tyler is still serving a life sentence without parole, and several groups believe that Tyler is innocent and may have been framed, just as he claims.

U.S. CAPITOL POLICE HIERARCHY IS UNDERREPRESENTED WITH MINORITIES

The U.S. Capitol Police Force comprised about 339 Black members, who were aggrieved that only one Black captain and three Black lieutenants were among the top sixty-five officers of the force. Black members contended that they did not receive fair and equal treatment in assignments and promotions and sought an end to "discrimination, cronyism, and nepotism," which had negatively affected their chances of promotion in the force.

VINCENT CROWNED MISS AMERICA

Marjorie Judith Vincent was crowned Miss America 1991. Vincent entered the pageant after being crowned Miss Illinois. She promised to concentrate on helping battered women.

WASHINGTON WINS ACADEMY AWARD

Denzel Washington won the Academy Award for best supporting actor for his performance in *Glory* — the story of the Black Fifty-fourth Massachusetts Regiment in the Civil War.

WATTS ELECTED OKLAHOMA COMMISSIONER

J. C. Watts, former University of Oklahoma football quarterback, became the first Black to hold statewide office in Oklahoma when he was elected Oklahoma corporation commissioner. In November 1994, Watts was elected as a Republican to the U.S. House of Representatives, the state's first Black Representative.

WILSON FIRED AS BOSTON SCHOOL SUPERINTENDENT

Laval Wilson, Boston's first Black school superintendent, was fired by the Boston School Committee. The committee's four Black members and one white member apparently disagreed with the decision and walked out in protest.

BROWN NAMED NEW YORK POLICE COMMISSIONER

In **JANUARY**, Dr. Lee Patrick Brown became commissioner of the New York Police Department, the nation's largest police force. Brown was the first Black to head this force. The recent racial problems in the city had put increased pressure on the commissioner.

HARRIS PROMOTED TO BRIGADIER GENERAL

In **JANUARY**, Marcelite Harris was promoted to brigadier general and commander of the 3300 Technical Training Wing at Keesler Air Force Base near Biloxi, Mississippi. Harris was the first Black woman to achieve this rank in the U.S. Air Force. She later became vice commander of Oklahoma City Air Logistics Center at Tinker Air Force Base in Oklahoma.

MAYOR BARRY ARRESTED

On **JANUARY 18**, Marion Barry, the mayor of Washington, D.C., was charged with possession of crack cocaine. Barry was arrested in a local hotel after being invited there by a woman who was part of an FBI sting operation. Barry, who had just announced his plans for reelection as mayor of the city, told the news media that he had been set up and entrapped. Barry was indicted in February on eight counts of cocaine use and possession and lying to a federal grand jury. Barry said "The whole mess is a continuation of the political lynching and excesses of the Justice Department." The court alleged that Barry had used cocaine on at least five occasions during the past two years.

On February 28, Mayor Barry pleaded not guilty in U.S. District Court to three perjury and five cocaine possession charges.

On June 19, Barry's trial began. The jurors were sequestered for the duration of the trial. On August 10, Barry was convicted of one misdemeanor count of drug possession and acquitted of another drug charge. Twelve charges remained undecided, including those concerning drug possession and perjury. Judge Thomas Jackson declares a mistrial on these twelve counts. Federal prosecutors did not seek a new trial. In October, Federal District Judge Thomas Jackson sentenced Barry to six months in prison and a year of probation for the cocaine possession conviction.

BASKETBALL HALL OF FAME WELCOMES THREE BLACK PLAYERS

In **FEBRUARY**, three former basketball greats who played for the Washington Bullets were elected to the Basketball Hall of Fame — Dave Bing, Elvin Hayes, and Earl Monroe. They were elected in their first year of eligibility and were inducted on May 15 in Springfield, Massachusetts.

Bing was NBA Rookie of the Year for the 1966–1967 season; Monroe received the award the next season. Hayes was considered one of the most consistent centers in the game. He was ranked third in most points during lifetime play, with 27,313 points, behind Wilt Chamberlain (31,419 points) and Kareem Abdul-Jabbar (38,387 points). In addition, Hayes was ranked fourth in most rebounds (16,279).

STUDENTS PROTEST IN SELMA

On **FEBRUARY 7**, high school students boycotted public schools in Selma, Alabama, and took to the streets, chanting "Soul Power" and "I Am Somebody" to protest the lack of Black representation in the leadership and administration of their schools. Selma was a majority Black school district, but its administrators and school board members were predominantly white. Students also protested the firing of Norward Roussell, the first Black school superintendent there. As many as 150 students occupied Selma High School as part of the protest. Norward Roussell was reinstated by the board of education, and the students ended their five-day sit-in at the school. When the school reopened, members of the National Guard, city police, and state troopers were present to ensure the safety of students, teachers, and administrators.

One of the positive outcomes of the student protest was an agreement that the school board would have ten voting members, five Black and five white, with the chair position alternating between races each year. This compromise brought calm to the school.

DOUGLAS DEFEATS TYSON TO WIN HEAVYWEIGHT BOXING TITLE

On **FEBRUARY 11**, James "Buster" Douglas defeated Mike Tyson in Tokyo to win the heavyweight boxing championship. Fight promoters were stunned by Tyson's defeat; many cited Tyson's lack of preparation and unwillingness to consider Douglas a serious challenger as the reasons for the fight's outcome.

BISHOP COLLEGE SITE BECOMES CAMPUS OF PAUL QUINN COLLEGE

On **FEBRUARY 23**, the Bishop College campus site was auctioned off to Comer Cottrell, president of Pro-Line Corporation. Cottrell paid $1.5 million for the site. He was later instrumental in relocating Paul Quinn College in Waco, Texas, to this Dallas site.

TENNESSEE CONGRESSMAN TRIED FOR CONSPIRACY

On **FEBRUARY 28**, Gary Humble, the assistant U.S. attorney, charged in his opening arguments at the trial of Harold E. Ford, the only Black U.S. representative from Tennessee, that Ford had created a "shell game" in which hundreds of thousands of dollars in bank loans had been funneled off to hide political payoffs. Ford was accused of conspiracy, bank fraud, and mail fraud. Ford's attorneys contended that the loans were legitimate and that Ford had already started to repay them. The case ended in a mistrial when deadlocked jurors were unable to render a decision. The charges were later dropped.

GIST WINS MISS USA PAGEANT

On **MARCH 2**, Carole Gist was crowned Miss USA, becoming the first Black American to win this beauty pageant. Gist, a twenty-year-old college student, would compete in the Miss Universe pageant to be held on April 15.

HALEY SWORN IN AS POSTAL RATE COMMISSION CHAIRPERSON

On **MARCH 20**, George Haley was sworn in as the chairperson of the U.S. Postal Rate Commission in Washington, D.C., becoming the first Black person to hold this position. Haley was the brother of Alex Haley, the author of *Roots.* Haley became responsible for contract and procurement decisions as well as hiring.

JENIFER NAMED PRESIDENT OF HOWARD UNIVERSITY

On **APRIL 1**, Howard University officials selected Dr. Franklyn Jenifer as president. He became the four-

teenth president of the university, succeeding Dr. James Cheek. Jenifer, although a native of Washington, D.C., was the former chancellor of higher education in Massachusetts. He was also the first alumnus to lead Howard University since its founding 124 years earlier. Jenifer resigned in 1994.

BLACK JOURNALISTS HALL OF FAME ESTABLISHED

On **APRIL 5**, the National Association of Black Journalists inducted seven African American journalists into its newly created Hall of Fame. These journalists, according to the association, were "pioneers of mainstream journalism." Those inducted included the following:

Dorothy Butler Gilliam, *Washington Post*
Malvin R. Goode, *ABC News*
Mal H. Johnson, Cox Broadcasting
Gordon Parks, *Life* magazine
Ted Poston, *New York Post*
Norma Quarles, Cable News Network
Carl T. Rowan, King Features Syndicate

At this ceremony, twelve Pulitzer Prize winners were honored for their contribution to excellence in journalism.

INVENTORS HALL OF FAME HONORS JULIAN AND CARVER

On **APRIL 8**, the National Inventors Hall of Fame honored two African Americans for the first time in its seventeen-year history. Percy L. Julian was honored as the inventor of drugs to cure glaucoma and methods for mass-producing cortisone. George Washington Carver was recognized for his many contributions as an agricultural and soil scientist. Julian and Carver were the only African Americans to receive this honor.

RACE RIOTING BREAKS OUT IN NEW JERSEY

On April 12, Governor James Florio called for calm after racial violence erupted in Teaneck, New Jersey, during a candlelight service for Phillip Pannell, a Black teenager who was shot by a white police officer. Although a grand jury was established to investigate the shooting, angry Blacks filled the streets to show their frustration with police brutality and the injustices of the criminal justice process. Blacks looted, burned cars, and threw stones at police and passing cars. On April 21, as many as nine hundred demonstrators marched to the Teaneck Police Headquarters to protest the fatal shooting of Pannell.

Few Blacks believed that anything would come of the grand jury investigation. The report, however, showed that Pannell was shot in the back by Officer Gary Spath. The rioting abated, but the anger and frustration within the Black community continued.

WILSON WINS PULITZER PRIZE

On **APRIL 12**, August Wilson, a successful Black playwright, won the Pulitzer Prize for drama for his new play, *The Piano Lesson*. Wilson thus became one of the few playwrights to have won two Pulitzer Prizes — the first was in 1987 for *Fences*. Wilson had also received the New York Drama Critics Award for *Fences*, *Ma Rainey's Black Bottom*, and *Joe Turner's Come and Gone*.

BLACK-OWNED BUSINESSES DECLINE

In **MAY**, *Black Enterprise* magazine reported that the nation's largest Black-owned businesses had performed sluggishly over the past year; that is, their employment fell and sales had declined. According to the magazine, Black-owned companies would face higher hurdles in the coming years as federal spending, particularly defense spending, was cut back, and affirmative action and minority programs were weakened. William Graves, the editor and publisher, said that Black businesses were "going to have to get leaner, stronger, better."

Among the one hundred largest Black-owned industrial and service companies, sales dropped by 3.8 percent, and employment fell by 10.4 percent. California still led the states with 23 of the top businesses. Michigan followed with 22; New York, with 19; Illinois, with 17; Ohio, with 13; Texas, with 11; and Maryland, with 6. Nineteen of the largest companies (two-thirds of them auto dealerships) sought bankruptcy court protection from creditors during the year. TLC Beatrice remained the top company, with $1.51 billion in revenues. TLC, which was to offer 35 percent of its stock in a public offering, withdrew the plan in December — TLC Beatrice would have become the first Black-controlled company on the New York Stock Exchange if the plan had been carried out.

SUPERINTENDENT ROUSSELL ACCEPTS SETTLEMENT

In **MAY**, Norward Roussell, the Black school superintendent in troubled Selma, Alabama, accepted a settlement of $150,000 from the city's board of education following his suit against the city for ten million dollars to compensate for racial discrimination.

It was rumored that Roussell had agreed to resign his post as superintendent. Roussell's dismissal by the city's white-controlled school board had triggered major student protests earlier in the year.

VIRGINIA GOVERNMENT DISPOSES OF HOLDINGS IN COMPANIES IN BUSINESS WITH SOUTH AFRICA

In **MAY**, Governor Douglas Wilder of Virginia ordered all state agencies and institutions to divest themselves of any financial holdings in companies doing business in South Africa. The order was directed primarily at the state's pension funds administration, which had invested four hundred million to seven hundred million dollars in stock of companies that did business with South Africa.

PRISON TERMS FOR KILLERS OF BLACK YOUTH

On **JUNE 11**, two white men involved in the August 1989 killing of Yusuf Hawkins, a Black teenager, were sentenced to maximum prison terms. Two others, sentenced in May, had received sentences of thirty-two years and eight months to life in prison; another had received a sentence of five years and four months to sixteen years.

BUSH VETOES CIVIL RIGHTS BILL

On **JULY 18**, the U.S. Senate passed the Civil Rights Bill of 1990. On August 11, the U.S. House of Representatives gave its approval. But according to the Bush administration, the president would veto it because it was a "quota" bill. The president was confident that his veto would not be overridden, as the Senate could muster only sixty-five votes to do so. When the bill was sent to the White House on October 20, for the president's signature, President Bush told the news media that the legislation would lead to job quotas for women and minorities and that he was forced to veto it. On October 24, the Senate failed by one vote to overturn Bush's veto.

ROCHON SETTLES FBI HARASSMENT CHARGES

On **AUGUST 8**, Donald Rochon, a Black FBI agent who charged racial harassment by white agents, signed an agreement with the FBI to settle his three-year-old legal battle. Rochon was to receive full pay and pension benefits (expected to be about one million dollars) as part of the settlement.

Rochon charged that he had been harassed by his white colleagues while working at Chicago's FBI office. As part of the settlement, the FBI promised to investigate allegations of widespread racial discrimination and cover-ups by white supervisors. Paul R. Philips, the highest-ranking Black field agent, was selected by FBI director William Sessions to further investigate Rochon's charges.

RODGERS BECOMES CBS DIVISION PRESIDENT
On **SEPTEMBER 3**, Jonathan A. Rodgers, general manager of Chicago's WBBM-TV, was selected as president of CBS's Television Stations Division, thus becoming the highest-ranking African American in network television.

STUDY FINDS THAT THE RICH GOT RICHER AND THE POOR GOT POORER
In **OCTOBER**, a new study for the Ford Foundation and the Rural Economic Policy Program of the Aspen Institute concluded that since the late 1970s, there had been a dramatic deterioration in the earnings of working African Americans — even those with college degrees. The report clearly blamed the Reagan administration for "nothing less than economic polarization of America." The report noted the following information regarding Blacks in America:

- One in three Black workers in the United States earned poverty-level wages in 1979, but by 1987, four out of ten were making a poverty-level wage of roughly $12,000 a year for a family of four;
- The "stable middle-class Black employee" who did not need equal opportunity protection was a myth;
- The number of well-educated Black men receiving wages below the poverty line had grown faster than the number earning more than $36,000 a year;
- Between 1979 and 1987, the number of college-educated Black women earning more than three times the poverty level declined by ten thousand, despite a net addition to the American labor pool of 407,000 Black women with at least four years of college education;
- The number of working Black men who earned wages below the poverty line had increased by 161 percent;
- Reasons for the increased suffering of Blacks included the devastation of much of the nation's manufacturing sector during the early 1980s, which hit Black men especially hard; the drastic increase in entrance requirements for the high-tech armed forces, resulting in a large decline in the number and percentage of Black recruits; cut-

backs in government jobs; and a series of administrative and U.S. Supreme Court decisions during the past decade, which made it difficult for Blacks to secure justice and redress of discrimination.

In conclusion, this study by Bennett Harrison and Lucy Gorham revealed that the deterioration in the earnings opportunities for Black Americans who worked for a living was a legacy of the politics and economics of the 1980s.

YOUNG RUNS FOR GOVERNOR IN GEORGIA
In **NOVEMBER**, Andrew Young made history as the first Black to seriously contend for the governor's office in Georgia. Although Blacks made up almost 27 percent of Georgia's population and nearly 40 percent of those registered to vote in the Democratic primary, Young's chances were doubtful. Some analysts believed that if Young could attract about 20 percent of registered white Democrats, he might be able to force a runoff. Young, however, was unsuccessful in the primary election.

BLACKS BOYCOTT MIAMI SCHOOLS
On **NOVEMBER 6**, Black leaders organized a boycott of Miami schools to protest the appointment of a white Hispanic American as superintendent. About 30 percent of the students boycotted classes, and as many as twenty-five hundred teachers and school-bus drivers honored the boycott. Black leaders demanded more involvement in choosing the superintendent, to ensure that the appointee would be more aware of Black issues and problems.

COLLINS ELECTED TO CONGRESS
On **NOVEMBER 6**, Barbara-Rose Collins was elected to the U.S. Congress from Michigan. She had served as a Detroit city councilor since 1982.

Collins was born in Detroit in 1939 and graduated from Wayne State University in 1957. She served on the Detroit Human Rights Commission and was a representative in the Michigan legislature from 1975 to 1981. In Congress, she served on the Post Office and Civil Service Committee, the Public Works and Transportation Committee, and the Select Committee on Children, Youth, and Families.

DUKE RUNS FOR U.S. SENATE
On **NOVEMBER 6**, David Duke, a former Ku Klux Klan wizard, ran for the U.S. Senate against three-term senator J. Bennett Johnston in Louisiana. Duke gar-

nered 55–60 percent of the white vote in the state, amounting to 44 percent of the total votes. As expected, Duke lost heavily in New Orleans, where he received less than one-third of the votes. Whites joined with Blacks (55 percent of the voters) to send Duke the message that he did not have their support. Other Republicans also tried to distance themselves from the Duke campaign. Words used negatively by Duke throughout the campaign included *welfare, affirmative action*, and *reverse discrimination*.

FREEDOM BANK DECLARED INSOLVENT

On **NOVEMBER 9**, federal bank auditors declared the Freedom Bank in Harlem insolvent. Ironically, the Freedom Bank was one of the largest African American–owned banks in the nation, but over the past several years, it had been losing money — $4.7 million in 1988–1989, and was predicted to lose approximately two million dollars in 1990. Regulators gave the bank a short time to raise the necessary cash to offset past and potential losses, but it failed to meet the federal deadline, and closure was enacted. Many poor Black depositors were badly hurt, losing their limited savings. Civil rights leaders and members of the Congressional Black Caucus made numerous attempts to find a bank willing to assume the assets and liabilities of Freedom National Bank, but they were unsuccessful. They did succeed, however, in getting the FDIC to honor the deposits of charitable and religious organizations after it was shown that many of these organizations — along with their community programs — would suffer or be completely destroyed if their funds were lost. Millions of dollars of "social conscience" money were lost, however. Civil rights leaders questioned the manner in which decisions had been made regarding the closure of this Black-owned bank, compared with those relating to white-owned banks.

GANTT FAILS TO UNSEAT HELMS

On **NOVEMBER 6**, Harvey Gantt, two-term mayor of Charlotte, North Carolina, was unsuccessful in his bid for the U.S. Senate seat against incumbent Republican senator Jesse Helms.

Gantt's political career started when he became the first Black to enter Clemson University in South Carolina. He was later elected to the Charlotte City Council and in 1983, as mayor. He was elected again in 1985 but lost in 1987. Gantt had been a successful mayor and over the years had received support from white and Black leaders in the state to enter the race. After a

"dirty" and "racially charged" campaign, Helms won. Negative advertisements and inaccuracies presented by the well-financed Helms campaign made many whites fear what they might expect from Gantt, who was portrayed as ultra liberal and concerned only with quotas for Blacks and with affirmative action.

NORTON ELECTED TO CONGRESS

On **NOVEMBER 6**, Eleanor Holmes Norton was elected as a nonvoting delegate to the U.S. House of Representatives from the District of Columbia.

WATERS ELECTED TO CONGRESS

On **NOVEMBER 6**, Maxine Waters was elected to the U.S. Congress from California. She represented District Twenty-nine, which included the economically

Maxine Waters was elected to represent south central Los Angeles in the U.S. Congress.

depressed South Central area of Los Angeles. She had served as a California state assemblywoman since 1976.

Waters was born in St. Louis, Missouri, and graduated from California State University in Los Angeles. In Congress, she sat on the Banking, Finance, and Urban Affairs Committee and the Veterans' Affairs Committee. Waters sponsored legislation on tenant and small business protection.

NJERI WINS AMERICAN BOOK AWARD

On **NOVEMBER 17**, Itabari Njeri was presented with the American Book Award for her "outstanding contribution in American literature." She was honored for her book *Every Good-bye Ain't Gone.*

HARVARD LAW SCHOOL STUDENTS FILE DISCRIMINATION SUIT

On **NOVEMBER 20**, a group of Harvard Law School students filed a suit in Boston, charging that their school discriminated against women and minorities in the hiring of professors.

JOHNSON WINS NATIONAL BOOK AWARD

On **NOVEMBER 27**, novelist Charles Johnson was selected to receive the National Book Award for his historical novel *Middle Passage,* the story of the voyage of a freed slave. Johnson, an English professor at the University of Washington, Seattle, was the fourth Black writer to win this award and the second Black man to achieve this distinction.

ARIZONA BOYCOTTS

On **NOVEMBER 29**, the International Association of Insurance Fraud Agencies canceled its convention in Phoenix because of the state's failure to honor the birthday of Martin Luther King, Jr., as a holiday. Several days later, the National League of Cities canceled its 1991 convention in Phoenix. A League of Cities spokesperson said that the nine thousand members canceled the convention to protest the state's reluctance to honor the slain civil rights leader. On November 7, the National Football League had chosen not to hold the 1993 Super Bowl in Arizona.

1991 AID TO CITIES MAY BE TRANSFERRED TO STATES

President Bush proposed to transfer twenty-two billion dollars in aid from cities to states, allowing governors and state legislatures to decide how to distribute the funds. Mayors of the nation's cities called the policy "fraud" and saw "a heavy component of racism

and a galling amount of 1992 reelection politics" in the president's proposal. They noted that "cities are largely populated with Blacks, Hispanics, and poor whites who do not support Bush, and their leaders are generally Democrats. On the other hand, state legislatures are generally white and controlled by Republicans." Thus, the billions of dollars in the hands of governors and state legislatures would be unlikely to benefit Black residents.

BARRIERS TO PROMOTION REMAIN IN LARGE CORPORATIONS

A U.S. Labor Department survey revealed that significant barriers still blocked the promotion of minority and women employees in nine large corporations. According to the survey, released in August, the following practices continued to slow or block the promotional paths of Blacks:

> Word-of-mouth recruiting
> Lack of access to management development and training
> Failure of executives to foster advancement for minorities and women

In addition, the report showed that the college education received by Blacks was less valued by the surveyed corporations than the same education received by whites. The Labor Department noted the following factors influencing this disparity:

- ◈ Urban residence — Jobs for many college-educated Blacks were no longer located in the cities but in the suburbs, where there were fewer Blacks;
- ◈ Type of company — College educated Blacks were most likely to find jobs in the service industries, where salaries were considerably lower than in other sectors;
- ◈ Company seniority — College-educated Blacks had generally spent considerably less time with the company and less time in any single department. Thus, they had less seniority to qualify them for promotions and higher salaries.

The Labor Department said that much of the bias was "unintentional" but recognized that the listed conditions were pervasive in large corporations throughout the United States.

BLACK MEMBERS ACCEPTED IN COLONIAL COUNTRY CLUB IN TEXAS

The Colonial Country Club in Fort Worth, Texas, protected its forty-five-year-old professional tournament by accepting its first Black members. The club had been in existence for fifty-five years, and until this year, had maintained a whites-only membership. Six Black applicants were accepted for golfing and nongolfing memberships in April.

BUREAU OF THE CENSUS SUED BY CITIES
Several big cities, led by New York City, sued the Bureau of the Census to force an adjustment of the population count. The bureau's own figures showed that minorities were much more likely to be missed in the count than whites. Thus, those cities with large minority populations were suspected to have large undercounts, which affected the number of aid dollars allocated to cities.

COSTS OF BEING BLACK IN AMERICA REVEALED
A Bureau of the Census report showed that college-educated Black men earned one-third less than white men with similar educational backgrounds. Other statistics, based on an interview survey of 111,000 people in 1989 and 1990, showed that Blacks lagged behind whites in almost every economic category. The survey revealed the following:

- Black men over age twenty-five with four or more years of college earned an average of $31,380 in 1989, but white men of equal education earned an average of $41,090;
- Black women over age twenty-five with four or more years of college earned less than white women, but the disparity was considerably less — $26,730 for Blacks and $27,440 for whites;
- Among persons over age twenty-five with only four years of high school, Black men earned $20,280 versus $26,510 for white men; Black women earned $16,440 versus $16,910 for white women.

The data showed that Blacks were more likely to have four years of college in 1990 than they had been a decade earlier. Sixteen percent of Blacks between the ages of thirty-five and forty-four had completed four or more years of college, compared with only 8 percent in 1980. About 80 percent of the same age group had completed four years of high school in 1990, compared with 63 percent in 1980. Discouragingly, however, the trend was toward fewer Black men enrolling in colleges at this time — 25 percent in 1988 versus 26 percent in 1980. As many as 31 percent of Black women were likely to attend college after high school in 1988, up from 29 percent in 1980.

Many Black social scientists believed that these findings discredited the "declining significance of race" thesis. On the contrary, some believed these data supported the thesis of "an increasing significance of race" in many aspects of everyday life in America.

DAVIS AWARDED LEGION OF HONOR
Miles Davis was awarded the French Legion of Honor for his influence on jazz. Davis had been one of the most influential jazz trumpet players for several decades and had pleased audiences throughout the world. Several of his albums had received widespread acclaim — *Sketches of Spain, Miles Smiles, Kind of Blue, We Want Miles, Decoy,* and *Tutu.* Davis was awarded a Grammy for each of these albums.

DRUG ARRESTS HIGHER AMONG BLACKS
A recent study of FBI arrest statistics found that although Blacks made up about 12 percent of the population, they accounted for more than 40 percent of drug arrests in 1989. Black leaders feared that such an imbalance fed public perceptions that drug use was concentrated among minorities.

DUBUQUE, IOWA, LAUNCHES RACIAL DIVERSITY PROGRAM
Dubuque, Iowa, a town that was 98 percent white (58,000 whites and about 221 Blacks), launched an experiment to attract Blacks, Asian Americans, and Hispanic Americans.

Three years earlier, two teenagers had burned a Black family's garage in the city. Well-meaning citizens began a program to purge racism from their community by learning how to live in a diverse society. The program called for local employers to connect with minority job applicants living elsewhere. It was initially proposed that one hundred minority families be brought to the city. A thirteen-member Council for Diversity was established to ensure cultural diversity in Dubuque. Minority employment, open housing, and educational programs were set as goals to "inoculate the young against bigotry." Karmen Hall Miller, the new executive director of the Council for Diversity, was responsible for the program. At stake was the city's economy. Several major firms that had recently located in the city had been affected by race-related boycotts, and new industries would be reluctant to move to a city boiling with racial turbulence.

Some Black leaders stated that the city's experiment was nothing but image building and had no substance. They questioned recruiting new minority workers with special favors, when no one was helping the people who were already residents. Dubuque's experiment must be given some time before it is deemed successful, or as some Blacks expect, "just another racist plan."

EXCLUSION OF BLACK PERSONS FROM JURIES UNDERMINES PUBLIC CONFIDENCE

Justice Anthony M. Kennedy wrote the majority opinion in *Edmonson* v. *Leesville Concrete Co.*, a case in which a man challenged his murder conviction because the prosecutor excluded Blacks from the jury. The exclusion of a juror on grounds of race has been illegal since 1875 and unconstitutional since 1880; challenges had caused the Supreme Court to reaffirm its unconstitutionality at least thirty times. Justice Kennedy wrote, "The opinion recognized that a prosecutor's discriminatory use of preemptory challenges harmed the excluded jurors and the community at large." Prosecutors used "peremptory challenges" — those for which no excuse had to be stated in court — to exclude Blacks from juries. In the 1985 opinion, Supreme Court justice Lewis F. Powell, Jr., wrote, "Even peremptory challenges are unacceptable if they are racially motivated." He concluded, "Selection procedures that purposely exclude Black persons from juries undermine public confidence in the fairness of our system."

FBI DISCRIMINATES IN PROMOTION

The Federal Bureau of Investigation opened negotiations with Black agents to settle a class action suit before it went to court. The 474 Black agents had submitted more than 122 equal opportunity complaints, many of them relating directly to personnel practices and procedures — particularly promotions. Thomas F. Jones, the bureau's highest-ranking Black official and an inspector who directed public affairs, indicated that Director William Sessions wanted to settle the issues.

HENDERSON NAMED NFL VICE PRESIDENT

Harold Henderson, vice president and attorney for Amtrak, was selected executive vice president for labor relations of the National Football League. He was the highest-ranking Black executive in NFL history.

HOWARD UNIVERSITY CREATES NEW PROGRAMS

Howard University president Franklyn Jenifer implemented a model to create "a new Howard" that would produce a generation of leaders to deal with Black community problems. This model included institutes for international faiths, an institute for entrepreneurial studies, a center for international affairs, and a center for urban affairs.

HYPERTENSION AMONG BLACKS LINKED TO RACISM

An article by a team of Johns Hopkins University researchers published in the *Journal of the American Medical Association* noted that the "high rate of hypertension among Blacks is attributed to the stresses of living with racism, poverty, and low educational levels — not to genes." Dr. Michael A. Klag, the lead investigator, emphasized that "we live in a race-conscious society, where darker skin color is probably a marker for exposure to psycho-social stress." Hypertension was most common among dark-skinned Blacks who lacked jobs or a high school education. Dark-skinned Blacks with higher education and income levels tended to have lower levels of hypertension. If genes were the predominant factor in determining this condition, the health problem would persist equally among both groups, regardless of economics or education.

INFANT MORTALITY RATE DOUBLE FOR BLACKS

Statistics confirmed that twice as many Black babies as white babies died within their first year.

JONES WINS GRAMMYS

Quincy Jones was awarded two Grammys, for producer of the year and for album of the year. The album was *Back on the Block*.

Jones (1933–) started his career as a trumpet player but excelled as a composer. He arranged, composed, and produced music for Billie Holiday, Count Basie, Duke Ellington, Sarah Vaughan, Frank Sinatra, Johnny Mathis, Lena Horne, George Benson, Michael Jackson, and Peggy Lee, among others. He recorded many albums and provided the background music for many of the successful records over the last couple of decades, including the two smash hits by Michael Jackson, the album *Thriller* and the single "Bad." Jones has received twenty Grammy Awards and over fifty Grammy nominations. He received the ABAA Music Award for his work to aid African famine victims, including the production of the album and video *We Are the World*. In 1986, he received the ASCAP Humanitarian Award.

KIDNEY TRANSPLANTS LESS LIKELY TO BE PERFORMED FOR BLACKS

According to a recent report by the American Society of Transplant Physicians, fewer Blacks than whites received kidney transplants or survived the procedure. In the United States, the risk of developing serious, or end-stage kidney disease was four times higher for Blacks than for whites. Statistics from the Health Care Financing Administration showed Blacks as accounting for 28 percent of patients with end-stage kidney disease in 1985.

KING BEATEN BY LOS ANGELES POLICE OFFICERS

National outrage erupted when Los Angeles police officers kicked and beat Rodney King, a Black motorist whom they had stopped for a traffic violation. A white citizen happened to capture the incident on videotape. Chief Daryl Gates of the Los Angeles Police Department was asked to resign by the police commission and Mayor Thomas Bradley. Gates refused, and because of civil service rules, he could not be forced to resign.

KLAN ACTIVITIES ATTRACT FEWER PARTICIPANTS

In Ida, Louisiana, a KKK leader berated whites for being too timid to join him in the name of bigotry. He shouted, "They don't have the guts to get off their butts and come out to a Klan rally. They sit at home and let us do the work. It's absolutely pitiful!" Only sixteen of the seventy-five people who showed up at a KKK gathering on a farm sixty miles north of Shreveport donned ceremonial robes and hoods for a ritual cross lighting.

Today, there are more than twenty-five different Klan organizations nationwide, according to Danny Welch, chief investigator for Southern Poverty Law Center's Klanwatch Project in Alabama.

MINIMUM WAGE RATES AFFECT BLACKS

Minimum hourly wage rates have changed relatively slowly over the past several decades. Businesses have supported small increases, whereas workers with few or no skills have been proponents of steeper increases. Blacks still occupy the lowest rung of the ladder in income, and many earn the minimum wage. The minimum hourly wage rates are set by the government and are based on inflation, purchasing power, and other economic indicators. The implementation of a minimum hourly wage rate has become a highly politicized decision, rather than a choice based on analyses of economic statistics.

NAACP SEEKS "FAIR SHARE" AGREEMENT WITH ENTERTAINMENT INDUSTRY

The NAACP announced a plan to establish a national office in Hollywood to oversee the entertainment industry and to negotiate "fair share" agreements with individual networks and studios. Fair share agreements had been signed with as many as sixty-five major corporations, including McDonald's, General Motors, Pacific Bell, and Safeway. After research revealed that Blacks had made few gains in trying to enter the Hollywood power structure, the NAACP planned to have more Blacks hired in many jobs, including positions of authority.

In 1987, the NAACP signed a fair share agreement with CBS Records, after threatening a boycott.

NEGRO BURIAL GROUNDS DISCOVERED IN MANHATTAN

On the southern tip of Manhattan, workers discovered Negro Burial Grounds, a cemetery dating to colonial times, while excavating a site for a new office tower. The cemetery contained the remains of at least four hundred slaves and white paupers. Archaeologists suggested that it was the most significant U.S. archaeological discovery of the century. It was the only pre-Revolutionary Black cemetery known in the United States. Analyses of the remains of children indicated that possibly 50 percent of New York City's slave population died at birth or within the first years of life.

PROFESSIONAL BLACK WOMEN FIND FEW COMPATIBLE BLACK MEN

Statistics published by the Population Reference Bureau revealed that Black women faced a dwindling pool of compatible Black men. Although Black women had made substantial professional and economic progress, Black men had not kept pace; thus, Black women saw their chances of meeting and marrying a Black professional man as growing increasingly slim. The statistics revealed the following details:

◈ The number of Black men enrolled in college in the past ten years had decreased by 5 percent and continued to fall, whereas Black women's enrollment had grown by 7 percent;

◈ Only 13 percent of Black men in the labor force held professional and managerial jobs, compared with 19 percent of Black women;

◈ One in four Black men between the ages of twenty and twenty-nine was on parole, on probation, or in jail;

◈ Seven out of ten interracial marriages in 1990 were between Black men and white women;

◈ Even if all Black men were eligible bachelors, there wouldn't be enough to go around — for every one hundred Black women between the ages of twenty and forty-nine, there were eighty-nine Black men;

◈ More than half of all Black women between twenty-five and twenty-nine years of age, and 35 percent of those age thirty to thirty-four, had never married — more than twice the rate for white women. In addition, about 17 percent of Black women remained unmarried at age forty, compared with only 7 percent in 1970.

RESEARCH ASSISTANTSHIPS FOR DOCTORAL STUDENTS GIVEN MORE OFTEN TO INTERNATIONAL STUDENTS THAN TO MINORITY STUDENTS

According to a Summary Report, the funding for doctoral research assistants had changed dramatically over the past decade or so; about 70 percent of funding for doctoral education derived from federally subsidized research assistantships. Research faculty were granting these subsidized awards more frequently to international students than to minority students.

In fact, the 1990 data showed that of the ninety-five hundred noncitizens who received doctorates in the United States, fully 70 percent of them incurred no debt in completing their degrees, whereas 70 percent of all Black Americans and 33 percent of Hispanic Americans who received their doctorates incurred debts of more than ten thousand dollars. An analysis of these same variables for this year showed that Blacks and Hispanic Americans were less favored as recipients of federally funded doctoral assistantships. That is, the gap between minority and international doctoral awardees had widened.

Johns Hopkins University was a case in point. According to data on doctorates awarded by American universities to African American students and international students, Johns Hopkins led all other universities in the receipt of federal research funding; about 27 percent of its doctoral degrees were awarded to international students, whereas only 1 percent of these

degrees went to African Americans. The disparity was particularly disconcerting because of Johns Hopkins University's location in Maryland, where fully one-quarter of the population was African American.

RIBBS ENTERS INDY 500

Willy T. Ribbs became the first Black to make the Indianapolis 500 lineup, but did not finish the race because of car trouble. Ribbs also qualified for the Indy 500 in 1993.

SUPREME COURT RULES THAT SCHOOL MAY REMAIN SEGREGATED IF SYSTEM MADE "GOOD FAITH" EFFORT

The U.S. Supreme Court ruled that a formerly legally segregated school system that had made a "good faith" effort to comply with court orders to desegregate could be freed from the Court's orders even if some of its schools remained racially segregated. Chief Justice William Rehnquist wrote the majority opinion: "From the very first, federal supervision of local school systems was intended as a temporary measure to remedy past discrimination." Justice Thurgood Marshall dissented, on the grounds that the survival of racially identifiable schools in places with a history of state-imposed segregation "perpetuates the message of racial inferiority associated with segregation. Therefore such schools must be eliminated wherever feasible."

TWO SOCIETIES EXIST WITHIN BLACK AMERICA

According to a recent study by the Population Reference Bureau — a private, nonprofit research organization based in Washington, D.C. — two distinct societies were emerging in Black America, one affluent and middle class, the other poor. As they both continued to grow, they were moving farther and farther apart. Of the thirty million Blacks in the country, fully 31 percent had incomes below the poverty level of twelve thousand dollars a year, but they were increasingly concentrated in high-poverty areas. Over the past decade, this population had increased by 19 percent, whereas the nation's Black population as a whole grew by 13 percent. In contrast, the number of Black families with incomes of fifty thousand dollars or more had doubled. Whereas one in seventeen Black families was middle class in 1967, the ratio in 1989 was one in seven. Growth in the middle class might be slower in the future because many spending programs, affirmative action programs, and civil rights gains made in the 1960s had been dismantled by the

Reagan and Bush administrations. The urban poor, sometimes referred to as the underclass, might see few ladders out of their predicament as unemployment, welfare, and crime continue to affect their well-being.

PRESIDENT'S BOARD OF ADVISERS ON HBCUs INAUGURATED

In **JANUARY**, the inaugural meeting of the President's Board of Advisers on Historically Black Colleges and Universities was held in Washington, D.C. President Bush created the board when he signed Executive Order 12677 to advise him and the secretary of education on how to strengthen Black colleges and universities. The board was composed of HBCU representatives, corporate foundations, community groups, and secondary education representatives. At their meeting, they declared that HBCUs were a "unique, critical, and essential component in the educational infrastructure" that had to be supported. The board agreed that there had to be an institutionalized mechanism of funding to ensure that these institutions continued to meet national educational goals. James E. Cheek, president emeritus of Howard University, was the chairperson of the board of advisers. In his opening remarks, Dr. Cheek noted, "Much of the language that defined the shape and direction of the American civil rights movement focused on the moral and social implications to come to the aid of disadvantaged Americans. But America's commitment to strengthening her historically Black colleges and universities is not a social or moral consideration, but a matter of national security and an economic imperative."

BURRIS BECOMES ATTORNEY GENERAL OF ILLINOIS

Roland W. Burris of Chicago was sworn in on **JANUARY 14** as the thirty-ninth attorney general of the state of Illinois, becoming the first Black Democratic attorney general of any state government in the nation. In his oath, Burris pledged to "become for the people of this state a shield of justice and righteousness, a shield which will not be moved by considerations of race, religion, national origin, gender or political affiliation." Burris was given the oath of office by Illinois Supreme Court justice Charles Freeman, who in the same November election became the first African American member of the state's highest court. Burris became the highest-ranking Democrat in Illinois government. He was not new to politics,

for he had been vice chair of the Democratic National Committee from 1985 through 1989 — a position giving him access to many of the most powerful Democrats in the country.

TUBERCULOSIS AMONG BLACKS DISPROPORTIONATELY HIGH

According to a study published in the **FEBRUARY** issue of the *New England Journal of Medicine,* Blacks in 165 racially integrated nursing homes in Arkansas were twice as likely as whites to be infected when exposed to mycobacterium tuberculosis. The high rate of tuberculosis among Blacks that had long been blamed on crowding and poverty could, they said, be due in part to a greater innate susceptibility to tuberculosis infection. According to the authors of this study, "certain cells appear to present a more penetrable first-line defense against tuberculosis infection in Blacks than in whites."

BLACKS LESS LIKELY TO USE DRUGS THAN WHITES

On **FEBRUARY 25**, a national drug survey conducted by the University of Michigan's Institute of Social Research found that Blacks were less likely than whites to use cocaine, marijuana, and other illicit drugs; to smoke cigarettes every day; and to engage in "binge" drinking of alcohol.

STEELE WINS BOOK AWARD

On **FEBRUARY 28**, Shelby Steele, a San Jose State University professor, was awarded the National Book Critics Circle Award for his controversial book on affirmative action and race relations in the United States, *The Content of Our Character,* which had become an immediate best-seller. It also won the 1992 National Book Award.

GOLDBERG WINS ACADEMY AWARD

In **MARCH**, Whoopi Goldberg won an Academy Award for best supporting actress in *Ghost.* Born Caryn Johnson on November 13, 1949, in New York City's Harlem ghetto, she fought drug addiction and poverty. Goldberg would later host her own late-night talk show, *Whoopi Plus One,* and star in more successful movies, including *Sister Act.*

WILLIAMS WINS ACADEMY AWARD

In **MARCH**, Russell Williams III was honored with an Academy Award for best sound editing for the film *Dances with Wolves.* Williams also received the award the past year for his sound editing in *Glory*. Williams was the first African American to win consecutive Oscars. This year was also the first one in which two African Americans received Oscars.

New Jack City PREMIERES

On **MARCH 8**, Mario Van Peebles, actor and director, premiered his film *New Jack City*. The movie was about the violence surrounding drugs and a drug lord, played by actor Wesley Snipes. The movie was produced by George Jackson and Doug McHenry, both African Americans. Its success suffered somewhat because violence among some moviegoers kept others from seeing the film.

CLEVER ELECTED MAYOR OF KANSAS CITY

On **MARCH 26**, the Reverend Emmanuel Clever was elected mayor of Kansas City, Missouri, becoming the first African American mayor of this large American city.

BALTIMORE ORIOLES EMPLOYS BLACK ASSISTANT GENERAL MANAGER

On **JUNE 4**, the Baltimore Orioles named Frank Robinson as assistant general manager of the Baltimore Orioles. Robinson was an outstanding player, and later manager, for the Baltimore Orioles. When Robinson was fired as manager of the Orioles, he was quickly named assistant general manager — some said to "quell the flap over his firing." Today, there are two other Black assistant general managers, Elaine Weddington (Boston Red Sox) and Bob Watson (Houston Astros).

WEBB ELECTED MAYOR OF DENVER

On **JUNE 18**, Wellington Webb, the city auditor, was elected mayor of Denver, Colorado, becoming the first African American to hold this position. Denver's population was about 12.8 percent Black.

THOMAS NOMINATED TO SUPREME COURT

On **JULY 1**, President Bush nominated Clarence Thomas, former chairperson of the Equal Employment Opportunity Commission (EEOC) and judge of the U.S. Court of Appeals, as associate justice of the U.S. Supreme Court. Thomas would replace Justice Thurgood Marshall, the first African American to sit on the U.S. Supreme Court. Thomas's confirmation hearings by the U.S. Senate ended in a drama that both enthralled and divided the nation, when he was accused by a former employee, law professor Anita

In 1991, Clarence Thomas became a member of the U.S. Supreme Court. Despite his conservative philosophy, several polls taken after his confirmation showed that the majority of African Americans supported him.

Hill, of sexual harassment during his term at the EEOC. Thomas, a conservative, was nevertheless confirmed by the U.S. Senate, 54–48. He replaced one of the most liberal justices on the U.S. Supreme Court and one who dedicated a most distinguished legal career to putting in place many of the processes and institutions that Thomas himself did not support — affirmative action, for example. It is ironic that Thomas had himself benefitted from afirmative action programs.

NATIONAL CIVIL RIGHTS MUSEUM OPENS

On **JULY 4**, the National Civil Rights Museum opened at the Lorraine Motel in Memphis, Tennessee, the site of the assassination of civil rights leader Martin Luther King, Jr.

Boyz N the Hood PROVOKES VIOLENT REACTION

On **JULY 12**, John Singleton's *Boyz N the Hood* premiered. Written and directed by Singleton, the film was a vivid exposé of gang violence in South Central Los Angeles. Its premiere was marred by rioting, prompted partly because there were too few seats for those who desired to see the movie.

WALT DISNEY, INC., PROMOTES BLACK TO HIGH CORPORATE POSITION

On **JULY 25**, Walt Disney, Inc., promoted Dennis Hightower to president of Disney Consumer Products — Europe/Middle East. Hightower thus became the highest-ranking African American in the Disney multinational corporation. In his new job, Hightower took responsibility for book and magazine publishing, merchandise licensing, children's records and music, film production, and television sponsorship.

HARRIS BECOMES ASTRONAUT

On **JULY 29**, Bernard Harris, Jr., qualified as an astronaut, having completed all training necessary to join future flights into space. Harris joined the NASA space program as a clinical scientist and flight surgeon.

MEMORIAL FOR BLACK UNION SOLDIERS PROPOSED

On **AUGUST 8**, Mayor Sharon Pratt Dixon of Washington, D.C., announced plans for a memorial for the 185,000 African Americans who fought with the Union army in the Civil War. The memorial was to include seventy granite slabs engraved with soldiers' names. The memorial, to be financed by the District of Columbia, the National Park Service, and private contributions, would be built in the U Street corridor, long the center of Black social and commercial life in Washington, D.C.

DETROIT'S ALL-MALE SCHOOLS VIOLATE EQUAL ACCESS

On **AUGUST 16**, a federal judge in Detroit ruled that Detroit public schools had to admit girls into three planned all-male academies because the separate schools would violate the right to equal education. The decision was being evaluated in a large number of cities where plans had been implemented to create all-male classes for Black youngsters as one means of enhancing self-esteem among Black males. To avoid the issue raised by the federal court, some schools planned to open all-girl classes with appropriate role models and curricula directed at "character building."

BLACK AND JEWISH VIOLENCE CONTINUES

On **AUGUST 22**, Black youths hurled rocks and bottles and scuffled with police in the Crown Heights section of Brooklyn. This was the third day of violence that was souring the relationships between Blacks and Jews, between Mayor David Dinkins and Blacks, and between Jews and Mayor Dinkins. Although Mayor Dinkins had tried to calm the violence earlier, he was ignored by Black youths, who had set out to avenge the death in a traffic accident of seven-year-old Gavin Cato, who was struck and killed by a car driven by a Hasidic Jew. Blacks had already retaliated by stabbing to death Yankel Rosenbaum, a visiting Australian Hasidic student.

The violence was exacerbated by a rumor that a private Hasidic ambulance had carried off three Hasidic men but had ignored the Black child and his severely injured cousin. Although more than two hundred Blacks had attended a meeting to hear Mayor Dinkins's response, the crowd did not let him talk. On the second night of violence, as many as seventeen were arrested. Hasidic leaders were quick to denounce Mayor Dinkins's handling of the entire situation. A grand jury was to be called to investigate the automobile crash that killed the Black child, and Lemerick Nelson, Jr., a sixteen-year-old Black youth, was arraigned on charges of second-degree murder in the stabbing of Rosenbaum.

EMMY AWARDS GO TO ELEVEN AFRICAN AMERICANS

On **AUGUST 25**, eleven Emmy Awards were presented to Blacks, the largest number ever given to African Americans at one ceremony. Included among those cited for their contributions were Thomas Carter, director, and Debbie Allen, choreographer. James Earl Jones won two Emmys for his roles in *Gabriel's Fire* and *Heatwave*, a television movie. He became only the second African American to win two awards in one year (Cicely Tyson did so in 1974 for her role in *The Autobiography of Miss Jane Pittman*). Other actors honored included Lynn Whitfield, Ruby Dee, and Madge Sinclair.

GASTON EXECUTED

On **SEPTEMBER 6**, Donald Gaston was put to death in Columbia, South Carolina, for the 1982 murder of a Black fellow inmate. Gaston was the first white person executed for killing a Black since 1944.

Gaston had already been convicted of murdering nine other people, all of them white. "That's apparently the sort of criminal record a white man needs to be executed for the murder of a Black," said David Bruck of the South Carolina office of the appellate defense. A 1989 study found that of 15,978 executions in the American colonies or the United States since 1608, only 30, one in every 533, were of whites who killed Blacks. Since 1977 (when executions were resumed), 42 of the 153 people executed had been Blacks who killed whites; none had been whites who killed Blacks. In 1944, a Kansas man was executed for killing a Black man in an attempted robbery.

SURVEY OF BLACK WOMEN'S REPRODUCTIVE HEALTH CARE

On **SEPTEMBER 11**, the National Council of Negro Women (NCNW) and the Communications Consortium Media Center (CCMC) in Washington, D.C., released findings from a survey on the attitudes of Black, Hispanic American, Asian American, and Native American women on reproductive health care issues. According to Dorothy I. Height, president and chief executive officer of the NCNW, women were "undervalued, underserved, underinsured and under the gun."

In general, the survey found that most minority women lacked basic knowledge about reproductive health care. The survey included these findings:

❖ Fifty-nine percent of minority women said they never used birth control;

❖ Among the minority women who never used birth control, 73 percent believed they did not "need" it;

❖ More than 60 percent of minority women believed they faced no risk of getting AIDS even though the Centers for Disease Control had reported that women, Blacks, and Hispanic Americans were attracting the AIDS virus at a higher rate than other groups;

❖ Seventy-three percent of all minority women believed that abortion should be a woman's personal choice;

❖ Sixty-four percent of minority women said they had health insurance.

HERENTON ELECTED MAYOR OF MEMPHIS

In **OCTOBER**, Memphis, Tennessee, elected its first Black mayor when Willie Herenton, a retired school superintendent, defeated the incumbent by 172 votes. Herenton received 122,585 votes, compared to 122,413 for Mayor Richard Hackett, in unofficial returns, according to the Shelby County Election Commission.

Herenton, fifty-one years of age, had been the first Black superintendent in Memphis history. He held this position in the state's largest school district for twelve years.

BET HOLDINGS, INC., GOES PUBLIC

On **OCTOBER 30**, Robert L. Johnson, president of BET Holdings, Inc., sold 4.2 million shares of stock of Black Entertainment Television in an initial public offering on the New York Stock Exchange. BET thus became the first African American company to be listed on the New York Stock Exchange. Twenty years earlier, in 1971, Johnsons Products had become the first Black-owned firm to be listed on a major stock exchange when it was listed on the American Exchange. Also in 1971, Daniels and Bell became the first Black brokerage on the New York Stock Exchange.

"MOST HATED JUDGE IN ALABAMA" RETIRES

In **NOVEMBER**, Judge Frank M. Johnson, Jr. (1918–), one of the most important persons in the social and civil rights movements in Alabama, retired at the age of seventy-three. As he finished active service on the U.S. Court of Appeals for the Eleventh Circuit, efforts were made to name the Montgomery courthouse in his honor.

For more than thirty-six years, Judge Frank M. Johnson heard cases on civil rights, voting rights, school desegregation, employment discrimination, and affirmative action. To the KKK, he was "the most hated man in Alabama," and to George Wallace, he was an "integrating, carpetbagging, scalawagging, baldfaced liar." To Dr. Martin Luther King, Jr., however, Judge Johnson had "given true meaning to the word justice."

◆ Johnson grew up in Winston County, in northwest Alabama, away from Alabama's Black Belt and plantations. He graduated from Alabama Law School and served in the U.S. Army, where he was awarded two Purple Hearts. When he returned from the war, he worked as a lawyer in Jasper until he was chosen U.S. attorney for northern Alabama. Two years later, at the age of thirty-seven, he was named to the Federal District Court as the youngest sitting federal judge. His appointment came one year after the U.S. Supreme Court's decision on *Brown* v. *Board of Education of Topeka*. Montgomery was also in the midst of a bus boycott sparked by Rosa Parks and led by Martin Luther King, Jr. Johnson eventually became a major player in the massive social revolution unfolding before him when he ruled that Montgomery's segregated public transportation system was, like segregated schools, unconstitutional. In 1965, he ruled that King could conduct the march from Selma to Montgomery over the objections of Governor Wallace. A number of his other decisions involving affirmative action, quotas, timetables, and goals would become central to the civil rights movement. Johnson's decisions regarding complex busing schemes in school desegregation cases confused both conservatives and liberals; he gave officials enough time to comply, but when they ignored his orders, he would step in to carry them out himself. Although he was a Republican, he was not cut from the same cloth as the conservatives of today. In fact, it was President Jimmy Carter who named Johnson to the U.S. Circuit Court of Appeals for the Eleventh District (covering Alabama, Georgia, and Florida). Judge Johnson's decisions on social issues made him the target of a number of racist groups, who in 1963 damaged the carport of his mother's Montgomery house. He had gathered names of just about every Klan member in the state, including lawyers, and although he did not bar them from his courtroom, he knew who they were.

JOHNSON RETIRES
On **NOVEMBER 7**, Magic Johnson, the star of the Los Angeles Lakers, announced his retirement from professional basketball because he had tested positive for HIV, the virus that causes AIDS. Johnson returned to play briefly for the Lakers but bowed to pressure from players who feared HIV infection and retired again in November 1992. In March 1994, Johnson was named head coach of the Los Angeles Lakers.

SETTLEMENT WILL INCREASE BLACK JUDGESHIPS
On **NOVEMBER 7**, a Federal district judge approved a settlement that would increase the number of Black judges in Arkansas. Judge Henry Woods approved ten new judicial seats in predominantly Black subdistricts that were carved from five of the state's twenty-four judicial districts. All twenty-four districts were now predominantly white, and judges were elected at large within each. Although white incumbents in the new Black subdistricts could serve for up to four more years as special judges, the number of Black judges was expected to increase.

The decision stemmed from a lawsuit in 1989, which stated that Arkansas officials had historically drawn judicial lines to dilute Black voting strength and that plaintiffs wished to petition for small districts that would allow for representation of Black residents. The first Black elected to an Arkansas judicial post in modern times was Joyce Williams Warren. She ran unopposed for the juvenile court judgeship in Pulaski. Judge Woods would retain jurisdiction over future changes in the judicial districts. In each of the districts, elections would be held in 1992, except for the district that had just elected Judge Warren. There was no residency requirement for the subdistricts; a candidate living in a predominantly white subdistrict could run for a seat in a predominantly Black subdistrict or for an at-large seat. The suit was filed on July 27, 1989, on behalf of Eugene Hunt, a Pine Bluff lawyer. The suit contended that twenty-three of the seventy-five counties had judicial districts that diluted Black voting strength.

JORDAN IS SPORTSMAN OF THE YEAR
On **DECEMBER 18**, *Sports Illustrated* selected Michael Jordan, the sensational guard of the Chicago Bulls, as the 1991 Sportsman of the Year. The magazine cited Jordan for leading his team to its first-ever NBA championship. His likeness appeared on the December 23 issue of *Sports Illustrated* in the form of a full-color holographic stereogram.

1992 ARRINGTON CITED FOR CONTEMPT OF COURT
Mayor Richard Arrington of Birmingham, Alabama, was cited for contempt of court by U.S. District Court judge Edwin Nelson. Arrington, the first Black mayor of Birmingham, was ordered to spend weekends in prison for eighteen months for refusing a January 2 order to hand over records (appointment logs for the 1986–1991 period) to a grand jury investigating city hall. Arrington accused prosecutors and the U.S. attorney of unfairly targeting him because he was Black.

BLACK CHILDREN ARE "BEING DAMAGED IN WAYS WE DON'T EVEN KNOW ABOUT YET"
George Buntin, executive director of the Baltimore branch of the NAACP, stated that "Our children are being damaged in ways we don't even know about yet. In my community, I see more helicopters flying around with searchlights than I ever saw in Vietnam." Close to half of all inner-city children personally knew of someone who had been murdered before the children had reached age eighteen — a traumatic

experience for them; its cumulative impact will not be known for some time.

Buntin was not alone in believing that the violence engulfing the Black community would be damaging its overall health for many years and decades to come. In Baltimore, almost 89 percent of all homicide and shooting victims were Black; three-quarters of these cases involved a Black suspect. These high levels of violence and victimization strained all resources in the Black community and their respective cities. Many crime victims did not seek medical treatment for their injuries, according to a University of Maryland study. According to Department of Health statistics, life expectancy for Blacks had decreased every year since 1984, whereas that of whites had risen steadily over the same period. Louis Sullivan, U.S. secretary of health, and other health officials and researchers blamed murder and AIDS for most of the decrease in life expectancy of Black men in particular, which had declined to 64.9 years in 1988.

BLACKS BRING HOME THE GOLD IN OLYMPIC COMPETITIONS AT BARCELONA, SPAIN

FIRST WOMAN TO WIN TWO OLYMPIC GOLD MEDALS IN MULTI-EVENTS On August 2, Jackie Joyner-Kersee became the first woman to earn two Olympic gold medals in multi-event competition, by winning the heptathlon. She had previously won a gold medal in the long-jump competition.

BLACKS SWEEP OLYMPIC LONG-JUMP COMPETITION On August 6, Carl Lewis won his third consecutive gold medal in the long-jump competition. Mike Powell, who had broken Bob Beamon's record and held the world record, came in second; Joe Greene, who placed third, provided the United States with a sweep of medals for the long jump.

BLACK ATHLETES SET RECORDS

On August 6, Kevin Young won the gold medal in the 400-meter hurdles, setting a world record of 46.78 seconds.

BLACK WOMEN TAKE GOLD IN TRACK EVENTS On August 6, Gwen Torrence won the gold medal in the 200-meter dash. On August 8, she contributed to the winning of a gold medal when she anchored the 4 x 100-meter women's relay. Evelyn Ashford, at the age of thirty-five, participated in the women's relay and won her fourth gold medal in sixteen years of Olympic competition.

BLACK MEN SET WORLD RECORD IN 4 X 100-METER RELAY Dennis Mitchell, Leroy Burrell, Mike Marsh, and Carl Lewis (as anchor) ran what many claim was the most beautifully executed men's relay yet. They ran the relay in 37.40 seconds, a new world record.

BLACK ATHLETE WINS GOLD IN 400-METER RUN Quincy Watts won the 400-meter run. Watts also won another gold medal as a participant in the 4 x 400-meter relay.

BLACKS SET RECORD IN RELAY In the 4 x 400-meter relay, Andrew Valmon, Quincy Watts, Michael Johnson, and Steve Lewis raced around the track to win the gold medal and set a new world record of 2 minutes, 55.74 seconds.

BLACKS INCREASINGLY SHUT OUT OF MILITARY

Between 1990 and 1991, the percentage of enlisted army recruits who were Black dropped from 25.2 percent to 20.3 percent. Throughout all branches of the U.S. armed forces, Black recruits dropped from 21 percent to 17 percent. Overall, Blacks made up a smaller percentage of army recruits than at any other time in at least a decade, and the downward trend was expected to continue. According to recruiters, Blacks might be physically fit, but they still could not make the score. In 1990, 17 percent of army recruits who scored in the top one-half of military entrance tests were Black. But nearly half of the new recruits who scored lowest were Black, and only about 2 percent of new recruits would come from this score range. The military was once viewed by many poor and unskilled Blacks as a way to gain skills and enter the middle class. The armed forces provided Blacks with "honorable jobs." A decade earlier, lower educational levels did not always exclude Blacks. New tougher standards, however, meant that poor Blacks who dropped out of high school or did not take algebra, geometry, or other demanding courses might find the doors of employment in the military locked.

BLACKS WANT CIVIL RIGHTS GROUPS TO HELP THEM

A recent *Detroit News* poll of 1,211 Black adults across the nation found that more than 94 percent wanted traditional civil rights groups like the NAACP to help provide jobs, assist the poor, improve education, and fight crime. The NAACP was perceived as the most powerful civil rights organization in the country, boasting twenty-two hundred chapters and as many as five hundred thousand members, but young Black professionals claimed that the group's leadership was too old and its civil rights agenda a relic of the past.

CIVIL RIGHTS COMMISSION FINDS BIAS WIDESPREAD IN MILITARY

According to *Stars and Stripes,* the U.S. armed forces newspaper, the U.S. Civil Rights Commission had found "hundreds of complaints about alleged discrimination in the U.S. military in Germany. Arthur A. Fletcher, the chairperson of the commission, made a thirteen-day visit to a number of army and air force bases and revealed that complaints included the distribution of Ku Klux Klan applications at military bases and communities.

COLE WINS GRAMMYS

Natalie Cole was awarded a number of Grammys for her much-acclaimed album *Unforgettable,* released in June 1991. Sales figures showed that the album had sold more than four million copies, her most successful to date. *Unforgettable* contained Cole's rendition of twenty-four songs made famous by her father, Nat King Cole. In the title track, their voices were mixed to create a sensational hit.

FORCED-RETURN POLICY FOR HAITIANS COMES UNDER ATTACK

For more than six months, the Bush administration had carried out its policy of picking up fleeing Haitians at sea and taking them back to their homeland without review of their pleas for asylum. The Supreme Court had voted 7–2 to reject a plea on behalf of the refugees to put the legal dispute on hold until President-elect Clinton evaluated the issue and set forth his own policy. The Court had been planning to decide whether President Bush had acted illegally in May to impose the forced-return policy on Haitians. Most observers expected the court to hear the issue in February. Lawyers for the refugees expected President Clinton, who by then would have been in office only one month, to develop a policy that would make the Supreme Court case irrelevant. Lawyers had long argued that President Bush's policy violated international law on refugee protection. Civil rights leaders called the policy "racist."

INDICATORS OF BLACK PROGRESS CONFLICTING

A recent report of the Bureau of the Census showed that Blacks had made progress in education, jobs, and family income. But when measures of progress are compared between Blacks and whites, the amount of progress becomes less clear. For example, in 1940, only 1 percent of Black persons age twenty-five years and older had four years of college or more. That figure had increased to 5 percent in 1971, and in 1991, about 12 percent of Blacks over twenty-five years of age had four years of college or more. Clearly, this showed progress. For whites, however, the comparable figures were 5 percent in 1940, 12 percent in 1971, and 22 percent in 1991. The proportion of Blacks with four years or more of college is about the same today as it was for whites in 1971 — progress had not yet led to parity for Blacks.

With regard to occupational change, Blacks had definitely moved into white-collar jobs, but so had everyone. Jobs in many blue-collar sectors had simply disappeared. And although statistics showed Blacks moving into white-collar jobs, they still lagged behind whites in proportion occupying such jobs. For example, 28 percent of whites were employed in professional managerial jobs, compared with 17 percent of Blacks, and in the technical/sales/administrative jobs, 32 percent of whites were employed, compared with 28 percent of Blacks.

Family income may reveal more about progress than the previously discussed indicators. In 1982, only about 9 percent of Blacks had incomes between $50,000 and $74,999 per year, compared with 19 percent of whites; in 1992, the number of Blacks in this category had increased to 11 percent, but the proportion of whites had increased to 21 percent. In essence, Blacks had not closed the gap in this income category. In 1982, only 2 percent of Blacks had incomes in the $75,000 to $99,999 category, as compared with 7 percent of whites. A decade later, the gap remained, as 3 percent of Blacks and 8 percent of whites had such incomes. In 1982, 1 percent of Blacks and 5 percent of whites had incomes over $100,000; in 1992, 2 percent of Blacks and 7 percent of whites had incomes in this category.

MORE THAN TWO MILLION MORE IN POVERTY IN 1991

According to a report released by the Bureau of the Census, the number of Americans living in poverty soared over the past year by 2.1 million to a total of 35.7 million. This was the second consecutive year that poverty had risen, representing the largest number of poor people since 1964, when President Lyndon Johnson declared the War on Poverty. A family of four was classified as poor if it had cash income less than $13,924 in 1991. Economists blamed the increase of 14.2 percent in poverty population on the recession, which began in July 1990; many victims were new to poverty. The census report made the following points:

◈ The poverty rate for whites rose to 11.3 percent over the past year, from 10.7 percent in 1990. The number of white married couples in the poverty population, traditionally low in number, had increased. Blacks in poverty increased from 31.9 percent in 1990 to 32.7 percent. Poverty among Hispanic Americans rose to 28.7 percent, up from 28.1 percent. For Asian Americans, the poverty rate rose to 13.8 percent, up from 12.2 percent in 1990;

◈ Over the past two years, household purchasing power declined to a total of 5.5 percent for whites, 5.3 percent of Blacks, 8.1 percent for Asian Americans, and 5.8 percent for Hispanic Americans;

◈ Poverty among children under eighteen years of age reached 21.8 percent, up from 19.6 percent in 1989 and 20.6 percent in 1990. Black children still suffered the highest rate of poverty;

◈ The South still had the nation's highest poverty rate, 16 percent; however, it was the only region without a significant increase in poverty in 1991. In seven of the ten most populous states, the poverty rate increased;

◈ The disparity between the rich and the poor widened in 1991, maintaining a long-term trend in income inequality between the "haves" and the "have-nots." The most affluent one-fifth of all households earned 46.5 percent of all household income in 1991, up from 43.5 percent in 1971 and 44.4 percent in 1981. The poorest one-fifth earned only 3.8 percent of all income over the past year, down from 4.1 percent in 1971 and 1981.

NUMBER OF MINORITY JUDGES AS INDEX OF JUDICIAL RACISM

Although there are many ways to measure judicial racism, the most common involve the absence of minority judges in the judicial system; the disparity in sentences for similar crime for Blacks and whites; differential sentences for possession of crack (drug of choice for minorities) versus possession of cocaine (drug of choice for wealthy whites); and, in general, differential sentences associated with types of offenses most frequently committed by minorities versus those committed by whites.

The first measure of judicial racism — absence of minority judges — was an area controlled by presidents. President Jimmy Carter made a major effort during his single term to redress some of the existing judicial imbalance by appointing Blacks to various benches in the judicial system. For example, in 1976, there were only two Black federal appellate judges on the bench. Carter appointed fifty-six judges to federal appellate courts, of whom nine (16 percent) were Black. During his two terms in office, President Ronald Reagan appointed a total of eighty-three judges to these courts but found only one African American suitable for the job. President George Bush had appointed thirty-two judges, of whom only one, Clarence Thomas, was African American.

POVERTY DECREASED SINCE 1960

According to data released this year, the number of Americans living in poverty dropped from 22.4 percent to 13.5 percent between 1960 and 1990. Both the Black and white populations experienced significant drops in their poverty levels. For whites, poverty dropped from 17.8 percent in 1960 to 10.7 percent in 1990. For Blacks, poverty dropped from 55.1 percent to 31.9 percent.

UNEQUAL JUSTICE FOR BLACKS CONFIRMED BY STUDIES

In a survey conducted by the UCLA Center for the Study of Urban Poverty, residents of Los Angeles County were asked how much confidence they had in the local police. They found that 52 percent of Blacks had "not much." About 13 percent of whites agreed. Two percent of Blacks, but 23 percent of whites, agreed with the first Rodney King trial verdict. A survey of African Americans taken after the Los Angeles riots following the acquittals in the Rodney King incident revealed that 84 percent believed that they did not receive fair or equal treatment in the courts. They concluded that the laws treated Blacks unequally. For example, Blacks made up 15 percent of all monthly drug users but accounted for 37 percent of drug-possession arrests; once caught, they were more likely than whites to serve time in prison.

Other research studies showed an equally clear pattern of unequal justice for Blacks. According to the *Dallas Times Herald*, murder or rape of whites in Dallas County was punished more severely than similar assaults on Blacks. Whites in California got better plea bargains than Blacks and Hispanic Americans accused of comparable crimes, according to the *San*

Jose Mercury News. A Harvard Law School professor cited statistics showing Blacks were ten times more likely than whites to be shot at by police because police in urban areas targeted minorities for searches.

RICH GOT RICHER IN 1980S

On **JANUARY 7**, the Federal Reserve Board released a report stating that the rich got richer while the middle class stagnated during the unprecedented economic boom of the past decade. According to the report, the incomes of affluent Americans rose more quickly throughout the decade than those of middle-class Americans. The disparity between the wealthiest Americans and the rest of the nation was even more evident in a comparison of net worth. Among whites, family income and net worth rose, whereas they fell among Blacks and Hispanic Americans.

KING'S BIRTHDAY CELEBRATED

On **JANUARY 16**, President George Bush celebrated the birthday of Martin Luther King, Jr., in Atlanta. Singing the civil rights anthem "We Shall Overcome," Bush, Coretta Scott King, and others demonstrated that the civil rights movement was not over. The ongoing nature of the struggle was echoed in the angry tone of the benediction delivered by the Reverend Bernice King, the slain civil right leader's daughter: "How dare we celebrate when tens of millions of Americans . . . are functionally illiterate or do not have health care. . . . How dare we celebrate when the ugly face of racism still peeks out at us. . . . How dare we celebrate in the midst of recession when nobody is even sure their job is secure."

"PAPA BEAR" NAMED TO HALL OF FAME

On **JANUARY 16**, Earl "Papa Bear" Banks, the head football coach of historically Black Morgan State University, was selected for induction in the College Football Hall of Fame. His accomplishments included putting forty players into the professional ranks.

Banks, sixty-seven years of age, was formally inducted on December 8 at a ceremony in New York. Banks joined Morgan State in 1960 and continued in his roles as coach and later as athletic director until 1987. In 1973, he gave up coaching football, having garnered impressive statistics that included finishing fourteen consecutive winning seasons, an overall record of 96–31–2, and four appearances in bowl games. Prior to his coming to Morgan State College, Banks was a line coach at Maryland State, now University of Maryland Eastern Shore.

"ENVIRONMENTAL RACISM" IS THEME OF CONFERENCE

On **JANUARY 23**, a conference on "environmental racism" provided evidence that hazardous waste was most often dumped in the nation's poor and minority neighborhoods. Proximity to the dumping of hazardous waste was clearly influenced by income and race, and example after example proved this relationship to be more than coincidental. Simple comparison of population statistics and the locations of facilities that contained or treated hazardous waste showed that minorities were far more likely to live within a mile of a hazardous-waste facility than were whites. Some researchers called this pattern "environmental racism."

PARKS SETS RECORD STRAIGHT IN *My Story*

In **FEBRUARY**, Rosa Parks, declaring that too many others had told her story, stated, "I want to set the record straight." Parks, seventy-nine years old, was on hand when Dial Press released her book, *My Story*, which explained that "it wasn't because my feet hurt and it wasn't because I was tired. The real reason of my not standing up was I felt that I had a right to be treated as any other passenger." In addition to promoting her book, Parks spoke about the Rosa & Raymond Parks Institute for Self-Development, which was headquartered in Detroit. The institute was created to motivate youths from age eleven to seventeen to reach their highest potential.

SINGLETON NOMINATED FOR TWO ACADEMY AWARDS

On **FEBRUARY 19**, John Singleton's celebrated first film, *Boyz N the Hood*, was nominated for two Academy Awards in the categories of best director and best screenplay. Singleton was the first African American film director to be nominated for an Academy Award.

HEAVYWEIGHT CHAMPION FOUND GUILTY OF RAPE

On **MARCH 26**, Mike Tyson, considered by many as one of the most gifted athletes of this decade, was sentenced to serve six years in the Indiana Youth Center, after being found guilty of raping an eighteen-year-old Miss Black America contestant. Tyson protested his innocence.

ASHE ANNOUNCES HE HAS AIDS VIRUS

On **APRIL 8**, Arthur Ashe, tennis star and civil rights advocate, announced that he had contracted AIDS from a blood transfusion he received during heart surgery. The following December, *Sports Illustrated* named Ashe Sportsman of the Year, citing him as the "Eternal example of good works, devotion to family and unwavering grace under pressure." On February 6, 1993, Ashe died of pneumonia at the age of forty-nine.

LOS ANGELES POLICE OFFICERS ACQUITTED IN BEATING OF KING

On **APRIL 29**, the four Los Angeles police officers charged with beating Rodney King in 1991 were acquitted by an all-white jury. By nightfall, rioting and looting began in South Central Los Angeles, a largely Black and Hispanic neighborhood. On May 1, President Bush ordered Marines and army troops into Los Angeles to try to restore order. When the federal troops left on May 10, fifty-two people had been killed and six hundred buildings set on fire.

JORDAN NAMED MOST VALUABLE PLAYER

On **MAY 18**, Michael Jordan was named the National Basketball Association's Most Valuable Player for the third time in his career. This was the second consecutive year in which he garnered the MVP award.

BLACKS RECEIVE DISCOURAGING HEALTH NEWS

In **JUNE**, a ten-year report on the nation's health showed that although whites had made significant progress, Blacks were faring relatively poorly. The life expectancy of Black men had decreased steadily from 1984 to 64.8 years. The infant mortality rate for Black babies — 18.6 for each one thousand live births — remained twice that for white babies. The report, called *Health, United States, 1991 and Prevention Profile*, also noted that homicide rates for Black men of ages fifteen to twenty-four had increased by 79 percent over the ten-year period and that AIDS death rates were three times higher for Black men than for white men, and nine times higher for Black women than for white women. Deaths from heart disease and strokes, however, had declined for both Blacks and whites.

SUPREME COURT RULES THAT KLAN CAN BURN CROSSES

On **JUNE 22**, the U.S. Supreme Court ruled that the Klan's burning of crosses was protected under the First Amendment, raising concern among Black civil rights leaders.

PUBLIC SCHOOL TEACHERS ARE OVERWHELMINGLY WHITE AND FEMALE

On **JULY 6**, the National Education Association (NEA) released a survey of public school teachers, which found that 86.8 percent were white, roughly the same proportion found twenty years earlier; 8 percent were Black and 3 percent Hispanic, and other minorities accounted for the remaining 2.2 percent. Three-quarters of public school teachers were women, and the percentage of male teachers was at its lowest level since the NEA first measured the female-male ratio in 1961. The NEA found it "disheartening" that elementary schools had failed to recruit male and minority teachers. They further acknowledged that "because students learn about life through both formal instruction and what they see around them, we need more male elementary teachers and more people of color at all grade levels to teach our children."

BUFFALO SOLDIER MONUMENT DEDICATED

On **JULY 25**, the U.S. Army commemorated a chapter of military history that had remained unpublicized and unacknowledged for many years: the contributions of the separate and unequal all-Black army regiments that had patrolled the harsh, uncharted West.

Four Black regiments — two infantry and two cavalry — were the first all-Black units commissioned in peacetime. They were called "buffalo soldiers" by the Native Americans against whom they fought, because of their bravery in battle. They also contributed greatly to westward migration as they guarded wagon trains, protected payrolls, and even helped to build towns throughout the West.

A twelve-foot bronze statue of a Black cavalryman pulling back the reins of his horse was erected in Fort Leavenworth, Kansas, to honor the Blacks who served their country in this way. It was fitting that General Colin L. Powell, the first Black chairman of the Joint Chiefs of Staff, addressed those attending the dedication. Powell and Commander Carlton G. Philpot, a navy historian, led the effort to establish this important monument. Philpot remarked that "one out of every five soldiers in the West was Black," and "above all else, the buffalo soldiers were patriots." Honored at the ceremony was Jones Morgan, who had joined the unit at age fifteen. He was 109 years old at the time of the ceremony.

MAJORITY OF YOUNG BLACK MEN IN TROUBLE WITH LAW

In **SEPTEMBER**, the National Center on Institutions and Alternatives (NCIA) of Alexandria, Virginia, reported that on an average day in 1991, 56 percent of Baltimore's Black men between the ages of eighteen and thirty-five were in prison, were on parole or probation, were being sought on arrest warrants, or were awaiting trial. The center blamed these high statistics on the war on drugs, stating that the war is "racially biased and its casualties are young, male and African American." The report went on to say that "African American men have been made the enemy." Critics of the NCIA report said that the statistics used in the report were strictly local or city arrest figures for 1991 — eleven thousand of the thirteen thousand people arrested for drugs were Black — whereas national estimates of drug users found only 15 percent to be Black.

CIVIL RIGHTS GROUPS IGNORED BY SENATE IN AFFIRMING FEDERAL JUDGE

On **SEPTEMBER 9**, civil rights leaders assailed the U.S. Senate for ignoring their concerns in voting to confirm Alabama assistant attorney general Edward Carnes to the Eleventh U.S. Circuit Court of Appeals. The Senate had voted 62–36 to confirm Carnes despite the efforts of civil rights groups throughout the eight-month confirmation process. The groups charged that Carnes was insensitive to African Americans and that he had defended Alabama prosecutors who excluded Blacks from trial juries that might impose the death penalty. President Bush selected Carnes to replace retiring U.S. circuit judge Frank M. Johnson, a revered supporter of civil rights since the 1960s. After the vote, Carnes refused to respond to allegations of racial bias leveled against him.

National Law Journal IMPLIES THAT EPA DISCRIMINATES

The **SEPTEMBER 21** issue of the *National Law Journal* reported that the Environmental Protection Agency (EPA) addressed problems of hazardous waste sites differently on the basis of whether the communities involved were white or minority. After examining thousands of environmental lawsuits filed by the U.S. government over the past seven years, the administrative enforcement actions by the EPA, and the agency's record in dealing with 1,777 Superfund toxic waste sites, the journal reported the following findings:

❖ Penalties under the hazardous waste laws were as much as 500 percent greater at sites in largely white communities than at sites in largely minority neighborhoods;

❖ The differences were not as dramatic for penalties involving other pollution laws, but fines for polluting still were higher by an average of 46 percent in largely white communities than in minority areas;

❖ Hazardous waste sites in largely minority areas took 20 percent longer to be placed on a national priority action list than did sites in largely white areas, and the start of Superfund cleanup efforts were generally delayed longer in minority locations;

❖ The EPA more often chose less-preferred methods of dealing with hazardous waste sites located in minority areas. The "containment" method of dealing with a hazardous waste site was used 7 percent more frequently in minority communities than in largely white communities, and the "treatment" process, which would eliminate wastes altogether, was used 22 percent more often in sites located in white communities.

Spokesperson of the journal, John Kasper, qualified the findings by stating that "certainly we would not agree that the government has a policy of racism as far as enforcing environmental laws."

BLACK CULTURAL CENTER ENDORSED BY CHANCELLOR AT UNIVERSITY OF NORTH CAROLINA

In **OCTOBER**, Chancellor Paul Hardin of the University of North Carolina at Chapel Hill endorsed a Black cultural center at the university. This endorsement was the second to be made (the first, in 1989, was never funded) and came after Black students protested and marched outside the chancellor's home. Black students requested a freestanding center to replace one in a refurbished snack bar at the student center. Although the chancellor endorsed the center, he cautioned against allowing a separate building to become a symbol of racial separation.

FUNDS RAISED FOR MONUMENT TO HONOR BLACKS OF REVOLUTIONARY WAR

In **OCTOBER**, the group raising funds to build the first national monument honoring Black soldiers of the Revolution and slaves who ran away to freedom announced that it needed $5.2 million by February 1993. The site for the monument would be between the Lincoln memorial and the Washington Monument. Of the 110 memorials in Washington, D.C., only the one to Mary McLeod Bethune was dedicated to an African American.

WILLIAMS NAMED SMALL BUSINESSPERSON OF THE YEAR

In **OCTOBER**, Ralph Williams, chief executive of ROW Sciences, a biotechnology company in Rockville, Maryland, was named by the Small Business

Administration as one of two minority small businesspersons of the year.

Williams, who started the company in the basement of his house, had successfully built a company with federal contracts of fifty million dollars. Williams had previously managed a consulting company, and served as chief of planning at the National Heart, Lung, and Blood Institute of the National Institutes of Health.

POVERTY AMONG WHITES GROWING FASTEST

On **OCTOBER 8**, the Center on Budget and Policy Priorities, a nonprofit organization, provided evidence that poverty was increasing faster among whites than among Blacks. In a report, the center noted that 51 percent of the 4.2 million people added to the ranks of the poor between 1989 and 1991 were non-Hispanic whites. Blacks and Hispanic Americans each accounted for 22 percent of the growth of poor people. The recent increases in poverty in the white segment of the population revealed a major snare in the safety net.

In 1991, a family of four with an income of $13,924 or less was considered below the poverty level. Whereas one in ten whites was poor in 1991, the poverty rates among Blacks and Hispanic Americans were still nearly triple this rate.

MORTGAGE LENDERS DISCRIMINATE AGAINST BLACKS

On **OCTOBER 27**, the Federal Reserve issued its second annual report on lending discrimination, stating that mortgage applications from Blacks and Hispanic Americans were rejected about twice as often as those from whites and Asian Americans. The findings by the Federal Reserve were based on 7.89 million loan applications submitted to 9,358 commercial banks, savings institutions, credit unions, and mortgage companies.

In 1991, lenders rejected 37.6 percent of applications for conventional mortgages from Blacks, 26.6 percent from Hispanic Americans, 15 percent from Asian Americans, and 17.3 percent from whites. In 1990, the rejection rates were 33.6 percent for Blacks, 21.4 percent for Hispanic Americans, 12.8 percent for Asian Americans, and 14.2 percent for whites. Rejection rates across population groups appeared in roughly the same proportions in 1991 as in 1990. The rejection rate for Blacks with low incomes was a staggering 48.2 percent, compared with 31.5 percent for whites, 20.2 percent for Asian Americans, and 37.1 percent for Hispanic Americans.

CINCINNATI REDS OWNER CONDEMNED FOR RACIST REMARKS

In **NOVEMBER**, Marge Schott, owner of the Cincinnati Reds, came under fire for racist remarks she was alleged to have made about Black players and employees. According to Sharon Jones, a former employee of the Oakland Athletics who brought the issue to the attention of the press and the Baseball Executive Council, Schott said, "I'd rather have a trained monkey working for me than a nigger." Hank Aaron, a senior vice president of the Atlanta Braves and baseball's home-run leader, and civil rights leaders called upon the council to oust Schott. Bill White, the National League president, made no comment on the matter. Aaron said, "This person has no business being involved in baseball or society at all with what she thinks of Blacks and Jews." The Reverend Al Sharpton, a political and social activist, sought a player boycott of Riverfront Stadium to protest Schott's racist remarks and to drive her out of baseball. Schott denied the allegations, and in a prepared statement said, "My actions as president and CEO of the Reds are an open book. They belie any charges of discrimination. I have nothing to hide."

JOHNSON PUBLISHING COMPANY CELEBRATES JUBILEE

In **NOVEMBER**, the company that publishes *Ebony* and *Jet* magazines celebrated its fiftieth anniversary.

In 1991, the company had sales of $261 million, and *Ebony*, the largest American magazine catering to Blacks, had a circulation of 1.8 million. Johnson Publishing also owned the Fashion Fair line of cosmetics, a travel agency, three radio stations, the syndicated television program *Ebony-Jet Showcase*, and *EM* magazine, a monthly men's publication. The company was started by John H. Johnson in Chicago with the publication of *Negro Digest*. Johnson, now seventy-four years old, was preparing to turn the management of the company over to his daughter, Linda Johnson Rice.

PAGE RUNS FOR PLACE ON MINNESOTA SUPREME COURT

In **NOVEMBER**, Alan Page was up for election to the Minnesota State Supreme Court. Page, an attorney, was a former Minnesota Viking football player and member of the Pro Football Hall of Fame.

BISHOP ELECTED TO CONGRESS

On **NOVEMBER 3**, Sanford Bishop became the new representative of Georgia's Second Congressional

District in the U.S. House of Representatives. Bishop, forty-five years of age, was a graduate of Morehouse College and Emory University. Bishop replaced Charles Hatcher, a white Democratic incumbent who was tainted in the House check-bouncing scandal.

Bishop came to the U.S. Congress with fourteen years of experience in the Georgia house and two years in the state senate. He was known for his effectiveness in getting results — particularly laws passed to reduce property taxes for local school districts and to create job training and employment programs for welfare recipients.

BRAUN BECOMES FIRST BLACK WOMAN IN U.S. SENATE

On **NOVEMBER 3**, voters elected Carol Mosely Braun as a Democratic senator for Illinois. Braun defeated her Republican opponent, Richard Williamson, by a ten-point margin — 55 percent to 45 percent of the

Politics in the U.S. Senate changed when Carol Moseley Braun joined what was at the time an all-white membership. The first Black woman ever to sit in the Senate, she was a symbol of Blacks' inexorable progress toward political equality.

total vote. Braun was not only the first African American woman senator but also the nation's first Black Democratic senator; she was the first Black senator since Senator Edward W. Brooke III lost his seat in 1979.

Previously, Braun, a Cook County recorder of deeds, had won an open seat held by the Democrats. She then campaigned hard, with high-profile women's support, to beat her opponent.

BROWN ELECTED TO CONGRESS

On **NOVEMBER 3**, Corrine Brown, a forty-five-year-old college professor, defeated a white Republican to capture the Third Congressional District in Florida, which encompassed fourteen counties and included Jacksonville and Orlando. Brown, a graduate of Florida A & M University, brought a wealth of experience to the U.S. House of Representatives — ten years as a member of Florida's state legislature and fifteen years as a faculty member at Florida Community College. She was one of three Blacks elected to the U.S. House of Representatives from Florida.

CLAYTON ELECTED TO CONGRESS

On **NOVEMBER 3**, Eva Clayton, a businesswoman and former Warren County commissioner, was elected to represent North Carolina's First District, which included twenty-eight counties. Clayton, the first woman to represent her state in Congress, won 68 percent of the vote against a white Republican. She was one of only two Blacks elected to Congress from North Carolina since Reconstruction. Although Clayton finished second in a seven-way primary race, she emerged the winner in the runoff election.

In 1968, she ran in the old Second Congressional District and won more than 40 percent of the vote. That same year, she helped antipoverty groups that ran daycare centers in vacant schools and churches.

CLYBURN ELECTED TO CONGRESS

On **NOVEMBER 3**, Jim Clyburn, a former human affairs commissioner, was elected to represent South Carolina's predominantly Black Sixth Congressional District, defeating a white Republican city councilor. He was the state's first Black congressman since George Washington Murray in 1897.

Clyburn, fifty-two years of age, represented a district that covered sixteen counties, including Florence and Charleston.

Clyburn was a high school teacher in Charleston after graduating from South Carolina State College in

1962. He later became director of Charleston's Neighborhood Youth Corps and New Careers projects. In 1968, he became executive director of the South Carolina Commission for Farm Workers, and in 1974, he was appointed human affairs commissioner.

FIELDS ELECTED TO CONGRESS

On **NOVEMBER 3**, Cleo Fields, thirty years of age, was the youngest person elected to the 103rd Congress. He defeated his opposition in the newly drawn Fourth Congressional District in Louisiana, representing twenty-four parishes and about 608,000 residents.

Fields was elected the nation's youngest state senator in 1987 at the age of twenty-four. He earned a law degree from Southern University while serving in the state senate. In 1990, Fields lost a bid for the Eighth District congressional seat.

HASTINGS ELECTED TO CONGRESS

On **NOVEMBER 3**, Alcee L. Hastings, a former federal judge, was elected to represent Florida's Twenty-third Congressional District in the U.S. House of Representatives. His district included parts of seven counties and the urban communities of West Palm Beach and Fort Lauderdale.

Born in Altamonte Springs, Florida, Hastings graduated from Fisk University and the Florida A & M University Law School. In 1977, Hastings was appointed a Florida circuit court judge, and in 1979, he was appointed a U.S. District Court judge — the first Black appointee in the state. He served in this capacity until he was impeached by the U.S. Congress in 1989 for bribery and perjury charges. Hastings claimed his innocence and turned his attention toward the U.S. Congress, the same body that had impeached him. Prior to his bid for the U.S. Congress, Hastings made an unsuccessful bid for the office of secretary of state of Florida.

HILLIARD ELECTED TO CONGRESS

On **NOVEMBER 3**, Earl F. Hilliard, a Birmingham attorney, was elected to the 103rd Congress to represent the Seventh Congressional District in Alabama. This district was predominantly Black and included parts of Birmingham, Tuscaloosa, Selma, and Montgomery. Hilliard became the first Black to represent the state since ex-slave Jeremiah Haralson held the office during Reconstruction. Hilliard had served almost twenty years as a state legislator.

Hilliard was a graduate of Morehouse College and held an M.B.A. from the Atlanta University School of Business and a law degree from Howard University.

As a state senator for almost four full terms, he sponsored several major bills, one on fluoride, another involving tax abatement, and a horse track bill. He was a strong advocate of educational reform, instrumental in helping low-income youth secure finances to attend local colleges.

JOHNSON ELECTED TO CONGRESS

On **NOVEMBER 3**, Eddie B. Johnson, a native of Waco, Texas, was elected to represent Texas's Thirtieth Congressional District, which encompassed part of Dallas. Johnson came to the U.S. Congress with varied experience, including roles as a state senator, businesswoman, and health-care administrator.

Johnson had joined the Texas House of Representatives almost twenty years earlier, becoming the first Black woman elected to public office in Dallas. She became the first woman to chair a major house committee during her second term. During the Carter administration, she was named regional director of the Department of Health, Education, and Welfare. In 1981, Johnson started a consulting business, but in 1986, she entered politics again by winning a decisive victory for the state senate seat. She was reelected in 1990.

McKINNEY ENTERS CONGRESS

On **NOVEMBER 3**, Cynthia Ann McKinney was elected to represent Georgia's new Eleventh Congressional District, which consisted of both rural and suburban areas outside Atlanta. McKinney had served two terms as a state legislator.

Born in Atlanta and educated at the University of Southern California, McKinney, age thirty-seven, was a professor at Agnes Scott College. Elected to the state legislature in 1988, McKinney represented the largest district in the state.

McKinney was the daughter of state representative Billy McKinney. They were the only father and daughter serving in the same legislature in the United States.

MEEK ELECTED TO CONGRESS

On **NOVEMBER 3**, Carrie Meek was elected to represent Florida's Seventeenth Congressional District, which included the northern part of Dade County. Meek was a graduate of Florida A & M University, held a master's degree in public health and physical education from the University of Michigan, and was working on a doctorate at Florida Atlantic University.

Meek won an overwhelming victory against her opponents. Meek, a great debater and a seasoned politician, had served thirteen years in the Florida legislature, where she successfully promoted causes related to women, minorities, the elderly, and the handicapped. Meek was the first Black woman elected to the Florida Senate.

REYNOLDS ELECTED TO CONGRESS

On **NOVEMBER 3**, Melvin J. Reynolds, a newcomer to politics, was elected to represent Illinois's Second Congressional District, which covered parts of Chicago's far south side and several southern suburbs. Reynolds defeated incumbent Black politician Gus Savage in the Democratic primary and encountered little opposition in the general election.

Reynolds was born in Mound Bayou, Mississippi, in 1952. He moved to Chicago in 1970 and attended Chicago city colleges and the University of Illinois. Reynolds, a Rhodes scholar, had a law degree from Oxford University in England. He had served as assistant professor at Chicago's Roosevelt University, special assistant to the vice president for academic affairs at the University of Illinois, and executive director of the Community Economic Development and Education Foundation.

RUSH ELECTED TO CONGRESS

On **NOVEMBER 3**, Bobby Rush, a former Black Panther, was elected to represent Illinois's historic First Congressional District, which had elected the nation's first Black representatives after Reconstruction — Oscar DePriest and Arthur Mitchell. Rush defeated Democrat incumbent Charles Hayes, another Black candidate, in the primary and encountered little opposition in the general election.

Born in Albany, Georgia, Rush was reared in Chicago. At the age of seventeen, Rush entered the U.S. Army, and after five years of service, he received an honorable discharge. He then cofounded the Illinois chapter of the Black Panther Party, in which he served as defense minister.

Rush received a bachelor's degree in political science form Roosevelt University in Chicago. He was elected to the Chicago City Council in 1983. He was an outspoken and effective city councilor, particularly concerned with issues related to energy and en-

vironmental protection. In March 1990, Rush was elected Democratic state central committeemember of Illinois's First Congressional District. A month later, he was appointed deputy chairperson of the Illinois Democratic Party.

SCOTT ELECTED TO CONGRESS

On **NOVEMBER 3**, Robert C. Scott, a forty-five-year-old politician and attorney, was elected to represent Virginia's Third Congressional District, which covered an area from Richmond to Portsmouth and Petersburg. He won the Democratic primary with 67 percent of the vote before going on to defeat his Republican opponent in the general election. During his campaign, Scott invoked the name of John M. Langston, Virginia's first Black congressman. Scott became the first Black Virginian in Congress since Congressman Langston was defeated in 1891.

Scott, born in 1947, graduated from Harvard University and Boston College Law School. Scott practiced law in Newport News from 1973 until 1978, when he defeated his opponent for a seat in the Virginia General Assembly. In 1982, he ran for the state senate and won, serving until his victory in the U.S. congressional campaign of November 1992.

TUCKER ELECTED TO CONGRESS

On **NOVEMBER 3**, Walter Tucker III was elected to represent California's Thirty-seventh Congressional District after having won the Democratic primary from Lynn Dymally, the daughter of Mervyn M. Dymally, the district's resigning Black representative and defeating an independent candidate in the general election.

Tucker was born and raised in Compton, California, one of the communities in his district. He was elected mayor there but held the position for only about a year until he was elected to Congress.

Tucker was an honors graduate from the University of Southern California at Los Angeles in 1978. He then earned a law degree from Georgetown Law Center in Washington, D.C. When he returned home to Los Angeles, he was appointed deputy district attorney for Los Angeles County. He later practiced criminal law.

WATT ELECTED TO CONGRESS

On **NOVEMBER 3**, Melvin Watt, a forty-seven-year-old attorney, was elected to represent North Carolina's Twelfth Congressional District. This predominantly

Black district (57 percent Black), included the urban areas of Charlotte, Greensboro, and Durham.

Watt graduated from the University of North Carolina and received his J.D. degree from Yale University Law School. In 1985, he was elected a state senator but declined to run for a second term. Watt managed Harvey Gantt's campaigns for mayor of Charlotte and for the U.S. Senate.

WYNN ELECTED TO CONGRESS

On **NOVEMBER 3**, Albert Wynn, an attorney and a ten-year veteran of the Maryland state legislature, captured more than 75 percent of the vote and defeated a Black Republican businesswoman to win the seat for Maryland's Fourth Congressional District.

Wynn had served in the state senate and the house and as the deputy majority whip; he took part in the judicial proceedings and the budget and taxation committees. As a Maryland legislative leader, Wynn worked hard to expand minority business loan programs.

Although he was born in Philadelphia, he was reared in Prince George's County. Wynn graduated from the University of Pittsburgh and received a law degree from Georgetown University. He was forty-one years old at the time of his election.

JORDAN BECOMES MEMBER OF PRESIDENT'S TRANSITION TEAM

On **NOVEMBER 7**, President-elect Bill Clinton selected former National Urban League president Vernon Jordan to serve as chairperson of the Clinton-Gore transition team. He was to work closely with Warren Christopher, the director of the team. Jordan, a Washington lawyer and former civil rights activist, assisted Christopher in selecting cabinet officers and other high-profile appointments. This was the first time that a Black person had been selected to chair a presidential transition team.

A native of Atlanta who began life in the city's public housing projects, Jordan attended all-Black schools in the segregated South and then attended DePauw University and Howard University, where he earned a law degree. He helped integrate the University of Georgia in 1961 by accompanying Charlayne Hunter into the university. In 1962, he was selected as Georgia's field secretary of the NAACP. In 1972, he succeeded Whitney Young, Jr., as the head of the National Urban League in New York City. He remained head of the National Urban League for almost

two decades before becoming a senior partner in a law firm in Washington, D.C.

KKK ALLOWED TO "ADOPT" STATE HIGHWAY

On **NOVEMBER 10**, the state of Arkansas decided not to appeal a federal judge's order to let the Ku Klux Klan adopt a one-mile section of a state highway. A U.S. district court had ruled that the state had curtailed the Klan's First Amendment rights to free expression by basing its decision on whether the Klan could adopt a highway solely on the group's political beliefs. The KKK had volunteered to clean up a section of Highway 65, but more important, a sign would be posted along this section, proclaiming the Klan's stewardship and giving free publicity to a racist institution. The Grand Knights of the KKK's tiny Arkansas chapter had sued the Arkansas Transportation Department after its initial refusal to allow the Klan to enroll in the program.

BLACK ATHLETE NAMED MOST VALUABLE PLAYER FOR SECOND TIME IN THREE YEARS

On **NOVEMBER 18**, National League all-star baseball player Barry Bonds was named the National League's Most Valuable Player for the second time in three years.

1993 "ABOLISHING THE SUBURBS" PUT FORWARD AS NEW URBAN POLICY

Perhaps the most discussed urban policy during this year had been "abolishing the suburbs," a policy introduced in *Cities Without Suburbs*, by David Rusk, former mayor of Albuquerque, New Mexico. In his book, Rusk emphasized that the basic economic unit in the nation was the metropolis: the central city and its surrounding communities. In 1950, the central cities were economically healthy, and only about 30 percent of the metropolitan residents lived outside them. By 1990, almost all metropolitan areas had grown, but most of the growth had occurred in suburban areas. In general, middle-class taxpayers had migrated from the cities to the suburbs, depriving the city of tax revenue to maintain schools and services. As this pattern solidified, the middle class (both white and Black populations) continued to flee the city, leaving behind the poor and a declining tax base.

Rusk and others believed that "if the real urban problem" was the Black and Hispanic underclass, then the right strategy was not central city development, but dispersion. He stated that if residents of South Central Los Angeles were desperate to escape the ghetto, the government should help them do so. Because the current separate suburbs would not be open to such an influx, Rusk suggested unifying suburb and city both economically and politically, to lessen racial and economic segregation. But although breaking the boundary between inner city and suburbs had obvious benefits, it would create new problems: (1) suburbanites would not want to pay higher taxes to support their poorer neighbors; (2) Blacks who had come to power in many central cities would be forced to give some power back to whites, who would outnumber and overpower them; (3) Blacks would be vulnerable to the same unequal status that existed for minorities before white flight to suburban areas.

Rusk offered the following incentive for middle-class suburbanites to accept his policy: give them extra deductions from local taxes if those taxes went to the new "consolidated" governments.

CAMPANELLA, HALL-OF-FAMER AND BASEBALL'S AMBASSADOR, DIES

Roy Campanella, the son of an Italian father and a Black mother, started his baseball career in the Negro leagues. He was twenty-six years of age and had played nine years in the Negro leagues before he signed with the majors, the Brooklyn Dodgers, in 1948. He joined Jackie Robinson, who had been called up the year before. He had already become a brilliant catcher with the Baltimore Elite Giants. It was as if he knew he had little time to prove himself — so he quickly became the winner of the National League's MVP award, three times. In 1953, he became the first catcher to hit more than forty homers in a season, and he led the league with 142 RBIs that same year.

Campanella's baseball career ended on a January night in 1958, when his automobile hit an icy patch, spun out of control, and rolled over. He suffered spinal injuries that left him paralyzed (with minimal movement of his hand) from the shoulders down. He became confined to a wheelchair. Campanella was inducted into the Baseball Hall of Fame in 1969. Doctors had given him about ten years to live, but he proved them wrong. He lived thirty-five years after the accident and was seventy-one years of age when he suffered a fatal heart attack in his Woodland Hills home in Los Angeles.

CUTTING ILLEGITIMACY COULD DRASTICALLY REDUCE WELFARE ROLLS

Statistics from the Bureau of the Census showed that during the 1982–1992 decade, the rate of illegitimate births soared from 15.8 percent to 24.2 percent. The illegitimacy rate had been about 3 percent in 1950 and 4 percent in 1960. African Americans had the highest illegitimacy rates, rising from 49 percent to 67 percent over the decade. Hispanic Americans experienced an increase in their rate, from 16 percent to 27 percent, but for whites, the rate grew from 10 percent to 17 percent, the steepest growth rate. The Congressional Research Service reported that 71 percent of the new cases in the Aid to Families with Dependent Children program between 1987 to 1991 were headed by a never-married mother.

MAJOR-LEAGUE BASEBALL LAGS BEHIND THE NBA AND NFL IN MINORITY HIRING

According to an annual report on minority participation in sports by Northeastern University's Center for the Study of Sport in Society, the hiring of minorities as coaches and front-office personnel differed among Major League Baseball (MLB), the National Basketball Association (NBA), and the National Football League (NFL). Baseball was given a grade of C in eleven areas; the NBA was awarded an A; and the NFL earned a B. The report noted that although baseball had made some improvements since 1987 — jumping from 2 percent front-office minority employment to 16 percent in 1991 — minority employment since 1991 had increased only from 16 to 17 percent. The NFL's league office employed minorities in 23 percent of its management positions, and the NBA employed 27 percent. Baseball was the only sport in which the majority of participants (67 percent) were white. Only 16 percent were Black, and another 16 percent were classified as Latin. For Blacks, this represented a decline from 24 percent in the early 1980s. Baseball had done relatively well in hiring minority coaches. At the start of this season, Dusty Baker became manager of the San Francisco Giants, and Don Baylor began to manage the Colorado Rockies. They joined Cito Gaston of Toronto and Hal McRae of Kansas City, making a total of four Black mangers among the twenty-eight in MLB. In the NFL, the Los Angeles Raiders and the Minnesota Vikings had Black head coaches — Art Shell and Dennis Green, respectively. Seven of the twenty-seven NBA teams had Black head coaches, up from two the previous season and six in the 1990–1991 season. In addition, the NBA had five teams with Black general managers and eight teams with minority vice presidents.

NATIONAL SECURITY AGENCY ACCUSED OF DISCRIMINATION

After a report revealed that the National Security Agency (NSA) lagged behind the rest of the federal government agencies in minority hiring, Senator Barbara A. Mikulski, a Democrat from Maryland, called for a probe of allegations of racial discrimination and sexual harassment against women. Vice Admiral John M. McConnell, NSA director, told the Congressional House Intelligence Committee, "It is clear to me there are imbalances in the representation of women and minorities. I am committed to identifying and eliminating the barriers, no matter how subtle, that help to perpetuate these imbalances." In addition, he indicated that the agency would redouble efforts to hire and promote women and minorities. The Pentagon inspector general was to begin an investigation of the agency in November.

NEW FORM OF SEGREGATION OCCURS AT COLLEGES

During the year, many universities across the country established residences strictly for minorities. On many campuses, university administrators allocated housing to racial groups, gays, and even female students of color, especially when these minorities were vastly outnumbered by the white majority. For example, Wesleyan University provided housing to twenty-six Black students in the Malcolm X house.

Some saw this effort as a new type of segregation. Still, Blacks at Wesleyan University defended their voluntary segregation as being a "refuge" for Black students overwhelmed on the predominantly white campus. Nonetheless, many minorities chose not to live in segregated or isolated housing. Freeman A. Hrabowski III, the Black president of the University of Maryland Baltimore County, resisted the trend, saying that the university should be teaching students "to learn how to be comfortable with people who are different than themselves."

PROJECT CONCERN'S ROLE CONTROVERSIAL IN RACIAL SEGREGATION OF HARTFORD SCHOOLS

In this year, a federal court was asked in *Sheff* v. *O'Neill* to provide educational opportunities to the poor and minority children in Hartford equal to those in neighboring towns. The suit contended that the concentration of poor and minority children in the city denied them equal educational opportunities to those in neighboring towns.

The context of this suit was a voluntary plan called Project Concern, one of the nation's earliest voluntary desegregation programs arranged between a city and its suburbs, that began more than twenty-six years ago. Project Concern was created to promote integration and to provide educational opportunities in the suburbs by busing children out of the city. Critics stated that the program never had enough students to resemble "integration," and that "one-way busing was biased in its conception." Started with state, federal, and foundation grants, the program quickly ran into financial difficulties, and according to critics, it constituted "window dressing." In 1965, when it began, a study had proposed integrating by building new middle schools across the city, but whites in the south end blocked the plan, which included a busing proposal. Instead, Project Concern began as a "two-year study" involving 266 students. It never became a large program, and the number of Project Concern students fell sharply in the 1980s as Hartford cut its support to redirect money to the children in its own schools. From its peak of serving 1,175 children in twelve grades in 1978 to 680 students today, Project Concern did not accomplish integration — in fact, Hartford schools are far more racially segregated today than ever before.

THOMAS NAMED MOST VALUABLE PLAYER

Frank Thomas, first baseman for the Chicago White Sox, was voted the Most Valuable Player in the American League by unanimous vote of the Baseball Writers Association of America.

Thomas's batting average was .317, he was second in the major leagues with 128 RBIs, and he had set a club record with forty-one homers. In addition to these impressive statistics, Thomas (only twenty-five years of age) ranked high in walks, runs, on-base percentage, and extra-base hits. Only seven other American League players had received unanimous votes, two of them African Americans — Frank Robinson (1966) and Reggie Jackson (1973).

O'LEARY CONFIRMED AS SECRETARY OF ENERGY

In **JANUARY**, Hazel O'Leary was confirmed as secretary of energy in the Clinton administration.
◆ O'Leary was born Hazel Reid on May 17, 1937, in Newport News, Virginia. After receiving a B.A. degree from Fisk University in 1959, she attended Rut-

gers University School of Law, where she was awarded a J.D. in 1966.

O'Leary was not a newcomer to the Washington, D.C., scene. She was a utilities regulator under Presidents Ford and Carter, and an effective Washington lobbyist as an executive vice president of the Northern States Power Company.

ANGELOU READS POEM AT CLINTON INAUGURATION

On **JANUARY 20**, Maya Angelou (1928–), the granddaughter of a slave, stood before thousands attending the inauguration of Bill Clinton as president of the United States and recited her poem, "On the Pulse of Morning."

Angelou was born in Stamp, Arkansas, about twenty-five miles from Hope, the birthplace of President Clinton. Angelou, a writer-historian and professor at Wake Forest University, is internationally known for her books and poetry. In a five-volume autobiography that began with *I Know Why the Caged Bird Sings*, she recounted growing up as an African American, being raped at the age of eight (which left her mute for five years), and having her only child at age sixteen. Angelou is also an accomplished actress. She played Kunta Kinte's grandmother in the television series *Roots*.

JUSTICE MARSHALL DIES

On **JANUARY 24**, Justice Thurgood Marshall, a member of the U.S. Supreme Court for twenty-four years, died. He was eighty-four years of age. Marshall dedicated his life to America's civil rights movement, human rights, and equal opportunity. He was mourned by millions of Blacks and whites whose lives had improved because of the brilliance, dedication, and raw courage of this great Black lawyer and justice. Lawrence Tribe, a constitutional scholar and professor at Harvard Law School, called Justice Marshall simply "the greatest lawyer in the twentieth century." Jesse Jackson commented, "For most of us who grew up under segregation, we have never known a day without Thurgood Marshall hovering over us to protect us." A. Leon Higginbotham, Jr., chief judge emeritus of the Third Circuit U.S. Court of Appeals, said, "For if he had not won the *Brown* v. *Board of Education* case, the door of equal opportunity would have been more tightly closed also to women, other minorities, and the poor."

◆ Thurgood Marshall was born in Baltimore to William Canfield Marshall and Normal Williams. His father was a Pullman car waiter and a steward at private clubs in Baltimore. His mother was a schoolteacher. He was initially named "Thoroughgood" by his parents, but his name was shortened to "Thurgood" during the second grade. Marshall graduated from Baltimore's Douglass High School with academic honors and attended Lincoln University in Oxford, Pennsylvania. When he graduated from Lincoln, he applied, but was denied admittance to the all-white University of Maryland Law School. He then commuted to Howard University Law School, from which he graduated in 1933. He was admitted to the Maryland bar the same year. In just two years, Marshall teamed up with two other lawyers to bring suit against the University of Maryland Law School on behalf of Donald G. Murray, a Black graduate of Amherst College who had been denied admission. They won the case. A year later, Marshall was encouraged to join the New York office of the NAACP.

As chief legal counsel for the NAACP, Marshall became one of the ablest lawyers in the country. He was responsible for ending the so-called white primary in the South in 1944 and for outlawing restrictive covenants in 1948. He argued school segregation cases in 1952 and 1953. President John F. Kennedy appointed him to the U.S. Court of Appeals for the Second Circuit in 1961. In 1965, President Lyndon Johnson appointed him solicitor general. As the government's chief advocate, Marshall secured the U.S. Supreme Court's acceptance of the Voting Rights Act of 1965. In 1967, he was nominated by President Johnson as the U.S. Supreme Court's first Black justice. Marshall expected and got a bitter fight in the Senate but was confirmed by a senate vote of 54–16. The opposition votes represented a Southern bloc that had made numerous efforts to stop Marshall's confirmation. Justice Marshall joined liberal justices William J. Brennan, Jr., William O. Douglas, and Abe Fortas. Over the years, Justice Marshall saw the makeup of the U.S. Supreme Court begin to reflect conservative Republican presidents and found himself a frequent dissenter. In 1978, he dissented in the 5–4 decision that directed the University of California at Davis to admit Allan Bakke, a white man who claimed he had been discriminated against because he was denied admission to the university's medical school while "less qualified" Blacks had been admitted. On June 27, 1991, Justice Marshall, angry, frustrated, and disillusioned by the Court, decided to retire. Some scholars stated that his retirement was prompted by his illness and his outrage by the Court's split decision in *Payne* v. *Tennessee*, a death sentence case. Justice Marshall left the Court with a powerful statement: "Power, not reason, is the new currency of this court's decision making."

BLACK MAYORS MEET AND IDENTIFY NEEDS

On **APRIL 7**, a panel of Black mayors, meeting in Baltimore as part of the tenth annual meeting of the National Forum for Black Public Administrators, identified the major challenges facing their cities as the creation of jobs and a work force skilled enough to perform them and providing help for small businesses, a major source of job growth, by providing investment capital and tax incentives and cutting governmental red tape. Mayor Sharon Pratt Kelly (formerly Dixon) of Washington, D.C., indicated that "the dysfunctional family" and "the changing economic environment" were the "linchpin challenges" she faced in her city. Baltimore Mayor Kurt Schmoke noted that jobs in the health-care field, the leading employer in the city, required a "much higher" level of literacy than industries that had earlier dominated the city's work force, putting greater demands on its educational institutions. Mayors attending the forum included James A. Sharpe, Jr., of Newark, New Jersey; Rodney Long of Gainesville, Florida; Paul H. Richards II of Lynwood, California; and James H. Sills of Wilmington, Delaware.

CHAVIS BECOMES NAACP CHIEF

On **APRIL 9**, Benjamin Chavis was selected to head the NAACP, the eighty-four-year-old civil rights organization. He was charged by the sixty-four-member board of directors to invigorate and provide new leadership to the civil rights organization.

◈ Chavis was born in Oxford, North Carolina. He received his first membership card in the NAACP after his twelfth birthday. As a child of thirteen, Chavis led his first protest when he marched into the all-white public library in Oxford to check out a book. At age fifteen, he took part in the 1963 March on Washington. At the age of forty-five, he accepted the challenge of guiding the NAACP into the next century. His goals included increasing membership, winning back 1.2 million inactive NAACP members, and recruiting Hispanic Americans and Asian Americans in order to make the organization "truly colored."

Although Chavis received the majority of the votes of the NAACP directors, many did not support him. Some did not want Chavis because of his past — he had spent more than four years in prison after being convicted in a 1971 firebombing of a white-

owned grocery store during racial unrest. Chavis and nine other civil rights activists (referred to later as the Wilmington Ten) were arrested for the incident and received sentences of twenty-nine to thirty-four years. Chavis's conviction was overturned when an appeals court ruled that the witnesses had lied.

After being paroled, Chavis taught high school chemistry, worked as a labor organizer (1969), a civil rights organizer (1967–1969), minister and director of the United Church of Christ's Commission for Racial Justice in Washington, D.C. (1972), and executive director of the Commission for Racial Justice (1985). Since 1977, when Chavis wrote *Let My People Go: Psalms from Prison*, he had received a number of awards for his service and activism in support of civil rights.

Chavis hoped to make the organization more relevant to the issues facing all people of color and to secure the civil rights of the more than thirty million Black Americans and the forty-one million other people of color in this country.

FITZGERALD CELEBRATES SEVENTY-FIFTH BIRTHDAY

On **APRIL 10**, Ella Fitzgerald celebrated her seventy-fifth birthday with the release of two new retrospective packages: *75th Birthday Celebration*, drawn from her Decca recordings, and *First Lady of Song*, a selection of her works for Verve. Fitzgerald had been dubbed the "First Lady of Song."

GUILTY VERDICTS HANDED DOWN IN KING'S BEATING

On **APRIL 17**, Police Sergeant Stacey C. Koon and Officer Laurence M. Powell were found guilty of violating Rodney King's civil rights after being tried again in federal court following their acquittal in April 1992. Officer Theodore Briseno and former officer Timothy E. Wind were cleared. The outcome of Los Angeles' most infamous police beating of a Black man was finally resolved.

Only a year earlier, the city had rioted when the four defendants were acquitted by an all-white jury, and the disturbances left fifty-three dead and almost one billion dollars in property damage. Los Angeles and the nation sighed with relief as the verdict caused no recurrence of violence, and the city remained peaceful.

BLACK-OWNED BUSINESSES OUTDOING OTHER COMPANIES

In **MAY**, *Black Enterprise* magazine reported that large Black-owned businesses had outperformed many companies over the past year, despite the cutbacks, layoffs, and downsizing that had affected many firms. According to Earl Graves, publisher, the nation's largest Black-owned businesses and their revenue for 1992 included the following:

TLC Beatrice International Holdings ($1.67 billion)
Johnson Publishing Co. ($247.2 million)
Philadelphia Coca-Cola Bottling ($266 million)
H. J. Russell & Co. ($145.6 million)
Anderson-Dubose ($110 million)
RMS Technologies ($103.3 million)
Gold Line Refining ($91.9 million)
Soft Sheen Products ($91.7 million)
Garden State Cable ($91 million)
CrossColours ($89 million)

To qualify for the list, a company had to be at least 51 percent Black-owned and had to manufacture or own the product it sold or provide industrial consumer services. Brokerages, real-estate firms, and firms that provided professional services, such as legal or accounting services, were ineligible.

BOSTON UNIVERSITY WINS RIGHT TO HOUSE KING'S PERSONAL PAPERS

On **MAY 6**, a Suffolk Superior Court jury ruled that Boston University was the rightful owner of the more than eighty-three thousand personal papers of the Reverend Dr. Martin Luther King, Jr. The jury decided that the combination of a 1964 letter from the civil rights leader to Boston University concerning the papers and the actual delivery of the papers to Boston University constituted a valid and enforceable charitable pledge.

Dr. King's widow, Coretta Scott King, had sued the university over ownership of the papers, noting that King had wanted the papers returned to Atlanta. The decision of the jury, which included two Blacks and a Hispanic American, came after seven hours over two days. The racial breakdown of the vote was not known.

RACIAL VIOLENCE CLOSES SOUTH BOSTON HIGH SCHOOL

On **MAY 6**, the Boston School Board ordered South Boston High School closed for a week after a street fight erupted between white and Black students. Racial tensions spread throughout the school, and more than two hundred students walked out. Police arrested no less than three at the incident.

CONNECTICUT TAKES ACTION ON RACE AND SCHOOLS

In **JUNE**, Governor Lowell P. Weicker, Jr., signed a school desegregation plan that would require Connecticut communities to take part in regional planning to end segregation. He stated that the new law, which he introduced, showed that the state was willing to confront a nationwide problem.

NAACP SIGNS FAIR SHARE AGREEMENTS

On **JULY 1**, the NAACP signed unprecedented fair share agreements with Flagstar Inc. and Richardson Sports Inc., which would provide over one billion dollars in direct economic benefits to African Americans throughout the United States. In addition to announcing the fair share agreements at a news conference, the Reverend Benjamin Chavis, the NAACP's executive director, reportedly endorsed Charlotte, North Carolina, over Baltimore for the new National Football League franchise. NAACP members and Baltimore citizens were outraged with the endorsement, particularly since the NAACP's headquarters was located in Baltimore, and the city had financially helped the civil rights organization move to Baltimore.

Although many officials of the state of Maryland publicly requested a retraction and apology from NAACP officials, the organization released the following statement from Dr. William F. Gibson, chairman, and Benjamin Chavis on July 3:

The National Association for the Advancement of Colored People reaffirms our strong commitments to equal justice and to the economic empowerment of the African American community.

We wish to clarify the issue of our stated support for these fair share agreements. Our support is guided by the principle of insuring economic empowerment of the African-American community. We are impressed with the written commitment of Flagstar and Richardson Sports to insure significant African-American involvement in the ownership, management, employment, corporate development and expansion and other tangible areas of these businesses. The NAACP does not favor any one city over others in the United States. We are committed, however, to supporting those corporations and businesses that are serious about the involvement of any empowerment of African Americans.

MARYLAND STATISTICS ON BLACK MEN MIRROR NATIONAL PROBLEM

On **JULY 6**, Elijah E. Cummings, the chairperson of the Maryland Governor's Commission on Black Males, issued a report that called for new approaches to problems that Black men face with health, education, jobs, and crime. According to the report, Black men were seven times more likely to die of homicide than white men and were more likely to suffer from heart disease, diabetes, and pneumonia. They were less likely to have health insurance and generally earned less money than white men. These and other problems confronting young Black men had resulted in low self-esteem. The report offered the following recommendations to improve this situation:

◈ Develop family support centers to offer programs in male mentoring and development, parenting skills, self-esteem, health maintenance, and mental health;
◈ Expand programs to prevent the spread of human immunodeficiency virus (HIV) and assist those already affected by it;
◈ Help communities establish health programs especially designed for Black men;
◈ Expand programs that teach values, character, and culture in the schools;
◈ Expand resources for education in poor communities;
◈ Develop new resources for Black business expansion;
◈ Expand education and job training programs for men at risk of going to prison;
◈ Expand the state's boot-camp program for nonviolent inmates.

SKINHEAD PLOT FOILED

On **JULY 15**, a federal and local FBI task force foiled a white supremacist plot when they arrested members of the Fourth Reich Skin Heads in four southern California counties. The plot involved bombing a Black church, spraying its members with machine-gun fire, and killing Rodney King and other well-known Black people. Other potential targets included the leaders of both the NAACP and the Urban League; Nation of Islam minister Louis Farrakhan; the Reverend Al Sharpton, a New York activist; Danny Bakewell of the Brotherhood Crusade in Los Angeles; and rap music stars. Christopher D. Fisher, age twenty, of Long Beach, was charged with conspiring to attack and destroy the First African Methodist Episcopal Church. Fisher was identified as the leader of the Fourth Reich Skin Heads, whose members included at least eighteen minors.

NAACP CHAPTER OFFICE IN SACRAMENTO DESTROYED BY FIREBOMB

On **JULY 27**, a fire destroyed the Sacramento office of the NAACP. Firefighters believed it was deliberately set. Although the NAACP chapter staff had not received any hate mail to forewarn them of the attack, somebody had broken a window and thrown a firebomb inside. Police had no suspects.

PAYTON INDUCTED INTO NATIONAL FOOTBALL HALL OF FAME

On **JULY 31**, Walter Payton, the National Football League's premier running back, was inducted into the Football Hall of Fame in Canton, Ohio. During his thirteen-year career, Payton gained 16,726 yards, more than any other professional back. He was presented at the ceremony by his twelve-year-old son, Jarrett. Larry Little, who had played most of his career with the Miami Dolphins in the 1970s and was famous for his pass and run blocking, was also inducted.

BLACK HEART PATIENTS GET KEY SURGERY LESS OFTEN THAN WHITES

In **AUGUST**, the *New England Journal of Medicine* published the findings of two reports that showed Blacks to be both significantly more likely to suffer and die from sudden heart failure than whites and less likely to undergo surgery to correct it than whites. One of the studies noted that these racial differences could not be attributed to socioeconomic factors, such as the ability to pay. Some experts believed that such differences resulted from racial prejudice among doctors (only 3 percent of the nation's doctors were Black). The study, conducted by researchers at the University of Chicago, revealed that Blacks were twice as likely as whites to suffer cardiac arrest and three times more likely to die from it. The second study, undertaken by the University of Pittsburgh Medical Center and the Pittsburgh Veterans' Affairs Medical Center, found that whites were two to three times more likely than Blacks to undergo heart procedures such as catheterization, angioplasty, and bypass surgery. Blacks and whites in the latter survey had equal access to medical care and the ability to pay for it.

BLACKS ARE AMONG HIGHEST-PAID FOOTBALL PLAYERS

In **AUGUST**, a salary survey by the National Football League Player Association showed that many players made up the "two million dollar club," earning salaries in excess of two million dollars annually. Although Steve Young, a white quarterback of the San Francisco 49ers, made the highest annual salary, seventeen Blacks were among the thirty-nine players of the two million dollar club. Of the Black players, Reggie White of the Green Bay Packers made the biggest salary ($4.25 million) followed by Warren Moon, Houston Oiler quarterback ($3.563 million). Black players made the highest salaries in five of the eleven positions — running back (Thurman Thomas), wide receiver (Jerry Rice), tight end (Keith Jackson), defensive lineman (Reggie White), and linebacker (Derrick Thomas).

UNITED NEGRO COLLEGE FUND MOVES FORWARD UNDER NEW LEADERSHIP

On **AUGUST 11**, data showed the United Negro College Fund (UNCF) had improved the chances for Black high school graduates to go to college. Much of the progress was attributed to former representative William Gray, who two years earlier had announced his sudden retirement (after more than twelve successful years) from the U.S. Congress. Gray immediately took the job as president and CEO at UNCF, the largest and oldest Black educational fundraising organization in the country. After about twenty-two months in this position, Gray pointed to his success by comparing the entire forty-eight years prior to his appointment at UNCF, when the organization had supported forty-one private historically Black colleges and universities by raising a total of $650 million. During Gray's twenty-two months as the head of UNCF, the organization had raised close to $200 million. Gray noted that "more than 60 percent of our students are the first members of their family to attend college. Fifty percent come from homes with family incomes below $25,000. Ten percent of all Black Ph.D.s attend Morehouse. Forty percent of all Black pharmacists attend Xavier. Last year, UNCF schools graduated 330 biology majors, 110 chemistry majors, 149 math majors, and 102 engineers."

MAYNARD DIES

On **AUGUST 17**, Robert C. Maynard (1937–1993), the former *Oakland Tribune* publisher, died after a six-year battle with prostate cancer.

Born in Brooklyn, Maynard had excelled in almost everything he attempted during his life. He was a high school dropout at age sixteen, but in 1965, he won a Nieman fellowship to Harvard University. Although he had worked in journalism in 1961 at the *Gazette and Daily* in York, Pennsylvania, and for a short time for the *Baltimore Afro-American*, his real break did not come until he had completed his studies at Harvard. In 1967, Maynard joined the *Washington Post* as a reporter. He worked his way up to associate editor–ombudsman and editorial writer before he left the *Post* for the job of editor of the *Oakland Tribune* in 1979. Within four years, Maynard and his wife (Nancy Hicks Maynard) had bought the *Tribune* from Gannett Co., Inc. The newspaper won a Pulitzer Prize for photojournalism for its coverage of the 1989 San Francisco–Oakland earthquake. It suffered bouts of debt under the Maynards, and they sold it in 1992 to the Alameda Newspaper Group. The *Oakland Tribune* was the nation's largest Black-owned daily newspaper. Maynard and his wife were instrumental in advancing Black writers, and in 1977, they founded the Institute for Journalism Education to train and promote minority journalists.

Black Wealth Through Black Entrepreneurship PUBLISHED

In **SEPTEMBER**, Robert Wallace's book *Black Wealth Through Black Entrepreneurship* argued that missed economic opportunities in Black communities were fundamental causes of much of the hopelessness found among Black youths. Wallace had an M.B.A. from the Amos Tuck School of Business at Dartmouth College and comanaged a computer systems integration company. Although he admitted that racism was the main reason that Blacks did not have a fair chance to succeed economically, he gave the following challenges for bolstering Black economic power:

◈ Recapture the local economies, encouraging business development and economic empowerment through Black ownership of drugstores, dry cleaners, record stores, and similar local businesses;

◈ Create joint ventures between mainstream companies and minority-owned businesses to provide a "win-win" situation for both;

◈ Aggressively match the financial strength and market appeal of Black athletes and entertainers with the Black community's entrepreneurial talent, utilizing the high concentration of financial strength among Black entertainers and athletes;

◈ Focus the "best" of Black youths on business and commerce opportunities and de-emphasize sports and entertainment careers — too many young people aspire to careers in sports and entertainment without even considering entrepreneurial business channels for their talent.

Wallace admitted that racism was "heavy baggage." Still, he encouraged Blacks to start with a positive mental attitude and to develop plans for success, including academic preparation, personal skills, and a support or advisory group.

ELDERS APPOINTED SURGEON GENERAL
In **SEPTEMBER**, Dr. Joycelyn Elders was at last confirmed by the U.S. Senate as Surgeon General of the United States. Dr. Elders was a controversial selection largely because of her support for sex education in the schools, the distribution of condoms to teenagers, and making the contraceptive implant Norplant available to drug-using prostitutes. In 1995 President Clinton bowed to pressure from conservatives and requested Elders's resignation.

FEW BLACK HEAD COACHES IN I-A FOOTBALL
As of **SEPTEMBER**, there were 107 head coaches of Division I-A football schools; only three Blacks were among their ranks.

Ron Dickerson, age forty-five, became Temple's head coach on November 24, 1992. A month later, Wake Forest hired Jim Caldwell, age thirty-seven; then Eastern Michigan employed Ron Cooper, age thirty-two. Throughout the whole history of Division I-A schools, there had been only nine Black head coaches. The paucity reflected a time when there were no Black head coaches to serve as role models for young talent.

These Black head coaches had credentials that surpassed most of their white counterparts. For example, Caldwell was an assistant coach for fifteen years, working under Minnesota Vikings head coach Dennis Green and a number of other notables, including Penn State's Joe Paterno. Dickerson had been an assistant coach since 1971 and had written a 103-page manual entitled *101 Defensive Back Drills and Techniques*. Twenty of his players went on to play in the NFL. Dickerson had worked under Joe Paterno, Colorado's Paul McCartney, and Louisville's Howard Schnellenberger. Although Cooper was the youngest and the least known of the three, he had been an assistant at Appalachian State, Minnesota, Austin Peay, Murray State, East Carolina, and Nevada–Las Vegas, before Lou Holtz hired him at Notre Dame. Equality of opportunity has been more elusive for the more than 163 Black assistant coaches in Division I-A schools. Ironically, about 46 percent of the schools' players were Black, but only 163 out of 900 assistant coaches were Black at this time; 15 held titles of head coach, assistant head coach, or offensive or defensive coordinator.

AIKEN WINS MISS AMERICA PAGEANT
On **SEPTEMBER 19**, Kimberly Clarice Aiken, an eighteen-year-old from South Carolina, was crowned Miss America 1994. The fourth African American Miss America, Aiken hoped to improve conditions for the homeless. She was founder and president of the Homeless Education and Resource Organization in Columbia, South Carolina.

MORRISON BECOMES FIRST AFRICAN AMERICAN NOBEL LAUREATE
In **OCTOBER**, Toni Morrison won the Nobel Prize for literature, becoming the first African American to win this prestigious award. She was honored for her "rhapsodic" novels depicting various aspects of the African American experience. She noted that the award was more than a personal victory; it "says something about the evolution of African American writing, that it's no longer outside the central enterprise, that it speaks about things that matter to anyone." Morrison had written six novels, including *The Bluest Eye* (1970) and *Jazz* (1992). She was awarded the Pulitzer Prize for *Beloved*, an internationally acclaimed novel that told the story of a mother who killed her child rather than allow her to live in slavery.

POVERTY RATE OUTPACES POPULATION GROWTH RATE
On **OCTOBER 5**, the Bureau of the Census reported that the number of poor people in the United States had increased by 1.2 million during the past year, to reach 36.9 million. Poverty increased by 3.3 percent, three times faster than the overall 1.1 percent population growth during the past year. The census attributed the growth in the number of poor to lingering unemployment and the recession of 1990–1991. For many years, the census had attributed the high poverty among Blacks to the dissolution of many Black families. But in the past year, the poverty rate for Black married couples increased significantly — from 11

Novelist Toni Morrison was the first Black person to win the Nobel Prize for literature. The Swedish Academy called her "a literary artist of first rank."

percent to 13 percent. The poverty rate for all Blacks in the past year had been 33.3 percent, in contrast to 11.6 percent for whites. Whites accounted for two-thirds of all poor. A family of four was classified as poor if it had a cash income that was less than $14,335. A family of three was considered poor if its income was less than $11,186.

JORDAN RETIRES FROM NBA

On **OCTOBER 6**, Michael Jordan of the Chicago Bulls, the league's most identifiable personality and biggest star, retired at the age of thirty. He contended that he was retiring because he had nothing left to prove as a basketball player. Some believed that it was the death

of his father the previous July, coupled with the unending media scrutiny of his life, particularly his gambling habits, that had driven him from the game. Jordan's career included three national championships with the Bulls, two Olympic gold medals, and an NCAA championship. His accomplishments in the NBA include the following:

> Led the NBA in scoring 7 times (tied for the record with Wilt Chamberlain)
> Scored 2,000 or more points during 8 seasons (1 season short of Kareem Abdul-Jabbar's record)
> Scored 50 or more points in 26 games (second to Wilt Chamberlain's record)
> Held NBA record in career scoring average (32.3 points)
> Held NBA record in playoff scoring average (34.7 points)
> Reached 20,000 points in 620 games (only Chamberlain did it faster, in 459 games)
> Scored 21,514 career points

Jordan received a salary of four million dollars a year from the Bulls but drew an estimated fifty million dollars a year from endorsements, particularly of Nike, Gatorade, and McDonald's. Jordan would be allowed to return to the NBA after a year if he wished to.

BLACK VOTE ALLEGEDLY SUPPRESSED IN NEW JERSEY

In **NOVEMBER**, Christine Todd Whitman defeated Democratic incumbent James Florio in New Jersey's gubernatorial election. Black turnout in the election was lower than expected. Blacks had traditionally backed the Democratic candidate in the state. Shortly after the election, Republican strategist, Edward Rollins, told reporters that Whitman's campaign organization had paid off Black ministers in an attempt to suppress the Black vote. He later recanted his statement, saying it was a lie designed to upset James Carville, the Democratic strategist who had worked for the defeated incumbent, James Florio. Rollins later testified for seven hours under oath that the campaign did not engage in any payoff. Democrats called for a new election because of the allegations.

NEW ERA IN BLACK POLITICS COMMENCES

In **NOVEMBER**, several cities would lose long-standing Black politicians who had shaped the political agenda for Blacks for decades. In Atlanta, Detroit, and Los Angeles, the longest-serving mayors in the country chose not to seek reelection. In Atlanta, Mayor Maynard

Jackson was prevented from seeking reelection because of term limitations. In Los Angeles, Mayor Thomas Bradley, who had guided the city for more than twenty-three years, chose not to run for reelection, perhaps because of his age and the exhaustion caused by the recent, sensational Rodney King incident, which had brought much criticism to his administration — many political analysts believed that he would not have survived a bitter mayoral contest. Perhaps the mayor who most symbolized Black power, Black pride, and the hope of urban rebirth, Coleman Young of Detroit, decided to call it quits. Young had been mayor of Detroit since 1970. Major increases in drug-related crime, widespread unemployment, and deteriorating schools and education would challenge the new mayors.

Although Black mayors were no longer novelties, it did seem that many of the nation's biggest cities that once had Black mayors were electing white mayors, for example, New York City, Los Angeles, Chicago, and Philadelphia. The issues that seemed to concern voters had also changed, to crime prevention and balanced budgets — a new pragmatism that did not completely resemble the ideology of the departing mayors.

BONDS NAMED MOST VALUABLE PLAYER
On **NOVEMBER 9**, Barry Bonds, outfielder for the San Francisco Giants, was chosen as the National League's Most Valuable Player. Bonds was perhaps the best baseball player in the nation at this time, a three-time winner of the National League MVP award. In 1993, Bond had the highest slugging percentage (.677) attained in the National League. In the slugging category, he was followed by three other African Americans — Hank Aaron (.669), Willie McCovey (.656), and Willie Stargell (.646).

COUNCILOR WINS MAYORAL RACE IN ATLANTA
On **NOVEMBER 23**, city councilor Bill Campbell beat his opponent, former Fulton County commissioner Michael Lomax, to win the mayoral runoff in Atlanta. Campbell won by 74 percent of the votes. The runoff occurred when Campbell was 831 votes short of a majority. Campbell had the endorsement of Mayor Maynard Jackson, who was retiring after serving three terms. Civil rights groups and former mayor Andrew Young supported Lomax. The mayor of Atlanta would be the leader of the 1996 Olympics, scheduled to take place in Atlanta.

The election was filled with unsubstantiated allegations by the press of Campbell's connection to the bribery scandal that had rocked the city. Several businesspeople, a city councilor, and a former airport commissioner had been indicted in the case, which involved kickbacks from concessions operators.

NAACP SAYS INSURER DISCRIMINATES AGAINST POOR AREAS
On **NOVEMBER 23**, the Montgomery County chapter of the NAACP charged that GEICO, the third largest auto insurer in the area and the fifth largest in the nation, refused to insure Blacks in poor areas of Baltimore and Washington, D.C.

RESEGREGATION OF BLACKS IS COMMON
In **DECEMBER**, a report entitled "The Growth of Segregation in American Schools: Changing Patterns of Separation and Poverty Since 1968," stated that racial isolation was increasing throughout the nation. The Northeast now had the most segregated schools in the country, and the South, the most integrated. But even in the South, racial isolation was increasing. In 1991–1992, only 39 percent of Black students attended predominantly white schools; the rate had been 44 percent three years earlier. Two-thirds of Black students attended predominantly minority schools in 1991–1992, the highest percentage since 1968, when it stood at 76 percent. Fifteen out of sixteen Black and Hispanic students in big city schools attended predominantly Black or Hispanic schools. In a more recent report released in 1994 from the Harvard Project on School Desegregation, it was noted that nationwide, one in three Black and Hispanic students went to schools with more than 90 percent minority enrollment. The underlying problem, the report noted, was segregated housing.

CHILDREN VICTIMIZED IN EPIDEMIC OF VIOLENCE
On **DECEMBER 13**, the Johns Hopkins Children's Center Pediatric Intensive Care Unit in Baltimore released data on the first ten months of 1993, which showed that thirty-one children, eighteen years of age and younger, were homicide victims, slightly more than 10 percent of the 295 murders recorded for that time period. More and more, children were becoming the victims of violence in cities across the nation. In Baltimore, 92 percent of all murder victims were Black. In the center's pediatric unit, the treatment of thirty-one children for gunshot injuries in ten months was considerably higher than the nineteen

treated in 1992 and the thirteen treated in 1991. Not only were these injuries preventable, but also they were extremely costly, economically and emotionally. In a national survey of children's hospitals in November, it was found that treating a child injured by gunfire cost an average of fourteen thousand dollars, excluding doctors' bills and rehabilitation costs. Because children are smaller and have a smaller blood volume, they are more difficult to treat than adults; therefore, any gunshot injury to a child must be considered life-threatening.

MORTGAGE COMPANY TO PAY FOR RACE-BASED DENIAL OF LOANS TO HOME BUYERS

On **DECEMBER 13**, the Justice Department released information stating that Shawmut Mortgage Company would pay $960,000 to settle federal charges that it had discriminated against Black and Hispanic homebuyers seeking loans. The settlement would compensate minorities who were unfairly denied loans by its mortgage unit between January 1990 and October 1992. Shawmut National Corporation, the parent company of the mortgage unit and the third largest bank in New England, denied any guilt as part of the settlement but was required to increase the fund if it was determined that more money would be needed to pay borrowers who had been turned down because of discrimination.

1994 SURVIVORS OF ROSEWOOD MASSACRE TO BE COMPENSATED

On **APRIL 8**, the Florida legislature agreed to pay up to $150,000 to each survivor of a weeklong rampage by a white mob that wiped out the Black town of Rosewood seventy-one years ago.

◈ On New Year's Day in 1923, a white mob formed and went on a rampage after hearing of a white woman's claim that she had been assaulted by a Black man. The white mob marched into the small Gulf Coast community of Rosewood in search of the Black man. Failing to find him, they burned nearly every house; at least eight people died, and many others fled the violence.

The 1994 bill, approved earlier by the House, established a fund of $1.5 million to pay anyone up to $150,000 who could prove he or she had lived in Rosewood and was evacuated during the violence. It also created a $500,000 fund for reimbursement of lost property and provided $100,000 a year for college scholarships for Rosewood family descendants and other minorities. As many as twenty-five students could receive up to $4,000 annually.

ILLUSTRATION CREDITS

Library of Congress: 3, 7, 14, 15, 23, 24, 25, 27, 29, 32, 38, 39, 43, 45, 46, 49, 51, 52, 56, 58, 59, 62, 65, 69, 70, 71, 73, 76, 78, 81, 83, 85, 87, 92, 95, 96, 99, 103, 104, 107, 109, 110, 113, 114, 115, 117, 123, 124, 125, 126, 127, 128, 132, 134, 135, 138, 139, 141, 146, 151, 152, 155, 156, 158, 162, 163, 164, 166, 168, 169, 170, 171, 177, 180, 181, 182, 186, 187, 190, 191, 193, 195, 197, 198, 199, 201, 203, 206, 207, 208, 209, 213, 214, 217, 218, 223, 224, 225, 235, 249, 260, 268, 272, 275, 277, 279, 282, 285, 290, 297, 304, 313, 321, 329, 330, 332, 333, 336, 338, 342, 348, 350, 351, 353, 354, 359, 362, 363, 368, 370, 371, 377, 382, 388, 389, 397, 409, 412, 414, 415, 416, 418, 419, 422, 423, 425, 426, 430, 431, 432, 435, 436, 438, 440, 441, 442, 443, 452, 453, 457, 468, 470, 472, 476, 498, 513, 517
Collection of the Maryland Historical Society, Baltimore: 40, 229
National Archives: 44, 50, 102, 165, 184, 188, 253, 272, 309, 312, 314, 357, 386
Sophia Smith Collection, Smith College: 143
University of Maryland Baltimore County: 120, 192
Courtesy of the Lynn Historical Society: 263
National Park Service, Maggie L. Walker, National Historic Site: 293
Walker Collection of A'Lelia Perry Bundles: 301
Reprinted with permissions of National Urban League, Inc.: 303, 408, 484, 491
Brown Brothers: 317, 344
Hogan Jazz Archive, Howard-Tilton Memorial Library, Tulane University: 328
Bettmann Archives: 340, 380
Hearst Corporation: 376
Courtesy of Johnson Publishing Company, Inc.: 374
Photo by Bill Tague: 381
AP/Wide World: 347, 391, 394, 396, 455
Movie Star News: 400
Courtesy of Vice Admiral Samuel L. Gravely, Jr., USN (Ret.)/U.S. Navy: 411
Photo by Charles Moore/Black Star: 417
New York Public Library: 427
Courtesy of Constance Baker Motley: 433
Courtesy of Ossie Davis/Photo by Tony Barboza: 444
Courtesy of Marian Wright Edelman/Photo by Katherine Lambert: 463
Urban Concerns Magazine: 464, 465
Spelman College: 493, 507
Courtesy of Kweisi Mfume: 506
Courtesy of NASA: 508
Courtesy of Mayor's Office, Baltimore City: 510
Courtesy of General Colin Powell, USA (Ret.): 512
Courtesy of Maxine Waters: 533
Collection, Supreme Court Historical Society: 540
Courtesy of Carol Mosely-Braun: 551
Globe Photos, Inc.: 563

SELECTED BOOKS
FOR FURTHER READING

Abrahams, Roger D. *Deep Down in the Jungle.* Chicago: Aldine, 1970.

Adamson, Alan H. *Sugar Without Slaves: The Political Economy of British Guiana, 1838 — 1904.* New Haven: Yale University Press, 1972.

Allen, Robert L. *Black Awakening in Capitalist America.* Garden City, N.Y.: Doubleday, 1970.

Angle, Paul M., ed. *Created Equal? The Complete Lincoln-Douglas Debates of 1858.* Chicago: University of Chicago Press, 1958.

Anstey, Roger T. *The Atlantic Slave Trade and British Abolition, 1760 — 1810.* Atlantic Highlands, N.J.: Humanities Press, 1975.

Aptheker, Bettina. *Woman's Legacy.* Amherst, Mass.: University of Massachusetts Press, 1982.

Aptheker, Herbert. *American Negro Slave Revolts.* New York: International Publishers, 1963.

——. *To Be Free: Studies in American Negro History.* New York: International Publishers, 1948.

Aptheker, Herbert, ed. *A Documentary History of the Negro People in the United States.* New York: Citadel, 1951.

Ashmore, Harry S. *The Negro and the Schools.* Chapel Hill, N.C.: University of North Carolina Press, 1954.

Atherton, Lewis E. *The Cattle Kings.* Bloomington, Ind.: Indiana University Press, 1961.

Baldwin, James. *Blues for Mister Charlie.* New York: Dial Publishing, 1964.

——. *The Fire Next Time.* New York: Dial Publishing, 1963.

——. *Go Tell It on the Mountain.* New York: Alfred Knopf, 1953.

Bardolph, Richard. *The Civil Rights Record: Black Americans and the Law, 1849 — 1970.* New York: Crowell, 1970.

——. *The Negro Vanguard.* New York: Holt, Rinehart and Winston, 1959.

Barney, William L. *The Successionist Impulse: Alabama and Mississippi in 1860.* Princeton: Princeton University Press, 1974.

Barrett, Russell H. *Integration at Ole Miss.* Chicago: Quadrangle, 1965.

Bateman, Fred. *A Deplorable Scarcity: The Failure of Industrialization in the Slave Economy.* Chapel Hill, N.C.: University of North Carolina Press, 1981.

Bennett, Lerone, Jr. *Before the Mayflower: A History of the Negro in America, 1619 — 1964.* Baltimore: Penguin Books, 1965.

——. *Confrontation: Black and White.* Baltimore: Penguin Books, 1965.

——. *What Manner of Man: A Biography of Martin Luther King, Jr.* Chicago: Johnson, 1965.

Bentley, George R. *A History of the Freedmen's Bureau.* Philadelphia: University of Pennsylvania Press, 1955.

Bergman, Peter M. *The Chronological History of the Negro in America.* New York: Harper & Row, 1969.

Berlin, Ira. *Slaves Without Masters.* New York: Pantheon, 1974.

Berry, Mary F. *Black Resistance — White Law.* New York: Appleton — Century Crofts, 1971.

Berwanger, Eugene H. *The Frontier Against Slavery: Western Anti-Negro Prejudice and the Slavery Extension Controversy.* Urbana, Ill.: University of Illinois Press, 1971.

Billingsley, Andrew. *Climbing Jacob's Ladder: The Enduring Legacy of African American Families.* New York: Simon & Schuster, 1992.

Blackett, R. J. M. *Building an Antislavery Wall: Black Americans in the Atlantic Abolitionist Movement, 1830 — 1860.* Baton Rouge, La.: Louisiana State University Press, 1983.

Blair, Lewis H. *A Southern Prophecy: The Prosperity of the South Dependent Upon the Elevation of the Negro.* Boston: Little, Brown, 1964.

Blassingame, Ike. *Dakota Cowboy: My Life in the Old Days.* New York: G. P. Putnam's Sons, 1958.

Blassingame, John W. *The Slave Community: Plantation Life in the Antebellum South.* New York: Oxford University Press, 1972.

——. *Slave Testimony.* Baton Rouge, La.: Louisiana University Press, 1977.

Blauner, Robert. *Racial Oppression in America.* New York: Harper & Row, 1972.

Blaustein, Albert P., and Clarence C. Ferguson. *Desegregation and the Law: The Meaning and Effects of the School Segregation Cases.* New Brunswick, N.J.: Rutgers University Press, 1957.

Bond, Horace M. *The Education of the Negro in the American Social Order.* New York: Prentice-Hall, 1934.

Bone, Robert A. *The Negro Novel in America.* New Haven: Yale University Press, 1958.

Bontemps, Arna. *100 Years of Negro Freedom.* New York: Dodd, Mead Publishing, 1961.

——. *Story of the Negro.* New York: Alfred Knopf, 1958.

Bontemps, Arna, and Jack Conroy. *They Seek a City.* Garden City, N.Y.: Doubleday, 1945.

Botkin, B. A., ed. *Lay My Burden Down: A Folk History of Slavery.* Chicago: University of Chicago Press, 1945.

Boyer, Paul. *Urban Masses and Moral Order in America, 1820 — 1920.* Cambridge, Mass.: Harvard University Press, 1978.

Bracey, John H., Jr., August Meier, and Elliott Rudwick, eds. *The Rise of the Ghetto.* Belmont, Calif.: Wadsworth, 1971.

Branch, Taylor. *Parting the Waters: America in the King Years, 1954 — 63.* New York: Touchstone, 1989.

Brawley, Benjamin. *A Short History of the American Negro.* New York: Macmillan, 1944.

——. *The Negro Genius: A New Appraisal of the Achievement of the American Negro in Literature and the Fine Arts.* New York: Dodd, Mead Publishing, 1937.

Breyfogle, William A. *Make Free: The Story of the Underground Railroad.* Philadelphia: Lippincott, 1958.

Brink, William J., and Louis Harris. *The Negro Revolution in America: What Negroes Want, Why, and How They Are Fighting, Whom They Support, What Whites Think of Them and Their Demands.* New York: Simon and Schuster, 1964.

Broderick, Francis L. *W. E. B. Du Bois: Negro Leader in a Time of Crisis.* Stanford, Calif.: Stanford University Press, 1959.

Brooks, Gwendolyn. *Annie Allen.* New York: Harper & Row, 1949.

——. *A Street in Bronzeville.* New York: Harper & Row, 1945.

Brown, Sterling A., Authur P. Davis, and Ulysses Lee, eds. *Negro Caravan: Writings by American Negroes.* New York: Dryden Press, 1941.

Brunn, Harry O. *The Story of the Original Dixieland Jazz Band.* Baton Rouge, La.: Louisiana State University Press, 1960.

Buckley, Roger N. *Slaves in Red Coats: The British West India Regiments, 1795 — 1815.* New Haven: Yale University Press, 1969.

Bureau of National Affairs. *The Civil Rights Act of 1964: Text, Analysis, Legislative History, What it Means to Employers, Businessmen, Unions, Employees, Minority Groups.* Washington, D.C.: Bureau of National Affairs, 1964.

———. *State Fair Employment Laws and Their Administration. Texts, Federal-State Cooperation, Prohibited Acts.* Washington, D.C.: Bureau of National Affairs, 1964.

Burgess, Margaret E. *Negro Leadership in a Southern City.* Chapel Hill, N.C.: University of North Carolina Press, 1962.

Burnham, W. Dean. *Presidential Ballots, 1836 — 1892.* Baltimore: Johns Hopkins University Press, 1955.

Butcher, Margaret. *The Negro in American Culture.* New York: Alfred Knopf, 1956.

Cairnes, J. E. *The Slave Power: Its Character, Career, and Probable Designs.* New York: Harper & Row, 1969.

Campbell, Ernest Q., Charles E. Bowerman, and Daniel O. Price. *When a City Closes Its Schools.* Chapel Hill, N.C.: Institute for Research in Social Science, University of North Carolina, 1960.

Campbell, R. B., and R. G. Lowe. *Wealth and Power in Antebellum Texas.* College Station, Tex.: Texas A & M University Press, 1977.

Carmichael, Stokely, and Charles V. Hamilton. *Black Power: The Politics of Liberation in America.* New York: Vintage, 1967.

Carter, Hodding. *The Angry Scar: The Story of Reconstruction.* Garden City, N.Y.: Doubleday, 1959.

Catterall, Helen. *Judicial Cases Concerning American Slavery and the Negro.* Washington, D.C.: Carney Institution Publications, 5 vols., 1926 — 1927.

Chadwick, Bruce. *When the Game Was Black and White: The Illustrated History of Baseball's Negro League.* New York: Abbeville Press Publishers, 1992.

Chalmers, David M. *Hooded Americanism: The First Century of the Ku Klux Klan, 1865 — 1965.* Garden City, N.Y.: Doubleday, 1965.

Chambers, Bradford. *Chronicles of Black Protest.* New York: New American Library, 1968.

Charters, Samuel B. *The Poetry of the Blues.* New York: Oak, 1963.

Cheek, William F., and Aimee L. Cheek. *John Mercer Langston and the Fight for Black Freedom, 1829 — 65.* Urbana, Ill.: University of Illinois Press, 1989.

Chisholm, Shirley. *Unbought and Unbossed.* Boston: Houghton Mifflin, 1970.

Chudacoff, Howard P. *The Evolution of American Urban Society.* Englewood Cliffs, N.J.: Prentice-Hall, 1975.

Clark, Kenneth. *Dark Ghetto.* New York: Harper & Row, 1965.

———. *Prejudice and Your Child.* Boston: Beacon, 1955.

———, ed. *The Negro Protest: James Baldwin, Malcolm X, Martin Luther King Talk With Kenneth B. Clark.* Boston: Beacon, 1963.

Clarke, John H., ed. *Harlem, A Community in Transition.* New York: Citadel, 1964.

Clift, Virgil A., Archibald W. Anderson, and H. G. Hullfish, eds. *Negro Education in America: Its Adequacy, Problems, and Needs.* 16th Yearbook of the John Dewey Society. New York: Harper, 1962.

Conant, James B. *Slums and Suburbs: A Commentary on Schools in Metropolitan Areas.* New York: McGraw-Hill, 1961.

Coles, Robert. *Migrants, Sharecroppers, Mountaineers.* Boston: Atlantic — Little Brown, 1973.

Conzen, Kathleen N. *Immigrant Milwaukee, 1836 — 1860: Accommodation and Community in a Frontier City.* Cambridge, Mass.: Harvard University Press, 1976.

Cook, James G. *The Segregationists.* New York: Appleton — Century Crofts, 1962.

Cooke, Jacob E. *Frederic Bancroft, Historian.* Norman, Okla.: University of Oklahoma Press, 1957.

Cooper, William J., Jr. *The South and the Politics of Slavery, 1828 — 1856.* Baton Rouge, La.: Louisiana State University Press, 1978.

Cornish, Dudley T. *The Sable Arm: Negro Troops in the Union Army, 1861 — 1865.* New York: Longmans, Green, 1956.

Coulter, Ellis M. *The South During Reconstruction, 1865 — 1877.* Baton Rouge, La.: Louisiana State University Press, 1947.

Courlander, Harold. *Negro Folk Music, U.S.A.* New York: Columbia University Press, 1963.

Cox, William R. *Luke Short and His Era.* Garden City, N.Y.: Doubleday, 1961.

Crain, Robert L. *The Politics of School Desegregation.* Garden City, N.Y.: Doubleday, 1969.

Cronon, Edmund D. *Black Moses: The Story of Marcus Garvey and the Universal Negro Improvement Association.* Madison, Wis.: University of Wisconsin Press, 1955.

Cruse, Harold. *Plural But Equal: Black and Minorities in America's Plural Society.* New York: William Morrow, 1987.

Cunliffe, Marcus. *Chattel Slavery and Wage Slavery: The Anglo-American Context, 1830 — 1860.* Athens, Ga.: University of Georgia Press, 1979.

Curry, Richard O., ed. *The Abolitionists: Reformers or Fanatics?* New York: Holt, Rinehart and Winston, 1965.

Curtin, Philip D. *The Atlantic Slave Trade: A Census.* Madison, Wis.: University of Wisconsin Press, 1969.

Cutler, John Henry. *Ed Brooke: Biography of a Senator.* Indianapolis: Bobbs-Merrill, 1972.

Dale, Edward E., and Morris L. Wardell. *History of Oklahoma.* New York: Prentice-Hall, 1948.

Daniel, Pete. *The Shadow of Slavery: Peonage in the South, 1901 — 1969.* New York: Oxford University Press, 1973.

David, Paul A., Herbert G. Gutman, Richard Sutch, Peter Temin, and Gavin Wright. *Reckoning with Slavery: A Critical Study in the Quantitative History of American Negro Slavery.* New York: Oxford University Press, 1975.

Davis, David B. *The Problem of Slavery in Western Culture.* Ithaca, N.Y.: Cornell University Press, 1975.

———. *Slavery and Human Progress.* New York: Oxford University Press, 1984.

Davis, George A., and O. Fred Donaldson. *Blacks in the United States: A Geographic Perspective.* Boston: Houghton Mifflin, 1975.

Degler, Carl N. *The Other South: Southern Dissenters in the Nineteenth Century.* Boston: Northeastern University Press, 1982.

Delta Prisons: Punishment for Profit, A Special Report. Atlanta: Southern Regional Council, 1968.

Detweiler, Frederick G. *The Negro Press in the United States.* Chicago: University of Chicago Press, 1922.

Dillion, Merton L. *The Abolitionists: The Growth of a Dissenting Minority.* New York: W. W. Norton, 1974.

Dionisopoulos, P. A. *Rebellion, Racism, and Representation: The Adam Clayton Powell Case and Its Antecedents.* DeKalb, Ill.: Northern Illinois University Press, 1970.

Donald, David H. *Charles Sumner and the Coming of the Civil War.* Chicago: University of Chicago Press, 1960.

Donald, Henderson H. *The Negro Freedman: Life Conditions of the American Negro in the Early Years After Emancipation.* New York: Schuman, 1952.

Donnan, Elizabeth, ed. *Documents Illustrative of the History of Slave Trade to America.* 4 vols. Washington, D.C.: Carnegie Institution Publications, 1930 — 35.

Dorson, Richard M. *Negro Folktales in Michigan.* Cambridge, Mass.: Harvard University Press, 1963.

Douglass, Frederick. *My Bondage and Freedom.* New York: Dover Publications, 1855.

Drake, Sadie D. St. Clair, and Horace R. Cayton. *Black Metropolis: A Study of Negro Life in a Northern City.* New York: Harper & Row, 1962.

Drake, Thomas E. *Quakers and Slavery in America.* Gloucester, Mass.: Peter Smith, 1950.

Duberman, Martin B., ed. *The Antislavery Vanguard: New Essays on the Abolitionist.* Princeton: Princeton University Press, 1965.

Du Bois, W. E. B. *Black Reconstruction in America*. New York: Russell and Russell, 1956.

———. *The Philadelphia Negro*. Philadelphia: University of Pennsylvania Press, 1899.

———. *The Souls of Black Folk: Essays and Sketches*. Chicago: McClurg, 1903.

———. *The Suppression of the African Slave — Trade to the United States of America, 1638 — 1870*. New York: Longmans, Green, 1896.

Dumond, Dwight L. *Antislavery: The Crusade for Freedom in America*. Ann Arbor, Mich.: University of Michigan Press, 1961.

———. *A Bibliography of Antislavery in America*. Ann Arbor, Mich.: University of Michigan Press, 1961.

Dunn, Richard S. *Sugar and Slaves: The Rise of the Planter Class in the British West Indies, 1624 — 1713*. New York: W. W. Norton, 1973.

Durham, Philip, and Everett L. Jones. *The Negro Cowboys*. New York: Dodd, Mead Publishing, 1965.

Duster, Alreda, ed. *Crusade for Justice: The Autobiography of Ida B. Wells*. Chicago: University of Chicago Press, 1970.

Ehle, John. *The Free Men*. New York: Harper & Row, 1965.

Elkins, Stanley M. *Slavery: A Problem in American Institutional and Intellectual Life*. Chicago: University of Chicago Press, 1959.

Eltis, David, and James Walvin, eds. *The Abolition of the Atlantic Slave Trade*. Madison, Wis.: University of Wisconsin Press, 1981.

Engerman, Stanley L., and Eugene D. Genovese, eds. *Race and Slavery in the Western Hemisphere: Quantitative Studies*. Princeton: Princeton University Press, 1975.

Escott, Paul D. *Slavery Remembered: A Record of Twentieth Century Slave Narratives*. Chapel Hill, N.C.: University of North Carolina Press, 1979.

Feagin, Joe R., and Harlan Hahn. *Ghetto Riots: The Politics of Violence in American Cities*. New York: Macmillan, 1973.

Fehrenbacher, Don E. *The Dred Scott Case: Its Significance in American Law and Politics*. New York: Oxford University Press, 1978.

Feldberg, Michael. *The Philadelphia Riots of 1844: A Study of Ethnic Conflict*. Westport, Conn.: Greenwood Press, 1975.

Fields, Barbara J. *Slavery and Freedom on the Middle Ground: Maryland During the Nineteenth Century*. New Haven: Yale University Press, 1985.

Filler, Louis. *The Crusade Against Slavery, 1830 — 1860*. New York: Harper, 1960.

Fishel, Leslie H., and Benjamin Quarles. *The Black American: A Documentary History*. New York: Morrow, 1967.

Floan, Howard R. *The South in Northern Eyes, 1831 — 1861*. Austin, Tex.: University of Texas Press, 1958.

Fogel, Robert W. *Time on the Cross: The Economics of American Negro Slavery*. 2 vols. Boston: Little, Brown, 1974.

———. *Without Consent or Contract: The Rise and Fall of American Slavery*. New York: W.W. Norton & Company, 1989.

Foner, Eric. *Free Soil, Free Labor, Free Men: The Ideology of the Republican Party Before the Civil War*. New York: Oxford University Press, 1970.

———. *Reconstruction: America's Unfinished Revolution*. New York: Harper Collins, 1988.

Foner, Philip S. *The Black Panthers Speak*. Philadelphia: Lippincott, 1970.

———. *Business and Slavery: The New York Merchants and the Irrepressible Conflict*. New York: Russell and Russell, 1968.

———. *Organized Labor and the Black Worker, 1619 — 1973*. New York: Praeger, 1974.

Forman, R. *Black Ghettoes, White Ghettoes, and Slums*. Englewood Cliffs, N.J.: Prentice-Hall, 1971.

Foster, William Z. *The Negro People in American History*. New York: International Publishers, 1954.

Franklin, John Hope. *The Emancipation Proclamation*. Garden City, N.Y.: Doubleday, 1963.

———. *The Free Negro in North Carolina, 1790 — 1860*. Chapel Hill, N.C.: University of North Carolina Press, 1943.

Franklin, John Hope. *From Slavery to Freedom: A History of Negro Americans*. New York: Vintage, Third Edition, 1968.

———. *The Militant South, 1800 — 1861*. Cambridge, Mass.: Harvard University Press, 1956.

———. *Reconstruction: After the Civil War*. Chicago: University of Chicago Press, 1961.

———. *A Southern Odyssey: Travellers in the Antebellum North*. Baton Rouge, La.: Louisiana State University Press, 1976.

Franklin, John Hope, and Isidore Starr. *The Negro in Twentieth Century America*. New York: Random House, 1967.

Frazier, E. Franklin. *Black Bourgeoisie*. Glencoe, Ill.: The Free Press, 1957.

———. *The Negro Church in America*. New York: Schocken, 1964.

———. *The Negro Family in the United States*. Chicago: University of Chicago Press, 1939.

———. *The Negro in the United States*. New York: Macmillan, 1957.

Friedland, William, and Dorothy Nelkins. *Migrants*. New York: Holt, Rinehart and Winston, 1972.

Frederickson, George M. *The Black Image in the White Mine: The Debate on Afro-American Character and Destiny, 1817 — 1914*. New York: Harper & Row, 1971.

Freehling, Alison G. *Drift Toward Dissolution: The Virginia Slavery Debate of 1831 — 1832*. Baton Rouge, La.: Louisiana State University Press, 1982.

Freyre, Gilberto. *The Master and the Slaves*. New York: Alfred Knopf, 1964.

Frye, Hardy T. *Black Parties and Political Power: A Case Study*. Boston: G. K. Hall & Co., 1980.

Galenson, David W. *Traders, Planters, and Slaves: Market Behavior in Early English America*. New York: Cambridge University Press, 1986.

———. *White Servitude in Colonial America: An Economic Analysis*. New York: Cambridge University Press, 1981.

Gara, Larry. *The Liberty Line: The Legend of the Underground Railroad*. Lexington, Ky.: University of Kentucky Press, 1961.

Gemery, Henry A., and Jan S. Hogendorn, eds. *The Uncommon Market: Essays in the Economic History of the Atlantic Slave Trade*. New York: Academic Press, 1979.

Genovese, Eugene D. *From Rebellion to Revolution: Afro-American Slave Revolts in the Making of the Modern World*. Baton Rouge, La.: Louisiana State University Press, 1979.

———. *In Red and Black: Mexican Exploration in Southern and Afro-American History*. New York: Vintage, 1971.

———. *The Political Economy of Slavery: Studies in the Economy and Society of the Slave South*. New York: Pantheon, 1965.

———. *Roll Jordan Roll: The World the Slaves Made*. New York: Pantheon, 1974.

———. *The World the Slaveholders Made*. New York: Vintage, 1969.

Geschwender, James A. *Racial Stratification in America*. Dubuque, Iowa: Wm. C. Brown Company Publishers, 1978.

Giddings, Joshua R. *Exiles of Florida*. New York: Arno Press, 1969.

Ginsberg, Ralph. *100 Years of Lynchings*. New York: Lancer Books, 1969.

Ginzberg, Eli, ed. *The Negro Challenge to the Business Community*. New York: McGraw-Hill, 1964.

Glazer, Nathan, and Daniel P. Moynihan. *Beyond the Melting Pot: The Negroes, Puerto Ricans, Jews, Italians, and Irish of New York City*. Cambridge, Mass.: MIT Press, 1970.

Golden, Claudie D. *Urban Slavery in the American South, 1820 — 1860: A Quantitative History*. Chicago: University of Chicago Press, 1976.

Golden, Harry L. *Mr. Kennedy and the Negroes*. Cleveland: World, 1964.

Good, Paul. *The American Serfs: A Report on Poverty in the Rural South*. New York: Ballantine Books, 1968.

Gosnell, Harold F. *Negro Politicians: The Rise of Negro Politicians in Chicago*. Chicago: University of Chicago Press, 1935.

Grant, Joanne. *Black Protest: History, Documents, and Analyses, 1619 to the Present*. New York: Ballantine Books, 1968.

Grant, Robert B. *The Black Man Comes to the City: A Documentary Account from the Great Migration to the Great Depression.* Chicago: Nelson-Hall, 1972.

Green, William A. *British Slave Emancipation: The Sugar Colonies and the Great Experiment, 1830 — 1865.* Oxford, U.K.: Clarendon Press, 1976.

Greenberg, Jack. *Race Relations and American Law.* New York: Columbia University Press, 1959.

Greene, Lorenzo J. *The Negro in Colonial New England, 1620 — 1776.* New York: Columbia University Press, 1942.

Greene, Lorenzo J., and Carter G. Woodson. *The Negro Wage Earner.* Washington, D.C.: The Association for the Study of Negro Life and History, 1930.

Gregory, Dick, with Robert Lipsyte. *Nigger: An Autobiography.* New York: Dutton, 1964.

Griffin, John H. *Black Like Me.* Boston: Houghton Mifflin, 1961.

Gutman, Herbert G. *The Black Family in Slavery and Freedom, 1750 — 1925.* New York: Pantheon, 1976.

———. *Slavery and the Numbers Game: A Critique of Time on the Cross.* Urbana, Ill.: University of Illinois Press, 1975.

Haber, Louis. *Black Pioneers of Science and Invention.* New York: Harcourt Brace Jovanovich, 1970.

Hacker, Andrew. *Two Nations: Black and White, Separate, Hostile, Unequal.* New York: Charles Scribner's Sons, 1992.

Haley, James E. *Charles Goodnight, Cowman & Plainsman.* Norman, Okla.: University of Oklahoma Press, 1949.

Hall, Gwendolyn. *Social Control in Slave Plantation Societies.* Baltimore: Johns Hopkins University Press, 1971.

Handlin, Oscar. *Fire-Bell in the Night: The Crisis in Civil Rights.* Boston: Little, Brown, 1964.

———. *The Newcomers: Negroes and Puerto Ricans in a Changing Metropolis.* Cambridge, Mass.: Harvard University Press, 1959.

Harlan, Louis R. *The Negro in American History.* Washington, D.C.: American Historical Society, 1965.

———. *Separate and Unequal: Public School Campaigns and Racism in the Southern Seaboard States, 1901 — 1915.* Chapel Hill, N.C.: University of North Carolina Press, 1958.

Harper, Francis E. W. *Sketches of Southern Life.* Philadelphia, 1872.

Harrington, Michael. *The Other America: Poverty in the United States.* New York: Macmillan, 1962.

Harris, Robert. *The Quest for Equality: The Constitution, Congress and the Supreme Court.* Baton Rouge, La.: Louisiana State University Press, 1960.

Harris, Sara, with Harriet Crittenden. *Father Divine: Holy Husband.* Garden City, N.Y.: Doubleday, 1953.

Hawkins, Hugh. *Booker T. Washington and His Critics: The Problem of Negro Leadership.* Lexington, Mass.: D. C. Heath and Company, 1962.

Hayes, Rutherford B. *Teach the Freeman: The Correspondence of Rutherford B. Hayes and the Slater Fund for Negro Education, 1881 — 1887.* Baton Rouge, La.: Louisiana State University Press, 1959.

Henderson, Vivian W. *The Economic Status of Negroes: In the Nation and in the South.* Atlanta: The Southern Regional Council, 1963.

Hentoff, Nat. *The New Equality.* New York: Viking, 1964.

Herskovits, Melville J. *The Myth of the Negro Past.* New York: Harper, 1941.

Hickey, Neil, and Ed Edwin. *Adam Clayton Powell and the Politics of Race.* New York: Fleet, 1965.

Hiestand, Dale L. *Economic Growth and Employment Opportunities for Minorities.* New York: Columbia University Press, 1964.

Higginson, Thomas W. *Army Life in a Black Regiment.* East Lansing, Mich.: Michigan State University Press, 1960.

Hill, Herbert, and Jack Greenberg. *Citizen's Guide to Desegregation.* Boston: Beacon, 1955.

Hine, Darlene Clark. *Black Women in American History: From Colonial Times through the Nineteenth Century.* Brooklyn, N.Y.: Carlson Publishing, 1990.

Holley, W. C., Ellen Winston, and T. J. Woofter. *The Plantation South: 1934 — 1937.* New York: DeCapo Press, 1940.

Howard, Warren S. *American Slavers and the Federal Law, 1837 — 1862.* Berkeley: University of California Press, 1963.

Huggins, Nathan I. *Black Odyssey: The Afro-American Ordeal in Slavery.* New York: Vintage, 1979.

Hughes, Langston. *Fight for Freedom: The Story of the NAACP.* New York: W. W. Norton, 1962.

Hughes, Langston, and Arna Bontemps, eds. *The Book of Negro Folklore.* New York: Dodd, Mead Publishing, 1958.

Hughes, Langston, and Milton Meltzer. *A Pictorial History of the Negro in America.* New York: Crown, 1963.

Humphrey, Hubert H., ed. *Integration vs. Segregation.* New York: Crowell, 1964.

Isaacs, Edith J. *The Negro in the American Theatre.* New York: Theatre Arts, 1947.

Isaacs, Harold R. *The New World of Negro Americans.* New York: Day, 1963.

Jacobs, Paul. *Prelude to Riot.* New York: Random House, 1966.

James, C. L. R. *The Black Jacobins.* New York: Vintage, 1963.

Janowitz, Morris. *The Social Control of Escalated Riots.* Chicago: University of Chicago Press, 1967.

Jaynes, Gerald D. *Branches Without Roots: Genesis of the Black Working Class in the American South, 1862 — 1882.* Oxford, U.K.: Oxford University Press, 1984.

Jenkins, William S. *Pro — Slavery Thought in the Old South.* Chapel Hill, N.C.: University of North Carolina Press, 1935.

Johnson, Charles S. *Patterns of Negro Segregation.* New York: Harper and Brothers, 1943.

———. *Shadow of the Plantation.* Chicago: University of Chicago Press, 1934.

Johnson, James Weldon. *The Book of American Negro Poetry.* New York: Harcourt, Brace & Company, 1922.

Johnson, James Weldon, and J. Rosamond Johnson, eds. *The Book of American Negro Spirituals.* New York: Viking, 1940.

Jones, Katherine M. *The Plantation South.* Indianapolis: Bobbs-Merrill, 1957.

Jones, LeRoi. *Blues People: Negro Music in White America.* New York: Morrow, 1963.

Katz, William. *Eyewitness: The Negro in American History.* New York: Pittman, 1969.

Kerner Commission. *Report of the National Advisory Commission on Civil Disorders.* New York: Bantam, 1968.

Kester, Howard. *Revolt Among Sharecroppers.* New York: Arno Press, 1969.

Killian, Lewis M., and Charles Grigg. *Racial Crisis in America: Leadership in Conflict.* Englewood Cliffs, N.J.: Prentice-Hall, 1964.

King, Martin Luther, Jr., *Strides Toward Freedom: The Montgomery Story.* New York: Harper, 1958.

———. *Why We Can't Wait.* New York: Harper & Row, 1964.

Kiple, Kenneth F. *Blacks in Colonial Cuba, 1774 — 1899.* Gainesville, Fla.: University Presses of Florida, 1976.

Klein, Herbert S. *African Slavery in Latin America and the Caribbean.* New York: Oxford University Press, 1986.

———. *The Middle Passage: Comparative Studies in the Atlantic Slave Trade.* Princeton: Princeton University Press, 1978.

———. *Slavery in the Americas: A Comparative Study of Virginia and Cuba.* Chicago: University of Chicago Press, 1967.

Klineberg, Otto, ed. *Characteristics of the American Negro.* New York: Harper, 1944.

Klingman, Peter D. *Josiah Walls: Florida's Black Congressman of Reconstruction.* Gainesville, Fla.: University Press of Florida, 1976.

Knowles, Louis L., and Kenneth Prewitt. *Institutional Racism in America.* Englewood Cliffs, N.J.: Prentice-Hall, 1969.

Kolchin, Peter. *American Slavery, 1619 — 1877.* New York: Hill and Wang, 1993.

Konvitz, Milton R. *A Century of Civil Rights: With a Study of State Law Against Discrimination by Theodore Leskes.* New York: Columbia University Press, 1961.

Kousser, J. Morgan, and James M. McPherson, eds. *Region, Race, and Reconstruction.* New York: Oxford University Press, 1982.

Kozol, Jonathan. *Savage Inequalities: Children in America's Schools.* New York: Crown Publishers, Inc., 1991.

Kraditor, Aileen S. *Means and Ends in American Abolitionism: Garrison and His Critics on Strategy and Tactics, 1834 — 1850.* New York: Vintage Books/Random House, 1970.

Kulikoff, Alan. *Tobacco and Slaves: The Development of Southern Cultures in the Chesapeake, 1680 — 1800.* Chapel Hill, N.C.: University of North Carolina Press, 1986.

Lamson, Peggy. *The Glorious Failure: Back Congressman Robert Brown Elliot and the Reconstruction in South Carolina.* New York: W. W. Norton, 1973.

Langston, John Mercer. *From the Virginia Plantation to the National Capitol.* New York: Arno Press, 1969 (reprint of 1884 edition).

Lerner, Gerda (ed.). *Black Women in White America: A Documentary History.* New York: Vintage Books, 1973.

Lester, Anthony. *Justice in the American South.* London: Amnesty International, 1965.

Levinson, Florence H. *Harold Washington: A Political Biography.* Chicago: Chicago Review Press, 1983.

Lewinson, Paul. *A Guide to Documents in the National Archives for Negro Studies.* Washington, D.C.: American Council of Learned Societies Committee on Negro Studies, 1947.

———. *Race, Class, and Party: A History of Negro Suffrage and White Politics in the South.* New York: Oxford University Press, 1932.

Lewis, Claude. *Adam Clayton Powell.* Greenwich, Conn.: Fawcett, 1963.

Lincoln, C. Eric. *The Black Muslims in America.* Boston: Beacon, 1961.

———. *The Negro Pilgrimage in America.* New York: Bantam, 1967.

Littlefield, Daniel C. *Rice and Slaves: Ethnicity and the Slave Trade in Colonial South Carolina.* Baton Rouge, La.: Louisiana State University Press, 1981.

Litwack, Leon F. *Been in the Storm So Long: The Aftermath of Slavery.* New York: Random House, 1978.

———. *North of Slavery: The Negro in the Free States, 1790 — 1860.* Chicago: University of Chicago Press, 1961.

Lloyd, Arthur Y. *The Slavery Controversy, 1831 — 1860.* Chapel Hill, N.C.: University of North Carolina Press, 1939.

Lloyd, Christopher. *The Navy and the Slave Trade: The Suppression of the African Slave Trade in the Nineteenth Century.* London: Longmans, Green, 1949.

Locke, Mary S. *Slavery in America from the Introduction of African Slaves to the Prohibition of the Slave Trade, (1619 — 1808).* Boston: Ginn, 1901.

Locke, Alain, ed. *The Negro in Art: A Pictorial Record of the Negro Artist and of the Negro Theme in Art.* Washington, D.C.: Associates in Negro Folk Education, 1940.

Loewenberg, Bert J., and Ruth Bogin, eds. *Black Women in Nineteenth-Century American Life: Their Words, Their Thoughts, Their Feelings.* University Park, Pa.: The Pennsylvania State University Press, 1976.

Logan, Rayford W. *The Negro in American Life and Thought: The Nadir, 1877 — 1901.* New York: Dial Publishing, 1954.

———. *The Negro in the United States: A Brief History.* Princeton: Van Nostrand, 1957.

Lomax, Louis E. *The Negro Revolt.* New York: Harper, 1962.

Lovejoy, Paul. *Transformations in Slavery: A History of Slavery in Africa.* Cambridge, U.K.: Cambridge University Press, 1983.

Lynch, John Roy. *Reminiscences of an Active Life.* Edited by John Hope Franklin. Chicago: University of Chicago Press, 1970.

McGarth, Earl J. *The Predominantly Negro Colleges and Universities in Transition.* New York: Teachers College, Columbia University Press, 1965.

McKay, Claude. *Harlem: Negro Metropolis.* New York: Dutton, 1940.

———. *Home to Harlem.* New York: Harper, 1928.

McKitrick, Eric L. *Andrew Johnson and Reconstruction.* Chicago: University of Chicago Press, 1960.

McKitrick, Eric L., ed., *Slavery Defended: The Views of the Old South.* Englewood Cliffs, N.J.: Prentice-Hall, 1963.

McKivigan, John K. *The War Against Proslavery Religion: Abolitionism and the Northern Churches, 1830 — 1865.* Ithaca, N.Y.: Cornell University Press, 1984.

McManus, Edgar J. *History of Negro Slavery in New York.* Syracuse, N.Y.: Syracuse University Press, 1966.

McPherson, James M. *The Negro's Civil War: How American Negroes Felt and Acted During the War for the Union.* New York: Pantheon, 1965.

———. *The Struggle for Equality: Abolitionist and the Negro in the Civil War and Reconstruction.* Princeton: Princeton University Press, 1964.

Maclachlan, John M. and Joe S. Floyd. *The Changing South.* Gainesville, Fla.: University of Florida Press, 1956.

Main, Gloria L. *Tobacco Colony: Life in Early Maryland, 1650 — 1720.* Princeton: Princeton University Press, 1982.

Mandel, Bernard. *Labor: Free and Slave.* New York: Associated Authors, 1955.

Mannix, Daniel P., with Malcolm Cowley. *Black Cargoes: A History of the Atlantic Slave Trade, 1518 — 1865.* New York: Viking, 1962.

Margolies, Jacob. *The Negro Leagues: The Story of Black Baseball.* New York: Franklin Watts, 1994.

Marshall, Herbert, and Mildred Stock. *Ira Aldridge: The Negro Tradition.* New York: Macmillan, 1958.

Martis, Kenneth C. *The Historical Atlas of United States Congressional Districts, 1789 — 1983.* New York: The Free Press, 1982.

Massey, Douglas S., and Nancy A. Denton. *American Apartheid.* Cambridge, Mass.: Harvard University Press, 1993.

Mathews, Basil. *Booker T. Washington, Educator and Interracial Interpreter.* Cambridge, Mass.: Harvard University Press, 1948.

Mathews, Donald R., and James W. Prothro. *Negroes and the New Southern Politics.* New York: Harcourt, Brace & World, 1966.

Meier, August. *Negro Thought in America, 1880 — 1915: Racial Ideologies in the Age of Booker T. Washington.* Ann Arbor, Mich.: University of Michigan Press, 1963.

Meier, August, and Elliot M. Rudwick. *From Plantation to Ghetto: An Interpretive History of American Negroes.* New York: Hill and Wang, 1969.

Meier, August, and Elliot M. Rudwick, eds. *The Making of Black America.* vol 2. New York: Atheneum, 1969.

Mendelson, Wallace, ed. *Discrimination: Based on the Report of the United States Commission on Civil Rights.* Englewood Cliffs, N.J.: Prentice-Hall, 1962.

Miers, Suzanne. *Britain and the Ending of the Slave Trade.* New York: Africana Publishing Co., 1975.

Mintz, Sidney W. *Sweetness and Power.* New York: Viking Penguin, 1985.

Morgan, Edmund S. *American Slavery, American Freedom: The Ordeal of Colonial Virginia.* New York: W. W. Norton, 1975.

Morgan, Philip D. *Slavery in Tennessee.* Bloomington, Ind.: Indiana University Press, 1957.

Morris, Aldon D. *The Origins of the Civil Rights Movement: Black Communities Organizing for Change.* New York: The Free Press, 1984.

Mossell, Gertrude. *The Work of the Afro-American Woman.* Philadelphia, 1894. Reprint. Freeport, N.Y.: Books for Libraries Press, 1971.

Moynihan, Daniel P. *Maximum Feasible Misunderstanding.* New York: The Free Press, 1969.

Mullin, Gerald W. *Flight and Rebellion: Slave Resistance in Eighteenth-Century Virginia.* New York: Oxford University Press, 1972.

Muse, Benjamin. *Ten Years of Prelude: The Story of Integration Since the Supreme Court's 1954 Decision.* New York: Viking, 1964.

Myrdal, Gunnar. *An American Dilemma: The Negro Problem and Modern Democracy.* New York: Harper & Row, 1962.

National Urban League. *The Racial Gap: 1955 — 1975.* New York: National Urban League, 1967.

Nearing, Scott. *Black America.* New York: Schocken, 1969.

Norfleet, Marvin B. *Forced School Integration in the U.S.A.* New York: Carlton Press, 1961.

Northrup, Solomon. *Twelve Years a Slave.* Auburn, N.Y.: Derby and Miller, 1853.

Nye, Russel B. *Fettered Freedom: Civil Liberties and the Slavery Controversy, 1830 — 1860.* East Lansing, Mich.: Michigan State University Press, 1949.

———. *Society and Culture in America, 1830 — 1860.* New York: Harper & Row, 1974.

Oakes, James. *The Ruling Race: A History of American Slaveholders.* New York: Alfred Knopf, 1982.

O'Connor, Ellen M. *Myrtilla Miner: A Memoir.* Boston: Houghton Mifflin, 1885.

Odum, Howard W., and Guy B. Johnson. *The Negro and His Songs: A Study of Typical Negro Songs in the South.* Chapel Hill, N.C.: University of North Carolina Press, 1925.

Ogden, Frederic D. *The Poll Tax in the South.* University, Ala.: University of Alabama Press, 1958.

Olmsted, Frederick Law. *The Cotton Kingdom: A Traveller's Observations on Cotton and Slavery in the American Slave States.* New York: Alfred Knopf, 1953.

———. *A Journey in the Seaboard Slave States.* New York: Negro Universities Press, 1968.

Osofsky, Gilbert. *Harlem: The Making of a Ghetto.* New York: Harper Torch Books, 1968.

———, ed. *Putting on Ole Massa.* New York: Harper Torch Books, 1966.

Ottley, Rio. *Black Odyssey: The Story of the Negro in America.* New York: Charles Scribner's Sons, 1948.

———. *The Lonely Warrior: The Life and Times of Robert S. Abbott.* Chicago: Regnery, 1955.

Packwood, Cyril. *Detour-Bermuda, Destination-U.S. House of Representatives: The Life of Joseph Haynes Rainey.* Hamilton, Bermuda: Baxter's Limited, 1977.

Painter, Nell Irvin. *Exodusters.* New York: Knopf, 1977.

Passel, Peter, and Gavin Wright. "The Effects of Pre–Civil War Territorial Expansion on the Price of Slaves." *Journal of Political Economy* 80 (1972): 1188 — 1202.

Patterson, Orlando. *Slavery and Social Death: A Comparative Study.* Cambridge, Mass.: Harvard University Press, 1982.

———. *The Sociology of Slavery.* New York: Academic Press, 1972.

Peck, James. *Freedom Ride.* New York: Simon and Schuster, 1962.

Pessen, Edward. *Riches, Class and Power Before the Civil War.* Lexington, Mass.: D. C. Heath and Company, 1973.

Pettigrew, Thomas F. *A Profile of the Negro American.* Princeton: Van Nostrand, 1964.

Postell, William D. *The Health of Slaves on Southern Plantations.* Gloucester, Mass.: Peter Smith, 1951.

Potter, David M. *Lincoln and His Party in the Succession Crisis.* New Haven: Yale University Press, 1962.

Powdermaker, Hortense. *After Freedom.* New York: Atheneum, 1968.

Powell, Adam Clayton, Jr. *Adam by Adam.* New York: The Dial Press, 1971.

Price, Hugh D. *The Negro and Southern Politics: A Chapter of Florida History.* New York: New York University, 1957.

Price, Margaret. *The Negro Voter in the South.* Atlanta: Southern Regional Council, 1957.

———. *The Negro and the Ballot in the South.* Atlanta: Southern Regional Council, 1959.

Proudfoot, Merrill. *Diary of a Sit-in.* Chapel Hill, N.C.: University of North Carolina Press, 1962.

Quarles, Benjamin. *Black Abolitionists.* New York: Oxford University Press, 1969.

———. *Lincoln and the Negro.* New York: Oxford University Press, 1962.

———. *The Negro in the American Revolution.* Chapel Hill, N.C.: University of North Carolina Press, 1961.

———. *The Negro in the Civil War.* Boston: Little, Brown, 1953.

———. *The Negro in the Making of America.* New York: Collier, 1964.

Randel, William P. *The Ku Klux Klan: A Century of Infamy.* Philadelphia: Chilton, 1965.

Raper, Arthur F. *Preface to Peasantry.* Chapel Hill, N.C.: University of North Carolina Press, 1936.

Redkey, Edwin S. *Black Exodus: Black Nationalist and Back-to-Africa Movements, 1889 — 1910.* New Haven: Yale University Press, 1969.

Redding, J. Saunders. *The Lonesome Road: The Story of the Negro's Part in America.* Garden City, N.Y.: Doubleday, 1958.

———. *On Being Negro in America.* Indianapolis: Bobbs-Merrill, 1951.

Reitzes, Dietrich C. *Negroes and Medicine.* Cambridge, Mass.: Harvard University Press, 1958.

Report of the National Advisory Commission on Civil Disorders. New York: Bantam, 1968.

Rice, Arnold S. *The Ku Klux Klan in American Politics.* Washington, D.C.: Public Affairs Press, 1962.

Roark, James L. *Masters Without Slaves: Southern Planters in the Civil War and Reconstruction.* New York: W. W. Norton, 1977.

Robert, Joseph C. *The Road from Monticello: A Study of the Virginia Slavery Debate of 1832.* Durham, N.C.: Duke University Press, 1941.

Robinson, Donald. *Slavery in the Structure of American Politics, 1765 — 1820.* New York: W. W. Norton, 1979.

Rodgers, Harrell R., Jr., and Charles S. Bullock III. *Law and Social Change.* New York: McGraw-Hill, 1972.

Rose, Arnold M. *The Negro in America.* New York: Harper, 1948.

Ross, Frank A., and Louise V. Kennedy. *A Bibliography of Negro Migration.* New York: Columbia University Press, 1934.

Ross, Steven J. *Workers on the Edge: Work, Leisure, and Politics in Industrializing Cincinnati, 1788 — 1840.* New York: Columbia University Press, 1985.

Rowan, Carl T. *Go South To Sorrow.* New York: Random House, 1957.

———. *South of Freedom.* New York: Alfred Knopf, 1952.

Russell, John H. *The Free Negro in Virginia, 1619 — 1865.* Baltimore: Johns Hopkins University Press, 1913.

Salk, Erwin A., ed. *A Layman's Guide to Negro History.* New York: McGraw-Hill, 1967.

Saunders, Doris E. *The Day They Marched.* Chicago: Johnson, 1963.

Saunders, Doris E., ed. *The Kennedy Years and the Negro: A Photographic Record.* Chicago: Johnson, 1964.

Savitt, Todd L. *Medicine and Slavery: The Diseases and Health Care of Blacks in Antebellum Virginia.* Urbana, Ill.: University of Illinois Press, 1978.

Scarborough, William K. *The Overseer: Plantation Management in the Old South.* Baton Rouge, La.: Louisiana State University Press, 1966.

Schlesinger, Arthur M. *The Rise of the City, 1878 — 1898.* New York: Macmillan, 1933.

Schleuter, Herman. *Lincoln, Labor and Slavery.* New York: Socialist Literature Co., 1913.

Schoenfeld, Seymour J. *The Negro in the Armed Forces.* Washington, D.C.: The Associated Publishers, 1945.

Schweninger, Loren. *James T. Rapier and Reconstruction.* Chicago: The University of Chicago Press, 1978.

Scott, Emmett. *Negro Migration During the War.* New York: Arno Press, 1969.

Scott, Rebecca J. *Slave Emancipation in Cuba: The Transition to Free Labor, 1860 — 1890.* Princeton: Princeton University Press, 1985.

Sellers, James B. *Slavery in Alabama.* University, Ala.: University of Alabama Press, 1950.

Semmes, Raphael. *Crime and Punishment in Early Maryland.* Baltimore: Johns Hopkins University Press, 1938.

Sewell, Richard H. *Ballots for Freedom: Antislavery Politics in the United States, 1837 — 1860.* New York: Oxford University Press, 1976.

Shapiro, Fred C., and James W. Sullivan. *Race Riots, New York, 1964.* New York: Crowell, 1964.

Sheridan, Richard B. *Sugar and Slavery: An Economic History of the British West Indies 1623 — 1775.* Aylesbury, U.K.: Ginn, 1974.

Sherman, Richard B., ed. *The Negro and the City.* Englewood Cliffs, N.J.: Prentice-Hall, 1970.

Shogan, Robert, and Tom Craig. *The Detroit Race Riot: A Study in Violence.* Philadelphia: Chilton, 1964.

Silberman, Charles E. *Crisis in Black and White.* New York: Random House, 1964.

Silver, James W. *Mississippi: The Closed Society.* New York: Harcourt, Brace & World, 1964.

Simmons, William J. *The Klan Unmasked.* Atlanta: Thompson, 1923.

Simpson, George E., and J. Milton Yinger. *Racial and Cultural Minorities: An Analysis of Prejudice and Discrimination.* New York: Harper & Row, 1972.

Singer, Benjamin D., Richard W. Osborn, and James A. Geschwender. *Black Rioters: A Study of Social Factors and Communication in the Detroit Riot.* Lexington, Mass.: D. C. Heath and Company, 1970.

Sitkoff, Harvard. *The Struggle for Black Equality.* New York: Hill and Wang, 1991.

Sitterson, J. C. *Sugar Country: The Cane Sugar Industry in the South, 1753 — 1950.* Lexington, Ky.: University of Kentucky Press, 1953.

Smith, Page. *The Nation Comes of Age: A People's History of the Ante-Bellum Years.* New York: Penquin Group, 1981.

Smith, Samuel D. *The Negro in Congress, 1870 — 1901.* Chapel Hill, N.C.: University of North Carolina Press, 1940.

Smith, William. *A Political History of Slavery.* New York: F. Ungar Publishing Co., 1966.

Soderland, Jean R. *Quakers & Slavery: A Divided Spirit.* Princeton: Princeton University Press, 1985.

Soltow, Lee. *Men and Wealth in the United States, 1850 — 1870.* New Haven: Yale University Press, 1975.

The South and Her Children. Atlanta: The Southern Regional Council, 1971.

Southern Education Reporting Service. *A Statistical Summary, State-by-State, of Segregation-Desegregation Activity Affecting Southern Schools from 1954 to Present.* Nashville: SERS, 1957.

Spangler, Earl. *Bibliography of Negro History: Selected and Annotated Entries, General and Minnesota.* Minneapolis: Ross and Haines, 1963.

Spear, Alan L. *Black Chicago: The Making of a Negro Ghetto, 1800 — 1920.* Chicago: University of Chicago Press, 1967.

Spencer, Samuel R., Jr. *Booker T. Washington and the Negro's Place in American Life.* Boston: Little, Brown, 1955.

Spero, Sterling D., and A. L. Harris. *The Black Worker: The Negro and the Labor Movement.* New York: Columbia University Press, 1968.

Stampp, Kenneth M. *And the War Came.* Baton Rouge, La.: Louisiana State University Press, 1970.

———. *The Peculiar Institution: Slavery in the Ante-Bellum South.* New York: Vintage, 1956.

Starobin, Robert. *Industrial Slavery in the Old South.* New York: Oxford University Press, 1970.

Staudenraus, P. J. *The African Colonization Movement, 1816 — 1865.* New York: Columbia University Press, 1961.

Steele, Shelby. *The Content of Our Character.* New York: St. Martin's Press, 1990.

Stephenson, George M. *A History of American Immigration, 1820 — 1924.* Boston: Ginn, 1926.

Sterling, Dorothy, ed. *We Are Your Sisters: Black Women in the Nineteenth Century.* New York: W. W. Norton, 1984.

Steward, Theophilus G. *The Colored Regulars in the United States Army.* Philadelphia: A.M.E. Book Concern, 1904.

Stewart, Maria W. *Meditations from the Pen of Mrs. Maria W. Stewart.* Washington, D.C., 1879.

Still, William. *The Underground Railroad.* Philadelphia: Porter and Coates, 1872.

Stuckey, Sterling. *Slave Culture: Nationalist Theory and the Foundations of Black America.* New York: Oxford University Press, 1988.

Suttles, Gerald D. *The Social Order of the Slum.* Chicago: University of Chicago Press, 1968.

Sydnor, Charles S. *Slavery in Mississippi.* New York: Appleton, 1965.

Taeuber, Karl and Alma Taeuber. *Negroes in Cities.* Chicago: Aldine, 1965.

Takaki, Ronald T. *A Pro-Slavery Crusade: The Agitation to Reopen the African Slave Trade.* New York: The Free Press, 1971.

Tannenbaum, Frank. *Slave and Citizen.* New York: Vintage, 1946.

Taper, Bernard. *Gomillion versus Lightfoot.* New York: McGraw-Hill, 1962.

Terkel, Studs. *Race: How Blacks and Whites Think and Feel About the American Obsession.* New York: The New Press, 1992.

Thomas, John L. *The Liberator: William Lloyd Garrison, A Biography.* Boston: Little, Brown, 1963.

———. *Slavery Attacked: The Abolitionist Crusade.* Englewood Cliffs, N.J.: Prentice-Hall, 1965.

Thompson, Edgar T. *Plantation Societies, Race Relations and the South: Selected Papers of Edgar T. Thompson.* Durham, N.C.: Duke University Press, 1970.

Thornton, J. Mills, III. *Politics and Power in a Slave Society: Alabama, 1800 — 1860.* Baton Rouge, La.: Louisiana State University Press, 1978.

Uya, Okon E. *From Slavery to Public Service: Robert Smalls, 1839 — 1915.* New York: Oxford University Press, 1971.

Von Hoffman, Nicholas. *Mississippi Notebook.* New York: David White, 1964.

Vincent, Theodore G. *Black Power and the Garvey Movement.* San Francisco: Ramparts Press, 1972.

Vose, Clement E. *Caucasians Only: The Supreme Court, the NAACP and the Restrictive Covenant Cases.* Berkeley: University of California Press, 1959.

Wade, Richard C. *Slavery in the Cities.* New York: Oxford University Press, 1964.

Walls, Dwayne E. *The Chickenbone Special.* New York: Harcourt Brace Jovanovich, 1971.

Warren, Robert P. *Who Speaks for the Negro?* New York: Random House, 1965.

Washington, Booker T. *Selected Speeches.* Edited by E. David Washington. Garden City, N.Y.: Doubleday, 1932.

———. *The Story of the Negro: The Rise of the Race from Slavery.* 2 vols. New York: Peter Smith, 1940.

———. *Up From Slavery: An Autobiography.* New York: Doubleday, 1901.

Washington, Joseph R. *Black Religion: The Negro and Christianity in the United States.* Boston: Beacon, 1964.

Watkins, James L. *King Cotton: A Historical and Statistical Review, 1790 — 1908.* New York: Negro Universities Press, 1908.

Weatherford, Willis D. *American Churches and the Negro: A Historical Study from Early Slave Days to the Present.* Boston: Christopher, 1957.

Weaver, Robert C. *The Negro Ghetto.* New York: Harcourt, Brace & Co., 1948.

Weinberg, Meyer. *Race and Place.* Washington, D.C.: U.S. Government Printing Office, 1967.

Weissbourd, Bernard. *Segregation Subsidies and Megalopolis.* Santa Barbara, Calif.: Center for the Study of Democratic Institutions, 1964.

Weld, Theodore D. *American Slavery As It Is: Testimony of a Thousand Witnesses.* New York: New York American Anti-Slavery Society, 1839.

West, Cornel. *Race Matters.* New York: Vintage Books, 1994.

Westin, Alan F., ed. *Freedom Now! The Civil Rights Struggle in America.* New York: Basic Books, 1964.

Weyl, Nathaniel. *The Negro in American Civilization.* Washington, D.C.: Public Affairs Press, 1960.

Wharton, Vernon L. *The Negro in Mississippi, 1865 — 1890.* Chapel Hill, N.C.: University of North Carolina Press, 1947.

White, Walter F. *A Man Called White: The Autobiography of Walter White.* New York: Viking, 1948.

Whiteman, Maxwell. *A Century of Fiction by American Negroes, 1853 — 1952: A Descriptive Bibliography.* Philadelphia: Saifer, 1955.

Who's Who in Colored America. 7 vols. New York: Who's Who in Colored America Corporation, 1927 — 1950.

Wiley, Bell I. *Southern Negroes, 1861 — 1965.* New Haven: Yale University Press, 1938.

Wilhelm, Sidney M. *Who Needs the Negro?* Garden City, N.Y.: Doubleday, 1971.

Williams, Eric. *Capitalism and Slavery.* New York: Capricorn Books, 1944.

Williams, George W. *History of the Negro Race from 1619 to 1880.* New York: G. P. Putnam's Sons, 1883.

Williams, Juan. *Eyes on the Prize: America's Civil Rights Years, 1954 — 1965.* New York: Viking Penguin Inc., 1987.

Wilson, Henry. *Rise and Fall of the Slave Power in America.* 3 vols. Boston: Houghton Mifflin, 1872 — 1877.

Wilson, James Q. *Negro Politics: The Search for Leadership.* Glencoe, Ill.: The Free Press, 1960.

Wilson, Theodore B. *The Black Codes of the South.* University, Ala.: University of Alabama Press, 1965.

Woodman, Harold. *King Cotton and His Retainers.* Lexington, Ky.: University of Kentucky Press, 1968.

Woodson, Carter G. *The Education of the Negro Prior to 1861: A History of the Educations of the Colored People of the United States from the Beginning of Slavery to the Civil War.* Washington, D.C.: The Associated Publishers, 1919.

———. *A Century of Negro Migration.* Washington, D.C.: Association for the Study of Negro Life and History, 1918.

———. *The History of the Negro Church.* Washington, D.C.: The Associated Publishers, 1921.

———. *The Rural Negro.* Washington, D.C.: Association for the Study of Negro Life and History, 1930.

Woodward, C. Vann. *American Counterpoint: Slavery and Racism in the North-South Dialogue.* Boston: Little, Brown, 1971.

Woodward, C. Vann. *The Burden of Southern History.* Baton Rouge, La.: Louisiana State University Press, 1968.

———. *The Strange Career of Jim Crow.* New York: Oxford University Press, 1974.

Woofter, T. J. Jr. *Landlord and Tenant on the Cotton Plantation.* New York: New American Library and Negro Universities Press, 1969.

———. *Negro Problems in Cities.* Garden City, N.Y.: Doubleday, 1928.

Work, Monroe N. *A Bibliography of the Negro in Africa and America.* New York: Wilson, 1928.

Workman, William D. *The Case for the South.* New York: Devin-Adair, 1960.

Wright, Gavin. *Old South, New South.* New York: Basic Books, 1986.

Wright, Richard R., Jr. *Black Boy: A Record of Childhood and Youth.* New York: Harper, 1945.

———. *Native Son.* New York: Harper, 1940.

———. *White Man. Listen!* Garden City, N.Y.: Doubleday, 1957.

Wyllys, Rufus K. *Arizona: The History of a Frontier State.* Phoenix: Hobson & Herr, 1950.

Wynes, Charles E. *Race Relations in Virginia, 1870 — 1902.* Charlottesville, Va.: University of Virginia Press, 1961.

Yette, Samuel. *The Choice: The Issue of Black Survival in America.* New York: G. P. Putnam's Sons, 1971.

Young, A. S. *Great Negro Baseball Stars and How They Made the Major Leagues.* New York: A. S. Barnes and Company, Inc., 1953.

Young, Whitney M. *To Be Equal.* New York: McGraw-Hill, 1964.

Zornow, William F. *Kansas: A History of the Jayhawk State.* Norman, Okla.: University of Oklahoma Press, 1957.

INDEX

Page numbers in **boldface** type refer to illustrations.

Aaron, Hank, 394, **394**, 395, 466, 550, 564
Abbott, Robert Sengstacke, 295, 381
Abdul-Jabbar, Kareem, 473, 529, 563
Abernathy, Rev. Ralph, 416, 427, **427**, 428, 441, 442, **442**, 445, 523
Abolition. *See* Emancipation
Abolitionism. *See* Antislavery movement/abolitionism
Abyssinian Baptist Church, 81, 367, 437
Adams, Maj. Charity, 372
Adams, Charles P., 292
Adams, Captain "Doc," 251–52
Adams, Gov. James H., 161
Adams, John, 59, 89
Adams, John Quincy, 109, 199, 125, 127, 136
Addams, Jane, 272
Advertisements for slaves, 122, 147
Affirmative action, 411, 445, 464, 526
    Bakke case, 474
    opposed/weakened, 489, 490, 492, 494, 502, 528
    "reverse discrimination," 474, 489, 495
    Supreme Court on, 474, 505, 508
AFL-CIO. *See* Labor unions
Africa, 2, 12, 89. *See also* Colonization; South Africa; West Africa
Africa House (Louisiana), 78
Afric-American Female Intelligence Society, 100, 110
African Aid Society, 184
"African Church," 60, 73
African Churches
    African American Catholic, 517
    Baptist (Philadelphia), 81
    Chapel for Methodists, 74
    First Baptist (Savannah), 64
    First Baptist of Gold Street (New York), 81
    First Church of Colored Baptists (Williamsburg), 33
    First Presbyterian (Philadelphia), 80, 116, 155
    Meetinghouse (Boston), 116
    Presbyterian (New York), 92, 96
    St. Benedict the Moor Catholic (New York), 264
    St. George's Episcopal (New York), 279
    St. George's ME (Philadelphia), 72, 73
    See also African Methodist Episcopal (AME), African Methodist Episcopal of Zion (AMEZ) Church
African Development Foundation, 475
African Free School (New York), 62, 95, 119, 196

African Kingdoms (map), 2
African Methodist Episcopal (AME), African Methodist Episcopal of Zion (AMEZ) Church, 72, 73, 93, 218, 222, 234, 285, 560
    Bethel (Philadelphia), 60, 72–73, 86, 107
    Church Review, 264
    colleges founded by, 161, 196, 232
    established nationally, 86
    membership of, 86, 87, 110, 240
    missionary work of, 206
    New Jersey Conference of, 240
    "Zion" added to name, 74
Africa Town (Tarkar village in Alabama), 167–68
Afro-American Democratic Leagues, 279
Afro-American League of the United States, 257, 276
Agnew, Spiro, 452
Agriculture
    backcountry, 41
    Black employment in, 274, 287, 299, 319, 320, 479–80, 487
    Black-owned farms, 240, 387, 320, 360
        dust storms and, 353
        white jealousy of, 323
    Colored Farmers' Alliance, 267–68, 278
    co-ops established, 190, 258
    Indian labor and, 4
    mechanization of, 372, 381
    plantation economy, 6, 8, 27, **27**, 29, 31, 43, 82
        changes suggested, 223
        crops change in importance, 67
        in *1860*, 169
        large-scale, 67, 171
        and "plantation culture," 147
        planters fix wages, 211
    sharecroppers, 215, 239–40, 254, 299, 320, 321, **321**, 347–48, 350, 358, 360
        protest, 316
    slave-grown or labor-intensive crops, *see* Cotton; Indigo; Rice production; Sugar; Tobacco
    wheat introduced into Americas, 4
    See also Land grant(s)
AIDS. *See* Disease
Aid to Families with Dependent Children, 488, 555
Ailey, Alvin, 397
Alabama, 142, 215, 231
    Blacks elected in, 232, 241, 243, 244, 440
    Black voting in, 219, 275, 289, 301, 374, 424, 426, 428, 463, 483

Constitutional Convention, 230, 241, 301
cotton production, 75, 82, 89, 90, 102, 177
lynchings/violence in, 314, 370, 428, 487, 519 (*see also* Birmingham, Ala.; Montgomery, Ala.; Selma, Ala.)
population, 90, 102, 105, 170, 173–74, 177, 256, 479, 521
racial quotas in, 509
rejects busing plan, 449
restrictions on Blacks, 97, 113, 217–18, 258, 302, 398, 401, 404
secedes, readmitted to Union, 185, 219, 226
slavery/peonage in, 88, 91, 147, 167–68, 214, 292–93
University of, 392, 416, 428, 434
Alabama Negro Labor Union, 237
Albany (Georgia) Movement, 410
Albany, N.Y., 88, 100
Alcohol sales to slaves prohibited, 20, 28, 30, 94
Alcorn College, 235
Aldridge, Ira F., 95, **95**
Alexander, Clifford Jr., 472
Alexander, John H., 269
Alexandria, La., as one of "worst" cities, 377
Ali, Muhammad (Cassius Clay), 404, 424, 429, 467, 469, 474, 485
Allen, Debbie, 464, 541
Allen, Ethan, 55
Allen, Macon B., 135, 242
Allen, Bishop Richard, 59, 60, 61, 71–77 *passim*, **73**, 86, 87, 146, 232
    and National Negro Convention, 98, 107
Allensworth, Col. Allen, and Allensworth, Calif., 297
Allen University, 73, 232
Almanacs, 68, 129
Alton Observer (antislavery newspaper), 123–24
Alvarado, Pedro de, 5
AME, AMEZ Church. *See* African Methodist Episcopal (AME), African Methodist Episcopal of Zion (AMEZ) Church
American Abolition Conventions, 72, 91, 115. *See also* American Anti-Slavery Society
American and Foreign Anti-Slavery Society, 92, 108
American Anti-Slavery Society, 92, 108, 118, 121, 200
    founding of, 107, 115, 125

American Anti-Slavery Society *(continued)*
lecturers for, 126, 127, 156
Black not allowed to speak, 119
publications of, 94, 139
quoted on "Reign of Terror," 178–81
women on executive committee, 115, 129, 168
American Baptist Convention, Black at head of, 443
American Baptist Free Mission and Home Mission societies, 141, 221, 259
American Baseball Association, 266
American Bible Society, 86
American Catholic Tribune, 268
American College of Surgeons, 305
American Colonization Society, 60, 86–87, 98, 105, 218
Blacks oppose, 74, 86–91 *passim,* 108, 112
and Liberia, 91, 164, 167, 222, 231
reports on activities, 204
See also Colonization
American Federation of Labor (AFL), 367.
See also Labor unions
American Freedmen's Aid Commission, 190
American Fund for Public Service, 350
American Labor Party, 289
American League of Colored Laborers, 147.
See also Labor unions
American Medical Association
Black heads unit of, 387
Blacks excluded from, later accepted, 264–65, 383
Journal of, 536
American Missionary Association, 138–39, 178, 183, 188–89, 215
American Muslim Mission, 347
American Negro Academy, 284
American Negro Theater, 362
American Society of Composers and Performers (ASCAP), 254
American Society of Free Persons of Colour, 107
American Tobacco Company, 494
Americas, 4–6, 15. *See also* Latin America; North America; West Indies
Ames, Gov. Adelbert, 232, 235
Amherst College, 95, 338
Amnesty Act (1872), 240
Amnesty International, 456, 528
Amoco Oil Company, 483
Amos, John, 469
Anderson, Garland, 335
Anderson, Marian, 331, 359, **359**, 364, 365, 385, 390, 420
Anderson, Osborne P., 169
Anderson, Maj. Robert, 183
Anderson, Robert Ball, 221
Anderson, Violette N., 339
Andersonville Prison, 200
Angelou, Maya, 454, 557
Angola, 462
Annapolis, Md., as one of "worst" cities, 377
Annapolis Naval Academy. *See* Navy, U.S.
Annenberg, Walter, 523
Anthony, Susan B., 168
Antislavery movement/abolitionism, 22, 35, 47, 89, 101, 135, 160
and aid to escaping slaves, 96, 137, 141, 152, 153, 261 (*see also* Underground Railroad)
in Boston, 132–33, **152**, 157–59

in Britain and Ireland, 62, 117, 131, 136, 156, 161
in Canada, 70, 106
centers of, 72, 97
churches and, 57–58, 79, 115, 135
Black churches, 110
colonies move toward, 12, 13, 47
Judge Sewell and, 25
and colonization, 88, 90, 112, 153
court view of, 92, 157
education of abolitionists, 114, 127
Garrison as leader of, *see* Garrison, William Lloyd
Jefferson and, 42, 52, 55–56, 58, 157
Lafayette and, 59, 62
members of Congress supporting, 126, 151
petitions to Congress, 68, 74, 77, 119, 125
"gag rule" on, repealed, 109, 119, 136
in presidential campaign, 157
Sojourner Truth and, 134, 220
speeches/lectures on, 86, 126, 127, 132, 136, 154, 156
violence against and by, 79, 134, 147, 155, 157, 162–63
women in, 129, 155, 168
excluded, 114, 115, 129
and women's rights, 114, 118, 220
writings on, 67, 79, 94, 127, 160, 238
abolitionist journals, *see* Newspapers
banned, 106, 109, 118, 129
children's books, 139
Jefferson's, 52, 55–56
pre-Revolutionary, 40, 42, 51
"Reign of Terror" described, 178–81
Uncle Tom's Cabin, 72, 94, 96, 106, 139, 154
Walker's Appeal, 98, **99**
See also Antislavery societies; Emancipation; Laws and Legislation; Quakers
Antislavery societies
American, 92 (*see also* American Anti-Slavery Society)
American and Foreign, 92, 129
American Convention, 72, 91, 115
Black female, 100, 108, 111–12, 113, 117, 155
and Congress, 73
Illinois, 124
international, 62, 114, 117, 128, 132, 156
membership in, 105
New England (later Massachusetts), 111, 126, 129, 132, 155, 163
New York and New Jersey, 58–59, 68, 72, 117–18, 129
Ohio, 119, 146
Pennsylvania, 48, 64, 68, 69, 72, 100, 108, 114, 125, 161, 339
Rhode Island, Connecticut, Vermont, 58, 67, 85, 115
secret, 135
southern, 64, 65–66, 68, 72, 79
Western Massachusetts, 155
Anti-Slave Trade Act (1819), 89
Appalachia, Black population in, 479
Arcaro, Eddie, 261
Arizona, 5, 521, 527, 534
Arkansas, 198, 230, 231, 288, 426
anti-Black and race laws of, 218, 258, 302
Black voting strength in, 543

Black settlement in, 215, 259
KKK in, 334, 554
racial violence in, 247, 314, 316
secedes, readmitted to Union, 185, 219, 226
slavery in, 100, 105, 147, 170
exile or, 165, 178
See also Little Rock, Ark.
Arkansas River Valley Immigration Company, 214
Armistead, James, 56
Arms and ammunition, 40
Blacks excluded from use of, 10, 17, 19, 212
See also Military service; Self-defense by Blacks
Armstrong, Louis "Satchmo," 288, 328, **328**, 333, 345
Armstrong, Robb, 518–19
Armstrong, Gen. Samuel Chapman, 224, 258, 280, 308
Army, Confederate, 183, 184, 194, 210, 237
veterans of, 219, 240, 241, 244
Army, Continental, 48–51 *passim,* 53–54, 56, 57. *See also* Revolutionary War
Army, U.S., 106, 132
Black commands, 507
Blacks in, *see* Military service, Blacks in
in Civil War, 182, 191, 192
Military Academy (West Point), 190
Blacks admitted, 233–34, 253, 269, 272–73, 361
Nurse Corps, 285, 315, 478
"Project Clear" integration study by, 387–88
protecting Blacks, 212, 235, 413 (*see also* Civil rights)
ROTC programs protested, 450
restricts enlistment, 90, 246
segregation of, *see* Segregation
south under command of, 212, 221, 226, 234, 245
terrorism and, 216, 225, 236, 247, 251, 252, 253
suppresses Arkansas "rebellion," 316
troops withdraw (1877), 230, 231, 253
Army Air Force, U.S., 363–64, 370–72 *passim,* 386, 413, 468–69, 495
Black four-star general, 508
segregation in, 363, 373
women with, 441–42, 476, 529
See also Astronauts, Black
Arson. *See* Crime
Arthur, Chester A., 161
Artisans. *See* Labor, Black (skilled)
Arts, the
architecture, African design, 78
painting and sculpture, 74, 275–76, 337, 454
promotion of African-American, 284
See also Awards and honors; Entertainment; Music; Poetry; Theater
Aryan Nations Church (white supremacy group), 509
Ashe, Arthur, 429, 442, 467, 547–48
Ashmun, Rev. Jehudi, 91, 157
Asian Americans, 514, 515, 558
Chinese denied rights, excluded, 149, 246
economic condition of, 496, 521, 523, 546, 550
employment of, 485, 518

Asiento (license for shipment of slaves), 4, 24
Associated Negro Press (ANP), 317
Associates of Dr. Bray (Anglican missionary group), 41. *See also* Missionaries
Association for the Study of Negro Life and History, Inc., 339
Astronauts, Black, 437, 473, 487, 500, 505, 520, 541
   woman, 507, 508
AT&T (American Telephone & Telegraph), 463
Athletes, Black. *See* Sports
Atlanta, Ga., 202, 302, 385, 489
   Black mayors of, 462, 464, 490, 498, 564
   as one of "worst" cities, 377
   population, 273, 288, 299, 446, 521
   racial violence in, 404, 405, 436
   "Sweet Auburn" district, 288–89
Atlanta Baptist Female Seminary, 259. *See also* Spelman College
Atlanta Baptist Seminary, 22. *See also* Morehouse College
"Atlanta Compromise" speech (B. T. Washington), 280
Atlanta Constitution (daily), 275
Atlanta University, 139, 178, 210, 259, 286
   chartered, 219
   new, formed by merger, 342
Attica prison riot, 454. *See also* Crime
Attucks, Crispus, 44, **44**
Augusta, Ga., 82, 273
Augusta Institute, 221. *See also* Morehouse College
Auxiliary of Redcaps, 389. *See also* Labor unions
Awards and honors
   arts and entertainment, 324, 337, 358, 359, 383, 454, 520 (*see also* Films; Music; Recordings; Television, Theater)
   Congressional Medal of Honor, 202–5 *passim*, 235–36, 249, 282, 298, 384, 433–34
   French (World War I), 309, 312, 314–15
   honorary degrees, 282, 324, 366
   for leadership and service, 463, 478, 558
   literature and journalism, 316, 337, 338, 347, 381–85 *passim*, 423, 467–68, 500, 501, 534, 539
   Medal of Freedom, 420, 424, 470, 472
   Nobel Prize, 382, 422, 478, 562
   Phi Beta Kappa, 244, 341, 384
   Pulitzer Prize, 381, 445, 446, 469, 471, 492, 494, 508, 511, 530, 531, 561, 562
   Spingarn Medal, 279, 285, 307, 384, 398, 469
   World War II, Korean and Vietnam wars, 363–69 *passim*, 382, 433, 473, 512, 542
   See also Monuments and memorials; entries for individual sports
Ayllon, Lucas Vasquez de, 5

Baez, Joan, 434
Bagby, Lucy (last fugitive slave), 185
Bailey, Frederick Augustus Washington, 126. *See also* Douglass, Frederick
Baker, Josephine, 326, 384
Baker, Monroe, 219
Bakke, Allan, 474, 557

Balboa, Vasco Núñez de, 4
Baldwin, James, 385, 414
Baldwin, Ruth Standish, 300
Baltimore, Md., 72, 83, 92, 229, 454
   Black mayors of, 510
   population, 66, 169, 171–72, **213**, 256, 273, 287, 299, 478
   racial violence in, 436
   segregation/integration in, 302, 388–89, 414
Baltimore Intelligencer, 74
Baltimore Sun, 140
Banking, 271, 273, 276, 281, 282, 287, 296
   bank failures, 246, 262, 271, 349, 533
   Black as CEO, 524
   Black woman opens bank, 293
   Freedmen's Bank 206, 237, 246, 296
   Freedom National Bank, 459, 533
   See also Business, Black-owned
Banks, Earl "Papa Bear," 547
Banks, Ernie, 398
Banneker, Benjamin, 40, **40**, 68
Baptism. *See* Christianity
Baptist church(es), 44, 141
   Abyssinian, 81, 367, 437
   Ebenezer (Atlanta), 289
   first Black, 33, 45, 64
   Mission Societies, 141, 221, 259
   National Conventions, 266, 280, 296, 443
   proslavery stance of, 79
   Southern, 93, 135
Barbados, 9, 12, 17, 18, 23, 27. *See also* West Indies
Barber, J. Max, 295
Barksdale, Don, 375
Barnett, Claude A., 317
Barnett, Marguerite Ross, 524
Barnett, Gov. Ross, 412
Barrow, Rev. David, 79
Barry, Marion, 525, 529
Baseball, 266, 335, 390, 448, 472, 517, 526–27
   Black managers, 467, 473, 485, 540, 555
   first all-Black major league team, 457
   first Black in major leagues, 375
   first Black umpires, 429, 463
   Hall of Fame, 324, 347, 375, 395, 413, 455, 459, 477, 492, 555
   MVP, 376, 385–98 *passim*, 407–8, 413, 432, 466, 477, 554–56 *passim*, 564
   racism in, 324, 459, 509, 550, 555–56
   Rookie of the Year, 375, 393, 413
   World Series, 378, 384, 455
Baseball Club of the First Baptist Church (white supremacy group), 222
Basie, William "Count," 323, 346, 395, 536
Basketball, 375, 411, 458, 563
   Black coaches, 406, 433, 446, 466, 503, 543, 555–56
   Black-owned team, 516
   Hall of Fame, 466, 473, 477, 529
   Harlem Globetrotters, 339–40, 473
   MVP, 398, 465, 466, 477, 501, 507, 548
   NBA teams, 382, 383, 407, 460, 543
   NCAA championship, 428
   New York Rens, 330, 348, 379
   racism in, 330, 555
   Rookie of the Year, 399, 407, 477, 501, 529
Bassett, Ebenezer Don Carlos, 227–28
Baton Rouge, La., 84, 287
Battle, Kathleen, 507

Baylor, Elgin, 399, 458
Beardsley, Samuel, 117, 118
Beasley, Delilah, 316
Beauregard, Gen. Pierre, 185
Beckwourth, James P., and Beckwourth Pass (Nevada), 147–49
Beecher, Catherine, 118
Beecher, Henry Ward, 179
Beecher, Lyman, 86
Belafonte, Harry, 362, 398, 405
Bell, Alexander Graham, 261
Bell, William, 489, 493
Benezet, Anthony, 42, 44, 146
Berea College, 139, 160
Berry, Chuck, 389
Berry, Mary Frances, 498, **498**
BET (Black Entertainment Television), 482, 542
Bethel AME Church. *See* African Methodist Episcopal (AME), African Methodist Episcopal of Zion (AMEZ) Church
Bethesda Congregational Church, 127
Bethlehem Steel Corporation, 337, 454
Bethune, Mary McLeod, 294, 351–52, **351**, 354, 355, 549
Bethune-Cookman College, 302, 370
Bibb, Henry Walton, 121, 151, **151**
Bibb, Mary, 100
Bicycling, 341. *See also* Sports
Biddle, Nicholas, 185
Bienville, Gov. Jean Baptiste, sieur de, 31
Bill of Rights (Virginia and Massachusetts), 52, 54
Bird (later Forten) School (Philadelphia), 92
Birmingham, Ala., 339, 495
   Black mayor of, 478, 498, 543
   Black population, 287, 299, 447–48
   as one of "worst" cities, 377
   racial violence in, 410, 416, 419–20, 472, 482, 519
   segregation/desegregation in, 302, 485
Birney, James, 118, 119, 123, 128, 135
Birth of a Nation (film), 308
Bishop, Sanford, 550–51
Bishop College closes, 514, 530
Black, Justice Hugo La Fayette, 354, 385
Black, Joe, 384
"Black" as term, 438
Black Belt. *See* Population (southern)
Black Codes. *See* Laws and legislation
Black colleges. *See* HBCUs (Historically Black Colleges and Universities)
"Black Eagles," 364
Black Enterprise Magazine. See Magazines, Black
"Black Expo," 454
Blackfeet tribe, 148. *See also* Native Americans
Black history, 150–51, 155, 377
   "nadir" in, 288
   Negro History Week, 339
Black History Month, 309
"Black labor" issue in South, 217–18. *See also* Labor, Black
Black Laws. *See* Laws and legislation
"Black List of the Confederacy," 178
Black magazines and newspapers. *See* Magazines, Black; Newspapers, Black
Black mayors
   California, 464, 488, 498, 558, 564
   choose not to run for re-election, 564

Black mayors (continued)
cited for contempt of court, 543
meet and discuss needs, 558
Midwest, 435, 519–20, 540
Chicago, 498, 499, 504
Michigan, 463, 498, 501, 519–20
Ohio, 389, 431, 451, 520, 524
North
Connecticut, 498, 520, 525
New Jersey, 451, 456, 470, 495, 527, 558
Philadelphia and New York, 498, 501, 520
numbers increase, 498, 503, 519–20, 524
Seattle, 520
South, 219, 236, 243, 498, 500, 501, 510, 542, 558
Atlanta, 462, 464, 490, 498, 564
Birmingham, 478, 498, 543
New Orleans, 80, 387, 459, 498
Washington, D.C., 460, 498, 525
women, 463, 464, 508, 525
Black Muslims, 414, 421, 447, 471
Black national anthem, 290–91, 304
Black nationalism, 266, 308, 324, 405, 421, 427
Chicago as center of, 347
Black Panther Party, 425, 429, 430, 438, 442, 449, 499, 553
charged with conspiracy, 445, 454
government conspiracy against, 467, 496
raided, members killed, 446, 456, 496
Black Power movement, 402, 429, 435, 438.
See also Political power
"Black Princeton." See Lincoln University
Black protest
against colonization, see Colonization
against disfranchisement, 126 (see also Voting rights)
against job discrimination, 305, 354, 362–63, 422, 524
against restriction of rights, 69
against segregation, see Segregation
against sharecropping (Arkansas), 316
against taxation, 55, 125, 135
against unequal army pay, 199–200
against violence, terrorism, lynchings, 99, 247, 265, 305, 311, 361, 434
antislavery, 64, 74, 77 (see also Antislavery societies)
convictions overturned, 413, 416
first in America, 10
march down Fifth Avenue (New York), 311
march from Selma to Montgomery, 427–28, 427, 457, 506, 543
retraced, 493
marches on Washington, 336–37, 361, 362–63, 389, 398, 414–15, 417–19, 418, 441, 441, 457, 499, 558
nonviolence urged, 397, 405
by organizations, 285, 286, 342, 346 (see also NAACP)
police and, 405, 406, 417, 483
retaliatory violence, see Violence (Black retaliatory)
right to protest denied, 98
in Scottsboro case, 343, 345
at statewide conventions, 98–99, 135, 205
traditional forms questioned, 410
See also Boycotts; Freedom rides; Racism; Sit-ins; Strikes

"Black revolution" advocated, 439
Black settlements and towns
encouraged, 159–60, 192, 203
Kansas issue and, 159–60
in Midwest and West, 110–11, 144–45, 154–55, 192, 221, 231, 269, 293–94, 297
in North, 53, 282, 339
in South, 78, 211, 269, 270
See also Colonization; Land grant(s); Migration
Blacks, freed. See Free Blacks; Freed slaves
Blacks, status of. See Status
"Black Swallow," 306
Blackwell, Dr. Elizabeth, 219
Blackwell, J. Kenneth, 525–25
Black women. See Women, Black
Blaine, James G., 237
Blair, Montgomery, 164
Blair (illiteracy) Bill defeated, 275
Blake, Eubie (James Hubert), 325–26
Blake, Rev. Eugene C., 414
Bland, James A., 254, 361
Bluford, Lt. Col. Guion S., 473, 500
Bluford, Lucille H., 316, 366
Bob Jones University, 493, 500
Boley, Okla., founded, 293–94
Bolin, Judge Jane M., 359–60
Bond, Julian, 424–25, 471
Bonds, Barry, 554, 564
Bontemps, Arna, 337, 347, 352
Bork, Judge Robert, 510
Boston, Mass., 151
anti-colonization protests in, 88
antislavery protest in, 132–33, 157–59
Black societies formed in, 60, 98, 110
Black soldiers ("Bucks of America") from, 54
first Black attorneys in, 135, 207, 227, 264
free Blacks in, 35, 60
population, 33, 66, 67, 100, 319
racial violence in, 117, 157–59, 437, 467, 469, 478, 559
schools, 31, 90
Black superintendent, 504, 529
closed by violence, 559
"Jim Crow" schooling ends, 160
as one of "best" cities, 375
parents seek "open access," 494
segregated, Blacks protest, 116–17, 135, 136–37
"separate but equal," 142
in slave trade, 9, 12, 22, 31
smallpox epidemic, 32–33
Stuart case, 525
Boston Massacre (Revolutionary War), 44
Boston Transcript, 266
Boston University, 439, 559
Boswell Amendment (Alabama, 1946), 374
Bouchet, Edward A., 244, 250
Bowdoin College, 72, 95
Boxing, 374, 383, 385, 393, 398, 413, 483, 530
at Olympics, 404, 424
racism in, 82, 297–98, 302, 356
See also Ali, Muhammad (Cassius Clay); Louis, Joe
Boxley, George, and Boxley Conspiracy, 86
Boycotts, 402
in Arizona, 534
bus, 375, 390–96 passim, 399, 415, 422, 542

economic, 107, 342, 397, 404, 420, 426, 450, 487, 495
of Nixon's address, by Black Caucus, 456
school, 406, 420, 424, 450, 529, 532, 559
Boylston, Dr. Zabdiel, 32–33
Bradley, Thomas, 413, 464, 465, 488, 497, 516, 537
chooses not to run for reelection, 564
Branagan, Thomas, 61
Brandeis University, 445
Braun, Carol Moseley, 551, 551
Bray, Thomas, 146
"Breaking in" or "seasoning," 15, 39. See also Slaves, treatment of
Breckenridge, John C., 181
Brennan, Justice William J. Jr., 470, 483, 557
Brice, Mary D., 182–83
Brimmer, Andrew F., 431, 439
Britain. See Great Britain
British West Indies. See West Indies
Brock, Lou, 472, 526
Brooke, Edward W. III, 204, 410–11, 431, 431, 443, 465, 474, 551
Brooklyn, N.Y., 10, 240, 432
Brooks, Clarence, 307, 318
Brooks, Gwendolyn, 381–82, 381, 454
Brooks, Preston, 162
Brotherhood of Sleeping Car Porters Union, 336, 337, 354, 356, 367
Brown, Albert Gallatin, 75
Brown, "Aunt Clara," 168, 168
Brown, Corrine, 551
Brown, Edgar, 355
Brown, H. Rap, 435, 437
Brown, Jim, 454
Brown, John, 107, 142, 162, 163, 163, 165, 168–69, 169, 181
financial backing of, 141, 206
memorial rally attacked, 183
raid commemorated, 296
Brown, Joseph E., 75
Brown, Lee Patrick, 494, 529
Brown, Morris, 72, 87, 87
Brown, Ronald H., 517, 517
Brown, Dr. Roscoe C., 355
Brown, S. Joe, 337
Brown, Tony, 448
Brown, Comm. Wesley A., 241, 253, 378
Brown, William H. III, 445
Brown, William Wells, 155, 155
Brown, Willie L., 481, 497
Brown Fellowship Society, 67–68
Brown v. Board of Education of Topeka. See Court cases
Browne, Roscoe Lee, 157
Bruce, Blanche K., 204, 246, 248, 252, 255, 276, 431
Bryan, Andrew, 64
Bryan, George, 55
Bryant, William Cullen, 94
Buchanan, James, 163, 183
"Bucks of America" (all-Black company), 54
Buffalo, N.Y., 100, 107, 151, 437, 485
as one of "best" cities, 375
"Buffalo soldiers," 259, 260, 260, 548
Bullard, Eugene, J., 306
Bunche, Ralph J., 376, 378, 382, 382, 383, 420, 428
Bunker Hill, Battle of, 49, 49, 50, 50, 61

Bureau of Refugees, Freedmen, and Abandoned Lands. *See* Freedmen's Bureau
Burke, Yvonne Brathwaite, 431, 461
Burleigh, Harry T., 279
Burns, Anthony, 157, **158**
Burr, Hetty, 114
Burris, Roland W., 539
Burrus, William, 481
Burton, LeVar, 469
Burton, Willie D., 513
Busby, Jheryl, 513, 524
Buses and streetcars, 141
 bus boycotts, *see* Boycotts
 busing in school integration, *see* Segregation (school)
 segregation on, 276, 296, 390–91
  Supreme Court decisions, 375, 393, 409–10
Bush, George Herbert Walker, 524, 534, 547, 548
 appointments by, 469, 517, 527, 540, 546, 549
 and civil rights, 531, 539, 545
Bush, George William, 145
Bushnell, Simon M., 165
Business, big. *See* Corporations
Business, Black-owned, 229, 308, 448, 454, 549–50
 federal funds aiding, 484, 486, 516
 increase/decline in, 289–90, 358, 444, 552, 531
  numbers of (1920, 1935), 320, 352
 life insurance, 284–85, 288, 295, 298, 305, 330, 335
  top ten companies, 456
 national organizations, 289–90, 460–61
 radio and TV stations, 288, 379, 464, 467, 482, 486, 542
 railroad, 229, **229**
 recording, 399, 513, 524
 on Stock Exchange, 446, 531, 542
 success of, 528, 558–59
 women as owners, 392, 301–2, 364
 See also Agriculture; Banking; Industry; Magazines, Black; Newspapers, Black; Professions
Butler, Andrew, 162
Butler, Gen. Benjamin, 183, 186, 194, 202–3, 226, 232
Butler, Octavia, 501
Butler, Pierce, 72
Butz, Earl, 470
Buxton, Ontario (experimental Black community), 241
Byrnes, Justice James, 364

Cabeza de Vaca, Álvar Núñez, 5
Cadoria, Brig. Gen. Sherian Grace, 503
Cain, Bishop Richard Harvey, 183–84, 233
 in Congress, 240, 242, 252
 supports colonization, 222, 231
Calhoun, John C., 75, 86, 119, 125–26, 137, 142
California, 149, 160–61, 316, 521
 Black population, 145, 149, 230, 299, 320, 379
  settlers, 154–55, 297
 Blacks hold office in, 136, 464, 470, 481, 558
 Fugitive Slave Law in, 145
 in Gold Rush, 141, 145, 154, 161

KKK in, 308
 and right to testify, 149, 153, 161
 Supreme Court of, 376, 474, 482
 See also Los Angeles, Calif.
California State University, 487
Caliver, Dr. Ambrose, 355
Calloway, Cab, 371
Campanella, Roy, 376, 385, 555
Campanis, Al, 509
Campbell, Bill, 564
Camp Nelson (Kentucky) phased out, 211
Canada, 161
 Black colonization in, 92, 108, 112, 117, 151, 241
 geographical distribution of Blacks in, 121
 passes antislavery law, 70
 refuses extradition, 121
 slaves flee to, 70, 85, 94, 100, 106, 107, 121, 134, 137, 147–53 *passim*, 159, 165
Cardozo, Francis L., 204, 223, **223**, 240
Caribbean islands. *See* West Indies
Carlos, John, 442, 443, **443**
Carmichael, Stokely, 429, 434, 437, 438, 506
Carnegie, Andrew, 224, 261
Carnes, Judge Edward, 549
Carney, Sgt. William H., 199, **199**
Carolina colony, 8, 16, 17–18, 19, 34. *See also* North Carolina; South Carolina
"Carpetbaggers," 221, 222, 230
Carroll, Charles, and Carrollton, 43
"Carry Me Back to Ole Virginny," 254, 361
Carson, Dr. Benjamin S., 509
Carswell, G. Harold, 448
Carter, Jimmy, 477, 486
 appointments by, 462, 469–72 *passim*, 476, 502, 543, 546, 557
Carver, Dr. George Washington, 261, 281, 358, 360, 365–66, 530
Cary, Mary Ann Shadd, 100, 149–50
Catechism School for Negroes (New York), 26, 28
Catholic Church. *See* Roman Catholic Church
Catholic Indigent Orphan's School (New Orleans), 154
Cato (leads slave revolt), 35
Cato, Minto, 367
Caulkers' Association, 229. *See also* Labor unions
Census figures. *See* Population
Central America. *See* Latin America
Centralia, Wash., 145
Central Tennessee College, 251
Chaffin's Farm (Virginia), Battle of, 202–3, 205
Challenger disaster, 505
Chamberlain, Wilt, 340, 411, 460, 473, 529, 563
Chambers, Adm. Lawrence C., 378
Chambliss, Robert Edward, 420, 472
Chaney, James E., 424, 435, 519
Chapman, Maria W., 129
Charles, Ezzard, 356, 379
Charles, Ray, 389–90
Charles I, king of Spain, 4, 5
Charles I, king of England, 8
Charles R. Drew University of Medicine and Science, 434

Charleston, S.C., 42, 67–68, 87, 98, 188, 145, 232
 Black as judge in, 153
 emigrants leave from, 164, 222, 252, 255
 housing conditions in, 287
 liberated by Black regiment, 207–8, **207**
 population, 17, 33, 66
  Black, 22, 67, 75, 169, 172, 256, 273, 287, 299
 race riots in, 252, 316
 slave revolts in, 32, 35, 37, 93
"Charleston Insurrection," 93. *See also* Slave revolts
Charlotte, N.C., 74, 498, 501
Chase, Anthony, 97
Chase, Salmon P., 128
Chavis, Rev. Benjamin, 456, 558, 559
Cheatham, Henry P., 270, 273, 277, 281–82
Cheek, Dr. James, 530, 538
Chenault, Kenneth I., 515
Cherokee tribe, 22, 82, 106, 181, 183, 238, 244. *See also* Native Americans
Chesapeake Female College, 138, 189
Chesnutt, Charles W., 285
Chester, Jane, 100
Cheyney University (formerly Institute for Colored Youth), 111, 146, 155, 178, 205–6
Chicago, Ill.
 Black mayor of, 498, 499, 504
 Black nationalism centered in, 347
 Black population, 273, 287, 317, 319, 320, 478
 DuSable first settler, 45–26
 Fire Department, 483
 and Fugitive Slave Law, 149
 as one of "best" cities, 375
 political machine of, 341–42, 350, 351, 453
 public school system, 488
 race riots in, 317–18, **317**, 325, 332, 425–26, 434, 436
 segregation
  school, defeated, 248, 272, 483
  residential, 499
 on Underground Railroad, 100, 107
Chicago *Daily News*, Chicago *Sun-Times*, 423
Chickasaw tribe, 22, 106, 181. *See also* Native Americans
Child, Lydia Maria, 129
Children
 of Black and white, prevailing view of, 23
 education of, 82, 219, 403, 481, 496 (*see also* Education)
  busing to school, *see* Segregation (school)
  working versus, 254
 damage to, 543–44
 drug-addicted, 510
 among exiled Blacks, 179
 first Black born in America, 8
 of freed slaves, 80, 150, 211, 219
 illegitimate, 20, 21, 407, 481, 490, 522, 555
 infant mortality rate, 505, 510, 522, 536, 537
 low-birth-weight, 511
 in poverty, 522
 registration of, 79
 of slaves, 57, 58, 74

Children *(continued)*
status of, 98, 142, 154
laws determining, 12, 17, 19, 26
teenage, 454
violence by, 318, 519, 525
violence against, 416, 419–20, 425, 450,
482, 564–65
parents accused of, 488
white, antislavery activities of, 139
Children's Defense Fund, 462, 505
Chimneysweeps (Black) form union, 42
Chinese. *See* Asian Americans
Chisholm, Shirley Anita St. Hill, 438–39,
438, 443, **453**, 459, 490
Choctaw tribe, 22, 106, 181. *See also* Native
Americans
Cholera, 145. *See also* Disease
Christian, Charlie, 358
Christian, Marcus, 352
Christianity
baptism/conversion and status, 4, 8, 14,
17, 18, 19, 27
Blacks converted to, convert owners, 64,
72, 146
Islam collides with, 4
and justification of slavery, 15, 51, 93
taught to Native Americans, 22
See also Missionaries
Christopher, Warren, 554
Chrysler Corporation, 435, 476
Church, Robert Sr., 296
Churches. *See* African Churches; Religion
Church of England, 8. *See also* Episcopal
Church
CIA (Central Intelligence Agency), 467
Cincinnati, Ohio, 67, 123, 188
antislavery in, 96, 135
Black mayors of, 389, 524
racial violence in, 95, 98, 119, 131, 424
refugees from, 121
Cincinnati Colonization Society, 98
Cincinnati *Commercial*, 179
Cinque, Joseph, 127, 129
CIO (Congress of Industrial Organizations).
See Labor unions (AFL-CIO)
Citizenship for Blacks
demanded, 296
denied, 98, 113, 163–64, 216, 276, 334
freed slaves, problems of, 195, 208
guaranteed, 226
"by necessity," 116
Citizens' Protective League (Black organiza-
tion), 295
City life. *See* Urbanization
Civil equality. *See* Equal rights
Civil rights
arguments for, 126, 142
Army protection of, 235, 238, 244, 247,
251, 413
refused, 225, 242, 245, 248, 250
Black activists for, 243, 306
Blacks protest restrictions on, 69 (*see also*
Black protest)
Citizens Committee on, 499
in court, *see* Courts
Crandall case as landmark, 113
filibuster against, 397
freed slaves lose or fear to use, 150, 221
Freedmen's Bureau and, 216 (*see also*
Freedmen's Bureau)
Howard University as cradle of, 220

laws on, *see* Laws and legislation
in Maine and California, 90, 141
Missouri Compromise, 90
National Civil Rights Museum, 540
new state constitutions guarantee, 230
presidential commissions on, 374, 399,
449
Supreme Court and, *see* Supreme Court,
U.S.
troops withdrawn, 253–54, 288
unprotected, lost, 211, 231, 248
violated by police, 466
white advocates of, 212, 218
See also Citizenship for Blacks; Freedom;
Slave rights; Voting rights
Civil Rights Bills
1866, 210, 216
1870, 233, 240, 241
1875, 242, 248–49, 264
1957 and *1960*, 396, 399, 404–5
1964, 390, 396, 411, 420, 447, 483, 489,
499
Restoration Act, 503, 512
Supreme Court on, 423, 502, 503
1968, 440–41, 454
1984, 503
1990 (vetoed), 531
Civil Rights Commission, U.S., 477, 482,
484, 494, 497, 498, 545
ends support of quota system, 502
Civil Rights Memorial, 519
Civil War, 183–84, 185
Blacks serving with Union, 134, 142, 153,
183–202 *passim*, **184**, 245, 297
all-Black units, *see* Military service,
Blacks in
captured, executed by Confederacy,
196, 202
casualties, 185, 194–205 *passim*
commissioned, 141, 153, 194, 200,
204–5, 224, 226, 239
court-martialed, 200
memorial planned, 541
in Navy, *see* Navy, U.S.
numbers of, at war's end, 205
as prisoners of war, 194, 200
protest pay inequality, 199–200
recruited, 193–94, 195–96, 199, 234
women, 189, 197, 256, 306
Blacks serving with Confederacy, 184,
210, 237
issues and events leading to, 90, 162–63,
164
Lincoln quoted on purpose of, 194
Native Americans in, 181, 183, 198
and slavery issue, 186
slaves set free at start of, 167, **190**
surrender at Appomattox, 202, 210–11
Union forces occupy, take southern
cities, 182, 191, 192, 202
as war of the poor, 195–96
draft riots, 198
Clark, Lewis, 154
Clark, Mark, 446, 456, 496
Clark College, 219
Clay, Cassius (boxer). *See* Ali, Muhammad
Clay, Cassius M. (abolitionist), 136, 160
Clay, Henry, 85, 90, 91, 135, 137, 149
Clay, William Lacy, 399, 410, 439
Clayton, Eva, 551
Cleaver, Eldridge (Leroy), 391, 425, 429, 440

Clement, Rufus E., 385
Cleveland, Grover, 245
Cleveland, Ohio, 436, 483, 499
Black mayor of, 519–20
as one of "best" cities, 375
racial violence in, 424, 434, 442, 519
Clinton, Bill, 545, 557
appointments by, 450, 452, 478, 506, 517,
554, 556
Clinton (Mississippi) massacre, 248, 250
Clyburn, Jim, 551
Coast Guard, Black, 258
Coast Guard, U.S., 372, 469
Cobb, Jewel P., 487
Coca-Cola boycotted, 487
Code noir, 73, 78. *See also* Laws and legisla-
tion
Coffin, Levi, 96, **96**, 107, 131
Coker, Daniel, 72
Cole, Johnetta B., 507, **507**, 514
Cole, Nat (Nathaniel Adams) "King," 373,
393–94, 452, 545
Cole, Natalie, 545
Cole, Dr. Rebecca, 200, 219
Cole-Alexander, Dr. Lenora, 487
Coleman, Bessie, 325
Coleman, William T., 378, 467, 468, **468**
Colfax Massacre, 243. *See also* Terrorism
Colleges. *See* Education; HBCUs (Histori-
cally Black Colleges and Universities)
Collins, Barbara-Rose, 532
Collins, Cardiss, **453**, 462
Collins, George Washington, 443–44, 462
Collins, Marva, 488
Colonization
advocated in Latin America, 153, 189
and anti-Black violence, 98
by British, 60, 90
in Canada, 92, 108, 112, 117, 151, 241
Delany and Turner crusade for, 167,
218–19, 228, 231
emigrant ships (*Mayflower of Liberia,
Golconda, Azor*), 90, 164, 167, 222,
255
in Ghana, 308
in or near Haiti, 92, 189, 192
in Liberia, *see* Liberia
Lincoln's view, 189
opposed, 74, 86–95 *passim*, 107, 108, 112,
117, 121, 125
proposed by Massachusetts slaves, 47
of Sea Islands, 184, 188,2 58
seen as impractical, 105
in Sierra Leone, *see* Sierra Leone
supported, 55, 84–98 *passim*, 112, 159,
167, 189, 222, 231, 240, 252, 308
UNIA and, 308
See also Black settlements and towns;
Land grant(s)
Colonization Council, 247
Colorado, 5, 168, 391, 449
Black officials in, 467, 540
"Colored" as term, 117
Colored Agricultural and Normal Univer-
sity, 283
Colored Association of Boston, 98
Colored Farmers' Alliance, 267–68, 278
Colored Female Charitable Society, 100
Colored Female Religious and Moral Soci-
ety of Salem, 113
Colored Independent Party, 263

Colored National Labor Union, 229, 238
Colored People's Convention (Charleston), 236
Colored Troops, Bureau of (Civil War), 196
Columbia, S.C., 253
  as one of "worst" cities, 377
Columbus, Christopher, 4
Columbus, Ohio, 319
Commission on Interracial Cooperation, 339
Communist Party, 343, 347, 381, 478, 486, 490
  Du Bois and Robeson join, 286, 341
Compromise
  of 1850, 149, 150, 166
  of 1877, 288
  See also Missouri Compromise; "Three-Fifths Compromise"
Compton State College, 300
Concord, Mass., 48–49
"Conditioning," 9. See also Slaves, treatment of
Confederate Congress, 184, 185, 196
Confederate States of America
  amnesty for veterans of, 240, 244
  declares war on U.S., 185
  split by Battle of Vicksburg, 197–98
  treatment by, of captured Blacks or disloyal slaves, 196, 202
  troops of, see Army, Confederate; Navy, Confederate
  veterans of, lose vote, 219, 241
  See also Civil War
Confiscation Act (1861), 186
Congregational Church, 55, 227
Congress, Confederate. See Confederate Congress
Congress, Continental. See Continental Congress
Congress, U.S.
  anti-discrimination legislation, 233, 261
  and antislavery issue
    and "gag rule," 109, 119, 136
    legislation introduced, 142
    petitions submitted, 68, 74, 77, 119, 125
  Blacks in
    1870–1880, 231, 242, 248, 252, 255
    1881–1901, 259, 262, 264, 266, 270–79 passim
    1915–1942, 307, 341, 342, 350, 368
    1950–1976, 404, 438–39, 443, 469
    no members (1887), 268
    refused seat, 223, 251
    representation declines, 277, 282, 283, 286, 289
    (see also House of Representatives, U.S.; Senate, U.S.)
  and civil rights, 211, 220, 503, 512 (see also Civil Rights Bills)
  Democrats rule (1874), 246
  Enforcement (KKK) Acts, 213, 234, 235, 238
  filibusters in, 331, 397
  first Black speaks before, 207
  14th Amendment, 218, 226
  and Freedmen's Bureau, 208, 210, 216
  Joint Reconstruction Committee and Reconstruction Acts, 212, 221, 226
  militia restrictions, 70, 193–94
  overrides vetoes, 210, 216, 218, 220, 221
  post-Reconstruction, 232

and slavery
  abolition of, 191, 212
  bans trade, 60, 61, 73, 78, 80, 81, 89, 90
  compensates owners of freed slaves, 191–92
  Confiscation Act, 186
  and Creole case, 132
  debates, reinforces, 119, 126, 151, 167, 182
  Fugitive Slave Law, 71–72, 202
  issues reports on violence, 225, 231
  leaves issue up to states or territories, 68, 78, 119, 137–38, 142, 159, 164
  Missouri Compromise, 90, 136, 147
  South represented in, 75, 212, 236, 423
    Amnesty Act, 240
  and War on Poverty, 420
  See also Laws and legislation
Congressional Black Caucus, 497, 533
  boycotts Nixon's address, 456
  chairpersons of, 452, 474, 486, 507
    woman, 462
  founded, 386
Congressional Medal of Honor. See Awards and honors
Connecticut, 67, 68, 142
  Black soldiers in Revolution, 48, 54
  population
    colonial, 18, 19, 26, 29, 30, 31, 42
    state, 67, 100, 525
  prejudice/violence in, 55, 113, 451
  and school desegregation, 556, 559
  slavery laws, 10, 20, 30, 47, 53
    manumission, 53, 57
    trade restricted, 60
  See also Hartford, Conn.; New Haven, Conn.
Conscription Act (1863), 195–96, 202
  draft riots, 131, 198, 202
  recruitment of Blacks, see Military service, Blacks in
Constitution, U.S., 53, 164
  and slavery, 68, 71–72, 126
Constitutional Amendments
  First, 548, 554
  Thirteenth, 206, 211, 212, 216, 282
    disregarded, 232, 248
  Fourteenth, 236, 282, 476
    courts and, 243, 259, 334, 340, 351
    disregarded, 232, 248
    ratification as condition of readmittance to Union, 212, 218, 219, 221, 240
    ratified, 226, 234
  Fifteenth, 238
    courts on, 251, 308, 374
    disregarded or circumvented, 232, 248, 301
    ratified, 204, 226, 234, 235
  Nineteenth, 527
  Twenty-fourth, 424
Constitutional Conventions
  Indiana, 147
  new southern, 280–81, 300–301
  New York, 92
  North Carolina, 116, 230
  Pennsylvania, 60, 61–62, 116
  post-Civil War southern states, 219–26 passim, 230
    Black delegates to, 230–37 passim, 240, 241, 244, 245, 262

Constitutions, state, 54, 68, 150
  Blacks disfranchised by, 300–301
    grandfather clauses, 283, 292, 308
  Reconstruction, 219, 221, 228, 230
Continental Congress
  bars extension of slavery into Northwest Territory, 62
  calls for end of slave trade, 48, 52
  debates on Blacks in Continental Army, 48, 49, 51
Continental troops. See Army, Continental; Navy, Continental
"Contraband" slaves, 190, 195. See also Freed slaves
Contract laws. See Laws and legislation
Conventions, Black, 142, 160–61, 236, 264
  Baptist, 266, 280, 296, 443
  and colonization issue, 112, 117, 159, 167
  of Colored Newspapermen, 250
  of Free Persons of Color, 108
  Freedmen's, 244
  National, of Colored Men, 134, 203, 227, 261
  National Emigration, 159, 167
  National Negro, 98, 107, 112, 117
  National Negro Labor, 229, 241
  National Political, 460
  petitions by, 98–99, 135, 205
  Southern States Negro, 241
  Tennessee State, 205
Convict labor. See Labor
Conway, Gen. Thomas, 255
Conyers, John Jr., 391, 420–21, 525
Conyers, John Henry, 241
Cook, Mercer, 429
Coolidge, Calvin, 309
Cooper, Anna Julia, 291
Cooper, Charles, 382
Cooper, Brig. Gen. Douglas, 198
Cooperatives. See Economic conditions
Copeland, John A., 169
Coppin, Fannie Jackson, 111, 205–6
Coppinger, William 222
Coppin State College, 287
CORE (Council of Racial Equality), 404, 410, 426, 432, 501
  founded, 368–69
  and freedom rides, 375, 409, 415
Cornell University, 296, 446
Cornish, Samuel, 92, 95–98 passim, 108, 113, 121
Cornwallis, Gen. Charles, 57
Coronado, Francisco Vásquez de, 5
Corporations
  Blacks in high positions at, 426, 455, 477, 515, 524, 541
  and denial of credit, 483
  hiring practices of
    back pay awarded, training programs set up, 463, 486, 515
    "fair share" agreements, 537
    protested, charges made against, 404, 422, 435, 494
    quota system adopted, 454
  Reynolds withdraws cigarette brand, 527
  as slave owners, 174, 175
  and working conditions for Blacks, 337
  See also Affirmative action
Cortés, Hernando, 4
Cosby, Bill, 259, 425, 434, 503, 514, 518
Cosby, Camille, 259, 514

Cotton, **268**
  cotton gin invented, 70, **70**, 71, 75
  cotton picker machine introduced, 372, 381
  crop failure, 299, 308, 320
  pickers strike, 267–68, 348
  production increases, shifts westward, 71, 75, 80–89 passim, 145, 172–77 passim, **177**
  profitability/prices, 59, 75, 76, 82, 89–90, 101–2, 121–23
  and slave labor, 31, **59**, 82, 85, 89, 102, 122, 144, 145, **146**, 147, 169
Cotton Belt, 82, 89, 299
  slaves exported to, 103–5, 117, 147, 177
Cotton Club (Harlem), 322, 340–41, 358, 362
Cotton States and International Exposition, 278, 280
Cottrell, Comer, 448
Court cases
  Ableman v. Booth, 168
  Alexander v. Holmes, 445
  Bob Jones University v. United States, 500
  Bolte v. Cohen, 334
  Boynton v. Virginia, 406, 409
  Bratton et al. v. Detroit, 502
  Brown v. Board of Education of Topeka, 387–97 passim, 436, 505, 542, 557
  Buchanan v. Warley, 310
  Chandler v. Neff, 331
  Commonwealth v. Jennison, 57
  Corrigan v. Buckley, 334
  Cotton v. Scotland Neck Board of Education, 459
  District of Columbia v. John R. Thompson Co., Inc. 389
  Dred Scott v. Sanford, 113, 163–64
  Edmonson v. Leesville Concrete Co., 536
  Firefighters v. Stotts, 502
  Florida ex rel Hawkins v. Board of Control, 393
  Fullilove v. Klutznick, 484
  Georgia v. United States, 463
  Gibbs v. Board of Education, 354
  Gomillion v. Lightfoot, 397, 408
  Gray v. Cincinnati and Southern Railroad Company, 261
  Griggs v. Duke Power, 456
  Grove City College v. Bell, 502, 503, 512
  Guinn v. United States, 308
  Hall v. DeCur, 254
  Hall v. Mullin, 91
  Hansberry v. Lee, 362
  Heart of Atlanta Motel v. U.S., 423
  Henderson v. United States, 383
  Hurd v. Hodge, 384
  Jenkins v. Missouri, 504, 528
  Johnson v. Transportation Agency, Santa Clara County, California, 508
  Jurek v. Texas, 470
  Keyes v. Denver School District, 463
  McClesky v. Kemp, 516
  McLaurin v. Oklahoma, 382–83
  Missouri ex rel Gaines v. Canada, 357, 384
  Moore v. Dempsey, 334
  Morgan v. Virginia, 375
  NAACP v. Alabama, 398
  NAACP v. Claiborne Hardware Co., 495
  Nixon v. Herndon, 340
  Payne v. Tennessee, 558
  Plessy v. Ferguson, 282, 388

  Powell v. Alabama and *Norris v. Alabama* (Scottsboro case), 343–45
  Presley v. Etowash County Commission, 516
  Prigg v. Commonwealth, 132
  Regents of the University of California v. Bakke, 474
  Roberts v. City of Boston, 141–42, 157
  Sheff v. O'Neill, 556
  Shelley v. Kramer, 377, 384
  Sipuel v. University of Oklahoma, 377
  Slaughterhouse, 233, 243
  Smith v. Allwright, 371–72
  State v. Bowen, 140
  State v. Mann, 97–98
  State v. Young, 317
  Steele v. Louisville & Nashville R.R., 384
  Strader v. Graham, 151
  Strauder v. West Virginia, 259
  Swan v. Charlotte-Mecklenburg, 456
  Sweatt v. Painter, 384
  Sweet, 337
  Thompson v. Wilmot, 79
  United States v. Cruikshank, 251
  United States v. Paradise, 508
  United States v. Reese, 251
  University of Maryland v. Murray, 384
  U.S. Steel v. Brian Weber, 477
  Watson v. Fort Worth Bank and Trust, 513
  Weber v. Kaiser Aluminum and Chemical Corporation, 492
  Wright v. City of Emporia, 459
Courts
  access to, denied, 23, 27, 29, 30, 206
  attitude of, toward antislavery, 92, 157
  Black judgeships, *see* Government service, Blacks in
  due process denied, violated, 28, 331, 343
  emancipation upheld by, 72
  jury service forbidden, 33, 77, 94, 99, 212, 364
    allowed, 230, 259, 317, 364, 501, 536
  jury trial forbidden, 20, 28, 31, 33, 69, 149
  KKK trials, *see* Ku Klux Klan
  racism in, 390, 516, 546–47
  right to testify
    allowed, 80, 141
    denied, 26, 31, 33, 69, 79, 149, 153, 161, 207, 212
    petitioned for, 153
    sale of slave ordered by, 150
    slaves or servants sue for freedom, *see* Emancipation
  See also Death penalty; Laws and legislation; Supreme Court, U.S.
Coushatta Massacre, 247. *See also* Terrorism
Couvent, Mme. Gabriel Bernard, 154
Craft, William and Ellen, 140–41
Crandall, Prudence, 113–14, **113**
Credit, denial of, 35, 483. *See also* Economic conditions
Creek-Seminole College and Agricultural Institute, 294
Creek tribe, 22, 82, 106, 116, 181, 294. *See also* Native Americans
Cresson, Sara Emlen, 157
Crime
  arson, 92, 113, 116, 263, 292, 329, 411, 560
  Attica prison riot, 454
  Blacks as perpetrators, 489, 522

  Blacks in prison, 283, 459, 522, 538, 546, 548–49
  Blacks as victims, 462–63, 485, 488, 510, 522, 544
  homicide rate, 485, 510, 511, 512, 544, 548, 560
  KKK and, 213–14
  under Mississippi law (1897), 283
  and sentencing reform, 522
  whites acquitted of, 464, 484, 496, 548, 558
  See also Drug addiction; Labor (convict); Terrorism; Violence
Crisis (NAACP magazine), 300, 317, 338, 390
  awards by, 337, 347
  Du Bois as editor, 286, 298, 302
  See also Magazines, Black
Crocket, Sergeant (last soldier killed in Civil War), 211
Crockett, Judge George W. Jr., 481
Cromwell, Oliver (Black soldier), 54, 57
Crow tribe, 148, 149. *See also* Native Americans
Crump, Edward H. "Boss," 305
Cuba, 4, 80, 284
  and *Amistad* case, 127, 130–31
Cuffe, Paul, 55, 60, 61, 83–84, 87
Cullen, Countee, 335, 337
Cultural development 67–68. *See also* Arts, the; Education
Curfew laws. *See* Laws and legislation
Curry, Jabez L. M., 163
Curtis, Dr. Austin M., 281
Curtus, Namahyoke Sockum, 285
Cushing, Chief Justice William, 57
Custer, Gen. George, 250

Dahomey, slave sales by the king of, 184–85
Daley, Richard J., 368, 426, 453, 486
Dallas, Texas, 299, 302, 334, 398, 521
Dallas Times Herald, 546
Dana, Richard Henry Jr., 157
Dance. *See* Entertainment
Daniel Payne College, 257
Daniels, John C., 520, 525
"Darling Nelly Gray," 161
Darrow, Clarence, 337, 342, 343
Dartmouth, earl of, 47
Daughters of Africa Society, 91
Daughters of the American Revolution (DAR), 359, 364, 365, 384–85, 473
Daughters of Zion, 189
Davidson, Maj. Gen. Frederick E., 460
Davis, Alexander K., 204, 243
Davis, Angela, 460
Davis, Gen. Benjamin O. Sr., 362, **362**, 386
Davis, Gen. Benjamin O. Jr., 362, 364, 373, 386, **386**
Davis, Doris A., 464
Davis, Gov. Edmund J., 242
Davis, Ernie, 406
Davis, Jefferson, 75, 210, 269
  as Confederate president, 167, 190–91, 211
  Revels fills unexpired Senate term of, 204, 234
Davis, Joseph Emory, 75
Davis, Miles, 535
Davis, Nathaniel, 462
Davis, Ossie, 444, **444**, 448
Davis, Sammy Jr., 391–92
Dawes, William, 48
Dawson, Mary Cardwell, 367

Dawson, William L., 313, 368, 452
Death penalty, 20, 27, 28, 106, 111
    execution of slaves permitted by law, see
        Laws and legislation
    race and, 525
    Supreme Court sets aside, later reverses
        decision, 461, 470
Death rate. See Mortality rate
DeBaptist, George, 107
Declaration of Independence, 52, 53, 64, 68,
    164
Declaration of Rights (Massachusetts,
    1780), 57
Dee, Ruby, 362, 541
Defense Department, U.S., 389
Defense industry. See Labor, Black
DeGrasse, Dr. John V., 141, 205
De La Beckwith, Byron, 417, 526
Delany, Dr. Martin R., 90, 107, 140, 153,
    159, 204
    and colonization, 167, 231, 252
DeLarge, Robert Carlos, 236, 237
Delaware, 16, 89, 149, 185, 558
    busing in, 483
    and emancipation/antislavery movement,
        53, 64, 68, 72
    population, 29, 37, 67, 89, 256
    and slavery, 19, 20, 28, 72, 74, 100
Delaware River, 116
    Washington crosses, 54, 57
Dellums, Ronald V., 452, 452, 458
Democratic National Conventions, 181,
    421, 424, 461, 462, 470
Democratic Party, 262, 453
    Black support of, 235, 307, 342, 350, 351,
        532, 534
        party bid for, 378
        switch from, 433
    Black vote suppressed by, 232–42 passim,
        245, 250, 331, 333
        later wooed, 378
    Black as whip, 475
    Blacks form Democratic clubs, 277, 279
    Blacks on National Committee, 461, 463,
        471, 517, 539
    Jackson as candidate of 501, 510, 513
    and KKK, see Ku Klux Klan
    post-Civil War power of, 212, 228, 231,
        237, 241, 245, 246
    sees Black migration as "plot," 254
    seizes control in South, 232, 242, 245,
        246–47, 248, 250, 253–54
    southern influence in, 423
    splits over slavery, 181–82
    See also Political power
Demographics. See Population
Denver, Colo., 449, 540
DePriest, Oscar, 294, 307, 324, 341–42, 342,
    350, 553
de Rens, Manuel de Gerrit de, 10, 12
Deslandes, Charles, 83
de Soto, Hernando, 5
De Sousa, Mathias, 10
Detroit, Mich., 121, 135, 464, 467
    all-male schools in, 541
    Black mayors of, 463, 498, 519–20
    Black population, 478, 485
    as "Motown," 399
    as one of "best" cities, 375
    police department quotas, 502
    racial violence in, 370, 436, 437–38, 449

Detroit News, 449, 544
Dett, Robert Nathaniel, 324
Dickey, Rev. John Miller, 157
Diego el Negro (James the Black), 4
Diggs, Charles C. Jr., 386, 481, 484
Dillard University, 139, 227, 377, 524
Dinkins, David, 520, 541
Discrimination
    against Blacks, see Racism; Segregation
    denial of credit, 35, 483
    in employment, see Labor; Labor, Black
    "intentional" (Supreme Court on), 483,
        494, 513
    reverse, see Affirmative action
Disease
    AIDS, 507, 511, 514, 542, 543, 544, 547,
        548
    Black "immunity" to, 71, 145, 285
    Blacks used as guinea pigs in syphilis
        study, 458–59
    cancer, 499, 524, 527
    Center for Control of, 481, 511, 515
    cholera, 145
    Civil War casualties from, 205
    heart problems, 560
    housing conditions and, 219, 229–30, 288
    hypertension, 536
    influenza epidemic (1918), 315
    kidney disease, 537
    malaria, 6, 145
    sickle cell anemia, 300
    smallpox, 32–33, 78
    tuberculosis, 219, 264, 539
    typhoid, 230, 28
    yellow fever, 21, 71, 145, 230, 271, 285,
        322
    See also Health concerns; Mortality rate
Disney Corporation, 541
District of Columbia. See Washington, D.C.
District of Columbia Bar Association, 365
Disunion Convention, 163
Divine, Father, 356
Divorce rate, 481
"Dixie" composed, 167
Dixon, Julian, 474
Dixon, Sharon Pratt. See Kelly, Sharon Pratt
    Dixon
Doby, Larry, 375, 473
Doctorates. See Education
Domestic service. See Labor, Black
Dominican Republic, 227, 228
Dorman, Isaiah, 250
Dorr Constitution (Rhode Island), 129
Dorsey, Gov. Hugh, 31, 323
Douglas, H. Ford, 159
Douglas, James "Buster," 504, 530
Douglas, Robert, 330
Douglas, Stephen A., 159, 166, 181
Douglas, Justice William O., 385, 557
Douglass, Aaron, 337
Douglass, Charles, 194, 234
Douglass, Frederick, 126, 126, 134, 180,
    199, 234, 246, 261, 276, 306
    attacked by mob, 133, 183
    autobiography/biography of, 133, 136, 160,
        227, 376
    on colonization/emigration, 159–60, 189,
        239, 255
    death of, 278, 280
    and future of Blacks, 200, 203, 215, 227
    and John Brown, 168

named to U.S. offices, 228, 252, 259
recruits for Union forces, 194
reward offered for capture of, 179, 180
ship named for, 360, 371
speeches of, 129, 132–33, 136, 200
    July Fourth, 116, 154
and Underground Railroad, 107, 140
at Women's Rights Convention, 140
Douglass, Grace Bustill, 100, 114, 129
Douglass, Lewis, 194, 234
Douglass, Margaret, 178
Douglass, Sara Mapps, 100, 114, 155
Dove, Rita, 508
Downing, George T., 215
Draft, the. See Conscription Act (1863)
Dred Scott v. Sanford, 113, 163–64. See also
    Court cases
Drew, Charles R., 338
Drug addiction, 346, 510, 515, 539
    and drug arrests, 535, 546, 549
    legislation regarding, 451
Drug (pharmaceutical) industry, 435
Drug research, 352, 365, 387, 530
Du Bois, W. E. B., 60, 196, 219, 285–86, 285,
    291, 303, 317, 337, 406
    credo of, 295
    on mob violence, 270, 315
    and NAACP, 286, 298, 302, 311
    opposes B. T. Washington, forms Niagara
        Movement, 280, 286, 292, 293, 295,
        296, 300
Dubuque, Iowa, diversity program, 535–36
Due process, denial of, 28, 331, 343. See
    also Constitutional Amendments
    (Fourteenth)
Duke, David, 532–33
Dunbar, Paul Laurence, 277 78, 277, 304,
    360
Duncan, Rev. James, 94
Dunham, Katherine, 349, 371
Dunmore, Lord, 49–50, 51
Dunn, Oscar J., 225–26, 239
DuSable, Jean-Baptiste Point, 45–46, 45
Dutch, the
    and New Amsterdam, 8, 10
    population in colonies, 9, 13, 15
    in slave trade, 6, 7, 78, 9, 13, 14, 29
        competition with, 18, 24, 34
Dwight, Theodore, 67
Dyer, L. C., and Dyer antilynching bill, 325,
    331
Dykes, Eva B., 323–24
Dymally, Mervyn M., 465, 485–86, 553

Earle, Thomas, 128
Early, Sarah, 162
Eastern Airlines, 455
Eastern North Carolina Immigration Asso-
    ciation, 214
East Orange, N.J., 479
East St. Louis, Ill., 310–11, 366, 479
East St. Louis Journal, 310
Eatonville, Fla., incorporated, 270
Ebony magazine, 352, 373–74, 550. See also
    Magazines, Black
Economic conditions
    and antislavery movement, 101
    Black business and farms (1920), 320–21
    Blacks considered threat, 35
    boycotts and, see Boycotts
    Carolina economy tied to Caribbean, 17

Economic conditions *(continued)*
  as cause and effect of racism, 485, 561
  co-ops and, 258, 356
  denial of credit, 35, 483
  economic progress for Blacks, 380–81,
    401, 446, 458, 498
  effect of Revolution on, 43
  employment discrimination and, 274, 276
  Great Depression, 325, 333, 342–43, 403
  income disparity (Black vs. white)
    1936–1955, 353, 358, 379, 389
    1960–1969, 401, 412
    1970–1979, 446, 458, 462, 477
    1980–1993, 480, 492, 513, 514–15, 521,
      545, 547, 550
  of migrants to West, 258–59, 268–69
  panics (1837, 1873, 1893), 122, 145, 271
  plantation economy, *see* Agriculture
  post-Civil War, 230–31
  poverty, 35, 255, 319, 513, 516
    Black vs. Hispanic, 491, 496, 521
    Black vs. white, 400, 403, 410, 446–47,
      458, 477, 480, 511–12, 523, 545–46
    Civil War as war of the poor, 196, 198
    cuts in aid, 488, 505, 538–39
    decreases/increases, 481, 495–96, 511,
      532, 546, 550, 562–63
    in families headed by women, 466, 481,
      522, 523
    and poll tax, 258
    Poor People's March, 441
    War on, 420, 545
  prices
    cotton, 75, 101–2, 121–23
    drop in, 16, 55, 121–23
    land, 43, 192, 237
    rice, 43, 67
    slave, 18, 31–32, 55, 81, 87, 89, 102,
      105, 147, 159, 169, 177, 185
    steamship ticket, 255
    tobacco, 16, 43, 55, 101
  rum and, 31–32
  slave wages, 8, 27 *(see also* Emancipation
    [purchase of freedom])
  slavery and, 14, 39–40, 51, **123,** 126
    cost of slaves, 6, 14, 29, 31, 43, 89
    demand for slaves, 15, 16, 103–5, 147,
      161
    monopoly broken, 9, 19–20
    profitability, 12, 16, 18, 24, 25, 34, 75
    shift of slaves to South, 41
    "triangular" trade, 12 *(see also* Slave
      trade)
    (see also prices, *below)*
  southern exports, 84, 174
    of slaves, 103–5, 117, 177
  stock market crash, 342–43
  "two societies," 538–39
  wages, *see* Labor, Black
  wealth, 296, 302, 518
  See also Business, Black-owned; Labor;
    Population; Population, slave
Economic Opportunity Act, 420
Edelman, Marian Wright, 462, 463, **463**
Edelman, Ramona, 448
Edison, Thomas A., 261, 268, 281
Education
  of abolitionists, 113, 127
  Afrocentric curriculum, 504, 516
  Black colleges, *see* HBCUs

Black doctorates, 206, 250, 280, 286, 296,
  332, 384, 421, 516, 525–26
  funding for, 523, 538, 561
  women, 323–24, 325
Black faculty at white colleges, 141, 239,
  523, 524
Black longing for, pursuit of, 146, 178,
  227, 348, 380
Black progress in, 288, 447, 468, 81, 489,
  496, 535, 545
  Black children lag, 403
  high school graduation rates remain the
    same, 510
Black teachers' associations, 267
Black women in, *see* Women, Black
Blacks in administration (Black and white
  colleges and schools), 204, 547
  chancellors, 246, 339, 449, 516, 526, 530
  superintendents, 451, 488, 504, 516, 529
Blacks admitted to white colleges, 55, 72,
  95, 105, 114, 127, 161, 178, 561
  barred, 153, 160, 270, 382
  first attorneys, 135, 157 *(see also*
    Lawyers, Black)
  first graduates, 94, 95
  first MDs, 119, 139, 141, 157
  first nursing graduate, 256
  first physicists, 157
  first Rhodes scholar, 296
  free tuition offered, 526
  opportunities expand, 288, 489
  Phi Beta Kappas, 244, 341, 384
  southern colleges, 383, 385, 407,
    412–13, 416, 526
  Supreme Court on, 377
  West Point and Annapolis, *see* Army,
    U.S.; Navy, U.S.
  (see also Black doctorates, *below)*
books banned, 367
Bowdoin College founded, 72
for clergy, 196, 250
decline in Black college enrollment, 504,
  517, 535, 537
equal/separate facilities, *see* Segregation
first Black high school, 233
of freed slaves, 138–39, 141, 190, **190,**
  195, 220–21, 227, 235
government funding for, 452, 495, 504
  disparity in, 307, 339, 518, 538
  refused or reduced, 261, 482, 523
individuals or societies promoting, 69, 88,
  97, 163, 262, 488
  Black women's groups, 100, 108, 298
  churches, 161, 196, 227, 232, 251
  (see also Missionaries)
integrated, 226, 388–89, 392, 404, 483, 491
  "open access," 482, 494
  peacefully, 405, 408, 450, 482, 485
  violence against, 434, 449
  (see also Segregation)
legislation on
  forbidding, 28, 36, 93, 94, 97, 98, 113,
    160, 178, 196, 244
  requiring or favoring, 64, 82, 142
and literacy, 209, 231, 241, 288, 346
  improves, 481
  in voting restrictions, 275, 276, 289,
    292, 450, 468
male v. female, 443, 447, 517, 535, 537
of Native Americans and servants, 8, 25

private funding of, 97, 111, 178, 220–21,
  257–62 *passim,* 271, 294, 295, 302,
  346, 486, 514, 523 *(see also* United
  Negro College Fund [UNCF])
public (for nonwhites) begins, 8 *(see also*
  public school system, *below)*
public school system, 196, 390, 482
  female-male ratio of teachers in, 548
  Massachusetts (1845), 136
  right to (Maine), 90
  salary disparities, 338, 354, 364, 366
  schools for Blacks
    Boston, 31, 90, 116–17, 135
    burned, 292
    Midwest, 123, 246
    New York, 26, 28, 62, **62,** 93, 95, 96,
      119, 150, 196
    Pennsylvania, 69, 150 *(see also*
      Philadelphia, *below)*
    Philadelphia, 41, 44, 92, 96, 111, 155,
      206
    Quakers and, *see* Quakers
    Rhode Island, 156
    South, 37, 80, 98, 138, 149, 154, 178,
      182–83, 189, 190, 196, 233
    of slaves and slave children, 25, 46, 82,
      93, 145–46, 183, 189, 246
    laws concerning, *see* legislation on,
      above
  standardized tests, 493, 496, 515
  Supreme Court on, 377 *(see also* Supreme
    Court, U.S.)
  tax-exempt status, 447, 451, 493, 494, 500
  Teacher of the Year, 460
  teacher training, 155, 260, 281, 287, 292,
    294
  vocational, 190, 205–6, 209, 257, 287,
    292, 302, 351
    proposed, 92, 106, 108, 156, 238
  whites object to or exclude Blacks, 37,
    125, 141–42, 145–46, 153, 155–56,
    270, 382
    by threats or violence, 113–14, 178,
      182, 238
    See also Student protest
Eighth Amendment, 470. *See also* Constitutional Amendments
Eisenhower, Dwight D. , 298, 390, 393, 395,
  482
  appointments by, 359, 362, 385–86, 387,
    388
  and civil rights, 306, 399, 404, 498
Elder, Lee, 465
Elders, Dr. Joycelyn, 562
Elections
  1848, 1852, 1855, 140, 160
  1860, 181–82, 183
  1874 congressional, 237, 238, 240, 241,
    244
  1876 (disputed), 288
  1896 national, 289
  1968, Black candidate for president nomi-
    nated, 439
  gerrymandering and, *see* Political power
  Congressional committees investigate,
    235–38 *passim,* 242, 244, 245, 276,
    278
  in post-Civil War southern states, 221,
    230, 235, 236
  redistricting and, 494, 495

violent environment of, 242, 245, 246 (see also Voting rights)
See also Political office, Blacks in
Elizabeth II, queen of England, 395
Ellington, Edward Kennedy "Duke," 340–41, **340**, 346, 362, 536
Elliott, Robert Brown, 233, 237, 242
Elliott, William, 276, 278–79
Ellis, Charles M., 157
Ellison, Ralph, 352, 384, 385
Emancipation
  and aid to freed slaves, 190, 195, 206, 208
  by baptism, in English law, 8, 14
    denied, 17
  of children of slave parents, 57, 58, 74, 150
  when Civil War begins, 167
  colonies for freed slaves, see Colonization
  without consent of governor, 40
  the Constitution and, 68, 126
  free Blacks returned to slavery, slavery reinstituted, see Slavery
  freed slaves lose rights (Virginia), 150
  by Frémont, of Missouri slaves, 186
  General Hunter orders (1862), 245
  gradual, 53, 55, 74–75, 185
    Lincoln calls for, 160, 191
  of indentured Blacks, 10
  Jefferson calls for, 42
  legislation regarding, see Laws and legislation, Antislavery
  by owner, 20, 28, 30, 58, 77
  petition for, in Massachusetts, 47, 61
  purchase of freedom, 4, 64
    by abolitionists, 133, 157, 261
    by Colonization Society, 105
    government refuses, 157
    by indentured servants, 15, 95
    Quakers aid in, 73, 74
    by slave wages, 47, 72, 105, 106, 145
  as reward for service, 61 (see also Military service, Blacks in)
  slavery abolished
    Blacks celebrate dates of, 116, 211
    Britain and colonies, 45, 80, 115, 127
    District of Columbia, 191–92
    France, 73
    northern states, 53, 55, 57, 58, 64–69, 97, 134, 137
    Texas, 211
    U.S., by 13th Amendment, 206, 212–13
    West Indies, 116
  of slave entering free state, 94
  of slaves or servants who sue for, 13–14, 18, 47, 79
  of slave who inherits property, 91
  by Spain, of Florida slaves, 5, 34, 35
  as state's right, 72 (see also States' rights)
  See also Antislavery movement/abolitionism; Free Blacks; Freed slaves
Emancipation Proclamation, 194–95
Emanuel AME Church, 222. See also African Methodist Episcopal (AME), African Methodist Episcopal of Zion (AMEZ) Church
Embry, Elroy, 405
Emigration. See Migration
Emmett, Dan, 167
Employment/unemployment. See Labor; Labor, Black

Enforcement (KKK) Acts, 213, 234, 235, 238
Enfranchisement. See Emancipation; Voting rights
England. See Great Britain
Entertainment
  all-Black nightclubs, 339, 340–41
  dance, 349, 394, 397, 445
  "fair-share" agreement in, 537
  highest-paid, 518
  radio, 288, 373, 379, 399
  at resorts, 303–4
  segregated facilities, 307
  vaudeville, 391
  See also Films; Miss Black America and Miss America pageants; Music; Recordings; Television; Theater
Environmental Protection Agency, 549
"Environmental racism," 528, 547, 549
Episcopal Church, 73, 266
  first female bishop, 516
  receives Black church, 88
  school for Blacks (New York), 26, 28
Equal Credit Opportunity Act, 483
Equal Employment Opportunity Act, 489
Equal Employment Opportunity Commission (EEOC), 411, 471, 489, 490, 492, 499
  investigations by, 463, 486, 514, 515
  Nixon and, 445, 472
  Thomas heads, 493, 514, 528
Equal Opportunity Council, 425, 435
Equal rights, 128, 205
  Massachusetts grants, 55, 136, 142
Equal Rights, Friends of (Charleston), 232
Equal Rights Amendment, 494
Equal Rights Association, 156
Equal Rights Convention (Georgia), 96
Equal Rights League, National, 203, 212, 271
Equal Suffrage Club, 196
Erving, Julius "Dr. J.," 465
Espy, Mike, 505–6
Estevanico (Esteban, Estevan de Dorantes), 5, 253
Ethiopia invaded by Italy, 351
Ethiopian Regiment (British army), 50. See also Revolutionary War
Evans, Joseph H., 355
Evans, Melvin, 474
Evanti, Lillian, 367
Everett, Edward, 200
Evers, James Charles, 444
Evers, Medgar, 417, 444, 519, 526
"Exodusters," 238, 241, 258–59. See also Migration
Explorers, Blacks and Native Americans as, 4, 5, 18, 147–49

Fahy, Charles, and Fahy Committee, 378
Fair Employment Practices Committee (FEPC), 363, 373, 481
Fairfax Resolve, 48
Fair Housing Act, 440–41
"Fair share" agreements, 537, 559
Fall, Albert, 253
Farmer, James, 368–69, **368**, 409, 421, 426, 434, 444
Farmer, Karen, 473
Farming. See Agriculture
Farragut, Adm. David, 205
Farrakhan, Louis, 347, 471, 560

Faubus, Gov. Orval, 395, 398, 400
Fauntroy, Walter, 457–58, 493, 525
Fauset, Crystal Bird, 356
Fauset, Jessie, 330
Fayetteville State University, 271
FBI (Federal Bureau of Investigation), 483
  v. KKK, 385, 482, 485
  racism of, 467, 476, 488, 531–32, 535, 536
Federal Drug Enforcement Agency, 494
Federal Elections Bill, 267
Federal Reserve Board, 431
Federal Revenue Sharing Act (1974), 483
Federal Trade Commission, 413
Federal troops. See Army, U.S.
Fee, John G., 160, 211
Female Anti-Slavery Society, 111–12, 117, 155
Female Literary Society, 100, 108
Feminism, Black, 157, 384. See also Women's rights
Fences (Wilson), 509
Ferdinand II, king of Spain, 4
Ferguson, Bishop Samuel D., 266
Fessenden, William, 212
Fields, Cleo, 552
Fifteenth Amendment. See Constitutional Amendments
Fillmore, Millard, 149
Films
  Blacks appearing in, 337, 341, 349, 350, 444, 448, 459, 516
  award-winning, 358, 454, 498, 502, 503, 513, 528
  made by Blacks, 303, 307, 313, 318, 337, 448, 454, 502, 516, 541
  award-winning, 520, 539–40, 547
  protested by NAACP, 275, 208
  See also Entertainment
Fines and penalties. See Penalties for:
First Amendment. See Constitutional Amendments
Fish, Hamilton, 228
Fisher, Gail, 445
Fisk University, 139, 210, 286, 312, 361, 374, 386
  founded, 178, 215
  Jubilee Singers of, 215, 224
Fitzgerald, Ella, 352, 558
Flake, Floyd, 505, 506, 525, 526
Fleetwood, Christian, 203, **203**
Fletcher, Arthur A., 445, 527, 545
Flipper, Henry O., 233, 253, **253**, 269
Florida, 215, 228, 521
  anti-Black laws, 217
  Black colleges founded in, 231
  Black voting in, 219, 257, 258
  Blacks elected or appointed to office in, 204, 238, 469, 558
  Constitutional Convention, 230
  death penalty upheld, 470
  enters Union, secedes, readmitted, 136, 185, 219, 226
  explorations of, 4, 5
  racial violence/lynchings in, 225, 231–32, 290, 314, 234, 383, 509, 517
  repays Rosewood survivors, 565
  segregation in, 258, 393, 401, 404
  rejects busing plan, 449
  Seminole Wars in, see Seminole Wars
  slavery in, 5, 28, 34, 35, 74, 87, 111

Florida *(continued)*
    maroon settlements destroyed, 37, 86
    as "slave" state, 136, 147
    slaves freed (1862), 245
    Supreme Court of, 500, 527–28
    University of, 383
    See also Jacksonville, Fla.; Miami, Fla.
Florida Atlantic University, 526
Foley, Lelia Smith, 463
Football, 277, 309, 341, 375, 534, 536
    Black coaches, 316, 503, 519, 547, 555, 562
    Hall of Fame, 454, 471, 547, 550, 560
    Heisman Trophy, 406, 407
    MVP, 512
    rushing record, 471, 501
    salaries, 560–61
Forbes, George, 280, 292
Ford, Gerald, 461, 468, 470
    appointments by, 378, 467, 527, 557
Ford, Harold E., 465, 525, 530
Ford Foundation, 448, 477, 489, 532
Ford Motor Company, 435, 486, 515
Forrest, Gen. Nathan B., 201, 213, 222
Fortas, Justice Abe, 557
Forten, Charlotte Sr., 100, 114
Forten, Charlotte (granddaughter of above),
    108, 155, 184
Forten, James, 73, 74, 85, 87–88, 92,
    114–115, 184
Forten, Margaretta and Sarah, 100, 114
Fort Pillow (Tennessee) massacre, 200–201,
    201, 213
Fortress Monroe, Va., 183, 186, 187, **187**
Fort Sumter, S.C., 183, 184, 185, **186**
Fort Ticonderoga, capture of, 55
Fortune, Amos, 74
Fortune, T. Thomas, 257, 265, 266, 276, 304
Fort Wagner (South Carolina), Battle of, 194,
    197, 198, 199
"Forty Acres and a Mule," 216. *See also*
    Freedmen's Bureau; Land grant(s)
Foster, Andrew "Rube," 324, 335
Foster, Stephen Collins, 156, 179
Fourteenth Amendment. *See* Constitutional
    Amendments
Fourth Reich Skin Heads, 560
Fowler, Wyche, 506
Fox, Col. Charles B., 207–8
France, 20–21, 24, 77
    and slavery, 6, 8, 17, 18, 31, 34
    code noir, 73, 78
    in World War I, 309, 310, 312–13
Franchise, the. *See* Emancipation; Voting
    rights
Francis, H. Minton, 253
Frankfurter, Justice Felix, 378, 467
Franklin, Ada Crogman, 316
Franklin, Benjamin, 40, 64, 68, 117, 146
Franklin, Chester, 315–16
Franklin, John Hope, 421
Franklin, Joseph Paul, 488, 496
Franklin, Martha M., 298
Frankoina and Armfield (slave-trading firm),
    104–5
Franks, Gary, 526
Fraternities, 95, 196, 303, 307
    Phi Beta Kappa, 386 (*see also* Awards and
    honors)
Frazier, E. Franklin, 348
Free African Society, 60, 72, 73, 155
Free Africa Schools, 96. *See also* Education

Free Blacks
    and choice between exile or slavery, 165,
    178
    colonization of, *see* Colonization
    education for, *see* Education
    emancipation dates celebrated by, 116, 211
    form Brown Fellowship Society, 67–68
    form union, 147 (*see also* Labor unions)
    in Gold Rush, 145
    government aid to, 208
    among Haitian refugees, 80
    hardships of, 35, 135
    kidnapping on, 53, 57, 59, 60, 79
    in labor force, 75, 89, 97, 129, 147, 167,
    206 (*see also* Labor, Black)
    legislation protecting, 53, 57, 163
    military service by, 49–50 (*see also* Mili-
    tary service, Blacks in)
    with Native Americans, 89, 106, 116, 124
    newly freed, *see* Freed slaves
    population, *see* Population
    protests by, *see* Black protest
    punishment of, 105, 108
    restrictions on, 20, 26, 28, 33, 68, 72, 88,
    113, 212
        barred or expelled, *see* Laws and legisla-
        tion
        education forbidden, 93, 97, 98
        freedom of assembly, 94, 105, 212
        white guardian required, 93
    returned to slavery, *see* Slavery
    settlements of, *see* Black settlements and
    towns
    as slaveowners, 100, 118
    southern fears of, hostility toward, 91, 93,
    105 (*see also* Racism)
    and taxes, 42, 55, 118, 125, 135
    violence against, 94, 113, 116, 128, 131
        self-defense recommended, 265, 268
        (*see also* Violence)
    voting rights of, 51, 53, 68, 90, 116, 204
        (*See also* Voting rights)
    See also Emancipation
Freedmen's Associations/Societies
    Affairs Committee, 237
    Aid Association (London), 156
    Aid Societies (U.S.), 195, 208, 251
    National Relief Association, 190
Freedmen's Bureau, 72, 153, 208–10, **208**,
    211, 214, 236, 255, 271
    closes (1872), 240
    creation and extension of, passed over
    veto, 210, 216
    helps found Black schools and colleges,
    178, 210, 215, 219, 224, 231
Freedmen's Convention of North Carolina,
    244
Freedmen's Hospital, 112, 125, 278, 281,
    285, 338
Freedmen's Savings and Trust Company
    (Freedmen's Bank). *See* Banking
Freedmen's Union Industrial School, 209,
    209
Freedom
    of assembly, restricted, 25, 33, 44, 80, 94,
    105, 212
    of movement, *see* Mobility
    as "natural state," 131
    purchase of, *see* Emancipation
    of religion, restricted, 44, 64, 72, 80 (*see
    also* Religion)

    of speech, restricted, 212
    See also Civil rights
"Freedom dues," 21
Freedom National Bank. *See* Banking
Freedom rides, 375, 402, 209–10, 413, 415,
    506
Freedom's Journal. *See* Newspapers, Black
Freed slaves
    aid to, 190, 195, 206
    and citizenship, 195, 208
    education of, *see* Education
    lose or fear to use civil rights, 150, 221
    statistics on killing of and by, 225
    See also Emancipation; Freedmen's Bureau
Freeman, Justice Charles, 539
Freeman, Morgan, 435
Freemasonry. *See* Masonic Order
Free School for Negroes (New York), 93
Free-Soil Party, 128, 140, 157
"Free Staters," 160. *See also* Antislavery
    movement/abolitionism
Frémont, Gen. John C., 157, 163, 184, 186,
    188
French and Indian War, 41
French Foreign Legion, 306
Friends of Equal Rights of Charleston, 232
Fugitive Slave Laws
    1793, 60, 71–72, 77, 79, 132
        Vermont blocks, 133
    1824 (Indiana), 94
    1832 (Virginia), 111
    1850, 137, 145, 147, 149, 154
        last slave returned under, 185
        policy changes (during Civil War), 186
        protested, 150, 152, 157
        repealed, 202
        Supreme Court on, 159, 164, 168
Fugitive slaves. *See* Slaves, runaway
Fuller, Charles, 494
Funding
    based on race, 484, 486, 516, 534
    for education, *see* Education; HBCUs
    Federal Revenue Sharing Act, 483
    See also Philanthropy
Fur-trading, 46, 148

Gage, Gov. Thomas, 47, 57
"Gag rule." *See* Congress, U.S.
Gaines, Col. Edmund, 86
Gaines, Ernest J., 454
Gaines, Lloyd, 357–58
Gallup polls, 459
Gambia, 12, 22
Gamble, Elizabeth, 330
Gamble, James, 294
Gantt, Harvey, 498, 501, 533, 554
Garfield, James A., 224, 246
Garnet, Rev. Henry Highland, 115, 128,
    135, 167, 196, 233, 260
    preaches to Congress, 207
    urges rebellion, 134–35
Garrison, William Lloyd, 84, 112, 114, 125,
    163, 261
    attached by mob, 117
    boycotts World Convention, 129
    followers decry violence, 134
    influence of, 105, 108, 109, 113, 126, 155
    Liberty Party opposes, 128
Garvey, Marcus, 266, 286, 308–9, 310, 323,
    324–25
    imprisoned, 337

Gary, Ind., 373, 435, 446, 460
Gates, Daryl, 494, 537
Gavagan, Joseph A., 361, 363
Gaye, Marvin, 399, 411, 501
General Motors Corporation, 422, 426, 455, 515
    "fair share" agreement with, 537
George III, king of England, 48
Georgetown University, 246, 250, 449
Georgia, 22, 164–65, 470
    Black colleges in, 257, 274
    Black voting in, 219, 257
        poll tax repealed 373
        restricted, 258, 275, 301, 395–96, 426, 463
    Blacks in legislature of, 226, 234, 412, 435
        denied seat, 218, 228, 424
    Constitutional Convention, 310, 301
    convict labor in, 214, 288
    cotton production in, 59, 75, 82, 89, 102, 320
    Equal Rights Convention in, 296
    population
        colonial, 34, 37, 41, 43, 55
        state, 67, 89, 170, 256, 319, 521
    in post-Civil War Congress, 212, 234
    racial violence in, 262, 285, 295, 296, 411, 450, 456, 483
    represented in Congress by Black, 461–62
    restricts Blacks, 48, 97, 113 (see also Black voting in, above)
    secedes, readmitted to Union, 185, 226, 234
    segregation in, 258, 276, 302, 401
        Justice Department sues, 445
        rejects busing plan, 449
        school desegregation, 408
    slavery in, 22, 48, 59, 82, 85, 87, 147, 245
        and antislavery, 98, 178
        laws, 10, 28, 39–40, 74, 77, 88, 97, 169
    University of, 366–67, 407
    See also Atlanta, Ga.; Savannah, Ga.
Gerrymandering. See Political power
Gettysburg Address, 200
Ghana, 1, 308, 406
Gibbs, Jonathan C., 204
Gibbs, Mifflin W., 153, 161, 243, 250
Gibson, Althea, 382, 392, 396, **396**
Gibson, Josh, 346–47, **347**, 459
Gibson, Kenneth A., 451, 470, 495
Gibson, Dr. William F., 559
Giddings, Joshua, 119, 132, 136, **180**
    reward offered for capture, 179, 180
Giles, Harriet E., 259
Gillem, Gen. A. C. Jr. and Gillem Board report, 373
Gillespie, Dizzy, 358
Gilliam, Dorothy Butler, 530
Gilliard, Nicholson, 72
Gilpin, Charles, 325
Giovanni, Nikki, 454
Glasgow, University of, 119, 223
Gleaves, Richard H., 204, 240
Glover, James, 476
Goetz, Bernhard, 503
Goldberg, Whoopi, 539
Golden Gate Male Quartet, 364
Gold Rush. See California
Goldsboro Christian Schools, 493, 500
Gomillion, Charles G., 397
Goode, Malvin R., 413, 530

Goode, W. Wilson, 498, 501
Gooding, Cpl. James Henry, 199–200
Goodman, Andrew, 424, 435, 519
Goodman, Benny, 333, 345, 358
Gordon, Brig. Gen. Fred A., 507
Gordone, Charles, 446
Gordy, Berry Jr., 399, 411
Gossett, Lou Jr., 498
Government service, Blacks in
    cabinet/subcabinet positions, 355, 439, 444–45, 467, 506, 528
        first holding, 277, 423, 426, 431
        women, 476, 487, 556
    consular/diplomatic service, 136, 161, 227–28, 239, 304, 398, 423, 428–30 passim, 439, 474, 505
        women, 476
        (see also Liberia)
    during Reconstruction, 204
    F. Douglass in, 228, 252, 259
    judgeships, 264, 468
        Circuit Court, 356, 378, 406, 528
        judge impeached, 513, 519, 552
        justices and chief justices, 236, 469, 500, 502, 539
        number of appointments, 469, 543
        racism and, 546
        in South, 153, 161, 242, 243, 248, 470
        Supreme Court Justices, 436, 470, 540, 546, 557–58
        women, 359–60, 433, 512, 543
    See also Congress, U.S.; Political office, Blacks in; Post Office, U.S.; Treasury Department, U.S.
Grambling College, 287, 292, 503
Grandfather clauses, 274–75, 283, 289, 292
    found unconstitutional, 308
"Grandparents' clause," 128. See also Miscegenation
Granger, Gen. Gordon, 211
Grant, Gen. Ulysses S., 197, 202, 210, 228, 239, 248, 271
    orders federal troops to South, 247, 251, 252
    refuses intervention, 242, 245, 250
    as presidential candidate, 225, 238
Gravely, Adm. Samuel L., 411, **411**
Gray, Rev. William, 474–75, 561
Great Britain, 6, 21, 37, 41
    Crafts escape to, 141
    establishes free Black colony, 60, 90
    "King of England's soldiers," 59
    offers freedom to Blacks who serve with, 43, 49–50, 51, 56–57
    sells Blacks back into slavery, 56, 86
    population of North American colonies, see Population
    in Revolutionary War, 43, 48–51, 54, 56–57
    and slavery, 5, 9, 16–18 passim, 28, 34, 133
        abolished, 45, 80, 115, 127
        and antislavery, 62, 117, 136, 156, 161
        colonies import slaves, 8, 12, 15
        monopoly revoked, 9, 19–20
        trading patterns, 23, 25, 31
    in War in 1812, 84, 85–86
    in West Indies, see West Indies
Great Depression. See Economic conditions
Greeley, Horace, 179, 194
Green, Shields, 168
Greene, Gen. Nathanael, 54

Greener, Richard T., 239, 255
Greenfield, Elizabeth ("the Black Swan"), 151–52
Green Mountain Boys, 55
Greenville, S.C., as one of "worst" cities, 377
Greenwich Village (New York), 10, 12, 67
Gregory, Dick, 426
Gregory, Lt. Col. Frederick, 473
Griffith, D. W., 308
Grimké, Angelina, 118, 128, 155
Grimké, Rev. Francis J., 184, 233
Grimké, John F., 118
Grimké, Sarah, 118, 155
Guinea Company, 24
Gulf Oil Company boycotted, 404
Gurley, R. R., 112
Gumbel, Bryant, 492

Haiti, 69–70, 81
    Black ministers to 227–28, 266, 271, 273
    refugees from, 78, 80, 545
    southern Blacks resettled in, 92, 192
    See also Hispaniola
Haley, Alex, 421, 469
Haley, George, 530
Hall, Charles E., 355
Hall, Juanita, 382
Hall, Katie Beatrice, 496
Hall, Primus, 90, 116, 146
Hall, Prince, 48, 49, 60–61
Hall, Maj. Gen. Titus, 494–95
Hambleton, James P., 178
Hamburg (South Carolina) massacre, 251–52
Hamer, Fannie Lou, 421
Hamilton, Alexander, 58
Hamilton, Charles, 429
Hamilton, Virginia, 467–68
Hamlin, Hannibal, 181, 182
Hammon, Jupiter, 41–42
Hampton, Fred, 429, 446, 456, 496
Hampton, Lionel, 345
Hampton Institute, 139, 189, 206, 210, **225**, 258, 280
    founded, 178, 224
Hanby, Benjamin, 161
Hancock, John, 49
Handy, W. C., 305, 322
Hansberry, Lorraine, 362, 399–400, 464
Haralson, Jeremiah, 241, 244, 248, 552
Harding, Warren G., 231
Harlan, Justice John Marshall, 281, 282
Harlem, 88, 352, 356, 445
    nation of Islam in, 471 (see also Islam)
    Renaissance era, 304, 332, 339, 362
        key figures in, 322, 325–31 passim, 335, 338, 340–41, 347, 358
Harlem Globetrotters. See Basketball
Harmon, Leonard Roy, 360, 369
Harper, Conrad, 526
Harper, Frances Ellen Watkins, 156–57, **156**, 169, 238
Harper, Robert Goodloe, and Harper, Liberia, 112
Harpers Ferry raid, 141, 142, 165, 168–69, 179, 183
Harris, Bishop Barbara, 516
Harris, Joel Chandler, 275
Harris, Brig. Gen. Marcelite, 529
Harris, Patricia Roberts, 428, 429, 476, **476**

Harris, Sara, 113
Harrison, Benjamin, 245, 246, 283
Hartford, Conn., 88, 451
  Black mayors of, 498, 508
  "Project Concern" of, 556
Harvard College/University, 90, 324
  Black athlete from, 277
  Black doctorates from, 280, 286, 296, 421
  Black graduates of, 226–27, 264, 384
  first honorary degree to Black, 282
  student protest at, 153, 365, 534
Harvard Law Review, 496
Hastie, Judge William H., 355, 356, 357,
  357, 378
Hastings, Alcee L., 513, 519, 552
Hatcher, Andrew, 406
Hatcher, Justice Joseph W., 469
Hatcher, Richard B., 435, **435**, 460, 496
Haviland, Laura, 99–100
Hawkins, Augustus F., 351, 411–12
Hawkins, Yusuf, 515, 531
Hayden, Harriet, 100
Hayden, Lewis, 107, 157
Hayden, Robert, 352
Hayes, Bob, 424
Hayes, Charles A., 499, 553
Hayes, Isaac, 454
Hayes, Marcella A., 476
Hayes, Roland, 331
Hayes, Rutherford B., 161, 254, 255, 271, 288
Hayne, Henry E., 240, 243
Haynes, Dr. George E., 300, 303
Haynes, Lemuel, 55, 56, **56**, 115
HBCUs (Historically Black Colleges and
    Universities), 350
  Black faculty at, 523, 547
  enrollment drops, 497
  first Black female presidents of, 157, 507
  first Black male president of, 162, 196
  first black woman lawyer, 240
  first Black women MDs, 200, 219
  first for Black women, 259–60
  first medical college, 251
  forced to close, 160, 514
  founded
    1832–1856, 111, 146, 157, 160, 161, 196
    1865–1880, 178, 215, 219, 221, 224,
      231, 232, 251, 495
    1881–1900, 257, 259, 260–61, 271, 274,
      276, 283, 287
    1901–1930, 293, 300, 302, 322, 342
    1947–1966, 375, 434
  funding of, 163, 193, 210, 251, 259, 292,
      346, 561
    federal aid, 452, 486, 495
  land grant, 235, 241, 259
  missionary support of, 139, 141
  President's Board of Advisers on, 539
  proposed, 107–8, 113
  See also Education; Fraternities; Sororities
"Headright" system, 13, 16. *See also* Land
    grant(s)
Health, U.S. Departments of, 449, 452, 495,
    517, 527, 544, 552
  and "Tuskegee Study," 458–59
Health concerns, 542, 548, 560. *See also*
    Disease; Life expectancy
Health Statistics, National Center for, 477,
    490, 522
Healy, Bishop James A., 159, 249–50, **249**,
    267

Healy, Fr. Patrick Francis, 206, **206**, 246,
    250, 267, 449
Heard, Rev. William H., 280
Height, Dorothy I., 542
Helms, Jesse, 486, 494, 500, 501, 533
Henderson, Harold, 536
Henderson, Rickey, 526–27
Hendricks, Caesar, 47
Henry, William "Jerry," 152, 153
Henson, Josiah, 94, 106, 154
Henson, Matthew, 298
Hentz, Caroline, 106
Herndon, Alonzo F., 295–96
Herrick, Dr. J. B., 300
Higginbotham, Judge A. Leon Jr., 413, 557
Higginson, Col. Thomas Wentworth, 157,
    189, 192
"Higher-law" doctrine, 131
Hill, Abram, 362
Hill, Anita, 540
Hill, Rev. Elias, 240
Hilliard, Asa, 504
Hilliard, Earl F., 552
Hines, Earl "Fatha," 371
Hispanics, 451, 481, 515, 520, 555, 558
  and AIDS, 514, 542
  discrimination against, 483, 497, 532,
    546
  on police force, 482, 489
  poverty/income of, 491, 496, 521, 523,
    546, 547, 550
  in urban population, 480, 534, 554
Hispaniola, 4, 5, 20–21, 70. *See also* West
    Indies
History. *See* Black History
Hitler, Adolf, 350, 354, 470
Hodges, Luther, 390, 415
Holden, Gov. William W., 232, 236
Holder, Geoffrey, 394
Holiday, Billie, 345–46, 459, 536
Holly, Ellen, 442
Holly, James T., 159
Holman, M. Carl, 448, 514
Holmes, Larry, 483, 485
Holmes, Justice Oliver Wendell Jr., 340
Home for Destitute Colored Women and
    Children (Washington, D.C.), 219
Homestead Acts. *See* Land grant(s)
Homicide rate. *See* Crime
Honors. *See* Awards and honors
Hood, James, 416
Hooks, Benjamin L. 392, 459, 471
Hoover, Herbert, 346, 352, 355
Hoover, J. Edgar, 445, 476, 482
Hope, John, 295, 296, 342, 360
Hopkins, Rev. Moses, 266
Hopkins, Samuel, 52
Horne, Dr. Frank, 355
Horne, Lena, 358, 362, 371, 536
Horse, Chief John, 124
Horton, George Moses, 106, 222–23
Houchins, Joseph R., 355
House of Representatives, U.S.
  addressed by Blacks, 224, 238
  and antilynching bill, 325
  Black demonstration at, 220
  Blacks elected to, 160, 192
    1896–1944, 281, 294, 371
    1950s–1960s, 386, 404, 420–21
    1970s, 431, 444, 450, 452, 461–62, 474,
      475

    1980s, 485–86, 490–91, 496, 497, 499,
      505–7, 514, 520
    1990s, 526, 527, 533, 551–54
  denied seat, 223–24, 251, 437
  increase in, 464–65, 514
  Reconstruction era, 204, 232–45 *passim*
  women, 438–39, 461, 465, 496, 551, 552
  and Civil Rights Bill, 503
  "gag rule" in, 119, 136
  and post–Civil War southern states, 212
  and slavery, 68, 69, 137
  state representation in, 61, 76
Housing
  discriminatory, 504, 565
    banned, 413, 441, 445
  fair housing ordinance, 395
  homeownership, 447, 480, 521–22, 550
    "redlining" and, 453
  police protection for, 396
  and racial violence, 325, 384
  segregation studied, 499
  substandard conditions, 521
    in "the alley," 287–88
    for Black employees, 337
    and disease, 219, 229–30, 288
    Urban League and, 303
  urban renewal and, 401
Housing and Urban Development (HUD),
    Department of, 426, 481–82
Houston, Charles H. 350, 360, 384
Houston, Whitney, 405
Houston, William, I., 355
Houston, Texas, 299, 311–12, 377, 494
Howard, Elston, 413
Howard, Gen. Oliver Otis, 72, 209, 211, 219
Howard University, 72, 163, 223, 348
  Black presidents of, 339, 530, 536
  engineering courses at, 363
  founded, 178, 219–20
  funding of, 210
  Law School, 239, 240, 271, 356
  Medical College, 251, 281, 434
  "new," 536
  ship named for, 361
  sororities and fraternities, 296, 303, 305,
    345
  students protest curriculum at, 440
  TV station of, 486
Howe, Cato, 53
Hrabowski, Freeman A. III, 556
Hubbard, DeHart, 334–35
Hughes, Justice Charles E., 365
Hughes, Langston, 338, **338**, 352, 381
Humphrey, Hubert, 411–12, 421, 425
Humphreys, Richard, 111
Hunt, Henry A., 355
Hunter, Charlayne, 407, 554
Hunter, Gen. David, 188, 189, 192, 245
Hunter, Jerry, 527
Hurston, Zora Neale, 270, 349–50, **350**, 352,
    492
Hutchinson, Gov. Thomas, 47, 57
Hyman, John A., 244, 248

Ickes, Harold 359
Idaho, 527
Idlewild, Mich., Black resort at, 303–4
Illinois, 94, 100, 107, 479
  Anti-Slavery Society, 124
  bars Black entry, 84, 147
  Black in legislature, 337

Black in state Supreme Court, 539
race riots in, 286, 298, 310–11, 366
repeals Black Laws, 206–7, 248
See also Chicago, Ill.
Immigrants, foreign
and Black migration, 299
competition between Blacks and, 128,
131, 149, 198, 230, 299
numbers decline, 306–7, 479–80
southern states fail to attract, 214
Immigration policies, 319
Chinese Exclusion Bill, 246
National Origins Act, 334
Import duties. *See* Taxes
Indentured servants, 21, 25, 78
Black, 6, 8, 9, 10, 18
become slaves, 15, 16
"headright" system, 13
sue for or purchase freedom, 18, 94
term of service extended, 13, 21
legislation concerning, 15, 16, 18, 21
Native American, 8
slavery distinguished from 6, 8, 13
in Virginia, 6, 8, 9, 16
white, 6, 9, 10, 13, 15, 20
free Black ownership of, 26
Irish or English, 14
term of service, 21
Independent (New York journal), 295
Independent Party, 232
Indiana, 148, 149
Constitutional Convention bars Blacks,
147
KKK in, 213, 308
slavery in, 78, 94, 133
Underground Railroad in, 96, 100, 107
See also Gary, Ind.; Indianapolis, Ind.
Indian Affairs, Committee on, and Appro-
priation Bill, 237. *See also* Native
Americans
Indianapolis, Ind., 256, 287, 319, 339
Indianapolis *World*, 271
Indian peoples, 4. *See also* Native Americans
Indian Territory. *See* Native Americans
Indigo, 37, 41, 42, 43
production drops, halts, 55, 67
Industry
Black-operated, 229
Blacks as strikebreakers in, *see* Strikes
Blacks in, 129, 167, 321–22, 477
defense, 361, 363, 369–70
integrated, 381
manufacturing jobs decline, 468
mechanization of, 372, 381, 479
mining, 479
music, 399, 524 (*see also* Recordings)
slave labor in, 64, 144
See also Business, Black-owned; Corpora-
tions; Inventions; Labor; Labor, Black
Institute for Colored Youth. *See* Cheyney
University
Institute for Southern Studies, 490
Integrated schools. *See* Education
Interdenominational Theological Center, 219
Intermarriage, 40, 538. *See also* Miscegena-
tion; Mulattos
International unions
Brotherhood of Red Caps, 356
Workers of the World (IWW), 229
See also Labor unions
Interstate Commerce Bill, 262, 406

Interstate Commerce Commission, 365,
383, 390
Inventions by Blacks, 40, 129, 133, 263–64,
286, 307, 369
agricultural tools, 116, 278
drug patents, 352, 387, 530
electrical, 261, 268, 333
first known patent held by Black, 91
railroad devices, 282, 291
slaves not allowed to hold patent, 116
Iowa, 136, 265–66
Constitutional Convention, 147
Ireland, 131
immigrants from, and job competition,
149, 299
riot against Blacks, 131, 198, 202, 295
Isham, John W., 281
Islam, 1, 4, 12, 424, 437
Black Muslims, 414, 421, 447, 471
Nation of, 347, 405, 471
Isle Brevelle (Louisiana), Black settlement
at, 78
Ithaca Journal, 487

Jack, Hulan, 386
Jack and Jill of America, Inc., 356
Jackson, Andrew, 75, 84, 89
free Blacks fight under, 85–86, 194
as president, 106, 118, 125
Jackson, Fannie, 111, 205–6
Jackson, Rev. Jesse, 435, 502, 509, **513**, 514,
557
as presidential candidate, 501, 507, 510,
513, 517
and PUSH, 454, 455, 487
Jackson, Jimmie L., 426, 519
Jackson, Keith, 561
Jackson, Maynard, 449, 464, 563–64
Jackson, Michael, 476–77, 492, 518, 527, 536
Jackson, Reggie, 556
Jackson, Miss., 519
as one of "worst" cities, 377
Jackson State University, 450
Jacksonville, Fla., 287, 295, 299, 304
racial violence in, 405, 456
Jacob, John E., 491–92, **491**
Jaffrey (New Hampshire) Social Library
founded by Black, 74
Jamaica, 12, 23, 56. *See also* West Indies
James, Gen. Daniel "Chappie," 468–69
James I, king of England, 6
James the Black (Diego el Negro or Diego
Mendez), 4
Jamestown, Va., 6 (and map), **7**, 8, 9, 13, 21
Jamison, Mae Carol, 507, 508, **508**
Japanese firms, racism of, 515
Jarboro, Caterina, 349
Jay, John, 58
sons and grandson of, 58–59
Jazz. *See* Music
Jeannes, Anna T., 295
Jefferson, Thomas, 53, 68, 91
opposes slavery, 42, 52, 55–56, 157
plan defeated, 58
as slaveowner, 58, 155
Jefferson, William and Andrea, 527
Jefferson Military College, 379. *See also*
White supremacy
Jenifer, Dr. Franklyn, 530, 536
Jet magazine, 352, 374, 550. *See also* Maga-
zines, Black

Jewett, Fidelia, 292
Jews, 322, 520
Black relationship with, 524, 541
"Jim Crow"
origin of term, 97
laws, *see* Segregation
Jocelyn, Simeon S., 107–8, **107**
John, Herschel V., 181
Johns Hopkins University, 538
Johnson, Andrew, 211, 212, 215, 221
opposes civil rights legislation, 210, 216,
218, 220
Johnson, Charles, 330, 534
Johnson, Dr. Charles Spurgeon, 215,
331–32, **332**, 374
Johnson, Earvin "Magic," 507, 543
Johnson, Eddie B., 552
Johnson, Judge Frank M. Jr., 428, 542–43, 549
Johnson, George, and Johnson Products
Company, 446
Johnson, Hall, 326
Johnson, Gen. Hazel Winifred, 478
Johnson, Henry, 312–13
Johnson, Jack, 297–98, **297**, 302, 445
Johnson, James Weldon, 291, 293, **304**, 310,
360, 381
with NAACP, 304–5, 311, 312, 325, 348
Johnson, John H., and Johnson Publishing
Company, 352, 369, 373–74, **374**, 550,
559
Johnson, Joshua, 74
Johnson, Lady Bird (Mrs. Lyndon B.), 439
Johnson, Lyndon B., 420, 424, 428, 440–41,
545
appointments by, 423–26 passim, 433–39
passim, 472
policy reversed, 487
Johnson, Mal H., 530
Johnson, Mordecai, W., 339
Johnson, Noble, 307, 318
Johnson, Pamela, 487
Johnson, Rafer, 404, 405–6
Johnson, Robert L., 482, 542
Johnson landholdings (Virginia), 13
Joint Center for Political and Economic
Studies, 448, 522
Jones, Rev. Absalom, 60, 61, 71–77 passim,
146
Jones, Alligator Sam, 124
Jones, Anna H., 291
Jones, Dewey R., 355
Jones, Dr. Edith Irby, 503
Jones, Eugene Kinckle, 303, **303**, 352, 355,
365
Jones, James Earl, 414, 445, 509, 541
Jones, James Warren "Rev. Jim," and Jones-
town affair, 475
Jones, John, 206–7, 215, 248
Jones, LeRoi, 460
Jones, Leroy, 483
Jones, Quincy, 472, 536
Jones, Judge Thomas G., 293
Joplin, Scott, 286, 326
Jordan, Barbara, 431, 461, 470, **470**, 475, 527
Jordan, Michael, 501, 543, 548, 563
Jordan, Vernon, 484, **484**, 488, 491, 496,
525, 554
Journal of Negro History, 309
"Journey of Reconciliation," 375. *See also*
Freedom rides
Joyner, Florence Griffith, 511

Joyner-Kersee, Jackie, 511, 516, 544
Jubilee Singers. *See* Fisk University
Judgeships. *See* Government service,
    Blacks in
Judson, Andrew T., 113
Julian, Percy L., 352, 387, 530
Jump Start comic strip, 518–19
Jury trial or service. *See* Courts
Just, Ernest Everett, 303, 307–8
Justice Department, U.S., 399, 458, 503, 522
    and affirmative action, 489, 490, 492
    Blacks with, 253, 471
    and police misconduct, 484
    and racial discrimination, 486, 565
    and segregated schools, 390, 445, 482,
        483, 485, 491
    and voting rights, 494, 516

Kansas, 5, 160, 165, 199, 324
    Black migration to, 231, 237–39 *passim*,
        254–59 *passim*, 269, 341
    and Civil War, 162–63, 183, 188
Kansas City, Mo., 323, 504, 528
    Black mayor of, 540
    Black population, 256, 273, 319
Kansas Herald, 257, 258
Kansas-Nebraska Act (1854), 157, 159, 160
Ka Zoola (Cudjoe Lewis), 167–68
Kelley, Abby, 129, 156
Kelly, Sharon Pratt Dixon, 525, 541, 558
Kennedy, Justice Anthony M., 536
Kennedy, Edward, 500, 507, 517
Kennedy, John F., 368, 404, 413–16 *passim*,
        420, 476
    appointments by, 406, 408, 557
Kennedy, Robert F., 404, 410, 416
Kentucky, 96, 105, 145, 183, 185
    Black colleges founded in, 160, 231
    population, 75, 89, 102, 172–73, 256
        Black emigrants from, 230, 231
    racial violence in, 314, 324, 392
    segregation in, 258, 302, 392
        struck down, 317
    slavery in, 147, 177
        escaping slaves, 79, 139, 140, 151
Kentucky Derby, 248, 259, 261, 279, 284
Kerner, Gov. Otto, and Kerner Commission,
        436, 440, **440**
Key, Elizabeth, 13–14
Kilgore, Thomas, 443
King, B. B., 448
King, Rev. Bernice, 547
King, Coretta Scott (Mrs. Martin Luther), 427,
        427, 445, 450, 452, 490, 511, 547, 559
    award named for, 468
King, Dr. Martin Luther Jr., 221, 288–89,
        414, **414**, **427**, 437, 466, 523, 542
    appointments by, 457, 462
    arrested, 404, 416, 420, 426
    assassination of, 440, 441, 445, 472, 476,
        497
    attacks on, 396–97, 399, 426, 434
    awards to, 422–23, 472
    birthday celebrated, 450, 464, 496, 500,
        505, 527, 534, 547
    FBI and, 467
    "I Have a Dream" speech, 419, 499, 519
    leads protests, 391, 392, 398, 405, 410,
        415, 434, 506
        other leaders split from, 421, 428, 433
    route retraced, 493

Library and Archives, memorials to, pa-
        pers of, 450, 490, 497, 540, 559
    mother slain, 466
King, Rodney, 464, 537, 546, 548, 558, 560,
        564
King, Susie, 189
Kitt, Eartha, 439, 467
Kittrell College, 257
Knights and Daughters of Tabor, Knights of
        Liberty (secret antislavery societies),
        135
Knights of Labor, 229, 256. *See also* Labor
        unions
Knights of the White Camellia (white su-
        premacy group), 222
Knox, Clinton, 431
Korean War, 381, 382, 384, 450, 460, 468, 473
Ku Klux Klan (KKK), 214, 224, 252, 254,
        336, 354, 369, 412, 420, 519
    activity against, 245, 331, 333, 478, 486
    arrests and trials, 239, 385, 424, 455, 478
        acquittals, 486, 494
        convictions and fines, 240, 335, 366,
            428, 439, 472
    countrywide, 325, 334, 335, 337, 537
    Court rulings favoring, 548, 554
    decrease in activity, 537
    Democratic Party and, 231–32, 233, 236,
        245, 247, 248, 250
    FBI v., 385, 482, 485
    federal response to, 213–14, 225, 234,
        236–39 *passim*, 252
    national convention, 222
    organized, revived, 213–14, 308, 350, 392,
        485, 545
    police link with, 490
    "Red Summer," 316–17

Labor
    convict, 21, 214, 217, 257, 283, 288
    discrimination against women and mi-
        norities, 240, 486, 497, 502, 518, 524,
        534, 556
    FEPC formed, 363, 373, 481
    Government Employment Committee,
        395
    Humphrey-Hawkins Act, 412, 421
    immigrant, 214, 299, 306–7
        competition between Black and, *see*
            Labor, Black
    import of white servants, 20
    Indian people as, 4
    minimum wage bill, 472
    occupations of Blacks, native and foreign
        whites (1890), 274
    "Philadelphia Plan," 445
    quota system approved, goals set, 482, 485
    seniority in, 471, 495, 502
    women employed, 274, 480, 486
    See also Business, Black-owned; Inden-
        tured servants; Industry; Labor,
        Black; Labor unions; Slave labor
Labor, Black
    child, 254
    competition between white/foreign im-
        migrant and, 26, 94, 128, 149, 230,
        299, 319, 443, 519
        occupations classified (1890), 274
        race riots over jobs, 94, 116, 128, 131,
            198, 202, 280, 286, 295, 298, 310–11,
            316–17, 370, 434

convict, 214, 217, 257, 283, 288
    as domestics, 149, 230
    in Harlem, 356
    job discrimination against, 97, 196, 274,
        343, 415–16, 432, 485
        contract and vagrancy laws, 217–18,
            222, 248, 254, 257, 283–84
        in defense industry, 361, 363, 366,
            369–70
        EEOC charges of, 435, 463
        in FBI, 536
        FEPC set up, 363, 373, 481
        and "intent to discriminate," 494, 513,
            534
        by Japanese, 515
        male v. female, 443
        on newspapers, 449, 485, 509
        on police force, 447–48, 482, 486, 489,
            494, 502, 528
        prohibited, 204, 456, 483, 486
        protested, 305, 354, 362–63, 422, 524
        racial quotas, 482, 488–89, 499, 502, 509
        settlements awarded, 463, 485, 494, 531
        Supreme Court rules on, 456, 471, 477,
            489
        (*see also* wages, *below*; Affirmative ac-
            tion; Corporations)
    in manufacturing (1920), 322
    mobility restricted, 217–18, 248, 254, 257,
        283–84
    northern demand for, 299, 307, 319, 334
    opportunities improve, 355, 404, 426,
        447, 454–55, 545
    and population concentration, 89
    on railroad, 131, 216, 227, 291, 299, 305,
        453
    recruitment of 231, 254, 256–57, 299,
        307, 319
    seniority v. minorities, 471, 495, 502
    shifts in, 379–80, 468
    skilled, 75, 147, 305, 447
        Blacks not considered for, 206, 230,
            263, 291, 403
    slave, *see* Slave labor
    South fears loss of, 254, 255–56
    as strikebreakers/strikes by, *see* Strikes
    and unemployment, 122, 343, 388, 401,
        454, 468, 496
    wages, 211, 258, 266, 472, 532
        disparities in, 206, 267–68, 338, 354,
            364, 366, 463, 480, 535, 537
        sharecropping v., 215, 239–40
    sports, 385, 433, 560–61, 563
    in whaling industry, 129, 167
    women, 274, 294, 299, 379–80, 388, 443,
        456, 480, 532, 535
    working and living conditions, 239–40,
        357, 337
    See also Agriculture; Industry; Labor;
        Labor unions; Professions
Labor Department, U.S., 331, 534
    Blacks with, 481, 487
    hiring goals of, 445, 485, 487, 490, 492
Labor unions
    AFL-CIO, 356, 367, 389, 404
    Blacks form, 42, 147, 234–41 *passim*, 336,
        347–48, 356, 389, 404
        membership declines, 350
        seen as "rebellion," 316, 348
    Blacks as members of, 229, 256, 267–68,
        389, 463

Black as head of, 481
excluded or discriminated against, 206, 274, 361, 367
Irish control of, 295
and wages, 472
See also Labor, Black; Strikes
Lafayette, Marquis de, 56, 59, 62
La Guardia, Fiorello, 359
Lamb, Pompey, 54
Land grant(s), 10, 136, 238, 246
Black hopes for, 216, 261
for Black settlements, 53, 92
as bonus with slave purchase, 16, 17–18
"headright" system and, 13, 16
Homestead Acts, 192, 215, 221, 231, 254
land grant colleges, 235, 241, 259
Morrill Land Grant Acts, 193, 276
See also Black settlements and towns
Land ownership. *See* Property
Land prices, 43, 192, 237
Lane, James H., 160, 183, 188, 194
Lane, Joseph, 181
Lane College, 257, 361
Langston, Charles, 165–66
Langston, John Mercer, 165, 166, 203, 255, 276, 553
in Congress, 160, 270–71, 273
town and school named for, 283
Langston University, 283
Las Casas, Bartolomé de, 4
Latimer, George, 132–33
Latimer, Lewis H., 261
Latimer Journal and North Star (abolitionist journal), 132
Latin America, 5, 6, 78, 153, 189, 462
Lawnside, N.J., incorporated, 339
Lawrence, Clarissa C., 113
Lawrence, Maj. Robert H. Jr., 437
Lawrence, Kans., 162, 199
Laws and legislation
affecting free Blacks, 26, 28, 33, 93, 113, 169
barring, 70, 78–79, 82, 84, 88, 90, 160, 206
forcing removal, 98, 107, 112
"Jim Crow," 189 (*see also* Segregation)
protecting, 53, 57, 163
antilynching, *see* Lynchings
antislavery, *see* Laws and legislation, Antislavery, *below*
on bearing arms/military service, 10, 13, 17, 19, 26, 51
Black Laws (Midwest and West), 78–79, 94, 98, 147, 161
repealed (by Illinois), 206, 248
civil rights, 210, 216, 233, 240–42 *passim*, 248–49
Black Codes, 212, 214, 217–18, 221
declared unconstitutional, 248, 264
concerning mulattos, 20, 36, 73, 78, 79, 111
contract and vagrancy, 217–18, 248, 254, 257, 283–84
on conversion to Christianity, 18
on convict labor, 214
curfew, 35, 212, 297, 370, 466, 484
dealing with runaways, *see* Slaves, runaway
defining slaves as property, 15, 26
determining status, 15, 16, 18, 21, 23, 182
"ending" Ku Klux Klan, 237

Enforcement Acts, 213, 234, 235
English, 8, 16, 17, 27
enlistment incentive, 55
execution of slaves allowed, 9, 17, 19, 20, 23, 26–28 *passim*, 36
forbidding or requiring education, *see* Education
foreign slave trade forbidden, 73, 90
after Haitian revolt, 69
harassing NAACP, 392, 398
immigration, 246, 334
keeping families together 64,
lien, 287
murder of slave made capital offense, 92
number of statutes increases, 14
prohibiting manumission, 88, 92–93
property ownership, 20, 36
race, 302 (*see also* Miscegenation)
slave codes
code noir, 73, 78
colonial, 9, 19, 20–21, 25–33 *passim*, 40
expanded (Virginia), 80, 94
state, 105–6, 109
slavery condoned, legalized, 10, 16, 17
legality questioned, 12
and slaves' rights, 23, 36, 60, 105, 163
in court, 23, 26, 31, 94 (*see also* Courts)
on treatment of slaves, 4, 9, 10, 13, 17–30 *passim*, 80, 94
cruel treatment prohibited, 36, 143–44
forbidding self-defense, 19
restricting movement, 19, 20, 21, 27, 30, 33, 36
Virginia changes law, 143–44
working-hour, 28, 36
See also Congress, U.S.; Court cases; Courts; Martial law, Penalties for:
Laws and legislation, Antislavery
abolition/emancipation, 53, 55, 57, 60, 74–75, 77, 80
manumission prohibited, 88, 92–93
in Canada, 70
confiscation of slave ships, 64, 81
difficulty in passing, 59
first colonial law, 13
Lincoln introduces into Congress, 142
restricting slave trade, 60, 73, 75, 90, 170
Anti-Slave Trade Act (1819), 89
disregarded, 167, 181, 184–85
slave importation
colonies/states, 28, 34, 46, 47, 48, 53, 57, 59, 74, 77, 105, 112
federal, 60, 61, 78, 80, 81, 87, 89
South Carolina seeks repeal, 161
Lawson, Edward H. Jr., 355
Lawyers, Black
denied admission to law school, discouraged from practice, 270, 295, 377
"firsts" in profession, 135, 226–27, 264, 304, 526
appear before Supreme Court, 207, 339, 384, 433
first women, 240, 325, 337, 339, 377, 433, 462
increase in numbers, 498
Lincoln University and, 157
NBA formed, 337
Washington, D.C. opens library to, 365
See also Government service, Blacks in (judgeships)

League for the Protection of Colored Women, 294, 300, 303
League of Nations, 332
Leary, Sherrard Lewis, 169
Lee, Dr. Rebecca, 200, 219
Lee, Gen. Robert E., 169, 184, 202, 210–11, 213
Lee, Spike, 221, 516
Legal Defense Fund of New York, 306
Leidesdorff, William A., 136
Leisure. *See* Entertainment; Resort communities; Sports
Leland, George Thomas "Mickey," 461, 475, 520
Lelia College, 302
LeMoyne Institute, 139
L'Enfant, Pierre Charles, 68
Leonard, "Sugar Ray," 518
Levittown, N.Y., first Black family in, 396. *See also* Housing
Lewis, Arthur, 478
Lewis, Cudjoe (Ka Zoola), 167–68
Lewis, Rev. John L., 409–10, 427, 506
Lewis, Sarah, 114
Lewis, William H., 277, 303
Lewis and Clark expedition, Black with, 79
Lexington, Ky., 145, 324
Lexington, Mass., 48, 49, 55
Liberator (antislavery newspaper), 84, 105, 111, 113, 133, 261
founded, 108
poetry published in, 106, 114, 331
Liberia, 247, 266, 332
Black ministers to, 238, 260, 266, 271, 273, 280, 362
colonization of, 87, 95, 164–65, 192, 204, 222, 240, 280
Delany's expedition fails, 167, 255
settlements and churches, 112, 218
declares independence, 139, 204, 252
founding of, 55, 91
population, 106, 204, 231
Liberty Party, 105, 128, 131, 134, 135, 140, 157
Liebowitz, Samuel, 343
Liele, George, 45, 64
Life expectancy, 477, 511, 522, 544, 548. *See also* Disease; Mortality rate
Life insurance. *See* Business, Black-owned
"Lift Every Voice and Sing," 290–91, 304
Lin, Maya, 519
Lincoln, Abraham
and antislavery legislation, 142, 191, 192
birthday celebrated, 271, 290
and Black colonization, 189
and Blacks in the Army, 134, 183, 184, 186, 188, 194
calls for more soldiers, 202
signs Conscription Act, 195
condemns Kansas-Nebraska Act, 160
debates Douglass, 166
Gettysburg Address by, 200
letter of protest to, 199–200
opposes revenge for Fort Pillow, 201
as presidential candidate, 167, 181, 182
elected, reelected, 183, 203
quoted on Civil War, 185, 194
quoted on Frederick Douglass, 280
signs Emancipation Proclamation, 194
signs land grant acts, 192, 193
visits Richmond, 210

Lincoln Parish Training School. *See* Grambling College
Lincoln University, 146, 157, 276, 366
Lind, Jenny, 151
Lindsay, John, 432, 440, **440**, 459, 491
Lindsay, Vachel, 338
Liston, Sonny, 413, 424
Literacy. *See* Education
Literacy tests (voting), 275, 289, 292
  abolished, 426, 450, 468
Little, Cleavon, 448
Little, Indiana, 339
Little, Larry, 560
Little Rock, Ark., 245, 287
  Central High School and "Little Rock Nine," 395–401 *passim*, **397**
  first Black judge in, 161, 243
Liuzzo, Viola Gregg, 428, 519
Locke, Alain, 296, 330
Locker, Jesse, 362
Loguen, J. W., 107
London abolition societies, 62, 117, 156
Long, Jefferson F., 234, 236, 238
Los Angeles, Calif., 434
  Black newspapers of, 250, 255, 349
  Bradley as mayor of, 464, 488, 498, 564
  founded by Blacks, 56
  as one of "best" cities, 375
  Police Department
    hiring practices, 486, 494
    in Rodney King case, 464, 537, 548, 558
  population, 319, 320, 343, 478
  Watts riot, 429
Louis, Joe, 353, 356, 362, 365, 383
Louis X. *See* Farrakhan, Louis
Louisiana, 145, 214, 215, 259
  abolitionist writings considered criminal, 106
  Black voting in, 426, 463
    as majority, declines, 219, 301
  Blacks in office, 204, 219, 225, 240, 244–45
  in Civil War, 196–97, 204, 205
  Colonization Society, 112
  Constitutional Convention, 226, 230, 301
  cotton production, 75, 82, 84, 89
  killings/lynchings in, 225, 246–47, 261, 262, 267
  population, 118, 170, 256, 287, 299, 521
    Black emigrants from, 112, 230
  Reconstruction in, 228, 250
  restrictions on Blacks, 97, 98, 217–18
    grandfather clause, 275, 283, 289
  secedes, readmitted to Union, 185, 219, 226
  segregation in, 258, 307, 401, 404
    prohibited, 230
    rejects busing plan, 449
  slavery in, 31, 147
    slave laws and *code noir*, 33, 73, 78, 80, 81
    slave revolts, 74, 83
    slaves in militia, 34
    trade reopened, 77, 105
  sugar production, 75–76, 133
    German labor imported for, 214
  See also New Orleans, La.
Louisiana Purchase, 90
Louisville, Ky., 96, 172–73, 302
Louisville Democrat, 139

Lovejoy, Elijah P., 123–24, 155
  Godfrey Gilman & Co. warehouse, **124**
Lowndes County Freedom Organization, 434
Lucas, Col. Ruth A., 441–42
Lucy, Autherine, 392
Lunceford, Lizzie, 364
Lundy, Benjamin, 91–92, **92**, 108
Lynch, John R., 204, 242–43, 248, 259, 505
Lynchings, 35, 232, 246, **275**
  1882–1950, 261–62, 270–77 *passim*, 280–89 *passim*, 297, 300, 305, 310–16 *passim*, 324, 325, 330, 352, 356, 366
  antilynching bills introduced, 289, 325, 331, 361, 363
  book on, 348
  county debt resulting from, 365
  court frees lynchers, 349
  as "entertainment," 278, 331, 335–36
  increase, decrease in numbers, 319, 341
  organized protests against, 305, 311, 361
  press and Tuskegee reports on, 257, 267, 268, 270, 271, 335–36, 361, 375, 385
  "Red Summer," 316–17
  of women (1889–1925), 337
  1952 (none recorded), 385
  1953–1959, 398, 401
  1981, 487, 519
  See also Terrorism; Violence
Lynk, Dr. Miles Vardahurst, 280

McAlpin, Harry S., 372
McCabe, Edwin P., 283
McClellan, Gen. George B., 203
MacColl, Ray O., 253
McCoy, Elijah, 291
McCree, Wade Jr., 439, 471
McCrummell, Sarah, 100, 114
McDaniel, Hattie, 358
McDonald's, "fair-share" agreement with, 537
McDuffie, Arthur, 478, 484
McFerrin, Robert 367, 379
McGee, James, 451
McHenry, Donald F., 472
McKay, Claude, 330–31, **330**, 352
McKinley, William, 243, 246, 270
McKinney, Cynthia Ann, 552
McKinney, Dr. Susan, 200
McKissick, Floyd, 432–33, **432**
McLaurin, G. W., 382–83
McLendon, John B., 406, 446
McNair, Ronald E., 473, 505
McWilliams, Sarah, 301–2
Madagascar, 22, 161
Maddox, Gov. Lese, 445
Madison, James 61
Magazines, Black
  Anglo-African Magazine, 166
  Church Review (AME), 264
  Ebony, 352, 373–74, 550
  EM, 550
  Emerge, 518
  Encore, 374
  Essence, 448
  Jet, 352, 374, 550
  Mirror of Liberty (first), 126
  Opportunity, 331–32, 335, 347
  See also Crisis (NAACP magazine); *Negro Digest*

Mahoney, Charles 387
Mahoney, Mary E., 256
Maine, 90
Maine (battleship), 284
Malaria. *See* Disease
Malcolm X, 414, **414**, 421, 422, **422**, 427, 469
Mali empire, 1, 2
Malone, Vivian, 416, 428
Mann Act, 297
Mansfield, Chief Justice Lord, 45
Manufacturing. *See* Industry
Manumission. *See* Emancipation
Manumission Society, 62
Marches, protest. *See* Black protest
Marie Thérèse (freed slave, founds Isle Brevelle), 78
Marine Corps, U.S., 369, 372, 381, 452, 473
  restricts enlistment, 74
Marino, Bishop Eugene A., 467, 511, 524
"Maroons." *See* Slaves, runaway
Marriage
  interracial, 40, 538 (*see also* Miscegenation)
  slaves' rights, 30, 81
  statistics (1990s), 523, 538
Marsalis, Wynton, 501–2
Marshall, Justice Thurgood, 157, 353, **353**, 377, 398, 406, 425, **436**
  death of, 557–58
  with NAACP, 360, 374, 377, 384, 388, 432, 557
  on Supreme Court, 436, 470, 476, 483, 538, 557
Martial law, 239, 296, 349, 410
  in Civil War and Reconstruction South, *see* Army, U.S.
Martin, J. Sella, 234, 250
Martineau, Harriet, 114
Maryland, 61, 258, 308
  Blacks elected in, 10, 453
  in Civil War, 185
  Colonization Society and Maryland in Liberia, 112
  free Blacks in, kidnapped, 79
  importance of tobacco in, 8, 42–43
  Inter-Racial Commission, 338
  one of "worst" cities in, 377
  population
    colonial, *see* Population (of North American British colonies)
    mulatto (1775), 51
    state, 67, 89, 256, 521
  race riot in, 438
  slavery in, 9, 74, 104, 177
    and antislavery, 41, 65–66, 72
    on escape route, 140
    manumission law, 80
    slave revolts, 88, 136
    slave/servant laws, 9, 10, 15–20 *passim*, 28–33 *passim*, 51, 60, 91
  Supreme Court of, 91
  University of, 353
  See also Baltimore, Md.
Mason, Biddy and Hannah, 154–55
Mason, George, 48, 52, **52**, 53, 54, 60
Mason-Dixon Line, 59, 125
Masonic Order, 48, 60–61
Massachusetts, 54, 68, 214
  and civil equality for Blacks, 55, 136, 142
  ends "Jim Crow" schooling, 160
  Constitutional Convention, 154

military service laws, 13, 154
miscegenation law, 16
population (state), 100 (see also Population [North American British colonies])
racial violence in, 451
and slavery, 9, 12, 22
  abolished, 53, 57, 68–69, 137
  Anti-Slavery Society, 111, 126, 129, 132, 155
  Bay Colony questions legality, 12–13
  laws on, 9, 10, 12–13, 20
  runaways aided, 100, 107, 159
  slaves petition Court, 47, 60, 61, 64
  trade prohibited, 57
  treatment of slaves, 30, 31
Supreme Court of, 57, 142
See also Boston, Mass.
Massachusetts Medical Society, 141
Massacres. See Boston Massacre; Fort Pillow (Tennessee) massacre; Terrorism
Massie, Dr. Samuel P., 431–32
Mather, Rev. Cotton, 31, 32–33, 146
Matzeliger, Jan, 263–64, **263**
Maynard, Robert C., 561
Maynor, Dorothy, 384
Mays, Benjamin, 221
Mays, Benjamin E., 449
Mays, Willie, 387, 394, **394**, 477
Meade, Gen. George, 202, 210
Mechanization. See Industry
Medal of Honor. See Awards and honors
Medical experiment ("Tuskegee Study"), 459
Medicine, Blacks in
Black medical society, 264–65, 280, 503
Blacks barred, 207
distribution of, in population (1930), 343
increase in numbers, 498
"firsts," 119, 139, 141, 281, 305
  first interracial hospital, 277, 278, 305
  first school, 251, 495
  first women, 200, 219, 298, 503
Lincoln University and, 157
surgery, 278, 509–10
veterinary, 261
Medico-Chirurgical Society, 264–65
Meek, Carrie, 552–53
Meharry, Samuel, 251
Meharry Medical College, 251, 434, 495
Melrose Plantation, 78
Memorials. See Monuments and memorials
Memphis, Tenn., 216–17, **217**, 322, 542
Black population, 256, **273**, 287
Memphis News Scimitar, 335
Menard, John W., 223–24
Mendez, Pedro, 5
Menéndez de Avilés, Pedro, 4
Mennonites. See Quakers
Meredith, James, 412–13, **412**, 433, 434
Messenger, The (socialist journal), 310, 336
Mestizos as slaves, 36. See also Mulattos
Metcalfe, Ralph H., 354, 452–53, 475
Methodist Episcopal Church, 44, 60, 106
aids education, 196, 227, 251
antislavery stance, 57–58
John Street (New York), 74, 93
segregation in, 240

See also African Methodist Episcopal (AME), African Methodist Episcopal of Zion (AMEZ) Church
Metoyer, Louis, 78
Metropolitan Opera (New York), 342, 349, 359, 385, 390, 394
Mexia, Peter, 4
Mexican War, 137, 140, 150
Mexico, 4, 5, 92, 136
Blacks escape to, 100, 116, 124 (see also Underground Railroad)
U.S. acquires land from, 137, 140, 149
Mfume, Kweisi, 506–7, **506**
Miami, Fla., 385
as one of "worst" cities, 377
racial violence in, 478, 484, 488, 489, 497
Micheaux, Oscar, 313, 337
Michigan, 137, 303–4, 482, 483, 501
racial violence in, 449, 455
See also Detroit, Mich.
Michigan State University, 449
Middlebury College, 55, 94, 95
Middle Passage (journey to West Indies), 14, 39. See also Slaves, treatment of
Mifflin, Warner, 64
Migration
to cities, see Urbanization
encouraged, 159, 215, 231, 239, 241, 255, 265–70 passim, 283, 299, 319
lien laws and, 287
National Emigration Convention, 159, 167
1910–1970, 299, 308, 319, 331, 343, 360, 379, 381, 403, 446, 479
restricted or discouraged, 237, 239, 254–59 passim, 319
slows or reverses, 479, 480, 521
three major streams of, 319–20
to the West, 144–47 passim, 154–55, 221, 238, 261, 265–70 passim, 283, 293–94, 297, 341
  barred, 84, 147
  debate on, 239
  funded, 110–11
white v. Black patterns of, 446
See also Mobility
Miles College, 287
Military rule of South. See Army, U.S.
Military service
Conscription Act (1863), 195–96, 202
  riots against, 131, 198, 202
militia, 14
mulattos barred from, 74, 90
Native Americans in, 181, 183, 198
  barred from, 13, 14, 198
racism in, 241, 245, 253, 269
regular army established, 216
slave offered as enlistment incentive, 55
See also Arms and ammunition; Army, Confederate; Army, U.S.; Civil War; Marine Corps, U.S.; National Guard; Navy, U.S.; Segregation; War of 1812; World War I; World War II
Military service, Blacks in, **85**, **197**, **198**
abilities questioned, later recognized, 84, 184, 188, 189, 192, 202
all-Black units
  abolished, 388, 389
  1775–1865, 49, 53–54, 85–86, 183, 185, 188, 189, 192–202 passim, 207–8, 211

1866–1918, 216, 219, 235, 253, 269, 272–73, 284, 296, 297, 309, 310, 314–15
1941–1954, 363–64, 368, 369, 372, 381
barred from, 13, 26, 48–51 passim, 70, 74, 90, 99, 147, 183–84, 188, 193, 544
bravery of, 34, 41, 196–200 passim, 312–13, 314–15, 433 (see also Awards and honors)
"Buffalo soldiers," 259, 260, 548
casualties, 185, 194–205 passim, 284, 401, 460, 466
and "Port Chicago mutiny," 372
commissioned, 273, 312, 361, 369, 381, 411, 447, 487, 508, 512
commander, 460
four-star general, heads Joint Chiefs, 512, 517–18
dishonorably discharged, 296, 298, 461
draft substitution allowed, 48, 51, 196, 198
in French and Indian War, 41
given or promised freedom for service, 34, 43, 48–51 passim, 56, 57, 86, 186
Indian wars, 216, 235–36
military history published, 150–51
militia
  for self-defense, 37, 254
  U.S., 242, 245, 251–52
peacetime, 447, 487
petition to join, 154
against rebelling slaves, 34, 35, 83
recruited, 193–94, **193**, 195–96, **195**, 199, 234
required to serve, 26 (see also recruited, above)
segregation ended, 373, 378, 458
slaves and Black women supporting, 184, 189, 197
volunteers, 51, 54, 184–204 passim, 219, 239, 256, 246, 250, 273, 284
See also Civil War; Korean War; Racism; Revolutionary War; Spanish-American War; Vietnam War; War of 1812; Women, Black; World War I; World War II
Militia
Black, for self-defense, 37, 354
pursues fugitive slaves, 14
U.S., Blacks in, 242, 245, 251–52
See also National Guard
Militia Act (1862), 193–94
Miller, Dorie, 360, 362
Miller, Thomas E., 270, 273, 276
Mills, Florence, 325–26
Milwaukee, Wis., Black migration to, 319
Mines, Janie L. and Gwen, 470
Mining, mechanization of, 479. See also Industry
Minneapolis Tribune, 423
Minnesota, lynching in, 324
Minstrel shows, 254. See also Theater
Miscegenation, 116
laws concerning, 9, 16, 20, 26, 31, 33, 40, 51, 128, 322–23
overturned, 376, 437
Miss Black America and Miss America pageants, 442, 500, 518, 528, 530, 547, 562
Missionaries, 35, 195
AMA (American Missionary Association) founded, 138–39

Missionaries *(continued)*
  Black, 81, 206
  open schools for Blacks
    Philadelphia and New York, 41, 141
    South, 37, 138–39, 178, 183, 188–89, 215, 221, 259
  racism of, 139
  slavery as viewed by, 4, 135
Mississippi, 145, 215, 231
  anti-Black laws, 94, 212, 217, 258
  contract labor, 283–84
  Blacks in office, 204, 233, 236, 243, 246, 440
  Black voting in, 219
    Court rulings on, 426, 463
    restricted, 258, 275, 300, 424
  Colonization Society, 112
  Constitutional Convention, 230, 300
  cotton production, 75, 82, 84, 89, 102
  one of "worst" cities in, 377
  population, 102, 105, 128, 170, 256, 320, 521
  and secession, 168, 185, 226, 234
  segregation in, 258, 401, 404
    school integration, 434, 450
    Supreme Court ruling, 445
  slavery in, 92–93, 147
    freed slaves must leave, 108, 178
  Supreme Court of, 93
  terrorism/lynchings in, 232, 262, 267, 314, 401, 405, 450
    civil rights workers murdered, 424, 435, 519
    federal troops v., 248
    KKK, 237, 239
    "Mississippi Plan," 242, 250
    protested, 247, 265, 434
  University of (Ole Miss), 412–13, 433
  See also Vicksburg, Miss.
Mississippi Freedom Democratic Party (MFDP), 421
Mississippi Industrial College, 287
Mississippi River, 5, 84, 197, 255
"Mississippi tests," 275. *See also* Voting rights
Missouri, 90, 142, 238
  Black education in, 246, 504
  in Civil War, 183–86 *passim,* 194
  slavery in, 147, 177
  proslavery violence, 124
  University of, 357
    state Supreme Court and, 366
  See also Kansas City, Mo.; St. Louis, Mo.
Missouri Compromise (1820), 90, 159, 164
Mitchell, Arthur, 445
Mitchell, Arthur W., 342, 350–51, 363, 365, 368
Mitchell, Charles L., 214
Mitchell, Clarence Jr., 454
Mitchell, Parren J., 453–54, **453**
Mizelle, Ralph E., 355
Mobile, Ala., 167–68, 297
  population, 173–74, 256, 483
  racial violence, 370, 487, 519
Mobility
  physical, restrictions on
    Black v. white, 403
    Black labor, 217–18, 248, 254, 257, 283–84

curfew laws and, 35, 212, 297, 370, 466, 484
  poverty and, 319
  slaves or indentured servants, 19, 20, 21, 27, 30, 33, 36 (*see also* Slaves, runaway)
  (*see also* Migration; Segregation)
social, 155–56, 231, 288–89, 302–4 *passim,* 322, 355, 380–81, 447, 523
  prevented, 35, 323, 358
  of women, 129
  (*see also* Business, Black-owned; Economic conditions; Education; Professions)
Molineaux, Tom, 82
Mondale, Walter, 421
Monk, Thelonius, 358
Monroe, James, 77, 91
Montana, 219, 527
Montgomery, Isaiah Thornton, 269, 300
Montgomery, Ala., 167, 241, 405, 410
  Black population, 256, 273, 287, 299
  bus boycott, 375, 390–93 *passim,* 396, 399, 415, 422, 542
  march from Selma to, 427–28, 457, 493, 506, 543
Montgomery Herald, 257
Monuments and memorials, 73, 352, 519
  to Black soldiers, 34, 548, 549
    for Union soldiers (planned), 541
  honorary shipmasters, 360, 369, 371, 460
  to Martin Luther King, 450, 490, 497, 540
  See also Awards and honors
Moon, Warren, 561
Moore, Acel, 469
Moore, Archie, 385, 393
Moore, Rt. Rev. Emerson Jr., 473
Moore, Harry T., 383
Moorhead, Scipio, 46
Morehouse, Rev. Henry L., 221
Morehouse College, 178, 221, 296, 561
  joins university system, 219, 342
Morgan, Garrett, 307, 309, 333
Morgan, J. P., 279
Morgan State College, 377, 547
Morial, Judge Ernest Nathan, 387, 459
Mormon Church, 160, 474
Morrill, Justin, and Morrill Land Grant Acts, 193, 276. *See also* Land grant(s)
Morris, Robert, 142, 157
Morris, Thomas, 126, 135
Morris Brown College, 219, 257
Morrison, Toni, 471, 511, 562, 563, **563**
Mortality rate, 9, 15, 38–39, 481
  from "fever," 145
  homicides and, 510, 511 (*see also* Crime)
  infant, 505, 510, 522, 536, 537, 548
  in slums, 219, 288
  See also Disease; Life expectancy; Slaves, treatment of
Morton, Azie Taylor, 471
Morton, Ferdinand Q., 289
"Moses." *See* Tubman, Harriet
Mossell, Sadi T., 324, 325
Moten, Etta, 350
Mother's Little Helpers (white supremacy group), 222
Motley, Constance Baker, 422, 433, **439**
Motown Record Corporation, 399, 408, 411, 477, 501, 513, 524

Mott, Lucretia, 114, **114**, 129, 155
Mound Bayou, Miss., founded, 269
MOVE (Black radical group), 504
Movies. *See* Films
Moynihan, Daniel Patrick, 451
Mozambique, 34
Muhammad, Elijah, 347, 405, 421, 471
Muhammad, Wallace J., 347
Mulattos, 42, 67, 161
  barred, 74, 90
  denied jury trial, 31
  laws concerning, 20, 36, 79, 111
    code noir, 73, 78
  population, 51, 116, 318–19
  southern definition of term, 142
  See also Miscegenation
Murchison, Rev. Abram, 192
Murphy, Eddie, 518
Murphy, Isaac, 261
Murray, Donald Gaines, 353, **353**, 557
Murray, Ellen, 190
Murray, George Washington, 276, 278–79, 551
Murray, John, Earl of Dunmore, 49–50, 51
Murray, Gov. Johnston C., 349
Music
  abolitionist songs, 161
  bandleaders and performers, 327, 340–441, 345, 395, 501–2, 535
    segregated, 326
  Black, as art form, 215, 279, 285
  Black control of industry, 524
  Black opera, 367, 379
  Black singers, 151–52, 326, 327, 333, 345, 349, 352, 358, 371, 379, 389, 393–94
    at Carnegie Hall, 331, 346
    Fisk Jubilee group, 215, 224
    at Idlewild (Mich.), 303–4
    at Inaugural Concert (1941), 364
    Metropolitan Opera and, 342, 359, 385, 390
    "Motown sound," 399, 408, 411, 477
    refused admission, 342, 359, 365, 384
    at White House (1934), 350
    win awards, 279, 395, 454, 520, 527, 535 (*see also* Recordings)
  composed by Blacks, 284, 324, 325–28, 340–41, 342, 383, 395
    Black national anthem, 290–91, 304
    popular songs, 161, 254, 286, 305
    Virginia state song, 254, 361
  "Dixie" composed, 167
  jazz, 326, 345–46, 352, 362, 371, 395, 502, 535
    emergence of, 288, 323, 325
    "swing" and "bebop," 341, 358
  musical comedies, 284, 325–26, 341, 342, 347, 371, 382, 448
  R&B, 438, 520
  See also Entertainment
Muslims. *See* Islam
Mussolini, Benito, 351
Mutiny
  of Black soldiers in Texas, 311–12
  "Port Chicago," 372
  See also Slave revolts; Violence (Black, retaliatory)
Myers, Isaac, 229, 238
Myrdal, Gunnar, 285–86, 369

NAACP (National Association for the Advancement of Colored People), 303, 323, 356
awards by, 279, 307, 384, 398, 411
Black criticisms of, 544–45
blamed for violence, 405
early officials of, 304–5, 325, 390
and "fair share" agreements, 537, 559
forerunner of, 276, 295
founding of, 272, 286, 298, 406
funding of, 302
leaders of, 298, 348, 363, 390, 415, 471, 557, 558
    killed, 383, 417
    targeted, 560
Legal Defense and Education Fund, 360, 378, 384, 433, 449, 462, 467
protests
    appointments, 346, 364, 448, 489
    films, 275, 308
    lynchings, riots, 311–12, 313, 361
    opposes King, 437
    police brutality, 295
    racial bias, 300, 350, 360, 361, 410, 564
    racial bias in education, 349, 374, 392, 413, 449
    racial bias in employment, 305, 354, 361, 369–70, 422
and Supreme Court, 308, 346, 354, 364, 374, 384, 398, 448, 495
survival threatened, 392, 398
Youth Council of, 398
"Nadir" in Black life and history, 288
Napoleon I, emperor of the French, 67, 70, 73, 78
Narváez, Panfilo de, 5
NASA. See Astronauts, Black
Nash, Charles E., 244–45, 248
Nashville, Tenn., 84, 191, 273, 383
Natchez, Miss., 84, 236, 243
Natchez Courier, 105
Natchez tribe, Blacks against, 34, 35. See also Native Americans
National Academy of Design, Black elected to, 276
National Academy of Recording Arts and Sciences, honors Black, 394
National Associations, Boards, Councils (Black)
    Afro-American Council, 285, 286
    Association of Black Journalists, 469, 530
    Association of Colored Graduate Nurses (NACGN), 298
    Association of Colored Women, 196, 279, 281, 296
    Bar Association, 337
    Board of Commissioners, 159
    Business League, 289
    Colored Labor Union, 234
    Council of Colored People, 156
    Council of Negro Women (NCNW), 351, 542
    Equal Rights League, 203, 212, 271
    Federation of Colored Women, 281
    League of Colored Women, 281
    League on Urban Conditions, 303 (see also National Urban League)
    Negro Baseball League, 324
    Negro Congress, 354
    Negro Labor Council, 463

Urban Coalition, 448
    See also Conventions, Black; Labor unions
National Baptist Convention, 280
National Committee to Combat Fascism, 449
National Education Association (NEA) survey, 548
National Emigrant Aid Society, 255
National Era (antislavery newspaper), 154
National Guard
    Blacks in, 310
    called to quell riots, 310, 328, 333, 428–45 passim, 450, 456, 467, 529
    federalized, 413, 416, 420, 428
    See also Militia
National Labor Relations Board, 527
National Liberty Party formed, 295
National Origins Act (1924), 334
National Security Agency, 556
National Security Council, 423
National Urban League, 292, 331, 343, 408–9, 415, 468, 484, 489, 491–92, 560
    founded, 300, 303
    and jobs for Blacks, 342, 361, 365, 369
    Reagan administration as viewed by, 508
National Women's Rights Convention. See Women's Rights Conventions
National Youth Administration, 355
    Negro Division, 352, 354
Native Americans, 18, 25, 45, 46, 514, 518, 521
    Black scouts in dealings with, 79, 148, 149
    Blacks against, 10, 26, 34, 35, 41
        post-Civil War (Indian wars), 216, 235–36, 250, 259, 548
    free Blacks serve with, 89, 124
    Indian Appropriation Bill (1872), 237
    Indian wars, 216, 235–36, 250
    intermarriage with, forbidden, 20
    military service of, 181, 183, 198
        barred from, 13, 74
    removed to Indian Territory ("trail of tears"), 22, 82, 116, 238, 244, 294
        Indian Removal Act (1830), 106, 132
    rights of, 77
        in court, denied, 31, 149
    as slaveowners, 22–23, 181, 294
    as slaves, 9, 10, 36
    slaves seek refuge among, 5, 82, 84, 106, 116, 131–32
    U.S. attacks on (Seminole Wars), 82, 86, 88–89, 116, 124, 131–32
    in Virginia colony, 8, 31
Navigation Acts (Britain), 16
Navy, Confederate, 183, 192
Navy, Continental, 48, 54, 84
Navy, U.S.
    Blacks barred from, 74
    Blacks serving in, 83, 83, 284, 502
        Civil War, 183–92 passim, 188, 205, 261, 297
        World War II, 362, 367, 369, 372, 382, 406, 411
    integration/segregation in, 189
    Naval Academy (Annapolis), 271, 361
        Black on faculty, 431–32
        Blacks at, 241, 253, 378, 481, 487
        refuses to let Black play on grounds, 365
        women admitted, 371, 450

Nurse Corps, 285
"Port Chicago mutiny," 372
ships named for Blacks and Black colleges, 360–61, 369, 371, 460
Naylor, Gloria, 500
Nazi Party, 311, 350, 490, 499
Neau, Elias, 26, 28
Nebraska, 147
    Blacks emigrate to, 221, 239, 265
    racial violence in, 316, 429
"Negro" as term, 438
"Negro act" (South Carolina), 36
Negro American Labor Council, 404
Negro banner, 323
Negro Burial Grounds (New York), 537
Negro Digest, 369, 373–74, 375, 377, 550.
    See also Magazines, Black
Negro Fort (Florida), 86
"Negro Hill" community (California), 145
Negro History Week established, 339. See also Black history
"Negro Mountain" (Maryland), 41
"Negro Watch" (Charleston, S.C., 1721), 32
Negro World, 266, 310, 324
Nell, William C., 150–51
New African Hall (Philadelphia) burned, 116
New Amsterdam, 8, 10, 16. See also New Netherland
Newark, N.J., 100, 446, 466
    Black mayor of, 451, 470, 495, 558
    racial violence in, 436, 437
New Bern, N.C., 256
Newby, Dangerfield, 169
Newcombe, Don, 393
New Deal, 342, 351, 363
New England, 25, 53
    antislavery in, 41
        and Underground Railroad, 100, 107
    Anti-Slavery Society, 111, 126, 129, 132, 163
    population, 22, 33, 35, 38, 42, 54
    slavery in, 9, 12, 20, 29, 30, 31
    See also entries for individual states
New England Confederation, 10
New England Female Medical College, 200, 219
New England Journal of Medicine, 539
New Hampshire, 30, 48, 117, 527
    and antislavery/emancipation, 53, 54
    population, 9, 19, 29, 33
    race or color not distinguished by law in, 53, 163
New Haven, Conn.
    Black college proposed for, 107–8, 113
    Black mayor of, 520, 525
New Jersey, 57, 142, 468
    antislavery movement, 59, 64, 68, 72, 142
    Blacks elected in, 456, 527
    Black towns in, 282, 339
    population
        colonial, 18–19, 29, 35, 37, 42
        state, 67, 100, 446, 479
    racial violence in, 449, 451, 530
    slavery in, 10, 16, 30, 53, 137
    voting rights, 51, 80
    See also Newark, N.J.
New Mexico, 5, 147, 149
New Netherland, 9, 10, 13, 15, 29. See also New York City

New Orleans, La., 31, 145, 161, 288, 334
  Battle of (War of 1812), 84, 85–86, 194
  Black mayors of, 80, 387, 459, 498
  in Civil War, 182, 184, 192
  exports through, 84, 174, 268
  population, 75, 80, 169, 174, 256, 273, 287, 299, 448
  racial violence in, 216, 219, 224, 280, 291–92
    troops withdrawn, 253
  school for Blacks in, 154, 182–83
  slavery in, 82, 102, 147, 169
  school integration in, 226, 406
New Orleans University, 227
Newport, R.I., 48, 52, 54, 60, 156
  in slave trade, 31, 32
  southerners summering in, bring slaves, 47
Newspapers
  abolitionist, 91, 96, 118, 129, 132, 136, 140, 153
    destroyed by mob, 119, 123–24
  employment discrimination by, 449, 485, 509
  northern, react to Black Codes, 212
  study of, reveals slaves' suffering, 119–20
  unfounded reports incite violence, 296, 311, 317
Newspapers, Black, 72, 272
  African Repository, 218
  American Citizen, 250, 267, 269
  Amsterdam News, 298–99
  Atlanta Daily World, 341, 372
  Baltimore Afro-American, 277, 377, 420, 561
  Baton Rouge Grand Era, 250
  Beaufort *Tribune*, 248
  Boston Guardian, 292
  Cairo, Illinois Gazette, 263
  Carroll Parish, 250
  Chicago Defender, 295, 299, 381
  Christian Recorder, 250, 264
  Cincinnati Colored Citizen, 250
  Citizen Newspapers chain, 486
  Cleveland Call & Post, 306
  Cleveland Gazette, 263, 284
  Colored American, 271
  Colored Citizen (Topeka), 254
  Colored Patriot, 258
  Concordia, 250
  Daily American, 304
  Daily Creole of New Orleans, 161
  Elevator, 250
  encourage migration, 265–66, 269–70
  first, *see Freedom's Journal, below*
  first convention of Black journalists, 250
  Freedom's Journal, 87, 92–98 *passim*, 106, 185
  Freeman (Florida), 268
  Galveston Spectator, 250
  Indianapolis Freeman, 271
  Kansas City Call, 315–16
  Lexington American Citizen, 250
  Liberia Herald, 95
  Los Angeles Eagle, 255
  Los Angeles Pacific Appeal, 250
  Los Angeles Sentinel, 349
  Memphis Free Speech, 262, 271
  Memphis Planet, 250
  Mirror of the Times, 161, 143
  Muhammad Speaks, 447

Mystery, 153
Negro World, 266, 310, 324
New Era (later *New National Era*), 234
New Orleans Louisianian, 239, 250
New Orleans Tribune, 203
New South, 248
New York Age, 88, 265, 266, 292, 295, 304
New York Freeman, 266
New York Progressive American, 250
Oakland Tribune, 561
oppose Farmers' Alliance, 267
Pacific Appeal, 250
People's Advocate, 265
People's Voice, 367
Philadelphia Tribune, 266
Provincial Freeman (Ontario), 149
report on lynchings, violence, 257, 267, 268, 271, 295
Right of All, 95, 96
Rumor (later *Globe*), 266
St. Louis Argus, 305
Selma *Independent*, 267
South Carolina Leader, 233, 240
State Journal of Harrisburg, 264
Tand Bonne Republican, 250
True Republican, 250
Union, 296
Washington Bee, 263
Weekly Advocate (later *Colored American*), 121, 127, 271
Weekly Anglo African, 295
Weekly Pelican, 268
World, 308
See also Press, the
Newton, Huey, 429, **430**, 442
New York, 61, 136, 150
  abolishes slavery, 97, 134
  antislavery movement in, 41, 58–59, 68, 72, 117–18, 129, 140
  Colonization Society, 112
  Constitutional Convention, 92
  and emancipation, 53, 74–75
  population
  proslavery violence in, 117–18
    colonial, 18, 19, 29, 35, 41, 42
    state, 67, 75, 76, 89, 100, 128, 379
  in Revolution, 48, 51
  slave revolts in, 26, 28, 37
  slavery laws, 10, 25, 26, 27, 30, 82
  Supreme Court of, 118
  voting rights, 53, 92
  See also Buffalo, N.Y.; New Amsterdam; New Netherland; New York City
New York African Bible Society, 93
New York Central College, 141
New York City, 60, 88, 395, 501
  Black churches in, 81, 88, 92, 93, 96, 264
  Black female societies in, 100, 112
  Black mayor, 520
  Black political machine in, 289
  Black protest march in (1917), 311
  Black superintendent of schools, 516
  Black theater in, 95, 156, 281
  Blacks on police force, 482, 489
    Black commissioner, 529
  draft riots in, 131, 198
  early Black cemetery found in, 537
  as one of "best" cities, 375
  population, 33, 66, 320
    Black migrants, 88, 265, 319–20

    slave or Black, 26, 67, 89, 100, 273, 287, 299, 319, 478
  racial violence in, 78, 115, 128, 292, 295, 432, 434, 436, 456
  schools for Blacks, 26, 28, 62, 96, 119
  slavery/antislavery in, 19, 28, 37, 152
  See also Harlem
New York City Bar Association, Black heads, 526
New York Daily News, 509
New York Evening Post, 94, 295
New York Globe, 257, 266, 295
New York Rens. *See* Basketball
New York Sun, 266
New York Times, 178, 252, 295, 325, 334, 438, 468
  Black employees of, 449, 485
New York Tribune, 164, 179, 194, 325
Niagara Movement, 272, 286, 292, 295, 296, 298
Nicholas Brothers, 371
Nicodemus, Kans., 231
"Nigger," suit over use of word, 471. *See also* Racism (racial slurs)
Nineteenth Amendment, 527. *See also* Constitutional Amendments
Niño, Pedro (Peter) Alonzo, 4
Nix, Robert N. C. Sr., 475
Nix, Robert N. C. Jr., 455, 502
Nixon, Richard M., 386, 433, 461
  appointments by, 368, 444–45, 448, 459, 474, 482, 527
  policy criticized, 449, 451, 452, 456, 472
Niza, Friar Marcos de, 5
Njeri, Itabari, 534
Nobel Prize. *See* Awards and honors
Norfolk, Va., 82, 145, 192, 273, 302
Norris, Clarence "Willie," 345, 470
North America, 5, 6, 8, 10–13. *See also* Canada; Population; United States; *individual states*
North Carolina
  bans miscegenation, 16
  Black emigration from, 283, 319
  Blacks elected in, 244, 501, 525
  Constitutional Convention, 116, 230, 244, 262, 301
  cotton production, 59, 82, 89, 102
  education for Blacks, 138, 231, 383
    barred, 97
  importance of tobacco in, 42–43
  "Jim Crow" laws, 258, 286
  KKK in, 239
  population
    colonial, 29, 37, 38, 41, 42, 54–55
    state, 67, 89, 256, 479, 521
  slavery in, 43, 147, 150, 177, 183
    freed slaves, 74, 92
    maroon community destroyed, 82
    secedes, readmitted to Union, 185, 219, 226
    sit-ins held in, 405
    slave laws, 10, 19, 20, 26, 28, 30, 54, 74
    slavery defined, 97–98
  Supreme Court of, 97
  University of, 106, 549
  violence in, 232, 236, 268, 285, 449, 456
  voting rights in, 116, 258, 275, 301, 426, 463
  See also Carolina colony

North Carolina State Teachers' Association for Negroes, 267
North Star (abolitionist newspaper), 140, 153
Northwest Ordinance of 1787, 62, 63 (map), 78, 137
Northwest Territory, 62, 77
Norton, Eleanor Holmes, 489, 533
Nova Scotia, 56
Noyes Academy (New Hampshire), 117

Oakland, Calif., 470, 499
Oberlin, Ohio, 160
Oberlin College, 105, 161, 205, 246, 270, 279
　founded, 114
　students rescue slave, 165
Oberlin rescuers, **166**
O'Connor, Justice Sandra Day, 516
Oglethorpe, James Edward, 34
O'Hara, James, 262, 264, 266
Ohio, 142, 308
　antislavery activity in, 137
　　Underground Railroad, 100, 107, 146
　　Society offices sacked, 119
　Black Laws of, 79–79, 94, 98
　Blacks deported, 107
　Blacks elected in, 389, 431, 451, 519–20, 524
　freed slaves move to, 110–11
　population, 105, 319
　slavery outlawed, 77
　See also Cincinnati, Ohio; Cleveland, Ohio
Oklahoma, 5, 183, 198, 274, 529
　Black migration to, 239, 261, 269–70, 283, 293–94
　Black voting rights in, 274, 301, 308
　as Indian Territory, see Native Americans
　KKK and violence in, 213, 308, 328–29, 331, 334
　　activity against, 331, 333
　　Supreme Court invalidates martial law, 349
　segregation laws, 258, 288, 296, 308, 382–83
Olano, Nuflo de, 4
O'Leary, Hazel Reid, 556–57
Olustee (Florida), Battle of, 200, 204
Olympic Games, Black winners of, 404, 424, **443**, 452–53, 544, 563, 564
　decathlon, 405–6
　first, 294, 334, 512
　Jesse Owens, 352, 354, 470
　13 medals, 354
　two winners suspended, 442
　women, 404, 442, 511, 512, 544
O'Neal, Frederick, 362
O'Neill, Eugene, 325
Onesimus (Mather's slave), 33
Operation Breadbasket, 455, 501
Operation PUSH, 454, 455, 487, 501
Opothayohola, Chief, 183
Opportunities Industrialization Center (OIC), 426
Ordinance of 1787, 62, 63, 78, 137
Oregon, 144–45, 147, 308
Oregon Trail, 144–45
Organization for Afro-American Unity, 421, 427
Orphanage established, 270
Osborn, Charles, 91
Osceola (Seminole leader), 116, 131

Ottley, Roi, 352
Owens, Charles, 310
Owens, Jesse, 352, 354, **354**, 470
Owens, Robert, 490–91
Ownership. *See* Property
Oxley, Lawrence A., 355

Pacific (San Francisco periodical), 149
Pacific Bell, "fair-share" agreement with, 537
Packard, Sophia B., 259
Page, Ruth, 349
Paige, Leroy Robert "Satchel," 378, 455–56, **455**
Paine, Thomas, 51, 55, 146
Paine College, 257
Painting and sculpture. *See* Arts, the
Pakenham, Gen. Sir Edward, 86
Pan-African Congress, 291, 317
Pankhurst, Sylvia, 331
Paris Peace Conference, 316
Paris Society (antislavery group), 62
Parker, Charlie "Bird," 323
Parker, Judge John J., 346
Parker, Theodore, 157
Parks, Gordon, 454, 530
Parks, Rosa, 390–91, **391**, 542, 547
Parrish, John, 79
Parsons, Judge James B., 406, 468
Parting Ways (free Black settlement), 53
Patents. *See* Inventions by Blacks
Patterson, Floyd, 393, 413, 429
Patterson, Frederick Douglass, 372
Patterson, Heywood, 343, 345, 354
Patterson, William L., 383
Paul, Susan, 100
Paul, Rev. Thomas, 81
Pauling, Dr. Linus, 300
Paul Quinn College, 240, 530
Payne, Bishop Daniel L., 98, 162, 196
Payne, Donald Alexander, 232
Payne, Donald M., 514
Payne Institute. *See* Allen University
Payton, Walter, 471, 560
Peabody Fund, 163, 220–21
Peace of Utrecht, 24
Peake, Mary S., 178, 183, 188–89
Peale, Charles Willson, 55
Peary, Adm. Robert E., 298
Peck, Dr. David John, 139, 141
Pemberton, Gen. Joseph, 197
Penalties for:
　aiding runaway slaves, 10, 27, 28, 30, 35–36, 79, 94, 99–100, 122, 140, 149, 168
　allowing slave to hire out, 60
　continuing foreign slave trade, 80
　differential, for slaves, 23
　educating Blacks, 28, 36, 93, 94, 97, 196
　employing Black without certificate of freedom, 79
　employing Black or slave as clerk, 28
　freeing slave, 77
　inciting revolt, 94, 98
　intentionally killing slave, 27, 28, 92
　kidnapping free Black, 53, 57
　killing Black, 541–52
　miscegenation, 9, 20, 31
　mistreatment of slave, 36, 80, 94
　publishing, distributing, or reading antislavery literature, 106, 108

selling alcohol to slaves, 28, 30, 94
　"unlawful assembly," 105
　violating contract/vagrancy laws, 217, 248, 257, 283–84
　violating curfew, 35, 212
　See also Death penalty; Slaves, treatment of
Pendleton, Clarence, 494
Penn, William, 19
Penn Normal Institute, 190
Pennsylvania, 73, 84, 126
　antislavery movement in, 55 (*see also* Antislavery societies)
　bans miscegenation, 16
　Black woman elected to legislature, 356
　Colonization Society, 112
　Constitutional Convention, 60, 61–62, 116
　and education for Blacks, 69, 150
　　"Black Princeton," 157
　　Cheyney University, 111
　emancipation in, 30, 53, 55, 72, 74
　population
　　colonial, 19, 29, 37, 41, 42, 54
　　state, 67, 75, 89, 100
　racial violence in, 131, 315
　slavery in, 19, 61, 86, 152
　　slave laws, 10, 23, 28, 33, 46
　Supreme Court of, 68, 512
　　first Black on, 455, 502
　See also Philadelphia, Pa.; Pittsburgh, Pa.
Pennsylvania Augustine Society, 88
Pennsylvania Hall (Philadelphia) burned, 92, 116
Peonage, federal report on, 292–93. See also Slavery (new forms of)
Peoria tribe, 46. See also Native Americans
Pepsi-Cola boycotted, 404
Perkins, Edward J., 505
Perry, Adm. Oliver H., 83, 84
Pershing, Gen. John "Black Jack," 309, 310
Perth Amboy, N.J., as port of entry, 16
Petersburg, Va., 82, 202, 256
Petersen, Gen. Frank E. Jr., 473
Peter the Great, tsar of Russia, 111
Philadelphia, Pa., 73, 126
　antislavery movement in, 48, 114, 141, 155, 161
　　Underground Railroad, 100, 107
　Black Conventions in, 107, 108, 112, 117
　Black institutions and churches in, 60, 61, 72, 73–74, 80, 81, 87–91 *passim*, 97, 100
　Black mayor of, 498, 501
　Black women's activities in, 100, 108, 155
　free Blacks in, 58, 77, 88
　as one of "best" cities, 375
　population, 33, 66
　　Black, 67, 89, 100, 256, 287, 299, 319, 320, 478
　racial violence in, 92, 116, 128, 315
　restricts movement of Blacks, 20
　schools for Blacks, *see* Education
　slave trade in, 19, 28
　　labor competition, slave v. white, 26
　　slave freed, 72
　yellow fever epidemics, 21, 71
"Philadelphia Plan," 445
Philadelphia Tribune, 266
Philanthropist (abolitionist newspaper), 91, 118, 119, 123

Philanthropy, 202, 280, 300
   aiding education, *see* Education; HBCUs
   Black, 154, 155, 227, 271, 281, 302, 514
   See also Funding
Philippe, duke of Orleans, 31
Phillips, Rev. Channing E., 439
Phillips, Wendell, 107, 126, 128, 155, 156, 157, **180**
   reward offered for capture of, 179, 180
Pickett, Gen. George, 210
Pico, Pio, 149
Pierce, Franklin, 157
Pierce, Samuel R., 481–82
Pierce, Capt. William, 9
Pilot, James, 80
Pinchback, Pinckney Benton Stewart, 225, 240, 246, 282
   Congress refuses to seat, 242, 251
   as governor, 204, 239, 242
Pinckney, Eliza Lucas, 37
Pioneers, Black, 147–49, 221. *See also* Black settlements and towns; Colonization; Explorers, Blacks and Native Americans as
Piracy, foreign slave trade as act of, 90, 181
Pitcairn, Maj. John, 49, 50
Pittsburgh, Pa., 100, 231, 287, 319
Pius IX (pope), 249
Pizarro, Francisco, 4
Planned Parenthood Federation of America, 473
Plantation economy. *See* Agriculture
Planter associations, 211
Pleasant, Mary Ellen, 141
Plessy, Homer Adolphe, and *Plessy* v. *Ferguson*, 282, 388. *See also* Court cases
Plinton, James O. Jr., 455
PLO (Palestine Liberation Organization), 477
Poage, George, 294
Poetry, 111, 114, 117
   by Blacks, 41–42, 46–47, 106, 156, 222, 238, 261, 266, 277, 310, 330, 335, 557
   awards for, 337, 338, 381–82
Poison Spring (Arkansas), Battle of, 201–2
Poitier, Sidney, 362, 400, **400**, 414
Police
   KKK linked with, 490
   Levittown Blacks protected by, 396
   minority representation among, 447–48, 482, 486, 489, 502, 528
      Black heads New York City Department, 529
      Black police chief (Houston), 494
      Black woman heads Pennsylvania Department, 528
   in Stuart case (Boston), 525
   studies of, 484, 546
   and violence, 547
      Blacks clash with, 216, 311, 318, 416, 423, 425–26, 437, 449
      Blacks targeted, killed by, 423, 450, 497, 547
      lack of intervention by, 291, 318, 410, 450, 503
      McDuffie case, 478, 484
      mob supported by, 183, 291, 292
      against protesters, 402, 405, 406, 416, 417, 420, 426–27, 428, 483
      riots caused by acquittal of, 464, 484, 548, 558

riots caused by actions of, 219, 295, 423, 497, 509, 517
   Rodney King case, 464, 537, 548, 558
   "Zebra" case, 466
Political office, Blacks in
   county or city councils, 294, 295, 307, 330, 376, 383, 399, 410, 440, 509
      power denied, 516
   delegates to National Conventions
      Republican, 225, 233–334, 239, 243
      Democrat, 421, 424, 461, 462, 470
   increase in numbers, 376, 383, 424, 435, 438, 443, 464–65, 469, 498, 503, 505
   lt. governors or governors, 467, 486, 504, 520
   post-Reconstruction, 204, 224, 233, 245, 252
   Reconstruction era, 204, 207, 214, 223–26 *passim*, 232–33, 239–48 *passim*
   refused seats, 218, 223–24, 226, 228, 251
   women, 330, 352, 356, 422, 438, 443, 463, 464, 465
      presidential candidate, 439, 459
   See also Black mayors; *entries for individual states*
Political parties (Independent, American Labor), 232, 289
   Black, 263, 295, 421, 434 (*see also* Black Panther Party)
   See also Communist Party; Democratic Party; Free-Soil Party; Liberty Party; Republican Party; Socialist Party
Political power
   Black, 204, 313
      aspirations for, 316–17
      denied, 516
      growth of, 243, 350, 368, 371, 372, 376, 383, 449, 543
      organization of, 241, 277, 289, 342, 390–91, 392
   Black emigration and, 255
   gerrymandering and, 245, 278, 289, 297, 408
   KKK and, 222, 231
   southern white, 61, 75, 76, 90, 132, 319, 423, 516
      white supremacy restored, 250, 288, 300, 379, 392
   See also Black protest; Boycotts; Political office, Blacks in; Political parties
Polk, James K., 137
Pollard, Fritz, 316
Polls, 459, 490
Poll taxes. *See* Taxes
Polygamy, 157
Ponce de León, Juan, 4
Poor, Salem, 49, 50
Poor People's Campaign/March on Washington, 441. *See also* Black protest
Popular songs. *See* Music
"Popular sovereignty" issue, 142, 164. *See also* States' rights
Population
   Black, among Native Americans, 22, 116
   Blacks in Canada, 121
   Blacks in western U.S.
      California, 145, 149, 230, 299
      Kansas City, Kans., 231,
      Kansas City, Mo., 256, 273

Tulsa, 329
   Census Report on (1969), 443
   cities sue Census Bureau for adjustment of figures, 535
   divorce rate data, 481
   elderly, 523
   farm, 274, 287, 299, 320, 360, 379–80, 487
   free Black
      farming, 320
      Liberia (1865), 204
      Louisiana (1836), 118
      male v. female, 174, 175
      troops in Civil War, 205
      1740, 1790–1820, 35, 67, 75, 81, 89
      1830–1860, 100, 118, 128, 144, 167, 169–70, 184
      1870–1900, 229, 230, 256, 273, 286–87
   growth of minorities, 479
   Liberia, 106, 204, 231
   marriage statistics, 523, 538
   mulatto, 51, 116, 318–19
   "nine-point" expression of wants of, 398
   North American British colonies
      1640–1690, 9, 13, 14–15, 17, 18–19
      1700–1733, 21–22, 26, 29–30, 31, 33, 34
      1740–1780, 35, 37–38, 41, 42, 43, 52, 54–55
      1783 (reaches 1 million), 57
   North American Dutch colonies, 9, 13, 15
   occupations of (1890), 274
   out-of-wedlock births, 407, 481, 490, 522
   and political representation (and "Three-Fifths Rule"), 61–62, 76, 226
   poverty statistics, 458 (*see also* Economic conditions)
   prison, 459, 522, 538, 548–59
   professional, distribution of (1930), 343
   race-riot statistics (1964–1968), 436 (*see also* Race riots)
   slaveholding (1829–1860), 175
   southern, 89–90, 128
      Appalachia, 479
      Black Belt, 319, 360, 446
      percentage of Black population in, 299, 483
      (*see also* Population, slave, *below*)
   United States
      Detroit census questioned, 485
      relocation of Blacks proposed, 379
      1790–1820, 66–67, 75, 81, 89
      1830–1860, 100, 128, 144–45, 169–75
      1870–1900, 229–30, 256, 273, 286–87
      1910–1940, 299, 318–19, 329, 343, 360
      1950–1990, 379, 402–3, 446, 478–80, 520–21, 525
   urban, 33, 66, 67, 89, 100, 169
      "alley," 287–88
      increase in, 287, 317, 379, 402, 446, 521
      post-Civil War, 229–30, 256, 273
      1900–1940, 286–87, 299, 319–20, 343, 360
      1950–1970, 379, 402, 403, 446, 447–48
      1980–1990, 478–79, 480–81, 492, 520–21, 525, 534
      suburban, 446, 473, 478, 479, 481, 489, 554–55
   Virginia colony (before 1640), 8, 9
   West Indies, 5
   See also Migration

Population, Slave
  northern, 26, 64–65, 67
  southern
    Appalachia (pre-Civil War), 479
    at end of Civil War, 192
    male v. female, 173, 175
    1715–1733, 29–30, 34
    1740–1780, 35, 37, 41, 42–43, 52, 55
    1783–1820, 57, 66–67, 75, 81, 82, 84–85, 89
    1830–1860, 102, 105, 117, 128, 144, 169–75, 184
  Virgin Islands, 354
"Port Chicago Mutiny," 372
Portugal, 4, 6, 15, 24
Post Office, U.S.
  Blacks employed by, 150–51, 292
  restrictions on, 97
  racial discrimination prohibited in, 204
  southern, and abolitionist literature, 109
Poston, Ted, 530
Potawatomi tribe, 45, 46. *See also* Native Americans
Poverty. *See* Economic conditions
Powell, Rev. Adam Clayton Sr., 81
Powell, Rev. Adam Clayton Jr., 81, 356, **371**, 378, 439
  in office, 367, 371, 407, 437
  defeated, 450
Powell, Gen. Colin L., 512, **512**, 517–18, 548
Powell, Justice Lewis F. Jr., 482, 536
Powell, Ozie, 354
Prejudice. *See* Racism
Prentiss Normal and Industrial College, 287
Presbyterian Church(es), 223, 414
  burned, 116
  first Black, 80, 92, 155
Prescott, J. Parker, 355
Press, the
  on "amalgamation," 155
  Black associations formed, 317, 469
  Black militant, 257, 266, 271
  racist words in, 258
  reports on lynchings, 257, 267, 268, 271, 335–36
  See also Magazines, Black; Newspapers; Newspapers, Black; Professions; Television
Price, John, 165
Price, Joseph C., 276, 304
Price, Leontyne, 385, 424
Prices. *See* Economic conditions
Pride, Charley, 436
Prince (rock star), 502, 518
Prince, Mary, 108
Princeton, N.J.
  Battle of, 57
  Black mayor of, 456
Princeton Theological Seminary and "Black Princeton," 157
Prisons. *See* Crime
Procter and Gamble, 294
Professions
  clergy, 343
  distribution of, in population (1930), 343
  engineering, 291, 363, 367 (*see also* Inventions by Blacks)
  first Black woman airline pilot, 325
  journalism, 366, 423, 496, 530, 561
    Black associations formed, 317, 469
    Black journalists hold Convention, 250

males v. females in 537
science/physics, 68, 157, 505
teaching (university), 141 (*see also* Education)
See also Astronauts, Black; Business, Black-owned; Corporations; Drug research; Government service, Blacks in; Industry; Lawyers, Black; Medicine, Blacks in
Progressive Farmers and Household Union, 316. *See also* Labor unions
"Project Clear" (Army integration study), 387–88
"Project Concern" (Hartford integration plan), 556
Property
  land ownership in the South, 320
    Blacks lose, 490
  ownership of, by slaves, 22, 30
    prohibited or property seized, 20, 36, 54, 105
  ownership of, and voting or public service, 92, 230, 276, 292
  slaves as heir to, 91
  white servants owned by free Blacks, 26
  See also Land grant(s); Slavery
Property holders' covenants, 300, 334
Prosser, Gabriel, 77, 347
Protest groups. *See* Black protest
Providence, R.I., 61, 94, 100
Provident Hospital (interracial), 277, 278, 305
Prussia, slave-trading by, 24
Public Health Service, U.S., 458–59
Public transportation, interstate, 390, 409. *See also* Buses and streetcars; Railroads
Public Works Employment Act (1977), 484
Puerto Rico, 5
Pulitzer Prize. *See* Awards and honors
Pullman Company, 336, 356
Punishment. *See* Penalties for:
Purple Rain (film), 502
Purvis, Dr. Charles B., 125, 205
Purvis, Harriet Forten, 114
Purvis, Robert, 107, 115, 125, **125**
PUSH (People United to Save Humanity). *See* Operation PUSH
Putnam, Caroline Remond, 156

Quakers
  antislavery activities and writings, 19, 40, 41, 48, 51, 64, 91, 115
  accused of inciting unrest, 74
  aid escaping slaves, 96, 100, 107
  aid slaves to purchase freedom, 73, 74
  curtail Philadelphia trade, 28
  Grimké opposes, 118
  petition Congress, 68
  and schools for Blacks, 44, 111, 146, 155, 190, 250
Quantrill's Raiders, 199
Quarles, Benjamin A., 376–77
Quarles, Norma, 530
Quota system. *See* Labor, Black (job discrimination against)

Race laws, 302, *See also* Miscegenation
Race riots, 98, 131, 264, 285, 438
  Black protest against, 99, **313**, **380**, (*see also* Black protest)

countrywide, 315, 324, 329, 270, 374
  "hot summer" (1967), 436
  "Red Summer" (1919), 316–18
Detroit, 437–38
East St. Louis, 310–11, 329, 366
over housing, 316, 317, 325, 384, 434, 451
incited by newspapers or by false accusations, 296, 298, 302, 317, 343
involving Black troops, 296, 298, 311–12, 461
National Guard called out to quell, *see* National Guard
in northern cities, 434, 436, 437, 451, 456
peaceful protest causes, 405, 416
provoked by movie, 541
over school integration/segregation, 407, 424, 434, 449
self-defense urged, 265
summary of and report on, 436, 489
Watts, 429, 461
"Wilmington Ten," 456, 558
See also Ku Klux Klan; Labor, Black; Police; Lynchings; Terrorism; Violence; Voting Rights; *entries for individual cities*
Racism
  acceptance, encouragement of, 282, 367, 379
  Anti-Slavery Society and, 115, 119
  Black "inferiority," 84, 87, 184, 189, 192, 210, 282, 538
  in the courts, 390, 516, 546–47
  and death penalty, 525
  decline in, 381
  denounced by Black press, 257, 271
  and discrimination
    in auto insurance, 564
    in housing, 413, 441, 445, 504, 565
    "intentional," 483, 494, 513, 554
    in issuing credit, 483
    legalized, 264, 282, 288
    and life in America, 481
    in newspaper industry, 449
    organized battles against, 360, 410
    policy reversed, 487
    prohibited by city ordinance, 410
    protested by students, 439–40, 534
    in standardized tests, 493, 515
    Supreme Court overturns law prohibiting, 248–49
  economic conditions and, 485, 561
  and emigration, 91, 287 (*see also* Migration)
  "environmental," 528, 547, 549
  of FBI, 467, 476, 488, 531–32, 535, 536
  government investigation of, 385, 440, 483
  of Haitian policy, 545
  and hypertension among Blacks, 536
  of Japanese firms, 515
  KKK and, 213–14 (*see also* Ku Klux Klan)
  in military service or training, 189, 253, 269, 310, 358, 378, 388, 401–2, 545
    Blacks protest, 226, 233–34, 239, 241, 243, 311–12, 441
  of missionary society, 139
  and poverty, 35, 441
  racial slurs, 258, 470, 471, 494, 509, 515
  Rotary Club, 495
  Texas country club overcomes, 534–35

Racism (continued)
  in the West, 146–47
  See also Labor, Black; Police; Political
    power; Race riots; Religion; Segrega-
    tion; Sports; White Supremacy
Radical Republicans. See Republican Party
Radio, Blacks in. See Entertainment
Railroads, 159, 175, 269, 294
  Black employment on, 131, 216, 227, 291,
    299, 305, 453
  Black-owned and -operated, 229
  Blacks invent devices for, 282, 291
  segregation on, 132, 245, 258, 261, 271,
    282–90 passim, 365
  Supreme Court decisions, 254, 282,
    351, 383
  as slave owners, 175
Raleigh Register, 222
Randolph, A. Philip, 310, 354, 367, 424
  Institute named for, 415
  leads marches on Washington, 336–37,
    361, 362–63, 398, 414, 419
  and unions, 336, 356, 389, 404
Randolph, Gen. Bernard P., 508
Randolph, John, 86, 110–11
Rangel, Charles, 371, 450–51
Ransier, Alonzo J., 232, 236, 242
Rapier, James Thomas, 241, 242, 244
Rawls, Lou, 471
Ray, Charles B., 121, 127, 134
Ray, Charlotte E., 240
Ray, James Earl, 440, 445, 472, 476
Razaf, Andy, 342
Reading Room Society (Philadelphia), 97
Reagan, Ronald, 489, 491, 495, 500, 505
  appointments by, 469, 481, 505, 546
    Senate rejects, 503, 510
  Blacks' opinion of, 488, 490, 499, 502,
    508–9, 527
  reverses policy, 469, 487–502 passim, 512,
    539
Reckless, Hetty, 114
Reconstruction, the, 154, 204, 218, 246
  "carpetbaggers" and "scalawags," 221,
    222, 230
  lynchings during, 261
  Reconstruction governments retained,
    224, 228
  ended, 245, 250, 255
  "Restoration" (Johnson's plan), 211, 212
  southern resistance to 213–14, 231 (see
    also Ku Klux Klan [KKK])
  state constitutions under, 219, 221, 228,
    230
Reconstruction Acts, 221, 226
Recordings
  Black artists, 292, 333, 341, 346, 371, 389
  Grammy awards, 394, 395, 405, 436,
    438, 448, 471, 492, 501, 502, 507,
    535, 536, 545
  other awards, 399, 411, 454, 535
  Blacks in recording industry, 399, 513, 524
    (see also Motown Record Corporation)
  See also Music
Redding, Otis, 438
Red Shirts (white supremacy group), 222
Reeb, Rev. James, 427, 428
Reed, Gov. Harrison, 225
Reed, Lt. Col. William N., 204
Reese, Della, 304
Reeves, Rev. Cornelius, 222

Registration
  of Blacks, required, 40, 79
  voter, see Voting rights
Rehnquist, Justice William, 482, 500, 538
"Reign of Terror," 178–81, 232. See also
    Terrorism
Religion
  Black churches
    burned or bombed, 116, 411, 419–20,
      424, 472, 482, 483, 519
    established in North, 60, 72, 73–74, 80,
      81, 88, 92, 93, 96, 155, 264
    established in South, 33, 64, 79
    functions of, 91
    restricted, opposed, 44, 64, 72
  Black clergy, 113, 115, 343
    arrested, killed in protests, 414, 426,
      427, 428, 440 (see also King, Dr.
      Martin Luther Jr.)
    education for, 196, 250
    female Episcopal bishop, 516
    first Catholic priests, first bishop, 159,
      249–50, 267, 467
  Black women's organizations and, 113
  church attendance, religious meetings
    forbidden, 64, 80
  church-founded school, 227 (see also Mis-
    sionaries)
    parochial schools integrated, 375, 413
  churches and antislavery, 57–58, 79, 115,
    135
  first Black Catholic sisterhood, 70
  racial prejudice within, 55, 88, 160, 474
    segregation/integration of Christian
      churches, 105, 115, 240, 267, 375,
      413, 469
  religious instruction required or advo-
    cated, 40, 82, 93
  separate meetinghouse for Blacks, 30, 33
  See also Christianity; entries for individ-
    ual denominations
Remond, Charles Lenox, 114, 129, 131, 132,
    132, 155, 156, 161, 184
Remond, Nancy, 100, 155
Remond, Sarah Parker, 155–56
Reno, Janet, 478
Republican Conventions
  National, 225, 233, 234, 239, 243
  State, 157, 226, 236, 241, 244, 245
Republican Party, 203, 251, 533, 534, 543
  Black migration as "plot" of, 254
  Blacks and
    abandoned by, 240, 288
    oppose or abandon, 235, 279, 341, 350,
      351, 355
    support, serve with, 224, 230–43 pas-
      sim, 266, 278–79, 330, 351
    switch to, 433
  founded, Free-Soil Party merges with,
    136, 140, 157
  Lincoln as candidate, elected, 167, 181,
    183, 188
  as majority, 212, 221, 237
    power declines, 223, 231, 246
    power increases, 313
  Radical, 188, 212, 218, 221
  southern view of, 168, 181, 221
  See also Violence
Resettlement. See Black towns and settle-
    ments; Colonization
Resort communities, 303–4, 322

"Restoration." See Reconstruction, the
"Resurrection City," 441. See also Black
    protest
Revels, Rev. Hiram R., 204, 234–35, 235,
    236, 431
Revere, Paul, 44, 48
Revolutionary War, 250
  Blacks in, 44, 48–61 passim, 70, 72, 84,
    90, 473
  on British side, 43, 48–51 passim,
    56–57, 86
  monument to, 549
  and slave labor shortage, 43
  Treaty of Paris ends, 57
Reynal, Gomes, 6
Reynolds, Melvin J., 486, 553
Reynolds, William Bradford, 491, 492, 503
Rhode Island, 61, 94, 129, 156
  antislavery/abolitionism, 13, 47, 53, 54,
    58, 68
  Black soldiers in Revolution, 48, 53, 54
  population, 17, 29, 30, 33, 37, 42, 100·
  slavery laws, 29, 30
Rhode Island Records, 13
Rhythm and Blues Foundation, 520. See
    also Awards and honors; Music
Ribicoff, Abraham, 456
Rice, Jerry, 561
Rice, Norm, 520
Rice, Thomas "Daddy," 97
Rice production, 22, 23, 29, 33–34, 40, 41,
    78, 144, 147
  indigo alternates with, 37
  prices/cost, 43, 55, 67
Richards, Lloyd, 400
Richmond, Va., 77, 210, 302
  Black mayor of, 500
  population, 169, 174–75
Rickey, Branch, 373, 376, 376
"Rifle clubs," 250, 255. See also White
    supremacy
Rillieux, Norbert, 133
Riots. See Race riots; Violence
Ritter, Archbishop Joseph E., 375
Rivers, Justice Prince, 251–52
R. J. Reynolds Tobacco Company, 527
Roberts, Adelbert H., 337
Roberts, Benjamin, 117, 141–42
Roberts, Joseph Jenkins, 139
Roberts, Needham, 312–13
Roberts, Sarah, 141–42
Robertson, Oscar, 407, 477
Robeson, Paul, 322, 326, 383
  discrimination against, 309, 341, 365
  in films and plays, 313, 337, 341, 349, 371
Robinson, Bill "Bojangles," 322, 365, 371
Robinson, Eddie G., 501
Robinson, Frank, 393, 407–8, 432, 492, 556
  first Black manager in major leagues, later
    fired, 467, 540
Robinson, J. (Black playwright), 70
Robinson, Jackie, 266, 373, 376, 379, 385,
    398, 555
  first Black in Hall of Fame, 413
  first Black to join major leagues, 375
Robinson, Marius, 123, 124
Robinson, Max, 469, 478
Robinson, "Sugar Ray," 374, 383, 398
Robinson, William "Smokey" Jr., 399
Rockville (Md.) Journal, 179
Rodgers, James M. Jr., 460

Rolfe, Capt. John, 6
Roman Catholic Church, 154, 246, 264, 524
  first Black bishops, 249–50, 467, 511
  first Black priests, 159, 246, 249–50, 267, 473
  first Black sisterhood, 70
  parochial schools integrated, 375, 413
  Stallings breaks with, 517
Roosevelt, Eleanor (Mrs. Franklin D.), 350, 359, 369
Roosevelt, Franklin D., 306, 358, 362–63, 364, 481
  "Black Cabinet" of, 303, 355, 356, 363
  and New Deal, 342, 352
  orders end of discrimination, 363, 366
Roosevelt, Theodore, 284, 292, 296, 304, 461
Roots (Haley), 469, 472, 557
Rosenwald, Julius, 346, 347, 366
Ross, Diana, 408, 459
Rotary Club (Birmingham), 495
ROTC programs protested, 450
Rough Riders (Spanish-American War), 284
Roussell, Norward, 529, 531
Rowan, Carl Thomas, 423, **423**, 530
Royal African Company, 18, 19–20, 24, 41
Royal Company of Adventurers, 16
Rudolph, Wilma, 404, 408
Ruffin, George L., 226–27, 264
Ruggles, David, 107, 126
Rum (in "triangular trade"), 22, 25, 31–32.
  See also Slave trade
Rush, Benjamin, 51, **51**, 60, 64, 71
Rush, Bobby, 499, 553
Rush, Gertrude E., 337
Rush Medical College, 139
Rusk, David, 554–55
Russell, Bill, 382, 398, 433, 466
Russell, Richard, 379
Russia, ambassador to, 136
Russwurm, John, 72, 87, 95, 96, 112
Rustin, Bayard, 375, 396, 414–15, 419, 421
Rutherford Gazette, 120
Ryan, Leo, 475

Safeway Stores, "fair-share" agreement with, 537
St. Augustine, Fla., 34, 35
  maroon settlement in, 5, 37
St. Louis, Mo., 135, 235, 399
  antidiscrimination law of, 410
  Black population, 319, 402
  Blacks warned away from, 256
  schools integrated, 485
  segregation in, 302, 342
St. Louis Observer (antislavery newspaper), 124
St. Philip's Protestant Episcopal Church (New York), 88
St. Thomas African Episcopal Church (Philadelphia), 60, 73
Salem, Peter, 45, 50
Salem, Mass., 9, 20, 113, 136, 184
  Female Anti-Slavery Society, 11–12, 155
Salem Methodist Episcopal Church (Harlem), 335
Sampson, Edith, 379
San Francisco, Calif., 136, 141, 153, 320
  as one of "best" cities, 375
San Jose Mercury News, 546–47
Sankore, University of, 3
Santo Domingo, 93, 271. See also Hispaniola

Santomee, Lucas and Peter, 10, 12
Saperstein, Abe, 339
Sargeant, Gov. Francis, 467
"Satraps," 221. See also Reconstruction, the
SAT scores, 496, 515
Savage, Gus, 486
Savannah, Ga., 34, 59, 64, 145, 165, 280
  Black population, 175, 256, 273, 287, 299
  Sherman captures, 203–4
  steam power in, 175
Savoy Ballroom opens (New York), 339
Sayers, Gale, 471
"Scalawags," 221. See also Reconstruction, the
Schmoke, Kurt, 510, **510**, 558
Schools. See Education
Schott, Marge, 550
Schwerner, Michael, 424, 435, 519
SCLC (Southern Christian Leadership Conference), 392, 410, 420, 428, 433, 435, 460, 493
  directors of, 441, 445, 457, 462, 523
  founded, 396, 414
  Jackson and, 455, 501
Scopes, John, and Scopes trial, 337
Scotland, Blacks study in, 119, 223, 291
Scott, Dred, 113, 163–64, **165**. See also Court cases
Scott, Dr. Hugh S., 451
Scott, Robert C., 553
Scottsboro case, 343–45, **344**, 354, 470
Sea Islands (Georgia)
  Black colony on, 184, 188, 258
  Union forces take, 189, 190, 192
Seale, Bobby, 429, **430**, 454
Seattle, Wash., as one of "best" cities, 375
Secession, 168, 183, 185, 191, 230
  readmission standards, 212, 219, 226, 234
Secret societies, 135, 256. See also Ku Klux Klan (KKK); Masonic Order; White supremacy
Segregation
  armed forces, 189
    desegregation urged, not acted upon, 246, 356
    post-Reconstruction, 253
    Truman ends, 373, 378, 458
    World Wars I and II, 286, 367–68, 371, 372, 373, 387–88
  banned at Democratic headquarters, 378
  in churches, 105, 115, 240, 375, 413, 469
  "Jim Crow" laws, 189, 231, 248, 258, 276, 281, 319, 328
    beginning of, 282
    protested, 305, 311
  legalized, ubiquitous, 288, 401
  of medical facilities, 277
  on public transportation, 248, 271, 390, 409, **409** (see also Buses and streetcars; Railroads)
  residential
    banned, 379
    city ordinances, 302, 305, 310, 334, 339, 342, 349
    NAACP on, 300, 349
    prevalence of, 499, 564
  restaurant, 219, 220, 245, 262, 384, 389, 398, 409

school
  Boston ends, 160
  busing opposed, 449, 457, 459, 467, 469, 482, 489, 494
  busing and redistricting as means of eliminating, 456, 476, 483, 486–87, 498, 543
  Connecticut integration plans, 556, 559
  court upholds, 149
  de facto, 393, 413, 420, 424, 456
  defeated (in D.C.), 234, 388
  federal funds denied, 482
  by gender, ruled against, 541
  policy changes, 491
  private schools opened as means of, 393, 447, 450, 451, 493, 500
  protested, 116–17, 135–38 passim
  segregation continues, 477, 482, 504, 564
  under state constitutions, 230
  voluntary, 556
school integration controversy, 141–42, 230, 414, 449
  Black schools founded, 375
  Black protest, 295, 420, 445
  "go slow" approach, 390, 393, 415
  leaders defy court orders, 386, 395–406 passim, 412, 445
  resistance groups formed, 387
  white protesters/violence in, 117, 373, 392, 393, 396, 400, 406, 412–13, 416, 450
"separate but equal" doctrine
  in education, 61, 90, 14, 261, 357–58, 374
  Supreme Court decisions (pro and con), 282, 357, 388, 477
  "two societies" (separate and unequal), 440
  social/recreational, 155, 156, 307, 308, 322, 326, 373, 385
    country club memberships at last accepted, 534
    prohibited/protested, 248–49, 390, 414, 439
  sports, 396, 437 (see also Sports)
  student protest against, 220, 363, 365, 367, 375, 405, 420
  Supreme Court rulings, 254, 310, 538 (see also Supreme Court, U.S.)
  voluntary, case for, 286, 556
  See also Military service, Blacks in; Racism
Self-defense by Blacks, 291, 429
  Black militia formed for, 37, 254
  forbidden by law (1682), 19
  recommended (1884), 265, 268
  See also Arms and ammunition
Seligman, Edwin R. A., 303
Selma, Ala., 426, 509, 529, 531
  march to Montgomery from, 427–28, 457, 493, 506, 543
Seminole tribe, 82, 84, 106, 132, 181
  as slaveowners, 22, 23
  See also Native Americans
Seminole Wars, 82, 84, 88–89, 116, 124, 131–32
Senate, U.S., 216, 235, 298
  Blacks elected to, 204, 234–35, 246, 248, 410, 506
  first since Reconstruction, 431, 474
  refused seat, 251
  woman, 551

Senate, U.S. *(continued)*
  Blacks petition, 205
  and Civil Rights Bill, 503
  Committee on Reconstruction, 212
  filibusters in, 331, 397
  rejects Reagan's appointees, 503, 510
  rejects Texas annexation, 135
  and slavery, 125, 159, 167, 191
  southern influence in, 423
  See also Congress, U.S.
Senegal Company, 24
Sentencing Project, 522. *See also* Crime
"Separate but equal" doctrine. *See*
    Segregation
Servants. *See* Indentured servants
Sessions, William, 532, 536
Seven Years War, 41
Seward, William H., 166–67, **180**, 181,
    226
  reward offered for capture of, 179, 180
Sewell, Judge Samuel, 20, 25
Shadd, Abraham, D., 115
Shadd, A. W., 239
Shadd, I. D., 239, 243
Sharecroppers. *See* Agriculture
Sharecroppers' Union, 347–48
Sharkey, Jack, 353
Sharp, James A. Jr., 498, 501
Sharpe, James A. Jr., 558
Sharpton, Rev. Al, 550, 560
Shaw, Artie, 346
Shaw, Justice Leander Jay Jr., 500, 527–28
Shaw, Chief Justice Lemuel, 68
Shaw, Col. Robert Gould, 194, 199, 219
Shawmut National Corporation, 565
Shaw University, 404
Shelley, Charles M., 241, 244
Sheridan, Gen. Philip, 210, 216, 226, 247
Sherman, Gen. William Tecumseh, 201,
    202, 203–4
Show Boat (musical comedy), 341
Shreveport, La., 287, 299
Shuttlesworth, Fred L., 395, 416, **416**
Sickle cell anemia, 300. *See also* Disease
Sierra Leone, 137
  colony for freed slaves, 55, 57, 60, 83–84,
    90, 218
Sifford, Charles, 396, 465
Simms, Willie, 279, 284
Simpson, Georgiana R., 324
Simpson, O. J., 501
Sims, Thomas, 152
Singleton, Benjamin "Pap," 231, 254,
    258–59
Singleton, John, 541, 547
Sioux tribe, 250. *See also* Native Americans
Sipuel, Ada Lois, 377, **377**
Sissle, Noble, 325, 326
Sit-ins, 375, 402, 410
  Black, 369, 398, 404, 405, 425, **425**,
    439–40, 529
  government interference banned, 415
  by white parents, 450
  See also Black protest; Student protest
Six Killer (Black Cherokee), 183
Sixteenth Street Baptist Church (Birming-
    ham, Ala.), bombing of, 419, **419**,
    472, 482
Skinhead plot, 560
Skinner, Elliot, 431
Slater, John F., and Slater Fund, 163, 262

Slaughterhouse cases, 233, 243. *See also*
    Court cases
Slave codes. *See* Laws and legislation
Slave conspiracies. *See* Slave revolts
Slave labor
  advantages of African, 14
  advertisements for, 147
  in Civil War, 184
  competition between whites and, 26
  "conditioning," "breaking in" of, 9, 15
    (*see also* Slaves, treatment of)
  dependence of North on southern, 41
  as domestics and in industry, 64, 144
  effect of *asiento* on, 4
  employment of, as clerk, penalized, 28
  Franklin's view of, 40
  gang, 177–78
  imported to West Indies, 8, 15
  Indians as, 4
  in the North, 64–65
  post-Revolution shortage of, 43
  skilled work by, 40, 43, 87
  slaves restricted from hiring themselves
    out, 60
  working hours, 28, 36, 145
  See also Cotton; Economic conditions; In-
    digo; Labor, Black; Rice production;
    Sugar; Tobacco
Slave owner(s)
  absentee, 28
  advertises for runaways, 122, **139**
  compensated for executed or freed slave
    or free Black sold back, 44, 86,
    191–92
  corporations as, 174, 175
  free Black or person of mixed ancestry as,
    100, 118
  "God's approval" of, 93
  Jefferson as, 58, 155
  missionary as, 135
  murders slave, 142–44
  Native Americans as, 22–23, 181, 294
  oppose education, 145–46
  paid by slave, 106
  slave relationship with, 28, 90, 98, 142,
    144
  slaves freed by, 20, 28, 30, 58, 77
  state sues, 140
  See also Slaves, runaway; Slaves, treat-
    ment of
Slave raids, 27. *See also* Slave revolts
Slave revolts
  blamed on colonization plans, 88
  Carolinas, 5, 32, 35, 37, 82, 93
  conspiracies, 16, 33, 37, 86, 87, 93, 183
  fears of, 13, 20, 43, 59, 87, 93, 98, 178
    and slave laws, 28, 32, 33, 69
  Garnet calls for, 134
  Georgia, 48, 82
  Hispaniola/Haiti, 4, 20–21, 69–70
  Latin America, 6
  Louisiana, 74, 83
  Maryland, 88, 136
  mini-revolts on plantation, 90
  mutinies at sea, 21, 34, 39, 127, **127**,
    129–30, 131, 132
  Nat Turner's, 108–9, **109**, 110, 178
  New York, 26, 28, 37
  penalty for inciting, 94, 98
  plots discovered, 33, 37, 74, 82, 93
  and slave raids, 27

Vesey's ("Charleston Insurrection"), 87,
    93, 178
Virginia, 56, 75, 77, 82, 108–9, 347
  See also Slaves, treatment of
Slave rights
  due process, denied, 28
  freedom restricted
    of assembly, 25, 33, 44, 80, 94
    of movement, 19, 20, 21, 27, 30, 33, 36
    of religion, 30, 64, 80
  marriage, 30, 81 (*see also* Miscegenation)
  "natural," 51
    disregarded, 47
  in New England, 29–30
  in Ohio and Northwest, 77
  See also Civil rights; Laws and legisla-
    tion; Property
Slavery
  children born into, 16, 17, 19, 26
  Christianity and, 4, 8, 14–19 *passim*, 27,
    51, 93
  debated, status clarified by Congress, 119,
    167, 182
  defined, 16–17, 97
  distribution of, 173 (map)
  of Europeans, 10
  or exile, free Blacks given choice, 165, 178
  free Blacks returned to, **29**, 48, 70, 77,
    108, 120, 178
    for aiding runaway, 35–36
    when captured in Civil War, 194
    for misconduct, 88, 111
    sold back by British, 56, 86
  in French colonies, 17, 31 (*see also*
    France)
  "ideal" slave, 144
  indentured servitude distinguished from,
    6, 8, 13 (*see also* Indentured servants)
  invention of cotton gin and, 71
  as issue in Civil War, 186
  as issue in 1860 election, 181–82
  last slave dies, 478
  legalized in North America, legislative
    protest against, slave status deter-
    mined, 10, 12, 15 (*see also* Laws and
    legislation)
  in Liberia, 332
  licensed in Americas, 4, 6
  lifelong, decreed, 36
  limited to Blacks, 26
  missionary view of, 4, 135
  murder of slave, 142–44
    becomes capital offense, 92
  of Native Americans, 9, 10, 36
  new forms of
    under Black Codes, 221
    convict-lease system, 257, 283
    lien laws and, 287
    peonage, 283, 292–93
    sharecropping, 215, 239–40, 254
    reinstituted, 77, 78, 119
    rejected by Illinois, 94
    Senate affirmation, 125, 159
  and separation of families, 64, 120, **138**
  and "slave" states, 136, 147, 160
  slaves as property, 15, 26, 58, 61, 80,
    105–6, 147
  and Civil War, 90
    (*see also* Slave owner[s])
  state/territorial rights and, 68, 72, 90,
    119, 126, 137–38, 142, 159, 164

and suicide, 12, 28, 120–21
in territories
  Congressional power over ("popular sovereignty" issue), 142, 164
  debate over Texas, 128, 131, 134
  Free-Soil Party opposes, 140
  Missouri Compromise, 90, 159, 164
  Ordinance of 1787 bars, is disregarded, 62, 63, 78, 137
  outlawed (1862), 192
  Wilmot Proviso and, 137–38
  "Three-Fifths Rule" revives, 61–62, 96
  Treaty of Paris and, 57
See also Antislavery movement/abolitionism; Economic conditions; Emancipation; Population, slave; Slaves, treatment of
Slaves, runaway
  advertisements for, **43**, 122
  ages of, 120
  aided, 100, 150, 159, 165–66
    by Quakers, 96, 100, 107
    legal defense of, 157, 185
  Crafts escape to England, 140–41
  extradition of, 60
    Canada refuses, 121
  flee to Canada or Mexico, 70, 100, 116, 124 (see also Canada; Underground Railroad)
  from Hispaniola, 21
  hiding places for, 73, 125
  from "insecure" property, 139–40
  intercolonial agreement on, 10
  join Native Americans, 5, 82, 84, 106, 116, 131–32
  killing of, permitted, 20, 120
  as "King of England's soldiers," 59
  and Latimer case, 132–33
  laws dealing with, 9, 10, 18–20 passim, 26–30 passim, 34
    Confiscation Act frees, 186
    last fugitive returned under law, 185
    militia established to pursue, 14
    return law protested, 75
    Supreme Court decisions, 132, 151, 159, 164, 168
  "maroons," 18
    settlements destroyed, 37, 82, 86
  numbers of, 71, 120, 125
  personal letter from slave, 97
  recapture of, 14, **102**
  reward for (bounty on), 18, 91, 122, 125, 142, 147, 149
  during Revolution, 48
  runaway servants liable for loss of, 14
  slavehunter patrols, **71**, 91, 103, 104, 116, 137, 140, 141, 152–53
  slave revolts and, 4, 5
  with Union Army, 141, 153, 185, 186–88, 190
See also Fugitive Slave Laws; Penalties for:; Slaves, treatment of
"Slave stealers," 99–100. See also Underground Railroad
Slaves, treatment of
  baptism confers privileges, 8, 14
    laws revoked, 17, 27
  change in owner-slave relationship and, 90
  "conditioning" or "breaking in," 9, 15, 39
  conditions aboard slave ships, 12, 14, 39, **39**, 64

by Confederacy, 202
cruel, prohibited by law, 36, 143–44
for curfew violation, 35
described, 52, 119–20, 151
education, see Education
on Hispaniola, 20–21
laws concerning, see Laws and legislation
marriages between slaves illegal, 81
missionary view of, 4
murder, 142–44
  by Native Americans, 22
"Negro Watch" and, 32
in New Amsterdam murder trial, 8
in New England, 30
owner absenteeism and, 28
patent restrictions on, 116
to produce "ideal" slave, 144
punishment
  for attending church, 64
  for congregating, 94
  "justified," 15
  for murder, burglary, rape, arson, 23, 28, 35, 144
  for poisoning, 28, 41
  for profanity, 30
  for revolt, 26–32 passim, 37, 39, 48, 74–77 passim, 82, 83, 93, 109
  of runaways, 9, 10, 19, 26–33 passim, 102–3, 120, 140
  for striking white person, 17, 20, 25, 28, 30, 33, 36
  for theft, 23, 27, 30, 35
punishment, types of
  barbarous/excessive, 33, 35, 44
  branding, 10, 17, 27, 33, 102–3, 120
  castration, 27, 103
  execution, 9, 17–28 passim, 36, 43–44, 75, 77, 82, 83, 140, 144 (see also hanging or burning alive, below)
  flogging or whipping, 10, 15–35 passim, 64, 94, **120**
  hamstringing, 33
  hanging or burning alive, 26, 28, 32, 33, 37, 41, 44, 48, 74, 109
  loss of ear, 27, 33
  lynching, 35
  "at master's discretion," 105, 120
  nose-slitting, 27
  retaliation against, 33, 69, 90
  at slave market, 32
  slaves sue for food and clothing, 140
  "sold down the river," 147
  Spanish licensing provisions, 6
  in tobacco fields, 9
  by Union Army, 186, 187
See also Courts; Religion; Slave rights; Slavery
Slave trade, 2 (map)
  advertisements, **78**, **104**, 147
  "breeding" and exporting of slaves, 61, 76, 102, 103–5, 117, 147, 177
  competition in, 9, 24, 34
    monopoly revoked, 9, 19–20
  confiscation of ships involved in, 64, 81
  Continental Congress calls for end of, 48, 52
  in D.C., 104
    abolished, 149, 167
    declared illegal, 64
    denied by British, 5 (see also Great Britain)

dominated by English and Anglo-Americans, 34
extended by Constitutional Convention, 60
foreign, forbidden by Congress, 73, 90, 170
  continues, 167, 181, 184–85
  intercepted by U.S. and Britain, 133
free Blacks kidnapped in, 59, 60, 79
growth in (1700–1775), 42
import duties on, 14, 28
interstate established, 147, 148 (map)
in Jamestown Colony, 6 (see also Virginia)
land bonus offered for purchase, 16, 17–18
in Latin America, 6
last slave ship at American port, 167–68
as major business, 3, 5–6
  becomes international, 24, **24**, **25**
New England enters, 9, 12, 31
ports of entry, 16
protested, curtailed, 12, 19, 28 (see also Antislavery movement/abolitionism)
Portugal and Spain control, 4, 5–6, 8, 24
reinstitution called for, 168
reopened, 77, 78
sale by court order, 150
slave auctions, 32, 36, 58, **81**, 102, **103**, 105
slave ships, 9, 12, 80, 165, 167, **171**, 181
  mutiny aboard, 21, 34, 39, 127, 129–30, 131, 132
slave sold eight times, 244
and smuggling, 80, 87, 89, 90, 133, **170**, **181**
Sullivan's Island as clearing-house, 76
taxation of, 15, 31, 46
traders attack antislavery activists, 92
triangular routes, 11 (map), 12, 22, 223, 25, 31–32
with West African empires, 4, 9 (see also West Africa)
See also Economic conditions; Laws and Legislation, Antislavery; Slaves, treatment of
Sleets, Moneta, 445
Smalls, Robert, 192, **192**, 262, 282
  in Congress, 204, 245, 248, 252, 259, 264, 266
Smith, Abiel, and Smith School (Boston), 116–17
Smith, Alfred Edgar, 355
Smith, Bessie, 333, **333**
Smith, Rev. Ezra E., 271
Smith, Gerrit, 118, 128, 136
Smith, Dr. James McCune, 119, 139, 141
Smith, James W., 233–34, 253
Smith, Morgan, 214
Smith, Tommie, 442, 443, **443**
Smithsonian Institution, 528
Smoking, incidence of, 515, 527
Smythe, Hugh, 431
SNCC (Student Non-Violent Coordinating Committee), 404, 410, 421, 424, 428, 429, 434–38 passim, 506
Snowden, Dan and Lew, 167
Socialist Party, 300, 336
Society for the Propagation of the Gospel in Foreign Parts, 25, 41
Society of Friends. See Quakers
"Sold down the river" as phrase, 147. See also Slaves, treatment of; Slave trade
Songhai (Songhay) empire, 1, 3–4

Songs. *See* Music
Sons of New York (Black group), 265
Sororities, 296, 305, 324, 331, 345, 348, 366
South Africa
  ambassador to, 518
  as political issue, 426, 439, 462, 474, 475, 499, 505, 531
South America. *See* Latin America
South Carolina, 45, 55
  anti-Black laws, 217, 258
    segregation, 285, 401, 404
  bans miscegenation, 16
  Black emigrants from, 39–40, 164, 283, 319
  Black voting in, 219, 224, 257, 277
    restricted, 258, 275, 276, 280, 301, 426, 463
  Blacks in office, 204, 240, 242, 245
  in Civil War, 184, 197, 237, 245
  Constitutional Convention, 223, 224, **224**, 230–37 *passim*, 240, 245
    new, 280–81, 301
  crops of
    cotton, 75, 82, 89, 102, 320
    indigo, 37, 42, 43, 67
    rice, 22, 29, 33–34, 37, 40
  education for Blacks in, 37
    barred, 97, 98, 196
    colleges founded, 232, 274
    disparity of funds, 307, 339
    segregation prohibited, 230
  foreign and convict labor in, 214, 283
  free Blacks in, 35–36, 88, 93
  population
    colonial, 29–37 *passim*, 41–43 *passim*, 54, 55
    state, 67, 89, 256, 320, 479, 521
  Reconstruction in, 228, 250
  secedes, readmitted to Union, **182**, 183, 185, 219, 226
  slavery in, 147, 177
    laws, 10, 27, 28, 35–36, 92
    proslavery forces, 118, 161
    revolts, raids, 5, 27, 32, 35, 82, 93
    slave owner sued by state, 140
    slave trade, 74, 78, 161
    slaves freed, 245
    slaves as soldiers, 48
  status of Blacks in, 142
  Supreme Court of, 118, 236, 276, 283
  terrorism and violence in, 231, 236, 239, 251–52, 284, 409, 450
  University of, 239, 243
  "worst" cities in, 377
  See also Carolina colony
South Carolina State College, 276
Southern Baptists. *See* Baptist church(es)
Southern Commercial Convention, 168
Southern Farmers' Alliance, 267
Southern Homestead Act (1866), 215. *See also* Land grant(s)
Southern Literary Messenger, Southern Citizen, Southern Confederacy, Southern Workman, Southern School News (periodicals), 106, 120, 178, 258, 401
"Southern Manifesto," 393
Southern Poverty Law Center, 424
Southern Regional Council, 385
Southern States Negro Convention, 241
Southern Tenant Farmers Union, 350

Southern University and A & M College, 257, 259
Southern University Conference, 367
South Seas Company, 24
Southwestern Christian Advocate, 235
Spain
  and *Amistad* case, 129–31
  Blacks in militia, 35
  California held by, 149
  cedes Louisiana to France, 77
  frees slaves in Florida, 5, 34, 35
  and Hispaniola, 20, 70
  slave trade by, 4, 6, 8, 15, 24, 127, 181
Spanish-American War, 216, 271, 273, 284, 285, 309, 362, 384
Spelman, Harvey Buel, 259
Spelman College, 219, 257, 259–60, 342, 507, 514
Spingarn, Joel, 304, 307, 312
Spingarn Medal. *See* Awards and honors
Sports
  auto-racing, 538
  bicycling, 341
  broad-jump record broken, 425
  "fair-share" agreements in, 559
  Female Athlete of the Year, 408, 516 (*see also* Women, Black)
  first Black all-American athlete, 277
  golf, 385, 396, 465, 535
  racism in
    baseball, 324, 459, 509, 550, 555–56
    basketball, 330
    boxing, 82, 297–98, 302, 356
    interracial athletics banned, 309, 365, 396, 437
    salaries, 385, 433, 560–61, 563
    tennis, 382, 392, 396, 429, 442, 467, 547–48
  See also Baseball; Basketball; Boxing; Football; Kentucky Derby; Olympic Games, Black winners of
Sports Illustrated, 543, 547–48
Spottswood, Bishop Stephen Gill, 451
Stallings, Bishop George Augustus, 517
Stance, Sgt. Emanual, 235–36
Stanton, Elizabeth Cady, 114, 129, 140
States' rights, 191, 243
  and slavery, 68, 72, 90, 119, 126, 142, 159
Status
  baptism/conversion and, *see* Christianity
  of children of slaves, *see* Children
  defined (1849), 142
  determination of, *see* Laws and legislation
  1970s, 474
  See also Economic conditions; Racism
Steele, Shelby, 539
Stephens, Alexander, H., 75, 212
Stephenson, D. C., 335
Stevens, Justice John P. III, 495, 500
Stevens, Thaddeus, 212, 232
Stevenson, Adlai, 384, 393
Steward, Susan Maria McKinney, 196
Stewart, Bennett McVey, 475–76
Stewart, Eliza, 239
Stewart, Maria W., 100, 112
Stewart, Ollie, 377
Stewart, Justice Potter, 482
Stiles, Ezra, 67
Still, William, 107, 326, 339, 379
Stokes, Carl B., 413, 435, 442
Storey, Moorfield, 298

Stork Club, 384
Story, Justice Joseph, 129–30
Stout, Justice Juanita Kidd, 512
Stowe, Harriet Beecher, 72, 86, 94, 96, 106, 151, 154
Straight University/College. *See* Dillard University
Strayhorn, Billy, 341
Strikes
  by Blacks, 42, 267–68, 284, 348, 445
  Blacks as strikebreakers, 230–31, 274, 298, 321
  protesting Black employment, 305, 370
Stuart, Charles, 525
Student protest, 446
  against discrimination, 439–40, 534
  against integration, 153, 373, 392
  against lack of Black programs and admissions, 440, 445, 450, 529, 549
  against segregation, 220, 363, 365, 367, 375, 405, 420
  against Vietnam War, 449
  See also Boycotts (school); SNCC (Student Non-Violent Coordinating Committee)
Stuyvesant, Peter, 16
Suburbs. *See* Population (urban)
Sudarkasa, Dr. Niara, 157
Sugar, 25, 75, 133
  grown by slave labor, 4, 12, 20, 31, 75–76, **76**, 77, 144, 147
Suicide of slaves, 12, 28, 120–21
Sullivan, Leon H., 426, **426**, 455, 517, 527, 544
Sumner, Charles, 141, **141**, 142, 151, 157, 208, 233, 237
  beaten in retaliation for speech, 162
  Civil Rights Bill of, 233, 240
  reward offered for capture of, 179
Sun Oil Company boycotted, 404
Supreme Court, U.S.
  and affirmative action, 474, 505, 508
  and aid to minority business, 484, 516
  allows cross-burning, 548
  appointments to, 354
    of Blacks, 378, 436, 540, 546, 557
    opposed, 346, 364, 448, 510, 540
  Black attorneys appear before, 207, 339, 384, 433
  and Civil Rights Bills, 248, 264, 265, 423, 502, 503
  on court racism, 516
  declines to rule, 334, 385, 502
  denies Black citizenship, 163–64
  on education, 377 (*see also* segregation decisions, *below*)
  on exclusion of jurors, 259, 364, 536
  and 14th Amendment (due process), 243, 259, 331, 340, 343, 351
  and fugitive slaves, 132, 151, 159, 164, 168
  on gerrymandering, 397, 408
  on "intent to discriminate," 483, 494, 513
  in mutiny case, 127, 129–31
  orders Bond seated (Georgia House), 424
  outlaws convict-lease system/peonage, 283
  overturns convictions of Blacks and freedom riders, 345, 364, 410, 413, 416
  overturns miscegenation laws, 376, 437
  rules on death penalty, 461, 470
  rules on employment, 456, 471, 477, 489

segregation decisions
  courtroom, 415
  public transportation and accommodations, 254, 282, 351, 375, 386, 389–93 *passim*, 406, 409, 423
  school, 382–83, 388, 399, 404, 456, 459, 463, 483, 528, 538
  school, "go slow" approach, 390, 393, 415, 445, 477
  school, state defiance of, 382, 390, 404
  separate but equal decisions (pro and con), 282, 357, 388, 477
  and voting rights, 251, 292, 308, 340, 371, 426, 483, 495, 516, 557
  See also Court cases; NAACP
Supreme Courts, State. *See entries for individual states*
Supremes, the, 399, 408, 459
Swails, Stephen A., 200, 242
Swanson, Howard, 383
Sweatt, Heman, 374, 383
Sweden, slave-trading by, 24
Sweet, Dr. Ossian, 337
Syracuse, N.Y., 153

Taft, William Howard, 224, 277
Talladega (Florida village), 84
Talladega College, 139
Talmadge, Gov. Eugene, 367
Taney, Chief Justice Roger, 113, 164
Tanner, Benjamin Tucker, 264
Tanner, Henry O., 275–76
Tappan, Arthur, 108, 113, 115, 121
Tappan, Lewis, 115, **115**, 129, 183
Tarkar people, 167–68
Tastee Baking Company boycotted, 404
Taxes
  Blacks refuse to pay, 125
  exemptions, 42
    school, 447, 451, 494
    school, denied, 493, 500
  Louisiana, paid by free Blacks, 118
  poll, 135, 257–58, 275, 289, 292, 301, 426, 519
    repealed, 373, 424
  on slave trade, 15, 31
    import duties, 14, 28, 46
  without representation, protested, 55, 135
Taylor, Marshal "Major," 341
Taylor, Susie King, 189
Television, 454, 469, 488, 500, 532, 550
  Black artists, 385, 392, 393–94, 425, 442, 452, 464, 473, 503, 557
    win awards, 405, 434, 444, 445, 448, 467, 472, 498, 503, 541
  Black newscasters, anchors, 407, 413, 469, 478, 492, 530
  Black-owned stations and network, 464, 467, 482, 486, 542
  MTV, 513–14
  shows civil rights struggles, 416, 420, 428
  See also Entertainment
Temple University, 516
Tennessee, 18, 92, 232, 383
  anti-Black laws, 218, 258
  Black colleges founded 231
  cotton production, 82, 84, 89, 177
  KKK formed in, 213
  lynchings/racial violence in, 246, 314, 316, 392, 456

population, 75, 84, 479
  Black emigrants from, 230, 231
  slavery in, 22, 147, 177, 183
  secedes, readmitted to Union, 185, 191, 218, 219
  University of, 382, 385
  voting restrictions lifted, 405
  See also Memphis, Tenn.
Tennessee State College, 300
Tennis. *See* Sports
Terrell, George, 275
Terrell, Mary Church, 279, **279**, 281, 296, 384
Territories, slavery in. *See* Slavery
Terrorism, 245–56 *passim*, 284, 295, 348
  assassinations, 383, 440, 485, 488, 496
  Black discussion of, 264, 265
  and Black migration, 231, 254, 287, 293–94
  bombings, 325, 383, 385, 395, 396–97, 427, 449, 455, 560
    of churches, 419–20, 424, 472, 482, 483, 519
  against integration, 325, 384, 392, 395
  massacres, 237, 243, 246–52 *passim*, 267, 285, 329, 565
  post-Reconstruction, 231–32, 233, 234, 251–52
  protested, 247, 265, 434
  "Reign of Terror," 178–81, 232
  "rifle clubs," 250, 255
  See also Ku Klux Klan (KKK); Lynchings; Race riots; Violence; White supremacy
Texas, 5, 82, 92, 149
  Black appointed police chief, 494
  Black college founded in, 274
  Black labor in, 214, 217–18
  Black voters barred, 340
  in Civil War, 197
  Constitutional Convention, 230
  country club accepts Blacks, 534–35
  Democratic Party in, 232, 243, 333
    armed forces of, seize capitol, 245
  Houston one of "worst" cities, 377
  lynchings/racial violence in, 262, 296, 298, 311–12, 314, 316, 392
  KKK and, 334
    against sit-in, 405
  secedes, readmitted to Union, 185, 226, 234
  segregation in, 258, 302, 374
    University of Texas, 374, 383
  as slave state, 119, 147, 154, 170
    annexation to Union debated, 128, 131, 135
    slavery abolished (1865), 211
  state Supreme Court and school financing in, 518
  upholds death penalty, 470
  See also Dallas, Texas
Texas Southern University, 375, 383
Theater
  Black performers, 70, 95, 214, 281, 322, 362, 435, 442, 464
    win awards, 383, 393, 414, 447, 459, 509
  Black playwrights, 70, 338–39, 352
    win awards, 399–400, 446, 509, 531
  Black spectators admitted, 155, 156
  Blackface, 97, 254

Harlem, 322, 362
  See also Music
"Third rail," invention of, 268
Thirteenth Amendment. *See* Constitutional Amendments
Thomas, Clarence, 493–94, 514, 528, 540, **540**, 546
Thomas, Debi, 512
Thomas, Derrick, 561
Thomas, Dorothy, 528
Thomas, Frank, 556
Thomas, Franklin, 477
Thomas, Marion Turner Stubbs, 356
Thomas, Thurman, 561
Thompkins, Dr. William J., 355
Thompson, George, 117
Thompson, Sarah, 196
Thompson, Pfc. William, 384
Thoms, Ada, 298, 315
Thoreau, Henry, 169
"Three-Fifths Compromise," 61–62, 76
Thurmond, Strom, 397
Tibbs, Lillian Evans, 342
Tilden, Samuel Jr., 288
Till, Emmett Louis, 385, 390, 519
Tillotson College, 139
Timbuktu, Mali, 1, 3, **3**
Times/CBS news poll, 490
TLC Beatrice, 528, 531, 559
Tobacco
  grown by slave labor, 5, 8, 9, 27, 29, 41, 42–43, 144, 147
  prices, 16, 43, 55, 101
  production peaks, declines, 67, 105
  value of, to colonies, 6, 8, 42–43
Tolton, Fr. Augustine, 267
Tougaloo College, 139
Toussaint L'Ouverture, François Dominique, 69, **69**
Towne, Laura, 190
Towns, Edolphus "Ed," 496–97
Townsend, Willard S., 356, 389
Toxic waste, 528, 547, 549
"Trail of tears," 106. *See also* Native Americans
Treasury, U.S. Department of, 493
  Blacks employed by, 184, 223, 233, 246, 482
  Black woman as Treasurer, 471
Treaties
  of Ghent (1814), 86
  of Paris (1783), 57
  of San Ildefonso (1800), 77
  Webster-Ashburton (1843), 133
Trent, William J., 355
Tribe, Lawrence, 557
"Triangular" trade. *See* Slave trade
Trinity Episcopal Church (New York), 26, 28, 88
Trotter, William Monroe, 280, 292, 295, 316
True American (antislavery journal), 136
Truman, Harry S., 326, 356, 374, 377, 379
  Executive Order of, 373, 378, 458
Truth, Sojourner, 133–34, **134**, 152, 220
Tubman, Harriet, 107, 142, 143, **143**, 197, 306, 360
Tucker, Walter III, 553
Tucker, William (first Black child born in America), 8
Tulane University, 416
Tulsa, Okla., 328–29, **729**

Turner, Benjamin S., 232–33, 237, 244
Turner, Carmen, 528
Turner, Henry, 167, 218–19, 228, 250
  and colonization, 231, 252
Turner, Nat, 108–9, 110, **110**, 178
Tuscarawas Valley strike (1880), 231
Tuscumbia Female Academy, conspiracy to
  burn, 241
Tuskegee Institute (now University), 206,
  281, 292
  Black pilots trained at, 363
  founding of, 224, 257, 260–61, 308
  funding of, 260–61, 346
  opposes NAACP, 286
  reports on lynchings, 270, 361, 375, 385
  ship named for, 361
"Tuskegee Study" (medical experiment), 459
Twenty-fourth Amendment, 424. See also
  Constitutional Amendments
Twilight, Alexander Lucius, 94, 95, 119
"Two societies"
  within Black America, 538–39 (see also
    Economic conditions)
  separate and unequal, 440 (see also Segre-
    gation)
Tyler, Gary, 528
Tyler, John, 131, 135, 183
Tyson, Cicely, 467, 469, 541
Tyson, Mike, 504, 518, 530, 547
Tyus, Wyomia, 442

Uncle Remus stories, 275
Uncle Tom's Cabin (Stowe), 72, 94, 96, 106,
  139, 154, 156
Underground Railroad, 85, 101 (map), 106,
  161, 206
  "conductors" on, 139, 142, 197, 306
  Purvis named "president" of, 107, 125
  stations on, 96, 99–100, 107, 114, 121,
    134, 140, 146, 248, 339
  white children and, 139
  See also Slaves, runaway
"Understanding Clause," 281, 292. See also
  Voting rights
UNIA (Universal Negro Improvement As-
  sociation), 308, 324–25, 337
United Church of Christ, 227, 558
United Color Democracy (New York Black
  political machine), 289
United Nations
  Blacks serving, 359, 374–79 passim, 383,
    387, 462, 472, 476, 477, 506
  petition to, 383
  UNESCO award, 411
United Negro College Fund (UNCF), 372,
  471, 475, 497, 523, 561
United States
  abolishes slavery by 13th Amendment,
    206, 212–13
  acquires land from Mexico, 137, 140, 149
  aids freed slaves, 206
  and colonization, 189 (see also Coloniza-
    tion)
  cost to, in Burns case, 159
  and government harassment of Blacks,
    525
  intercepts slave trade, 133, 167
  recognizes Liberia, 112
  in War of 1812, 85 (see also War of 1812)
  See also Citizenship for Blacks, Civil
    War; Congress, U.S.; Elections; Gov-

ernment service, Blacks in; Popula-
  tion; Secession, Seminol War;
  Supreme Court, U.S.
U.S. Route 27, 96. See also Underground
  Railroad
United Transport Service Employees of
  America, 356. See also Labor unions
Universities, Black. See HBCUs (Histori-
  cally Black Colleges and Universities)
Unrest, Black. See Black protest; Slave re-
  volts; Violence
"Upper Country," 82
Urban coalition groups, 436, 448, 514, See
  also National Urban League
Urbanization, 67, 287, 319–20, 402, 521
  "best" and "worst" cities, 375, 377–78
  and Blacks in office, 435
  Committee on, 300, 303
  and group solidarity, 381
  suburbs v., 480–81, 554–55
  urban renewal, 400–401
  See also Migration; National Urban
    League; Population (urban)
Usry, James, 527
Utah, 147, 149

Vagrancy laws. See Laws and legislation
Van Buren, Martin, 129, 135, 140
Vance, Cyrus, 477
Van Peebles, Melvin, 454
Varick, Bishop James, 93
Vassa, Gustavus, 64, 65, **65**
Vaughan, Sarah, 304, 371, 536
Vermont, 53, 67, 115, 119, 133
Vesey, Denmark, 87, 93, 178
Vicksburg, Miss., 247, 248, 255
  Battle of, 197–98
  Black population, 256, 287, 299
Vicksburg Herald, 247
Victoria, queen of England, 106, 254
Victor Talking Machine Company, 292
Vietnam War
  Blacks in, 401–2, 433–34, 466, 469, 473
  opposition to, 385, 424, 433, 437, 449
Vigilance Association, 100
Villa, Francisco "Pancho," 309
Violence
  antislavery, 134, 157, 162, 163
  Attica prison riot, 454
  Black, 78, 98, 296, 298, 352 (see also
    Black retaliatory, *below*)
  Black retaliatory, 328–29, 449
    after acquittals, 417, 484, 488, 489, 548
    after deaths, 440, 517, 530–31, 541
    postwar, 317, 402
    (see also Mutiny)
  Congressional statistics on, 225, 231
  draft riots, 131, 198, 202
  at elections, 241, 246
  Enforcement Acts against, 213, 234, 235
  against freed slaves, 221, 225
  against freedom riders, 409–10
  memorial to victims of, 519
  "Mississippi Plan" (rifle clubs, etc.), 242,
    250
  mob, 95, 284, 290, 295, 504, 509, 525
    anti-abolition, 116, 119
    refugees from, 121
    (see also Race riots)
  and nonviolent protest (450, 483, 506 (see
    also Black protest)

organized protests against, 286 (see also
  NAACP)
proslavery, 79, 92, 105, 115–18 passim,
  133, 162, 178–81, 185
  abolitionists attacked, 123–24, 133, 183
  Burns case (Boston), 157–59
  Irish immigrants join, 131, 198
  in Kansas, 162–63
  by Quantrill's Raiders, 199
  against Republican Party, 222, 224, 232,
    234, 239, 246–50 passim
restitution for, 565
  refused, 282
Rodney King case, 464
skinhead plot, 560
students, civil rights workers killed, 424,
  435, 450, 519
teenage, 318, 519, 525
See also Children; Crime; Lynchings; Police; Slave revolts; Slaves, treatment
  of; Terrorism
Virginia, 202, 211, 214, 494
  admits Blacks to juries, 317
  African settlement in, 6, 7, 21
  becomes royal colony, 8
  Bill of Rights, 52, 54
  Black governor of, 520
  Black voting in, 275, 292, 301, 426, 463
  constitution of, 150, 301
  cotton production, 82, 89, 102
  and free Blacks, 70, 78, 79, 111, 142
    schools for, 178, 183, 189
    win tax exemption, 42
  indentured servants in, 6, 8, 9, 13, 15, 18
  miscegenation laws, 9, 16, 20, 26
    overturned, 437
  population
    colonial, 8, 9, 57 (see also Population
      [of North American British colonies])
    state, 67, 75, 76, 89, 105, 128, 230, 256,
      273, 479
  racial violence in, 232, 264
  secedes, readmitted to Union, 185, 226,
    234
  segregation in, 258, 290, 302, 305, 393,
    401
    schools integrated, 405
  slavery in, 33, 48, 49–50, 56, 58, 157
    and antislavery, 41, 45, 47, 57, 68
    conspiracy/revolts, 16, 33, 56, 75, 77,
      82, 108–9, 347
    legislation, 10, 14–20 passim, 26–31
      passim, 40, 42, 47, 53, 74, 80, 93, 105,
      111, 143–44
    slave trade, 6, 18, 24, 102–5, 117, 169,
      177
  state song of, 254, 361
  tobacco crop in, 6, 8, 42–43, 101
  See also Norfolk, Va.
Virginia Times, 104
Virgin Islands, 353–54, 356, 474
Vivant, Constance, 133
Voting rights
  Black efforts for, 126, 129, 203, 241, 244,
    339, 398
    "right to vote" petition, 212
  Blacks as majority, 204, 219, 224
  Confederate veterans lose, 219, 241
  debated (North Carolina), 116
  in District of Columbia, 220
  Federal Elections Bill, 267

for free white males only, 51, 54, 55, 68, 77, 80, 99, 128, 147
for males only, 6, 53, 68, 90, 92
Justice Department and, 494, 516
"natural," 215
property qualifications, 92, 276, 292
in Reconstruction era, 204, 218, **218**, 234, 235, 238, 251
suppression of Black/Republican
  federal court upholds, 331
  grandfather clauses, 274–75, 283, 289, 292, 308
  by law, 280, 300–301, 333, 395
  literacy/understanding requirements, 275, 276, 281, 289, 292, 300, 374, 396, 426, 450, 468
  "Mississippi tests," 275
  poll taxes imposed, 257–58, 275, 289, 292, 301, 426, 519
  registration drives, 399, 404, 410, 424, 426, 501, 506, 519
  restoration of, 399, 405
  grandfather clauses barred, poll tax repealed, literacy test banned, 308, 373, 424, 450, 468
  Supreme Court requires proof of, 483
  by violence and intimidation, 204, 218, 232–42 *passim*, 245, 247, 250, 268, 288, 428
vote fraud charges, 493
See also Civil Rights; Elections; Supreme Court, U.S.; Women
Voting Rights Act
1870, 1960, 271, 404
1965, 396, 421, 428, 557
  extension of, 450, 461, 462, 491, 493, 494, 495
  Supreme Court upholds, 426, 463
1968, 444
1975, 468, 516

Wages, *See* Labor, Black
Wagner, Robert, 361
Walden University, 251
Waldon, Alton R. Jr., 505, 506
Walker, Alice, 350, 492, 493, **493**
Walker, Madame C. J., 301–2, **301**
Walker, David, and *Walker's Appeal,* 98, 214
Walker, Edward (Edwin), 214
Walker, George, 292
Walker, Maggie Lena, 293, **293**
Walker, Margaret, 352
Walker, Moses Fleetwood, 266
Walker, Quaco, 57
Walker, William O., 306
Wallace, Gov. George C., 345, 428, 460, 470, 542
  blocks integration, 416, 419, 543
Wallace, Robert, 561–62
Waller, Thomas Wright "Fats," 341, 342, 371
Walls, Josiah T., 237, 238, 242, 248
Walters, Bishop Alexander, 285, 291
Walton, Gov. J. C., 333
Ward, Rev. Samuel Ringgold, 115, 126, 128, 134, 147
War Department, U.S., 208, 250, 273
  in Civil War, 186, 196, 199
  discrimination in, 356
  open facilities to Blacks, 361, 363, 369
Warmoth, Gov. Henry C., 226, 239, 242
War of 1812, 83, 84, 85–86, 90, 194

War on Poverty, 420, 545
Warren, Justice Earl, 386, 388, **388**
Warren, Judge Joyce Williams, 543
Warrentown (Va.) *Flag,* 179
Warwick, Dionne, 405
Washington, Booker T., 224, **290**, 295, **301**
  "Atlanta Compromise" speech, 280
  honorary degree from Harvard, 289–90
  influence of, 266, 280, 293, 303, 304, 308
  opposition to, 286, 292, 296, 300
  ships named for, 360, 368
  and Tuskegee, 224, 260–61
Washington, Judge Bushrod, 86
Washington, Craig A., 520
Washington, Denzel, 528
Washington, Gen. George, 47, 48, 55
  in Revolutionary War, 49, 50, 53, 54, 57
Washington, George (former slave), 145
Washington, Harold, 476, 498, 499, 504, 509
Washington, Kenny, 375
Washington, Walter E., 438, 445, 459–60, 472
Washington, D.C., 61, 68, 155
  and antislavery movement, 108, 109, 119, 125, 126, 142
  Bar Association library opened to Blacks, 365
  Black officeholders in, 246, 252, 270
  Black population, 67, 89, 169, 171, 256, 273, 287, 299, 319, 478
    reaches majority, 403, 446, 521
  Blacks allowed to testify, given voting rights, 80, 220
  first Black schools in, 80, 233
  first Black superintendent, 451
  integration in, 234, 245, 388
    segregationist "policy," 359
  one of "worst" cities, 377
    housing conditions, 287
    racial violence, 315, 316, 436
    as "murder capital," 512
  police force of, 528
  self-government for, 386, 458
    Black mayors, 459–60, 498, 525
    representative from, 457
  slavery abolished, 191–92, **191**
  slave-trading in, 104, 149, 167
  See also Black protest
Washington, Territory and State of, 145, 147, 520
Washington Post, 515
  Blacks employed by, 449, 561
Waters, Ethel, 322, 365
Waters, Maxine, 533–34, **533**
Watt, Melvin, 553–54
Wattleton, Faye, 473
Watts, J. C., 529
Watts riots, 429, 461. *See also* Race riots
Wayne, Gen. Anthony, 54
WBBM-TV (Chicago), 532
Weaver, Dr. Robert C., 355, 363, **363**, 408, 426
Webster, Daniel, 91, 126, 132
Webster, Noah, 67
Webster, William, 485, 488
Webster-Ashburton Treaty (1843), 133
Wedgwood, Josiah, 114, **117**
Weicker, Gov. Lowell P. Jr., 489, 559
Weinberger, Caspar, 518
Weiseger, Arthur, 355
Welcome, Verda F., 420
Weld, Theodore, 115, 118, 127–28, **128**, 155

Wells, Mary, 399, 411, 520
Wells-Barnett, Ida, 262, 271–72, **272**
WERD-AM (Atlanta), 288, 379
Wesley, Bishop John, 57
Wesleyan University, 127, 556
West Africa, 1, 3, 4
  colonies of free Blacks in, *see* Colonization
  slave trade in, 9, 11 (map), 12, 22, 23, 167, 184–85
    "slave area," 34
Western Reserve College, 105
West Indies
  "breaking in" of slaves in, 15, **15**, 39
  British, 17, 56, 70, 127 (*see also* Barbados)
  Dutch, 8
  Free Blacks taken back to slavery in, 56, 86
  French, 8, 24, 20–21, 69–70
    population, 5, 52
    slave code in, 9
    slavery abolished, 116
  slaves imported from, 74, 75
  slaves taken to, 4, 9, 12, 15, 19, 354
  slave trade reopened, 78
  sugar and tobacco produced in, 4, 5, 6, 12
  on trade routes, 11 (map), 12, 22
    Middle Passage, 14, 39
  See also Haiti; Jamaica; Santo Domingo; Virgin Islands
West Point. *See* Army, U.S.
West Virginia, 185, 274, 479
Wewoka, Mexico, 124
WGPR-TV (Detroit), 464, 467
Whaling industry, 129, 167
Wharton, Clifton R. Sr., 398, 408
Wharton, Clifton R. Jr., 449–50
Wheat, Alan, 497
Wheat, cultivation of introduced, 4
Wheatley, Phillis, 46–47, **46**
Whig (Richmond journal), 179
Whig Party, 157
Whipper, William J., 97, 115, 231, 242, 248
Whipple, Prince, 54
White, Bill, 517, 550
White, Justice Byron, 483
White, George H., 270, 281–82, 282, **282**, 286, 289, 296, 341
White, Gov. Hugh L., 390
White, Kevin, 467
White, Reggie, 561
White, Sonny, 346
White, Walter, 305, 317, **348**
  with NAACP, 348, 363, 390
White Citizens' Councils, 387, 392, 410. *See also* White supremacy
White Knights (white supremacy group), 424
White League (white supremacy group), 246
White supremacy, 285, 410
  individuals convicted or acquitted, 483, 488, 496
  organizations, 222, 237, 246, 250, 255, 379, 387, 424, 509, 560 (*see also* Ku Klux Klan [KKK])
  power restored, 250, 288, 300, 379, 392
  self-defense against, 254
  See also Racism; Violence
Whitfield, James M., 159
Whitman, Christine Todd, 563
Whitney, Eli, 70, 71
Whitten, John W., 355
Whittier, John Greenleaf, 114, 117
WHMM-TV (Howard University), 486

Wilberforce, William, 161
Wilberforce, Ontario, Canada, 121
Wilberforce University, **162**, 184, 269, 273
  founded, 146, 161, 162, 196
Wild Cat (commander in Seminole War), 124
Wilder, Gov. L. Douglas, 242, 504, 520, 531
Wilkins, James Ernest Jr., 388
Wilkins, Roy, 316, 389, **389**, 390, 415, 421, 471
Williams, Bert, 292, 360
Williams, Dr. Daniel Hale, 277, 278, 303, 305
Williams, Doug, 512
Williams, Franklin, 431
Williams, Rev. George Washington, 266
Williams, Hosea, 427
Williams, H. Sylvester, 291
Williams, Gov. John Bell, 450
Williams, Ralph, 549
Williams, Russell III, 539–40
Williams, Wayne B., 489, 494
Williamsburg, Va., 33, 56
Wilmington, Del., 72, 558
Wilmington, N.C., 256, 285
  and "Wilmington Ten," 456, 558
Wilmot, David, and Wilmot Proviso, 137
Wilson, August, 509, 531
Wilson, Charles E., 377
Wilson, Flip, 452
Wilson, Harriet, 169
Wilson, Henry, 179, 205
Wilson, Laval, 504, 529
Wilson, William J., 473–74
Wilson, Woodrow, 311
Winfrey, Oprah, 500, 503–4, 518
Winston-Salem, N.C., 302
Winthrop, Gov. John, 9
Wisconsin decision overturned, 168
Witchcraft trials (Salem), 20
Witnesses, slaves denied right to serve as.
  See Courts
Women
  at Annapolis, 470
  antislavery activities of, 129, 155, 168
    Blacks excluded, 119
    women excluded, 114, 115, 129
  denied credit, 483
  educate Blacks, 178, 227
  employment of, 274, 480
    discrimination against, 240, 486, 497, 502, 524, 534, 556
    gains in, 518
    as teachers, male-female ratio, 548
  first female Episcopal bishop, 516
  first physician, 219
  Hall of Fame, 527
  as heads of households, 481, 522, 523
  life expectancy of, 477
  lung cancer among, 499
  suffrage for, 140, 150, 220, 226, 238, 527
  See also Women, Black; Women's rights

Women, Black
  associations for the protection of, 294, 300, 303
  as astronaut, 507, 508
  athletes, 404, 408, 442, 511, 512, 516, 544
  in Civil War, 189, 197, 256, 306
  in education, 111, 162, 178, 188–89, 316, 351, 438
    college enrollment, 517, 535, 537
    compared to Black men, 537
    equal access ruling, 541
    "firsts" in, 112, 196, 256, 296, 323–24
    first university presidents, 157, 487, 504, 524
    in public school system, 196, 548
    teach freed Blacks, 227
    teach white students, 184
    vocational training for, 106, 209, 302, 351
    (*see also* Sororities)
  first air pilot, 325
  first female Episcopal bishop, 516
  as head of police department, 528
  as heads of families, 466, 481, 522, 523, 555
  health concerns of, 499, 542, 548
  Industrial Exchange for, 206
  influential, 473
  in law, 240, 325, 337, 339, 377, 462
    appear before Supreme Court, 339, 433
    appointed judges, 359–60, 433, 512, 543
  life expectancy of, 477
  lynched, 337
  magazine for, 448
  in medicine, 200, 219, 298, 503
  in military service, 371, 372
    commissioned, 441–42, 476, 478, 487, 503, 529
    as nurses, 285, 315, 478
  Miss America pageants, 442, 500, 518, 528, 547, 562
  organized activities of
    1820s–1860s, 91, 100, 108–14 *passim*, 117, 129, 189, 196
    1890s–1910, 196, 279, 281, 296
    1930s, 351, 356
    first professional, 298
  owning and operating business, 293, 301–2, 364
  percentage of population, 172, 174, 175, 179
  in politics, 330, 352, 354, 356, 422, 431, 433
    cabinet/subcabinet positions, 476, 487, 556
    in Congress, 438–39, 461, 465, 496, 551, 552
    first ambassador, 476
    first presidential candidate, 459
    mayors, 463, 464, 508, 525
    U.S. Treasurer, 471
  professional, compared to Black men, 537–38

"slave status" of, 156
  upward mobility of, 443
  writings by, 46, 108, 156–57, 169, 189
  See also Labor, Black; Women's rights
Women's Christian Temperance Union, 238
Women's Medical College of Pennsylvania, 219
Women's Relief Corps, 189
Women's rights
  abolitionists and, 114, 118, 220
  activists for, 108, 112, 128, 140, 150, 156, 279
  U.S. movement founded, 114
Women's Rights Conventions, 114, 140, 152, 156, 168
Wonder, Stevie, 399, 502
Wood, Robert H., 236, 243
Woodruff, Hale, 337
Woods, Granville, T., 268
Woodson, Dr. Carter G., 309, **309**, 339
Woodson, George H., 337
Woolman, John 40
World Anti-Slavery Convention (London, 1840), 114, 128, 132
  women denied seats at, 114, 129
World War I, 272, 286, 319, 367, 384
  Blacks with French Forces, 306, 309–15 *passim*, **314**
World War II
  Black anti-war sentiments, 311, 415
  Blacks serving in, 361–72 *passim*, **370**, 386, 387–88, 411, 432
  postwar period, 373, 403
WPA (Works Progress Administration), 352, 355
Wright, Justice Jonathan Jasper, 236
Wright, Richard, 352, 361
Wynn, Albert, 554

Yale College/University, 67
  Black graduates from, 244, 250
Yang, C. K., 405–6
Yardley, Sir George and Lady, 6, 8
Yazoo City (Mississippi) violence, 248, 250, 265
Yerby, Frank, 352
YMCA (Young Men's Christian Association), first Black, 155, **301**
Yorktown, Battle of, 56, 57
Yoruba people, 1, 167
Young, Andrew, 234, 461–62, **472**, 532, 564
  as mayor, 462, 464, 490
  at UN, 462, 472, 477, 506
Young, Brigham, 160
Young, Col. Charles, 272–73, **272**, 312
Young, Coleman, 463, 464, **464**, 519–20, 564
Young, Steve, 561
Young, Whitney Jr., 408–09, **408**, 554

"Zebra" case, 466. *See also* Police
Zuni Pueblo Indians, 5. *See also* Native Americans